MATHEMATICAL REASONING
for Elementary Teachers

SECOND EDITION

MATHEMATICAL REASONING for Elementary Teachers

SECOND EDITION

Calvin T. Long
Washington State University

Duane W. DeTemple
Washington State University

 **ADDISON-WESLEY**

An imprint of Addison Wesley Longman, Inc.

Reading, Massachusetts • Menlo Park, California • New York • Harlow, England
Don Mills, Ontario • Sydney • Mexico City • Madrid • Amsterdam

Sponsoring Editor: Bill Poole

Project Editor: Christine O'Brien

Text Design: The Davis Group

Cover Design: Barbara Atkinson

Cover Photo: © 1999 Scott Barrow, Inc.

Senior Production Supervisor: Peggy McMahon

Production Services: Elm Street Publishing Services, Inc.

Compositor: Typo-Graphics, Inc.

To my wife and constant helpmate, Jean.

C.T.L.

To my wife, Janet, and my daughters, Jill
    and Rachel.

D.W.D.

For permission to use copyrighted material, grateful acknowledgment is made to the copyright holders on pp. A-57 and A-58, which are hereby made part of this copyright page.

Library of Congress Cataloging-in-Publication Data

Long, Calvin T.
    Mathematical reasoning for elementary teachers / Calvin Long,
  Duane DeTemple.— 2nd ed.
      p.   cm.
    Includes index.
    ISBN 0–321–04333–2
    1. Mathematics—Study and teaching (Elementary)   I. DeTemple,
  Duane W.   II. Title.
  QA135, 5.L63   2000
  510—dc21   99–22166
                                                        CIP

ISBN 0–321–04333–2

1 2 3 4 5 - DOW - 010099

CONTENTS

Preface   ix

To the Student   xix

Chapter 1 **Thinking Critically**   1

1.1   Some Surprising Tidbits   4
1.2   An Introduction to Problem Solving   11
1.3   Pólya's Problem-Solving Principles   16
1.4   More Problem-Solving Strategies   27
1.5   Additional Problem-Solving Strategies   48
1.6   Problem Solving in the Real World   58

Chapter 1 Summary   72
Chapter Review Exercises   74
Chapter Test   77

Chapter 2 **Sets, Whole Numbers, and Functions**   78

2.1   Sets and Operations on Sets   80
2.2   Sets, Counting, and the Whole Numbers   92
2.3   Addition and Subtraction of Whole Numbers   103
2.4   Multiplication and Division of Whole Numbers   117
2.5   Functions   136

Chapter 2 Summary   150
Chapter Review Exercises   153
Chapter Test   154

Chapter 3 **Numeration and Computation**   156

3.1   Numeration Systems Past and Present   158
3.2   Nondecimal Positional Systems   176
3.3   Algorithms for Adding and Subtracting Whole Numbers   184

3.4   Algorithms for Multiplication and Division of Whole Numbers   199
3.5   Mental Arithmetic and Estimation   213
3.6   Getting the Most Out of Your Calculator   225

Chapter 3 Summary   240
Chapter Review Exercises   241
Chapter Test   242

Chapter 4   **Number Theory**   **244**

4.1   Divisibility of Natural Numbers   247
4.2   Tests for Divisibility   261
4.3   Greatest Common Divisors and Least Common Multiples   270
4.4   Clock Arithmetic   283

Chapter 4 Summary   297
Chapter Review Exercises   298
Chapter Test   299

Chapter 5   **Integers**   **300**

5.1   Representations of Integers   302
5.2   Addition and Subtraction of Integers   313
5.3   Multiplication and Division of Integers   334

Chapter 5 Summary   346
Chapter Review Exercises   348
Chapter Test   350

Chapter 6   **Fractions and Rational Numbers**   **351**

6.1   The Basic Concepts of Fractions and Rational Numbers   354
6.2   The Arithmetic of Rational Numbers   371
6.3   The Rational Number System   390

Chapter 6 Summary   407
Chapter Review Exercises   409
Chapter Test   410

Chapter 7   **Decimals and Real Numbers**   **412**

7.1   Decimals   415
7.2   Computations with Decimals   436
7.3   Ratio and Proportion   449
7.4   Percent   460

Chapter 7 Summary   473
Chapter Review Exercises   474
Chapter Test   476

Chapter 8 **Statistics: The Interpretation of Data**   **477**

8.1   **The Graphical Representation of Data**   479
8.2   **Measures of Central Tendency and Variability**   500
8.3   **Statistical Inference**   518

Chapter 8 Summary   531
Chapter Review Exercises   532
Chapter Test   533

Chapter 9 **Probability**   **534**

9.1   **Empirical Probability**   536
9.2   **Principles of Counting**   550
9.3   **Theoretical Probability**   567

Chapter 9 Summary   588
Chapter Review Exercises   589
Chapter Test   591

Chapter 10 **Geometric Figures**   **592**

10.1   **Figures in the Plane**   596
10.2   **Curves and Polygons in the Plane**   616
10.3   **Figures in Space**   637
10.4   **Networks**   656

Chapter 10 Summary   668
Chapter Review Exercises   670
Chapter Test   672

Chapter 11 **Measurement**   **674**

11.1   **The Measurement Process**   676
11.2   **Area and Perimeter**   692
11.3   **The Pythagorean Theorem**   712
11.4   **Surface Area and Volume**   721

Chapter 11 Summary   742
Chapter Review Exercises   744
Chapter Test   745

Chapter 12   **Transformations, Symmetries, and Tilings**   **748**

12.1   Rigid Motions and Similarity Transformations   751
12.2   Patterns and Symmetries   775
12.3   Tilings and Escher-like Designs   789

Chapter 12 Summary   804
Chapter Review Exercises   806
Chapter Test   807

Chapter 13   **Congruence, Constructions, and Similarity**   **810**

13.1   Congruent Triangles   812
13.2   Constructing Geometric Figures   830
13.3   Similar Triangles   849

Chapter 13 Summary   865
Chapter Review Exercises   866
Chapter Test   868

Chapter 14   **Coordinate Geometry**   **870**

14.1   The Cartesian Coordinate System   872
14.2   Lines and Their Graphs   885
14.3   Solving Geometric Problems Using Coordinates   906
14.4   Graphing Functions   915

Chapter 14 Summary   925
Chapter Review Exercises   926
Chapter Test   928

Appendices

Appendix A   Manipulatives in the Mathematics Classroom   929
Appendix B   Spreadsheets   933
Appendix C   Graphing Calculators   939
Appendix D   A Brief Guide to *The Geometer's Sketchpad*   953

Answers to Selected Problems   A-1

Acknowledgments   A-57

Mathematical Lexicon   A-59

Index and Pronunciation Guide   A-61

PREFACE

This text is for use in mathematics content courses for prospective elementary and middle school teachers. We assume the students enrolled in these courses have completed two years of high school algebra and one year of high school geometry. We do not assume that the students will be highly proficient in algebra and geometry but that they have a basic knowledge of these subjects and reasonable arithmetic skills. Typically, students bring widely varying backgrounds to these courses, and this text is written to accommodate this diversity.

It is perhaps not overstating the case to assert that many people have at least a mild aversion to mathematics and that many find it quite difficult and daunting—something to be avoided if at all possible. This view is also shared by many of those who aspire to be elementary or middle school teachers. It is not surprising then that school teachers with this perception of mathematics soon impart similar attitudes to their students. If we are to change this pervasive negative view of mathematics, it seems clear that we must begin by producing teachers who see mathematics in a different, more favorable light.

With a positive attitude toward mathematics comes confidence and an increased willingness to learn the mathematical content, skills, and effective teaching techniques necessary to become a competent teacher of mathematics. One of the principal goals of this text is to impart that positive attitude to those who aspire to be elementary or middle school teachers.

Guiding Philosophy and Approach

The content and processes of mathematics are presented in an appealing and logically sound manner with these three principal goals in mind:

- **to develop positive attitudes toward mathematics and mathematics teaching,**
- **to develop mathematical knowledge and skills, and**
- **to develop students as competent mathematics teaching professionals.**

In short, the goals of this text seek to implement the recommendations in the National Council of Teachers in Mathematics (NCTM) *Standards,* published in the late 1980s and early 1990s. In light of recent research in teaching mathematics and ten years' experience since the first of the NCTM *Standards* documents was published, the *Standards* are now being combined, refined, and updated into *Principles and Standards for School Mathematics* (the *Principles and Standards*) and are expected in final form in the year 2000.

Principles and Standards is not yet official NCTM policy, but it effectively unifies, explains, and builds upon the original *Standards,* continuing the original thrust to "ensure quality, indicate goals, and promote positive changes in mathematics education in grades preK–12." Our approach to achieving our goals in this text reflects the recommendations of the NCTM *Standards,* now reformulated in the *Principles and Standards,* which we cite throughout the text.

Aside from mastering **content and skills,** teachers often pattern their own teaching after the ways they have been taught. This text models effective teaching by emphasizing

- activities,
- manipulatives,
- investigations,
- written projects,
- discussion questions,
- appropriate use of technology,

and above all else,

- **problem solving and mathematical reasoning.**

It is our hope that this book will provide future elementary school teachers with the positive attitudes and mathematical skills and techniques they need to convey the beauty, usefulness, and power of mathematics to their own students.

Content Features

- **Problem Solving**   We begin the text with an extensive introduction to problem solving in Chapter 1. This theme is continued throughout the text in special problem-solving examples and featured in the exercises in the problems grouped under the headings *Understanding Concepts, Thinking Critically, Thinking Cooperatively, Communicating, Using a Calculator, Using a Computer,* and *Making Connections.*
- **Number Systems**   Chapters 2, 3, 5, 6, and 7 focus on the various number systems and make use of discussion, pictorial and graphical representations, and manipulatives to promote understanding of the systems, their properties, and the various modes of computation. Students are given plenty of opportunity for drill and practice as well as for individual and cooperative problem solving, reasoning, and communication.
- **Number Theory**   Chapter 4 contains much material that is new and interesting to students. Notions of divisibility, divisors, multiples, greatest common divisors, and least common multiples are first developed via informative diagrams and then through the use of manipulatives, sets, prime factor representations, and the Euclidean algorithm. A final section deals with clock arithmetic (modular arithmetic) and contains interesting applications to zip codes and the ISBN book number codes in common use.
- **Statistics**   Chapter 8 on statistics is designed not only to give the students an appreciation of the basic measures and graphical representations of data but also of the uses and misuses of statistics. This last issue is particularly important since we are confronted daily with a stream of "facts and figures" seductively intended to influence our thinking. The informed citizen needs not only to be aware of the legitimate predictive and descriptive power of statistics but also to be wary of the way statistics can mislead.

- **Probability**   In Chapter 9, we first study empirical probability—probability based on experience and repeated trials. This prepares the way for the subsequent study of the elements of theoretical probability of an event based on counting and other *a priori* considerations. The great surprise for the students is how closely the results agree, particularly when the number of trials is large. Of course, it is necessary to consider various methods of counting in order to compute theoretical probabilities. At the same time counting is an important topic in its own right, and we have made it accessible through the use of tree diagrams, Venn diagrams, and careful explanation of the use of the words *or* and *and.*

- **Geometry**   The creative and inductive nature of geometric discovery is emphasized in Chapters 10, 11, 12, 13, and 14, and students who acquire a distaste for the subject from a heavily axiomatic and deductive course will often see geometry in a positive new way. The text's approach to geometry is constructive and visual. Students are often asked to draw, cut, fold, paste, count, and so on, making geometry an experimental science. While the traditional construction and measurement tools continue to have a place, the visual and dynamic scope of geometry is enhanced with computer geometry software. Problem solving and applications permeate the geometry chapters, and sections on tilings and symmetry provide an opportunity to highlight the aesthetic and artistic aspects of geometry. Examples are often taken from culturally diverse sources.

Special Pedagogical Features

The teacher of mathematics should be aware of the historical development of mathematics, have some knowledge of the principal contributors to mathematics, and realize that mathematics continues to be a lively area of research. Moreover, the teacher must always be alert to ways to foster mathematical power in the elementary or middle school classroom. This text contains a number of features that prospective teachers will find to be valuable resources.

- **Highlights from History** illustrate the contributions individual men and women have made to mathematics and provide a cultural, historical, and personal perspective on the development of mathematical concepts and thought.

- **Into the Classroom** provides insights on teaching the topics in this text to elementary and middle school children. These tips often come from current elementary or middle school teachers.

- **Schoolbook Pages** are taken from actual elementary or middle school textbooks and show how topics from the text are made meaningful to schoolchildren. They also show that the topics are central to the elementary or middle school curriculum.

- **Did You Know** provides examples of recent advancements in mathematics, often demonstrating the important role mathematics has in today's world and in our personal lives. This feature also highlights excerpts from mathematical literature that have relevance to the classroom teacher.

- **Just for Fun** shows the lighter side of mathematical problem solving, with engaging puzzles and teasers that have an element of surprise and humor.

- **Window on Technology** contains explanations of special applications of graphing calculators, spreadsheets, and dynamic geometry software.

Chapter Structure

Each chapter is structured consistently and meaningfully according to the following pattern.

- **Chapter Opener**   A class activity called **Hands On** introduces the chapter topic. The activity is followed by **Connections,** a feature that reveals the interconnections between the various parts of mathematics and between mathematics and the real world.
- **Examples** are presented in a *problem-solving mode,* asking the reader to independently obtain a solution that can be compared with the solution presented in the text. Solutions are frequently structured in the Pólya four-step format.
- **Figures and Tables**   A large number of figures visually reinforce the concepts, problems, and solutions. Many figures and all tables include informative captions.
- **From the NCTM *Principles and Standards***   Extensive excerpts from the *Principles and Standards* help students understand the timeliness and relevance of topics.
- **Think Clouds**   These notes serve as quick reminders and clarify key points in discussions.
- **Cooperative Investigations** provide activities, open-ended problems, and opportunities for *cooperative learning.*
- **Problem Sets** are grouped according to the following categories:
  - *Understanding Concepts* exercises provide drill and reinforce basic concepts.
  - *Thinking Critically* exercises offer problem-solving practice related to the section topic. Many of these problems can be used as classroom activities or with small groups.
  - *Thinking Cooperatively* exercises provide cooperative problem-solving experiences specifically for small groups.
  - *Making Connections* exercises apply the section concepts to solving real-life problems and to other parts of mathematics.
  - *Communicating* exercises offer students opportunities to write about mathematics and to investigate mathematics as a language.
  - *Using a Calculator* exercises provide problems that are best solved using a calculator. These problems are highlighted by suitable icons.
  - *Using a Computer* gives students the opportunity to use various types of software. Again a suitable icon is used to indicate when use of a computer would be helpful or desirable.
  - *From State Student Assessments* provides examples of problems from tests now in use in many states to assess student progress. These problems help make future teachers aware of the types of knowledge that their future students will be asked to master.
  - *For Review* exercises offer students continual reinforcement of concepts covered earlier in the text.
- **Epilogue**   This is a brief concluding essay that discusses the importance of the materials just covered and provides a helpful summarizing overview.

- **End of Chapter Material**   Each chapter closes with the following features:
  - Chapter Summary
    - Key Concepts
    - Vocabulary and Notation
  - Chapter Review Problems
  - Chapter Test

End-of-Text Material

- Appendix A, "Manipulatives in the Mathematics Classroom," offers a brief overview of the use of manipulatives in the mathematics classroom. It provides succinct answers to such questions as: What are manipulatives? Why are they used? When should they be used?
- Appendix B, "Spreadsheets," provides an introduction to spreadsheet software, highlighting those features that are especially useful in the mathematics classroom. In particular, it is shown how number sequences and statistical calculations can be treated with spreadsheet technology.
- Appendix C, "Graphing Calculators," provides detailed examples to help illustrate some of the capabilities of graphing calculators useful for the elementary school classroom. For example, it is shown
  - how functions can be entered, graphed, and analyzed;
  - how lists of data can be entered, examined statistically, and represented graphically; and
  - how programs can be written and used to solve problems.
- Appendix D, "A Brief Guide to *The Geometer's Sketchpad*," provides an introduction to some of the basic features of this popular dynamic geometry software. Students are shown how the toolbox and menu commands are used to construct, measure, and transform geometric figures. The dynamic capability of the software, which allows figures to be manipulated, is used to examine properties of classes of geometric shapes.
- Answers to Selected Problems. Exercise problems identified with a colored problem number are answered at the back of the text.
- Mathematical Lexicon
- Pronunciation Guide and Index

Course Flexibility

Course Options

This text contains ample material for at least two semester-length courses. At Washington State University, elementary education majors are required to take two three-semester-hour courses, with the option for an elective third course that is particularly suited to the needs of upper elementary and middle school teachers. Our text is used in all three courses. The suggestions below are for semester-length courses, but instructors should have little difficulty selecting material that fits the coverage needed for courses in a quarter system.

- A First Course, *Problem Solving and Number Systems*, covers Chapters 1 through 7. Our own first course devotes at least five weeks to Chapter 1. The

problem-solving skills and enthusiasm developed in this chapter make it possible to move through most of the topics in Chapters 2 through 6 more quickly
than usual. There is considerable latitude in which topics an instructor might
choose to give lighter or heavier emphasis.

- A Second Course, *Statistics, Probability, and Basic Geometry,* covers Chapters
  8 through 12 with optional inclusion of computer geometry software.
  (Appendix D gives a brief introduction to *The Geometer's Sketchpad.*)
- An Alternative Second Course, *Informal Geometry,* covers Chapters 10
  through 14, with optional inclusion of computer geometry software.

Once the basic notions and symbolism of geometry have been covered in Sections 10.1 and
10.2, the remaining chapters in geometry can be taken up in any order. Section 10.3 on figures in space should receive some coverage before taking up surface area and volume in
Section 11.4.

Supplements

•

For the Instructor

- **Instructor's Guide**
  ISBN 0-321-04326-X
  Offers:
    - A brief statement of teaching philosophy
    - Suggestions for planning time for coverage of the chapter and its vari-
      ous sections
    - Ideas for teaching the subject of the chapter
    - Discussion of *Hands On* activities
    - Specific teaching tips for each section
    - Transparency masters
- **Instructor's Solution Manual**
  ISBN 0-321-04327-8
    - Provides solutions to all of the problems
- **Printed Test Bank**
  ISBN 0-321-06836-X
    - Provides prepared tests for each chapter
- **TestGen-EQ with QuizMaster-EQ**
  Windows ISBN 0-321-04329-4
  Macintosh ISBN 0-321-04330-8
    - Can easily view, edit, and add questions, transfer questions to tests, and
      print tests in a variety of fonts and forms
    - Built-in question editor gives the ability to create graphs, import graph-
      ics, insert mathematical symbols and templates, and insert variable
      numbers or text
    - Can create and save tests using TestGen-EQ so students can take them
      for practice or a grade on a computer network using QuizMaster-EQ
    - Can set preferences for how and when tests are administered with
      QuizMaster-EQ
    - Free to departments with textbook adoption

- **Videotapes**
  - A set of videotapes keyed to the text and featuring an experienced instructor, utilizes worked-out examples to provide reinforcement of all basic concepts.

For the Student

- **Mathematics Activities for Elementary School Teachers**
  by Dolan, Williamson, Muri
  ISBN 0-321-04328-6
  - Provides hands-on, manipulative-based activities keyed to the text that involve future elementary teachers in discovering mathematical concepts, solving problems, and exploring mathematical concepts in interesting, stimulating, real-world settings.
  - Activities can be adapted for use with elementary students at a later time.
  - *Purpose* outlines the major mathematical concepts developed in the activity.
  - *Materials* provides a list of supplies needed for the activity.
  - *Grouping* describes classroom setting for the activity.
  - *Getting Started* provides an introduction to the activity and explains the preparation needed.
  - *Reflections* help students bring closure to ideas.
  - *Extensions* present suggestions and ideas for extending the activity to other mathematical topics or for making connections.
  - *Manipulatives* in color and on heavy paper stock are included.
  - *Activity Masters* contain models, activity recording sheets, graph paper, nets for polyhedra, activity cards, and so on.
- **Student's Solution Manual**
  ISBN 0-321-04325-1
  - Contains detailed, worked-out solutions to exercises that are answered in the back of the text
- **Web site**
  - Additional resources for instructors and students

Acknowledgments

We would like to thank the following individuals who reviewed either the current or previous edition of our text:

Richard Anderson-Sprecher
University of Wyoming

James E. Arnold
University of Wisconsin–Milwaukee

Bill Aslan
Texas A & M–Commerce

James K. Bidwell
Central Michigan University

James R. Boone
Texas A & M University

Peter Braunfeld
University of Illinois–Urbana

Jane Buerger
Concordia College

Louis J. Chatterley
Brigham Young University

Phyllis Chinn
Humboldt State University

Lynn Cleary
University of Maryland

Max Coleman
Sam Houston State University

Lynn D. Darragh
San Juan College

Allen Davis
Eastern Illinois University

Gary A. Deatsman
West Chester University

Sheila Doran
Xavier University

Arlene Dowshen
Widener University

Stephen Drake
Northwestern Michigan College

Joseph C. Ferrar
Ohio State University

Marjorie A. Fitting
San Jose State University

Gina Foletta
Northern Kentucky University

Grace Peterson Foster
Beaufort County Community College

Fay Jester
Pennsylvania State University

Wilburn C. Jones
Western Kentucky University

Jane Keiser
Miami University

Mark Klespis
Sam Houston State University

Martha Ann Larkin
Southern Utah University

Charlotte K. Lewis
University of New Orleans

Jim Loats
Metropolitan State College of Denver

Jennifer Luebeck
Sheridan College

Eldon L. Miller
University of Mississippi

F.A. Norman
University of North Carolina–Charlotte

Jon Odell
Richland Community College

Anthony Piccolino
Montclair State College

Buddy Pierce
Southeastern Oklahoma University

Jane Pinnow
University of Wisconsin–Parkside

Jane M. Rood
Eastern Illinois University

Lisa M. Scheuerman
Eastern Illinois University

Carol J. Steiner
Kent State University

Many of the best aspects of the book are due to the creative suggestions of others. Also, we would especially like to thank Aron Cummings who helped prepare the graphing calculator programs. We assume all responsibility for the weaknesses and errors that may unfortunately remain in the text. We hope these are few in number and earnestly request that users of this text write or call with suggestions for improvements and corrections of errors.

Calvin Long can be reached at 2120 N. Timberline Road, Flagstaff, AZ 86004-7548; 520-527-4047. Duane DeTemple can be reached at the Department of Pure and Applied Mathematics, Washington State University, Pullman, WA 99164–3113, 509-335-3161. Our e-mail addresses are ctl@bmol.com and detemple@wsu.edu

C.T.L.

D.W.D.

About the Authors

Both Calvin Long and Duane DeTemple have been extensively involved in mathematics education throughout their careers. They have taught the content for elementary teachers at Washington State University for many years. In addition, they have served as invited speakers at international, national, and regional mathematics education meetings; conducted extensive in-service programs for elementary, middle school, and high school teachers; taught in and directed numerous summer institutes designed for teachers; served as educational consultants to publishers, to the National Science Foundation, to the National Assessment of Educational Progress, to the State Superintendent of Public Instruction, and other organizations; and served on numerous committees of the National Council of Teachers of Mathematics and the Mathematical Association of America. Calvin Long also served on NCTM and MAA committees that drew up guidelines for the preparation for teachers of mathematics.

TO THE STUDENT

You may be wondering what to expect from a college course in mathematics for prospective elementary school teachers. Will this course simply repeat arithmetic and other material that you already know, or will the subject matter be new and interesting? We will try to answer that question here and at the same time provide a useful orientation to the text.

Problem Solving and Mathematical Reasoning

The entire first chapter of this text is devoted to developing skills in problem solving and critical thinking, and this theme is continued throughout the book. At first, problem solving may seem daunting, but as you gain experience and begin to acquire an arsenal of strategies, you will become increasingly comfortable and will begin to find the challenge of solving a unique problem stimulating and even fun. Quite often, and much to their surprise, this has been the experience of students in our classes as they successfully match wits with challenging problems and gain insight that leads to even more success.

You should not expect to see instantly to the heart of a problem or to know immediately how it can be solved. This text contains many exercises that check your understanding of basic concepts and build basic skills, but you will continually encounter problems characterized by the following couplet.

Problems worthy of attack
prove their worth by hitting back

These problems are not unreasonably hard (indeed, many would be suitable with only a minor modification for use in classes you will subsequently teach). However, they do require thought. Expect to try a variety of approaches, be willing to discuss possibilities with your classmates, and form a study group to engage in cooperative problem solving. Don't be afraid to try and perhaps fail, but then try again. This is the way mathematics is done, even by professionals, and as you gain experience you will increasingly experience the real pleasure of success. Also, you will greatly improve your thinking and problem-solving skills if you take time to write carefully worded solutions that explain your methods and reasoning. Similarly, it will help to engage in verbal mathematical discourse with your instructor and with other students. Finally, remember as little as possible, but be able to figure out as much as possible. Mechanical skills learned by rote without understanding are soon forgotten and guarantee failure, both for you now, and for your students later. Conversely, the ability to think creatively makes it more likely that the task can be successfully completed.

How to Read This Book

> *Mathematics is not a spectator sport.*
> *Learning is an inside job.*

No mathematics textbook can be read passively. To understand the concepts and to benefit from the examples, you must be an active participant in a dialog with the text. Often this means you need to check a calculation, make a drawing, take a measurement, construct a model, or use a calculator or computer. If you first attempt to answer questions raised in the examples on your own, the solutions written in the text will be more meaningful and useful than they would be without your personal involvement.

Many of the problems are fully or partially answered in the back of the book, including all of the Chapter Review problems and Chapter Test problems. This gives you an additional source of worked examples, but again you will benefit most fully by attempting to solve the problems on your own (or in a study group) before you check your reasoning by looking up the answer provided in the text. Other special features are described earlier in the Preface for this book.

CHAPTER

1

Thinking Critically

1.1 Some Surprising Tidbits

1.2 An Introduction to Problem Solving

1.3 Pólya's Problem-Solving Principles

1.4 More Problem-Solving Strategies

1.5 Additional Problem-Solving Strategies

1.6 Problem Solving in the Real World

HANDS ON

One Sided Paper

Materials Needed

1.   At least six strips of adding machine tape about 2 feet long for each student.
2.   Scotch tape and scissors for each student.

Directions

Step 1. Take two of the strips. Give each strip a half twist and tape its two ends together to form a loop as shown. These two loops are called **Möbius strips.**

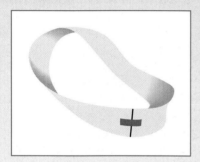

Step 2. Draw a line down the middle of one of the strips stopping only when there is a unique and compelling reason to do so. How many sides does the strip have?

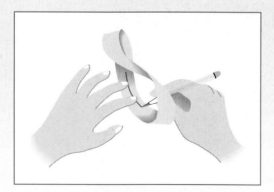

Step 3. Cut a notch out of one edge of the strip used in Step 2 and two notches out of the other edge as shown. Decide if these notches are really cut out of opposite edges of the strip. (*Hint:* Think of what was done in Step 2.)

Step 4. Use the scissors to cut the strip of Step 3 in half lengthwise as shown. Are you surprised at the result?

Step 5. Predict what will happen if you cut the second Möbius strip lengthwise as in Step 4 but one-third of the way in from one edge. Now make the cut. Are you surprised again?

Step 6. Möbius strips are not just curiosities. If you had a belt twisted to form a Möbius strip running over pulleys as shown, would it last longer than an untwisted belt? Why or why not?

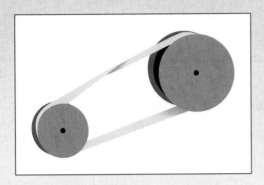

Step 7. Now start again and make two strips of adding machine tape into untwisted loops taped together at right angles as shown. Cut both strips in half lengthwise. Are you surprised at the result?

Step 8. Repeat Step 7 but make several twists in the second strip before taping it into a loop. Again cut both strips in half. Are you again surprised at the result? Try it again with a different number of twists in the second strip.

Connections   Mathematics Is Problem Solving

One of the most prominent features of current efforts to reform and revitalize mathematics instruction in American schools is the recommendation that such instruction should stress problem solving and quantitative reasoning. That this emphasis continues is borne out by the fact that it appeared as **Standard 1** in the document *Curriculum and Evaluation Standards for School Mathematics* published by the National Council of Teachers of Mathematics (NCTM) in 1989 and as **Standard 6,** the first of the process standards, in the draft form of NCTM's *Principles and Standards for School Mathematics,* expected to be published in the year 2000. The conviction is that children need to learn to *think* about quantitative situations in insightful and imaginative ways, and that mere rote memorization of seemingly arbitrary rules for computation is largely unproductive.

from The NCTM Principles and Standards

Standard 6: Problem Solving

Mathematics instructional programs should focus on solving problems as part of understanding mathematics so that all students—

- build new mathematical knowledge through their work with problems;
- develop a disposition to formulate, represent, abstract, and generalize in situations within and outside mathematics;
- apply a wide variety of strategies to solve problems and adapt the strategies to new situations;
- monitor and reflect on their mathematical thinking in solving problems.

Elaboration: Pre-K–12

The ability to solve problems is not only a purpose for learning mathematics but also a major means of doing so. As students use problem-solving approaches in their investigations of mathematical content, they can develop new mathematical understandings and strengthen their abilities to use the mathematics that they know. Problem solving means engaging in a task for which the solution method is not known in advance. In order to find a solution, students must use their knowledge in different ways and, through this process, may develop new knowledge. Problem solving is an integral part of all mathematics learning, not an isolated part of the mathematics program. It should be a well-integrated part of the curriculum that supports the development of mathematical understanding. Students should have frequent opportunities to formulate, grapple with, and solve complex problems that require a significant amount of effort.

Problem-solving strategies are part of a student's mathematical tool kit. When a solution to a problem is not readily available, students will benefit from having a repertoire of strategies available to help them make progress. Problem-solving strategies should be treated like any part of the mathematical tool kit. Students should be provided with enough instruction in, and practice with, a range of strategies to enable them to use them. Their use must be embedded in the curriculum so that students develop skill at recognizing when various strategies are appropriate to use and are capable of deciding when and how to use them.

SOURCE: Reprinted with permission from *Curriculum and Evaluation Standards for School Mathematics: Discussion Draft*, copyright 1998 by the National Council of Teachers of Mathematics. All rights reserved.

Of course, if children are to learn problem solving, their teachers must themselves be competent problem solvers and teachers of problem solving. Professor Robert Davis, a prominent mathematics educator, once said, "All too often we involve our students in a rhetoric of conclusions when, in fact, we ought to be involving them in a rhetoric of inquiry." This is true not only of elementary and secondary school students, but of college students as well. Thus, the purpose of this chapter, and indeed of this entire book, is to help you to think more critically and thoughtfully about mathematics, and to be more comfortable with mathematical reasoning and discourse.

We begin with some "mathematical tidbits" that we hope you will find interesting and surprising. You may also find many of these tidbits useful in your own classroom.

After the tidbits, we spend the remainder of the chapter studying problem-solving strategies, and how to use them to solve problems. Strategies for problem solving are legion, and we cannot begin to discuss them all in a single chapter. However, we introduce the most basic strategies, which you will be able to use and refine as you continue your study of this book.

1.1   Some Surprising Tidbits

Tidbit Number 1

Follow these directions.

> For example, May would be 5.

Step 1. Write down the number of the month in which you were born.
Step 2. Double the number in Step 1.

Step 3. Add 5 to the result of Step 2.
Step 4. Multiply the result of Step 3 by 50.
Step 5. Subtract 250 from the present year.
Step 6. Add the result from Step 5 to the result from Step 4.
Step 7. Subtract the year of your birth from the result from Step 6.
Step 8. Circle the last two digits of the result from Step 7. The circled number should give your age on your birthday this year!
Step 9. The uncircled part of the number from Step 8 should be the number of your birth month!

Did the process work? Are you somewhat puzzled? Surprised? Pleased? Do you think your future students might find this trick interesting?

Tidbit Number 2

Let's try another one.

> A digit is one of
> 0, 1, 2, 3, 4, 5, 6, 7, 8, or 9.

Step 1. Write down your favorite digit.
Step 2. Multiply your favorite digit by 101.
Step 3. Multiply 110011 by the result from Step 2. (Use a calculator if you like.)

Are you surprised at the result? Do you think this will always work? Perhaps you should try a different favorite digit. Compute 101×110011. Clearly 101 and 110011 are "magic" numbers. Are 73 and 152207 "magic"?

Tidbit Number 3

See how quickly you can perform each of these multiplications. (Use a calculator if you like.)

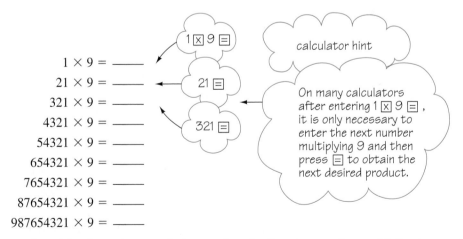

$1 \times 9 =$ _____
$21 \times 9 =$ _____
$321 \times 9 =$ _____
$4321 \times 9 =$ _____
$54321 \times 9 =$ _____
$654321 \times 9 =$ _____
$7654321 \times 9 =$ _____
$87654321 \times 9 =$ _____
$987654321 \times 9 =$ _____

calculator hint

On many calculators after entering 1 ⨯ 9 ⊟, it is only necessary to enter the next number multiplying 9 and then press ⊟ to obtain the next desired product.

Neat, isn't it? All you have to do is complete the first three or four multiplications and notice the emerging pattern. But the pattern only suggests; it may not continue as you expect. You may want to check your guess by calculating the last product. Can you do this on your calculator? (Some calculators have too little display space.) Is the result what you expected? How about 10987654321×9?

Tidbit Number 4

Draw two nonparallel nonintersecting line segments and three points on each segment labeled as shown.

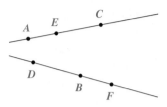

Consider the three *X*s formed by the line segments $\overline{AB}$ and $\overline{DE}$, $\overline{EF}$ and $\overline{BC}$, and $\overline{AF}$ and $\overline{DC}$. Let *P*, *Q*, and *R* be the "centers" of these *X*s. What appears to be the case about points *P*, *Q*, and *R*?

The exercise set that follows contains more surprising examples. Elementary students enjoy problems like these and teachers report that using such activities in their classes helps to create interest and enthusiasm for doing mathematics that were missing before.

This is not to say that mathematics is all "fun and games." It requires diligence and perseverance, but the effort need not be distasteful. Mathematics is full of unexpected and pleasing results that will continually excite and interest both you and your students. As a student in this course, you are preparing to teach. You want to teach well and with success. Experience and research have shown that you are much more likely to succeed if you are confident in the subject matter you teach and actually find it pleasing and personally satisfying.

PROBLEM SET 1.1

In doing these problems the use of calculators is encouraged. Problem numbers in color indicate that the answer to the problem can be found at the back of the book.

1. (a) Compute the products:

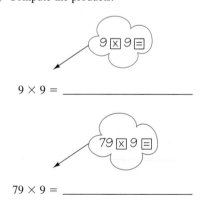

$9 \times 9 =$ _____

$79 \times 9 =$ _____

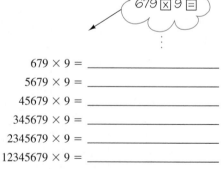

$679 \times 9 =$ _____

$5679 \times 9 =$ _____

$45679 \times 9 =$ _____

$345679 \times 9 =$ _____

$2345679 \times 9 =$ _____

$12345679 \times 9 =$ _____

(b) Did you have to complete all the multiplications in part (a) to be pretty sure you knew what all the answers would be? Explain in two *carefully* written sentences.

2. (a) Perform these computations being careful to multiply first and then add.

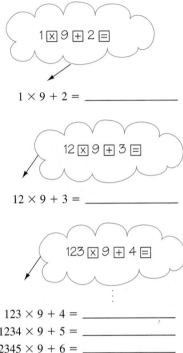

$1 \times 9 + 2 = $ _____

$12 \times 9 + 3 = $ _____

$123 \times 9 + 4 = $ _____
$1234 \times 9 + 5 = $ _____
$12345 \times 9 + 6 = $ _____
$123456 \times 9 + 7 = $ _____
$1234567 \times 9 + 8 = $ _____
$12345678 \times 9 + 9 = $ _____
$123456789 \times 9 + 10 = $ _____

(b) Did you have to complete all the work in part (a) to be pretty sure you knew all the answers? Explain in two *carefully* written sentences.

3. (a) Perform these computations:

$1 \times 8 + 1 = $ _____
$12 \times 8 + 2 = $ _____
$123 \times 8 + 3 = $ _____

(b) Guess the results of these computations:

$1234 \times 8 + 4 = $ _____
$123456789 \times 8 + 9 = $ _____

(c) Check the last answer to part (b) by some means.

4. (a) The numbers 3 and 37,037 are "magic." Pick your favorite digit from among 1, 2, . . . , 9 and multiply it by 3. Now multiply the result by 37,037. What is the result?

(b) Are 13 and 8547 "magic"?

(c) Find two other pairs of "magic" numbers.
   (*Hint:* Compute 3 × 37,037 and 13 × 8547.)

5. (a) Compute these products:

$67 \times 67 = $ _____
$667 \times 667 = $ _____
$6667 \times 6667 = $ _____

(b) Guess the result of multiplying 6,666,667 by itself. Are you sure your guess is correct? Explain in one *carefully* written sentence.

6. (a) This is a magic square. Compute the sums of the numbers in each row, column, and diagonal of the square and write your answers in the appropriate circles.

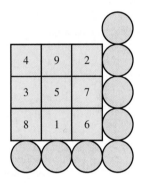

(b) Interchange the 2 and 8 and the 4 and 6 in the array in part (a) to create this magic *subtraction* square. Add the two end entries and subtract the middle entry from this sum for each row, column, and diagonal.

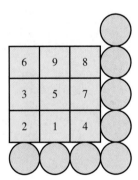

7. (a) Write the digits 0, 1, 2, 3, 4, 5, 6, 7, and 8 in the small squares to create another magic square. (*Hint:* Relate this to problem 6. Also, you may want to write these digits on nine small squares that you can move around easily to check various possibilities.)

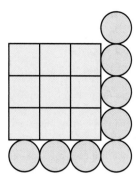

(b) Make a magic subtraction square using the numbers 0, 1, 2, 3, 4, 5, 6, 7, 8.

8. Flow charts are frequently used in computer science since they make it possible to chart a sequence of operations or events in a visual format that is easily followed and understood.

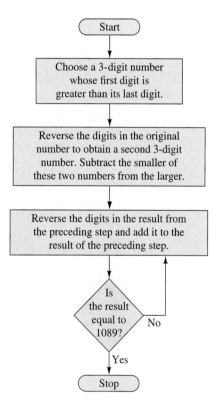

(a) Follow the steps indicated by this flow chart. All the work can be done on your calculator without writing anything down, though you may find it interesting to record the result of each step. Repeat the process with several different starting numbers.

(b) Do you believe that the process always stops? Explain briefly.

GARFIELD by Jim Davis © 1989 United Feature Syndicate, Inc. All Rights Reserved.

9. **(a)** Compute these products:

$1 \times 1089 = $ _____

$2 \times 1089 = $ _____

$3 \times 1089 = $ _____

$4 \times 1089 = $ _____

$5 \times 1089 = $ _____

$6 \times 1089 = $ _____

$7 \times 1089 = $ _____

$8 \times 1089 = $ _____

$9 \times 1089 = $ _____

(b) Did you have to compute all the products in part (a) to be pretty sure you knew what all the answers would be? Explain briefly.

(c) Do you see any other interesting patterns in part (a)? Explain briefly.

10. **(a)** Compute these products:

$1 \times 142857 = $ _____

$2 \times 142857 = $ _____

$3 \times 142857 = $ _____

$4 \times 142857 = $ _____

$5 \times 142857 = $ _____

(b) Predict the product of 6 and 142857. Now calculate the product and see if your prediction was correct.

(c) Predict the result of multiplying 7 times 142857, then compute this product.

(d) What does part (c) suggest about apparent patterns? Explain.

11. (a) Compute these products:

1 × 76923	4 × 76923	5 × 76923
9 × 76923	10 × 76923	11 × 76923
12 × 76923	2 × 76923	6 × 76923
3 × 76923	7 × 76923	8 × 76923

(b) Compute 13 × 76923.

(c) What patterns do you see in part (a)? Explain briefly but carefully.

12. (a) Using the bottom of a paper cup as a pattern, *very carefully* draw a circle and place six points on it labeled as shown here. Draw the chords $\overline{AB}$, $\overline{BC}$, $\overline{CD}$, $\overline{DE}$, $\overline{EF}$, and $\overline{FA}$. Let P, Q, and R be the points of intersection of $\overline{AB}$ and $\overline{DE}$, $\overline{BC}$ and $\overline{EF}$, and $\overline{CD}$ and $\overline{FA}$, respectively. What seems to be true of the points P, Q, and R?

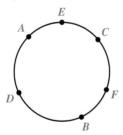

(b) Would the result of part (a) still hold if the six points were labeled in a different order? Try some cases being careful to locate the points so that the line segments, or their extensions if needed, intersect on the paper on which you are drawing.

13. Draw three line segments l, m, and n from a common point O and draw two triangles $\triangle ABC$ and $\triangle A'B'C'$ with corresponding vertices on l, m, and n respectively as shown. Let P, Q, and R be the points where the lines $\overleftrightarrow{AB}$ and $\overleftrightarrow{A'B'}$, $\overleftrightarrow{AC}$ and $\overleftrightarrow{A'C'}$, and $\overleftrightarrow{BC}$ and $\overleftrightarrow{B'C'}$ respectively intersect. What seems to be true about P, Q, and R?

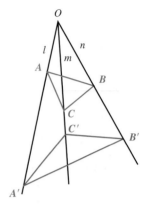

14. Use a quarter as a pattern to *very carefully* draw a circle and use a ruler or straightedge to draw six tangent lines l, m, n, o, p, and q that form a hexagon around the circle, as shown below. Let A, B, C, D, E, and F respectively be the points where the consecutive tangent lines l and m, m and n, n and o, o and p, p and q, and q and l respectively intersect. What appears to be true about the line segments $\overline{AD}$, $\overline{BE}$, and $\overline{CF}$?

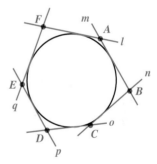

The next four problems can all be done automatically on a graphing calculator like the TI-73 using programs available in Appendix C. This technology enables you to do many examples in just a few minutes. However, in each case, it is instructive to do one or two examples by hand or using a simple calculator like the TI *Math Explorer*.

15. (a) **Sums of Squares of Digits.** Carry out the activities explained in the flow chart on the next page. You can do this by hand or on a calculator. If you use a calculator, be sure to record your result at each step as shown here. Try this several times. Do you think the process always stops no matter what whole number you start with?

(b) It takes six steps for the process to stop if you start with 98. How many steps are required if you start with 248? with 999? with 9999?

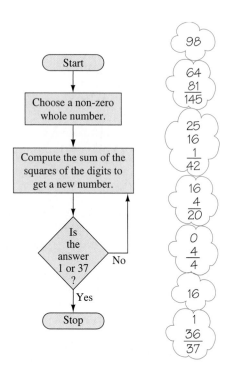

16. (a) Palindromes. A number palindrome is a number like 242 or 3113 that reads the same both forward and backward. A famous palindrome in words, attributed to Napoleon, is "Able was I ere I saw Elba." Complete the activity of this flow chart. This can be done with a calculator. If you use a calculator, be sure to record your results at each step as shown here. Try this several times.

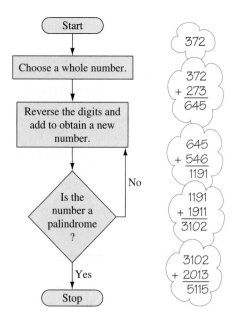

(b) It takes four steps for the process to stop if we start with 372. Will it stop if we start with 98? If so, in how many steps?

(c) Do you think the process will always stop?

17. (a) Kaprekar's Number. Complete this activity. If you use your calculator, be sure to record the intermediate steps as shown here.

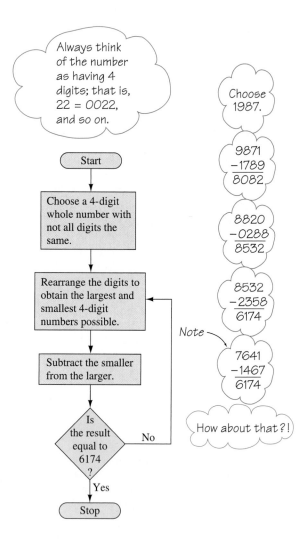

(b) Will the process stop if you start with 1999? If so, in how many steps?

(c) Starting with any 4-digit number, do you think the process will always stop?

(d) What happens if you start with a 3-digit number? A 5-digit number? Explain briefly.

18. (a) **Collatz's Problem.** Complete this activity. This can be done easily on a calculator, but, if you do, be sure to write down all the steps shown as here. Try this for a number of different starting values. Do you think the process will always stop?

    (b) How many steps are required if you start with 9?

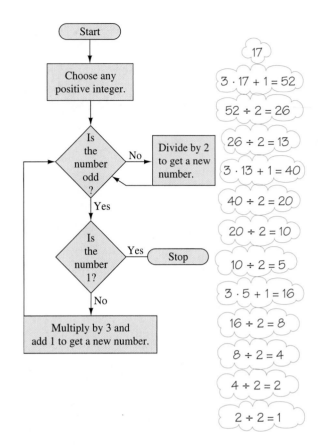

1.2   An Introduction to Problem Solving

When the children arrived in Frank Capek's fifth grade class one day, this "special" problem was on the blackboard.

> Old MacDonald had a total of 37 chickens and pigs on his farm. All together they had 98 feet. How many chickens were there and how many pigs?

After organizing the children into problem-solving teams, Mr. Capek asked them to solve the problem. "Special" problems were always fun and the children got right to work. Let's listen in on the group with Mary, Joe, Carlos, and Sue.

> "I'll bet there were 20 chickens and 17 pigs," said Mary.
> "Let's see," said Joe. "If you're right there are 2×20 or 40 chicken feet and 4×17 or 68 pigs feet. This gives 108 feet. That's too many feet."
> "Let's try 30 chickens and 7 pigs," said Sue. "This should give us less feet."
> "Hey," said Carlos. "With Mary's guess we got 108 feet and Sue's guess gives us 88 feet. Since 108 is 10 too much and 88 is 10 too few, I'll bet we should guess 25 chickens—just half way between Mary's and Sue's guesses!"

These children are using a **guess and check** strategy. If their guess gives an answer that is too large or too small they adjust the guess to get a smaller or larger answer as needed. This can be a very effective strategy. By the way, is Carlos's guess right? Let's look in on another group.

"Let's make a table," says Nandita. "We've had good luck that way before."

"Right, Nani," responded Ann. "Let's see. If we start with 20 chickens and 17 pigs, we have 2 × 20 or 40 chicken feet and 4 × 17 or 68 pig feet. If we have 21 chickens . . . "

> This is a powerful refinement of guess and check.

Chickens	Pigs	Chicken Feet	Pig Feet	Total
20	17	40	68	108
21	16	42	64	106
22	15	44	60	104
.	.	.	.	.
.	.	.	.	.
.	.	.	.	.

Making a table to look for a pattern is often an excellent strategy. Do you think the group with Nandita and Ann will soon find a solution? How many more rows of the table will they have to fill in? Can you think of a shortcut?

Mike says, "Let's draw a picture. We can draw 37 circles for heads and put two lines under each circle to represent feet. Then we can add two extra feet under enough circles to make 98. That should do it."

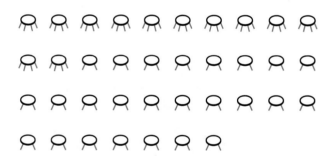

Drawing a picture is often a good strategy. Does it work in this case?

JUST FOR FUN

For Careful Readers

1. Two engineers were standing on a street corner. The first engineer was the second engineer's father but the second engineer was not the first engineer's son. How could this be?

2. If an electric train is traveling 40 miles an hour due west and a wind of 30 miles per hour is blowing due east, which way is the smoke from the train blowing?

3. At noon a rope ladder with rungs 1 foot apart is hanging over the side of the ship and the 12th rung down is even with the water surface. Later, after the tide has risen 3 feet, which rung of the ladder is just even with the surface of the water?

"Oh! The problem is easy," says Jennifer. "If we have all the pigs stand on their hind legs then there are 2×37 or 74 feet touching the ground. That means the pigs must be holding 24 front feet up in the air. This means there must be 12 pigs and 25 chickens!"

It helps if you can be ingenious like Jennifer, but it is not essential, and children *can* be taught strategies like

Guess and check

Make a table

Look for a pattern

Draw a picture

Other useful strategies will be discussed later but for now let's try some problems on our own.*

EXAMPLE 1.1 **Guessing Toni's Number**

Toni is thinking of a number. If you double the number and add 11, the result is 39. What number is Toni thinking of?

Solution 1 Guessing and Checking

Guess 10.	$2 \cdot 10 + 11 = 20 + 11 = 31.$	This is too small.
Guess 20.	$2 \cdot 20 + 11 = 40 + 11 = 51.$	This is too large.
Guess 15.	$2 \cdot 15 + 11 = 30 + 11 = 41.$	This is a bit large.
Guess 14.	$2 \cdot 14 + 11 = 28 + 11 = 39.$	This checks!

Toni's number must be 14.

Solution 2 Making a Table and Looking for a Pattern

Trial Number	Result Using Toni's Rule	
5	$2 \cdot 5 + 11 = 21$	
6	$2 \cdot 6 + 11 = 23$	2 larger
7	$2 \cdot 7 + 11 = 25$	2 larger
8	$2 \cdot 8 + 11 = 27$	2 larger
.	.	.
.	.	.
.	.	.

We need to get to 39 and we jump by 2 each time we take a step of 1. Therefore, we need to take

$$\frac{39 - 27}{2} = \frac{12}{2} = 6$$

more steps; we should guess $8 + 6 = 14$ as Toni's number as before.

---

*Note that algebra students might solve this problem by solving the equation $2x + 4(37 - x) = 98$ where x denotes the number of chickens. But this approach is not available to fifth graders and it is certainly not as quick as Jennifer's solution!

EXAMPLE   1.2 | **Guessing and Checking**

(a) Place the digits 1, 2, 3, 4, and 5 in these circles so that the sums across and vertically are the same. Is there more than one solution?

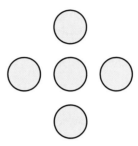

(b) Can part (a) be accomplished if 2 is placed in the center? Why or why not?

Solution

(a) Using the guess and check strategy, suppose we put the 3 in the center circle. Since the sums across and down must be the same, we must pair the remaining numbers so that they have equal sums. But this is easy since $1 + 5 = 2 + 4$. Thus, one solution to the problem is as shown here.

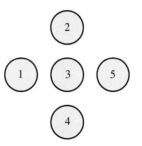

Checking further, we find other solutions like these.

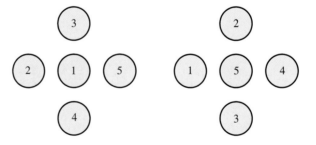

(b) What about putting 2 in the center? The remaining digits are 1, 3, 4, and 5 and these cannot be grouped into two pairs with equal sums since one sum is necessarily odd and the other even. Therefore, there is no solution with 2 in the center circle.

PROBLEM SET 1.2

1. Levinson's Hardware has a number of bikes and trikes for sale. There are 27 seats and 60 wheels all told. Determine how many bikes there are and how many trikes.

   (a) Use the guess and check strategy to find a solution.

   (b) Complete this table to find a solution.

Bikes	Trikes	Bike Wheels	Trike Wheels	Total
17	10	34	30	64
18	9	36	27	63
.	.	.	.	.
.	.	.	.	.
.	.	.	.	.

   (c) Find a solution by completing this diagram.

   (d) Would Jennifer's method work for this problem? Explain briefly.

2. (a) Mr. Aiken has 32 18-cent and 27-cent stamps all told. The stamps are worth $7.65. How many of each kind of stamp does he have?

   (b) Summarize your solution method in one or two *carefully* written sentences.

3. Make up a problem similar to problems 1 and 2.

4. (a) Place the digits 4, 6, 7, 8, and 9 in the circles to make the sum across and vertically equal 19.

   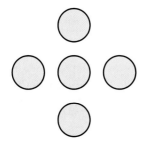

   (b) Is there more than one answer to part (a)? Explain briefly.

5. Who am I? If you multiply me by 5 and subtract 8, the result is 52.

6. Who am I? If you multiply me by 15 and add 28, the result is 103.

7. Make up a problem like problems 5 and 6.

8. Melissa Dietz has nine coins with a total value of 48 cents. What coins does Melissa have?

9. (a) Using each of 1, 2, 3, 4, 5, and 6 once and only once, fill in the circles so that the sums of the numbers on each of the three sides of the triangle are equal.

   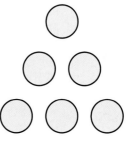

   (b) Does part (a) have more than one solution?

   (c) Write up a brief but careful description of the thought process you used in solving this problem.

10. In this diagram, the sum of any two horizontally adjacent numbers is the number immediately below and between them. Using the same rule of formation, complete these arrays.

   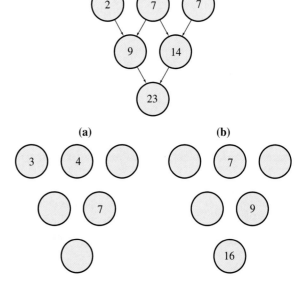

(c)

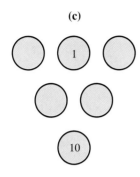

(d) Is there more than one solution to part (a), (b), or (c)?

11. Study the sample diagram. Note that

$$2 + 8 = 10,$$
$$5 + 3 = 8,$$
$$2 + 5 = 7,$$
$$3 + 8 = 11.$$

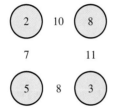

If possible, complete each of these diagrams so that the same pattern holds.

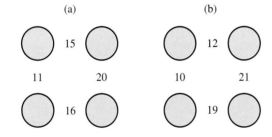

(c) 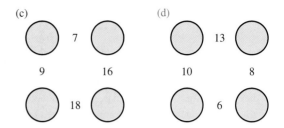 **(d)**

12. Study this sequence of numbers: 3, 4, 7, 11, 18, 29, 47, 76. Note that $3 + 4 = 7, 4 + 7 = 11, 11 + 18 = 29$, and so on. Use the same rule to complete these sequences.

(a) 1, 2, 3, _____, _____, _____, _____

(b) 2, _____, 8, _____, _____, _____, _____

(c) 3, _____, _____, 13, _____, _____, _____

(d) 2, _____, _____, _____, _____, 26

(e) 2, _____, _____, _____, _____, 11

13. **(a)** Use each of the numbers 2, 3, 4, 5, and 6 once and only once to fill in the circles so that the sum of the numbers in the three horizontal circles equals the sum of the numbers in the three vertical circles.

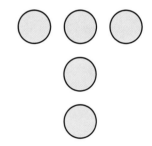

(b) Can you find more than one solution?

(c) Can you have a solution with 3 in the middle of the top row? Explain in two *carefully* written sentences.

14. Make up a guess and check problem of your own and solve it.

1.3   Pólya's Problem-Solving Principles

Strategies

- *Guess and check.*
- *Make an orderly list.*
- *Draw a diagram.*

In *How to Solve It**, George Pólya identifies four principles that form the basis for any serious attempt at problem solving. He then proceeds to develop an extensive list of questions that teachers should ask students who need help in solving a problem, questions students can and should ask themselves as they seek solutions to problems.

_____

*George Pólya, *How to Solve it* (Princeton, N.J.: Princeton University Press, 1988.)

Pólya's First Principle: Understand the problem

This principle seems so obvious that it need not be mentioned. However, students are often stymied in their efforts to solve a problem because they don't understand it fully, or even in part. Teachers should ask students such questions as:

- Do you understand all the words used in stating the problem? If not, look them up in the index, in a dictionary, or wherever they can be found.
- What are you asked to find or show?
- Can you restate the problem in your own words?
- Is there yet another way to state the problem?
- What does *(key word)* really mean?
- Could you work out some numerical examples that would help make the problem clear?
- Could you think of a picture or diagram that might help you understand the problem?
- Is there enough information to enable you to find a solution?
- Is there extraneous information?
- What do you really need to know to find a solution?

Pólya's Second Principle: Devise a plan

Devising a plan for solving a problem once it is fully understood may still require substantial effort. But don't be afraid to make a start—you may be on the right track. There are often many reasonable ways to try to solve a problem, and the successful idea may emerge only gradually after several unsuccessful trials. A partial list of strategies include:

- guess and check
- make an orderly list
- think of the problem as partially solved
- eliminate possibilities
- solve an equivalent problem
- use symmetry
- consider special cases
- use direct reasoning
- solve an equation
- look for a pattern
- draw a picture
- think of a similar problem already solved
- solve a simpler problem
- solve an analogous problem
- use a model
- work backward
- use a formula
- be ingenious!

Skill at choosing an appropriate strategy is best learned by solving many problems. As you gain experience, you will find choosing a strategy increasingly easy—and the satisfaction of making the right choice and having it work is considerable! Again, teachers can turn the above list of strategies into appropriate questions to ask students in helping them learn the art of problem solving.

Pólya's Third Principle: Carry out a plan

Carrying out the plan is usually easier than devising the plan. In general, all you need is care and patience, given that you have the necessary skills. If a plan does not work immediately, be persistent. If it still doesn't work, discard it and try a new strategy. Don't be misled, this is the way mathematics is done, even by professionals.

HIGHLIGHT FROM HISTORY
George Pólya (1887–1985)

*H*ow does one most effi-
ciently proceed to solve a
problem? Can the art
of problem solving be taught or is it a
talent possessed by only a select few?
Over the years, many have thought
about these questions but none so
effectively and definitively as the late
George Pólya, and he maintained that
the skill of problem solving can be
taught.

Pólya was born in Hungary in 1887
and received his Ph.D. in mathematics
from the University of Budapest. He
taught for many years at the Swiss
Federal Institute of Technology in

Zurich and would no doubt have continued to do so but for the advent of
Nazism in Germany. Deeply concerned
by this threat to civilization, Pólya
moved to the United States in 1940 and
taught briefly at Brown University and
then, for the remainder of his life, at
Stanford University. He was extraordinarily capable both as a mathematician
and as a teacher. He also maintained a
life-long interest in studying the
thought processes that are productive in
both learning and doing mathematics.
Indeed, among the numerous books
that he wrote he seemed most proud of
How to Solve It (1945), which has sold
nearly one million copies and has been
translated into 17 languages. This
book, along with his two two-volume
treatises, *Mathematics and Plausible
Reasoning* (1954) and *Mathematical*

Discovery (1962), form the definitive
basis for the current thinking in mathematics education and are as timely and
important today as when they were
written.

Pólya's Fourth Principle: Look back

Much can be gained by looking back at a completed solution to analyze your thinking and ascertain just what was the key to solving the problem. This is how we gain "mathematical power," the ability to come up with good ideas for solving problems never
encountered before. The French mathematician and philosopher, Henri Poincaré
(1854–1912), put this rather strongly when he wrote

> *Suppose I apply myself to a complicated calculation and with much difficulty
> arrive at a result. I shall have gained nothing by my trouble if it has not enabled
> me to foresee the results of other analogous calculations, and to direct them with
> certainty, avoiding the blind groping with which I had to be content the first time.*

Clearly, Poincaré felt that merely solving a problem was essentially meaningless if he did
not also gain experience and insight that increased his "mathematical power." Often the
connection between very dissimilar problems is tenuous at best. Yet, in working on a problem, there is something lurking in the back of your mind from a previous effort that says,
"I'll bet if . . . ," and the plan does indeed work!

Questions to ask yourself in looking back after you have successfully solved a problem include:

- What was the key factor that allowed me to devise an effective plan for solving
  this problem?
- Can I think of a simpler strategy for solving this problem?
- Can I think of a more effective or powerful strategy for solving this problem?
- Can I think of *any* alternative strategy for solving this problem?
- Can I think of any other problem or class of problems for which this plan of
  attack would be effective?

Looking back is an often overlooked but extremely important step in developing problem-solving skills.

Let's now look at some examples.

Guess and Check

PROBLEM-SOLVING STRATEGY 1   Guess and Check

Make a guess and check to see if it satisfies the demands of the problem. If it doesn't, alter the guess appropriately and check again. When the guess finally checks, a solution has been found.

Students often feel that it is not "proper" to solve a problem by guessing. And they are right if the guess is not accompanied by a check. However, a process of guessing, checking, altering the guess if it does not check, guessing again in light of the preceding check, and so on, is a legitimate and effective strategy. When a guess finally checks, there can be no doubt that a solution has been found. If we can be sure that there is only one solution, *the* solution has been found. Moreover, the process is often quite efficient and it may be the only approach available.

EXAMPLE   1.3   **Guess and Check**

In the first diagram the numbers in the big circles are found by adding the numbers in the two adjacent smaller circles as shown. Complete the second diagram so that the same pattern holds.

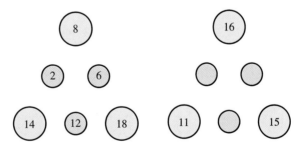

Solution   *Understand the problem*

Considering the example, it is pretty clear that we must find three numbers—a, b, and c—such that

$$a + b = 16,$$
$$a + c = 11,$$
$$b + c = 15.$$

How should we proceed?*

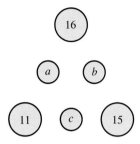

Devise a plan

Let's try the *guess and check* strategy. It worked on several problems somewhat like this in the last problem set. Also, even if the strategy fails, it may at least suggest an approach that will work.

Carry out the plan

We start by guessing a value for *a*. Suppose we guess that *a* is 10. Then, since $a + b$ must be 16, *b* must be 6. Similarly, since $b + c$ must be 15, *c* must be 9. But then $a + c$ is 19 instead of 11 as it is supposed to be. This does not check.

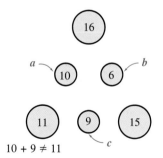

Since 19 is too large, we try again with a smaller guess for *a*. Guess that *a* is 5. Then, *b* is 11 and *c* is 4. But then $a + c$ is 9 and this is too small, but by just a little bit. We should guess that *a* is just a bit larger than 5.

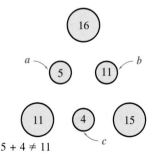

---

*Students who know algebra could solve this system of simultaneous equations, but elementary school students don't know algebra.

Guess that $a = 6$. This implies that b is 10 and c is 5. Now $a + c$ is 11 as desired and we have the solution.

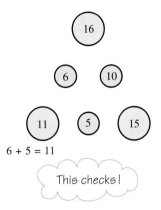

$6 + 5 = 11$

This checks!

Look back

Guess and check worked fine. Our first choice of 10 for a was too large so we chose a smaller value. Our second choice of 5 was too small, but quite close. Choosing $a = 6$, which was between 10 and 5 but quite near 5, we obtained a solution that checked. Surely this approach would work equally well on other similar problems.

But wait. Have we fully understood this problem? Might there be an easier solution?

Look back at the initial example and also at the completed solution to the problem. Do you see any special relationship between the numbers in the large circles and those in the small circles?

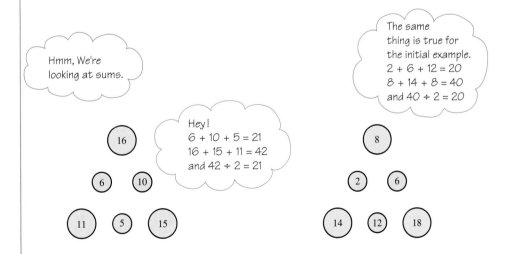

Hmm, We're looking at sums.

Hey!
$6 + 10 + 5 = 21$
$16 + 15 + 11 = 42$
and $42 \div 2 = 21$

The same thing is true for the initial example.
$2 + 6 + 12 = 20$
$8 + 14 + 8 = 40$
and $40 \div 2 = 20$

That's interesting; the sum of the numbers in the small circles in each case is just half the sum of the numbers in the large circles. Could we use this to find another solution method?

Sure! Since $16 + 15 + 11 = 42$ and $a + b + c$ is half as much, $a + b + c = 21$. But $a + b = 16$, so c must equal 5; that is,

$$c = 21 - 16 = 5$$
$$b = 21 - 11 = 10, \quad \text{and}$$
$$a = 21 - 15 = 6.$$

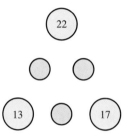

This is much easier than our first solution and, for that matter, the algebraic solution. Quickly now, does it work on this diagram? Try it.

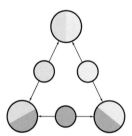

But there's one more thing. Do you understand *why* the sum of the numbers in the little circles equals half the sum of the numbers in the big circles? This diagram might help.

Make an Orderly List

PROBLEM-SOLVING STRATEGY 2   **Make an Orderly List**

For problems that require consideration of many possibilities, make an orderly list or a table to make sure that no possibilities are missed.

Sometimes a problem is sufficiently involved that the task of sorting out all the possibilities seems quite forbidding. Often these problems can be solved by making a carefully structured list so that you can be sure that all of the data and all of the cases have been considered. Consider the next example.

EXAMPLE 1.4

Make an Orderly List

How many different total scores could you make if you hit the dart board shown with three darts?

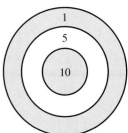

Solution

Understand the problem

Three darts hit the dart board and each scores a 1, 5, or 10. The total score is the sum of the scores for the three darts. There could be three 1s, two 1s and a 5, one 5 and two 10s, and so on. The fact that we are told to find the total score when throwing three darts at a dart board is just a way of asking what sums can be made using three numbers, each of which is either 1, 5, or 10.

It's often helpful to restate the problem in a different way.

Devise a plan

If we just write down sums hit or miss, we will almost surely overlook some of the possibilities. Using an orderly scheme instead, we can make sure that we obtain all possible scores. Let's make such a list. We first list the score if we have three 1s, then two 1s and one 5, then two 1s and no 5s, and so on. In this way, we can be sure that no score is missed.

Carry out the plan

Number of 1s	Number of 5s	Number of 10s	Total score
3	0	0	3
2	1	0	7
2	0	1	12
1	2	0	11
1	1	1	16
1	0	2	21
0	3	0	15
0	2	1	20
0	1	2	25
0	0	3	30

The possible total scores are listed.

Look back

Here the key to the solution was in being very systematic. We were careful first to obtain all possible scores with three 1s, then two 1s, then no 1s. With two 1s there could be either a 5 or a 10 as shown. For one 1 the only possibilities are two 5s and no 10s, one 5 and one 10, or no 5s and two 10s. Constructing the table in this orderly way makes it clear that we have not missed any possibilities.

Draw a Diagram

PROBLEM-SOLVING STRATEGY 3   Draw a Diagram

Draw a diagram or picture that represents the data of a problem as accurately as possible.

The aphorism "a picture is worth a thousand words" is certainly applicable to solving many problems. Language used to describe situations and state problems often can be clarified by drawing a suitable diagram, and unforeseen relationships and properties often become clear. As with the problem of the pigs and chickens on Old MacDonald's farm, even problems that do not appear to have pictorial relationships can sometimes be solved using this technique. Would you immediately draw a picture in attempting to solve the problem in the next example? Some would and some wouldn't, but it's surely the most efficient approach.

EXAMPLE   1.5   Draw a Diagram

In a stock car race the first five finishers in some order were a Ford, a Pontiac, a Chevrolet, a Buick, and a Dodge.

(a) The Ford finished seven seconds before the Chevrolet.

(b) The Pontiac finished six seconds after the Buick.

(c) The Dodge finished eight seconds after the Buick.

(d) The Chevrolet finished two seconds before the Pontiac.

In what order did the cars finish the race?

Solution   *Understand the problem*

We are told how each of the cars finished the race relative to one other car. The question is, "Can we use just this information to determine the order in which the five cars finished the race?"

Devise a plan

Imagine the cars in a line as they race toward the finish. If they do not pass one another, this is the order in which they will finish the race. We can draw a line to represent the track at the finish of the race and place the cars on it according to the conditions of the problem. Mark the line off in time intervals of one second. Then, using the first letter of each car's name to represent the car, see if we can line up B, C, D, F, and P according to the given information.

Carry out the plan

Here is a line with equally spaced points to represent one second time intervals. Pick some point and label it C to represent the Chevrolet's finishing position.

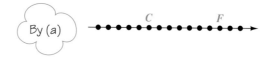

Then *F* is seven seconds ahead of *C* by condition (a) as shown above. Conditions (b) and (c) cannot yet be used since they do not relate to the positions of either *C* or *F*. However, (d) allows us to place *P* two seconds behind (to the left) of *C* as shown.

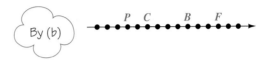

Since (b) relates the finishing position of *B* to *P*, we place *B* six seconds ahead of *P*.

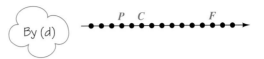

Similarly, (c) relates the finishing positions of *D* and *B* and allows us to place *D* eight seconds behind (to the left) of *B*. Since this accounts for all the cars, a glance at the last diagram reveals the order in which the cars finished the race. We repeatedly drew the line for pedagogical purposes in order to show the placement of the cars as each new condition was used. Ordinarily, all the work would be done on a single line since it is not necessary to show what happens at each stage as we did here.

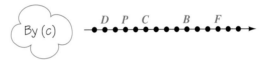

Look back

Like the problem of the pigs and chickens on Old MacDonald's farm, this problem did not immediately suggest drawing a picture. However, having seen pictures used to solve these problems will help you to see how pictures can be used to solve other even vaguely related problems.

PROBLEM SET 1.3

1. Diedre is thinking of a number. If you multiply it by 5 and add 13 you get 48. Could Diedre's number be 10? Why or why not?

2. John is thinking of a number. If you divide it by 2 and add 16, you get 28. What number is John thinking of?

3. Lisa is thinking of a number. If you multiply it by 7 and subtract 4, you get 17. What is the number?

4. Vicky is thinking of a number. Twice the number increased by 1 is 5 less than three times the number. What is the number? (*Hint:* For each guess, compute two numbers and compare.)

5. In Mrs. Garcia's class they sometimes play a game called **Guess My Rule**. The student who is IT makes up a rule for changing one number into another. The other students then call out numbers and the person who is IT tells what number the rule gives back. The first person in the class to guess the rule then becomes IT and gets to make up a new rule.

(a) For Juan's rule the results were:

Numbers chosen	2	5	4	0	8
Numbers Juan gave back	7	22	17	−3	37

Could Juan's rule have been, "multiply the chosen number by 5 and subtract 3?" Could it have been, "reduce the chosen number by 1, multiply the result by 5 and then add 2?" Are these rules really different? Discuss briefly.

(b) For Mary's rule, the results were:

Numbers chosen	3	7	1	0	9
Numbers Mary gave back	10	50	2	1	82

What is Mary's rule?

(c) For Peter's rule, the results were:

Numbers chosen	0	1	2	3	4
Numbers Peter gave back	7	10	13	16	19

Observe that the students began to choose the numbers in order starting with 0. Why is that a good idea? What is Peter's rule?

6. As in Example 1.3, the numbers in the big circles are the sums of the numbers in the two small adjacent circles. Place numbers in the empty circles in each of these arrays so that the same scheme holds.

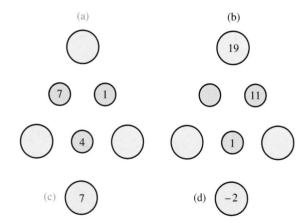

(a)

(b)

(c)

(d)

7. How many different amounts of money can you pay if you use four coins including only nickels, dimes, and quarters?

8. How many different ways can you make change for a 50 cent coin using quarters, nickels, dimes, and pennies?

9. List the 3-digit numbers that can be written using each of the digits 2, 5, and 8 once and only once.

10. List the 4-digit numbers that can be written using each of 1, 3, 5, and 7 once and only once.

11. When Anita made a purchase she gave the clerk a dollar and received 21 cents in change. Complete this table to show what Anita's change could have been.

Number of Dimes	Number of Nickels	Number of Pennies
2	0	1

12. Julie has 25 pearls. She put them in three velvet bags with an odd number of pearls in each bag. What are the possibilities?

13. A rectangle has an area of 120 cm². Its length and width are whole numbers.
    (a) What are the possibilities for the two numbers?
    (b) Which possibility gives the smallest perimeter?

14. The product of two whole numbers is 96 and their sum is less than 30. What are the possibilities for the two numbers?

15. Peter and Jill each worked a different number of days but earned the same amount of money. Use these clues to determine how many days each worked:
    Peter earned $20 a day.
    Jill earned $30 a day.
    Peter worked five more days than Jill.

16. Bob can cut through a log in one minute. How long will it take Bob to cut a 20 foot log into 2-foot sections? (*Hint:* Draw a diagram.)

17. How many posts does it take to support a straight fence 200 feet long if a post is placed every 20 feet?

18. How many posts does it take to support a fence around a square field measuring 200 feet on a side if posts are placed every 20 feet?

19. Albright, Badgett, Chalmers, Dawkins, and Ertl all entered the primary to seek election to the city council. Albright received 2000 more votes than Badgett and 4000 less than Chalmers. Ertl received 2000 votes less than Dawkins and 5000 votes more than Badgett. In what order did each person finish in the balloting?

20. Nine square tiles are laid out on a table so that they make a solid pattern. Each tile must touch at least one other tile along an entire edge. The squares all have sides of length one.

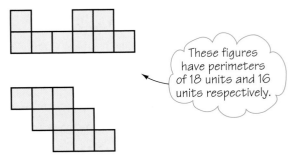

These figures have perimeters of 18 units and 16 units respectively.

(a) What are the possible perimeters of the figures that can be formed? (The perimeter is the distance around the figure.)

(b) Which figure has the least perimeter?

21. A 9 meter by 12 meter rectangular lawn has a concrete walk one meter wide all around it outside the lawn. What is the area of the walk?

From State Student Assessments

22. (Washington State, Grade 4)

Pat needs 30 ounces of chocolate chips to make cookies. He finds the two brands below in a store.

$1.20

$1.75

Pat wants to buy 30 ounces of chocolate chips for the least amount of money. Which is a good first step he could use to solve this problem?

A. Find the total price of the bags he decides to buy.

B. Find how many bags of each brand would be needed.

C. Find the price-per-ounce for each bag.

23. (Washington State, Grade 4)

Four students create their own Good Fitness Games. The students run their fastest and do as many sit-ups and pull-ups as they can. Below are their results.

	50-Meter Dash	Sit-Ups	600-Meter Run	Pull-Ups
Sarah	10 seconds	42	3 minutes, 15 seconds	4
Jan	7 seconds	37	3 minutes, 50 seconds	2
Angel	8 seconds	38	3 minutes, 20 seconds	6
Mike	9 seconds	27	3 minutes, 30 seconds	8

The students want to pick an overall winner. They decide that all the events are equally important. Tell who you think the overall winner is. Explain your thinking using words, numbers, or pictures.

1.4   More Problem-Solving Strategies

Strategies

- *Look for a pattern.*
- *Make a table.*
- *Use a variable.*
- *Consider special cases.*
- *Solve an equivalent problem.*
- *Solve an easier, simpler problem.*
- *Argue from special cases.*

Look for a Pattern

> **PROBLEM-SOLVING STRATEGY 4   Look for a Pattern**
>
> Consider an ordered sequence of particular examples of the general situation described in a problem. Then carefully scrutinize these results, looking for a pattern that may be the key to the problem.

It is no overstatement to assert that this strategy is the most important of all problem-solving strategies. In fact, mathematics is often characterized as the study of patterns, and patterns occur in some form in almost all problem-solving situations. Think about the problems we have already considered and you will see patterns everywhere—numerical patterns, geometrical patterns, counting patterns, listing patterns, rhetorical patterns—patterns of all kinds.

Some problems, like those in the next examples, are plainly pattern problems, but looking for a pattern is almost never a bad way to start solving a problem.

EXAMPLE   1.6 | **Look for Patterns in Numerical Sequences**

Continue these numerical sequences. Fill in the next three blanks in each part.

(a)   1, 4, 7, 10, 13, _____ , _____ , _____

(b)   19, 20, 22, 25, 29, _____ , _____ , _____

(c)   1, 1, 2, 3, 5, _____ , _____ , _____

(d)   1, 4, 9, 16, 25, _____ , _____ , _____

Solution | *Understand the problem*

In each case we are asked to discover a reasonable pattern suggested by the first five numbers and then to continue the pattern for three more terms.

Devise a plan

Questions we might ask ourselves and answer in search of a pattern include: Are the numbers growing steadily larger? Steadily smaller? How is each number related to its predecessor? Is it perhaps the case that a particular term depends on its two predecessors? On its three predecessors? Perhaps each term depends in a special way on the number of the term in the sequence; can we notice any such a dependence? Are the numbers in the sequence somehow special numbers that we recognize? This is rather like playing *Guess My Rule*. Let's see how successful we can be.*

Carry out the plan

In each of (a), (b), (c), and (d) the numbers grow steadily larger. How is each term related to the preceding term or terms in each case? Are the terms related to their numbered place in the sequence? Do they have a special form we can recognize?

(a)   For the sequence in part (a), each number listed is three larger than its predecessor. If this pattern continues, the next three will be 16, 19, and 22.

(b)   Here the numbers increase by 1, by 2, by 3, and by 4. If we continue this scheme, the next three numbers will be 5 more, 6 more, and 7 more than their predecessors. This would give 34, 40, and 47.

(c)   If we use the idea of (a) and (b) for this sequence, we should check how much larger each entry is than its predecessor. The numbers that must be added are *0, 1, 1,* and *2;* that is, $0 + 1 = 1, 1 + 1 = 2, 1 + 2 = 3, 2 + 3 = 5$. This just amounts to adding any two consecutive terms of the sequence to obtain the next term. Continuing this scheme, we obtain 8, 13, and 21.

   The sequence 1, 1, 2, 3, 5, 8, 13, 21, . . . , where we start with 1 and 1 and add any two consecutive terms to obtain the next, is called the **Fibonacci sequence** and the numbers are called the **Fibonacci numbers.** Using function notation, with F_i in place of $F(i)$, we denote the Fibonacci numbers by $F_1 = 1$, $F_2 = 1, F_3 = 2, F_4 = 3,$ . . . , $F_n =$ the nth Fibonacci number and so on. In particular, observe that

---

*Actually, there is a touchy point here. To be strictly accurate, any three numbers you choose in each case can be considered correct. There are actually infinitely many different rules that will give you any first five numbers followed by any three other numbers. What we seek here are relatively simple rules that apply to the given numbers and tell how to obtain the next three in each case.

$$F_3 = 2 = 1 + 1 = F_2 + F_1,$$
$$F_4 = 3 = 2 + 1 = F_3 + F_2,$$
$$F_5 = 5 = 3 + 2 = F_4 + F_3,$$

and so on. In general, any particular entry in the sequence is the sum of its two predecessors. The Fibonacci numbers first appeared in A.D. 1202 in the book *Liber Abaci* by Leonardo of Pisa (Fibonacci), the leading mathematician of the thirteenth century.

(d)   Here 4 is 3 larger than 1, 9 is 5 larger than 4, 16 is 7 larger than 9, and 25 is 9 larger than 16. The terms seem to be increasing by the next largest **odd** number each time. Thus, the next three numbers should probably be $25 + 11 = 36$, $36 + 13 = 49$, and $49 + 15 = 64$. Alternatively, in this case, we may recognize that the numbers 1, 4, 9, 16, and 25 are special numbers. Thus, $1 = 1^2$, $4 = 2^2$, $9 = 3^2$, $16 = 4^2$, and $25 = 5^2$. The sequence appears to be just the sequence of **square numbers.** The 6th, 7th, and 8th terms are just $6^2 = 36$, $7^2 = 49$, and $8^2 = 64$ as before.

Look back

In all four sequences, we checked to see how much larger each number was than its predecessor. In each case we were able to discover a pattern that allowed us to write the next three terms of the sequence. In part (d), we also noted that the first term was 1^2, the second term was 2^2, the third term was 3^2, and so on. Thus, it was reasonable to guess that each term was the square of the number of its position in the sequence. This allowed us to write the next few terms with the same result as before.

We have already seen in earlier examples how making a table is often an excellent strategy, particularly when combined with the strategy of looking for a pattern. Like drawing a picture or making a diagram, making a table often reveals unexpected patterns and relationships that help to solve a problem.

Make a Table

> ### PROBLEM-SOLVING STRATEGY 5   **Make a Table**
>
> Make a table reflecting the data in a problem. If done in an orderly way, such a table will often reveal patterns and relationships that suggest how the problem can be solved.

EXAMPLE   1.7 | **Make a Table**

(a)   Draw the next two diagrams to continue this dot sequence.

_____ , _____

(b)   How many dots are in each figure?

_____ , _____ , _____ , _____ , _____ , _____

(c)   How many dots would be in the one hundredth figure?

(d)   How many dots would be in the one millionth figure?

Chapter 6 Lesson 9

Problem Solving

Compare Strategies: Look for a Pattern and Draw a Picture

You Will Learn

how to solve the same problem using different strategies

Learn

Plan a class picnic for 29 people! Decide how many blankets to bring. Each blanket seats 4 people. How many blankets do you need?

Maura's Way

I made a table and looked for a pattern.

Blankets	People
1	4
2	8
3	12
4	16
5	20
6	24
7	28
8	32

I could bring 7 blankets for 28 people. But 29 people are coming, so I'll need 8 blankets.

Freddy's Way

I drew a picture.

Each square is one blanket.

Each x is one person.

I drew 29 xs. Then I counted to see how many blankets were used.

There were 8 squares. So, I'll need to bring 8 blankets.

Talk About It

1. How did finding a pattern help Maura to solve the problem?

2. How did Freddy's picture help him find an answer?

262 Chapter 6 • More Multiplication Facts

SOURCE: From *Scott Foresman – Addison Wesley Math*, Grade 3, p. 262, by Randall I. Charles et al. Copyright © 1999, Addison Wesley Longman, Inc.

Questions for the Teacher

1. Pose three additional questions you might ask your students if you were teaching this class.

2. You are planning a party for 34 people. You must buy paper plates in packages of 8. How many packages of plates will you need?

(a) Show the table you might make to answer this question.

(b) Show a picture you might draw to answer this question.

Solution

Understand the problem

What is given?

In part (a), we are given an ordered sequence of arrays of dots. We are asked to recognize how the arrays are being formed and to continue the pattern for two more steps. In part (b), we are asked to record the number of dots in each array in part (a). In parts (c) and (d) we are asked to determine specific numerical terms in the sequence of part (b).

Devise a plan

In part (a), we are asked to continue the pattern of a sequence of arrays of dots. As with numerical sequences, our strategy will be to see how each array relates to its predecessor or predecessors hoping to discern a pattern that we can extend 2 more steps.

In part (b), we will simply count and record the numbers of dots in the successive arrays in part (a).

In parts (c) and (d), we will study the numerical sequence of part (b) just as we did in Example 1.6 hoping to discern a pattern and understand it sufficiently well that we can determine its one hundredth and one millionth terms.

Carry out the plan

In part (a), we observe that the arrays of dots are similar but that each one has one more 2-dot column than its predecessor. Thus, the next two arrays are

For part (b), we count the dots in each array of part (a) to obtain

$$1, 3, 5, 7, 9, 11, \cdots$$

These are just the odd numbers, and we could write out the first 1 million odd numbers and so answer parts (c) and (d). But surely there's an easier way.

Let's review how the successive terms were obtained. A table may help.

Reviewing this carefully, we finally experience an Aha!

Number of Entry	Entry
1	$1 = 1$
2	$3 = 1 + 2$
3	$5 = 1 + 2 + 2 = 1 + 2 \times 2$
4	$7 = 1 + 2 + 2 + 2 = 1 + 3 \times 2$
5	$9 = 1 + 2 + 2 + 2 + 2 = 1 + 4 \times 2$

The *second* term is $1 + 1 \times 2$ 2 − 1

The *third* term is $1 + 2 \times 2$ 3 − 1

The *fourth* term is $1 + 3 \times 2$ 4 − 1

The number of twos added is one less than the number of the term. Therefore, the one hundredth term is

$$1 + 99 \times 2 = 199$$ 100 − 1

and the one millionth term is

$$1 + (1{,}000{,}000 - 1) \times 2 = 1 + 999{,}999 \times 2 = 1{,}999{,}999.$$

Look back

The basic observation was that each diagram could be obtained by adding an additional column of two dots to its predecessor. Hence, the successive terms in the numerical sequence were obtained by adding 2 to each entry to get the next entry. Using this notion, we examined the successive terms and discovered that any entry could be found by subtracting 1 from the number of the entry, doubling the result, and adding 1. But this last sentence is rather cumbersome and we have already seen that using *symbols* can make it easier to make mathematical statements. If we use n for the number of the term, the above sentence can be translated into this mathematical sentence:

$$e_n = (n - 1) \times 2 + 1 = 2n - 2 + 1 = 2n - 1.*$$

$2n - 1$ is the nth odd number.

Here e_n, read "e sub n," is the formula that gives the nth entry in the sequence of part (b). All we have to do is replace n by 1, 2, 100, and so on, to find the first entry, the second entry, the one hundredth entry, and so on. Thus,

$$e_1 = 2 \times 1 - 1 = 1,$$
$$e_2 = 2 \times 2 - 1 = 3,$$
$$e_{100} = 2 \times 100 - 1 = 199,$$

and so on.

Calculator Note

Many electronic calculators have a constant function. Pressing the keys 1 $+$ 2 $=$ $=$ $=$ causes the calculator to add 2 to 1 three times. With such a calculator, the successive terms of the sequence of part (b) in the preceding example can be obtained by pressing keys 1 $+$ 2 and then pressing $=$ for each new term. Try this to show that 49 is the twenty-fifth odd number.

---

*The formula $e_n = 2n - 1$ is an example of a function. Functions are of considerable importance in mathematics and will be discussed in detail in Chapter 2.

Use a Variable

In the preceding example, and even earlier, we saw how using symbols or variables often makes it easier to express mathematical ideas and so to solve problems.

EXAMPLE 1.8

Use a Variable—Gauss's Trick

Carl Gauss (1777–1855) is generally acknowledged as one of the three greatest mathematicians of all time. When Gauss was just a young school boy, the teacher instructed the students in his class to add all the numbers from 1 to 100, expecting this to take a long time. To the teacher's surprise, young Gauss completed the task in about half a minute.

Solution

Gauss's strategy was to use a variable. If

$$s = 1 + 2 + 3 + \ldots + 100,$$

then

$$s = 100 + 99 + 98 + \ldots + 1.$$

$$\begin{array}{l} 1 + 100 = 101 \\ 2 + 99 = 101 \\ 3 + 98 = 101 \\ \vdots \\ 100 + 1 = 101 \end{array}$$

a sum with 100 terms

Therefore,

$$2s = 101 + 101 + 101 + \ldots + 101,$$
$$2s = 100 \times 101,$$

and

$$s = \frac{100 \times 101}{2} = 5050.$$

> **DEFINITION** *A Variable*
>
> A **variable** is a letter that can represent any of the numbers of some set of numbers.

Sometimes we want to use a variable in representing the general term in a sequence. Thus, as we saw in Example 1.7, $2n - 1$ is the nth odd number. In the expression $2n - 1$, n is the variable and it can be replaced by any natural number.

Other times we want to find the numerical replacement for a variable that makes a statement true. For example, if we want to know which odd number 85 is, we need to determine n such that

$$2n - 1 = 85.$$

This implies that $2n = 86$ and so $n = 43$. Hence, 85 is the 43rd odd number.

> ### PROBLEM-SOLVING STRATEGY 6   Use a Variable
>
> Often a problem requires that a number be determined. Represent the number by a variable and use the conditions of the problem to set up an equation that can be solved to ascertain the desired number.

EXAMPLE   1.9

Use a Variable to Determine a General Formula

Look at these corresponding geometrical and numerical sequences.

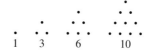

For fairly obvious reasons, the numbers 1, 3, 6, and 10 are called **triangular numbers** (the diagram with a single dot is considered a *degenerate triangle*). The numbers 1, 3, 6, and 10 are the first four triangular numbers. Find a formula for the nth triangular number.

Solution   *Understand the problem*

Having just gone through a similar problem in Example 1.7, we understand that we are to find a formula for t_n, the nth triangular number.

Devise a plan

The geometrical and numerical sequences in the statement of the problem suggest that we look for a pattern. How is each diagram related to its predecessor? How is each triangular number related to its predecessor?

Carry out the plan

We add a diagonal of 2 dots to the first diagram to obtain the second, a diagonal of 3 dots to the second diagram to obtain the third, and so on. Thus, the next two diagrams should be as shown here. Numerically, we add 2 to the first triangular number to obtain the second, 3 to the second triangular number to obtain the third, and so on. To make this even more clear, we can construct the following table.

Number of Entry	Entry
1	$t_1 = 1$
2	$t_2 = 1 + 2 = 3$
3	$t_3 = 1 + 2 + 3 = 6$
4	$t_4 = 1 + 2 + 3 + 4 = 10$
5	$t_5 = 1 + 2 + 3 + 4 + 5 = 15$

Indeed, it appears that

$$t_n = 1 + 2 + 3 + \cdots + n.$$

$$\begin{aligned} 1 + n &= n + 1 \\ 2 + (n-1) &= n + 1 \\ 3 + (n-2) &= n + 1 \\ &\vdots \\ n + 1 &= n + 1 \end{aligned}$$

Then, using Gauss's trick,

$$t_n = n + (n - 1) + (n - 2) + \cdots + 1.$$

So,

$$2t_n = (n + 1) + (n + 1) + (n + 1) + \cdots + (n + 1)$$

A sum with n terms

$$= n(n + 1)$$

and

$$t_n = \frac{n(n + 1)}{2}$$

as required.

Look back

Looking back, the key to our solution lay in considering the sequence of special cases t_1, t_2, t_3, t_4, and t_5 and in looking for a pattern. This approach deserves special recognition as a problem-solving strategy. We call it **considering special cases.**

Consider Special Cases

PROBLEM-SOLVING STRATEGY 7   Consider Special Cases

In trying to solve a complex problem, consider a sequence of special cases. This will often show how to proceed naturally from case to case until one arrives at the case in question. Alternatively, the special cases may reveal a pattern that makes it possible to solve the problem.

Pascal's Triangle

One of the most interesting and useful patterns in all of mathematics is the numerical array called Pascal's triangle.

Consider the problem of finding how many different paths there are from A to P on the grid shown in Figure 1.1 if you can only move *down* along edges in the grid. If we start to trace out paths willy-nilly, our chances of finding all possibilities are not good. A better approach is to notice that any path from *A* to *P* must contain four moves downward and to the left along the edges of small squares in the grid and six moves downward and to the right. Thus, the question becomes one of finding the number of different ways we can arrange 4 Ls (for left) and 6 Rs (for right) in order. This, by the way, illustrates another important problem-solving strategy, the strategy of **solving an equivalent problem.** The idea is to find a problem that is equivalent to the original problem that may be easier to solve. Here, finding how many ways you can put four Ls and six Rs in order using the strategy *make an orderly list* is easier than the original problem of finding the number of paths from *A* to *P* on the grid. Even this approach with four Ls and six Rs is sufficiently complicated that it is probably better to see if we can find yet another strategy.

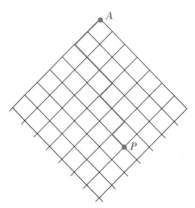

Figure 1.1
A path from A to P

A strategy that is often helpful is to **solve an easier similar problem.** It would certainly be easier if *P* were not so far down in the grid. Consider the easier similar problem of finding the number of paths from *A* to *E* in Figure 1.2.

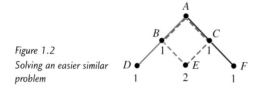

Figure 1.2
Solving an easier similar
problem

Or, consider solving a similar *set* of easier problems all at once. How many different paths are there from *A* to each of *B, C, D, E,* and *F?* (Note that this is an example of considering a series of special cases.) Clearly, there is only one way to go from *A* to each of *B* and *C,* and we indicate this by the 1s under *B* and *C* in Figure 1.2. Also, the only route to *D* is through *B,* so there is only one path from *A* to *D* as indicated. For the same reason, there is one path from *A* to *F.* On the other hand, thereare two ways to go from *A* to *E*— one route through *B* and one through *C.* We indicate this by placing a 2 under *E* on the diagram. This certainly doesn't solve the original problem, but it gives us a start and even suggests how we might proceed. Consider the diagram of Figure 1.3.

Having determined the number of paths from *A* to each of *B, C, D, E,* and *F,* could we perhaps determine the number of paths to *G, H, I,* and *J* and then continue on down the grid to eventually solve the original problem?

1.   Always moving downward, the only way to get to *G* from *A* is via *D.* But there is only one path to *D* and only one path from *D* to *G.* Thus, there is only one path from *A* to *G* and we enter a 1 under *G* on the diagram as shown.

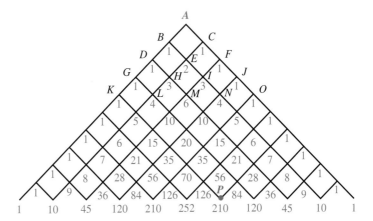

Figure 1.3
The number of paths from
A to P

2. The only way to get to *H* from *A* is via *D* or *E*. Since there is only one path from *A* to *D* and one from *D* to *H,* there is only one path from *A* to *H* via *D*. However, since there are two paths from *A* to *E* and one path from *E* to *H,* there are two paths from *A* to *H* via *E*. The number of paths from *A* to *H* is the number via *D* plus the number via *E* for $1 + 2 = 3$ paths, and we enter 3 under *H* on the diagram as shown.

3. The arguments for *I* and *J* are the same as for *H* and *G,* so we enter 3 and 1 under *I* and *J* on the diagram.

4. But this reveals a very nice pattern that enables us to solve the original problem with ease. There can be only one path to any edge vertex on the grid since we have to go straight down the edge to get to such vertex. For interior points on the grid, however, we can always reach the grid by paths through the points immediately above and to the left and right of such a point. Since there is only one path from each of these points to the point in question, the total number of paths to this point is the *sum* of the number of paths to these preceding two points. Thus, we easily generate the number of paths from *A* to any given point in the grid by simple addition. In particular, there are 210 different paths from *A* to *P* as we initially set out to determine.

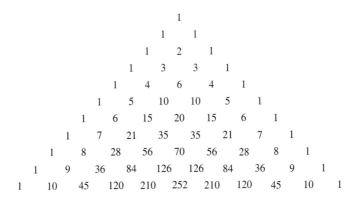

Without the grid and with an additional 1 at the top to complete a triangle, the number array of Figure 1.4 is called **Pascal's triangle.**

The array is named after the French mathematician Blaise Pascal (1623–1662) who showed that these numbers play an important role in the theory of probability. However, the triangle was certainly known in China as early as the twelfth century. An interesting and clear depiction of the famous triangle from a fourteenth century manuscript is shown in Figure 1.5.

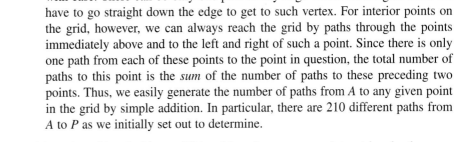

Figure 1.4
Pascal's triangle

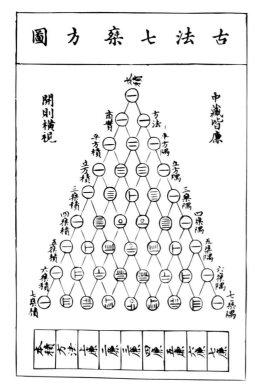

Figure 1.5

Pascal's triangle from Chu Shih—Chieh's Ssu Yuan Yii
Chien, A.D. 1303

Pascal's triangle is rich with remarkable patterns and is also extremely useful.

Before discussing the patterns, we observe that it is customary to call the single 1 at the top of the triangle the 0th row (since, for example, in the path counting problem discussed above, this 1 would represent a path of length 0). For consistency, we will also call the initial 1 in any row the 0th element in the row, and the initial diagonal of 1s the 0th diagonal. (See Figure 1.6.) Thus, 1 is the zeroth element in the fourth row, 4 is the first element, 6 the second element, and so on.

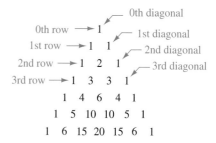

Figure 1.6

Numbered rows and diagonals in Pascal's triangle

EXAMPLE 1.10   Find a Pattern in the Row Sums of Pascal's Triangle

(a) Compute the sum of the elements in each of rows zero through four of Pascal's triangle.

(b) Look for a pattern in the results of part (a) and guess a general rule.

(c) Use Figure 1.4 to check your guess for rows five through eight.

(d) Give a convincing argument that your guess in part (b) is correct.

Solution   *Understand the problem*

For part (a), we must add the elements in the indicated rows. For part (b), we are asked to discover a pattern in the numbers generated in part (a). For part (c), we must compute the sums for four more rows and see if the results obtained continue the pattern guessed in part (b). In part (d), we are asked to argue convincingly that our guess in part (b) is correct.

Devise a plan

Part (a) is certainly straightforward; we must compute the desired sums. To find the pattern requested in part (b) we should ask the question, "Have we ever seen a similar problem before?" The answer, of course, is a resounding yes—all the problems in this section, but particularly Example 1.6, have involved looking for patterns. Surely, the techniques that succeeded earlier should be tried here. Appropriate questions to ask and answer include: "How are the successive numbers related to their predecessors?" "Are the numbers special numbers that we can easily recognize?" "Can we relate the successive numbers to their numbered location in the sequence of numbers being generated?" Answering these questions should help us make the desired guess. For part (c) we will compute the sums of the elements in rows five through eight to see if these numbers agree with our guess in part (b). If they *don't* agree, we will go back and modify our guess. If they *do* agree we will proceed to part (d) and try to make a convincing argument that our guess is correct. About all we have to go on is the fact that the initial and terminal elements in each row are 1s and that the sum of any two consecutive elements in a row is the element between these two elements but in the next row down.

Carry out the plan

(a) $1 = 1$
$1 + 1 = 2$
$1 + 2 + 1 = 4$
$1 + 3 + 3 + 1 = 8$
$1 + 4 + 6 + 4 + 1 = 16$

(b) It appears that each number in part (a) is just twice its predecessor. The numbers are just

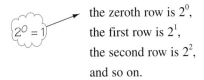

$1, 2 \cdot 1 = 2, 2 \cdot 2 = 2^2, 2 \cdot 2^2 = 2^3, 2 \cdot 2^3 = 2^4.$

It appears that the sum of the elements of

the zeroth row is 2^0,

$2^0 = 1$

the first row is 2^1,

the second row is 2^2,

and so on.

Our guess is that the sum of the elements in the nth row is 2^n.

(c) Computing these sums for the next four rows, we have

5th row $\qquad\qquad\qquad 1 + 5 + 10 + 10 + 5 + 1 = 32 = 2^5$

6th row $\qquad\qquad\qquad 1 + 6 + 15 + 20 + 15 + 6 + 1 = 64 = 2^6$

7th row $\qquad\qquad 1 + 7 + 21 + 35 + 35 + 21 + 7 + 1 = 128 = 2^7$

8th row $\qquad 1 + 8 + 28 + 56 + 70 + 56 + 28 + 8 + 1 = 256 = 2^8$

Since these results do not contradict our guess, we proceed to try to make a convincing argument that our guess is correct.

(d) What happens as we go from one row to the next? How is the next row obtained? Consider the third and fourth rows shown here. The arrows show how the fourth row is obtained from the third, and we see that each of the 1, 3, 3, and 1 in the third row appears *twice* in the sum of the elements in the fourth row. Since this argument would hold for any two consecutive rows, the sum of the numbers in any row is just twice the sum of the numbers in the preceding row. Hence, from above, the sum of the numbers in the 11th row must be $2 \cdot 2^{10} = 2^{11}$, in the 12th row it must be $2 \cdot 2^{11} = 2^{12}$, and so on. Thus, the result is true in general as claimed.

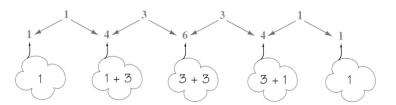

Look back

Several aspects of our solution merit special comment. Beginning with the strategies of considering special cases and looking for a pattern, we were led to guess that the sum of the elements in the nth row of the triangle is 2^n. In an attempt to argue that this guess was correct, we considered the special case of obtaining the fourth row from the third. This showed that the sum of the elements in the fourth row was twice the sum of the elements in the third row. *Since the argument did not depend on the actual numbers appearing in the third and fourth rows but only on the general rule of formation of the triangle,* it would hold for any two consecutive rows and so actually proves that our conjecture was correct. This type of argument is called **arguing from a special case,** and is an important problem-solving strategy.

In considering Pascal's triangle we found it helpful to use three additional problem-solving strategies that are well worth highlighting.

PROBLEM-SOLVING STRATEGY 8   **Solve an Equivalent Problem**

Try to recast the problem in totally different terms that change it into a new, different, but completely equivalent problem. Solving the equivalent problem also solves the original problem, but it may be easier.

PROBLEM-SOLVING STRATEGY 9   **Solve an Easier Similar Problem**

Instead of attempting immediately to solve a problem in general or for a reasonably large value like 10 or 20, try first to solve it for small values like 2 or 3, or even 1, 2, and 3. This may show how to solve the larger problem.

PROBLEM-SOLVING STRATEGY 10   **Argue from Special Cases**

A convincing argument for a general case can often be made by discussing a special case but only using those features of the special case that are typical of the general case.

WINDOW ON TECHNOLOGY
Exploring Number Patterns on a Spreadsheet

Spreadsheets were originally designed with business applications in mind, but they are also ideally suited to create and investigate number patterns. Instructions to use a spreadsheet, together with several mathematical applications, are given in Appendix B and the accompanying exercises.

As a specific example of a spreadsheet application to a number pattern exploration, let's generate rows 0, 1, 2, . . . , 10 of Pascal's triangle.

Steps to generate Pascal's triangle on a spreadsheet:

Column A. Select cell A1, type 1 and click the accept button (or just press Return or Enter). The remaining 1s in column A can be entered by the familiar **Copy** and **Paste** commands: select cell A1 and **Copy,** then select the cell range A2:A11 and **Paste.** (Alternatively, you may use the **Fill** command, or the "copy handle" at the lower right corner of the cell.) This fills in the first eleven cells of column A with 1s.

Column B. Enter a 0 in cell B1. Select cell B2, enter the formula "= B1 + A1", and then click the accept button

(or press **Return** or **Enter**). Fill in the rest of column B with **Copy** and **Paste:** select cell B2 and **Copy,** then select cells B3:B11 and **Paste.** The entries 0, 1, 2, . . . , 10 will appear now in column B.

Columns C through K. Select the cell range B1:B11 and **Copy.** Then select the rectangular cell range with cell B1 at the upper left and cell K11 at the lower right. Executing **Paste** will complete Pascal's triangle.

Once Pascal's triangle has been created on the spreadsheet, it becomes easy to explore some of its patterns. To be specific, let's investigate the sum of the entries of each row and the sum of the squares of the entries of each row. To accomplish this, enter the formula "=SUM(A1:K1)" in cell L1. Next copy this formula and paste it into cells L1 through L11. The sums of the rows, 1, 2, 4, 8, . . . , are then displayed in column L. The sums of the squares of the entries of each row can be placed in column M in an analogous way. Enter the function "=SUMSQ(A1:K1)" in cell M1, and then copy it into the cells M2:M11. Can you describe where to find the entries 1, 2, 6, 20, . . . within Pascal's triangle? Can you check your guess by adding additional rows to Pascal's triangle using spreadsheet procedures?

	B2	▼		=B1+A1								
								Pascal				
	A	**B**	**C**	**D**	**E**	**F**	**G**	**H**	**I**	**J**	**K**	**L**	**M**
1	1	0	0	0	0	0	0	0	0	0	0	1	1
2	1	1	0	0	0	0	0	0	0	0	0	2	2
3	1	2	1	0	0	0	0	0	0	0	0	4	6
4	1	3	3	1	0	0	0	0	0	0	0	8	20
5	1	4	6	4	1	0	0	0	0	0	0	16	70
6	1	5	10	10	5	1	0	0	0	0	0	32	252
7	1	6	15	20	15	6	1	0	0	0	0	64	924
8	1	7	21	35	35	21	7	1	0	0	0	128	3432
9	1	8	28	56	70	56	28	8	1	0	0	256	12870
10	1	9	36	84	126	126	84	36	9	1	0	512	48620
11	1	10	45	120	210	252	210	120	45	10	1	1024	184756

DID YOU KNOW?

Aha!

E xperimental psychologists like to tell a story about a professor who investigated the ability of chimpanzees to solve problems. A banana was suspended from the center of the ceiling, at a height that the chimp could not reach by jumping. The room was bare of all objects except several packing crates placed around the room at random. The test was to see whether a lady chimp would think of first stacking the crates in the center of the room, and then of climbing on top of the crates to get the banana.

The chimp sat quietly in a corner, watching the psychologist arrange the crates. She waited patiently until the professor crossed the middle of the room. When he was directly below the fruit, the chimp suddenly jumped on his shoulder, then leaped into the air and grabbed the banana.

The moral of this anecdote is: *A problem that seems difficult may have a simple, unexpected solution. In this case* the chimp may have been doing no more than following her instincts or past experience, but the point is that the chimp solved the problem in a direct way that the professor had failed to anticipate.

This quotation is from the introduction to Martin Gardner's delightful book, *Aha! Insight* (Scientific American, Inc./W. H. Freeman and Company, 1978). It is full of interesting, thought-provoking problems as well as insightful solutions and analyses of the problem-solving process.

PROBLEM SET 1.4

1. Look for a pattern and fill in the next three blanks with the most likely choices for each sequence.
    (a) 2, 5, 8, 11, _____, _____, _____
    (b) −5, −3, −1, 1, _____, _____, _____
    (c) 1, 1, 3, 3, 6, 6, 10, _____, _____, _____
    (d) 1, 3, 4, 7, 11, _____, _____, _____
    (e) 2, 6, 18, 54, _____, _____, _____

2. (a) Draw three diagrams to continue this dot sequence.
    $$\cdot, \quad \cdot\cdot, \quad \cdot\cdot\cdot,$$
    (b) What number sequence corresponds to the pattern of part (a)?
    (c) What is the tenth term in the sequence of part (b)? The one hundredth term?
    (d) Which even number is $2n$?
    (e) What term in the sequence is 2402?
    (f) Compute the sums $2 + 4 + 6 + \ldots + 2402$. (*Hint:* Use Gauss's trick.)

3. (a) Fill in the blanks to continue this dot sequence in the most likely way.
    $$\cdot, \quad \cdot\cdot, \quad \cdot\cdot\cdot, \quad \cdot\cdot\cdot\cdot, \quad \text{\_\_\_\_\_}, \quad \text{\_\_\_\_\_}$$
    (b) What number sequence corresponds to the sequence of dot patterns of part (a)?
    (c) What is the tenth term in the sequence of part (b)? The one hundredth term?
    (d) Which term in the sequence is 101? (*Hint:* How many 3s must be added to 2 to get 101?)
    (e) Compute the sum $2 + 5 + 8 + \cdots + 101$. (*Hint:* Use Gauss's trick and the result of part (d).)

4. Sequences like 2, 5, 8, . . . , where each term is greater (or less) than its predecessor by a constant amount, are called **arithmetic** (a-rith-mé-tic) **progressions.** Find the number of terms in each of these arithmetic progressions.
    (a) 5, 7, 9, . . . , 35
    (b) −4, 1, 6, . . . , 46
    (c) 3, 7, 11, . . . , 67

5. Compute the sum of each of these arithmetic progressions.
    (a) $5 + 7 + 9 + \cdots + 35$
    (b) $-4 + 1 + 6 + \cdots + 46$
    (c) $3 + 7 + 11 + \cdots + 67$
    (d) $1 + 7 + 13 + \cdots + 73$

6. Consider the arithmetic progression: 2, 9, 16, 23, . . . , 86.
    (a) How many 7s must be added to 2 to obtain 86?
    (b) Compute the sum $2 + 9 + 16 + \cdots + 86$.
    (c) What is the nth number in the progression?
    (d) Compute the sum
    $$2 + 9 + 16 + \cdots + (7n - 5).$$

7. (a) Fill in the blanks to continue this sequence of equations.
    $$1 = 1$$
    $$1 + 2 + 1 = 4$$
    $$1 + 2 + 3 + 2 + 1 = 9$$
    $$1 + 2 + 3 + 4 + 3 + 2 + 1 = 16$$
    $$\text{_____} = \text{_____}$$
    $$\text{_____} = \text{_____}$$

(b) Compute this sum.

$$1 + 2 + 3 + \cdots + 99 + 100 + 99$$
$$+ \cdots + 3 + 2 + 1 = \underline{\qquad}$$

(c) Fill in the blank to complete this equation.

$$1 + 2 + 3 + \cdots + (n - 1)$$
$$+ n + (n - 1) + \cdots + 3$$
$$+ 2 + 1 = \underline{\qquad}$$

8. (a) Fill in the blanks to continue this sequence of equations.

$$1 = 0 + 1$$
$$1 + 3 + 1 = 1 + 4$$
$$1 + 3 + 5 + 3 + 1 = 4 + 9$$
$$\underline{\qquad} = \underline{\qquad}$$
$$\underline{\qquad} = \underline{\qquad}$$

(b) What expression, suggested by part (a), should be placed in the blank to complete this equation?

$$1 + 3 + 5 + \cdots + (2n - 3) + (2n - 1) +$$
$$(2n - 3) + \cdots + 5 + 3 + 1 = \underline{\qquad}$$

(*Hint:* The number preceding n is $n - 1$.)

9. Writers of standardized tests often pose questions like, "What is the next term in the sequence 2, 4, 8, . . . ?"

(a) How would you answer this question?

(b) Evaluate the expressions 2^n, $n^2 - n + 2$, and $n^3 - 5n^2 + 10n - 4$ in the following chart by replacing n successively by 1, 2, 3, and 4.

n	1	2	3	4
2^n				
$n^2 - n + 2$				
$n^3 - 5n^2 + 10n - 4$				

(c) In light of the results in (b), what criticism would you make of the test writer who would write a test question like that above? Compare the wording above with that in problem 1.

10. Here is the start of a 100 chart.

1	2	3	4	5	6	7	8	9	10
11	12	13	14	15	16	17	18	19	20
21	22	23	24	25	26	27	28	29	30
31						37	38	39	40

Shown below are parts of the chart. Without extending the chart, determine which numbers should go in the lavender squares.

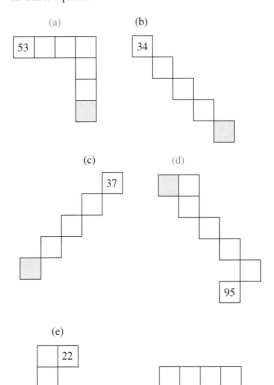

11. Five blue and five red discs are lined up in the B B B B B R R R R R arrangement shown.

Switching just two adjacent discs at a time, what is the least number of moves you can make to achieve the B R B R B R B R B R arrangement shown here?

(*Hint:* How many moves are required to rearrange B B R R to B R B R? B B B R R R to B R B R B R? And so on.)

12. (a) Complete the next two of this sequence of equations.

$$1 = 1$$
$$1 - 4 = -3$$
$$1 - 4 + 9 = 6$$
$$1 - 4 + 9 - 16 = -10$$

$$\underline{\hspace{4cm}} = \underline{\hspace{2cm}}$$
$$\underline{\hspace{4cm}} = \underline{\hspace{2cm}}$$

    (b) Write the seventh and eighth equations in the sequence of equations of part (a).
(*Hint:* Have you encountered the number sequence 1, 3, 6, 10, . . . before?)

    (c) Write general equations suggested by parts (a) and (b) for even n and for odd n where n is the number of the equation.

13. (a) How many rectangles are there in each of these figures? (*Note:* Rectangles may measure 1 by 1, 1 by 2, 1 by 3, and so on.)

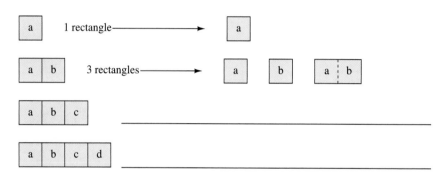

    (b) How many rectangles are in this figure?_____

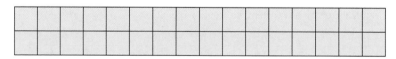

    (c) How many rectangles are in a $1 \times n$ strip?

    (d) Argue that your guess in part (c) is correct, giving a lucid and careful write-up. (*Hint:* How many of each type of rectangle begin with each small square?)

14. (a) In how many ways can you exactly cover this diagram with "dominoes" that are just the size of two small squares?

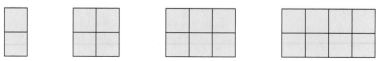

(*Hint:* This is too complicated as is. Consider this sequence of simpler arrays and look for a pattern.)

    (b) Argue carefully that your solution in part (a) is correct.
(*Hint:* A covering must start with one vertical domino or two horizontal dominoes.)

15. If one must always move downward along lines of the grid shown, how many different paths are there from point *A* to each of these points?

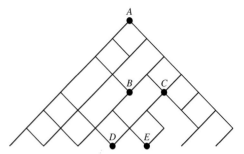

16. If one must always move upward or to the right on each of the grids shown, how many paths are there from *A* to *B?*

(a)

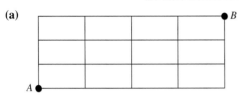

(b)

17. If one must follow along the paths of the following diagram in the direction of the arrows, how many paths are there from *C* to *E?*

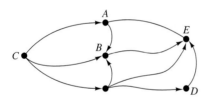

18. How many line segments are determined by joining dots on a circle if there are

(a) four dots?   (b) ten dots?

(c) 100 dots?   (d) *n* dots?

(e) Argue that your solution to part (d) is correct.

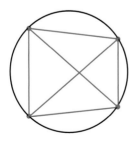

19. (a) How many games are played in a round robin tournament with ten teams if every team plays every other team once?

(b) How many games are played if there are 11 teams?

(c) Is this problem related to problem 18? If so how?

20. Here is an addition table.

+	0	1	2	3	4	5	6	7	8	9
0	0	1	2	3	4	5	6	7	8	9
1	1	2	3	4	5	6	7	8	9	10
2	2	3	4	5	6	7	8	9	10	11
3	3	4	5	6	7	8	9	10	11	12
4	4	5	6	7	8	9	10	11	12	13
5	5	6	7	8	9	10	11	12	13	14
6	6	7	8	9	10	11	12	13	14	15
7	7	8	9	10	11	12	13	14	15	16
8	8	9	10	11	12	13	14	15	16	17
9	9	10	11	12	13	14	15	16	17	18

(a) Find the sum of the entries in these squares of entries from the addition table.

2	3
3	4

5	6
6	7

11	12
12	13

15	16
16	17

Look for a pattern and write a clear and simple rule for finding such sums almost at a glance.

(b) Find the sum of the entries in these squares of entries from the table.

4	5	6
5	6	7
6	7	8

10	11	12
11	12	13
12	13	14

14	15	16
15	16	17
16	17	18

(c) Write a clear and simple rule for computing these sums.

(d) Write a clear and simple rule for computing the sum of the entries in any square of entries from the addition table.

21. Consider the following sequence of equations.

$$1 = 1$$
$$3 + 5 = 8$$
$$7 + 9 + 11 = 27$$
$$13 + 15 + 17 + 19 = 64$$
$$\underline{\quad} + \underline{\quad} + \underline{\quad} + \underline{\quad} + \underline{\quad} = \underline{\quad}$$

(a) Fill in the blanks to continue the sequence of equations.

(b) Guess a formula for the number on the right of the *n*th equation.

(c) Check that the expression $n^2 - n + 1$ generates the first number in the sum on the left of each equation and that $n^2 + n - 1$ generates the last number in these sums.

(d) Use the result of part (c) to prove that your guess to part (b) is correct. (*Hint:* How many terms are in the sum on the left of the *n*th equation?)

22. We have already considered the triangular numbers:

and the square numbers:

(a) Draw the next two figures to continue this sequence of dot patterns.

(b) List the sequence of numbers that corresponds to the sequence of part (a). These are called **pentagonal numbers.**

(c) Complete this list of equations suggested by parts (a) and (b).

$$1 = 1$$
$$1 + 4 = 5$$
$$1 + 4 + 7 = 12$$
$$1 + 4 + 7 + 10 = 22$$
$$\underline{\qquad} = \underline{\qquad}$$
$$\underline{\qquad} = \underline{\qquad}$$

Observe that each pentagonal number is the sum of an arithmetic progression.

(d) Compute the 10th term in the arithmetic progression 1, 4, 7, 10, ...

(e) Compute the 10th pentagonal number.

(f) Determine the *n*th term in the arithmetic progression 1, 4, 7, 10, ...

(g) Compute the *n*th pentagonal number, p_n.

23. (a) The **hexagonal numbers** are associated with this sequence of dot patterns. Complete the next two diagrams in the sequence.

(b) Write the first five hexagonal numbers.

(c) What is the tenth hexagonal number?

(d) Compute a formula for h_n, the *n*th hexagonal number.

24. Compute the sum of the numbers in the "handle" of each "hockey stick" in Pascal's triangle. Explain what you observe. Does the pattern always appear to hold?

```
                    1
                 1     1
              1     2     1
           1     3     3     1
        1     4     6     4     1
     1     5    10    10     5     1
  1     6    15    20    15     6     1
1   7    21    35    35    21    7     1
  1   8   28    56   70   56   28    8    1
```

25. Find and correct the error in the rod numerals appearing in the Chinese rendition of Pascal's triangle shown in Figure 1.5.

26. (a) Compute the square root of the product of the six elements surrounding an element in Pascal's triangle. In particular, do this for the six entries surrounding each of 4, 15, and 35.

(b) Does the limited amount of data from part (a) suggest a general conjecture? What appears to be true in general?

Using a Computer

The next two problems are not difficult to do by hand or with a calculator. At the same time, they are much more quickly done using a spreadsheet on a computer. See Appendix B for help with a spreadsheet. Sample commands that may be suitable for your spreadsheet are given below in the problems.

27. In the following array the first row is just the infinite sequence of whole numbers. (On your spreadsheet enter 1 in A1. Enter "=1 + A1" in B1 and use **Copy** and **Paste** or the **Fill** commands to extend the first row at least as far as Z1. Each entry in subsequent rows is the sum of the three consecutive entries in the row above the desired entry starting with the entry immediately above. Thus, $9 = 2 + 3 + 4$, $45 = 12 + 15 + 18$, and so on. (Enter " $= A1 + B1 + C1$" in A2 and use **Copy** and **Paste** or the **Fill** commands to extend row two to the right and also to extend the array downward and to the right.)

1	2	3	4	5	6	___	___	___	. . .
6	9	12	15	18		___	___	___	___	. . .
27	36	45	54	63		___	___	___	___	. . .
108	___	___	___	___	___	___	___	___	. . .

(a) Extend the array by filling in at least the blanks shown.

(b) Find a simpler rule than stated in the problem for producing the same array.

(c) Give a rule for determining the first entry in each row independent of the remaining columns in the array.

(d) Give a rule for determining the entries in row two independent of the rule of formation in the statement of the problem or the rule determined in part (b). Do the same for row three. Row four. The nth row.

28. In the array shown, the first row is just the infinite sequence of whole numbers and the first column is an infinite sequence of 1s. (On your spreadsheet, enter 1 in A1 and use **Copy** and **Paste** or the **Fill** commands to extend the first column downward. Extend the first row to the right by entering "$1 + A1$" in B1 and using **Copy** and **Paste** or the **Fill** commands.) Every other entry in the array is the sum of the second entry in the preceding column and the entry immediately above the desired entry. Thus, $9 = 3 + 6$, $22 = 6 + 16$, and so on. (In your spreadsheet, enter " $= A\$2 + B1$" in B2 and use **Copy** and **Paste** or the **Fill** commands to extend the array both down by columns and to the right by rows.)

1	2	3	4	5	6	___	___	___	. . .
1	3	6	10	15		___	___	___	___	. . .
1	4	9	16	25		___	___	___	___	. . .
1	5	12	22	___	___	___	___	___	. . .
1	___	___	___	___	___	___	___	___	. . .
___	___	___	___	___	___	___	___	___	. . .
. . .	. . .	. . .	. . .	. . .	. . .	. . .	. . .	. . .	. . .

(a) Extend the array by filling in the blanks shown.

(b) What kind of sequences are the columns in the array?

(c) Determine the 10th entry in the fourth column. The nth entry.

(d) Note that the second row of the array is just the sequence of triangular numbers and the third row is the sequence of square numbers. Can you identify the sequences of numbers in the fourth row? The fifth row? Suggestion: Refer to problems 22 and 23.

29. (Washington State, Grade 4)

Look at the following list of numbers. Describe two different patterns you see in these numbers.

| 9 | 18 | 27 | 36 | 45 | 54 | 63 | 72 | 81 | 90 |

1.5   Additional Problem-Solving Strategies

Strategies

- *Work backward.*
- *Eliminate possibilities.*
- *Use the pigeonhole principle.*

Working Backward

PROBLEM-SOLVING STRATEGY 11   **Work Backward**

Start from the desired result and work backward step-by-step until the initial conditions of the problem are achieved.

Many problems require that a sequence of events occur that result in a desired final outcome. These problems at first seem obscure and intractable, and one is tempted to try a guess and check approach. However, it is often easier to work backward from the end result to see how the process would have to start to achieve the desired end. To make this more clear, consider the following example.

EXAMPLE   1.11

Working Backward—The Gold Coin Game

This a two-person game. Place 15 golden coins (markers) on a desk top. The players play in turn and, on each play, can remove one, two, or three coins from the desk top. The player who takes the last coin wins the game. Can one player or the other devise a strategy that guarantees a win?

Solution

Understand the problem

The assertion that the game is played with gold coins is just so much window dressing. What is important is that the players start with 15 objects; that they can remove one, two, or three objects on each play; and that the player who takes the last object wins the game. The question is, how can one play in such a way that he or she is sure of winning?

Devise a plan

Since it is not clear how to begin to play or how to continue as the play proceeds, we turn the problem around to see how the game must end. We then work backwards step-by-step to see how we can guarantee that the game ends as we desire.

Carry out the plan

We carry out the plan by presenting an imaginary dialogue that you could have with yourself to arrive finally at the solution to the problem.

Q.   What must be the case just before the last person wins the game?

A.   There must be 1, 2, or 3 markers on the desk.

Q.   So how can I avoid leaving this arrangement for my opponent?

A.   Clearly, I must leave at least 4 markers on the desk in my next to last move. Indeed, if I leave precisely 4 markers, my opponent must take 1, 2, or 3 leaving me with 3, 2, or 1. I can remove all of these on my last play to win the game.

Q.   So how can I be sure to leave precisely 4 markers on my next to last play?

A.   If I leave 5, 6, or 7 markers on my previous play, my opponent can leave *me* with 4 markers and he or she can then win. Thus, I must be sure to leave my opponent 8 markers on the previous play.

Q.   All right. So how can I be sure to leave 8 markers on the previous play?

A.   Well, I can't leave 9, 10, or 11 markers on the next previous play or my opponent can take 1, 2, or 3 markers as necessary and so leave me with 8 markers. But then, as just seen, my opponent can be sure to win the game. Therefore, at this point, I must leave 12 markers on the desk.

Q.   Can I be sure of doing this?

A.   Only if I play first and remove 3 markers the first time. Otherwise, I have to be lucky, and hope that my opponent will make a mistake and still allow me to leave 12, 8, or 4 markers at the end of one of my plays. The following outlines the play if I get to play first.

- I take 3 markers, leaving 12.
- My opponent takes 1, 2, or 3 markers, leaving 11, 10, or 9.
- I take 3, 2, or 1 marker as needed to make sure that I leave 8.
- My opponent takes 1, 2, or 3 markers, leaving 7, 6, or 5.
- I take 3, 2, or 1 marker as needed to assure leaving 4 markers on the desk.
- My opponent takes 1, 2, or 3 markers, leaving 3, 2, or 1.
- I take the remaining markers and win the game!

Look back

In looking back, it is important to ask such questions as these.

- What was the key feature that led me to eventually solve this problem?
- Could I use this strategy to solve variations of this problem? For example, suppose the game started with 21 coins or 37 coins or, in general, with n coins.
- Suppose that each player could take up to five coins at a time. How would that affect the strategy?
- Could I use the successful strategy I just employed to solve other similar (or not so similar) problems?
- Could I devise other problems for which this strategy would lead to a solution?

JUST FOR FUN

How many pages in the book?

If it takes 867 digits to number the pages of a book starting with page 1, how many pages are in the book?

Working backward is a must in many problem-solving situations, and particularly so with a problem like this. The desired strategy to win the game described is not at all clear. Here the strategy of working backward is somewhat similar to considering special cases and looking for a pattern. It is as if we started with just a few counters where the strategy was more apparent and gradually increased the number of counters until we reached the given number of 15. Working backward is a powerful strategy that ought to be in every problem solver's repertoire.

Eliminate Possibilities

One way of determining what must happen in a given situation is to determine what the possibilities are and then to eliminate them one by one. If you can eliminate all but one possibility in this way, then that possibility must, in fact, prevail. Suppose that either John, Jim, or Yuri is singing in the shower. Suppose also that you are able to recognize both John's voice and Yuri's voice but that you do not recognize the voice of the person singing in the shower. Then the person in the shower must be Jim. This is another important problem-solving strategy that should not be overlooked.

PROBLEM-SOLVING STRATEGY 12   Eliminate Possibilities

Suppose you are guaranteed that a problem has a solution. Use the data of the problem to decide which outcomes are impossible. Then at least one of the possibilities not ruled out must prevail. If all but one possibility can be ruled out, then it must prevail.

Of course, if you use this strategy on a problem and **all** possibilities can be correctly ruled out, the problem has no solution. Don't be misled. It is certainly possible to have problems with no solution! Consider the problem of finding a number such that three more than twice the number is 15 and six more than four times the number is 34. This problem has no solution since the first condition is only satisfied by 6 and the second is only satisfied by 7. Yet $6 \neq 7$.

However, if we know that a problem has a solution, it is sometimes easier to determine what can't be true than what must be true. In this approach to problem solving one eliminates possibilities until the only one left must yield the desired solution.

Consider the following problem.

EXAMPLE   1.12

Eliminate Possibilities

Saturday afternoon, Aaron, Boyd, Carol, and Donna stopped by the soda fountain for treats. Altogether they ordered a chocolate malt, a strawberry shake, a banana split, and a double-dip walnut ice cream cone. Given the following information, who had which treat?

(a)   Both boys dislike chocolate.
(b)   Boyd is allergic to nuts.
(c)   Carol bought a malt and a milkshake for Donna and herself.
(d)   Donna shared her treat with Boyd.

Solution   *Understand the problem*

Given the clues in (a), (b), (c), and (d), we are to determine which youth had which confection.

Make a table.

Devise a plan

At best, the problem is confusing. Perhaps if we make a table of all possibilities, we can make some order out of the chaos and so arrive at a conclusion.

Carry out the plan

While one table would suffice, to facilitate the explanation we exhibit two diagrams showing how we are able to X out possibilities step-by-step on the basis of the given information. We use X_a, X_b, and so on to indicate impossibilities due to statements (a), (b), (c), and (d). It would be helpful to make a table of your own to see how all the work can be done on a single table as we go along.

	Choc. Malt	Straw. Shake	Banana Split	Walnut Cone
Aaron	X_a			
Boyd	X_a			X_b
Carol				
Donna				

Statements (a) and (b)

	Choc. Malt	Straw. Shake	Banana Split	Walnut Cone
Aaron	X_a	X_c	X_c	O
Boyd	X_a	X_c	O	X_b
Carol	O	$X_{c,d}$	$X_{c,d}$	$X_{c,d}$
Donna	$X_{c,d}$	O	X_c	X_c

Statements (c) and (d)

Statement (a) says that both boys dislike chocolate. This justifies placing an X_a in the chocolate malt column in Aaron's and Boyd's rows as shown. Statement (b) justifies placing an X_b in the walnut cone column in Boyd's row. Statement (c) says that Carol and Donna had a chocolate malt and strawberry shake or vice versa. But statement (d) says that Donna shared her treat with Boyd, who doesn't like chocolate. Therefore, Donna didn't have the malt and this justifies putting an $X_{c,d}$ in the chocolate malt column in Donna's row. But then, the only possibility for the chocolate malt is that it was Carol's treat and we indicate this by putting an O in her row as shown. Moreover, if she had the malt, she didn't have any other treat and this justifies Xing out the other possibilities in her row. Also, since Carol had the malt, Donna had the shake and this justifies placing an O in the shake column in Donna's row and Xing out the other possibilities in that row and column. Now, the only empty space in the cone column is in Aaron's row. This justifies placing O in that row and column, and placing X_c in the only other remaining spot in that row. Finally, we place an O in the only remaining cell in the table. Thus, Aaron, Boyd, Carol, and Donna respectively had the walnut cone, the banana split, the chocolate malt, and the strawberry shake as we were to determine.

Look back

In this problem, we were confronted with a wealth of data simply too extensive to analyze readily. To bring order into this chaos, it seemed reasonable to make a table allowing for all possibilities and then to use the given statements to decide which possibilities could be ruled out. In this way we were able to delete possibilities systematically until the only remaining possibilities completed the solution.

Eliminating possibilities is often a successful approach to solving a problem.

Check

Use logical reasoning to solve the problem.

Problem Solving
Understand
Plan
Solve
Look Back

1. Anna, Gary, Mark, and Tina are from Alabama, Georgia, Mississippi, and Tennessee. None comes from a state that begins with the same letter as his or her name. Neither Anna nor Tina is from Georgia. Gary is from Tennessee.

   Which person comes from each state?

	AL	GA	MS	TN
Anna				
Gary				
Mark				
Tina				

Gary lives Here!

Problem Solving Practice

Use logical reasoning or any strategy to solve each problem.

2. **Logic** Ivan always answers in riddles. Daniella asked him what his address is on Chestnut Street. Ivan answered "It's a 3-digit number. The digit in the tens place is twice the digit in the ones place. The digit in the hundreds place is 3 times as great as the tens digit." What is Ivan's address?

3. **Time** Chantelle gets home from school each day at 4:40 P.M. On her way home she first walks to her friend's home. This takes 15 minutes. After chatting for 15 min, she walks to the library in 10 min. She stays there 45 min, doing her homework. The walk home from the library takes 15 min. What time does she leave school? What strategy did you use to solve this problem?

4. **Write Your Own Problem** Write a problem using the data shown in the table.

5. **Journal** When you can use either logical reasoning or draw a picture, which do you prefer? Give your reasons.

Problem Solving Strategies
- Use Objects/Act It Out
- Draw a Picture
- Look for a Pattern
- Guess and Check
- Use Logical Reasoning
- Make an Organized List
- Make a Table
- Solve a Simpler Problem
- Work Backward

Choose a Tool

School

Friend's house

Library

Chantelle's house

Pizza Toppings				
	Cheese	Mushroom	Sausage	Broccoli
Ali	yes	no	no	no
Ben	no	no	yes	no
Cass	no	no	no	yes
Dee	no	yes	no	no

Skills Practice Bank, page 573, Set 6   Lesson 9-9   **427**

PROBLEM SOLVING PRACTICE

SOURCE: From *Scott Foresman – Addison Wesley Math*, Grade 5, p. 427, by Randall I. Charles et al. Copyright © 1999, Addison Wesley Longman, Inc.

Questions for the Teacher

1. Solve problem 1 above. Students may wonder if it makes a difference in which order they use the clues. Does the order matter?

2. In order to help your students solve problem 2, would it help to ask if 1 could serve as the units digit of Ivan's house number (guess and check)? Could 2 be the units digit of the house number? Could any digit other than 1 be the units digit?

3. Formulate your own answer to problem 4.

The Pigeonhole Principle

If 101 guests are staying at a hotel with 100 rooms, can we make any conclusion about how many people there are in a room? It is probable that a number of the rooms are empty since some of the guests probably include married couples, families with children, and friends staying together to save money. But suppose most of the hotel's guests desire single rooms? How many such persons could the hotel possibly accommodate? Putting just one person per room, all 100 rooms would be occupied with one person left over. Thus, if *all* 101 guests are to be accommodated, there must be at least two persons in one of the rooms. To summarize:

> If 101 guests are staying in a hotel with 100 guest rooms, then at least one of the rooms must be occupied by at least two guests.

This reasoning is essentially trivial, but it is also surprisingly powerful. Indeed, it is so often useful that we name it **the pigeonhole principle,** which is stated here.

PROBLEM-SOLVING STRATEGY 13 The Pigeonhole Principle

If m pigeons are placed in n pigeonholes and $m > n$, then there must be at least two pigeons in one pigeonhole.

For example, if we place three pigeons in two pigeonholes, then there must be at least two pigeons in one pigeonhole. To make this quite clear, consider all possibilities as shown here:

Pigeonhole Number 1	Pigeonhole Number 2
3 pigeons	0 pigeons
2 pigeons	1 pigeon
1 pigeon	2 pigeons
0 pigeons	3 pigeons

In every case there are at least two pigeons in one of the pigeonholes.

A second useful way to understand this reasoning is to try to avoid the conclusion by spreading out the pigeons as much as possible. Suppose we start by placing one pigeon in each pigeonhole as indicated below. Then we have one more pigeon to put in a pigeonhole, and it must go in either hole number one or hole number two. In either case, one of the holes must contain a second pigeon and the conclusion follows.

Pigeonhole Number 1	Pigeonhole Number 2
1	1

EXAMPLE 1.13 | **Using the Pigeonhole Principle**

An electrician working in a tight space in an attic can barely reach a box containing twelve 15-amp fuses and twelve 20-amp fuses. If her position is such that she cannot see into the box, how many fuses must she select to be sure that she has at least two fuses of the same strength?

Solution | *Understand the problem*

The box contains twelve 15-amp fuses and twelve 20-amp fuses. The electrician is in a tight spot and can barely reach the box into which she cannot see. In one attempt, she wants to select enough fuses to be sure that she has at least two fuses of the same strength. We must determine how many fuses she must select to insure the desired result.

Devise a plan

Let's consider possibilities. To make sure we don't miss one, we make an orderly list.

Make an orderly list.

Carry out the plan

If the electrician chooses two fuses she must have:

two 15-amp fuses	and	zero 20-amp fuses, or
one 15-amp fuse	and	one 20-amp fuse, or
zero 15-amp fuses	and	two 20-amp fuses.

Two fuses are **not** enough; she might get one of each kind. But if she selects a third fuse, it must either be a third 15-amp fuse, a second 15-amp fuse, a second 20-amp fuse, or a third 20-amp fuse. In any case, she has two fuses of the same strength and the condition of the problem is satisfied. Therefore, she only needs to select three fuses from the box.

Look back

We certainly solved the problem considering possibilities. But might there be an easier solution? Choosing fuses of two kinds is much like putting pigeons into two pigeonholes. Thus, if we select three fuses, at least two must be the same kind by the pigeonhole principle, and we have the same result as before.

Observe that the number 12 in the statement of the preceding problem is misleading (only two fuses of each kind in the box are really needed), and it causes many students to respond that the answer is 13. This is incorrect as we have just seen, but the good teacher will make use of this error to stimulate further study. For example, one might ask, "What question can I ask about the electrician for which 13 is the correct answer? What question might I ask for which 14 is the correct answer? How many fuses must the electrician select to be sure that she has twelve 20-amp fuses?" Also, one might repeat the problem with twelve 15-amp fuses, twelve 20-amp fuses, and twelve 30-amp fuses. The possibilities are almost limitless.

PROBLEM SET 1.5

1. Play this game with a partner. The first player marks down 1, 2, 3, or 4 tallies on a sheet of paper. The second player then adds to this by marking down 1, 2, 3, or 4 more tallies. The first player to exceed a total of 30 loses the game. Can one player or the other devise a surefire winning strategy? Explain carefully.

2. Consider this mathematical machine.

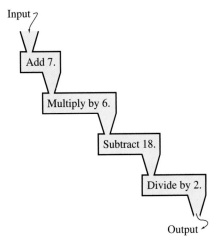

(a) What number would you have to use as input if you wanted 39 as the output?

(b) What would you have to input to obtain an output of 57?

(c) Describe a strategy for attacking this problem different from the one you used for parts (a) and (b).

3. Josh wanted to buy a bicycle but didn't have enough money. After telling his troubles to Sam Slick, Sam said, "I can fix that. See that fence? Each time you jump that fence, I'll double your money. There's one small thing though. You must give me $32 each time for the privilege of jumping." Josh agreed, jumped the fence, received his payment from Sam Slick and paid him $32. Repeating the routine twice more, Josh was distressed to find that, on the last jump after Sam had made his payment to Josh, Josh had only $32 with which to pay Sam and so had nothing left. Sam, of course, went merrily on his way leaving Josh wishing that he had known a little more about mathematics.

(a) How much did Josh have before he made his deal with Sam?

(b) Suppose the problem is the same but this time Josh jumps the fence five times before running out of money. How much did Josh start with this time?

4. Lola is thinking of a number. If you multiply her number by 71, add 29, and divide by 2, you obtain 263. What is Lola's number? Solve this problem by working backward.

5. A stack of ten cards numbered 0, 1, 2, . . . , 9 in some order lies face up on a desk. Form a new stack as follows: Place the top card face up in your hand, place the second card face up **under** the first card, place the third card face up **on top** of the new stack, place the fourth card face up **on the bottom** of the new stack, and so on. Arrange the cards in the original stack so that they appear in the new stack numbered in increasing order from the top down.

6. Moe, Joe, and Hiram are brothers. One day, in some haste, they left home with each one wearing the hat and coat of one of the others. Joe was wearing Moe's coat and Hiram's hat. Whose hat and coat was each one wearing?

7. Lisa Kosh-Granger likes to play number games with the students in her class since it improves their skill at both mental arithmetic and critical thinking. Solve each of these number riddles she gave to her class.

(a) I'm thinking of a number.

The number is odd.

It is more than 1 but less than 100.

It is greater than 20.

It is less than $5 \cdot 7$.

The sum of its digits is 7.

It is evenly divisible by 5.

What is the number? Was all the information needed?

(b) I'm thinking of a number.

The number is not even.

The sum of its digits is divisible by 2.

The number is a multiple of 11.

It is greater than $4 \cdot 5$.

It is a multiple of 3.

It is less than $7 \cdot 8 + 23$.

What is the number? Is more than one answer possible?

(c) I am thinking of a number.

The number is even.

It is not divisible by 3.

It is not divisible by 4.

It is not greater than 9^2.

It is not less than 8^2.

What is the number? Is more than one answer possible?

8. Beth, Jane, and Mitzi play on the basketball team. Their positions are forward, center, and guard.

Beth and the guard bought a milk shake for Mitzi.

Beth is not the forward.

Who plays each position?

9. Four married couples belong to a bridge club. The wives' names are Kitty, Sarah, Josie, and Anne. Their husbands' names (in some order) are David, Will, Gus, and Floyd.

Will is Josie's brother.

Josie and Floyd dated some, but then Floyd met his present wife.

Kitty is married to Gus.

Anne has two brothers.

Anne's husband is an only child.

Use this table to sort out who is married to whom.

	Kitty	Sarah	Josie	Anne
David				
Will				
Floyd				
Gus				

10. (a) Katrina chose one of the numbers 1, 2, 3, . . . , 1024 and challenged Sherrie to determine the number by asking no more than 10 questions to which Katrina would respond truthfully either 'yes' or 'no.' Determine the number she chose if the questions and answers are as follows:

Questions	Answers
Is the number greater than 512?	no
Is the number greater than 256?	no
Is the number greater than 128?	yes
Is the number greater than 192?	yes
Is the number greater than 224?	no
Is the number greater than 208?	no

Is the number greater than 200?	yes
Is the number greater than 204?	no
Is the number greater than 202?	no
Is the number 202?	no

(b) In part (a), Sherrie was able to dispose of 1023 possibilities by asking just ten questions. How many questions would Sherrie have to ask to determine Katrina's number if it is one of 1, 2, 3, . . . , 8192? If it is one of 1, 2, 3, . . . , 8000? Explain briefly but clearly. (*Hint:* Determine the differences between 512, 256, 128, 192, and so on.)

(c) How many possibilities might be disposed of with 20 questions?

11. (a) How many students must be in a room to be sure that at least two are of the same sex?

(b) How many students must be in a room to be sure that at least six are boys or at least six are girls?

12. (a) How many people must be in a room to be sure that at least two people in the room have the same birthday (not birth date)? Assume that there are 365 days in a year.

(b) How many people must be in a room to be sure that at least three have the same birthday?

13. In any collection of 11 natural numbers, show that there must be at least two whose difference is evenly divisible by ten. Helpful question: When is the difference of two natural numbers divisible by ten?

14. (a) In any collection of seven natural numbers, show that there must be two whose sum or difference is divisible by ten. (*Hint:* Try a number of particular cases. Try to choose numbers that show that the conclusion is false. What must be the case if the sum of two natural numbers is divisible by ten?)

(b) Find six numbers for which the conclusion of part (a) is false.

15. Show that, if five points are chosen in or on the boundary of a square with a diagonal of length $\sqrt{2}$ inches, at least two of them must be no more than $\sqrt{2}/2$, inches apart. (*Hint:* Consider this figure.)

16. Show that if five points are chosen in or on the boundary of an equilateral triangle with sides one meter long, at least two of them must be no more than 1/2 meter apart.

17. Think of ten cups with one marble in the first cup, two marbles in the second cup, three marbles in the third cup, and so on. If the cups are arranged in a circle in any order whatsoever, show that some three adjacent cups in the circle must contain a total of at least 17 marbles.

18. A fruit grower packs apples in boxes. Each box contains at least 240 apples and at most 250 apples. How many boxes must be selected to be certain that at least three boxes contain the same number of apples?

19. Show that at a party of 20 people, there are at least two people with the same number of friends at the party. Presume that the friendship is mutual. (*Hint:* Consider the following three cases! (i) Everyone has at least one friend at the party; (ii) Precisely one person has no friends at the party; (iii) At least two people have no friends at the party.)

20. Argue convincingly that at least two people in New York have precisely the same number of hairs on their heads. (*Hint:* You may need to determine a reasonable figure for the number of hairs on a human head.)

From State Student Assessments

21. (Washington State, Grade 4)

    Dan baked some cookies. Sam took half of the cookies. Then Sue took half of the remaining cookies. Later, Lisa took half of the cookies that were left. When Dan came home, he saw only three cookies. Tell how you could figure out many cookies Dan baked altogether. Explain your thinking using words, numbers, or pictures.

22. (Washington State, Grade 4)

    Emily, Mei, and Andrew go to the same camp. They each like different games. Use the information below to find out which game Mei likes best.

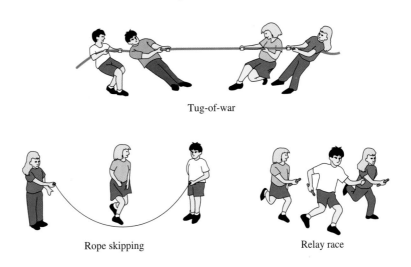

Tug-of-war

Rope skipping   Relay race

Their favorites are tug-of-war, rope skipping, and relay race.

   Emily's favorite game does *not* use a rope.

   Andrew does *not* like tug-of-war.

Which is Mei's favorite game?

A. Tug-of-war

B. Relay race

C. Rope skipping

1.6   Problem Solving in the Real World

For most people it is the practical aspect of mathematics that makes it an important part of their educational background. Many of the advances in science and technology have depended on contributions from mathematics and, in contemporary society, applications of mathematics have become increasingly numerous, complex, and essential. In the workplace, many new jobs require advanced education and even so-called blue-collar jobs require substantial mathematical expertise. In personal life, decisions we face as consumers, financial planners, environmental caretakers, and informed voters can be approached more confidently using mathematical methods and skills.

Many problems of the "real world" (that is, the world beyond the school walls) involve large and complex systems. To solve such problems, a company or governmental agency will often turn to the mathematical scientist, a person who can bring the most advanced methods and latest technology to bear. Even so, the professional uses strategies of problem solving that are no different from those which school children should learn in their mathematics classes.

The examples that follow are simplified but otherwise representative of real problems encountered in today's world.

Two Problems on Routes of Shortest Time

In a world of limited resources and finite available time, companies are understandably interested in operating at maximal efficiency. Accomplishing a task in the shortest time and at a minimum cost brings success, whereas inefficient designs and procedures send business to competitors. The mathematics of **optimization** is concerned with the study of doing the most for the least expenditure of time, space, or money.

EXAMPLE   1.14

Solving a Minimum-Time Routing Problem

Four city blocks are shown in the figure. The minutes required to travel each block are shown; the times vary because of different amounts of traffic and congestion on each block. If you must head either north, N, or east, E, at each corner, what route from point A will enable you to reach point B in the shortest time?

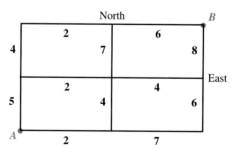

Solution   *Understand the problem*

Each route from A to B must cover blocks headed north or east; no block can be traveled heading west or south. The travel time for each route is computed by adding the times to cover each block. We need to find a route that reaches B in the shortest possible time.

Devise a plan

Plan 1. Direct search   One approach is to make an orderly list of all routes and times. An objection to this plan is that it requires lots of computation. Also, most of the routes examined are far from being the best so much of the work is wasted. If we had 30 blocks instead of just four, a direct search might be overwhelming to carry out.

Plan 2. Work backward   Starting at *B,* the point to the west of *B* is 6 minutes from *B* and the point to the south of *B* is 8 minutes from *B.* The circled numbers give the time to reach *B* from the corresponding corners.

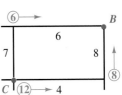

At corner *C,* heading north 7 minutes takes you to a point 6 minutes from *B,* and so *C* is 7 + 6 = 13 minutes from *B* along the north-east route. However, the east-north route takes 4 + 8 = 12 minutes. If you find yourself at *C* then it is 12 minutes from *B,* and the shortest route heads east. The shortest time and best direction are shown by a circled arrow at corner *C.* Plan 2 is to continue working backward, placing a circled number and an arrow at each intersection. The number gives the least time to reach *B* from that intersection and the arrow indicates the direction one must go to reach *B* in that time. When *A* is finally reached in this way, the circled number there gives the least time from *A* to *B* and the arrows show the path that must be followed to achieve this time.

Carry out the plan

Plan 1.   The six routes and their times are easy to list (since there are just four blocks!). There is one route, NNEE, which connects *A* to *B* in 17 minutes. The other routes all require more time.

Route	Time in Minutes
EENN	23
ENEN	18
ENNE	19
NEEN	19
NENE	20
NNEE	17

Plan 2.   The work backward plan, when fully carried out as indicated below, also shows that point *A* is 17 minutes from *B.* By following the route corresponding to the arrows, the optimal route NNEE is again discovered as shown.

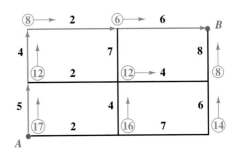

Plan 1 required 18 additions (three for each of the six routes from *A* to *B*). Then it was necessary to compare the six travel times to pick out the least. Plan 2 required only 10 additions and four comparisons. For a larger problem, the working backward method offers the better hope for success.

EXAMPLE   1.15

Solving a Larger Minimum-Time Routing Problem

Find the route of least time from A to B for the 3 by 4 block system shown in the figure.

North

	6		3		5		2		B
4		4		5		6		4	
1	3	5	2	4	7	2	6	4	East
5	4	3	2	5	8	6	1	3	
A	6		9		2		4		

Solution

There are 35 routes from *A* to *B*. To compute the time of one route takes six additions, so there would be 210 additions all together. Let's try the work backward solution shown below instead. The circled values and arrows in the figure take only 29 additions and 12 comparisons between pairs of numbers.

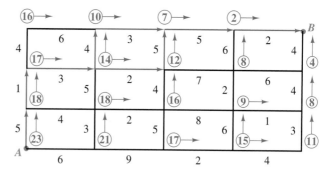

We quickly find that the shortest time from *A* to *B* is 23 minutes. There are two routes that have the smallest possible travel time, NNENEEE and NNEENEE.

The work backward solution is a special case of **dynamic programming,** a branch of mathematics created about 1950 by the mathematician Richard Bellman. Problems of shortest routes, quickest routes, or cheapest routes are real problems faced in today's world. A telecommunications network should direct its signal over routes with the smallest total rental fees. A power company will try to deliver service to its customers with the

The most remarkable mathematician at the beginning of the twentieth century was Henri Poincaré, born in Nancy, France, on August 29, 1854. Poincaré was the last person to take all of mathematics as his province. It is certainly true today that this would be impossible for any single individual and, even in 1880, it was generally believed that Gauss was the last mathematician of whom this could be said. But it was true of Poincaré, whose work was monumental—including over 500 landmark papers and some 30 important books.

Among Poincaré's many interests was the psychology of mathematical invention and discovery, or, as we have phrased it in this text, the psychology of problem solving. Poincaré thought and wrote extensively about this subject. One idea he expressed is akin to Pólya's look-back principle. One learns to solve problems by solving problems and each time remembering the key to the solution so that it can be utilized again and again to solve other problems. As in any other endeavor, the key to success in problem solving is practice.

shortest number of miles of transmission lines. It is easy to add other examples from the airline industry, shipping companies, and so forth.

Two Fair Division Problems

An interesting application of elementary mathematics is the problem of **fair division.**

EXAMPLE 1.16	**Fairly Dividing a Gift**

When Joyce joined the army, she decided to give her boom box to Ron and Jim, her two high-school age brothers. After she heard Ron and Jim quarrel over using the boom box, Joyce told them they had better figure out a fair method of division so that one of them would get the stereo and the other would get a fair payment. Determine a method that is fair to Ron and Jim.

Solution

The following method allows for the possibility that, while both Ron and Jim want the boom box, they have different assessments of its worth. Independently Ron and Jim are asked to write down what they think the stereo is worth. Let's say that Jim thinks it's worth $90, but Ron thinks it's worth $120. Since Ron places a higher value on the stereo, it should be his, and the question now is—how much should Ron pay Jim?

A reasonable answer is $52.50. To see why this is fair, recall that each brother feels he should get half of the value of Joyce's gift. Thus Ron should expect to pay $60 for the $120 boom box, leaving him with a net $60 gain, which he feels is fair to him. If Jim receives $45 of this $60, he too thinks he has been treated fairly since he expected to get half of the $90 value he placed on the boom box. This leaves $60 − $45 = $15 dollars excess, which (temporarily) can be put in a "pot." The final settlement is reached by distributing the $15 pot equally to Ron and Jim; that is, each is awarded $15 ÷ 2 = $7.50. This reduces Ron's payment to $60 − $7.50 = $52.50, and increases Jim's cash to $45 + $7.50 = $52.50. Both Ron and Jim feel they have been treated even better than fairly—each received $7.50 more value than expected.

The work to reach a fair settlement can be organized in a table. The payments required of Ron are shown in parentheses.

	Ron	Jim	Pot
Value of boom box	$120	$90	
Fair share	$60	$45	
Value of object awarded	$120	$0	
Cash received (or payment made) to receive fair share	($60)	$45	$15
Initial settlement (before distribution of pot)	Boom box & ($60 payment)	$45	$15
Share of pot	$7.50	$7.50	$0
Final settlement	Boom box & ($52.50 payment)	$52.50	$0

The solution just described works equally well when several people must divide any number of items among themselves. The method is a legally accepted process in many states for settling estate claims.

EXAMPLE   1.17   Settling an Estate Claim*

Alice, Bill, and Carl have jointly inherited a piano, a car, a boat, and $20,000 in cash. The lawyer has asked each of them to bid on the value of the four items. Their bids are shown in this table. Decide which person receives each item, and what cash payments are made so that Alice, Bill, and Carl all feel they have received at least what each considers to be his or her fair share of the inheritance.

Bids Alice, Bill, and Carl Have Made on the Four Items of Their Inheritance		
	Alice	Bill	Carl
Piano	$1900	$1500	$2000
Car	5000	5200	6000
Boat	2500	1800	2000
Cash	20,000	20,000	20,000
Total	$29,400	$28,500	$30,000
Fair share	9800	9500	10,000

---

*This scheme for estate division is due to Hugo Steinhaus, who published it in 1948.

Solution	Each heir expects to receive one-third of the value he or she places on the estate. Giving each person the item on which he or she made the highest bid, indicated in bold-face type below, determines the value of the estate, $30,500. The fair share for each heir is one-third of his or her valuation of the estate. The sum of the fair shares is $29,300, leaving $1200 to be distributed equally among the heirs. This means that each should receive $400 more than what they consider their fair share including the item(s) they won in bidding. Organized as in the solution to the preceding example, we have the following, where the $20,000 is temporarily placed in the "pot."	

	Alice	Bill	Carl	Pot
Piano	$1900	$1500	**$2000**	
Car	$5000	$5200	**$6000**	
Boat	**$2500**	$1800	$2000	
Cash	$20,000	$20,000	$20,000	$20,000
Total	$29,400	$28,500	$30,000	
Fair share	$9800	$9500	$10,000	
Value of objects awarded	$2500	0	$8000	
Cash received (or payment made) to arrive at fair share	$7300	$9500	$2000	$1200
Initial settlement (before distribution of pot)	Boat + $7300	$9500	Piano + Car + $2000	$1200
Share of pot	$400	$400	$400	0
Final settlement	Boat + $7700	$9900	Piano + Car + $2400	0

$20,000 - (7300 + 9500 + 2000)$

Each heir receives $400 more than his or her perceived fair share.

For a spreadsheet solution, see the Window on Technology on page 64.

Mathematics has made many contributions to the general notion of fairness. The equitable allocation of resources and funding is one example. Other examples relate to the democratic process—how many representatives is each state entitled to have in Congress? How can voters fairly rank candidates in a race contested by more than two contenders for office? As one can see, mathematics reaches into arenas far beyond the natural sciences.

A Problem in Correcting Errors*

Making errors is sometimes viewed as a uniquely human attribute, but computers, memory banks, and communications equipment are also susceptible to error. For example,

---

*Additional information on binary coding and error-corrections can be found in Chapter 10 of *For All Practical Purposes,* 4th ed., (New York: W. H. Freeman and Company, 1997).

WINDOW ON TECHNOLOGY
Estate Division on a Spreadsheet

It is interesting to set up an estate division settlement on a spreadsheet. For example, let's reexamine Example 1.17. First, using the procedures described in Appendix B, the bids of the heirs are entered into rows 2 through 5. If the estate includes cash, this is also assigned to the "pot" in cell E5. In cell B6, Alice's assessment of the total value of the estate is computed by entering the formula

"=SUM(B2:B5)". Her fair share is computed with the formula "=B6/3" entered in cell B7. Similar formulas complete rows 6 and 7. Enter the formula "=IF(B2< MAX($B2:$D2),0,B2)" into cell B8 and then copy and paste the formula into the rectangular range B8:D10. You should see that the logical "IF" function correctly assigns each item to the highest bidder.

B8	▼	=	=IF(B2<MAX($B2:$D2),0,B2)		
	A	B	C	D	E
1		Alice	Bill	Carl	"Pot"
2	Piano	$ 1,900	$ 1,500	$ **2,000**	
3	Boat	$ 5,000	$ 5,200	$ **6,000**	
4	Car	$ **2,500**	$ 1,800	$ 2,000	
5	Cash	$ 20,000	$ 20,000	$ 20,000	$ 20,000
6	Total	$ 29,400	$ 28,500	$ 30,000	
7	Fair share	$ 9,800	$ 9,500	$ 10,000	
8	Value of assigned items	$ -	$ -	$ 2,000	
9		$ -	$ -	$ 6,000	
10		$ 2,500	$ -	$ -	
11	Total value of objects awarded	$ 2,500	$ -	$ 8,000	
12	Cash award (payment) to get fair share	$ 7,300	$ 9,500	$ 2,000	$ 1,200
13	Distribution of "pot"	$ 400	$ 400	$ 400	
14	Final distribution (payments) of cash	$ 7,700	$ 9,900	$ 2,400	
15	Final distribution of objects	-	-	Piano	
16		-	-	Boat	
17		Car	-	-	

The following formulas will complete your spreadsheet document:

Cell	Formula
B11	=SUM(B8:B10)
B12	=B7 − B11
E12	=E5-SUM(B12:D12)
B13	=$E12/3
B14	=B12 + B13
B15	=IF(B2=MAX($B2:$D2),$A2, "-")

The formulas in B11 through B14 are copied into columns C and D, and the formula in cell B15 is copied into the rectangle of cells B15:D17.

Once your spreadsheet is set up, try answering these questions by editing the amount bid:

1. Suppose Bill learns that Carl has bid $2000 on the piano. Would Bill get more out of the estate by increasing his bid to $1995? What effect does this have on Alice and Carl?

2. Suppose Alice realizes she has bid too much for the car. If she wants the car, what should she do? (Try adjusting her bid to $2020 say.) What if she doesn't want the car and knows that Carl's bid is $2000? (Adjust her bid to, say, $1980 and see what effect this has on each of the three heirs.)

the telemetry data sent by a spacecraft from the far reaches of the solar system will surely be affected by background radiation.

Most signals are coded into strings of pulses that can be viewed as strings of zeros and ones. At first glance this may appear to be overly confining, but even as complex a signal as music can be coded in this way—this is why the compact disc is "digital." Although longer strings are needed for most applications, even strings of four 0s and 1s—0000, 0001, 0010, . . . , 1111—provide a vocabulary of 16 words. The use of 0s and 1s to store, transmit, and receive data is called **binary coding.** Each 0 or 1 is a **binary digit,** or **bit** in the shorthand parlance of computing.

It is hoped that errors will be infrequent. But even when a single 0 or 1 is misread as a 1 or 0, the intended word is replaced by a different word. In 1948, Richard Hamming, a mathematician at Bell Laboratories, proposed an efficient method to detect errors. As an added bonus, the **Hamming code** can correct the error if just one 0 or 1 has been misread as a 1 or 0.

A simple way to describe Hamming's idea is with the diagrams shown in Figure 1.7. A 4-bit word, say 1001, is stored in the 4 regions of intersection of three circles as shown.

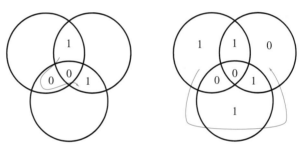

Figure 1.7
Extending the 4-bit "word" 1001 to the Hamming 7-bit 1001110

Next, starting with the upper left hand circle and proceeding counterclockwise, the empty region of each circle is assigned a 0 or 1 so that each circle contains an even number of 1s. The 4-bit word 1001 becomes, in the Hamming code, the 7-bit word 1001110.

More generally, any 4-bit word abcd can be completed to its 7-bit Hamming code abcdefg as shown in Figure 1.8.

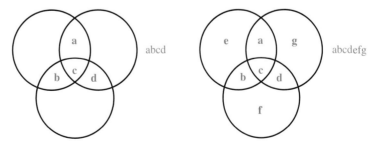

Figure 1.8
Hamming's scheme for extending a 4-bit code word to a 7-bit error-correcting word.

The redundancy of the 7-bit representation provides an **error-correcting code,** since any single error of one of the seven bits can be corrected. The following example shows how this works.

EXAMPLE   1.18

Correcting Errors with the Hamming Code

The following 7-bit representations have *at most* a single bit in error. Determine if an error is present and, if so, correct it.

(a)

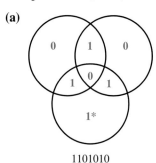

1101010

(b)

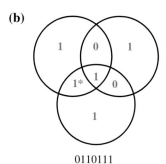

0110111

(c)

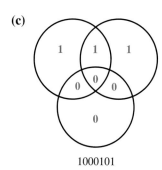

1000101

Solution

(a)   The upper two circles contain two 1s and are "good," but the lower circle is "bad" since it contains three 1s. Thus, one of the four bits in the lowest circle is in error. If the 0 is changed to a 1, the "good" circles become "bad." For the same reason, neither of the uppermost 1s in the lowest circle can be replaced by a 0. This leaves just the lowest 1 (marked with an asterisk) that can be changed. Thus, the corrected word is 1101000.

(b)   The upper right circle is good but the remaining circles are bad. Because both bad circles must be changed to good, but we don't want the good circle to become bad, it follows that the 1 marked by the asterisk is the single bit in error. The corrected word is 0010111.

(c)   Each of the three circles has evenly many 1s so we assume the word 1000101 is correct.

If two errors occur in a 7-bit word, the error-correction procedure can actually make things worse by introducing yet a third error. Fortunately, if single errors are relatively infrequent, the chances of two errors in the same word are quite rare.

In situations where an error may be critical—imagine the flight control system of an airplane, for example—redundant computing units may be required to reduce the chance of error to an acceptably low value. In more critical applications, more complex error-correcting codes are used. Many compact disc players can correct up to 14,000 consecutive errors. Even so, the ratio of error-correcting bits to sound bits is just 1 to 3, so there is a modest 33 percent overhead to provide error-correction capability.

Coded information—zip code codes, uniform price codes, book number codes, and others—plays an increasingly important role in what has become the "age of information."

Much of the mathematics involved is accessible and exciting and provides opportunities for problem solving in the real world.

PROBLEM SET 1.6

1. Find the least amount of time to go from A to B. The times are in minutes. One must travel east or north from each corner. Use the work backward method of Example 1.15.

North

7	2 1	4 3	6 4	B

(grid figure)

```
        North
      2       4       6      • B
   7     1      3       4
      5       2       5    East
   4     3      7       6
      2       1       5
   1     4      3       4
   A
      5       2       6
```

2. Find the quickest route from A to B in this diagram. You must head north or east at each corner.

```
            North
                          • B
                      4    3  2
         3         3  6   5  5
      2        2  4   1      1   East
   4     3
      1   3   2  4   3   3  1  3
   2                             
   A   1      1      3      1
```

3. The rental costs of natural gas pipelines are shown (in thousands of dollars per month). What is the cheapest route from A to B? The direction of flow is indicated by the arrows.

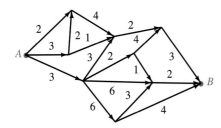

4. Sara and Ken are given a tennis racket by their uncle. Sara values the racket at $25 and Ken thinks the racket

is worth $20. Who should get the racket? What payment should be made?

5. Suppose Ken, in problem 4, already has a tennis racket and is not interested in the racket from his uncle.

   (a) Assuming Ken would like his sister to pay him as much as possible, what strategy should he follow when making his bid? Should he bid at all?

   (b) If he guesses that Sara thinks the racket is worth $20 to $30, what bid would be best?

   (c) What can Sara do, knowing that Ken isn't much interested in the racket?

6. La'Tiece, Mike, and Nancy wish to divide fairly a bike, a stereo, and a computer game. They have submitted bids as shown. Who should receive each item and what payments do they need to make so that they all feel they received a fair share?

	La'Tiece	Mike	Nancy
Bike	$40	$50	$45
Stereo	$75	$60	$40
Game	$44	$40	$50

7. Suppose La'Tiece learns that Mike only bid $60 for the stereo in problem 6. If La'Tiece also knows that Nancy isn't very interested in the stereo, can she adjust her bid to take advantage of her knowledge? How does this affect Mike and Nancy? Discuss briefly.

8. At most one bit is in error in the following 7-bit Hamming code representations. Determine if the representation is correct; if not, correct the error.

(a)

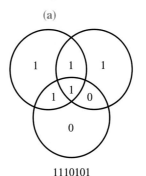

1110101

(b)

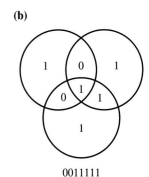

0011111

(c)   **(d)**

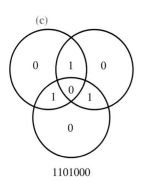

1101000

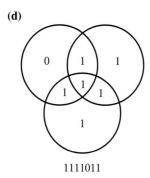

1111011

9. (a) Correct the single error in the following 7-bit Hamming code representation.

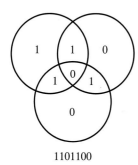

1101100

(b) If all three circles are "bad" and there is an error in a single bit, why is it easy to correct the error?

10. Suppose the bits marked by an asterisk are incorrect. Show that the error-correction procedure makes things worse by introducing a third error changing just one bit.

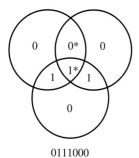

0111000

11. There are four 2-bit words: 00, 01, 10, 11. A *Gray code* is a circular ordering of the four words with the property that adjacent words differ by just one bit.

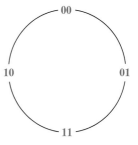

(a) Find a Gray code for the eight 3-bit words. (*Hint:* Try adding a 0 on the left of each of the 2-bit words. Then add a 1 on the left of each 2-bit word and see if the two sequences of 3-bit words can be properly joined together.)

(b) Find a Gray code for the sixteen 4-bit words.

12. Burger Boy has three stores along Division Street, all doing the same volume of business. Store B is 4 miles east of store A and store C is 2 miles east of store B. Burger Boy would like to build a warehouse somewhere along Division Street to supply all three stores as inexpensively as possible. It costs $3 per mile to run the truck that is to supply the stores.

(a) If the warehouse is located 3 miles from A toward B, what is the cost of running the truck to each store once? Consider the drawing shown.

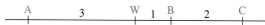

(b) If the warehouse is located halfway from B to C, what is the cost of running the truck to each store once?

(c) If the warehouse is located d miles east of A with $0 \le d \le 4$ (i.e.; at or between A and/or B), what is the cost of running the truck to each store once? In this case where should the warehouse be located to make this cost least and what is this least cost?

(d) If the warehouse is located d miles east of B with $0 \le d \le 2$ (i.e.; at or between B and/or C), what is the cost of running the truck to each store once? In this case where should the warehouse be located to make this cost least and what is this least cost?

(e) Considering the results of (c) and (d), what location of the warehouse will make the cost of running the truck to each store least?

13. The Acme Yardstick Company frequently sends boxes of yardsticks measuring $\frac{1}{4}$ by $1\frac{1}{2}$ by 36 inches to distribution centers. Naturally the boxes are a yard long, but postal regulations limit the girth of the box to 72 inches. The girth is the perimeter of the box when viewed from an end. Acme has been using boxes 12 inches high and 24 inches wide, but wonders if a different shaped box might hold more of their rulers. What shape do you believe may be better? (*Hint:* Complete the table at the top of the next page.)

Height *h* (Inches)	Width *w* (Inches)	Area = *hw* (Square Inches)
12	24	288
13		
14		
15		
16		
17		
18		
19		
20		

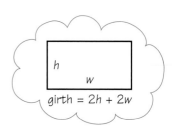

girth = 2h + 2w

 Using a Computer

Problems 4, 5, 6, and 7 above were intended to be done by hand. However, when done on a spreadsheet, it is a simple matter to change a given bid and see immediately how this affects the outcome. Suggestion: See the Window on Technology on page 64 for help in setting up a spreadsheet.

14. (a) Set up a spreadsheet to solve problem 4 above.

    (b) What payment is made if Ken fails to bid (i.e., bids $0) for the racket?

    (c) What payment is made if he bids $24 for the racket? What if he bids $24.99?

15. (a) Set up a spreadsheet to solve problem 6 above.

    (b) What payment is made if La'Tiece bids $61 for the stereo? What if she bids $60.01?

16. (a) Set up a spreadsheet to determine the dimensions of the rectangular field of maximum area that can be enclosed with 1600 feet of fencing.

    (b) Repeat part (a) but suppose that the fence is to be built along a long existing stone wall.

From State Student Assessments

17. (Washington State, Grade 4)

Ana and Deval are planning to meet at school and walk to the library together.

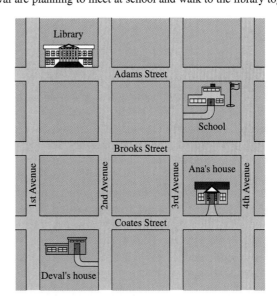

If they take the shortest routes, which of the following is true?

A. Deval has to walk farther than Ana.   B. Ana has to walk farther than Deval.

C. Deval and Ana walk the same distance.

INTO THE CLASSROOM

Teaching Problem Solving

Here are some bits of advice for teaching problem solving.

- Set out now to develop a store of interesting and challenging problems appropriate to the skill levels of the students in your class. This process should continue over your professional lifetime. A good start is to keep your present textbook and to use many of the problems you find here as is or modified to be more accessible to your students.

- Really listen to your students. They often have good ideas. They also frequently find it difficult to express their ideas clearly. Listening carefully and helping your students to communicate clearly are skills you should continually seek to improve.

- Don't be afraid of problems you don't already know how to solve. Say, "Well, I don't know. Let's work together and see what we can come up with." You needn't be the oracle who "knows all." Indeed, many students will be excited and motivated by the prospect of "working with my teacher" to solve a problem. They also learn not to be afraid to tackle the unknown, and to make mistakes and yet persevere until a solution is finally achieved.

- Don't be too quick to help your students or to simply tell them how to solve a problem.

- Develop a long list of leading questions you can ask of your students, and that they can ask themselves, to help clarify their thinking and eventually arrive at a solution.

- Don't be afraid of having students in your class who are brighter and better at solving problems than you are. Just be happy to have such students; give them all the encouragement you can, and use them to help teach the others. Your ego should not be on the line—we have all taught students who are brighter than we are!

EPILOGUE   Fascination with Mathematics—Past and Present

The fascination of individuals with mathematical problems, both real world and fanciful, goes back at least as far as recorded history. The reason for the interest in real-world problems, then and now, is obvious. The successful conduct of many human activities requires mathematical understanding. Thus, much of ancient mathematics was developed to meet particular needs and to enable individuals to accomplish desired tasks. The not-so-simple matter of making a reliable calendar, for example, requires reasonably sophisticated understanding of mathematics, and the Babylonians had this ability by approximately 4700 B.C. Similarly, many practical notions from geometry, including formulas for areas and volumes of geometrical figures and the properties of right triangles, were known at least 1000 years before Pythagoras and Euclid.

But it is also true that much of mathematics was studied for its own sake, simply because it was interesting. It is even true that many of the problems still popular today are of extraordinarily ancient origin. One of the most interesting of ancient mathematical documents is the Rhind papyrus purchased by the Scottish Egyptologist, Henry Rhind, in a small shop in Egypt in 1858. The scroll dates from approximately 1650 B.C. and is something of a mathematical handbook. However, it also contains a number of fanciful problems including this cryptic set of data.

Estate		
Houses	7	7^1
Cats	49	7^2
Mice	343	7^3
Heads of wheat	2401	7^4
Hekat measures	16807	7^5

The problem is not explained, but one can guess that the challenge was to compute the sum

$$7 + 7^2 + 7^3 + 7^4 + 7^5. \quad \longleftarrow \; 19{,}607$$

This problem reappears in A.D. 1202 in *Liber abaci* by the celebrated thirteenth century mathematician, Leonardo of Pisa or Fibonacci. In translation, Fibonacci's rendition of the problem runs as follows

> There are seven old women on the road to
> Rome. Each woman has seven mules; each mule
> carries seven sacks; each sack contains seven
> loaves; with each loaf are seven knives and
> sheaths. How many are there in all on the
> road to Rome?

The modern version of the problem is the well-known nursery rhyme

> As I was going to St. Ives,
> I met a man with seven wives,
> Each wife had seven sacks,
> Each sack had seven cats,
> Each cat had seven kits.
> Kits, cats, sacks, and wives,
> How many were going to St. Ives?

It has been conjectured that the original problem in the Rhind papyrus might have been: "An estate consisted of seven houses; each house had seven cats; each cat ate seven mice; each mouse ate seven heads of wheat; each head of wheat when planted would produce seven hekats of grain. How many of all these items were in the estate?" However that may be, here is a problem, still popular in children's literature, that was already ancient when Fibonacci copied it nearly 800 years ago. One even wonders if the O'Henry twist in the nursery rhyme version of the problem (where the answer is 1 and not $7 + 7^2 + 7^3 + 7^4 + 7^5 = 19{,}607$) might not have existed in some form in the ancient Egyptian version.

In any case, mathematical problems and puzzles have piqued the curiosity and challenged the ingenuity of individuals for millennia and this is no less true today. Introducing problem solving into the curriculum improves students' skills and their ability to think creatively and carefully; it also greatly enhances both student and teacher enjoyment of the entire educational process.

Finally, listing all possible strategies for solving problems is not possible. Those presented in this chapter are some of the most basic. But all have variants that we have not mentioned, all can be mixed and matched in many ways, and other methods, approaches, ideas, and schemes will occur both to you and to your students over the years.

CHAPTER 1 SUMMARY

Key Concepts

The thrust of this chapter has been to introduce the basic ideas of problem solving or critical mathematical thinking. Fundamental to this entire process are Pólya's Principles:

- Understand the problem
- Devise a plan
- Carry out the plan
- Look back

Understand the problem

Students are often stymied because they don't understand a problem fully or even in part. To help, teachers should ask such questions as:

- Do you understand all the words in the problem? If not, look them up in your book, in a dictionary, and so on.
- What are you given?
- What are you asked to find or show?
- Can you restate the problem in your own words?
- What does *(key word)* really mean?
- Could you work out some numerical problems that might clarify the problem at hand?
- Would a picture or diagram help?
- If you knew *(key word)* could you solve the problem?
- Could you determine *(key word)*?

As a teacher, your entire professional life should be spent adding to and refining this list. Students can't solve a problem unless they understand it.

Devise a plan

Devising a plan involves seeking an appropriate strategy that will ultimately lead to a solution. A list of such strategies includes:

- guess and check
- make an orderly list
- think of the problem as partially solved
- eliminate possibilities
- solve an equivalent problem
- use symmetry
- consider special cases
- work backward
- use direct reasoning
- be ingenious

- look for a pattern
- draw a picture
- think of a similar problem already solved
- solve a simpler problem
- solve an analogous problem
- solve an equation
- use a diagram or model
- use a formula (function)
- use indirect reasoning

Not all of these strategies have been discussed in this chapter. But problem solving pervades this text, and these strategies will occur and be discussed further in examples from time to time.

Carry out the plan

Having decided on a strategy, try to carry it out. Don't give up too soon. But if your strategy doesn't work, give it up and try another strategy. With practice, you are increasingly apt to choose a successful strategy the first time.

Look back

An important part of problem solving is looking back at a completed solution to see what the key ideas were, what ultimately led you to a solution, and how your approach might be modified to solve other even remotely related problems. Solving problems begets problem-solving skill. If we do not learn by our successes *and failures,* we are not apt to make much progress as problem solvers. Conversely, success at solving problems improves our chances of solving additional problems more easily.

Questions and ideas you should consider when looking back include these:

- What was the key idea that eventually led me to devise a successful strategy for solving this problem?
- Now that I understand the problem better, can I discover other successful strategies and thus increase my problem-solving ability?
- My first several attempts were unsuccessful but they did help me to understand the problem and eventually devise the successful strategy that led to the solution. I must not be afraid to try and fail and try again and again.
- How else might I view the problem that would lead to a successful strategy?
- Can I think of other similar problems that I have solved whose solutions might be modified to solve the present problem?
- Can I think of simpler similar problems that I can solve and that might suggest a successful strategy for solving the problem at hand?

Be thoughtful. Be expectant. Like Poincaré, you should expect to gain more than just a solution when you solve a problem. You also expect to gain increased *mathematical power.*

Problem-solving ability is learned by solving problems!

Vocabulary and Notation

Hands On

Möbius strip

Section 1.1

Palindrome
Kaprekar's number
Collatz's problem

Sections 1.2 and 1.3

Guess and check
Make a table
Look for a pattern

Make an orderly list
Draw a picture or diagram
Guess my rule

Section 1.4

Look for a pattern
Make a table
Variable
Use a variable
Triangular numbers
Fibonacci numbers
Consider special cases
Pascal's triangle

Solve an equivalent problem
Solve an easier similar problem
Argue from special cases

Section 1.5

Work backward
Eliminate possibilities
The pigeonhole principle

Section 1.6

Optimization
Dynamic programming
Fair division
Binary code
Binary digit
Hamming code
Error-correcting code

CHAPTER REVIEW EXERCISES

Section 1.1

1. (a) See how quickly you can compute these products. You may use a calculator if you like.

    $1 \cdot 8 =$ ————————
    $21 \cdot 8 =$ ————————
    $321 \cdot 8 =$ ————————
    $4321 \cdot 8 =$ ————————
    $54321 \cdot 8 =$ ————————
    $654321 \cdot 8 =$ ————————
    $7654321 \cdot 8 =$ ————————
    $87654321 \cdot 8 =$ ————————
    $987654321 \cdot 8 =$ ————————

    (b) Did you have to perform all the multiplications to complete the problem?
    (c) Does the pattern you noticed hold for the first product?
    (d) Does the pattern you noticed hold for the last product? What general principle about guessing does this suggest?

2. (a) Multiply your favorite digit by 239. Now multiply the product by 4649. The numbers 239 and 4649 are "magic" numbers as discussed in Section 1.1, Tidbit Number 2.
    (b) To see why 239 and 4649 are "magic," compute $239 \cdot 4649$.
    (c) Use the graphing calculator program FACTOR to show that there are no other magic numbers whose product is a 7-digit integer.

3. (a) Form a magic addition square using the numbers 1, 7, 13, 31, 37, 43, 61, 67, and 73.
    (b) Form a magic subtraction square using the numbers in part (a).

4. Generate a palindrome starting with the number 87. (See Problem 16 in Problem Set 1.1.)

Sections 1.2 and 1.3

5. Standard Lumber has 8' and 10' two-by-fours. If Mr. Zimmermann bought 90 two-by-fours with a total length of 844 feet, how many were eight feet long? Give two solutions, (a) and (b), using different strategies. (*Note:* Zimmermann is the German word for carpenter. Have you ever known anyone with this last name?)

6. (a) Using each of 1, 2, 3, 4, 5, 6, 7, 8, and 9 once and only once, fill in the circles in this diagram so that the sum of the three-digit numbers formed is 999.

    (b) Is there more than one solution to this problem? Explain briefly.
    (c) Is there a solution to this problem with the digit 1 not in the hundreds column? Explain briefly.

7. Bill's purchases at the store cost $4.79. In how many ways can Bill receive change if he pays with a five dollar bill?

8. How many 3-letter code words can be made using the letters a, e, i, o, and u at most once each time?

9. A flower bed measuring 8' by 10' is bordered by a concrete walk two feet wide. What is the area of the concrete walk?

10. Karen is thinking of a number. If you double it and subtract 7 you obtain 11. What is Karen's number?

11. (a) Chanty is IT in a game of *Guess My Rule*. If you give her a number, she uses her rule to determine another number. The numbers the other students gave Chanty and her responses are as shown. Can you guess her rule?

Student Input	Chanty's Responses
2	8
7	33
4	18
0	−2
3	13
⋮	⋮

(b) Can you suggest a better strategy for the students to use in attempting to determine Chanty's rule? Explain briefly.

Section 1.4

12. Study this sequence: 2, 6, 18, 54, 162, ... Each number is obtained by multiplying the preceding number by 3. The sequences in (a) through (e) are formed in the same way but with a different multiplier. Complete each sequence.

(a) 3, 6, 12, _____, _____, _____

(b) 4, _____, 16, _____, _____,
_____

(c) 1, _____, _____, 216, _____,
_____

(d) 2, _____, _____, _____, 1250,
_____

(e) 7, _____, _____, _____,
_____, 7

13. Because of the high cost of living, Kimberly, Terry, and Otis each holds down two jobs, but no two have the same occupation. The occupations are doctor, engineer, teacher, lawyer, writer, and painter. Given the following information, determine the occupations of each individual.

(a) The doctor had lunch with the teacher.

(b) The teacher went fishing with Kimberly, who is not the writer.

(c) The painter is related to the engineer.

(d) The doctor hired the painter to do a job.

(e) Terry lives next door to the writer.

(f) Otis beat Terry and the painter at tennis.

(g) Otis is not the doctor.

14. (a) Write down the next three rows to continue this sequence of equations.

$$2 = 1^3 + 1$$
$$4 + 6 = 2^3 + 2$$
$$8 + 10 + 12 = 3^3 + 3$$
$$\underline{\hspace{2cm}} = \underline{\hspace{1cm}}$$
$$\underline{\hspace{2cm}} = \underline{\hspace{1cm}}$$
$$\underline{\hspace{2cm}} = \underline{\hspace{1cm}}$$

(b) Write down the tenth row in the sequence in part (a).

15. (a) How many terms are in the arithmetic progression 7, 10, 13, 16, . . . , 79?

(b) Compute the sum of the terms in part (a).

16. (a) A **geometric progression** is a sequence of numbers where each term is a constant multiple of the preceding term. Thus, 3, 6, 12, 24, . . . , 3072 is a geometric progression since each term is twice its predecessor.

Analyzing these terms, we have

$$3 = 3$$
$$6 = 2^1 \cdot 3,$$
$$12 = 2 \cdot 6 = 2(2^1 \cdot 3) = 2^2 \cdot 3,$$
$$24 = 2 \cdot 12 = 2(2^2 \cdot 3) = 2^3 \cdot 3,$$
$$\bullet$$
$$\bullet$$
$$\bullet$$

Which term in the sequence is 3072?

(b) Let $S = 3 + 6 + 12 + 24 + \cdots + 1536 + 3072$ denote the sum of the progression. Compute S.

(c) Note that $2S = 6 + 12 + 24 + \cdots + 3072 + 6144.$

(d) Note that $2S - S = S$ and use (b) and (c) to compute S a second time.

17. Compute the sum of this geometric progression:

$$5, 15, 45, . . . , 295{,}245$$

18. Consider a circle divided by n chords in such a way that every chord intersects every other chord interior to the circle and no three chords intersect in a common point. Complete this table and answer these questions.

(a) Into how many regions is the circle divided by the chords?

(b) How many points of intersection are there?

(c) Into how many segments do the chords divide one another?

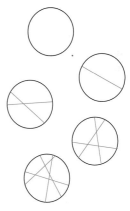

Number of Chords	Number of Regions	Number of Intersections	Number of Segments
0	1	0	0
1	2	0	1
2	4	1	4
3			
4			
5			
6			
⋮			
n			

19. Recall Pascal's triangle.

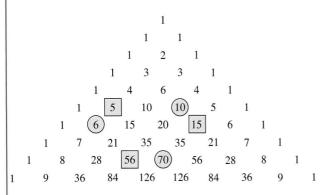

Consider the pattern of circled and squared entries in the diagram. Compute the product of the circled entries in Pascal's triangle and the product of the squared entries for several placements of this pattern in the triangle. Does your work suggest a plausible conjecture? Explain briefly. Find other hexagonal patterns of entries with the observed property.

20. Compute the following sums associated with Pascal's triangle.

(a) $1 + 1 \cdot 2$

(b) $1 + 2 \cdot 2 + 1 \cdot 2^2$

(c) $1 + 3 \cdot 2 + 3 \cdot 2^2 + 1 \cdot 2^3$

(d) What do these sums suggest? Explain briefly.

(e) Compute the sums

$$1 + 1 \cdot 3$$
$$1 + 2 \cdot 3 + 1 \cdot 3^2$$
$$1 + 3 \cdot 3 + 3 \cdot 3^2 + 1 \cdot 3^3$$

(f) What do (a), (b), (c), (d), and (e) together suggest? What might you do to check your guess further? Explain briefly.

Section 1.5

21. How many cards must be drawn from a standard deck of 52 playing cards to be sure that:

(a) at least two are of the same suit?

(b) at least three are of the same suit?

(c) at least two are aces?

22. How many books must you choose from among a collection of 7 mathematics books, 18 books of short stories, 12 chemistry books, and 11 physics books to be certain that you have at least 5 books of the same type?

Section 1.6

23. The numbers on the railroad network shown give the cost (in hundreds of dollars) of moving a trainload of coal along various links between junctions in the system.

(a) Determine the least possible cost of moving a load of coal from *A* to *M*.

(b) Starting with *A*, list the junctions through which the least cost route of part (a) passes.

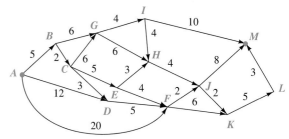

24. Judy, John, Joshua, and JoAnn are bequeathed a motor home, a car, a house, and a painting by a wealthy uncle. Since the items are clearly of unequal value and the executor of the estate wants to fairly divide the bequest, she asks the four siblings to submit statements of the value they place on the items. Given the list of values shown, who should inherit which items and what financial adjustments should be made so that each inheritee receives what he or she considers at least a fair share of the bequest?

	Judy	John	Joshua	JoAnn
Motor home	27,000	32,000	35,000	30,000
Automobile	19,000	18,000	23,000	24,000
House	250,000	200,000	220,000	230,000
Painting	900,000	800,000	1,000,000	700,000

25. Write the 7-bit Hamming code representation for each of these 4-bit binary words.

(a) 1101   (b) 1000   (c) 1010

26. The following 7-bit Hamming code words contain at most one error. Determine if an error is present and, if so, correct it.

(a) 1110001   (b) 0101101   (c) 1000010

CHAPTER TEST

1. Perform these multiplications as quickly as possible.

   $2345679 \times 9 = $ _____

   $1345679 \times 9 = $ _____

   $1245679 \times 9 = $ _____

   $1235679 \times 9 = $ _____

   $1234679 \times 9 = $ _____

   $1234579 \times 9 = $ _____

   $1234569 \times 9 = $ _____

   $1234568 \times 9 = $ _____

2. Consider the following equations.

$$1 = 0 + 1 = 1 - 0$$
$$2 + 3 + 4 = 1 + 8 = 9 - 0$$
$$5 + 6 + 7 + 8 + 9 = 8 + 27 = 36 - 1$$
$$10 + 11 + 12 + 13$$
$$+ 14 + 15 + 16 = 27 + 64 = 100 - 9$$

   (a) Continue this sequence for two more equations.

   (b) What is the tenth row in the sequence?

   (c) What is the nth row in the sequence?

3. While three watchmen were guarding an orchard, a thief slipped in and stole some apples. On his way out, he met the three watchmen one after another, and to each in turn he gave half the apples he had and two besides. In this way he managed to escape with one apple. How many had he stolen originally?

4. If five pigeons are placed in two pigeonholes, what is the least possible number of pigeons in the pigeonhole with the greatest number of pigeons?

5. (a) Make a magic square using each of the numbers 2, 7, 12, 27, 32, 37, 52, 57, 62 once and only once.

   (b) Make a magic subtraction square using each of the numbers in part (a) once and only once.

6. A frog is in a well 12 feet deep. Each day he climbs up 3 feet and each night he slips back 2 feet. How many days will it take the frog to get out of the well?

7. (a) Write the next two lines in this sequence of equations.

$$2 = 2 = 0^2 + 2 \cdot 1^2$$
$$2 + 5 + 2 = 9 = 1^2 + 2 \cdot 2^2$$
$$2 + 5 + 8 + 5 + 2 = 22 = 2^2 + 2 \cdot 3^2$$
$$\underline{\hspace{4cm}} = \underline{\hspace{2cm}}$$
$$\underline{\hspace{4cm}} = \underline{\hspace{2cm}}$$

   (b) Write the tenth line in the sequence of part (a).

8. Consider these equations.

$$s_1 = 1 = 1$$
$$s_2 = 1 - 3 = -2$$
$$s_3 = 1 - 3 + 6 = 4$$
$$s_4 = 1 - 3 + 6 - 10 = -6$$
$$s_5 = 1 - 3 + 6 - 10 + 15 = 9$$
$$s_6 = 1 - 3 + 6 - 10 + 15 - 21 = -12$$

   (a) Guess the values of s_{20} and s_{21}.

   (b) Guess the value of s_n. (*Hint:* You may want to consider n even and n odd separately.)

9. (a) Write the Hamming 7-bit code word for the 4-bit word 1101.

   (b) Correct the error in the Hamming code word 0101111.

10. Find the cost of the shortest path from A to B on the following network if you can only move east or north.

	7		1		4		6	
7		8		3		3		2
	6		5		2		4	
2		7		3		7		5
	1		6		6		4	
3		5		3		1		5
	2		4		3		2	

CHAPTER

2

Sets, Whole Numbers, and Functions

2.1 Sets and Operations on Sets

2.2 Sets, Counting, and the Whole Numbers

2.3 Addition and Subtraction of Whole Numbers

2.4 Multiplication and Division of Whole Numbers

2.5 Functions

HANDS ON
Counting Cars and Trains

Materials Needed

A set of Cuisenaire® rods (or colored number strips) for each cooperative group of three or four students. The rods, which have lengths from 1 to 10 centimeters, are color coded as follows.

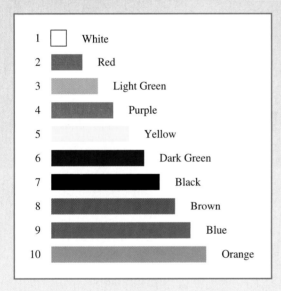

1	☐	White
2	▬	Red
3	▬	Light Green
4	▬	Purple
5	▬	Yellow
6	▬	Dark Green
7	▬	Black
8	▬	Brown
9	▬	Blue
10	▬	Orange

Directions

Form a train by placing one or more rods end-to-end: each rod in a train is a car. For example, in the figure at the top of the next column there are four ways to form trains which have the same overall length as the light green (LG) rod:

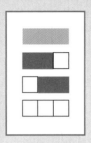

The order in which the cars appear is taken into account, so we consider the red-white and white-red trains as two different trains (imagine that the engine is the right-most car, and the caboose is the left-most car).

1. How many trains can you form that have the same length as the purple rod?

2. How many trains can you form that have the same length as the yellow rod?

3. What pattern do you observe in the number of trains of length 3, 4, and 5? On the basis of this pattern, predict the number of trains of length 8.

4. How many trains can be formed of length n, where n is any whole number and you use cars of lengths I up to n? Can you justify your conjecture? Can you give more than one justification?

5. A train made up of only red and white cars is called an RW-train. Answer questions 1 through 4 for RW-trains.

6. Call a train with no white cars a $\overline{W}$-train. Answer questions 1 through 4 for $\overline{W}$-trains.

CONNECTIONS Counting and Thinking Mathematically

> *When you can measure what you are speaking about and express it in numbers, you know something about it; but when you cannot measure it, when you cannot express it in numbers, your knowledge is of a meager and unsatisfactory kind.*
>
> —Sir William Thomson (Lord Kelvin)*

Number systems, since the very beginnings of civilization, have been an essential tool in people's ability to understand the world. We measure the distance between towns,

*Popular Lectures and Addresses (New York, NY: Macmillan and Co., 1891, 1894).

HIGHLIGHT FROM HISTORY
The Early Origins of Mathematics

"The history of mathematics should really be the kernel of the history of culture."

—George Sarton

The transition from simply gathering food to actually producing it occurred some 10,000 years ago, marking the change from the Paleolithic to the Neolithic age. Agriculture required farmers to stay in one place for long periods, so people designed and constructed permanent dwellings. Laying out fields, tending flocks, measuring the amount of grain that should be stored over the winter, knowing whether excess grain could be traded to neighboring villages—all gave rise to problems dealing with quantity and form. Thus, the two important branches of mathematics—number and geometry—have origins concurrent with the dawn of civilization.

Until about 600 B.C., mathematics was pursued primarily for its practical, decorative, and religious values. Problems in land apportionment, inter-

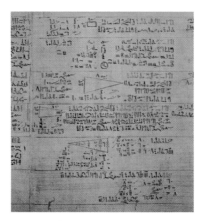

A portion of the Rhind papyrus that discusses the measurement of the area of a triangle and the slopes of pyramids. The papyrus, which contains 85 mathematical problems, was copied c. 1575 B.C. by the scribe Ahmes from a work written almost three centuries earlier.

est payments, and tax rates required solution for the development of commerce. Many problems of a mathematical nature were successfully solved during the construction of irrigation canals, temples, and pyramids. Interest in astronomy grew out of the need for calendars sufficiently accurate to forecast flood and growing seasons. Number systems and notations were developed, and even some empirically derived formulas from algebra and

geometry were known. However, little use was made of symbolism, scant attention was given to abstraction and general methods, and nowhere was the notion of proof or even informal justification to be found.

The Incas recorded and communicated quantitative data with quipus. A quipu is an assemblage of cords, with numerical values determined by the colors of the cords, the way the cords are spaced and interconnected, and the type and placement of knots tied in the cords. The quipu shown is in the Museo Nacional de Antropologia y Arqueologia, Lima, Peru.

the area of fields, the volume of a reservoir; we record and predict temperatures and the length of growing seasons; we are interested in the size of a profit or loss. Perhaps the most basic mathematical questions of all times are these: How many? How much?

In this chapter we introduce the concept of **sets,** discuss how sets may be related to each other, and define **operations** on sets by which two or more sets can be combined to form new sets. The **whole numbers**—0, 1, 2, 3, and so on—are then defined in terms of sets. The relations and operations on sets give meaning to the order of the whole numbers and the definitions and properties of the basic arithmetic operations of addition, subtraction, multiplication, and division. In the concluding section, we explore functions.

2.1   Sets and Operations on Sets

The notion of a set originated with the German mathematician Georg Cantor (1845–1918) in the last half of the nineteenth century. Sets have now become indispensable to nearly every branch of mathematics. Sets make it possible to organize, classify, describe, and communicate. For example, each number system that we will investigate—the whole numbers, the integers, the rationals, and the real numbers—is best viewed as a set together with a list of operations and properties that the numbers in the system possess.

Intuitively, a set is a collection of objects. An object that belongs to the collection is called an **element** or **member** of the set. Words like *collection, family,* or *class* are frequently used interchangeably with set. In fact, a set of dishes, a collection of stamps, and the class of 2001 at Harvard University are all examples of sets.

Cantor requires that a set be **well-defined.** This means two things. First, there is a **universe** of objects which are allowed into consideration. Second, any object in the universe is either an element of the set or it is not an element of the set. For example, "the first few presidents of the United States" does not well-define a set, since "few" is a matter of varying opinion. On the other hand, "the first three presidents of the United States" does provide an adequate verbal description of a set, with the understanding that the universe is all people who have ever lived.

There are three ways to define a set:

Word Description:	The set of the first three presidents of the U.S.
Listing in Braces:	{George Washington, Thomas Jefferson, John Adams}
Set Builder Notation:	$\{x \mid x$ is one of the first three presidents of the United States$\}$

The order in which elements in a set are listed is arbitrary, so listing Jefferson, the third president, before Adams is permissible. However, each element should be listed just once. In set builder notation, $\{x \mid x \ . \ . \ .\}$ is read "the set of all x such that x is . . . ." The letter x used in set builder notation can be replaced with any convenient letter.

Capital letters, A, B, C . . . are generally used to denote sets. Membership is symbolized by $\in$, so that if P designates the above set of three U.S. presidents, then John Adams $\in P$, where $\in$ is read "is a member of." The symbol $\notin$ is read "is not a member of," so James Monroe $\notin P$. It is sometimes useful to choose letters that suggest the set being designated. For example, the set of **natural,** or **counting,** numbers will be written

$$N = \{1, 2, 3, \ . \ . \ .\}$$

where " . . ." indicates "and so on."

HIGHLIGHT FROM HISTORY
Georg Cantor (1845–1918)

Georg Cantor was born in St. Petersburg, Russia, but at age 12 moved with his family to Germany. Cantor excelled in mathematics, and in 1867 completed his doctorate from the prestigious University of Berlin. His research soon led him to sets and the comparison of the size of various infinite sets. Today, this work is regarded as fundamental to mathematical thought, but at the time of its development it generated considerable controversy. In particular, Leopold Kronecker exhibited an unpleasant animosity toward Cantor and his work. This stifled Cantor's dream of a professorship at the University of Berlin, and may also have contributed to the onset of the mental breakdowns that plagued Cantor from age 40 until his death at age 73 in a mental hospital. Eventually, Cantor's work was widely recognized and appreciated. The mathematician David Hilbert proclaimed that "no one shall expel us from the paradise which Cantor has created for us."

EXAMPLE   2.1

Describing Sets

Each set below is taken from the universe N of the natural numbers, and has been described either in words, by listing in braces, or with set builder notation. Provide the two remaining types of description of each set.

(a)   The set of natural numbers greater than 12 and less than 17.
(b) $\{x \mid x = 2n \text{ and } n = 1, 2, 3, 4, 5\}$
(c) $\{3, 6, 9, 12, \ldots\}$
(d)   The set of the first ten odd natural numbers.
(e) $\{1, 3, 5, 7, \ldots\}$
(f) $\{x \mid x = n^2 \text{ and } n \in N\}$

Solution

(a) $\{13, 14, 15, 16\}$
      $\{n \mid n \in N \text{ and } 12 < n < 17\}$
(b) $\{2, 4, 6, 8, 10\}$
      The set of the first five even natural numbers.
(c)   The set of all natural numbers that are multiples of 3.
      $\{x \mid x = 3n \text{ and } n \in N\}$
(d) $\{1, 3, 5, 7, 9, 11, 13, 15, 17, 19\}$
      $\{x \mid x = 2n - 1 \text{ and } n = 1, 2, \ldots, 10\}$
(e)   The set of the odd natural numbers.
      $\{x \mid x = 2n - 1 \text{ and } n \in N\}$
(f) $\{1, 4, 9, 16, 25, \ldots\}$
      The set of the squares of the natural numbers.

Venn Diagrams

Sets can be represented pictorially by **Venn diagrams,** named for the English logician John Venn (1834–1923). The universal set, which we denote by U, is represented by a rectangle. Any set within the universe is represented by a closed loop lying within the rectangle. The region inside the loop is associated with the elements in the set. An example is given in Figure 2.1, which shows the Venn diagram for the set of vowels $V = \{a, e, i, o, u\}$ in the universe $U = \{a, b, c, \ldots, z\}$.

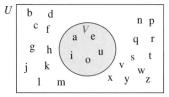

Figure 2.1
The Venn diagram showing the set of vowels in the universe of the 26-letter alphabet

Coloring, shading, or cross-hatching are also useful devices to distinguish the sets in a Venn diagram. For example, set A is blue in Figure 2.2 and the set of elements of the universe that do not belong to A is colored red.

The elements in the universe that are not in set A form a set called the **complement** of A, which is written $\overline{A}$.

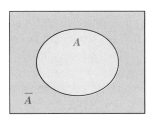

Figure 2.2
The Venn diagram of set A (shown in blue), its complement $\overline{A}$ (shown in red), and the universal set U (the region within the rectangle)

DEFINITION *The Complement of a Set* A

The **complement of set A,** written $\overline{A}$, is the set of elements in the universal set U which are not elements of A. That is,

$$\overline{A} = \{x \mid x \in U \quad \text{and} \quad x \notin A\}.$$

EXAMPLE   2.2 | **Finding Set Complements**

Let $U = N = \{1, 2, 3, \ldots\}$ be the set of natural numbers. For the sets E and F given below, find the complementary sets $\overline{E}$ and $\overline{F}$.

(a) $E = \{2, 4, 6, \ldots\}$
(b) $F = \{n \mid n > 10\}$

Solution

(a) $\overline{E} = \{1, 3, 5, \ldots\}$. That is, the complement of the set E of even natural numbers is the set $\overline{E}$ of odd natural numbers.
(b) $\overline{F} = \{1, 2, 3, 4, 5, 6, 7, 8, 9, 10\}$.

Relationships and Operations on Sets

Consider several sets, labeled $A, B, C, D, \ldots$, whose members all belong to the same universal set U. It is useful to understand how sets may be related to one another, and how two or more sets can be used to define new sets.

DEFINITION *Subset*

The set A is a **subset** of B, written $A \subseteq B$, if, and only if, every element of A is also an element of B.

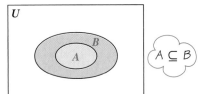

If A is a subset of B, every element of A also belongs to B. In this case it is useful in the Venn diagram to place the loop for representing A within the loop representing set B, as shown in Figure 2.3.

Figure 2.3
A Venn diagram when it is known that A is a subset of B

If two sets A and B have precisely the same elements then they are **equal** and we write $A = B$. If $A \subseteq B$ but $A \neq B$, we say that A is a **proper subset** of B and write $A \subset B$. If $A \subset B$, there must be some element of B which is not also an element of A; that is, there is some x for which $x \in B$ and $x \notin A$.

> **DEFINITION** *Intersection of Sets*
>
> The **intersection** of two sets A and B, written $A \cap B$, is the set of elements common to both A and B. That is,
>
> $$A \cap B = \{x \mid x \in A \text{ and } x \in B\}.$$

For example, $\{a, b, c, d\} \cap \{a, d, e, f\} = \{a, d\}$. The symbol $\cap$ is a special mathematics symbol called a **cap.**

Two sets with no element in common are said to be **disjoint.** The intersection of disjoint sets is then the set with no members, which is called the **empty set.** The empty set is given the special mathematical symbol $\varnothing$, which should not be mistaken for the Greek letter ϕ (phi). In symbols, two sets C and D are disjoint if and only if $C \cap D = \varnothing$. See Figure 2.4.

Figure 2.4

(a) *A Venn diagram whose shaded region shows the intersection $A \cap B$.*

(b) *A Venn diagram for sets C and D that are disjoint. That is, $C \cap D = \varnothing$.*

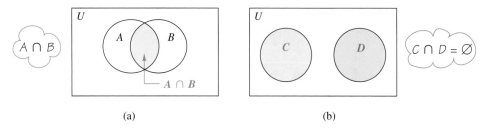

(a)   (b)

> **DEFINITION** *Union of Sets*
>
> The **union** of sets A and B, written $A \cup B$, is the set of all elements that are in A or B. That is,
>
> $$A \cup B = \{x \mid x \in A \text{ or } x \in B\}.$$

For example, if $A = \{a, e, i, o, u\}$ and $B = \{a, b, c, d, e\}$ then $A \cup B = \{a, b, c, d, e, i, o, u\}$. Elements such as a and e that belong to both A and B are listed just once in $A \cup B$. The word *or* in the definition of union is taken in the inclusive sense of and/or. The symbol for union is the **cup,** $\cup$. The cup symbol must be carefully distinguished from the letter U used to denote the universal set. See Figure 2.5.

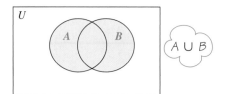

Figure 2.5
The shaded region corresponds to the union, $A \cup B$, of sets A and B

EXAMPLE   2.3

Performing Operations on Sets

Let $U = \{p, q, r, s, t, u, v, w, x, y\}$ be the universe, and let $A = \{p, q, r\}$, $B = \{q, r, s, t, u\}$, $C = \{r, u, w, y\}$. Locate all ten elements of U in a three loop Venn diagram, and then find the following sets:

(a) $A \cup C$ **(b)** $A \cap C$ **(c)** $A \cup B$ **(d)** $A \cap B$

(e) $\overline{B}$ **(f)** $\overline{C}$ **(g)** $A \cup \overline{B}$ **(h)** $A \cap \overline{C}$

Solution

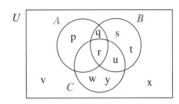

(a) $A \cup C = \{p, q, r, u, w, y\}$ **(b)** $A \cap C = \{r\}$

(c) $A \cup B = \{p, q, r, s, t, u\}$ **(d)** $A \cap B = \{q, r\}$

(e) $\overline{B} = \{p, v, w, x, y\}$ **(f)** $\overline{C} = \{p, q, s, t, v, x\}$

(g) $A \cup \overline{B} = \{p, q, r, v, w, x, y\}$ **(h)** $A \cap \overline{C} = \{p, q\}$

Using Sets for Problem Solving

The notions of sets and their operations are often used to understand a problem and communicate its solution. Moreover, Venn diagrams provide a means of visual understanding and representation.

EXAMPLE   2.4

Using Sets to Solve a Problem in Color Graphics

The cathode ray tube (CRT) on a color monitor uses three types of phosphors, each of which when excited by an electron beam produces one of the three primary colors—red, blue, or green. By exciting different combinations of phosphors a wider range of colors is possible. Use a Venn diagram to show what combinations are possible.

Solution

Introduce three loops in a Venn diagram—one for each of the primary colors. As shown below, eight colors can be achieved. Most computers also allow the intensity of each color to be specified. In this way even more colors can be obtained.

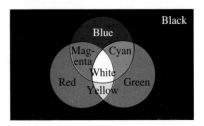

INTO THE CLASSROOM

Sets Education for Elementary School Children

Sets provide a theoretical basis for defining the whole numbers. The operations and properties of the system of whole numbers can be defined and understood through their connection with corresponding operations and properties of sets. However, it is not appropriate to use *abstract* notions of set theory to teach young children. Instead, the teacher should use activities with physical collections of objects to give concrete hands-on experiences with set ideas and associated number concepts. It is critically important to use an approach that has meaning in the child's world. Colored chips, attribute pieces, tiles, beans, and so on, all become useful concrete embodiments of elements that may be organized and classified into sets—sets that can be seen, touched, and manipulated. The older child can later move successfully to pictorial representation. Later still, the student will become comfortable dealing with abstract models, represented entirely in words and symbols.

Notice that if red and green are excited, then including blue will produce white. On the other hand, if red is excited then including both green and blue will also produce white. In symbols, this becomes

$$(R \cap G) \cap B = R \cap (G \cap B).$$

Since the result is independent of where the parentheses are placed, this illustrates what is called the **associative property** of the intersection operation. Since the order in which the intersections are taken has no effect on the outcome, we do not need parentheses and it is meaningful to write $R \cap G \cap B$. Similarly, union is associative and it is meaningful to write $R \cup G \cup B$ without parentheses.

The associative property is just one example of a number of useful properties that hold for set operations and relations. The properties listed in the following theorem can be proved by reasoning directly from the definitions given earlier. They can also be justified by considering appropriately shaded Venn diagrams.

THEOREM   *Properties of Set Operations and Relations*

1. Transitivity of inclusion
$$\text{If } A \subseteq B \text{ and } B \subseteq C \text{ then } A \subseteq C.$$

2. Commutativity of union and intersection
$$A \cup B = B \cup A$$
$$A \cap B = B \cap A$$

3. Associativity of union and intersection
$$A \cup (B \cup C) = (A \cup B) \cup C$$
$$A \cap (B \cap C) = (A \cap B) \cap C$$

4. Properties of the empty set
$$A \cup \varnothing = \varnothing \cup A = A$$
$$A \cap \varnothing = \varnothing \cap A = \varnothing$$

5. Distributive properties of union and intersection
$$A \cap (B \cup C) = (A \cap B) \cup (A \cap C)$$
$$A \cup (B \cap C) = (A \cup B) \cap (A \cup C)$$

EXAMPLE 2.5 **Verifying Properties with Venn diagrams**

(a) Verify the distributive property $A \cap (B \cup C) = (A \cap B) \cup (A \cap C)$.

(b) Show that $A \cup B \cap C$ is not meaningful without parentheses.

Solution

(a) To shade the region corresponding to $A \cap (B \cup C)$, we intersect the A loop with the "figure 8" loop of $B \cup C$.

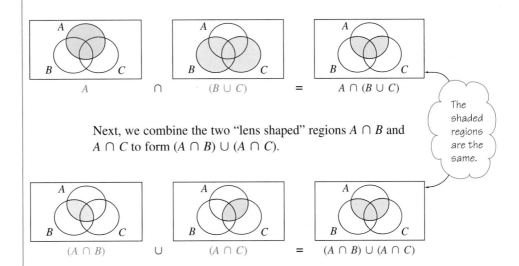

Next, we combine the two "lens shaped" regions $A \cap B$ and $A \cap C$ to form $(A \cap B) \cup (A \cap C)$.

The shaded regions are the same.

The shaded regions at the right agree, which verifies that intersection distributes over union; that is, that

$$A \cap (B \cup C) = (A \cap B) \cup (A \cap C).$$

(b) If the union is taken first, we have the expression $(A \cup B) \cap C$, corresponding to the region shaded at the left in the following figure. If the intersection is taken first, we have the expression $A \cup (B \cap C)$, corresponding to the region shaded in the Venn diagram at the right. The shaded regions are different, so in general $(A \cup B) \cap C \neq A \cup (B \cap C)$.

The shaded regions are different.

We can also consider the explicit case $A = \{a\}$, $B = \{a, b\}$, $C = \{b, c\}$, for which $(A \cup B) \cap C = \{b\}$ and $A \cup (B \cap C) = \{a, b\}$. We see that $(A \cup B) \cap C \neq A \cup (B \cap C)$ since $\{b\} \neq \{a, b\}$. Such an example that shows that a statement is false is called a **counterexample**.

PROBLEM SET 2.1

Understanding Concepts

Problem numbers in color indicate that the answer to this problem can be found at the back of the book.

1. Write the following sets by listing their elements.

   (a) The set of states in the U.S. which border Nevada.

   (b) The set of states in the U.S. whose names begin with the letter M.

   (c) The set of states in the U.S. whose names contain the letter Z.

2. Write the following sets.

   (a) The set of letters used in the sentence "list the elements in a set only once."

   (b) The set of letters that are needed to spell these words: team, meat, mate, tame.

3. Let $U = \{1, 2, 3, \ldots, 20\}$. Write these sets by listing the elements in braces.

   (a) $\{x \in U \mid 7 < x \le 12\}$

   (b) $\{x \in U \mid x \text{ is odd and } 4 \le x \le 13\}$

   (c) $\{x \in U \mid x \text{ is divisible by } 3\}$

   (d) $\{x \in U \mid x = 3n \text{ for some } n \in N\}$

   (e) $\{x \in U \mid x = n^2 \text{ for some } n \in N\}$

4. Write these sets in set builder notation, where $U = \{1, 2, \ldots, 20\}$.

   (a) $\{11, 12, 13, 14\}$

   (b) $\{6, 8, 10, 12, 16\}$

   (c) $\{4, 8, 12, 16, 20\}$

   (d) $\{2, 5, 10, 17\}$

5. Use set builder notation to write the following subsets of the natural numbers.

   (a) The even natural numbers larger than 12.

   (b) The squares of the odd numbers larger than or equal to 25.

   (c) The natural numbers divisible by 3.

6. Discuss whether or not the following descriptions describe well-defined sets:

   (a) Moscow, Lima, Paris, Duluth

   (b) Moscow ID, Lima MT, Paris TX, Duluth GA

   (c) The smart students in my math class.

   (d) The students in my class with a 3.5 GPA.

> ## Trucker rolls to right city, but wrong state
>
> DULUTH, Minn. (AP)
> A truck driver made a longer trip than he bar–gained for when he ended up in the right town – but the wrong state.

SOURCE: From "Trucker rolls to right city, but wrong state" from *The Daily Evergreen*, Vol. 97, No. 92, January 21, 1991. Reprinted by permission of The Daily Evergreen.

7. Decide if the following set relationships are *true* or *false*.

   (a) $\{s, c, r, a, m, b, l, e, d\} = \{a, b, c, d, e, l, m, r, s\}$

   (b) $\{2\} \subset \{1, 2, 3\}$

   (c) $\{1, 2, 3\} = \{3, 1, 2\}$

   (d) $\{2\} \subseteq \{1, 2, 3\}$

   (e) $\{1, 2, 3\} \subseteq \{3, 2, 1\}$

   (f) $\{3\} \subset \{2\}$

8. Let $U = \{a, b, c, d, e, f, g, h\}$, $A = \{a, b, c, d, e\}$, $B = \{a, b, c\}$, and $C = \{a, b, h\}$. Locate all eight elements of U in a three loop Venn diagram, and then list the elements in the following sets.

   (a) $B \cup C$ (b) $A \cap B$ (c) $B \cap C$

   (d) $A \cup B$ (e) $\overline{A}$ (f) $A \cap C$

   (g) $A \cup (B \cap C)$

9. Let $L = \{6, 12, 18, 24, \ldots\}$ be the set of multiples of 6 and let $M = \{45, 90, 135, \ldots\}$ be the set of multiples of 45.

   (a) Use your calculator to find four more elements of set M.

   (b) Describe $L \cap M$.

   (c) What is the smallest element in $L \cap M$?

10. Let $G = \{n \mid n \text{ divides } 90\}$ and $D = \{n \mid n \text{ divides } 144\}$. In listed form $G = \{1, 2, 3, 5, 6, 9, 10, 15, 18, 30, 45, 90\}$.

   (a) Find the listed form of the set D.

   (b) Find $G \cap D$.

   (c) Which element of $G \cap D$ is largest?

11. Draw and shade Venn diagrams that correspond to the following sets.

(a) $A \cap B \cap C$ (b) $A \cup (B \cap \overline{C})$

(c) $(A \cap B) \cup C$ (d) $\overline{A} \cup (B \cap C)$

(e) $A \cup B \cup C$ (f) $\overline{A} \cap B \cap C$

12. For each part, draw a Venn diagram whose loops for set A, B, and C show that the conditions listed must hold.

(a) $A \subseteq C, B \subseteq C, A \cap B = \emptyset$

(b) $C \subseteq (A \cap B)$

(c) $(A \cap B) \subseteq C$

13. If $A \cup B = A \cup C$, is it necessarily true that $B = C$? Give a proof, or provide a counterexample.

14. Let U be the set of natural numbers 1 through 20, let A be the set of even numbers in U, and let B be the set of numbers in U that are divisible by 3.

(a) Find $\overline{A \cap B}, \overline{A} \cup \overline{B}, \overline{A \cup B}, \overline{A} \cap \overline{B}$.

(b) What two pairs of the four sets of part (a) are equal?

15. The 12 shapes in the Venn diagram below are described by the following attributes.

Shape: circle, hexagon, or triangle

Size: small or large

Color: red or blue

Let C, H, and T denote the respective sets of circular, hexagonal, and triangular shapes. Similarly, let S, L, R, and B denote the sets of small, large, red, and blue shapes, respectively. The set A contains the shapes that are small and not a triangle, so $A = S \cap \overline{T}$.

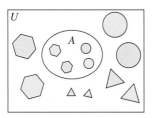

Describe which shapes are found in these sets.

(a) $R \cap C$ (b) $L \cap H$ (c) $T \cup H$

(d) $L \cap T$ (e) $B \cap \overline{C}$ (f) $H \cap S \cap R$

16. Let C, H, T, S, L, R, and B denote the sets of attribute shapes described in problem 15. The set of small hexagons can be written $S \cap H$ in symbolic form. Express these sets in symbolic form.

(a) The large triangles.

(b) The blue polygonal (that is, noncircular) shapes.

(c) The small or triangular shapes.

(d) The shapes that are either blue circles or are red.

Thinking Critically

17. The set {a} has two subsets, $\emptyset$ and {a}. The set {a, b} has four subsets: $\emptyset$, {a}, {b}, {a, b}.

(a) How many subsets are there of {a, b, c}? (*Hint:* Make an orderly list of the subsets.)

(b) How many subsets are there of {a, b, c, d}?

(c) How many of the subsets of {a, b, c, d} do not contain the element d? Contain element d?

(d) If a set has n elements, guess a formula for the number of subsets. Explain carefully, on the basis of consideration of parts (a), (b), and (c).

(e) How many subsets does the set of 26 letters {a, b, . . . , z} of the alphabet have?

(f) A set has exactly 524,288 subsets. How many elements does it have?

18. Circular loops in a Venn diagram divide the universe U into distinct regions.

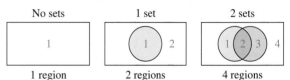

(a) Draw a diagram for three circles that gives the largest number of regions.

(b) How many regions do the four circles define in this figure?

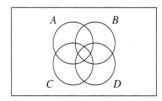

(c) Verify that the four circle diagram is missing a region corresponding to $A \cap \overline{B} \cap \overline{C} \cap D$. What other set has no corresponding region?

(d) Will this Venn diagram allow for all possible combinations of four sets? Explain briefly but carefully.

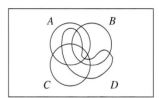

19. The English mathematician Augustus DeMorgan (1806–1871) showed that

$$\overline{A \cap B} = \overline{A} \cup \overline{B} \quad \text{and} \quad \overline{A \cup B} = \overline{A} \cap \overline{B}$$

These identities are now called DeMorgan's Laws.

(a) Use a sequence of Venn diagrams to explain, in words and pictures, how to shade in the regions corresponding to $\overline{A \cap B}$ and $\overline{A} \cup \overline{B}$. The final shaded regions obtained should be identical, justifying DeMorgan's First Law.

(b) Carefully explain how to justify DeMorgan's Second Law by shading Venn diagrams.

20. Columnist Marilyn vos Savant was asked by a reader "If some quizzles are quozzles, and all quazzles are quozzles, then some quizzles are definitely quazzles. True or false." Draw a three loop Venn diagram that satisfies the conditions between the sets of quizzles, quozzles, and quazzles, and then use the diagram to answer the reader's question.

21. Each of the objects depicted in problem 15 is described by its attributes: shape (three choices), size (two choices), and color (two choices). The number of pieces in a full set of shapes can be varied by changing the number of attributes and the number of possible choices of an attribute. How many pieces are contained in these attribute sets?

(a) Shape: circle, hexagon, equilateral triangle, isosceles right triangle, rectangle, square

Size: large, small

Color: red, yellow, blue

(b) As in part (a), but also include this attribute:
Thickness: thick, thin

Thinking Cooperatively

22. Obtain (or make) a 12-piece attribute shape set as described in problem 15, one set per small group. Let *C, H, T, S, L, R,* and *B* denote the sets of attribute shapes described in problem 15. Each loop in the Venn diagrams below corresponds to one of the above sets. Just some of the twelve attribute pieces are depicted in each figure. Determine how to label the loops. Is there more than one correct way to label each diagram?

(a)

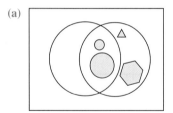

(b)

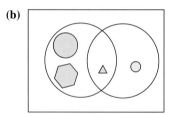

(c)

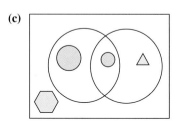

(d)

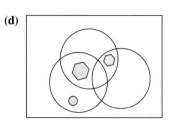

(e) Have each group invent its own "missing label" puzzles similar to those shown. In turn, have each group challenge the other groups to label its puzzles.

23. Attribute cards can be made by drawing various shapes on cards, varying the figure shown, the color used, and so on. Here are some examples of a few attribute cards.

(a) Conjecture how many cards make a full deck. Explain how you get your answer.

(b) Form groups of 3 to 5 students. Each group is to design and make a set of attribute cards, drawing simple figures on small rectangles of cardstock with colored pens.

(c) Exchange decks of attribute cards among the cooperative groups. Shuffle each deck and turn over just a few of the cards. Can your group predict the number of cards in the complete deck? Carefully explain the reasoning used.

Making Connections

24. The ABO System of Blood Typing. Until the beginning of the twentieth century, it was assumed that all human blood was identical. About 1900, however, the Austrian-American pathologist Karl Landsteiner discovered that blood could be classified into four groups according to the presence of proteins called antigens. This discovery made it possible to transfuse blood safely. A person with the antigens A, or B, or both A and B, has the respective blood type A, B, or AB. If neither antigen is present the type is O. Draw and label a Venn diagram which illustrates the ABO system.

25. The Rh System of Blood Typing. In 1940, Karl Landsteiner (see problem 24) and the American pathologist Alexander Wiener discovered another protein which coats the red blood cells of some persons. Since the initial research was on rhesus monkeys, a person with the protein is classified as Rh positive (Rh+), and a person whose blood cells lack the protein is classified as Rh negative (Rh−). Draw and label a Venn diagram illustrates the classification of blood in the eight major types A+, A−, B+, B−, AB+, AB−, O+, O−.

Communicating

26. The word "set" has been given precise mathematical meaning. The same word is also used as part of our ordinary language. For example, you may own a set of golf clubs. Make a list of other examples where "set," or "family," "aggregate," "class," or "collection" is used, and discuss to what extent their usage corresponds to the mathematical concept of set.

27. Many of the terms introduced in this section also have meaning in nonmathematical contexts. For example, "complement," "union," and "intersection" are used in ordinary speech. Other terms, such as "transitive," "commutative," "associative," and "distributive" are rare in everyday usage but there are closely related words that are quite common, such as "transit," "commute," "associate," and "distribute." Discuss the differences and similarities in meanings of the words, and word roots, of the terms introduced in this section.

From State Student Assessments

28. (Washington State, Grade 4) Ms. Yonan took a survey in her class to see how many students like hamburgers, pizza, or hot dogs. The results of the survey are shown in the chart.

NUMBER OF STUDENTS WHO LIKE:		
Only 1 of These Foods	Only 2 of These Foods	All 3 of These Foods
14	10	4

Look at the three Venn diagrams below. Choose the diagram that best represents the results of this survey.

A.

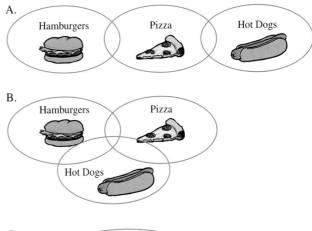

B.

C.

For Review

29. Show that the natural numbers 1, 2, . . ., 15 can be arranged in a list so that the sum of each adjacent pair is a square number. Write your solution to illustrate Pólya's four steps of problem solving.

30. A power company intends to number its power poles from 1 to 10,000. Each numeral is formed by gluing stamped-metal digits to the poles. How many metal 2s should the company order? Write your solution to illustrate Pólya's four steps of problem solving.

2.2   Sets, Counting, and the Whole Numbers

If you attended a student raffle, you might hear the following announcement when the entry forms are drawn:

> *"The student with identification number 50768–973 has just won second prize—four tickets to the big game this Saturday."*

There are three types of numbers.

This sentence contains three numbers, each of a different type, and each serving a different purpose.

First, a number can be an **identification,** or **nominal number.** A nominal number is a sequence of digits used as a name or label. Telephone numbers, social security numbers, account numbers with stores and banks, serial numbers, and driver's license numbers are just a few examples of the use of numbers for identification and naming. The role such numbers play in contemporary society has expanded rapidly with the advent of computers.

The next type of number used by the raffle announcer is an **ordinal number.** The words first, second, third, fourth, and so on, are used to describe the relative position of the objects in an ordered sequence. Thus, ordinal numbers communicate location in an ordered collection. First class, second rate, third base, Fourth of July, fifth page, sixth volume, and twenty-first century are all familiar examples of ordinal numbers.

The final use of a number by the raffle announcer was to tell how many tickets had been won. That is, the prize is a set of tickets and *four* tells us *how many* tickets are in the set. More generally, a **cardinal number** of a set is the number of objects in the set. Thus cardinal numbers help communicate the basic notion of "how many."

It should be noticed that numbers, of whatever type, can be expressed verbally (in a language) or symbolically (in a numeration system). For example, the number of moons of Mars is "two" in English, "zwei" in German, and "dos" in Spanish. Symbolically, we could write 2 in the Indo-Arabic* (or Hindu-Arabic) system or II in Roman numerals. Numeration, as a system of symbolic representation of numbers, is closely related to algorithms for computation. Numeration systems, both historic and contemporary, are described in Chapter 3.

In the remainder of this section, we explore the notion of cardinal numbers more fully. Of special importance is the set of whole numbers, which can be viewed as the set of cardinal numbers of finite sets.

One-to-one Correspondence and Equivalent Sets

Suppose, when you come to your classroom, each student is seated at his or her desk. You would immediately know, *without counting,* that the number of children and the number of occupied desks are the same. This example illustrates the concept of a **one-to-one correspondence** between sets in which each element of one set is paired with exactly one element of the second set, and each element of either set belongs to exactly one of the pairs.

> **DEFINITION** *One-to-One Correspondence*
>
> A **one-to-one correspondence** between sets A and B is a pairing of the elements of A with the elements of B in such a way that each element of A and B belongs to one, and only one, pair.

---

*Indo refers to India, the region of origination of the symbols. Hindu refers to the predominant religion of India.

Figure 2.6 illustrates a one-to-one correspondence between the sets of board members and officers of the Math Club.

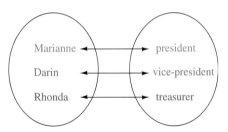

Figure 2.6

A one-to-one correspondence between the set of board members {Marianne, Darin, Rhonda} and officers {president, vice-president, treasurer} of the Math Club

Because there is a one-to-one correspondence between the sets {m, d, r} and {p, v, t}, we say that they are **equivalent sets** and write {m, d, r} ∼ {p, v, t}.

More generally we have the following definition.

> **DEFINITION**   *Equivalent Sets*
>
> Sets A and B are **equivalent** if there is a one-to-one correspondence between A and B. When A and B are equivalent, we write $A \sim B$. We also say that equivalent sets **match.** If A and B are not equivalent we write $A \nsim B$.

It is easy to see that equal sets match. To see why, suppose that $A = B$. Since each x in A is also in B, the natural matching $x \leftrightarrow x$ is a one-to-one correspondence between A and B. Thus $A \sim B$. On the other hand, there is no reason to believe equivalent sets must be equal. For example, $\{\square, \bigstar\} \sim \{1, 2\}$ but $\{\square, \bigstar\} \neq \{1, 2\}$.

EXAMPLE   2.6

Investigating Sets for Equivalence

Let $A = \{x \mid x \text{ is a moon of Mars}\}$

   $B = \{x \mid x \text{ is a former U.S. president whose last name is Adams}\}$

   $C = \{x \mid x \text{ is one of the Brontë sisters of nineteenth century literary fame}\}$

   $D = \{x \mid x \text{ is a satellite of the fourth closest planet to the sun}\}$

Which of these relationships, $=, \neq, \sim, \nsim$, holds between distinct pairs of the four sets?

Solution

It is useful to write the sets in listed form:

   $A = D = \{\text{Deimos, Phobos}\}, B = \{\text{John Adams, John Quincy Adams}\},$
   $C = \{\text{Anne, Charlotte, Emily}\}$

$$A \neq B, A \neq C, A = D, B \neq C, B \neq D, C \neq D$$
$$A \sim B, A \nsim C, A \sim D, B \nsim C, B \sim D, C \nsim D$$

The Whole Numbers

The sets {a, b, c}, {□, ○, △}, {Mercury, Venus, Earth}, {Larry, Moe, Curly} are distinct, but they do share the property of "threeness." The English word "three," and the Indo-Arabic numeral 3, are used to identify this common property of all sets that are equivalent to $\{1, 2, 3\}$. In a similar way, we use the word "two," and the symbol 2, to convey the idea that all of the sets that are equivalent to the set $\{1, 2\}$ have the same cardinality.

Some sets are quite large and it is difficult to know how large n must be for the set to be equivalent to the set $\{1, 2, 3, \ldots, n\}$. For example, the set of people alive in the world in the year 2000 would require n to be around 6×10^9 (that is, n is about 6 billion). Even so, this is an example of a finite set. In general, a set is said to be **finite** if it is either the empty set or is equivalent to a set $\{1, 2, 3, \ldots, n\}$ for some natural number n. Sets which are not finite are called **infinite.** For example, the set N of all of the natural numbers is an infinite set. It is usually easy to know whether a set is finite or infinite, but not always. In Chapter 4, we'll see Euclid's clever proof that the set of prime numbers $\{2, 3, 5, 7, 11, 13, 17, 19, 23, 29, 31, \ldots\}$ is an infinite set. Many of these prime numbers come in pairs of adjacent odd numbers known as **twin primes,** such as $(3, 5)$, $(5, 7)$, $(11, 13)$, $(17, 19)$, and $(29, 31)$. However, it is unknown if the set of twin primes is finite or infinite.

The whole numbers, as defined below, allow us to classify any finite set according to how many elements the set contains. It is useful to adopt the symbol $n(A)$ to represent that cardinality of the finite set A. If A is not the empty set, then $n(A)$ is a counting number. The cardinality of the empty set, however, requires a new name and symbol: we let **zero** designate the cardinality of the empty set, and write $0 = n(\varnothing)$.

> Use $n(A)$ to denote the number of elements in set A.

A common error is made by omitting the $n(\ )$ symbol: be sure not to write "$A = 4$" when your intention is to state that $n(A) = 4$.

DEFINITION   *The Whole Numbers*

The **whole numbers** are the cardinal numbers of finite sets; that is, the numbers of elements in finite sets. If $A \sim \{1, 2, 3, \ldots, m\}$ then $n(A) = m$, and $n(\varnothing) = 0$, where $n(A)$ denotes the cardinality of set A. The set of whole numbers is written $W = \{0, 1, 2, 3, \ldots\}$.

EXAMPLE   2.7   **Determining Whole Numbers**

For each set find the whole number that gives the number of elements in the set.

(a) $M = \{x \mid x \text{ is a month of the year}\}$
(b) $A = \{a, b, c, \ldots, z\}$
(c) $B = \{n \in N \mid n \text{ is a square number smaller than } 200\}$
(d) $Z = \{n \in N \mid n \text{ is a square number between 70 and 80}\}$
(e) $S = \{0\}$

Solution

(a) $n(M) = 12$ since $M \sim \{1, 2, 3, \ldots, 12\}$, and this amounts to counting the elements in M.
(b) $n(A) = 26$
(c) $n(B) = 14$ since $B = \{1, 4, 9, 16, 25, 36, 49, 64, 81, 100, 121, 144, 169, 196\}$ and contains 14 elements.
(d) $n(Z) = 0$ since there are no square numbers between 70 and 80 and therefore $Z = \varnothing$.
(e) $n(S) = 1$ since the set $\{0\}$ contains one element. This shows that zero is *not* the same as "nothing"!

I t required thousands of years of mathematical thought for the concept of zero to emerge and its importance be recognized. Zero, as is true of any whole number, expresses a quantity. Thus zero *is* something, and it should not be mistaken as synonymous with nothing. (Ask any student who gets a zero on a test if it means nothing to his or her grade!) The contemplation of the void was an important aspect of ancient Eastern philosophy, and it is possible to trace the idea, and even the word zero, to this tradition. The Hindu word *sunya,* meaning "void" or "empty," was translated into Arabic as *sifr.* In its Latinized form sifr became *zephirum,* from which the word *zero* ultimately evolved.

EXAMPLE   2.8

Problem Solving with Whole Numbers and Venn Diagrams

In a recent survey, the 60 students living in Harris Hall were asked about their enrollments in science, engineering, and humanities classes. The results were as follows:

24 are taking a science class
22 are taking an engineering class
17 are taking a humanities class
5 are taking both science and engineering classes
4 are taking both science and humanities classes
3 are taking both engineering and humanities classes
2 are taking classes in all three areas.

How many students are not taking classes in any of the three areas? How many students are taking a class in just one area? Use a Venn diagram, indicating the number of students in each region of the diagram.

Solution

Let S, E, and H denote the set of students in science, engineering, and humanities classes, respectively. Since $n(S \cap E \cap H) = 2$, begin by placing the 2 in the region of the Venn diagram corresponding to the subset $S \cap E \cap H$. Then, by comparing $n(S \cap E \cap H) = 2$ and $n(E \cap H) = 3$, we conclude there is one student who is taking both engineering and humanities, but not a science class. This allows us to fill in the 1 in the Venn diagram. Analogous reasoning leads to the entries within the loops of the following Venn diagram.

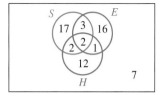

The values within the loops account for 53 of the 60 students, so it follows that 7 students are not taking classes in any of the three areas. Also, since $17 + 16 + 12 = 45$, we conclude that 45 students are taking a class in just one area.

Physical and Pictorial Representations for Whole Numbers

Here are just a few physical and pictorial representations useful for explaining whole and natural number concepts. It should be noticed that we have not yet introduced repre-

JUST FOR FUN

Red and Green Jellybeans

Caralee has two jars of jellybeans, labeled R and G. The jellybeans in one jar R are all red, and those in the other jar G are all green. Caralee removed 20 red jellybeans, mixed them up with the green jellybeans in jar G and then without looking grabbed 20 jellybeans from the mixed jar and put them back in jar R. How does the number of green jellybeans in jar R compare to the number of red jellybeans in jar G?

sentations that require grouping, number base, or place value. In the next chapter, additional representations are introduced that help illustrate connections to numeration and algorithms for the operations of arithmetic.

Tiles   Tiles are congruent squares, each about 2 centimeters (3/4 inch) on a side. They should be sufficiently thick to be easily picked up and moved about. Colored plastic tiles are available from suppliers, but tiles are easily homemade from vinyl tile or cardboard. Of course, beans, circular discs, and other objects can be used as well. However, square tiles can be arranged into rectangular patterns, and such patterns reveal many of the fundamental properties of the whole numbers. See Figure 2.7.

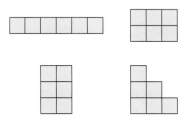

Figure 2.7
Some representations of six with square tiles

Cubes   Cubes are much like tiles, but they can form both three-dimensional and two-dimensional patterns. Several attractive versions are commercially available. Unifix™ Cubes can be snapped together to form linear groupings. Multilink™ Cubes permit planar and spatial patterns as we see in Figure 2.8.

Figure 2.8
Some representations of twelve with cubes

Number Strips and Rods   Colored strips of cardboard or heavy paper, divided into squares, can be used to demonstrate and reinforce whole number properties and operations. The squares should be ruled off, and colors can be used to visually identify the number of squares in a strip, as indicated in Figure 2.9. Number strips can be used nearly interchangeably with Cuisenaire® rods, which have been used effectively for many years. The colors shown in the figure correspond to those of Cuisenaire® rods. Whole numbers larger than ten are illustrated by placing strips, or rods, end-to-end to form a "train."

Number Line   The number line is a pictorial model in which two distinct points on a line are labeled 0 and 1, and then the remaining whole numbers are laid off in succession with the same spacing (see Figure 2.10). Any whole number is interpreted as a distance from 0,

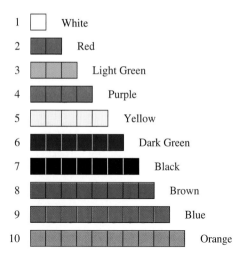

Figure 2.9
Number strips for the natural numbers 1 through 10

which can be shown by an arrow. The number line model is particularly important because it can also be used to visualize the number systems that are developed later. In this way, it can be seen how the whole numbers are extended to the integers, and how the integers are related to the rational and real number systems.

> The number line begins at 0, not at 1.

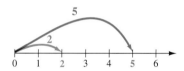

Figure 2.10
Illustrating two and five on the number line model of the whole numbers

Ordering the Whole Numbers

We often wish to relate the number of elements in two given sets. For example, if each child in the class is given one cupcake, and there are some cupcakes left over, we would know that there are more cupcakes for the party than children. Notice that children have been matched to a *proper* subset of the set of cupcakes.

The order of the whole numbers can be defined in the following way.

DEFINITION   *Ordering the Whole Numbers*

Let $a = n(A)$ and $b = n(B)$ be whole numbers, where A and B are finite sets. If A matches a *proper* subset of B, we say that a **is less than** b and write $a < b$.

The expression $b > a$ is read "b is greater than a," and is equivalent to $a < b$. Also, $a \leq b$ means "a is less than or equal to b." The sets A and B used in checking the definition are arbitrary, and it is sometimes useful to choose $A \subset B$.

HIGHLIGHT FROM HISTORY
**The Equality and
Inequality Symbols**

M any of the mathematical symbols we commonly use today originated in Renaissance times or shortly thereafter. The sign = was introduced in 1557 by Robert Recorde (1510–1558) of Cambridge. It appeared in *The Whetstone of Witte,* the first English book on algebra. According to Recorde, no two things are so alike as two parallel lines, and hence the symbol of equality. The symbols > and < , for "greater" and "less," first appeared in 1631 in a posthumous publication of Thomas Harriot (1560–1621). The equality sign in Harriot's book was very long, looking like this: ═════

EXAMPLE   2.9

Showing the Order of Whole Numbers

Show that $4 < 7$ using (a) sets; (b) tiles; (c) rods; and (d) the number line.

Solution

(a)   The following diagram shows that a set with 4 elements matches a proper subset of a set with 7 elements. Therefore, $4 < 7$.

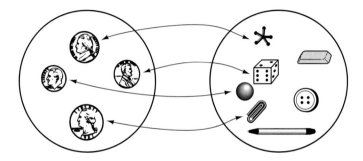

(b)   By setting tiles side by side, it is seen that the 4 colored tiles match a proper subset of the 7 uncolored tiles.

(c)   With rods, the order of whole numbers is interpreted by comparing the lengths of the rods.

Numbers larger than ten are compared by forming side by side trains of rods.

(d)   On the number line, $4 < 7$ because 4 is to the left of 7.

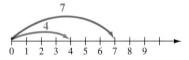

PROBLEM SET 2.2

Understanding Concepts

1. Classify by type—cardinal, ordinal, or nominal—the numbers that appear in these sentences.

   (a) On June 13, Mary was promoted to first vice-president.

   (b) On the eleventh hole, Joe's second shot with a 6-iron went 160 yards.

   (c) Erin's bowling partner left the 7 pin in the sixth frame, which added 9 to her score.

2. For each pair of sets, decide if the sets are equivalent to one another.

   (a) $\{1, 2, 3, 4, 5\}$ and $\{x \mid x$ is a letter in the phrase "PANAMA BANANA MAN"$\}$

   (b) $\{a, b, c\}$ and $\{w, x, y, z\}$.

   (c) $\{o, n, e\}$ and $\{t, w, o\}$

   (d) $\{0\}$ and $\varnothing$

3. Kelly plans to attend the concert at Smith Auditorium. The concert is free so Kelly is surprised to learn that a ticket must be obtained for admission. Why do you think this is so?

4. Let A, B, and C be finite sets, with $A \subset B \subseteq C$ and $n(B) = 5$.

   (a) What are the possible values of $n(A)$?

   (b) What are the possible values of $n(C)$?

5. Use counting to determine the whole number that corresponds to the cardinality of these sets.

   (a) $A = \{x \mid x \in N$ and $20 \leq x < 35\}$

   (b) $B = \{x \mid x \in N$ and $x + 1 = x\}$

   (c) $C = \{x \mid x \in N$ and $(x - 3)(x - 8) = 0\}$

   (d) $D = \{x \mid x \in N, 1 \leq x \leq 100, x$ is divisible by both 4 and 6$\}$

6. Let $A = \{n \mid n$ is a cube of a natural number and $1 \leq n \leq 100\}$

   $B = \{s \mid s$ is a state in the U.S. which borders Mexico$\}$

   Is $A \sim B$?

7. Let $N = \{1, 2, 3, 4, \ldots\}$ be the set of natural numbers and $S = \{1, 4, 9, 16, \ldots\}$ be the set of squares of the natural numbers. Then $N \sim S$, since we have the one-to-one correspondence $1 \leftrightarrow 1$, $2 \leftrightarrow 4$, $3 \leftrightarrow 9$, $4 \leftrightarrow 16, \ldots, n \leftrightarrow n^2$ (This example is interesting since it shows that an infinite set can be equivalent to a proper subset of itself.) Show that each of the following pairs of sets are equivalent by carefully describing a one-to-one correspondence between the sets.

   (a) The whole numbers and natural numbers: $W = \{0, 1, 2, 3, \ldots\}$ and $N = \{1, 2, 3, 4, \ldots\}$

   (b) The sets of odd and even natural numbers: $D = \{1, 3, 5, 7, \ldots\}$ and $E = \{2, 4, 6, 8, \ldots\}$

   (c) The set of natural numbers and the set of powers of 10: $N = \{1, 2, 3, 4, \ldots\}$ and $\{10, 100, 1000, \ldots\}$

8. Decide which of the following sets are finite.

   (a) {grains of sand on all the world's beaches}

   (b) {whole numbers divisible by 46182970138}

   (c) {points on a line segment that is one inch long}

9. The figure below shows two line segments, L_1 and L_2. The rays through point P give, geometrically, a one-to-one correspondence between the points on L_1 and the points on L_2, for example, $Q_1 \leftrightarrow Q_2$.

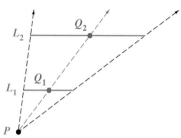

   Use similar geometric diagrams to show that the following figures are equivalent sets of points. Describe all possible locations of point P.

   (a) Two concentric circles

   (b) A circle and an inscribed square

   (c) A triangle and its circumscribing circle

   (d) A semicircle and its diameter

10. Decide whether or not the following statements are true or false. If false, give a counterexample; that is, give two sets which satisfy the hypothesis but not the conclusion of the statement. A and B designate finite sets.

   (a) If $A \subseteq B$ then $n(A) \leq n(B)$

   (b) If $n(A) < n(B)$ then $A \subset B$

(c) If $n(A \cup B) = n(A)$, then $B \subseteq A$

(d) If $n(A \cap B) = n(A)$, then $A \subseteq B$

11. Let A and B be finite sets.

   (a) Explain why $n(A \cap B) \leq n(A)$.

   (b) Explain why $n(A) \leq n(A \cup B)$.

   (c) Suppose $n(A \cap B) = n(A \cup B)$. What more can be said about A and B?

12. A survey of 700 households revealed that 300 had only a TV, 100 had only a computer, and 100 had neither a TV nor a computer. How many households have both a TV and a computer? Use a two-loop Venn diagram to find your answer.

13. Finish labeling the number of elements in the regions in the Venn diagram shown, where the subsets A, B, and C of the universe U satisfy the conditions listed.

$n(U) = 100$

$n(A) = 40$

$n(B) = 50$

$n(C) = 30$

$n(A \cap B) = 17$

$n(B \cap C) = 12$

$n(A \cap C) = 15$

$n(A \cap B \cap C) = 7$

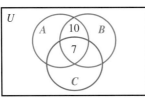

14. A poll of students showed that 55 percent liked basketball, 40 percent liked soccer, 55 percent liked football, 25 percent liked both basketball and soccer, 20 percent liked both soccer and football, 20 percent liked both basketball and football, and 10 percent liked all three sports. Use a Venn diagram to answer these questions: What percentage of students like only one sport? What percentage do not like any of the three sports?

15. Number tiles can be arranged to form patterns which relate to properties of the numbers.

   (a) Arrange number tiles to show why 1, 4, 9, 16, 25, . . . are called the "square" numbers.

   (b) Arrange number tiles to show why 1, 3, 6, 10, 15, . . . are called "triangular" numbers.

16. Suppose the square number tiles are replaced by regular hexagons. Instead of building rectangular patterns, it is natural to build "hex" patterns with 6-fold symmetry. The first three **hex** numbers are 1, 7, and 19.

1

7

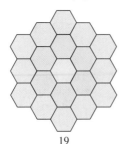

19

(a) Find the next two hex numbers.

(b) Use number cubes to form corner shapes, as shown. The two walls and the floor are the thickness of one cube. What connection do you see to hex numbers?

(c) Draw the next corner shape.

Thinking Critically

17. Joe Freespender makes $10 per week, but his extravagant lifestyle requires $100 per week. After ten weeks, Joe has earned $100 and so he can pay off the bills he accumulated during the first week. Fortunately Joe lives forever.

   (a) Will he have any bills which he can never pay?

   (b) At the end of what week can Joe pay off the bills for week 100?

18. An infinite pile of coconuts, numbered 1, 2, 3, . . ., are neatly stacked on a beach. There is also a stretchy rubber barrel on the beach that can hold any number of coconuts. On the morning of the first day, a monkey on the beach tosses coconuts 1 and 2 into the barrel, waking up a lazy monkey sleeping inside the barrel, who throws coconut number 1 into the ocean at noon. The morning of the second day, the monkey on the beach throws coconuts 3 and 4 into the barrel, and at noon, the monkey inside the barrel throws coconut number 2 into the ocean. The process continues forever: the monkey on the beach throws the next two lowest numbered coconuts into the barrel each morning, and at noon the monkey inside the barrel throws the lowest numbered coconut inside the barrel out into the ocean.

   (a) Which coconuts are in the barrel on the afternoon of day two? Day three? Day 100? At the "end of time" when no coconuts are left on the beach?

   (b) Suppose the monkey inside the barrel only throws the lowest *odd* numbered coconut into the ocean, so on the afternoon of day two coconut 3 is tossed into the ocean and coconuts 2 and 4 are still inside the barrel. Now re-answer the questions of part (a).

   (c) Suppose you are spying on the monkeys from a high cliff overlooking the beach, too far away to read the numbers on the coconuts. Could you tell if the monkey in the barrel throws out the lowest numbered coconut or the lowest odd numbered coconut? Would you agree infinite sets can be pretty strange?

19. Show that set equivalence satisfies the following properties. Carefully describe the one-to-one correspondences you choose.

    (a) The reflexive property: $A \sim A$

    (b) The symmetric property: If $A \sim B$, then $B \sim A$.

    (c) The transitive property: If $A \sim B$ and $B \sim C$, then $A \sim C$.

20. Evelyn's Electronics Emporium hired Sloppy Survey Services (SSS) to poll 100 households at random. Evelyn's report from SSS contained the following data on ownership of a TV, VCR, or stereo:

TV only	8
TV and VCR	70
TV, VCR, and stereo	65
Stereo only	3
Stereo and TV	74
No TV, VCR, or stereo	4

    Evelyn, who assumes anyone with a VCR also has a TV, is wondering if she should believe the figures are accurate. Should she?

21. At a school with 100 students, 35 students were taking Arabic, 32 Bulgarian, and 30 Chinese. Twenty students take only Arabic, 20 take only Bulgarian, and 14 take only Chinese. In addition, 7 students are taking both Arabic and Bulgarian. How many students are taking all three languages? None of these three languages?

22. A political polling organization sent out a questionnaire that asked the following question: "Which taxes—income, sales, excise—would you be willing to have raised?" Sixty voters' opinions were tallied by the office clerk:

Tax	Number Willing to Raise the Tax
Income	20
Sales	28
Excise	29
Income and sales	7
Income and excise	8
Sales and excise	10
Unwilling to raise any tax	5

    The clerk neglected to count how many, if any, of the 60 voters are willing to raise all three of the taxes. Can you help the pollsters? Explain how.

23. There are 40 students in the Travel Club. They discovered that 17 members have visited Mexico, 28 have visited Canada, 10 have been to England, 12 have visited both Mexico and Canada, 3 have been only to England, and 4 have been only to Mexico. Some club members have not been to any of the three foreign countries and, curiously, an equal number have been to all three countries.

    (a) How many students have been to all three countries?

    (b) How many students have been only to Canada?

24. There are two ways to match the sets {a, b} and {1, 2}, namely by the one-to-one correspondences a $\leftrightarrow$ 1, b $\leftrightarrow$ 2 and a $\leftrightarrow$ 2, b $\leftrightarrow$ 1.

    (a) Find the six different one-to-one correspondences between the equivalent sets {a, b, c} and {1, 2, 3}.

    (b) Use informal but careful reasoning to explain why a set with n elements can be matched in $n!$ ways to the set {1, 2, 3, . . . , n}. Here $n!$ [read "n factorial"] is defined by $n! = n \times (n - 1) \times \cdots \times 3 \times 2 \times 1$, so $1! = 1$, $2! = 2 \times 1 = 2$, $3! = 3 \times 2 \times 1 = 6$, and so on. [*Suggestion:* Consider a list of the n elements in the given set, say a, b, c, ... How many choices of elements from {1, 2, 3, . . . , n} are there to match with a? Once a has been matched, how many elements are left from {1, 2, 3, . . . , n} to match with b? And so on.]

    (c) How many different ways can you put a dozen eggs in the carton?

    (d) A set of history books can be placed on the shelf in 362,880 ways. How many volumes are there?

25. Consider a 3-element set $C = $ {a, b, c}. It has 1 subset with no elements—namely $\varnothing$, 3 subsets with one element—{a}, {b}, {c}, 3 subsets with two elements—{a, b}, {b, c}, {a, c}, and 1 subset with 3 elements—{a, b, c}. This fills in row $n = 3$ of the following table, where the entry in row n and column r gives the number of ways to choose a subset of r elements from a set of n elements.

	$r = 0$	$r = 1$	$r = 2$	$r = 3$	$r = 4$	$r = 5$	$r = 6$
$n = 0$							
$n = 1$							
$n = 2$							
$n = 3$	1	3	3	1			
$n = 4$							
$n = 5$							
$n = 6$							

(a) Find all of the subsets of $\varnothing$, $A = \{a\}$, $B = \{a, b\}$, and $D = \{a, b, c, d\}$ and fill in the table through row $n = 4$.

(b) What pattern of numbers do you see in the table? Use the pattern to fill in the next two rows.

(c) A steering committee for the class play consists of Amy, Byron, Clea, Don, Edie, and Franco. How many ways can they choose a 3-member subcommittee to arrange publicity?

---

26. Use the ideas of sets and the definition of the order relation on the whole numbers to justify the transitive property of "less than." That is, if k, l, and m are whole numbers satisfying $k < l$ and $l < m$, then $k < m$. [*Suggestion:* Consider sets satisfying $K \subset L \subset M$.]

Making Connections

27. In the late twentieth century, modern society entered what some observers have called "the information age." People are now accustomed to being identified by number as often as by name. Make a list of your own identification numbers—social security, credit cards, telephone, and so on. It may be helpful to look through your billfold!

28. Blood tests of 100 people showed that 45 had the A antigen and 14 had the B antigen (see problem 24 of Section 2.1). Another 45 had neither antigen, and so are of type O. How many people are of type AB, having both the A and B antigens? Draw and label a Venn diagram that shows the number of people with blood type A, B, AB, and O.

Communicating

29. The English words for the whole numbers are zero, one, two, three, and so on. Make similar lists in other languages. For example, your list in German would begin *Null, eins, zwei, drei,* . . . . Do you notice any common roots of the words?

30. Describe how you might teach a very young child the idea of "color" and the words—"blue" or "red" for example—that describe particular colors.

(a) Do you see any similarities in teaching the idea of "number" and such words as "two" or "five"?

(b) Suggest a method to convey the notion of "zero" to a young child.

31. Imagine yourself teaching a third-grader the transitive property of "less than" discussed in problem 26. Write an imagined dialogue with the student, using number strips (or colored rods) as a manipulative.

From State Student Assessments

32. (Washington State, Grade 4)

What numbers do W, X, and Y probably represent on the number line?

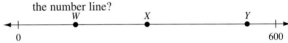

A. $W = 100$, $X = 200$, $Y = 500$

B. $W = 150$, $X = 300$, $Y = 400$

C. $W = 150$, $X = 300$, $Y = 525$

For Review

33. Let $U = \{0, 1, 2, \ldots, 25\}$, $A = \{n \mid n \text{ is even}\}$, $B = \{m \mid m = n^2 \text{ for some } n \in U\}$, $C = \{p \mid p \in U \text{ and } p \text{ divides into 48 with no remainder}\}$. Make a Venn diagram that shows the location of all the elements of U.

34. The elements of a universal set $U = \{a, b, c, d, e, f, g\}$ with two subsets A and B are shown in the following Venn diagram.

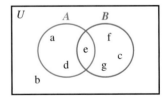

List the elements in the following sets.

(a) $\overline{A}$ (b) $A \cap B$

(c) $A \cup \overline{B}$ (d) $A \cap \overline{B}$

(e) $\overline{A} \cap \overline{B}$ (f) $\overline{A \cup B}$

(g) $\overline{A \cap B}$ (h) $(A \cup B) \cap (\overline{A \cap B})$

35. Draw a three-loop Venn diagram for each set given, shading the region corresponding to the set.

(a) $(A \cap \overline{B}) \cup C$

(b) $\overline{(A \cup B \cup C)}$

(c) $(A \cup B \cup C) \cap (\overline{A \cap B \cap C})$

2.3 Addition and Subtraction of Whole Numbers

In this section we introduce the operations of addition and subtraction on the set of whole numbers $W = \{0, 1, 2, 3, \ldots\}$. In each operation, two whole numbers are combined to form another whole number. Because *two* whole numbers are added to form the sum, addition is called a **binary operation.** Similarly, subtraction is defined on a pair of numbers, so subtraction is also a binary operation.

The definitions of addition and subtraction are accompanied by a variety of conceptual models that give the operations both intuitive and practical meaning. A corresponding variety of physical and pictorial models are described which reinforce these conceptual notions at the concrete and visual levels. It is vitally important that children be able to interpret and express the operations and their properties through manipulatives and visualization. These activities prepare them to understand the algorithms of computation and build confidence in their ability to select the appropriate operations for problem solving.

The Set Model of Whole Number Addition

The whole numbers answer the basic question "how many?" For example, if Alok collects baseball cards and A is the set of cards in his collection, then $a = n(A)$ is the number of cards he owns. Suppose his friend Barbara also has a collection of baseball cards, forming a set B with $b = n(B)$ cards. If Alok and Barbara decide to combine their collections, the new collection would be the set $A \cup B$ and would contain $n(A \cup B)$ cards. The **addition,** or **sum,** of a and b can be defined as the number of cards in the combined collection. That is, the sum of two whole numbers a and b is given by $a + b = n(A \cup B)$, where A and B are disjoint sets and $a = n(A)$, $b = n(B)$.

Addition answers the question "how many elements are in the union of two disjoint sets?" Figure 2.11 shows how the set model is used to show that $3 + 5 = 8$. First, disjoint

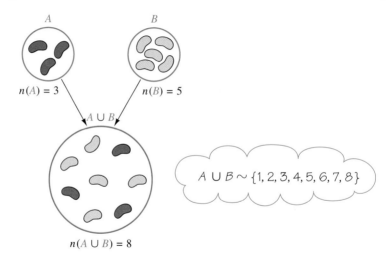

Figure 2.11
Showing $3 + 5 = 8$ with the set model of addition

sets A and B are found, with $n(A) = 3$ and $n(B) = 5$. Since $n(A \cup B) = 8$, we have shown that $3 + 5 = 8$. Using physical objects such as beans to form the sets, there is no question about disjointness.

Here is the general definition.

DEFINITION   *The Addition of Whole Numbers*

Let a and b be any two whole numbers. If A and B are any two disjoint sets for which $a = n(A)$ and $b = n(B)$, then the **sum of a and b,** written $a + b$, is given by

$$a + b = n(A \cup B).$$

The expression $a + b$ is read "a plus b" and a and b are called the **addends** or **summands.**

$$a + b$$

 addends

---

EXAMPLE   2.10

Using the Set Model of Addition

The University Math Club membership includes 14 women and 11 men. There are 21 club members with a major in mathematics, and 6 with a major in physics.

(a)   How many students belong to the Math Club?

(b)   How many club members have a double major in mathematics and physics?

Solution

(a)   If C denotes the set of members of the club, then $C = M \cup W$ where M and W denote the sets of men and women members, respectively. Since M and W are disjoint sets, the number of club members is

$$n(C) = n(M \cup W) = n(M) + n(W) = 11 + 14 = 25.$$

(b)   Let P denote the set of club members with a math major, and Q the set of club members with a physics major. Since $n(P) + n(Q) = 6 + 21 = 27$ is 2 more than the 25 members of the club, this means 2 club members belong to both sets P and Q. That is, $n(P \cap Q) = 2$ club members have a double major. Notice the equation $n(P \cup Q) = n(P) + n(Q) - n(P \cap Q)$ (see problem 21).

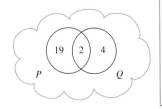

The set model of addition can be illustrated with manipulatives such as those described in the last section. Many addition facts and patterns become evident when they are discovered and visualized by means of concrete embodiments. An example is the triangular numbers $t_1 = 1, t_2 = 3, t_3 = 6, \ldots$ introduced in Chapter 1. Recall that t_n denotes that nth triangular number, where the name refers to the triangular pattern which can be formed with t_n objects. By using number tiles, as shown in Figure 2.12, we see that the sum of any two successive triangular numbers forms a square number. Indeed, we have the general formula:

$$t_{n-1} + t_n = n^2, \quad n = 1, 2, \ldots .$$

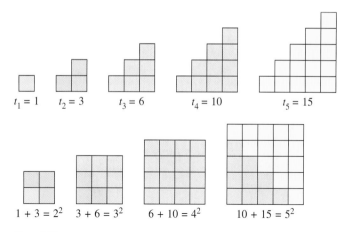

Figure 2.12
The sum of two successive triangular numbers is a square number

The Measurement Model of Addition

On the number line, whole numbers are geometrically interpreted as distances. Addition can be visualized as combining two distances to get a total distance. Right pointing arrows are used to indicate distances. Figure 2.13 illustrates $3 + 5$ on the number line. It is important to notice that the two distances are not overlapping, and the tail of the arrow representing 5 is placed at the head of the arrow representing 3. The result of the addition is 8, which will be indicated on the number line by circling the 8.

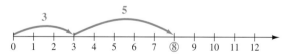

Figure 2.13
Illustrating $3 + 5$ on the number line

Properties of Whole Number Addition

The sum of any two whole numbers is also a whole number, so we say that the set of whole numbers has the **closure property** under addition. This property is so obvious for addition it may seem unnecessary to mention it. However, the set of whole numbers is not closed under subtraction or division. Even under addition, many subsets of whole numbers do not have the closure property. For example, if $D = \{1, 3, 5, \ldots\}$ denotes the subset of the odd whole numbers, then D does *not* have the closure property under addition. For example, the sum of 1 and 3 is not in D. On the other hand, the set of even whole numbers, $E = \{0, 2, 4, 6, \ldots\}$, is closed under addition; this is so because the sum of any two even whole numbers is also an even whole number.

Some other important properties of whole number addition correspond to properties of operations on finite sets. For example, the commutative property of union, $A \cup B = B \cup A$, proves that $a + b = b + a$ for all whole numbers a and b. Similarly, the associative property $A \cup (B \cup C) = (A \cup B) \cup C$ tells us that $a + (b + c) = (a + b) + c$. Since $A \cup \varnothing = \varnothing \cup A = A$, we obtain the additive identity property of zero, $a + 0 = 0 + a = a$. Zero is said to be the **additive identity** because of this property.

THEOREM   *Properties of Whole Number Addition*

Closure Property	If a and b are any two whole numbers, then $a + b$ is a unique whole number.
Commutative Property	If a and b are any two whole numbers, then $a + b = b + a$.
Associative Property	If a, b, and c are any three whole numbers, then $a + (b + c) = (a + b) + c$.
Additive Identity Property of Zero	If a is any whole number, then $a + 0 = 0 + a = a$.

The properties of whole number addition can also be illustrated with any of the physical and pictorial models of the whole numbers. Figure 2.14 shows how the associative property can be demonstrated with number strips.

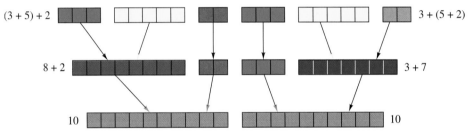

Figure 2.14
Illustrating the associative property $(3 + 5) + 2 = 3 + (5 + 2)$ with number strips or Cuisenaire® rods

The addition properties are very useful when adding several whole numbers, since we are permitted to rearrange the order of the addends and the order in which pairs of addends are summed.

EXAMPLE 2.11

Using the Properties of Whole Number Addition

(a) Which property justifies each of the following statements?
   (i) $8 + 3 = 3 + 8$
   (ii) $(7 + 5) + 8 = 7 + (5 + 8)$
   (iii) A million plus a quintillion is not infinite.

(b) Justify each equality below:

$$(20 + 2) + (30 + 8) = 20 + [2 + (30 + 8)] \tag{i}$$
$$= 20 + [(30 + 8) + 2] \tag{ii}$$
$$= 20 + [30 + (8 + 2)] \tag{iii}$$
$$= (20 + 30) + (8 + 2) \tag{iv}$$

Solution

  (a) (i) Commutative property, (ii) associative property, (iii) the sum is a whole number by the closure property, and is therefore a finite value.

  (b) (i) associative property, (ii) commutative property, (iii) associative property, (iv) associative property.

INTO THE CLASSROOM

Using Addition Properties to Learn Addition Facts

As children learn addition, the properties of whole number addition should become a habit of thought from the very beginning. Indeed, the properties are useful even for learning and recalling the sums of one digit numbers, as found in the addition table shown. The commutative property $a + b = b + a$ means the entries above the diagonal repeat the entries below the diagonal. Also, the first column of addition by zero is easy by the additive identity property. The next four columns, giving addition by 1, 2, 3, and 4, can be learned by "counting on." For example, $8 + 3$ is viewed as "8 plus 1 makes 9, plus 1 more makes 10, plus 1 more makes 11." The diagonal entries $1 + 1 = 2$, $2 + 2 = 4, \ldots$, are the "doubles," which are readily learned by knowing how to count by twos: $2, 4, \ldots, 18$. The remaining entries in the table can be obtained by combining "doubles" and "counting on." For example, $6 + 8$ is viewed as $6 + (6 + 2)$, which is $(6 + 6) + 2$; knowing that 6 doubled is 12 and counting on 2 gives the answer 14.

Other effective strategies include:

Making tens: For example, $8 + 6 = (8 + 2) + 4 = 10 + 4 = 14$.

Counting back: For example, 9 is 1 less than 10, so $6 + 9$ is 1 less than $6 + 10 = 16$, giving 15. In symbols, this amounts to

$$6 + 9 = (6 + 10) - 1 = 16 - 1 = 15.$$

> Look for patterns. They also help you learn the facts!

+	0	1	2	3	4	5	6	7	8	9
0	0	1	2	3	4	5	6	7	8	9
1	1	2	3	4	5	6	7	8	9	10
2	2	3	4	5	6	7	8	9	10	11
3	3	4	5	6	7	8	9	10	11	12
4	4	5	6	7	8	9	10	11	12	13
5	5	6	7	8	9	10	11	12	13	14
6	6	7	8	9	10	11	12	13	14	15
7	7	8	9	10	11	12	13	14	15	16
8	8	9	10	11	12	13	14	15	16	17
9	9	10	11	12	13	14	15	16	17	18

EXAMPLE   2.12 | **Illustrating Properties on the Number Line**

What properties of whole number addition are shown below?

(a)

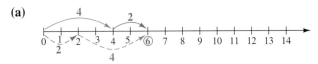

(b)

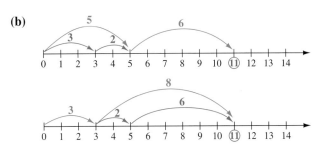

(c)

Solution | (a)   The commutative property: $4 + 2 = 2 + 4$.

(b)   The associative property: $(3 + 2) + 6 = 3 + (2 + 6)$.

(c)   The additive identity property: $5 + 0 = 5$.

Subtraction of Whole Numbers

Subtraction can be defined in a brief statement.

DEFINITION *Subtraction of Whole Numbers*

Let a and b be whole numbers. The **difference,** written $a - b$, is the unique whole number c such that $a = b + c$. That is, $a - b = c$ if, and only if, there is a whole number c such that $a = b + c$.

The expression $a - b$ is read "a minus b." The a is the **minuend** and b is the **subtrahend**.

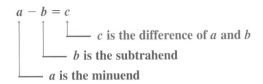

$$a - b = c$$

c is the difference of a and b
b is the subtrahend
a is the minuend

This definition relates subtraction to addition, and is the definition most easily extended to the integers, rationals, and real numbers.

Since $8 = 5 + 3$ the definition tells us that $8 - 5 = 3$. However, the practical value of subtraction is not revealed in the definition above. To understand the nature and value of subtraction, we will introduce four conceptual models: **take-away, missing addend, comparison,** and **number-line** (or **measurement**). The following four problems illustrate each of the four conceptual models.

Take-away:
Eroll has $8 and spent $5 for a ticket to the movies. How much money does Eroll have left?

Missing addend:
Alice has read 5 chapters of her book. If there are 8 chapters in all, how many more chapters must she read to finish the book?

Comparison:
Georgia has 8 mice and Tonya has 5 mice. How many more mice does Georgia have than Tonya?

Number-line:
Mike hiked up the mountain trail 8 miles. Five of these miles were hiked after lunch. How many miles did Mike hike before lunch?

In all four problems, the answer is 3 because we know that $8 = 5 + 3$. For example, Eroll's $8, when written as $5 + $3, shows that a $5 movie ticket and the $3 still in his pocket account for all of the $8 he had originally. The cashier at the box office "took away" 5 of Eroll's 8 dollars, leaving him with $3. Thus the problem is an example of the **take-away model** of subtraction. Alice, having read 5 chapters, wants to know how many more chapters she must read; the emphasis now is on what number is to be added to 5 to get 8, so the second problem illustrates the **missing addend model** of subtraction. Similarly, the remaining problems illustrate the **comparison model** and the **number-line** (or **measurement**) **model** of subtraction.

JUST FOR FUN

Paper Clip Comparison

In full view of a group of people, show them that you have ten paper clips on the table. Still in plain sight, divide the paper clips into two groups of five and put a piece of cardboard on the table which hides one group. Next move one clip from the hidden pile in the back, to the pile in sight in the front. Now ask, "How many more paper clips are in the front than in the back?" Don't be surprised if more than just a few people say there is just one more in front!

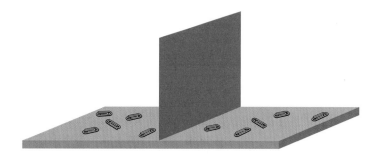

The four basic conceptual models of the subtraction 8 − 5 are visualized as follows.

Take-away Model

    1. Start with 8 objects.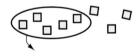

    2. Take away 5 objects.
    3. How many objects are left?

Missing Addend Model

    1. Start with 5 objects.
    2. How many more objects are needed to give a total of 8 objects?

Comparison Model

    1. Start with two collections, with 8 objects in one collection and 5 in the other.

        ◻ ◻ ◻ ◻ ◻ ◻ ◻ ◻   8 objects

        △ △ △ △ △   5 objects

    2. How many more objects are in the larger collection?

Number-line Model

    1. Move forward (to the right) 8 units.

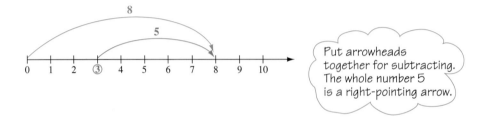

Put arrowheads together for subtracting. The whole number 5 is a right-pointing arrow.

    2. Remove a jump to the right of 5 units.
    3. What is the distance from 0?

Notice that the head of the arrow representing 5 is positioned at the head of the arrow representing 8. The result of the subtraction, namely 3, is shown by circling the 3.

Notice that the whole numbers 8, 5, and 3 are all represented with right pointing arrows. In Chapter 5, negative integers will always be identified with left pointing arrows on the number line.

EXAMPLE 2.13	**Identifying Conceptual Models of Subtraction**

Identify the conceptual model of subtraction that best fits these problems.

(a) Mary got 43 pieces of candy trick-or-treating on Halloween. Karen got 36 pieces. How many more pieces of candy does Mary have than Karen?

(b) Mary gave 20 pieces of her candy to her sick brother Jon. How many pieces of candy does Mary have left?

(c) Karen's older brother Ken collected 53 pieces of candy. How many more pieces of candy would Karen need to have as many as Ken?

(d) Ken left home and walked 10 blocks east along Grand Avenue trick-or-treating. The last 4 blocks were after crossing Main Street. How far is Main Street from Ken's house?

Solution

(a) Comparison model

(b) Take-away model

(c) Missing addend model

(d) Number-line model

The set of whole numbers is not closed under subtraction. For example, $2 - 5$ is undefined since there is no whole number n which satisfies $2 = 5 + n$. Similar reasoning shows subtraction is not commutative, so the order in which a and b are taken is important. Neither is subtraction associative, which means that parentheses must be placed with care in expressions involving subtractions. For example,

$$5 - (3 - 1) = 5 - 2 = 3 \text{ but } (5 - 3) - 1 = 2 - 1 = 1.$$

HIGHLIGHT FROM HISTORY

The Origins of the + and − Symbols

The + and − symbols first appeared in an arithmetic book by Johannes Widman, published in Leipzig in 1489. The signs were not used as symbols of operation, but simply to indicate excess or deficiency. Widman states, "What is −, that is minus, what is +, that is more." The + symbol is thought to be a contraction of the Latin word *et,* which often indicated addition. The minus symbol may be a contraction of the abbreviation $\overline{m}$ for minus. The + and − symbols were used to designate algebraic operations by the Dutch mathematician Vander Hoecke in 1514.

Diffy

The process in this activity is sometimes called *Diffy.* The name comes from the process of taking successive differences of whole numbers, and the activity provides an interesting setting for practicing skills in subtraction. The activity can be done on a spreadsheet (see Example B.2 of Appendix B) or with a graphing calculator program (see Appendix C). Work in pairs to check each other's calculations.

Directions

Step 1. Make an array of circles as shown and choose four whole numbers to place in the top four circles.

Step 2. In the first three circles of the second row write the differences of the numbers above and to the right and left of the circle in question, always being careful to subtract the smaller of these two numbers from the larger. In the fourth circle of the second row place the difference of the numbers in the first and fourth circles in the preceding row, again always subtracting the smaller number from the larger.

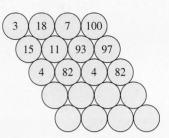

Step 3. Repeat Step 2 to fill in successive rows of circles in the diagram. You may stop if you obtain a row of zeros.

Step 4. Replace the four numbers in the top row, and then repeat steps 1, 2, and 3 several times, each time replacing the four numbers in the top row with different numbers.

Questions

1. Do you think the process will always stop?
2. Can you find four numbers such that the process terminates at the first step? The second step? The third step? Try several sets of starting numbers.
3. On the basis of your work so far, what do you guess is the largest number of steps needed for the process to stop?
4. Can you find four starting numbers such that the process requires eight steps to reach termination?
5. Try DIFFY with the starting numbers 17, 32, 58, and 107.

PROBLEM SET 2.3

Understanding Concepts

1. Let $A = \{\text{apple, berry, peach}\}$, $B = \{\text{lemon, lime}\}$, $C = \{\text{lemon, berry, prune}\}$.

    (a) Find (i) $n(A \cup B)$, (ii) $n(A \cup C)$, (iii) $n(B \cup C)$,

    (b) In which case is the number of elements in the union *not* the sum of the number of elements in the individual sets?

2. Let $n(A) = 5$, $n(B) = 8$, and $n(A \cup B) = 10$. What can you say about $n(A \cap B)$?

3. Let $n(A) = 4$ and $n(A \cup B) = 8$.

    (a) What are the possible values of $n(B)$?

    (b) If $A \cap B = \varnothing$, what is the only possible value of $n(B)$?

4. Draw number strips (or rods) to illustrate

    (a) $4 + 6 = 10$;

    (b) $2 + 8 = 8 + 2$; and

    (c) $3 + (2 + 5) = (3 + 2) + 5$

5. Illustrate each of these additions with a number line diagram. Circle the value on the number line that corresponds to the sum.

    (a) $3 + 5$ **(b)** $5 + 3$

    (c) $4 + 2$ **(d)** $0 + 6$

    (e) $3 + (5 + 7)$ (e) $(3 + 5) + 7$

6. Make up a word problem which uses the set model of addition to illustrate $30 + 28$.

7. Make up a word problem which uses the measurement model of addition to illustrate $18 + 25$.

8. Which of the following sets of whole numbers are closed under addition? If the set is not closed, give an example of two elements from the set whose sum is not in the set.

    (a) $\{10, 15, 20, 25, 30, 35, 40, \ldots\}$

    (b) $\{1, 2, 3, \ldots, 1000\}$

    (c) $\{0\}$ **(d)** $\{1, 5, 6, 11, 17, 28, \ldots\}$

    (e) $\{n \in N: n \geq 19\}$

    (f) $\{0, 3, 6, 9, 12, 15, 18, \ldots\}$

9. What properties of addition are used in these equalities?

    (a) $14 + 18 = 18 + 14$

    (b) $12345678 + 97865342$ is a whole number

    (c) $18 + 0 = 18$

    (d) $(17 + 14) + 13 = 30 + 14$

    (e) $(12 + 15) + (5 + 38) = 50 + 20$

10. Carefully explain why the parentheses on the left side of this expression can be overlooked and the addends rearranged as on the right side:
    $$(8 + (3 + (4 + 2))) + (7 + 6)$$
    $$= (8 + 2) + (3 + 7) + (4 + 6)$$

11. An easy way to add $1 + 2 + 3 + 4 + 5 + 6 + 7 + 8 + 9 + 10$ is to write the sum as $(1 + 10) + (2 + 9) + (3 + 8) + (4 + 7) + (5 + 6) = 11 + 11 + 11 + 11 + 11 = 55$.

    (a) Compute $1 + 2 + 3 + \cdots + 20$. Describe your procedure.

    (b) What properties of addition are you using to justify why your procedure works?

12. Illustrate each of these subtractions with a number line diagram. Remember to put the heads of the minuend and subtrahend arrows together.

    (a) $7 - 3$ **(b)** $7 - 4$ (c) $7 - 7$ **(d)** $7 - 0$

13. If it is known that $5 + 9 = 14$, then it follows that $9 + 5 = 14$, $14 - 9 = 5$ and $14 - 5 = 9$. Many elementary texts call such a group of four basic facts a "fact family."

    (a) What is the fact family that contains $5 + 7 = 12$?

    (b) What is the fact family that contains $12 - 4 = 8$?

14. (a) Draw four number line diagrams to illustrate each of the number facts in the fact family (see problem 13) $5 + 9 = 14$, $9 + 5 = 14$, $14 - 9 = 5$, $14 - 5 = 9$.

    (b) Repeat part (a), but for the fact family that contains $11 - 4 = 7$.

15. Here are some subtraction problems found in *Exploring Mathematics, Grade 2* (From *Scott Foresman Exploring Mathematics* Grades 1–7 by L. Carey Bolster et al. Copyright © 1994 Scott, Foresman and Company. Reprinted by permission of Scott, Foresman and Company.). Which subtraction model—take-away, missing addend, comparison, or measurement—corresponds best to each problem?

    (a) The second graders have 38 more books than the first graders. The second graders have 87 books. How many books do the first graders have?

    (b) Jodi's book has 75 pages. On Monday she read 32 pages. How many pages did she have left to read?

    (c) Lee took 65¢ to the swimming pool. He spent 33¢ for a waterslide ticket. How much did Lee have left?

    (d) Amy's book has 124 pages. Steve's book has 133 pages. How many more pages are in Steve's book than Amy's?

16. Make up a word problem which corresponds well to each of the four conceptual models for subtraction.

   (a) Take-away   **(b)** Missing addend

   (c) Comparison   **(d)** Measurement (number-line)

17. Jeff must read the last chapter of his book. It begins on the top of page 241 and ends at the bottom of page 257. How many pages must he read?

18. Notice that $(6 + (8 - 5)) - 2 = 7$, but a different placement of parentheses on the left side would give the statement $(6 + 8) - (5 - 2) = 11$. Place parentheses to turn these into *true* statements.

   (a) $8 - 5 - 2 - 1 = 2$

   (b) $8 - 5 - 2 - 1 = 4$

   (c) $8 - 5 - 2 - 1 = 0$

   (d) $8 + 5 - 2 + 1 = 12$

   (e) $8 + 5 - 2 + 1 = 10$

19. Each circled number is the sum of the adjacent row, column, or diagonal of the numbers in the square array.

Fill in the missing entries in these patterns.

(a)

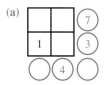

(b)

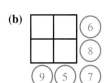

20. The first figure below shows that the numbers 1, 2, 3, 4, 5, 6 can be placed around a triangle in such a way that the three numbers along any side sum to 9, which is shown circled. Arrange the numbers 1, 2, 3, 4, 5, 6 to give the sums circled in the next three figures.

(a)

(b)

(c)

Thinking Critically

21. If $A = \{a, b, c, d\}$ and $B = \{c, d, e, f, g\}$, then $n(A \cup B) = n(\{a, b, c, d, e, f, g\}) = 7$, $n(A) = 4$, $n(B) = 5$, and $n(A \cap B) = n(\{c, d,\}) = 2$. Since $7 = 4 + 5 - 2$, this suggests that

$$n(A \cup B) = n(A) + n(B) - n(A \cap B).$$

Use Venn diagrams to justify this formula for arbitrary finite sets A and B.

22. Since $12 \times 16 = 192$ and $5 \times 40 = 200$, it follows that among the first 200 natural numbers $\{1, 2, \ldots, 200\}$ there are 16 that are multiples of 12 and 40 that are multiples of 5. Just 3 are multiples of *both* 5 and 12, namely 60, 120, and 180. Use the formula of problem 21 to find how many natural numbers in the set $\{1, 2, \ldots, 200\}$ are divisible by *either* 12 or 5 or both.

23. (a) Notice that $1 + 2 + 3 + 2 + 1 = 9 = 3^2$, a square number. Explain how this number fact is evident from a square pattern of circles.

   (b) Draw a pattern of circles that makes it apparent that the sum $1 + 2 + 3 + 4 + 3 + 2 + 1$ is a square number.

   (c) What pattern allows you to know quickly the value of $1 + 2 + 3 + \cdots + 99 + 100 + 99 + \cdots + 3 + 2 + 1$?

24. The odd whole numbers 1, 3, 5, 7, . . . can be represented by number tiles arranged in an angle shape. For example, the first four odd numbers correspond to these shapes.

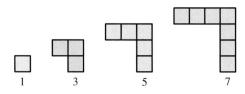

   (a) Draw number tile arrangements to represent the odd whole numbers 9, 11, and 13.

   (b) Use your angular shapes to show that the sum of the first five odd whole numbers, $1 + 3 + 5 + 7 + 9$, is the square number 25.

   (c) The one-hundredth odd whole number is 199. What is the sum $1 + 3 + 5 + \cdots + 197 + 199$?

(d) Find a formula for $1 + 3 + 5 + \cdots + (2n - 1)$, which is the sum of the first n odd whole numbers.

25. Begin with a single small cube. The original small cube can be covered with 26 more small cubes like the first one to form a larger solid cube with three small cubes on each edge as shown.

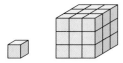

(a) Now cover the larger cube with a layer of small cubes to form a solid cube with five small cubes on each edge. How many small cubes must be added to form this next larger cube?

(b) If the large cube of part (a) is now covered by a layer of cubes to form a solid cube with seven cubes on each edge, how many small cubes must be added?

(c) How many small cubes must be added next to obtain a solid cube with nine small cubes on an edge?

26. There is a nonempty subset of the whole numbers that is closed under subtraction. Find this subset.

27. The set C contains 2 and 3 and is closed under addition.

(a) What whole numbers must be in C?

(b) What whole numbers may not be in C?

(c) Are there any whole numbers definitely not in C?

(d) How would your answers to (a), (b), and (c) change if 2 and 4 were contained in C instead of 2 and 3?

28. The triangular numbers $t_1 = 1, t_2 = 3, t_3 = 6, \ldots$, are shown in Figure 2.12

(a) Complete the following table of the first fifteen triangular numbers:

n	1 2 3 4 5 6 7 8 9 10 11 12 13 14 15
t_n	1 3 6 10

(b) The first ten natural numbers can be expressed as sums of triangular numbers. For example, $1 = 1$, $2 = 1 + 1, 3 = 3, 4 = 1 + 3, 5 = 1 + 1 + 3$, $6 = 6, 7 = 1 + 6, 8 = 1 + 1 + 6, 9 = 3 + 6$, $10 = 10$. Show that the natural numbers 11 through 25 can be written as a sum of triangular numbers. Use as few triangular numbers as possible each time.

(c) Choose five more numbers at random (don't look at your table!) between 26 and 120 and write each of them as a sum of as few triangular numbers as

possible. What is the largest number of triangular numbers needed?

(d) On July 10, 1796, the 19-year-old Carl Friedrich Gauss wrote in his notebook "EUREKA! NUM = $\triangle + \triangle + \triangle$." What theorem do you think Gauss had proved?

Thinking Cooperatively

29. The following table represents a partially complete scrambled addition table. The rows and columns have both been mixed up. See if your cooperative team can complete the table.

+	5				2			3
3								
				18				
			12					
		5		6				
					0			
		8					14	
5								
				3				
8						16		

30. Have your cooperative team make up its own incomplete scrambled addition table puzzle, similar to the one in problem 29. It may be helpful to use two colors, to separate the entries which are given from the entries which are determined by what is given. Trade puzzles among groups and see which presents the most challenge.

31. Three numbers (not necessarily all different) are determined by rolling three dice. Using either two or three of these numbers (not just one), together with parentheses and $+$ and $-$ symbols, the objective of the game is to form expressions equalling the seven numbers 0, 1, 2, 3, 4, 5, 6, 7 on a hex board as shown. The team filling in all seven positions on the board first is the winning team. If no team fills in all seven positions, the dice are rolled again. For example, a roll of 3, 3, and 4 would allow you to fill in 0 (as $3 - 3$), 1 (as $4 - 3$), 2 (as $(3 + 3) - 4$), 4 (as $(3 - 3) + 4$ or $(3 + 4) - 3$ say), and 6 (as $3 + 3$). Your team would hope to fill in the 3 and 5 on the next roll of the dice. Play the game in class, and practice with these questions:

(a) Show that you should be able to win the game with the roll 1, 4, 5.

(b) Can you win the game with a single roll of 2, 3, 5?

(c) Can you win the game with a single roll of 2, 4, 6?

Making Connections

32. Addition and subtraction problems arise frequently in everyday life. Consider such activities as scheduling time, making budgets, sewing clothes, making home repairs, planning finances, modifying recipes, and making purchases. Make a list of five addition and five subtraction problems you have encountered at home or in your work. Which conceptual model of addition or subtraction corresponds best to each problem?

From State Student Assessments

33. (Washington State, Grade 4)

Look at the picture below. The letter c stands for the number of chips in the cup.

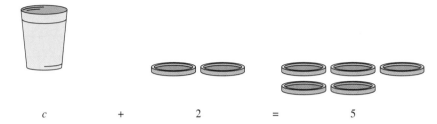

$$c \qquad + \qquad 2 \qquad = \qquad 5$$

The cup contains 3 chips. Therefore, the letter c stands for the number 3.

Look at the picture below.

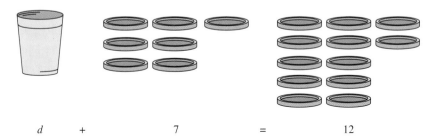

$$d \qquad + \qquad 7 \qquad = \qquad 12$$

How many chips does the letter d stand for?

A. 5   B. 6   C. 7

For Review

34. The Venn diagram shows the number of elements in each region. Find the numbers of elements in the sets indicated.

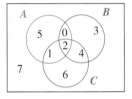

(a) $n(A \cap B)$ (b) $n(B \cup C)$ (c) $n(\overline{A} \cup C)$

(d) $n(B \cap C)$ (e) $n(A \cap \overline{C})$ (f) $n(\overline{A \cup B} \cup C)$

35. A school of 300 students has 100 students in each of algebra, geometry, and statistics, with 30 students enrolled in each pair of classes and 10 students in all three classes. How many students are taking only geometry? How many students are not taking any of these three classes?

2.4   Multiplication and Division of Whole Numbers

Multiplication as Repeated Addition

Misha has an after-school job at a local bike factory. Each day she has a 3-mile round trip walk to the factory. At her job she assembles 4 hubs and wheels. How many hubs and wheels does she assemble in 5 afternoons? How many miles does she walk to and from her job each week?

These two problems can be answered by repeated additions. Misha assembles

$$4 + 4 + 4 + 4 + 4 = 20$$ Sum of 5 fours, written $5 \cdot 4$

hubs and wheels. This can be illustrated with the set model as shown in Figure 2.15.

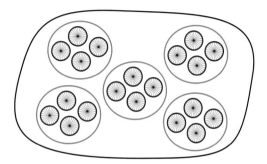

Figure 2.15
Set model to show 5 times 4 is 20

Misha walks

$$3 + 3 + 3 + 3 + 3 = 15$$ Sum of 5 threes, written $5 \cdot 3$

miles each week. This can be illustrated by the measurement model as in Figure 2.16.

Figure 2.16
Measurement model to show 5 times 3 is 15

If Misha only worked one day in the week, she would assemble $1 \cdot 4 = 4$ wheels. If she were sick all week and missed work entirely, she would not assemble any wheels; therefore $0 \cdot 4 = 0$.

Since multiplication is defined for all pairs of whole numbers, and the outcome is also a whole number, we see that multiplication is a binary operation on the set of whole numbers. The dot symbol for multiplication is often replaced by a cross $\times$ (not to be mistaken for the letter x) or by a star * (asterisk), the symbol computers use most often.

DEFINITION   *Multiplication of Whole Numbers as Repeated Additions*

Let a and b be any two whole numbers. Then the **product** of a and b, written $a \cdot b$, is defined by:

$$a \cdot b = \underbrace{b + b + \cdots + b}_{a \text{ addends}} \text{ when } a \neq 0;$$

and by:

$$0 \cdot b = 0.$$

Sometimes no symbol at all is used, or parentheses are placed around the factors. Thus, the expressions

$$a \cdot b, \quad a \times b, \quad a * b, \quad ab, \quad (a)(b)$$

all denote the multiplication of a and b. Each whole number, a and b, is a **factor** of the product $a \cdot b$, and often $a \cdot b$ is read "a times b."

In addition to the set model and the measurement model, there are two other useful models of multiplication, the *array model* and the *Cartesian product model.*

The Array Model for Multiplication

Suppose Lida, as part of her biology research, planted 5 rows of bean seeds and each row contains 8 seeds. How many seeds did she plant in her rectangular plot?

The 40 seeds Lida planted form a 5 by 8 rectangular array, as shown in Figure 2.17. The arrays can also be drawn with squares, giving an important connection with the measurement model of the whole numbers. This measurement model for multiplication is especially important because it extends from the whole numbers to the rational numbers, the integers, and even the real number system.

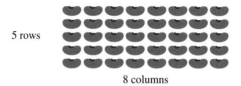

5 rows

8 columns

Figure 2.17
Array model to show $5 \cdot 8 = 40$

The Cartesian Product Model of Multiplication

At Sonya's Ice Cream Shop, a customer can order either a sugar or a waffle cone and one of four flavors of ice cream—vanilla, chocolate, mint, or raspberry. Any ice cream cone order can be written as an **ordered pair (a, b),** where the first component a of the ordered pair indicates the type of cone and the second component b of the ordered pair indicates the flavor. For example, if $C = \{s, w\}$ and $F = \{v, c, m, r\}$ are the respective sets of cone types and flavors, then an order for raspberry ice cream in a waffle cone corresponds to the ordered pair (w, r). The total set of ice cream orders can be pictured in a rectangular array much like the figures used to model multiplication as a rectangular array.

		Flavor			
		v	c	m	r
Type of cone	s	(s, v)	(s, c)	(s, m)	(s, r)
	w	(w, v)	(w, c)	(w, m)	(w, r)

The set of ordered pairs shown in the table is called the **Cartesian product** of C and F, written as $C \times F$ where the cross symbol $\times$ should not be confused with the letter x. The name Cartesian honors the French mathematician and philosopher René Descartes (1596–1650). Here is the general definition of the Cartesian product of two sets.

DEFINITION *Cartesian Product of Sets*

The **Cartesian product** of sets A and B, written $A \times B$, is the set of all ordered pairs whose first component is an element of set A and whose second component is an element of set B. That is,

$$A \times B = \{(a, b) \mid a \in A \text{ and } b \in B\}.$$

At Sonya's, there are $n(C) = 2$ ways to choose the type of cone and $n(F) = 4$ ways to choose the flavor of ice cream. This gives $n(C \times F) = 2 \cdot 4 = 8$ ways to order an ice cream cone. More generally, the Cartesian product of sets gives us an alternative way to define the multiplication of whole numbers.

ALTERNATIVE DEFINITION *Multiplication of Whole Numbers via the Cartesian Product*

Let a and b be whole numbers, and A and B be any sets for which $a = n(A)$ and $b = n(B)$. Then $a \cdot b = n(A \times B)$.

Since $\varnothing \times B = \varnothing$ (there are no ordered pairs in $\varnothing \times B$ since no first component can be chosen from $\varnothing$) and $0 = n(\varnothing)$, this definition of multiplication is consistent with the earlier definition of multiplication by 0; that is, $0 \cdot b = b \cdot 0 = 0$.

EXAMPLE   2.14

Using the Cartesian Product Model of Multiplication

To get to work, Juan either walks, bikes, or takes a cab from his house to downtown. From downtown, he either continues on the bus the rest of the way to work or catches the train to his place of business. How many ways can Juan get to work?

Solution

If $A = \{w, b, c\}$ is the set of possibilities for the first leg of his trip, and $B = \{b, t\}$ is the next set of choices, then Juan has altogether

$$3 \cdot 2 = n(A \times B) = n(\{(w, b), (w, t), (b, b), (b, t), (c, b), (c, t)\}) = 6$$

ways to commute to work. We notice that it doesn't matter whether or not A and B have an element in common.

Properties of Whole Number Multiplication

It follows from the definition that the set of whole numbers is **closed under multiplication:** the product of any two whole numbers is a unique whole number. We have also observed earlier that $0 \cdot b = 0$ and $1 \cdot b = b$ for all whole numbers b.

By rotating a rectangular array through 90°, we interchange the number of rows and the number of columns in the array, but we do not change the total number of objects in the array. Thus $a \cdot b = b \cdot a$, which demonstrates the **commutative property of multiplication.** An example is shown in Figure 2.18.

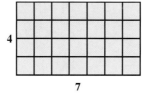
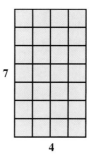

Figure 2.18
Multiplication is commutative: 4 · 7 = 7 · 4

Since we already know that $1 \cdot b = b$ for any whole number b, the commutative property tells us $1 \cdot b = b \cdot 1 = b$. This makes 1 a **multiplicative identity.**

A three-dimensional model, as shown in Figure 2.19, shows that multiplication is **associative,** so that $a \cdot (b \cdot c) = (a \cdot b) \cdot (c)$ This means that an expression such as $4 \cdot 3 \cdot 5$ is meaningful without parentheses: the product is the same for both ways in which parentheses can be placed.

There is one more important property, the **distributive property,** which relates multiplication and addition. This property is the basis for the multiplication algorithm discussed in the next chapter. The distributive property can be nicely visualized by the array model. In Figure 2.20, it is seen that $4 \cdot (6 + 3) = (4 \cdot 6) + (4 \cdot 3)$; that is, the factor 4 *distributes* itself over each term in the sum $6 + 3$.

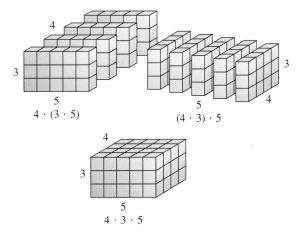

Figure 2.19
Multiplication is associative: $4 \cdot (3 \cdot 5) = (4 \cdot 3) \cdot 5$

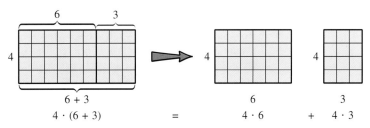

Figure 2.20
Multiplication is distributive over addition: $4 \cdot (6 + 3) = (4 \cdot 6) + (4 \cdot 3)$

Here is a summary of the properties of multiplication on the whole numbers.

THEOREM   *Properties of Whole Number Multiplication*

Closure Property	If a and b are any two whole numbers, then $a \cdot b$ is a unique whole number.
Commutative Property	If a and b are any two whole numbers, then $a \cdot b = b \cdot a$
Associative Property	If a, b, and c are any three whole numbers, then $a \cdot (b \cdot c) = (a \cdot b) \cdot (c)$
Multiplicative Identity Property of One	The number 1 is the unique whole number for which $b \cdot 1 = 1 \cdot b = b$ holds for all whole numbers b.
Multiplication by Zero Property	For all whole numbers b, $0 \cdot b = b \cdot 0 = 0$.
Distributive Property of Multiplication over Addition	If a, b, and c are any three whole numbers, then $a \cdot (b + c) = (a \cdot b) + (a \cdot c)$ and $(a + b) \cdot c = (a \cdot c) + (b \cdot c)$.

Understanding the Meaning and Relationships of the Operations in Grades K–5

As they develop computational fluency, students must understand the meaning of arithmetic operations. This includes deciding which operations should be used for a particular problem, how the same operation can be applied to problem situations that appear to be quite different from one another, how operations relate to one another, and what kind of result to expect.

During the primary grades, students encounter a variety of meanings for addition and subtraction. Subtraction can be viewed through a "take away" interpretation or as a comparison of two sets. Missing-addend situations highlight the relationship between addition and subtraction. Multiplication and division can begin to have meaning for students in grades pre-K–2 as they solve problems that arise within their environment. Such problems might include these: How many slices of bread are needed to make four sandwiches? How can this bag of raisins be shared fairly among four people? Although the major instructional emphasis in pre-K–2 is on addition and subtraction, students who naturally encounter and are curious about situations involving other operations, such as multiplication and division, should be encouraged.

Focusing on the meaning of multiplication and division, particularly with whole numbers, becomes central in grades 3–5. By creating representations of multiplication and division situations, either with diagrams or concrete objects, students gain a sense of the relationships among addition, subtraction, multiplication, and division. By inventing strategies for computing as well as by using conventional computational strategies, students use and recognize such properties as associativity, commutativity, and distributivity and recognize 0 and 1 as identities. The development and comparison of computational strategies provide a chance to focus on the nature of algorithms. For example, many multiplication algorithms illustrate distributivity, and division strategies sometimes involve an iterative process.

EXAMPLE   2.15 | **Multiplying Two Binomial Expressions**

(a) Use the properties of multiplication to justify the formula $(a + b)(c + d) = ac + ad + bc + bd$. The factors $(a + b)$ and $(c + d)$ are called **binomials** since each factor has two terms.

(b) Illustrate the expansion $(a + b)(c + d) = ac + ad + bc + bd$ with the array model of multiplication.

(c) Visualize $16 \cdot 28 = (10 + 6) \cdot (20 + 8) = 200 + 80 + 120 + 48$ with an array diagram.

(d) Show that $(x + 7) \cdot (2x + 5) = 2x^2 + 5x + 14x + 35$ with an array diagram.

Solution

(a) $(a + b)(c + d) = (a + b)c + (a + b)d$ Distributive property
$\qquad\qquad\qquad = ac + bc + ad + bd$ Distributive property
$\qquad\qquad\qquad = ac + ad + bc + bd$ Commutative property of addition

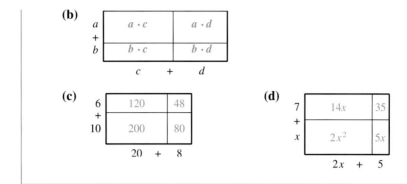

Division of Whole Numbers

There are three conceptual models for the division $a \div b$ of a whole number a by a nonzero whole number b: the **repeated subtraction** model, the **partition** model, and the **missing-factor** model.

The Repeated Subtraction Model of Division

Ms. Rislov has 28 students in her class that she wishes to divide into cooperative learning groups of 4 students per group. If each group requires a set of Cuisenaire® rods, how many sets of rods must Ms. Rislov have available? The answer, 7, is pictured in Figure 2.21, and is obtained by counting how many times groups of 4 can be formed, starting with 28. Thus, $28 \div 4 = 7$. The repeated subtraction model can be realized easily with physical objects; the process is called **division by grouping.**

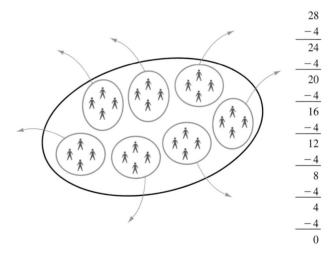

Figure 2.21
Division as repeated subtraction: $28 \div 4 = 7$ because seven 4s can be subtracted from 28.

The Partition Model of Division

When Ms. Rislov checked her supply cupboard, she discovered she had only 4 sets of Cuisenaire® rods to use with the 28 students in her class. How many students must she assign to each set of rods? The answer, 7 students in each group, is depicted in Figure 2.22. The partition model is also realized easily with physical objects, in which case the process is called **division by sharing.**

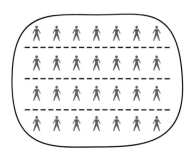

Figure 2.22
Division as a partition:
28 ÷ 4 = 7 because when
28 objects are partitioned into
4 equal-sized sections, there
are 7 objects in each partition.

The Missing-Factor Model of Division

In the repeated subtraction model, $28 \div 4 = 7$ because, when grouped by fours, seven groups will be formed. That is, $28 = 4 + 4 + 4 + 4 + 4 + 4 + 4 = 7 \cdot 4$. However, in the partition model, $28 \div 4 = 7$ because $28 = 7 + 7 + 7 + 7 = 4 \cdot 7$. In both cases, the division $28 \div 4$ can be viewed as finding the factor c for which $28 = 4 \cdot c$ or $28 = c \cdot 4$. The missing-factor model is usually the concept adopted to define division formally.

> **DEFINITION**   *Division in Whole Numbers*
> Let a and b be whole numbers with $b \neq 0$. Then $a \div b = c$ if, and only if, $a = b \cdot c$ for a unique whole number c.

The symbol $a \div b$ is read "a divided by b," where a is the **dividend** and b is the **divisor.** If $a \div b = c$, then we say that b **divides** a or is a **divisor** of a, and c is called the **quotient.**

$$a \div b = c$$
$$\text{dividend} \longrightarrow \quad \uparrow \quad \uparrow \quad \sqsubset \longrightarrow \text{quotient}$$
$$\text{divisor}$$

Division is also symbolized by a/b or $\dfrac{a}{b}$; the slash notation is used by most computers.

Any multiplication fact with nonzero factors, say $3 \cdot 5 = 15$, is related to four equivalent facts which form a **fact family** such as

$$3 \cdot 5 = 15 \qquad 15 \div 3 = 5$$
$$5 \cdot 3 = 15 \qquad 15 \div 5 = 3$$

With the array model in mind, a fact family is associated with rectangular arrays of 15 objects:

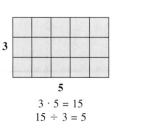

$3 \cdot 5 = 15$
$15 \div 3 = 5$

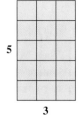

$5 \cdot 3 = 15$
$15 \div 5 = 3$

The three division models are nicely illustrated in the School Book Page in this section. Studying these examples and the accompanying Questions for the Teacher will help you understand the meaning of division.

EXAMPLE 2.16	**Computing Quotients with Manipulatives**

Suppose you have 78 number tiles. Describe how to illustrate $78 \div 13$ with the tiles, using each of the three basic conceptual models for division.

Solution

(a) **Repeated subtraction.** Remove groups of 13 tiles each. Since 6 groups are formed, $78 \div 13 = 6$.

(b) **Partition.** Partition the tiles into 13 equal-sized parts. Since each part contains exactly 6 tiles, $78 \div 13 = 6$.

(c) **Missing factor.** Use the 78 tiles to form a rectangle with 13 rows. Since it turns out there are 6 columns in the rectangle, then $78 \div 13 = 6$.

Division by Zero Is Undefined

The definition of division tells us that $12 \div 3 = 4$ since 4 is the unique whole number for which $12 = 3 \times 4$. Division *into zero* is also defined. For example, $c = 0$ is the unique whole number for which $0 = 5 \times c$ so $0 \div 5 = 0$. However, division *by zero* (or "$a \div 0$") is not defined for any whole number a. The reason for this can best be explained by taking the cases $a \neq 0$ and $a = 0$ separately.

Case 1: $a \neq 0$. In this case, "$a \div 0$" would be equivalent to finding the missing factor c that makes $a = c \cdot 0$. But $c \cdot 0 = 0$ for all whole numbers c, so there is no solution when $a \neq 0$. Thus $a \div 0$ is undefined for $a \neq 0$.

Case 2: $a = 0$. In this case "$0 \div 0$" is equivalent to finding a unique whole number c for which $0 = 0 \cdot c$. This equation is satisfied by every choice of the factor c. Since no *unique* factor c exists, the division of 0 by 0 is also undefined.

In the division $a \div b$, there is no restriction on the dividend a. For all $b \neq 0$, we have that $0 \div b = 0$ since $0 = b \cdot 0$.

The multiplicative identity 1 has two simple but useful relationships to division:

$$\frac{b}{b} = 1 \qquad \text{for all } b, \qquad \text{where } b \neq 0;$$

$$\frac{a}{1} = a \qquad \text{for all } a.$$

Division with Remainders

Consider the division problem $27 \div 6$. There is no whole number c that satisfies $c \cdot 6 = 27$, so $27 \div 6$ is not defined in the whole numbers. That is, the set of whole numbers is *not closed* under division.

By allowing the possibility of a **remainder,** we can extend the division operation. Consider $27 \div 6$, where division is viewed as repeated subtraction. Four groups of 6 can

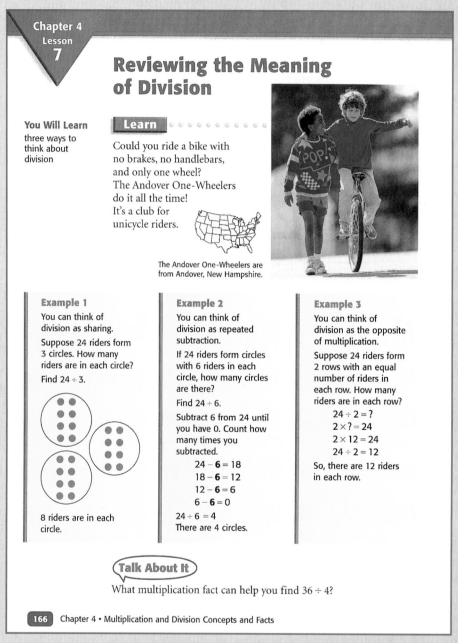

Chapter 4
Lesson
7

Reviewing the Meaning of Division

You Will Learn
three ways to think about division

Learn

Could you ride a bike with no brakes, no handlebars, and only one wheel? The Andover One-Wheelers do it all the time! It's a club for unicycle riders.

The Andover One-Wheelers are from Andover, New Hampshire.

Example 1

You can think of division as sharing.

Suppose 24 riders form 3 circles. How many riders are in each circle? Find 24 ÷ 3.

8 riders are in each circle.

Example 2

You can think of division as repeated subtraction.

If 24 riders form circles with 6 riders in each circle, how many circles are there?

Find 24 ÷ 6.

Subtract 6 from 24 until you have 0. Count how many times you subtracted.

$24 - 6 = 18$
$18 - 6 = 12$
$12 - 6 = 6$
$6 - 6 = 0$

$24 ÷ 6 = 4$
There are 4 circles.

Example 3

You can think of division as the opposite of multiplication.

Suppose 24 riders form 2 rows with an equal number of riders in each row. How many riders are in each row?

$24 ÷ 2 = ?$
$2 × ? = 24$
$2 × 12 = 24$
$24 ÷ 2 = 12$

So, there are 12 riders in each row.

Talk About It

What multiplication fact can help you find 36 ÷ 4?

166   Chapter 4 • Multiplication and Division Concepts and Facts

SOURCE: From Scott Foresman–Addison Wesley, *Math Grade 4*, p. 166, by Randall I. Charles et al. Copyright © 1999.

Questions for the Teacher

1. The red arrays of dots represent unicycle riders. What other arrangement of dots in each loop might a fourth grader form to make the pictorial model correspond more closely to the problem posed in Example 1?

2. Describe how to use a set of red counters to illustrate the repeated subtraction model in Example 2 to fourth graders?

3. How would you use 24 red counters to illustrate the missing-factor model in Example 3?

4. What help could you offer to fourth graders who wish to respond to the "Talk About It" question at the bottom of the school book page?

be removed from 27. This leaves 3, which are too few to form another group of 6. This can be written

$$27 = 4 \cdot 6 + 3.$$

Here 4 is called the **quotient** and 3 is the **remainder.** This information is also written

$$27 \div 6 = 4 \text{ R } 3,$$

where R separates the quotient from the remainder. A visualization of division with a remainder is shown in Figure 2.23

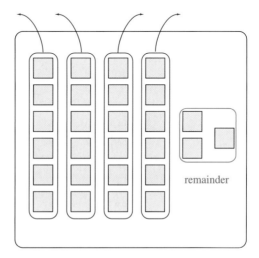

remainder

Figure 2.23
Visualizing division with a remainder: 27 ÷ 6 = 4 R 3

In general, we have the following result.

THEOREM   *The Division Algorithm*

Let a and b be whole numbers with $b \neq 0$. Then there is a unique whole number q called the **quotient** and a unique whole number r called the **remainder** such that

$$a = q \cdot b + r, \quad 0 \leq r < b.$$

It is common to write

$$a \div b = q \text{ R } r$$

if $a = q \cdot b + r$, $0 \leq r < b$. The quotient q is the largest whole number of groups of b objects that can be formed from a objects, and the remainder r is the number of objects that are left over. The remainder is 0 if, and only if, b divides a according to the definition of division in whole numbers. This important case is explored fully in Chapter 4.

EXAMPLE   2.17

Using the Division Algorithm to Solve the Marching Band Problem

Mr. Garza was happy to see that so many students in the school band had turned out for the parade. He had them form into rows of 6, but it turned out that just one tuba player was in the back row. To his dismay, when he reformed the band into rows of 5, there was still a lone tuba player in the back row. In desperation, Mr. Garza had the band reassemble into rows of 7. To his relief, every row was filled! How many students are marching in the parade band?

Solution

If we let n denote the number of students marching in the band, then we know that when n is divided by 6 the remainder is 1. Thus $n = 6q + 1$ for some whole number $q = 0$, 1, 2, ... This means n is somewhere in the list:

$$1, 7, 13, 19, 25, 31, 37, 43, 49, 55, 61, 67, 73, 79, 85, 91, 97, 103, \ldots .$$

Similarly, $n \div 5$ has a remainder of 1, so n is also a number in this list:

$$1, 6, 11, 16, 21, 26, 31, 36, 41, 46, 51, 56, 61, 66, 71, 76, 81, 86, 91, 96, 101, \ldots .$$

Finally, 7 is a divisor of n so n is one of these numbers:

$$7, 14, 21, 28, 35, 42, 49, 56, 63, 70, 77, 84, 91, 98, 105, \ldots .$$

Comparing the three lists, we find that 91 is the smallest number common to all three lists, so it is possible there are 91 band members. By extending the lists (it helps to notice that the numbers 1, 31, 61, 91, . . . common to the first two lists jump ahead by 30 each step), we find that the next smallest number in all three lists is 301, since $301 = 50 \cdot 6 + 1 = 60 \cdot 5 + 1 = 43 \cdot 7$. It seems pretty unlikely the band is this large, so we conclude that there are 91 members of the band. Mr. Garza has arranged them in 13 rows, since $91 \div 7 = 13$.

Exponents and the Power Operation

Instead of writing $3 \cdot 3 \cdot 3 \cdot 3 \cdot 3$ we can follow a notation introduced by René Descartes and write 3^5. This operation is called "taking 3 to the fifth power." The general definition is described as follows.

DEFINITION   *The Power Operation for Whole Numbers*

Let a and m be whole numbers, where $m \neq 0$. Then a **to the mth power,** written a^m, is defined by:

$$a^1 = a, \quad \text{if } m = 1,$$

and

$$\overbrace{a^m = a \cdot a \cdots \cdot a}^{m \text{ factors}}, \quad \text{if } m > 1.$$

The number a is called the **base**, m is called the **exponent** or **power**, and a^m is called an **exponential.** Special cases include squares and cubes. For example, 7^2 is read "7 squared," and 10^3 is read "10 cubed." On most computers, 7^2 and 10^3 would be typed in as $7 \wedge 2$ and $10 \wedge 3$, where the circumflex $\wedge$ separates the base from the exponent. Calculators often have a $\boxed{\wedge}$ or $\boxed{y^x}$ key to compute powers. For example, $3 \boxed{y^x} 2 \boxed{=}$ will give the answer 9.

EXAMPLE 2.18

Working with Exponents

Compute the following products and powers, expressing your answers in the form of a single exponential a^m.

(a) $7^4 \cdot 7^2$ (b) $6^3 \cdot 6^5$ (c) $2^3 \cdot 5^3$

(d) $3^2 \cdot 5^2 \cdot 4^2$ (e) $(3^2)^5$ (f) $(4^2)^3$

Solution

(a) $7^4 \cdot 7^2 = (7 \cdot 7 \cdot 7 \cdot 7) \cdot (7 \cdot 7) = 7 \cdot 7 \cdot 7 \cdot 7 \cdot 7 \cdot 7 = 7^6$

(b) $6^3 \cdot 6^5 = (6 \cdot 6 \cdot 6) \cdot (6 \cdot 6 \cdot 6 \cdot 6 \cdot 6)$
$= 6 \cdot 6 \cdot 6 \cdot 6 \cdot 6 \cdot 6 \cdot 6 \cdot 6 = 6^8$

(c) $2^3 \cdot 5^3 = (2 \cdot 2 \cdot 2) \cdot (5 \cdot 5 \cdot 5) = (2 \cdot 5) \cdot (2 \cdot 5) \cdot (2 \cdot 5)$
$= (2 \cdot 5)^3 = 10^3$

(d) $3^2 \cdot 5^2 \cdot 4^2 = (3 \cdot 3) \cdot (5 \cdot 5) \cdot (4 \cdot 4) = (3 \cdot 5 \cdot 4) \cdot (3 \cdot 5 \cdot 4)$
$= (3 \cdot 5 \cdot 4)^2 = 60^2$

(e) $(3^2)^5 = (3)^2 \cdot (3)^2 \cdot (3)^2 \cdot (3)^2 \cdot (3)^2$
$= (3 \cdot 3) \cdot (3 \cdot 3) \cdot (3 \cdot 3) \cdot (3 \cdot 3) \cdot (3 \cdot 3)$
$= 3 \cdot 3 \cdot 3 \cdot 3 \cdot 3 \cdot 3 \cdot 3 \cdot 3 \cdot 3 \cdot 3 = 3^{10}$

(f) $(4^2)^3 = (4^2) \cdot (4^2) \cdot (4^2) = (4 \cdot 4) \cdot (4 \cdot 4) \cdot (4 \cdot 4)$
$= 4 \cdot 4 \cdot 4 \cdot 4 \cdot 4 \cdot 4 = 4^6$

Example 2.18 reveals that multiplying exponentials follows useful patterns that can be used to shorten calculations. For example, $7^4 \cdot 7^2 = 7^{4+2}$ and $6^3 \cdot 6^5 = 6^{3+5}$ are two

HIGHLIGHT FROM HISTORY
Symbols for Multiplication, Division, and Power

W illiam Oughtred introduced the symbol $\times$ for multiplication in 1631. Gottfried Leibniz objected to the $\times$,

writing to Bernoulli in 1698 that it ". . . is easily confounded with *x*." Leibniz preferred the dot $\cdot$ symbol which Thomas Harriot had introduced in the same year 1631. The symbol $\div$ was introduced in 1659 by the Swiss mathematician J. H. Rohn. It was adopted into the English-speaking countries by John Wallis and others, but on the European continent the

colon symbol a : b of Leibniz was the symbol of regular choice. The slanted line /, and the horizontal line, gradually became more common. Exponential notation became common with its systematic use by Descartes (1596–1650) in *La Geometrie*. For use with computers, where it is best to keep expressions on one line, the circumflex $\wedge$ is used: thus $4 \wedge 7$ denotes 4^7.

special cases of the general rule $a^m \cdot a^n = a^{m+n}$ for multiplying exponentials with the same base. Similarly, $2^3 \cdot 5^3 = (2 \cdot 5)^3$ is a special case of $a^n \cdot b^n = (a \cdot b)^n$, and $(3^2)^5 = 3^{2 \cdot 5}$ is a special case of $(a^m)^n = a^{m \cdot n}$.

THEOREM *Multiplication Rules of Exponentials*

Let a, b, m, n be whole numbers, where $m \neq 0$ and $n \neq 0$. Then:

(i) $a^m \cdot a^n = a^{m+n}$
(ii) $a^m \cdot b^m = (a \cdot b)^m$
(iii) $(a^m)^n = a^{m \cdot n}$.

Proof of (i): $a^m \cdot a^n = a^{m+n}$

$$a^m \cdot a^n = \underbrace{a \cdot a \cdots \cdots a}_{m \text{ factors}} \cdot \underbrace{a \cdot a \cdots \cdots a}_{n \text{ factors}}$$

$$= \underbrace{a \cdot a \cdots \cdots a}_{m + n \text{ factors}}$$

$$= a^{m+n}.$$

The proofs of (ii) and (iii) follow similarly.

If the formula $a^m \cdot a^n = a^{m+n}$ were extended to allow $m = 0$, it would state that $a^0 \cdot a^n = a^{0+n} = a^n$. This suggests that it is reasonable to define $a^0 = 1$ when $a \neq 0$.

DEFINITION *Zero as an Exponent*

Let a be any whole number, $a \neq 0$. Define $a^0 = 1$.

To see why 0^0 is not defined, notice that there are two conflicting patterns:

$$3^0 = 1, \quad 2^0 = 1, \quad 1^0 = 1, \quad 0^0 = ?$$

$$0^3 = 0, \quad 0^2 = 0, \quad 0^1 = 0, \quad 0^0 = ?$$

The multiplication formula $a^m \cdot a^n = a^{m+n}$ can also be converted to a corresponding division fact. For example,

$$a^{5-3} \cdot a^3 = a^{(5-3)+3} = a^5$$

so

$$a^5/a^3 = a^{5-3}.$$

In general, we have the following theorem.

> **THEOREM** *Rules for Division of Exponentials*
> Let a, b, m, n be whole numbers, where $m \geq n > 0$, $b \neq 0$, and $a \div b$ is defined. Then
>
> **(i)**
> $$b^m/b^n = b^{m-n}$$
>
> and
>
> **(ii)**
> $$(a^m/b^m) = (a/b)^m.$$

EXAMPLE   2.19   **Working with Exponents**

Rewrite these expressions in exponential form a^m.

(a) $5^{12} \cdot 5^8$ (b) $7^{14}/7^5$ (c) $3^2 \cdot 3^5 \cdot 3^8$
(d) $8^7/4^7$ (e) 2^{5-5} (f) $(3^5)^2/3^4$

Solution

(a) $5^{12+8} = 5^{20}$ (b) $7^{14-5} = 7^9$ (c) $3^{2+5+8} = 3^{15}$
(d) $(8/4)^7 = 2^7$ (e) $2^0 = 1$ (f) $3^{5 \cdot 2 - 4} = 3^6$

COOPERATIVE INVESTIGATION

The Krypto Game

The Krypto game, which is available commercially or which can be homemade, consists of 25 cards numbered 1 through 25. Each player, or cooperative group, is dealt a hand of 5 cards plus a sixth card which designates the target number. Here is an example:

Hand: | 21 | 5 | 17 | 8 | 3 | Target: | 12 |

The object of the game is to combine the cards in the hand, using any of the operations $+$, $-$, $\times$, $\div$ and using each card once and only once, to obtain the target number. Here is one solution:

$$21 - 5 = 16$$
$$16 \div 8 = 2$$
$$2 + 3 = 5$$
$$17 - 5 = 12 \leftarrow \text{Target}$$

That is, $17 - (((21 - 5) \div 8) + 3) = 12$. Other solutions are $((17 + 8) \div 5) + (21 \div 3) = 12$ and $(5 + 17 + 8 + 3) - 21 = 12$

In this game, guess and check and working backwards are useful problem-solving strategies. Parentheses are needed to show the order in which operations are performed.

PROBLEM SET 2.4

Understanding Concepts

1. What multiplication fact is illustrated in each of these diagrams?

    (a)
    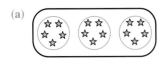

    (b)
    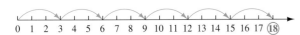

    (c)

    (d)

    (e)

    (f)

2. Discuss which model of multiplication—set model, measurement, rectangular array, Cartesian product—best fits the following problems:

    (a) A set of dominoes came in a box containing eleven stacks of five dominoes each. How many dominoes are in the set?

    (b) Marja has 3 skirts which she can "mix or match" with 6 blouses. How many outfits does she have to wear?

    (c) Harold hiked 10 miles each day, and crossed the mountains after 5 days. How long was his hike?

    (d) Ace Widgit Company makes 35 widgits a day. How many widgits are made in a 5-day workweek?

3. Multiplication as repeated addition can be illustrated on most calculators. For example, $4 \cdot 7$ is computed by $7\ \boxed{+}\ 7\ \boxed{+}\ 7\ \boxed{+}\ 7\ \boxed{=}$. Each press of the $\boxed{+}$ key completes any pending addition and sets up the next one, so the intermediate products $2 \cdot 7 = 14$ and $3 \cdot 7 = 21$ are displayed along the way. Many calculators have a constant feature, which avoids having to reenter the same addend over and over. For example, $\boxed{+}\ 734\ \boxed{=}\ \boxed{=}\ \boxed{=}$, or $734\ \boxed{+}\ \boxed{+}\ \boxed{+}$, may compute $3 \cdot 734$; it all depends on how your particular calculator operates.

    (a) Explain carefully how repeated addition is best accomplished on your calculator.

    (b) Use repeated additions on your calculator to compute these products. Check your result by using the $\boxed{\times}$ button.

    (i) $4 \cdot 9$ **(ii)** 7×536
    (iii) 6×47819 **(iv)** 56108×6 (What property may help?)

4. The Cartesian product of finite and nonempty sets can be illustrated by the intersections of a crossing-line pattern, as shown.

    $$\{ f, \quad g, \quad h \} \ \times \ \{ x, \quad y \}$$

    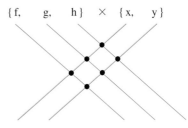

    (a) Explain why the number of intersection points in the crossing-line pattern for $A \times B$ is $a \cdot b$, where $a = n(A)$ and $b = n(B)$.

    (b) Draw the pattern for $\{\square, \triangle\} \times \{\heartsuit, \blacklozenge, \clubsuit, \spadesuit\}$.

5. Which of the following sets of whole numbers are closed under multiplication? Explain your reasoning.

    (a) $\{1, 2\}$ **(b)** $\{0, 1\}$ **(c)** $\{0, 2, 4\}$
    (d) $\{0, 2, 4, \dots\}$ (the even whole numbers)
    (e) $\{1, 3, 5, \dots\}$ (the odd whole numbers)
    (f) $\{1, 2, 2^2, 2^3\}$ **(g)** $\{1, 2, 2^2, 2^3, \dots\}$
    (h) $\{1, 7, 7^2, 7^3, \dots\}$

6. Which of the following subsets of the whole numbers $W = \{0, 1, 2, \ldots\}$ are closed under multiplication? Explain carefully.

(a) $\{0, 1, 2, 3, 4, 6, 7, \ldots\}$ (that is, the whole numbers except for 5)

(b) $\{0, 1, 2, 3, 4, 5, 7, 8, \ldots\}$

(c) $\{0, 1, 4, 5, 6, \ldots\}$

7. What properties of whole number multiplication justify these equalities?

(a) $4 \cdot 9 = 9 \cdot 4$

(b) $4 \cdot (6 + 2) = 4 \cdot 6 + 4 \cdot 2$

(c) $0 \cdot 439 = 0$ (d) $7 \cdot 3 + 7 \cdot 8 = 7 \cdot (3 + 8)$

(e) $5 \cdot (9 \cdot 11) = (5 \cdot 9) \cdot 11$ (f) $1 \cdot 12 = 12$

---

8. What property of multiplication is illustrated in each of these diagrams?

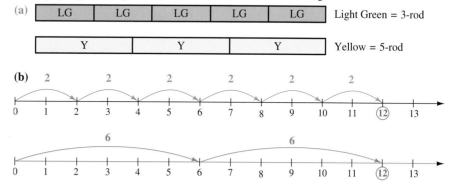

9. Use the rectangular array model to illustrate each of the following statements. Make drawings similar to Figure 2.20.

(a) $(2 + 5) \cdot 3 = 2 \cdot 3 + 5 \cdot 3$

(b) $3 \cdot (2 + 5 + 1) = 3 \cdot 2 + 3 \cdot 5 + 3 \cdot 1$

(c) $(3 + 2) \cdot (4 + 3) = 3 \cdot 4 + 3 \cdot 3 + 2 \cdot 4 + 2 \cdot 3.$

10. Use the figure below to show that the product of trinomials, $(a + b + c) \cdot (d + e + f)$, can be written as a sum of nine products.

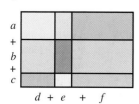

11. Modify Figure 2.19 to show how the associative property $3 \cdot (2 \cdot 4)$ can be illustrated with arrays of cubes in 3-dimensional space.

12. Shannon bought 18 nuts and 18 bolts. The bolts were 86¢ each, and the nuts were 14¢ each. The store clerk computed the bill as shown below. How did Shannon already know the answer by simple mental math?

$$
\begin{array}{cc}
\overset{4}{86} & \overset{3}{14} \\
\times\ 18 & \times\ 18 \\
\hline
688 & 112 \\
86 & 14 \\
\hline
1548 & 252
\end{array}
\qquad
\begin{array}{c}
\overset{1\ 1}{} \\
15.48 \\
+\ 2.52 \\
\hline
18.00
\end{array}
$$

13. What properties of multiplication make it easy to compute these values mentally?

(a) $7 \cdot 19 + 3 \cdot 19$

(b) $24 \cdot 17 + 24 \cdot 3$

(c) $36 \cdot 15 - 12 \cdot 45$

14. What division facts are illustrated below?

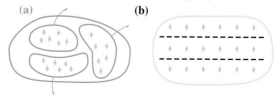

15. A 2 by 3 rectangular array is associated with the fact family $2 \cdot 3 = 6, 3 \cdot 2 = 6, 6 \div 2 = 3, 6 \div 3 = 2$. What fact family is associated with each of these rectangular arrays?

(a) 4 by 8   (b) 6 by 5

16. Discuss which of three conceptual models of division—repeated subtraction, partition, missing-factor—best corresponds to the following problems. More than one model may fit.

(a) Preston owes $3200 on his car. If his payments are $200 a month, how many more months will Preston make car payments?

(b) An estate of $76,000 is to be split among 4 heirs. How much can each heir expect to inherit?

(c) Anita was given a grant of $375 to cover expenses on her trip. She expects that it will cost her $75 a day. How many days can she plan to be gone?

17. Use repeated subtraction on your calculator to compute the following division problems, where remainders are possible. Be sure to take advantage of the constant feature of your calculator.

(a) $78 \div 13$ (b) $832 \div 52$

(c) $96 \div 14$ (d) $548245 \div 45687$

18. Show that the following statements are not always true, where a, b, and c represent nonzero whole numbers. In each part, choose specific values of a, b, c which provide a counterexample.

(a) $a \div b$ is a whole number

(b) $a \div b = b \div a$

(c) $(a \div b) \div c = a \div (b \div c)$

19. (a) Show that if a/b and d/b are defined, then $(a + d)/b$ is defined and $(a + d)/b = (a/b) + (d/b)$.

(b) Show by an example that division is *not* distributive over addition from the left; that is, it is not always true that $a/(b + c) = (a/b) + (a/c)$.

20. Solve for the unknown whole number in the following expressions.

(a) $y \div 5 = 5 \text{ R } 4$

(b) $20 \div x = 3 \text{ R } 2$

21. Rewrite the following in the form of a single exponential.

(a) $3^{20} \cdot 3^{15}$ (b) $4^8 \cdot 7^8$ (c) $(3^2)^5$

(d) $x^7 \cdot x^9$ (e) $y^3 \cdot z^3$ (f) $(t^3)^4$

22. Write the following as 2^m for some whole number m.

(a) 8   (b) $4 \cdot 8$ (c) 1024   (d) 8^4

23. (a) Show that $2^4 = 4^2$. Does this mean that the power operation is commutative?

(b) Is the power operation associative on the nonzero whole numbers? That is, is $(a^b)^c = a^{(b^c)}$ for *all* a, b, and c? Explain carefully.

 24. Find the exponents that make the following equations true.

(a) $3^m = 81$ (b) $3^n = 531,441$

(c) $4^p = 1,048,576$ (d) $2^q = 1,048,576$

Thinking Critically

25. Let a and b be whole numbers. Explain why the square array shown below illustrates the formula $(a + b)^2 = a^2 + 2ab + b^2$.

26. Let a and b be whole numbers, with $a > b$. Explain how the square array shown below illustrates the formula $(a + b)^2 - (a - b)^2 = 4ab$.

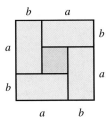

27. (a) The Math Club wants to gross $500 on its raffle. Raffle tickets are $2 each and 185 tickets have been sold so far. The answer is 65. What is the question?

(b) A total of 67 eggs were collected from the hen house and placed in standard egg cartons. If the answer is 5, what is the question? If the answer is 7, what is the question?

28. There are 318 folding chairs being set up in rows in an auditorium, with 14 chairs being put in each row starting at the front of the auditorium.

(a) If the answer is 22, what is the question?

(b) If the answer is 10, what is the question?

29. (a) Verify that $4 \cdot (5 - 2) = 4 \cdot 5 - 4 \cdot 2$.

(b) Prove that multiplication distributes over subtraction. That is, for all whole numbers a, b, and c, with $b \geqslant c$, show that $a \cdot (b - c) = a \cdot b - a \cdot c$.

30. **Adams' Magic Hexagon.** In 1957 Clifford W. Adams discovered a magic hexagon, in which the sum of the numbers in any "row" is 38. Fill in the empty cells of the partially completed hexagon shown, using the whole numbers 6, 7, . . . , 15, to recreate Adams' discovery. When completed, each cell is assigned one of the numbers 1, 2, . . . , 19.

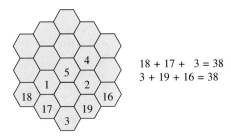

$18 + 17 + 3 = 38$
$3 + 19 + 16 = 38$

31. A clock chimes on the hour, once at 1 o'clock, twice at 2 o'clock and so on. How many times does it chime every 24-hour period?

32. How many total spots are on the 28 dominoes of a "double-six" domino set? (*Suggestion:* Imagine you have *two* sets of dominoes, and each domino of one set has been matched with its "complementary" domino from the other set. The figure below shows two pairs of complementary dominoes.)

33. A certain whole number less than 100 leaves the remainders 1, 2, 3, and 4 when divided respectively by 2, 3, 4, and 5. What is the whole number?

Thinking Cooperatively

34. Each team is given a game sheet as shown. The teacher rolls 3 dice (or a die 3 times) to determine three numbers x, y, and z. Each team uses whole number operations, including power, involving all three numbers exactly once, to obtain expressions equal to as many of the numbers 0, 1, 2, . . . , 18 as possible. The team filling all regions of the game board first is the winner. If no team has won at the end of the first roll, the numbers x, y, and z are replaced by rolling the dice again. Each team now fills in remaining empty positions on the game board using the new set of three numbers. The dice are rolled again until there is a winning team. Example: Suppose the dice turn up the numbers 2, 3, 3. Show that at least 13 of the regions on the board can be filled.

Using a Calculator

35. Let T_n denote the sum of first n triangular numbers, so that

$$T_n = 1 + 3 + 6 + 10 + \ldots + t_n,$$

where

$$t_n = 1 + 2 + 3 + \ldots + n.$$

Now observe that

$$T_1 = 1 = 1 \cdot 2 \cdot 3/6$$
$$T_2 = 1 + 3 = 4 = 2 \cdot 3 \cdot 4/6$$
$$T_3 = 1 + 3 + 6 = 10 = 3 \cdot 4 \cdot 5/6$$

(a) See if the pattern continues to hold for T_4, $T_5, \ldots, T_{12}$.

(b) What is T_{100}?

36. **A Magic Multiplication Square.** Consider the square shown. This is a Magic Addition Square, since the sum of three numbers in any row, column, or diagonal is the same magic constant 30. Show the square also has this amazing property: the sum of the row products (that is $11 \times 2 \times 17 + 16 \times 10 \times 4 + 3 \times 18 \times 9$), the sum of the column products, and the sum of the diagonal products are all the same.

11	2	17
16	10	4
3	18	9

37. The eighth triangular number is $t_8 = (8 \cdot 9)/2 = 36$, which is also a square number since $6^2 = 36$. Verify that the triangular numbers t_{49}, t_{288}, and t_{1681} are also square numbers. Recall that $t_n = n(n + 1)/2$.

From State Student Assessments

38. (Washington State, Grade 4)

Juan and Bill worked together to unload bags of food from a van. On each trip, Juan carried 6 bags and Bill carried 4 bags. They each made a total of 3 trips.

Which number sentence would you use to find how many bags they unloaded in all?

A. $3 \times 6 \times 4 = \square$

B. $(3 \times 6) + 4 = \square$

C. $(3 \times 6) + (3 \times 4) = \square$

For Review

39. What addition-subtraction fact family contains $2 + 7 = 9$?

40. Let $n(A) = 2$, $n(B) = 7$, and $n(A \cup B) = 9$. What is $n(A \cap B)$?

41. What basic facts are illustrated by these number strip trains?

2.5   Functions

The earlier sections of this chapter have introduced the whole numbers and described their basic properties. In the chapters that follow, we will investigate computational procedures, and extend the whole numbers to the integers, rational numbers, and real numbers. Independently of what number system we work with, our mathematical understanding and problem-solving powers are greatly enhanced by the concept of a **function.**

Defining Functions

Imagine yourself at the service station, filling your tank with gasoline priced at $1.299 per gallon. If you purchase 10 gallons of gas, your bill will be $12.99, and if you put 13.28 gallons in your tank, your bill (rounded to the penny) will be $17.25. The general principle is that your bill that day at the station is a *function* of the amount of gasoline you purchase. If we let the letter x represent the number of gallons of gasoline purchased and let the letter y represent the final bill, then y is given by the simple rule $y = \$1.299x$. Nicely enough, the pump carries out this calculation right before our eyes and, as the values of x whirl by on one display of the pump, we can simultaneously watch the corresponding values of y on another display.

It is easy to make a list of functions used in our lives. Here are a few samples:

- The amount of postage on a first-class letter is a function of the weight of the envelope rounded upward to the nearest ounce.
- The amount of lawn fertilizer applied is a function of the number of square feet of lawn area.
- The amount of federal income tax you will owe is a function of your taxable income the previous year.

These examples should help you understand the general definition of a function

> **DEFINITION** *Function*
> A **function** on a set D is a rule that assigns to each element $x \in D$ precisely one value y. The set D is called the **domain** of the function.

A function is often denoted by a letter such as f, and we write $y = f(x)$ to indicate that the element y is assigned to element x by the function f. Often a function is denoted by a word or abbreviation to help remember its definition. For example, the function that computes the square root of a positive number is frequently denoted by Sqrt, so that Sqrt(49) = 7.

If a function assigns the value y to an element x in the domain then y is called the **image,** or **value,** of f at x. For example, if f denotes the function giving our bill at the gasoline station and we have purchased $x = 10$ gallons of gas, then $\$12.99 = f(10)$ is the value of the function at $x = 10$. We can also write that $f(x) = \$12.99 \cdot x$ and $D = \{x \mid x \geq 0\}$, which describes the gasoline-buying function by a computational rule and the domain of permissible values of x.

DID YOU KNOW?

A Provocative Perspective on a Disturbing Modern Problem

In the following excerpt, writer and mathematician John Allen Paulos delivers a compelling and passionate treatise on the phenomenon of "innumeracy" in the modern world.

"Although few students get past elementary school without knowing their arithmetic tables, many do pass through without understanding that if one drives at 35 mph for four hours, one will have driven 140 miles; that if peanuts cost 40 cents an ounce and a bag of them costs $2.20, then there are 5.5 ounces of peanuts in the bag; that if 1/4 of the world's population is Chinese and 1/5 of the remainder is Indian, then 3/20 or 15 percent of the world is Indian. This sort of understanding is, of course, not the same as simply knowing that $35 \times 4 = 140$; that $(2.2)/(.4) = 5.5$; that $1/5 \times (1 - 1/4) = 3/20 = .15 = 15$ percent. And since it doesn't come naturally to many elementary students, it must be furthered by doing numerous problems, some practical, some more fanciful . . . .

"Some of the blame for the generally poor instruction in elementary schools must ultimately lie with teachers who . . . too often have little interest in or appreciation of mathematics. In turn, some of the blame for that lies, I think, with schools of education in colleges and universities which place little or no emphasis on mathematics in their teacher training courses . . .

"If mathematics education communicated [the] playful aspect of the subject, formally at the elementary, secondary, or college level or informally via popular books, I don't think innumeracy would be as widespread as it is."

SOURCE: John Allen Paulos, *Innumeracy: Mathematical Illiteracy and Its Consequences.* New York: Hill and Wang, pp. 73–74, 75, and 77.

The definition of function requires that precisely one image value y be assigned to each x value in the domain. This should seem reasonable, since it would seem strange to buy 10 gallons of gas and be given two bills, say one for $12.99 and another bill for $14.75. The set of all image values is called the **range** of the function.

> **DEFINITION**   *Range of a Function*
> The **range** of a function f on a set D is the set of images of f. That is,
> $$\text{range } f = \{y \mid y = f(x) \text{ for some } x \in D\}.$$

For example, a first class letter mailed in the U.S. costs $0.33 for the first ounce and $0.22 for each additional ounce. Therefore, the range of the function that gives the cost of mailing a first class letter is $\{\$0.33, \$0.55, \$0.77, \ldots\}$.

EXAMPLE   2.20

Finding the range of a function

Let f be the function defined by the formula $f(x) = x(10 - x)$ on the domain $D = \{1, 2, 3, 4, 5, 6, 7, 8, 9, 10\}$. Find the range of f.

Solution

The image of f at $x = 1$ is $f(1) = 1 \cdot (10 - 1) = 9$. Similarly, $f(2) = 2 \cdot 8 = 16$, $f(3) = 3 \cdot 7 = 21, f(4) = 4 \cdot 6 = 24, f(5) = 5 \cdot 5 = 25, f(6) = 6 \cdot 4 = 24, f(7) = 7 \cdot 3 = 21$, $f(8) = 8 \cdot 2 = 16, f(9) = 9 \cdot 1 = 9$, and $f(10) = 10 \cdot 0 = 0$. Thus, the range of f is $\{0, 9, 16, 21, 24, 25\}$. Some image values, such as 9, 16, and 21, correspond to more than one x in the domain, but any x yields a unique y value in the range.

One of the most popular ways to introduce function concepts to elementary school children is to play the game "Guess My Rule."

EXAMPLE   2.21   **Guessing Erica's Rule**

Erica is "it" in a game of Guess My Rule. As the children pick an input number, Erica tells what number her rule gives back as shown in this table. Can you guess Erica's rule?

Children's Choice	Result of Erica's Rule (function)
2	−1
5	8
6	11
0	−7
1	−4

Solution   *Understand the problem*

The rule Erica has chosen is a function—given an input number, she uses her function to determine the output number that she reveals to the class. We must guess her function. We will express the formula in terms of a variable x or n as in the above examples.

Devise a plan

The children's choices are somewhat random. Perhaps a pattern will become more apparent if we arrange their input numbers in order of increasing size. We anticipate that Erica's function is given by a formula.

Rearranging the children's choices in order of increasing size, we have the following table.

Children's Choice	Result of Erica's Rule (function)
0	−7
1	−4
2	−1
5	8
6	11

When 0 is input the formula yields −7. This suggests that −7 is a separate term in the formula; when $n = 0$ all the other terms are zero. Also, we observe that when n increases by 1 from 0 to 1, from 1 to 2, and from 5 to 6, the output number increases by 3. This suggests that the formula also contains the term $3n$, since this quantity increases by 3 each time n increases by 1. Combining these observations, we guess that Erica's function (rule), E, is given by the formula:

$$E(n) = 3n - 7.$$

Checking, we see that $E(0) = 3 \cdot 0 - 7 = -7$, $E(1) = 3 \cdot 1 - 7 = -4$, $E(2) = -1$, $E(5) = 8$, and $E(6) = 11$ as in Erica's table. When challenged, Erica reveals that we have guessed correctly.

Erica's rule is really a function—given a single input, her rule returns a single output. We guessed the rule by arranging the data in a more orderly way, noting that her rule associated −7 with 0, and that the output number increased by 3 each time the input number increased by 1. Thus, we correctly guessed Erica's function to be $E(n) = 3n - 7$.

Describing and Visualizing Functions

There are several useful ways to describe and visualize functions.

- **Functions as formulas.** Consider, for example, a circle of radius r, where r is any positive number. The formula $area(r) = \pi r^2$ defines the function *area* that expresses the area of the circle as a function of the radius r. Similarly, the formula $circum(r) = 2\pi r$ defines the function *circum* that gives the circumference of a circle of radius r. Several interesting formulas were encountered in Chapter 1, each of which can be viewed as a function defined on the domain N, the set of natural numbers. For example, the nth odd number is given by the formula

$h(n) = 2n - 1$, so that the 50th odd number is $h(50) = 2(50) - 1 = 99$. Another example is the sum $1 + 2 + 3 + \cdots + n$ of the first n natural numbers (that is, the nth triangular number), which is given by the formula $t(n) = n(n + 1)/2$. Thus, the sum of the first 100 natural numbers is $1 + 2 + 3 + \cdots + 99 + 100 = t(100) = 100(100 + 1)/2 = 100 \cdot 101/2 = 5050$. Functions that are defined on the domain N of the natural numbers are called **sequences,** and it is common to use the notation f_n instead of $f(n)$. For example, the nth triangular number is given by $t_n = n(n + 1)/2$, and in particular $t_{100} = 5050$.

- **Functions as tables.** The following table gives the grades of three students on an essay question.

Student	Grade
Raygene	8
Sergei	7
Leticia	10

No algebraic formula connects the student to the grade. Even so, as long as the table assigns a unique grade to each student, then a function is completely described.

- **Functions as machines.** Viewing a function as a machine gives students an attractive dynamic visual model. The machine has an input hopper which accepts any domain element x, and an output chute which gives the image $y = f(x)$. A few machines are shown in Figure 2.24.

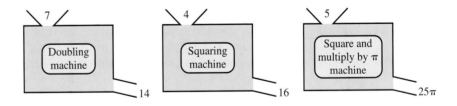

Figure 2.24
Three function machines

- **Functions as graphs.** A function whose domain and range are sets of numbers can be graphed on a two-dimensional coordinate system: if $f(x) = y$, plot the points (x, y) for all x in the domain. The Fibonacci sequence $F_1 = 1$, $F_2 = 1$, $F_3 = 2$, $F_4 = 3, \ldots$ and the doubling function $y = 2x$ are plotted in Figure 2.25.

It is still instructive to make graphs by "hand," using squared paper, rulers, and colored pencils. Begin by making a table of selected values of x from the domain and calculating the corresponding image values y. The table of values will help you to choose an appropriate range of x and y values to include on the axes. Next plot the points (x, y) from your table onto your graph. Finally, fill in the rest of the graph. Additional information on graphing will be taken up in Chapter 14.

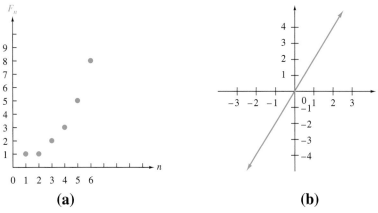

(a)   **(b)**

Figure 2.25
Graphs of (a) the Fibonacci sequence and (b) the doubling function

Graphs can also be made by machine, either with a computer program or with a graphing calculator. Information about the graphing calculator can be found in Appendix C.

An Application of Functions and Graphs

The following example illustrates how functions and graphs can be used to investigate and solve meaningful problems

EXAMPLE   2.22   **Making the Biggest Rabbit Pen**

The third grade class wants to make pens for its pet rabbits and guinea pigs. A parent has donated 24 feet of chain link fencing material, which will be used to make two side-by-side rectangular pens along a wall, as shown in the figure. What dimensions of x and w will give the pens their largest total area?

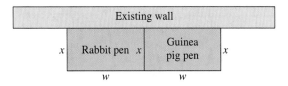

Solution   As seen in the figure, the pens form a rectangle x feet across and $2w$ feet long. Therefore, the total area of the pens is given by $A = 2wx$. The pens will require $3x + 2w$ feet of fencing. Since 24 feet of fencing is available, this gives the equation $3x + 2w = 24$, which can be rewritten as $2w = 24 - 3x$. Thus the area A of the pens is given by the following equation of x.

$$A = 2wx = (24 - 3x)x = 24x - 3x^2$$

The following table of values indicates that the largest area occurs when $x = 4$. The total area of the two pens is 48 square feet and $2w = 24 - 3 \cdot 4 = 12$. Therefore, $w = 6$, so each pen is 4 feet by 6 feet.

x	0	1	2	3	4	5	6	7	8
Area A	0	21	36	45	48	45	36	21	0

The following graph of the function $y = 24x - 3x^2$ also shows that the maximum area occurs when $x = 4$

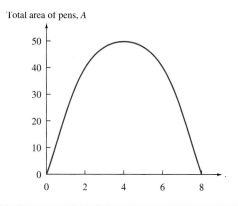

DID YOU KNOW?

The Mathematical Brain

One of the brain's specialized mental organs is a primitive number processor that prefigures, without quite matching it, the arithmetic that is taught in our schools. Improbable as it may seem, numerous animal species that we consider stupid or vicious, such as rats and pigeons, are actually quite gifted at calculation. They can represent quantities mentally and transform them according to some of the rules of arithmetic. The scientists who have studied these abilities believe that animals possess a mental module, traditionally called the "accumulator," that can hold a register of various quantities. We shall see later how rats exploit this mental accumulator to distinguish series of two, three, or four sounds or to compute approximate additions of two quantities. The accumulator mechanism opens up a new dimension of sensory perception through which the cardinal of a set of objects can be perceived just as easily as their color, shape, or position. This "number sense" provides animals and humans alike with a direct intuition of what numbers mean.

SOURCE: From the introduction to *The Number Sense* by Stanislas Dehaene, Oxford University Press, 1997.

WINDOW ON TECHNOLOGY
Investigating Functions with a Graphing Calculator

A calculator of any type is helpful to compute the values of a function $y = f(x)$ for various choices of the domain variable x. For dealing with more complex functions, however, the graphing calculator provides a truly powerful tool for problem solving and classroom demonstrations. An introduction to the graphing calculator is found in Appendix C.

Functions are entered into the graphing calculator using the $\boxed{Y=}$ key to open the function editor. Once a function is entered, next set the x and y ranges of values using the $\boxed{\text{WINDOW}}$ key. Finally, display the graph by pressing the $\boxed{\text{GRAPH}}$ key. Further explorations of the function are aided with the $\boxed{\text{TRACE}}$ and $\boxed{\text{ZOOM}}$ features of the calculator.

As an example, consider the function $f(x) = x(24 - 3x)$. This function arose in Example 2.22, where the values of the function represent the total area of the two animal pens being constructed. Since the area should be positive, the function will be defined on the domain $0 < x < 8$. The three basic steps to graphing the function are shown in these three screens.

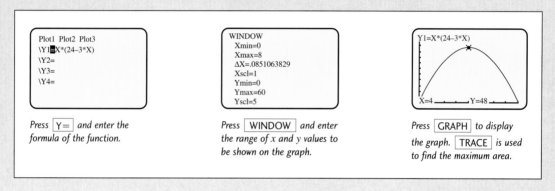

Press $\boxed{Y=}$ *and enter the formula of the function.*

Press $\boxed{\text{WINDOW}}$ *and enter the range of x and y values to be shown on the graph.*

Press $\boxed{\text{GRAPH}}$ *to display the graph.* $\boxed{\text{TRACE}}$ *is used to find the maximum area.*

It is also easy to make a table of values of the function. Press $\boxed{2^{nd}}$ $\boxed{\text{TblSet}}$ to set up the table parameters, and then press $\boxed{2^{nd}}$ $\boxed{\text{Table}}$ to see the table of values of the function.

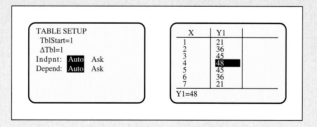

The graphing calculator makes it a simple process to see that the maximum total area of the two pens is 48 square feet, and occurs when x is 4 feet.

PROBLEM SET 2.5

Understanding Concepts

1. Which of the following describe functions from set *A* to set *B*? If your answer is "not a function," explain why not.

    (a) *A* is the set of students in a university and *B* is the set of classes offered. Each student is associated with a class in which the student is enrolled.

    (b) *A* is the set of classes offered by a university and *B* is the set of whole numbers. Each class is associated with the number of students enrolled in the class.

    (c) *A* is the set of students in a classroom and *B* is the set of letter grades A through F. Each student is associated with the grade earned on the first midterm.

    (d) *A* is the set of letter grades A through F and *B* is the set of 25 students in a math class. Each grade is associated with a student who earned that grade on the first midterm.

2. Is a one-to-one correspondence from set *A* to set *B* a function from *A* to *B*? If so, what is the range of the function?

3. Each arrow in the following diagrams indicates that the element in set *A* at the tail of the arrow is associated with the element in set *B* at the head of the arrow. Decide which of these arrow diagrams corresponds to a function with domain *A*. If the diagram does not define a function, explain why. If a function is defined, give the range of the function.

    (a)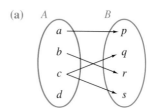

    (b)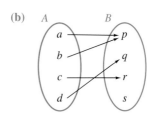

    (c)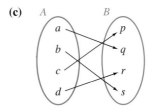

4. Each of the axes systems shows a plot of points. Identify those plots which represent the graph of a function $y = f(x)$. If the plot cannot be a graph of a function, explain why not. If a function graph is depicted, give both the domain and the range of the function.

    (a)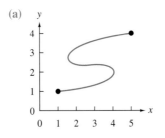

    (b)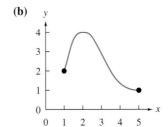

    (c)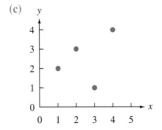

    (d)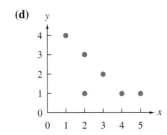

5. Let f be the function given by the formula
$f(x) = 8 - 2x$ on the domain $D = \{x \mid x = 2, 3, 4, 5\}$.
   (a) Make a table of the x and y values.
   (b) What is the range of f?
   (c) Sketch the graph of f.

6. Let g be the function given by the formula
$g(x) = 2x - 2$, defined for all the real (decimal)
numbers x in the interval $-2 \le x \le 3$.
   (a) Make a table of values of $g(x)$ for $x = -2, -1, 0,$
   1, 2, 3.
   (b) Plot the points in your table of part (a), and then
   sketch the entire graph.
   (c) What is the range of g?

7. Let g be the function from $S = \{0, 1, 2, 3, 4\}$ to the
whole numbers W given by the formula
$g(x) = 5 - 2x + x^2$.
   (a) Find $g(0), g(1), g(2), g(3), g(4)$.
   (b) What is the range of g?

8. Let h be the function defined by $h(x) = x^2 - 1$, where
the domain is the set of real numbers (that is, the set of
positive and negative decimal numbers).
   (a) Find $h(2)$.
   (b) Find $h(-2)$.
   (c) If $h(t) = 15$, what are the possible values of t?
   (d) Find $h(7.32)$.

9. Karalee made a trip to the store one afternoon. Her trip is shown below, where her distance
(in miles) from home is graphed as a function of the hours past noon. Refer to the graph to
answer these questions about her trip:

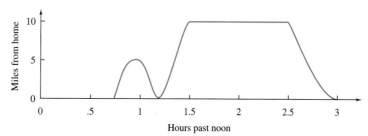

   (a) What time did she leave home?
   (b) When did she realize she forgot her checkbook?
   (c) What did she do about the forgotten checkbook?
   (d) When did Karalee park the car at the store?
   (e) How long did she shop?
   (f) How far away was the store?
   (g) Did Karalee encounter slower traffic going to or coming from the store? Explain how
   you can determine this from the graph.

10. Four graphs are shown, labeled G1, G2, G3, and G4. Which of these graphs matches the
function described?

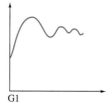
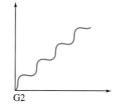
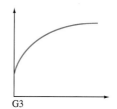
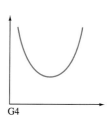

G1   G2   G3   G4

   (a) Temperature of a pan of water placed on a hot burner
   (b) Height of a flag being run up the flag pole
   (c) Height of a weight hung from a Slinky
   (d) Length of the shadow of a flag pole throughout a sunny day in Dallas

11. Make simple approximate sketches of graphs (such as those in problem 10) that correspond to these functions of time.

    (a) Temperature of a forgotten cup of hot tea

    (b) Pitch of a train whistle as the train passes

    (c) Height of the water in a bathtub, during the time someone takes a bath

    (d) Hours of daylight in Chicago during a calendar year; that is, domain = $\{1, 2, \ldots , 365\}$

12. Consider the "double-square" rectangles of height x and width $2x$, as shown.

    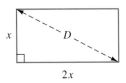

    (a) Find a formula that gives the area A of a double-square of width x.

    (b) Find a formula that gives the perimeter P of a double-square of width x.

    (c) Use the Pythagorean theorem to obtain a formula for the diagonal D of a double-square of width x.

13. Solve each of these "Guess My Rule" games.

    (a)

Guess	4	7	2	0	10	1
Response	9	12	7	5	15	6

    (b)

Guess	4	2	0	7	3	9
Response	10	6	2	16	8	20

    (c)

Guess	4	5	7	3	0	10
Response	17	26	50	10	1	101

14. Che is "it" in a game of Guess My Rule. The students' inputs, and Che's outputs, are shown in the table below.

Input given to Che	5	2	4	0	−2	−5
Output reported by Che	24	3	15	−1	3	24

    (a) Guess Che's rule (function), $y = C(x)$.

    (b) Antonio says that Che's rule is $C(x) = x^2 - 1$, but Claudette claims that it is $C(x) = (x + 1)(x - 1)$. Who is correct, Antonio or Claudette? Explain.

15. Carpet remnants are sold by the square yard of area. To keep the unfinished cut edges from fraying, edging material must be applied at a cost that depends on the total length of the edges (that is, the perimeter) of the remnant.

    (a) Define a remnant cost function $C = f(l, w)$ that depends on *two* variables, the length l and the width w of the remnant, each given in feet. Your function should give the cost (in dollars) to buy an edged remnant l feet long and w feet wide. Assume remnants are sold for $8 a square yard and edging costs 15 cents per foot.

    (b) Use your cost function of part (a) to show that a 6 foot by 8 foot remnant with edging will cost $46.87.

16. Suppose two function machines are hooked up in sequence, so the output chute of machine g empties into the input hopper of machine f. Such a coupling of machines, which is defined if the range of g is a subset of the domain of f, is called the **composition** of f and g, and can be written $F(x) = f(g(x))$.

    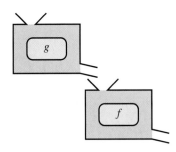

    (a) Suppose f is the doubling function $f(x) = 2x$ and g is the "add 3" function $g(t) = t + 3$. Then $F(4) = f(g(4)) = f(4 + 3) = f(7) = 2 \times 7 = 14$. Evaluate $f(g(x))$ for $x = 0, 1, 2, 3$.

    (b) Suppose the doubling and "add 3" function machines are coupled in reverse order to define the composition of g and f given by $G(x) = g(f(x))$. Then $G(4) = g(f(4)) = g(2 \times 4) = g(8) = 8 + 3 = 11$. Evaluate $g(f(x))$ for $x = 0, 1, 2, 3$.

17. The statement that "There are six times as many students as professors at this university" can be written symbolically as $S = 6P$, where S denotes the number of students and P denotes the number of professors. Some years ago, incoming freshmen at a certain university were challenged to convert the given statement to an equation, and a large percentage mistakenly answered with "$6S = P$." Convert each of these statements into simple formulas, using the letters suggested.

   (a) There are 10 times as many female nurses as male nurses at the hospital. (F and M)

   (b) Sean has 4 more dollars than Gunther. (S and G)

(c) With 10 more points, LeAnn's score will be twice that of Itzhak. (L and I)

Thinking Critically

18. Shaquita noticed the following pattern when summing the squares of the successive natural numbers.
$$S_1 = 1^2 = 1 = 2 \cdot 3 \cdot 4/24$$
$$S_2 = 1^2 + 2^2 = 5 = 4 \cdot 5 \cdot 6/24$$
$$S_3 = 1^2 + 2^2 + 3^2 = 14 = 6 \cdot 7 \cdot 8/24$$

   (a) Does Shaquita's pattern hold for S_5 and S_6?

   (b) Find a formula that gives Shaquita's function S_n.

19. The 3×3 square array shown contains nine unit 1×1 squares, four 2×2 squares, and one 3×3 square, making $1 + 4 + 9 = 14$ squares in all.

   (a) Fill in this partially completed table counting the squares of various sizes in a given square array.

Size of the Array	Number of Squares of Size					Total Number of Squares
	1×1	2×2	3×3	4×4	5×5	
1×1	1					1
2×2	4	1				5
3×3	9	4	1			14
4×4						
5×5						

   (b) Make a conjecture about the number of squares, S_6, that can be found in a 6×6 array.

   (c) Give a formula for S_n, the number of squares in an $n \times n$ array.

20. Investigate the sum of the cubes function $C_n = 1^3 + 2^3 + 3^3 + \cdots + n^3$. Make a table of values of C_n and see if you can discover a connection between C_n and the triangular number function t_n given by $t_n = n(n + 1)/2$. [*Suggestion:* enter values of t_n in a new row of your table for easy comparison.]

Making Connections

Linear functions. *A function f is called **linear** if there are two numbers m and b so that f(x) = mx + b for all x in the domain of the function. Some useful linear functions are investigated in problems 21 through 25.*

21. **Hooke's Law.** If a (small) weight w is suspended from a spring, the length L of the stretched spring is a linear function of w. Find m and b in the formula $L = mw + b$ if the unstretched spring has length $10''$ and a weight of 2 pounds stretches it to $14''$.

22. Temperature Conversion. The temperature at which water freezes is 32 degrees Fahrenheit and 0 degrees Celsius, and the temperature at which water boils is 212 degrees Fahrenheit and 100 degrees Celsius. Find the constants m and b in the formula $F = mC + b$ to express the Fahrenheit temperature F as a function of the Celsius temperature C.

23. Speed of a Dropped Object. Neglecting the resistance of air, the (downward) speed of an object t seconds after being dropped is given by $v = 32t$ feet per second. How many seconds does it take an object to reach a downward speed of 100 miles per hour? Recall that there are 5280 feet in one mile, since you'll need to express 100 mph in feet per second.

24. Straight Line Depreciation. Suppose a car originally valued at $18,500 is worth $10,400 after 5 years. Express the value V of the car as a linear function $V = mt + b$ of the age t of the car, where t is measured in years. Use the formula to determine the value of the car after three years of service.

25. The Lightning Distance Function. The speed of sound is about 760 miles per hour. Assuming the lightning flash takes no appreciable time to be seen, and the peal of thunder is heard after t seconds, show that $d = t/5$ gives the approximate distance d (in miles) to the strike.

26. Taxi Fare. The Evergreen Taxi Company in Pullman, Washington, charges $2.15 for the first mile (or fraction thereof), and $1.25 for each additional mile. What is the charge for these trips?

(a) From Pullman to the airport, which is 4.3 miles.

(b) From Pullman to Moscow, Idaho, a 7.8-mile trip.

27. The U.S. Post Office calls the perimeter of a cross-section of a package the "girth." The combined girth plus length of a package cannot exceed 108 inches.

(a) Find a formula for the girth, g, of a rectangular box whose cross-section is of width w and height h.

(b) What is the maximum length of a rectangular box whose cross-section is 10" by 18" that can be mailed at the U.S. Post Office?

28. First Class Postage. First class postage in the United States is 33 cents for the first ounce, and 22 cents for each additional ounce or fraction of an ounce. What does it cost to mail a package weighing **(a)** 1 1/2 ounces? **(b)** half a pound? **(c)** 2 ounces?

29. Tax Tables. A portion of the 1998 Tax Table is shown.

(a) Demitrius had a taxable income of $41,162 in 1998. If Demitrius is single, what is his tax?

(b) How many of the last $100 of Demitrius' 1998 earnings were paid in income tax?

(c) Kay and Andres filed a joint return on $41,127 of taxable income. What is their tax?

(d) How much of Andres and Kay's last $100 of income went to taxes?

(e) Is Demitrius, or Kay and Andres, in the higher tax bracket?

If line 39 (taxable income) is—		And you are—			
At least	But less than	Single	Married filing jointly *	Married filing sepa- rately	Head of a household
			Your tax is—		
41,000					
41,000	41,050	8,192	6,154	8,734	7,074
41,050	41,100	8,206	6,161	8,748	7,088
41,100	41,150	8,220	6,169	8,762	7,102
41,150	41,200	8,234	6,176	8,776	7,116

Using a Calculator

30. Tax rate schedules. Tax Tables (see problem 29) apply to incomes less than $100,000. Those with higher taxable incomes determine their tax by a Tax Rate Schedule. For example, a single person would use Schedule X on the next page for 1998. Notice that the schedule is shown for *all* levels of income, so that all taxpayers can see the rate that applies to them.

Schedule X—Use if your filing status is Single			
If the amount on Form 1040, line 39, is: Over—	But not over—	Enter on Form 1040, line 40	of the amount over—
$0	$25,350	.........15%	$0
25,350	61,400	$3,802.50 + 28%	25,350
61,400	128,100	13,896.50 + 31%	61,400
128,100	278,450	34,573.50 + 36%	128,100
278,450	....	88,699.50 + 39.6%	278,450

(a) If Demitrius, a single person with $41,162 of taxable income, could use Schedule X, what would his tax be?

(b) Cyndi is a single person whose 1998 taxable income is $134,520. What is her income tax?

---

31. Matt has a cartoon measuring 1.25 by 1.75 inches that he wishes to enlarge to make an overhead transparency for his class. He has a copier that can make enlarged copies 144% the size of the original.

    (a) Describe an "enlargement" function that gives the size after n copies are made at the 144% setting.

    (b) How many times must the cartoon be enlarged to fill an 8.5" by 11" overhead?

32. The department of vehicle licensing in a certain state charges a yearly fee of $20 plus 1.75% of the retail value of the vehicle. Evaluate the fee for cars of value $2000, $4000, $6000, . . . , $20,000. Sketch a graph of the license fee function, and give a formula for the fee as a function of the vehicle's value.

33. **World Population.** The table below gives the world population (in billions) every 20 years since 1900, and an estimate of the population for 2020.

Year	1900	1920	1940	1960	1980	2000	2020
Pop.	1.6	1.9	2.3	3.0	3.7	6.0	7.6

    (a) Make a graph of the world population as given in the table.

    (b) Letting x denote the number of decades (ten-year periods) since 1900, plot the graph of the function $y = (1.45)1.14^x$ on the graph drawn in part (a). Does the formula mimic the population data well in your opinion?

    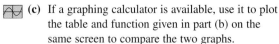 (c) If a graphing calculator is available, use it to plot the table and function given in part (b) on the same screen to compare the two graphs.

34. **The Windchill Index.** In windy cold weather, the increased rate of heat loss makes the temperature feel colder than the actual temperature. To describe an equivalent temperature that more closely matches how it "feels," weather reports often give a windchill index, WCI. The WCI is a function of both the temperature F (in degrees Fahrenheit) and the wind speed v (in miles per hour). For wind speeds v between 4 and 45 miles per hour, the WCI is given by the formula

    $$\text{WCI} = 91.4 - \frac{(10.45 + 6.69\sqrt{v} - 0.447v)(91.4 - F)}{22}$$

    (a) Verify that a temperature of 10°F in a wind of 20 miles per hour produces a windchill index of −25°F.

    (b) A weather forecaster claims that a wind of 36 miles per hour has resulted in a WCI of −50°. What is the actual temperature to the nearest degree?

35. **Day of Week Function.** The following function gives the number Y_1 of the day of the week (1 = Sunday, 2 = Monday, etc.) as a function of the date (D, M, Y) in the Gregorian calendar introduced in 1582. The three variables in the function are:

    D = number of the day of the month,

    M = number of the month (with 13 = January, 14 = February, 3 = March, . . . , 12 = December)

    Y = year.

    The function, in graphing calculator form, is:

    $Y_1 = 7 * $ fPart$((D + 2M + $ iPart$(.6M + .6) + Y + $ iPart$(Y/4) - $ iPart$(Y/100) + $ iPart$(Y/400) + 2)/7)$

The functions "*fPart*" (fractional part) and "*iPart*" (integer part) are built-in functions on your graphing calculator. As an example, to find the day of the week of July 4th, 1776, enter the function Y_1 and then return to the home screen and enter on one line

$$7 \rightarrow M:4 \rightarrow D:1776 \rightarrow Y:Y_1.$$

Pressing $\boxed{\text{ENTER}}$ returns a 5, showing us the day of the week was Thursday. Using $\boxed{\text{2nd}}$ $\boxed{\text{ENTRY}}$, you can edit the entry lines to investigate new dates.

(a) Verify that President Lincoln signed the Emancipation Proclamation on Friday, January 1, 1863. [*Reminder:* for January use M = 13]

(b) What day of the week was July 20, 1969, the day astronaut Neil Armstrong became the first person to set foot on the moon?

(c) What day of the week is January 1, 2001, the first day of the new millennium?

For Review

36. In each of 10,000 boxes of Cracker Smacks one of the following prizes is placed: a ring, a top, a ball, or a marble. How many boxes must be purchased to be absolutely certain you receive a prize of each type? Assume there are equally many prizes of each type, one per box.

37. Let $A = \{a, b, c, d\}$, $B = \{b, d, e, f\}$, and $C = \{a, b, e, g, h\}$. Draw a Venn diagram of A, B, and C in the universe of the first half of the alphabet, $U = \{a, b, \ldots, l, m\}$.

38. For the sets listed in problem 37, give
   (a) $n(A \cup B)$ (b) $n(B \cap C)$
   (c) $n(\overline{B})$ (d) $n(C \cap \overline{A})$

39. What fact family contains $42 \div 7 = 6$?

EPILOGUE   From Counting to Numbers

The simplest mathematical idea of all is counting, a skill possessed by our ancient human ancestors even before the rise of civilization. The value of counting as a survival tool is also apparent in terms of evolutionary development. Indeed, recent research has identified areas of the brain associated with basic number processing and even a vestigial number line. Remarkably, mathematical brain structures have also been found in pigeons, rats, chimpanzees, and other animals. Humans, being in possession of complex language and symbolic skills, have the means to refine rudimentary and approximate number ideas into a sophisticated and precise system of numbers and calculations. This chapter has examined the first steps of this development. The idea of counting was taken to a new level of abstraction, namely the whole numbers. The arithmetic operations—addition, subtraction, multiplication, division—were then developed, together with the properties of these operations.

CHAPTER 2 SUMMARY

Key Concepts

1. Sets and operations on sets
   (a) A set is a collection of objects from a stated universe. A set can be described either verbally, by a list, or with set builder notation.
   (b) Sets can be visualized with Venn diagrams, in which the universe is a rectangle and closed loops correspond to sets. Elements of the set are associated with points within the loop.
   (c) Sets are combined and related by set complement $\overline{A}$, subset $A \subseteq B$, proper subset $A \subset B$, intersection $A \cap B$, union $A \cup B$, and the Cartesian product $A \times B$.

2. Sets, counting, and the whole numbers
   (a) Numbers are used in three ways: to name (nominal numbers), to indicate position in an order (ordinal numbers), and to indicate how many elements are in a set (cardinal numbers).

(b) Two sets that have a one-to-one correspondence of their elements are equivalent sets.

(c) The whole numbers are the cardinal numbers of the finite sets, with zero the cardinal number of the empty set. The whole numbers can be represented and visualized by a variety of manipulatives and diagrams, including tiles, cubes, number strips, rods, and the number line.

(d) The whole numbers are ordered, so that m is less than n if a set with n elements has a proper subset which matches a set with m elements.

3. Addition and subtraction of whole numbers

(a) Addition of whole numbers is defined in the set model by $a + b = n(A \cup B)$, where $a = n(A)$, $b = n(B)$ and A and B are disjoint finite sets. Addition can also be visualized on the number line with the measurement model.

(b) Addition of whole numbers is a closed binary operation. Addition satisfies the commutative property $a + b = b + a$ and the associative property $a + (b + c) = (a + b) + c$. Zero is an additive identity: $a + 0 = 0 + a = a$.

(c) Subtraction of whole numbers is defined by $a - b = c$, where c is the unique whole number for which $a = b + c$. There are four conceptual models: take-away, missing addend, comparison, and number-line.

4. Multiplication and division of whole numbers

(a) Multiplication is defined as a repeated addition, so that $a \cdot b = b + b + \cdots + b$, where there are a addends. Alternatively, multiplication is defined by the Cartesian product, $a \cdot b = n(A \times B)$, and can be visualized as the number of objects in an a row by b column rectangular array.

(b) Multiplication is closed; is commutative $a \cdot b = b \cdot a$; is associative $a \cdot (b \cdot c) = (a \cdot b) \cdot c$; distributes over addition, $a \cdot (b + c) = a \cdot b + a \cdot c$; has 1 as a multiplicative identity, $1 \cdot a = a \cdot 1 = a$; and satisfies the multiplication by zero property $0 \cdot a = a \cdot 0 = 0$.

(c) Division $a \div b$, where $b \neq 0$, is defined in whole numbers if, and only if, $a = b \cdot c$ for a unique whole number c. Division is modeled as repeated subtraction (grouping), as a partition (sharing), and as the missing factor c in the equation $a = b \cdot c$.

(d) The division algorithm extends the division operation to all nonzero whole number divisors by allowing remainders. By the division algorithm, given whole numbers a and b, $b \neq 0$, there is a quotient q and remainder r so that $a = b \cdot q + r$, $0 \leq r < b$.

5. Functions

(a) A function is a rule that assigns a unique value to an element of a set D called the domain of the function. A function is written as $y = f(x)$, where $x \in D$ is an element of the domain and y is the value, or image, of x.

(b) The set of images of a function is the range of the function.

(c) Functions are defined by formulas and tables, and can be interpreted as a machine which converts an input x into an output $y = f(x)$.

(d) The correspondence between x and y values of a function can be visualized with a graph of the function in the coordinate plane.

Vocabulary and Notation

Section 2.1

Universe U
Element of $\in$
List in braces $\{a, b, \ldots\}$
Set builder notation $\{x \mid x \text{ is } (condition)\}$
Venn diagram
Complement $\bar{A}$
Subset $A \subseteq B$
Equal sets $A = B$
Proper subset $A \subset B$
Intersection $A \cap B$
Disjoint sets $A \cap B = \varnothing$
Empty set $\varnothing$
Union $A \cup B$
Transitive property of set inclusion
Commutative property of union and intersection
Associative property of union and intersection
Distributive properties of union and intersection

Section 2.2

Nominal (naming, identification) number
Ordinal number
Cardinal number
One-to-one correspondence
Equivalent sets $A \sim B$
Finite set
Infinite set
Whole number $n(A)$
Zero $0 = n(\varnothing)$
Number tiles, cubes, strips, rods
Number line
Less than: $a < b$, greater than: $a > b$

Section 2.3

Binary operation
Addition (sum) $a + b$
    Addend
    Summand
    Set model: $a + b = n(A \cup B)$ for $A \cap B = \varnothing$
    Measurement (number-line) model
Properties of addition
Closure, commutative, associative, additive identity
    property of zero
Subtraction (difference) $a - b$

Minuend
Subtrahend
Take-away model
Missing addend model
Comparison model
Measurement (number-line) model
Addition-subtraction fact family

Section 2.4

Multiplication (product) $a \cdot b$
    Factor
    Repeated addition model
    Array model
    Cartesian product model
Properties of multiplication
    Closure, commutative, associative property
    Multiplicative identity property of 1
    Multiplication by zero property
    Distributivity over addition
Division $a \div b$ (or a/b)
    Repeated subtraction (grouping) model
    Partition (sharing) model
    Missing-factor model
Dividend
Divisor
Multiplication-division fact family
Division with remainders
    Division algorithm $a \div b = q \text{ R } r$ or
        $a = bq + r, 0 \leq r < b$
    Power operation
    Base and exponent a^m
Division by grouping
Division by sharing
Quotient
Exponential

Section 2.5

Function f
Image (or value) of f at x, $f(x)$
Domain of a function
Range of a function
Table of values of a function
Graph of a function
Function machine
Sequence

CHAPTER REVIEW EXERCISES

Section 2.1

1. Let $U = \{n \mid n$ is a whole number and $2 \le n \le 25\}$
   $S = \{n \mid n \in U$ and n is a square number$\}$
   $P = \{n \mid n \in U$ and n is a prime number$\}$
   $T = \{n \mid n \in U$ and n is a power of 2$\}$
   (a) Write S, P, T in listed form.
   (b) Find the following sets: $\overline{P}, S \cap T, S \cup T, S \cap \overline{T}$
2. Draw a Venn diagram of the sets S, P, T in problem 1.
3. Replace each box $\square$ with one of the symbols $\cap$, $\cup$, $\subset$, $\subseteq$, or $=$ to give a correct statement for general sets A, B, C.
   (a) $A \;\square\; A \cup B$
   (b) If $A \subseteq B$ and $A \subset B$, then $A \;\square\; B$.
   (c) $A \;\square\; (B \cup C) = (A \cap B) \cup (A \cap C)$
   (d) $A \;\square\; \varnothing = A$

Section 2.2

4. Let $S = \{s, e, t\}$ and $T = \{t, h, e, o, r, y\}$. Find $n(S)$, $n(T)$, $n(S \cup T)$, $n(S \cap T)$, $n(S \cap \overline{T})$, $n(T \cap \overline{S})$.
5. Show that the set of square natural numbers less than 101 is in one-to-one correspondence with the set $\{a, b, c, d, e, f, g, h, i, j\}$.
6. Show that the set of cubes $\{1, 8, 27, \ldots\}$ is equivalent to the set of natural numbers.

Section 2.3

7. Explain how to illustrate $5 + 2$ with
   (a) the set model of addition;
   (b) the number line (measurement) model of addition.
8. What properties of whole number addition are illustrated on the number lines below?
   (a)

   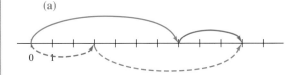

   (b)

9. Draw figures that illustrate $6 - 4$
   (a) using sets
   (b) using the number line.

Section 2.4

10. Whiffle balls 2″ in diameter are packed individually in cubical boxes and then in cartons of 3 dozen balls. What are the dimensions of a suitable rectangular carton?
11. A drill sergeant lined up 92 soldiers in rows of 12, except for a partial row in the back. How many rows are formed? How many soldiers are in the back row?
12. Draw figures that illustrate the division problem $15 \div 3$, using these models:
    (a) repeated subtraction (grouping objects in a set)
    (b) partition (sharing objects)
    (c) missing factor (rectangular array)

Section 2.5

13. For each table, decide whether it is the table of a function $y = f(x)$. If not, state why not. If so, give the domain and range.

    (a)

x	3	6	7	8	3
y	4	3	5	1	0

    (b)

x	3	6	7	8	4
y	4	3	5	1	2

    (c)

x	3	6	7	8	4
y	4	3	3	4	3

14. Solve these two "Guess My Rule" games. Carefully describe a function that agrees with the table of values.

    (a)

x	4	2	0	5	1
y	14	8	2	17	5

(b)

x	4	2	5	0	1
y	20	6	30	0	2

15. Let f be a function defined by the formula
$f(x) = 2x(x - 3)$.
    (a) Find $f(3), f(0.5), f(-2)$
    (b) If $f(x) = 0$, what are the possible values of x?

16. When light passes into two face-to-face layers of glass, it is either reflected or transmitted when it strikes the glass surfaces. There is 1 path with no reflections, 2 paths with 1 reflection, and 3 paths with 2 reflections.
    (a) Show that there are 5 paths with 3 internal reflections.
    (b) Conjecture a formula which gives the number of paths which have n internal reflections.

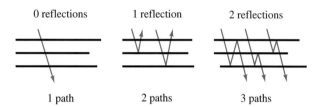

0 reflections   1 reflection   2 reflections

1 path   2 paths   3 paths

CHAPTER TEST

1. The following sentence contains three types of numbers:

   "On the *15th* of April, Joe Taxpayer sent in form *1040* and a money order for *$253*."

   Name and describe the three kinds of numbers.
2. Shade regions in Venn diagrams which correspond to the following sets.
    (a) $A \cap (B \cup C)$
    (b) $A \cup B$
    (c) $(A \cap \overline{B}) \cup (B \cap \overline{A})$
3. Suppose $A \cap B = A$. What can you say about $A \cap \overline{B}$
4. Let $A = \{w, h, o, l, e\}$, $B = \{n, u, m, b, e, r\}$, $C = \{z, e, r, o\}$. Find:
    (a) $n(A \cup B)$ (b) $n(B \cap \overline{C})$
    (c) $n(A \cap C)$ (d) $n(A \times C)$
5. What property of whole numbers justifies the following equalities?

    (a) $4 + (6 + 2) = (4 + 6) + 2$
    (b) $8 \cdot (4 + x) = 8 \cdot 4 + 8x$
    (c) $3 + 0 = 0 + 3 = 3$
    (d) $2 \cdot (8 \cdot 5) = (2 \cdot 8) \cdot 5$

6. Althea made 5 gallons of root beer and wishes to bottle it in 10 ounce bottles.
    (a) How many bottles does she need? Remember that a quart contains 32 ounces.
    (b) Discuss which model of division—grouping or sharing—corresponds best to your answer for part (a).

7. Let A and B be two sets in the universe $U = \{a, b, c, \ldots, z\}$. If $n(A) = 12$, $n(B) = 14$, and $n(A \cup B) = 21$, find $n(A \cap B)$ and $n(\overline{A \cap B})$.

8. Let $n(A \times B) = 21$. Are all the possible numbers in the set A?

9. What operation on whole numbers is being illustrated in the following diagrams?

    (a)

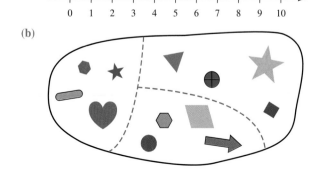

    (b)

(c)

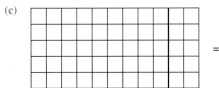 = 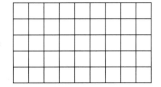 +

(d)

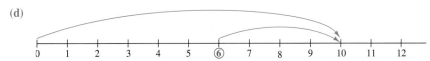

10. Let $S = \{1, 2, 4, 8, 16, \ldots\}$ denote the set of powers of 2.
    (a) Is S closed under multiplication?
    (b) Is S closed under addition?
    Explain why you answered as you did.

11. Show how to illustrate the following properties of whole number multiplication with the rectangular array model.
    (a) $2 \cdot (4 + 3) = 2 \cdot 4 + 2 \cdot 3$
    (b) $2 \cdot 5 = 5 \cdot 2$

12. Discuss which conceptual model of subtraction you feel best corresponds to each of the following problems.

    (a) On Monday, Roberto hiked 11 miles to the lake. On Friday at noon he had hiked 6 miles back down the trail. How much farther does Roberto have to hike to get back to the trailhead?
    (b) Kerri has 56 customers on her paper route, but her manager only left her 48 papers. How many extra papers should she have brought over before starting her delivery?
    (c) All but 7 of the 3 dozen picnic plates were used. How many people came to the picnic?

13. Match these graphs to the hike described. Each graph shows the elevation as a function of time into the hike

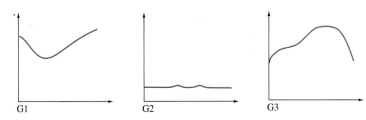

G1   G2   G3

    (a) A hike up Mount Shasta and return to base camp.
    (b) A round-trip hike into the Grand Canyon.
    (c) A hike along the wilderness beach in Olympic National Park.

14. Let f be the function given by $f(x) = x^2 - 4x + 5$ on the domain $\{1, 2, 3, 4, 5\}$. Give the range of the function.

15. A bee starts in cell 1, and moves by crawling over cell walls. Assume that the bee always moves to the right, from one cell to one of the two adjacent cells.

There is one path to cell 2, two paths to cell 3, and three paths to cell 4.
    (a) How many paths are there to cell 5?
    (b) Let F be the function for which $F(n)$ is the number of paths from cell 1 to cell n. Explain why $F(n + 2) = F(n + 1) + F(n)$ for $n = 1, 2, 3, \ldots$.
    (c) How many paths can the bee follow to cell 12?

CHAPTER

3

Numeration and Computation

3.1 Numeration Systems Past and Present

3.2 Nondecimal Positional Systems

3.3 Algorithms for Adding and Subtracting Whole Numbers

3.4 Algorithms for Multiplication and Division of Whole Numbers

3.5 Mental Arithmetic and Estimation

3.6 Getting the Most Out of Your Calculator

HANDS ON

Numbers from Rectangles

Materials Needed

1. One rectangle of each of these shapes for each student.

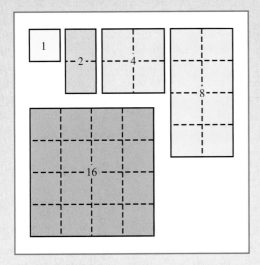

2. One record sheet like this for each student.

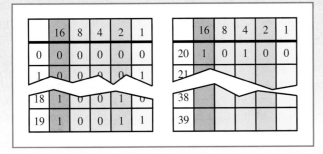

Directions

Step 1. Use the rectangles to determine representations of each of the numbers 0, 1, 2, . . . , 39 as a sum of the numbers 1, 2, 4, 8, or 16 with each of these numbers used at most once.

Step 2. For each representation determined in Step 1, record the numbers (rectangles) used by placing a 0 or a 1 in the appropriate columns of the record sheet. The rows for 0, 1, 18, 19, and 20 have been done for you.

    (a) Do all the numbers from 0 through 39 have such a representation?

    (b) What additional numbers could be represented if you had a 32 rectangle?

    (c) Describe any interesting patterns you see on your record sheet.

CONNECTIONS   Counting and Calculating

In Chapter 2, we introduced whole numbers as the cardinal numbers of finite sets. For example, if A is the set shown, then $n(A) = 5$; that is, the number five is an abstract idea which represents the count of the elements in A and in each set equivalent to A.

Historically, the notion of number developed over many years from people's need to count objects—sheep, goats, arrows, warriors, beads, and so on. Indeed, the need to count collections of concrete objects to develop an understanding of numbers was not just true historically; it remains equally true for individuals today. Research has shown that it is essentially impossible for children to understand the abstract notion of "five" without counting many sets of five objects—five beans, five fingers, five pennies, five concrete objects of any kind. Thus, the need to use a variety of manipulative devices in the elementary school classroom to help children develop an understanding of numerousness—or number—cannot be ignored.

In this chapter we consider how we write numbers and how this is reflected in the methods used to perform calculations both by hand and with calculators and computers. We begin with a brief look at some of the earlier numeration systems and then consider the Indo-Arabic system we use today.

It is essential for children's understanding that these notions be introduced with extensive use of hands-on manipulative devices and copious pictorial representations. To do otherwise is to condemn students to rote memorization and meaningless manipulation of symbols. Put positively, students who are allowed to work with appropriate devices—to handle, to manipulate, and to experience—are much more likely to develop real understanding of concepts and skills, and also to develop enthusiasm for the study of mathematics.

3.1   Numeration Systems Past and Present

To appreciate the power of the Indo-Arabic (or Hindu-Arabic) numeration system, or decimal system as we call it, it is important to know something about numeration systems of the past. Just as the idea of number historically arose from the need to determine "how many," the demands of commerce in an increasingly sophisticated society stimulated the development of convenient symbolism for writing numbers and methods for calculating. The symbols for writing numbers are called **numerals** and the methods for calculating are called **algorithms.** Taken together, any particular system of numerals and algorithms is called a **numeration system.**

The earliest means of recording numbers consisted of creating a set of tallies—marks on stone, stones in a bag, notches in a stick—one-for-one for each item being counted. Indeed, the original meaning of the word "tally" was a stick with notches cut into it to record debts owed or paid. Often such a stick was split in half with one half going to the debtor and the other half to the creditor. It is still common practice today to keep count by making tallies or marks with the minor but useful refinement of marking off the tallies in groups of five. Thus,

is much easier to read as twenty-three than

But such systems for recording numbers were much too simplistic for large numbers and for calculating.

Of the various systems used in the past, we consider here only four—the Egyptian, the Roman, the Babylonian, and the Mayan.

The Egyptian System

As early as 3400 B.C., the Egyptians developed a system for recording numbers on stone tablets using hieroglyphics (Table 3.1). This system was based on ten, as is our modern system, and probably for the same reason. That is, we humans come with a built-in "digital" calculator, as it were, with 10 convenient keys. Of course, for the same reason, other systems were often based on five or twenty. The French word for eighty, for example, is *quatre-vingts,* which literally means "four twenties" and suggests the early use of a system based on twenty. Other systems were based on two, three, and even sixty.

The Egyptians had symbols for the first few powers of ten, and then combined symbols to represent other numbers. (See Table 3.2.)

TABLE 3.1	Egyptian Symbols for One Through Nine								
Egyptian Symbol	|	||	|||	||||	|| ||	||| |||	||| |||	|||| ||||	||||| ||||
Modern Equivalent	1	2	3	4	5	6	7	8	9

TABLE 3.2	Egyptian Symbols for Powers of Ten	
Power of 10	Egyptian Symbol	Description
$10^0 = 1$	|	a vertical staff
$10^1 = 10$	∩	a heel bone or yoke
$10^2 = 100$	℆	a scroll or coil of rope
$10^3 = 1,000$		a lotus flower
$10^4 = 10,000$		a pointing finger
$10^5 = 100,000$		a fish
$10^6 = 1,000,000$		an amazed person

The Egyptian system was an *additive* system since the values of the various symbols were simply added together to obtain the desired number as the following example shows.

| EXAMPLE 3.1 | **Writing a Number in Egyptian Notation** |

Write 4293 using Egyptian notation.

Solution   Since this is an additive system, it suffices to write the symbols for four thousands, two hundreds, nine tens, and three ones. Referring to Tables 3.1 and 3.2, we see that 4293 is written in Egyptian symbols as

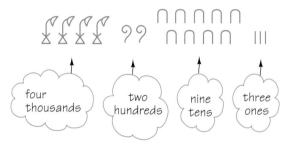

| EXAMPLE 3.2 | **Converting from Egyptian to Standard Notation** |

What number does this Egyptian numeral represent?

Solution

From Tables 3.1 and 3.2 we see that

⌐	represents	10,000
⌐⌐	represents	2000
999	represents	300
∩∩	represents	20
‖‖‖	represents	7

and this all adds up to 12,327.

Arithmetic in the Egyptian system was cumbersome but, at least for addition and subtraction, not conceptually difficult. Since it was an additive system, to add two numbers all one had to do was to draw all the numerals used to represent both numbers and then simplify using the fact that ten 10s give 100, ten 100s give 1000, and so on. Subtraction could be done in much the same way except that it was necessary to "take away" the symbols needed to represent the number being subtracted. Of course, as with our present system, this might first require some exchanging or regrouping; that is, writing 100 as ten 10s, and so on.

EXAMPLE 3.3	**Adding in the Egyptian System**

Add $999 \cap\cap\cap \;{}^{|||}_{|||}$ to $9 \cap\cap \;{}^{|||}_{||}$ using Egyptian notation only.

Solution

$999 \cap\cap\cap \;{}^{|||}_{|||} + 9 \cap\cap \;{}^{|||}_{||}$

$= 9999 \;{}^{\cap\cap\cap}_{\cap\cap}\cap \;{}^{||||||}_{|||||}$

$\left({}^{|||||}_{|||||} = \cap \right)$

$\begin{array}{r} 336 \\ +125 \\ \hline 461 \end{array}$

$= 9999 \;{}^{\cap\cap\cap}_{\cap\cap\cap}|$

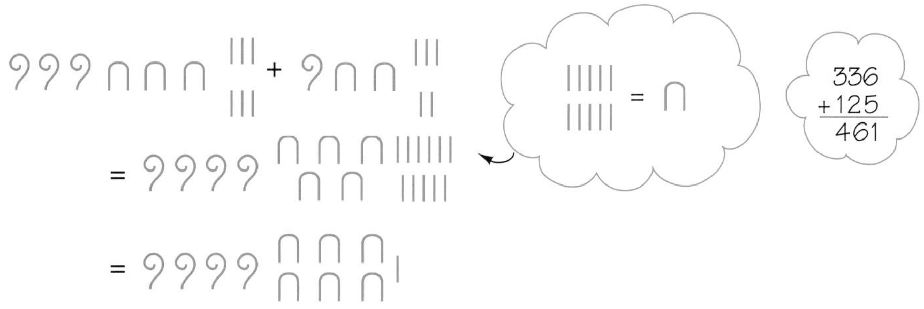

EXAMPLE 3.4	**Subtracting in the Egyptian System**

Subtract $99 \cap {}^{\cap\cap}_{\cap\cap}\cap |||$ from $999 \cap \;{}^{||||}_{|||}$ using Egyptian notation only.

Solution

$999 \;\cap\;{}^{||||}_{|||} - 99 \;{}^{\cap\cap\cap}_{\cap\cap}\cap ||| $

$\begin{array}{r} 317 \\ -253 \\ \hline 64 \end{array}$

$\left(9 = {}^{\cap\cap\cap\cap\cap}_{\cap\cap\cap\cap\cap} \right)$

$= 99 \;{}^{\cap\cap\cap\cap\cap\cap}_{\cap\cap\cap\cap\cap}\; {}^{||||}_{|||} - 99 \;{}^{\cap\cap\cap}_{\cap\cap}\; |||$

$= {}^{\cap\cap\cap}_{\cap\cap\cap}\; ||||$

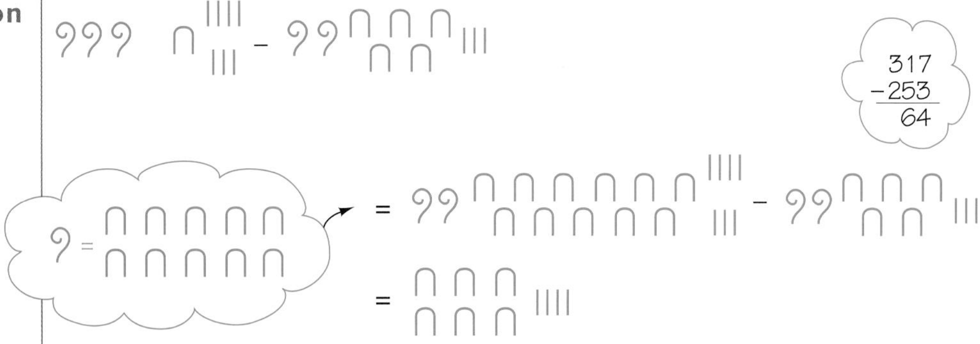

Multiplication and division in the Egyptian system were quite difficult since these operations had to be treated as repeated addition and repeated subtraction. This would normally involve considerable simplifying and combining of symbols and substantial mental arithmetic.

The Roman System

The Roman system of numeration is already somewhat familiar from its current usage on the faces of analog watches and clocks, on cornerstones, and on the façades of buildings to record when they were built. Originally, the system was completely additive, like the Egyptian system, with the familiar symbols as shown in Table 3.3.

TABLE 3.3	Roman Numerals and Their Modern Equivalents
Roman Symbols	Modern Equivalent
I	1
V	5
X	10
L	50
C	100
D	500
M	1000

Using these symbols, 1959 originally was written as

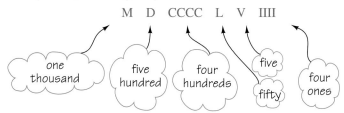

Later a subtractive principle was introduced to shorten the notation. If a single symbol for a lesser number was written to the left of a symbol for a greater number then the lesser number was to be *subtracted* from the greater number. In particular, the common representations were as shown here.

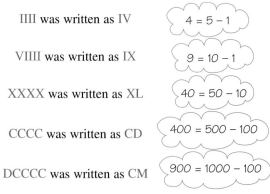

IIII was written as IV   4 = 5 − 1

VIIII was written as IX   9 = 10 − 1

XXXX was written as XL   40 = 50 − 10

CCCC was written as CD   400 = 500 − 100

DCCCC was written as CM   900 = 1000 − 100

Using this principle, 1959 could then be written more succinctly as

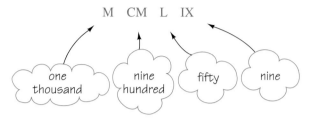

As with the Egyptian system, addition and subtraction in the Roman system was cumbersome but not conceptually difficult as these examples show.

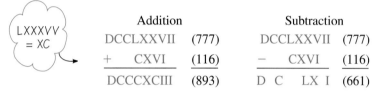

	Addition			Subtraction	
	DCCLXXVII	(777)		DCCLXXVII	(777)
+	CXVI	(116)	−	CXVI	(116)
	DCCCXCIII	(893)	D C	LX I	(661)

As with the Egyptian system, however, multiplication and division were quite cumbersome. For this reason, much of the commercial calculation of the time was performed on devices like abacuses, counting boards, sand trays, and the like.

EXAMPLE 3.5

Writing a Number in the Roman System

Write 1999 in Roman numerals.

Solution

One could write

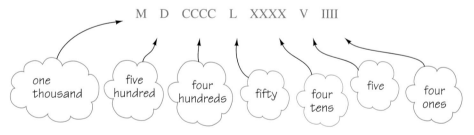

or, using the subtraction principle,

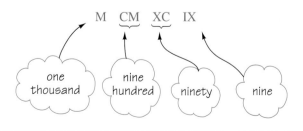

EXAMPLE   3.6

Solution

Converting from Roman to Standard Notation

Write MDCXLIII using modern notation.

M	represents	1000
D	represents	500
C	represents	100
XL	represents	40
III	represents	3

Adding, we obtain 1643.

The Babylonian System

Developed about the same time as the Egyptian system and much earlier than the Roman system, the Babylonian system was more sophisticated than either in that it introduced the notion of **place value,** in which the position of a symbol in a numeral determined its value. In particular, this made it possible to write numerals for even very large numbers using very few symbols. Indeed, the system utilized only two symbols, ▼ for 1 and ❮ for 10, and combined these additively to form the "digits" 1 through 59. Thus,

❮❮▼   and   ❮❮❮▼▼▼▼

respectively, represented 21 and 34. Beyond 59, the system was positional to base sixty (a sexigesmal system), where the positions from right to left represented multiples of successive powers of 60 and the multipliers (digits) were the composite symbols for 1 through 59. Thus,

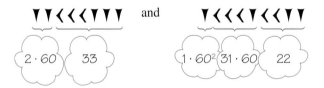

represented $2 \cdot 60^1 + 33 = 153$ and $1 \cdot 60^2 + 31 \cdot 60^1 + 22 = 5482$.

A difficulty with the Babylonian system was the lack of a symbol for zero. In writing numerals, scribes simply left a space if a certain position value was not to be used and, since spacing was not always uniform, this often made it necessary to infer values from context. For example, the Babylonian notation for 83 and 3623 originally were

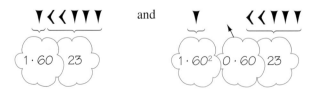

and these could easily be confused if the spacing were not clear. Indeed, there was no way even to indicate missing position values on the extreme right of a numeral so that ▼ could represent 1 or $1 \cdot 60^1 = 60$ or $1 \cdot 60^2 = 3600$, and so on. Eventually the Babylonians employed the symbol ⬧ as a place holder to indicate missing position values though they never developed the notion of zero as a number. Using this symbol, ▼❮❮▼▼▼ was clearly understood as $1 \cdot 60 + 23 = 83$ and ▼⬧❮❮▼▼▼ was unmistakably $1 \cdot 60^2 + 23 = 3623$.

EXAMPLE   3.7   **Writing a Number in the Babylonian System**

Write each of these in the Babylonian system.

(a)   45   **(b)**   145   **(c)**   7345

Solution

(a)   Since the Babylonian representation of the numbers from 1 through 59 is additive, we simply need four 10s and five 1s. Thus, $45 =$ ❮❮❮❮▼▼▼▼▼.

(b)   Since $145 = 2 \cdot 60 + 25$, in Babylonian notation 145 is represented by
▼▼❮❮▼▼▼▼▼.

(c)   Since $60^3 = 216{,}000$, $60^2 = 3600$, and $60^1 = 60$, the question is, "How many of each position value must we use?" Since 216,000 is clearly too large we consider 3600. Since $2 \cdot 3600 = 7200$, we can use two 60^2 and still have 145 left over to represent. Thus, using part (b), 7345 is represented by

EXAMPLE   3.8   **Converting from Babylonian to Standard Notation**

Write ❮❮▼▼❮❮❮▼ in standard notation.

Solution   Since ❮❮▼▼ represents 22 and ❮❮❮▼ represents 31, the number represented is $22 \cdot 60 + 31 = 1351$.

The Mayan System

One of the most interesting of the ancient systems of numeration was developed by the Mayans in the region now known as the Yucatan Peninsula in southeastern Mexico. As early as A.D. 200, these resourceful people had developed a remarkably advanced society. They were the first Native Americans to develop a system of writing and to manufacture paper and books. Their learned scholars knew more about astronomy than was known at that time anywhere else in the world. Their calendar was very accurate with a 365 day year and a leap year every fourth year. In short, many scholars believe that the Mayans very early developed the most sophisticated society ever attained by early residents of the Western Hemisphere.

Like their other achievements, the Mayan system of numeration was remarkably advanced. It contained a symbol for zero, which did not appear elsewhere until about A.D. 800. Also, it was a positional system of notation, like our current system, which made it possible to write very large numbers with relatively few symbols. Unlike our present system, the Mayan system was essentially a *vigesimal* or base twenty system, although the positions from the third on were for $18 \cdot 20$, $18 \cdot 20^2$, $18 \cdot 20^3$, and so on, rather than 20^2, 20^3, 20^4, and so on, as might be expected.* As with any fully developed positional system, the Mayans needed symbols for the numbers 0 through 19, the base minus one. It was then possible to write any whole number in positional notation in one and only one way using only these 20 symbols. Their symbols for 0 through 19 were as shown in Table 3.4.

TABLE 3.4   Mayan Numerals for 0 Through 19

JUST FOR FUN

For Careful Readers

1. How much dirt is there in a hole 10 meters long, 5 meters wide, and 3 meters deep?
2. The outer track of a phonograph record is a circle of radius 6 inches. The unused center of the disk is a circle of radius 3 inches. If the record has 20 grooves per inch, how far, to the nearest inch, does the needle travel while the record plays from beginning to end?
3. Joni has two U.S. coins in her pocket. One of the coins is not a quarter. The total value of the coins is 26¢. What are the two coins?

The Mayans wrote their numerals in a vertical style with the unit's position on the bottom. For example, the number 43,487 would appear as

$$6 \cdot 18 \cdot 20^2 = 43,200$$
$$0 \cdot 18 \cdot 20 = 0$$
$$14 \cdot 20 = 280$$
$$7 \cdot 1 = 7$$
$$43,487$$

*It is conjectured that this was because $18 \cdot 20 = 360$, approximately the number of days in a year.

All that is needed to convert a Mayan numeral to modern notation is a knowledge of the digits and the value of the position each digit occupies as shown in Table 3.5.

TABLE 3.5	Position Values in the Mayan System
Position Level	**Position Value**
.	.
.	.
.	.
fifth	$18 \cdot 20^3 = 144{,}000$
fourth	$18 \cdot 20^2 = 7200$
third	$18 \cdot 20 = 360$
second	20
first or lowest	1

EXAMPLE 3.9

Writing a Number Using Mayan Notation

Write 27,408 in Mayan notation.

Solution

We will not need the fifth or any higher position since $18 \cdot 20^3 = 144{,}000$ is already greater than 27,408. How many 7200s, 360s, 20s, and 1s are needed? This can be answered by repeated subtraction or, more simply, by division. From the arithmetic shown,

$$
\begin{array}{cccc}
3 & 16 & 2 & 8 \\
7200\overline{)27{,}408} & 360\overline{)5808} & 20\overline{)48} & 1\overline{)8} \\
21{,}600 & 360 & 40 & 8 \\
\overline{5\ 808} & \overline{2208} & \overline{8} & \overline{0} \\
 & 2160 & & \\
 & \overline{48} & &
\end{array}
$$

it follows that we need three 7200s, sixteen 360s, two 20s and eight 1s. Thus, in Mayan notation, 27,408 appears as

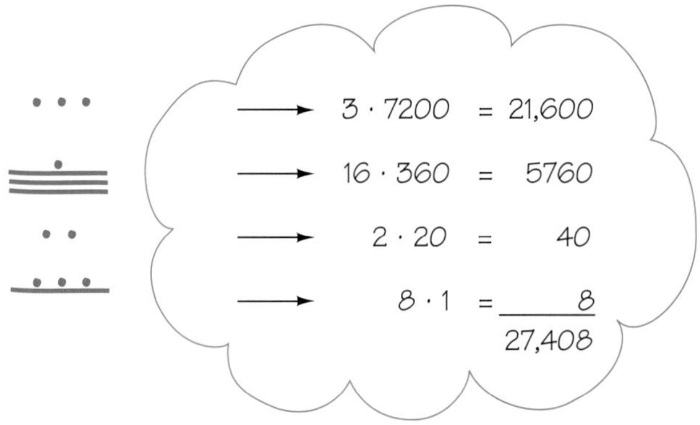

$$
\begin{array}{rcr}
3 \cdot 7200 & = & 21{,}600 \\
16 \cdot 360 & = & 5760 \\
2 \cdot 20 & = & 40 \\
8 \cdot 1 & = & 8 \\
\hline
 & & 27{,}408
\end{array}
$$

The ingenuity of this system, particularly since it involves the 18s, is easy to overlook. It turns out that such a positional system *will not work* unless the value of each position is a number that evenly divides the value of the next higher position. This fact is not at all obvious!

The Indo-Arabic System

Today the most universally used system of numeration is the **Indo-Arabic,** or **decimal system.** The system was named jointly for the East Indian scholars, who invented it at least as early as 800 B.C., and for the Arabs who transmitted it to the Western world. Like the Mayan, it is a positional system. Since its **base** is ten, it requires special symbols for the numbers zero through nine. Over the years various notational choices have been made, as shown in Table 3.6.

TABLE 3.6   Symbols for Zero Through Nine, Ancient and Modern

Tenth century East Indian	0	୧	୨	୩	୪	୫	୬	୭	୮	୯
Current Arabic	•	١	٢	٣	٤	٥	٦	٧	٨	٩
Fifteenth century European	0	1	2	3	4	4	6	∧	8	9
Modern cursive	0	1	2	3	4	5	6	7	8	9
Modern print	0	1	2	3	4	5	6	7	8	9
Lighted scoreboard	0	1	2	3	4	5	6	7	8	9
Calculator display	0	1	2	3	4	5	6	7	8	9
Machine readable	0	1	2	3	4	5	6	7	8	9

The common symbols 0, 1, 2, 3, 4, 5, 6, 7, 8, and 9 are called **digits,** as are our fingers and toes, and it is easy to imagine the historical significance of this terminology. With these ten symbols and the idea of positional notation, all that is needed to write the numeral for any whole number is the value of each digit and the value of the position the digit occupies in the numeral. In the decimal system, the positional values as shown in Table 3.7 are well known.

TABLE 3.7	Positional Values in Base Ten					
Position Names	$\cdots$	Hundred Thousands	Ten Thousands	Thousands	Hundreds	Tens	Units
Decimal Form	$\cdots$	100,000	10,000	1000	100	10	1
Powers of Ten	$\cdots$	10^5	10^4	10^3	10^2	10^1	10^0

As our number words suggest, the symbol 2572 means two thousands plus five hundreds plus seven tens plus two ones. In so-called **expanded notation** we write

$$2572 = 2 \cdot 1000 + 5 \cdot 100 + 7 \cdot 10 + 2 \cdot 1$$
$$= 2 \cdot 10^3 + 5 \cdot 10^2 + 7 \cdot 10^1 + 2 \cdot 10^0$$

> 2000 + 500 + 70 + 2

The amount each digit contributes to the number is the value of the digit times the value of the position the digit occupies in the representation.

Physical Models for Positional Systems

The classroom abacus   The Indo-Arabic scheme for representing numbers derived historically from the use of counting boards and abacuses of various types to facilitate computations in commercial transactions. Such devices are still useful today in helping children to understand the basic concepts. One such device, commercially available for classroom use, is shown in Figure 3.1.

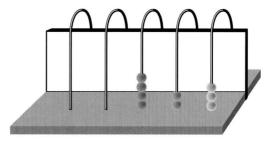

Figure 3.1
A classroom demonstration abacus

The device consists of a series of wire loops fixed into a wooden base and with a vertical shield affixed to the center of the base under the wire loops so that the back is hidden from the students. On each wire loop are beads that can be moved from the back of the shield to the front and *vice versa*.

To demonstrate counting and positional notation one begins by moving beads from the back of the shield to the front on the wire to the students' right (the instructor's left) counting 1, 2, 3, and so on, as the beads are moved to the front of the shield. Once ten beads on the first wire are counted, all ten are moved back behind the shield and the fact that ten beads on this wire have all been counted once is recorded by moving a single bead to the front of the shield on the second wire. The count 11, 12, 13, and so on, then continues with a single bead on the first wire again moved forward with each count. When the count reaches 20, ten beads on the first wire will have been counted a second time and this is recorded by moving a second bead forward on the second wire and moving the beads to the back again on the first wire. Then the count continues. When the count reaches 34, for example, the children will see the arrangement of beads shown schematically in Figure 3.2 with three beads showing on the second wire and four beads showing on the first wire. A natural way to record the result is to write 34; that is, three tens and four ones. Note that we never leave ten beads up on any wire.

Figure 3.2
Thirty-four on the classroom abacus

What happens if we count to 100; that is, if we count ten beads on the first wire ten times? Since we move one bead on the second wire forward each time we count ten beads on the first wire once, we will have ten beads showing on the second wire. But we record this on the abacus by moving one bead forward on the third wire and moving all beads on the second wire back behind the shield. Thus, each bead showing on the first wire counts for 1, each bead showing on the second wire counts for 10, each bead showing on the third wire counts for 100, and so on. If we count to 423, for example, the arrangement of beads is as illustrated earlier in Figure 3.1 and the count is naturally recorded as 423.

HIGHLIGHT FROM HISTORY
Fibonacci

The most talented mathematician of the Middle Ages was Leonardo of Pisa (ca. 1170–1250), the son of a Pisan merchant named Bonaccio. The Latin, *Leonardo Filius Bonaccio* (Leonardo son of Bonaccio) was soon contracted to Leonardo Fibonacci. This was further shortened simply to Fibonacci, which is still popularly used today. The young Fibonacci was brought up in Bougie—still an active port in modern Algeria—where his father served for many years as customs manager. It was here and on numerous trips throughout the Mediterranean region with his father that Fibonacci became acquainted with the Indo-Arabic numerals and the algorithms for computing with them which we still use today. Fibonacci did outstanding original work in geometry and number theory and is best known today for the remarkable sequence

1, 1, 2, 3, 5, 8, 13, 21, 34, 55, 89, . . .

which bears his name. However, his most important contribution to Western civilization remains his popularization of the Indo-Arabic numeration system in his book *Liber abaci* written in 1202. This book so effectively illustrated the vast superiority of this system over the other systems then in use that it soon was widely adopted not only for use in commerce but also in serious mathematical studies. Its use so simplified computational procedures that its effect on the rapid growth of mathematics during the Renaissance and beyond can only be characterized as profound.

INTO THE CLASSROOM

Mary Cavanaugh Discusses the Use of Manipulatives

Teaching for meaning in mathematics is a major focus of math educators. The work of Piaget and others suggests that students begin their exploration of mathematical concepts through hands-on experiences with manipulatives. Manipulatives appeal to several senses and are used to physically involve students in a learning situation. Students manipulate the objects with actions such as forming, ordering, comparing, tracing, joining, or separating groups. By these actions they gain an understanding of the meanings of number and various operations in mathematics.

Research points to multi-digit numeration as the pivotal concept that students must learn with the help of manipulatives before they can succeed in learning computational algorithms. A comfortable progression through representing numbers, trading, and computing with manipulatives is developmentally appropriate for providing a solid foundation for understanding arithmetic concepts. Premature introduction of paper-and-pencil procedures pushes students into memorizing a complex sequence of mathematical acts before the acts have meaning.

Manipulating objects allows students to develop internal images of number and the relative magnitude of number that can be recalled when needed. Pictures of concrete materials that follow manipulative experiences form a connection between the internal images, the pictures, and abstract symbols. The guidance of teachers is needed to help bridge the gap between what is learned from manipulatives and what is written using mathematical symbols.

A research recommendation, easily realized with manipulatives, is that teachers can and should expect students to enjoy the learning of mathematics. Concrete materials appeal to a variety of senses and motivate students. The frequent use of manipulatives in the classroom helps make the expectation of enjoyment evident.

SOURCE: From *ScottForesman Exploring Mathematics,* Grades 1–7, by L. Carey Bolster et al. Copyright © 1994 Scott, Foresman and Company. Reprinted by permission of Scott, Foresman and Company. Mary Cavanaugh is the coordinator of "Math, Science, and Beyond" for Solana Beach School District, Solana Beach, California.

Approached in this way, the notion of place value becomes much more concrete. One can actually experience the fact that each bead on the second wire counts for 10, each bead on the third wire counts for 100, and so on—particularly if allowed to handle the device and move the beads while counting. One can also see that the counting process on the abacus can proceed as far as desired though more and more wire loops would have to be added to the device. It follows that any whole number can be represented in one and only one way in our modern system using only the digits 0, 1, 2, 3, 4, 5, 6, 7, 8, and 9.

Other physical devices can also be used to illustrate positional notation and many are even more concrete than the historical abacus mimicked above.

Sticks in bundles   One simple idea for introducing positional notation is to use bundles of small sticks which can be purchased inexpensively at almost any craft store. Single sticks are ones. Ten sticks can be bound together in a bundle to represent ten. Ten bundles can be banded together to represent 100, and so on. Thus, 34 would be represented as shown in Figure 3.3.

Figure 3.3
Representing 34 with sticks and bundles of sticks

Unifix™ cubes   Here single cubes represent ones. Ten cubes snapped together to form a stick represent ten. Ten sticks bound together represent 100, and so on. Again, 34 would be represented as shown in Figure 3.4.

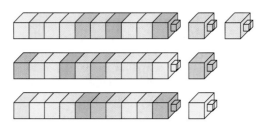

Figure 3.4
Representing 34 with Unifix™ cubes

Units, strips, and mats   Pieces for this concrete realization of the decimal system are easily cut from graph paper with reasonably large squares. A unit is a single square, a strip is a strip of ten squares, and a mat is a square ten units on a side as illustrated in Figure 3.5. To make the units, strips, and mats more substantial and hence easier to manipulate, the graph paper can be pasted to a substantial tag board or it can be copied on reasonably heavy stock. Using units, strips, and mats, 254 would be represented as shown in Figure 3.6.

Base ten blocks   These commercially prepared materials include single cubes that represent ones, sticks called "longs" made up of ten cubes that represent ten, "flats" made up of ten longs that represent 100, and "blocks" made up of ten flats that represent 1000 as shown in Figure 3.7.

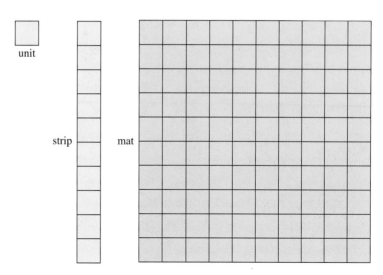

Figure 3.5
A unit, a strip, and a mat

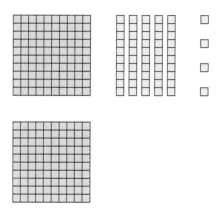

Figure 3.6
Representing 254 with units, strips, and mats

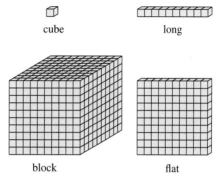

Figure 3.7
Base ten blocks for 1, 10, 100, and 1000

PROBLEM SET 3.1

Understanding Concepts

1. Write the Indo-Arabic equivalent of each of the following.

   (a)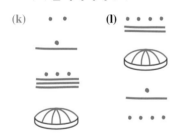

   (b)

   (c)

   (d) MDCCXXIX

   (e) DCXCVII

   (f) CMLXXXIV

   (g) **(h)**

   (i)

   (j)

   (k)   (l)

2. Write the following in Egyptian notation.
   (a) 11   (b) 597   (c) 1949

3. Write the following in Roman notation using the subtraction principle as appropriate.
   (a) 9   (b) 486   (c) 1945

4. Write these in Babylonian notation.
   (a) 251   (b) 3022   (c) 18,741

5. Write these in Mayan notation.
   (a) 12   (b) 584   (c) 12473

6. Add

   and

   using only Egyptian notation. Write your answer as simply as possible.

7. Add MDCCCXVI and MCCCLXIV using only Roman notation. Write your answer as simply as possible.

8. Add ———•——— and ══•══ using only Mayan

   notation. Write your answer as simply as possible.

9. Subtract

   from

   using only Egyptian notation.

10. Subtract MCCXCV from MDCCCXVI using only Roman notation.

11. (a) Write 1999, 2000, and 2001 in Roman numerals.

    (b) To date, what year has had the Roman numeral with the most symbols? Give your answer in both Roman and Indo-Arabic numerals.

12. Subtract ══•══ from ———•——— using only

    Mayan notation.

13. The ancient Chinese "rod system" of numeration was a base ten positional system like our modern system with two possible arrangements for the digits 1 through 9:

1	2	3	4	5	6	7	8	9

    For easy reading, the vertical arrangement was used in the columns corresponding to the even powers of ten and the horizontal arrangement for the columns corresponding to the odd powers of ten. A blank space was used for the digit zero. Thus, 12,462 would appear as | = |||| ⊥ || . Write the modern equivalent of the following

    (a) ≡ 𝕋 ≐ |||| (b) = 𝕋 ≐ ||||

    (c) ⊥   ≡ 𝕋𝕋   (d) ||| ≛   ≐ 𝕋

14. Write each of the following using the Chinese rod system of notation.

    (a) 2763   **(b)** 38,407   (c) 804   **(d)** 7561

15. Perform each of the following computations using the Chinese rod system of notation. Check using modern notation.

    (a) ||| ⊥ |||| + || ≐ | **(b)** ≡ 丅 ≐ 丅 + ||| ⊥ ||

    (c) ⊥ || = |||| − 丅 ≡ || **(d)** 丅 ≐ ||||| − || ≐ ||||

16. Draw a sketch to illustrate 452 using units, strips, and mats. Use dots to represent units, vertical line segments to represent strips, and squares to represent mats.

17. Draw a sketch to illustrate 234 using base ten blocks.

18. Draw a sketch of the exposed side of a classroom abacus to illustrate 2475.

19. Write 24,872 and 3071 in expanded notation.

20. Suppose you have 3 mats, 24 strips, and 13 units for a total count of 553. Briefly describe the exchanges you would make to keep the same total count but have the smallest possible number of manipulative pieces.

21. Suppose you have 2 mats, 7 strips, and 6 units in one hand and 4 mats, 5 strips, and 9 units in the other.

    (a) Put all these pieces together and describe the exchanges required to keep the same total count but with the smallest possible number of manipulative pieces.

    (b) Explain briefly but clearly what mathematics the manipulation in part (a) represents.

22. Suppose you have 3 mats and 6 units on your desk and want to remove a count represented by 3 strips and 8 units.

    (a) Describe briefly but clearly the exchange that must take place to accomplish the desired task.

    (b) After removing the 3 strips and 8 units, what manipulative pieces are left on your desk?

    (c) What mathematics does the manipulation in part (a) represent?

Thinking Critically

23. Suppose the discussion of the classroom abacus on pages 169 to 170 were repeated with "five" playing the role of "ten." Then forty-two would be represented on the abacus as shown here. Moreover, it would be recorded as 132 and read as "one three two" and *not* as "one hundred thirty-two".

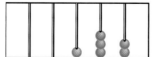

What numbers would be represented if the beads on the abacus described are as shown in these diagrams?

(a)

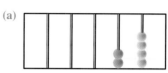

Fourteen, since 2 · 5 + 4 = 14

(b)

(c)

(d)

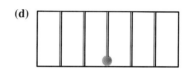

(e)

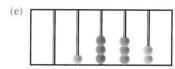

24. The number represented in the diagram of problem 23, part (b) would be recorded as 10 ("one-zero"). How would the numbers for parts (a), (c), (d), and (e) naturally be recorded?

25. Suppose the abacus of problem 23 is configured as shown here.

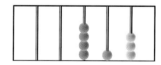

    (a) What number does this arrangement represent?

    (b) How would this number naturally be recorded?

    (c) Suppose the number shown in part (a) is increased by seven. Draw a diagram to show how the abacus will then be configured.

26. Suppose the abacus of problem 23 is as shown here.

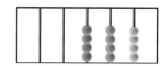

How will it appear if the number represented is increased by 1? Draw a suitable diagram.

27. Draw diagrams of the abacus of problem 23 for each of these numbers.

    (a) five   (b) seven   (c) ten   (d) twenty-five

    (e) thirty-two   (f) one hundred four

    (g) one hundred twenty-five

    (h) one hundred forty-seven

28. The right-most wire on the abacus of problem 23 is called the units wire. What would be appropriate names for

    (a) the second wire from the right?

    (b) the third wire from the right?

29. If the number represented on the abacus of problem 23 is recorded as 132, what is the count?

Communicating

30. Suppose the abacus of problem 23 had been invented by a race of one-handed, five-fingered aliens.

    (a) Could they represent any number, however large, on such an abacus with suitably many wires? Explain.

    (b) Carefully describe the numeration system that the aliens of part (a) might use.

31. Write a two-page paper describing one of these ancient numeration systems: Greek or Japanese.

For Review

32. Given sets $U = \{1, 2, 3, 4, 5, 6, 7, 8, 9\}$, $A = \{1, 3, 5, 7, 9\}$, $B = \{1, 2, 3, 4\}$, and $C = \{2, 4, 6, 8\}$, complete the following.

    (a) $A \cup B =$ _____   (b) $A \cap B =$ _____

    (c) $\overline{A} =$ _____   (d) $A \cap C =$ _____

    (e) $A \cap (B \cup C) =$ _____

    (f) $(A \cap B) \cup (A \cap C) =$ _____

    (g) $n(A) =$ _____, $n(C) =$ _____,

    $n(A \cup C) =$ _____

    (h) $n(A) =$ _____, $n(B) =$ _____,

    $n(A \cup B) =$ _____,

    $n(A) + n(B) - n(A \cap B) =$ _____

    (i) Explain in two carefully written sentences the reason for the difference between the results of parts (g) and (h).

33. Name the property that justifies each of the following.

    (a) $3x + 5x = (3 + 5)x$

    (b) $4\pi + 7\pi = 7\pi + 4\pi$

    (c) $3x + (4y + z) = 3x + (z + 4y)$

    (d) $21 + 7 = 20 + (1 + 7)$

34. Write two subtraction equations corresponding to each of these equations.

    (a) $3 + 7 = 10$ (b) $11 + 5 = 16$

    (c) $21 + 19 = 40$

35. Write one addition equation and a second subtraction equation that corresponds to each of these equations.

    (a) $17 - 8 = 9$ (b) $23 - 15 = 8$

    (c) $23 - 5 = 18$

3.2   Nondecimal Positional Systems

In the preceding section we discussed several numeration systems including the decimal system in common use today. As already mentioned, the decimal system is a positional system based on ten. This is probably so because we have ten fingers and, as now, people often counted on their fingers. Suppose that there are little green aliens on Mars who have only one hand with five fingers. If Martians were to go through essentially the same process of developing a number system as occurred in ancient India, how would their system work?

Base Five Notation

For our purposes, perhaps the quickest route to understanding **base five notation** is to reconsider the abacus of Figure 3.1. This time, however, we suppose that we allow only five beads to be moved forward on each wire. As before, we start with the wire to the students' right (our left) and move one bead forward each time as we count one, two, three, and so on. When we reach five, we have counted the first wire once and we record this on the abacus by moving one bead forward on the second wire while moving all five beads on the first wire to the back. Continuing to count, when the count reaches ten we will have counted all the beads on the first wire a second time. We move a second bead forward on the second wire and again move all the beads on the first wire to the back as indicated in Figure 3.8.

$$5^0 = 1$$
$$5^1 = 5$$
$$5^2 = 25$$
$$5^3 = 125$$
$$5^4 = 625$$

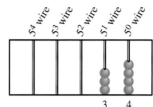

Figure 3.8
A count of nineteen on a
5-bead abacus

3   4

Thus, each bead on the second wire counts for five; that is, the second wire is the "fives" wire. Continuing the count, when it reaches 19, the abacus will appear as in Figure 3.8 and

$$19 = 3 \cdot 5 + 4.$$

If we continue the count to 25, all the beads on the first wire will have been counted five times. This means that we have moved all five beads to the front on the *second* wire. This is recorded on the abacus by returning these beads to the back of the abacus and moving one bead forward on the *third* wire. Thus, the third wire becomes the $25 = 5^2$ wire. The count can be continued in this way, and it is apparent that any whole number will eventually be counted and can be recorded on the abacus with only 0, 1, 2, 3, or 4 beads per wire showing at the front; that is, we need only the digits 0, 1, 2, 3, and 4 in base five. For example, if we continue the counting process up to 113, the abacus will have three beads on the units wire, two on the fives wire, and four on the twenty-fives wire; that is,

$$113 = 4 \cdot 5^2 + 2 \cdot 5 + 3.$$

Just as we shorten $4 \cdot 10^2 + 2 \cdot 10 + 3$ to 423, the little green Martian might also shorten $4 \cdot 5^2 + 2 \cdot 5 + 3$ to 423. Thus, the three-digit sequence 423 can represent many different numbers depending on which base is chosen. To the average American, who doesn't even

think about it, it means "four hundred twenty-three." To our Martian friend it means *flug globs zeit-tab;* that is, Martian for $4 \cdot 5^2 + 2 \cdot 5 + 3$. Note that our Martian friend certainly would **not** say "one hundred thirteen" since that is decimal, or base ten, language. To avoid confusion in talking about base five numeration, we agree that we will *not* say "four hundred twenty-three" when we read 423 as a base five numeral. Instead, we will say "four two three base five" and will write 423_{five} where the subscript five indicates the base. In base six, we understand that

$$423_{\text{six}} = 4 \cdot 6^2 + 2 \cdot 6 + 3$$

$423_{\text{six}} = 159_{\text{ten}}$ *since*
$4 \cdot 6^2 + 2 \cdot 6 + 3 = 159_{\text{ten}}$

and read the numeral as "four two three base six." As an additional example, 423_{twelve} should be read "four two three base twelve," and in expanded form, we have

$$423_{\text{twelve}} = 4 \cdot 12^2 + 2 \cdot 12 + 3 = 603_{\text{ten}}.$$

Unless expressly stated to the contrary a numeral written *without* a subscript should be read as a base ten numeral.

Observe that, in base five, we need the digits 0, 1, 2, 3, and 4 and we need to know the values of the positions in base five. In base six, the digits are 0, 1, 2, 3, 4, and 5 and we need to know the positional values in base six. In base twelve, we use the digits 0, 1, 2, 3, 4, 5, 6, 7, 8, 9, T, and E where T and E are, respectively, the digits for ten and eleven. For these bases, the positional values are given in Table 3.8.

TABLE 3.8	Digits and Positional Values in Bases Five, Six, and Twelve						
Base	Digits			DECIMAL VALUES OF POSITIONS			
b	used	$\cdots$	b^4	b^3	b^2	b^1	units ($b^0 = 1$)
Five	0, 1, 2, 3, 4	$\cdots$	$5^4 = 625$	$5^3 = 125$	$5^2 = 25$	$5^1 = 5$	$5^0 = 1$
Six	0, 1, 2, 3, 4, 5	$\cdots$	$6^4 = 1296$	$6^3 = 216$	$6^2 = 36$	$6^1 = 6$	$6^0 = 1$
Twelve	0, 1, 2, 3, 4, 5, 6, 7, 8, 9, T, E	$\cdots$	$12^4 = 20{,}736$	$12^3 = 1728$	$12^2 = 144$	$12^1 = 12$	$12^0 = 1$

EXAMPLE 3.10 **Converting from Base Five to Base Ten Notation**

Write the base ten representation of 3214_{five}.

Solution

We use the place values of Table 3.8 along with the digit values. Thus,

$$3214_{\text{five}} = 3 \cdot 5^3 + 2 \cdot 5^2 + 1 \cdot 5^1 + 4 \cdot 5^0$$
$$= 3 \cdot 125 + 2 \cdot 25 + 1 \cdot 5 + 4 \cdot 1$$
$$= 375 + 50 + 5 + 4$$
$$= 434.$$

Therefore, "three two one four" base five is four hundred thirty-four.

EXAMPLE   3.11

Solution

Converting from Base Ten to Base Five Notation

Write the base five representation of 97.

Recall that 97 without a subscript has its usual meaning as a base ten numeral.

We begin with the notion of grouping. Suppose that we have 97 beans and want to group them into groups of single beans (units), groups of five beans (fives), groups of five groups of five beans each (twenty-fives), and so on. The problem is to complete the grouping using the least possible number of groups. This means that we must use as many of the larger groups as possible. Diagrammatically, we have

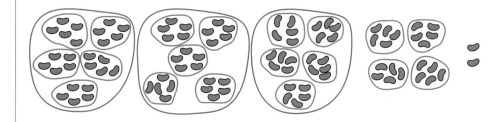

so that $97_{\text{ten}} = 342_{\text{five}}$. Arithmetically, this corresponds to determining how many of each position value in base five are required to represent 97. This can be determined by successive divisions as in Example 3.8 in Section 3.1. Referring to Table 3.8 for position values, we see that 125 is too big. Thus, we begin with 25 and divide successive remainders by successively lower position values.

$$
\begin{array}{ccc}
\dfrac{3}{25\overline{)97}} & \dfrac{4}{5\overline{)22}} & \dfrac{2}{1\overline{)2}} \\
\dfrac{75}{22} & \dfrac{20}{2} & \dfrac{2}{0}
\end{array}
$$

These divisions reveal that we need 3 25s, 4 5s, and 2 1s or, in tabular form,

25s	5s	1s
3	4	2

Thus,

$$97_{\text{ten}} = 342_{\text{five}}.$$

As a check, we note that

$$
\begin{aligned}
342_{\text{five}} &= 3 \cdot 25 + 4 \cdot 5 + 2 \\
&= 75 + 20 + 2 \\
&= 97_{\text{ten}}.
\end{aligned}
$$

DID YOU KNOW?

The Utility of Other Bases

At first thought it might appear that positional numeration systems in bases other than base ten are merely interesting diversions. Quite the contrary, they are extremely important in today's society. This is particularly true of the base two or binary system, the base eight or octal system, and the base sixteen or hexadecimal system. The degree to which calculators and computers have affected modern life is simply enormous, and the basic notion

that allows these devices to operate is base two arithmetic. A switch is either on or off, a spot on a magnetic grid is either magnetized or not magnetized, a spot on a compact disc is activated or it is not. All of these devices are capable of recording two states—either 0 or 1—and so can be programmed to do base two arithmetic and to record other data in code "words" consisting of strings of 0s and 1s. A drawback of base two notation is that numerals for relatively small numbers become quite long. Thus,

$$60_{\text{ten}} = 111100_{\text{two}}$$

and this makes programming a computer somewhat cumbersome. The notation is greatly simplified by using

octal or hexadecimal notation, since these are intimately related to binary notation. Thus, triples of binary digits become single octal digits and vice versa, and quadruples of digits in binary notation correspond to single digits in hexadecimal. For example, since

$$111_{\text{two}} = 7 \quad \text{and} \quad 100_{\text{two}} = 4,$$

it follows that

$$60_{\text{ten}} = 111100_{\text{two}} = 74_{\text{eight}}.$$

For this reason, computer programmers often work in octal or hexadecimal notation.

PROBLEM SET 3.2

Understanding Concepts

1. In a long column write the base five numerals for the numbers from zero through twenty-five.

2. Briefly describe the pattern or patterns you observe in the list of numerals in problem 1.

3. Here are the base six representations of the numbers from zero through thirty-five arranged in a rectangular array. Briefly describe any patterns you observe in this array.

0	1	2	3	4	5
10	11	12	13	14	15
20	21	22	23	24	25
30	31	32	33	34	35
40	41	42	43	44	45
50	51	52	53	54	55

4. What would be the entries in the next two rows of the table of problem 3?

5. Write the base ten representations of each of the following.
   (a) 413_{five} (b) 2004_{five} (c) 10_{five}
   (d) 100_{five} (e) 1000_{five} (f) 2134_{five}

6. Write the base ten representations of each of the following.
   (a) 413_{six} (b) 2004_{six} (c) 10_{six}
   (d) 100_{six} (e) 1000_{six} (f) 2134_{six}

7. Write the base ten representations of each of these. Remember that in base twelve the symbols for the digits ten and eleven are T and E.
   (a) 413_{twelve} (b) 2004_{twelve} (c) 10_{twelve}
   (d) 100_{twelve} (e) 1000_{twelve} (f) $2TE4_{\text{twelve}}$

8. Determine the base five representation for each of the following. Remember that a numeral with no subscript is understood to be in base ten.
   (a) 362   (b) 27   (c) 5   (d) 25

9. Determine the base six representation for the following.
   (a) 342   (b) 21   (c) 6   (d) 216

10. Determine the base twelve representation for each of the following.
    (a) 2743   (b) 563   (c) 144   (d) 1584

11. Base two is a very useful base. Since it only requires two digits, 0 and 1, it is the system on which all calculators and computers are based.

(a) Make a table of position values for base two up as far as $2^{10} = 1024$.

(b) Write each of these in base ten notation.

(i) 1101_{two} (ii) 111_{two} (iii) 1000_{two}

(iv) 10101_{two}

(c) Write each of these in base two notation.

(i) 24   (ii) 18   (iii) 2   (iv) 8

(d) Write the numbers from zero to thirty-one in base two notation in a vertical column and discuss any pattern you observe in a short paragraph.

(e) In three or four sentences compare part (d) of this problem with the *Hands On* activity at the beginning of the chapter.

Thinking Critically

12. Here's an interesting trick. Consider these pictures of cards you might make for use in your class.

1 3 5 7 9 11	2 3 6 7 10 11	4 5 6 7 12 13	8 9 10 11 12 13	16 17 18 19 20 21
13 15 17 19 21	14 15 18 19 22	14 15 20 21 22	14 15 24 25 26	22 23 24 25 26
23 25 27 29 31	23 26 27 30 31	23 28 29 30 31	27 28 29 30 31	27 28 29 30 31

(a) Record the first number on each card that shows the day of the month on which you were born.

(b) Add the numbers in part (a).

(c) Surprised? Our experience is that elementary school students are too and that they immediately want to know how the trick works. See if you can discover the secret by carefully comparing the cards with your answer to problem 11, part (d).

---

13. (a) Add $11,111,111_{two}$ and 1_{two} in base 2.

(b) What are the base two numerals for 2^n and $2^n - 1$? Explain briefly, describing a pattern.

14. Recall that the rows of Pascal's triangle (see Section 1.4) are numbered 0, 1, 2, 3, ... Thus, row 5 is 1, 5, 10, 10, 5, 1, which has four odd entries. Also, the base two representation of 5 is 101_{two}, with 2 ones and $2^2 = 4$. Remarkably, if f is the number of ones in the base two representation of n, then 2^f gives the number of odd entries in the nth row of Pascal's triangle. Verify that this is true for the following rows of Pascal's triangle.

(a) row $n = 7$, whose entries are 1, 7, 21, 35, 35, 21, 7, 1.

(b) row $n = 8$, whose entries are 1, 8, 28, 56, 70, 56, 28, 8, 1.

(c) row $n = 11$, whose entries are 1, 11, 55, 165, 330, 462, 462, 330, 165, 55, 11, 1.

15. The two 1-digit sequences of 0s and 1s are 0 and 1. The four 2-digit sequences of 0s and 1s are 00, 10, 01, and 11.

(a) Write down all of the 3-digit sequences of 0s and 1s. Can you think of an easy way to do this? Explain.

(b) Write down all of the 4-digit sequences of 0s and 1s. Can you think of an easy way to do this? Explain.

(c) How many 5-digit sequences of 0s and 1s are there?

(d) How many n-digit sequences of 0s and 1s are there? Explain why this is so.

16. (a) Think of each 3-digit sequence of 0s and 1s in problem 15(a) as a base two numeral. What are the base ten equivalents of these numerals?

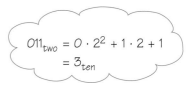

$$011_{two} = 0 \cdot 2^2 + 1 \cdot 2 + 1$$
$$= 3_{ten}$$

(b) Think of each 4-digit sequence of 0s and 1s in problem 15(b) as a base two numeral. What are the base ten equivalents of these numerals?

(c) Think of each n-digit sequence of 0s and 1s as a base two numeral. What do you think are the base ten equivalents of these numerals? Explain.

17. There are one thousand base ten numerals using three or fewer digits, namely 0, 1, 2, . . . , 999. Another way to count these numerals is to note that there are ten choices for the units digit, ten choices for the tens digit, and ten choices for the hundreds digit giving $10 \cdot 10 \cdot 10 = 1000$ 3-digit numerals as just noted. This counts such 3-digit numerals as 006 and 083, which would be written simply as 6 and 83.

(a) How many base two numerals are there with three or fewer digits?

(b) Consider the 3-element universal set $U = \{a, b, c\}$. The subset $A = \{a, c\}$ can be associated with the 3-digit base two numeral 101 since A contains a, does not contain b, and does contain c. Similarly, the empty subset is associated with 000, and the subset $\{b\}$ is associated with 010. In view of your answer to part (a), how many subsets are there of $\{a, b, c\}$?

(c) How many subsets are there of $\{a, b, c, d\}$?

(d) How many subsets are there of an n-element set?

18. The diagram below shows a Cuisenaire rod train of length four (see the Hands On of Chapter 2), consisting of a red 2-rod caboose at the left, a 1-rod car, and a 1-rod engine. This train can be associated with the 3-digit base two numeral 011 where the digit 0 indicates a single car

of length two, and each 1 indicates a break from one car to the next. Similarly, two consecutive 0s indicate a single car of length three, and three consecutive 0s indicate a single car of length four. Thus, two red rods form a train of length four associated with the base two numeral 010.

(a) Draw all trains of length four and write their corresponding base two numerals. Explain how you know that there are $2^3 = 8$ of these trains.

(b) Using the same reasoning as in part (a), determine the number of different trains of length five.

(c) How many trains of length n can be formed if cars come in all lengths—1, 2, 3, . . . , n?

Communicating

19. Read the article "Counting" by L. L. Conant in *The World of Mathematics,* vol. 1 (New York: Simon and Schuster, 1956), and write a brief two-page summary.

Using a Calculator

20. (a) Lyudmila discovered a method to convert a numeral in any base to its equivalent in base ten using her calculator. For example, to convert 423_{five}, she used the entry string

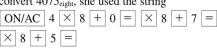

to obtain the correct result of 113. Similarly, to convert 4075_{eight}, she used the string

$$\boxed{\text{ON/AC}}\ 4\ \boxed{\times}\ 8\ \boxed{+}\ 0\ \boxed{=}\ \boxed{\times}\ 8\ \boxed{+}\ 7\ \boxed{=}$$
$$\boxed{\times}\ 8\ \boxed{+}\ 5\ \boxed{=}$$

to obtain the correct result of 2109. Lydumila isn't quite sure why her procedure works. Write an imaginary dialogue with her to help her understand why the method is valid.

(b) Would this method succeed on an ordinary 4-function calculator?

For Review

21. Write two division equations corresponding to each of these multiplication equations.

(a) $3 \cdot 17 = 51$ (b) $11 \cdot 91 = 1001$

(c) $9 \cdot 121 = 1089$

22. Write a multiplication equation and a second division equation corresponding to each of these division equations.

(a) $341 \div 11 = 31$ (b) $455 \div 65 = 7$

(c) $124857 \div 13873 = 9$

23. Lida Lee has three sweaters, four blouses, and two pairs of slacks that mix and match beautifully. How many different outfits can she wear using these nine items of clothing?

24. (a) If n represents Shane Stagg's age six years ago, how old is Shane now?

(b) If m represents Shane's age now, how old was Shane six years ago?

COOPERATIVE INVESTIGATION

A Remarkable Base Three Trick

Mathematical magic certainly has a place in the classroom. Students find it interesting, fun, and highly motivational. Consider the following problem: You are given 12 coins that appear identical but one of the coins is false and is either heavy or light, you don't know which. You have a balance scale and are to find the false coin and to determine whether it is heavy or light in just three weighings. This is a difficult problem that is usually solved by considering a whole series of cases. However, if you know base three arithmetic you can determine the false coin so quickly right in front of your class that you appear to be a real wizard! Here's how it can be done.

1. Number the coins from 1 through 12.
2. With your back turned, ask your class to agree on the number of the coin they want to be false and to decide whether it is to be heavy or light.
3. Indicate that you are going to make these three weighings and ask the class what the movement of the *left hand* pan on each weighing will be. If the left hand pan goes up, record a 2. If it balances, record a 1. If it goes down, record a 0. Now use the results of these weighings to form a 3-digit base three numeral. The first weighing determines the *nines* digit, the second weighing determines the *threes* digit, and the third weighing determines the *units* digit. If the base ten number determined in this way is less than 13, it names the false coin. If the number is more than 13, then 26 minus the number generated names the false coin. You can tell, by knowing the false coin, whether it is heavy or light by noting how the left hand pan moved on a weighing involving the false coin.

For example, suppose the class chooses coin 7 as the false coin and decides that it should be heavy. Then on the three weighings the left hand pan goes down, goes up, and balances and we generate $021_{three} = 7$, the number of the false coin. Moreover, since coin 7 was in the left hand pan, which went down on the first weighing, coin 7 must be heavy. On the other hand, suppose that coin 7 is light. Then on the three weighings the left hand pan goes up, goes down, and balances, and we generate $201_{three} = 19$. But then $26 - 19 = 7$, so coin 7 is the false coin and must be light since the left hand pan went up on the first weighing.

Our experience is that children like the trick very much and are strongly motivated to learn base three notation in order to pull the trick on their friends and parents. Note also that to do the trick well students must be able to perform mental calculations quickly—itself a worthy goal.

3.3   Algorithms for Adding and Subtracting Whole Numbers

Today's predominant opinion, as summarized in NCTM's *Curriculum and Evaluation Standards for School Mathematics,* is that we spend much more time than necessary trying to teach youngsters the intricacies of pencil and paper calculations. The time would be much better spent helping students learn to think critically about quantitative situations, to develop thoughtful mathematical behavior as opposed to rote memorization of rules, and to learn effective techniques for solving thought-provoking problems while handling the arithmetic details by appropriate use of a calculator.

The calculation skills and essential knowledge for school mathematics include:

- knowledge of the 1-digit arithmetic facts,
- the meaning of the arithmetic operations,
- the properties of numbers,
- the meaning of positional notation,
- the ability to perform mental arithmetic,
- the ability to use pencil and paper algorithms with small numbers,
- an understanding of why the algorithms give correct results,
- the ability to calculate correctly and efficiently with a calculator,
- the ability to estimate the results of calculations.

We address these essentials here.

The Addition Algorithm

Consider the addition shown.

$$\begin{array}{r} \overset{1}{}28 \\ +\ 45 \\ \hline 73 \end{array}$$

This process depends entirely on our positional system of notation. But why does it work this way? Why "carry" the "one"? Why add by columns? To many young people, these procedures remain a great mystery—you add this way because you were told to—it's simply done by rote with no understanding.

As noted earlier, children learn abstract notions by first experiencing them concretely with devices they can actually see, touch, and manipulate. Thus, one should introduce the addition algorithm with manipulatives like base ten blocks; sticks and bundles of sticks; units, strips, and mats; abacuses; or, better yet, by using a number of these devices. For illustrative purposes here we use units, strips, and mats.

After cutting out their strips and mats, students will be aware that there are ten units on a strip and ten strips or 100 units on a mat, and they will be aware that, in manipulating these materials, they can make these exchanges back and forth as needed.

EXAMPLE   3.12   **Making Exchanges with Units, Strips, and Mats**

Suppose a number is represented by 15 units, 11 strips, and 2 mats. What exchanges must be made in order to represent the same number but with the smallest number of manipulative pieces?

Solution

Understand the problem

We are given the mats, strips, and units indicated in the statement of the problem and are asked to make exchanges that reduce the number of loose pieces of apparatus while keeping the same number of units in all.

Devise a plan

Since we know that 10 units form a strip and 10 strips form a mat, we can reduce the number of loose pieces by making these exchanges.

Carry out the plan

If we actually had in hand the pieces described we would physically make the desired exchanges. Here in the text, we illustrate the exchanges pictorially.

We reduce the number of pieces by replacing 10 units by 1 strip and 10 strips by 1 mat. This gives 3 mats, 2 strips, and 5 units for 325 units as shown.

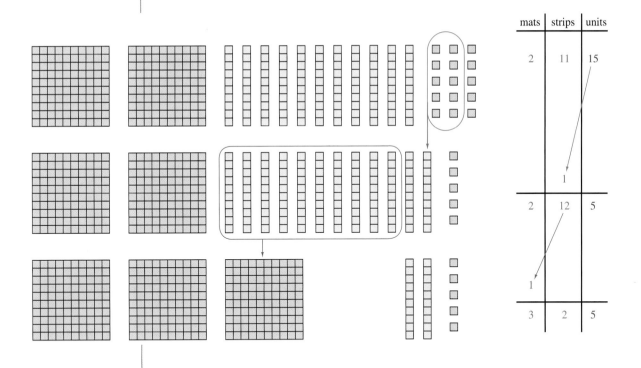

mats	strips	units
2	11	15
	1	
2	12	5
1		
3	2	5

Look back

No more combining can take place because it takes 10 units to make a strip and 10 strips to make a mat. Thus, we finish with 3 mats, 2 strips, and 5 units for a total of 325 units. Moreover, we have not changed the total number of units since

$$2 \cdot 100 + 11 \cdot 10 + 15 = 200 + 110 + 15 = 325.$$

EXAMPLE   3.13

Developing the Addition Algorithm
Find the sum of 135 and 243.

Solution

With units, strips, and mats
One hundred thirty-five is represented by 1 mat, 3 strips and 5 units, and 243 is represented by 2 mats, 4 strips and 3 units, as shown. All told this gives a total of 3 mats, 7 strips, and 8 units. Therefore, since no exchanges are possible, the sum is 378. Note how this illustrates the column by column addition algorithm typically used in pencil and paper calculation.

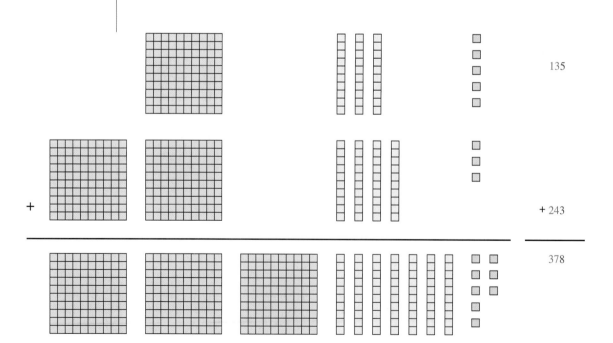

135

+ 243

378

With place value cards

A somewhat more abstract approach to this problem is to use **place value cards;** that is, cards marked off in squares labeled 1s, 10s, and 100s right to left, and with the appropriate number of markers placed in each square to represent the desired number. A marker on the second square is worth 10 markers on the first square; a marker on the third square is worth 10 markers on the second square, and so on. The addition of this example is illustrated as follows.

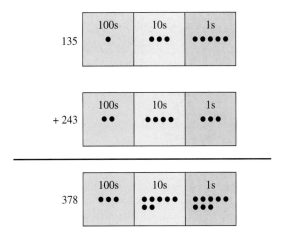

With place value diagrams and instructional algorithms

An even more abstract approach leading finally to the usual algorithm is provided by the following place value diagrams and instructional algorithms.

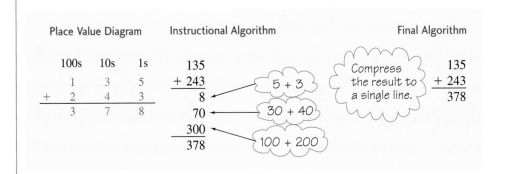

Notice how the degree of abstraction steadily increases as we move through the various solutions. If the elementary school teacher goes directly to the final algorithm, many students will be lost along the way. The approach from the concrete gradually moving toward the abstract is more likely to impart the desired understanding.

EXAMPLE 3.14

Adding with Exchanging

Find the sum of 357 and 274.

Solution

With units, strips, and mats

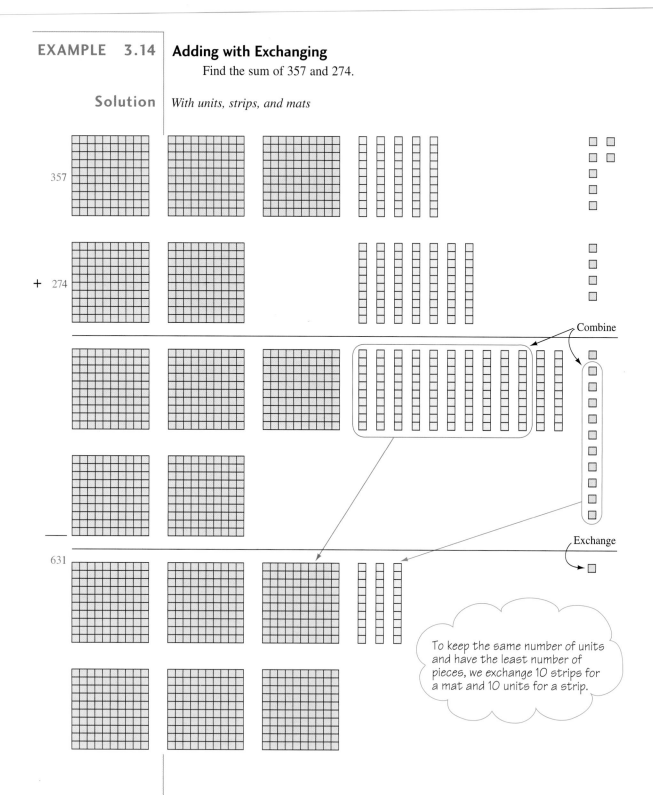

357

+ 274

Combine

Exchange

631

To keep the same number of units and have the least number of pieces, we exchange 10 strips for a mat and 10 units for a strip.

Note how the above not only illustrates the usual column by column addition of pencil and paper arithmetic, but also "carrying" or, more appropriately, "exchanging." The 1 "carried"

1 1
357
+ 274
631

from the first column to the second indicates the exchange of ten units for one ten (represented by one strip) and the 1 carried from the second column to the third indicates the exchange of ten tens (i.e., ten strips) for one hundred (represented by one mat). Many teachers try to avoid the traditional word "carry" since it encourages students to perform the algorithms by rote with no understanding of what they are actually doing. Words like "exchange," "trade," or "regroup" are much more descriptive and actually describe what is being done.

With place value cards

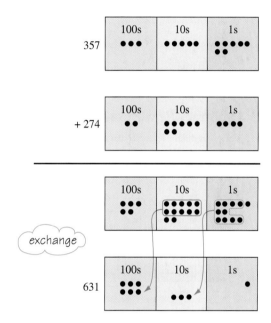

exchange

With place value diagrams and instructional algorithms

exchange

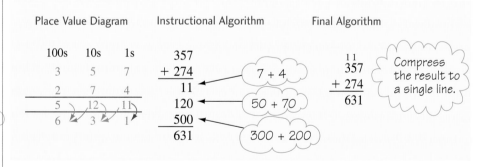

Notice again how the level of abstraction steadily increases as we move through these solutions. This example and the various solutions should make it clear to students that at no point are they "carrying a one." It is always the case of exchanging ten ones from the ones column for one ten in the tens column, 10 tens from the tens column for one hundred in the hundreds column, and so on.

The Subtraction Algorithm

We can illustrate the subtraction algorithm in much the same way as the addition algorithm. For primary children, the idea of subtraction is often understood in terms of "take away." Thus, if you have 9 apples and I take away 5, you have 4 left as in Figure 3.9.

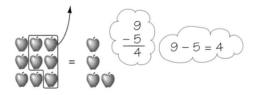

Figure 3.9
Subtraction as "take away"

EXAMPLE   3.15

Subtracting without Exchanging

Subtract 243 from 375.

Solution   *With units, strips, and mats*

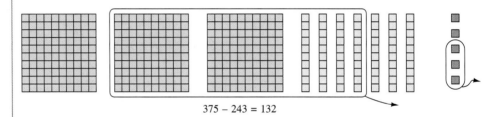

$$375 - 243 = 132$$

With place value cards

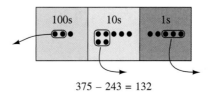

$$375 - 243 = 132$$

With place value diagrams and instructional algorithms

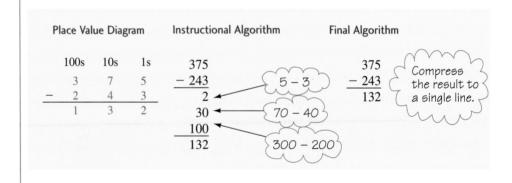

Place Value Diagram			Instructional Algorithm	Final Algorithm	
100s	10s	1s	375	375	
3	7	5	− 243	− 243	Compress
− 2	4	3	2 ← 5 − 3	132	the result to a single line.
1	3	2	30 ← 70 − 40		
			100 ← 300 − 200		
			132		

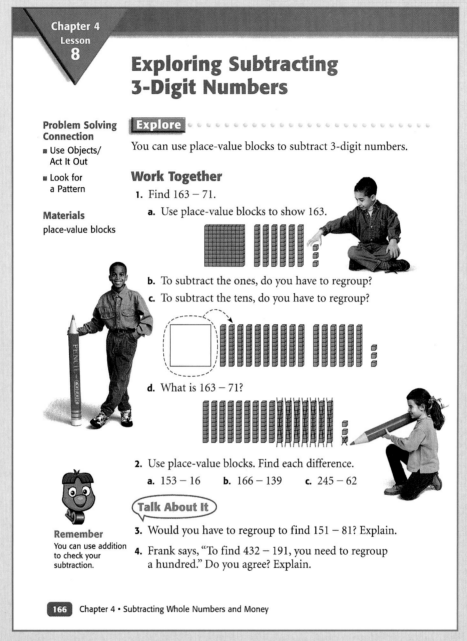

Chapter 4
Lesson
8

Exploring Subtracting 3-Digit Numbers

Problem Solving Connection

■ Use Objects/ Act It Out

■ Look for a Pattern

Materials
place-value blocks

Explore

You can use place-value blocks to subtract 3-digit numbers.

Work Together

1. Find 163 − 71.

  a. Use place-value blocks to show 163.

  b. To subtract the ones, do you have to regroup?

  c. To subtract the tens, do you have to regroup?

  d. What is 163 − 71?

2. Use place-value blocks. Find each difference.

  a. 153 − 16   **b.** 166 − 139   **c.** 245 − 62

Talk About It

Remember
You can use addition to check your subtraction.

3. Would you have to regroup to find 151 − 81? Explain.

4. Frank says, "To find 432 − 191, you need to regroup a hundred." Do you agree? Explain.

166 Chapter 4 • Subtracting Whole Numbers and Money

SOURCE: From *Scott Foresman – Addison Wesley Math*, Grade 3, p. 166, by Randall I. Charles et al. Copyright © 1999, Addison Wesley Longman, Inc.

Questions for the Teacher

1. In the lesson above, place value blocks were used to illustrate regrouping in subtracting 3-digit numbers. Carefully explain how you could use money—dollars, dimes, and pennies—to accomplish the same purpose.

2. On the sample page, the word "regroup" was used instead of "borrow." Why is it better to use words like regroup, exchange, or trade than borrow and phrases like "borrow 1 from the tens column"?

EXAMPLE   3.16 | **Subtracting with "Exchanging"**

Subtract 185 from 362.

Solution | *With units, strips, and mats*

We start with 3 mats, 6 strips, and 2 units.

362

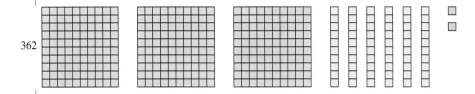

We want to take away 1 mat, 8 strips, and 5 units. Since we cannot pick up 5 units from our present arrangement, we exchange a strip for 10 units to obtain 3 mats, 5 strips and 12 units.

35(12)

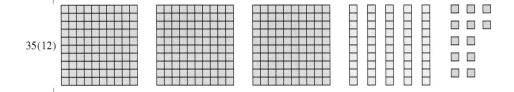

We can now take away 5 units, but we still cannot pick up 8 strips. Therefore, we exchange a mat for 10 strips to obtain 2 mats, 15 strips, and 12 units. Finally we are able to take away 1 mat, 8 strips, and 5 units (that is, 185 units) as shown. This leaves 1 mat, 7 strips, and 7 units. So

$$362 - 185 = 177.$$

2(15)(12)

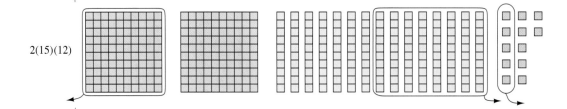

With place value cards

We must take away 1 marker from the 100s square, 8 markers from the 10s square, and 5 markers from the 1s square. To make this possible we trade 1 marker from the 10s square for 10 markers on the 1s square and 1 marker on the 100s square for 10 markers on the 10s square. Now, taking away the desired markers, we have 1 marker left on the 100s square, 7 markers left on the 10s square, and 7 markers left on the 1s square for 177.

With place value cards

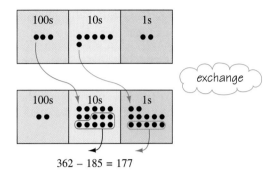

exchange

$$362 - 185 = 177$$

With place value diagrams and instructional algorithms

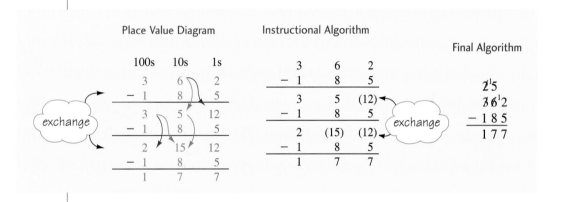

| Place Value Diagram | Instructional Algorithm | Final Algorithm |

JUST FOR FUN

What's the Difference?

Perform these subtractions.

91	95	42	62	74
− 19	− 59	− 24	− 26	− 47

61	82	81	32	54
− 16	− 28	− 18	− 23	− 45

(a)   What do you notice about the answer in each case?

(b)   Can you predict the answers to all problems like this just by looking at the two digits involved?

(c)   What seems to be true about the sums of the digits in the answers to all such 2-digit problems?

Algorithms in Other Bases

It is interesting to note that the algorithms for addition and subtraction are just as valid in base five or any other base as they are in base ten, and that the notions can be developed with manipulatives just as for base ten. Indeed, it is reasonable to consider other bases right along with base ten. Studied together this way, students gain a greater understanding of the whole idea of positional notation and the related algorithms. In base five, for example, the place value cards would have a units or 1s square, a 5s square, a 5^2 or 25s square, and so on. With sticks, we could use loose sticks, bundles of 5 sticks, bundles of 5 bundles of sticks, and so on. With units, strips, and mats, we would have units, strips with 5 units each, and mats with 5 strips per mat.

Adding in Base Five

The next example shows us how the addition algorithm works in base five. Let's see how the process works using place value cards.

EXAMPLE 3.17

Adding in Base Five

Compute the sum of 143_{five} and 234_{five} in base five notation.

Solution

With place value cards

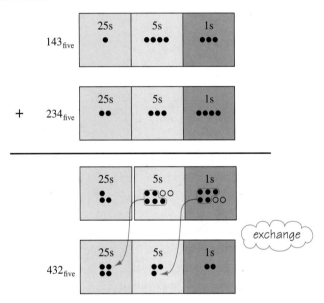

With place value diagrams and instructional algorithms

So the sum is 432_{five}.

To check the addition, we convert everything to base ten where we feel comfortable.

$$143_{\text{five}} = 1 \cdot 25 + 4 \cdot 5 + 3 \cdot 1 = 48_{\text{ten}}$$
$$234_{\text{five}} = 2 \cdot 25 + 3 \cdot 5 + 4 \cdot 1 = 69_{\text{ten}}$$
$$432_{\text{five}} = 4 \cdot 25 + 3 \cdot 5 + 2 \cdot 1 = 117_{\text{ten}}$$

The result is confirmed since $48_{\text{ten}} + 69_{\text{ten}} = 117_{\text{ten}}$.

The difficulty in doing base five arithmetic is unfamiliarity with the meaning of the symbols—we do not recognize at a glance, for example, that $8_{\text{ten}} = 13_{\text{five}}$. On the other hand, thinking of units, strips with 5 units per strip, and so on, it is not hard to think of 1 strip and 3 units as 8. In fact, doing arithmetic in another base gives good practice in mental arithmetic, which is a desirable end in itself. Of course, elementary school children memorize the addition and multiplication tables in base ten so that the needed symbols are readily recalled and we could do the same thing here. The addition table in base five, for example, is as shown.

+	0	1	2	3	4
0	0	1	2	3	4
1	1	2	3	4	10
2	2	3	4	10	11
3	3	4	10	11	12
4	4	10	11	12	13

These numerals are in base five.

This could be used to make the above addition easier and more immediate. From the table we see that $3 + 4 = 12_{\text{five}}$ so we write down the 2 and exchange the five 1s for a five in the fives column as shown in the final algorithm above. Next, $4 + 3 = 12_{\text{five}}$ and the 1 from the exchange gives 13_{five}. Thus, we write down the 3 and exchange the five 5s for one 25 in the next column. Finally, $1 + 2 = 3$ and 1 from the exchange makes 4, so we obtain 432_{five} as before. However, there is no merit in memorizing the addition table in base five; it is far better just to think carefully about what is going on.

Subtracting in Base Five

EXAMPLE 3.18

Subtracting in Base Five

Subtract 143_{five} from 234_{five} in base five notation.

Solution

With place value cards

There is no problem in taking away 3 markers from the 1s square, but we cannot remove 4 markers from the 5s square without exchanging 1 marker on the 25s square for 5 markers on the 5s square. Taking away the desired markers, we are left with zero 25s, four 5s, and one 1 for 41_{five}.

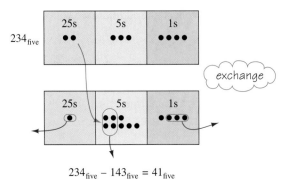

$$234_{\text{five}} - 143_{\text{five}} = 41_{\text{five}}$$

With place value diagrams and instructional algorithms

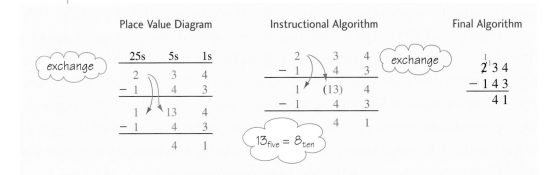

So the answer is 41_{five}.

As a check, we already know that $243_{\text{five}} = 69_{\text{ten}}$ and $143_{\text{five}} = 48_{\text{ten}}$. Since $69 - 48 = 21$ and $41_{\text{five}} = 4 \cdot 5 + 1 \cdot 1 = 21$, the calculation checks.

PROBLEM SET 3.3

Understanding Concepts

1. Sketch the solution to $36 + 75$ using:
   (a) mats, strips, and units. Draw a square for a mat, a vertical line segment for a strip, and a dot for a unit.
   (b) place value cards marked 1s, 10s, and 100s from right to left.

2. Use the addition Instructional Algorithm to perform the following additions:
   (a) $23 + 44$ (b) $57 + 84$ (c) $324 + 78$

3. The hand calculation of the sum 279 and 84 involves two exchanges and might appear as follows.

$$\begin{array}{r} {}^{11} \\ 279 \\ \underline{84} \\ 363 \end{array}$$

Carefully describe each of the exchanges. How would you explain these to a third grader?

4. While Sylvia was trying to balance her checkbook, her calculator battery went dead. When she added up the

outstanding checks by hand, her work looked like this. Is the addition correct? Discuss each of the exchanges shown. Is this how you would have proceeded? How else might you have done it?

$$
\begin{array}{r}
{}^{11} \\
2109 \\
308 \\
19 \\
207 \\
129 \\
208 \\
219 \\
307 \\
29 \\
108 \\
17 \\
209 \\
\underline{118} \\
3987
\end{array}
$$

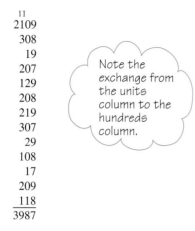

Note the exchange from the units column to the hundreds column.

5. Sketch the solution to $275 - 136$ using:

(a) mats, strips, and units.

(b) place value cards marked 1s, 10s, and 100s from right to left.

6. Use the subtraction Instructional Algorithm to perform these subtractions:

(a) $78 - 35$ **(b)** $75 - 38$ **(c)** $414 - 175$

7. The calculation of the difference $523 - 247$ might look like this.

$$
\begin{array}{r}
{}^{4}{}^{11} \\
\cancel{5}\ \cancel{2}{}^{1}3 \\
-\ 2\ 4\ 7 \\
\hline
2\ 7\ 6
\end{array}
$$

Carefully discuss the exchanges indicated. How would you explain these to a third grader?

8. The calculation of the difference $30007 - 1098$ might look like this.

$$
\begin{array}{r}
2\ 9\ 9\ 9 \\
\cancel{3}{}^{1}\cancel{0}{}^{1}\cancel{0}{}^{1}\cancel{0}{}^{1}7 \\
-\ \ \ 1\ 0\ 9\ 8 \\
\hline
2\ 8\ 9\ 0\ 9
\end{array}
$$

Carefully discuss the exchanges indicated.

---

9. Perform these additions and subtractions being careful not to leave more than 59 seconds or 59 minutes in your answers.

(a)   3 hours, 24 minutes, 54 seconds
     + 2 hours, 47 minutes, 38 seconds

(b)   7 hours, 56 minutes, 29 seconds
     + 3 hours, 27 minutes, 52 seconds

(c)   5 hours, 24 minutes, 54 seconds
     − 2 hours, 47 minutes, 38 seconds

(d)   7 hours, 46 minutes, 29 seconds
     − 3 hours, 27 minutes, 52 seconds

---

10. Julien spent one hour and 45 minutes mowing the lawn and two hours and 35 minutes trimming the hedge and some shrubs. How long did he work all together?

11. **(a)** Mr. Arronson has four pieces of oak flooring left over from a job he just completed. If they are 3' 8", 4' 2", 6' 10", and 5' 11" long, respectively, what total length of flooring does he have left over? Make sure the number of inches in your answer is less than 12.

(b) If Mr. Arronson uses 9'10" of the flooring left over in part (a) to make a picture frame, how much flooring does he have left over then?

12. The column by column addition of numbers can be justified as follows. State the property of the whole numbers that justifies each of these steps. We begin with expanded notation.

$$
\begin{aligned}
36 + 52 &= (3 \cdot 10 + 6) + (5 \cdot 10 + 2) \quad \text{expanded notation} \\
&= 3 \cdot 10 + [6 + (5 \cdot 10 + 2)] \quad \textbf{(a)} \underline{} \\
&= 3 \cdot 10 + [(6 + 5 \cdot 10) + 2] \quad \textbf{(b)} \underline{} \\
&= 3 \cdot 10 + [(5 \cdot 10 + 6) + 2] \quad \textbf{(c)} \underline{} \\
&= 3 \cdot 10 + [5 \cdot 10 + (6 + 2)] \quad \textbf{(d)} \underline{} \\
&= (3 \cdot 10 + 5 \cdot 10) + (6 + 2) \quad \textbf{(e)} \underline{} \\
&= (3 + 5) \cdot 10 + (6 + 2) \quad \textbf{(f)} \underline{} \\
&= 8 \cdot 10 + 8 \quad \text{addition facts} \\
&= 88 \quad \text{expanded notation}
\end{aligned}
$$

13. **(a)** In a single column, write the base four representations of the numbers from 0 to 15 inclusive.

(b) Briefly discuss any pattern you noticed in part (a).

14. Complete the addition table for base four arithmetic shown by placing the sum of $a + b$ at the intersection of the ath row and the bth column. The subscript "four" may be omitted here.

+	0	1	2	3
0				
1				
2				
3				

15. Complete the following computations in base four notation. The numerals are written in base four and the subscript indicating base four may be omitted from your work. Check your work by converting to base ten notation.

(a)
$$\begin{array}{r} 231 \\ +\ 121 \\ \hline \end{array}$$

(b)
$$\begin{array}{r} 303 \\ +\ \ 33 \\ \hline \end{array}$$

(c)
$$\begin{array}{r} 1223 \\ +\ \ 231 \\ \hline \end{array}$$

(d)
$$\begin{array}{r} 333 \\ +\ 101 \\ \hline \end{array}$$

(e)
$$\begin{array}{r} 32 \\ +\ 13 \\ \hline \end{array}$$

(f)
$$\begin{array}{r} 302 \\ -\ 103 \\ \hline \end{array}$$

(g)
$$\begin{array}{r} 212 \\ -\ \ 33 \\ \hline \end{array}$$

(h)
$$\begin{array}{r} 3102 \\ -\ 1033 \\ \hline \end{array}$$

Thinking Critically

16. On his way to school, Peter dropped his arithmetic paper in a puddle of water blotting out some of his work. What digits should go under the blots on these problems? (The base is ten.)

(a)
$$\begin{array}{r} 6\blacksquare 3 \\ +\blacksquare 51\blacksquare \\ \hline \blacksquare 2282 \end{array}$$

(b)
$$\begin{array}{r} 77\blacksquare \\ +\ \blacksquare\blacksquare 2 \\ \hline 871 \end{array}$$

(c)
$$\begin{array}{r} 8\blacksquare \\ +\ 362 \\ \hline \blacksquare 43 \end{array}$$

(d)
$$\begin{array}{r} 248\blacksquare \\ -1\blacksquare 22 \\ \hline \blacksquare 1\blacksquare 9 \end{array}$$

(e)
$$\begin{array}{r} 4\blacksquare 2 \\ -1843 \\ \hline \blacksquare 15\blacksquare \end{array}$$

(f)
$$\begin{array}{r} 34\blacksquare 5 \\ -\blacksquare 748 \\ \hline \blacksquare 2\blacksquare \end{array}$$

17. Find the missing digits in each of these base ten addition problems.

(a)
$$\begin{array}{r} \_437 \\ 2\_1 \\ +\ 347\_ \\ \hline 6\_94 \end{array}$$

(b)
$$\begin{array}{r} \_721 \\ 901\_ \\ +\ 71\_3 \\ \hline \_0\_26 \end{array}$$

(c)
$$\begin{array}{r} 38\_1 \\ 24\_3 \\ +\ 512\_ \\ \hline \_\_5\_9 \end{array}$$

(d)
$$\begin{array}{r} 5\_4 \\ 612\_ \\ +\ 8\_1 \\ \hline 76\_6 \end{array}$$

18. Fill in the missing digits in each of these base ten subtraction problems.

(a)
$$\begin{array}{r} \_3\_ \\ -\ 2\_1 \\ \hline 594 \end{array}$$

(b)
$$\begin{array}{r} 3\_\_4 \\ -\ \ 346 \\ \hline 175\_ \end{array}$$

(c)
$$\begin{array}{r} 7\_4\_ \\ -\ \_5\_4 \\ \hline 808 \end{array}$$

(d)
$$\begin{array}{r} 63\_\_4 \\ -\ 2\_12\_ \\ \hline \_6209 \end{array}$$

19. These additions and subtractions are written in different bases. Determine the base used in each case. (*Hint:* There may be more than one correct answer.)

(a)
$$\begin{array}{r} 231 \\ +\ 414 \\ \hline 1200 \end{array}$$

(b)
$$\begin{array}{r} 231 \\ +\ 414 \\ \hline 1045 \end{array}$$

(c)
$$\begin{array}{r} 231 \\ +\ 414 \\ \hline 645 \end{array}$$

(d)
$$\begin{array}{r} 344 \\ +\ 143 \\ \hline 1042 \end{array}$$

(e)
$$\begin{array}{r} 523 \\ -\ 254 \\ \hline 236 \end{array}$$

(f)
$$\begin{array}{r} 523 \\ -\ 254 \\ \hline 247 \end{array}$$

(g)
$$\begin{array}{r} 523 \\ -\ 254 \\ \hline 28E \end{array}$$

(h)
$$\begin{array}{r} 1020 \\ -\ 203 \\ \hline 312 \end{array}$$

20. There is a rather interesting addition algorithm called the **scratch** method that proceeds as follows. Consider this sum.

$$\begin{array}{r} 2\ 834 \\ 3\not7\not6 \\ 4\ \not835 \\ \underline{2\ 743} \\ 10,988 \end{array}$$

Begin by adding from the top down in the units column. When you add a digit that makes your sum 10 or more, scratch out the digit as shown and make a mental note of the units digit of your present sum. Start with the digit noted and continue adding and scratching until you have completed the units column, writing down the units digit of the last sum as the units digit of the answer as shown. Now, count the number of scratches in the units column and, starting with this number, add on down the tens column repeating the scratch process as you go. Continue the entire process until all the columns have been added. This gives the desired answer. Explain why the algorithm works.

Thinking Cooperatively

21. Form two 4-digit numbers using each of 1, 2, 3, 4, 5, 6, 7, and 8 once, and only once, so that

(a) the sum of the two numbers is as large as possible.

(b) the sum of the two numbers is as small as possible.

(c) You can do better than guess and check on parts (a) and (b). Explain your solution strategy briefly.

(d) Is there only one answer to each of parts (a) and (b)? Explain in two sentences.

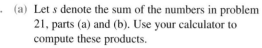 **22.** **(a)** Let s denote the sum of the numbers in problem 21, parts (a) and (b). Use your calculator to compute these products.

$$1 \cdot s = \underline{\hspace{2cm}}$$
$$2 \cdot s = \underline{\hspace{2cm}}$$
$$3 \cdot s = \underline{\hspace{2cm}}$$
$$4 \cdot s = \underline{\hspace{2cm}}$$
$$5 \cdot s = \underline{\hspace{2cm}}$$
$$6 \cdot s = \underline{\hspace{2cm}}$$
$$7 \cdot s = \underline{\hspace{2cm}}$$
$$8 \cdot s = \underline{\hspace{2cm}}$$
$$9 \cdot s = \underline{\hspace{2cm}}$$
$$10 \cdot s = \underline{\hspace{2cm}}$$

(b) Briefly discuss any patterns you notice in part (a).

(c) See if you can predict the product $41 \cdot s$ and then check the result with a calculator.

(d) Compute $14 \cdot s$, $23 \cdot s$, and $32 \cdot s$.

(e) Compute $6 \cdot s$, $17 \cdot s$, $28 \cdot s$, and $39 \cdot s$.

(f) What kind of sequences are 14, 23, 32, 41 and 6, 17, 28, 39?

23. Form two 4-digit numbers using each of the digits 1, 2, 3, 4, 5, 6, 7, and 8 precisely once so that:

(a) the difference of the two numbers is a natural number that is as small as possible.

(b) the difference of the two numbers is as large as possible.

(c) Briefly explain the strategy you used in solving this problem.

(d) Is there more than one solution to parts (a) and (b)? Why or why not?

For Review

24. Write two division equations and a second multiplication equation corresponding to each of these multiplication equations.

(a) $11 \cdot 91 = 1001$ **(b)** $7 \cdot 84 = 588$

(c) $13 \cdot 77 = 1001$

25. Write a multiplication equation and a second division equation corresponding to each of these division equations.

(a) $1001 \div 7 = 143$ **(b)** $323 \div 19 = 17$

(c) $899 \div 31 = 29$

26. If Jennifer Hurwitz had four sweaters, three blouses, and two pairs of slacks that all mixed and matched, how many different outfits consisting of a sweater, blouse, and pair of slacks could she wear?

27. Let $A = \{1, 2, 3, 4, 5\}$, $B = \{2, 4, 6, 8\}$, and $C = \{3, 4, 5, 6, 7\}$.

(a) Determine $A \cup B \cup C$, $A \cap B$, $A \cap C$, $B \cap C$, and $A \cap B \cap C$.

(b) Determine $n(A \cup B \cup C)$.

(c) Compute $n(A) + n(B) + n(C) - n(A \cap B) - n(A \cap C) - n(B \cap C) + n(A \cap B \cap C)$.

28. **(a)** Repeat problem 27 with three different sets A, B, and C of your own choosing.

(b) What general result do problems 27 and 28(a) suggest?

(c) Write a paragraph of argument that the result guessed in part (b) is true. (*Hint:* Consider an element x not in any of A, B, or C; y in A but not B or C, and so on.)

3.4 Algorithms for Multiplication and Division of Whole Numbers

Multiplication and division in most ancient numeration systems were quite complicated. The decimal system makes these processes much easier, but many people still find them confusing. At least part of the difficulty is that the ideas are often presented as a collection of rules to be learned by rote, with little or no effort made to impart understanding. In this section we endeavor to strip away some of the mystery.

Multiplication Algorithms

Multiplication is repeated addition. Thus, $2 \cdot 9$ means $9 + 9$, $3 \cdot 9$ means $9 + 9 + 9$, and so on. But repeated addition is slow and tedious and easier algorithms exist. As with addition and subtraction, these should be introduced starting with concrete approaches and gradually becoming more and more abstract. The development should proceed through units, strips, and mats; place value cards; classroom abacuses; and so on. Let's consider the product $9 \cdot 3$.

EXAMPLE 3.19	## Developing the Multiplication Algorithm

Compute the product of 9 and 3.

Solution

Using units, strips, and mats

Since $9 \cdot 3 = 3 + 3 + 3 + 3 + 3 + 3 + 3 + 3 + 3$, we can illustrate this as shown with 9 rows of 3 units each. Simplifying the original array by appropriately exchanging units for strips, we eventually have 2 strips and 7 units which is recorded as 27. Of course, elementary school children should actually handle the materials, making the necessary exchanges of units for strips.

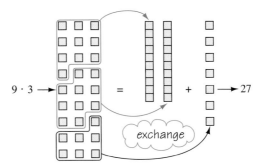

Using place value cards

With place value cards students should start with 9 rows of 3 markers each on the 1s square of their place value cards as shown here. They then exchange 10 markers on the 1s square for 1 marker on the 10s square as many times as possible, and record the fact that this gives 2 tens plus 7 units or 27.

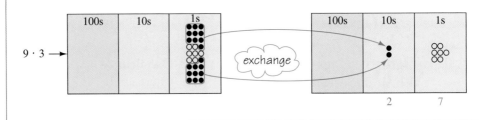

Using manipulatives as illustrated, children can experience, learn and actually *understand* all the one-digit multiplication facts. It should not be the case that $9 \cdot 3 = 27$ is a string of meaningless symbols memorized by rote. This basic fact must be understood.

Once the 1-digit facts are thoroughly understood *and memorized,* as they must be, even for intelligent use of a calculator, one can move on to more complicated problems. Consider, for example, $3 \cdot 213$. This could be illustrated with units, strips, and mats but, for brevity, we will go directly to place value cards, expanded notation, and then to an algorithm as illustrated in the following figure. Again we make use of the understanding that $3 \cdot 213 = 213 + 213 + 213$.

EXAMPLE   3.20

Computing a Product with a Multi-digit Number

Compute the product of 3 and 213.

Solution   *Using place value cards, expanded notation, and algorithms*

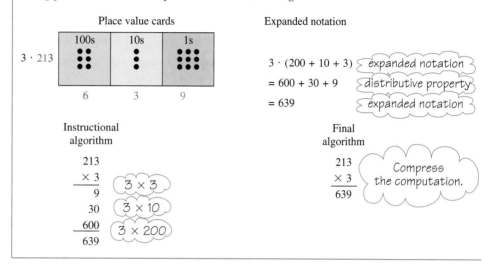

The product $3 \cdot 213$ did not require exchanging. Consider the product $4 \cdot 243$. Presentation of this product proceeds from the concrete representation to the final algorithm.

EXAMPLE   3.21

Multiplying with Exchanging

Compute the product of 4 and 243.

Solution   *Using place value cards, expanded notation, and algorithms*

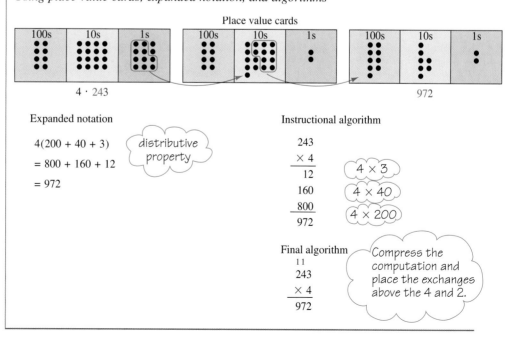

The preceding development represents many lessons. However, the various demonstrations should clearly be tied together and enough time should be spent to assure that each level of the chain of reasoning is understood before proceeding to the next.

Finally, consider the product 15 · 324. Unquestionably, the most efficient algorithm is that provided by the calculator. The pencil and paper algorithm, however, is not unusually difficult as the following series of calculations show.

EXAMPLE   3.22

Multiplying Multi-digit Numbers

Compute the product of 15 and 324.

Solution   *Using expanded notation, an instructional algorithm, and the final algorithm*

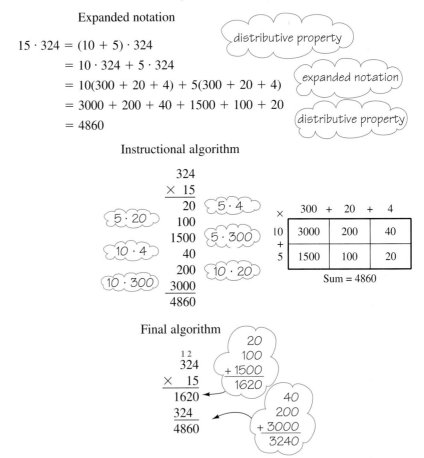

Expanded notation

$$15 \cdot 324 = (10 + 5) \cdot 324$$
$$= 10 \cdot 324 + 5 \cdot 324$$
$$= 10(300 + 20 + 4) + 5(300 + 20 + 4)$$
$$= 3000 + 200 + 40 + 1500 + 100 + 20$$
$$= 4860$$

distributive property

expanded notation

distributive property

Instructional algorithm

Multiplication in Other Bases

As with the algorithms for addition and subtraction, the multiplication algorithm depends on the idea of positional notation but is independent of the base. The arithmetic is more awkward since we do not think in other bases as we do in base ten, but the ideas are the same. However, working in other bases not only enhances understanding of base ten but also provides an interesting activity that helps to improve mental arithmetic skills. Let's consider an example.

EXAMPLE   3.23

Multiplication in Base Six

Compute the product $24_{six} \cdot 315_{six}$ in base six.

Solution

We use the base six positional values from Table 3.8 and the instructional algorithm of Example 3.22. To simplify notation, we will write all *numerals* in base six notation so that the subscripts will be omitted. Finally, the numeral *words* will have their usual base ten meaning. The work proceeds as shown, with descriptive comments in the "think cloud."

$$
\begin{array}{r}
324 \\
\times\ 15 \\
\hline
32 \\
140 \\
2300 \\
40 \\
200 \\
3000 \\
\hline
10152
\end{array}
$$

Think

$5 \times 4 = \text{twenty} = 3 \text{ sixes} + 2 \text{ units} = 3 \cdot 6^1 + 2 \cdot 6^0 = 32_{six}$

$5 \times 20 = 5 \times 2 \text{ sixes} = \text{ten sixes} = (1 \cdot 6 + 4) \cdot 6^1 = 1 \cdot 6^2 + 4 \cdot 6^1 + 0 \cdot 6^0 = 140_{six}$

$5 \times 300 = 5 \times 3 \text{ thirty-sixes} = 15 \text{ thirty-sixes} = (2 \cdot 6 + 3) \cdot 6^2 = 2 \cdot 6^3 + 3 \cdot 6^2 + 0 \cdot 6^1 + 0 \cdot 6^0 = 2300_{six}$

$10 \times 4 = 1 \text{ six} \times 4 = 4 \cdot 6^1 + 0 \cdot 6^0 = 40_{six}$

$10 \times 20 = 1 \text{ six} \times 2 \text{ sixes} = 2 \cdot 6^2 + 0 \cdot 6^1 + 0 \cdot 6^0 = 200_{six}$

$10 \times 300 = 1 \text{ six} \times 3 \text{ thirty-sixes} = 3 \cdot 6^3 + 0 \cdot 6^2 + 0 \cdot 6^1 + 0 \cdot 6^0 = 3000_{six}$

To check, we convert all numerals to base ten.

$$324_{six} = 3 \cdot 6^2 + 2 \cdot 6^1 + 4 \cdot 6^0$$
$$= 3 \cdot 36 + 2 \cdot 6 + 4 \cdot 1$$
$$= 108 + 12 + 4 = 124_{ten}$$
$$15_{six} = 1 \cdot 6^1 + 5 \cdot 6^0$$
$$= 1 \cdot 6 + 5 \cdot 1$$
$$= 6 + 5 = 11_{ten}$$
$$10152_{six} = 1 \cdot 6^4 + 0 \cdot 6^3 + 1 \cdot 6^2 + 5 \cdot 6^1 + 2 \cdot 6^0$$
$$= 1 \cdot 1296 + 0 \cdot 216 + 1 \cdot 36 + 5 \cdot 6 + 2 \cdot 1$$
$$= 1296 + 36 + 30 + 2 = 1364_{ten}$$

Since $11_{ten} \cdot 124_{ten} = 1364_{ten}$, the check is complete.

Division Algorithms

An approach to division discussed in Chapter 2 was repeated subtraction. This ultimately led to the so-called **division algorithm,** which we restate here for easy reference.

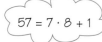
$57 = 7 \cdot 8 + 1$

THEOREM   *The Division Algorithm*

If a and b are whole numbers with b not zero, there exists precisely one pair of whole numbers q and r with $0 \le r < b$ such that $a = bq + r$.

The Long Division Algorithm

Suppose we want to divide 941 by 7. Doing this by repeated subtraction will take a long time even with a calculator. But suppose we subtract several sevens at a time and keep track of the number we subtract each time. Indeed, since it is so easy to multiply a number by 10, 100, 1000, and so on, let's subtract hundreds of sevens, tens of sevens, and so on. The work might be organized like this.

```
7)941
  700       Subtract  100 sevens
  241
   70       Subtract   10 sevens
  171
   70       Subtract   10 sevens
  101
   70       Subtract   10 sevens
   31
   28       Subtract    4 sevens
    3                  134 number of sevens subtracted
```

Since $3 < 7$, the process stops and we see that 941 divided by 7 gives a quotient of 134 and a remainder of 3. As a check we note that $941 = 7 \cdot 134 + 3$. The above work could have been shortened if we had subtracted the three tens of sevens all at once and then the four sevens all at once like this.

```
7)941
  700       100
  241
  210        30
   31
   28         4
    3       134
```

A slightly different form of this algorithm, sometimes called the **scaffold** algorithm, is obtained by writing the 100, 30, and 4 above the divide symbol like this.

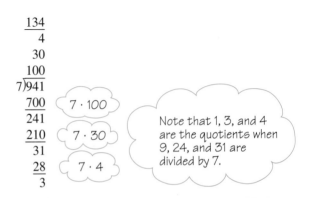

```
    134
      4
     30
    100
  7)941
    700    7 · 100
    241
    210    7 · 30
     31
     28    7 · 4
      3
```

Note that 1, 3, and 4 are the quotients when 9, 24, and 31 are divided by 7.

Many teachers prefer the scaffold algorithm as the final algorithm for division since it fully displays the mathematics being done. Others still cling to the following, which is easily obtained from the scaffold algorithm, even though it seriously masks the mathematics and forces many students to rely on rote memorization rather than understanding.

$$
\begin{array}{r}
134 \\
7\overline{)941} \\
\underline{7} \\
24 \\
\underline{21} \\
31 \\
\underline{28} \\
3
\end{array}
$$

A further example with a larger divisor may be helpful.

EXAMPLE 3.24

Using the Long Division Algorithm

Divide 28,762 by 307.

Solution

Scaffold algorithm   Standard algorithm

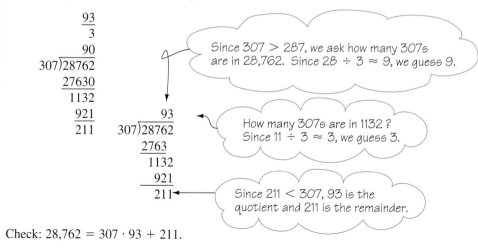

Check: $28{,}762 = 307 \cdot 93 + 211$.

JUST FOR FUN

What's the Sum?

Perform these additions.

$$
\begin{array}{ccccc}
91 & 95 & 42 & 62 & 74 \\
\underline{+\ 19} & \underline{+\ 59} & \underline{+\ 24} & \underline{+\ 26} & \underline{+\ 47} \\
\end{array}
$$

$$
\begin{array}{ccccc}
61 & 82 & 81 & 32 & 54 \\
\underline{+\ 16} & \underline{+\ 28} & \underline{+\ 18} & \underline{+\ 23} & \underline{+\ 45} \\
\end{array}
$$

(a) Investigate the results of dividing the answers to the above additions by 11.

(b) Can you predict the answers to all problems just by looking at the two digits involved?

The Short Division Algorithm

A division algorithm that is quite useful, even in this calculator age, is the **short division** algorithm. This is a much simplified version of the long division algorithm and is quite useful and quick when the divisor is a single digit. This can be developed using the scaffold method as above. Also, it follows directly from the long division algorithm if that is already known.

EXAMPLE 3.25	**Using the Short Division Algorithm**

Divide 2834 by 3 and check your answer.

Solution   Consider the following divisions which show how the short division algorithm derives from the long division algorithm.

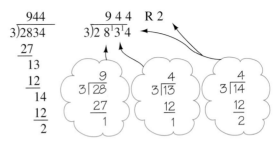

$$
\begin{array}{r}
944 \\
3\overline{)2834} \\
27 \\
\hline
13 \\
12 \\
\hline
14 \\
12 \\
\hline
2
\end{array}
$$

PROBLEM SET 3.4

Understanding Concepts

(Note: Problems 1 through 11 are all base ten problems.)

1. (a) Make a suitable drawing of units and strips to illustrate the product $4 \cdot 8 = 32$.

    (b) Make a suitable sketch of place value cards to illustrate the product $4 \cdot 8 = 32$.

2. Make a suitable sketch of place value cards to illustrate the product $3 \cdot 254 = 762$.

3. (a) In the product shown, what does the colored 2 actually represent?

$$
\begin{array}{r}
2 \\
274 \\
\times \quad 34 \\
\hline
1\,096 \\
8\,22 \\
\hline
9,316
\end{array}
$$

    (b) In the product shown in part (a) when multiplying $4 \cdot 7$ one "exchanges" a 2. What is actually being exchanged?

4. The diagram shown illustrates the product $27 \cdot 32$. Discuss how this is related to finding the product by the Instructional Algorithm.

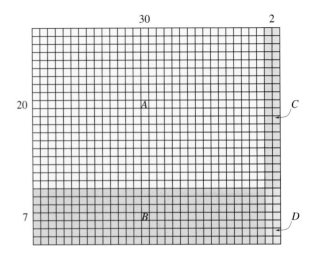

5. What property of the whole numbers justifies each step in this calculation?

    $17 \cdot 4 = (10 + 7) \cdot 4$ expanded notation
    $= 10 \cdot 4 + 7 \cdot 4$ **(a)** _____
    $= 10 \cdot 4 + 28$ 1-digit multiplication fact
    $= 10 \cdot 4 + (2 \cdot 10 + 8)$ expanded notation
    $= 4 \cdot 10 + (2 \cdot 10 + 8)$ **(b)** _____
    $= (4 \cdot 10 + 2 \cdot 10) + 8$ **(c)** _____
    $= (4 + 2) \cdot 10 + 8$ **(d)** _____
    $= 6 \cdot 10 + 8$ 1-digit addition fact
    $= 68$ expanded notation

6. Draw a sequence of sketches of units, strips, and mats to illustrate dividing 429 by 3.

7. What calculation does this sequence of sketches illustrate? Explain briefly.

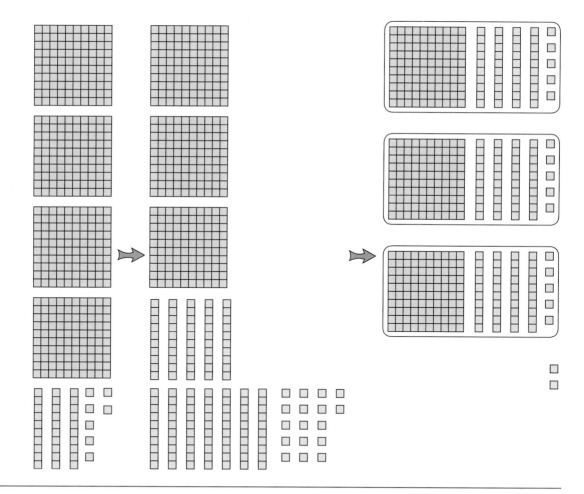

8. Multiply 352 by 27 using the Instructional Algorithm.

9. Find the quotient q and a remainder r when a is divided by b and write the result in the form $a = bq + r$ of the division algorithm for each of these choices of a and b.

    (a) $a = 27$, $b = 4$ **(b)** $a = 354$, $b = 29$
    (c) $a = 871$, $b = 17$

10. Perform each of the following divisions by the scaffold method. In each case check your results by using the equation of the division algorithm.

   (a) $351\overline{)7425}$ (b) $23\overline{)6814}$ (c) $213\overline{)3175}$

11. Use short division to find the quotient and remainder for each of these. Check each result.

   (a) $5\overline{)873}$ (b) $7\overline{)2432}$ (c) $8\overline{)10,095}$

(Note: Problems 12 through 15 are in bases other than ten.)

12. Construct base five addition and multiplication tables.

13. What is being illustrated by the following sequence of sketches of place value cards? Explain briefly.

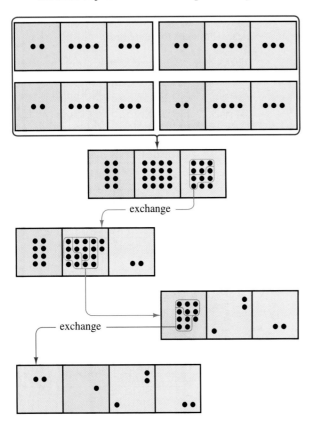

14. Carry out these multiplications using base five notation. All the numerals are already written in base five so that no subscript is needed.

   (a) $\begin{array}{r} 23 \\ \times\ 3 \\ \hline \end{array}$ (b) $\begin{array}{r} 432 \\ \times\ 41 \\ \hline \end{array}$ (c) $\begin{array}{r} 2013 \\ \times\ 23 \\ \hline \end{array}$

   (d) Convert the numerals in parts (a), (b), and (c) to base ten and check the results of your base five computations.

15. Carry out these divisions using base five notation. All numerals are already in base five so that the subscripts are omitted.

   (a) $4\overline{)231}$ (b) $32\overline{)2342}$ (c) $213\overline{)34122}$

(d) Convert the numerals in parts (a), (b), and (c) to base ten and check the results of your base five computations.

Thinking Critically

16. The **Egyptian algorithm** for multiplication was one of the interesting subjects explained in the Rhind papyrus mentioned in Chapters 1 and 2. We will explain the algorithm by giving the following example. Suppose we want to compute 19 times 35. Successively doubling 35 we obtain this list.

$$
\begin{array}{rl}
\rightarrow & 1 \cdot 35 = 35 \\
\rightarrow & 2 \cdot 35 = 70 \\
 & 4 \cdot 35 = 140 \\
 & 8 \cdot 35 = 280 \\
\rightarrow & 16 \cdot 35 = 560
\end{array}
$$

$19 = 1 + 2 + 16$

Adding the results in the indicated rows gives us 665 as the desired product.

(a) After carefully considering the above computation, write a short paragraph explaining how and why the process always works.

(b) This scheme is also known as the **duplation algorithm.** Use duplation to find the product of 24 and 71.

17. The **Russian peasant algorithm** for multiplication is similar to the duplation algorithm described in problem 16. To find the product of 34 and 54, for example, successively divide the 34 by 2 (ignoring remainders if they occur) and successively multiply 54 by 2. This gives the following lists.

34	54
17	108
8	216
4	432
2	864
1	1728
	1836

Now cross out the even numbers in the left-hand column and the companion numbers in the right-hand column. Add the remaining numbers in the right-hand column to obtain the desired product. To see why the process works, consider the products $34 \cdot 54 = 1836$ and $17 \cdot 108 = 1836$. Also, consider $8 \cdot 216$, $4 \cdot 432$, and $2 \cdot 864$.

(a) Why are $34 \cdot 54$ and $17 \cdot 108$ the same?

(b) Why are $17 \cdot 108$ and $8 \cdot 216$ different? How much do they differ?

(c) Why are $8 \cdot 216$, $4 \cdot 432$, $2 \cdot 864$, and $1 \cdot 1728$ all the same?

(d) Write a short paragraph explaining why the Russian peasant algorithm works.

(e) Use the Russian peasant algorithm to compute $29 \cdot 81$ and $11 \cdot 243$.

18. Another multiplication algorithm is the **lattice algorithm.** Suppose, for example, you want to multiply 324 by 73. Form a two by three rectangular array of boxes with the 3, 2, and 4 across the top and the 7 and 3 down the right side as shown. Now compute the products $3 \cdot 7 = 21$, $2 \cdot 7 = 14$, $4 \cdot 7 = 28$, $3 \cdot 3 = 9$, $2 \cdot 3 = 6$, and $4 \cdot 3 = 12$. Place the products in the appropriate boxes ($3 \cdot 7$ is in the 3 column and the 7 row) with the units digit of the product below the diagonal in each box and the tens digit (if there is one) above the diagonal. Now add down the diagonals and add any "exchanges" to the sum in the next diagonal. The result of 23,652 is the desired product.

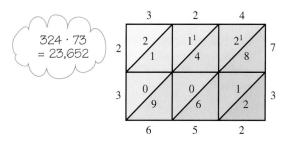

(a) Multiply 374 by 215 using the lattice algorithm.

(b) Write a short paragraph comparing the lattice algorithm with the standard pencil and paper algorithm.

19. Consider the following computation.

$$\begin{array}{r} 374 \\ \times\ \ 23 \\ \hline 748 \\ 1122 \\ \hline 8602 \end{array}$$

(a) Is the algorithm correct? Explain briefly.

(b) Multiply 285 by 362 by this method.

20. Earlier in this chapter we showed how to convert a base ten numeral for a number into a numeral in another base. The process was described as it was to impart proper understanding. However, the conversion can be completed much more easily. The trouble with showing this new scheme (at least in the beginning) is that it can be carried out with absolutely no understanding. Using the earlier method, we find that $583_{\text{ten}} = 4313_{\text{five}}$. Now let's see how the new scheme works. Divide 583 by 5 to obtain a quotient and a remainder, then divide the quotient by 5 and record the next remainder, and so on like this:

Remarkably, $4313_{\text{five}} = 583_{\text{ten}}$ as we have just seen. But why does the method work? If we write each of the above divisions in the form of the division algorithm, we have

$$583 = 5 \cdot 116 + 3$$
$$116 = 5 \cdot 23 + 1$$

and

$$23 = 5 \cdot 4 + 3.$$

Combining these, we obtain

$$\begin{aligned} 583 &= 5 \cdot 116 + 3 \\ &= 5(5 \cdot 23 + 1) + 3 \\ &= 5^2 \cdot 23 + 5 \cdot 1 + 3 \\ &= 5^2(5 \cdot 4 + 3) + 5 \cdot 1 + 3 \\ &= 5^3 \cdot 4 + 5^2 \cdot 3 + 5 \cdot 1 + 3 \end{aligned}$$

and this is the expanded form of 4313_{five}. Thus, $583_{\text{ten}} = 4313_{\text{five}}$ as noted. Write 482_{ten} in each of these bases and check by reconverting the numeral obtained to base ten.

(a) base seven   **(b)** base four

(c) base two   **(d)** base twelve

Thinking Cooperatively

Divide into small groups to work each of the next three problems. In each case, discuss possible strategies among your group and develop an answer agreed upon by the entire group

21. Use each of 1, 3, 5, 7, and 9 once, and only once, in the boxes to obtain the largest possible product in each case.

(a)

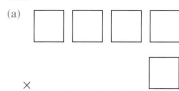

(b)

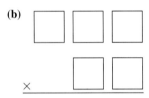

22. Use each of 1, 3, 5, 7, and 9 once, and only once, in the boxes to obtain the smallest possible product in each case.

(a)

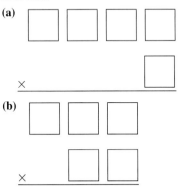

(b)

23. A druggist has a balance scale to weigh objects. She also has two 1-gram weights, two 3-gram weights, two 9-gram weights, and two 27-gram weights. She places an object to be weighed in one pan and her weights in the other.

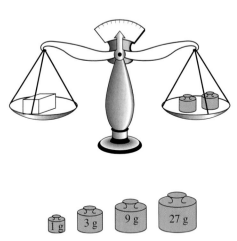

(a) What weights can she weigh in this way?

(b) What mathematics would this activity be illustrating if you did it in one of your classes?

24. Suppose you had only one of each type of weight and that you could put weights in both scales, some along with the object being weighed.

(a) What weights of objects could you possibly weigh in this way?

(b) Could you "weigh" a balloon filled with helium that was tied to one of the pans of the scales and exerted an upward pull of 11 grams on the pan? What balloons could you "weigh" in this way?

Using a Calculator

25. **(a)** Compute 375×2432.

(b) Examine the following calculation where certain zeros are suppressed.

		24	32
$\times$		3	75
1	1		
		24	00
	18	00	
		96	
	72		
91	20	00	

$$75 \cdot 32$$
$$75 \cdot 2400$$
$$300 \cdot 32$$
$$300 \cdot 2400$$

Note that this agrees with your answer to part (a). Use the same idea to compute the following product which would ordinarily exceed the capacity of your calculator.

	3748	2325
$\times$	263	1473

26. **Computing quotients on a calculator with Integer Divide.** Some calculators, like the Texas Instruments *Math Explorer,* have an integer divide key, $\boxed{\text{INT} \div}$, that gives the quotient and remainder when one integer is divided by another. Use the integer divide key to find the quotient and remainder when

(a) 723 is divided by 37.

(b) 34,723 is divided by 508.

27. **Computing quotients and remainders on a standard calculator.** On most calculators, the remainder of a division of integers is expressed as the decimal part of the display. Thus, dividing 34,678 by 44 gives the answer 788.13636 on a calculator that displays eight digits. The quotient is the integer part of the displayed answer and the decimal part of the display is $R \div 44$ where R is the remainder. To compute the remainder, subtract the quotient, 788, leaving 0.1363636 in the display (since the calculator actually works with greater accuracy than it shows). Since 0.1363636 represents $R \div 44$, just multiply by 44 to obtain the remainder.

Actually, because of round off error, the *Math Explorer* gives 5.9999997, which you should interpret as 6 since R is a whole number. To check, note that 34,678 = 788 · 44 + 6. Note that other calculators may well give something different from 5.9999997 depending on their built-in accuracy, but it will be a number quite close to 6 and should be so interpreted. Without using the integer divide key, use your calculator to compute the quotient and remainder when

(a) 276,523 is divided by 511.

(b) 347,285 is divided by 87.

(c) 374,821 is divided by 357.

28. The integer divide capability of the *Math Explorer* and some other calculators makes it particularly easy to change from base ten notation to notation in another base using the method described in problem 20 above. For example, 583_{ten} can be converted to base five by entering the following string in the calculator and noting the remainder after each division.

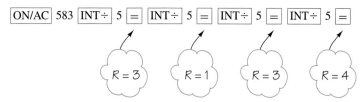

Writing the remainders in reverse order we find that the base five representation of 583_{ten} is 4313_{five}. Use a calculator (and the method of problem 26 if necessary) to determine the representation of 5781_{ten} in each of the following bases.

(a) base five   (b) base seven   (c) base twelve   (d) base six

From State Student Assessments

29. (Washington State, Grade 4)

When Lori tries multiplying with her calculator, she gets the following results.

$$8 \times 3 = 34 \qquad 4 \times 2 = 18$$
$$9 \times 5 = 55 \qquad 8 \times 4 = 42$$

Lori knows her multiplication facts and knows that something is wrong with her calculator. She wants to multiply 9×6. Explain what is wrong with Lori's calculator and tell what she needs to do to get the correct answer. Use words, numbers, or pictures.

For Review

30. An alternative to using expanded form in explaining addition and subtraction algorithms is to write out in words what numerals mean. For example, we could write

$$232 = 2 \text{ hundreds} + 3 \text{ tens} + 2 \text{ ones}$$

which we might call **word expanded form.** Then, we could write

$$232 = 2 \text{ hundreds} + 3 \text{ tens} + 2 \text{ ones}$$
$$+ 465 = 4 \text{ hundreds} + 6 \text{ tens} + 5 \text{ ones}$$
$$\overline{\qquad 6 \text{ hundreds} + 9 \text{ tens} + 7 \text{ ones}}$$
$$= 697$$

Use word expanded form to perform these additions and subtractions.

(a)   634   (b)   247   (c)   383
    + 163   + 332   + 532

(d)   674   (e)   725   (f)   544
    − 122   − 413   − 432

31. Note that

2 hundreds + 14 tens + 5 ones

$$= 2 \text{ hundreds} + 10 \text{ tens} + 4 \text{ tens} + 5 \text{ ones}$$
$$= 2 \text{ hundreds} + 1 \text{ hundred} + 4 \text{ tens} + 5 \text{ ones}$$
$$= 3 \text{ hundreds} + 4 \text{ tens} + 5 \text{ ones}$$

Now perform these additions and subtractions using word expanded form.

(a)   374   (b)   264   (c)   724
    + 483   + 327   + 532

(d)   418   (e)   367   (f)   642
    − 237   − 249   − 246

32. In base five, the word expanded form of 231 is 2 twenty-fives + 3 fives + 1 one. Use the base five word expanded form to perform each of these additions and subtractions.

(a)   213   (b)   332   (c)   142
    + 131   + 12   + 123

(d)   231   (e)   344   (f)   342
    − 130   − 232   − 104

33. Write 495_{ten} and 7821_{ten} in base six

   (a) using the positional value method and Table 3.8, in Section 3.2.

   (b) using the short division with remainder method of problem 20 above.

34. Perform these computations entirely in base five. The numerals are already written in base five, so the subscripts are omitted.

(a)	34 + 23	(b)	243 + 22	(c)	312 − 21

(d)	423 − 234	(e)	32 × 4	(f)	241 × 22

(g) $23\overline{)344}$ (h) $32\overline{)2341}$

Calvin and Hobbes   by Bill Watterson

COOPERATIVE INVESTIGATION

Magic in Base Three

Materials Needed

A deck of cards.

Discussion

This is an extremely effective card trick that surprises and excites students. They immediately want to know how the trick is done, and this provides great motivation for learning. Doing the trick well in front of a group requires only basic knowledge of base three numeration, a quick eye, and the ability to do just a small amount of arithmetic while keeping up a steady stream of chatter about mind reading and other psychic nonsense. For students the activity is a great skill and understanding builder with many times the benefit of dull drill and practice. To pull the trick off, proceed as follows.

Step 1. Shuffle a deck of playing cards several times and then count off 27 cards from the top of the deck setting the remaining 25 cards aside.

Step 2. Ask someone to volunteer as your assistant. With your back turned, ask the assistant to

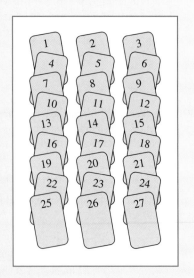

select one of the 27 cards and show it to the audience so that all can see. Then move off to the side where you cannot possibly see individual cards and ask the assistant to lay out the cards face up on the desk in the order shown. Note that the numbers in the drawing only indicate the order in which the cards are to be distributed. Thus, 1 might be the queen of spades, 2 the three of diamonds, and so on.

Step 3. Ask the assistant to tell you which column contains the chosen card and then to scoop up the cards by columns and place them face up in his or her hand. At this point you must be especially aware of the way in which the cards are picked up. Carefully watch where the column containing the selected card is placed. There are three positions in the assistant's hand. The column in question can be placed in

the 0 position—next to the palm
the 1 position—in the middle
the 2 position—away from the palm

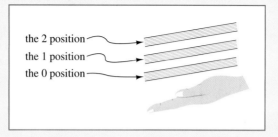

the 2 position
the 1 position
the 0 position

as indicated in the diagram. Using this numbering, the first time the cards are picked up determines the units digit in the base three representation of a number n and you make a mental note of 0, 1, or 2 as appropriate.

Step 4. After the cards are picked up, ask the assistant to turn the assembled pack of all 27 cards face down in his or her hand and then to redistribute them as in step 2.

Step 5. Again ask the assistant to tell you in which column the selected card lies and then to pick them up as in step 3. Carefully watch to see where the critical column is placed. This determines the 3s digit of n. Note 0, 3, or 6 as appropriate and add it to the number you are remembering from step 3.

Step 6. Ask the assistant to repeat steps 4 and 5 once more, thus determining the 9s digit of n. Note 0, 9, or 18 as appropriate and add it to the sum determined in step 5. This determines n.

Step 7. Finally, ask the assistant to place the assembled cards face down in his or her hand and count down to the card numbered $n + 1$. Everyone will be surprised to see that this is the chosen card!

But there is more. What if you had 9 cards? 81 cards? 243 cards? Could the trick be modified so that it would still work? Could a similar trick be worked out for other bases? A little experimenting would suggest answers to these questions. *Note:* An equally effective alternative form of this trick is explained in the Instructor's Solution Manual.

3.5 Mental Arithmetic and Estimation

The ability to make accurate estimates and do mental arithmetic is increasingly important in today's society. When buying several items in a store it is helpful to know before you go to the cashier that you have enough money to pay for your purchase. It is also worthwhile to keep a mental check on the cashier to make sure that you are charged correctly.

More importantly, as we increase our use of calculators and computers, it has become essential that we be able to tell if an answer is "about right." Because of their quickness and the neatness with which they display answers, it is tempting to accept as true whatever answer your calculator or computer gives. It is quite easy to enter an incorrect number or press an incorrect operation key and so obtain an incorrect answer. Care must be exercised, and this requires estimation skills.

The One-Digit Facts

It is essential that the basic addition and multiplication facts be memorized since all other numerical calculations and estimations depend on this foundation. At the same time, this should not be rote memorization of symbols. Using a variety of concrete objects students should actually *experience* the fact that $8 + 7 = 15$, that $9 \cdot 7 = 63$, and so on. Moreover, rather than having children simply memorize the addition and multiplication tables, these should be learned by the frequent and long-term use of manipulatives, games, puzzles, oral activities, and appropriate problem-solving activities. In the same way, children learn the basic properties of the whole numbers which, in turn, can be used to recall some momentarily forgotten arithmetic fact. For example, $7 + 8$ can be recalled as $7 + 7 + 1, 6 \cdot 9$ can be recalled as $5 \cdot 9 + 9$, and so on. In the same way, the properties of whole numbers along with the one-digit facts form the basis for mental calculation. Here are several strategies for mental calculation.

Easy Combinations

Always look for **easy combinations** in doing mental calculations. The next example shows how this works.

EXAMPLE 3.26	**Using Easy Combinations**

Use mental processes to perform these calculations.

(a) $35 + 7 + 15$ (b) $8 + 3 + 4 + 6 + 7 + 12 + 4 + 3 + 6 + 3$
(c) $25 \cdot 8$ (d) $4 \cdot 99$ (e) $57 - 25$ (f) $47 \cdot 5$

Solution

(a)   Using the commutative and associative properties, we have

$$35 + 7 + 15 = 35 + 5 + 10 + 7 = 40 + 10 + 7 = 50 + 7 = 57$$

Think   35, 40, 50, 57   The answer is 57.

(b)   Note numbers that add to 10 or multiples of 10.

$$8 + 3 + 4 + 6 + 7 + 12 + 4 + 3 + 6 + 3 = 56$$

Think   20, 30, 40, 50, 53, 56   The answer is 56.

(c) $25 \cdot 8 = 25 \cdot 4 \cdot 2 = 100 \cdot 2 = 200.$

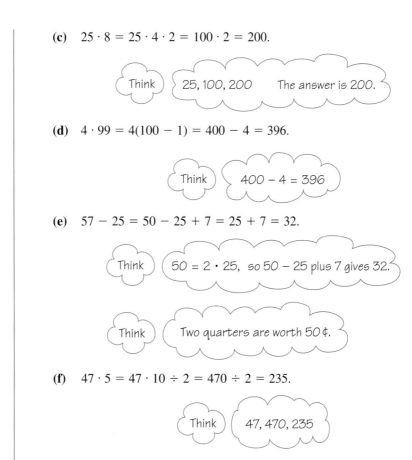

Think   25, 100, 200   The answer is 200.

(d) $4 \cdot 99 = 4(100 - 1) = 400 - 4 = 396.$

Think $400 - 4 = 396$

(e) $57 - 25 = 50 - 25 + 7 = 25 + 7 = 32.$

Think $50 = 2 \cdot 25,$ so $50 - 25$ plus 7 gives 32.

Think   Two quarters are worth 50¢.

(f) $47 \cdot 5 = 47 \cdot 10 \div 2 = 470 \div 2 = 235.$

Think   47, 470, 235

Adjustment

In parts (d) and (e) of Example 3.26, we made use of the fact that 99 and 57 were close to 100 and 50, respectively. This is an example of adjustment. **Adjustment** simply means that we modify numbers in a calculation to minimize the mental effort required.

EXAMPLE   3.27

Using Adjustment in Mental Calculation

Use mental processes to perform these calculations.

(a) $57 + 84$	**(b)** $83 - 48$	**(c)** $286 + 347$
(d) $493 \cdot 7$	**(e)** $2646 \div 9$	**(f)** $639 \div 7$

Solution

(a) $57 + 84 = (57 + 3) + (84 - 3)$
$= 60 + 81 = 60 + 80 + 1$
$= 140 + 1 = 141$

Think $57 + 84,$ $60 + 81,$ 140,   141

(b) $83 - 48 = (83 + 2) - (48 + 2) = 85 - 50 = 35.$

Think $83 - 48,\ \ 85 - 50,\ \ 35$

(c) $286 + 347 = (286 + 14) + (347 - 14)$
$$= 300 + 300 + 47 - 14$$
$$= 600 + 33 = 633$$

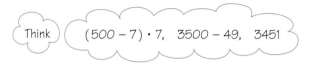

Think $300,\ \ 647 - 14,\ \ 633$

(d) $493 \cdot 7 = (500 - 7) \cdot 7 = 3500 - 49 = 3451.$

Think $(500 - 7) \cdot 7,\ \ 3500 - 49,\ \ 3451$

(e) $2646 \div 9 = (2700 - 54) \div 9 = 300 - 6 = 294.$

Think $\div 9,\ \ 2700 - 54,\ \ 300 - 6,\ \ 294$

(f) $639 \div 7 = (630 + 7 + 2) \div 7 = 90 + 1 \text{ R } 2 = 91 \text{ R } 2.$

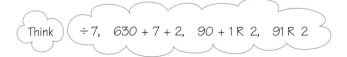

Think $\div 7,\ \ 630 + 7 + 2,\ \ 90 + 1\text{ R } 2,\ \ 91\text{ R } 2$

Working from Left to Right

Because it tends to reduce the amount one has to remember, many expert mental calculators **work from left to right** rather than the other way around as in most of our standard algorithms.

EXAMPLE   3.28 | **Working from Left to Right**

Use mental processes to perform these calculations.

(a) $352 + 647$ **(b)** $739 - 224$ **(c)** $4 \cdot 235$

Solution

(a) $352 + 647 = (300 + 50 + 2) + (600 + 40 + 7)$
$= (300 + 600) + (50 + 40) + (2 + 7)$
$= 900 + 90 + 9 = 999$

(b) $739 - 224 = (700 + 30 + 9) - (200 + 20 + 4)$
$= (700 - 200) + (30 - 20) + (9 - 4)$
$= 500 + 10 + 5 = 515$

(c) $4 \cdot 235 = 4(200 + 30 + 5)$
$= 800 + 120 + 20$
$= 920 + 20$
$= 940$

Left to right methods often combine nicely with an understanding of positional notation to simplify mental calculation. Since $4200 = 42 \cdot 100$, for example, we might compute the sum

$$
\begin{array}{r}
3700 \\
900 \\
2800 \\
+\ 5600 \\
\end{array}
$$

by thinking of

$$
\begin{array}{r}
37 \\
9 \\
28 \\
+\ 56 \\
\end{array}
$$

Then, working from left to right, we think

30, 50, 100, 107, 116, 124, 130
times 100. The answer is 13,000.

Rounding

Often we are **not** interested in exact values. This is certainly true when *estimating* the results of numerical calculations, and it is often the case that exact values are actually unobtainable. What does it mean, for example, to say that the population of California in 1998 was 28,874,293? Even if this is supposed to be the actual count on a given day, it is almost surely in error because of the sheer difficulty in conducting a census. How many illegal immigrants were not counted? How many homeless people? How many transients? In gross terms, it is probably accurate to say that the population of California was approximately 29,000,000 or 29 million people. To obtain this figure we **round** to the nearest million. This is accomplished by considering the digit in the hundred thousands position. If this digit is 5 or more, we increase the digit in the millions position by one and replace all the digits to the right of this position by zeros. If the hundred thousands digit is 4 or less, we leave the millions digit unchanged and replace all the digits to its right by zeros.

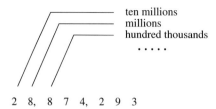

Rounding Using the 5-up Rule

1. Determine to which position you are rounding.
2. If the digit to the right of this position is 5 or more, add one to the digit in the position to which you are rounding. Otherwise leave the digit unchanged.
3. Replace by zeros all digits to the right of the position to which you are rounding.

EXAMPLE   3.29

Using the 5-up Rule to Round Whole Numbers

Round 27,250 to the position indicated.

(a) the nearest ten thousand   (b) the nearest thousand
(c) the nearest hundred   (d) the nearest ten

Solution

(a) The digit in the ten thousand position is 2. Since the digit to its right is seven and $7 > 5$, we add 1 to 2 and replace all digits to the right of the rounded digit by zeros. This gives 30,000.

(b) This time 7 is the critical digit and 2 is the digit to its right. Thus, to the nearest thousand, 27,250 is rounded to 27,000.

(c) Here 2 is the digit in the hundreds position and 5 is to its right. Thus 27,250 is rounded to 27,300 to the nearest hundred.

(d) This time 5 is the critical digit and zero is the digit on its right. Thus, no change need be made and 27,250 is already rounded to the nearest ten.

HIGHLIGHT FROM HISTORY
Emmy Noether (1882–1935)

Emmy Noether was born in Erlangen, Germany, to a family noted for mathematical talent. Much of her life was spent at the University of Göttingen, exploring, teaching, and writing about algebra. This university—where Carl Gauss had taught a century earlier—was the first in Germany to grant a doctoral degree to a woman. Yet Noether met with frustrating discrimination there. For many years she was denied appointment to the faculty; finally she was given an impressive title as "extraordinary professor"—with no salary. But her abilities overcame the obstacles that daunted many other women in mathematics. Her work in the 1920s brought invitations to lecture throughout Europe and in Moscow. In 1933, as the Nazi party came to power in Germany, Emmy Noether met with persecution not only as a woman but as an intellectual, a Jew, a pacifist, and a political liberal. She fled to the United States, where she taught and lectured at Bryn Mawr and Princeton until her death in 1935.

"How can it be allowed that a woman become . . . a professor . . . ? What will our soldiers think when they return to the University and find that they are expected to learn at the feet of a woman?"

—Faculty member at Göttingen, in 1918

". . . for two of the most significant sides of the theory of relativity, she gave at that time [1919] the genuine and universal mathematical formulation."

—Hermann Weyl, colleague at Göttingen

"In the judgement of the most competent living mathematicians, Fraulein Noether was the most significant creative mathematical genius thus far produced since the higher education of women began. In the realm of algebra . . . she discovered methods which have proved of enormous importance . . . ."

—Albert Einstein, 1935

"She was the most creative abstract algebraist in the world."

—Eric Temple Bell in *Men of Mathematics*

SOURCE: Biographical information is from Lynn Osen, *Women in Mathematics* (MIT Press, 1974). Quotations are cited in that source, original references including: Einstein, *New York Times*, May 4, 1935; Weyl, *Scripta Mathematica*, Vol. 3, 1935; *Men of Mathematics*, p. 261. Simon and Schuster, 1965; anonymous faculty member, Constance Reid, *Hilbert* (Springer-Verlag, 1970, p. 143). From Mathematics in Modules, *Intermediate Algebra*, A5, Teachers Edition. Reprinted by permission.

Estimation

The ever increasing use of calculators and computers makes it essential that students develop skill at estimation. How large an answer should I expect? Is this about the right answer? These are questions students should ask and be able to answer. And they can be answered reasonably effectively on the basis of a good understanding of 1-digit arithmetic facts and positional notation. To be effective, the estimator must also be adept at mental arithmetic.

Approximating by Rounding

Rounding is often used in finding estimates. The advantage of **approximating by rounding** is that it gives a single estimate that is reasonably close to the desired answer. The idea is to round the numbers involved in a calculation to the position of the left-most one or two digits and to use these rounded numbers in making the estimate. For example, consider $467 + 221$. Rounding to the nearest hundreds, we have

$$467 \approx 500 \quad \text{and} \quad 221 \approx 200,$$

Chapter 2
Lesson
14

Estimating Sums and Differences

You Will Learn
how to estimate sums and differences of whole numbers and decimals

Vocabulary
front-end estimation
a way to estimate a sum by adding the first digit of each addend and adjusting the result based on the remaining digits

Math Tip
You can use ≈ to show about or "approximately equal."

Learn • • • • • • • • • • •

John collected 1,004,024 pennies. They were worth $10,040.24 and weighed almost 7,000 lb.

This table shows the weights and values of some pennies.

Weights and Values of Pennies		
Number	(lb)	($)
144	1	$1.44
288	2	$2.88
576	4	$5.76
1,152	8	$11.52

John Tregembo, from Plymouth, Michigan, collected his pennies from 1982 to 1995.

If you have 6 lb of pennies, about how many pennies do you have? You can find 6 pounds of pennies by subtracting 2 from 8 or by adding 4 and 2. You can estimate by rounding or **front-end estimation**.

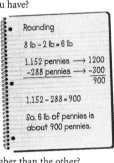

Rounding

8 lb – 2 lb = 6 lb

1,152 pennies ⟶ 1200
–288 pennies ⟶ –300
900

1,152 – 288 ≈ 900

So, 6 lb of pennies is about 900 pennies.

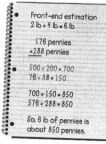

Front-end estimation
2 lb + 4 lb = 6 lb

576 pennies
+288 pennies

500 + 200 = 700
76 + 88 = 150

700 + 150 = 850
576 + 288 ≈ 850

So, 6 lb of pennies is about 850 pennies.

Talk About It
Why was one estimate higher than the other?

Check •

Estimate each sum or difference.

1.	520	**2.**	884	**3.**	$7.07	**4.**	621	**5.**	$9.82
	+ 375		– 406		– 3.59		432		+ 3.12
							+ 561		

6. Reasoning If you round $9.75 and $25.82 to the nearest dollar, will your estimated sum be more or less than the actual sum?

82 Chapter 2 • Whole Numbers and Decimals

SOURCE: From *Scott Foresman – Addison Wesley Math*, Grade 5, p. 82, by Randall I. Charles et al. Copyright © 1999, Addison Wesley Longman, Inc.

Questions for the Teacher

1. The above rounding estimate for 1152 − 288 was obtained by rounding to the nearest hundred as opposed to rounding to the left-most digit. Which method seems preferable here? Explain.

2. Using "front-end estimation" twice on the addition problem in the notebook on the right above gives an even closer estimate than rounding. Explain why this is likely to be the case.

where we use the symbol $\approx$ to mean "is approximated by." Thus, we obtain the approximation

$$500 + 200 \approx 700.$$

The actual answer is 688, so the approximation is reasonably good. Rounding to the nearest ten usually gives an even closer approximation if it is needed. Thus,

$$467 \approx 470, \qquad 221 \approx 220,$$

and $470 + 220$ gives the very close approximation 690.

EXAMPLE 3.30 | **Approximating by Rounding**

Round to the left-most digit to find approximate answers to each of these. Also, compute the exact answer in each case.

     (a) $681 + 241$ **(b)** $681 - 241$
     (c) $681 \cdot 241$ **(d)** $57{,}801 \div 336$

Solution

To the nearest hundred $681 \approx 700$ and $241 \approx 200$. Also, $57{,}801 \approx 60{,}000$ and $336 \approx 300$. Using these, we obtain the approximations shown.

Approximation   *Exact Answer*

(a) $681 + 241 \approx 700 + 200 = 900$ $681 + 241 = 922$
(b) $681 - 241 \approx 700 - 200 = 500$ $681 - 241 = 440$
(c) $681 \cdot 241 \approx 700 \cdot 200 = 140{,}000$ $681 \cdot 241 = 164{,}121$
(d) $57{,}801 \div 336 \approx 60{,}000 \div 300 = 200$ $57{,}801 \div 336 = 172$ R 9

Here the quotient is approximately 200.

PROBLEM SET 3.5

Understanding Concepts

1. Calculate mentally, using easy combinations. Write a sequence of numbers indicating intermediate steps in your thought process. The first one is done for you.

  (a) $7 + 11 + 5 + 3 + 9 + 16 + 4 + 3.$

Think   10, 30, 50, 55, 58

  (b) $6 + 9 + 17 + 5 + 8 + 12 + 3 + 6$
  (c) $27 + 42 + 23$ **(d)** $47 - 23$
  (e) $48 \cdot 5$ **(f)** $21{,}600 \div 50$

2. Calculate mentally using adjustment. Write down a sequence of numbers indicating intermediate steps in your thought process. The first one is done for you.
  (a) $78 + 64$

Think   80 + 62,   140,   142

  (b) $294 + 177$ **(c)** $306 - 168$ **(d)** $294 - 102$
  (e) $479 + 97$ **(f)** $3493 \div 7$ **(g)** $412 \cdot 7$

3. Perform these calculations mentally from left to right. Write down a sequence of numbers indicating intermediate steps in your thought process.
  (a) $425 + 362$ **(b)** $363 + 274$ **(c)** $572 - 251$
  (d) $764 - 282$ **(e)** $3 \cdot 342$
  (f) $47 + 32 + 71 + 9 + 26 + 32$

4. Round 235,476 to the
   (a) nearest ten thousand.
   (b) nearest thousand.
   (c) nearest hundred.

5. Round each of these to the position indicated.
   (a) 947 to the nearest 100.
   (b) 850 to the nearest 100.
   (c) 27,462,312 to the nearest million.
   (d) 2461 to the nearest thousand.

6. Rounding to the left-most digit, calculate approximate values for each of these:
   (a) $478 + 631$ (b) $782 + 346$ (c) $678 - 431$
   (d) $257 \cdot 364$ (e) $7403 \cdot 28$ (f) $28,329 \div 43$
   (g) $71,908 \div 824$

7. Compute exact answers to parts (a) through (g) of problem 6.

8. Rounding to the nearest thousands and using mental arithmetic, estimate each of these sums and differences.

   (a)
   ```
       17,281
        6 564
       12,147
        2 481
     + 13,671
   ```
   (b)
   ```
       2734
       3541
       2284
       3478
     + 7124
   ```

   (c)
   ```
       28,341
          942
        2 431
        4 716
     + 12,824
   ```
   (d)
   ```
       4270
     − 1324
   ```

   (e)
   ```
       21,243
     −  7 824
   ```
   (f)
   ```
       37,481
     − 16,249
   ```

   (g) Use your calculator to compute the exact value of the answer to parts (a) through (f).

9. Using rounding to the left-most digit, estimate these products.
   (a) $2748 \cdot 31$ (b) $4781 \cdot 342$ (c) $23,247 \cdot 357$
   (d) Use your calculator to determine the exact value of the products in parts (a) through (c).

10. Use rounding to the left-most digit to estimate the quotient in each of the following.
    (a) $29,342 \div 42$ (b) $7431 \div 37$
    (c) $79,287 \div 429$
    (d) Use your calculator to determine the exact value of the quotients in each of parts (a) through (c).

Thinking Critically

11. Theresa and Fontaine each used their calculators to compute $357 + 492$. Fontaine's answer was 749 and Theresa's was 849. Who was most likely correct? In two brief sentences tell how estimation can help you decide whose answer was probably correct.

12. Use rounding to estimate the results of each of the following.
    (a) $\dfrac{452 + 371}{281}$ (b) $\dfrac{3 \cdot 271 + 465}{74 + 9}$
    (c) $\dfrac{845 \cdot 215}{416}$
    (d) Use your calculator to determine the exact answer to each problem in parts (a) through (c).

13. Sometimes the last digits of numbers can help you decide if calculator computations are correct.
    (a) Given that one of 27,453; 27,587; or 27,451 is the correct result of multiplying 283 by 97, which answer is correct?
    (b) In two brief sentences, tell how consideration of last digits helped you answer part (a).

14. Since 25,781; 24,323; 26,012; and 25,243 are all about the same size, about how large is their sum? Explain briefly.

Thinking Cooperatively

Solve each of the next three problems as a group, discussing the ideas and strategies that eventually led to correct solutions. Arrive at a solution agreed upon by all the members of your group.

15. Note that $(2)(4678) = 9356$. Place parentheses in each of the following strings of digits to make the equality true.
    (a) $2\ 4\ 6\ 7\ 8 = 16,272$
    (b) $2\ 4\ 6\ 7\ 8 = 19,188$
    (c) $2\ 4\ 6\ 7\ 8 = 19,736$
    (d) $2\ 4\ 6\ 7\ 8 = 11,232$

16. Place parentheses and plus signs in each string of digits to make these equalities true. (*Hint:* $(88) + (88) + (88) + (88) = 352$.)
    (a) $8\ 8\ 8\ 8\ 8\ 8\ 8\ 8 = 136$
    (b) $8\ 8\ 8\ 8\ 8\ 8\ 8\ 8 = 17,776$
    (c) $8\ 8\ 8\ 8\ 8\ 8\ 8\ 8 = 928$
    (d) $8\ 8\ 8\ 8\ 8\ 8\ 8\ 8 = 9064$
    (e) $8\ 8\ 8\ 8\ 8\ 8\ 8\ 8 = 8920$

17. Place parentheses and divide signs in each of these strings of digits so that the equalities are true. Remember that it is **not** generally the case that $(a \div b) \div c = a \div (b \div c)$. (*Hint:* $(844 \div (4 \div 2)) \div (2 \div 1) = 211$.)

(a) 8 4 4 4 2 2 1 = 844,422

(b) 8 4 4 4 2 2 1 = 42,221

(c) 8 4 4 4 2 2 1 = 42

(d) 8 4 4 4 2 2 1 = 38 R 46

Connections

18. While grocery shopping with $40, you buy the following items at the price listed:

2 gallons of milk	$2.29 a gallon
1 dozen eggs	$1.63 per dozen
2 rolls of paper towels	$1.21 per roll
1 5-pound pork roast	$1.47 per pound
2 boxes of breakfast cereal	$3.19 each
1 azalea	$9.95 each

(a) About how much will all of this cost?

(b) If you don't buy the azalea, about how much change should you receive?

From State Student Assessments

19. (Washington State, Grade 4)

Kaitlin's dad bought 6 gallons of white paint for the house. He also bought 3 gallons of yellow paint for the garage. Each can of paint costs $14.98. About how much did Kaitlin's dad have to pay for the paint?

A. $80   B. $100   C. $140

20. (Washington State, Grade 4)

Solve 52×40.

A. 2800   B. 2080   C. 280   D. 208

21. (Washington State, Grade 4)

Estimate the answer. Show how you found your estimate.

$$9\overline{)820}$$

22. (Washington State, Grade 4)

Solve the problem.

$$\begin{array}{r} 254 \\ + 67 \\ \hline \end{array}$$

A. 211   B. 221   C. 311   D. 321

For Review

23. In a college mathematics class all the students are also taking anthropology, history, or psychology and some of the students are taking two or even all three of these courses. If (i) forty students are taking anthropology, (ii) eleven students are taking history, (iii) twelve students are taking psychology, (iv) three students are taking all three courses, (v) six students are taking anthropology and history, and (vi) six students are taking psychology and anthropology,

(a) how many students are taking only anthropology?

(b) how many students are taking anthropology or history?

(c) how many students are taking history and anthropology but not psychology?

24. Fill in the missing digits in each of these addition problems.

(a)
$$\begin{array}{r} \_742 \\ 41\_ \\ 69\_3 \\ + \ 2\_18 \\ \hline \_2,818 \end{array}$$

(b)
$$\begin{array}{r} 2341 \\ 4\_30 \\ 1\_\_\_ \\ + \ 3\_18 \\ \hline \_3,100 \end{array}$$

(c)
$$\begin{array}{r} \_21\_ \\ \_0\_ \\ 41\_ \\ + \ 777\_ \\ \hline 9666 \end{array}$$

25. Fill in the missing digits in each of these subtraction problems.

(a)
$$\begin{array}{r} 27\_4 \\ - \ \_64\_ \\ \hline 91 \end{array}$$

(b)
$$\begin{array}{r} 7\_01 \\ - \ 192\_ \\ \hline \_8\_9 \end{array}$$

(c)
$$\begin{array}{r} \_22\_ \\ - \ 2333 \\ \hline 1\_\_9 \end{array}$$

26. Fill in the missing digits in each of these multiplication and division problems.

(a)
$$\begin{array}{r} 34\_ \\ \times \ \_\_ \\ \hline 6\_4 \\ \_\_8 \\ \hline \_\_,57\_ \end{array}$$

(b)
$$\begin{array}{r} 3\_\_7 \\ \times \ 1\_ \\ \hline \_\_296 \\ \_7\_\_\_ \\ \hline \_6\_,6\_\_ \end{array}$$

(c)
$$\begin{array}{r} 1\_ \\ \_61\overline{)3\_24} \\ \_6\_ \\ \hline 121\_ \\ \_\_\_\_ \\ \hline \_\_0 \end{array}$$

OPERATIVE INVESTIGATION

Multiplication Tic-Tac-Toe

Materials Needed

1.   A calculator for each student.
2.   A multiplication Tic-Tac-Toe handout for each pair of students.

Procedure

This is like regular tic-tac-toe except that on each play the player chooses two numbers from the list and places his or her mark (X or O) on the square containing the product of the numbers chosen. Thus, in part (a), if the first player's symbol is X, and 11 and 23 are chosen on the first play, an X is placed on 253 on the diagram and also the notation 11 · 23. As usual, the player to get three Xs or Os in a row wins the game. If a player chooses a product not in a square, (s)he loses that turn.

(a) 11, 12, 15, 19, 23

345	132	285
228	209	437
253 (11 · 23)	276	180

(b) 13, 14, 17, 19, 21

221	266	273
247	238	182
323	399	357

(c) 7, 23, 341, 2706, 4123

94,829	2,387	11,156,838
1,405,943	7,843	18,942
28,861	62,238	922,746

Parts (d) and (e) are the same as parts (a) through (c) except that the numbers in the squares are the approximations of the true products obtained by rounding each number to the left position.

(d) 23, 27, 36, 47, 55

600 (= 23 · 27)	800	1800
2000	1500	1200
1000	2400	3000

(e) 143, 254, 361, 2391, 2511

40,000	800,000	300,000
600,000	200,000	1,200,000
120,000	6,000,000	900,000

(f) For parts (a) through (c), discuss how looking at the last digits in the numerals can help you play the game.

(g) For part (c), discuss how estimation can help you play the game.

Strategy

- *Use algorithmic thinking.*

Figure 3.10
The Math Explorer Calculator

3.6 Getting the Most Out of Your Calculator

It's a safe bet that almost everyone who reads these words is the owner of at least one calculator. It's also a safe bet that almost every reader knows how to add, subtract, multiply, and divide with his or her calculator. However, most calculators have useful features that are not well understood and are not employed by some users. In this section, we discuss some of these special features.

First, we note that there are three common types of logic that determine how your calculator operates—arithmetic (á-rith-me-tic), algebraic, and reverse Polish. **Reverse Polish notation** is a powerful system used on sophisticated scientific calculators and is not suitable for elementary school students. Machines utilizing **arithmetic logic** are too simplistic and again are not recommended for classroom use. Machines using **algebraic logic** (such machines are easily identified by the presence of left and right parenthesis keys) are the most appropriate for student use and have built-in features that make calculations easier and more natural. Of course, your instruction manual is the basic source of information about the operation of your particular calculator. We will discuss the features of the *Math Explorer* calculator. This machine, shown in Figure 3.10, is made by Texas Instruments especially for use by elementary school students. The *Math Explorer* uses algebraic logic, does arithmetic both with fractions and decimals, and also does integer division with remainders. Most of the discussion here applies equally well to other algebraic machines, but your instruction manual is the final arbiter. We will also refer briefly to the graphing calculator (see Appendix C), which is becoming increasingly useful to both mathematics and science teachers in the upper elementary grades.

from **The NCTM Principles and Standards**

The Place of Calculators

Calculators are accessible and reliable tools for computing. All students should use calculators at appropriate times as computational tools. The calculator should be considered a legitimate tool within the mathematics classroom for computing, particularly when many or cumbersome computations are necessary for solving problems. However, when the instructional focus is on developing student-generated or conventional computational algorithms, the calculator should be set aside to allow for this focus. Today, the calculator is a commonly used computational tool outside the classroom. The environment inside the classroom should reflect this reality.

Computation, in this draft, as was also the case in the *Curriculum and Evaluation Standards* (1989), involves a broadening of the traditional view to include not only paper-and-pencil computation but also mental computation and the use of calculators and other calculation tools. Because of this expanded definition, computation must be tightly linked to reasoning and estimating. In any particular situation, students need to decide whether an exact answer or an estimate is appropriate, and also whether it makes sense to solve the problem mentally, with paper and pencil, or with a calculator. For example, the cost of 1 1/4 pounds of nuts at $2.40 per pound could be found mentally, whereas the cost of 1.37 pounds of bulk candy at $1.17 a pound might be estimated, although a calculator would probably be the preferred tool if an exact answer were needed. Students also should be able to do this computation with paper and pencil, if necessary. Helping students decide when exact answers or estimates are appropriate, which computational method to use, and how to judge the reasonableness of answers are part of the teaching and learning.

Priority of Operations

Suppose you enter

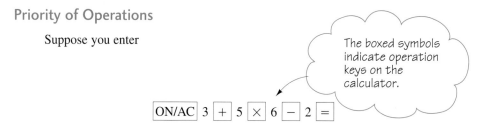

> The boxed symbols indicate operation keys on the calculator.

$$\boxed{\text{ON/AC}}\; 3 \;\boxed{+}\; 5 \;\boxed{\times}\; 6 \;\boxed{-}\; 2 \;\boxed{=}$$

into your calculator. A calculator with arithmetic logic would perform each operation in exactly the order entered and would give the answer 46; that is,

$$3 + 5 = 8$$
$$8 \times 6 = 48$$
$$48 - 2 = 46.$$

In contrast, a calculator with algebraic logic multiplies and divides *before* adding and subtracting. Also, if there are pending operations of equal priority, these calculators execute them from left to right. Since these priorities are those generally accepted in mathematics, algebraic machines correspond well to the standard rules and properties of arithmetic. Thus, the above sequence of entries in an algebraic calculator gives the answer 31, obtained as follows:

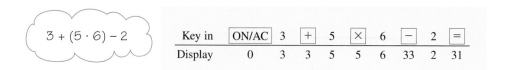

$$3 + (5 \cdot 6) - 2$$

Key in	ON/AC	3	+	5	×	6	−	2	=
Display	0	3	3	5	5	6	33	2	31

When the $\boxed{-}$ was pressed, the calculator *first* multiplied 5 × 6 to get 30, *then* completed the pending addition to 3 giving 33. When 2 and $\boxed{=}$ were pressed, it then subtracted the 2 to give 31.

While we have not yet discussed the use of all of these keys, the priority of operations for machines with algebraic logic is as shown in Table 3.9.

TABLE 3.9	Priority of Operations on Calculators with Algebraic Logic	
Priority	Keys	Explanation
1	$\boxed{(}\,\boxed{)}$	Operations in parentheses are performed before other operations.
2	$\boxed{x^2}\,\boxed{\surd}$ $\boxed{10^n}\,\boxed{1/x}$ $\boxed{\%}$	Operations performed on a single number.
3	$\boxed{y^x}$	Exponentiation.
4	$\boxed{\times}\,\boxed{\div}$	Multiplications and divisions are completed before additions and subtractions.
5	$\boxed{+}\,\boxed{-}$	Additions and subtractions are completed last.
6	$\boxed{=}$	Terminates a calculation.

EXAMPLE   3.31

Understanding the Order of Calculator Operations

(a) Indicate what should be entered into a calculator with algebraic notation to compute

$$27 \div 3 + 24 \cdot 4.$$

(b) Actually key the sequence in part (a) into your calculator and complete the computation.

Solution

(a) Because of the priority of operations, it is only necessary to key in the following:

$$\boxed{\text{ON/AC}}\ 27\ \boxed{\div}\ 3\ \boxed{+}\ 24\ \boxed{\times}\ 4\ \boxed{=}.$$

(b) On a machine with algebraic logic, the calculator makes the following sequence of calculations:

$$27 \div 3 = 9,\ 24 \cdot 4 = 96,\ 9 + 96 = 105.$$

Using the Parentheses Keys $\boxed{(}$ and $\boxed{)}$

It is possible to override the priority of operations built into the calculator by use of the parentheses keys. Suppose you want to compute

$$(789 + 364) \cdot (863 + 939).$$

This is accomplished by keying the sequence

$\boxed{\text{ON/AC}}$ $\boxed{(}$ 789 $\boxed{+}$ 364 $\boxed{)}$ $\boxed{\times}$ $\boxed{(}$ 863 $\boxed{+}$ 939 $\boxed{)}$ $\boxed{=}$

into the calculator. The desired answer is 2,077,706. If we keyed in

$\boxed{\text{ON/AC}}$ 789 $\boxed{+}$ 364 $\boxed{\times}$ 863 $\boxed{+}$ 939 $\boxed{=}$

(the same entries but omitting the parentheses) the calculator would show 315,860 determined by computing the product of 364 and 863 and then adding 789 and 939 in that order.

EXAMPLE   3.32   **Using the $\boxed{\text{ON/AC}}$, $\boxed{=}$, and Parentheses Keys**

Perform this computation on your calculator.

$$216 \div (3 + 24) \cdot 4$$

Solution   Key in $\boxed{\text{ON/AC}}$ 216 $\boxed{\div}$ $\boxed{(}$ 3 $\boxed{+}$ 24 $\boxed{)}$ $\boxed{\times}$ 4 $\boxed{=}$ to obtain the answer 32. Remember that divide and multiply are operations of the same priority. Thus, the calculator first computes the sum in parentheses, divides 216 by that sum, and multiplies the result by 4. Using clearer notation, what the calculator is computing is

$$(216 \div (3 + 24)) \cdot 4$$

but the built-in priority of operations makes it unnecessary to key the expression into the calculator this way.

Before proceeding, several observations should be made.

1. It is always a good idea to begin each calculation by pressing the $\boxed{\text{ON/AC}}$ key. This key turns the calculator on. Equally importantly, it clears all preceding data from all parts of the calculator so that present work will not be rendered incorrect by the presence of unexpected and unwanted information from a preceding calculation. As a reminder, in all our examples we indicate starting by pressing this key.

2. Pressing the $\boxed{=}$ key causes the calculator to complete all entered calculations up to that point. This can be used on occasion to simplify calculation. For example, to compute $(29 + 37) \div 11$, one could use parentheses or alternatively enter

$\boxed{\text{ON/AC}}$ 29 $\boxed{+}$ 37 $\boxed{=}$ $\boxed{\div}$ 11 $\boxed{=}$

to obtain the correct answer of 6. As a check, key in

$$\boxed{\text{ON/AC}} \quad \boxed{(} \quad 29 \quad \boxed{+} \quad 37 \quad \boxed{)} \quad \boxed{\div} \quad 11 \quad \boxed{=}$$

to see that you obtain the same answer.

3. Parentheses must always be entered in pairs; that is, for each left parenthesis entered a right parenthesis must be entered later. Otherwise, when $\boxed{=}$ is entered, the expression *Error P* will appear in the display to inform you of an error in entering parentheses. Other common error messages are:

Error A   Arithmetic error. For example, attempting to divide by zero.

Error O   Overflow error. The number is too large for the calculator.

Error U   Underflow error. The number is too small for the calculator.

Error 4   You have entered four or more pending operations. The limit for the *Math Explorer* is three.

If, in the midst of a calculation, you obtain an error message of any kind, you must press the $\boxed{\text{ON/AC}}$ key to clear the machine. Then repeat the calculation being careful to restructure your procedure to avoid the previous error.

It may be useful to consider one more example concerning priority of operations.

EXAMPLE   3.33 | **Prioritizing Operations**

Compute $\dfrac{323 - 4 \cdot 38}{19}$.

Solution | If you enter

$$\boxed{\text{ON/AC}} \quad 323 \quad \boxed{-} \quad 4 \quad \boxed{\times} \quad 38 \quad \boxed{\div} \quad 19 \quad \boxed{=}$$

into the calculator, you obtain the incorrect answer 315. Because of the priority of operations, this sequence of commands computes $4 \cdot 38 \div 19$ and subtracts this from 323. However, the problem requires that the entire quantity $323 - 4 \cdot 38$ be divided by 19. This can be accomplished in several ways but perhaps the following are easiest. Using parentheses:

$$\boxed{\text{ON/AC}} \quad \boxed{(} \quad 323 \quad \boxed{-} \quad 4 \quad \boxed{\times} \quad 38 \quad \boxed{)} \quad \boxed{\div} \quad 19 \quad \boxed{=}$$

Using $\boxed{=}$ twice:

$$\boxed{\text{ON/AC}} \quad 323 \quad \boxed{-} \quad 4 \quad \boxed{\times} \quad 38 \quad \boxed{=} \quad \boxed{\div} \quad 19 \quad \boxed{=}$$

Key in each of these sequences and note that each gives the correct answer of 9.

Using the x^2, $\sqrt{}$, 10^n, and $1/x$ Keys

Each of these keys causes the calculator to perform an operation on a single number, and all but 10^n operate in the same way. To compute

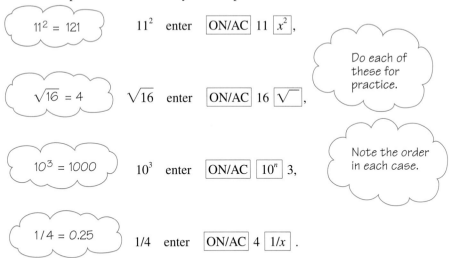

$11^2 = 121$

11^2 enter $\boxed{\text{ON/AC}}$ 11 $\boxed{x^2}$,

Do each of these for practice.

$\sqrt{16} = 4$

$\sqrt{16}$ enter $\boxed{\text{ON/AC}}$ 16 $\boxed{\sqrt{}}$,

Note the order in each case.

$10^3 = 1000$

10^3 enter $\boxed{\text{ON/AC}}$ $\boxed{10^n}$ 3,

$1/4 = 0.25$

$1/4$ enter $\boxed{\text{ON/AC}}$ 4 $\boxed{1/x}$.

In each case, the operation is carried out immediately; it is not necessary to use the $\boxed{=}$ key to complete the computation.

Using the $\boxed{y^x}$ Key

To compute 10^3 on the calculator you enter the string $\boxed{\text{ON/AC}}$ $\boxed{10^n}$ 3. To compute 5^3 we proceed similarly but with the $\boxed{y^x}$ key. Here we have to tell the calculator what number we want to raise to a power and what power to raise it to. For 5^3, $y = 5$, $x = 3$, and we enter 5 $\boxed{y^x}$ 3 $\boxed{=}$ to obtain 125. Check to see that the entry strings

$$\boxed{\text{ON/AC}}\ 2\ \boxed{y^x}\ 5\ \boxed{=}$$

and

$$\boxed{\text{ON/AC}}\ 2\ \boxed{\times}\ 2\ \boxed{\times}\ 2\ \boxed{\times}\ 2\ \boxed{\times}\ 2\ \boxed{=}$$

both give 32 as the value of 2^5.

Using the Memory Keys— $\boxed{\text{M+}}$, $\boxed{\text{M−}}$, $\boxed{\text{MR}}$, and $\boxed{x\ \circlearrowleft\ \text{M}}$

The *Math Explorer* has a memory that is accessed with the $\boxed{\text{M+}}$, $\boxed{\text{M−}}$, $\boxed{\text{MR}}$, and $\boxed{x\ \circlearrowleft\ \text{M}}$ keys. Other good algebraic calculators will have similar capabilities though the keys may bear different symbols like $\boxed{\text{M}}$, $\boxed{\text{RCL}}$, and so on.

Using the $\boxed{\text{M+}}$ or $\boxed{\text{M−}}$ keys adds or subtracts respectively the number in the calculator display to the number in the memory. If nothing has been placed in the memory, it will be assumed to contain a zero. Also, when you place a number in the memory, the display will show a small M to remind you that the memory is not empty. The $\boxed{\text{MR}}$ key recalls what is in the memory and shows it in the display. The $\boxed{x \, \circlearrowleft \, M}$ key exchanges the number in the display, *x,* with the number in the memory, M. These capabilities are useful in elementary ways but, with a little imagination, they are also useful in more surprising and powerful ways.

EXAMPLE 3.34

Using the $\boxed{M+}$ and $\boxed{MR}$ Keys

Compute the quotient

$$\frac{\sqrt{158{,}404} - 200}{6019 - 5986}$$

without using parentheses.

Solution

The idea is to compute $6019 - 5986$ and store it in the memory. Then compute $\sqrt{158{,}404} - 200$ and divide the result by the number stored in the memory using the divide, $\boxed{\div}$, and recall memory, $\boxed{MR}$, keys. We enter the following to obtain the correct answer of 6.

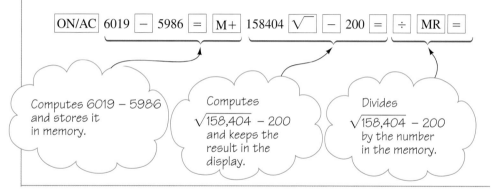

$\boxed{ON/AC}$ 6019 $\boxed{-}$ 5986 $\boxed{=}$ $\boxed{M+}$ 158404 $\boxed{\sqrt{}}$ $\boxed{-}$ 200 $\boxed{=}$ $\boxed{\div}$ $\boxed{MR}$ $\boxed{=}$

Computes $6019 - 5986$ and stores it in memory.

Computes $\sqrt{158{,}404} - 200$ and keeps the result in the display.

Divides $\sqrt{158{,}404} - 200$ by the number in the memory.

EXAMPLE 3.35

Using the $\boxed{M+}$ and $\boxed{M-}$ Keys

Compute

$$329 \cdot 742 - 3 \cdot 8914 + 2 \cdot 2175.$$

Solution

The idea is to compute the products and add them to or subtract them from the contents of the memory. We then obtain the answer by using the $\boxed{MR}$ key. The desired string entered in the calculator is

$\boxed{ON/AC}$ 329 $\boxed{\times}$ 742 $\boxed{=}$ $\boxed{M+}$ 3 $\boxed{\times}$ 8914 $\boxed{=}$ $\boxed{M-}$ 2 $\boxed{\times}$ 2175 $\boxed{=}$ $\boxed{M+}$ $\boxed{MR}$.

This gives the correct answer of 221,726. However, in this simple case, it is easier to enter the string

$\boxed{ON/AC}$ 329 $\boxed{\times}$ 742 $\boxed{-}$ 3 $\boxed{\times}$ 8914 $\boxed{+}$ 2 $\boxed{\times}$ 2175 $\boxed{=}$

to obtain 221,726 as before. Be sure to check both entry sequences to see that they give this result.

EXAMPLE   3.36

Using the $x \circlearrowright M$ **Key**

Compute this quotient.

$$\frac{2927 + 8976 - 3417}{3154 + 1089}$$

Solution

The idea is to compute the numerator and place it in memory using the $\boxed{M+}$ key. Then compute the denominator which will be in the display. Use $\boxed{x \circlearrowright M}$ to exchange the two numbers. Then use $\boxed{\div}$ $\boxed{MR}$ to perform the desired division. The entry string

$\boxed{ON/AC}$ 2927 $\boxed{+}$ 8976 $\boxed{-}$ 3417 $\boxed{=}$ $\boxed{M+}$ 3154 $\boxed{+}$ 1089

$\boxed{=}$ $\boxed{x \circlearrowright M}$ $\boxed{\div}$ $\boxed{MR}$ $\boxed{=}$

yields the answer 2. Check to see that the entry string

$\boxed{ON/AC}$ $\boxed{(}$ 2927 $\boxed{+}$ 8976 $\boxed{-}$ 3417 $\boxed{)}$ $\boxed{\div}$ $\boxed{(}$ 3154 $\boxed{+}$ 1089 $\boxed{)}$ $\boxed{=}$

with parentheses gives the same answer.

Using the $\boxed{INT \div}$ **Key to Compute Integer Division with Remainders**

Since the *Math Explorer* calculator is designed for use in elementary classrooms, it was thought appropriate to give it the capability of dividing one natural number by another and displaying the quotient as well as the remainder. Because of limited space in the display, there is a limitation on the size of the numbers that can be used. If either the quotient or the remainder is more than a 4-digit number, the Error O (overflow) message will appear in the calculator display and the problem will have to be completed by some other method.

EXAMPLE   3.37

Using the $\boxed{INT \div}$ **Key**

(a) Using the $\boxed{INT \div}$ key, compute the quotient and the remainder when 89,765 is divided by 78.

(b) Using the $\boxed{INT \div}$ key, compute the quotient and the remainder when 897,654 is divided by 81.

Solution

(a) Entering $\boxed{ON/AC}$ 89765 $\boxed{INT \div}$ 78 $\boxed{=}$ into your calculator, you see the quotient, 1150, and the remainder, 65, in the display. Use your calculator to check this result by showing that

$$1150 \cdot 78 + 65 = 89765.$$

(b) Entering $\boxed{ON/AC}$ 897654 $\boxed{INT \div}$ 81 $\boxed{=}$ into your calculator, the display reads *Error O* since the quotient is a 5-digit number.

Using the Built-in Constant Function

Consider the arithmetic progression

$$3, 7, 11, 15, 19, \ldots, 67.$$

It is easy to use your calculator to compute all the terms in this progression. Simply enter
$\boxed{\text{ON/AC}}$ 3 $\boxed{+}$ 4 and then repeatedly press the $\boxed{=}$ key to repeatedly add 4. This utilizes
the built-in constant function of most calculators with algebraic logic.

EXAMPLE 3.38

Finding the Sum of an Arithmetic Progression

Compute the sum $3 + 7 + 11 + \cdots + 67$ of the first 17 terms in the arithmetic progression above.

Solution

1. If we remember young Gauss's trick, then

$$
\begin{aligned}
S &= 3 + 7 + 11 + \cdots + 67 \\
S &= 67 + 63 + 59 + \cdots + 3 \\
2S &= 70 + 70 + 70 + \cdots + 70 = 17 \cdot 70
\end{aligned}
$$

so

$$S = \frac{17 \cdot 70}{2} = 595.$$

2. An alternative approach to this problem is to use the $\boxed{\text{M+}}$ and the constant function of your calculator. Thus, we enter

$$\boxed{\text{ON/AC}} \; 3 \; \boxed{\text{M+}} \; \boxed{+} \; 4 \; \boxed{=} \; \boxed{\text{M+}} \; \boxed{=} \boxed{\text{M+}} \; \boxed{=} \cdots,$$

repeating the $\boxed{\text{M+}}$ $\boxed{=}$ sequence until the display shows 67. We then press
$\boxed{\text{M+}}$ once more and $\boxed{\text{MR}}$ to again obtain 595 as the answer.

EXAMPLE 3.39

Finding the Sum of a Geometric Progression

Find the sum of the first 15 terms of the geometric progression whose first 4 terms are 4, 12, 36, 108.

Solution

The consecutive terms of the progression can be found on your calculator by entering 4 $\boxed{\times}$ 3 $\boxed{=}$ and then pressing $\boxed{=}$ repeatedly.

As with the arithmetic progression, this problem can also be solved on algebraic notation machines with a built-in constant. Thus, if we enter

$$\boxed{\text{ON/AC}} \; 4 \; \boxed{\text{M+}} \; \boxed{\times} \; 3 \; \boxed{=} \; \boxed{\text{M+}} \; \boxed{=} \boxed{\text{M+}} \; \boxed{=} \cdots \boxed{=} \; \boxed{\text{M+}} \; \boxed{\text{MR}}$$

where we use the $\boxed{=}$ key 14 times (to add 15 terms), we obtain the desired answer of 28,697,812. Check this on your calculator.

Using the $\boxed{+ \circlearrowright -}$ Key

The $\boxed{+ \circlearrowright -}$ key is used to change the sign of a number in the calculator's display. Thus, if 23 is in the display, pressing $\boxed{+ \circlearrowright -}$ causes -23 to appear. Similarly, if -23 is in the display, pressing $\boxed{+ \circlearrowright -}$ causes 23 to appear.

EXAMPLE   3.40

Using the $\boxed{+ \circlearrowright -}$ Key

Compute $281 - \sqrt{133 \div 19 + 7914}$.

Solution

Here we compute the square root first and then subtract it from 281. This could be done using the memory, but suppose there is a number in the memory that we want to use later. Using the fact that

$$281 - \sqrt{133 \div 19 + 7914} = -(\sqrt{133 \div 19 + 7914} - 281)$$

we enter the following command string.

$$\boxed{\text{ON/AC}} \ 133 \ \div \ 19 \ \boxed{+} \ 7914 \ \boxed{=} \ \boxed{\sqrt{\ }} \ \boxed{-} \ 281 \ \boxed{=} \ \boxed{+ \circlearrowright -}$$

to obtain the desired answer of 192.

Check that the entry string

$$\boxed{\text{ON/AC}} \ 133 \ \boxed{\div} \ 19 \ \boxed{+} \ 7914 \ \boxed{=} \ \boxed{\sqrt{\ }} \ \boxed{\text{M+}} \ 281 \ \boxed{-} \ \boxed{\text{MR}} \ \boxed{=},$$

which performs the subtraction in the reverse order, gives the same answer.

Algorithmic Thinking

An approach to doing mathematics that is particularly important when working with calculators and computers is **algorithmic thinking**—the doing of mathematical tasks by means of a sequential and often repetitive set of steps. This was illustrated modestly in the preceding examples explaining the repeated use of the $\boxed{=}$ and $\boxed{\text{M+}}$ keys. But much more can be done with your calculator to illustrate this approach to problem solving. To make the idea more clear consider the following example.

EXAMPLE   3.41

Generating the Fibonacci Sequence Algorithmically

Develop an efficient algorithm for generating successive terms of the Fibonacci sequence $(1, 1, 2, 3, 5, \ldots)$ using the special capabilities of your calculator.

Solution

The Fibonacci numbers can be computed with the straightforward use of the $\boxed{+}$ and $\boxed{=}$ keys on your calculator. But this requires repeatedly entering the proper numbers. More efficient algorithmic approaches can be devised which only require entering one or two numbers initially and then repetitively using the special keys on your calculator to complete the task. **Note:** Since not all calculators with algebraic logic operate exactly the same, great care must be exercised in devising an algorithm suitable for your machine.

The following algorithm generates the Fibonacci numbers by making particularly effective use of the $\boxed{\text{MR}}$ and $\boxed{\text{M+}}$ keys found on most calculators. The table below gives the Entry (a number or keystroke), the value x seen in the display, and the value M contained in the memory.

Entry	$\boxed{\text{ON/AC}}$	1	$\boxed{\text{M+}}$	$\boxed{+}$	$\boxed{\text{M+}}$	$\boxed{\text{MR}}$	$\boxed{+}$	$\boxed{\text{M+}}$	$\boxed{\text{MR}}$	$\boxed{+}$	$\boxed{\text{M+}}$	$\boxed{\text{MR}}$	$\boxed{+}$	$\cdots$
x	0	1	1	1	1	2	3	3	5	8	8	13	21	$\cdots$
M	0	0	1	1	2	2	2	5	5	5	13	13	13	$\cdots$

The Fibonacci numbers generated by the algorithm are shown in red. Each repetition of the three keystroke pattern $\boxed{\text{M+}}$ $\boxed{\text{MR}}$ $\boxed{+}$ first repeats the last number displayed and then generates the next two numbers of the Fibonacci sequence. Since two of each three successive keystrokes generate a new Fibonacci number, the algorithm is highly efficient.

EXAMPLE   3.42

Computing $1 + 2 + \cdots + n$ and $1^2 + 2^2 + \cdots + n^2$ Simultaneously

Write an algorithm that simultaneously computes

$$t_{10} = 1 + 2 + 3 + 4 + 5 + 6 + 7 + 8 + 9 + 10$$

and

$$s_{10} = 1^2 + 2^2 + 3^2 + 4^2 + 5^2 + 6^2 + 7^2 + 8^2 + 9^2 + 10^2.$$

Solution

The entry string

$\boxed{\text{ON/AC}}$ 1 $\boxed{\text{M+}}$ $\boxed{x^2}$ $\boxed{+}$ 2 $\boxed{\text{M+}}$ $\boxed{x^2}$ $\boxed{+}$ 3 $\boxed{\text{M+}}$ $\boxed{x^2}$

$\boxed{+}$ $\cdots$ $\boxed{+}$ 10 $\boxed{\text{M+}}$ $\boxed{x^2}$ $\boxed{=}$ $\boxed{\text{MR}}$

does the job quite nicely. Check to see that when the last $\boxed{=}$ is pressed you obtain $s_{10} = 385$, and, when the last $\boxed{\text{MR}}$ is pressed, you obtain $t_{10} = 55$.

PROBLEM-SOLVING STRATEGY   •   **Use Algorithmic Thinking**

Sometimes a problem or set of problems can be solved by devising a set of operations that can be carried out repetitively on a calculator or computer. Doing the problem by hand may be prohibitively time-consuming.

WINDOW ON TECHNOLOGY
Automating Algorithms on a Graphing Calculator

Graphing calculators can display graphs of functions and plots of statistical data (see Appendix C). Graphing calculators are also **programmable,** which means that the steps of an algorithm can be entered into the calculator as a **program.** Several useful programs can be found in Appendix C. Programs for the calculator can be quite sophisticated, using a wide variety of input/output and control instructions; in fact, the calculator is really a small computer. Many upper elementary and middle school teachers are finding that learning to program a calculator can pay large dividends for classroom use. Many mathematical "What if?" explorations can be pursued using a program to automate the laborious calculations, allowing students to focus on the higher level aspects of the investigation.

Consider the following problem:

> *Given any two numbers* A *and* B, *generate the Fibonacci-type sequence in which each successive number of the sequence is the sum of the two preceding numbers. What seems to be happening to the ratio of successive numbers in the sequence?*

For example, when $A = B = 1$, we generate the Fibonacci sequence 1, 1, 2, 3, 5, 8, . . . , and compute the successive ratios 1/1, 2/1, 3/2, 5/3, 8/5, ... When $A = 1$ and $B = 3$, we generate the Lucas sequence 1, 3, 4, 7, 11, 18, ... (named for Edouard Lucas, 1842–1891) and then examine the ratios 3/1, 4/3, 7/4, 11/7, ... This investigation would be tedious using an ordinary calculator, especially if we wanted to compute the sequence and ratios for lots of choices of A and B. The following program, however, written for the TI-73 (and other TI graphing calculators) allows the user to compute Fibonacci-type sequences easily. It is essential to try many choices of A and B to see what pattern emerges.

PROGRAM:FIB	[Name the program]
Input "INPUT A",A	[The user inputs the
Input "INPUT B",B	initial values of A and B]
2→K	[K counts the number of terms in the sequence so far]

Lbl 1	[Label a line in the program to return to later]
ClrScreen [ClrHome on TI-82]	[Clear the home screen]
Disp"NO. TERMS SO FAR",K	[Display the number of terms computed so far]
Disp "LAST 2 TERMS",A,B	[Display the last two values computed in the sequence]
Disp "RATIO",B/A	[Display the ratio of the last 2 terms]
Pause	[Pause to look at the displayed text and numbers]
A+B→C	[Add the last two numbers of the sequence]
B→A	[Move down the sequence to the next two values to be considered]
C→B	
K+1→K	[Update the number of terms computed so far]
Goto 1	[Return to the Label 1 line in the program]

The screen below shows the result of executing the program for $A = 1$, $B = 3$, and $N = 20$, which generates the first 20 Lucas numbers. The 19th and 20th Lucas numbers are 9349 and 15,127, and their ratio, 15,127/9349, is 1.618034014.

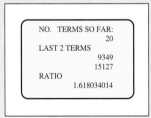

```
    NO.  TERMS SO FAR:
                      20
    LAST 2 TERMS
                    9349
                   15127
    RATIO
               1.618034014
```

The ratio should begin to look familiar after you try other choices of the starting values A and B.

PROBLEM SET 3.6

Understanding Concepts

1. Use your calculator to compute each of the following.
   - (a) $284 + 357$
   - (b) $357 - 284$
   - (c) $284 \cdot 357$
   - (d) $284 \div 71$
   - (e) $781 - 35 + 24$
   - (f) $781 - (35 + 24)$
   - (g) $781 - (35 - 24)$
   - (h) $861 - 423 - 201$
   - (i) $861 - (423 + 201)$

2. Compute the following using your calculator.
   - (a) $271 \cdot 365$
   - (b) $1183 \div 91$
   - (c) $1024 \div 16 \div 2$
   - (d) $1024 \div (16 \div 2)$

3. Use your calculator to calculate each of these division problems.
   - (a) $\dfrac{420 + 315}{15}$
   - (b) $423 + 315 \div 15$
   - (c) $\dfrac{4441 + 2332}{220 + 301}$
   - (d) $\dfrac{16{,}157 + 17 \cdot 13}{722 - 291}$

4. Evaluate the following using your calculator.
   - (a) 29^2
   - (b) $\sqrt{1849}$
   - (c) $\sqrt{2569 - 1480}$
   - (d) $\sqrt{1444} - \sqrt{784}$

5. Write out an entry string to compute
   $$\frac{\sqrt{784} - 91 \div 13}{8 \cdot 49 - 11 \cdot 35}$$
   - (a) using parentheses.
   - (b) not using parentheses.

6. Use the $\boxed{M+}$, $\boxed{M-}$, and $\boxed{MR}$ keys to compute
   $$\frac{4041 + 1237}{91} + \frac{3381 + 2331}{84} - \frac{2113 + 2993}{46}$$
   (*Note:* You should be able to do this entirely with your calculator. Nothing need be (should be) written down but the answer.)

7. (a) Write out the expression you are evaluating if you enter $\boxed{ON/AC}$ 1831 $\boxed{-}$ 17 $\boxed{\times}$ 28 $\boxed{+}$ 34 $\boxed{=}$ into a calculator with algebraic logic.
   (b) Write the numerical answer to part (a).

8. (a) Write out the expression you are evaluating if you enter
   $\boxed{ON/AC}$ 42 $\boxed{\times}$ 34 $\boxed{-}$ 14 $\boxed{\times}$ 6 $\boxed{=}$ $\boxed{\div}$ 28 $\boxed{=}$
   into your calculator.
   (b) What expression does this string evaluate?
   $\boxed{ON/AC}$ 42 $\boxed{\times}$ 34 $\boxed{-}$ 14 $\boxed{\times}$ 6 $\boxed{x^2}$ $\boxed{=}$ $\boxed{\div}$ 28 $\boxed{=}$

9. (a) Make your calculator count by 2s by entering
   $\boxed{ON/AC}$ 0 $\boxed{+}$ 2 $\boxed{=}$ $\boxed{=}$ $\boxed{=}$ $\cdots$.

   (b) Make your calculator generate the odd numbers by entering
   $\boxed{ON/AC}$ 1 $\boxed{+}$ 2 $\boxed{=}$ $\boxed{=}$ $\boxed{=}$ $\cdots$.

10. (a) Make your calculator count by 17s by entering
    $\boxed{ON/AC}$ 0 $\boxed{+}$ 17 $\boxed{=}$ $\boxed{=}$ $\boxed{=}$ $\cdots$.
    (b) If you count by 17s do you ever get to 323? If so when?

11. Use the constant function to generate the first 10 terms of the arithmetic progression whose first four terms are 2, 6, 10, 14; that is, use the $\boxed{=}$ key repeatedly.

12. Use the constant function to generate the first 10 terms of the geometric progression whose first four terms are 3, 15, 75, 375.

13. Use the $\boxed{=}$ and $\boxed{M+}$ keys to compute the sum of the arithmetic progression
    $$5 + 8 + 11 + \cdots + 47.$$

14. Use the $\boxed{=}$ and $\boxed{M+}$ keys to compute the sum of the geometric progression
    $$3 + 15 + 75 + \cdots + 234{,}375.$$

15. Compute 2^{20} using the built-in constant and mentally keeping track of the times you multiply by 2. (*Hint:* Enter $\boxed{ON/AC}$ 2 $\boxed{\times}$ 2 $\boxed{=}$ $\boxed{=}$ $\cdots$, repeating the $\boxed{=}$ as long as necessary.)

Thinking Critically

16. (a) The Lucas numbers are 1, 3, 4, 7, 11, 18, . . . where we start with 1 and 3 and, like for the Fibonacci numbers, add any two consecutive terms to obtain the next. Notationally, we will set $L_1 = 1$, $L_2 = 3$, $L_3 = 4$, . . . , L_n = the nth Lucas number, and so on, In Example 3.41, we developed an algorithm for successively generating the Fibonacci numbers. Modify the algorithm to obtain an algorithm the generates the Lucas numbers. *Suggestion:* Try inserting a 3 after the first $\boxed{M+}$ in the algorithm of Example 3.41.
    (b) Use the algorithm of part (a) to compute the first ten Lucas numbers.

17. (a) Write the expression your calculator will evaluate if you enter the string

    $\boxed{ON/AC}$ 1 $\boxed{+}$ 5 $\boxed{\sqrt{}}$ $\boxed{=}$ $\boxed{\div}$ 2 $\boxed{=}$ $\boxed{M+}$
    and tell where in your calculator the computed number (called the Golden Ratio) can be found.
    (b) Write in general terms the series of expressions your calculator will evaluate if you enter the string

| ON/AC | 1 | + | 5 | $\sqrt{}$ | = | ÷ | 2 | = | M+ |

| × | MR | = | = | = | $\cdots$,

repeatedly pressing the = key. Enter in the following table the expressions and the whole numbers *nearest* (either smaller than or larger than) the computed numbers. The first line has been completed for you.

n	Expression	Nearest Whole Number
2	$\left(\dfrac{1 + \sqrt{5}}{2}\right)^2$	3
3		
4		
5		
6		
7		
8		

(c) Make a conjecture based on the results in part (b).

(d) Compute $(1 + \sqrt{5})/2$ and, using the y^x key, check your conjecture in part (c) for $n = 35$. Note that $L_{35} = 20{,}633{,}239$ is the 35th Lucas number. See problem 16.

18. (a) Use the constant function of your calculator to compute the values of the expressions in the following table filling in the column "Nearest whole number" as you repeatedly press the = key. The first line has been completed for you.

n	Expression	Nearest Whole Number
1	$\left(\dfrac{1 + \sqrt{5}}{2}\right)/\sqrt{5}$	1
2	$\left(\dfrac{1 + \sqrt{5}}{2}\right)^2/\sqrt{5}$	
3	$\left(\dfrac{1 + \sqrt{5}}{2}\right)^3/\sqrt{5}$	
4	$\left(\dfrac{1 + \sqrt{5}}{2}\right)^4/\sqrt{5}$	
5	$\left(\dfrac{1 + \sqrt{5}}{2}\right)^5/\sqrt{5}$	
6	$\left(\dfrac{1 + \sqrt{5}}{2}\right)^6/\sqrt{5}$	
7	$\left(\dfrac{1 + \sqrt{5}}{2}\right)^7/\sqrt{5}$	
8	$\left(\dfrac{1 + \sqrt{5}}{2}\right)^8/\sqrt{5}$	

(b) Make a conjecture based on the results obtained in part (a).

(c) Compute $(1 + \sqrt{5})/2$ and use your y^x key to check your conjecture for $n = 36$. Note that $F_{36} = 14{,}930{,}352$.

▦ Thinking Cooperatively

For these next problems, divide your class into groups of about four students.

19. (a) Use the definition of the Fibonacci and Lucas numbers (see problem 16) to complete this table.

n	1	2	3	4	5	6	7	8	9
F_n	1	1							
L_n	1	3							

(b) Compute the sums $F_1 + F_3$, $F_2 + F_4$, $F_3 + F_5$, ... What result do these sums suggest?

(c) Compute the sums $L_1 + L_3$, $L_2 + L_4$, $L_3 + L_5$, ... What result do these sums suggest?

(d) Compute the sums $F_1 + L_1$, $F_2 + L_2$, $F_3 + L_3$, ... What result do these sums suggest?

20. (a) Use the function $y = \sqrt{5x^2 - 4}$ to compute the values of y in the following table. If the computed value of y is not a whole number, do not enter it into the table.

x	1	2	3	4	5	6	7	8	. . .
y									

(b) What values of x in part (a) yield whole number values for y? Identify these x and y values (they should be familiar).

(c) Guess what value of x will next yield a whole number value for y. Also guess the y value it should yield and check your guess with your calculator.

21. **(a)** Use the function $y = \sqrt{5x^2 + 4}$ to compute the values of y in the following table. If the computed value of y is not a whole number, do not enter it into the table.

x	1	2	3	4	5	6	7	8	...
y									

(b) What values of x in part (a) yield whole number values for y? Identify these values of x and y (they should be familiar).

(c) Guess what value of x will next yield a whole number value for y. Also guess what y value it should yield and check your guess with your calculator.

22. **(a)** Simultaneously compute $t_6 = 1 + 2 + 3 + 4 + 5 + 6$ and $c_6 = 1^3 + 2^3 + 3^3 + 4^3 + 5^3 + 6^3$.

(b) Repeat part (a) for t_{10} and c_{10}.

(c) Make a guess relating t_n and c_n for any n.

(d) Do your examples prove that your guess is correct? Explain briefly.

For Review

23. Write a second addition equation and two subtraction equations equivalent to $18 + 17 = 35$.

24. Write two addition equations and a second subtraction equation equivalent to $27 - 9 = 18$.

25. Write a second multiplication equation and two division equations equivalent to $27 \cdot 11 = 297$.

26. Write two multiplication equations and a second division equation equivalent to $96 \div 12 = 8$.

27. Draw a rectangular array to illustrate the product $5 \cdot 7$.

28. Draw an appropriate diagram to illustrate the equation $5(3 + 4) = 5 \cdot 3 + 5 \cdot 4$; that is, to illustrate the distributive property for whole numbers.

EPILOGUE   Calculating Today

In this chapter we have considered the art of writing numbers and performing calculations using methods extending from ancient to modern times. Our algorithms range from pencil and paper procedures to the use of modern calculators and computers. History shows that the development of the art of calculation has been a tortuous task extending over several thousands of years, but that it has finally reached a stage of extraordinary speed and accuracy. Electronic calculators perform ordinary arithmetic at the touch of a few buttons and the speed of the latest high-speed computing machines is measured in nano* seconds.

But speed is not the purview of machines alone. History is replete with the names of calculating prodigies who could perform the most astounding feats of mental arithmetic quickly and accurately. Be that as it may, with command of the ideas discussed in this chapter, every child can become a calculating prodigy in his or her own right.

These important notions include the following:

- the basic number facts,
- positional notation in base ten and other bases,
- the basic algorithms,
- estimation and approximation,
- the use of a calculator with algebraic notation.

This puts great arithmetic power within easy reach of everyone and makes it possible for students to spend a great deal more time thinking about and doing more significant and meaningful mathematics. We consider some of these more important ideas, starting in the next chapter with notions from number theory.

---

*A nano second is one billionth of a second.

CHAPTER 3 SUMMARY

Key Concepts

1. Numeration systems
   (a) Ancient systems like the Egyptian and Roman were additive systems that made it difficult to record large numbers and to calculate.
   (b) Positional systems like the Mayan and our modern Indo-Arabic, or decimal, system make it possible to record large numbers with only a few symbols and to devise relatively easy algorithms for addition, subtraction, multiplication, and division.
   (c) Studying positional systems in bases other than base ten makes positional notation more clear and also helps to clarify computational algorithms.

2. Mental arithmetic and estimation
   (a) It is important that students develop skill at mental arithmetic. Children find mental arithmetic exciting (in games, contests, and so on), and it promotes greater confidence in doing mathematics generally.
   (b) With calculators and computers giving quick and easy solutions, it is crucial that students be able to make good estimates so that they can reliably assess the correctness of results obtained. This not only requires a complete understanding of 1-digit facts but also a good understanding of positional notation.

3. Getting the most out of your calculator
   (a) Calculators take the drudgery out of everyday arithmetic.
   (b) Calculators free students to spend considerably more time on problem solving and critical mathematical thinking.
   (c) Beyond simple arithmetic, it is possible to use special capabilities of calculators to devise ingenious methods or algorithms for acomplishing numerous mathematical tasks.

Vocabulary and Notation

Section 3.1

Additive systems
    The Egyptian system
    The Roman system
Positional systems
    The Babylonian system
    The Mayan system
    The Indo-Arabic (decimal) system
        Base
        Digits
        Place value
        Expanded notation
        Models for positional notation
            The classroom abacus
            Sticks in bundles
            Unifix™ cubes
            Units, strips, and mats
            Base 10 blocks

Section 3.2

Nondecimal positional systems
    Base five notation
    Converting from base five to base ten notation
    Converting from base ten to base five notation

Section 3.3

Algorithms for addition
    Using units, strips, and mats
    Using place value cards
    Using pencil and paper
Algorithms for subtraction
    Using units, strips, and mats
    Using place value cards
    Using pencil and paper
Algorithms in other bases

Addition in base five
Subtraction in base five

Section 3.4

Algorithms for multiplication
    Using units, strips, and mats
    Using place value cards
    Using expanded notation
    Using algorithms
Multiplication in other bases
    Multiplication in base six
Algorithms for division
    The division algorithm
    The long division algorithm
    The short division algorithm

Section 3.5

Mental arithmetic
    One-digit facts
    Easy combinations
    Adjustment
    Working from left to right
    Rounding
    The 5-up rule
Estimation
    Approximating by rounding

Section 3.6

Types of calculators
    Reverse Polish notation
    Arithmetic logic
    Algebraic logic
Priority of operations
    Order for machines using arithmetic logic
    Order for machines using algebraic logic
    Use of parentheses
Special capabilities
    Use of the $\boxed{\text{ON/AC}}$ key
    Use of the $\boxed{=}$ key
    Pairing of parentheses
    Error messages
    Using the $\boxed{x^2}$, $\boxed{\sqrt{}}$, $\boxed{10^n}$, and $\boxed{1/x}$ keys
    Using the $\boxed{y^x}$ key
    Using the $\boxed{\text{M}+}$, $\boxed{\text{M}-}$, $\boxed{\text{MR}}$, and $\boxed{x \circlearrowright \text{M}}$ keys
    Using the $\boxed{\text{INT}\div}$ key
    Using the built-in constant function
        The sum of an arithmetic progression
        The sum of a geometric progression
    Using the $\boxed{+ \circlearrowright -}$ key
Algorithmic thinking

CHAPTER REVIEW EXERCISES

Section 3.1

1. Write the Indo-Arabic equivalent of each of these.

    (a)

    ![Egyptian hieroglyphic numeral symbols]

    (b)

    (c) MCMXCVIII

2. Write 234,572 in Mayan notation.

3. Suppose you have 5 mats, 27 strips, and 32 units for a total count of 802. Briefly describe the exchanges that must be made to represent this number with the smallest possible number of manipulative pieces. How many mats, strips, and units result?

Section 3.2

4. Find the base ten equivalent of each of the following.
    (a) 101101_{two} (b) 346_{seven} (c) $2T9_{\text{twelve}}$

5. Write 287_{ten} as a numeral in each base indicated.
    (a) base five   (b) base two   (c) base seven

Section 3.3

6. Sketch the solution to 47 + 25 using mats, strips, and units. Draw a square for each mat, a vertical line segment for each strip, and a dot for each unit.

7. Use the Instructional Addition Algorithm to perform the following additions.
    (a) 42 + 54   (b) 47 + 35   (c) 59 + 63

8. Use sketches of place value cards to illustrate each of these subtractions.
   (a) $487 - 275$ (b) $547 - 152$
9. Perform the following calculations in base five notation. Assume that the numerals are already written in base five.
   (a) $\begin{array}{r} 2433 \\ + \ 141 \\ \hline \end{array}$ (b) $\begin{array}{r} 2433 \\ - \ 141 \\ \hline \end{array}$ (c) $\begin{array}{r} 243 \\ \times \ 42 \\ \hline \end{array}$

Section 3.4

10. Perform these multiplications using the Instructional Multiplication Algorithm.
    (a) 4×357 (b) 27×642
11. Use the scaffold method to perform each of these divisions.
    (a) $7\overline{)895}$ (b) $347\overline{)27483}$
12. Use the short division algorithm to perform each of these divisions.
    (a) $5\overline{)27436}$ (b) $8\overline{)39584}$
13. Carry out each of these multiplications in base five. Assume that the numerals are already written in base five.
    (a) $23 \cdot 42$ (b) $2413 \cdot 332$
14. Use the Russian peasant method to compute the product $42 \cdot 35$.

Section 3.5

15. Round 274,535
    (a) to the nearest one hundred thousand.
    (b) to the nearest ten thousand.
    (c) to the nearest thousand.
16. Rounding to the left-most digit, compute approximations to the answers to each of these.

(a) $657 + 439$ (b) $657 - 439$
(c) $657 \cdot 439$ (d) $1657 \div 23$

Section 3.6

17. Compute the following using your calculator.
$$\frac{\sqrt{1444} - 152 \div 19}{2874 - 2859}$$
18. (a) Compute the sum of this arithmetic progression.
$$4 + 11 + 18 + \cdots + 333$$
    (b) Compute the sum of this geometric progression.
$$3 + 6 + 12 + 24 + \cdots + 24576$$
19. (a) Compute each of the following. (*Suggestion:* Compute $(1 + \sqrt{5})/2$ and store it in the memory for repeated use or use the constant feature of your calculator.)

Nearest Integer

$\left(\dfrac{1 + \sqrt{5}}{2}\right) \cdot 7,$ _____

$\left(\dfrac{1 + \sqrt{5}}{2}\right) \cdot 11,$ _____

$\left(\dfrac{1 + \sqrt{5}}{2}\right) \cdot 18,$ _____

$\left(\dfrac{1 + \sqrt{5}}{2}\right) \cdot 29,$ _____

Remember: The Lucas numbers are 1, 3, 4, 7, 11, 18, 29, ...

(b) Make a conjecture on the basis of part (a).
(c) Does your conjecture hold for all Lucas numbers? How about L_1, L_2, and L_3?
(d) How might you mofidy your conjecture in view of part (c)? Note that $L_{34} = 12,752,043$ and $L_{35} = 20,633,239$.

CHAPTER TEST

1. Write the base ten equivalents of each of the following.
   (a) 21022_{three} (b) 317_{eight} (c) 4213_{five}
2. Write 281_{ten} as a numeral in each of these bases.
   (a) base five   (b) base two   (c) base twelve
3. Perform each of the following calculations entirely in base five. The numerals are already written in base five.
   (a) $\begin{array}{r} 242 \\ + \ 43 \\ \hline \end{array}$ (b) $\begin{array}{r} 242 \\ - \ 43 \\ \hline \end{array}$ (c) $\begin{array}{r} 242 \\ \times \ 43 \\ \hline \end{array}$

4. Make a schematic drawing using mats, strips, and units to illustrate the addition of 74 and 48. Draw squares for mats, straight line segments for strips, and dots for units.
5. Write 39,485 in Mayan notation.

6. Fill in the missing digits in this addition problem.
$$\begin{array}{r} 2\_37 \\ + \ \_22\_ \\ \hline \_0{,}0\_1 \end{array}$$
7. Fill in the missing digits in this subtraction problem.
$$\begin{array}{r} \_23\_ \\ - \ 35\_2 \\ \hline 4\_94 \end{array}$$
8. Round 3,376,500 to the
   (a) nearest million.
   (b) nearest one hundred thousand.
   (c) nearest ten thousand.
   (d) nearest one thousand.

9. Round each number to the left-most digit to find an estimate for the sum

$$378 + 64 + 291 + 39 + 3871.$$

10. Place the digits 1, 3, 5, 7, 9, in the proper boxes to achieve the maximum product.

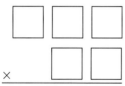

11. Place the digits 0, 2, 4, 6, 8 in the proper boxes to obtain the least product given that 0 cannot be placed in either of the left-hand boxes.

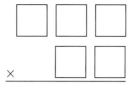

12. (a) Compute the integers nearest to each of

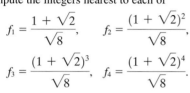

$$f_1 = \frac{1 + \sqrt{2}}{\sqrt{8}}, \qquad f_2 = \frac{(1 + \sqrt{2})^2}{\sqrt{8}},$$

$$f_3 = \frac{(1 + \sqrt{2})^3}{\sqrt{8}}, \qquad f_4 = \frac{(1 + \sqrt{2})^4}{\sqrt{8}}.$$

(b) Guess the most likely choices for f_5 and f_6.

(c) Guess what rule (other than that of part (a)) might be used to obtain the successive values of f_n.

13. (a) Compute the quantities:

1^3	and 1^2
$1^3 + 2^3$	and $(1 + 2)^2$
$1^3 + 2^3 + 3^3$	and $(1 + 2 + 3)^2$
$1^3 + 2^3 + 3^3 + 4^3$	and $(1 + 2 + 3 + 4)^2$

(b) Compute the square roots of the answers to the computations of part (a).

(c) Guess a formula for $1^3 + 2^3 + \cdots + n^3$ and for $(1 + 2 + 3 + \cdots + n)^2$.

14. Compute the sum of this arithmetic progression.

$$3 + 8 + 13 + \cdots + 123$$

15. Compute the sum of this geometric progression.

$$3 + 15 + 75 + \cdots + 1{,}171{,}875$$

16. Write an algorithm to generate the sequence

$$2, 5, 7, 12, 19, \ldots$$

where we start with 2 and 5 and add any two consecutive terms to obtain the next term.

CHAPTER

4

Number Theory

4.1 Divisibility of Natural Numbers

4.2 Tests for Divisibility

4.3 Greatest Common Divisors
and Least Common Multiples

4.4 Clock Arithmetic

HANDS ON
Representing Integers as Sums

Materials Needed

One copy of the sheet outlined below for each student.

Directions

Divide the class into groups of three or four students each and have them carry out the directions on the handout.

Investigation 1. Representing Natural Numbers as a Sum of Consecutive Integers

Some numbers can be written as a sum of two or more consecutive positive integers. For example, $3 = 1 + 2$, and $15 = 4 + 5 + 6$ (alternatively, $15 = 1 + 2 + 3 + 4 + 5$). On the other hand, 2 cannot be written as the sum of two or more consecutive integers. Fill in the rest of this table, and then conjecture what pattern is revealed in your table.

n		n		n		n	
1	X	11		21		31	
2	X	12		22		32	
3	1 + 2	13		23		33	
4		14		24		34	
5		15		25		35	
6		16		26		36	
7		17		27		37	
8		18		28		38	
9		19		29		39	
10		20		30		40	

Investigation 2. Representing Numbers with Sums of Consecutive Evens or Odds

Some numbers can be written as a sum of two or more consecutive even or consecutive odd positive integers. For example, $6 = 2 + 4$, and $45 = 5 + 7 + 9 + 11 + 13$ (alternatively, $45 = 13 + 15 + 17$). On the other hand, 2 cannot be written as the sum of two or more consecutive integers that are all even or all odd. Fill in this table, and then conjecture what pattern is revealed in your table.

n		n		n		n	
1	X	11		21		31	
2	X	12		22		32	
3		13		23		33	
4		14		24		34	
5		15		25		35	
6	2 + 4	16		26		36	
7		17		27		37	
8		18		28		38	
9		19		29		39	
10		20		30		40	

Number Theory

As students in grades 3–5 study numbers, they also learn about classes of numbers and their characteristics, such as which numbers are odd, even, prime, composite, or square. Recognizing such characteristics lays a foundation for checking divisibility rules, finding prime factors, or understanding functional relationships.

Students also work with whole numbers in their study of number theory concepts. Problems concerning divisibility (e.g., show that the product of any four consecutive integers is always divisible by 24), prime numbers (e.g., show that the sum of two primes is not necessarily prime), or figurate numbers (find the 20th triangular number) not only build on students' knowledge of whole numbers but also provide rich opportunities for problem solving, reasoning, and the use of algebraic thinking. Moreover, students' learning about prime factorization and relatively prime numbers helps them understand some aspects of their work with fractions (e.g., procedures for simplifying or adding fractions).

Some mathematical conjectures have gained notoriety for their simplicity as well as for the challenge they have provided many mathematicians over many years. A famous open problem is known as Goldbach's Conjecture. Goldbach predicted that every even number greater than 4 can be written as the sum of two (not necessarily different) odd primes. For example, "$6 = 3 + 3, 8 = 3 + 5, 10 = 3 + 7 = 5 + 5, \ldots$" The conjecture has been tested and found true for numbers into the trillions, but it has not yet been proved or disproved in general.

The point is that doing mathematics involves *discovery*. Conjecture—that is, informed guessing—is a major pathway to discovery. Teachers and researchers agree that students can learn to make, refine, and test conjectures in elementary school. For example, one lesson from a third-grade class includes conversations among students as they looked for patterns when adding even and odd numbers. The students conjectured that the sum of two even numbers will always be even, as will the sum of two odd numbers.

SOURCE: Reprinted with permission from *Curriculum and Evaluation Standards for School Mathematics: Discussion Draft*, copyright 1998 by the National Council of Teachers of Mathematics. All rights reserved.

CONNECTIONS   The Fascination with Numbers

In Chapter 2, we considered the whole numbers, operations with whole numbers, and some of their properties. In Chapter 3, we studied various systems for writing whole numbers and a variety of algorithms for calculating. Initially, these ideas arose in response to people's needs—the need to count, the need to record counts, and the need of merchants to calculate in the course of doing business. However, very early on, people began to be fascinated with numbers themselves and their many interesting properties. For example, the Greeks called 6 a **perfect number** since

$$6 = 1 + 2 + 3$$

$1 \cdot 6 = 6$
$2 \cdot 3 = 6$

and 1, 2, and 3 are all the natural numbers that divide 6 evenly except for 6 itself.

It turns out that 28 also has this property since

$$28 = 1 + 2 + 4 + 7 + 14$$

$1 \cdot 28 = 28$
$2 \cdot 14 = 28$
$4 \cdot 7 = 28$

and 1, 2, 4, 7, and 14 are all the natural numbers that divide 28 evenly except for 28 itself. The next two perfect numbers are 496 and 8128. As of this writing, 33 perfect numbers are known. It is conjectured that there are infinitely many perfect numbers, but there is no proof that this is so.

In this chapter, we consider divisibility properties of the natural numbers. These ideas are necessary and useful (in working with fractions, for example), and are a rich source of interesting problems and puzzles that can be used to heighten student interest in learning mathematics.

4.1 Divisibility of Natural Numbers

Divides, Divisors, Factors, Multiples

In Chapter 3 we considered the division algorithm. If a and b are whole numbers with b not zero, when we divide a by b we obtain a unique quotient q and remainder r such that $a = bq + r$ and $0 \leq r < b$. Thus, the division

$$\begin{array}{r} 4 \ \ R \ \ 2 \\ 3\overline{)14} \end{array}$$

is equivalent to the equation

$$14 = 3 \cdot 4 + 2.$$

Of special interest in this chapter, because it is important in dealing with fractions, is the case when the remainder r is zero. Then $a = bq$ and we say that **b divides a evenly** or, more simply, **b divides a.** This is expressed in other terminology as indicated here.

DEFINITION *Divides, Divisor, Factor, Multiple*

If a and b are whole numbers with $b \neq 0$ and there is a whole number q such that $a = bq$, we say that b **divides** a. We also say that b is a **factor** of a or a **divisor** of a and that a is a **multiple** of b. If b divides a and b is less than a, it is called a **proper divisor** of a.

A useful model for the ideas "b divides a" and "a is a multiple of b" has already been provided by the array models for multiplication of natural numbers in Chapter 2. Thus, the five by seven rectangular array in Figure 4.1 illustrates the fact that 5 and 7 are both divisors of 35 and that 35 is a multiple of 5 and also of 7.

Figure 4.1
Array model showing that 5 and 7 are factors of 35 and that 35 is a multiple of both 5 and 7.

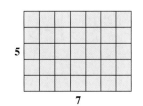

$5 \cdot 7 = 35$
$35 \div 5 = 7$
$35 \div 7 = 5$

EXAMPLE 4.1

The Multiples of 2

Write the multiples of 2.

Solution

According to the above definition, the multiples of 2 are the numbers of the form $2q$ where q is a whole number. Taking $q = 0, 1, 2, 3, \ldots$, we obtain the multiples

$$0 = 2 \cdot 0, \ 2 = 2 \cdot 1, \ 4 = 2 \cdot 2, \ 6 = 2 \cdot 3, \ldots$$

which are just the **even** whole numbers. These multiples could also be obtained by starting with 0 and counting by 2s. Also, except for 0, the multiples of 2 can be illustrated by this series of rectangles

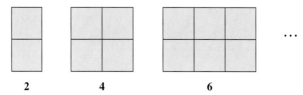

As in the preceding example, the multiples of 3 are

$$0 = 3 \cdot 0, \ 3 = 3 \cdot 1, \ 6 = 3 \cdot 2, \ 9 = 3 \cdot 3, \ldots$$

which can be obtained by starting with 0 and counting by 3s. In general, the multiples of m are

$$0 = m \cdot 0, \ m = m \cdot 1, \ 2m = m \cdot 2, \ 3m = m \cdot 3, \ldots$$

obtained by starting with 0 and counting by m's.

EXAMPLE 4.2

The Divisors or Factors of 6

List all the factors of 6.

Solution

We must determine all natural numbers b for which there is a whole number q such that $6 = bq$. This means that we must find all rectangular arrays with six small squares. By trial and error, we find that there are only four such rectangles and that the desired factors of 6 are 1, 2, 3, and 6. Note, by the way, that as b runs through the divisors of 6—1, 2, 3, 6—so does the quotient q but in the reverse order—6, 3, 2, 1. Finally, it is correct to say that 1, 2, 3, and 6 are factors of 6 and that 6 is a multiple of each of 1, 2, 3, and 6. It is also correct to write 1 divides 6, 2 divides 6, 3 divides 6, and 6 divides 6.

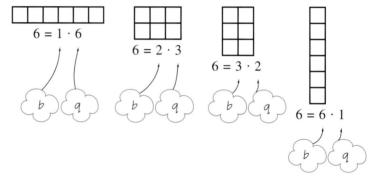

Prime and Composite Numbers

Since $1 \cdot a = a$, 1 and a are *always* factors of a for every natural number a. For this reason, 1 and a are often called trivial factors of a and $1 \cdot a$ and $a \cdot 1$ are trivial factorings. Some numbers, like 2, 3, 5, and 7, have only trivial factorings. Other numbers, like 6, have nontrivial factorings. The number 1 stands alone since it has only one factor, 1 itself. All this is summarized in this definition.

DEFINITION   *Units, Primes, and Composite Numbers*

A natural number that possesses exactly two different factors, itself and 1, is called a **prime number.** A natural number that possesses more than two different factors is called a **composite number.** The number 1 is called a **unit;** it is neither prime nor composite.

The primes are sometimes called the building blocks of the natural numbers since every natural number other than 1 is either a prime or a product of primes. For example, consider a number like 180. This is composite since, for example, we can write $180 = 10 \cdot 18$. Moreover, 10 and 18 are both composite since $10 = 2 \cdot 5$ and $18 = 2 \cdot 9$. Now 2 and 5 are both primes and cannot be factored further. But $9 = 3 \cdot 3$ and 3 is a prime. We simply continue to factor a composite number into smaller and smaller factors and stop when this can proceed no further; that is, when the factors are all primes. In the case of 180, we see that

$$180 = 10 \cdot 18$$
$$= 2 \cdot 5 \cdot 2 \cdot 9$$
$$= 2 \cdot 5 \cdot 2 \cdot 3 \cdot 3,$$

and this is a product of primes.

A convenient way of organizing this work is to develop a **factor tree,** as shown in Figure 4.2, to keep track of each step in the process. But there are other ways to factor 180 as these factor trees show.

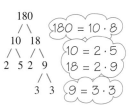

Figure 4.2
A factor tree for 180

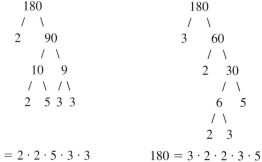

Another, perhaps even more convenient, scheme for finding the prime factors of a number should be mentioned as well. Repeatedly use prime divisors and short division until arriving at a quotient that is a prime. For 180 we might have these divisions.

$$180 = 2 \cdot 2 \cdot 3 \cdot 3 \cdot 5 \qquad 180 = 5 \cdot 2 \cdot 2 \cdot 3 \cdot 3 \qquad 180 = 3 \cdot 3 \cdot 2 \cdot 2 \cdot 5$$

In making a factor tree most of the arithmetic is done mentally. The short division scheme makes for a bit more writing while still leaving a written record of the results. Thus, some find the short division approach more helpful.

The most important thing about all the factorings shown for 180 is that, no matter what scheme is used and no matter how it is carried out, the *same prime factors always result*. That this is always the case is stated here without proof.

THEOREM   *Simple Product Form of the Fundamental Theorem of Arithmetic*
Every natural number greater than 1 is a prime or can be expressed as a product of primes in one and only one way apart from order.

The preceding theorem is the reason that we do not think of 1 as either a prime or composite number. If 1 were considered a prime, the theorem would not be true. For example, we could multiply 180 by any number of factors of 1 and the prime factorization of 180 would not be unique.

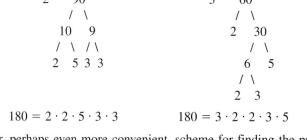

EXAMPLE 4.3

The Prime Factors of 600

Represent 600 as a product of prime factors.

Solution

Using a factor tree:

$$
\begin{array}{c}
600 \\
/\ \ \backslash \\
30 \quad 20 \\
/\ \backslash \ /\ \backslash \\
15 \ \ 2\ \ 2 \quad 10 \\
/\ \backslash \qquad /\ \backslash \\
3\ \ 5 \qquad 2\ \ 5
\end{array}
$$

Using short division:

$$
\begin{array}{r}
5 \\
5\overline{)25} \\
2\overline{)50} \\
2\overline{)100} \\
3\overline{)300} \\
2\overline{)600}
\end{array}
$$

$$600 = 2 \cdot 2 \cdot 2 \cdot 3 \cdot 5 \cdot 5$$

In Example 4.3, we can also write 600 as a product of primes by collecting like primes together and writing their products as powers; i.e., we write $600 = 2^3 \cdot 3^1 \cdot 5^2$. Since this could be done for any natural number, it is useful to give an alternative version of the **fundamental theorem of arithmetic.**

> **THEOREM** *Prime Power Form of the Fundamental Theorem of Arithmetic*
>
> Every natural number n greater than 1 is a power of a prime or it can be expressed as a product of powers of different primes in one and only one way apart from order. This representation is called the **prime power representation of n.**

EXAMPLE 4.4

The Prime Power Representation of 675

Determine the prime power representation of 675.

Solution

$$
\begin{array}{r}
3 \\
3\overline{)9} \\
3\overline{)27} \\
5\overline{)135} \\
5\overline{)675}
\end{array}
$$

Using the short division method we see that $675 = 3^3 \cdot 5^2$.

The Divisors of a Natural Number

An important feature of the prime power representations of numbers is that they make it possible to tell at a glance if one number divides another. In Example 4.4, we saw that $675 = 3^3 \cdot 5^2$. Suppose that r divides 675, then there is an integer s such that

$$rs = 675 = 3^3 \cdot 5^2.$$

Then those primes that divide r must be among the primes that divide 675 and they must appear to no higher power. For example, $r = 15 = 3^1 \cdot 5^1$ divides 675. Moreover, the quotient s must be $3^2 \cdot 5^1 = 45$ so that the product of r and s contains three 3s and two 5s. In fact, all the divisors of 675 can be written down by making a systematic list as shown here.

$$
\begin{array}{lll}
1 = 3^0 \cdot 5^0 & 5 = 3^0 \cdot 5^1 & 25 = 3^0 \cdot 5^2 \\
3 = 3^1 \cdot 5^0 & 15 = 3^1 \cdot 5^1 & 75 = 3^1 \cdot 5^2 \\
9 = 3^2 \cdot 5^0 & 45 = 3^2 \cdot 5^1 & 225 = 3^2 \cdot 5^2 \\
27 = 3^3 \cdot 5^0 & 135 = 3^3 \cdot 5^1 & 675 = 3^3 \cdot 5^2
\end{array}
$$

In determining r above, there are four choices for the exponent on 3—0, 1, 2, or 3—and three choices for the exponent on 5—0, 1, or 2. Thus, there are $3 \cdot 4 = 12$ possible factors of 675 as the above list shows. This argument can be repeated in general and the result stated as a theorem that tells which numbers divide a given number.

> **THEOREM**   *The Divisors of a Natural Number*
>
> Let $n = p_1^{a_1} p_2^{a_2} \cdots p_r^{a_r}$ be the prime power representation of n. Then m divides n if, and only if, $m = p_1^{b_1} p_2^{b_2} \cdots p_r^{b_r}$ where $0 \le b_1 \le a_1, 0 \le b_2 \le a_2, \ldots, 0 \le b_r \le a_r$. Moreover, the number of factors or divisors of a is given by $N = (a_1 + 1)(a_2 + 1) \ldots (a_r + 1)$.

EXAMPLE 4.5

The Divisors of 600

List all the divisors of 600.

Solution

The divisors must be all the numbers of the form $2^r \cdot 3^s \cdot 5^t$ with $0 \le r \le 3, 0 \le s \le 1$, and $0 \le t \le 2$. We make a systematic list of the divisors as follows.

$$
\begin{array}{lll}
1 = 2^0 \cdot 3^0 \cdot 5^0 & 5 = 2^0 \cdot 3^0 \cdot 5^1 & 25 = 2^0 \cdot 3^0 \cdot 5^2 \\
2 = 2^1 \cdot 3^0 \cdot 5^0 & 10 = 2^1 \cdot 3^0 \cdot 5^1 & 50 = 2^1 \cdot 3^0 \cdot 5^2 \\
4 = 2^2 \cdot 3^0 \cdot 5^0 & 20 = 2^2 \cdot 3^0 \cdot 5^1 & 100 = 2^2 \cdot 3^0 \cdot 5^2 \\
8 = 2^3 \cdot 3^0 \cdot 5^0 & 40 = 2^3 \cdot 3^0 \cdot 5^1 & 200 = 2^3 \cdot 3^0 \cdot 5^2 \\[6pt]
3 = 2^0 \cdot 3^1 \cdot 5^0 & 15 = 2^0 \cdot 3^1 \cdot 5^1 & 75 = 2^0 \cdot 3^1 \cdot 5^2 \\
6 = 2^1 \cdot 3^1 \cdot 5^0 & 30 = 2^1 \cdot 3^1 \cdot 5^1 & 150 = 2^1 \cdot 3^1 \cdot 5^2 \\
12 = 2^2 \cdot 3^1 \cdot 5^0 & 60 = 2^2 \cdot 3^1 \cdot 5^1 & 300 = 2^2 \cdot 3^1 \cdot 5^2 \\
24 = 2^3 \cdot 3^1 \cdot 5^0 & 120 = 2^3 \cdot 3^1 \cdot 5^1 & 600 = 2^3 \cdot 3^1 \cdot 5^2
\end{array}
$$

Note that the four choices for r, the two choices for s, and the three choices for t show that there are $4 \cdot 2 \cdot 3 = 24$ divisors of 600 as shown in the list.

Two Questions About Primes

Since we have just seen how important the primes are as "building blocks" for the natural numbers, it is reasonable to ask at least two questions:

- How many primes are there?
- How does one determine if a given number is a prime?

We answer these questions in the order asked.

There Are Infinitely Many Primes

The answer to the first of the questions just posed is that there are infinitely many primes. To see this we describe a step-by-step process that determines at least one new prime at each step. Since the process can be continued without end, it follows that the set of primes is infinite. The argument proceeds as follows.

Since 1 is the only natural number less than 2, the only factors of 2 are 1 and 2 itself. Thus, 2 is a prime. Consider $3 = 2 + 1$. Since 2 does not divide 3, the only divisors of 3 are 1 and 3. So 3 is also a prime. Consider $7 = 2 \cdot 3 + 1$. Recalling the division algorithm, this says that, if you divide 7 by either 2 or 3, there is a remainder of 1. Thus, 2 does not divide 7 and 3 does not divide 7. But, by the fundamental theorem of arithmetic, 7 must have a prime divisor. Therefore, 7 has a prime factor different from both 2 and 3. In fact, 7 is itself a prime. Similarly, $43 = 2 \cdot 3 \cdot 7 + 1$ leaves a remainder of 1 when divided by 2, 3, or 7. Thus, 43 is divisible by a prime different from 2, 3, and 7. In fact, 43 is also a prime. We next consider $1807 = 2 \cdot 3 \cdot 7 \cdot 43 + 1$. As before, 1807 is not divisible by any of 2, 3, 7, or 43 (since all leave a remainder of 1) so there must exist a prime other than these primes. In this case, $1807 = 13 \cdot 139$ and both 13 and 139 are primes. In any event, if we multiply all the known primes together and add 1, we obtain a number that must be divisible by at least one new prime. Since this process can be continued *ad infinitum,* it follows that there is no end to the list of primes; that is, there are infinitely many primes.

THEOREM   *The Number of Primes*

There are infinitely many primes.

HIGHLIGHT FROM HISTORY
Euclid of Alexandria

One of the great mathematicians of the ancient world was Euclid of Alexandria. Little is known of Euclid's life. The dates of his birth and death are not even known (though he lived about 300 B.C.) nor is his birth place or any of the other little details one might find of interest. What is known is that he was a first rate teacher/scholar at the great university at Alexandria under Ptolemy II and that he authored some dozen books on mathematics. The most important of these is his *Elements (Stoichia)* which set a new standard of rigor for mathematical thought that persists to this day. It is almost certain that no book, save the Bible, has been more used, studied, or edited than the *Elements* and none has had a more profound effect on scientific thought.

This monumental work is divided into 13 books and is more popularly known for its remarkable treatment of geometry—an approach that set the pattern for what is taught in schools even today. However, books VII, VIII, and IX deal with number theory and contain many interesting results. Euclid was the first to prove that there are infinitely many primes, and his proof is essentially the one given in this text. He also invented the Euclidean algorithm for determining the greatest common divisor of two natural numbers, which we consider shortly.

Another fascinating result is Euclid's formula for even perfect numbers. Recall that a number is considered perfect if it is the sum of its proper divisors. Thus, as observed earlier,

$$6 = 1 + 2 + 3$$

and

$$28 = 1 + 2 + 4 + 7 + 14$$

are the first two perfect numbers. The next three perfect numbers are 496, 8128, and 33,550,336. That Euclid was able to devise a formula for all even perfect numbers was truly remarkable.

So impressed was she by Euclid's work that the American poet, Edna St. Vincent Millay, was moved to write, "Euclid alone has looked at beauty bare!"

Determining if a Given Integer Is a Prime

We now answer the second question posed above. Observe that if n is composite it must have at least one nontrivial factor (and hence at least one prime factor) not greater than its own square root. For, suppose $n = bc$ with $b > \sqrt{n}$ and $c > \sqrt{n}$. Then,

$$n = bc > \sqrt{n} \cdot \sqrt{n} = n.$$

But this says that $n > n$ which is nonsense. Thus, either $b \leq \sqrt{n}$ or $c \leq \sqrt{n}$ and we have this theorem.

THEOREM *Prime Divisors of* n
If n is composite, then there is a prime p such that p divides n and $p \leq \sqrt{n}$, (that is, $p^2 \leq n$).

To use this theorem, we still need to know all the primes less than or equal to $\sqrt{n}$. Remarkably, a systematic method for determining all the primes up to a given limit was devised by the Greek mathematician, Eratosthenes (276–195 B.C.). Aptly called the **sieve of Eratosthenes,** the method depends only on counting. Suppose we want to determine all the primes up to 100. Since 1 is neither prime nor composite, we write down all the whole numbers from 2 to 100. Note that 2 is a prime since its only possible factors are itself and 1. However, every second number after 2 is a multiple of 2 and so is composite. Thus, we delete or "sieve out," these numbers from our list. The next number not deleted is 3. It must be a prime since it is not a multiple of the only smaller prime. We now "sieve out" all multiples of 3 after 3 itself; that is, we strike from the list every third number after 3 whether it has been struck out before or not. The next number not already deleted must also be a prime since it is not a multiple of 2 or 3, the only smaller primes. Thus, 5 is a prime and every fifth number after 5 must be deleted as a multiple of 5. In the same way, we determine that 7 is a prime and delete every seventh number after 7. Similarly, 11 is the next prime, but, when we delete every eleventh number after 11, no new numbers are deleted. In fact, all the remaining numbers at this point are primes and the sieve, as shown in Figure 4.3, is complete.

	(2)	(3)	~~4~~	(5)	~~6~~	(7)	~~8~~	~~9~~	~~10~~
(11)	~~12~~	(13)	~~14~~	~~15~~	~~16~~	(17)	~~18~~	(19)	~~20~~
~~21~~	~~22~~	(23)	~~24~~	~~25~~	~~26~~	~~27~~	~~28~~	(29)	~~30~~
(31)	~~32~~	~~33~~	~~34~~	~~35~~	~~36~~	(37)	~~38~~	~~39~~	~~40~~
(41)	~~42~~	(43)	~~44~~	~~45~~	~~46~~	(47)	~~48~~	~~49~~	~~50~~
~~51~~	~~52~~	(53)	~~54~~	~~55~~	~~56~~	~~57~~	~~58~~	(59)	~~60~~
(61)	~~62~~	~~63~~	~~64~~	~~65~~	~~66~~	(67)	~~68~~	~~69~~	~~70~~
(71)	~~72~~	(73)	~~74~~	~~75~~	~~76~~	~~77~~	~~78~~	(79)	~~80~~
~~81~~	~~82~~	(83)	~~84~~	~~85~~	~~86~~	~~87~~	~~88~~	(89)	~~90~~
~~91~~	~~92~~	~~93~~	~~94~~	~~95~~	~~96~~	(97)	~~98~~	~~99~~	~~100~~

Figure 4.3
The sieve of Eratosthenes for $n = 100$

The primes have been circled to make them stand out. To see why the sieve is complete at this point, note that if $n < 100$, then $\sqrt{n} < \sqrt{100} = 10$. Hence, if n is composite and is in the list, it must have a prime factor less than or equal to 10 by the preceding theorem. Thus, the sieve is complete by the time we have deleted all multiples of 2, 3, 5, and 7.

Chapter 4
Lesson
14

Exploring Prime and Composite Numbers

Problem Solving Connection
- Look for a Pattern
- Use Logical Reasoning

Materials
hundred chart

Vocabulary
prime number
whole number with exactly two different factors

composite number
whole number greater than 1 that is not prime

Explore • • • • • • • • • • • • • •

Eratosthenes (*ehr uh TAHS thuh neez*) was a mathematician from Cyrene (now known as Libya) who lived about 2,200 years ago. He studied **prime numbers**. The number 3 is an example of a prime number. It has only two factors, 1 and 3.

Composite numbers have more than two factors. An example of a composite number is 8. Its factors are 1, 2, 4, and 8.

Cyrene was the capital of ancient Cyrenaica.

1×8 • • • • • • • • 2×4 • • • •
                                              • • • •

You tell whether a number is prime by testing possible factors. There are no other factors for 7 besides 7 and 1. So, 7 is a prime number.

1×7 • • • • • • •

Eratosthenes' Sieve is a process that "strains" out composite numbers and leaves prime numbers behind. Use it to find the prime numbers between 1 and 100.

Did You Know?
A computer has been used to find a prime number that, if printed in a newspaper, would fill 12 pages.

Work Together

1. Use a hundred chart. Follow the directions to cross out composite numbers and circle prime numbers.

   a. Cross out 1. It has only 1 factor.

   b. Circle 2, the least prime number. Cross out all numbers divisible by 2.

   c. Repeat this step with 3, the next prime number.

2. Continue this process until you reach 100.

3. List all of the circled numbers. There should be 25.

Talk About It

What pattern can you see in the list of prime numbers?

204 Chapter 4 • Dividing Whole Numbers and Decimals: 1-Digit Divisors

Questions for the Teacher

1. Is the discussion of the sieve of Eratosthenes above fully adequate? How are students to tell if 2, 3, 5, . . . are primes? Must they draw a rectangular array each time? Is there any other way to tell? How would you help them at this point?

2. Students will wonder why no more numbers are sieved out of the hundred chart after the multiples of 7. How would you help them to understand why this is so and why all the numbers not crossed out at this point are primes?

EXAMPLE   4.6 | **Determining the Primality of 439**

Show that 439 is a prime.

Solution

This is also easily determined with your calculator (or the program FACTOR on a graphing calculator) in just a couple of minutes. Since $\sqrt{439} \doteq 21$, we see from the sieve of Eratosthenes that, if 439 is composite, it is a multiple of one of 2, 3, 5, 7, 11, 13, 17, or 19. Putting 439 in the memory of our calculator, we easily complete the necessary divisions and determine that 439 is a prime since it is not divisible by 2, 3, 5, 7, 11, 13, 17, or 19.

JUST FOR FUN

The Chinese Remainder Problem

Find the least positive integer having remainders of 2, 3, and 4 when divided by 5, 7, and 9 respectively. What is the next larger integer having this property? Problems like these were studied by Chinese mathematicians like Sun-Tse as early as the first century A.D.

EXAMPLE   4.7 | **A Prime Different from 2, 3, 7, and 13**

Determine a prime different from 2, 3, 7, and 13 that divides $2 \cdot 3 \cdot 7 \cdot 13 + 1 = 547$.

Solution

Since $\sqrt{547} \doteq 23.4$, we must check for divisibility by 2, 3, 5, 7, 11, 13, 17, 19, and 23. Placing 547 in $\boxed{M+}$, and using $\boxed{MR}$, the divisions are easily carried out, or you can use the program FACTOR on a graphing calculator. Either way, it is quickly determined that 547 is itself a prime.

DID YOU KNOW?

The largest prime known at this writing is $2^{3,021,377} - 1$, a huge number with 909,526 digits in its decimal representation. Normally, determining the primality of such a large number would be beyond the power of even the largest and fastest modern computers. However, the special form of this number, $2^n - 1$, makes it especially susceptible to attack by a relatively fast algorithm. Numbers of the form $2^n - 1$ are called Mersenne numbers after the French monk, Father Marin Mersenne, who discovered the first few primes of this form early in the seventeenth century. Checking such numbers for primality has now become a test of the speed of new computers and also a pastime for computer buffs who are willing to let their personal computers work at the task for almost countless hours. If you want to keep up with the latest on these large primes, you can check the World Wide Web at www.utm.edu/research/primes/largest.html.

WINDOW ON TECHNOLOGY
Prime Power Factorizations with a Graphing Calculator

The algorithm to compute the prime factorization of a given whole number N is easy to describe in a general way:

Step 1. Set $P = 2$, the smallest possible prime that may be a factor of N.

Step 2. See if P divides N and, if so, continue to see if higher powers P^2, P^3, . . . also divide N. If the largest exponent is E (that is, P^E divides N but P^{E+1} does not), then P is a prime factor of N with corresponding power E.

Step 3. Let the quotient N/P^E become the new value N to be factored, let $P + 1$ become the new lowest possible factor P of N to be checked out, and return to Step 2 (unless $P > \sqrt{N}$, in which case you are done).

Step 4. Continue to repeat Steps 2 and 3 until $P > \sqrt{N}$, at which time the program is done.

The program FACTOR for the TI-73 graphing calculator (or TI-8X or other machines) can be found in Appendix C. This program automates the algorithm outlined. It is made efficient by checking only for odd factors $P = 3, 5, 7, . . .$ once the even prime factor $P = 2$ has been examined. The user's guide accompanying your graphing calculator will explain how to enter and edit the FACTOR program. Once you have the program available, it can be a helpful and fun program for you to use.

The result of factoring $N = 134{,}483{,}440$ is shown on the screen depicted below. Being careful to match each prime factor with its corresponding power, we see in just a few moments of calculator time that $N = 2^4 \times 5^1 \times 7^3 \times 13^2 \times 29^1$. The primes and corresponding powers can also be viewed in the List Editor; press $\boxed{\text{ON}}$ 1 to quit the program and then press $\boxed{\text{LIST}}$. The side-by-side lists of prime factors and powers are then easily viewed.

> $2\hat{\ }(2\hat{\ }5) + 1$ is calculator notation for $2^{(2^5)} + 1$.

```
N=?134483440              ⋮
PRIME FACTORS
   {2 5 7 13 29}
POWERS
   {4 1 3 2 1}
```

L1	L2	L3	2
2	**4**	------	
5	1		
7	3		
13	2		
29	1		
------	------		
L2(1)=4			

You might like to try factoring the quite large number $N = 2\hat{\ }(2\hat{\ }5) + 1$ (that is, $N = 4{,}294{,}967{,}297$). The great 17th century mathematician Pierre Fermat thought this number was prime since replacing the exponent 5 with any of 0, 1, 2, 3, or 4 gives the respective numbers 3, 5, 17, 257, 65537, which are all prime. In about a minute and a half, your calculator will tell you Fermat was mistaken that $2\hat{\ }(2\hat{\ }5) + 1$ is prime. What is the factorization of N?

PROBLEM SET 4.1

Understanding Concepts

1. Draw array diagrams to show that
   (a) 4 is a factor of 36.
   (b) 6 is a factor of 36.

2. Draw array diagrams to illustrate all the factorings of 35 taking order into account; that is, think of $1 \cdot 35$ as different from $35 \cdot 1$.

3. (a) List the first ten multiples of 8 starting with $0 \cdot 8 = 0$.
   (b) List the first ten multiples of 6 starting with $0 \cdot 6 = 0$.
   (c) Use parts (a) and (b) to determine the least natural number that is a multiple of both 8 and 6.

   O is not a natural number.

4. Complete this table of all factors of 18 and their corresponding quotients.

Factors of 18	1	2							
Corresponding quotients	18	9							

5. Construct factor trees for each of these numbers.
   (a) 72   (b) 126   (c) 264   (d) 550

6. Use short division to find all the prime factors of each of these numbers.
   (a) 700   (b) 198   (c) 450   (d) 528

7. (a) List all the divisors (factors) of 48.
   (b) List all the divisors (factors) of 54.
   (c) Use parts (a) and (b) to find the largest common divisor of 48 and 54.

8. (a) Determine the prime power representations of both 136 and 102.
   (b) Determine the set of all divisors (factors) of 136.
   (c) Determine the set of all divisors of 102.
   (d) Determine the greatest divisor of both 136 and 102.

9. Determine the prime power representation of each of these numbers.
   (a) 48   (b) 108   (c) 2250   (d) 24,750

10. Let $a = 2^3 \cdot 3^1 \cdot 7^2$.
    (a) Is $2^2 \cdot 7^1 = 28$ a factor of a? Why or why not?
    (b) Is $2^1 \cdot 3^2 \cdot 7^1 = 126$ a factor of a? Why or why not?
    (c) One factor of a is $b = 2^2 \cdot 3^1$. What is the quotient when a is divided by b?

(d) How many different factors does a possess?

(e) Make an orderly list of all of the factors of a.

11. To determine if 599 is a prime, which primes must you check as possible divisors?

 12. Use your calculator and information from the sieve of Eratosthenes in Figure 4.3 to determine if 1139 is prime. If it is not prime, give its prime factors.

13. If n is composite, is it true that all prime factors of n must not exceed $\sqrt{n}$? Explain briefly.

Thinking Critically

14. (a) List all the distinct factors of $9 = 3^2$.
    (b) Find three natural numbers (other than 9) that have precisely three distinct factors.
    (c) Find three natural numbers that have precisely four distinct factors.

15. Earlier we observed that 6 and 28 were perfect numbers; i.e., numbers equal to the sum of their proper divisors.
    (a) Determine the prime power representation of 496.
    (b) Show that 496 is a perfect number.
    (c) Determine the prime power representation of 8128.
    (d) Show that 8128 is a perfect number.
    (e) Write 31 and 127 in the form $2^n - 1$.
    (f) Recalling that 6 and 28 are perfect numbers and considering the results of parts (a), (b), (c), and (d), make a conjecture about the prime power representation of an even perfect number.
    (g) Given that 8191 is a prime, determine the prime factorization of 33,550,336 and show that this number is perfect. Does this result strengthen your confidence in your conjecture in part (f)?

16. A number is said to be **deficient** if the sum of its proper divisors is less than the number. Similarly, a number is said to be **abundant** if the sum of its proper divisors is greater than the number. Thus 14 is deficient since $1 + 2 + 7 < 14$, and 12 is abundant since $1 + 2 + 3 + 4 + 6 > 12$. Classify each of the following as deficient or abundant.
    (a) 10   (b) 18   (c) 20   (d) 16   (e) 468
    (f) 2^n where n is a natural number
    (g) p where p is a prime

17. A pair of natural numbers *m* and *n* are called **amicable** if the sum of the proper divisors of *m* equals *n* and the sum of the proper divisors of *n* equals *m*. Show that 220 and 284 are an amicable pair.

18. A prime *p* such that $2p + 1$ is also a prime is called a **Germain prime** after the eminent nineteenth century German mathematician, Sophie Germain (see the Highlight from History in Chapter 11). Which of 11, 13, 97, 241, and 359 are Germain primes?

19. Which of the following are *true* or *false*? Justify your answer in each case.

   (a) *n* divides 0 for every natural number *n*.

   (b) 0 divides *n* for every natural number *n*.

   (c) 1 divides *n* for every natural number *n*.

   (d) *n* divides *n* for every natural number *n*.

   (e) 0 divides 0

20. Assume that *a* divides *b* and *b* divides *c* where *a, b,* and *c* are natural numbers. Give a carefully written three sentence argument showing that *a* divides *c*.

21. If *p* is a prime, *b* and *c* are natural numbers, and *p* divides *bc,* is it necessarily the case that *p* divides *b* or *p* divides *c*? Justify your answer.

22. If *n, b,* and *c* are natural numbers and *n* divides *bc,* is it necessarily the case that *n* divides *b* or *n* divides *c*? Justify your answer.

23. Assume that *p* and *q* are different primes and that *n* is a natural number. If *p* divides *n* and *q* divides *n,* argue briefly that *pq* divides *n*.

24. Let N_n be the natural number whose decimal representation consists of *n* consecutive 1s. For example, $N_2 = 11$, $N_7 = 1,111,111$, and $N_9 = 111,111,111$.

   (a) Show that N_2 divides N_4, N_2 divides N_6, and N_2 divides N_8.

   (b) Guess the quotient when N_{18} is divided by N_2 and check your guess by multiplication by hand.

25. Let N_n be as in problem 24.

   (a) Show that N_3 divides N_6, N_3 divides N_9, and N_3 divides N_{12}.

   (b) Guess the quotient when N_{18} is divided by N_3 and check your guess by multiplication by hand.

26. Let N_n be as in problems 24 and 25.
   (a) Does N_3 divide N_5?   (b) Does N_3 divide N_7?
   (c) Does N_3 divide N_{15}?
   (d) Guess conditions on *m* and *n* that guarantee that N_m divides N_n.

27. Draw a square measuring 10 centimeters on a side. Draw vertical and horizontal line segments dividing the square into rectangles of areas 12, 18, 28, and 42 square centimeters respectively. Where should *A, B, C,* and *D* be located?

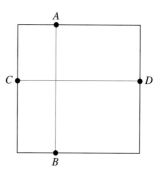

28. When the students arrived in Mr. Gowing's classroom one day there were 28 three by five cards neatly propped up in the chalk tray. They were numbered from 1 through 28 and arranged in order with the numbers facing the chalkboard. After the students were seated Mr. Gowing asked the first student in the first row of seats to go to the board and turn each card so that they all faced the classroom. He then asked the second student to go to the board and turn every second card back facing the board. The third student was to turn every third card whether it had been turned before or not. Thus, for example, the sixth card would have been turned toward the class by the first student, toward the board by the second, and toward the class again by the third student. The process continues until the twenty-eighth student turns the twenty-eighth card for the last time.

   (a) When the process is complete, which numbers are left facing the students?

   (b) Show why the answer to part (a) is as it is. (*Hint:* You may also want to make a table to exhibit what is happening.)

Thinking Cooperatively

29. Work with members of your cooperative group to complete this activity. The Fibonacci numbers, 1, 1, 2, 3, 5, 8, 13, . . . , were defined in Section 1.4, Example 1.6.

   (a) Extend the following table so that it shows the first 30 Fibonacci numbers.

n	1	2	3	4	5	6	7	8	9	10	. . .
F_n	1	1	2	3	5	8	13	21	34	55	. . .

   (b) Which Fibonacci numbers, F_m, are divisible by $F_3 = 2$? Carefully describe the pattern you discover.

(c) Which Fibonacci numbers, F_m, are divisible by $F_4 = 3$? By $F_5 = 5$? Describe the patterns you discover.

(d) If r is a natural number, conjecture which Fibonacci numbers are divisible by F_r on the basis of your observations in parts (b) and (c).

Using a Calculator

30. Use FACTOR to determine the prime power representation of each of these numbers.

   (a) 548   **(b)** 936   **(c)** 274   **(d)** 45,864

   (e) Use the results of parts (a), (b), (c), and (d) to determine which, if any, of these numbers divides another of these numbers.

31. Use FACTOR to determine the prime power representation of each of these integers.

   (a) 894,348   **(b)** 245,025   **(c)** 1,265,625

   (d) Which of the numbers in parts (a), (b), and (c) are squares?

   (e) What can you say about the prime power representation of a square? Explain briefly.

   (f) Guess how you might see from a glance at its prime power representation that 93,576,664 is the cube of a natural number. Explain.

For Review

32. Let $S = \{1, 3, 5, \ldots\}$ be the set of all odd natural numbers. Which of the following are *true* and which are *false*? Justify your answer in each case.

(a) S is closed with respect to addition.

(b) S is closed with respect to multiplication.

(c) The commutative property for addition holds for elements of S.

(d) The commutative property for multiplication holds for elements of S.

(e) The associative property for addition holds for elements of S.

(f) The associative property for multiplication holds for elements of S.

(g) The distributive property for multiplication over addition holds for elements of S.

(h) S possesses an additive identity.

(i) S possesses a multiplicative identity.

33. (a) Compute the one hundredth term in the arithmetic sequence 2, 5, 8, 11, ...

   (b) Compute the sum of the first one hundred terms in the sequence of part (a).

34. Write the most likely choices for the next three terms in each of these sequences.

   (a) 3, 7, 11, 15, _____, _____, _____

   (b) 1, 3, 7, 17, 41, _____, _____, _____

   (c) 1, 3, 6, 10, _____, _____, _____

   (d) 1, 0, 1, 0, 2, 0, 3, 0, 5, _____ _____, _____

   (e) 3, 6, 12, 24, _____, _____, _____

   (f) 2, 9, 13, 31, 57, 119, _____, _____, _____

35. Compute the sum of the terms in each of these arithmetic progressions.

   (a) 2, 5, 8, . . . , 155

   (b) 7, 12, 17, . . . , 152

   (c) 3, 10, 17, . . . , 689

COOPERATIVE INVESTIGATION

A Neat Fibonacci Trick

Materials Needed

1. A calculator for each student.

2. A Fibonacci Sum record sheet for each student as below.

Directions

1. Start the activity by placing any two natural numbers in the first two rows of column one of the record sheet and then complete the column by adding any two consecutive entries to obtain the next entry in the Fibonacci manner. Finally, add the ten entries obtained and divide the sum by 11.

2. Repeat the process to complete all but the last column of the record sheet. Then look for a pattern and make a conjecture. Lastly, prove that your conjecture is correct by placing *a* and *b* in the first and second positions in the last column and then repeating the process as before.

FIBONACCI SUM RECORD SHEET

	1	2	3	4	5	General Case
1						*a*
2						*b*
3						
4						
5						
6						
7						
8						
9						
10						
Sum						
Sum ÷ 11						

4.2 Tests for Divisibility

It is convenient for both teachers and students to have simple tests that show when one number is divisible by another. Relatively easy tests exist for the primes 2, 3, 5, 7, 11, and 13; for 9, 10, and powers of 2; and for products of numbers in the preceding list. Indeed, tests for divisibility by every prime exist but they become quite cumbersome and are not useful. In general, for larger primes, we are reduced to using technology and/or trial and error. Also, all the tests depend on using base ten notation.

Because it is so useful in answering divisibility questions, we first develop a result about the divisibility of sums and differences of numbers. Since

$$84 = 66 + 18 = 3 \cdot 22 + 3 \cdot 6 = 3(22 + 6) = 3 \cdot 28$$

and

$$48 = 66 - 18 = 3 \cdot 22 - 3 \cdot 6 = 3(22 - 6) = 3 \cdot 16,$$

it is clear that 3 divides both 84 and 48 because it divides both 66 and 18. Moreover, since the same argument could be repeated in general, we have the following theorem.

THEOREM *Divisibility of Sums and Differences*

If n, a, and b are natural numbers and n divides both a and b, then n divides both $a + b$ and $a - b$.

Now consider a number like

$$9276 = 927 \cdot 10 + 6 \qquad \text{or, equivalently,} \qquad 9276 - 927 \cdot 10 = 6.$$

Since 2 divides 10, it follows from the theorem on divisibility of sums and differences that 2 divides 9276 if, and only if, 2 divides 6. Therefore, 2 does divide 9276.

In general, when we divide any natural number n by 10 we obtain a quotient q and a remainder r (the units digit in the decimal representation of n), such that

$$n = 10q + r \qquad \text{or, equivalently,} \qquad n - 10q = r.$$

> 6 is the units digit in the decimal representation of 9276

Hence, as above, 2 divides n if, and only if, 2 divides r. Moreover, since 5 divides 10, these same equations assure that 5 divides n if, and only if, 5 divides r. Thus, since 0, 2, 4, 6, and 8 are the only digits divisible by 2 and 0 and 5 are the only digits divisible by 5, we have the following theorem.

THEOREM *Divisibility by 2 and 5*

Let n be a natural number. Then n is divisible by 2 if, and only if, its units digit is 0, 2, 4, 6, or 8. Similarly, n is divisible by 5 if, and only if, its units digit is 0 or 5.

The test for divisibility by $10 = 2 \cdot 5$ follows immediately from the tests for divisibility by 2 and 5.

THEOREM *Divisibility by 10*

Let n be a natural number. Then n is divisible by 10 if, and only if, 2 and 5 divide n; that is, if, and only if, the units digit of n is 0.

Proof   By definition 10 divides n if, and only if, $10q = n$ for some q. But, since $2 \cdot 5 = 10$, this is so if, and only if, $2(5q) = n$ and $5(2q) = n$; that is, if, and only if, 2 divides n and 5 divides n. Thus, the divisibility tests for both 2 and 5 must be satisfied, and this is so if, and only if, the units digit of n is 0.

It is important to note that the preceding theorem is a special case of a much more general result.

THEOREM *Divisibility by Products*

Let a and b be natural numbers with no common factor other than 1. Then, if a divides c and b divides c, it follows that ab divides c.

Proof   From section 4.1 all the prime factors of a must appear in c and to at least as high a power as they appear in a. Similarly, all prime factors of b must appear in c and to at least as high a power as they appear in b. But, since a and b have no factors in common, they can have no prime factors in common and this implies that all primes appearing in either a or b must appear in c and to at least as high a power as they appear in ab. Therefore, ab divides c as claimed.

EXAMPLE   4.8

Solution

Divisibility by Products

Using the fundamental theorem of arithmetic, show that $18 \cdot 25$ divides 22,050.

Since $18 = 2^1 \cdot 3^2$, $25 = 5^2$, and $22{,}050 = 2^1 \cdot 3^2 \cdot 5^2 \cdot 7^2$, it is clear that 18 divides 22,050 and that 25 divides 22,050. Moreover, since 18 and 25 have no common factor other than 1, it follows from the preceding theorem that $18 \cdot 25$ divides 22,050. In fact, $22{,}050 \div (18 \cdot 25) = 7^2 = 49$.

THEOREM   *Tests for Divisibility by 3 and 9*
A natural number is divisible by 3 if, and only if, the sum of its digits is divisible by 3. Similarly, a natural number is divisible by 9 if, and only if, the sum of its digits is divisible by 9.

Instead of a formal proof, we use an example to reveal why these tests hold. Consider $n = 27{,}435$ and let $s = 2 + 7 + 4 + 3 + 5$ denote the sum of the digits of n. Then

$$n - s = 27{,}435 - (2 + 7 + 4 + 3 + 5)$$
$$= (20{,}000 - 2) + (7{,}000 - 7) + (400 - 4) + (30 - 3)$$
$$= 2(10{,}000 - 1) + 7(1{,}000 - 1) + 4(100 - 1) + 3(10 - 1)$$
$$= 2 \cdot 9999 + 7 \cdot 999 + 4 \cdot 99 + 3 \cdot 9$$
$$= 9(2 \cdot 1111 + 7 \cdot 111 + 4 \cdot 11 + 3 \cdot 1)$$
$$= 9q$$

$$q = 2 \cdot 1111 + 7 \cdot 111 + 4 \cdot 11 + 3 \cdot 1$$

and

$$n = s + 9q.$$

Therefore, by the theorem on divisibility of sums and differences, 9 divides n if, and only if, 9 divides s. Since $9 = 3 \cdot 3$, the same argument holds for divisibility by 3. Moreover, since in this case $s = 21$, n is divisible by 3 and not by 9.

EXAMPLE   4.9

Divisibility by 2, 3, 5, 9, and 10

State whether each of the following is *true* or *false* without actually dividing. Give a reason for your answer.

(a) 2 divides 43,826   **(b)** 3 divides 111,111   **(c)** 10 divides 26,785
(d) 9 divides 10,020,006 **(e)** 6 divides 111,111   **(f)** 5 divides (287 + 78)

Solution

(a) True, since the units digit of 43,826 is 6 (that is, even).
(b) True, since $1 + 1 + 1 + 1 + 1 + 1 = 6$ and 3 divides 6.
(c) False, since 10 divides a number if, and only if, its units digit is 0. Here it is 5.
(d) True, since $1 + 0 + 0 + 2 + 0 + 0 + 0 + 6 = 9$ and 9 divides 9.
(e) False. If 6 divides 111,111, then 2 divides 111,111 since 2 divides 6. But 2 does not divide 111,111 since the units digit is not even.
(f) True. 5 does not divide 287 and 5 does not divide 78. Yet $287 + 78 = 365$, and 5 divides 365 since the units digit is 5.

COOPERATIVE INVESTIGATION

Two Interesting Division Patterns

Materials Needed

1. Pencil and paper for each student.
2. A calculator for each student would be useful but it is not necessary.

Directions

1. Complete the following divisions.
2. After each set of quotients is determined, look for a pattern and state a conjecture.

Division Pattern Number 1	Division Pattern Number 2
$99 \div 11 =$ _____	$11 \div 11 =$ _____
$9999 \div 11 =$ _____	$1001 \div 11 =$ _____
$999,999 \div 11 =$ _____	$100,001 \div 11 =$ _____
$99,999,999 \div 11 =$ _____	$10,000,001 \div 11 =$ _____
Conjecture: _____	Conjecture: _____
_____	_____
_____	_____
Test your conjecture by multiplying a suitable 15-digit number by 11.	Test your conjecture by multiplying a suitable 14-digit number by 11.

Proceeding by example, we now develop a test for divisibility by 11. Consider the numbers 8,571,937 and $t = 8 - 5 + 7 - 1 + 9 - 3 + 7 = (8 + 7 + 9 + 7) - (5 + 1 + 3)$ where 8, 7, 9, and 7 are the 7th, 5th, 3rd, and 1st digits in 8,571,937 and 5, 1, and 3 are the 6th, 4th, and 2nd digits. Since

$8,571,937 - t$

> $8,000,000 - 8$
> $= 8(1,000,000 - 1)$

> $500,000 + 5$
> $= 5(100,000 + 1)$

> etc.

$= 8,000,000 + 500,000 + 70,000 + 1000 + 900 + 30 + 7 - 8 + 5 - 7 + 1 - 9 + 3 - 7$

$= 8(1,000,000 - 1) + 5(100,000 + 1) + 7(10,000 - 1) + 1(1000 + 1) + 9(100 - 1) + 3(10 + 1)$

$= 8 \cdot 999,999 + 5 \cdot 100,001 + 7 \cdot 9999 + 1 \cdot 1001 + 9 \cdot 99 + 3 \cdot 11$

$= 8 \cdot 90,909 \cdot 11 + 5 \cdot 9091 \cdot 11 + 7 \cdot 909 \cdot 11 + 1 \cdot 91 \cdot 11 + 9 \cdot 9 \cdot 11 + 3 \cdot 11$

> By the preceding Cooperative Investigation

$= (8 \cdot 90,909 + 5 \cdot 9091 + 7 \cdot 909 + 1 \cdot 91 + 9 \cdot 9 + 3) \cdot 11$

$= 11q$

where q is a natural number, $8,571,937 - t = 11q$ is divisible by 11. Since $8,571,937 = t + 11q$, it follows from the theorem on the divisibility of sums and differences that 8,571,937 is divisible by 11 if, and only if, t is divisible by 11. In the present case, $t = 22$ so 8,571,937 is divisible by 11 as one can easily check.

Since the preceding argument is essentially general, we have the following theorem.

THEOREM *Divisibility Test for 11*

A natural number is divisible by 11 if, and only if, the difference of the sums of the digits in the even and odd positions in the number is divisible by 11.

HIGHLIGHT FROM HISTORY
Eratosthenes of Cyrene (276–195 B.C.)

Much has been written about the remarkable scholarly accomplishments of the ancient Greeks. Such accounts are sprinkled with names like Pythagoras, Thales, Euclid, Archimedes, Aristarchus, Eudoxus, Hypatia, Theano, and Apollonius. Another extraordinarily able contributor to Greek thought was Eratosthenes, who was remarkably gifted not only in mathematics but also in poetry, astronomy, geography, history, philosophy, and even athletics. Eratosthenes was born in Cyrene on the south shore of the Mediterranean, lived most of his early life in Athens, and, later, was invited to Alexandria by Ptolemy III of Egypt to tutor his son and to serve as librarian of the great Alexandrian University. We have already mentioned his remarkable sieve for determining all the prime numbers up to any given limit, but he is perhaps best known for his unusually accurate determination that the circumference of the earth was very nearly 25,000 miles—a figure much nearer the actual value than that of any of the ancients either before or after. In old age, Eratosthenes became almost totally blind and it is said that he died of voluntary starvation in about 195 B.C.

EXAMPLE 4.10 | **Testing for Divisibility by 11**

Show that $n = 8,193,246,781,053,476,109$ is divisible by 11 and that $m = 76,124,738,465,372,103$ is not divisible by 11.

Solution

First consider n. Using mental arithmetic, we find that

$$8 + 9 + 2 + 6 + 8 + 0 + 3 + 7 + 1 + 9 = 53$$

and

$$1 + 3 + 4 + 7 + 1 + 5 + 4 + 6 + 0 = 31.$$

Since $53 - 31 = 22$ and 11 divides 22, it follows that 11 divides n. In fact,

$$8,193,246,781,053,476,109 \div 11 = 744,840,616,459,406,919.$$

Now consider m. Using mental arithmetic, we find that

$$7 + 1 + 4 + 3 + 4 + 5 + 7 + 1 + 3 = 35$$

and

$$6 + 2 + 7 + 8 + 6 + 3 + 2 + 0 = 34.$$

Since $35 - 34 = 1$ and 11 does not divide 1, it follows that 11 does not divide m. Here

$$76,124,738,465,372,103 \div 11 = 6,920,430,769,579,282 \text{ R } 1.$$

A Combined Test for Divisibility by 7, 11, and 13

We now describe a test for divisibility by 7, 11, and 13 all at the same time. Consider a number like

$$n = 92,252,191,213$$

Break n up into the series of 3-digit numbers

$$092, 252, 191, 213$$

determined by the 3-digit groups starting from the right in n. Now, as in the test for divisibility by 11, compute the sum of the numbers in the odd-numbered positions in the above list and the sum of the numbers in the even-numbered positions. This gives

$$
\begin{array}{cc}
\begin{array}{r} 092 \\ +\ 191 \\ \hline 283 \end{array}
& \text{and} \quad
\begin{array}{r} 252 \\ +\ 213 \\ \hline 465 \end{array}
\end{array}
$$

as shown. The difference in these sums is

$$465 - 283 = 182$$

and n will be divisible

by 7 if, and only if, 182 is divisible by 7,

by 11 if, and only if, 182 is divisible by 11, and

by 13 if, and only if, 182 is divisible by 13.

Since $182 = 7 \cdot 26$ and $182 = 13 \cdot 14$, it follows that 7 divides n and 13 divides n. On the other hand, 11 does not divide 182 and so 11 does not divide n. Find the quotients when n is divided by 7 and by 13 and also find the quotient and remainder when n is divided by 11.

EXAMPLE   4.11

Divisibility by 7, 11, and 13

Test to see if $n = 8,346,261,059,482,647$ is divisible by 7, 11, or 13.

Solution

Breaking n up into 3-digit numbers and computing the sums of those in even positions and odd positions we have

$$
\begin{array}{ccc}
008 & \text{and} & 346 \\
261 & & 59 \\
\underline{482} & & \underline{647} \\
751 & & 1052
\end{array}
$$

The test number is $1052 - 751 = 301$. Since $7 \cdot 43 = 301$, 7 divides 301 and hence 7 divides n. However,

$$301 = 11 \cdot 27 + 4 \qquad \text{and} \qquad 301 = 13 \cdot 23 + 2.$$

Thus, 11 does not divide 301 and 13 does not divide 301, so neither divides n.

A Test for Divisibility by Powers of Two

> **THEOREM** *A Test for Divisibility by 4, 8, and Other Powers of 2*
> Let n be a natural number. Then 4 divides n if, and only if, 4 divides the number named by the last two digits of n. Similarly, 8 divides n if, and only if, 8 divides the number named by the last three digits of n. In general, 2^r divides n if, and only if, 2^r divides the number named by the last r digits of n.

This theorem can be understood by looking at an example. Consider a number like $28,476,324$. This can be written in the form

$$
\begin{aligned}
28,476,324 &= 284,763 \cdot 100 + 24 \\
&= 4 \cdot 25 \cdot 284,763 + 24.
\end{aligned}
$$

Thus, by the theorem on divisibility of sums and differences, 4 divides $28,476,324$ if, and only if, 4 divides 24. Therefore, 4 does indeed divide $28,476,324$.

In general, when we divide any natural number n by 100, we obtain a quotient q and a remainder r such that

$$n = 100q + r = 4(25q) + r$$

and by the argument above 4 divides n if, and only if, 4 divides r.

A similar argument holds for divisibility by 8 since $n = 1000q + s$ where s is the number represented by the last three digits of n and 8 divides 1000. For higher powers of 2, the test depends on the fact that 16 divides 10,000, 32 divides 100,000, and so on.

EXAMPLE 4.12

Testing for Divisibility by 4 and 8

Test the following for divisibility by 4 and 8.

(a) 2452   (b) 3849   (c) 7672   (d) 39,000

Solution

Since 2 divides 4, 4 divides 8, 8 divides 16, and so on, divisibility of a number by any power of 2 guarantees divisibility by any lower power. Thus, it follows that if 2 does not divide n, then 2^k does not divide n for any k.

(a) Since $452 = 8 \cdot 56 + 4$, 8 does not divide 452. Thus 8 does not divide 2452. However, 4 divides 52 and so 4 divides 2452 and 2 divides 2452.

(b) Since 2 does not divide 9, it follows that 2 does not divide 3849, 4 does not divide 3849, and 8 does not divide 3849.

(c) Since $672 = 8 \cdot 84$, it follows that 8 divides 7672, 4 divides 7672, and 2 divides 7672.

(d) Since 8 divides 1000, it follows that 8 divides 39,000, 4 divides 39,000, and 2 divides 39,000.

PROBLEM SET 4.2

Understanding Concepts

1. Test each number for divisibility by each of 2, 3, and 5. Do the work mentally.
   (a) 1554   (b) 1999
   (c) 805   (d) 2450

2. Use the results of problem 1 to decide which, if any, of the numbers in problem 1 are divisible by
   (a) 6   (b) 10
   (c) 15   (d) 30

3. Test each of these for divisibility by 7, 11, and 13.
   (a) 253,799   (b) 834,197   (c) 1,960,511

4. Use the results of problem 3 to decide which of the numbers in problem 3 are divisible by
   (a) 77   (b) 91
   (c) 143   (d) 1001

5. Is 1,927,643,001,548 divisible by 11? Explain briefly.

6. (a) At a glance, determine the digit d so that $87{,}543{,}24d$ is divisible by 4. Is there more than one answer? Explain.
   (b) Can you choose the digit d so that $87{,}543{,}24d$ is divisible by 8 and not 16? Explain.

7. Determine the digit d so that $6{,}34d{,}217$ is divisible by 11.

8. (a) Fill in the missing digit so that $897{,}650{,}243{,}28\_\_$ is divisible by 6. Can this be done in more than one way?
   (b) Fill in the missing digit so that the number in part (a) is divisible by 11.

9. A palindrome is a number like 2,743,472 that reads the same forward and backward.
   (a) Give a clear but brief argument to show that every palindrome with an even number of digits is divisible by 11.
   (b) Is it possible for a palindrome with an odd number of digits to be divisible by 11? Explain.

Thinking Critically

10. Show that every number whose decimal representation has the form $abc{,}abc$ is divisible by 7, 11, and 13.

11. (a) Reverse the digits in a two-digit number to obtain a second number and then subtract the smaller of these two numbers from the larger. What possible numbers can result? Can you tell at a glance what number will result? Explain carefully.
    (b) Repeat part (a) for 3-digit numbers.

12. A common error in banking is to make an interchange or transposition of some of the digits in a number involved in a transaction. For example, a teller may pay out $43.34 on a check actually written for $34.43 and so be short by $8.91 at the end of the day. Show that such a mistake always causes the teller's balance sheet to show an error in pennies, here 891, that is divisible by 9. (*Hint:* Recall that, in the proof of the divisibility test for 9, we showed that every number differs from the sum of its digits by a multiple of 9.)

13. If a teller's record of the day's work is out of balance by an amount, in pennies, that is a multiple of 9, is it necessarily the case that he or she has made a transposition error in the course of the day's work? Explain.

 14. **(a)** Consider a 6-digit number like 142,857 that is divisible by 27. Show by actually dividing that each of 428,571; 285,714; 857,142; 571,428; and 714,285 is also divisible by 27.

(b) 769,230 and 153,846 are two other numbers divisible by 27. See if the pattern of part (a) holds for these numbers.

(c) What general property is suggested by parts (a) and (b) of this problem? State it carefully.

(d) Find another 6-digit number that is divisible by 27. Does it have the property you guessed in part (c)?

(e) Check to see that all the numbers in parts (a) and (b) are also divisible by 11. Is this true of all 6-digit numbers divisible by 27?

Thinking Cooperatively

15. The first thirty Fibonacci numbers are displayed in the following table.

n	1	2	3	4	5	6	7	8	9	10
F_n	1	1	2	3	5	8	13	21	34	55

n	11	12	13	14	15	16	17	18	19	20
F_n	89	144	233	377	610	987	1597	2584	4181	6765

n	21	22	23	24	25	26	27	28	29	30
F_n	10,946	17,711	28,657	46,368	75,025	121,393	196,418	317,811	514,229	832,040

Do the following in cooperation with three or four other students. In each case come to a consensus on the conjectures you make.

(a) In problem 29, Problem Set 4.1, you were asked to conjecture which Fibonacci numbers were divisible by 2, by 3, and by 5. If you did not do that problem, do it now.

(b) List the first few Fibonacci numbers that are divisible by 4.

(c) On the basis of the limited data of part (b), guess what must be true of n if 4 divides F_n.

(d) Use the results of part (a) to guess what must be true of n if 6 divides F_n.

(e) Note that 7 divides F_8, 7 divides F_{16}, and 7 divides F_{24}. Conjecture what must be true about n if 7 divides F_n.

(f) What do the results of parts (a) through (e) suggest about the divisibility of Fibonacci numbers by natural numbers?

For Review

16. Use short division to determine the prime power representation of these natural numbers.

(a) 8064   **(b)** 2700   **(c)** 19,602

17. Construct a factor tree for each of these natural numbers and write their prime power representations.

(a) 7000   **(b)** 6174   **(c)** 6237

18. How many factors does each number in problem 17 possess? Be sure to show your work on this problem.

19. What is the quotient when a is divided by b if $a = 2^3 \cdot 3^4 \cdot 5^1 \cdot 7^2$ and $b = 2^1 \cdot 3^2 \cdot 7^1$?

20. **(a)** Is $2^4 \cdot 3^2 \cdot 5^1 \cdot 7^2$ divisible by $2^3 \cdot 3^1 \cdot 7^2$? Why or why not?

  (b) Is $2^4 \cdot 3^2 \cdot 5^1 \cdot 7^2$ divisible by $2^2 \cdot 5^2 \cdot 7^2$? Why or why not?

4.3   Greatest Common Divisors and Least Common Multiples

An architect is designing an elegant display room for an art museum. One wall is to be covered with large square marble tiles. To obtain the desired visual effect the architect wants to use the largest tiles possible. If the wall is to be 12 feet high and 42 feet long, how large can the tiles be?

If the tiles measure 4 feet on a side, the possible height of the wall must be a multiple of 4 (i.e., 4 must be a divisor of 12). Indeed, the length of the side of a tile must be a divisor of both the height and length of the wall; i.e., a common divisor of both 12 and 42. Since the sets of divisors of 12 and 42 are $D_{12} = \{1, 2, 3, 4, 6, 12\}$ and $D_{42} = \{1, 2, 3, 6, 7, 14, 21, 42\}$, the tile size must be chosen from the set $D_{12} \cap D_{42} = \{1, 2, 3, 6\}$, the set of common divisors of both 12 and 42. Thus, if the tiles are to be as large as possible, they must measure 6 feet on a side since 6 is the largest of the common divisors of 12 and 42.

Considerations like these lead to the notion of the greatest common divisor of two natural numbers defined formally as follows.

> **DEFINITION** *Greatest Common Divisor*
>
> Let m and n be natural numbers. The greatest natural number d that divides both m and n is called their **greatest common divisor** and we write $d = \text{GCD}(m, n)$.

We note that divisors are often called **factors**, that the greatest common divisor is often called the **greatest common factor**, and that $\text{GCD}(m, n)$ is often written as **GCF**(m, n).

JUST FOR FUN   Making a Chain

Here are six sections of chain, each containing four links. What is the *least* number of links you can open and close to join these sections into a single chain of 24 links?

A Weighty Matter

If a basketball weighs 21 ounces plus half its own weight, how much does it weigh?

Before proceeding further, we note in particular that greatest common divisors and, later, least common multiples play an important role in elementary school in helping students to understand the arithmetic of fractions.

Greatest Common Divisors by Intersection of Sets

This method, suggested by the above discussion, works well when the numbers involved are small and all the divisors of both numbers are easily written down. By way of explanation, it is probably best to do an example.

EXAMPLE 4.13

Finding the Greatest Common Divisor by Intersection of Sets

Find the greatest common divisor of 18 and 45.

Solution

Let D_{18} and D_{45} denote the sets of divisors of 18 and 45. Since

$$D_{18} = \{1, 2, 3, 6, 9, 18\} \quad \text{and} \quad D_{45} = \{1, 3, 5, 9, 15, 45\},$$

$D_{18} \cap D_{45} = \{1, 3, 9\}$ is the set of common divisors of 18 and 45. Thus, GCD(18, 45) = 9.

Greatest Common Divisors from Prime Power Representations

The greatest common divisor of two numbers can also be found by using their prime power representations. Consider

$$54 = 2^1 \cdot 3^3 \quad \text{and} \quad 45 = 3^2 \cdot 5^1.$$

Since $2^0 = 5^0 = 1$, we can write these representations so that they *appear* to be products of powers of the same primes. Thus,

$$54 = 2^1 \cdot 3^3 \cdot 5^0 \quad \text{and} \quad 45 = 2^0 \cdot 3^2 \cdot 5^1.$$

From the theorem on the divisors of a natural number (just preceding Example 4.5), the divisors of 54 are numbers of the form

$$d = 2^a \cdot 3^b \cdot 5^c \qquad \begin{cases} 0 \leq a \leq 1 \\ 0 \leq b \leq 3 \\ 0 \leq c \leq 0 \end{cases}$$

and the divisors of 45 are numbers of the form

$$d = 2^a \cdot 3^b \cdot 5^c. \qquad \begin{cases} 0 \leq a \leq 0 \\ 0 \leq b \leq 2 \\ 0 \leq c \leq 1 \end{cases}$$

Thus, we obtain the largest common divisor by choosing a, b, and c as large as possible while still satisfying both the above sets of inequalities. Hence, a must be the smaller of 0 and 1, b must be the smaller of 3 and 2, and c must be the smaller of 0 and 1. Therefore,

$$\text{GCD}(54, 45) = 2^0 \cdot 3^2 \cdot 5^0 = 9.$$

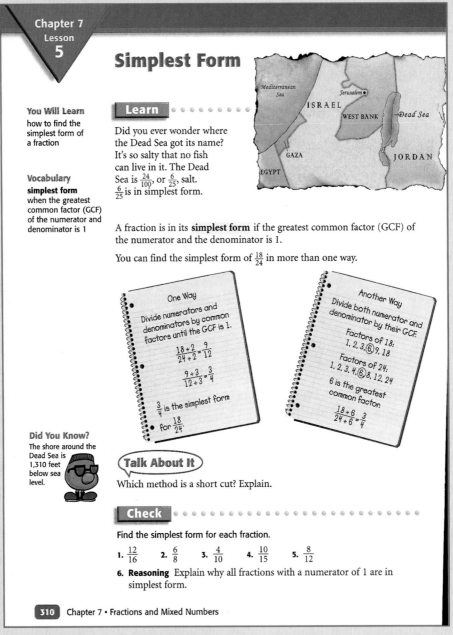

Chapter 7
Lesson
5

Simplest Form

You Will Learn
how to find the simplest form of a fraction

Vocabulary
simplest form
when the greatest common factor (GCF) of the numerator and denominator is 1

Learn • • • • • • • • • •

Did you ever wonder where the Dead Sea got its name? It's so salty that no fish can live in it. The Dead Sea is $\frac{24}{100}$, or $\frac{6}{25}$, salt. $\frac{6}{25}$ is in simplest form.

A fraction is in its **simplest form** if the greatest common factor (GCF) of the numerator and the denominator is 1.

You can find the simplest form of $\frac{18}{24}$ in more than one way.

One Way
Divide numerators and denominators by common factors until the GCF is 1.

$$\frac{18 \div 2}{24 \div 2} = \frac{9}{12}$$

$$\frac{9 \div 3}{12 \div 3} = \frac{3}{4}$$

$\frac{3}{4}$ is the simplest form for $\frac{18}{24}$.

Another Way
Divide both numerator and denominator by their GCF.

Factors of 18:
1, 2, 3, ⑥, 9, 18
Factors of 24:
1, 2, 3, 4, ⑥, 8, 12, 24

6 is the greatest common factor.

$$\frac{18 \div 6}{24 \div 6} = \frac{3}{4}$$

Did You Know?
The shore around the Dead Sea is 1,310 feet below sea level.

Talk About It

Which method is a short cut? Explain.

Check •

Find the simplest form for each fraction.

1. $\frac{12}{16}$ **2.** $\frac{6}{8}$ **3.** $\frac{4}{10}$ **4.** $\frac{10}{15}$ **5.** $\frac{8}{12}$

6. Reasoning Explain why all fractions with a numerator of 1 are in simplest form.

310   Chapter 7 • Fractions and Mixed Numbers

Questions for the Teacher

1. Two different methods are shown above for writing a fraction in simplest form. Students may wonder why they both work. How would you explain to a student that they are equivalent?

2. To use the first of the above methods for simplifying a fraction, it is necessary to recognize common factors. How would you answer a student who asked you how to use the first method to simplify $\frac{143}{253}$? Could you use divisibility tests?

> **THEOREM** *GCDs from Prime Power Representations*
>
> Let
>
> $$a = p^{a_1} p^{a_2} \cdots p_r^{a_r} \quad \text{and} \quad b = p_1^{b_1} p_2^{b_2} \cdots p_r^{b_r}$$
>
> be the prime power representations of a and b. Then
>
> $$\text{GCD}(a, b) = p_1^{c_1} p_2^{c_2} \cdots p_r^{c_r}$$
>
> where $c_1 =$ the smaller of (a_1, b_1), $c_2 =$ the smaller of (a_2, b_2), . . . , and $c_r =$ the smaller of (a_r, b_r).

EXAMPLE 4.14

Finding the Greatest Common Divisor by Using Prime Power Representations

Compute the greatest common divisor of 504 and 3675.

Solution

We first find the prime power representation of each number.

$$
\begin{array}{c}
3 \\
3\overline{)9} \\
7\overline{)63} \\
2\overline{)126} \\
2\overline{)252} \\
2\overline{)504}
\end{array}
\qquad
\begin{array}{c}
3 \\
7\overline{)21} \\
7\overline{)147} \\
5\overline{)735} \\
5\overline{)3675}
\end{array}
$$

$$504 = 2^3 \cdot 3^2 \cdot 5^0 \cdot 7^1 \qquad 3675 = 2^0 \cdot 3^1 \cdot 5^2 \cdot 7^2$$

Choosing the smaller of the exponents on each prime, we see that

$$\text{GCD}(504, 3675) = 2^0 \cdot 3^1 \cdot 5^0 \cdot 7^1 = 21.$$

As a check, we note that $504 \div 21 = 24$, that $3675 \div 21 = 175$, and that 24 and 175 have no common factor other than 1.

The Euclidean algorithm

This method for finding greatest common divisors is found in Book IV of Euclid's *Elements* written in about 300 B.C. It has the distinct advantage of working unfailingly no matter how large the two numbers are or how complicated the arithmetic. It all depends on the division algorithm.

Dividing a by b, we obtain a quotient q and a remainder r such that

$$a = bq + r, \quad 0 \le r < b.$$

But then

$$r = a - bq.$$

Therefore, by the theorem on divisors of sums and differences, d divides a and d divides b if, and only if, d divides b and d divides r. Thus, a and b must have the same set of divisors as b and r and, hence, the same greatest common divisor.

The long struggle for women's rights is certainly reflected in mathematics. From Hypatia (370?–A.D. 415) to the twentieth century, few women worked in mathematics—long considered a male domain. Though strides still need to be made, many women now ply the trade and there is even an Association of Women in Mathematics (AWM). One of the most successful women mathematicians of our time was Professor Julia Bowman Robinson, solver of the tenth in David Hilbert's famous list of problems. Professor

Robinson was born in St. Louis in 1919. Her graduate work in logic was done at the University of California where she received her Ph.D. in 1948. It was also at Berkeley that she met her husband to be, number theorist Raphael Robinson. After solving Hilbert's tenth problem in 1970, she was made a member of the prestigious National Academy of Sciences as well as the American Academy of Arts and Sciences and was promptly awarded the rank of Professor at UC Berkeley. Professor Robinson served as President of the American Mathematical Society and was also active in the Association of Women in Mathematics. She died on July 30, 1985, hoping that she would not be remembered "as the first woman this or that, I would prefer to be

remembered, as a mathematician should, simply for the theorems I have proved and the problems I have solved." There is little doubt but that her hope will be realized.

THEOREM *The GCD and the Division Algorithm*

Let a and b be any two natural numbers and let q and r be determined by the division algorithm. Thus,

$$a = bq + r, \quad 0 \leq r < b.$$

Then, $\text{GCD}(a, b) = \text{GCD}(b, r)$.

This theorem is the basis of the **Euclidean algorithm,** which we illustrate by determining GCD(1539, 3144). We begin by dividing 3144 by 1539 and then continue by dividing successive divisors by successive remainders. It turns out that the last nonzero remainder is the desired greatest common divisor. Of course, these divisions can be performed by hand or with a calculator. (They are particularly easy using the $\boxed{\text{INT} \div}$ key as discussed in Section 3.6.) We obtain these divisions.

$$\begin{array}{cccc}
2\text{ R }66 & 23\text{ R }21 & 3\text{ R }3 & 7\text{ R }0 \\
1539\overline{)3144} & 66\overline{)1539} & 21\overline{)66} & 3\overline{)21}
\end{array}$$

In the form of the division algorithm, these give

$$3144 = 2 \cdot 1539 + 66$$
$$1539 = 23 \cdot 66 + 21$$
$$66 = 3 \cdot 21 + 3$$
$$21 = 3 \cdot 7.$$

Hence, from the preceding theorem,

$$\text{GCD}(1539, 3144) = \text{GCD}(66, 1539) = \text{GCD}(21, 66) = \text{GCD}(3, 21) = 3$$

since 3 divides 21. Thus, the last nonzero remainder is the greatest common divisor of 1539 and 3144 as asserted.

THEOREM   *The Euclidean Algorithm*

Let a and b be any two natural numbers. Using the division algorithm, determine natural numbers $q_1, q_2, \ldots, q_s$ and $r_1, r_2, \ldots, r_{s-1}$ such that

$$
\begin{aligned}
a &= bq_1 + r_1, && 0 \le r_1 < b \\
b &= r_1q_2 + r_2, && 0 \le r_2 < r_1 \\
r_1 &= r_2q_3 + r_3, && 0 \le r_3 < r_2 \\
&\qquad\vdots \\
r_{s-3} &= r_{s-2}q_{s-1} + r_{s-1}, && 0 \le r_{s-1} < r_{s-2} \\
r_{s-2} &= r_{s-1}q_s.
\end{aligned}
$$

Then, $\text{GCD}(a, b) = r_{s-1}$.

EXAMPLE   4.15

Using the Euclidean Algorithm

Compute $\text{GCD}(18{,}411, 1649)$ using the Euclidean algorithm.

Solution

Using the Euclidean algorithm, we have

$$
\begin{array}{ccc}
11 \text{ R } 272 & 6 \text{ R } 17 & 16 \text{ R } 0 \\
1649\overline{)18{,}411} & 272\overline{)1649} & 17\overline{)272}
\end{array}
$$

and it follows that $\text{GCD}(18{,}411, 1649) = 17$.

The Least Common Multiple

In fourteenth century France, the style of choral motet writing called *Ars Nova* was such that, while the tenor line was written in a repeated pattern of a fixed number of measures (an isorythmic pattern), the other three parts were written in an isorythmic pattern with a different number of measures. Moreover, the motets were designed so that the end of the motet, the end of a tenor pattern, and the end of a pattern for the other three parts all coincided. How short might such a motet be? Or, more generally, how long might such a motet need to be?

If the length of the tenor pattern is eight measures, the length of the motet must be a multiple of eight—8, 16, 24, 32, 40, 48, 56, 64, . . . measures—and so on. Also, if the length of the pattern of the other three parts is six measures, the possible lengths of the motet must be a multiple of six—6, 12, 18, 24, 30, 36, 42, 48, 54, 60, . . . measures. Indeed, the length of the motet must be a multiple of both six and eight and so must appear in both lists. Such a number is called a **common multiple** of 6 and 8. Thus, in the present case, the possible lengths of the motet are the common multiples of 6 and 8—24, 48, 72, 96, . . . measures; and the shortest such motet is 24 measures long. Quite reasonably, the smallest number in a list of common multiples of two numbers is called their **least common multiple.**

In general, we have the following definition.

DEFINITION   *Least Common Multiple*

Let a and b be natural numbers. The least natural number m that is a multiple of both a and b is called their **least common multiple** and we write $m = \text{LCM}(a, b)$.

DID YOU KNOW?

Eureka!

"At last, shout of 'Eureka!' in age-old math mystery," so read the headline in the *New York Times* on June 24, 1993. The following article then proceeded to detail the announcement of the proof of Fermat's last theorem, a problem that has plagued mathematicians for over 350 years. It has been known since the time of the Babylonians (ca. 1600 B.C.) that there are infinitely many triples of natural numbers x, y, and z for which $x^2 + y^2 = z^2$. However, Pierre de Fermat, the greatest French

mathematician of the seventeenth century, in 1637 noted in the margin of his copy of Diophantus's *Arithmetica*, "that the equation $x^n + y^n = z^n$ has **no** solution in natural numbers if n is greater than two." And he went on to write, ". . . and I have assuredly found an admirable proof of this, but the margin is too narrow to contain it." This produced a frenzy on the part of others to find the proof and much first rate mathematics has been produced in the process. However, the proof resisted all efforts for over three centuries until Dr. Andrew Wiles, a British mathematician at Princeton University, using the most sophisticated of the accumulated methods, finally produced a proof. In view of the great effort required to construct it, it is seriously doubted that

Fermat actually had a valid proof. Nevertheless, he had the insight to guess the result, and the efforts to provide a proof have greatly enriched mathematics.

Least common multiples by intersection of sets

As with the greatest common divisor, the preceding discussion suggests a method for finding the least common multiple of two natural numbers. The following method is simple and works particularly well if the two numbers are not large. Let a and b be any two natural numbers. The sets of natural number multiples of a and b are

$$M_a = \{a, 2a, 3a, \ldots\} \quad \text{and} \quad M_b = \{b, 2b, 3b, \ldots\}.$$

Therefore, $M_a \cap M_b$ is the set of all natural number common multiples of a and b, and the least number in this set is the least common multiple of a and b. Incidentally, it should be noted that ab is clearly a common multiple of both a and b so, in using this method to find LCM(a, b), one need not extend the sets beyond this product.

EXAMPLE   4.16

Finding a Least Common Multiple by Set Intersection

Find the least common multiple of 9 and 15.

Solution

$$M_9 = \{9, 27, 36, 45, 54, 63, 72, 81, 90, \ldots\}$$
$$M_{15} = \{15, 30, 45, 60, 75, 90, 105, \ldots\}$$
$$M_9 \cap M_{15} = \{45, 90, \ldots\}$$

Since, $M_9 \cap M_{15}$ is the set of all natural number common multiples of 9 and 15, the least element of this set is LCM(9, 15). Therefore, LCM(9, 15) = 45. Notice that GCD(9, 15) = 3, so GCD(9, 15) $\cdot$ LCM(9, 15) = 3 $\cdot$ 45 = 135 = 9 $\cdot$ 15.

Least common multiples from prime power representations

Suppose we want to find the least common multiple of 54 and 45. Computing the prime power representations of these numbers, we obtain

$$54 = 2^1 \cdot 3^3 \cdot 5^0 \qquad \text{and} \qquad 45 = 2^0 \cdot 3^2 \cdot 5^1$$

where we use the zero exponents to make it *appear* that 54 and 45 are products of powers of the same primes. By the theorem just preceding Example 4.5, the multiples of 54 are numbers of the form

$$m = 2^a \cdot 3^b \cdot 5^c \qquad \begin{cases} a \geq 1 \\ b \geq 3 \\ c \geq 0 \end{cases}$$

and the multiples of 45 are numbers of the form

$$m = 2^a \cdot 3^b \cdot 5^c \qquad \begin{cases} a \geq 0 \\ b \geq 2 \\ c \geq 1. \end{cases}$$

We obtain the least common multiple of 54 and 45 by choosing a, b, and c as small as possible while still satisfying both the above sets of inequalities. It follows that we must choose a to be the larger of 1 and 0, b the larger of 3 and 2, and c the larger of 0 and 1. Hence,

$$m = 2^1 \cdot 3^3 \cdot 5^1 = 270 = \text{LCM}(54, 45).$$

Since this argument could be repeated in general, we have the following theorem.

THEOREM   *LCMs from Prime Power Representations*
Let

$$a = p_1^{a_1} p_2^{a_2} \cdots p_s^{a_s} \qquad \text{and} \qquad b = p_1^{b_1} p_2^{b_2} \cdots p_s^{b_s}$$

be the prime power representations of a and b. Then

$$\text{LCM}(a, b) = p_1^{d_1} p_2^{d_2} \cdots p_s^{d_s}$$

where d_1 = larger of (a_1, b_1), d_2 = larger of (a_2, b_2), . . . , and d_s = larger of (a_s, b_s).

EXAMPLE   4.17

Finding LCMs and GCDs Using Prime Power Representations

Compute the least common multiple and greatest common divisor of $r = 2^2 \cdot 3^4 \cdot 7^1$ and $s = 3^2 \cdot 5^2 \cdot 7^3$.

Solution

Both the least common multiple and the greatest common divisor will be of the form $2^a \cdot 3^b \cdot 5^c \cdot 7^d$. For the greatest common divisor we choose the *smaller* of the two exponents with which each prime appears in r and s, and for the least common multiple we choose the *larger* of each pair of exponents. Thus, since

$$r = 2^2 \cdot 3^4 \cdot 5^0 \cdot 7^1 = 2268 \qquad \text{and} \qquad s = 2^0 \cdot 3^2 \cdot 5^2 \cdot 7^3 = 77{,}175,$$

$5^0 = 1$
$2^0 = 1$

we have that

$$GCD(r, s) = 2^0 \cdot 3^2 \cdot 5^0 \cdot 7^1 = 63$$

and

$$LCM(r, s) = 2^2 \cdot 3^4 \cdot 5^2 \cdot 7^3 = 2{,}778{,}300.$$

Since both exponents on each prime were used in finding $GCD(r, s)$ and $LCM(r, s)$, it follows that

$$rs = GCD(r, s) \cdot LCM(r, s).$$

Thus,

$$rs = 2268 \cdot 77{,}175 = 175{,}032{,}900$$

and

$$GCD(r, s) \cdot LCM(r, s) = 63 \cdot 2{,}778{,}300 = 175{,}032{,}900.$$

Since the last part of the solution in Example 4.17 showing that $rs = GCD(r, s) \cdot LCM(r, s)$ could be repeated in general, we have the following important theorem.

> **THEOREM** $ab = GCD(a, b) \cdot LCM(a, b)$
> If a and b are any two natural numbers, then $ab = GCD(a, b) \cdot LCM(a, b)$.

Least common multiples using the Euclidean algorithm

As noted above, if a and b are natural numbers, then $GCD(a, b) \cdot LCM(a, b) = ab$. Thus,

$$LCM(a, b) = \frac{ab}{GCD(a, b)}$$

and we have already learned that $GCD(a, b)$ can always be found using the Euclidean algorithm.

EXAMPLE   4.18

Finding a Least Common Multiple by Use of the Euclidean Algorithm
Find the least common multiple of 2268 and 77,175 by using the Euclidean algorithm.

Solution   These are the same two numbers treated in Example 4.17. However, here our procedure is totally different. Using the Euclidean algorithm we have these divisions.

$$\begin{array}{r} 34 \text{ R } 63 \\ 2268\overline{)77{,}175} \end{array} \qquad \begin{array}{r} 36 \text{ R } 0 \\ 63\overline{)2268} \end{array}$$

Since the last nonzero remainder is 63, $GCD(2268, 77{,}175) = 63$ and

$$LCM(2268, 77{,}175) = \frac{2268 \cdot 77{,}175}{63}$$

$$= 2{,}778{,}300$$

as before.

Using Technology to Find GCDs and LCMs

Graphing calculators often have built-in GCD and LCM programs. For example, on the TI-73, the functions **lcm** and **gcd** are found by pressing $\boxed{\text{MATH}}$. These work quickly at the press of just a few buttons and are very handy. Also, the program EUCLID in Appendix C finds both the GCD and LCM of two numbers in a single series of steps. The GCD and LCM functions are also available on spreadsheets like Excel.

PROBLEM SET 4.3

Understanding Concepts

1. Find the greatest common divisor of each of these pairs of numbers by the method of intersection of sets of divisors.

   (a) 24 and 27   (b) 14 and 22   (c) 48 and 72

2. Find the least common multiple of each of these pairs of numbers by the method of intersection of sets of multiples.

   (a) 24 and 27   (b) 14 and 22   (b) 48 and 72

3. Use the results of problems 1 and 2 to show that:

   (a) $24 \cdot 27 = \text{GCD}(24, 27) \cdot \text{LCM}(24, 27)$

   (b) $14 \cdot 22 = \text{GCD}(14, 22) \cdot \text{LCM}(14, 22)$

   (c) $48 \cdot 72 = \text{GCD}(48, 72) \cdot \text{LCM}(48, 72)$

4. Use the method based on prime power representations to find the greatest common divisor and least common multiple of each of these pairs of numbers.

   (a) $r = 2^2 \cdot 3^1 \cdot 5^3$ and $s = 2^1 \cdot 3^3 \cdot 5^2$

   (b) $u = 5^1 \cdot 7^2 \cdot 11^1$ and $v = 2^2 \cdot 5^3 \cdot 7^1$

   (c) $w = 2^2 \cdot 3^3 \cdot 5^2$ and $x = 2^1 \cdot 5^3 \cdot 7^2$

5. Use the Euclidean algorithm to find each of the following.

   (a) GCD(3500, 550) and LCM(3500, 550)

   (b) GCD(3915, 825) and LCM(3915, 825)

   (c) GCD(624, 1044) and LCM(624, 1044)

Thinking Critically

6. The following problem is from Claudia Zaslavsky's *The Multicultural Classroom* (Heineman, Portsmouth, NH, 1996, p. 113). "Challenge upper-grade students to calculate the interval in days between the two successive New Year's Days that coincide in both Mayan calendars—the 365-day everyday calendar and the 260-day ritual calendar. What is the greatest common divisor (GCD) of both numbers? What is the lowest common multiple?" Solve Claudia's problem.

7. The notions of the greatest common divisor and the least common multiple extend naturally to more than two numbers. Moreover, the prime power method extends naturally to finding GCD(a, b, c) and LCM(a, b, c).

   (a) If $a = 2^2 \cdot 3^1 \cdot 5^2$, $b = 2^1 \cdot 3^3 \cdot 5^1$ and $c = 3^2 \cdot 5^3 \cdot 7^1$, compute GCD($a$, b, c) and LCM(a, b, c).

   (b) Is it necessarily true that GCD(a, b, c) · LCM(a, b, c) = abc?

   (c) Find numbers r, s, and t such that GCD(r, s, t) · LCM(r, s, t) = rst.

8. Use the method of intersection of sets to compute the following.

   (a) GCD(18, 24, 12) and LCM(18, 24, 12)

   (b) GCD(8, 20, 14) and LCM(8, 20, 14)

   (c) Is it true that GCD(8, 20, 14) · LCM(8, 20, 14) = 8 · 20 · 14?

9. (a) Compute GCD(6, 35, 143) and LCM(6, 35, 143).

   (b) Is it true that GCD(6, 35, 143) · LCM(6, 35, 143) = 6 · 35 · 143?

   (c) Guess under what conditions GCD(a, b, c) · LCM(a, b, c) = abc.

10. (a) Compute GCD(GCD(24, 18), 12) and LCM(LCM(24, 18), 12) and compare with the results of problem 8(a).

    (b) Compute GCD(GCD(8, 20), 14) and LCM(LCM(8, 20), 14) and compare the results with those of problem 8(b).

    (c) In one or two written sentences, state a conjecture based on parts (a) and (b).

11. Cuisenaire® rods are colored rods one centimeter square and of lengths 1 cm, 2 cm, 3 cm, . . . , 10 cm as shown here.

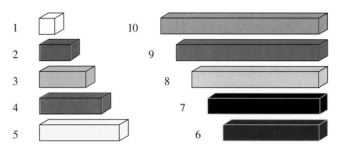

We say that a smaller rod *measures* a longer rod if a number of the smaller rods placed end to end are the same length as the given rod.

(a) Which rods will measure the 9 rod?

(b) Which rods will measure the 6 rod?

(c) What is the greatest common divisor of 9 and 6?

(d) Place the 10 rod and the 8 rod end to end to form an "18 train" as in the HANDS ON in Chapter 2. Which rods or trains will measure the "18 train"?

(e) Place the 7 rod and the 5 rod end to form a "12 train." Which rods or trains will measure the "12 train"?

(f) What is the greatest common divisor of 12 and 18?

(g) Briefly describe how you might use Cuisenaire® rods to demonstrate the notion of greatest common divisor to children.

12. Cuisenaire® rods are described in the preceding problem.

(a) What is the shortest train or length that can be measured by both 4-rods and 6-rods?

(b) What is the least common multiple of 4 and 6?

(c) What is the shortest train or length that can be measured by both 6-rods and 9-rods?

(d) What is the least common multiple of 6 and 9?

(e) Briefly describe how you could use Cuisenaire® rods to demonstrate the notion of least common multiple to children.

13. (a) Indicate how you could use a number line to illustrate the notion of greatest common divisor to children.

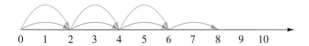

(b) Indicate how you could use a number line to illustrate the notion of least common multiple to children.

14. The greatest common divisor machine of Andres Zavrotsky (U.S. patent number 2 978 816, April 11, 1961) is described in Martin Gardner's *The Sixth Book*

of Mathematical Games from Scientific American (San Francisco: W. H. Freeman, 1971). For example, build a 6 by 8 "billiard table" out of mirrors and shine a light at 45° from a corner, *P*. The beam will bounce around the "table" and will eventually be absorbed at a corner. Let *Q* be the point on the long side of the "table" closest to *P* where the light beam "bounces." Then

$$GCD(6, 8) = (1/2) \cdot PQ = (1/2) \cdot 4 = 2.$$

Use graph paper and draw a similar diagram to determine GCD(9, 15).

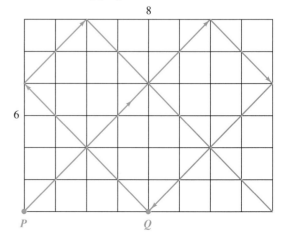

15. A simple graphical scheme for finding the greatest common divisor of two numbers is illustrated below. Suppose again that we want to compute GCD(6, 8). Draw a 6 by 8 rectangle and draw a diagonal from corner to corner.

In this case, the diagonal passes through just one point *P* that is a corner of squares on the graph paper. *P* divides the diagonal into 2 parts and 2 = GCD(6, 8). Use graph paper and draw a similar diagram to determine GCD(15, 25).

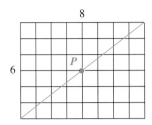

Thinking Cooperatively

16. Work through this problem as a group project. You will particularly want to consult with the members of your group as you respond to parts (e), (f), (g), and (h). Recall that the Fibonacci sequence was defined in Example 1.6 in Section 1.4. For easy reference, the first 30 numbers in the sequence are listed here. Also recall that we use the notation F_n to designate the *n*th Fibonacci number. Thus, $F_1 = F_2 = 1$, $F_3 = 2$, and so on.

n	1	2	3	4	5	6	7	8	9	10
F_n	1	1	2	3	5	8	13	21	34	55

n	11	12	13	14	15	16	17	18	19	20
F_n	89	144	233	377	610	987	1597	2584	4181	6765

n	21	22	23	24	25	26	27	28	29	30
F_n	10,946	17,711	28,657	46,368	75,025	121,393	196,418	317,811	514,229	832,040

(a) In problem 29 of Problem Set 4.1, you should have guessed that, for $m > 2$, F_m divides F_n if, and only if, m divides n. Compute each of these quotients: $F_{12} \div F_6$, $F_{18} \div F_9$, $F_{30} \div F_{15}$.

(b) If n is composite must F_n be composite? Explain briefly.

(c) If n is a prime must F_n be a prime? Explain briefly.

(d) Complete the following list.

GCD(F_6, F_9) = GCD(8, 34) = 2 = F_3 GCD(6, 9) = 3

GCD(F_{14}, F_{21}) = GCD(377, 10,946) = 13 = F_7 GCD(14, 21) = 7

GCD(F_{10}, F_{15}) =   GCD(10, 15) =

GCD(F_{20}, F_{30}) =   GCD(20, 30) =

GCD(F_{16}, F_{24}) =   GCD(16, 24) =

GCD(F_{12}, F_{18}) =   GCD(12, 18) =

(e) On the basis of the calculations in part (c), make a conjecture about GCD(F_m, F_n).

(f) Test your conjecture by computing GCD(F_{24}, F_{28}).

(g) Does the result of part (f) prove that your conjecture in part (e) is correct?

(h) If GCD(F_{16}, F_{20}) were to equal 4, what could you conclude about your conjecture in part (e)?

(i) Actually compute GCD(F_{16}, F_{20}).

Making Connections

17. The front wheel of a tricycle has a circumference of 54 inches and the back wheels have a circumference of 36 inches.

If points P and Q are both touching the sidewalk when Marja starts to ride, how far will she have ridden when P and Q first touch the sidewalk at the same time again?

18. Sarah Speed and Hi Velocity are racing cars around a track. If Sarah can make a complete circuit in 72 seconds and Hi completes a circuit in 68 seconds,

(a) how many seconds will it take for Hi to first pass Sarah at the starting line?

(b) how many laps will Sarah have made when Hi laps her the first time?

19. In a machine, a gear with 45 teeth is engaged with one with 96 teeth, with teeth A and B on the small and large gears respectively in contact as shown. How many more revolutions will the small gear have to make before A and B are again in the same position?

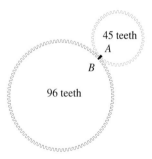

20. The musical notes A and E just below and above middle C have fundamental frequencies of 220 and 330 cycles per second (cps) respectively. Whenever these notes are sounded, overtones whose frequencies are multiples of the fundamental frequencies are also generated. A and E harmonize because many of their overtones have the same frequencies (660, 1320, 1980, . . .). The closer the least common multiple of the fundamental frequencies is to the fundamental frequencies, the better the harmony.

(a) A, C, and C sharp have frequencies of 220, 264, and 275 cps respectively. Compute LCM(220, 264), LCM(220, 275), and LCM(264, 275).

(b) On the basis of part (a), which pair of these three notes will produce the most pleasing harmony?

(c) Compute GCD(220, 264), GCD(220, 275), and GCD(264, 275).

(d) How can the results of part (c) tell you if two notes harmonize nicely?

Using a Graphing Calculator

21. Compute the following using DIVISORS.

(a) GCD(45, 48)   (b) GCD(48, 54)

22. Use MULTPLS to compute each of these numbers.

(a) LCM(45, 48)   (b) LCM(48, 54)

23. Use FACTOR to compute each of the following.

(a) The prime power representation of 205800, 31460, and 25840.

(b) GCD(31460, 205800)

(c) LCM(31460, 205800)

(d) GCD(205800, 31460, 25840)

(e) LCM(205800, 31460, 25840)

24. Compute the following using EUCLID.

(a) GCD(36461, 33269)

(b) GCD(16583, 16377)

(c) LCM(36461, 33269)

(d) LCM(16583, 16377)

For Review

25. (a) Check to see if $n^2 - 81n + 1681$ is prime for $n = 1, 2, 3, 4,$ and 5.

(b) On the basis of part (a), make a conjecture about the values of $n^2 - 81n + 1681$.

(c) Does the fact that your conjecture is true for $n = 1, 2, 3, 4,$ and 5 mean that the conjecture is always true? Explain briefly.

(d) Check your conjecture for $n = 6, 7,$ and 8. What do you conclude? Explain briefly.

(e) Check your conjecture for $n = 80$. How does this affect your belief in your conjecture? Explain.

(f) Check your conjecture for $n = 81$. What do you conclude? Explain briefly.

26. Let $n = 2 \cdot 5 \cdot 7 + 1$.

(a) Could 2, 5, or 7 divide n evenly? Why or why not?

(b) Is n prime or composite?

27. Let $n = 2 \cdot 3 \cdot 5 + 7 \cdot 11 \cdot 13$.

(a) Do any of 2, 3, 5, 7, 11, or 13 divide n evenly? Explain briefly.

(b) Must n have a prime divisor different from 2, 3, 5, 7, 11, or 13? Explain briefly.

(c) Is n prime or composite? (*Hint:* Use the program FACTOR on a graphing calculator.)

28. Let $n = 2 \cdot 3 \cdot 5 + 7 \cdot 11 \cdot 13 + 17 \cdot 19 \cdot 23$.

    (a) Do any of 2, 3, 5, 7, 11, 13, 17, 19, or 23 divide n evenly? Explain briefly.

(b) Can you argue as in problem 27(b) that n must have a prime divisor different from 2, 3, 5, 7, 11, 13, 17, 19, and 23?

(c) Find the prime power representation of n using the program FACTOR on a graphing calculator.

4.4   Clock Arithmetic

Mathematics is all around us. Making use of such naturally occurring mathematical ideas is an important and useful teaching strategy. What, for example, is the mathematics of an ordinary clock as depicted in Figure 4.4?

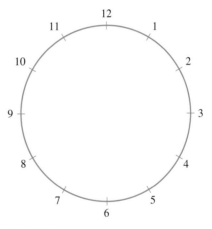

Figure 4.4
A 12-hour clock

Clock Addition and Multiplication

What is the point on the number line 9 units to the right of 7?

This is an addition problem that can be solved on the number line by "counting on." Starting at 0, we first count out to 7 and then count on 9 more to 16. Thus, $7 + 9 = 16$. Now, thinking of the clock, we might ask "what time is it 9 hours after 7 o'clock?" Again this can be answered by counting, but this time we count clockwise around the face of a clock. Starting at 12 on the clock diagrammed in Figure 4.4, we count to 7 and then count on 9 more to arrive at 4. Thus, in **12-hour clock arithmetic,** it is reasonable to say that 7 plus 9 is 4 and to write

$$7 +_{12} 9 = 4$$

where we indicate 12-hour clock addition by the symbol $+_{12}$.

Proceeding in the same way, we find that $9 +_{12} 12 = 12 +_{12} 9 = 9$. Indeed, since counting on 12 steps takes us all the way around the clock, it is clear that $n +_{12} 12 = 12 +_{12} n = n$ for every n on the clock. Thus, 12 plays the role of zero in 12-hour clock arithmetic and it will suit our purposes to replace 12 by 0 and to number the clock as shown in Figure 4.5. Thus, the numbers in the arithmetic are those in the set $T = \{0, 1, 2, 3, 4, 5, 6, 7, 8, 9, 10, 11\}$, and the arithmetic for the clock is determined as for whole numbers except that we count around the clock instead of on the number line.

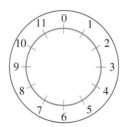

Figure 4.5
The 12-hour clock with 12 replaced by 0

A simple but effective manipulative for visualizing addition (and subtraction) in clock arithmetic is easily made from two circular discs marked as shown in Figure 4.6 and joined at the center so that they can rotate against one another. (Paper plates with one trimmed down a bit are reasonably durable and work well.) To add 9 to 7 in 12-hour clock arithmetic, for example, set the 0 on the inner circle under the 7 on the outer circle. Then count around to 9 on the inner circle. Since 9 on the inner circle lies under 4 on the outer circle, $7 +_{12} 9 = 4$ as noted above.

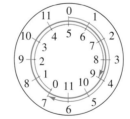

Figure 4.6
Illustrating $7 +_{12} 9 = 4$ with two rotatable discs

Now consider the sum $7 +_{12} 9 +_{12} 11 +_{12} 5 +_{12} 10 +_{12} 8 +_{12} 6$. Starting at 0 and counting to 7, then counting on 9 more, then 11 more, then 5 more, then 10 more, then 8 more, and then 6 more, gets us to 8. Thus, we have

$$7 +_{12} 9 +_{12} 11 +_{12} 5 +_{12} 10 +_{12} 8 +_{12} 6 = 8.$$

In whole number arithmetic this sum would be 56. Since $56 = 4 \cdot 12 + 8$, we would have counted four times around the clock and then on 8 more, obtaining the result shown. In a similar way, we determine that

$$7 \times_{12} 9 = 9 +_{12} 9 +_{12} 9 +_{12} 9 +_{12} 9 +_{12} 9 +_{12} 9 = 3$$

and, in ordinary whole number arithmetic, $7 \cdot 9 = 63 = 5 \cdot 12 + 3$. These considerations lead to the following definition.

> **DEFINITION**   *Computing 12-hour Clock Sums and Products*
> To compute sums and products in 12-hour clock arithmetic, perform the same computation
> in whole number arithmetic, divide by 12, and take the remainder, r, as the answer.

EXAMPLE   4.19

Computing 12-Hour Clock Sums and Products

Perform the following computations in 12-hour clock arithmetic.

(a) $7 +_{12} 8$ (b) $3 +_{12} 9$ (c) $11 +_{12} 7 +_{12} 6 +_{12} 10$

(d) $7 \times_{12} 8$ (e) $4 \times_{12} 9$ (f) $5 \times_{12} 5 \times_{12} 5$

Solution

Using the division algorithm, we have the following.

(a) $7 + 8 = 15 = 1 \cdot 12 + 3$, so $7 +_{12} 8 = 3$.
(b) $3 + 9 = 12 = 1 \cdot 12 + 0$, so $3 +_{12} 9 = 0$.
(c) $11 + 7 + 6 + 10 = 34 = 2 \cdot 12 + 10$, so $11 +_{12} 7 +_{12} 6 +_{12} 10 = 10$.
(d) $7 \cdot 8 = 56 = 4 \cdot 12 + 8$, so $7 \times_{12} 8 = 8$.
(e) $4 \cdot 9 = 36 = 3 \cdot 12 + 0$, so $4 \times_{12} 9 = 0$.
(f) $5 \cdot 5 \cdot 5 = 125 = 10 \cdot 12 + 5$, so $5 \times_{12} 5 \times_{12} 5 = 5$.

It follows from the above definition that the properties for addition and multiplication of whole numbers also hold in 12-hour clock arithmetic. For example, in whole number arithmetic, $(a + b) + c = a + (b + c)$. Since we obtain 12-hour clock sums by taking
ordinary sums, dividing by 12, and taking the remainder as the answer, it follows that
$(a +_{12} b) +_{12} c = a +_{12} (b +_{12} c)$. Since the other properties are treated in the same way,
it follows that, in 12-hour clock arithmetic

- the closure properties for both addition and multiplication hold,
- addition and multiplication are both commutative,
- addition and multiplication are both associative, and
- 0 is the additive identity and 1 is the multiplicative identity.

DID YOU KNOW?

Public Key Encryption

Number theory is usually
considered a part of pure
mathematics; that is,
mathematics studied for its own sake
with no thought that it might be, or
even could be, applied to real world
problems. Who would have guessed
that the notions of primality and
factoring would turn out to provide the
basis for a simple and remarkably
secure method of sending secret
messages in code? The idea is to
determine two, 100-digit primes, p and
q, and to publish the product pq for all
to see. Using this "key" anyone can
send you a message, but no one can
read the message unless they know p
and q; that is, unless they are able to
factor the 200-digit product, pq. While
it is a three or four minute job to
determine two 100-digit primes on one
of today's fastest computers, it would
take one of these same machines on the
order of 10^9 years (that is, 1 billion
years), to factor the product pq. Thus,
unless someone has discovered a way
to break the code without determining
p and q—a very unlikely
circumstance—it is effectively
unbreakable. The importance of the
existence of such a code in our modern
society, with its need to keep masses of
data (financial records, industrial
secrets, computer data bases of all
sorts) secret, cannot be overstated.

Clock Subtraction

Like whole number subtraction, subtraction in clock arithmetic is defined in terms of addition. In whole number subtraction, $a - b = c$ if, and only if, $a = b + c$. In like manner, we have this definition.

> **DEFINITION**   *Clock Subtraction*
>
> Let $T = \{0, 1, 2, 3, \ldots, 11\}$. For all $a \in T$ and $b \in T$, $a -_{12} b = c$ if, and only if, $a = b +_{12} c$.

EXAMPLE 4.20

12-Hour Clock Subtraction

Compute the following clock "differences."

(a) $11 -_{12} 4$ (b) $4 -_{12} 7$ (c) $8 -_{12} 5$ (d) $5 -_{12} 8$

Solution

(a) Since $4 +_{12} 7 = 11$, it follows that $11 -_{12} 4 = 7$.
(b) Since $7 +_{12} 9 = 4$, it follows that $4 -_{12} 7 = 9$.
(c) Here $8 = 5 +_{12} 3$ and so $8 -_{12} 5 = 3$.
(d) Since $8 +_{12} 9 = 5$, it follows that $5 -_{12} 8 = 9$.

Since any point on the clock can be reached from any other point by counting in either the clockwise direction or the counterclockwise direction, clock subtraction can always be performed as clock addition. For example, $5 -_{12} 9 = 8$ since, starting at 0, if we count 5 in the clockwise direction and 9 in the counterclockwise direction, we arrive at 8. However, 8 can also be reached by starting at 0 and counting 5 in the clockwise direction and then 3 more in the clockwise direction. Thus,

$$5 -_{12} 9 = 5 +_{12} 3 = 8$$

as illustrated in Figure 4.7. Indeed, since the counts of 9 and 3 have to reach all the way

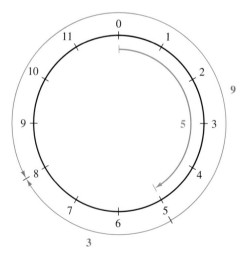

Figure 4.7
Illlustrating clock subtraction as clock addition.

$$5 -_{12} 9 = 5 +_{12} 3 = 8$$

around the circle, it is clear that $9 + 3 = 12$. This is always the case, and we have the following theorem.

> **THEOREM**   *Clock Subtraction as Clock Addition*
> Let $T = \{0, 1, 2, 3, \ldots , 11\}$. For all a and b in T, $a -_{12} b = a +_{12} (12 - b)$.

EXAMPLE   4.21

Subtracting by Adding in Clock Arithmetic

Perform the following subtractions as additions.

    (a) $3 -_{12} 8$ **(b)** $11 -_{12} 7$ **(c)** $9 -_{12} 11$ **(d)** $2 -_{12} 6$

Solution

    (a) Since $12 - 8 = 4$, $3 -_{12} 8 = 3 +_{12} 4 = 7$. Check: $8 +_{12} 7 = 3$
    (b) Since $12 - 7 = 5$, $11 -_{12} 7 = 11 +_{12} 5 = 4$. Check: $7 +_{12} 4 = 11$
    (c) Since $12 - 11 = 1$, $9 -_{12} 11 = 9 +_{12} 1 = 10$. Check: $11 +_{12} 10 = 9$
    (d) Since $12 - 6 = 6$, $2 -_{12} 6 = 2 +_{12} 6 = 8$. Check: $6 +_{12} 8 = 2$

In the preceding theorem and example, we saw that we can subtract by b in 12-hour clock arithmetic by *adding $12 - b$*. We call $12 - b$ the **additive inverse** of b and note that we can subtract b from a by *adding the additive inverse of b to a*.

DID YOU KNOW?

Fascinating Fibonaccis

"For many years I have been captivated and intrigued by Fibonacci numbers. It has been enormously satisfying to share what I know about them with my young . . . students. Their responses have run the gamut from profound disbelief to patronizing good humor, sprinkled with scientific inquisitiveness. Invariably they ask for more information that they might take home to share with family and friends, demonstrating a confidence in others' interest in the subject and thus revealing their own. Unfortunately the information they seek has been deeply buried in scientific journals or aging mathematical literature, occasionally surfacing as one perfunctory page in a textbook or as a scholarly article in a popular periodical.

"It seemed to me that the time had come to collect and sort out what is currently known about this fascinating subject, to make it understandable and to excite the curiosity of believers and skeptics alike. What is so special about these numbers? Where did they come from? Why do they keep popping up in unlikely, unrelated places? Where might they be that no one has yet thought to look? What answers might they hold for the world, if not the universe?"

This is the preface to the book by middle school teacher Trudi Hammel Garland, *Fascinating Fibonaccis: Mystery and Magic in Numbers*. The book brims with great ideas that will not only stimulate your imagination but will do the same for your students.

SOURCE: From *Fascinating Fibonaccis: Mystery and Magic in Numbers* by Trudi Hammel Garland. Copyright © 1987 by Dale Seymour Publications, Palo Alto, CA 94303. Reprinted by permission.

DEFINITION   *The Additive Inverse*

Let $T = \{0, 1, 2, \ldots, 11\}$. If $a \in T$ and $a +_{12} b = b +_{12} a = 0$, then b is called the **additive inverse** of a. Also, a is the **additive inverse** of b.

Using this terminology, the preceding theorem can now be written as follows.

THEOREM   *Clock Subtraction as Clock Addition*

To subtract b from a in clock arithmetic, add the additive inverse of b to a.

Since clock subtraction can always be performed as clock addition and clock arithmetic is closed under clock addition, it follows that clock arithmetic is also closed under clock subtraction. However, parts (c) and (d) of Example 4.20 make it clear that subtraction is not commutative in clock arithmetic, and the fact that $8 -_{12} (7 -_{12} 5) = 6$ and $(8 -_{12} 7) -_{12} 5 = 8$ makes it clear that clock subtraction is not associative. In summary

- clock arithmetic *is* closed under addition,
- clock arithmetic *is* closed under subtraction,
- subtraction *is not* commutative in clock arithmetic, and
- subtraction *is not* associative in clock arithmetic.

Division in Clock Arithmetic

Division without remainder is defined in clock arithmetic just as it is for whole numbers.

Note: the word "unique" is important here.

DEFINITION   *Clock Division*

Let $T = \{0, 1, 2, 3, \ldots, 11\}$. For $a \in T$ and $b \in T$, we say that b **divides** a in clock arithmetic, and write $a \div_{12} b = c$, if, and only if, there exists a *unique* $c \in T$ such that $a = b \times_{12} c$.

EXAMPLE   4.22

12-Hour Clock Division

Perform these divisions if possible.

(a) $8 \div_{12} 5$ **(b)** $7 \div_{12} 8$ **(c)** $4 \div_{12} 10$

Solution

Division in clock arithmetic is greatly facilitated if one has a complete multiplication table as shown on the next page.

12-hour Clock Multiplication Table

$\times_{12}$	0	1	2	3	4	5	6	7	8	9	10	11
0	0	0	0	0	0	0	0	0	0	0	0	0
1	0	1	2	3	4	5	6	7	8	9	10	11
2	0	2	4	6	8	10	0	2	4	6	8	10
3	0	3	6	9	0	3	6	9	0	3	6	9
4	0	4	8	0	4	8	0	4	8	0	4	8
5	0	5	10	3	8	1	6	11	4	9	2	7
6	0	6	0	6	0	6	0	6	0	6	0	6
7	0	7	2	9	4	11	6	1	8	3	10	5
8	0	8	4	0	8	4	0	8	4	0	8	4
9	0	9	6	3	0	9	6	3	0	9	6	3
10	0	10	8	6	4	2	0	10	8	6	4	2
11	0	11	10	9	8	7	6	5	4	3	2	1

   (a)   From the table, 4 is the only element a in T such that $8 = 5 \times_{12} a$. Therefore, $8 \div_{12} 5 = 4$.

   (b)   From the table, there is no $c \in T$ such that $7 = 8 \times_{12} c$. Therefore, this division is not defined.

   (c)   From the table, $10 \times_{12} 4 = 10 \times_{12} 10 = 4$. Since there is *more than one number* $c \in T$ such that $10 \times_{12} c = 4$, this division is *not* defined.

INTO THE CLASSROOM

Clock Arithmetic

Clock arithmetic should be considered a worthwhile enrichment topic for the elementary classroom. Our experience is that children like mathematical ideas drawn from their immediate surroundings, and that they are intrigued and interested by this arithmetic generated by an ordinary clock; an arithmetic that is both similar to yet different from ordinary arithmetic. As usual, the arithmetic should be introduced via manipulatives (in this case an ordinary clock or a device like that illustrated in Figure 4.6 and, later, diagrams of n-hour clocks for other values of n), and then students should be led to develop the resulting arithmetic pretty much on their own. The teacher should ask only occasional pertinent questions and make occasional suggestions as the development proceeds. Of special importance is the difference between the arithmetics generated by n-hour clocks when n is prime and when n is composite. In particular, n-hour clock arithmetic where n is a prime number is closed under division except for division by zero and, as we have seen, this is not so when n is composite. Other interesting questions and properties of clock arithmetic that can be turned into classroom activities will be seen in Problem Set 4.4.

Also, this material should not be presented to students in a vacuum. Classroom activities involving zip codes are attractive to students as are other codes, like ISBN numbers in books, that rely at least partly on clock arithmetic.

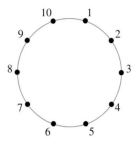

Figure 4.8
A 10-hour clock

A Post Office Application of Clock Arithmetic

Suppose we had a "10-hour" clock as shown in Figure 4.8 instead of a 12-hour clock. The resulting arithmetic is like 12-hour clock arithmetic except that to find the 10-hour sum or product of two elements of

$$T = \{0, 1, 2, 3, 4, 5, 6, 7, 8, 9\},$$

we find the sum as in ordinary arithmetic, divide the answer by 10, and use the resulting remainder, r.

Subtraction and division are then defined in terms of addition and of multiplication as above.

EXAMPLE   4.23

Calculating in 10-Hour Clock Arithmetic

Perform each of these 10-hour clock computations.

(a) $6 +_{10} 9$ **(b)** $6 -_{10} 9$ **(c)** $6 \times_{10} 9$ **(d)** $6 \div_{10} 9$

Solution

(a)   Since $6 + 9 = 15 = 1 \cdot 10 + 5$, $6 +_{10} 9 = 5$.

(b)   Here we must find $c \in T$ such that $6 = 9 +_{10} c$. Since the remainder on dividing a number by 10 is just its units digit and $9 + 7 = 16$, it follows that $c = 7$.

(c)   Since $6 \cdot 9 = 54 = 5 \cdot 10 + 4$, $6 \times_{10} 9 = 4$.

(d)   Here we must find $c \in T$ such that $9 \times_{10} c = 6$. Since $4 \cdot 9 = 36 = 3 \cdot 10 + 6$, it follows that $c = 4$. Thus, $6 \div_{10} 9 = 4$.

Have you ever wondered what all the strange marks mean that appear so often on mail (particularly junk mail) that you regularly receive? Consider the following problem.

EXAMPLE   4.24

The Bar Code on Envelopes and Postal Cards

Discover the meaning of bar codes like those appearing below the address on the postal cards shown on the next page.

Solution   *Understand the problem*

Surely the markings are placed on the cards and envelopes for a purpose. They must mean something; they must convey some sort of information.

That means the string of marks must be a code of some sort. But what is secret about business reply cards and other pieces of mail? Why should there be coded information on each such card? Since it is unlikely that the information is intended to be kept secret, it is no doubt coded for some other purpose. Do you suppose that it is encoded in this way so that it is machine readable? Actually, given the ever increasing use of automation coupled with the steady increase in the amount of mail being processed, it is quite likely that this has something to do with the automatic sorting of mail.

The first bit of information needed to deliver a piece of mail is the post office to which the mail must be sent, and this is determined by the 5-digit zip code. Actually, we all have a 9-digit zip code as on the post cards shown, with the first two of the last four digits indicating a portion of a delivery area (for example, a specific delivery route) and the last two digits indicating a specific business or organization, a specific building, or a specific portion (say a part of a street) of a delivery route. Do you suppose the bar code in question gives the zip code in machine readable form? Let's analyze the bar codes and see if we can associate them with the zip codes.

Carry out the plan

To simplify the work, we repeat here the two zip codes and what we guess are the associated bar codes.

07713-0001

III₁₁₁I₁₁₁III₁₁₁I₁₁₁III₁₁IIIIII₁₁IIII₁₁IIIIᵢₙᵢIIₙᵢIII

20077-9964

I₁₁I₁IIIₙᵢII₁₁ᵢII₁₁IIᵢₙIIIᵢIₙIₙIᵢₙₙIIᵢₙIᵢIᵢII₁I

Looking for patterns and trying to associate the numbers with the bar code, we note that each string begins and ends with a long bar. In fact, this is always true as you can easily check by finding other examples in your mail box. These two bars probably tell the machine when the code starts and stops. Doing a count, we find that there are 52 bars in each code. Thus, deleting the start and stop bars, there are 50 bars to determine the zip code. Since there are nine numbers and a dash in the zip code, this may mean that all code groups are of length five. Thus, we break the bar code up into 5-bar groups as shown below and try to associate the successive numbers in the zip code with the successive groups. As a check, we can use the fact that several digits are repeated both within and between the two codes. For the first code we obtain the pairings shown. But this can't make sense because then 0 and the dash correspond to the same code group.

$$0 \quad 7 \quad 7 \quad 1 \quad 3 \quad – \quad 0 \quad 0 \quad 0 \quad 1$$

Indeed, given the four 0s in this code, it appears that no code group corresponds to the dash and that ‖ıı corresponds to zero. This means that the last two code groups both correspond to 1s so there must be additional information in the code. Let's look again at both codes, this time leaving out the dash. We obtain these pairings.

$$0 \quad 7 \quad 7 \quad 1 \quad 3 \quad 0 \quad 0 \quad 0 \quad 1 \quad 1$$

$$2 \quad 0 \quad 0 \quad 7 \quad 7 \quad 9 \quad 9 \quad 6 \quad 4 \quad 6$$

Note that each of 0, 1, and 7 appear more than once in these codes and that each time they appear, they have the same representation in bar code! This is very strong evidence that we are correct, that the bar code represents the zip code, and that the code representations are as shown here. Of course, the last 1 and 6 in the above diagrams were determined by the earlier appearance of the same 5-bar patterns in each zip code. Finally, it is not clear from the illustration what code group should correspond to each of 5 and 8, though it might be guessed with careful study of the following patterns. Otherwise, these can be determined by looking at other pieces of mail whose zip codes contain these digits.

1 ← ııı‖		6 ← ı‖ıı	
2 ← ıı‖ı		7 ← ‖ııı	
3 ← ıı‖ı		8 ←	
4 ← ı‖ıı		9 ← ‖ı‖ıı	
5 ←		0 ← ‖ıııı	

Look back

We first guessed that the bar code must indeed be a code and that it likely gave the zip code in machine readable form. We then noticed that both codes had 52 bars beginning and ending with a long bar. Ignoring the first and last bars, we had a bar code with 50 bars. Our guess was that each five consecutive bars represented a digit which, in turn, could be determined by looking at the printed zip code.

This gave us 10 digits and a question remains regarding the tenth digit. Trying a variety of possibilities, we find that

$$0 + 7 + 7 + 1 + 3 + 0 + 0 + 0 + 1 + 1 = 20$$

and

$$2 + 0 + 0 + 7 + 7 + 9 + 9 + 6 + 4 + 6 = 50.$$

It appears that the tenth digit in each case, here 1 and 6 respectively, has been chosen so that the sum of all the digits is a multiple of 10; that is, 0 in 10-hour clock arithmetic. This suggests that the tenth digit is a *check digit* and that it is included so that incorrect codes can be detected by machine. In fact, this is the case, and, if an error is detected in this way, the piece of mail is automatically shunted aside for human inspection and correction of the zip code.

PROBLEM SET 4.4

Understanding Concepts

1. Compute these 12-hour clock sums.
   (a) $5 +_{12} 9$ (b) $8 +_{12} 7$ (c) $8 +_{12} 4$
   (d) $4 +_{12} 7$ (e) $10 +_{12} 10$ (f) $7 +_{12} 8$

2. Compute these *n*-hour clock sums, where $+_n$ denotes *n*-hour clock addition; that is, $5 +_7 3$ indicates the 7-hour clock addition of 5 and 3.
   (a) $3 +_5 4$ (b) $17 +_{26} 13$ (c) $2 +_{10} 7$
   (d) $7 +_9 4$ (e) $12 +_{16} 10$ (f) $2 +_7 7$

3. In 12-hour clock arithmetic, $a -_{12} b$ can be computed by starting at *a* and counting *b* steps *counterclockwise* around the clock. Use this method to compute each difference.
   (a) $9 -_{12} 7$ (b) $8 -_{12} 11$ (c) $5 -_{12} 9$
   (d) $8 -_{12} 12$ (e) $2 -_{12} 11$ (f) $8 -_{12} 8$

4. Recall that 0 is the additive identity in 12-hour clock arithmetic and that *b* is the additive inverse of *a* if, and only if, $a +_{12} b = b +_{12} a = 0$. Compute the additive inverses of each of these numbers in 12-hour clock arithmetic.
   (a) 7   (b) 11   (c) 9   (d) 8

5. Compute each of these differences by adding. Be sure to show what you are adding each time.
   (a) $9 -_{12} 7$ (b) $8 -_{12} 11$ (c) $5 -_{12} 9$
   (d) $8 -_{12} 12$ (e) $2 -_{12} 11$ (f) $8 -_{12} 8$

6. Compute these products in 12-hour clock arithmetic.
   (a) $5 \times_{12} 7$ (b) $9 \times_{12} 11$ (c) $8 \times_{12} 9$
   (d) $8 \times_{12} 6$ (e) $4 \times_{12} 6$ (f) $4 \times_{12} 9$

7. Perform these divisions if they are defined. (*Suggestion:* See Table 4.1.)
   (a) $5 \div_{12} 7$ (b) $7 \div_{12} 10$ (c) $8 \div_{12} 4$
   (d) $8 \div_{12} 5$ (e) $9 \div_{12} 5$ (f) $6 \div_{12} 11$

8. Two numbers are said to be **relatively prime** if their greatest common divisor is 1.
   (a) List the numbers in $T = \{0, 1, 2, \ldots, 11\}$ that are relatively prime to 12.
   (b) List the numbers in $T = \{0, 1, 2, \ldots, 11\}$ that are not relatively prime to 12.
   (c) Compare the results of parts (a) and (b) with the results of Example 4.22. What conjecture does this comparison suggest?

9. Construct complete addition and multiplication tables for 5-hour clock arithmetic.

10. Perform these computations in 5-hour clock arithmetic.
    (a) $3 +_5 4$ (b) $2 +_5 3$ (c) $4 +_5 4$
    (d) $3 \times_5 4$ (e) $2 \times_5 3$ (f) $4 \times_5 4$
    (g) $3 -_5 4$ (h) $2 -_5 3$ (i) $4 -_5 4$
    (j) $3 \div_5 4$ (k) $2 \div_5 3$ (l) $4 \div_5 4$

11. (a) What is the additive identity in 5-hour clock arithmetic? Why?
    (b) What is the multiplicative identity in 5-hour clock arithmetic? Why?

12. If $a +_5 b = b +_5 a = 0$, then *b* **is the additive inverse of** *a* **and** *a* **is the additive inverse of** *b* in 5-hour clock arithmetic; that is, $a = -_5 b$ and $b = -_5 a$. *Note:* $-_5 b = 5 - b$. Why?

(a) Compute the additive inverse of each of 1, 2, 3, 4, and 0 in 5-hour clock arithmetic.

As in 12-hour clock arithmetic, we can subtract b from a in 5-hour clock arithmetic by *adding* the additive inverse of b to a. Perform each of these subtractions in two ways—(i) by counting backwards on a 5-hour clock and (ii) by adding the additive inverse of the number being subtracted.

(b) $2 -_5 4$　　(c) $3 -_5 2$　　(d) $1 -_5 3$

13. If $a \times_5 b = b \times_5 a = 1$, then a **is called the multiplicative inverse of b** and b **is called the multiplicative inverse of a** in 5-hour clock arithmetic; that is, we write $a = b^{-1}$ and $b = a^{-1}$.

　(a) Which numbers in 5-hour clock arithmetic possess multiplicative inverses? (*Hint:* Check the results of problem 9 above.)

　(b) Which numbers in 12-hour clock arithmetic possess multiplicative inverses? (*Hint:* Check Table 4.1.)

14. Just as we can subtract in clock arithmetic by adding the additive inverse, we can divide by multiplying by the multiplicative inverse. Use the definition of clock division to compute each of the following.

(a) $4 \div_{12} 7$　　(b) $3 \div_{12} 11$　　(c) $3 \div_5 2$

(d) $2 \div_5 2$　　(e) $2 \div_5 4$　　(f) $4 \div_5 3$

Compute each of the quantities in parts (g) through (l) by multiplying by the multiplicative inverse; that is, compute each of these products.

(g) $4 \times_{12} 7^{-1}$　　(h) $3 \times_{12} 11^{-1}$　　(i) $3 \times_5 2^{-1}$

(j) $2 \times_5 2^{-1}$　　(k) $2 \times_5 4^{-1}$　　(l) $4 \times_5 3^{-1}$

15. Using Table 4.1 solve the following equations in 12-hour clock arithmetic. The first one is done for you.

(a) $(3 \times_{12} y) +_{12} 7 = 4$　　*Solution:*

(b) $(7 \times_{12} y) -_{12} 4 = 8$　　$3 \times_{12} y = 4 +_{12} 5$

(c) $(y +_{12} 2) \div_{12} 11 = 3$　　$3 \times_{12} y = 9$

(d) $(2 \div_{12} y) -_{12} 4 = 3$　　$y = 3, 7,$ or 11

16. Write the bar code for each of these zip codes.

(a) 99164–3113　　(b) 18374–2147

(c) 38423–1747

---

17. Write the zip code given by each of these bar codes unless the code is necessarily incorrect. If it is necessarily incorrect, tell why.

(a) ||⸱⸱|||||⸱⸱⸱⸱|⸱|⸱|⸱⸱⸱|⸱|⸱⸱|||⸱|⸱|⸱⸱||⸱⸱|⸱|⸱⸱⸱||⸱|⸱|⸱⸱||

(b) |⸱|⸱|⸱⸱|⸱|⸱|⸱⸱|⸱|⸱|⸱⸱|||⸱⸱⸱⸱|⸱|⸱|⸱⸱||⸱⸱⸱⸱|||⸱⸱||⸱|⸱|⸱|

(c) |||⸱⸱⸱|⸱⸱⸱|||⸱⸱⸱⸱||⸱|⸱|⸱⸱|⸱|⸱⸱|⸱|⸱⸱⸱|||⸱⸱|⸱⸱⸱||||⸱⸱|

Thinking Critically

18. **Powers in *n*-Hour Clock Arithmetic.** Since $a^s = a \cdot a \cdots a$ with s factors of a, we can compute a^s in n-hour clock arithmetic in the usual way. That is, $a^s = r$ in n-hour clock arithmetic where r is the remainder when a^s is divided by n. Moreover, it follows that the usual rules

$$a^s a^t = a^{s+t} \quad \text{and} \quad (a^s)^t = a^{st}$$

hold in clock arithmetic just as they do in ordinary arithmetic. Compute these in 12-hour clock arithmetic. Do parts (e), (f), (g), and (h) in order using the result of each part to compute the result required in the next part. (*Note:* To compute 3^5, for example, using your calculator, enter the string $3 \boxed{y^x} 5 \boxed{=}$. Then reenter the answer and use $\boxed{\text{INT} \div}$ to determine the result in 12-hour clock arithmetic.)

(a) 3^3　　(b) 3^4　　(c) $3^3 \cdot 3^4$

(d) 3^{3+4}　　(e) 4^2　　(f) $(4^2)^5$

(g) $4^{2 \cdot 5}$　　(h) 4^{10}

19. (a) Complete the following table. The first two rows have been completed for you. *Note:* In using your calculator to compute $2^n - 2$ in n-hour clock arithmetic, you may have to enter the string $\boxed{\text{ON/AC}} \; 2 \; \boxed{y^x} \; n \; \boxed{-} \; 2 \; \boxed{=}$, record the result in the second column of

the table, then *reenter* the result and use $\boxed{\text{INT} \div}$ to determine the correct result for column three.

n	$2^n - 2$	$2^n - 2$ in n-hour clock arithmetic
2	2	0
3	6	0
4		
5		
6		
7		
8		
9		
10		
11		
12		
13		

(b) What seems to be the case when n is a prime in the table of part (a)? Make a conjecture.

(c) Compute $2^{23} - 2$ in 23-hour arithmetic. Note that you cannot use the $\boxed{\text{INT} \div}$ key on a *Math Explorer* to determine the remainder when dividing by 23 since the quotient is too large. Instead, enter the sequence $\boxed{\text{ON/AC}}$ 2 $\boxed{y^x}$ 23 $\boxed{-}$ 2 $\boxed{=}$ $\boxed{\div}$ 23 $\boxed{=}$ $\boxed{-}$ 364722 $\boxed{=}$ $\boxed{\times}$ 23 $\boxed{=}$. (Did you actually have to perform the last six steps in this sequence to know what the remainder was in this case?) Does this result strengthen your belief in the conjecture you made in part (b)? Does it prove that it is correct?

---

20. (a) Repeat problem 19 (a) with 2 replaced by 3.

    (b) Make a conjecture on the basis of part (a).

21. You have little to go on, but make a conjecture generalizing the conjectures for problems 19 and 20. If you need more data, repeat 19(a) and (b) with 2 replaced by 4, by 5, by 6, etc.

Thinking Cooperatively

In the next three problems divide the work among the members of your group, discuss the results obtained, and determine conjectures agreed upon by the group.

22. Make a conjecture concerning the value of $1 \cdot 2 \cdot 3 \cdots (p - 1) + 1$ in p-hour clock arithmetic where p is a prime. Suggestion: Consider a number of examples using the first few primes.

23. Make a conjecture concerning the value of $a^{p-1} - 1$ in p-hour clock arithmetic if p is a prime and p does not divide a.

24. Fill in the following table for a number of choices of a and b in $T = \{0, 1, 2, 3, \ldots, 11\}$ and endeavor to discover when $a \times_{12} y = b$ is solvable and how many solutions this equation has. (*Hint:* Use Table 4.1.)

a	b	GCD $(a, 12)$	b/GCD $(a, 12)$	12/GCD $(a, 12)$	No. of solutions of $a \times_{12} y = b$

Making Connections

25. Since about 1972 all books published anywhere in the world have been given an identifying number called an International Standard Book Number (ISBN). These numbers greatly facilitate buying

and selling books, inventory control, and so on. A typical ISBN number is

$$0\text{--}13\text{--}257502\text{--}7$$

and, somewhat like the zip code, the last digit is a check digit. It works like this. There are 10 digits in the code and the check digit is chosen so that 10 times the first digit plus 9 times the second digit, plus 8 times the third digit, . . . , plus 1 times the check digit is 0 in 11-hour clock arithmetic. Thus, for the above, $(10 \times_{11} 0) +_{11} (9 \times_{11} 1) +_{11} (8 \times_{11} 3) +_{11} (7 \times_{11} 2) +_{11} (6 \times_{11} 5) +_{11} (5 \times_{11} 7) +_{11} (4 \times_{11} 5) +_{11} (3 \times_{11} 0) +_{11} (2 \times_{11} 2) +_{11} (1 \times_{11} 7) = 0$ since the result in ordinary arithmetic is 143 and 11 divides 143. The check digit may be an X, denoting a ten.

(a) Which of these ISBN numbers is correct?

   (i) 0–70–808228–7

   (ii) 0–201–30722–7

(b) Supply the check digit to complete each of these correct ISBN numbers.

   (i) 5–648–00738–

   (ii) 3–540–11200–

26. Supply the correct check digit for each of these zip codes.

(a) 24763–8117–

(b) 35992–1712–

Using a Computer

27. The following commands set up a spreadsheet to check an ISBN code.

(i) Put "10" in A1.

(ii) Put " = A1 − 1" in B1 and **COPY** and **PASTE** or **FILL** right to J1.

(iii) Put the digits of the ISBN code in A2 through J2. If X appears in the code, replace it by 10.

(iv) Put " = A1*A2" in A3 and **COPY** and **PASTE** or **FILL** right to J3.

(v) Put " = SUM(A3:J3)" in K3.

(vi) Put " = MOD(K3,11)" in L3. This places the 11-hour clock value of the sum in K3 in L3. If L3 contains 0, the code is correct.

Set up such a spreadsheet and use it to determine if the following codes are correct. Note that once a sheet is set up all you need do to immediately see if a given code is correct is enter the digits of the code in A2 through J2.

(a) 0–673–46483–0   (b) 0–321–01330–2

28. Use guess and check and the computer program of problem 27 to determine the check digit that should be added to complete these 9-digit ISBN codes.

(a) 0–13–257–502   (b) 0–88133–836

For Review

29. Draw rectangular diagrams to illustrate all the factorings of 12 taking order into account; that is, think of $1 \cdot 12$ as different from $12 \cdot 1$.

30. Use the method of intersection of sets to determine the following.

(a) GCD(60, 150)   (b) LCM(60, 150)

31. (a) Use a factor tree to determine all the prime divisors of 540.

(b) How can you tell at a glance if 540 is or is not divisible by 9?

32. (a) Write the prime power representations of 540 and 600.

(b) Use part (a) to determine GCD(540, 600).

(c) Use part (a) to determine LCM(540, 600).

33. Does $2^3 \cdot 3^5 \cdot 7^2 \cdot 11^6$ evenly divide $2^4 \cdot 3^7 \cdot 5^2 \cdot 7^1 \cdot 11^8$? Explain briefly.

34. To determine if 427 is a prime, which primes must you check as possible divisors?

EPILOGUE   Number Theory, the Queen of Mathematics

Almost 200 years ago Carl Gauss wrote, "Mathematics is the queen of the sciences, but number theory is the queen of mathematics." What Gauss was really saying is that our modern technology, and work in science generally, depends so heavily on mathematics that progress in these areas would be essentially impossible without mathematical skill. This assertion is increasingly true in the social sciences as well. Beyond that, Gauss was saying that mathematics is also intrinsically interesting and intellectually satisfying and that this is particularly true of number theory.

    In this chapter we have introduced the basic number theoretic notions of divisibility, factoring, factors and multiples, primes and composite numbers, least common multiples and greatest common divisors, and related ideas from clock arithmetic. These ideas are not only useful in other parts of mathematics and in disciplines like computer science but they also provide interesting and stimulating motivational material for the elementary mathematics classroom. In particular, number theory is replete with interesting and challenging problems which provide additional opportunities to further develop problem-solving skills. It is increasingly the case that number theoretic notions appear in elementary school texts and that these ideas must be understood by teachers.

Chapter 4 Summary

Key Concepts

The main objectives of this chapter have been to introduce the fundamental ideas of number theory and clock arithmetic most likely to appear in modern elementary school texts. The central ideas are these.

- divisibility
- composite numbers
- multiples
- least common multiples
- the fundamental theorem of arithmetic
- primes
- factors or divisors
- greatest common divisors
- clock arithmetic
- the Euclidean algorithm

Vocabulary and Notation

Section 4.1

Perfect number
Divides
Divisor, proper divisor
Factor
Multiple
Prime number
Composite number
Unit
Factor tree
Fundamental theorem of arithmetic
Prime power representation of n
Number of divisors of a number

Section 4.2

Divisibility by 2 and 5
Divisibility by 10
Divisibility by products

Divisibility by 3 and 9
Divisibility by 11
Divisibility by 7, 11, and 13
Divisibility by 4, 8, and other powers of 2

Section 4.3

Factor
Greatest common divisor, greatest common factor
GCD(a, b), GCF(a, b)
Finding the GCD by intersection of sets
Finding the GCD from prime power representations
Finding the GCD by the Euclidean algorithm
Common multiple
Least common multiple
Finding least common multiples by intersection of sets
Finding the LCM from prime power representations
GCD(a, b) · LCM(a, b) = ab
Finding the LCM using the Euclidean algorithm

Section 4.4

12-hour clock arithmetic
12-hour clock addition, $+_{12}$
12-hour clock multiplication, $\times_{12}$
12-hour clock subtraction, $-_{12}$

Additive inverse
12-hour clock subtraction by 12-hour clock addition
12-hour clock division, $\div_{12}$
10-hour clock arithmetic
Zip codes, bar codes, and 10-hour clock arithmetic

CHAPTER REVIEW EXERCISES

Section 4.1

1. Draw rectangular diagrams to illustrate the factorings of 15 taking order into account; that is, think of $1 \cdot 15$ as different from $15 \cdot 1$.
2. Construct a factor tree for 96.
3. (a) Determine the set D_{60} of all divisors of 60.
   (b) Determine the set D_{72} of all divisors of 72.
   (c) Use $D_{60} \cap D_{72} =$ to determine GCD(60, 72).
4. (a) Determine the prime power representation of 1200.
   (b) Determine the prime power representation of 2940.
   (c) Use parts (a) and (b) to determine GCD(1200, 2940) and LCM(1200, 2940).
5. Use information from the sieve of Eratosthenes in Figure 4.3 to determine if 847 is prime or composite.
6. (a) Determine a composite natural number n with a prime factor greater than $\sqrt{n}$.
   (b) Does the n in part (a) have a prime divisor less than or equal to $\sqrt{n}$? If so what is it?
7. Determine natural numbers r, s, and m such that r divides m and s divides m, but rs does not divide m.
8. Use the number $n = 3 \cdot 5 \cdot 7 + 11 \cdot 13 \cdot 17$ to determine a prime different from 3, 5, 7, 11, 13, or 17.

Section 4.2

9. Using mental methods, test each number for divisibility by 2, 3, 5, and 11.
   (a) 9310   (b) 2079
   (c) 5635   (d) 5665
10. Test each number for divisibility by 7, 11, and 13.
    (a) 10,197   (b) 9373   (c) 36,751
11. Use the results of problem 9 to decide which of these are *true*.
    (a) 15 divides 9310   (b) 33 divides 2079
    (c) 55 divides 5635   (d) 55 divides 5665
12. Let $m = 3^4 \cdot 7^2$.
    (a) How many divisors does m have?
    (b) List all the divisors of m.

13. Determine d so that $2{,}765{,}301{,}2d3$ is divisible by 11.
14. (a) Determine the least natural number divisible by both q and m if $q = 2^3 \cdot 3^5 \cdot 7^2 \cdot 11^1$ and $m = 2^1 \cdot 7^3 \cdot 11^3 \cdot 13^1$.
    (b) Determine the largest number less than the q of part (a) that divides q.

Section 4.3

15. (a) Find the greatest common divisor of 63 and 91 by the method of intersection of sets of divisors.
    (b) Find the least common multiple of 63 and 91 by the method of intersection of sets of multiples.
    (c) Demonstrate that GCD(63, 91) · LCM(63, 91) = $63 \cdot 91$.
16. If $r = 2^1 \cdot 3^2 \cdot 5^1 \cdot 11^3$, $s = 2^2 \cdot 5^2 \cdot 11^2$, and $t = 2^3 \cdot 3^1 \cdot 7^1 \cdot 11^3$, determine each of the following.
    (a) GCD(r, s, t)   (b) LCM(r, s, t)
17. Determine each of the following using the Euclidean algorithm.
    (a) GCD(119,790, 12,100)
    (b) LCM (119,790, 12,100)
18. Seventeen-year locusts and thirteen-year locusts both emerged in 1971. When will these insect's descendants next emerge in the same year?

Section 4.4

19. Perform the indicated clock calculations if they are defined.
    (a) $4 +_{12} 9$ (b) $9 -_{12} 4$ (c) $4 \times_{12} 9$
    (d) $4 \div_{12} 9$ (e) $9 +_{12} 8$ (f) $9 \times_{12} 0$
    (g) $4 \div_{12} 0$ (h) $9 \div_{12} 7$ (i) $9 \times_{12} 7$
20. Perform these clock calculations.
    (a) $5 +_7 6$ (b) $6 -_7 5$
    (c) $6 \times_7 5$ (d) $6 \div_7 5$
21. List the numbers in 10-hour clock arithmetic for which 10-hour clock division is *not* defined.
22. Determine the check digit for each of these zip codes.
    (a) 87243–1772   (b) 22001–8941

23. Write out the zip code named by each of these bar codes. Which one, if either, is incorrect?

    (a) ||ıılıl|lıııll||ıılılıılıılıılllılılılılılılıılllıl

    (b) l|lııllıııll|ıılıllılılılılılılılılıılllıllıııılıll

CHAPTER TEST

1. Indicate whether each of these is *always true* (T) or *not always true* (F).
    (a) If a divides c and b divides c, then ab divides c.
    (b) If r divides s and s divides t, then r divides t.
    (c) If a divides b and a divides c, then a divides $(b + c)$.
    (d) If a does not divide b and a does not divide c, then a does not divide $(b + c)$.
2. (a) Make a factor tree for 8532.
    (b) Write the prime power representation of 8532.
    (c) Name the largest natural number smaller than 8532 that divides 8532.
    (d) Name the smallest number larger than 8532 that is divisible by 8532.
3. Using mental methods, test each of these for divisibility by 2, 3, 9, 11, and 33.
    (a) 62,418   (b) 222,789
4. Use the Euclidean algorithm to determine each of the following.
    (a) GCD(13,534, 997,476)
    (b) LCM(13,534, 997,476)
5. Let $m = 2^3 \cdot 5^2 \cdot 7^1 \cdot 11^4$ and $n = 2^2 \cdot 7^2 \cdot 11^3$.
    (a) Does r divide m if $r = 2^2 \cdot 5^1 \cdot 7^2 \cdot 11^3$? Why or why not?
    (b) How many divisors does m have?
    (c) Determine GCD(m, n).
    (d) Determine LCM(m, n).
6. Draw diagrams of Cuisenaire ® rods to illustrate all the divisors of 21.
7. Perform the indicated clock calculations.
    (a) $7 +_8 5$ (b) $7 +_{12} 5$ (c) $5 -_7 7$
    (d) $7 \times_8 5$ (e) $7 \div_8 5$
    (f) 7^5 (in 8-hour clock arithmetic)
8. Classify each of these zip codes as correct or incorrect and tell why.
    (a) 06992–7548   (b) 84232–7612
9. Use the Euclidean algorithm to determine GCD(154, 553) and LCM(154, 553).
10. Determine if 281 is a prime.

CHAPTER

5

Integers

5.1 Representation of Integers

5.2 Addition and Subtraction
of Integers

5.3 Multiplication and Division
of Integers

HANDS ON

Black–Red Game

Materials Needed

1. Fifty cards for each pair of students—four of each type shown plus six with 2 red discs and four with 3 black discs.

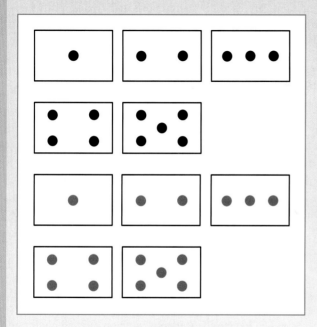

2. Sheets for each group of students to keep score on.

Directions

This is a two- to four-person game played as follows:

1. The cards are shuffled and then laid out face down in a 5 by 10 array.

2. A player plays by picking up two cards and recording the score using the rule that each red disc cancels a black disc and vice versa. Thus, if a player turns up a red 4 and a black 5, the score is 1B. If, on the other hand, a red 4 and a black 2 are turned up, the score is 2R. The player records his or her score and also the cumulative score obtained by combining the score on a play with the cumulative score on the preceding play. (On the first play for each player the cumulative score is the same as the score.) After a player's score is recorded, the chosen cards are set aside and the play shifts to the next player.

3. To start the play, each player turns over a card and the player with the greatest black score, or, if none has a black score, the player with the least red score, goes first.

4. Play continues for six full rounds. The player with the greatest cumulative black score, or, if none has a cumulative black score, the player with the least cumulative red score, is the winner. The privilege of going first rotates between the players from game to game. Also, the cards are shuffled and redistributed after each game.

CONNECTIONS   A Further Extension of the Number System

In Chapter 2 we discussed the whole numbers and operations with whole numbers. In particular, we observed that the whole numbers and their operations were developed as a direct result of people's need to count. But a modern society has many quantitative needs aside from counting and these often require numbers other than whole numbers.

In this chapter, we consider the set *I* of **integers** which consists of:

- the **natural numbers** or **positive integers** denoted by 1, 2, 3, . . . ,
- the number **zero**, 0, and
- the **negative integers** denoted by $-1, -2, -3, \ldots$.

We note immediately that

$$N \subset W \subset I.$$

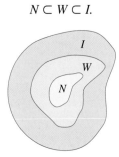

In today's society, these numbers are used to record debits and credits, profits and losses, changes in prices in the stock market, degrees above zero and degrees below zero in measuring temperature, yards lost and yards gained in football, points won or points "in the hole" in many card and board games, and so on.

As usual, we introduce the set of integers by means of manipulatives, pictures, and diagrams with steadily increasing levels of abstraction to suggest, in turn, how these ideas might be presented to elementary school children.

5.1   Representations of Integers

Businesspeople of all kinds regularly use the phrases "in the black" and "in the red" to indicate whether a given business has experienced a profit or a loss or to indicate whether a bank account still has money available or if it has been overdrawn. Since accountants often note these states of affairs with black and red ink, we adopt that same convention here.

Representing Integers by "Drops" of Colored Counters

Mark Garza gives each student in his class a collection of about 25 counters colored black on one side and red on the other. These are easily made by duplicating the desired shapes on red construction paper and then having the students cut them out and color one side of each counter black.

Mr. Garza has each student drop several counters on his or her desk top, match the black and red counters, and record as the score for the drop the number of unmatched black or red counters. This could be viewed as recording the results of playing a game against two opponents and winning points (black counters) from one opponent and losing points (red counters) to the other opponent. The score is then the net gain or loss on a given play, and this can be used to represent positive or negative integers. For example, Figure 5.1 shows a drop of 6 black and 4 red counters for a score of 2B. We interpret this as representing *positive two* and write 2. Similarly, we interpret a score of 2R as *negative two* and write −2.

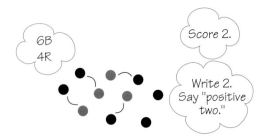

Figure 5.1
A drop of 6 black and 4 red counters. The score is 2B and represents positive two.

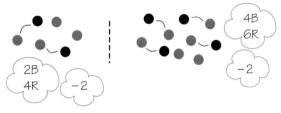

It is important to observe that different drops can result in the same score. For example, the two diagrams in Figure 5.2 both represent -2. Moreover, -2 could also be represented by a diagram with only 2 red counters. A drop with counters of only one color is the simplest of all such representations and we will have occasion to use such drops in what follows. Mr. Garza discusses this at length with his students and asks particularly how to increase or decrease the number of counters in a drop without changing the score. A moment's reflection makes it clear that adding or taking away the same number each of black and red counters does not change the score of a drop. In summary, two drops of colored counters are *equivalent* and represent the same integer if one can be obtained from the other by adding (or deleting) the same number each of black and red counters. The simplest representation of the positive integer n is a drop of n black counters. The simplest representation of the negative integer $-n$ is a drop of n red counters.

Figure 5.2
Two drops representing -2

A drop consisting of an equal number of black and red counters is of special interest. Since no counters remain unmatched, such a drop represents 0, which is therefore *neither positive nor negative.* Moreover, as we have just seen, adding such a drop to an existing drop does not change its score and this corresponds numerically to the fact that

$$0 + n = n + 0 = n$$

for *any* integer n—positive, negative, or zero. Finally, any such drop can be viewed as a combination of two drops—one of s black counters and one of s red counters for some natural number s. Separately these drops would score sB and sR and represent s and $-s$, respectively. Since together they score 0, we have the following definition.

DEFINITION   *The Integers*

The **positive integers** are the natural numbers.

The **negative integers** are the numbers $-1, -2, -3, \dots$, where $-s$ is defined by the equality

$$s + (-s) = (-s) + s = 0.$$

The integer 0 is neither positive nor negative and has the property

$$0 + n = n + 0 = n$$

for every integer n. The **integers** consist of the positive integers, the negative integers, and zero.

A Comment on Notation

Observe that it is standard to use the same sign in writing $8 - 6$ and -5. The expression $8 - 6$ is often read "8 minus 6" and the sign, $-$, is often called the *minus sign*. However, there is a double meaning in the usage that must be clearly understood. In $8 - 6$, the sign is used to indicate the *operation of subtraction*, and, in writing -5, it is used to indicate the *negative* or *additive inverse* of 5. This distinction is made on your calculator with two separate keys, one for subtraction and one for negation. To compute $8 - 6$ on the calculator one keys in the sequence

$$8 \boxed{-} \; 6 \boxed{=}$$

and to enter -5 in the display one keys in the sequence

$$5 \; \boxed{+ \bigcirc -}.$$

Indeed, keying in the sequence

$$5 \boxed{+ \bigcirc -} \; \boxed{+ \bigcirc -} \; \boxed{+ \bigcirc -} \; \boxed{+ \bigcirc -}$$

shows 5, -5, 5, -5, and 5 in the calculator display since the $\boxed{+ \bigcirc -}$ key changes the sign of the number in the display each time it is pressed. This suggests that the negative of negative 5 is 5 (that $-(-5) = 5$), and we will see later that this is so. Indeed, as we will show, $-(-n) = n$ for every integer n.

The distinction between the operation of subtraction and the notion of negation is also made with two different keys on graphing calculators like the TEXAS INSTRUMENTS TI-73. The $\boxed{-}$ key is used to indicate subtraction and the $\boxed{(-)}$ key is used to indicate "the negative of." Indeed, if you key $\boxed{(-)} \; 2 \; \boxed{\text{ENTER}}$ into a TI-73 or similar calculator, the display shows $^-2$ rather than -2. And if $5 \boxed{-} \; \boxed{(-)} \; 2 \; \boxed{\text{ENTER}}$ is keyed in, the display shows $5 - {}^-2$ and the answer 7, indicating that subtracting the negative of 2 from 5 gives 7 as we will show later.

We observe that, like the TI-73, many texts for elementary school try to avoid the difficulty noted above by using a raised minus sign to indicate the negative of a number. Thus, they write $^-5$ in place of -5. And some even write $^+2$ in place of 2. However, these texts invariably ultimately change to the standard notation of -5 and 2 used here. We feel that it causes less confusion to do this at the outset, stressing that the context makes it clear when "subtract" is meant as opposed to "the negative of."

Finally, note that when a symbol like n is written to represent a number, it is *not* implied that n is necessarily positive. For example, n might represent negative 3 (that is,

from **The NCTM Principles and Standards**

Integers

Middle grades students also work with integers. Typically they already have intuitive understandings of these numbers from experiences in their everyday lives: temperatures in winter that drop below zero, games such as football where teams gain or lose yards on each play, news reports regarding stock market fluctuations, or their own speculation about what happens when 7 is subtracted from 5. The school curriculum needs to build and expand on these informal experiences. For example, to help students understand that -12 is less than -5, it may be useful to refer to temperatures and their location on a thermometer, which then leads to extending the number line to include negative numbers.

SOURCE: Reprinted with permission from *Curriculum and Evaluation Standards for School Mathematics: Discussion Draft*, copyright 1998 by the National Council of Teachers of Mathematics. All rights reserved.

−3) and then −*n* is −(−3) or 3. *Thus, the negative of n is negative or positive according as n is positive or negative.* If we mean *n* to be positive, we must say so by calling it a natural number, a positive integer, a positive rational number, or simply a positive number. Otherwise, we must allow for the possibility that *n* represents either a positive or negative number or zero.

EXAMPLE   5.1

Scoring Drops of Colored Counters

Determine the score and the integer represented by each of these drops.

(a)

(b)

(c)

(d)

Solution

(a)   Matching the two red counters with two of the black counters, we see that the score is 3B representing 3.

(b)   Matching the red counter with a black counter, we see that the score is 2B representing 2.

(c)   Matching the 3 red with the 3 black counters, we see that the score is 0; we have no red or black counters unmatched.

(d)   Since there are no black counters, the score is 3R and the integer represented is −3.

EXAMPLE   5.2

Drops for Given Integers

Illustrate two different drops for each of these integers.

(a)   2   (b)   −3   (c)   0   (d)   5

Solution

(a)   Here the drops must have 2 more black counters than red counters. Two possibilities are

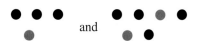

(b)   Here the drop must have 3 less black counters than red counters. Possibilities include

(c)   Here the drop must contain the same number of red and black counters or no counters at all. Possibilities include

(d)   Here the drop must have 5 more black than red counters. Possibilities include

and

Mail-time Representations of Integers

Integers can also be represented in other real-life situations. The following examples illustrate how the mail delivery of a check or a bill affects your overall net worth, or the value of your assets at any given time.

At mail time suppose that you are delivered a check for $20. What happens to your net worth? Answer: It goes up by $20.

At mail time you are delivered a bill for $35. What happens to your net worth? Answer: It goes down by $35.

At mail time, you received a check for $10 and a bill for $10. What happens to your net worth? Answer: It stays the same.

EXAMPLE 5.3 | **Interpreting Mail-time Situations**

(a)   At mail time you are delivered a check for $27. What happens to your net worth?

(b)   At mail time you are delivered a bill for $36. Are you richer or poorer? By how much?

Solution

(a)   Your net worth goes up $27.

(b)   Poorer. Your net worth goes down by $36.

EXAMPLE 5.4 | **Describing Mail-time Situations for Given Integers**

Describe a mail-time situation corresponding to each of these integers.

(a) −42   **(b)** 75   **(c)** 0

Solution

(a)   At mail time the letter carrier brought you a bill for $42. Are you richer or poorer and by how much?

(b)   At mail time you were delivered a check for $75. What happens to your net worth?

(c)   Quite to your surprise, at mail time the mail carrier skipped your house so you received no checks and no bills. Are you richer or poorer and by how much?

Number Line Representations of Integers

We have already used a number line to illustrate whole numbers, and it can be used equally effectively to represent integers. Choose an arbitrary point on the number line for 0. Then successively measure out unit distances on each side of 0 and label successive

points on the right of 0 with successive positive integers and points on the left with successive negative integers as shown in Figure 5.3.

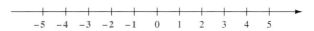

Figure 5.3
Representing integers on a number line

This corresponds nicely to marking thermometers with degrees above zero and degrees below zero, and with the practice in most parts of the world (with the notable exceptions of North America and Russia) of numbering floors above ground and below ground in a skyscraper. It also corresponds to the countdown of the seconds to lift-off and beyond in a space shuttle launch. The count 9, 8, 7, 6, 5 4, 3, 2, 1, lift-off!, 1, 2, 3, . . . is not really counting backward and then forward but forward all the time. The count is actually

9 seconds before lift-off	-9
8 seconds before lift-off	-8
.	.
.	.
.	.
1 second before lift-off	-1
Lift-off!	0
1 second after lift-off	1
2 seconds after lift-off	2

and so on. This is very real to space-age children and helps to make positive and negative numbers real and understandable.

In this connection it is also often helpful to represent positive and negative integers by curved arrows. For example, an arrow from any point to a point 5 units to the right represents 5, and an arrow from any point to a point 5 units to the left represents -5 as illustrated in Figure 5.4.

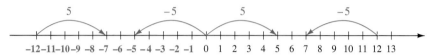

Figure 5.4
Using arrows to represent integers

Thus, the arrow for -5 has the same length as the arrow for 5 but is directed in the opposite direction and vice versa. This is indicated in some elementary school texts by writing *opp 5* to indicate -5. Since opp means that you simply change the direction of the arrow, it follows that opp (opp n) $= n$ for any integer n. In our notation, this would be written $-(-n) = n$ for any integer n.

THEOREM   *The Negative of the Negative of an Integer*
For any integer n, $-(-n) = n$.

EXAMPLE   5.5   **Determining Negatives**

Determine the negative of each of these integers.

(a) 4   (b) -2 (c) 0   (d) -320

Solution

(a)   The negative of 4 is -4.
(b)   The negative of -2 is $-(-2) = 2$.
(c)   The negative of 0 is $-0 = 0$ since 0 is neither positive nor negative.
(d)   The negative of -320 is $-(-320) = 320$.

Note that the negative of a negative integer is positive.

Absolute Value of an Integer

While discussing number line representations it is convenient to introduce the notion of absolute value of an integer. We have just observed that the integer 5 can be illustrated by the point numbered 5 on the number line. Similarly, -5 is represented by the point numbered -5. On the other hand both 5 and -5 are five units from 0 on the number line as shown in Figure 5.5. The **absolute value** of an integer n is defined to be the distance of the corresponding point on the number line from 0. We indicate the absolute value of n by writing $|n|$.

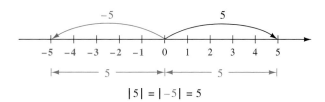

Figure 5.5
The absolute value of both 5
and −5 is 5.

$$|5| = |-5| = 5$$

EXAMPLE   5.6 | **Determining Absolute Values**

Determine the absolute values of these integers.

(a)   −11   (b)   13   (c)   0   (d)   −9

Solution

We plot the numbers on the number line and determine the distance of the points from 0.

(a) $|-11| = 11 = -(-11)$ since −11 is 11 units from 0.
(b) $|13| = 13$ since 13 is 13 units from 0.
(c) $|0| = 0$ since 0 is 0 units from 0.
(d) $|-9| = 9 = -(-9)$ since −9 is 9 units from 0.

Careful examination of the results of Example 5.6 suggests an alternative definition that makes it possible to avoid drawing diagrams to find absolute values.

DEFINITION   *Absolute Value of an Integer*

If a is an integer, then

$$|a| = \begin{cases} a \text{ if } a \text{ is positive or zero} \\ -a \text{ if } a \text{ is negative.} \end{cases}$$

EXAMPLE   5.7 | **Determining Absolute Values**

Determine the absolute values of these integers.

(a)   −71   (b)   29   (c)   0   (d)   −852

Solution

(a)   Since −71 is negative, $|-71| = -(-71) = 71$.
(b)   Since 29 is positive, $|29| = 29$.
(c)   Since 0 is 0, $|0| = 0$.
(d)   Since −852 is negative, $|-852| = -(-852) = 852$.

9-1 Using Integers to Represent Quantities

You'll Learn ...
- to use integers to represent real-world quantities
- to find the opposite of an integer
- to find the absolute value of an integer

... How It's Used

Sailors need to know ocean and harbor depths to prevent their ships from running aground.

Vocabulary

negative numbers

origin

opposite numbers

integers

absolute value

▶ **Lesson Link** Most of the numbers you've studied so far have been greater than zero. Now you'll explore numbers that are less than zero. ◀

Explore Numbers Less than Zero

Hills and Valleys

In Plaquemines Parish, Louisiana, a borehole was drilled to 22,570 ft below sea level. Sea level is the average height of the earth's oceans.

1. Which landmarks are below sea level? Above sea level?

2. Which is closer to sea level, the deepest point in the Gulf of Mexico or Mt. Whitney? How much closer?

3. Which is farther from sea level, Mt. McKinley or the Plaquemines borehole? How much farther?

4. Describe a way to show the difference between numbers of feet above sea level and below sea level.

Learn Using Integers to Represent Quantities

A vertical number line can be used to compare heights and depths.

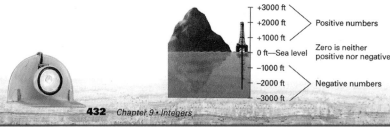

432 Chapter 9 • Integers

SOURCE: *Scott Foresman–Addison Wesley Middle School Math, Course 2*, p. 432, by Randall I. Charles et al. Copyright © 1999, Addison Wesley Longman, Inc.

Questions for the Teacher

1. This lesson uses elevations above and below sea level to introduce negative numbers. What other situations illustrate positive and negative numbers?

2. Number lines help students understand negative and positive numbers. This lesson also uses *opposite numbers* and the number line as shown here.

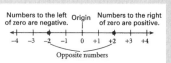

Opposite numbers are the same distance from zero. −2 and 2 are opposites because they are both 2 units from zero.

Could you use the operation of addition to help students understand opposites? Explain.

PROBLEM SET 5.1

Understanding Concepts

1. Draw two colored counter diagrams to represent each of these scores or integers.
   (a) 5B   (b) 2R   (c) 0   (d) −3   (e) 3

2. Draw a colored counter diagram with the least number of counters to represent each of the following.
   (a) 3   (b) −4   (c) 0   (d) 2

3. (a) Draw a colored counter diagram to represent 5.
   (b) Draw what you would see if you turned over all the colored counters in your diagram for part (a). What integer would this new diagram represent?
   (c) We could quite reasonably call the diagram of part (b) the opposite of the diagram of part (a). Thus, we might reasonably call −5 the opposite of 5 and write opp 5. As noted earlier, some elementary texts actually use this terminology. What would these texts write in place of −17?

(d) Using the opp idea with colored counters, write an argument that −(−5) = 5.
(e) Use the colored counter model to argue convincingly that −(−n) = n for any integer n.

4. (a) Describe a mail-time situation that illustrates 14.
   (b) Describe a mail-time situation that illustrates −27.

5. At mail time you are delivered a check for $48 and a bill for $31.
   (a) Are you richer or poorer and by how much?
   (b) What integer does this situation illustrate?

6. (a) At mail time you are delivered a check for $27 and a bill for $42. What integer does this situation illustrate?
   (b) Describe a different mail-time situation that illustrates the same integer as in part (a).

7. Draw a number line and plot the points representing these integers.
   (a) 0   (b) 4   (c) −4   (d) 8   (e) (4 + 8)/2
   (f) Where is (4 + 8)/2 relative to 4 and 8?

---

8. What integers are represented by the curved arrow on each of these number line diagrams?

   (a)
   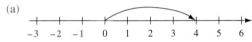

   (b)

   (c)
   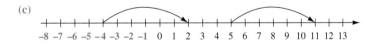

   (d)

---

9. Draw number line diagrams to represent each of these integers.
   (a) 7   (b) 0   (c) −9   (d) 9

10. In Europe, the floor of a building at ground level is called the ground floor. What in America is called the second floor is called the first floor in Europe and so on.
    (a) If an elevator in a tall building in Paris, France, starts on the fifth basement level below ground, B5, and goes up 27 floors, on which numbered floor does it stop?
    (b) What would the answer to part (a) be if the building were located in New York?

11. If an elevator starts on basement level B3 and goes down to B6, how far down has it gone?

12. Find the absolute values of these quantities.
    (a) 34   (b) 4 − 4
    (c) −76   (d) 17 − 5
    (e) How far is it between 5 and 17 on the number line?

13. For what values of x are these equations true?
    (a) $|x| = 13$ (b) $|x| + 1 = 2$ (c) $|x| + 5 = 0$

14. Determine all pairs (x, y) of integer values of x and y for which $|x| + |y| = 2$.

Thinking Critically

15. (a) What colored counters would have to be added to this array in order to represent −3?

(b) Could the question in part (a) be answered in more than one way?

(c) How many different representations of −3 can be made with 20 or fewer counters?

16. If all the counters are used each time, list all the integers that can be represented using

(a) 12 counters.   (b) 11 counters.

17. (a) If all the counters are used each time, describe the set of integers that can be represented using n counters.

(b) How many different integers are representable using n counters as in part (a)?

18. If some or all of the counters are used each time, describe the set of integers that can be represented

(a) using 12 counters.   (b) using 11 counters.

(c) using n counters.

Thinking Cooperatively

Do the next three problems with a group of two or three other students. At each step, discuss your solution with the other members of your group and determine a consensus answer for your group.

19. (a) What integers are represented by these arrays of counters?

(b) Considering the pattern of answers to part (a), what integer would be represented by a similar array with n rows and columns?

20. (a) How many different appearing rows of counters can you make using all of 20 counters each time? Remember that each counter has a black side and a red side. Two possibilities with only 4 counters are shown here.

(b) How many different appearing rows of counters can you make with at least 1 and at most 20 counters?

(c) How many different appearing rows of counters can you make with n counters (all used each time) if precisely 2 of the counters show red and the others show black?
(*Suggestion:* Consider the special cases $n = 2, 3, 4,$ and 5.)

21. (a) How many black and how many red counters are there in a triangular array like this but with 20 rows?

You should not actually need to make a diagram with 20 rows in order to answer this question.

(b) Write a brief explanation of your solution to part (a).

(c) Repeat part (a) but with a triangular array with 21 rows.

(d) What integers are represented by the triangular arrays in parts (a) and (c)?

(e) Make a table of integers represented by triangular arrays like those in parts (a) and (c) but with n rows for $n = 1, 2, 3, 4, 5, 6, 7,$ and 8.

(f) Carefully considering the table of part (e), conjecture what integer is represented in a triangular array like those in parts (a) and (c) but with n rows where n is any natural number. (*Suggestion:* Consider n odd and n even separately.)

From State Student Assessments

22. (Massachusetts, Grade 8. Note that students were *not* allowed to use calculators to solve this problem.)
Use the number line below to answer the question.

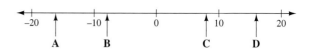

Which point represents the number $(^-2)^4$?

A. Point A

B. Point B

C. Point C

D. Point D

For Review

23. How many different factors does each of these numbers have?

(a) $2310 = 2^1 \cdot 3^1 \cdot 5^1 \cdot 7^1 \cdot 11^1$

(b) $5,336,100 = 2^2 \cdot 3^2 \cdot 5^2 \cdot 7^2 \cdot 11^2$

24. If $a = 2^1 \cdot 3^3 \cdot 5^2$ and $b = 2^3 \cdot 3^2 \cdot 5^1 \cdot 7^1$, compute each of the following.

  (a) GCD(a, b)   (b) LCM(a, b)

  (c) GCD(a, b) · LCM(a, b)   (d) $a \cdot b$

25. (a) Does c divide a if a is as in problem 24 and $c = 2^1 \cdot 3^4 \cdot 5^1$? Why or why not?

  (b) Is d a multiple of b if b is as in problem 24 and $d = 2^4 \cdot 3^2 \cdot 5^2 \cdot 7^1$? Why or why not?

26. Determine the prime power representation of each of these numbers.

  (a) 1400   (b) 5445   (c) 4554

27. Determine each of the following using the Euclidean algorithm.

  (a) GCD(4554, 5445)   (b) LCM(4554, 5445)

5.2   Addition and Subtraction of Integers

Addition of Integers

In the preceding section we introduced the integers using devices like colored counters, mail-time stories, and number lines. In this section we consider adding and subtracting integers and it is helpful to students to use these same devices to illustrate how these operations should be performed in this enlarged number system.

Addition of Integers Using Sets of Colored Counters

We discussed integers in the preceding section in terms of sets of colored counters. Also, in Chapter 2, addition of whole numbers was defined in terms of sets. If $a = n(A)$, $b = n(B)$, and $A \cap B = \varnothing$, then $a + b$ was defined as $n(A \cup B)$.

This idea works equally well for integers using **sets of colored counters.** Notice that when working with actual sets of counters, the counters are necessarily different so that any two distinct sets A and B clearly satisfy the condition $A \cap B = \varnothing$. In what follows, we presume that the diagrams show actual physical sets of counters so that the condition $A \cap B = \varnothing$ is automatically satisfied. Moreover, we avoid using set notation by drawing a loop around two sets we wish to combine into a single set. Suppose, for example, that we wish to illustrate the addition of 8 and −3. We draw the diagram shown in Figure 5.6 and interpret this as a drop consisting of all the counters in the combined set.

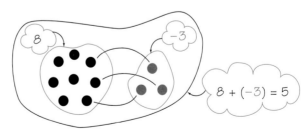

Figure 5.6
Diagram of colored counters illustrating 8 + (−3) = 5

The score of this drop, 5B, illustrates that the desired sum is 5 as shown. Of course, in Figure 5.6 we used the simplest possible representation of 8 and −3. However, as shown in Figure 5.7, the result is the same if we use other, equivalent, representations for 8 and

−3. In both Figures 5.6 and 5.7 the total number of black counters exceeds the total number of red counters by 5. Thus, in each case, the score of the combined set is 5B representing 5.

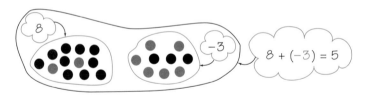

Figure 5.7
Another representation of 8 + (−3) = 5 using sets of colored counters

EXAMPLE   5.8

Representing Sums of Integers Using Colored Counter Diagrams

Draw appropriate diagrams of colored counters to illustrate each of these sums.

(a)   (−3) + 5   (b)   (−2) + (−4)   (c)   5 + (−7)   (d)   4 + (−4)

Solution

(a)   Using the simplest representations of −3 and 5, we draw this diagram.

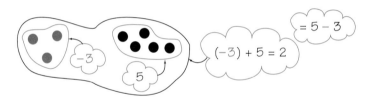

Since the combined set has a score of 2B, this represents 2. Thus, (−3) + 5 = 2 and we note that 2 = 5 − 3 as well. Hence, (−3) + 5 = 5 − 3 = 2.

(b)   This sum can be represented as shown.

Since the combined set has a score of 6R, this illustrates the sum

$$(−2) + (−4) = −6,$$

and we note that −6 = −(2 + 4). Thus,

$$(−2) + (−4) = −(2 + 4) = −6.$$

(c)   5 + (−7) = −2 = −(7 − 5)

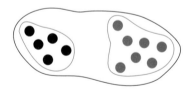

(d) $4 + (-4) = 0 = 4 - 4$

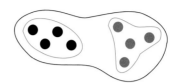

The results of Example 5.8 are entirely typical and we state them here as a theorem.

THEOREM   *Adding Integers*

Let m and n be positive integers so that $-m$ and $-n$ are negative. Then the following are true:

- $(-m) + (-n) = -(m + n)$
- If $m > n$, then $m + (-n) = m - n$.
- If $m < n$, then $m + (-n) = -(n - m)$.
- $n + (-n) = (-n) + n = 0$

EXAMPLE   5.9

Adding Integers

Compute these sums.

(a) $7 + 11$ **(b)** $(-6) + (-5)$ **(c)** $7 + (-3)$
(d) $4 + (-9)$ **(e)** $6 + (-6)$ **(f)** $(-8) + 3$

Solution

(a) $7 + 11 = 18$
(b) $(-6) + (-5) = -(6 + 5) = -11$
(c)   Since $7 > 3$, $7 + (-3) = 7 - 3 = 4$.
(d)   Since $4 < 9$, $4 + (-9) = -(9 - 4) = -5$
(e) $6 + (-6) = 0$
(f) $(-8) + 3 = 3 + (-8)$ and since $8 > 3$,
$3 + (-8) = -(8 - 3) = -5$. Therefore, $(-8) + 3 = -5$.

As with the properties of whole number addition, except for the existence of additive inverses, the properties of integer addition derive from the corresponding properties of sets.

THEOREM   *Properties of the Addition of Integers*

Let m, n, and r be integers. Then the following hold.

Closure Property	$m + n$ is an integer
Commutative Property	$m + n = n + m$
Associative Property	$m + (n + r) = (m + n) + r$
Additive identity	$0 + m = m + 0 = m$
Additive inverse	$(-m) + m = m + (-m) = 0$

Proof   Since we have defined integers in terms of unions of sets of colored counters, the first four properties in the theorem follow from the fact that, for any sets M, N, and R,

$$M \cup N \text{ is a set,}$$
$$M \cup N = N \cup M,$$
$$M \cup (N \cup R) = (M \cup N) \cup R, \text{ and}$$
$$\varnothing \cup M = M \cup \varnothing = M.$$

The existence of the additive inverse of m for every integer m follows as a generalization of part (d) of Example 5.8.

Addition of Integers Using Mail-time Stories

Bringing something to you is adding.

A second useful approach to addition of integers is by means of **mail-time stories.**

At mail time suppose you receive a check for $13 and another check for $6. Are you richer or poorer and by how much? Answer: Richer by $19. This illustrates $13 + 6 = 19$.

EXAMPLE   5.10 | **Adding Integers Using Mail-time Stories**

Write the addition equation illustrated by each of these stories.

(a)   At mail time you receive a check for $3 and a check for $5. Are you richer or poorer and by how much?

(b)   At mail time you receive a bill for $2 and another bill for $4. Are you richer or poorer and by how much?

(c)   At mail time you receive a check for $5 and a bill for $7. Are you richer or poorer and by how much?

(d)   At mail time, you receive a check for $4 and a bill for $4. Are you richer or poorer and by how much?

Solution

(a)   Receiving a check for $3 and a check for $5 makes you $8 richer. This illustrates $3 + 5 = 8$.

(b)   Receiving a bill for $2 and another bill for $4 makes you $6 poorer. This illustrates $(-2) + (-4) = -6$.

(c)   Receiving a check for $5 makes you richer by $5, but receiving a bill for $7 makes you $7 poorer. The net effect is that you are $2 poorer. This illustrates $5 + (-7) = -2$.

(d)   Receiving a $4 check and a $4 bill exactly balances out and you are neither richer nor poorer. This illustrates $4 + (-4) = 0$.

Note that these results are exactly the results of Example 5.8 above. Moreover, the arguments hold in general and we are again led to the theorem immediately preceding Example 5.9.

Addition of Integers Using a Number Line

Suppose we want to illustrate $5 + 4$ on a number line. The addition can be thought of as starting at 0 and counting five units to the right (in the positive direction on the number line) and then counting on 4 more units to the right. Figure 5.8 shows that this is the same as counting 9 units to the right from 0 straight away. Thus, $5 + 4 = 9$.

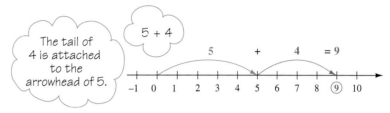

Figure 5.8
Illustrating $5 + 4 = 9$ on a number line

If 4 is depicted by counting four units to the right, then -4 should be depicted by counting four units to the left. Thus, the addition $5 + (-4)$ is depicted on the number line as in Figure 5.9.

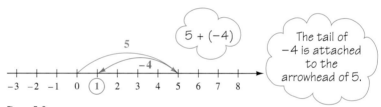

Figure 5.9
Illustrating $5 + (-4) = 1$ on a number line

We count five units to the right from 0 and then count "on" 4 units to the left in the direction of the -4 arrow. As seen on the diagram this justifies $5 + (-4) = 1$.

EXAMPLE 5.11

Adding Integers on a Number Line

What addition fact is illustrated by each of these diagrams?

(a)

(b)

(c)

(d)

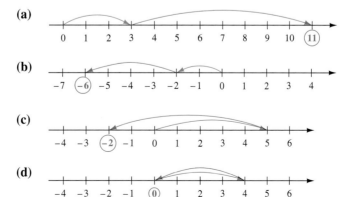

Solution   Since counting in the direction indicated by an arrow means adding, these diagrams represent the following sums.

(a) $3 + 8 = 11$ (b) $(-2) + (-4) = -6$
(c) $5 + (-7) = -2$ (d) $4 + (-4) = 0$

Note that these are again precisely the same results as in Example 5.8.

EXAMPLE   5.12   **Drawing a Number Line Diagram for a Given Sum**

Draw a number line diagram to illustrate $(-7) + 4$.

Solution   Since -7 is indicated by counting 7 units to the left from 0 (in the direction indicated by the minus sign on the -7), and adding 4 is indicated by counting on to the right (in the positive direction since 4 is a positive integer), we have this diagram.

Thus, $(-7) + 4 = -3 = -(7 - 4)$.

Ordering the Set of Integers

Since the set with 3 black counters as shown in Figure 5.10 contains fewer counters than the set with 7 black counters, we say that *3 is less than 7* and write $3 < 7$. We also observe that $3 + 4 = 7$ and say that 7 is 4 more than 3.

Figure 5.10
Comparing 3 and 7; $3 < 7$

This idea is also easily illustrated on a number line as shown in Figure 5.11. In particular, we note again that $3 + 4 = 7$ and this implies that 3 *is to the left of* 7 on a number line. With this in mind, we extend the notion of less than to the set of all integers. In particular, if a is to the left of b on a number line, then there is a positive integer c such that $a + c = b$ and so $a < b$.

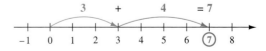

Figure 5.11
Comparing 3 and 7 on a number line; $3 < 7$

INTO THE CLASSROOM

Nancy Rolsen On Comparing and Ordering Integers

Students seem to gain a better understanding of positive and negative numbers through active participation. When comparing and ordering integers, I give each student a large index card with an integer written on it and have them form a human number line by standing in the order of their integers. I put masking tape on the floor to make a number line and we mark off the integers in equal intervals. At the beginning of the unit I use the number line for comparing and ordering integers. Later I have students show addition of integers on this number line.

To introduce graphing ordered pairs of integers, I separate the room into four quadrants with masking tape and use students' desks as coordinate points. Then I call on students by giving the coordinates of their desks. I also give directions such as, "Will all students with *y*-coordinate of 2 stand." I note that a horizontal row of students is standing.

Source: *Scott Foresman–Addison Wesley Middle School Math,* Course 2, p. 428, by Randall I. Charles et al. Copyright © 1999 Addison Wesley Longman, Inc.

DEFINITION   *Less Than and Greater Than for the Set of Integers*

Let a and b be integers. We say that a **is less than** b, and write $a < b$, if, and only if, there is a positive integer c such that $a + c = b$. We say that b **is greater than** a, and write $b > a$, if, and only if, $a < b$.

Notions similar to less than and greater than are **less than or equal to** and **greater than or equal to,** and these mean just what they say. That is, we say that a is less than or equal to b and write $a \leq b$ if, and only if, $a < b$ or $a = b$. Similarly, we say that a is greater than or equal to b and write $a \geq b$ if, and only if, $a > b$ or $a = b$. Moreover, it is important to note that if a and b are any two points on a number line, either a is to the left of b, or $a = b$, or a is to the right of b. Thus, the integers satisfy the so-called law of trichotomy.

THEOREM   *The Law of Trichotomy*

If a and b are any two integers, then precisely one of these three possibilities must hold:

$$a < b \quad \text{or} \quad a = b \quad \text{or} \quad a > b.$$

Since the law of trichotomy holds for the integers, they are said to be *ordered;* that is, they can be lined up on a number line in order of increasing size.

EXAMPLE   5.13   **Ordering Pairs of Integers**

Place a less than or greater than sign in the circle as appropriate.

(a)   17 ◯ 121   **(b)**   2 ◯ −7   **(c)**   −7 ◯ −27   **(d)**   0 ◯ −6

Solution

(a) $17 < 121$ since $17 + 104 = 121$.
(b) $2 > -7$ since $-7 + 9 = 2$.
(c) $-7 > -27$ since $-27 + 20 = -7$.
(d) $0 > -6$ since $-6 + 6 = 0$.

> 104, 9, 20, and 6 are all positive.

EXAMPLE   5.14   **Ordering a Set of Integers**

Plot each of these integers on a number line and then list them in increasing order: $-5, -9, 7, 0, 12, -8$.

Solution

Reading from left to right, we see that

$$-9 < -8 < -5 < 0 < 7 < 12.$$

EXAMPLE   5.15   **Operating with Inequalities**

If a, b, and c are integers and $a < b$, prove that $a + c < b + c$.

Solution   *Understand the problem*

We are told that a, b, and c are integers with $a < b$. We're asked to show that $a + c < b + c$.

Devise a plan

Imagine the following internal dialogue that reveals how a plan emerges:
Perhaps I should ask and answer some questions of myself to see if I can come up with a plan.

Q.   What am I given?
A.   That $a < b$ where a and b are integers.
Q.   What must I show?
A.   That $a + c < b + c$ where c is also an integer.
Q.   What does it mean to say that $a + c < b + c$? Can I say this in another way?
A.   I guess so. According to the definition, $a + c < b + c$ if, and only if, some natural number added to $a + c$ gives $b + c$.
Q.   Okay. So how could I find such a natural number? Do I have anything to go on?
A.   Well, I'm given that $a < b$. This means that there is some natural number r such that $a + r = b$. Perhaps I can use this.

> Say it in another way.

Carry out the plan

Since $a < b$, there is some natural number r such that $a + r = b$. Therefore, add c to both sides,

$$a + r + c = b + c.$$

Then, by the commutative property for addition,

$$a + c + r = b + c.$$

This shows that adding the natural number r to $a + c$ gives $b + c$ and that means that $a + c < b + c$ as was to be shown.

Look back

Basically, we obtained the solution just by making sure we understood the problem. Key questions answered were: What is given? What must be shown? Can we say all this in a different way (that is, what does $a < b$ mean, and so on)? With answers to these questions clearly in mind, a little arithmetic finished the job.

Subtraction of Integers Using Sets of Colored Counters

As with the subtraction of whole numbers, one approach to the subtraction of integers is the notion of "take away." Consider the subtraction

$$7 - (-3).$$

Modeling 7 with counters, we must "take away" a representation of -3. Since any representation of -3 must have at least 3 red counters, we must use a representation of 7 with at least 3 red counters. The simplest representation of this subtraction is shown in Figure 5.12.

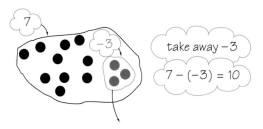

Figure 5.12
Colored counter representation of $7 - (-3) = 10$

Thus, $7 - (-3) = 10$. Also, the result does not change if we use another representation of 7 with at least three red counters since equivalent representations are obtained by adding (or deleting) the same number of counters of each color from a given representation. A second representation of $7 - (-3) = 10$ is shown in Figure 5.13.

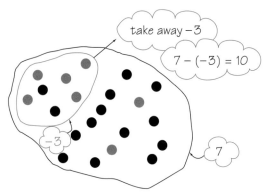

Figure 5.13
A second colored counter representation of 7 − (−3) = 10

<table>
<tr><td>EXAMPLE 5.16</td><td>

Subtracting Using Colored Counters

Write out the subtraction equation illustrated by each of these diagrams.

(a)

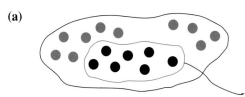

(b)

(c)

(d)

</td></tr>
</table>

Solution

(a) Since the large loop contains 10 red counters and 7 black counters, it represents −3. The small loop contains 7 black counters and so represents 7. If we remove the small loop of counters as indicated, we are left with 10 red markers representing −10. Thus, this diagram illustrates the subtraction $(-3) - 7 = -10$.

(b) This diagram represents the subtraction $(-3) - (-1) = -2$.

(c) This diagram represents the subtraction $(-3) - 1 = -4$.

(d) This diagram represents the subtraction $(-5) - (-2) = -3$.

EXAMPLE   5.17 | **Drawing Diagrams for Given Subtraction Problems**

Draw a diagram of colored counters to illustrate each of these subtractions and determine the result in each case.

(a) $7 - 3$ (b) $(-7) - (-3)$ (c) $7 - (-3)$ (d) $(-7) - 3$

Solution | (a) Many different diagrams could be drawn, but the simplest is shown here.

(b) As in part (a) we can use a diagram with counters of only one color.

(c) This is illustrated in Figures 5.12 and 5.13.

(d) Here, in order to remove 3 black counters (that is, subtract 3), the representation for -7 must have at least 3 black counters. The simplest diagram is as shown.

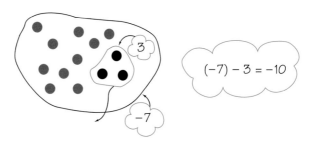

Notice that we can interpret any subtraction diagram as an addition diagram and *vice versa*. For example, if we interpret the diagram of Figure 5.14 on the next page as taking away the four red counters, the diagram represents the subtraction

$$5 - (-4) = 9.$$

On the other hand, if we view it as a diagram showing the combining of the set of black counters with the set of red counters, it illustrates the addition

$$5 = (-4) + 9.$$

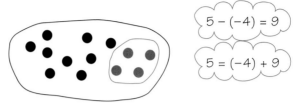

Figure 5.14
Diagram illustrating both $5 - (-4) = 9$ *and* $5 = (-4) + 9$

Since all the subtraction diagrams can be interpreted in this way, we have the following definition.

DEFINITION   *Subtraction of Integers*

If a, b, and c are integers, then

$$a - b = c$$

if, and only if, $a = b + c$.

This was also the definition of subtraction of whole numbers. Thus, as before, we have a family of equivalent facts; that is,

$$a - b = c, \qquad a = b + c, \qquad a = c + b, \qquad \text{and} \qquad a - c = b$$

all express essentially the same relationship among the integers a, b, and c. If we know that any one of these equations is true, then all are true.

Another important fact about subtraction of integers is illustrated in Figure 5.15.

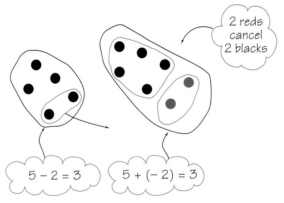

Figure 5.15
Subtracting by adding the negative

Note that the diagram on the left illustrates the subtraction

$$5 - 2 = 3$$

while the diagram on the right illustrates the addition

$$5 + (-2) = 3.$$

Since the effect of adding the negative of 2 to 5 is the same as subtracting 2 from 5 we see that

$$5 - 2 = 5 + (-2).$$

Moreover, since the opposite of an integer represented by a set of counters is always represented by the set with all the counters turned over, this proposition is true in general and can be expressed as a theorem.

To subtract, add the negative.

> **THEOREM**   *Subtracting by Adding the Negative*
>
> Let a and b be any integers. Then
>
> $$a - b = a + (-b).$$

Finally, since we have already seen that the set of integers is closed under addition, an immediate consequence of this theorem is that, unlike the set of whole numbers, *the set of integers is closed under subtraction.*

> **THEOREM**   *Closure Property for the Subtraction of Integers*
>
> The set of integers is closed under subtraction.

EXAMPLE   5.18

Subtracting by Adding

Perform each of these subtractions as additions.

(a) $7 - 3$ **(b)** $(-7) - (-3)$ **(c)** $7 - (-3)$ **(d)** $(-7) - 3$

Solution

We make use of the theorem stating that $a - b = a + (-b)$ for any integers a and b.

(a) $7 - 3 = 7 + (-3) = 4$
(b) $(-7) - (-3) = (-7) + 3 = -4$
(c) $7 - (-3) = 7 + 3 = 10$
(d) $(-7) - 3 = -7 + (-3) = -10$

Subtraction of Integers Using Mail-time Stories

For this model of subtraction to work we must imagine a situation where checks and bills are immediately credited or debited to your account as soon as they are delivered whether or not they are really intended for you. If an error has been made by the mail carrier, he or she must return and reclaim delivered mail and take it to the intended recipient. Thus,

bringing a check adds a positive number,
bringing a bill adds a negative number,
taking away a check subtracts a positive number, and
taking away a bill subtracts a negative number.

EXAMPLE 5.19 | **Subtraction Facts from Mail-time Stories**

Indicate the subtraction facts that are illustrated by each of the following mail-time stories.

(a) The mail carrier brings you a check for $7 and takes away a check for $3. Are you richer or poorer and by how much?

(b) The mail carrier brings you a bill for $7 and takes away a bill for $3. Are you richer or poorer and by how much?

(c) The mail carrier brings you a check for $7 and takes away a bill for $3. Are you richer or poorer and by how much?

(d) The mail carrier brings you a bill for $7 and takes away a check for $3. Are you richer or poorer and by how much?

Solution

(a) You are $4 richer. This illustrates $7 - 3 = 4$.

(b) You are $4 poorer. This illustrates $(-7) - (-3) = -4$.

(c) You are $10 richer. This illustrates $7 - (-3) = 10$.

(d) You are $10 poorer. This illustrates $(-7) - 3 = -10$.

Note that these are precisely the same subtractions that were illustrated in Example 5.17 on page 323 with diagrams of colored counters and in Example 5.18 by adding negatives.

Subtraction of Integers Using the Number Line

The addition $5 + 3 = 8$ is illustrated on a number line in Figure 5.16.

Figure 5.16
The sum $5 + 3 = 8$ on the number line

Now consider the subtraction

$$5 - 3.$$

In this instance we start at 0 and count 5 units to the right as before, and then we count *backwards* 3 units in the direction *opposite from that indicated by the 3 arrow.* Figure 5.17 on the following page shows us that the result is then 2 as we already know from the subtraction of whole numbers. In particular, this diagram accurately models the missing addend approach to subtraction. Here the dashed red arrow (for 2) shows what must be added to 3 to obtain 5. (Recall that arrows representing positive integers are directed from left to right and those representing negative integers are directed from right to left.)

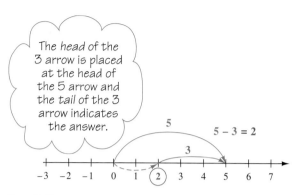

Figure 5.17
The subtraction 5 − 3 = 2 on the number line

EXAMPLE 5.20	**Drawing Diagrams to Illustrate Subtraction on the Number Line**

Illustrate each of these subtractions on a number line and give the result in each case.

(a) $7 − 3$ **(b)** $(−7) − (−3)$ **(c)** $7 − (−3)$ **(d)** $(−7) − 3$

Solution

(a)

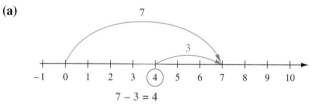

(b)

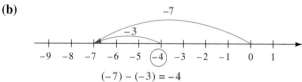

(c)

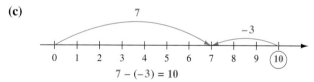

(d)

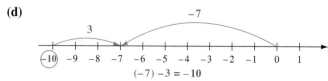

The number line is particularly useful in demonstrating the result

$$a − b = a + (−b)$$

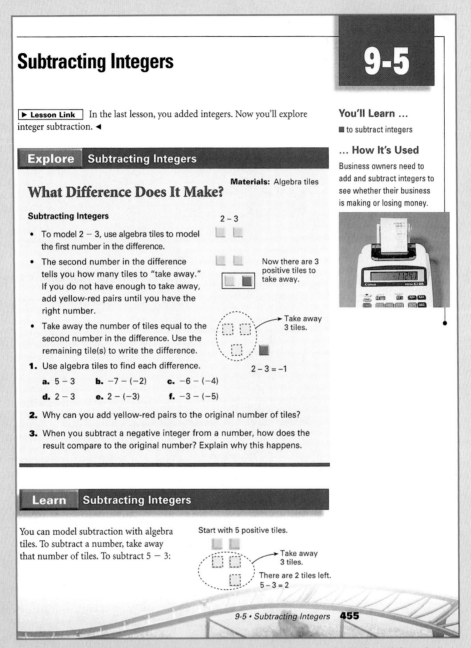

Subtracting Integers

9-5

▶ **Lesson Link** In the last lesson, you added integers. Now you'll explore integer subtraction. ◀

You'll Learn ...

■ to subtract integers

... How It's Used

Business owners need to add and subtract integers to see whether their business is making or losing money.

Explore Subtracting Integers

What Difference Does It Make?

Materials: Algebra tiles

Subtracting Integers

2 − 3

- To model 2 − 3, use algebra tiles to model the first number in the difference.

- The second number in the difference tells you how many tiles to "take away." If you do not have enough to take away, add yellow-red pairs until you have the right number.

Now there are 3 positive tiles to take away.

- Take away the number of tiles equal to the second number in the difference. Use the remaining tile(s) to write the difference.

Take away 3 tiles.

2 − 3 = −1

1. Use algebra tiles to find each difference.

  a. 5 − 3   **b.** −7 − (−2)   **c.** −6 − (−4)

  d. 2 − 3   **e.** 2 − (−3)   **f.** −3 − (−5)

2. Why can you add yellow-red pairs to the original number of tiles?

3. When you subtract a negative integer from a number, how does the result compare to the original number? Explain why this happens.

Learn Subtracting Integers

You can model subtraction with algebra tiles. To subtract a number, take away that number of tiles. To subtract 5 − 3:

Start with 5 positive tiles.

Take away 3 tiles.

There are 2 tiles left.

5 − 3 = 2

9-5 • Subtracting Integers **455**

SOURCE: *Scott Foresman–Addison Wesley Middle School Math, Course 2*, p. 455, by Randall I. Charles et al. Copyright © 1999, Addison Wesley Longman, Inc.

Questions for the Teacher

1. The above lesson continues on the next page with this poser.

> The Drop Zone™ Stunt Tower at Paramount's Great America® has a free-fall altitude change of −129 ft. It replaces the Edge™, which had a −60 ft change. How much farther do you free-fall in the Drop Zone? **−69 feet**

How would you help a student to understand that this translates into the equation $(-129) - (-60) = -69$ as desired by the teacher's edition of the text?

2. What would you say to a student who models the preceding problem with the equation $129 - 60 = 69$ and says that you free-fall 69 feet farther on the Drop Zone? Is the student wrong? Explain.

noted earlier. The diagram illustrating that $(-7) - 3 = -10$ of part (d) in the preceding example is essentially the same as that in Figure 5.18 which illustrates $(-7) + (-3) = -10$. Thus, as in the theorem,

$$(-7) - 3 = (-7) + (-3).$$

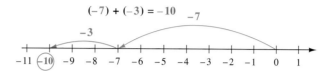

Figure 5.18
The sum $(-7) + (-3) = -10$ *on the number line*

Adding and Subtracting Integers with a Calculator

Calculator addition and subtraction of natural numbers has already been discussed. Integers can also be added and subtracted on a calculator but care must be taken since integers are both positive and negative.

Using the Change of Sign Key, $\boxed{+\ \circlearrowleft\ -}$

We observed earlier that to enter -5 into the display of your calculator you enter

$$5\ \boxed{+\ \circlearrowleft\ -}\ .$$

Thus, $27 + (-83)$ can be found by keying into your calculator the string

$$\boxed{\text{ON/AC}}\ 27\ \boxed{+}\ 83\ \boxed{+\ \circlearrowleft\ -}\ \boxed{=}$$

and the result is -56. Similarly, entering the string

$$\boxed{\text{ON/AC}}\ 71\ \boxed{+\ \circlearrowleft\ -}\ \boxed{-}\ 93\ \boxed{+\ \circlearrowleft\ -}\ \boxed{=}$$

performs the subtraction

$$(-71) - (-93) = 22.$$

EXAMPLE   5.21   ## Adding and Subtracting Integers Using the $\boxed{+\ \circlearrowleft\ -}$ Key

Perform these computations using the $\boxed{+\ \circlearrowleft\ -}$ key.

(a) $(-27) + (-95)$ **(b)** $(-27) - (-95)$ **(c)** $3250 + (-4729)$

Solution   In each case we indicate the key string entered into the calculator and the resulting answer.

(a) $\boxed{\text{ON/AC}}\ 27\ \boxed{+\ \circlearrowleft\ -}\ \boxed{+}\ 95\ \boxed{+\ \circlearrowleft\ -}\ \boxed{=}$, -122

(b) $\boxed{\text{ON/AC}}\ 27\ \boxed{+\ \circlearrowleft\ -}\ \boxed{-}\ 95\ \boxed{+\ \circlearrowleft\ -}\ \boxed{=}$, 68

(c) $\boxed{\text{ON/AC}}\ 3250\ \boxed{+}\ 4729\ \boxed{+\ \circlearrowleft\ -}\ \boxed{=}$, -1479

Alternatively, one can use the theorems in this section to write

$$(-27) + (-95) = -(27 + 95),$$
$$(-27) - (-95) = (-27) + 95 = 95 - 27, \text{ and}$$
$$3250 + (-4729) = 3250 - 4729.$$

Then these can be calculated as follows.

(a) $\boxed{\text{ON/AC}}$ 27 $\boxed{+}$ 95 $\boxed{=}$ $\boxed{+\bigcirc -}$, -122

(b) $\boxed{\text{ON/AC}}$ 95 $\boxed{-}$ 27 $\boxed{=}$, 68

(c) $\boxed{\text{ON/AC}}$ 3250 $\boxed{-}$ 4729 $\boxed{=}$, -1479

PROBLEM SET 5.2

Understanding Concepts

1. Draw diagrams of colored counters to illustrate these computations and state the answer in each case.

   (a) $8 + (-3)$ (b) $(-8) + 3$ (c) $(-8) - (-3)$
   (d) $8 - (-3)$ (e) $9 + 4$ (f) $9 + (-4)$
   (g) $(-9) + 4$ (h) $(-9) - (-4)$

2. Describe mail-time situations that illustrate each computation and state the answer in each case.

   (a) $(-27) + (-13)$ (b) $(-27) - 13$
   (c) $27 + 13$ (d) $27 - 13$
   (e) $(-41) + 13$ (f) $(-41) - 13$
   (g) $(-13) + 41$ (h) $13 - 41$

3. Draw number line diagrams that illustrate each computation and state the answer in each case.

   (a) $8 + (-3)$ (b) $8 - (-3)$ (c) $(-8) + 3$
   (d) $(-8) - (-3)$ (e) $4 + (-7)$ (f) $4 - (-7)$
   (g) $(-4) + 7$ (h) $(-4) - (-7)$

4. Write each of these subtractions as an addition.

   (a) $13 - 7$ (b) $13 - (-7)$
   (c) $(-13) - 7$ (d) $(-13) - (-7)$
   (e) $3 - 8$ (f) $8 - (-3)$
   (g) $(-8) - 13$ (h) $(-8) - (-13)$

5. Perform each of these computations.

   (a) $27 - (-13)$ (b) $12 + (-24)$
   (c) $(-13) - 14$ (d) $-81 + 54$
   (e) $(-81) - 54$ (f) $(-81) - (-54)$
   (g) $(-81) + (-54)$ (h) $27 + (-13)$
   (i) $(-27) - 13$

6. By 2 P.M. the temperature in Cutbank, Montana, had risen $31°$ from a nighttime low of $41°$ below zero.

   (a) What was the temperature at 2 P.M.?
   (b) What computation does part (a) illustrate?

7. (a) If the high temperature on a given day was $2°$ above zero and the morning's low was $27°$ below zero, how much did the temperature rise during the day?
   (b) What computation does part (a) illustrate?

8. (a) If the high temperature for a certain day was $8°$ above zero and that night's low temperature was $27°$ below zero, how much did the temperature fall?
   (b) What computation does part (a) illustrate?

9. During the day Sam's Soda Shop took in $314. That same day Sam paid a total of $208 in bills.

   (a) Was Sam's net worth more or less at the end of the day? By how much?
   (b) What computation does part (a) illustrate?

10. During the day Sam's Soda Shop took in $284. Also, Sam received a check in the mail for $191 as a refund for several bills that he had inadvertently paid twice.

    (a) Was Sam's net worth more or less at the end of the day? By how much?
    (b) What computation does part (a) illustrate?
    (c) If you think of the $191 check as removing or taking away the bills previously paid, what computation does this represent? Explain.

11. Place a less than or greater than sign in each circle to make a *true* statement.

   (a) $-117 \bigcirc -24$ (b) $0 \bigcirc -4$ (c) $18 \bigcirc 12$

   (d) $18 \bigcirc -12$ (e) $-5 \bigcirc 1$ (f) $-5 \bigcirc -9$

12. List these numbers in increasing order from least to greatest: $-5, 27, 5, -2, 0, 3, -17$.

Thinking Critically

13. Which of the following are *true?*

   (a) $3 < 12$ (b) $-3 < -12$

   (c) $-3 < 12$ (d) $3 < -12$

14. If $a < b$, is $a \le b$ true? Explain.

15. If $a \ge b$, is $a > b$ true? Explain.

16. Is $2 \ge 2$ true? Explain.

17. For which integers x is it true that $|x| < 7$?

18. For which integers x is it true that $|x| > 99$?

19. (a) Compute each of these absolute values.

   (i) $|5 - 11|$ (ii) $|(-4) - (-10)|$

   (iii) $|8 - (-7)|$ (iv) $|(-9) - 2|$

   (b) Draw a number line and determine the distance between the points on the number line for each of these pairs of integers.

   (i) 5 and 11   (ii) -4 and -10

   (iii) 8 and -7 (iv) -9 and 2

   (c) Since parts (a) and (b) are completely representative of the corresponding general cases, state a general theorem summarizing these results.

20. (a) Compute each of these pairs of expressions.

   (i) $|7 + 2|$ and $|7| + |2|$

   (ii) $|(-8) + 5|$ and $|-8| + |5|$

   (iii) $|7 + (-6)|$ and $|7| + |-6|$

   (iv) $|(-9) + (-5)|$ and $|-9| + |-5|$

   (v) $|6 + 0|$ and $|6| + |0|$

   (vi) $|0 + (-7)|$ and $|0| + |-7|$

   (b) Since the results of part (a) are completely typical, place one of the signs $>$, $<$, $\ge$, or $\le$ in the circle to make the following a *true* statement. For any integers a and b,

   $$|a + b| \bigcirc |a| + |b|.$$

21. Let a and b be positive integers, with $a < b$. If c is a negative integer, prove that $ac > bc$. (*Suggestion:* Try using specific numbers first.)

22. (a) Make a magic square using the numbers $-4, -3, -2, -1, 0, 1, 2, 3, 4$.

   (b) Make a magic subtraction square using the numbers $-4, -3, -2, -1, 0, 1, 2, 3, 4$.

23. Place the numbers $-2, -1, 0, 1, 2,$ in the circles in the diagram so that the sum of the numbers in each direction is the same.

   (a) Can this be done with 0 in the middle of the top row? If so, show how. If not, why not?

   (b) Can this be done with 2 in the middle of the top row? If so, show how. If not, why not?

   (c) Can this be done with -2 in the middle of the top row? If so, show how. If not, why not?

   (d) Can this be done with 1 or -1 in the middle of the top row? If so, show how. If not, why not?

24. Perform these pairs of computations.

   (a) $7 - (-3)$ and $(-3) - 7$

   (b) $(-2) - (-5)$ and $(-5) - (-2)$

   (c) Does the commutative law for subtraction hold for the set of integers? Explain briefly.

25. Does the associative law for subtraction hold for the set of integers (that is, is $a - (b - c) = (a - b) - c$ true for all integers a, b, and c)? If so, explain why. If not, give a counter example.

26. The equation $a(b - c) = ab - ac$ expresses the distributive law for multiplication over subtraction. Is it true for all integers a, b, and c? If so, explain why. If not, give a counter example.

Thinking Cooperatively

Do the next five problems in a group with two or three other students. At each step discuss your solution with the other members of your group and determine a consensus answer for your group.

27. Recall that the triangular numbers are the numbers 1, 3, 6, 10, 15, . . . generated by the formula

$$t_n = \frac{n(n+1)}{2}$$

(a) Fill in the blanks to complete these equations and to extend the pattern.

$$1 = \underline{\hspace{2cm}}$$
$$1 - 3 = \underline{\hspace{2cm}}$$
$$1 - 3 + 6 = \underline{\hspace{2cm}}$$
$$1 - 3 + 6 - 10 = \underline{\hspace{2cm}}$$
$$\underline{\hspace{2cm}} = \underline{\hspace{2cm}}$$
$$\underline{\hspace{2cm}} = \underline{\hspace{2cm}}$$

(b) What would the nth equation in this pattern be? (*Hint:* You may have to consider two cases—n odd and n even.)

28. Recall that the Fibonacci numbers are the numbers $F_1 = 1, F_2 = 1, F_3 = 2, F_4 = 3,$ $F_5 = 5, . . .$ where we start with 1 and 1 and then add any two successive terms to obtain the next term in the sequence.

(a) Fill in the blanks to continue this pattern.

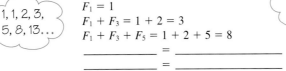

$$F_1 = 1$$
$$F_1 + F_3 = 1 + 2 = 3$$
$$F_1 + F_3 + F_5 = 1 + 2 + 5 = 8$$
$$\underline{\hspace{2cm}} = \underline{\hspace{2cm}}$$
$$\underline{\hspace{2cm}} = \underline{\hspace{2cm}}$$

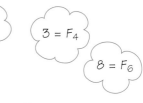

(b) Guess a formula for the general result suggested by part (a).

29. Continue each of these patterns two more steps and guess a general result in each case.

(a) $F_2 = 1$
$$F_2 + F_4 = 1 + 3 = 4$$
$$F_2 + F_4 + F_6 = 1 + 3 + 8 = 12$$
$$\underline{\hspace{2cm}} = \underline{\hspace{2cm}}$$
$$\underline{\hspace{2cm}} = \underline{\hspace{2cm}}$$

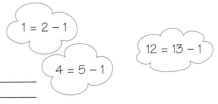

General result: _____

(b) $F_1 = 1$
$$F_1 + F_2 = 1 + 1 = 2$$
$$F_1 + F_2 + F_3 = 1 + 1 + 2 = 4$$
$$\underline{\hspace{2cm}} = \underline{\hspace{2cm}}$$
$$\underline{\hspace{2cm}} = \underline{\hspace{2cm}}$$

General result: _____

30. Note that the successive powers $(-1)^1 = -1, (-1)^2 = 1, (-1)^3 = -1, (-1)^4 = 1$ alternate between 1 and -1. Thus, $(-1)^n = 1$ if n is even and -1 if n is odd. Using this idea, continue each of these patterns two more steps and guess a general result in each case.

(a) $F_1 = 1$
$$F_1 - F_3 = 1 - 2 = -1$$
$$F_1 - F_3 + F_5 = 1 - 2 + 5 = 4$$
$$\underline{\hspace{2cm}} = \underline{\hspace{2cm}}$$
$$\underline{\hspace{2cm}} = \underline{\hspace{2cm}}$$

General result: _____

(b) $F_2 = 1$

$F_2 - F_4 = 1 - 3 = -2$

$F_2 - F_4 + F_6 = 1 - 3 + 8 = 6$

$$\underline{\hspace{4cm}} \quad = \quad \underline{\hspace{3cm}}$$

$$\underline{\hspace{4cm}} \quad = \quad \underline{\hspace{3cm}}$$

General result: $\underline{\hspace{6cm}}$

(c) $1 = 1$

$1 - 1 = 0$

$1 - 1 + 2 = 2$

$1 - 1 + 2 - 3 = -1$

$1 - 1 + 2 - 3 + 5 = 4$

$1 - 1 + 2 - 3 + 5 - 8 = -4$

$1 - 1 + 2 - 3 + 5 - 8 + 13 = 9$

$$\underline{\hspace{6cm}} \quad = \quad \underline{\hspace{3cm}}$$

$$\underline{\hspace{6cm}} \quad = \quad \underline{\hspace{3cm}}$$

General result: $\underline{\hspace{5cm}}$

(*Suggestion:* To guess the general result, think very carefully about the last three equations in part (c).)

31. **(a)** The general result guessed in problem 30, part (c) does not hold for $n = 1$ unless we define F_0 to be 0. Would this be consistent with the definition of the Fibonacci numbers as given in problem 28? Explain.

(b) Determine F_{-1}, F_{-2}, F_{-3}, and F_{-4} so that the pattern established by the definition of problem 28 still holds.

(c) Determine F_{-n} so that the definition of problem 28 holds for all integer values of n. (*Hint:* Use $(-1)^n$ as in problem 30.)

(d) Recall that the Lucas numbers are the numbers $L_1 = 1, L_2 = 3, L_3 = 4, \ldots$ where we start with 1 and 3 and then add any two successive terms to obtain the next term in the sequence. As in part (c), determine L_0 and L_{-n} so that this definition holds for all integer values of n.

Making Connections

32. One day Anne had the flu. At 8 A.M. her temperature was 101°. By noon her temperature had increased by 3° and then it fell 5° by six in the evening.

(a) Write a single addition equation to determine Anne's temperature at noon.

(b) Write a single equation using both addition and subtraction to determine Anne's temperature at 6 P.M.

33. Vicky was 12 years old on her birthday today.

(a) How old was Vicky on her birthday 7 years ago?

(b) How old will Vicky be on her birthday 7 years from now?

(c) Write addition equations that answer both parts (a) and (b) of this problem.

34. Greg's bank balance was $4500. During the month he wrote checks for $510, $87, $212, and $725. He also made deposits of $600 and $350. What was his balance at the end of the month?

35. A ball is thrown upward from the top of a building 144 feet high. Let h denote the height of the ball above the top of the building t seconds after it was thrown. It can be shown that $h = -16t^2 + 96t$ feet.

(a) Complete this table of values of h.

t	h
0	0
1	80
2	
3	
4	
5	
6	
7	

(b) Give a carefully worded plausibility argument (not a proof) that the greatest value of h in the table is the greatest height the ball reaches.

(c) Carefully interpret (explain) the meaning of the value of h when $t = 7$.

36. The velocity of the ball in problem 35 in feet per second is given by the equation $v = -32t + 96$.

(a) Complete the table of values of v shown below.

(b) Carefully interpret (explain) the value of v when $t = 0$.

(c) Interpret the value of v when $t = 3$.

t	v
0	96
1	64
2	
3	
4	
5	
6	
7	

(d) Carefully interpret the meaning of the values of v for $t = 4, 5, 6,$ and 7.

(e) Compare the values of v for $t = 0$ and 6, 1 and 5, and 2 and 4. What do these values tell you about the motion of the ball?

Communicating

37. In playing Simon Says, children line up along a line on the floor, sidewalk, or ground and move steps forward or backward as directed by the person who is "it."

(a) How could you use this game to introduce the notion of a negative integer to children?

(b) Describe how you could use your version of Simon Says to help students understand addition and subtraction of positive and negative integers.

Using a Calculator

38. If we write $a - b + c - d$, it is understood to mean $(((a - b) + c) - d)$. The operations are performed from left to right as on a calculator with algebraic logic.

(a) Compute $1 - 2 + 3 - \cdots + 99$.

(b) Could you think of an easy way to complete part (a) without a calculator?

(c) Compute $1 - 2 + 3 - \cdots + 99 - 100$.

39. Use your calculator to perform these calculations.

(a) $3742 + (-2167)$ (b) $(-2751) + (-3157)$

(c) $(-2167) - 3742$ (d) $(-3157) - (-2751)$

(e) $-(3571 - 5624)$ (f) $-[49{,}002 + (-37{,}621)]$

From State Student Assessments

40. (Massachusetts, Grade 8. Calculators are not allowed here because one can obtain the correct answer without understanding.)

Compute: $(^-2)(^-5)(^-1) =$

41. (Massachusetts, Grade 8. Calculators are not allowed here because one can obtain the correct answer without understanding.)

Compute: $4 + 2 \cdot 3 - 3^2 + (^-6) =$

For Review

42. Test the following numbers for divisibility by each of 2, 3, 5, and 11.

(a) 214,221   (b) 106,090   (c) 1,092,315

43. Test each of the following for divisibility by 7, 11, and 13.

(a) 965,419   (b) 1,140,997   (c) 816,893

44. Test each of the following for divisibility by 4, 6, and 8.

(a) 62,418   (b) 83,224   (c) 244,824

45. Show that each of 271,134; 427,113; 342,711; 134,271; 113,427; and 711,342 is divisible by 27.

46. Let $r, s, t,$ and u be natural numbers. If $r = s + t, u$ divides s, and u does not divide t, use the method of proof by contradiction to prove that u does not divide r.

5.3   Multiplication and Division of Integers

Multiplication of Integers

Just as the set of integers is an extension of the set of natural numbers, multiplication and division in the set of integers is a direct extension of these operations for natural numbers. Recall that multiplication of natural numbers was originally defined in Chapter 2 as repeated addition. Thus, by definition,

$$4 \cdot 3 = 3 + 3 + 3 + 3 = 12.$$

In like manner, we have that

$$4 \cdot (-3) = (-3) + (-3) + (-3) + (-3) = -12.$$

In general, if m and n are positive integers, so that $-m$ and $-n$ are negative, we have that

$$m \cdot (-n) = -mn.$$

Well and good, but this approach does not make clear what the products $(-m) \cdot (-n)$ and $(-m) \cdot n$ should be. To understand, we consider patterns of products.

Multiplication of Integers Using Patterns of Products

Consider the following pattern of equalities. Note that the second factors in the successive products

$$4 \cdot 3 = 12$$
$$4 \cdot 2 = 8$$
$$4 \cdot 1 = 4$$
$$4 \cdot 0 = 0$$

decrease by 1 each time and that the successive results decrease by 4. Continuing the pattern, we obtain this sequence of equalities.

$$4 \cdot 3 = 12$$
$$4 \cdot 2 = 8$$
$$4 \cdot 1 = 4$$
$$4 \cdot 0 = 0$$
$$4 \cdot (-1) = -4$$
$$4 \cdot (-2) = -8$$
$$4 \cdot (-3) = -12$$

Since these results agree with what would be obtained by repeated addition, the pattern of products is an appropriate guide. In general, it suggests that

$$m \cdot (-n) = -mn.$$

positive times negative gives negative

Using this result, we can now construct the following two additional patterns that suggest what to make of the products $(-m) \cdot (-n)$ and $(-m) \cdot n$.

$3 \cdot (-3) = -9$	$(-3) \cdot (-3) = 9$
$2 \cdot (-3) = -6$	$(-3) \cdot (-2) = 6$
$1 \cdot (-3) = -3$	$(-3) \cdot (-1) = 3$
$0 \cdot (-3) = 0$	$(-3) \cdot 0 = 0$
$(-1) \cdot (-3) = 3$	$(-3) \cdot 1 = -3$
$(-2) \cdot (-3) = 6$	$(-3) \cdot 2 = -6$
$(-3) \cdot (-3) = 9$	$(-3) \cdot 3 = -9$

Charlotte Scott is an example of a woman who has overcome great obstacles in the field of mathematics. Born in England, she attended Girton College of Cambridge University at a time when women were barred from receiving degrees and from even attempting the examinations for honors. She took the exams "informally," however, and besides two first places won eighth place in math, a field "too difficult for women." As the honors lists were read, shouts for "*Scott of Girton!*" cheered her achievement. Scott received her doctoral degree from the University of London and was called to the United States to become the only woman on the founding faculty of Bryn Mawr College in Pennsylvania. A long record of scholarship, writing, and contributions to the field of analytic geometry followed. Scott's students found her classes exciting, her mathematical style "elegant," and her own gift for clear explanation combined nicely with her quick understanding of their "stupidity." In later years, her record at Cambridge opened new doors for women; and many of her women students joined her in the lists of distinguished mathematicians and teachers.

Source: From *Mathematics in Modules, Algebra, A3*, Teacher's Edition. Reprinted by permission.

Thus, the patterns suggest that

$$(-m) \cdot (-n) = mn \qquad \text{and} \qquad (-m) \cdot (n) = -mn.$$

negative times negative gives positive

negative times positive gives negative

Collecting these results together, we have the following theorem.

> **THEOREM** *The Rule of Signs*
> Let m and n be positive integers so that $-m$ and $-n$ are negative integers. Then the following are true:
> - $m \cdot (-n) = -mn$
> - $(-m) \cdot n = -mn$
> - $(-m) \cdot (-n) = mn$
>
> and,
> - $a \cdot 0 = 0 \cdot a = 0$
>
> for any integer a.

EXAMPLE   5.22   **Multiplying Integers**

Compute these products.

(a) $(-7) \cdot (-8)$ (b) $(-8) \cdot (-7)$ (c) $3 \cdot (-7)$

(d) $(-7) \cdot 3$ (e) $[8 \cdot (-5)] \cdot 6$ (f) $8 \cdot [(-5) \cdot 6]$

(g) $(-4) \cdot [(-5) + 7]$ (h) $(-4) \cdot (-5) + (-4) \cdot 7$

Solution

(a) $(-7) \cdot (-8) = 7 \cdot 8 = 56$ (b) $(-8) \cdot (-7) = 8 \cdot 7 = 56$
(c) $3 \cdot (-7) = -(3 \cdot 7) = -21$ (d) $(-7) \cdot 3 = -(7 \cdot 3) = -21$
(e) $[8 \cdot (-5)] \cdot 6 = [-(8 \cdot 5)] \cdot 6 = (-40) \cdot 6 = -(40 \cdot 6) = -240$
(f) $8 \cdot [(-5) \cdot 6] = 8 \cdot [-(5 \cdot 6)] = 8 \cdot (-30) = -(8 \cdot 30) = -240$
(g) $(-4) \cdot [(-5) + 7] = (-4) \cdot 2 = -8$
(h) $(-4) \cdot (-5) + (-4) \cdot 7 = 4 \cdot 5 + [-(4 \cdot 7)] = 20 + (-28) = -8$

The results of the preceding example illustrate that the closure, commutative, associative, and distributive properties of multiplication hold for the set of integers. Since these results are typical, we have the following theorem.

THEOREM *Multiplication Properties of Integers*

Let *r*, *s*, and *t* be any integers.

Closure Property	rs is an integer.
Commutative Property	$rs = sr$.
Associative Property	$r(st) = (rs)t$.
Distributive Property	$r(s + t) = rs + rt$.

Multiplication of Integers Using Mail-time Stories

Recall that in mail-time stories the mail carrier bringing checks and bills corresponds to adding positive and negative numbers, respectively. Similarly, taking away checks and bills corresponds to subtracting positive and negative numbers.

Suppose the letter carrier brings 5 bills for $11 each. Are you richer or poorer and by how much? Answer: Poorer by $55. Since this is repeated addition, this illustrates the product

$$5 \cdot (-11) = -55.$$

Suppose the mail carrier takes away 4 bills for $13 each. Are you richer or poorer and by how much? Answer: Richer by $52. This illustrates the product

$$(-4) \cdot (-13) = 52$$

since 4 bills for the same amount are *taken away*.

JUST FOR FUN

Three on a Bike?

Three teenagers arrived at a rental agency each desiring to rent a bicycle for the day. There was only one bicycle left, but the teenagers finally agreed to share equally the $30 charge for the one day and also to share equally in the bicycle's use. Later the manager of the agency decided that his charge was excessive and sent his helper to return $5 to the teenagers. Being dishonest, the helper pocketed $2 and only returned $3 to the teenagers. Thus, each paid $9 for the use of the bicycle. But $27 plus the $2 the helper took makes only $29. What happened to the other dollar?

EXAMPLE 5.23   **Writing Mail-time Stories for Multiplication of Integers**

Write a mail-time story to illustrate each of these products.

(a) $(-4) \cdot 16$ **(b)** $(-4) \cdot (-16)$ **(c)** $4 \cdot (-16)$ **(d)** $4 \cdot 16$

Solution

(a)   The letter carrier takes away 4 checks for $16 each. Are you richer or poorer and by how much? Answer: $64 poorer, $(-4) \cdot 16 = -64$.

(b)   The letter carrier takes away 4 bills for $16 each. Are you richer or poorer and by how much? Answer: $64 richer, $(-4) \cdot (-16) = 64$.

(c)   The letter carrier brings 4 bills for $16 each. Are you richer or poorer and by how much? Answer: Poorer by $64, $4 \cdot (-16) = -64$.

(d)   The letter carrier brings you 4 checks for $16 each. Are you richer or poorer and by how much? Answer: Richer by $64, $4 \cdot 16 = 64$.

Multiplication of Integers Using a Number Line

Think of $3 \cdot 4$ as $4 + 4 + 4$,

$3 \cdot (-4)$ as $(-4) + (-4) + (-4)$,

$(-3) \cdot (4)$ as $-4 - 4 - 4$, and

$(-3) \cdot (-4)$ as $-(-4) - (-4) - (-4)$.

These can be illustrated on the number line as follows.

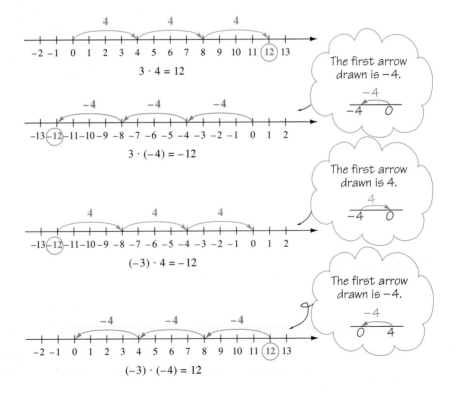

EXAMPLE 5.24	**Multiplying Integers Using a Number Line**

What products do each of these diagrams illustrate?

(a)

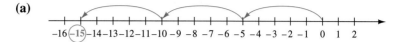

(b)

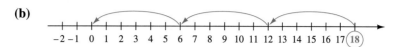

Solution

(a) Starting with the tail of the right-most arrow at 0, we move in the direction of the arrows 5 units to the left, then 5 more units to the left, and finally five more units to the left. Thus, we are *adding* -5 to -5 to -5 and the result is $3 \cdot (-5) = -15$.

(b) Here we start with the head of the left more arrow at 0 and move in the direction *opposite* to the direction of the arrows, 6 units to the right, 6 more units to the right, and finally 6 more units to the right. Since the arrows are directed from right to left, we are *subtracting* -6 and -6 and -6. The result is $(-3) \cdot (-6) = 18$.

Division of Integers

When discussing division of natural numbers, we considered families of facts. Thus, the equations

$$12 = 3 \cdot 4 \qquad 12 \div 3 = 4$$
$$12 = 4 \cdot 3 \qquad 12 \div 4 = 3$$

all express the same relationship between the numbers 12, 3, and 4. Indeed, one definition of division of whole numbers was the following:

If a, b, and c are whole numbers with $b \neq 0$, then $a \div b = c$ if, and only if, $a = bc$.

Thus, to find the quotient $143 \div 11$, we determine c such that $143 = 11 \cdot c$. Since $c = 13$ satisfies this equation, $143 \div 11 = 13$.

Applying the same ideas to integers, we have the following fact families.

(a) $12 = (-3) \cdot (-4)$ $12 \div (-3) = -4$
          $12 = (-4) \cdot (-3)$ $12 \div (-4) = -3$

(b) $-12 = 3 \cdot (-4)$ $(-12) \div 3 = -4$
         $-12 = (-4) \cdot 3$ $(-12) \div (-4) = 3$

These equations are typical and, as in the case of the natural numbers, lead to the following definition of division in the set of integers.

DEFINITION   *Division of Integers*

If a, b, and c are integers with $b \neq 0$, then $a \div b = c$ if, and only if, $a = b \cdot c$.

EXAMPLE 5.25

Dividing Integers

Perform the following divisions.

(a) $28 \div 4$ (b) $28 \div (-4)$ (c) $(-28) \div 4$ (d) $(-28) \div (-4)$

Solution

The solution depends entirely on the preceding definition.

(a) $28 \div 4 = 7$ since $28 = 4 \cdot 7$.
(b) $28 \div (-4) = -7$ since $28 = (-4) \cdot (-7)$.
(c) $(-28) \div 4 = -7$ since $-28 = 4 \cdot (-7)$.
(d) $(-28) \div (-4) = 7$ since $-28 = (-4) \cdot 7$.

Since these results are entirely typical, we state here the rule of signs for division.

THEOREM   *Rule of Signs for Division of Integers*

Let m and n be positive integers so that $-m$ and $-n$ are negative integers and suppose that n divides m. Then the following are true:

- $m \div (-n) = -(m \div n)$
- $(-m) \div n = -(m \div n)$
- $(-m) \div (-n) = m \div n$

Thus, *given that n divides m*, we see that:

- a positive integer divided by a negative integer is a negative integer,
- a negative integer divided by a positive integer is a negative integer,
- a negative integer divided by a negative integer is a positive integer, and
- a positive integer divided by a positive integer is a positive integer.

EXAMPLE   5.26

Performing Division of Integers

If possible, compute each of these quotients.

(a) $(-24) \div (-8)$ (b) $24 \div (-8)$ (c) $48 \div 12$
(d) $(-48) \div 12$ (e) $(-57) \div 19$ (f) $(-12) \div 0$
(g) $(-51) \div (-17)$ (h) $28 \div (9 - 5)$ (i) $(27 + 9) \div (-4)$

Solution

We use the preceding theorem and the definition of division of integers.

(a) $(-24) \div (-8) = 3$. Check: $-24 = (-8) \cdot 3$
(b) $24 \div (-8) = -3$. Check: $24 = (-8) \cdot (-3)$
(c) $48 \div 12 = 4$. Check: $48 = 12 \cdot 4$
(d) $(-48) \div 12 = -4$. Check: $-48 = 12 \cdot (-4)$
(e) $(-57) \div 19 = -3$. Check: $-57 = 19 \cdot (-3)$
(f) $(-12) \div 0$ is not defined since there is no number c such that $-12 = 0 \cdot c = 0$.
(g) $(-51) \div (-17) = 3$. Check: $-51 = (-17) \cdot 3$
(h) $28 \div (9 - 5) = 28 \div 4 = 7$. Check: $28 = 4 \cdot 7$
(i) $(27 + 9) \div (-4) = 36 \div (-4) = -9$. Check: $36 = (-4) \cdot (-9)$.

PROBLEM SET 5.3

Understanding Concepts

1. Perform these multiplications.
   - (a) $7 \cdot 11$
   - (b) $7 \cdot (-11)$
   - (c) $(-7) \cdot 11$
   - (d) $(-7) \cdot (-11)$
   - (e) $12 \cdot 9$
   - (f) $12 \cdot (-9)$
   - (g) $(-12) \cdot 9$
   - (h) $(-12) \cdot (-9)$
   - (i) $(-12) \cdot 0$

2. Perform these divisions.
   - (a) $36 \div 9$
   - (b) $(-36) \div 9$
   - (c) $36 \div (-9)$
   - (d) $(-36) \div (-9)$
   - (e) $(-143) \div 11$
   - (f) $165 \div (-11)$
   - (g) $(-144) \div (-9)$
   - (h) $275 \div 11$
   - (i) $72 \div (21 - 19)$

3. Write another multiplication equation and two division equations that are equivalent to $(-11) \cdot (-25{,}753) = 283{,}283$.

4. Write two multiplication equations and another division equation that are equivalent to $(-1001) \div 13 = -91$.

5. What computation does each of these mail-time stories illustrate?
   - (a) The mail carrier brings you 6 checks for $13 each. Are you richer or poorer? By how much?
   - (b) The mail carrier brings you 4 bills for $23 each. Are you richer or poorer? By how much?
   - (c) The mail carrier takes away 3 bills for $17 each. Are you richer or poorer? By how much?
   - (d) The mail carrier takes away 5 checks for $20 each. Are you richer or poorer? By how much?

6. What computation does each of these number line diagrams represent?

   (a)

   (b)
   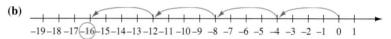

   (c)
   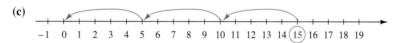

7. Draw a number line diagram to illustrate $(-4) \cdot 3 = -12$.

Thinking Critically

8. If we assume that the integers obey the distributive property as illustrated earlier in this section, then a proof of the rule of signs is available. Fill in the blanks to justify steps of these proofs.

   (a) $3 \cdot 0 = 0$ _____
   $3 \cdot [5 + (-5)] = 0$ Definition of additive inverse
   $3 \cdot 5 + 3 \cdot (-5) = 0$ _____
   $3 \cdot (-5) = -(3 \cdot 5)$ _____

   (b) If a and b are any positive integers, then
   $a \cdot 0 = 0$ _____
   $a[b + (-b)] = 0$ _____
   $ab + a(-b) = 0$ _____
   $a \cdot (-b) = -(ab)$ _____

   (c) $0 \cdot 5 = 0$ _____
   $[3 + (-3)] \cdot 5 = 0$ Definition of additive inverse
   $3 \cdot 5 + (-3) \cdot 5 = 0$ _____
   $(-3) \cdot 5 = -(3 \cdot 5)$ _____

(d) If a and b are any positive integers, then

$0 \cdot b = 0$ _____

$[a + (-a)] \cdot b = 0$ _____

$ab + (-a)b = 0$ _____

$(-a)b = -(ab)$ _____

(e) $(-3) \cdot 0 = 0$ _____

$(-3) \cdot [5 + (-5)] = 0$ _____

$(-3) \cdot 5 + (-3) \cdot (-5) = 0$ _____

$-(3 \cdot 5) + (-3) \cdot (-5) = 0$ By part (c)

$(-3) \cdot (-5) = 3 \cdot 5$ _____

(f) $(-a) \cdot 0 = 0$ _____

$(-a) \cdot [b + (-b)] = 0$ _____

$(-a)b + (-a)(-b) = 0$ _____

$-(ab) + (-a)(-b) = 0$ _____

$(-a)(-b) = ab$ _____

(g) Would parts (b), (d), and (f) be appropriate for an elementary school classroom? Why or why not?

(h) Might parts (a), (c), and (e) be appropriate for an upper elementary or middle school classroom? Discuss.

---

9. In the diagram below, the sum of the numbers in any two small circles is the number in the large circle between them.

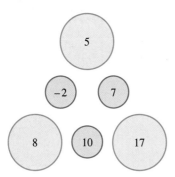

Complete the following so that the same pattern holds in each case.

(a)

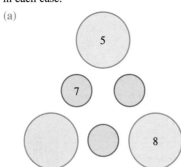

(b)

(c)

(d)

10. This problem is like the preceding one except that there are 5 large and 5 small circles. Again the sum of the numbers in two small circles is the number in the large circle between them.

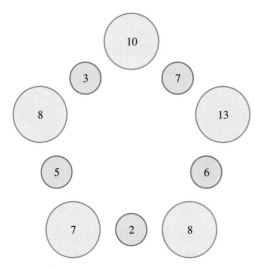

Complete each of the following so that the same pattern holds in each case. Indicate if the solution to each of these is unique.

(a)

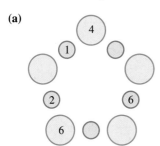

(b)

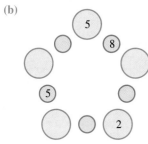

(c)

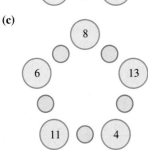

(d) Is a puzzle like these always solvable? Explain. (*Hint:* Let *u*, *v*, *w*, *x*, and *y* be the numbers in the small circles.) Use variables

11. Consider a four large circle version of problem 10 as shown below.

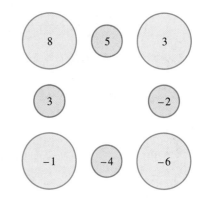

(a) Complete the following diagram so that the same relationships hold.

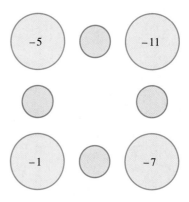

(b) Is a puzzle like this always solvable? Explain. (*Hint:* Let *x*, *y*, *z*, and *w* be the numbers in the small circles.)

(c) What must be the case to ensure that a puzzle with 6 large circles is solvable? Explain carefully.

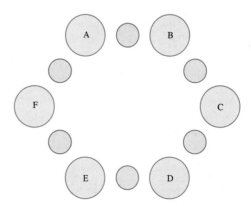

12. Use the numbers $-8, -6, -4, -2, 0, 2, 4, 6, 8$ to make a magic square. What should the sum in each row, column, and diagonal be? What should the middle number be?

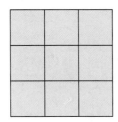

13. Use the numbers $-7, -6, -5, -1, 0, 1, 5, 6, 7$ to make a magic square.

14. **(a)** Using each of $-3, -1, 1,$ and 3 at most once, what sums can be found? For example, three such sums are

$$3 + (-1) = 2, (-3) + (-1) = -4, \text{ and } 1 = 1.$$

(b) What strategy did you use to solve part (a)? Explain.

Thinking Cooperatively

Work with two or three other students to complete this problem.

15. **(a)** Complete the following table for values of r and s such that $r + s = 3, 4, 5, 6, 7,$ and 8 with $r > s > 0$ by dividing the work among members of the group.

r	s	$r+s$	$x = 2rs$	$y = r^2 - s^2$	$z = r^2 + s^2$	$x^2 + y^2$	z^2
2	1	3					
3	1	4					
4	1	5					
3	2	5					
5	1	6					
4	2	6					
6	1	7					
5	2	7					
4	3	7					
7	1	8					
6	2	8					
5	3	8					

(b) Discuss the results of part (a) and agree on a conjecture for your group.

Making Connections

16. The Pep Club tried to raise money by raffling off a pig, agreeing that if they actually lost money on the enterprise the members would share the loss equally.

(a) If they lost $105 and there are 15 members in the club, how much did each club member have to pay?

(b) What arithmetic might be used to illustrate this story? Explain.

17. It cost $39 each to buy sweatshirts for members of the Pep Club.

(a) If there are 15 members in the Pep Club, what was the total cost?

(b) What arithmetic might be used to illustrate this story? Explain.

Using a Calculator

18. Calculate each of these without using the $\boxed{\text{M}+}$, $\boxed{\text{M}-}$, or $\boxed{\text{MR}}$ keys on your calculator.

(a) $31 - 47 + 88 + 16 - 5$

(b) $57 + 165 \div (-11) + 17$

(c) $(47 + 81 - 56 + 9) \div (67 - 31 - 9)$

19. **(a)** Use the $\boxed{\text{M}+}$, $\boxed{\text{M}-}$, and $\boxed{\text{MR}}$ keys to simultaneously calculate

$$a_n = 1^2 - 2^2 + 3^2 - \ldots + (-1)^{n-1} n^2$$

and
$$s_n = 1^2 + 2^2 + 3^2 + \cdots + n^2$$
for $n = 1, 2, 3, 4, 5,$ and 6.

(b) Compute $3s_n \div a_n$ from part (a) for $n = 1, 2, 3, 4,$ 5, and 6.

(c) Make a conjecture based on the results of part (b).

20. The Diffy process described in the Cooperative Investigation in Section 2.3 employed whole numbers. Explain why the process is essentially unchanged if we start with all negative or a mixture of positive and negative integers.

For Review

 21. Use the constant function on a calculator to compute the twentieth term in each of these sequences.

(a) 5, 8, 11, 14, 17, . . .

(b) 5, 10, 20, 40, 80, . . .

 22. Let $a_1 = 1$, $a_2 = 2$, and $a_{n+2} = 2a_{n+1} + a_n$ for $n \geq 1$.

(a) Compute a_3, a_4, a_5, and a_6.

(b) Recall that x refers to the number in the display of your calculator and M refers to the number in memory. Complete this table using symbols and the facts from part (a)—that $a_3 = 2a_2 + a_1$, $a_4 = 2a_3 + a_2$, $a_5 = 2a_4 + a_3$, and so on. Notice that, from step 8 on, the indicated operations in this algorithm occur in a repeating pattern.

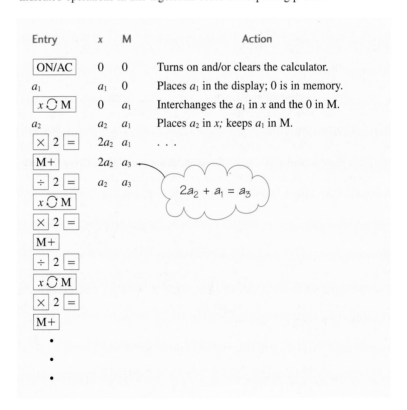

(c) List the entries that appear in the display, x, each time you press $\boxed{x \mathbin{\bigcirc} M}$ after the first time.

(d) Carry out the above algorithm starting with $a_1 = 1$ and $a_2 = 2$. List the first six terms of the sequence being generated.

(e) Start with $b_1 = 2$ and $b_2 = 6$ and compute the sequence b_1, b_2, b_3, b_4, b_5, and b_6 using the algorithm of part (a).

(f) Compute $a_1 + a_3$, $a_2 + a_4$, $a_3 + a_5$, and $a_4 + a_6$ and compare with the results of part (e). Make a conjecture based on your observations.

(g) Compute $(b_1 + b_3) \div 8$, $(b_2 + b_4) \div 8$, $(b_3 + b_5) \div 8$, and $(b_4 + b_6) \div 8$. Make a conjecture based on these computations.

(h) Compute $b_1 + 2a_1$, $b_2 + 2a_2$, $b_3 + 2a_3$, $b_4 + 2a_4$, $b_5 + 2a_5$, and $b_6 + 2a_6$. Make a conjecture based on these computations.

EPILOGUE   Developing the Number System

In the struggle to develop numbers, history shows that it took a very long time for people to develop the natural numbers and even longer to develop the notion of zero. Even then, zero was first introduced only as a placeholder in positional systems like the Mayan, and it was not until much later that it was considered to be a number.

Somewhat surprisingly, negative numbers made their appearance on the mathematical scene before zero did. No evidence of the recognition of negative numbers, as distinct from subtrahends, appears in ancient Egyptian, Babylonian, Hindu, Chinese, or Greek mathematics. Still, the rules of signs, considered at length in this chapter, were established early on by considering such products as $(8 - 4) \cdot (7 - 5)$. The Chinese made use of such subtractions at least as early as 200 B.C., but the rules of signs in Chinese mathematics were not stated explicitly until A.D. 1299. The first mention of negative numbers in western mathematics occurred in *Arithmetica* by the Greek mathematician, Diophantus, in about A.D. 275, though spoken of there in disparaging terms. Diophantus called the equation $4x + 20 = 4$ *absurd* since it would require that $x = -4$. The first substantial use of negative numbers occurred in the work of the Hindu mathematician, Brahmagupta, in about A.D. 628, and after that time they appear in all Indian works on the subject.

In this chapter, we have used various devices to introduce the notions of negative numbers and the rules for operating with them. The fact that these numbers were considered absurd or nonnumbers by early mathematicians notwithstanding, negative numbers, like all the other numbers, are simply ideas in our minds. They are in constant use to solve problems that occur daily in modern technological society.

CHAPTER 5 SUMMARY

Key Concepts

The thrust of this chapter has been to introduce the notion of negative numbers and the rules for operating with these numbers. Various physical and diagrammatic devices were used. The essential feature of negative numbers is that, if a is a natural number, then $-a$ is the number having the property

$$a + (-a) = (-a) + a = 0;$$

that is, $-a$ was introduced primarily as the additive inverse of a.

Properties of the Integers

The integers satisfy these properties:

- The closure properties for addition, subtraction, and multiplication

  If r and s are any integers, then

  $r + s$, $r - s$, and rs are integers.

- The commutative properties for addition and multiplication

    If *r* and *s* are any integers, then

    $r + s = s + r$, and $rs = sr$.

- The associative properties for addition and multiplication

    If *r*, *s*, and *t* are any integers, then

    $(r + s) + t = r + (s + t)$ and $(rs)t = r(st)$.

- The distributive property for multiplication over addition and subtraction

    If *r*, *s*, and *t* are any integers, then

    $r(s + t) = rs + rt$ and

    $(s + t)r = sr + tr$. Also,

    $r(s - t) = rs - rt$ and

    $(s - t)r = sr - tr$.

- 0 is the additive identity for the integers.

    If *r* is any integer, then

    $0 + r = r + 0 = r$.

- 1 is the multiplicative identity for the integers.

    If *r* is any integer, then

    $1 \cdot r = r \cdot 1 = r$.

- $r \cdot 0 = 0 \cdot r = 0$ for any integer *r*.

Rules for Integer Computation

If *r*, *s*, and *t* are positive integers so that $-r$, $-s$, and $-t$ are negative, then:

- $r + (-s) = r - s$ if $r > s$,
- $r + (-s) = -(s - r)$ if $r < s$,
- $(-r) + (-s) = -(r + s)$,
- $r \cdot (-s) = -(rs)$,
- $(-r) \cdot s = -(rs)$,
- $(-r) \cdot (-s) = rs$.

Also, if *s* divides *r*, then:

- $r \div (-s) = -(r \div s)$,
- $(-r) \div s = -(r \div s)$,
- $(-r) \div (-s) = r \div s$.

Vocabulary and Notation

Section 5.1

Integers
The set of integers consists of
　　—the natural numbers or positive integers 1, 2,
　　　　3, . . .
　　—the number 0
　　—the negative integers −1, −2, −3, . . .
Representing integers by drops of colored counters
Representing integers using mail-time stories
Representing integers on the number line
Absolute value

Section 5.2

Addition of integers
　　—using sets of colored counters
　　—using mail-time stories
　　—using the number line
Ordering the set of integers
　　—less than
　　—greater than

　　—less than or equal to
　　—greater than or equal to
　　—the law of trichotomy
Subtraction of integers
　　—using sets of colored counters
　　—using mail-time stories
　　—using the number line
　　—using a calculator
　　—using the ⎡ + ◯ − ⎤ key

Section 5.3

Multiplication of integers
　　—using patterns
　　—the rule of signs
　　—using mail-time stories
　　—using a number line
Division of integers

CHAPTER REVIEW EXERCISES

Section 5.1

1.　You have 15 counters colored black on one side and
　　red on the other.
　　(a) If you drop them on your desk top and 7 come
　　　　up black and 8 come up red, what integer is
　　　　represented?
　　(b) If you drop them on your desk top and twice as
　　　　many come up black as red, what number is
　　　　being represented?
　　(c) What numbers are represented by all possible
　　　　drops of the 15 counters?
2.　(a) If the mail carrier brings you a check for $12,
　　　　are you richer or poorer and by how much?
　　　　What integer does this situation illustrate?
　　(b) If the mail carrier brings you a bill for $37, are
　　　　you richer or poorer and by how much? What
　　　　integer does this situation illustrate?
3.　(a) 12° above zero illustrates what integer?
　　(b) 24° below zero illustrates what integer?
4.　(a) List five different "drops" of colored counters
　　　　that represent the integer −5.
　　(b) List five different drops of colored counters that
　　　　represent the integer 6.
5.　(a) Give a mail-time story that illustrates −85.
　　(b) Give a mail-time story that illustrates 47.

6.　(a) What number must you add to 44 to obtain 0?
　　(b) What number must you add to −61 to obtain 0?

Section 5.2

7.　What addition is represented by this diagram?

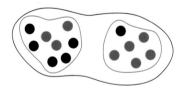

8.　What subtraction is represented by this diagram?

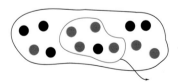

9.　What additions and subtractions are represented by
　　these mail-time stories?
　　(a) At mail time the letter carrier brings you a check
　　　　for $45 and a bill for $68. Are you richer or
　　　　poorer and by how much?

(b) At mail time the letter carrier brings you a check for $45 and takes away a bill for $68 left previously. Are you richer or poorer and by how much?

---

10. What additions and/or subtractions do these number line diagrams represent?

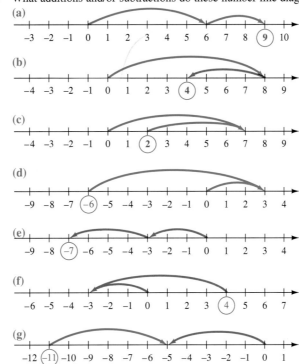

(a)

(b)

(c)

(d)

(e)

(f)

(g)

---

11. Perform these additions and subtractions.
    (a) $5 + (-7)$ (b) $(-27) - (-5)$
    (c) $(-27) + (-5)$ (d) $5 - (-7)$
    (e) $8 - (-12)$ (f) $8 - 12$

12. (a) If it is 15° below zero and the temperature falls 12°, what temperature is it?
    (b) What arithmetic does this situation illustrate?

13. (a) Dina's bank account was overdrawn by $12. What was her balance after she deposited $37 she earned working at a local pizza parlor?
    (b) What arithmetic does this situation illustrate?

14. (a) Plot these numbers on a number line: $-2, 7, 0, -5, -9,$ and 2.
    (b) List the numbers in part (a) in increasing order.
    (c) Determine what integer must be added to each number in your list from part (b) to obtain the next.

Section 5.3

15. What products do these number line diagrams represent?

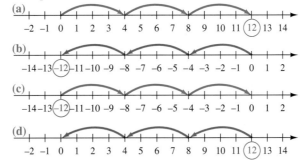

(a)

(b)

(c)

(d)

16. (a) Show that $3 \cdot 5 + 3 \cdot (-5) = 0$. Suggestion: Begin with the fact that $3 \cdot 0 = 0$.
    (b) If $3 \cdot 5 + 3 \cdot (-5) = 0$, what can you conclude about the product $3 \cdot (-5)$?
    (c) Show that $-(3 \cdot 5) + (-3) \cdot (-5) = 0$. Suggestion: Begin with the fact that $0 \cdot (-5) = 0$ and use the result of part (a).
    (d) If $-(3 \cdot 5) + (-3) \cdot (-5) = 0$, what can you conclude about the product $(-3) \cdot (-5)$?

17. Perform each of these computations
    (a) $(-8) \cdot (-7)$ (b) $8 \cdot (-7)$
    (c) $(-8) \cdot 7$ (d) $84 \div (-12)$
    (e) $(-84) \div 7$ (f) $(-84) \div (-7)$

18. Write a mail-time story to illustrate each of these products.
    (a) $7 \cdot (12)$ (b) $(-7) \cdot (13)$ (c) $(-7) \cdot (-13)$

19. If d divides n, prove that d divides $-n$, $-d$ divides n, and $-d$ divides $-n$.

20. If a and b are integers, the greatest common divisor of a and b is the largest positive integer dividing both a and b. Compute each of the following.
    (a) GCD$(255, -39)$ (b) GCD$(-1001, 2651)$

21. If n is an integer not divisible by 2 or 3, show that $n^2 - 1$ is divisible by 24. (*Hint:* By the division algorithm, n must be of one of these forms: $6q$, $6q + 1$, $6q + 2$, $6q + 3$, $6q + 4$, or $6q + 5$.)

CHAPTER TEST

1. Perform each of these computations.
   (a) $(-7) + (-19)$ (b) $(-7) - (-19)$
   (c) $7 - (-19)$ (d) $7 + (-19)$
   (e) $(-6859) \div 19$ (f) $(-24) \cdot 17$
   (g) $36 \cdot (-24)$ (h) $(-1155) \div (-11)$
   (i) $0 \div (-27)$

2. The least common multiple of integers a and b is the least positive integer divisible by both a and b. Compute LCM$(-240, 54)$

3. At mail time, if the mail carrier took away 5 bills for $27 each, are you richer or poorer and by how much? What calculation does this illustrate?

4. Draw a number line diagram to illustrate each of these calculations
   (a) $(-7) + 10$ (b) $10 - (-7)$ (c) $7 \cdot (-5)$

5. Write a mail-time story to illustrate the subtraction $7 - (-4) = 11$.

6. Mary Lou's checkbook balance was $129. What was it after she deposited $341 and then wrote checks for $13, $47, and $29? What arithmetic does this illustrate?

7. Tammie, Jody, and Nora formed a small club. After a party celebrating the first anniversary of the club's existence they owed the local pizzeria $27. The bill was paid and shared equally by the three girls. Was each one richer or poorer and by how much? What arithmetic does this illustrate?

8. The Fibonacci sequence is formed by adding any two consecutive numbers in the sequence to obtain the next. If the same rule is followed in each of these, correctly fill in the blanks.
   (a) $-5, -3,$ _____, _____, _____, _____
   (b) $7,$ _____, $2,$ _____, _____, _____
   (c) $6,$ _____, _____, _____, $-12,$ _____

9. (a) Use your calculator to compute these sums.
$$1 =$$
$$1 - 4 =$$
$$1 - 4 + 9 =$$
$$1 - 4 + 9 - 16 =$$
$$1 - 4 + 9 - 16 + 25 =$$
   (b) Make a conjecture suggested by the pattern of part (a).

10. (a) What sums can be obtained using only the numbers $-10, -5, -2, -1, 1, 2, 5,$ and $10,$ each at most once and without using any number with its double?
    (b) Do the representations in part (a) appear to be unique?

Fractions and Rational Numbers

6.1   The Basic Concepts of
      Fractions and Rational
      Numbers
6.2   The Arithmetic of Rational
      Numbers
6.3   The Rational Number System

HANDS ON
Folded Fractions

Materials Needed

Each student (or cooperating pair of students) should have about six paper squares (4- to 5-inch side length) and several colored pencils.

Example: Folding Quarters

A unit of area is defined as the area of a square.

Fold the square in half vertically, then again horizontally, and finally unfold the square to its original size.

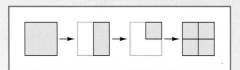

The fractions $\frac{1}{4}$, $\frac{2}{4}$, or $\frac{3}{4}$ can be illustrated by shading 1, 2, or 3 of the small squares within the unit square.

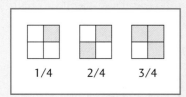

| 1/4 | 2/4 | 3/4 |

The two small shaded squares can be rearranged to show the fraction equivalence $\frac{2}{4} = \frac{1}{2}$.

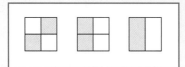

Fraction Folding Activities and Problems

1. **Eighths.** Fold a square into quarters as in the example, and also fold along the two diagonals.

   (a) Identify these fractions.

   (b) How many *different* ways can two of the eight regions be colored to give a representation of $\frac{2}{8}$? Two colorings are considered identical if one pattern can be rotated to become identical to the second pattern.

2. **Sixths.** "Roll" the paper square into thirds and flatten, and then fold in half in the opposite direction to divide the square into six congruent rectangles.

   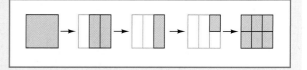

   How many *different* ways can you represent the fraction $\frac{3}{6}$? Remember that two patterns are different only if one cannot be rotated to become identical to another.

3. **Identifying fractions.** The leftmost shaded region shown in the figure at the top of the next page is bounded by segments joining successive midpoints of the sides of the square. What is the area of the shaded region? The region can be divided into smaller regions that are easy to rearrange into a pattern that shows $\frac{1}{2}$ of the square is shaded. Use

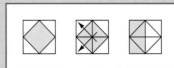

similar multiple representations of the same amount of shaded region to identify the fractions represented by these colored regions.

(a) The shaded region obtained by joining the midpoints of the vertical edges of the square with the $\frac{1}{3}$ and $\frac{2}{3}$ points along the horizontal edges.

(b) The shaded region obtained by joining the $\frac{1}{3}$ and $\frac{2}{3}$ points along the vertical and horizontal edges.

(c) The shaded square whose corners are the intersections of the segments joining the corners of the unit square to the midpoint of an opposite side of the unit square. [*Suggestion:* Rearrange the small regions to create squares, all congruent to the shaded square.]

C O N N E C T I O N S   Numbers for Parts and Pieces

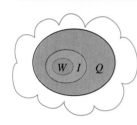

In Chapter 5 the set of whole numbers, $W = \{0, 1, 2, \ldots\}$ was extended to the set of integers $I = \{\ldots, -2, -1, 0, 1, 2, 3, \ldots\}$. In the set of integers it becomes possible to solve problems that are more difficult or even impossible to solve in the whole number system. In particular, the integers are closed under subtraction. Therefore, the equation $x + a = b$ has the unique solution $x = b - a$ for any integers a and b. However, even in the integers, equations like $ax = b$, $a \neq 0$, may not have a solution. Thus, it is necessary to extend the integers to an even larger set of numbers, the rational number system Q.

A rational number is represented by an ordered pair of integers a and b, $b \neq 0$, which is written as $\frac{a}{b}$ and called a fraction. Section 6.1 introduces the basic concepts of fractions and rational numbers. Pictorial and physical models are used to illustrate equivalent fractions, fractions in simplest form, common denominators, and inequality. In Section 6.2, the arithmetic operations—addition, subtraction, multiplication, and division—are defined for rational numbers by introducing corresponding operations for fractions. The properties of the rational number system are explored in the concluding Section 6.3. This section also discusses estimations and mental arithmetic, the use of calculators, and practical applications of the rational numbers.

The rational numbers have two new important properties that do not hold in the integers. First, *the rational numbers are closed under division.* For example, the equation $3x = 2$ has no solution in the integers. However, the division $2 \div 3$ is defined in the rational numbers, so the equation has the solution $x = \frac{2}{3}$. The second new property is called the *density property of the rational numbers:* between any two rational numbers there are infinitely many more rational numbers. For example, between 0 and 1 there are no integers, but the rational numbers $\frac{1}{2}, \frac{2}{3}, \frac{1}{5}, \frac{4}{17}$ and infinitely many others lie between 0 and 1. These new properties bring powerful new tools to solving problems in both the mathematical and the real world.

6.1 The Basic Concepts of Fractions and Rational Numbers

The whole numbers, as suggested by the word "whole," arise most often in *counting* problems, where the units or objects being counted cannot be subdivided into smaller parts. For example, Earth has one moon and Mars has two moons, but no planet can have some number of moons between one and two. If Earth's moon were to split into two parts, we would have two moons! In many situations, however, the objects or quantities of interest can be meaningfully subdivided. For example, when just one cookie remains, two young children may well display a good understanding of what "one half" of a cookie is all about.

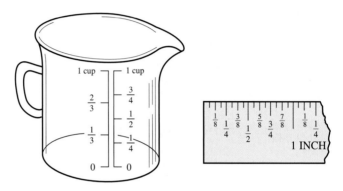

Figure 6.1

Fractions are used on measuring cups and rulers to indicate subdivisions of the basic unit.

Fractions were first introduced in *measurement* problems, to express a quantity that is less than a whole unit. Indeed, the word "fraction" comes from the Latin word *fractio,* meaning "the act of breaking into pieces." Figure 6.1 shows a measuring cup and a ruler, two common items on which fractions appear.

Fractions may be used to indicate capacity, length, weight, area, or indeed any quantity for which it is sensible to subdivide the fundamental unit of measure into any number of equal-sized parts. To interpret the meaning of any fraction $\dfrac{a}{b}$, we must:

- agree on the **unit** (for example, the unit is a cup, an inch, the area of the hexagon in a set of pattern blocks, and so on);
- understand that the unit is **subdivided in b parts of equal size;** and
- understand that we are considering a **of the parts of the unit.**

The number b is called the **denominator** of the fraction, a word derived from the Latin *denominare,* meaning "namer." The number a is called the **numerator,** derived from the Latin *numeros,* meaning "number."

For example, suppose the unit is one pizza, as shown in Figure 6.2. The pizza has been divided into 8 parts and 3 parts have been consumed. Using fractions, we can say that $\dfrac{3}{8}$ of the pizza was eaten, and $\dfrac{5}{8}$ of the pizza remains.

The notion of a subdivided unit of measure motivates the following formal definition of a fraction.

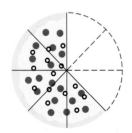

Figure 6.2

$\dfrac{3}{8}$ *of the pizza has been eaten and* $\dfrac{5}{8}$ *remains*

Hagar The Horrible   Dik Browne

DEFINITION *Fractions*

A **fraction** is an ordered pair of integers a and b, $b \neq 0$, written $\dfrac{a}{b}$ or a/b. The integer a is

called the **numerator** of the fraction, and the integer b is called the **denominator** of the
fraction.

This definition, it should be noticed, permits the numerator or denominator to be a nega-

tive integer. For example, $\dfrac{-3}{-8}, \dfrac{-4}{12}, \dfrac{31}{-4}, \dfrac{0}{1}$ are all fractions according to the definition just

given. Both negative and positive integers are allowed to ensure that additive inverses exist
in the rational number system Q.

Any integer m is viewed as the fraction $\dfrac{m}{1}$. Usually the denominator 1 is not writ-

ten explicitly. For example, we write 3 instead of $\dfrac{3}{1}$.

Models for Fractions

Several physical and pictorial models are useful in the elementary school classroom to illustrate fraction concepts. These include colored regions, fraction strips, and
the fraction number line. These models foster the development of deep understanding,
as distinct from formulas and rules of calculation that are devoid of meaning. Any
model must make three things clear: What is the unit? How many parts (the denominator)
has the unit been divided into? How many of these parts are under consideration (the
numerator)?

Colored Regions

A shape is chosen to represent the unit and is then subdivided into subregions of
equal size. A fraction is visualized by coloring some of the subregions. Three examples are
shown in Figure 6.3. Colored region models are sometimes called **area** models.

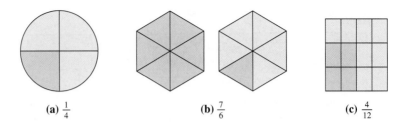

Figure 6.3
Some colored region models
for fractions

(a) $\frac{1}{4}$ (b) $\frac{7}{6}$ (c) $\frac{4}{12}$

The Set Model

The unit is a finite set of objects, U, divided naturally into $n(U)$ parts by its elements. Each subset A of U corresponds to the fraction $\frac{n(A)}{n(U)}$. For example, the set of 10 apples shown in Figure 6.4 contains a subset of 3 which are wormy. Therefore, we would say that $\frac{3}{10}$ of the apples are wormy. In Chapter 9 we will see that the set model of fractions is particularly useful in probability. An apple drawn at random from the ten apples has a $\frac{3}{10}$ probability of being wormy.

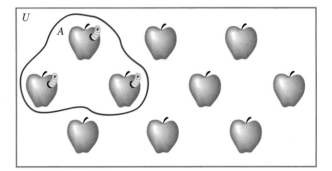

Figure 6.4

The set model depicts that $\frac{3}{10}$

of the apples are wormy.

Fraction Strips

Here the unit is defined by a rectangular strip of cardstock. A fraction, such as $\frac{3}{6}$, is modeled by shading 3 of 6 equally sized subrectangles of the card. Sample fraction strips are shown in Figure 6.5. A set of fraction strips typically contains strips for the denominators 1, 2, 3, 4, 6, 8, and 12.

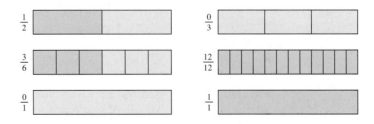

Figure 6.5
Examples of fractions modeled
by fraction strips

The Number Line Model

Once the points corresponding to 0 and 1 are assigned on a number line, all of the points corresponding to the integers are determined. A fraction such as $\frac{5}{4}$ is assigned to a point along the number line by subdividing the unit interval into 4 equal parts, and then counting off 5 of these lengths to the right of 0. Typical fractions are shown in Figure 6.6. It should be noticed that the same distance from 0 can be named by different fractions. For example $\frac{1}{2}$ and $\frac{2}{4}$ both correspond to the same distance. The number line model has the advantage of allowing negative fractions such as $-\frac{3}{4}$ to be visualized.

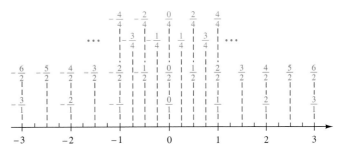

Figure 6.6
Fractions on the number line model

from The NCTM Principles and Standards

Reasoning and Problem Solving with Fractions in Grades 3–5

With the grounding students have developed in the meaning and relationships of fractions and decimals, they can begin to solve a variety of problems involving familiar fractions and decimals. At these grades, the emphasis is not on developing general procedures to solve all fraction problems but on developing solutions based on students' sense of number and using area and number line models. For example, in a fifth-grade class, students worked on this problem: Jamal invited 7 of his friends to lunch on Saturday. He thinks that each of the 8 people will eat $1\frac{1}{2}$ sandwiches. How many sandwiches should he make? Students might draw a picture and count up the number of sandwiches or might use reasoning based on their knowledge of number and operations: That would be 8 whole sandwiches and 8 half sandwiches; since two halves make a whole sandwich, the 8 halves will make 4 more sandwiches, so Jamal needs to make 12 sandwiches. Students should also use their knowledge of fraction relationships to estimate a reasonable result (e.g., $\frac{1}{3} + \frac{2}{5}$ must be less than 1 since both fractions are less than one half).

Equivalent Fractions

In Figure 6.7, the fraction strip representing $\frac{2}{3}$ is further subdivided by the vertical dashed lines to show that $\frac{4}{6}, \frac{6}{9}$, and $\frac{8}{12}$ are other fractions which express the *same* shaded portion of a whole strip.

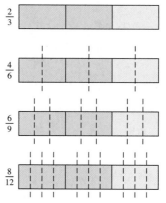

Figure 6.7
The fraction strip model showing that
$\frac{2}{3}, \frac{4}{6}, \frac{6}{9}$, *and* $\frac{8}{12}$ *are equivalent fractions*

Fractions that express the same quantity are called **equivalent fractions.** The equality symbol, $=$, is used to signify that fractions are equivalent, so we write

$$\frac{2}{3} = \frac{4}{6} = \frac{6}{9} = \frac{8}{12}.$$

The number of additional dashed lines between each vertical pair of solid lines shown in Figure 6.6 can be increased arbitrarily; therefore,

$$\frac{2}{3} = \frac{2 \cdot n}{3 \cdot n}$$

for $n = 1, 2, \ldots$. In this way, beginning with one fraction $\frac{a}{b}$, an infinite list, $\frac{2a}{2b}, \frac{3a}{3b}, \frac{4a}{4b}, \ldots$, of equivalent fractions is obtained.

In summary, we have the following important property.

PROPERTY   *The Fundamental Law of Fractions*

Let $\frac{a}{b}$ be a fraction. Then

$$\frac{a}{b} = \frac{an}{bn}, \text{ for any integer } n \neq 0.$$

Equivalent fractions can also be obtained by dividing both the numerator and denominator by a common factor. For example, the numerator and denominator of $\dfrac{35}{21}$ are each divisible by 7, so by the fundamental law

$$\frac{35}{21} = \frac{5 \cdot 7}{3 \cdot 7} = \frac{5}{3}$$

Now suppose we are given two fractions, say $\dfrac{3}{12}$ and $\dfrac{2}{8}$, and wish to know if they are equivalent. From the fundamental law of fractions we know that

$$\frac{3}{12} = \frac{3 \cdot 8}{12 \cdot 8} = \frac{24}{96} \quad \text{and} \quad \frac{2}{8} = \frac{2 \cdot 12}{8 \cdot 12} = \frac{24}{96}.$$

Thus, $\dfrac{3}{12}$ and $\dfrac{2}{8}$ are equivalent fractions. More generally, two given fractions $\dfrac{a}{b}$ and $\dfrac{c}{d}$ are respectively equivalent to $\dfrac{ad}{bd}$ and $\dfrac{bc}{bd}$. These are equivalent if, and only if, the numerators are equal, so we get the following theorem.

THEOREM   *A Characterization of Equivalent Fractions*

The fractions $\dfrac{a}{b}$ and $\dfrac{c}{d}$ are **equivalent** if, and only if, $ad = bc$.

EXAMPLE   6.1

Showing the Equivalence of Fractions

(a)   Show that $\dfrac{6}{14} = \dfrac{9}{21}$.

(b)   Show that $\dfrac{-23}{47} = \dfrac{2231}{-4559}$.

(c)   Find m if $\dfrac{m}{6} = \dfrac{10}{15}$.

(d)   Find *all* fractions that are equivalent to $\dfrac{2}{3}$.

Solution

(a)   Since $6 \cdot 21 = 126 = 9 \cdot 14$, $\dfrac{6}{14} = \dfrac{9}{21}$ by the preceding theorem.

(b)   Using a calculator (or paper and pencil), $(-23) \cdot (-4559) = 104{,}857$ and $2231 \cdot 47 = 104{,}857$.

(c) $\dfrac{m}{6} = \dfrac{10}{15}$ if, and only if, $m \cdot 15 = 10 \cdot 6$. Thus, $m = 60 \div 15 = 4$.

(d)   Suppose $\dfrac{2}{3} = \dfrac{a}{b}$. Then $2b = 3a$. Since 3 is a factor of $3a$, 3 must also be a factor of $2b$. Since 3 is not a factor of 2, it must be a factor of b, so $b = 3 \cdot n$

for some integer n. This gives us $3a = 2(3 \cdot n)$, so $a = 2 \cdot n$. This shows that any fraction $\dfrac{a}{b}$ equivalent to $\dfrac{2}{3}$ can be written as $\dfrac{2 \cdot n}{3 \cdot n}$ for some integer n.

Altogether, the set of fractions equivalent to $\dfrac{2}{3}$ is

$$\left\{ \cdots, \frac{-6}{-9}, \frac{-4}{-6}, \frac{-2}{-3}, \frac{2}{3}, \frac{4}{6}, \frac{6}{9}, \cdots \right\}.$$

Fractions in Simplest Form

Often it is preferable to use the simplest equivalent form of a fraction instead of a more complicated fraction. For example, it may be best to use $\dfrac{2}{3}$ instead of $\dfrac{400}{600}$, and to use $\dfrac{-3}{4}$ instead of $\dfrac{75}{-100}$.

Here is the definition of a fraction in **simplest** or **reduced form** or in **lowest terms.** The term *reduced* is best avoided, since this mistakenly suggests a "reduced" fraction is smaller than the unreduced one.

DEFINITION *Fractions in Simplest Form*

A fraction $\dfrac{a}{b}$ is in **simplest form** if a and b have no common divisor larger than 1 and b is positive.

There are several ways to determine the simplest form of a fraction $\dfrac{a}{b}$.

Method 1. Divide successively by common factors.   Suppose we want to write $\dfrac{560}{960}$ in simplest form. Using the fundamental law of fractions, we successively divide both numerator and denominator by common factors. Since 560 and 960 are both divisible by 10, it follows that

$$\frac{560}{960} = \frac{56 \cdot 10}{96 \cdot 10} = \frac{56}{96}.$$

But both 56 and 96 are even (that is, divisible by 2), so

$$\frac{56}{96} = \frac{28 \cdot 2}{48 \cdot 2} = \frac{28}{48}.$$

Again, 28 and 48 are easily seen to be divisible by 4 so that

$$\frac{28}{48} = \frac{7 \cdot 4}{12 \cdot 4} = \frac{7}{12}.$$

Finally, since 7 and 12 have no common factor other than 1, $\dfrac{7}{12}$ is the simplest form of $\dfrac{560}{960}$. Indeed, one might quickly and efficiently carry out this simplification as here

$$\dfrac{\overset{\displaystyle 7}{\overset{28}{\cancel{560}}}}{\underset{12}{\underset{48}{\cancel{960}}}} \quad \text{or} \quad \dfrac{560}{960} = \dfrac{56}{96} = \dfrac{28}{48} = \dfrac{7}{12}$$

to obtain the desired result.

Method 2. Divide a and b by GCD(a, b). Using the ideas of Chapter 4, we determine that GCD(560, 960) = 80. Therefore, $\dfrac{560}{960} = \dfrac{7 \cdot 80}{12 \cdot 80} = \dfrac{7}{12}$.

Method 3. Divide by the common factors in the prime power representation of a and b. Using this method,

$$\dfrac{560}{960} = \dfrac{2^4 \cdot 5 \cdot 7}{2^6 \cdot 3 \cdot 5} = \dfrac{7}{2^2 \cdot 3} = \dfrac{7}{12}.$$

Method 4. Use a fraction calculator. On the *Math Explorer*, the fraction $\dfrac{560}{960}$ can be entered by pressing 560 $\boxed{/}$ 960. To simplify, pressing $\boxed{\text{Simp}}$ $\boxed{=}$ gives 280/480 in the display. Pressing $\boxed{x \bigcirc y}$ displays the common factor 2 that was divided into both 560 and 960. Pressing $\boxed{x \bigcirc y}$ returns 280/480 to the display, and $\boxed{\text{Simp}}$ $\boxed{=}$ gives 140/240, where a second factor of 2 has been divided out. Continuing the sequence $\boxed{\text{Simp}}$ $\boxed{=}$ three more steps gives the final result of 7/12. By making a list of the common factors, 2, 2, 2, 2, 5, the *Math Explorer* makes it easy to compute GCD (560, 960) = $2 \cdot 2 \cdot 2 \cdot 2 \cdot 5 = 80$.

EXAMPLE 6.2	**Simplifying Fractions**

Find the simplest form of each fraction.

(a) $\dfrac{240}{72}$ (b) $\dfrac{-450}{1500}$ (c) $\dfrac{294}{-84}$ (d) $\dfrac{399}{483}$.

Solution

(a) By Method 1, $\dfrac{240}{72} = \dfrac{120}{36} = \dfrac{60}{18} = \dfrac{10}{3}$, where the successive common factors 2, 2, and 6 were divided into the numerator and denominator.

(b) Since $1500 = 3 \cdot 450 + 150$ and $450 = 3 \cdot 150 + 0$, the Euclidean algorithm shows that GCD(450, 1500) = 150. Thus, by Method 2,

$$\dfrac{-450}{1500} = \dfrac{-3 \cdot 150}{10 \cdot 150} = \dfrac{-3}{10}.$$

(c) Using Method 3 this time, we find

$$\dfrac{294}{-84} = \dfrac{2 \cdot 3 \cdot 7^2}{(-2) \cdot 2 \cdot 3 \cdot 7} = \dfrac{7}{-2} = \dfrac{-7}{2}.$$

(d)   If 399 $\boxed{/}$ 483 is entered on the *Math Explorer,* then pressing $\boxed{\text{Simp}}$ $\boxed{=}$ repeatedly gives first 133/161 and next 19/23. Therefore $\dfrac{399}{483} = \dfrac{19}{23}$. The common factors are 3 and 7, so GCD(399, 483) = 3 · 7 = 21.

Common Denominators

When working with two fractions, it is important to know how they can be replaced with equivalent fractions with the *same* denominator. For example, $\dfrac{5}{8}$ and $\dfrac{7}{10}$ can each be replaced by equivalent fractions with the **common denominator** 8 · 10 = 80 so that

$$\frac{5}{8} = \frac{5 \cdot 10}{8 \cdot 10} = \frac{50}{80} \qquad \text{and} \qquad \frac{7}{10} = \frac{7 \cdot 8}{10 \cdot 8} = \frac{56}{80}.$$

In the same way any two fractions $\dfrac{a}{b}$ and $\dfrac{c}{d}$ can be rewritten with the common denominator $b \cdot d$, since $\dfrac{a}{b} = \dfrac{a \cdot d}{b \cdot d}$ and $\dfrac{c}{d} = \dfrac{c \cdot b}{d \cdot b}$.

It is sometimes worthwhile to find the common positive denominator which is as small as possible. Assuming $\dfrac{a}{b}$ and $\dfrac{c}{d}$ are in simplest form, we require a common denominator that is a multiple of both b and d. The least such common multiple is called the **least**

JUST FOR FUN

Playing Card Fractions

Shuffle an ordinary deck of playing cards, and deal them out face down into two hands of 26 cards each. For one of the hands, form the fraction $\dfrac{r}{b}$, where r is the number of red cards and b the number of black cards in the hand. Similarly, for the second hand, form the fraction $\dfrac{b'}{r'}$ where

b' and r' are the respective number of black and red cards in the second hand. What relationship holds between the two fractions $\dfrac{r}{b}$ and $\dfrac{b'}{r'}$? Try the experiment several times. Can you explain why it works?

common denominator and is the least common multiple of b and d. For the example $\dfrac{5}{8}$ and $\dfrac{7}{10}$, we would calculate LCM(8, 10) = 40, so 40 is the least common denominator. Therefore,

$$\frac{5}{8} = \frac{5 \cdot 5}{8 \cdot 5} = \frac{25}{40} \quad \text{and} \quad \frac{7}{10} = \frac{7 \cdot 4}{10 \cdot 4} = \frac{28}{40}.$$

The least common denominator can often be determined by mental arithmetic. Consider, for example, $\dfrac{5}{6}$ and $\dfrac{3}{8}$. With a little practice, it won't take long to notice that $4 \cdot 6 = 24$ and $3 \cdot 8 = 24$, and that 24 is the least common denominator.

EXAMPLE   6.3

Finding Common Denominators

Find equivalent fractions with a common denominator.

(a) $\dfrac{5}{6}$ and $\dfrac{1}{4}$

(b) $\dfrac{9}{8}$ and $\dfrac{-12}{7}$

(c) $\dfrac{14}{-16}$ and $\dfrac{11}{12}$

(d) $\dfrac{3}{4}, \dfrac{5}{8},$ and $\dfrac{2}{3}$

Solution

(a)   By mental arithmetic, the least common denominator of $\dfrac{5}{6}$ and $\dfrac{1}{4}$ is 12.

Therefore, $\dfrac{5}{6} = \dfrac{10}{12}$ and $\dfrac{1}{4} = \dfrac{3}{12}$. This can be shown with fraction strips.

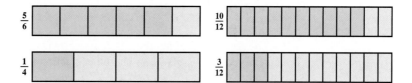

(b)   Since 8 and 7 have no common factors other than 1, $8 \cdot 7 = 56$ is the least common denominator:

$$\frac{9}{8} = \frac{9 \cdot 7}{8 \cdot 7} = \frac{63}{56}, \quad \frac{-12}{7} = \frac{-12 \cdot 8}{7 \cdot 8} = \frac{-96}{56}.$$

(c)   First we simplify $\dfrac{14}{-16}$ to $\dfrac{-7}{8}$. Since 8 and 12 have 4 as their greatest common divisor, we see that LCM(8, 12) = $8 \cdot 12$/GCD(8, 12) = 96/4 = 24. Thus,

$$\frac{14}{-16} = \frac{-7}{8} = \frac{-7 \cdot 3}{8 \cdot 3} = \frac{-21}{24}, \quad \frac{11}{12} = \frac{11 \cdot 2}{12 \cdot 2} = \frac{22}{24}.$$

(d)   With three fractions, it is still possible to use the product of all of the denominators as a common denominator. Since $4 \cdot 8 \cdot 3 = 96$, we have

$$\frac{3}{4} = \frac{3 \cdot 8 \cdot 3}{4 \cdot 8 \cdot 3} = \frac{72}{96}, \quad \frac{5}{8} = \frac{5 \cdot 4 \cdot 3}{8 \cdot 4 \cdot 3} = \frac{60}{96}, \quad \frac{2}{3} = \frac{2 \cdot 4 \cdot 8}{3 \cdot 4 \cdot 8} = \frac{64}{96}.$$

Alternatively, LCM(4, 8, 3) = 24, so we have

$$\frac{3}{4} = \frac{3 \cdot 6}{4 \cdot 6} = \frac{18}{24}, \quad \frac{5}{8} = \frac{5 \cdot 3}{8 \cdot 3} = \frac{15}{24}, \quad \frac{2}{3} = \frac{2 \cdot 8}{3 \cdot 8} = \frac{16}{24}.$$

This expresses the three fractions as equivalent fractions with the least common denominator.

Rational Numbers

We have seen that different fractions can nevertheless express the same amount or correspond to the same point on a number line. For example, the fraction strips in Figure 6.7 each show that two-thirds of a whole strip has been shaded, but the fraction which represents this amount can be any one of the choices $\frac{2}{3}, \frac{4}{6}, \frac{6}{9}, \ldots$. Similarly, in Figure 6.6 the single point on the number line at a distance of one half of a unit to the left of the origin can be expressed by any of the equivalent fractions $\frac{-1}{2}, \frac{1}{-2}, \frac{-2}{4}, \frac{2}{-4}, \ldots$.

Numbers such as "two-thirds" and "negative one half" which can be represented by fractions are examples of **rational numbers.** The following definition is suitable for use in the elementary school classroom.*

DEFINITION   *Rational Numbers*

A **rational number** is a number that can be represented by a fraction a/b, where a and b are integers, $b \neq 0$. Two rational numbers are **equal** if, and only if, they can be represented by equivalent fractions.

The set of rational numbers is denoted by Q. A rational number such as 3/4 can also be represented by 6/8, 30/40, or any other fraction that is equivalent to 3/4.

EXAMPLE   6.4   **Representing Rational Numbers**

How many different rational numbers are given in this list?

$$2/5, \quad 3, \quad -4/-10, \quad 39/13, \quad 7/4$$

Solution   Since $2/5 = -4/-10$ and $3 = 39/13$, there are three different rational numbers: 2/5, 3, and 7/4.

---

*In advanced mathematics a **rational number** is defined to be a set containing all of the fractions that are equivalent to some given fraction. The informal definition given above conveys the proper intuitive meaning of rational number however.

Ordering Fractions and Rational Numbers

By placing the fraction strips for $\frac{3}{4}$ and $\frac{5}{6}$ side by side, as shown in Figure 6.8(a), it becomes geometrically apparent that $\frac{3}{4}$ represents a smaller shaded portion of a whole strip than $\frac{5}{6}$. The comparison can be made even clearer by replacing the strips $\frac{3}{4}$ and $\frac{5}{6}$ by the equivalent strips $\frac{9}{12}$ and $\frac{10}{12}$, as shown in Figure 6.8(b). Since $9 < 10$, we see that $\frac{9}{12}$ is less than $\frac{10}{12}$, and therefore why $\frac{3}{4}$ is less than $\frac{5}{6}$.

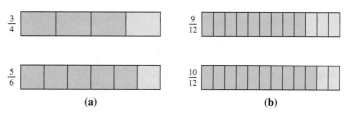

Figure 6.8
Showing $\frac{3}{4} < \frac{5}{6}$ and $\frac{9}{12} < \frac{10}{12}$ with fraction strips

More generally, let two rational numbers be represented by the fractions $\frac{a}{b}$ and $\frac{c}{d}$ with positive denominators b and d. These numbers can be compared by first rewriting them in equivalent form $\frac{ad}{bd}$ and $\frac{bc}{bd}$. Then $\frac{ad}{bd} < \frac{bc}{bd}$ if, and only if, $ad < bc$. This leads us to the following definition.

DEFINITION   *Inequality of Rational Numbers*

Let two rational numbers be represented by fractions $\frac{a}{b}$ and $\frac{c}{d}$, with b and d positive. Then $\frac{a}{b}$ is **less than** $\frac{c}{d}$, written $\frac{a}{b} < \frac{c}{d}$, if, and only if, $ad < bc$.

The corresponding relations, less than or equal to, $\leq$, greater than, $>$, and greater than or equal to, $\geq$, are defined similarly.

EXAMPLE   6.5   **Comparing Rational Numbers**

Replace the box by the proper relation $<$, $=$, $>$ for each pair of rational numbers.

(a) $\frac{3}{4} \ \square \ \frac{2}{5}$ (b) $\frac{15}{29} \ \square \ \frac{6}{11}$

(c) $\dfrac{2106}{7047} \,\square\, \dfrac{234}{783}$ **(d)** $\dfrac{-10}{13} \,\square\, \dfrac{22}{-29}$

Solution

(a) Since $3 \cdot 5 = 15 > 8 = 2 \cdot 4$, we have $\dfrac{3}{4} > \dfrac{2}{5}$.

(b) Since $15 \cdot 11 = 165 < 174 = 6 \cdot 29$, we have $\dfrac{15}{29} < \dfrac{6}{11}$.

(c) Using a calculator, $2106 \cdot 783 = 1648998 = 7047 \cdot 234$. Thus, the two fractions are equivalent: $\dfrac{2106}{7047} = \dfrac{234}{783}$.

(d) First write $\dfrac{22}{-29}$ as $\dfrac{-22}{29}$ so that its denominator is positive. Then, since $-10 \cdot 29 = -290 < -286 = -22 \cdot 13$, we conclude that $\dfrac{-10}{13} < \dfrac{22}{-29}$.

PROBLEM SET 6.1

Understanding Concepts

1. What fraction is represented by the darker shaded portion of the following figures?

   (a)
   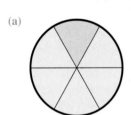

   (b)
   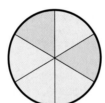

   (c)

   (d)
   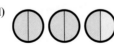
   Unit = one disc

   (e)

   (f)

2. Subdivide and shade the unit octagons shown to represent the given fraction.

   (a)   **(b)**   **(c)**   **(d)**

   $\dfrac{1}{8}$ $\dfrac{6}{8}$ $\dfrac{3}{4}$ $\dfrac{11}{8}$

3. For each lettered point on the number lines below, express its position by a corresponding fraction.

   (a)

   (b)
   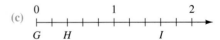

   (c)

   (d)
   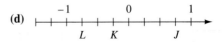

   (e)

4. Depict the fraction $\frac{4}{6}$ with the following models.

   (a) Colored region model   **(b)** Set model

   (c) Fraction strip model   **(d)** Number line model

5. Express the following quantities by a fraction placed in the blank space.

   (a) 20 minutes is _____ of an hour.

   (b) 30 seconds is _____ of a minute.

   (c) 5 days is _____ of a week.

   (d) 25 years is _____ of a century.

   (e) A quarter is _____ of a dollar.

   (f) 3 eggs is _____ of a dozen.

   (g) 2 feet is _____ of a yard.

   (h) 3 cups is _____ of a quart.

6. In Figure 6.7, fraction strips show that $\frac{2}{3}, \frac{4}{6}, \frac{6}{9}$, and $\frac{8}{12}$ are equivalent fractions. Use a similar drawing of fraction strips to show that $\frac{3}{4}, \frac{6}{8}$, and $\frac{9}{12}$ are equivalent fractions.

7. What equivalence of fractions is shown in these pairs of colored region models?

    (a)   **(b)**   **(c)**

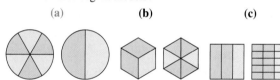

8. Find four different fractions equivalent to $\frac{4}{9}$.

9. Subdivide and mark the unit square on the right to illustrate that the given fractions are equivalent.

    (a)   **(b)**   **(c)**

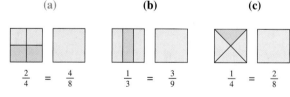

$\frac{2}{4} = \frac{4}{8}$ $\frac{1}{3} = \frac{3}{9}$ $\frac{1}{4} = \frac{2}{8}$

10. Fill in the missing integer to make the fractions equivalent.

   (a) $\frac{4}{5} = \frac{}{30}$ **(b)** $\frac{6}{9} = \frac{2}{}$

   (c) $\frac{-7}{25} = \frac{}{500}$ **(d)** $\frac{18}{3} = \frac{-6}{}$

11. Determine if each set of two fractions is equivalent by calculating equivalent fractions with a common denominator.

   (a) $\frac{18}{42}$ and $\frac{3}{7}$ **(b)** $\frac{18}{49}$ and $\frac{5}{14}$

   (c) $\frac{9}{25}$ and $\frac{140}{500}$ **(d)** $\frac{24}{144}$ and $\frac{32}{96}$

12. Determine which of these pairs of fractions are equivalent.

   (a) $\frac{78}{24}$ and $\frac{546}{168}$ **(b)** $\frac{243}{317}$ and $\frac{2673}{3487}$

   (c) $\frac{412}{-864}$ and $\frac{-308}{616}$

13. (a) Is it true that $\frac{4 \cdot 3}{9 \cdot 3} = \frac{12}{27}$?

   (b) Is it true that $\frac{4 \cdot 3}{9 \cdot 3} = \frac{4}{9}$?

   (c) Is it true that $\frac{4 + 3}{9 + 3} = \frac{7}{12}$?

   (d) Is it true that $\frac{4 + 3}{9 + 3} = \frac{4}{9}$?

14. Rewrite the following fractions in simplest form.

   (a) $\frac{84}{144}$ **(b)** $\frac{208}{272}$ (c) $\frac{-930}{1290}$ **(d)** $\frac{325}{231}$

15. Find the prime factorizations of the numerators and denominators of these fractions and use them to express the fractions in simplest form.

   (a) $\frac{96}{288}$ **(b)** $\frac{247}{-75}$ (c) $\frac{2520}{378}$

16. For each of these sets of fractions, determine equivalent fractions with a common denominator.

   (a) $\frac{3}{11}$ and $\frac{2}{5}$ **(b)** $\frac{5}{12}$ and $\frac{2}{3}$

   (c) $\frac{4}{3}, \frac{5}{8}$, and $\frac{1}{6}$ **(d)** $\frac{1}{125}$ and $\frac{-3}{500}$

17. For each of these determine equivalent fractions with the least common denominator.

   (a) $\frac{3}{8}$ and $\frac{5}{6}$ **(b)** $\frac{1}{7}, \frac{4}{5}$, and $\frac{2}{3}$

   (c) $\frac{17}{12}$ and $\frac{7}{32}$ **(d)** $\frac{17}{51}$ and $\frac{56}{42}$

18. Order the rational numbers from least to greatest in each part.

   (a) $\frac{2}{3}, \frac{7}{12}$ **(b)** $\frac{2}{3}, \frac{5}{6}$ (c) $\frac{5}{6}, \frac{29}{36}$

   (d) $\frac{-5}{6}, \frac{-8}{9}$ (e) $\frac{2}{3}, \frac{5}{6}, \frac{29}{36}, \frac{8}{9}$

19. Decide if each statement is *true* or *false*. Explain your reasoning in a brief paragraph.

   (a) There are infinitely many ways to replace two fractions with two equivalent fractions which have a common denominator.

(b) There is a unique least common denominator for a given pair of fractions.

(c) There is a least positive fraction.

(d) There are infinitely many fractions between 0 and 1.

20. For each, determine the set of all fractions that are equivalent to the given fraction.

(a) $\dfrac{3}{5}$ **(b)** $\dfrac{-7}{4}$ (c) 0   **(d)** $\dfrac{39}{65}$

21. How many different rational numbers are given by this list:

$$\dfrac{27}{36}, \quad 4, \quad \dfrac{21}{28}, \quad \dfrac{24}{6}, \quad \dfrac{3}{4}, \quad \dfrac{-8}{-2}.$$

Thinking Critically

22. What fraction represents the part of the whole region which has been shaded? Draw additional lines to make your answer visually clear. For example, $\dfrac{2}{6}$ of the regular hexagon on the left is shaded, since the entire hexagon can be subdivided into six congruent regions as shown on the right.

(a)   **(b)**

(c)

(d)

(e)

The right angle is at the center of the square.

(f)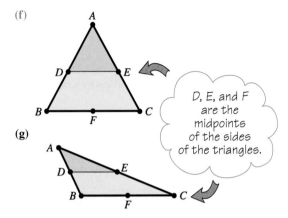

D, E, and F are the midpoints of the sides of the triangles.

(g)

23. Beginning with $a = 1$ and $b = 1$, the Fibonacci numbers 1, 1, 2, 3, 5, 8, 13, . . . are defined by adding the two previous numbers in the sequence to give the next number.

(a) Locate the first five Fibonacci fractions $\dfrac{1}{1}, \dfrac{2}{1}, \dfrac{3}{2}, \dfrac{5}{3}, \dfrac{8}{5}$ on a number line. Describe what pattern you observe. Does your pattern allow you to predict the location of the next Fibonacci fraction, $\dfrac{13}{8}$?

(b) Use the starting values $a = 1$ and $b = 3$ to form the Lucas numbers 1, 3, 4, 7, 11, 18, 29, . . . , and locate the first five Lucas fractions $\dfrac{3}{1}, \dfrac{4}{3}, \dfrac{7}{4}, \dfrac{11}{7}, \dfrac{18}{11}$. What pattern do you observe now? Can you predict the location of the next Lucas fraction, $\dfrac{29}{18}$?

(c) Repeat part (b) but for your own Fibonacci-like sequence beginning with any two positive integer values of a and b you wish to choose. Carefully describe what you see happening.

24. The **mediant** of two fractions $\dfrac{a}{b}$ and $\dfrac{c}{d}$ is $\dfrac{a + c}{b + d}$, where b and d are positive denominators. For example, the mediant of $\dfrac{1}{4}$ and $\dfrac{1}{2}$ is $\dfrac{1 + 1}{4 + 2} = \dfrac{2}{6} = \dfrac{1}{3}$. Notice that the mediant is between the two starting fractions, since $\dfrac{1}{4} < \dfrac{1}{3} < \dfrac{1}{2}$.

(a) Find the mediant of $\dfrac{3}{4}$ and $\dfrac{4}{5}$, and show it is between the two given fractions.

(b) Show that the mediant is always between the given two fractions; that is, show that if $\frac{a}{b} < \frac{c}{d}$, then
$$\frac{a}{b} < \frac{a + c}{b + d} < \frac{c}{d}.$$

(c) Carefully explain why the result of the property shown in part (b) guarantees there are infinitely many fractions between any two given fractions.

25. The row of Pascal's triangle (see Section 4 of Chapter 1) shown below has been separated by a vertical bar drawn between the 15 and the 20, with 3 entries of the row on the left of the bar and 4 entries on the right of the bar.

$$1 \quad 6 \quad 15 \mid 20 \quad 15 \quad 6 \quad 1$$

Notice that $\frac{15}{20} = \frac{3}{4}$. That is, the two fractions formed by the entries adjacent to the dividing bar and by the number of entries to the left and the right of the bar are equivalent fractions. Was this an accident, or is this a general property of Pascal's triangle? Investigate the property further, by placing the dividing bar in new locations and examining other rows of Pascal's triangle.

Thinking Cooperatively

The following two problems develop the concept of a fraction with pattern blocks, a popular and versatile manipulative that is used successfully in many elementary school classrooms. The following four shapes should be available to students working in groups of two or three:

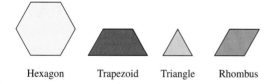

Hexagon   Trapezoid   Triangle   Rhombus

26. Use your pattern blocks to answer these questions.
  (a) Choose the hexagon as the unit. What fraction is each of the other three pattern blocks?
  (b) Choose the trapezoid as the unit. What fraction is each of the other three pattern blocks?
  (c) Choose the rhombus as the unit. What fraction is each of the other three pattern blocks?

27. **(a)** A hexagon and six triangles are used to form a six-pointed star. Choose the star as the unit. Next, form pattern block shapes corresponding to each of these fractions: $\frac{1}{6}, \frac{1}{4}, \frac{1}{3}, \frac{2}{3}, \frac{3}{4}$. Use as few pieces as you can for each shape.

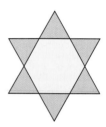

(b) Create a pattern block shape that will be defined as the unit and for which you may form other pattern block shapes corresponding to the fractions $\frac{1}{8}$ and $\frac{5}{8}$.

Making Connections

28. Francisco's pickup truck has a 24 gallon gas tank and an accurate fuel gauge. Estimate the number of gallons in the tank at these readings.

(a)   (b)   (c)

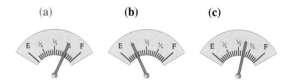

29. If 153 of the 307 graduating seniors go on to college, it is likely that a principal would claim that $\frac{1}{2}$ of the class is collegebound. Give simpler convenient fractions that approximately express the data in these situations.
  (a) Esteban is on page 310 of a 498 page novel. He has read _____ of the book.
  (b) Myra has saved \$73 toward the purchase of a \$215 plane ticket. She has saved _____ of the amount she needs.
  (c) Nine students in Ms. Evaldo's class of 35 students did perfect work on the quiz. _____ of the class scored 100% on the quiz.
  (d) The Math Club has sold 1623 of the 2400 raffle tickets. They have sold _____ of the available tickets.

30. Lakeside High won 19 of their season's 25 baseball games. Rival Shorecrest High School lost just 5 of the 21 games they played. Can Shorecrest claim to have had the better season? Explain.

31. **Basketball Math.** If a basketball player makes m free throws in n attempts, the rational number $\frac{m}{n}$ gives a measure of the player's skill at the foul line. Suppose, going into the playoffs, Carol and Joleen have the following records over the first and second halves of the regular season. For example, Carol made 38 free throws in 50 attempts during the first half of the season.

$\dfrac{m}{n}$	Carol	Joleen
Nov.–Jan.	$\dfrac{38}{50}$	$\dfrac{30}{40}$
Jan.–Mar.	$\dfrac{42}{70}$	$\dfrac{14}{24}$
Entire Season		

(a) Who was the more successful free throw shooter during the first half of the regular season? During the second half?

(b) Combine the data for each half-season. For example, Carol hit 80 free throws in 120 attempts. Which player had the higher success rate over the entire season?

(c) Suppose the data in the table represents the success rate of two drugs: drug C versus drug J. Which drug is best in each half of the 5 month trial period? Which drug looks most promising overall?

32. **Fractions in Probability.** If a card is picked at random from an ordinary deck of 52 playing cards, there are 4 ways it can be an ace, since it could be the ace of hearts, diamonds, clubs, or spades. To measure the chances of drawing an ace, it is common to give the probability as the rational number $\dfrac{4}{52}$. In general, if n equally likely outcomes are possible and m of these outcomes are successful for an event to occur, then the probability of the event is $\dfrac{m}{n}$. As another example, $\dfrac{5}{6}$ is the probability of rolling a single die and having more than one spot appear. Give fractions which express the probability of the following events:

(a) Getting a head in the flip of a fair coin.

(b) Drawing a face card from a deck of cards.

(c) Rolling an even number on a single die.

(d) Drawing a green marble from a bag which contains 20 red, 30 blue, and 25 green marbles.

(e) Drawing either a red or a blue marble from the bag of marbles described in part (d).

Communicating

33. **Fraction squares** are another popular manipulative for teaching the basic concepts of fractions. The unit is represented by a square. The unit can be divided into vertical or horizontal strips, or a combination of vertical and horizontal divisions are used to partition the unit square into congruent rectangles. Coloring or shading indicates the corresponding fraction. Here are some examples.

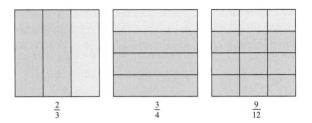

$$\frac{2}{3} \qquad \frac{3}{4} \qquad \frac{9}{12}$$

Write a report outlining how fraction squares can be used to illustrate these basic concepts:

(a) equivalence of fractions,

(b) common denominator,

(c) the fundamental law of fractions.

34. A set of classroom materials for children makes the following claim: "If you use the lowest common denominator to add fractions, your answer will be in lowest terms." Write an imaginary dialogue with a youngster who has questioned you (the teacher) about this statement. Anticipate what questions the child might ask, and form responses that you believe will help the child's understanding.

From State Student Assessments

35. (Minnesota, Grade 5) Four children drew fraction pictures. Which drawing is $\dfrac{2}{3}$ shaded? A. Aaron's B. Betsy's C. Carla's D. Daisy's

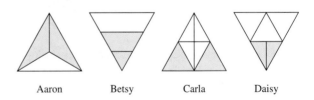

Aaron   Betsy   Carla   Daisy

For Review

36. The Fibonacci sequence 1, 1, 2, 3, 5, . . . , is formed by adding the two successive terms to obtain the next one, beginning with 1 and 1. Suppose subtraction is used in place of addition, to get

$$1, 1, 0, 1, -1, 2, -3, \ldots$$

(a) Obtain the next ten terms of this sequence.

(b) If you know $F_{24} = 46,368$ and $F_{25} = 75,025$ are the twenty-fourth and twenty-fifth Fibonacci numbers, what do you think the twenty-seventh and twenty-eighth numbers in the subtractive sequence are? Explain your reasoning.

37. (a) Find integers m and n which solve the equation $8m - 11n = 1$. It may be helpful to compare a list of multiples of 8 to a list of multiples of 11.

(b) Explain why it is not possible to find integers x and y which satisfy the equation $8x - 12y = 1$. (*Hint:* Is there an integer which divides the left side of the equation but cannot divide the right side?)

38. Find the digit d so that $49,d84$ is divisible by 24. (*Hint:* Use divisibility tests for 3 and 8.)

6.2 The Arithmetic of Rational Numbers

In this section we consider addition, subtraction, multiplication, and division in the set of rational numbers. The geometric and physical models of fractions serve to motivate the definition of each operation. The primary goal here is to learn how manipulatives and visualizations are used to convey the meaning of each arithmetic operation to children.

Addition of Rational Numbers

The sum of $\frac{3}{8}$ and $\frac{2}{8}$ is illustrated in Figure 6.9. The colored region and number-line models both show that $\frac{3}{8} + \frac{2}{8} = \frac{5}{8}$. The colored region visualization corresponds to the set model of addition, and the number line visualization corresponds to the measurement model of addition.

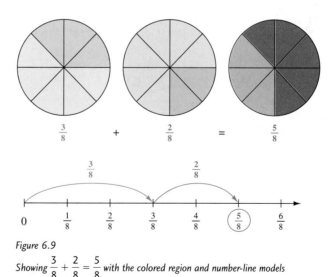

Figure 6.9

Showing $\frac{3}{8} + \frac{2}{8} = \frac{5}{8}$ *with the colored region and number-line models*

The models suggest that the sum of two rational numbers represented by fractions with a common denominator should be found by adding the two numerators. This motivates the following definition.

> **DEFINITION** *Addition of Rational Numbers*
>
> Let two rational numbers be represented by fractions $\frac{a}{b}$ and $\frac{c}{b}$ with a common denominator. Then their **sum** is the rational number given by
>
> $$\frac{a}{b} + \frac{c}{b} = \frac{a+c}{b}.$$

To add rational numbers represented by fractions with unlike denominators, we first rewrite the fractions with a common denominator. For example, to add $\frac{1}{4}$ and $\frac{2}{3}$, we rewrite them with 12 as a common denominator:

$$\frac{1}{4} = \frac{1 \cdot 3}{4 \cdot 3} = \frac{3}{12}, \qquad \frac{2}{3} = \frac{2 \cdot 4}{3 \cdot 4} = \frac{8}{12}.$$

According to the definition above, we then have

$$\frac{1}{4} + \frac{2}{3} = \frac{1 \cdot 3}{4 \cdot 3} + \frac{2 \cdot 4}{3 \cdot 4} = \frac{1 \cdot 3 + 2 \cdot 4}{4 \cdot 3} = \frac{3 + 8}{12} = \frac{11}{12}.$$

The procedure just followed can be modeled with fraction strips as shown in Figure 6.10.

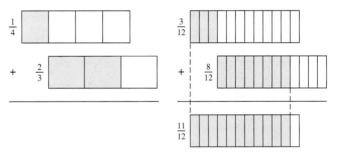

Figure 6.10

The fraction strip model showing $\dfrac{1}{4} + \dfrac{2}{3} = \dfrac{3}{12} + \dfrac{8}{12} = \dfrac{11}{12}$

The same procedure can be followed to add any two rational numbers $\frac{a}{b}$ and $\frac{c}{d}$. We have

$$\frac{a}{b} + \frac{c}{d} = \frac{a \cdot d}{b \cdot d} + \frac{c \cdot b}{d \cdot b} = \frac{ad + bc}{bd}.$$

Rewrite the fractions with a common denominator.

Add the numerators, retain the common denominator.

EXAMPLE 6.6

Adding Rational Numbers

Show the steps followed to compute these sums, as if you were showing a fifth grader.

(a) $\dfrac{3}{10} + \dfrac{4}{7}$

(b) $\dfrac{3}{8} + \dfrac{-7}{24}$

(c) $\left(\dfrac{3}{4} + \dfrac{5}{6}\right) + \dfrac{2}{3}$

(d) $\dfrac{3}{4} + \left(\dfrac{5}{6} + \dfrac{2}{3}\right)$

Solution

(a) $\dfrac{3}{10} + \dfrac{4}{7} = \dfrac{3 \cdot 7}{10 \cdot 7} + \dfrac{4 \cdot 10}{7 \cdot 10} = \dfrac{21}{70} + \dfrac{40}{70} = \dfrac{61}{70}$

(b) $\dfrac{3}{8} + \dfrac{-7}{24} = \dfrac{3 \cdot 24}{8 \cdot 24} + \dfrac{8 \cdot (-7)}{8 \cdot 24} = \dfrac{72}{192} + \dfrac{-56}{192} = \dfrac{72 - 56}{192} = \dfrac{16}{192}$

A better method is to use the least common denominator. Thus, $\dfrac{3}{8} + \dfrac{-7}{24} =$

$\dfrac{3 \cdot 3}{8 \cdot 3} + \dfrac{-7}{24} = \dfrac{9}{24} + \dfrac{-7}{24} = \dfrac{2}{24}$. To see that the two answers are equivalent we rewrite each fraction in simplest form:

$$\dfrac{16}{192} = \dfrac{8}{96} = \dfrac{4}{48} = \dfrac{1}{12}, \quad \dfrac{2}{24} = \dfrac{1}{12}.$$

(c) The parentheses tell us to compute first

$$\dfrac{3}{4} + \dfrac{5}{6} = \dfrac{9}{12} + \dfrac{10}{12} = \dfrac{19}{12}$$

Then,

$$\left(\dfrac{3}{4} + \dfrac{5}{6}\right) + \dfrac{2}{3} = \dfrac{19}{12} + \dfrac{2}{3} = \dfrac{19}{12} + \dfrac{8}{12} = \dfrac{19 + 8}{12} = \dfrac{27}{12},$$

which simplifies to $\dfrac{9}{4}$ when written in simplest form.

(d) The sum in parentheses is

$$\dfrac{5}{6} + \dfrac{2}{3} = \dfrac{5}{6} + \dfrac{4}{6} = \dfrac{9}{6} = \dfrac{3}{2}.$$

Then $\dfrac{3}{4} + \left(\dfrac{5}{6} + \dfrac{2}{3}\right) = \dfrac{3}{4} + \dfrac{3}{2} = \dfrac{3}{4} + \dfrac{6}{4} = \dfrac{9}{4}.$

Parts (c) and (d) of Example 6.6 show that

$$\left(\dfrac{3}{4} + \dfrac{5}{6}\right) + \dfrac{2}{3} = \dfrac{3}{4} + \left(\dfrac{5}{6} + \dfrac{2}{3}\right),$$

since each side represents the rational number $\dfrac{9}{4}$. This result is a particular example of the associative property for the addition of rational numbers. The properties of the arithmetic operations on the rational numbers will be explored in the next section.

Proper Fractions and Mixed Numbers

The sum of a natural number and a fraction is most often written as a **mixed number.** For example, $2 + \frac{3}{4}$ is written $2\frac{3}{4}$ and is read "two and three quarters." It is important to realize that it is the addition symbol $+$ which is suppressed, since the common notation xy for multiplication might suggest, incorrectly, that $2\frac{3}{4}$ is $2 \cdot \frac{3}{4}$. Thus, $2\frac{3}{4} = 2 + \frac{3}{4}$, not $\frac{6}{4}$.

A mixed number can always be rewritten in the standard form $\frac{a}{b}$ of a fraction. For example,

$$2\frac{3}{4} = 2 + \frac{3}{4} = \frac{8}{4} + \frac{3}{4} = \frac{11}{4}.$$

Mixed numbers and their equivalent forms as a fraction can be visualized this way:

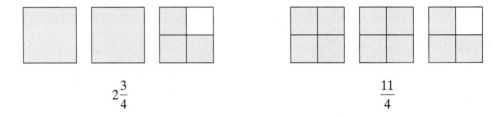

$$2\frac{3}{4} \qquad\qquad\qquad \frac{11}{4}$$

Since $A\frac{b}{c} = \frac{Ac}{c} + \frac{b}{c} = \frac{Ac + b}{c}$, we see that it is an easy calculation to write a mixed number as a fraction: $A\frac{b}{c} = \frac{Ac + b}{c}$.

A fraction $\frac{a}{b}$ for which $0 \le |a| < b$ is called a **proper fraction.** For example, $\frac{2}{3}$ is a proper fraction, but $\frac{3}{2}, \frac{-8}{5}$, and $\frac{6}{6}$ are not proper fractions. It is common, though not necessary, to rewrite fractions which are not proper as mixed numbers. For example, to express $\frac{439}{19}$ as a mixed number we first use the division algorithm (division with remainder) to find that $439 = 23 \cdot 19 + 2$. Then

$$\frac{439}{19} = \frac{23 \cdot 19 + 2}{19} = \frac{23}{1} + \frac{2}{19} = 23 + \frac{2}{19} = 23\frac{2}{19}.$$

In mixed number form, it is obvious that $23\frac{2}{19}$ is just slightly larger than 23; this fact was not as evident in the original fraction form $\frac{439}{19}$. Nevertheless, it is perfectly acceptable to express rational numbers as "improper" fractions. In general, the fractional form $\frac{a}{b}$ is the more convenient form for arithmetic and algebra, and the mixed number form is easiest to understand for practical applications. For example, it would be more common to buy $2\frac{1}{4}$ yards of material than to request $\frac{9}{4}$ yards.

EXAMPLE 6.7 | **Working with Mixed Numbers**

(a) Give an improper fraction for $3\frac{17}{120}$.

(b) Give a mixed number for $\frac{355}{113}$.

(c) Give a mixed number for $\frac{-15}{4}$.

(d) Compute $2\frac{3}{4} + 4\frac{2}{5}$.

Solution

(a) $3\frac{17}{120} = \frac{3}{1} + \frac{17}{120} = \frac{3 \cdot 120 + 1 \cdot 17}{120} = \frac{360 + 17}{120} = \frac{377}{120}$.

This rational number was given by Claudius Ptolemy around A.D. 150 to approximate π, the ratio of the circumference of a circle to its diameter. It has better accuracy than $3\frac{1}{7}$, the value proposed by Archimedes in about 240 B.C.

(b) Using the division algorithm, $355 = 3 \cdot 113 + 16$. Therefore,

$$\frac{355}{113} = \frac{3 \cdot 113 + 16}{113} = \frac{3}{1} + \frac{16}{113} = 3\frac{16}{113}$$

which corresponds to a point somewhat to the right of 3 on the number line. The value $\frac{355}{113}$ was used around A.D. 480 in China to approximate π; as a decimal it is correct to six places!

(c) $\frac{-15}{5} = \frac{-(3 \cdot 4 + 3)}{4} = -\left(3 + \frac{3}{4}\right) = -3\frac{3}{4}$.

(d) $2\frac{3}{4} + 4\frac{2}{5} = 2 + 4 + \frac{3}{4} + \frac{2}{5} = 6 + \frac{15}{20} + \frac{8}{20} = 6 + \frac{23}{20} = 7\frac{3}{20}$.

Subtraction of Rational Numbers

Figure 6.11 shows how the take-away, measurement, and missing-addend conceptual models of the subtraction operation can be illustrated with colored regions, the number line, and fraction strips. In each case we see that $\frac{7}{6} - \frac{3}{6} = \frac{4}{6}$.

Take-away model:

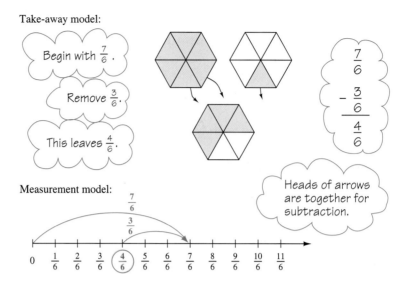

Measurement model:

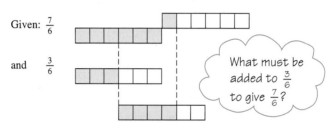

Heads of arrows are together for subtraction.

Missing-addend model:

Given: $\frac{7}{6}$

and $\frac{3}{6}$

What must be added to $\frac{3}{6}$ to give $\frac{7}{6}$?

Since $\frac{3}{6} + \frac{4}{6} = \frac{7}{6}$, then $\frac{7}{6} - \frac{3}{6} = \frac{4}{6}$.

Figure 6.11

Models that show $\dfrac{7}{6} - \dfrac{3}{6} = \dfrac{4}{6}$

Subtraction of whole numbers and integers was defined on the basis of the missing-addend approach, which emphasizes that subtraction is the inverse operation to addition. Subtraction of rational numbers is defined in the same way.

> **DEFINITION** *Subtraction of Rational Numbers*
>
> Let $\dfrac{a}{b}$ and $\dfrac{c}{d}$ be rational numbers. Then $\dfrac{a}{b} - \dfrac{c}{d} = \dfrac{e}{f}$ if, and only if, $\dfrac{a}{b} = \dfrac{c}{d} + \dfrac{e}{f}$.

For rational numbers expressed by fractions $\dfrac{a}{b}$ and $\dfrac{c}{b}$ with the same denominator, the formula $\dfrac{a}{b} - \dfrac{c}{b} = \dfrac{a-c}{b}$ follows easily from the definition. For fractions with unlike denominators, it is necessary first to find a common denominator.

The hieroglyphic numerals of ancient Egypt were described in Chapter 3. Fractions were likewise expressed with hieroglyphs. For example, the symbol ⬭ originally indicated $\frac{1}{320}$ of a bushel, but later it came to denote a fraction in general. Here are some hieroglyphic fractions and their modern equivalents:

Some common fractions were denoted by special symbols:

With $\frac{2}{3}$ as an exception, Egyptian fractions were written as sums of fractions with numerator 1 and distinct denominators, though no summation sign appeared. For example, $\frac{2}{5}$ would be written

$\frac{1}{3} + \frac{1}{15}$

With more effort the Egyptians expressed $\frac{7}{29}$ as

$$\frac{1}{6} + \frac{1}{24} + \frac{1}{58} + \frac{1}{87} + \frac{1}{232}.$$

The Egyptians assumed every fraction could be written as a sum of unit numerator fractions, but no record has been found that justifies this assumption. In A.D. 1202, Leonardo of Pisa—otherwise known as Fibonacci—gave the first proof of this theorem: *Every fraction between 0 and 1 can be written as a sum of distinct fractions with numerator 1.*

EXAMPLE   6.8   **Subtracting Rational Numbers**

Show, as you might to a student, the steps to compute these differences.

(a) $\dfrac{4}{5} - \dfrac{2}{3}$ (b) $\dfrac{103}{24} - \dfrac{-35}{16}$ (c) $4\dfrac{1}{4} - 2\dfrac{2}{3}$

Solution

(a) $\dfrac{4}{5} - \dfrac{2}{3} = \dfrac{4\cdot3}{5\cdot3} - \dfrac{5\cdot2}{5\cdot3} = \dfrac{12}{15} - \dfrac{10}{15} = \dfrac{12-10}{15} = \dfrac{2}{15}$

(b) Since LCM(24, 16) = 48, the least common denominator, 48, can be used to give

$$\frac{103}{24} - \frac{-35}{16} = \frac{206}{48} - \frac{-105}{48} = \frac{206 - (-105)}{48} = \frac{311}{48}.$$

(c) $4\dfrac{1}{4} - 2\dfrac{2}{3} = \dfrac{17}{4} - \dfrac{8}{3} = \dfrac{17\cdot3}{4\cdot3} - \dfrac{4\cdot8}{4\cdot3} = \dfrac{51}{12} - \dfrac{32}{12} = \dfrac{51-32}{12} = \dfrac{19}{12} = 1\dfrac{7}{12}$

Alternatively, subtraction of mixed numbers can follow the familiar regrouping algorithm:

$$\begin{array}{r} 4\frac{1}{4} \\ -\,2\frac{2}{3} \\ \hline \end{array} \quad \Rightarrow \quad \begin{array}{r} 4\frac{3}{12} \\ -\,2\frac{8}{12} \\ \hline \end{array} \quad \Rightarrow \quad \begin{array}{r} 3\frac{15}{12} \\ -\,2\frac{8}{12} \\ \hline 1\frac{7}{12} \end{array}$$

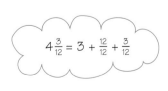

$4\frac{3}{12} = 3 + \frac{12}{12} + \frac{3}{12}$

This can also be visualized with the area model of fractions.

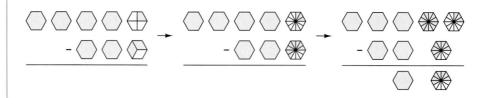

Multiplication of Rational Numbers

In earlier chapters, the array model provided a useful visualization of multiplication for both the whole numbers and the integers. The array model also serves well to motivate the definition of multiplication of rational numbers.

In Figure 6.12, we see that $2 \cdot 3 = 6$, since shading a 2 by 3 rectangle covers exactly 6 unit (that is, 1 by 1) squares. In (b), the vertical dashed lines divide the unit squares into congruent halves, and $2 \cdot \dfrac{3}{2} = \dfrac{6}{2}$ since 6 half-units form the shaded rectangle. We also see that $2 \cdot \dfrac{3}{2} = \dfrac{3}{2} + \dfrac{3}{2} = \dfrac{6}{2}$, and so multiplication as repeated addition is retained when a whole number multiplies a rational number. Parts (c) and (d) of Figure 6.12 show that we can just as well multiply a rational number times either a whole number or another fraction.

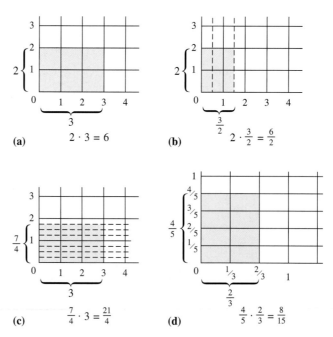

Figure 6.12

Extending the array model of multiplication to fractions

In general, if $\dfrac{a}{b}$ and $\dfrac{c}{d}$ are any two fractions, each unit square is divided into bd congruent rectangles and ac of the small rectangles are shaded. This shows that $\dfrac{ac}{bd}$ units are shaded. Thus, extending the array model of multiplication to fractions leads to the following definition.

DEFINITION *Multiplication of Rational Numbers*

Let $\dfrac{a}{b}$ and $\dfrac{c}{d}$ be rational numbers. Then their **product** is given by

$$\frac{a}{b} \cdot \frac{c}{d} = \frac{ac}{bd}.$$

Often a product, say $\dfrac{4}{5} \cdot \dfrac{2}{3}$, is read as four-fifths "of" two-thirds. The association between "of" and "times" is natural for multiplication by whole numbers and extends naturally to multiplication by rational numbers. For example, "I'll buy three *of* the half-gallon size bottles" is equivalent to buying $3 \cdot \dfrac{1}{2} = \dfrac{3}{2} = 1\dfrac{1}{2}$ gallons.

EXAMPLE 6.9 | **Calculating Products of Rational Numbers**

Practice your fraction multiplication skills with these examples. Look for ways to shorten your work, and express each answer in simplest form.

(a) $\dfrac{5}{8} \cdot \dfrac{2}{3}$ **(b)** $\dfrac{56}{88} \cdot \dfrac{-4}{7}$ **(c)** $3\dfrac{1}{7} \cdot 5\dfrac{1}{4}$

Solution

It is useful to look for common factors in the numerator and denominator before doing any multiplications, applying the Fundamental Law of Fractions.

(a) $\dfrac{5}{8} \cdot \dfrac{2}{3} = \dfrac{5 \cdot 2}{8 \cdot 3} = \dfrac{5 \cdot 2}{2 \cdot 4 \cdot 3} = \dfrac{5}{4 \cdot 3} \cdot \dfrac{2}{2} = \dfrac{5}{12}$

(b) $\dfrac{56}{88} \cdot \dfrac{-4}{7} = \dfrac{56 \cdot (-4)}{88 \cdot 7} = \dfrac{7 \cdot 8 \cdot (-4)}{8 \cdot 11 \cdot 7} = \dfrac{-4}{11} \cdot \dfrac{7 \cdot 8}{8 \cdot 7} = \dfrac{-4}{11}$

(c) $3\dfrac{1}{7} \cdot 5\dfrac{1}{4} = \dfrac{22}{7} \cdot \dfrac{21}{4} = \dfrac{22 \cdot 21}{7 \cdot 4} = \dfrac{2 \cdot 11 \cdot 3 \cdot 7}{7 \cdot 2 \cdot 2} = \dfrac{11 \cdot 3}{2} \cdot \dfrac{2 \cdot 7}{7 \cdot 2} = \dfrac{33}{2}.$

EXAMPLE 6.10 | **Computing the Area and Cost of a Carpet**

The hallway in the Bateks' house is a rectangle 4 feet wide and 20 feet long; that is, in yards it measures $\dfrac{4}{3}$ yards by $\dfrac{20}{3}$ yards. What is the area of the carpet in square yards? Mrs. Batek wants to know how much she will pay to buy carpet priced at $18 per square yard.

Multiplying by a Fraction

7-3

▶ **Lesson Link** In the last lesson, you learned to multiply fractions and mixed numbers by whole numbers. Now you'll multiply fractions and mixed numbers by fractions. ◀

You'll Learn ...
■ to multiply a fraction by another fraction

... How It's Used
Consumers multiply fractions by fractions when calculating the price of an item with multiple discounts.

Explore **Multiplying by a Fraction**

Inner Sections

Materials: Colored pencils

Multiplying a Fraction by a Fraction

- Draw a rectangle. Divide it vertically into equal sections. There should be as many sections as the denominator of the first number.
- Divide the rectangle horizontally into equal sections. There should be as many sections as the denominator of the second number.
- Color in a number of vertical strips equal to the numerator in the first number.
- Use a different color to shade a number of horizontal strips equal to the numerator in the second number.
- Describe the area where both colors overlap.

$\frac{2}{5} \times \frac{3}{4} = \frac{6}{20}$

1. Model these problems.

a. $\frac{1}{2} \times \frac{1}{3}$ **b.** $\frac{1}{4} \times \frac{2}{5}$ **c.** $\frac{5}{6} \times \frac{2}{3}$

d. $\frac{2}{7} \times \frac{2}{7}$ **e.** $\frac{1}{5} \times \frac{3}{5}$ **f.** $\frac{1}{2} \times \frac{5}{8}$

2. Describe the pattern between the numerators in the problem and the numerator in the answer.

3. Describe the pattern between the denominators in the problem and the denominator in the answer.

4. Is your answer bigger or smaller than both of the fractions you started with? Why?

7-3 • Multiplying by a Fraction **375**

SOURCE: From *Scott Foresman – Addison Wesley Middle School Math Course 1*, p. 375, by Randall I. Charles et al. Copyright © 1999 Addison Wesley Longman, Inc.

Questions for the Teacher

1. The instructions for coloring the rectangle say "color in a number of vertical strips equal to the numerator in the first number." A student wonders what would happen if, when coloring the rectangle illustrating $\frac{2}{5} \times \frac{3}{4}$, the second and fourth strip were shaded yellow instead of the first and second strip. How would you respond?

2. What advantage is there to coloring the leftmost vertical strips and the lowermost horizontal strips?

3. On page 373 of the School Book, the students discovered that $3 \times 1\frac{7}{12} = 4\frac{3}{4}$. Since the answer is bigger than both the fractions being multiplied, a student is perplexed about how to answer Question 4 of the School Book page. How would you help the student out?

Solution

Since $\frac{4}{3} \cdot \frac{20}{3} = \frac{80}{9} = 8\frac{8}{9}$, the area is $8\frac{8}{9}$ square yards, or nearly 9 square yards. This can be seen in the diagram below, which shows the hallway divided into six full square yards, six $\frac{1}{3}$-square yard rectangular regions, and eight square regions which are each $\frac{1}{9}$ of a square yard. This gives the total area of $6 + \frac{6}{3} + \frac{8}{9} = 8\frac{8}{9}$ square yards. The cost of the carpet will be $8\frac{8}{9} \cdot 18 = 160$ dollars.

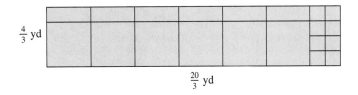

$\frac{4}{3}$ yd

$\frac{20}{3}$ yd

Division of Rational Numbers

As with division in whole numbers and integers, the missing-factor model is the basis for the definition of division of rational numbers.

DEFINITION *Division of Rational Numbers*

Let $\frac{a}{b}$ and $\frac{c}{d}$ be rational numbers, where $\frac{c}{d}$ is not zero. Then $\frac{a}{b} \div \frac{c}{d} = \frac{e}{f}$ if, and only if, $\frac{a}{b} = \frac{c}{d} \cdot \frac{e}{f}$.

This definition stresses that division is the inverse operation of multiplication. However, it continues to be important to understand division as repeated subtraction, and to be able to visualize the division operation with the measurement model. For example, the division $2\frac{1}{8} \div \frac{3}{4}$ answers the question "How many three-quarters are there in two and one-eighth?" This is the division concept necessary to solve the map reading problem in the next example.

EXAMPLE   6.11

Scale of a Map: Illustrating Division of Rational Numbers with a Measurement Model

Colton and Uniontown are $2\frac{1}{8}''$ apart on the map. The map is scaled so that $\frac{3}{4}''$ on the map corresponds to 1 mile of actual distance. How far is it between the two towns?

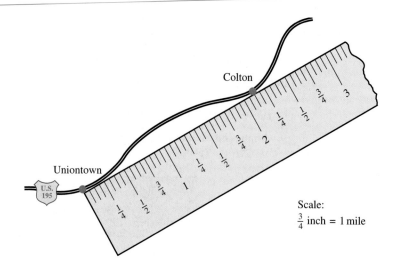

Colton

Uniontown

U.S.
195

Scale:
$\frac{3}{4}$ inch = 1 mile

Solution   Each $\frac{3''}{4}$ on the map represents 1 mile of distance. To find the number of miles between Uniontown and Colton, we must know how many segments of length $\frac{3''}{4}$ lie between the two points on the map.

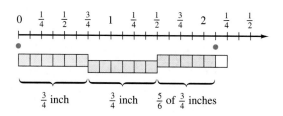

$\frac{3}{4}$ inch $\frac{3}{4}$ inch $\frac{5}{6}$ of $\frac{3}{4}$ inches

1 mile + 1 mile + $\frac{5}{6}$ of 1 mile = $2\frac{5}{6}$ miles

The figure shows that there are $1 + 1 + \frac{5}{6} = 2\frac{5}{6}$ segments of length $\frac{3''}{4}$ in a segment $2\frac{1''}{8}$ long. Thus it is $2\frac{5}{6}$ miles between Uniontown and Colton.

This example has shown us that

$$\frac{17}{8} \div \frac{3}{4} = 2\frac{5}{6} = \frac{17}{6} = \frac{17}{8} \cdot \frac{4}{3}.$$

This computation suggests that the quotient $\frac{a}{b} \div \frac{c}{d}$ can be computed by performing the related multiplication $\frac{a}{b} \cdot \frac{d}{c}$. To check that this is generally true, first notice that $\frac{c}{d} \cdot \left(\frac{a}{b} \cdot \frac{d}{c} \right) = \frac{c \cdot a \cdot d}{d \cdot b \cdot c} = \frac{a}{b}$. According to the definition of division, this is equivalent to $\frac{a}{b} \div \frac{c}{d} = \frac{a}{b} \cdot \frac{d}{c}$, so we have proved the following important theorem about the division of rational numbers.

INTO THE CLASSROOM

Charlotte Jenkins Discusses Addition and Subtraction of Fractions

I use paper plate activities to introduce adding and subtracting fractions with different denominators. To find $\frac{5}{8} + \frac{1}{4}$, I give each student two paper plates. I ask students to draw lines to divide one plate into fourths and the other into eighths. Then I have them cut the plates to join $\frac{1}{4}$ of one to $\frac{5}{8}$ of the other, and ask them to describe the result. To find $\frac{5}{8} - \frac{1}{4}$, I give each student one paper plate. I ask students to draw lines to divide the plate into eighths and shade five of the eighths. Then I have them cut $\frac{1}{4}$ of the plate from the shaded area and describe the shaded amount that is left. I have students repeat the activities to find other sums and differences.

SOURCE: *Scott Foresman–Addison Wesley Middle School Math Course 1 Teacher's Edition*, p. 320, © 1999 Addison Wesley Longman, Inc.

THEOREM   *An Algorithm for Division of Rational Numbers*

Let $\frac{a}{b}$ and $\frac{c}{d}$ be rational numbers where $\frac{c}{d}$ is not zero. Then $\frac{a}{b} \div \frac{c}{d} = \frac{a}{b} \cdot \frac{d}{c}$.

It is instructive to derive the algorithmic formula in alternative ways. For example, the formula follows easily by using common denominators in this way.

$$\frac{a}{b} \div \frac{c}{d} = \frac{ad}{bd} \div \frac{bc}{bd} = ad \div bc = \frac{ad}{bc} = \frac{a}{b} \cdot \frac{d}{c}$$

For obvious reasons the algorithm is called the **invert the divisor and multiply rule.** To "invert" $\frac{c}{d}$ means to form the rational number $\frac{d}{c}$, which is called the **reciprocal** of $\frac{c}{d}$.

DEFINITION   *Reciprocal of a Rational Number*

The **reciprocal** of a nonzero rational number $\frac{c}{d}$ is $\frac{d}{c}$.

Since

$$\frac{c}{d} \cdot \frac{d}{c} = \frac{c \cdot d}{d \cdot c} = 1,$$

$\dfrac{d}{c}$ is also known as the **multiplicative inverse** of $\dfrac{c}{d}$. The importance of the multiplicative inverse is investigated in Section 3 of this chapter.

Sometimes the invert and multiply rule is mistaken for a definition of division of fractions. This is unfortunate; the algorithm does not relate directly to any conceptual model of division, and division becomes a meaningless and unpleasant process of following abstract and seemingly arbitrary rules.

The algorithm for division tells us that the rational numbers are closed under division, since every quotient $\dfrac{a}{b} \div \dfrac{c}{d}$ with $c \neq 0$ defines the unique fraction $\dfrac{ad}{bc}$. The whole numbers are not closed under division. For example, 3 is not divisible by 8. On the other hand, if we view 3 and 8 as rational numbers, then we see that

$$3 \div 8 = \frac{3}{1} \div \frac{8}{1} = \frac{3 \cdot 1}{1 \cdot 8} = \frac{3}{8}.$$

In general, if a and b are any integers, with $b \neq 0$, then interpreting a and b as *rational numbers* we find that

$$a \div b = \frac{a}{b}.$$

This shows that extending the set of integers to the rational numbers gives us a set of numbers for which division is closed.

EXAMPLE 6.12

Dividing Rational Numbers

Show, as if you are working with a fifth grader, the steps to follow to compute these division problems.

(a) $\dfrac{3}{4} \div \dfrac{1}{8}$ (b) $\dfrac{-7}{4} \div \dfrac{2}{3}$ (c) $3 \div \dfrac{4}{3}$

(d) $39 \div 13$ (e) $13 \div 39$ (f) $4\dfrac{1}{6} \div 2\dfrac{1}{3}$

Solution

(a) $\dfrac{3}{4} \div \dfrac{1}{8} = \dfrac{3}{4} \cdot \dfrac{8}{1} = \dfrac{24}{4} = 6$ (b) $\dfrac{-7}{4} \div \dfrac{2}{3} = \dfrac{-7}{4} \cdot \dfrac{3}{2} = \dfrac{-21}{8}$

(c) $3 \div \dfrac{4}{3} = \dfrac{3}{1} \cdot \dfrac{3}{4} = \dfrac{9}{4}$ (d) $39 \div 13 = \dfrac{39}{1} \cdot \dfrac{1}{13} = \dfrac{39}{13} = 3$

(e) $13 \div 39 = \dfrac{13}{1} \cdot \dfrac{1}{39} = \dfrac{13}{39} = \dfrac{1}{3}$

(f) $4\dfrac{1}{6} \div 2\dfrac{1}{3} = \dfrac{25}{6} \div \dfrac{7}{3} = \dfrac{25}{6} \cdot \dfrac{3}{7} = \dfrac{25 \cdot 3}{6 \cdot 7} = \dfrac{25}{2 \cdot 7} = \dfrac{25}{14}$

In the next example, both the repeated-subtraction and missing-factor models are used to solve a real-life problem.

| EXAMPLE   6.13 | **Bottling Root Beer: A Division Problem** |

Bottling Root Beer: A Division Problem

Ari is making homemade root beer. The recipe he followed nearly fills a 5-gallon glass jug, and he estimates it contains $4\frac{3}{4}$ gallons of root beer. He is now ready to bottle his root beer. How many $\frac{1}{2}$ gallon bottles can he fill?

Solution

The repeated-subtraction approach. In the language of the repeated-subtraction model, the division problem $4\frac{3}{4} \div \frac{1}{2}$ is phrased in the form of a question: "How many $\frac{1}{2}$ gallons are in $4\frac{3}{4}$ gallons?" Since

$$4\frac{3}{4} = \left(\frac{1}{2} + \frac{1}{2} + \frac{1}{2} + \frac{1}{2} + \frac{1}{2} + \frac{1}{2} + \frac{1}{2} + \frac{1}{2} + \frac{1}{2} \right) + \left(\frac{1}{2} \right) \cdot \frac{1}{2}$$

$$= 9 \cdot \left(\frac{1}{2} \right) + \frac{1}{2} \cdot \frac{1}{2} = \left(9 + \frac{1}{2} \right) \cdot \frac{1}{2},$$

we see that there are $9\frac{1}{2}$ "halves" in $4\frac{3}{4}$. Thus, Ari can fill 9 half-gallon bottles, and half of another one. This is shown in the figure below. Ari will need 9 half-gallon bottles, and he will probably see if he can also find a quart bottle to use.

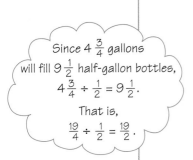

Since $4\frac{3}{4}$ gallons will fill $9\frac{1}{2}$ half-gallon bottles, $4\frac{3}{4} \div \frac{1}{2} = 9\frac{1}{2}$. That is, $\frac{19}{4} \div \frac{1}{2} = \frac{19}{2}$.

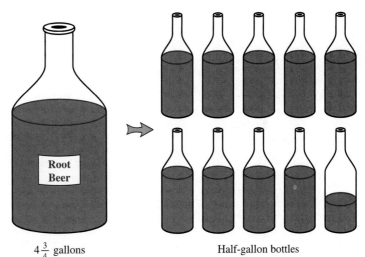

$4\frac{3}{4}$ gallons   Half-gallon bottles

The missing-factor approach. Let x denote the number of half-gallon bottles required, where x will be allowed to be a fraction since we expect some bottle may be only partially filled. We must then solve the equation

$$x \cdot \frac{1}{2} = 4\frac{3}{4},$$

since this is the missing-factor problem that is equivalent to the division problem $4\frac{3}{4} \div \frac{1}{2}$.

Since

$$4\frac{3}{4} = \frac{19}{4} = \frac{19}{2} \cdot \frac{1}{2},$$

we see that the missing factor is $x = \dfrac{19}{2} = 9\dfrac{1}{2}$.

Using a Fraction Calculator

Some calculators, such as the Texas Instrument *Math Explorer,* are capable of performing "rational arithmetic." That is, fractions can be added, subtracted, multiplied, and divided, with the result displayed as a fraction. For example, consider the expression

$$\left(2\frac{3}{4} + \frac{2}{3}\right) \div \left(\frac{4}{5} - \frac{1}{2}\right).$$

The entry string

| ON/AC | | (| 2 Unit 3 | / | 4 | + | 2 | / | 3 |) | ÷ | (| 4 | / | 5 | − | 1 | / | 2 |) | = |

yields the fractional answer 410/36. Pressing Simp   = expresses the answer in simplest form, 205/18. Pressing Ab/c then converts the fraction to mixed number form, 11 ⊔ 7/18, where ⊔ separates the units to the left from the fractional part at the right. Pressing F ↻ D gives the decimal number 11.388889 that approximates the fraction $11\dfrac{7}{18}$. The F ↻ D key switches the display from fraction to decimal form, and vice versa.

PROBLEM SET 6.2

Understanding Concepts

1. (a) What addition fact is illustrated by the following fraction strip model?

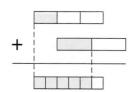

   (b) Illustrate $\dfrac{1}{6} + \dfrac{1}{4}$ with the fraction strip model.

   (c) Illustrate $\dfrac{2}{3} + \dfrac{3}{4}$ with the fraction strip model.

      (The sum will require two strips.)

2. Use the colored region model to illustrate these sums, with the unit given by a circular disc.

   (a) $\dfrac{2}{5} + \dfrac{6}{5}$ (b) $\dfrac{1}{4} + \dfrac{1}{2}$ (c) $\dfrac{2}{3} + \dfrac{1}{4}$.

3. Represent each of these sums with a number-line diagram.

   (a) $\dfrac{1}{8} + \dfrac{3}{8}$ (b) $\dfrac{1}{4} + \dfrac{5}{4}$ (c) $\dfrac{2}{3} + \dfrac{1}{2}$

4. Use the number-line model to illustrate these sums.

   (a) $\dfrac{3}{4} + \dfrac{-2}{4}$ (b) $\dfrac{-3}{4} + \dfrac{2}{4}$ (c) $\dfrac{-3}{4} + \dfrac{-1}{4}$.

5. Perform these additions. Express each answer in simplest form.

   (a) $\dfrac{2}{7} + \dfrac{3}{7}$ (b) $\dfrac{6}{5} + \dfrac{4}{5}$ (c) $\dfrac{3}{8} + \dfrac{11}{24}$

   (d) $\dfrac{6}{13} + \dfrac{2}{5}$ (e) $\dfrac{5}{12} + \dfrac{17}{20}$ (f) $\dfrac{6}{8} + \dfrac{-25}{100}$

   (g) $\dfrac{-57}{100} + \dfrac{13}{10}$ (h) $\dfrac{213}{450} + \dfrac{12}{50}$

6. Express these fractions as mixed numbers.

   (a) $\dfrac{9}{4}$ (b) $\dfrac{17}{3}$ (c) $\dfrac{111}{23}$ (d) $\dfrac{3571}{-100}$

7. Express these mixed numbers as fractions.

    (a) $2\dfrac{3}{8}$ (b) $15\dfrac{2}{3}$ (c) $111\dfrac{2}{5}$ (d) $-10\dfrac{7}{9}$.

8. (a) What subtraction fact is illustrated by this fraction strip model?

    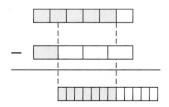

    (b) Use the fraction strip, colored region, and number-line models to illustrate $\dfrac{2}{3} - \dfrac{1}{4}$.

9. Compute these differences, expressing each answer in simplest form.

    (a) $\dfrac{5}{8} - \dfrac{2}{8}$ (b) $\dfrac{3}{5} - \dfrac{2}{4}$ (c) $2\dfrac{2}{3} - 1\dfrac{1}{3}$

    (d) $4\dfrac{1}{4} - 3\dfrac{1}{3}$ (e) $\dfrac{6}{8} - \dfrac{5}{12}$ (f) $\dfrac{1}{4} - \dfrac{14}{56}$

    (g) $\dfrac{137}{214} - \dfrac{-1}{3}$ (h) $\dfrac{-23}{100} - \dfrac{198}{1000}$

10. What multiplication facts are illustrated by these colored rectangular region models?

    (a)   (b)

    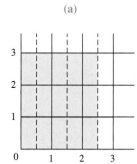   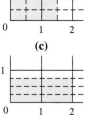

                            (c)

11. Illustrate these multiplications with the model used in problem 10.

    (a) $2 \times \dfrac{3}{5}$ (b) $\dfrac{3}{2} \times \dfrac{3}{4}$ (c) $1\dfrac{2}{3} \times 2\dfrac{1}{4}$

12. A rectangular plot of land is $2\dfrac{1}{4}$ miles wide and $3\dfrac{1}{2}$ miles long. What is the area of the plot, in square miles? Draw a sketch that verifies your answer.

13. Find the reciprocals of the following rational numbers.

    (a) $\dfrac{3}{8}$ (b) $\dfrac{4}{3}$ (c) $2\dfrac{1}{4}$

    (d) $\dfrac{1}{8}$ (e) 5   (f) 1

14. Compute these divisions, expressing each answer in simplest form.

    (a) $\dfrac{2}{5} \div \dfrac{3}{4}$ (b) $\dfrac{6}{11} \div \dfrac{4}{3}$ (c) $\dfrac{100}{33} \div \dfrac{10}{3}$

    (d) $2\dfrac{3}{8} \div 5$ (e) $3 \div 5\dfrac{1}{4}$ (f) $\dfrac{21}{25} \div \dfrac{7}{25}$

15. Compute the fraction with simplest form that is equivalent to the given expression.

    (a) $\dfrac{2}{3} \cdot \left(\dfrac{3}{4} + \dfrac{9}{12} \right)$ (b) $\left(\dfrac{3}{5} - \dfrac{3}{10} \right) \div \dfrac{6}{5}$

    (c) $\left(\dfrac{2}{5} \div \dfrac{4}{15} \right) \cdot \dfrac{2}{3}$

16. Set up and evaluate expressions to solve these map problems.

    (a) Each inch on a map represents an actual distance of $2\dfrac{1}{2}$ miles. If the map shows Helmer $3\dfrac{3}{4}$ inches due east of Deary, how far apart are the two towns?

    (b) A map shows that Spokane is 60 miles north of Colfax. A ruler shows the towns are $3\dfrac{3}{4}$ inches apart on the map. How many actual miles are represented by each inch on the map?

17. An alternative, but equivalent, definition of rational number inequality is the following:

    $$\dfrac{a}{b} < \dfrac{c}{d} \text{ if, and only if, } \dfrac{c}{d} - \dfrac{a}{b} > 0$$

    Use the alternative definition to verify these inequalities.

    (a) $\dfrac{2}{3} < \dfrac{3}{4}$ (b) $\dfrac{4}{5} < \dfrac{14}{17}$ (c) $\dfrac{19}{10} < \dfrac{99}{50}$

Thinking Critically

18. Reread the Just For Fun, "The Sultan's Estate" in Section 6.2. Can you determine the sum $\dfrac{1}{2} + \dfrac{1}{3} + \dfrac{1}{9}$ just by the outcome of the story, with no need to do the calculations explicitly? Explain carefully. Now check your answer by actually computing the sum.

19. Find the missing fractions in the Magic Fraction Squares below, so that the entries in every row, column, and diagonal add to 1.

(a)

$\frac{1}{2}$	$\frac{1}{12}$	
	$\frac{1}{3}$	

(b)

	$\frac{1}{3}$	$\frac{3}{5}$
		$\frac{2}{15}$

20. The positive rational numbers 3 and $1\frac{1}{2}$ are an interesting pair since their sum is equal to their product: $3 + \frac{3}{2} = \frac{6}{2} + \frac{3}{2} = \frac{9}{2}$ and $3 \cdot \frac{3}{2} = \frac{9}{2}$

   (a) Show that $3\frac{1}{2}$ and $1\frac{2}{5}$ have the same sum and product.

   (b) Show that $2\frac{3}{5}$ and $1\frac{5}{8}$ have the same sum and product.

   (c) If two positive rational numbers $\frac{a}{b}$ and $\frac{c}{d}$ have the same sum and product, what must be true of the sum of their reciprocals?

21. Three children had just cut their rectangular cake into three equal parts as shown to share when a fourth friend joined them. Describe how to make one additional straight cut through the cake so all four can share the cake equally.

22. **Other Algorithms for Division.** The "invert and multiply" algorithm, $\frac{a}{b} \div \frac{c}{d} = \frac{a}{b} \cdot \frac{d}{c}$, transforms a division of rational numbers into a multiplication. Here are two other useful algorithms:

   Common-denominators: $\frac{a}{b} \div \frac{c}{b} = \frac{a}{c}$

   Divide-numerators and denominators:

   $$\frac{a}{b} \div \frac{c}{d} = \frac{a \div c}{b \div d}$$

   Thus,

   $$\frac{3}{19} \div \frac{15}{19} = \frac{3}{15} = \frac{1}{5} \quad \text{and} \quad \frac{24}{35} \div \frac{6}{5} = \frac{24 \div 6}{35 \div 5} = \frac{4}{7}.$$

Choose one of the two new algorithms to perform these calculations:

   (a) $\frac{7}{12} \div \frac{11}{12}$,   (b) $\frac{4}{15} \div \frac{2}{3}$,   (c) $\frac{19}{210} \div \frac{19}{70}$

23. With the exception of $\frac{2}{3}$, which was given the hieroglyph , the ancient Egyptians attempted to express all rational numbers as a sum of different *unit* fractions, fractions with 1 as the numerator.

   (a) Verify that $\frac{3}{25} = \frac{1}{2} + \frac{1}{3} + \frac{1}{15} + \frac{1}{50}$.

   (b) Verify that $\frac{7}{29} = \frac{1}{6} + \frac{1}{24} + \frac{1}{58} + \frac{1}{87} + \frac{1}{232}$.

   (c) Verify that $\frac{7}{29} = \frac{1}{5} + \frac{1}{29} + \frac{1}{145}$.

   (d) If $|\quad|$ represents $1\frac{1}{2}$, and $\bigcirc$ is interpreted as "one over," does the symbol seem reasonable for $\frac{2}{3}$?

24. The Rhind (or Ahmes) papyrus of about 1650 B.C. opens with the words "Directions for Obtaining the Knowledge of All Dark Things." The papyrus solves 85 problems, and includes a table expressing the fractions with numerator 2 and an odd denominator 5 through 101 as a sum of unit (numerator 1) fractions. For example, the first two entries in the table are

   $$\frac{2}{5} = \frac{1}{3} + \frac{1}{15} \quad \text{and} \quad \frac{2}{7} = \frac{1}{4} + \frac{1}{28}.$$

   (a) Verify the next entry of the table: $\frac{2}{9} = \frac{1}{5} + \frac{1}{45}$.

   (b) Verify the general formula

   $$\frac{2}{2n-1} = \frac{1}{n} + \frac{1}{n(2n-1)}.$$

   (c) Let $n = 51$ in the formula of part (b) to find the last entry in the table.

25. Solve this problem found in the Rhind papyrus: "A quantity and its $\frac{1}{7}$ th added together become 19. What is the quantity?"

Using a Calculator

26. **DIFFY with Fractions.** The DIFFY game, described in Section 2.3, was played with whole numbers. Here are the beginning lines of DIFFY where the entries are

fractions. A new line is formed by subtracting the smaller fraction from the larger. The DIFFY graphing calculator program (see Appendix C) can also be used for fraction entries.

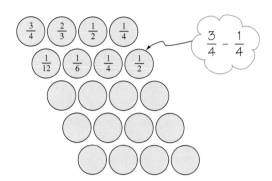

(a) Fill in additional lines of the DIFFY array started above. Does it terminate?

(b) Try fraction DIFFY with these fractions in your first row: $\dfrac{2}{7}, \dfrac{4}{5}, \dfrac{3}{2}, \dfrac{5}{6}$.

(c) Suppose that you know DIFFY with whole number entries always terminates with 0, 0, 0, 0. Does it necessarily follow that DIFFY with fractions must terminate? Explain your reasoning carefully.

27. **DIVVY.** The process called DIVVY is like DIFFY (see problem 26) except that the larger fraction is *divided* by the smaller. The first few rows of DIVVY are shown.

(a) Continue to fill in additional rows, using a calculator if you like.

(b) Try DIVVY with $\dfrac{2}{7}, \dfrac{4}{5}, \dfrac{3}{2}, \dfrac{5}{6}$ in the first row. Don't let complicated fractions put you off! Things should get better if you persist.

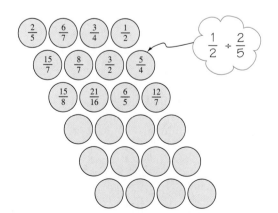

Making Connections

28. At a certain university, a student's senior thesis is acceptable if at least $\dfrac{3}{4}$ of the student's committee votes in its favor. What is the smallest number of favorable votes needed to accept a thesis if the committee has 3 members? 4 members? 5 members? 6 members? 7 members? 8 members?

29. A sign on a roll-end of canvas says it contains 42 square yards. The width of the canvas, which is easily measured without unrolling, is 14 feet (or $4\dfrac{2}{3}$ yards). What is the length of the piece of canvas, in yards?

30. Tongue-and-groove decking boards are each $2\dfrac{1}{4}''$ wide. How many boards must be placed side by side to do a deck 14 feet in width?

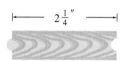

31. Six bows can be made from $1\dfrac{1}{2}$ yards of ribbon. How many bows can be made from $5\dfrac{3}{4}$ yards of ribbon?

32. Andre has 35 yards of material available to make aprons. Each apron requires $\dfrac{3}{4}$ yard. How many aprons can Andre make?

33. Gisela paid $28 for a skirt that was "$\dfrac{1}{3}$ off." What was the original price of the skirt?

34. A soup recipe calls for $2\dfrac{3}{4}$ cups of chicken broth, and will make enough to serve 8 people. How much broth is required if the recipe is modified to serve 6 people?

Communicating

35. For each fraction operation below, make up a realistic word problem whose solution requires the computation shown. Try to create an interesting and original situation.

(a) $\dfrac{19}{32} + \dfrac{1}{4}$ (b) $3\dfrac{1}{4} - 1\dfrac{1}{16}$

(c) $\dfrac{4}{5} \times \dfrac{7}{8}$ (d) $\dfrac{9}{10} \div \dfrac{3}{5}$

36. Respond to a student who asks "should fractions always be written in simplest form, or are there situations where it would be better not to simplify?"

From State Student Assessments

37. (Kentucky, Grade 4) **Mowing the Yard.** The green shaded area of the picture below shows what part of the yard Jessie mowed in 30 minutes.

She wonders about how long it takes her to mow the whole yard. Write a note to Jessie

A. telling her about how long it takes to mow her whole yard and

B. explaining to her how you found your answer. Be sure to include a drawing of the yard in your explanation.

For Review

38. Represent these rational numbers by fractions in simplest form.

(a) $\dfrac{168}{48}$ (b) $\dfrac{945}{3780}$

39. Arrange these rational numbers in increasing order:

$$\frac{31}{90}, \quad \frac{1}{3}, \quad \frac{19}{60}, \quad \frac{4}{13}$$

40. Find the least common denominator of $\dfrac{4}{9}, \dfrac{5}{12}, \dfrac{4}{15}$ and then find the sum of the three numbers.

6.3   The Rational Number System

This section explores the properties of the rational numbers. Many properties will be familiar, since the integers have the same properties. However, we will also discover some important new properties of rational numbers which have no counterpart in the integers. This section also gives techniques for estimation and computation, and presents additional examples of the application of rational numbers to the solution of practical problems.

Properties of Addition and Subtraction

To add two rational numbers, the definition introduced in the preceding section tells us to "represent the rational numbers by fractions with a common denominator, and then add the two numerators." For example, to add $\dfrac{5}{6}$ and $\dfrac{3}{10}$ we could use the common denominator 30; thus

$$\frac{5}{6} + \frac{3}{10} = \frac{25}{30} + \frac{9}{30} = \frac{34}{30}.$$

We could also have used the common denominator 60 to find,

$$\frac{5}{6} + \frac{3}{10} = \frac{50}{60} + \frac{18}{60} = \frac{68}{60}.$$

The two answers, namely $\dfrac{34}{30}$ and $\dfrac{68}{60}$, are different fractions. However, they are equivalent fractions, and both represent the *same* rational number, $\dfrac{17}{15}$, when expressed by a fraction in simplest form. More generally *any* two rational numbers have a unique rational number which is their sum. That is, the rational numbers are closed under addition.

It is also straightforward to check that addition in the rational numbers is commutative and associative. For example, $\frac{5}{6} + \frac{3}{10} = \frac{3}{10} + \frac{5}{6}$ and $\frac{3}{4} + \left(\frac{-1}{3} + \frac{2}{5}\right) = \left(\frac{3}{4} + \frac{-1}{3}\right) + \frac{2}{5}$. Similarly, 0 is the additive identity. For example, $\frac{7}{9} + 0 = \frac{7}{9}$ since $0 = \frac{0}{9}$.

The rational numbers share one more property with the integers, namely the existence of **negatives,** or **additive inverses.** We have the following definition.

> **DEFINITION**   *Negative or Additive Inverse*
>
> Let $\frac{a}{b}$ be a rational number. Its **negative,** or **additive inverse,** written $-\frac{a}{b}$, is the rational number $\frac{-a}{b}$.

For example, $-\frac{4}{7} = \frac{-4}{7}$. This is the additive inverse of $\frac{4}{7}$, since we see that

$$\frac{4}{7} + \left(-\frac{4}{7}\right) = \frac{4}{7} + \frac{-4}{7} = \frac{4 + (-4)}{7} = \frac{0}{7} = 0.$$

As another example, $-\left(-\frac{3}{4}\right) = -\left(\frac{-3}{4}\right) = \frac{-(-3)}{4} = \frac{3}{4}$, which illustrates the general property $-\left(-\frac{a}{b}\right) = \frac{a}{b}$.

A negative is also called an **opposite.** This term describes how a rational number and its negative are positioned on the number line: $-\frac{a}{b}$ is on the opposite side of 0 from $\frac{a}{b}$.

The properties of addition on the rational numbers are listed in the following theorem.

> **THEOREM**   *Properties of Addition of Rational Numbers*
>
> Let $\frac{a}{b}, \frac{c}{d}$, and $\frac{e}{f}$ be rational numbers. The following properties hold.
>
> | | |
> |---|---|
> | **Closure Property** | $\frac{a}{b} + \frac{c}{d}$ is a rational number. |
> | **Commutative Property** | $\frac{a}{b} + \frac{c}{d} = \frac{c}{d} + \frac{a}{b}$ |
> | **Associative Property** | $\left(\frac{a}{b} + \frac{c}{d}\right) + \frac{e}{f} = \frac{a}{b} + \left(\frac{c}{d} + \frac{e}{f}\right)$ |
> | **Zero Is an Additive Identity** | $\frac{a}{b} + 0 = \frac{a}{b}$ |
> | **Existence of Additive Inverses** | $\frac{a}{b} + \left(-\frac{a}{b}\right) = 0$, where $-\frac{a}{b} = \frac{-a}{b}$. |

In the integers we discovered that subtraction was equivalent to the addition of the negative. The same result holds for the rational numbers. Since the rational numbers are closed under addition and every rational number has a negative, this means that the rational numbers are closed under subtraction.

THEOREM *Formulas for Subtraction of Rational Numbers*

Let $\dfrac{a}{b}$ and $\dfrac{c}{d}$ be rational numbers. Then $\dfrac{a}{b} - \dfrac{c}{d} = \dfrac{a}{b} + \left(-\dfrac{c}{d}\right) = \dfrac{ad - bc}{bd}$.

Subtraction is neither commutative nor associative, as examples such as $\dfrac{1}{2} - \dfrac{1}{4} \neq \dfrac{1}{4} - \dfrac{1}{2}$ and $1 - \left(\dfrac{1}{2} - \dfrac{1}{4}\right) \neq \left(1 - \dfrac{1}{2}\right) - \dfrac{1}{4}$ show. This means that subtraction requires that careful attention be given to the order of the terms and the placement of parentheses.

EXAMPLE   6.14   **Subtracting Rational Numbers**

Compute the following differences.

(a) $\dfrac{3}{4} - \dfrac{7}{6}$ (b) $\dfrac{2}{3} - \dfrac{-9}{8}$ (c) $\left(-2\dfrac{1}{4}\right) - \left(4\dfrac{2}{3}\right)$

Solution

(a) $\dfrac{3}{4} - \dfrac{7}{6} = \dfrac{3 \cdot 6}{4 \cdot 6} - \dfrac{4 \cdot 7}{4 \cdot 6} = \dfrac{18 - 28}{24} = \dfrac{-10}{24} = \dfrac{-5}{12} = -\dfrac{5}{12}.$

(b) $\dfrac{2}{3} - \dfrac{-9}{8} = \dfrac{2}{3} + \dfrac{9}{8} = \dfrac{2 \cdot 8}{3 \cdot 8} + \dfrac{3 \cdot 9}{3 \cdot 8} = \dfrac{16}{24} + \dfrac{27}{24} = \dfrac{43}{24}.$

(c) $\left(-2\dfrac{1}{4}\right) - \left(4\dfrac{2}{3}\right) = (-2 - 4) - \left(\dfrac{1}{4} + \dfrac{2}{3}\right) = -6 - \left(\dfrac{3}{12} + \dfrac{8}{12}\right) = -6\dfrac{11}{12}.$

Properties of Multiplication and Division

Multiplication of rational numbers includes all of the properties of multiplication for the integers. For example, let's investigate the distributive property of multiplication over addition by considering a specific case:

$$\dfrac{2}{5} \cdot \left(\dfrac{3}{4} + \dfrac{7}{8}\right) = \dfrac{2}{5} \cdot \left(\dfrac{6}{8} + \dfrac{7}{8}\right) = \dfrac{2}{5} \cdot \dfrac{13}{8} = \dfrac{26}{40} \quad \longleftarrow \text{Add first, then multiply.}$$

$$\dfrac{2}{5} \cdot \dfrac{3}{4} + \dfrac{2}{5} \cdot \dfrac{7}{8} = \dfrac{6}{20} + \dfrac{14}{40} = \dfrac{12}{40} + \dfrac{14}{40} = \dfrac{26}{40} \quad \longleftarrow \text{Multiply first, then add.}$$

These computations show that multiplication by $\dfrac{2}{5}$ distributes over the sum $\dfrac{3}{4} + \dfrac{7}{8}$. A similar calculation proves the general distributive property $\dfrac{a}{b} \cdot \left(\dfrac{c}{d} + \dfrac{e}{f}\right) = \dfrac{a}{b} \cdot \dfrac{c}{d} + \dfrac{a}{b} \cdot \dfrac{e}{f}.$

There is one important new property of multiplication of rational numbers that is *not* true for the integers: the existence of multiplicative inverses. For example, the nonzero rational number $\frac{5}{8}$ has the multiplicative inverse $\frac{8}{5}$, since

$$\frac{5}{8} \cdot \frac{8}{5} = 1.$$

This property does not hold in the integers. For example, since there is no integer m for which $2 \cdot m = 1$, the integer 2 does not have a multiplicative inverse in the set of integers.

THEOREM *Properties of Multiplication of Rational Numbers*

Let $\frac{a}{b}, \frac{c}{d}$, and $\frac{e}{f}$ be rational numbers. The following properties hold.

Closure Property $\frac{a}{b} \cdot \frac{c}{d}$ is a rational number.

Commutative Property $\frac{a}{b} \cdot \frac{c}{d} = \frac{c}{d} \cdot \frac{a}{b}$

Associative Property $\left(\frac{a}{b} \cdot \frac{c}{d} \right) \cdot \frac{e}{f} = \frac{a}{b} \cdot \left(\frac{c}{d} \cdot \frac{e}{f} \right)$

Distributive Property of Multiplication over Addition and Subtraction

$$\frac{a}{b} \cdot \left(\frac{c}{d} + \frac{e}{f} \right) = \frac{a}{b} \cdot \frac{c}{d} + \frac{a}{b} \cdot \frac{e}{f} \quad \text{and} \quad \frac{a}{b} \cdot \left(\frac{c}{d} - \frac{e}{f} \right) = \frac{a}{b} \cdot \frac{c}{d} - \frac{a}{b} \cdot \frac{e}{f}$$

Multiplication by Zero $0 \cdot \frac{a}{b} = 0$

One Is a Multiplicative Identity $1 \cdot \frac{a}{b} = \frac{a}{b}$

Existence of Multiplicative Inverse If $\frac{a}{b} \neq 0$, then there is a unique rational number, namely $\frac{b}{a}$, for which $\frac{a}{b} \cdot \frac{b}{a} = 1$.

$0 = \frac{0}{1}$

$1 = \frac{1}{1}$

EXAMPLE 6.15 | **Solving an Equation with the Multiplicative Inverse**

Consuela paid \$36 for a pair of shoes at the "one-fourth off" sale. What was the price of the shoes before the sale?

Solution | Let x be the original price of the shoes, in dollars. Consuela paid $\frac{3}{4}$ of this price, so $\frac{3}{4} \cdot x = 36$. To solve this equation for the unknown x, multiply both sides by $\frac{4}{3}$ to get

$$\frac{4}{3} \cdot \frac{3}{4} \cdot x = \frac{4}{3} \cdot 36.$$

But $\frac{4}{3} \cdot \frac{3}{4} = 1$ by the multiplicative inverse property, so

$$1 \cdot x = \frac{4 \cdot 36}{3} = 48.$$

Since 1 is a multiplicative identity we find that $1 \cdot x = x = 48$. Therefore, the original price of the pair of shoes was \$48.

In the last section, we discovered that the rational numbers are closed under division, since any division $\dfrac{a}{b} \div \dfrac{c}{d}$ (where $c \neq 0$) is given by the rational number $\dfrac{a \cdot d}{b \cdot c}$. Nevertheless, division in the rational numbers is neither commutative nor associative, which means it is important to place terms in their proper order and to use parentheses to avoid ambiguities. For example, $\dfrac{1}{3} \div \dfrac{1}{2} = \dfrac{2}{3}$ but $\dfrac{1}{2} \div \dfrac{1}{3} = \dfrac{3}{2}$ shows that division is not commutative. Since division is not associative, an expression such as 2/3/4 requires us to place parentheses to know if we wish to compute $(2/3)/4 = 2/12 = 1/6$ or $2/(3/4) = 8/3$.

Properties of the Order Relation

The order relation has many useful properties that are not difficult to prove.

THEOREM   *Properties of the Order Relation on the Rational Numbers*

Let $\dfrac{a}{b}, \dfrac{c}{d}, \dfrac{e}{f}$ be rational numbers.

Transitive Property

$$\text{If } \frac{a}{b} < \frac{c}{d} \quad \text{and} \quad \frac{c}{d} < \frac{e}{f}, \quad \text{then } \frac{a}{b} < \frac{e}{f}.$$

Addition Property

$$\text{If } \frac{a}{b} < \frac{c}{d}, \quad \text{then } \frac{a}{b} + \frac{e}{f} < \frac{c}{d} + \frac{e}{f}.$$

Multiplication Property

$$\text{If } \frac{a}{b} < \frac{c}{d} \quad \text{and} \quad \frac{e}{f} > 0, \quad \text{then } \frac{a}{b} \cdot \frac{e}{f} < \frac{c}{d} \cdot \frac{e}{f}.$$

$$\text{If } \frac{a}{b} < \frac{c}{d} \quad \text{and} \quad \frac{e}{f} < 0, \quad \text{then } \frac{a}{b} \cdot \frac{e}{f} > \frac{c}{d} \cdot \frac{e}{f}.$$

Trichotomy Property Exactly one of the following holds:

$$\frac{a}{b} < \frac{c}{d}, \qquad \frac{a}{b} = \frac{c}{d}, \qquad \text{or} \qquad \frac{a}{b} > \frac{c}{d}.$$

The Density Property of Rational Numbers

By the definition of inequality, we know that

$$\frac{1}{2} < \frac{2}{3}.$$

Alternatively, using 6 as a common denominator, we have

$$\frac{3}{6} < \frac{4}{6}$$

and with 12 as a common denominator, we have

$$\frac{6}{12} < \frac{8}{12}.$$

In the last form, we see that $\frac{7}{12}$ is a rational number which is between $\frac{6}{12}$ and $\frac{8}{12}$. That is,

$$\frac{1}{2} < \frac{7}{12} < \frac{2}{3},$$

as shown in Figure 6.13.

Figure 6.13

The rational number $\frac{7}{12}$ is between $\frac{1}{2}$ and $\frac{2}{3}$

The idea used to find a rational number that is between $\frac{1}{2}$ and $\frac{2}{3}$ can be extended to show that between *any* two rational numbers there is some other rational number. This interesting fact is called the **density property** of the rational numbers. The analogous property does not hold in the integers. For example, there is no integer between 1 and 2.

> **THEOREM**   *The Density Property of Rational Numbers*
>
> Let $\frac{a}{b}$ and $\frac{c}{d}$ be any two rational numbers, with $\frac{a}{b} < \frac{c}{d}$. Then there is a rational number $\frac{e}{f}$
>
> between $\frac{a}{b}$ and $\frac{c}{d}$; that is, $\frac{a}{b} < \frac{e}{f} < \frac{c}{d}$.

EXAMPLE   6.16   **Finding Rational Numbers Between Two Rational Numbers**

Find a rational number between the two given fractions.

(a) $\frac{2}{3}$ and $\frac{3}{4}$ (b) $\frac{5}{12}$ and $\frac{3}{8}$

Solution

(a) Using $2 \cdot 3 \cdot 4 = 24$ as a common denominator, we have $\frac{2}{3} = \frac{16}{24}$ and $\frac{3}{4} = \frac{18}{24}$.

Since $\frac{16}{24} < \frac{17}{24} < \frac{18}{24}$, this shows that $\frac{17}{24}$ is one answer.

(b) If we use 48 as a common denominator, we have $\frac{5}{12} = \frac{20}{48}$ and $\frac{3}{8} = \frac{18}{48}$. Thus $\frac{19}{48}$ is one answer. Alternatively, we could use 480 as a common denominator, writing $\frac{5}{12} = \frac{200}{480}$ and $\frac{3}{8} = \frac{180}{480}$. This makes it clear that $\frac{181}{480}, \frac{182}{480}, \ldots, \frac{199}{480}$ are all rational numbers between $\frac{3}{8}$ and $\frac{5}{12}$. Using a larger common denominator allows us to identify even more rational numbers between the two given rationals.

Computations with Rational Numbers

To work confidently with rational numbers, it is important to develop skills in estimation, rounding, mental arithmetic, efficient paper-and-pencil computation, and the use of the calculator.

Estimations

In many applications, the exact fractional value can be rounded off to the nearest integer value; if more precision is required, values can be rounded to the nearest half, third, or quarter.

EXAMPLE 6.17

Using Fraction Rounding to Convert a Brownie Recipe

Krishna's recipe, shown in the box, makes two dozen brownies. He'll need five dozen for the Math Day picnic, so he wants to adjust the quantities of his recipe. How should this be done?

Solution

Since Krishna needs $2\frac{1}{2}$ times the number of brownies given by his recipe, he'll multiply the quantities by $\frac{5}{2}$. For example, $\frac{5}{2} \times 4 = 10$, so he'll use 10 squares of chocolate. Similarly, he'll use $\frac{5}{2} \times 2 = 5$ cups of sugar, $2\frac{1}{2}$ teaspoons of vanilla, and $2\frac{1}{2}$ cups of flour. On the other hand, $\frac{5}{2} \times \frac{3}{4} = \frac{15}{8} = 1\frac{7}{8}$, so Krishna will use "just short" of 2 cups of butter. Similarly, $\frac{5}{2} \times \frac{5}{4} = \frac{25}{8} = 3\frac{1}{8}$, so Krishna will use "about" 3 cups of chopped walnuts. Finally, $\frac{5}{2} \times 3 = \frac{15}{2} = 7\frac{1}{2}$, so he will use either 7 or 8 eggs.

Brownie Recipe
(2-dozen)

4 squares chocolate

$\frac{3}{4}$ cup butter

2 cups sugar

3 eggs

1 teaspoon vanilla

1 cup flour

$1\frac{1}{4}$ cups chopped walnuts

Mental Arithmetic

By taking advantage of the properties, formulas, and algorithms associated with the operations, it is often possible to simplify the computational process. Some useful strategies are demonstrated in the following example.

DID YOU KNOW?
The Importance of Generalization

*E*xtending a domain by introducing new symbols in such a way that the laws which hold in the original domain continue to hold in the larger domain is one aspect of the characteristic mathematical process of *generalization.* The generalization from the natural to the rational numbers satisfies both the theoretical need for removing the restrictions on subtraction and division, and the practical need for numbers to express the results of measurement. It is the fact that the rational numbers fill this two-fold need that gives them their true significance. As we have seen, this extension of the number concept was made possible by the creation of new numbers in the form of abstract symbols like 0, −2, and 3/4. Today, when we deal with such numbers as a matter of course, it is hard to believe that as late as the seventeenth century they were not generally credited with the same legitimacy as the positive integers, and that they were used, when necessary, with a certain amount of doubt and trepidation. The inherent human tendency to cling to the "concrete," as exemplified by the natural numbers, was responsible for this slowness in taking an inevitable step. Only in the realm of the abstract can a satisfactory system of arithmetic be created.

SOURCE: Richard Courant and Herbert Robbins, *What Is Mathematics? An Elementary Approach to Ideas and Methods* (New York: Oxford University Press, 1941), p. 56.

EXAMPLE   6.18

Computational Strategies for Rational Number Arithmetic

Perform these computations mentally.

(a) $53 - 29\dfrac{3}{5}$

(b) $\left(2\dfrac{1}{8} - 4\dfrac{2}{3}\right) + 7\dfrac{7}{8}$

(c) $\dfrac{7}{15} \times 90$

(d) $\dfrac{3}{8} \times 14 + \dfrac{3}{4} \times 25$

(e) $4\dfrac{1}{6} \times 18$

(f) $\dfrac{5}{8} \times \left(\dfrac{7}{10} \times \dfrac{24}{49}\right)$

Solution

(a) Adding $\dfrac{2}{5}$ to each term gives $53 - 29\dfrac{3}{5} = 53\dfrac{2}{5} - 30 = 23\dfrac{2}{5}.$

(b) $\left(2\dfrac{1}{8} - 4\dfrac{2}{3}\right) + 7\dfrac{7}{8} = \left(2 + 7 + \dfrac{1}{8} + \dfrac{7}{8}\right) - 4\dfrac{2}{3}$

$$= 10 - 4\dfrac{2}{3} = 10\dfrac{1}{3} - 5 = 5\dfrac{1}{3}$$

(c) $\dfrac{7}{15} \times 90 = 7 \times \dfrac{90}{15} = 7 \times 6 = 42$

(d) $\dfrac{3}{8} \times 14 + \dfrac{3}{4} \times 25 = \dfrac{3}{8} \times 14 + \dfrac{3}{8} \times 50$

$$= \dfrac{3}{8} \times (14 + 50) = \dfrac{3}{8} \times 64$$

$$= 3 \times \dfrac{64}{8} = 3 \times 8 = 24$$

(e) $4\dfrac{1}{6} \times 18 = \left(4 + \dfrac{1}{6}\right) \times 18 = 4 \times 18 + \dfrac{1}{6} \times 18 = 72 + 3 = 75$

(f) $\dfrac{5}{8} \times \left(\dfrac{7}{10} \times \dfrac{24}{49}\right) = \dfrac{5}{10} \times \dfrac{7}{49} \times \dfrac{24}{8} = \dfrac{1}{2} \times \dfrac{1}{7} \times 3 = \dfrac{3}{14}$

HIGHLIGHT FROM HISTORY
Rational Numbers and the Pythagorean Musical Scale

One of the earliest applications of mathematics was made to music. The Pythagoreans (c. 500 B.C.) noticed that two tones plucked on stretched strings sounded pleasing together if the length of the shorter string was a simple fraction of the length of the longer string. For example, if the longer string, say of length 1, is the note C (the middle white key on a piano), then a string of length $\frac{1}{2}$ sounds C′, the note an octave higher than C. Similarly, a string of length $\frac{2}{3}$ produces the note G, which is the fifth note in the scale C-D-E-F-G. Thus, to raise the pitch by a "fifth," the length of the string is multiplied by $\frac{2}{3}$. In particular, a "fifth" above G is the note D′ sounded by a string of length $\frac{2}{3} \cdot \frac{2}{3} = \frac{4}{9}$. Doubling this length to $\frac{8}{9}$ gives D, the pitch an octave below D′. By ascending by fifths (mutiplying by $\frac{2}{3}$) and lowering by octaves (multiplying by 2), the lengths of the strings which sound the white key pitches C, G, D′, D, A, E′, E, and B are obtained.

A string of length $\frac{3}{4}$ produces the pitch of F, the fourth note of the scale.

A "fourth" above F is B♭ (B flat), a black key on the piano sounding the pitch of a string of length $\frac{3}{4} \cdot \frac{3}{4} = \frac{9}{16}$.

By ascending by fourths (multiplying by $\frac{3}{4}$) and lowering by octaves, the pitches C, F, B♭, E♭′, E♭, A♭, D♭′, D♭, G♭, C♭ are obtained. The diagram shows how the Pythagoreans filled in the notes of their scale.

Ascending by fifths eventually reaches the note B:$\frac{128}{243}$, and ascending by fourths reaches C♭:$\frac{2187}{4096}$. These notes are assumed to be the same on a piano, but in fact C♭ is a slightly lower pitch than B, as the following calculation shows.

$$\frac{2187}{4096} \div \frac{128}{243} = \frac{531441}{524288} = 1.0136\ldots.$$

Amazingly, the Pythagoreans were aware of this difference in pitch; it is called the *Pythagorean Comma*. To avoid the comma, a number of different tunings have been used throughout musical history. Modern pianos are tuned to the "equal tempered" scale, in which the intervals from one pitch to the next are made equal.

D♭ : $\frac{243}{256}$ ⟶ G♭ : $\frac{729}{1024}$ ⟶ C♭ : $\frac{2187}{4096}$ ascending by fourths from

E♭ : $\frac{27}{32}$ ⟶ A♭ : $\frac{81}{128}$ ⟶ D♭′: $\frac{243}{512}$ C to C♭

C:1 ⟶ F : $\frac{3}{4}$ ⟶ B♭ : $\frac{9}{16}$ ⟶ E♭′ : $\frac{27}{64}$

C:1 ⟶ G : $\frac{2}{3}$ ⟶ D′ : $\frac{4}{9}$

D : $\frac{8}{9}$ ⟶ A : $\frac{16}{27}$ ⟶ E′ : $\frac{32}{81}$

E : $\frac{64}{81}$ ⟶ B : $\frac{128}{243}$ ascending by fifths from C to B

Rational Numbers on a Calculator

Some special purpose calculators, such as the *Math Explorer,* can perform arithmetic on fractional values and display the result as a fraction. Most calculators, however, perform calculations only in decimal form, and it takes special care to represent the final answer as a fraction.

EXAMPLE   6.19

Computing with Rational Numbers on a Calculator

Use a calculator to find $\dfrac{3}{8} \times \left(\dfrac{-7}{12} + \dfrac{9}{5} \right)$.

Solution

On a fraction calculator. On the *Math Explorer* the steps are

| ON/AC | 3 | / | 8 | × | (| 7 | + | ↻− | / | 12 | + | 9 | / | 5 |) | = |

which gives 219/480 in the display. Pressing | Simp | | = | gives the simplified form 73/160.

On a decimal calculator. We can first obtain a decimal answer by pressing

| ON/AC | 3 | ÷ | 8 | × | (| 7 | + | ↻− | ÷ | 12 | + | 9 | ÷ | 5 |) | = |,

obtaining 0.45625. To express this as a fraction, we first observe that 8, 12, and 5 are the denominators of the terms which appear in the problem. Thus, the answer can be written as a fraction with $8 \cdot 12 \cdot 5 = 480$ as a denominator. Multiplying by 480 we get $0.45625 \times 480 = 219$, so the decimal answer 0.45625 is equivalent to the fraction 219/480; in simplest form this is 73/160.

We conclude with a real-life application of the use of rational numbers and their arithmetic.

EXAMPLE   6.20

Designing Wooden Stairs

A deck is 4' 2" above the surface of the patio. How many steps and risers should there be in a stairway which connects the deck to the patio? The decking is $1\dfrac{1}{2}''$ thick, the stair treads are $1\dfrac{1}{8}''$ thick, and the steps should each rise the same distance, from one to the next. Calculate the vertical dimension of each riser.

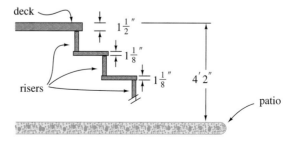

Solution

Understand the problem

We have been given some important dimensions, including the thickness of the treads and the deck. We have *not* been told what dimension to cut the risers. This, we see from the figure, depends on the number of steps we choose, with a lower rise corresponding to a greater number of steps. We must choose a number of steps which feels natural to walk on. We must also be sure each step rises the same amount.

Devise a plan

If we know what vertical rise from step to step is customary, we can first get a reasonable estimate of the number of steps to use. Once it is agreed what number of steps to incorporate in the design, we can calculate the height of each riser. The riser meeting the deck must be adjusted to account for the decking being thicker than the stair tread.

Carry out the plan

A brief survey of existing stairways shows that most steps rise 5" to 7" from one to the next. Since 4' 2" = 50" and $\frac{50}{5} = 10$ and $\frac{50}{7} = 7\frac{1}{7}$, this suggests that 8, or perhaps 9, steps will work well, including the step onto the deck itself. Let's choose 8. Then $\frac{50"}{8} = 6\frac{2"}{8} = 6\frac{1"}{4}$; that is, each combination of riser plus tread is to be $6\frac{1"}{4}$. Since the treads are $1\frac{1"}{8}$ thick, the first seven risers require the boards to be cut $6\frac{1"}{4} - 1\frac{1"}{8} = 5\frac{1"}{8}$ wide. Since the decking is $1\frac{1"}{2}$ thick, the uppermost riser is $6\frac{1"}{4} - 1\frac{1}{2}" = 4\frac{3"}{4}$ wide.

Look back

If we were concerned that the steps will take up too much room on the patio, we might use a steeper 7-step design. Each riser plus tread would rise $7\frac{1"}{7}$. Experienced carpenters would think of this as a "hair" more than $7\frac{1"}{8}$, and cut the lower six risers from a board 8" wide for a total rise of $7\frac{1"}{8}$. The last riser is cut to make any final small adjustment.

PROBLEM SET 6.3

Understanding Concepts

1. Explain what properties of addition of rational numbers can be used to make this sum very easy to compute.

$$\left(3\frac{1}{5} + 2\frac{2}{5}\right) + 8\frac{1}{5}$$

2. What properties can you use to make these computations easy?

   (a) $\dfrac{2}{5} + \left(\dfrac{3}{5} + \dfrac{2}{3}\right)$ (b) $\dfrac{1}{4} + \left(\dfrac{2}{5} + \dfrac{3}{4}\right)$

   (c) $\dfrac{2}{3} \cdot \dfrac{1}{8} + \dfrac{2}{3} \cdot \dfrac{7}{8}$ (d) $\dfrac{3}{4} \cdot \left(\dfrac{5}{9} \cdot \dfrac{4}{3}\right)$

3. Find the negatives (that is, the additive inverses) of the following rational numbers. Show each number and its negative on the number line.

   (a) $\dfrac{4}{5}$ (b) $\dfrac{-3}{2}$ (c) $\dfrac{8}{-3}$ (d) $\dfrac{4}{2}$

4. Compute these sums of rational numbers. Explain what properties of rational numbers you find useful. Express your answers in simplest form.

   (a) $\dfrac{1}{6} + \dfrac{2}{-3}$ (b) $\dfrac{-4}{5} + \dfrac{3}{2}$

   (c) $\dfrac{9}{4} + \dfrac{-7}{8}$ (d) $\dfrac{3}{4} + \dfrac{-5}{8} + \dfrac{7}{-12}$

5. Compute these differences of rational numbers. Explain what properties you find useful. Express your answers in simplest form.

   (a) $\dfrac{2}{5} - \dfrac{3}{4}$ (b) $\dfrac{-6}{7} - \dfrac{4}{7}$ (c) $\dfrac{3}{8} - \dfrac{1}{12}$

   (d) $3\dfrac{2}{5} - \dfrac{7}{10}$ (e) $2\dfrac{1}{3} - 5\dfrac{3}{4}$ (f) $-4\dfrac{2}{3} - \dfrac{-19}{6}$

6. Calculate these products of rational numbers. Explain what properties of rational numbers you find useful. Express your answers in simplest form.

   (a) $\dfrac{3}{5} \cdot \dfrac{7}{8} \cdot \left(\dfrac{5}{3}\right)$ (b) $\dfrac{-2}{7} \cdot \dfrac{3}{4}$

   (c) $\dfrac{-4}{3} \cdot \dfrac{6}{-16}$ (d) $3\dfrac{1}{8} \cdot 2\dfrac{1}{5} \cdot (40)$

   (e) $\dfrac{14}{15} \cdot \dfrac{60}{7}$ (f) $\left(\dfrac{4}{11} \cdot \dfrac{22}{7}\right) \cdot \left(\dfrac{-3}{8}\right)$

7. Find the reciprocals (that is, the multiplicative inverses) of these rational numbers. Show each number and its reciprocal on the number line.

   (a) $\dfrac{3}{2}$ (b) $\dfrac{4}{-9}$

   (c) $\dfrac{-4}{-11}$ (d) 5

   (e) -2 (f) $2\dfrac{1}{2}$

8. Use the properties of the operations of rational number arithmetic to perform these calculations. Express your answers in simplest form.

   (a) $\dfrac{2}{3} \cdot \dfrac{4}{7} + \dfrac{2}{3} \cdot \dfrac{3}{7}$

   (b) $\dfrac{4}{5} \cdot \dfrac{2}{3} - \dfrac{3}{10} \cdot \dfrac{2}{3}$

   (c) $\dfrac{4}{7} \cdot \dfrac{3}{2} - \dfrac{4}{7} \cdot \dfrac{6}{4}$

   (d) $\left(\dfrac{4}{7} \cdot \dfrac{2}{5}\right) \div \dfrac{2}{7}$

9. Justify each step in the following proof of the distributive property of multiplication over addition. The two addends have a common denominator, but this is always possible by using a common denominator for two fractions.

   $$\dfrac{a}{b} \cdot \left(\dfrac{c}{d} + \dfrac{e}{d}\right) = \dfrac{a}{b} \cdot \dfrac{c+e}{d} \qquad \text{(a) Why?}$$

   $$= \dfrac{a \cdot (c+e)}{b \cdot d} \qquad \text{(b) Why?}$$

   $$= \dfrac{a \cdot c + a \cdot e}{b \cdot d} \qquad \text{(c) Why?}$$

   $$= \dfrac{a \cdot c}{b \cdot d} + \dfrac{a \cdot e}{b \cdot d} \qquad \text{(d) Why?}$$

   $$= \dfrac{a}{b} \cdot \dfrac{c}{d} + \dfrac{a}{b} \cdot \dfrac{e}{d}. \qquad \text{(e) Why?}$$

10. If $\dfrac{a}{b} \cdot \dfrac{4}{7} = \dfrac{2}{3}$, what is $\dfrac{a}{b}$? Carefully explain how you obtain your answer. What properties do you use?

11. Solve each equation for the rational number x. Show your steps, and explain what property justifies each step.

    (a) $4x + 3 = 0$ (b) $x + \dfrac{3}{4} = \dfrac{7}{8}$

    (c) $\dfrac{2}{3}x + \dfrac{4}{5} = 0$ (d) $3\left(x + \dfrac{1}{8}\right) = -\dfrac{2}{3}$

12. The Fahrenheit and Celsius temperature scales are related by the formula F = $\frac{9}{5}$C + 32. For example, a temperature of 20° Celsius corresponds to 68° Fahrenheit since

$$\frac{9}{5} \cdot 20 + 32 = 36 + 32 = 68.$$

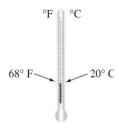

68° F⟶   ⟵20° C

(a) Explain what properties of rational number arithmetic permit you to deduce the equivalent formula C = $\frac{5}{9}$ (F − 32) relating the two temperature scales.

(b) Fill in the missing entries in this table.

°C	−40°			0°	10°	20°		
°F		−13°				68°	104°	212°

(c) Electronic signboards frequently give the temperature in both Fahrenheit and Celsius. What is the temperature if both readings are the same (that is, F = C)? The negative of one another (that is, F = −C)? Answer the latter question with an exact rational number and the approximate integer that would be seen on the signboard.

13. Arrange each group of rational numbers in increasing order. Show, at least approximately, the numbers on the number line.

(a) $\frac{4}{5}$, $-\frac{1}{5}$, $\frac{2}{5}$ (b) $\frac{-3}{7}$, $\frac{4}{7}$, $\frac{-5}{7}$

(c) $\frac{3}{8}$, $\frac{1}{2}$, $\frac{3}{4}$ (d) $\frac{-7}{12}$, $\frac{-2}{3}$, $\frac{3}{-4}$

14. Verify these inequalities.

(a) $\frac{-4}{5} < \frac{-3}{4}$ (b) $\frac{1}{10} > -\frac{1}{4}$ (c) $-\frac{19}{60} > \frac{-1}{3}$

15. The properties of the order relation can be used to solve inequalities. For example, if $-\frac{2}{3}x + \frac{1}{4} < -\frac{1}{2}$, then

$-8x + 3 < -6$ (multiply by 12)

$-8x < -9$ (subtract 3 from both sides)

$8x > 9$ (multiply by −1, which reverses the direction of inequality)

$x > \frac{9}{8}$ (divide both sides by 8)

That is, all rational numbers x greater than $\frac{9}{8}$, and only these, satisfy the given inequality. Solve these inequalities. Show all of your steps.

(a) $x + \frac{2}{3} > -\frac{1}{3}$ (b) $x - \left(-\frac{3}{4}\right) < \frac{1}{4}$

(c) $\frac{3}{4}x < -\frac{1}{2}$ (d) $-\frac{2}{5}x + \frac{1}{5} > -1$.

16. Find a rational number which is between the two given rational numbers.

(a) $\frac{4}{9}$ and $\frac{6}{11}$ (b) $\frac{1}{9}$ and $\frac{1}{10}$

(c) $\frac{14}{23}$ and $\frac{7}{12}$ (d) $\frac{141}{568}$ and $\frac{183}{737}$

17. Find three rational numbers between $\frac{1}{4}$ and $\frac{2}{5}$.

18. For each given rational number, choose the best estimate from the list provided.

(a) $\frac{104}{391}$ is approximately $\frac{1}{3}$, $\frac{1}{4}$, $\frac{1}{2}$.

(b) $\frac{217}{340}$ is approximately $\frac{1}{3}$, $\frac{1}{2}$, $\frac{2}{3}$.

(c) $\frac{-193}{211}$ is approximately $-\frac{1}{2}$, -1, 1, $\frac{1}{2}$.

(d) $\frac{453}{307}$ is approximately $\frac{3}{4}$, 1, $1\frac{1}{3}$, $1\frac{1}{2}$.

19. Use estimations to choose the best approximation of the following expressions.

(a) $3\frac{19}{40} + 5\frac{11}{19}$ is approximately 8, $8\frac{1}{2}$, 9, $9\frac{1}{2}$.

(b) $2\frac{6}{19} + 5\frac{1}{3} - 4\frac{7}{20}$ is approximately 3, $3\frac{1}{3}$, $3\frac{1}{4}$, 4.

(c) $17\frac{8}{9} \div 5\frac{10}{11}$ is approximately 2, 3, $3\frac{1}{2}$, 4.

20. Do the following calculations mentally.

(a) $\frac{1}{2} + \frac{1}{4} + \frac{3}{4}$ (b) $\frac{5}{2} \cdot \left(\frac{2}{5} - \frac{2}{10}\right)$

(c) $\dfrac{3}{4} \cdot \dfrac{12}{15}$ (d) $\dfrac{2}{9} \div \dfrac{1}{3}$

(e) $2\dfrac{2}{3} \times 15$ (f) $3\dfrac{1}{5} - 1\dfrac{1}{4} + 7\dfrac{4}{5}$

(g) $6\dfrac{1}{8} - 8\dfrac{1}{4}$ (h) $\dfrac{2}{3} \cdot \dfrac{7}{4} - \dfrac{2}{3} \cdot \dfrac{1}{4}$

21. (a) Hal owns $3\dfrac{1}{2}$ acres and just purchased an adjacent plot of $\dfrac{3}{4}$ acres. The answer is $4\dfrac{1}{4}$. What is the question?

(b) Janet lives $1\dfrac{3}{4}$ mile from school. On the way to school, she stopped to walk the rest of the way with Brian, who lives $\dfrac{1}{2}$ of a mile from school. The answer is $1\dfrac{1}{4}$. What is the question?

(c) A family room is $5\dfrac{1}{2}$ yards wide and 6 yards long. The answer is 33 square yards. What is the question?

(d) Clea made $3\dfrac{1}{2}$ gallons of ginger ale, which she intends to bottle in "fifths" (that is, bottles that contain a fifth of a gallon). The answer is 17 full bottles and $\dfrac{1}{2}$ of another bottle. What is the question?

22. Invent interesting word problems that lead you to the given expression.

(a) $\dfrac{3}{4} + \dfrac{1}{2}$ (b) $4\dfrac{1}{2} \div \dfrac{3}{4}$ (c) $7\dfrac{2}{3} \times \dfrac{1}{4}$

Thinking Critically

23. Problem 31 of the Rhind papyrus, if translated literally, reads: "A quantity, its $\dfrac{2}{3}$, its $\dfrac{1}{2}$, its $\dfrac{1}{7}$, its whole, amount to 33." That is, in modern notation, $\dfrac{2}{3}x + \dfrac{1}{2}x + \dfrac{1}{7}x + x = 33$. What is the quantity?

24. Solve this problem from the Rhind papyrus: "Divide 100 loaves among five men in such a way that the share received shall be in arithmetic progression and that one seventh of the sum of the largest three shares shall be equal to the sum of the smallest two." [*Suggestion.* Denote the shares as s, $s + d$, $s + 2d$, $s + 3d$, $s + 4d$]

25. The ancient Egyptians measured steepness of a slope by the fraction $\dfrac{x}{y}$, where x is the number of hands of horizontal "run" and y is the number of cubits of vertical "rise." Seven hands form a cubit. Problem 56 of the Ahmes Papyrus asks for the steepness of the face of a pyramid 250 cubits high and having a square base 360 cubits on a side. The papyrus gives the answer $5\dfrac{1}{25}$. Show why this is correct.

26. **The Law of the Lever.** One of Archimedes (c. 225 B.C.) great achievements was the law of the lever. The law can be described in terms of a condition under which weights hung from a beam pivoting at 0 will be in balance. For example, the two beams shown below are in balance.

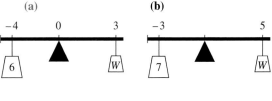

$$-3 \cdot 5 + 5 \cdot 3 = 0 \qquad -2 \cdot 9 + 3 \cdot 4 + 6 \cdot 1 = 0$$

In general, if weights W_1, W_2, . . . , W_n are hung at positions x_1, x_2, . . . , x_n, then the beam is balanced if, and only if, $x_1 \cdot W_1 + x_2 \cdot W_2 + \ldots + x_n \cdot W_n = 0$.

For each diagram below, find the missing weight W or unknown position x which will balance the beam. You can expect rational number answers.

(a) (b)

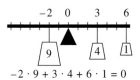

(c) (d)

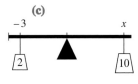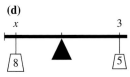

(e) (f)

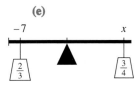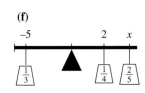

27. **(a)** Let x, y, and z be arbitrary rational numbers. Show that the sums of the three entries in every row, column, and diagonal in the Magic Square are the same.

$x - z$	$x - y + z$	$x + y$
$x + y + z$	x	$x - y - z$
$x - y$	$x + y - z$	$x + z$

(b) Let $x = \dfrac{1}{2}$, $y = \dfrac{1}{3}$, $z = \dfrac{1}{4}$. Find the corresponding Magic Square.

(c) Here is a partial Magic Square that corresponds to the form shown in part (a). Find x, y, z, and then fill in the remaining entries of the square.

$-\dfrac{5}{12}$		1
$-\dfrac{1}{3}$		

(*Hint:* $2x = (x + y) + (x - y)$.)

Making Connections

28. The earth revolves about the sun once in 365 days, 5 hours, 48 minutes, and 46 seconds. Since this *solar year* is more than 365 days long, it is important to have 366-day-long *leap* years to keep the seasons in the same months of the calendar year.

(a) The solar year is very nearly 365 days and 6 hours, or $365\dfrac{6}{24} = 365\dfrac{1}{4}$ days long. Explain why having the years divisible by 4 as leap years is a good rule to decide when leap years should occur.

(b) Show that a solar year is $365\dfrac{20926}{24 \cdot 60 \cdot 60}$ days long.

(c) Estimate the value given in part (b) with $365\dfrac{20952}{24 \cdot 60 \cdot 60}$, and then show that this can also be written as $365\dfrac{1}{4} - \dfrac{1}{100} + \dfrac{1}{400}$.

(d) What rule for choosing leap years is suggested by the approximation $365\dfrac{1}{4} - \dfrac{1}{100} + \dfrac{1}{400}$ to the solar year?

[*Hint:* 1900 was not a leap year, but 2000 is a leap year.]

29. Fractions have a prominent place in music, where the time value of a note is given as a fraction of a whole note. The note values and their corresponding fractions are shown in this table:

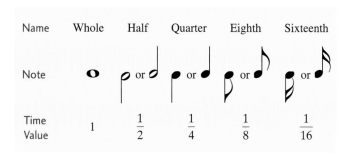

Name	Whole	Half	Quarter	Eighth	Sixteenth
Note					
Time Value	1	$\dfrac{1}{2}$	$\dfrac{1}{4}$	$\dfrac{1}{8}$	$\dfrac{1}{16}$

The time signature of the music can be interpreted as a fraction that gives the time duration of the measure. Here are two examples:

$$\frac{3}{4} = \frac{1}{4} + \frac{1}{2} \qquad \frac{6}{8} = \frac{1}{4} + \frac{1}{8} + \frac{2}{16} + \frac{1}{4}$$

In each measure shown, fill in the upper number of the time signature by adding the note values shown in the measure.

(a)

(b)

(c)

30. Stock prices are quoted in dollars and fractions (to the nearest $\frac{1}{16}$) of a dollar. For example, AAR Corporation was $13\frac{7}{8}$ at the close of the New York Stock Exchange on Wednesday, meaning that shares last sold for $13\frac{7}{8}$ each. On Thursday, the closing price increased to 14, which is reported as a change of $+\frac{1}{8}$. Similarly the closing prices of ACMin dropped from $11\frac{7}{8}$ to $11\frac{3}{4}$, for a change of $11\frac{3}{4} - 11\frac{7}{8} = -\frac{1}{8}$.

Company	Wed. Close	Change	Thurs. Close	Change
AAR	$13\frac{7}{8}$		14	$+\frac{1}{8}$
ACELln	$30\frac{3}{8}$	$+\frac{1}{8}$	$31\frac{1}{2}$	$+1\frac{1}{8}$
ACMin	$11\frac{7}{8}$	$+\frac{1}{8}$	$11\frac{3}{4}$	$-\frac{1}{8}$
ACMOp	$9\frac{5}{8}$		$9\frac{5}{8}$	
ACM Scl	$11\frac{5}{8}$		$11\frac{5}{8}$	

Fill in the missing entries in this table.

Company	Wed. Close	Change	Thurs. Close	Change
(a) Chrysler	$55\frac{1}{4}$	$+\frac{3}{8}$	$54\frac{1}{2}$	?
(b) Compaq	$34\frac{3}{16}$	$+2\frac{1}{4}$	?	$+\frac{5}{8}$
(c) DuPont	?	$-\frac{1}{8}$	$60\frac{1}{2}$	$-\frac{1}{2}$
(d) Ford	$51\frac{5}{16}$	$+\frac{7}{8}$	?	$1\frac{1}{8}$

31. Design a stairway which connects the patio to the deck (see Example 6.20).

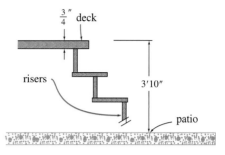

Assume the tread of each stair is $\frac{1}{2}$" thick.

32. This recipe makes six dozen cookies. Adjust the quantities to have a recipe for four dozen cookies.

1 cup shortening	$1\frac{1}{2}$ cup sugar
1 tsp baking soda	3 eggs
3 cups unsifted flour	$\frac{1}{2}$ tsp salt 9 oz mincemeat

33. Anja has a box of photographic print paper. Each sheet measures 8 by 10 inches. She could easily cut a sheet into four 4 by 5 inch rectangles. However, to save money, she wants to get six prints, all the same size, from each 8 by 10 inch sheet. Describe how she can cut the paper.

34. Krystoff has an 8' piece of picture frame molding, shown in cross section below.

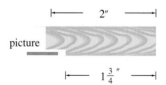

Is this 8' piece sufficient to frame a 16" by 20" picture? Allow for saw cuts and some extra space to ensure that the picture fits easily into the frame.

Using a Calculator

35. Use a calculator to evaluate the following expressions. Express your answers in simplest form.

   (a) $\frac{4}{5} \times \left(\frac{18}{25} - \frac{3}{4} \right)$ (b) $\left(\frac{-7}{3} + \frac{4}{9} \right) \div \frac{1}{5}$

36. Mathematicians from ancient times hoped to find a rational number $\frac{a}{b}$ equal to the square root of 2. A rather inaccurate choice is $\frac{3}{2}$, which is too large since $\left(\frac{3}{2} \right)^2 = \frac{9}{4} = 2 + \frac{1}{4}$. An improved estimate is obtained

by replacing the fraction $\frac{a}{b}$ with the fraction $\frac{a+2b}{a+b}$.

For example, $\frac{3}{2}$ is replaced with $\frac{3+2\cdot2}{3+2}=\frac{7}{5}$. Since $\left(\frac{7}{5}\right)^2=\frac{49}{25}=2-\frac{1}{25}$, we see that $\frac{7}{5}$ is a better approximation to $\sqrt{2}$ than $\frac{3}{2}$.

(a) Start with $\frac{7}{5}$, and use the replacement rule

$\frac{a}{b}\Rightarrow\frac{a+2b}{a+b}$ to obtain another rational

number. Is it a better approximation to

$\sqrt{2}$ than $\frac{7}{5}$?

(b) Use the replacement rule once more, starting with the rational number obtained in part (a). Do you obtain an even better approximation of $\sqrt{2}$?

(c) Set up a graphing calculator or spreadsheet program to automate the replacement rule $\frac{a}{b}\Rightarrow\frac{a+2b}{a+b}$. Begin with any fraction you wish and carry out the rule several times. Describe any pattern or properties of the sequence of rational numbers you generate.

From State Student Assessments

37. (Minnesota, Grade 5) Which figure shows $\frac{3}{5}$ shaded?

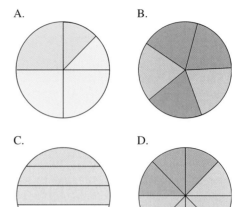

A.   B.

C.   D.

For Review

38. (a) The Ahmes papyrus is about 6 yards long and $\frac{1}{3}$ of a yard wide. What is its area in square yards?

(b) The Moscow papyrus, another source of mathematics of ancient Egypt, is about the same length as the Ahmes papyrus, but has $\frac{1}{4}$ the area. What is the width of the Moscow papyrus?

39. A TV, regularly priced at \$345, is offered on sale at "up to one-third off." What range of prices would you expect to pay?

40. The triangular shape shown to the right is $\frac{1}{4}$ of a whole figure. What does the whole figure look like? Give several answers.

EPILOGUE   Fractions and Technology

The equation $x+m=n$ cannot always be solved in the whole numbers. However, by extending the whole numbers to the integers, this equation always has a unique solution. Computationally, going from whole number to integer arithmetic comes at a modest cost, since the algorithms used to perform calculations on integers are essentially the same as those for whole numbers; the only added step is determining if the answer is positive or negative.

In the rational number system, the greatest gain is that the equation $rx+p=q$ can always be solved uniquely for the unknown x, whatever values are given for the rational numbers r, p, and q (although r must be nonzero).

However, going to rational number arithmetic comes with a high cost in the complexity of the computations. For example, adding two rationals $\frac{a}{b}+\frac{c}{d}$ requires three integer multiplications and an integer addition to produce the answer $\frac{ad+bc}{bd}$. Even then, the answer may not be in simplest form. It is scarcely surprising that school children (and adults) often find fractions and the arithmetic of fractions difficult.

When calculators and computers first became widely available, there was some talk of diminishing, or even removing, fractions from the curriculum. After all, these machines were based on decimal fractions, not on common fractions. There are many good reasons this did not and should not occur, including:

- fractions, as expressions of ratios and rates, convey a dynamic sense of number which is absent in decimal fractions;
- the algebraic concepts used in rational number arithmetic provide important readiness skills for learning algebra.

At the present time, technology is moving in a direction which supports teaching, learning, and using fractions. For example, inexpensive calculators with fraction arithmetic capabilities are now becoming common in the classroom. Also, computer algebra systems for both calculators and computers can now perform rational number arithmetic in the blink of an eye to unlimited precision. With these devices, problem solving and critical thinking in the realm of rational numbers can actually be a source of pleasure.

In this chapter, we have discussed the properties and arithmetic of fractions and rational numbers, both from a concrete and pictorial point of view and from a more theoretical standpoint. We have also seen how the operations with fractions often depend on notions from number theory. Many of the examples illustrated the practical side of fractions, in which the solution of real-life problems led naturally to operations with rational numbers.

CHAPTER 6 SUMMARY

Key Concepts

1. The Basic Concepts of Fractions and Rational Numbers

(a) A fraction is an ordered pair of integers a and b, $b \neq 0$, written $\frac{a}{b}$ or a/b.

Fractions are physically and pictorially modeled with colored regions, sets, fraction strips, and the number line.

(b) Two fractions that express the same quantity, or correspond to the same point on a number line, are called equivalent fractions. In particular $\frac{a}{b} = \frac{a \cdot n}{b \cdot n}$ for all integers n, $n \neq 0$ (the fundamental law of fractions), and $\frac{a}{b} = \frac{c}{d}$ if, and only if, $ad = bc$.

(c) Any fraction is equivalent to a fraction in simplest form. Two or more fractions can always be replaced by equivalent fractions with a common denominator.

(d) A rational number is a number represented by a common fraction $\frac{a}{b}$. The same rational number can also be represented by any fraction equivalent to $\frac{a}{b}$.

(e) If two rational numbers are represented by $\frac{a}{b}$ and $\frac{c}{d}$, with $b > 0$ and $d > 0$, then $\frac{a}{b} < \frac{c}{d}$ if, and only if, $ad < bc$.

2. The Arithmetic of Rational Numbers

(a) The sum of two rational numbers represented by fractions $\dfrac{a}{b}$ and $\dfrac{c}{b}$ with a common denominator is defined by $\dfrac{a}{b} + \dfrac{c}{b} = \dfrac{a+c}{b}$. The definition is motivated by colored region and number-line models. From this definition it follows that $\dfrac{a}{b} + \dfrac{c}{d} = \dfrac{ad}{bd} + \dfrac{bc}{bd} = \dfrac{ad+bc}{bd}$.

(b) Subtraction is defined by the missing-addend approach: $\dfrac{a}{b} - \dfrac{c}{d} = \dfrac{e}{f}$ if, and only if, $\dfrac{a}{b} = \dfrac{c}{d} + \dfrac{e}{f}$. The subtraction formula $\dfrac{a}{b} - \dfrac{c}{d} = \dfrac{ad}{bd} - \dfrac{bc}{bd} = \dfrac{ad-bc}{bd}$ follows from the definition of subtraction.

(c) Multiplication is defined by $\dfrac{a}{b} \cdot \dfrac{c}{d} = \dfrac{ac}{bd}$. This definition is motivated by extending the rectangular array model of multiplication.

(d) Division is defined by the missing-factor approach: $\dfrac{a}{b} \div \dfrac{c}{d} = \dfrac{e}{f}$ if, and only if, $\dfrac{a}{b} = \dfrac{c}{d} \cdot \dfrac{e}{f}$. The "invert the divisor and multiply" algorithm follows from this definition, so that $\dfrac{a}{b} \div \dfrac{c}{d} = \dfrac{a}{b} \cdot \dfrac{d}{c}$.

(e) A nonzero rational number, $\dfrac{a}{b}$, has a unique multiplicative inverse, the reciprocal $\dfrac{b}{a}$, which when multiplied by $\dfrac{a}{b}$ gives the product 1. That is, $\dfrac{a}{b} \cdot \dfrac{b}{a} = 1$.

3. The Rational Number System

(a) The rational numbers are closed under addition. Addition is commutative and associative, and zero is the additive identity.

(b) Each rational number, $\dfrac{a}{b}$, has a unique negative, $-\dfrac{a}{b}$, given by $\dfrac{-a}{b}$, which is the additive inverse of $\dfrac{a}{b}$. Subtraction is equivalent to adding the negative, so $\dfrac{a}{b} - \dfrac{b}{d} = \dfrac{a}{b} + \left(-\dfrac{b}{d} \right)$.

(c) Multiplication is closed, commutative, and associative; one is the multiplicative identity; and multiplication distributes over addition and subtraction.

(d) Each nonzero rational number $\dfrac{a}{b}$ has a unique multiplicative inverse given by the reciprocal $\dfrac{b}{a}$. Division is equivalent to multiplication by the multiplicative inverse of the divisor, so $\dfrac{a}{b} \div \dfrac{c}{d} = \dfrac{a}{b} \cdot \dfrac{d}{c}$.

(e) The rational numbers have the density property; that is, there is a rational number between any two rational numbers.

(f) Computational skills—estimations, rounding, mental arithmetic, paper and pencil and electronic calculations—are as useful and necessary for work with the rational numbers as for any other number system.

Vocabulary and Notation

Section 6.1

Fraction
Numerator
Denominator
Models for fractions:
    Colored regions
    Sets
    Fraction strips
    Number line
Equivalent fraction
Fundamental law of fractions
Simplest (or reduced) form
Common denominator
Least common denominator
Rational number
Set of rational numbers, Q

Section 6.2

Operations on fractions:

    Addition $\dfrac{a}{b} + \dfrac{c}{d}$

    Subtraction $\dfrac{a}{b} - \dfrac{c}{d}$

    Multiplication $\dfrac{a}{b} \cdot \dfrac{c}{d}$ or $\dfrac{a}{b} \times \dfrac{c}{d}$

    Division $\dfrac{a}{b} \div \dfrac{c}{d}$

Mixed number
Proper fraction
Invert the divisor and multiply algorithm
Reciprocal, or multiplicative inverse

Section 6.3

Negative (or opposite, or additive inverse)
Transitive property of order
Density property

CHAPTER REVIEW EXERCISES

Section 6.1

1. What fraction is represented by the darker blue shading in each of the colored region models shown? In (d) the unit is the region inside one circle.

    (a)   (b)

    (c)   (d)

    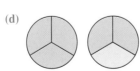

2. Label the points on the number line which correspond to these rational numbers:

    (a) $\dfrac{3}{4}$ (b) $\dfrac{12}{8}$

    (c) 1 (d) $2\dfrac{3}{8}$

3. Express each rational number by a fraction in simplest form.

    (a) $\dfrac{27}{81}$ (b) $\dfrac{100}{825}$

    (c) $\dfrac{378}{72}$ (d) $\dfrac{3^5 \cdot 7^2 \cdot 11^3}{3^2 \cdot 7^3 \cdot 11^2}$

4. Order these fractions from smallest to largest.

    $$\frac{1}{2}, \ \frac{13}{27}, \ \frac{25}{49}, \ \frac{13}{30}, \ \frac{26}{49}$$

5. Find a common denominator of each set of fractions.

    (a) $\dfrac{4}{9}, \dfrac{5}{12}$ (b) $\dfrac{7}{18}, \dfrac{5}{6}, \dfrac{1}{3}$

Section 6.2

6. Illustrate $\dfrac{3}{4} + \dfrac{7}{8}$ on the number line.

7. Illustrate $\dfrac{3}{4} - \dfrac{1}{3}$ with fraction strips.

8. Compute these sums and differences.

    (a) $\dfrac{3}{8} + \dfrac{1}{4}$ (b) $\dfrac{2}{9} + \dfrac{-5}{12}$

    (c) $\dfrac{4}{5} - \dfrac{2}{3}$ (d) $5\dfrac{1}{4} - 1\dfrac{5}{6}$

9. Illustrate these products by labeling and coloring appropriate rectangular regions.

   (a) $3 \times \dfrac{1}{3}$ (b) $\dfrac{2}{3} \times 4$ (c) $\dfrac{5}{6} \times \dfrac{3}{2}$

10. On a map, it is $7\dfrac{1}{8}{}''$ from Arlington to Banks. If the scale of the map is $1\dfrac{1}{4}{}''$ per mile, how far is it between the two towns?

Section 6.3

11. Perform these calculations, expressing your answers in simplest form.

    (a) $\dfrac{-3}{4} + \dfrac{5}{8}$ (b) $\dfrac{4}{5} - \dfrac{-7}{10}$

   (c) $\left(\dfrac{3}{8} \cdot \dfrac{-4}{27}\right) \div \dfrac{1}{9}$ (d) $\dfrac{2}{5} \cdot \left(\dfrac{3}{4} - \dfrac{5}{2}\right)$

12. Solve each equation. Give the rational number x as a fraction in simplest form.

    (a) $3x + 5 = 11$ (b) $x + \dfrac{2}{3} = \dfrac{1}{2}$

    (c) $\dfrac{3}{5}x + \dfrac{1}{2} = \dfrac{2}{3}$ (d) $-\dfrac{4}{3}x + 1 = \dfrac{1}{4}$

13. Find two rational numbers between $\dfrac{5}{6}$ and $\dfrac{10}{11}$.

14. Do the following calculations mentally. Explain your method.

    (a) $1\dfrac{1}{3} + 2\dfrac{5}{12} + \dfrac{1}{4}$ (b) $\dfrac{6}{7} \cdot \dfrac{28}{3} \cdot \dfrac{5}{8}$ (c) $\dfrac{36}{5} \div \dfrac{9}{25}$

CHAPTER TEST

1. Illustrate $\dfrac{2}{3}$ (a) on the number line, (b) with a fraction strip, (c) with a colored region model, and (d) with the set model.

2. Give three different fractions each equivalent to $-\dfrac{3}{4}$.

3. Order these rational numbers from least to greatest.
   $\dfrac{16}{5},\ \dfrac{2}{3},\ -1\dfrac{1}{2},\ 0,\ \dfrac{5}{8},\ 3,\ -3.$

4. Perform these calculations:

   (a) $\dfrac{1}{3} + \dfrac{5}{8} - \dfrac{5}{6}$ (b) $\left(\dfrac{2}{3} - \dfrac{5}{4}\right) \div \dfrac{3}{4}$

   (c) $\dfrac{4}{7} \cdot \left(\dfrac{35}{4} + \dfrac{-42}{12}\right)$ (d) $\dfrac{123}{369} \div \dfrac{1}{3}$

5. (a) Define division in the rational number system.

   (b) Justify the invert and multiply algorithm; that is, prove that $\dfrac{a}{b} \div \dfrac{c}{d} = \dfrac{a}{b} \cdot \dfrac{d}{c}$, where $c \neq 0$.

6. (a) Invent a realistic problem whose solution requires the calculation $\dfrac{4}{5} \cdot \dfrac{2}{3}$.

   (b) Make up a realistic problem which leads to $\dfrac{3}{8} \div \dfrac{3}{10}$.

7. Solve the following equations and inequalities for all possible rational numbers x. Show all of your steps.

   (a) $2x + 3 > 0$ (b) $\dfrac{3}{4}x + \dfrac{1}{2} = \dfrac{1}{3}$

   (c) $\dfrac{5}{4}x > -\dfrac{1}{3}$ (d) $\dfrac{1}{2} < 4x + \dfrac{5}{6}$

8. Carefully explain why $\dfrac{a+b}{b} = \dfrac{c+d}{d}$ if, and only if, $\dfrac{a}{b} = \dfrac{c}{d}$.

9. An acre is $\dfrac{1}{640}$ of a square mile.

   (a) How many acres are in a rectangular plot of ground $\dfrac{1}{8}$ mile wide by $\dfrac{1}{2}$ mile long?

   (b) A rectangular piece of property contains 80 acres and is $\dfrac{1}{2}$ mile long. What is the width of the property?

10. (a) What is the density property of the rational numbers?

    (b) Find a rational number between $\dfrac{3}{5}$ and $\dfrac{2}{3}$.

11. What is the best approximate answer listed for each of these problems?

    (a) $2\dfrac{1}{48} + 3\dfrac{1}{99} + 6\dfrac{13}{25}$ is approximately

    $11, \quad 11\dfrac{1}{2}, \quad 12, \quad 12\dfrac{1}{4}.$

(b) $8 \cdot \left(2\frac{1}{2} + 3\frac{7}{15} \right)$ is approximately

40, 44, 48, 56.

(c) $11\frac{9}{10} \div \frac{21}{40}$ is approximately

20, 23, 26, 30.

12. (a) Define *additive inverse*.

(b) Find the additive inverses of the following rational numbers: $\dfrac{3}{4}, \dfrac{-7}{4}, \dfrac{8}{-2}$.

13. (a) Define *multiplicative inverse*.

(b) Find the multiplicative inverses of these rational numbers: $\dfrac{3}{2}, \dfrac{-4}{5}, -5$.

14. Describe how the following calculations can be performed efficiently with "mental math."

(a) $\dfrac{19}{111} \cdot \left(\dfrac{2}{3} + \dfrac{-4}{6} \right)$

(b) $\dfrac{5}{6} \cdot \dfrac{36}{15}$

(c) $\dfrac{5}{8} \cdot \left(\dfrac{9}{5} - \dfrac{1}{5} \right)$

(d) $\dfrac{2}{3} \cdot \dfrac{3}{4} \cdot \dfrac{4}{5} \cdot \dfrac{5}{6}$

CHAPTER

7

Decimals and Real Numbers

7.1 Decimals
7.2 Computations with Decimals
7.3 Ratio and Proportion
7.4 Percent

HANDS ON
On Triangles and Squares

Materials Needed

One 3" × 5" card, scissors, a sharp pencil, and one sheet of plain white paper.

Directions

Step 1. Cut a triangle with unequal sides off the corner of the card and denote the lengths of the three sides by a, b, and c as shown.

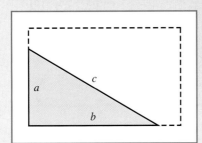

Step 2. With the lettering on the triangle always facing up, carefully trace around the triangle four times to form a square as shown here.

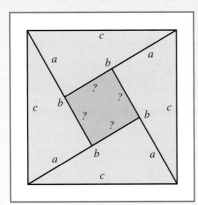

Step 3. Determine the dimensions of the small square in the center and then find its area. Remember that, using the distributive property of multiplication over subtraction and the commutative property,

$$(x - y)(x - y) = (x - y)x - (x - y)y$$
$$= x^2 - yx - xy + y^2$$
$$= x^2 - 2xy + y^2.$$

Step 4. The area of the large square is clearly four times the area of the triangle plus the area of the small square; it is also equal to c^2. Express these two ways of finding the area of the large square by an equation and simplify it as much as possible.

Step 5. Relate the equation in Step 4 to the diagram shown here. What does the equation reveal about triangles with one square corner (that is, one right angle)? Explain briefly.

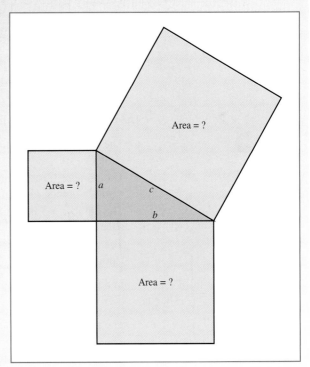

Step 6. If c is the length of the diagonal of a square one unit on a side, then the formula of Step 4 gives $c^2 = 2$. Remarkably, as we will see later, this number c is not a rational number.

CONNECTIONS   Further Enlarging the Number System

In the preceding chapters we have considered:

- the set of natural numbers, N,
- the set of whole numbers, W,
- the set of integers, I, and
- the set of rational numbers, Q.

The fact that each succeeding set is an extension of the immediately preceding set can be expressed in a Venn diagram as shown in Figure 7.1.

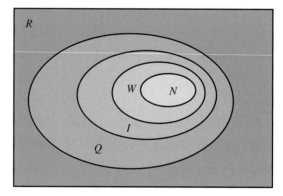

Figure 7.1
Venn diagram for the natural numbers, whole numbers, integers, and rational numbers

The following statements illustrate the relationships between these sets:

- The number 2 is a natural number, a whole number, an integer, and a rational number.
- The number 0 is a whole number, an integer, and a rational number; it is *not* a natural number.
- The number −5 is an integer and a rational number; it is not a whole number or a natural number.
- The number 3/4 is a rational number; it is not an integer, a whole number, or a natural number.

From a practical point of view, each number system was created to meet a specific need:

- The natural numbers came into being as a result of people's need to count.
- The number 0, which with the natural numbers comprises the set of whole numbers, was first introduced simply as a place holder in positional number systems, but it also allows us to count the number of elements in the empty set and has other useful arithmetic properties.
- The integers allow us to keep track of debits and credits, gains and losses, degrees above zero and degrees below zero, and so on.
- The rational numbers are needed to make accurate measurements of lengths, areas, volumes, and other quantities.

From a more mathematical point of view the natural numbers allow us to solve equations like

$$x - 3 = 0 \quad \text{and} \quad 7x - 21 = 0.$$

The whole numbers allow us to solve equations like

$$3x = 0 \quad \text{and} \quad (x - 5)(x - 7) = 0.$$

Extending the number system to include all integers allows us to solve equations like

$$x + 4 = 0 \quad \text{and} \quad 9x + 36 = 0.$$

Extending the number system to include the rational numbers allows us to solve equations like

$$3x - 4 = 0 \quad \text{and} \quad (2x + 1)(5x - 4) = 0.$$

In summary, the rational number system permits us to deal with a wide range of practical and theoretical problems. However, remarkably, there remain simple questions that ought to have simple answers but do not if we do not extend the number system beyond the rationals. For example, if we stopped with the rationals, we would be unable to answer such a simple question as, "How long is the diagonal of a square measuring 1 unit on a side?" (See Figure 7.2.) Thus, it is necessary to extend the number system at least once more. In this chapter, we consider the system of numbers called the real numbers.* We do so by means of decimals.

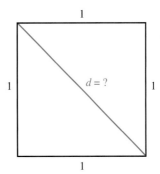

Figure 7.2
The length of the diagonal of a square 1 unit on a side is not a rational number.

7.1 Decimals

Since it is a positional system based on ten, we have used the term decimal system (from the Latin *decimus* meaning tenth) to refer generally to the Indo-Arabic system of numeration in common use today. However, more colloquially, people often refer to expressions like 0.235 or 2.7142 as **decimals** as opposed to 24, 98, 0, or 2478, which they more often speak of as whole numbers or integers. In fact, both are part and parcel of the same system. Just as the **expanded form** of 2478 is

$$2478 = 2 \cdot 10^3 + 4 \cdot 10^2 + 7 \cdot 10^1 + 8 \cdot 10^0$$
$$= 2000 + 400 + 70 + 8,$$

*The word *real,* when applied to numbers, is used to distinguish these numbers from those called *imaginary* in a final extension of the number system to the system of *complex numbers.* We do not consider the complex number system in this book.

the expanded form of 0.235 is

$$0.235 = 2 \cdot \frac{1}{10^1} + 3 \cdot \frac{1}{10^2} + 5 \cdot \frac{1}{10^3}$$

$$= \frac{2}{10} + \frac{3}{100} + \frac{5}{1000},$$

and the expanded form of 23.47 is

$$23.47 = 2 \cdot 10^1 + 3 \cdot 10^0 + 4 \cdot \frac{1}{10^1} + 7 \cdot \frac{1}{10^2}$$

$$= 20 + 3 + \frac{4}{10} + \frac{7}{100}.$$

Representations of Decimals

For beginning grade school students, it is helpful to introduce the study of decimals by considering concrete physical manipulative devices and pictorial representations. We discuss three such representations here.

Using mats, strips, and units   As in the introduction of fractions in chapter 6, if a mat represents one unit or 1, then a strip represents one-tenth or $\frac{1}{10}$ and a unit represents one

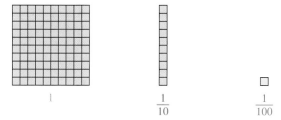

Figure 7.3

Representation of 1, $\frac{1}{10}$, and $\frac{1}{100}$ using a mat, a strip, and a unit

one-hundredth or $\frac{1}{100}$ as shown in Figure 7.3. Thus, a display of 3 mats, 2 strips, and 5 units as shown in Figure 7.4, represents $3 \cdot 1 + 2 \cdot \frac{1}{10} + 5 \cdot \frac{1}{100} = 3 + \frac{2}{10} + \frac{5}{100} = \frac{325}{100}$, which we write using the shorthand notation 3.25. Conversely, the expanded notation for 3.25 is $3 + \frac{2}{10} + \frac{5}{100}$. The decimal point is used to separate the integer part of the numeral from the fractional part.

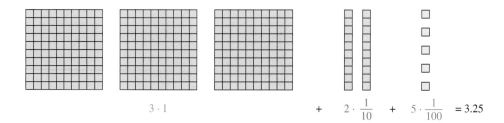

Figure 7.4

Representation of 3.25 using mats, strips, and units

The development of mathematics over time has been paralleled by the development of good mathematical notation that facilitates doing mathematics. One of these developments was that of the Indo-Arabic or decimal system of notation as already observed. Related to this is the use of a period (the decimal point) to separate the integer part and the fractional part of a numeral.

Thus,

$$25.423 = 25\frac{423}{1000}.$$

As we have seen, use of the decimal point makes possible the easy extension of the algorithms for integer computation to decimal computation. Though it seems natural to us now, the decimal point was developed rather late in the history of mathematics and even today its use is not completely standardized. To illustrate the development, we list here various notations of the past and present.

3.4813	modern American
3 · 4813	modern English
3,4813	modern continental Europe
3 ǀ 4813	Rudolph, 1530
34813	F. Vieta, 1579
3 ⓪ 4 ① 8 ② 1 ③ 3 ④	S. Stevin, 1585
$\overset{\text{o i ii iii iv}}{3 \,.\, 4\ 8\ 1\ 3}$	J. Beyer, 1603
3 4813	J. Beyer, 1603
$3^{(0)}4^{(1)}8^{(2)}1^{(3)}3^{(4)}$	R. Norton, 1608
34813 ④	W. Kalcheim, 1629

Using base ten blocks   Consider the base ten blocks depicted in Figure 7.5. Suppose the block is chosen as the unit. Then, since ten flats are equivalent to a block, a flat represents $\frac{1}{10}$. Similarly, ten longs are equivalent to a flat and $10 \cdot 10 = 100$ longs are equivalent

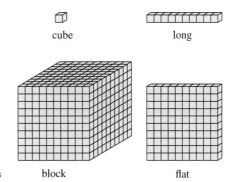

cube   long

Figure 7.5
Base ten blocks   block   flat

to a block. Thus, a long represents $\frac{1}{100}$. Finally, since there are $10 \cdot 10 \cdot 10 = 1000$ cubes in a block, a cube represents $\frac{1}{1000}$. With this in mind, a display of 2 blocks, 1 flat, 3 longs, and 2 cubes, as shown in Figure 7.6, would represent $2 \cdot 1 + 1 \cdot \frac{1}{10} + 3 \cdot \frac{1}{100} + 2 \cdot \frac{1}{1000} = 2 + \frac{1}{10} + \frac{3}{100} + \frac{2}{1000} = \frac{2132}{1000}$, which we write using the shorthand notation 2.132. Conversely, the expanded notation for 2.132 is $2 + \frac{1}{10} + \frac{3}{100} + \frac{2}{1000}$.

On the other hand, if the flat is chosen as the unit, then the above reasoning dictates that the block represents 10, the flat represents 1, the long represents $\frac{1}{10}$, and the cube $\frac{1}{100}$.

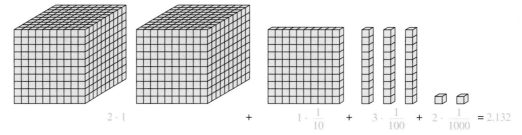

Figure 7.6
Representing 2.132 using base ten blocks

In this case, the display in Figure 7.6 would represent $2 \cdot 10 + 1 \cdot 1 + 3 \cdot \dfrac{1}{10} + 2 \cdot \dfrac{1}{100} =$ $20 + 1 + \dfrac{3}{10} + \dfrac{2}{100}$, which we would write as 21.32.

Using dollars, dimes, and pennies   A particularly apt manipulative, already familiar to children, is provided by money. Since ten dimes are worth one dollar and one hundred pennies are also worth one dollar, a dollar represents 1, a dime represents $\dfrac{1}{10}$, and a penny represents $\dfrac{1}{100}$. Thus, the 3.25 of Figure 7.4 would be represented as in Figure 7.7. This representation is particularly useful since students are already familiar with the fact that this set of coins is worth three dollars and twenty-five cents as well as the fact that this is written $3.25, thus making the understanding of the above expanded notation for 3.25 quite natural.

Figure 7.7
Representing 3.25 using dollars, dimes, and pennies

EXAMPLE   7.1

Using Money to Represent Decimals

How would you use money in attempting to explain the decimal 23.75 to elementary students?

Solution

Use 2 ten-dollar bills, 3 dollars, 7 dimes, and 5 pennies. The students will easily see that this collection of bills and coins is worth $23.75 and this makes it relatively easy to explain the expanded notation

$$23.75 = 2 \cdot 10 + 3 \cdot 1 + 7 \cdot \frac{1}{10} + 5 \cdot \frac{1}{100}$$

since a dime is one-tenth of a dollar and a penny is one one-hundredth of a dollar.

3-1 Place Value: Comparing and Ordering Decimals

You'll Learn ...

■ to compare and order decimals

... How It's Used

Environmental scientists need to compare the decimal values of pollutants that they find in the air or in water.

▶ **Lesson Link** ◀ You have worked with whole numbers. Now you'll begin to study decimals by deciding which of two decimals is greater. ◀

Explore   Comparing and Ordering Decimals

Model Behavior

Materials: Graph paper, Colored pencils

Modeling Decimals

The graph paper shows a model of the number 1.47. To model a decimal:

- Color a complete 10-by-10 grid for each whole in the decimal.

- Draw another 10-by-10 grid next to the last complete grid.

- In this grid, color one 10-by-1 strip for each tenth in the decimal. Color a small square for each hundredth.

1. Draw a grid model for each decimal.

   a. 1.3   **b.** 1.29   **c.** 0.8   **d.** 1.30   **e.** 0.51   **f.** 0.99

2. What do you notice about the models for 1.3 and 1.30? What does this tell you about these numbers? Explain.

3. Rank the decimals from smallest to largest. Explain your reasoning.

4. The number 51 is greater than 8. Why is 0.8 greater than 0.51?

5. Could you use this method to model 1.354? Explain.

Learn   Comparing and Ordering Decimals

The place value of each digit of a whole number is one-tenth of the value of the place to its left. Moving to the right of a decimal point, you can create the place values *tenths, hundredths, thousandths,* and so on.

106 *Chapter 3 • Number Sense: Decimals and Fractions*

SOURCE: *Scott Foresman–Addison Wesley Middle School Math,* Course 2, p. 106, by Randall I. Charles et al. Copyright © 1999, Addison Wesley Longman, Inc.

Questions for the Teacher

1. The above lesson models decimals. Each 10-by-10 square represents one unit. Each column of ten small squares represents one tenth. Each small square represents one one-hundredth. Since this is the language of fractions, how would you explain the notation 1.47 to a student?

2. How would you assist a student having trouble with problem 4 above?

3. How would you help a student understand how to answer problem 5 above? Would it help to have a set of base ten blocks that includes a 1000 cube? Explain.

Fractions and Decimals

In grades 6–8, students expand their work with fractions, decimals, and percents, so that they are able to move flexibly among equivalents and apply a range of strategies to order and compare rational numbers. The shift in thinking of fractions as "parts of" specific units to understanding fractions as numbers is completed in the middle grades. Students' knowledge about, and use of, decimals in the base-ten system also extends in these grades. In addition to estimating with rational numbers, students in grades 6–8 also develop computational strategies for fractions and decimals.

SOURCE: Reprinted with permission from *Curriculum and Evaluation Standards for School Mathematics: Discussion Draft*, copyright 1998 by the National Council of Teachers of Mathematics. All rights reserved.

Using the representations discussed, students can be led to understand that the shorthand notation for $\frac{1}{10}$ is 0.1, for $\frac{1}{100}$ is 0.01, for $\frac{1}{1000}$ is 0.001, for $\frac{2}{10}$ is 0.2, for $\frac{3}{100}$ is 0.03, etc., and also to understand that each digit of a decimal numeral contributes an amount to the number being represented that depends both on the digit and on its position in the number as shown in Table 7.1.

TABLE 7.1   Positional Values in the Decimal System

Position Names ...	Hundreds	Tens	Units	Tenths	Hundredths	Thousandths	Ten Thousandths ...
Decimal Form ...	100	10	1	0.1	0.01	0.001	0.0001 ...
Rational Form ...	100	10	1	$\frac{1}{10}$	$\frac{1}{100}$	$\frac{1}{1000}$	$\frac{1}{10,000}$ ...
Power of 10 ...	10^2	10^1	10^0	10^{-1}	10^{-2}	10^{-3}	10^{-4} ...

The pattern in expanded notation becomes even more clear if we use negative exponents.

Negative Exponents and Expanded Exponential Form

We have already observed that, for a natural number n,

$$\overbrace{}^{n \text{ factors}}$$

a^n is shorthand for the product $a \cdot a \cdots a$

and therefore

$$\overset{\overbrace{n \text{ factors}}}{a^n} \cdot \overset{\overbrace{m \text{ factors}}}{a^m} = a \cdot a \cdots a \cdot a \cdot a \cdots a = a^{m+n}.$$

Moreover, if this rule is to hold for $m = 0$, then

$$a^n \cdot a^0 = a^{n+0} = a^n$$

and we must define $a^0 = 1$ as we did in Chapter 2. Now suppose that n is a positive integer so that $-n$ is negative. What shall we mean by a^{-n}? If we require that the above rule of exponents holds for **negative exponents** as well as for 0, then

$$a^n \cdot a^{-n} = a^{n+(-n)} = a^0 = 1.$$

$$\left(r \cdot \frac{1}{r} = 1 \right)$$

This implies that we should define a^{-n} to be $1/a^n$.

DEFINITION   *Negative Numbers and Zero as Exponents*

If n is a positive integer and $a \neq 0$, then $a^0 = 1$ and $a^{-n} = \dfrac{1}{a^n}$.

Using this definition, we complete the last row of Table 7.1 as shown. We also write the decimals at the beginning of this section in **expanded exponential form** as follows:

$$0.235 = 0 + 2 \cdot \frac{1}{10^1} + 3 \cdot \frac{1}{10^2} + 5 \cdot \frac{1}{10^3}$$

$$= 2 \cdot 10^{-1} + 3 \cdot 10^{-2} + 5 \cdot 10^{-3}$$

$$23.47 = 2 \cdot 10^1 + 3 \cdot 10^0 + 4 \cdot \frac{1}{10^1} + 7 \cdot \frac{1}{10^2}$$

$$= 2 \cdot 10^1 + 3 \cdot 10^0 + 4 \cdot 10^{-1} + 7 \cdot 10^{-2}$$

In this form, the pattern of decreasing exponents is both clear and neat.

EXAMPLE   7.2

Writing Decimals in Expanded Exponential Form

Write each of these in expanded exponential form.

(a)   234.72   **(b)**   30.0012

Solution

(a) $234.72 = 2 \cdot 10^2 + 3 \cdot 10^1 + 4 \cdot 10^0 + 7 \cdot 10^{-1} + 2 \cdot 10^{-2}$
(b) $30.0012 = 3 \cdot 10^1 + 0 \cdot 10^0 + 0 \cdot 10^{-1} + 0 \cdot 10^{-2} + 1 \cdot 10^{-3} + 2 \cdot 10^{-4}$

Multiplying and Dividing Decimals by Powers of 10

There is an emphasis in elementary textbooks on what happens notationally (to the decimal point) when a number is multiplied by a power of ten. Consider the decimal

$$25.723 = 2 \cdot 10^1 + 5 \cdot 10^0 + 7 \cdot 10^{-1} + 2 \cdot 10^{-2} + 3 \cdot 10^{-3}.$$

If we multiply by 10^2 using the distributive property and the above rule for multiplying powers, we obtain

$$(10^2)(25.723) = (10^2)(2 \cdot 10^1 + 5 \cdot 10^0 + 7 \cdot 10^{-1} + 2 \cdot 10^{-2} + 3 \cdot 10^{-3})$$
$$= 2 \cdot 10^{2+1} + 5 \cdot 10^{2+0} + 7 \cdot 10^{2+(-1)} + 2 \cdot 10^{2+(-2)} + 3 \cdot 10^{2+(-3)}$$
$$= 2 \cdot 10^3 + 5 \cdot 10^2 + 7 \cdot 10^1 + 2 \cdot 10^0 + 3 \cdot 10^{-1}$$
$$= 2572.3$$

and the notational effect is to move the decimal point two places to the right. Note that 2 is the exponent of the power of 10 we are multiplying by and also the number of zeros in 100.

$10^2 = 100$

The result is analogous if we divide 25.723 by 10^2 except that the notational effect is to move the decimal point two places *to the left*. To see this, recall that we can divide by multiplying by the multiplicative inverse. Thus,

$$(25.723) \div 10^2 = (25.723) \cdot (1/10^2)$$
$$= (25.723) \cdot 10^{-2}$$
$$= (2 \cdot 10^1 + 5 \cdot 10^0 + 7 \cdot 10^{-1} + 2 \cdot 10^{-2} + 3 \cdot 10^{-3}) \cdot (10^{-2})$$
$$= 2 \cdot 10^{1+(-2)} + 5 \cdot 10^{0+(-2)} + 7 \cdot 10^{(-1)+(-2)} + 2 \cdot 10^{(-2)+(-2)}$$
$$\quad + 3 \cdot 10^{(-3)+(-2)}$$
$$= 2 \cdot 10^{-1} + 5 \cdot 10^{-2} + 7 \cdot 10^{-3} + 2 \cdot 10^{-4} + 3 \cdot 10^{-5}$$
$$= 0.25723.$$

$10^{-2} = \dfrac{1}{10^2}$

These results are typical of the general case, which we state here as a theorem.

> **THEOREM** *Multiplying and Dividing Decimals by Powers of 10*
> The notational effect of multiplying a decimal by 10^r is to move the decimal point r places to the right. The notational effect of dividing a decimal by 10^r (that is, multiplying by 10^{-r}) is to move the decimal point r places to the left.

EXAMPLE 7.3 | **Multiplying and Dividing Decimals by Powers of 10**

Compute each of the following.

(a) $(10^3)(253.26)$ (b) $(253.26) \div 10^3$
(c) $(100)(34.764)$ (d) $(34.764) \div 10{,}000$

Solution | The preceding theorem gives the desired results.

(a) $(10^3)(253.26) = 253{,}260$
(b) $(253.26) \div 10^3 = 0.25326$
(c) $(100)(34.764) = (10^2)(34.764) = 3476.4$
(d) $(34.764) \div 10{,}000 = 34.764 \div (10^4) = 0.0034764$

Terminating Decimals as Fractions

From grade school we know that

$$\frac{1}{3} = 0.333\ldots$$

where the ellipsis dots indicate that the string of 3s continues without end. Such a decimal is called a **nonterminating decimal.** A decimal like 24.357 which has only finitely many digits is called a **terminating decimal.** The preceding discussion concerning expanded notation shows that every terminating decimal represents a rational number; that is, any terminating decimal can be represented by a fraction with integers in the numerator and denominator. For example, using expanded notation

$$24.357 = 20 + 4 + \frac{3}{10} + \frac{5}{100} + \frac{7}{1000}$$

$$= \frac{20{,}000}{1000} + \frac{4000}{1000} + \frac{300}{1000} + \frac{50}{1000} + \frac{7}{1000}$$

$$= \frac{24{,}357}{1000}.$$

Alternatively,

$$24.357 = 24.357 \cdot \frac{1000}{1000}$$

$$= \frac{24{,}357}{1000}$$

$$a \cdot \frac{b}{c} = \frac{ab}{c}$$

as before. In each case, the denominator is determined by the position of the right-most digit (in this case, the 7 is in the thousandths position).

The preceding discussion shows how to convert a terminating decimal into a ratio of two integers, that is, into a fraction. Not all rational numbers have finite decimal expansions, but those that do can be converted to decimal form as follows. Consider

$$\frac{17}{40} = \frac{17}{2^3 \cdot 5^1}.$$

Since the prime factor representation of the denominator contains only 2s and 5s, the fraction, can be written so that the denominator is a power of 10. Thus,

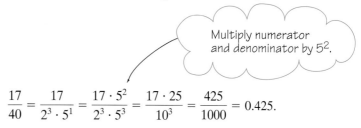

Multiply numerator and denominator by 5^2.

$$\frac{17}{40} = \frac{17}{2^3 \cdot 5^1} = \frac{17 \cdot 5^2}{2^3 \cdot 5^3} = \frac{17 \cdot 25}{10^3} = \frac{425}{1000} = 0.425.$$

Since the numbers in the preceding discussion are typical of the general case, the results can be summarized as a theorem.

THEOREM *Terminating Decimals and Rational Numbers*

If *a* and *b* are integers with $b \neq 0$, if *a/b* is a simplest form, and if the prime factor representation of *b* contains only 2s and 5s, then *a/b* can be represented as a terminating decimal and conversely.

EXAMPLE   7.4   **Writing a Terminating Decimal as a Ratio of Two Integers**

Express each of these in the form a/b where the fraction is in simplest form.

(a)   31.75   **(b)**   4.112   **(c)** -0.035

Solution

(a) $31.75 = 31.75 \cdot \dfrac{100}{100} = \dfrac{3175}{100} = \dfrac{127}{4}$

(b) $4.112 = 4.112 \cdot \dfrac{1000}{1000} = \dfrac{4112}{1000} = \dfrac{514}{125}$

(c) $-0.035 = -0.035 \cdot \dfrac{1000}{1000} = \dfrac{-35}{1000} = \dfrac{-7}{200}$

We just saw how to write 17/40 as a finite decimal by multiplying both numerator and denominator by powers of 2 or 5. But the task can also be accomplished by division. Thus, by hand or using a calculator, we have that

$$\frac{17}{40} = 0.425$$

$\dfrac{17}{40} = 17 \div 40$

EXAMPLE   7.5   **Converting Certain Fractions to Decimals**

Convert each of these fractions to decimals by writing each as an equivalent fraction whose denominator is a power of 10. Check by dividing using a calculator.

(a) $\dfrac{37}{40}$ **(b)** $-\dfrac{29}{200}$

Solution

(a) $\dfrac{37}{40} = \dfrac{37}{2^3 \cdot 5^1} = \dfrac{37 \cdot 5^2}{2^3 \cdot 5^3}$

$5^1 \cdot 5^2 = 5^3$

$= \dfrac{37 \cdot 25}{10^3}$

$= \dfrac{925}{1000}$

$5^2 = 25,\ 37 \cdot 25 = 925$

$= 0.925$

Also, by calculator, $37 \div 40 = 0.925$.

(b) $-\dfrac{29}{200} = -\dfrac{29}{2^3 \cdot 5^2} = -\dfrac{29 \cdot 5}{2^3 \cdot 5^3}$

$= -\dfrac{145}{10^3}$

$= -\dfrac{145}{1000}$

$= -0.145.$

Also, by calculator, $-(29 \div 200) = -0.145$.

HIGHLIGHT FROM HISTORY
Simon Stevin (1548–1620)

The most influential mathematician from the Low Countries in the sixteenth century was the Flemish mathematician, Simon Stevin. Stevin served in the Dutch army as quartermaster and was something of an expert on military engineering and the building of fortifications. His most significant contribution to mathematics was the extension of the use of the positional Indo-Arabic system of numeration to the rational and real numbers, thus greatly facilitating numerical calculation. To the local Dutch he was most famous for his invention of a carriage powered by sails and capable of carrying more than a score of people at speeds up to twenty miles per hour.

Nonterminating Decimals and Rational Numbers

Somewhat surprisingly not all rational numbers have decimal expansions that terminate. For example, as noted earlier

$$\frac{1}{3} = 0.333\ldots = 0.\overline{3}$$

where the three dots indicate that the decimal continues *ad infinitum* and the bar over the 3 indicates the digit or group of digits that repeats. To see why this is so, set

$$x = 0.333\ldots.*$$

Then, using the preceding theorem,

$$10x = 3.333\ldots$$

so that

$$10x - x = 9x = 3.$$

> $3.333\ldots$
> $-\ 0.333\ldots$
> $3.000\ldots$

But this implies that

$$x = \frac{3}{9} = \frac{1}{3}.$$

Notice that the decimal expansion of 1/3 is a nonterminating but *repeating* decimal; that is, the stream of 3s repeats without end. In general, we have the following definition.

DEFINITION   *A Repeating Decimal*

A nonterminating decimal that has the property that a digit or group of digits repeats *ad infinitum* from some point on is called a **periodic** or **repeating decimal.** The number of digits in the repeating group is called the **length of the period.**

Just as $0.333\ldots = .\overline{3}$ represents the rational number 1/3, so every repeating decimal represents a rational number.

---

*Actually there is a touchy point here that we gloss over. The question is whether $0.333\ldots = 3/10 + 3/100 + 3/1000 + \ldots$ means anything at all since it is the sum of an *infinite* number of numbers. That the answer is yes really depends on ideas from calculus!

EXAMPLE   7.6   **Repeating Decimals as Rational Numbers**

Write each of these repeating decimals in the form a/b where a and b are integers and the fraction is in simplest form. Check by dividing a by b with your calculator.

(a) $0.242424\ldots = 0.\overline{24}$ **(b)** $3.14555\ldots = 3.14\overline{5}$

Solution

(a)   Let $x = 0.242424\ldots$.

a decimal of period 2

Then,

Multiply by $10^2 = 100$ to move the decimal point two places to the right.

$$100x = 24.242424\ldots$$

and

$$100x - x = 99x = 24.$$

$\begin{array}{r} 24.242424\ldots \\ -\ 0.242424\ldots \\ \hline 24.000000\ldots \end{array}$

But then,

$$x = \frac{24}{99} = \frac{8}{33}.$$

Also, by calculator, $8 \div 33 \doteq 0.2424242$.

Here the calculator answer is only approximate since only finitely many digits can appear in the calculator display.

(b)   Let $x = 3.14555\ldots$.

Multiply by 10^2 to move the decimal point two places to the right where the period starts.

Then,

$$100x = 314.555\ldots$$

and

a decimal of period 1

$$1000x = 3145.555\ldots$$

$10 \cdot 100 = 1000$

Multiply by 10 again to move the decimal point one more place (the length of the period) to the right.

Then,

$$1000x - 100x = 900x = 2831$$

$\begin{array}{r} 3145.555\ldots \\ -\ 314.555\ldots \\ \hline 2831.000\ldots \end{array}$

and

$$x = \frac{2831}{900}.$$

Also, by calculator, $2831 \div 900 \doteq 3.1455556$. Explain why the decimal is finite and ends with a 6.

Example 7.6 is typical of the general case and so we have the following theorem.

> **THEOREM** *Rational Numbers and Periodic Decimals*
> Every repeating decimal represents a rational number a/b. If a/b is in simplest form, b must contain a prime factor other than 2 or 5. Conversely, if a/b is such a rational number its decimal representation must be repeating.

" I THOUGHT IT WAS A BREAKTHROUGH, BUT IT WAS ONLY A MISPLACED DECIMAL."

Ordering Decimals

Elementary textbooks also lay stress on properly ordering decimals. Ordering decimals is much like ordering integers. For example, to determine the larger of 247,761 and 2,326,447 write both numerals as if they had the same number of digits; that is, write

$$0{,}247{,}761 \quad \text{and} \quad 2{,}326{,}447.$$

Then determine the first place from the *left* where the digits differ. It follows from the idea of positional notation that the larger integer is the integer with the larger of these two different digits. In the present case, the first digits differ and so

$$0{,}247{,}761 < 2{,}326{,}447.$$

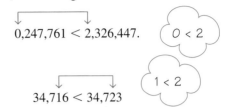

In a similar example,

$$34{,}716 < 34{,}723$$

since the first pair of corresponding digits that differ are the 1 and the 2 and $1 < 2$.

Now consider the decimals,

$$0.2346612359 \quad \text{and} \quad 0.2348999.$$

Suppose we multiply both numbers by 10^{10} so that both become integers. We obtain

$$2{,}346{,}612{,}359 \quad \text{and} \quad 2{,}348{,}999{,}000.$$

We order these as integers in the manner just discussed to obtain

$$2{,}346{,}612{,}359 < 2{,}348{,}999{,}000.$$ ($6 < 8$)

Thus,

$$(10^{10})(0.2346612359) < (10^{10})(0.2348999000).$$

But this implies that

$$0.2346612359 < 0.2348999$$

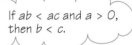
Divide both sides by 10^{10}.

and we are done.

These arguments could be repeated in general with the following result.

If $ab < ac$ and $a > 0$, then $b < c$.

THEOREM   *Ordering Decimals*

To order two positive decimals, add zeros on the left if necessary so that there are the same number of digits to the left of the decimal point, and then determine the first digits from the left that differ. The decimal with the lesser of these two digits is the lesser decimal.

EXAMPLE   7.7

Ordering Decimals

In each case, decide which of the decimals represents the lesser number.

(a)   2.35714 and 2.35709   (b)   23.45 and $23.4\overline{5}$

Solution

(a)   Here the first digits from the left that differ are 1 and 0. Since $0 < 1$, it follows that $2.35709 < 2.35714$.

(b)   Since $23.4\overline{5} = 23.4555\ldots$, the first digits from the left that differ are 0 and 5. Since $0 < 5$, it follows that $23.45 < 23.4\overline{5}$.

EXAMPLE   7.8

Ordering Decimals and Fractions

Arrange these numbers in order from least to greatest.

$$\frac{11}{24}, \quad \frac{3}{8}, \quad 0.37, \quad 0.4584, \quad 0.37666\ldots, \quad 0.4583$$

Solution

The easiest approach is to write all these numbers as decimals. Since

$$\frac{11}{24} = 0.458333\ldots \qquad \text{and} \qquad \frac{3}{8} = 0.375,$$

it follows that

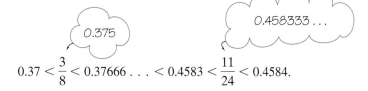

$$0.37 < \frac{3}{8} < 0.37666\ldots < 0.4583 < \frac{11}{24} < 0.4584.$$

The Set of Real Numbers

Earlier we showed that

the decimal expansion of a rational number either terminates or is nonterminating and repeating.

This raises an interesting question. What kind of numbers are represented by nonterminating nonrepeating decimals like 0.101001000100001 . . . ? Such numbers cannot be represented as ratios of integers, and so are called **irrational numbers.** This distinguishes them from the rational numbers considered in Chapter 6. The set consisting of all rational and irrational numbers is called the set of **real numbers.**

> **DEFINITION**   *Irrational and Real Numbers*
> Numbers represented by nonterminating nonperiodic decimals are called **irrational numbers.** The set R consisting of all rational numbers and all irrational numbers is called the set of **real numbers.**

Thus, the set of real numbers is another extension of the number system. This number system contains all the earlier systems as illustrated by the Venn diagram in Figure 7.1.

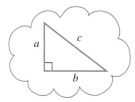

Irrationality of $\sqrt{2}$

Like the set of rational numbers, the set of irrational numbers is an infinite set. To give but a single example, we show that the length of the diagonal of a square measuring 1 unit on a side is not a rational number. Recall that the equation $c^2 = a^2 + b^2$ relates the length of the long side of a triangle with one square corner to the lengths of the other two

HIGHLIGHT FROM HISTORY
Pythagoras and Irrational Numbers

The great Greek mathematician Pythagoras (c. 585–497 B.C.) is best known because of the Pythagorean theorem considered in the HANDS ON at the beginning of this chapter. Actually, it is doubtful that Pythagoras discovered this theorem or even proved the result true. At best, the theorem may be due to one of the members of the religious, philosophical, and scientific society founded by Pythagoras and called the Pythagorean School. The Pythagoreans said that "all is number" (and by numbers they meant natural numbers) and made numbers the basis for their entire system of thought. It is true that the Pythagoreans considered ratios and were able to deal with situations like measurement that required rational numbers. However, the discovery by Hippasus of Metapotum that the diagonal and side of a square are incommensurable (that is, have no common unit of measure), which amounts to showing that $\sqrt{2}$ is not rational and so cannot be expressed as a ratio of integers, struck a serious blow to the Pythagorean system. The story goes that Hippasus made his discovery while on a sea voyage with his fellow Pythagoreans who were so distressed that Hippasus was promptly thrown overboard and drowned.

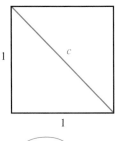

$c = \sqrt{2}$

sides as discovered in the HANDS ON* at the beginning of this chapter. If c is the length of the diagonal of a square 1 unit on a side, it follows that

$$c^2 = 1^2 + 1^2 = 2.$$

Recall that if $c^2 = 2$, then c is called the square root of 2 and we write $c = \sqrt{2}$. We now show that $\sqrt{2}$ is not a rational number.

> **THEOREM** *Irrationality of* $\sqrt{2}$
>
> If $c^2 = 2$, then c is not a rational number.

Proof (By Contradiction)   Suppose, to the contrary, that there is a rational number c for which $c^2 = 2$. Since any rational number can be expressed as a fraction in simplest form, let

$$c = \frac{u}{v}$$

where u and v have no common factors other than 1. But $c^2 = 2$, so

$$2 = \frac{u^2}{v^2}.$$

Thus,

$$2v^2 = u^2.$$

---

*A triangle with one square corner (that is, a corner forming a 90° angle) is called a **right** triangle. The fact that $c^2 = a^2 + b^2$ for such a triangle is called the **Pythagorean theorem.**

This says that 2 is a prime factor of u^2. Hence, by the fundamental theorem of arithmetic, 2 is a prime factor of u. But then $u = 2k$ for some integer k and

$$2v^2 = u^2 = (2k)^2 = 4k^2.$$

This implies that

$$v^2 = 2k^2$$

and so 2 is also a factor of v^2 and hence of v. But then u and v have a factor of 2 in common and u/v is not in simplest form. This contradicts the fact that *u/v is in simplest form.* In view of this contradiction, the assumption that c was rational that started this chain of reasoning must be false. Therefore, c is irrational as was to be proved.

EXAMPLE 7.9

Proving a Number Irrational

Show that $3 + \sqrt{2}$ is irrational.

Solution

Understand the problem

We have just seen that $\sqrt{2}$ is irrational. We must show that $3 + \sqrt{2}$ is irrational.

Devise a plan

Does the assertion even make sense? Is it possible that $3 + \sqrt{2}$ is rational? If so, then $3 + \sqrt{2} = s$ where s is some rational number. Perhaps we can use this equation, and the fact that we already know that $\sqrt{2}$ is irrational, to arrive at the desired conclusion.

Carry out a plan

Since $3 + \sqrt{2} = s$, it follows that $\sqrt{2} = s - 3$. But 3 and s are rational and we know that the rational numbers are closed under subtraction. This implies that $\sqrt{2}$ is rational, and we know that that is not so. Therefore, the assumption that $3 + \sqrt{2} = s$ where s is rational must be false. Hence, $3 + \sqrt{2}$ is irrational as was to be shown.

Look back

Initially, it was not clear that the assertion of the problem had to be true, so we assumed briefly that it was not true. But this led directly to the contradiction that $\sqrt{2}$ was rational and so the assumption that $3 + \sqrt{2}$ was rational had to be false; that is $3 + \sqrt{2}$ had to be irrational as we were to prove.

The preceding argument could be repeated exactly with 3 replaced by any rational number r. Thus, since there are infinitely many rational numbers, the preceding example shows that there are infinitely many irrational numbers. Moreover, in a very precise sense, which we will not discuss here, there are many more irrational numbers than rational numbers. One such number which is well-known but not usually known to be irrational is the number

$$\pi = 3.14159265 \ldots$$

occurring in the formula $A = \pi r^2$ for the area of a circle of radius r or the formula $C = 2\pi r$ for the circumference of a circle. Moreover, if the natural number m is not a perfect square, it can be shown that $\sqrt{m}$ is also irrational. Indeed, if m is not a perfect nth power, $\sqrt[n]{m}$ is irrational, where by $\sqrt[n]{m}$ we mean a number c such that $c^n = m$.

Real Numbers and the Number Line

When we discussed the length of the diagonal of the square measuring 1 unit on a side and proved that $\sqrt{2}$ is irrational, we made a tacit assumption that is easily overlooked. Simply put, the assumption was that to every possible length there corresponds exactly one real number that names the length in question. Figure 7.8 illustrates how we can accurately plot the length $\sqrt{2}$ on the number line.

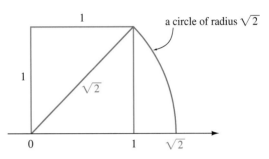

Figure 7.8
$\sqrt{2}$ on the number line

Also, the decimal expansion of $\sqrt{2}$ can be found step-by-step as follows. Using a calculator and trial and error, we find that

$$1^2 = 1 < 2 < 4 = 2^2,$$
$$1.4^2 = 1.96 < 2 < 2.25 = 1.5^2,$$
$$1.41^2 = 1.9881 < 2 < 2.0164 = 1.42^2,$$
$$1.414^2 = 1.999396 < 2 < 2.002225 = 1.415^2,$$

and so on. Thus, the decimal expansion of $\sqrt{2}$ is

$$\sqrt{2} = 1.414\ldots$$

> Note that this is determined by the lower estimates above.

where successive digits are found by catching $\sqrt{2}$ between successive units, between successive tenths, between successive hundredths, and so on. To show that this can be done for any real number is somewhat tricky but the following theorem can be proved.

THEOREM *Real Numbers and the Number Line*
There is a one-to-one correspondence between the set of real numbers and the set of points on a number line. The absolute value of the number associated with any given point gives the distance of the point to the right or left of the 0.

PROBLEM SET 7.1

Understanding Concepts

1. Write the following decimals in expanded form and in expanded exponential form.

    (a) 273.412   (b) 0.000723   (c) 0.20305

2. Write these decimals as fractions in lowest terms and determine the prime factorization of the denominator in each case.

    (a) 0.324   (b) 0.028   (c) 4.25

3. Write these fractions as terminating decimals.

    (a) $\dfrac{7}{20}$ (b) $\dfrac{7}{16}$ (c) $\dfrac{3}{75}$ (d) $\dfrac{18}{2^2 \cdot 5^4}$

4. Determine the rational fraction in lowest terms represented by each of these periodic decimals.

    (a) $0.321321\ldots = 0.\overline{321}$

    (b) $0.12414141\ldots = 0.12\overline{41}$

    (c) $3.262626\ldots = 3.\overline{26}$

    (d) $0.999\ldots = 0.\overline{9}$

    (e) $0.24999\ldots = 0.24\overline{9}$

    (f) $0.666\ldots = 0.\overline{6}$

    (g) $0.142857142857142857\ldots = 0.\overline{142857}$

    (h) $0.153846153846153846\ldots = 0.\overline{153846}$

5. (a) Give an example of a fraction whose decimal expansion is repeating and the length of the period is 3.

    (b) Use your calculator to check your answer to part (a). Is this check really complete? Explain.

    (c) Check your answer to part (a) by some other means.

6. In each of these, write the numbers in order of increasing size (from least to greatest).

    (a) $0.017, 0.007, 0.01\overline{7}, 0.027$

    (b) $25.412, 25.312, 24.999, 25.41\overline{2}$

    (c) $\dfrac{9}{25}, 0.35, 0.36, \dfrac{10}{25}, 0.3\overline{5}$

    (d) $\dfrac{1}{4}, \dfrac{5}{24}, \dfrac{1}{3}, \dfrac{1}{6}$

7. Show that $\sqrt{3}$ is irrational. (*Hint:* Have you ever seen a similar result proved?)

8. Show that $3 - \sqrt{2}$ is irrational.

9. Show that $2\sqrt{2}$ is irrational.

Thinking Critically

10. In problem 4, parts (d) and (e) you may have been surprised to discover that some rational numbers have two *different* decimal representations.

    (a) What rational number is represented by the periodic decimal $0.0999\ldots = 0.0\overline{9}$?

    (b) Write two other decimals that are different but represent the same rational number.

    (c) What rational numbers possess two different decimal expansions? Explain briefly.

11. Compute the decimal expansions of each of the following.

    (a) $\dfrac{1}{11}$ (b) $\dfrac{1}{111}$ (c) $\dfrac{1}{1111}$

    (d) Guess the decimal expansion of $1/11111$.

    (e) Check your guess in part (d) by converting the decimal of your guess back into a ratio of two integers.

    (f) Carefully describe the decimal expansion of $1/N_n$ where $N_n = 111\ldots 1$ with n 1s in its representation.

12. What rational number corresponds to each of these periodic decimals? (Refer to Example 7.6 if you need help.)

    (a) $0.747474\ldots = 0.\overline{74}$ (b) $0.777\ldots = 0.\overline{7}$

    (c) $0.235235235\ldots = 0.\overline{235}$

    (d) If a, b, and c are digits, what rational numbers are represented by each of these periodic decimals? You should be able to guess these results on the basis of patterns observed in parts (a), (b), and (c).

    (i) $0.aaa\ldots = 0.\overline{a}$

    (ii) $0.ababab\ldots = 0.\overline{ab}$

    (iii) $0.abcabcabc\ldots = 0.\overline{abc}$

13. Write the decimal representing each of these rational numbers without doing any calculation or at most doing only mental calculation.

    (a) $\dfrac{5}{9}$ (b) $\dfrac{22}{99}$ (c) $\dfrac{317}{999}$

    (d) $\dfrac{17}{33}$ (e) $\dfrac{14}{11}$

    (f) Check the answers in parts (a) through (e) using your calculator. Is this check foolproof? Explain.

14. **(a)** Give an example that shows that the sum of two irrational numbers is sometimes rational.

    (b) Give an example that shows that the sum of two irrational numbers is sometimes irrational.

15. Give an example that shows that the product of two irrational numbers is sometimes rational.

16. Is $2/\sqrt{2}$ rational or irrational? Explain.

17. Give an example that shows that the quotient of two irrational numbers is sometimes rational.

18. What real numbers are represented by points A, B, and C in this diagram? Explain your answer in a brief paragraph.

19. Find a rational number between the irrational number π and $2 + \sqrt{2}$.

---

20. **(a)** If a is an integer, what are the possibilities for the last digit of the decimal representation of a^2?

Last digit of a	0	1	2	3	4	5	6	7	8	9
Last digit of a^2										

    (b) If b is an integer, what are the possibilities for the last digit of the decimal representation of $2b^2$?

Last digit of b	0	1	2	3	4	5	6	7	8	9
Last digit of $2b^2$										

    (c) Using the results of parts (a) and (b), make a careful argument that $\sqrt{2} = a/b$, with a and b integers, is impossible.

Thinking Cooperatively

21. Dividing the work between members of your group, compute the decimal representations of these rational numbers and also compute the prime power representations of their denominators.

(a) $\dfrac{23}{6}$ **(b)** $\dfrac{7}{24}$ **(c)** $\dfrac{11}{9}$ **(d)** $\dfrac{23}{18}$ **(e)** $\dfrac{7}{22}$

(f) $\dfrac{23}{22}$ **(g)** $\dfrac{13}{110}$ **(h)** $\dfrac{311}{88}$ **(i)** $\dfrac{37}{220}$ **(j)** $\dfrac{29}{5500}$

(k) Discuss the results of (a) through (j) and arrive at a consensus prediction about how many digits there are between the decimal point and the repeating part of the decimal expansion of a rational number r/s.

Communicating

22. Write a proof that $\sqrt{6}$ is irrational.

23. If r is rational and $r \neq 0$, write a proof that $r \cdot \sqrt{2}$ is irrational.

▣ Using a Computer

24. **(a)** Choose any two positive integers a and b and compute the first 20 terms in the sequence $f_1 = a$, $f_2 = b$, $f_3 = 2a + 2b$, $f_4 = 4a + 6b$, . . . where every term after the second is twice the sum of its two predecessors. This is most easily done on a spreadsheet.

    (b) Compute the quotients $f_2/f_1, f_3/f_2, f_4/f_3, \ldots, f_{20}/f_{19}$.

    (c) Compute $1 + \sqrt{3}$.

    (d) Consider the results of parts (b) and (c), and then write up a brief analysis of what seems to be the case.

From State Student Assessments

25. (Connecticut, Grade 6)

    (a) The shaded portion of this picture represents the number

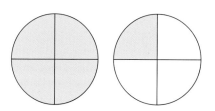

      A. 1   B. 2   C. 1.5   D. 1.25

    (b) Which of the following shows 1.63?

      A.

      B.
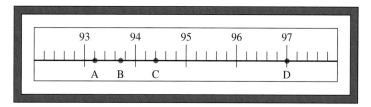

      C.

      D.

26. (Minnesota, Grade 5)

Use the picture below to answer the question.

Radio station **WMTH** can be found at 93.7 on your radio dial. Which letter shown above represents where you would find **WMTH**?

    A. letter A   B. letter B   C. letter C   D. letter D

For Review

27. Arrange these fractions in order from least to greatest:

3/5, 3/4, −2/3, 27/29, 7/8, 1/2

28. The *mediant* of *a/b* and *c/d* is the fraction $(a + c)/(b + d)$.

Consider the following sequences of fractions where each new sequence is obtained by adding to the previous sequence the mediants of that sequence.

$$\frac{0}{1}, \frac{1}{1}$$

$$\frac{0}{1}, \frac{1}{2}, \frac{1}{1}$$

$$\frac{0}{1}, \frac{1}{3}, \frac{1}{2}, \frac{2}{3}, \frac{1}{1}$$

  (a) List the next two sequences found in this way.

(b) For any two adjacent fractions $\dfrac{a}{b}$ and $\dfrac{c}{d}$, in any of these sequences, compute $ad - bc$.

(c) Make a conjecture based on the results of part (b).

29. Perform the following computations leaving all answers as fractions in simplest form.

(a) $\dfrac{1}{2} + \dfrac{2}{3}$ (b) $\dfrac{1}{2} - \dfrac{2}{3}$

(c) $\dfrac{1}{2} \cdot \dfrac{2}{3}$ (d) $\dfrac{1}{2} \div \dfrac{2}{3}$

(e) $\dfrac{3}{4} \cdot \left(1 + \dfrac{3}{5}\right)$ (f) $\dfrac{3}{4} \div \left(1 - \dfrac{3}{5}\right)$

30. Find two rational numbers between 1/2 and 1/3.

31. In a certain population, 2/3 of the men are married and 1/2 of the women are married. What fraction of the adult population is unmarried?

7.2   Computations with Decimals

It is essential that elementary students develop a sense of *numeracy*; i.e., an idea of what numbers *mean* and what makes *sense* when dealing with numbers. For example, is it practically useful to consider a decimal like 0.7342061? The answer, in general, is *no*. Even in scientific work where considerable accuracy is required, a decimal correct to seven significant digits is rarely meaningful. It is much more likely that an approximation like 0.73, or 0.734, or even simply 0.7 is all that can be used effectively. This naturally leads to the question of approximation and rounding of decimals.

Rounding Decimals

Suppose a *couturiere* wants to buy material to make into a dress for her upcoming fashion show. The material comes in 40-inch widths and she needs a piece 3.75 yards long. If the material costs $15.37 per yard, how much will she have to pay? Using a calculator, the price would be

$$(3.75)(\$15.37) = \$57.6375$$

and the *couturiere* would be charged $57.64, the cost rounded to the nearest cent. The process of rounding here is precisely the same as it was for integers. Thus, 2.3254071 rounded

- to the nearest integer is 2,
- to the nearest tenth is 2.3,
- to the nearest hundredth is 2.33,

and so on. As before, we are using the 5-up rule.

> **RULE**   *The 5-up Rule for Rounding Decimals*
>
> To round a decimal to a given place, consider the digit in the next place to the right. If this digit is less than 5, leave the digit in the place under consideration unchanged and replace all digits to its right by 0s. If the digit to the right of the place in question is 5 or more, increase the digit in the place under consideration by 1 and replace all digits to the right by 0s.

EXAMPLE 7.10 | **Rounding Decimals**

Round each of these to the indicated position.

(a) 23.2047 to the nearest integer
(b) 3.6147 to the nearest tenth.
(c) 0.015 to the nearest hundredth.

Solution

23.000 . . .
= 23

(a) Since we are asked to round 23.2047 to the nearest integer, we consider the digit to the right of 3. Since this digit is 2 and $2 < 5$, we leave the 3 unchanged and replace the digits to its right by 0s. Thus, 23.2047 rounded to the nearest integer is 23.

3.6000 . . .
= 3.6

(b) In rounding 3.6147 to the nearest tenth, we note that the digit to the right of the 6 is 1. Since $1 < 5$, we leave the 6 unchanged and replace the digits to its right by 0s. Thus, 3.6147 rounded to the nearest tenth is 3.6.

0.02000 . . .
= 0.02

(c) Here the digit in question is 1 and the digit to its right is 5. Thus, we increase the 1 by 1 and replace the digits to its right by 0s. Hence, 0.015 rounded to the nearest hundredth is 0.02.

Adding and Subtracting Decimals

To do some repair work at the Louvre in Paris, plumber Jean Ferre estimated that he needed 17.5 meters of copper tubing. After a plan change, he decided that he needed an additional 15.75 meters of tubing. When he finished the job, Ferre discovered that he had 2.34 meters of tubing left over. How much tubing did Ferre purchase and how much did he use to complete the job? Answers to questions such as these require that we consider the addition and subtraction of decimals.

Suppose we wish to add 2.71 and 37.762. Converting these decimals to fractions we have

$$2.71 = \frac{271}{100} = \frac{2710}{1000} \quad \text{and} \quad 37.762 = \frac{37{,}762}{1000}.$$

Thus,

$$2.71 + 37.762 = \frac{2710}{1000} + \frac{37{,}762}{1000}$$

$$= \frac{40{,}472}{1000}$$

$$= 40.472.$$

```
  2710
+ 37,762
  40,472
```

```
 02.710
+ 37.762
  40.472
```

```
  2.71
+ 37.762
  40.472
```

To add decimals by hand, write the numbers in vertical style lining up the decimal points and then add essentially just as we add integers. With a calculator, we enter the string

$$\boxed{\text{ON/AC}} \;\; 2.71 \;\; \boxed{+} \;\; 37.762 \;\; \boxed{=}$$

and automatically obtain the desired sum 40.472. The important thing with a calculator is to recognize that we are adding approximately 3 to approximately 38 so the sum should be approximately 41. The estimation and mental arithmetic should proceed right along with the calculator manipulation to be sure that we recognize if we have inadvertently made a calculator error.

Suppose now that we want to subtract 2.71 from 37.762. The calculation is much the same as above and we have

$$37.762 - 2.71 = \frac{37{,}762}{1000} - \frac{2710}{1000}$$

$$= \frac{35{,}052}{1000}$$

$$= 35.052$$

$$\begin{array}{r} 37{,}762 \\ -\ 2710 \\ \hline 35{,}052 \end{array}$$

$$\begin{array}{r} 37.762 \\ -\ 2.710 \\ \hline 35.052 \end{array}$$

As before, in hand calculation, we write the problem in vertical style lining up the decimal points and then subtract essentially as we subtract integers.

If done with a calculator, we should estimate and perform mental calculation as well. Thus, we think

approximately 38 minus approximately 3 gives approximately 35

and thus avoid gross calculator errors.

EXAMPLE   7.11

Adding and Subtracting Decimals

Compute each of these by estimating, by calculator, and by hand.

   (a)   23.47 + 7.81   **(b)**   351.42 − 417.815

Solution

   (a)   By estimating: Approximately 23 plus approximately 8 gives approximately 31.

   By calculator: [ON/AC] 23.47 [+] 7.81 [=] 31.28

   By hand:
$$\begin{array}{r} {\scriptstyle 1\ 1} \\ 23.47 \\ +\ 7.81 \\ \hline 31.28 \end{array}$$

   (b)   By estimating: Approximately 350 minus approximately 400 gives approximately −50.

   By calculator: [ON/AC] 351.42 [−] 417.815 [=] −66.395

   By hand:
$$\begin{array}{r} {\scriptstyle 3\quad 7} \\ 417.815 \\ -\ 351.42 \\ \hline 66.395 \end{array}$$

   Therefore, since 417.815 > 351.42, the desired answer is −66.395

Multiplying Decimals

Tom Swift wanted to try out his new Ferrari on a straight stretch of highway. If he drove at 91.7 miles per hour for 15 minutes, how far did he go? Since 15 minutes equals 0.25 hours and distance traveled equals rate times elapsed time, Tom traveled $(91.7) \cdot (0.25)$ miles. For a more explicit answer, we need to be able to multiply decimals. Converting these decimals to fractions we have

$$91.7 = \frac{917}{10} \quad \text{and} \quad 0.25 = \frac{25}{100}.$$

Thus,

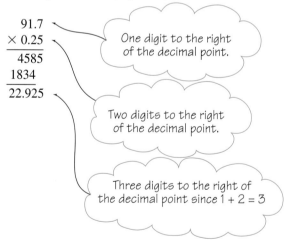

$$(91.7) \cdot (0.25) = \frac{917}{10} \cdot \frac{25}{100}$$

$$= \frac{917 \cdot 25}{10 \cdot 100}$$

$$= \frac{22,925}{1000}$$

$$= 22.925$$

Three digits to the right of the decimal point since we are dividing by 1000 = 10³

$$917$$
$$\times 25$$
$$\overline{4585}$$
$$1834$$
$$\overline{22925}$$

and the multiplication is performed just as in the multiplication of integers except for the placement of the decimal point. Indeed, by hand, it is common to write the following:

$$91.7$$
$$\times 0.25$$
$$\overline{4585}$$
$$1834$$
$$\overline{22.925}$$

One digit to the right of the decimal point.

Two digits to the right of the decimal point.

Three digits to the right of the decimal point since 1 + 2 = 3

Since this is typical of the general case, we summarize it as a theorem.

THEOREM   *Multiplying Decimals*

To multiply two decimals:

1.   Multiply as with integers.
2.   Count the number of digits to the right of the decimal point in each number in the product, add these numbers, and call their sum t.
3.   Finally, place the decimal point in the product obtained so that there are t digits to the right of the decimal point.

Finally, we note that, since Tom's odometer only gives mileage to the nearest tenth, it actually shows that Tom traveled approximately 22.9 miles. Thus, the accuracy to three decimal places in the preceding multiplication is hardly useful to Tom. Also, Tom's estimated speed of 91.7 miles per hour as well as his measurement of the 15 minute time interval were almost surely not entirely accurate. Hence, the accuracy to three decimal places is surely not warranted; it is certainly much more reasonable in this case to round the answer to 22.9 or even to 23 miles.

EXAMPLE   7.12

Multiplying Decimals

Compute these products by estimating, by calculator, and by hand.

(a) $(471.2) \cdot (2.3)$ **(b)** $(36.34) \cdot (1.02)$

Solution

(a)   By estimating: Approximately 500 times approximately 2 gives approximately 1000.

By calculator: $\boxed{\text{ON/AC}}$ 471.2 $\boxed{\times}$ 2.3 $\boxed{=}$ 1083.76

By hand:
$$
\begin{array}{r}
471.2 \\
\times \quad 2.3 \\
\hline
14136 \\
9424 \\
\hline
1083.76
\end{array}
$$

two digits to the right of the decimal point $1 + 1 = 2$

(b)   By estimating: Approximately 36 times approximately 1 gives approximately 36.

By calculator: $\boxed{\text{ON/AC}}$ 36.34 $\boxed{\times}$ 1.02 $\boxed{=}$ 37.0668

By hand:
$$
\begin{array}{r}
36.34 \\
\times \quad 1.02 \\
\hline
7268 \\
36340 \\
\hline
37.0668
\end{array}
$$

Dividing Decimals

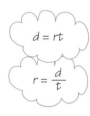

Tom Swift also has his own airplane. If Tom traveled 537.6 miles in 2.56 hours in his airplane, how fast did he travel? Again, since distance traveled equals rate times elapsed time, rate equals distance traveled divided by time. Therefore, we need to compute the quotient $537.6 \div 2.56$. Converting these decimals to fractions, we have

$$
\begin{aligned}
537.6 \div 2.56 &= \frac{5376}{10} \div \frac{256}{100} \\
&= \frac{5376}{10} \cdot \frac{100}{256} \\
&= \frac{537{,}600}{2560} \\
&= \frac{53{,}760}{256} \\
&= 210
\end{aligned}
$$

and the problem is reduced to that of dividing 53,760 by 256; that is, to dividing integers. Recall that, when confronted by a division like

$$2.56\overline{)537.6},$$

students are often told to "move the decimal point in both the divisor and the dividend 2 places to the right so that the divisor becomes an integer." The preceding calculation with fractions justifies this rule and, by hand, we have

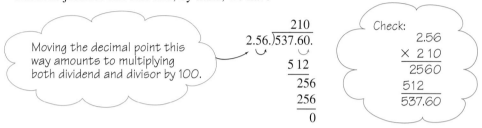

Moving the decimal point this way amounts to multiplying both dividend and divisor by 100.

$$
\begin{array}{r}
210 \\
2.56\overline{)537.60.} \\
\underline{5\,12} \\
256 \\
\underline{256} \\
0
\end{array}
$$

Check:
$$
\begin{array}{r}
2.56 \\
\times\ 2\,10 \\
\hline
2560 \\
512 \\
\hline
537.60
\end{array}
$$

More on Periodic Decimals

Earlier we claimed that the decimal expansion of a fraction a/b in simplest form, where b has prime factors other than 2 and 5, is necessarily nonterminating but repeating. We are now in a position to give a justification and we do so by example.

EXAMPLE   7.13

The Decimal Expansion of 3/7

Use long division to find the decimal expansion of 3/7.

Solution

Since $3/7 = 3 \div 7$, we obtain the desired decimal expansion by dividing 3 by 7. We have

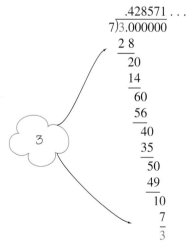

$$
\begin{array}{r}
.428571\ldots \\
7\overline{)3.000000} \\
\underline{2\,8} \\
20 \\
\underline{14} \\
60 \\
\underline{56} \\
40 \\
\underline{35} \\
50 \\
\underline{49} \\
10 \\
\underline{7} \\
3
\end{array}
$$

and, since the remainder at this stage is 3, the number with which we began, the division will continue *ad infinitum* with this repeating pattern. Thus,

$$\frac{3}{7} = 0.428571428571428571\ldots = 0.\overline{428571}.$$

Moreover, since we are dividing by 7, the only possible remainders at each step are 0, 1, 2, 3, 4, 5, and 6. Thus, if the division does not terminate, it must repeat after at most 6 steps. This is true in general and so essentially proves the theorem mentioned.

As a check of the preceding result, we compute the rational number determined by the decimal

$$x = 0.428571428571428571 \ldots = 0.\overline{428571}.$$

It follows that

$$1{,}000{,}000x - x = 999{,}999x = 428{,}571.$$

So

$$x = \frac{428{,}571}{999{,}999} = \frac{3}{7}$$

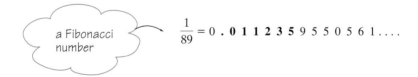

Divide both numerator and denominator by 142,857.

as claimed.

JUST FOR FUN

The Decimal Expansion of 1/89

Recall that the Fibonacci numbers are the numbers 0, 1, 1, 2, 3, 5, 8, 13, 21, 34, 55, 89, 144, 233, ... Computing the decimal expansion of 1/89, we obtain

a Fibonacci number

$$\frac{1}{89} = 0 . \mathbf{0\ 1\ 1\ 2\ 3\ 5}\ 9\ 5\ 5\ 0\ 5\ 6\ 1 \ldots.$$

After starting with the digits 0, 1, 1, 2, 3, 5, we expect the next digit to be 8, the next Fibonacci number. But it is 9. Have we made an error? No. But all is not lost. By hand, compute this sum.

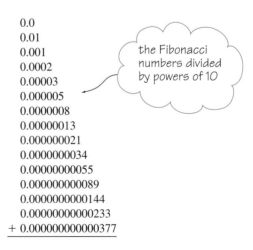

the Fibonacci numbers divided by powers of 10

```
   0.0
   0.01
   0.001
   0.0002
   0.00003
   0.000005
   0.0000008
   0.00000013
   0.000000021
   0.0000000034
   0.00000000055
   0.000000000089
   0.0000000000144
   0.00000000000233
+  0.000000000000377
```

Surprised?! In fact, it is not too difficult to show that

$$\frac{1}{89} = \frac{0}{10^1} + \frac{1}{10^2} + \frac{1}{10^3} + \frac{2}{10^4} + \frac{3}{10^5} + \frac{5}{10^6} + \frac{8}{10^7} + \frac{13}{10^8} + \cdots + \frac{F_n}{10^{n+1}} + \cdots$$

This gives a repeating decimal of period 44.

just as the nonterminating sum

$$\frac{3}{10^1} + \frac{3}{10^2} + \frac{3}{10^3} + \frac{3}{10^4} + \cdots = 0.3333\ldots = \frac{1}{3}.$$

Scientific Notation

Some products and quotients cannot be calculated directly on a nonscientific calculator because the results are either too large or too small. For example, attempting to calculate either

$$876592 \cdot 7654 \qquad \text{or} \qquad 0.0011 \div 65536$$

results in an error message on many calculators. On scientific calculators, the display for these two calculations shows something like

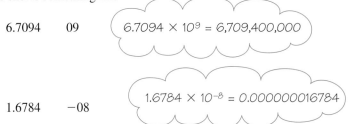

6.7094   09

6.7094 × 10⁹ = 6,709,400,000

and

1.6784   −08

1.6784 × 10⁻⁸ = 0.000000016784

respectively and these are understood to mean

$$6.7094 \times 10^9 \qquad \text{and} \qquad 1.6784 \times 10^{-8}.$$

What these calculators are doing is giving an **approximate** answer in each case, using a form of what is called **scientific notation.*** That is, they give the correct first few digits of the answer in each case as a number between 1 and 10 and then tell what power of 10 to multiply this by, to correctly place the decimal point.

In computing answers like

$$6709435168 \qquad \text{and} \qquad 0.00000001678466796875\ldots,$$

it is highly unlikely that we are interested in, or, because of inaccuracy of measurements, for example, that we are very sure of the last several digits of each result. Thus, the first answer is much more informative if we understand it as essentially 6.7 billion or as 6.7×10^9 and the second answer is more readily appreciated as 1.7×10^{-8}. We usually *round off* the number either to the number of digits we are interested in or the number of digits we are sure of and then use scientific notation. The digits we write before writing the power of ten are called **significant digits.** Thus, we might write the first answer above as

$$6.7 \times 10^9 \text{ to 2 significant digits}$$

---

*The actual answers respectively are 6709435168 and 0.00000001678466796875 . . . .

or

$$6.7094 \times 10^9 \text{ to 5 significant digits.}$$

Similarly, the second answer would be written as

$$1.7 \times 10^{-8} \text{ to 2 significant digits}$$

and

$$1.6784 \times 10^{-8} \text{ to 5 significant digits.}$$

DEFINITION *Scientific Notation*

To write a number in **scientific notation,** write it as the product of a number greater than or equal to 1 and less than 10 times the appropriate power of 10 to correctly place the decimal point. The digits in the number multiplying the power of 10 are called **significant digits.**

EXAMPLE 7.14

Writing Numbers in Scientific Notation

Write each of these in scientific notation using the number of significant digits indicated.

    (a)   93000000 using 2 significant digits
    (b)   93000000 using 3 significant digits
    (c)   0.000027841 using 2 significant digits
    (d)   0.000027841 using 3 significant digits

Solution

    (a)   First write $93000000 = 9.3000000 \times 10^7$. Then round this to 9.3×10^7 to obtain the answer to 2 significant digits.
    (b)   This is the same as part (a) and we proceed as before except that we round the answer to 9.30×10^7 to obtain 3 significant digits.
    (c)   Here $0.000027841 = 2.7841 \times 10^{-5}$ and this is rounded to 2.8×10^{-5} to obtain the answer correct to 2 significant digits.
    (d)   This is the same as part (c) but 2.7841×10^{-5} is rounded to 2.78×10^{-5} to obtain the answer correct to 3 significant digits.

Some calculators have a key marked $\boxed{\text{EXP}}$ or $\boxed{\text{E}}$ or $\boxed{\text{EE}}$, and one can calculate in exponential notation using this key. For example, to calculate the product

$$(8.77 \times 10^7) \cdot (7.65 \times 10^3)$$

and write the answer to 3 significant figures, enter the string

$$\boxed{\text{ON/AC}}\ 8.77\ \boxed{\text{EXP}}\ 7\ \boxed{\times}\ 7.65\ \boxed{\text{EXP}}\ 3\ \boxed{=}\ .$$

In the display we read something like 6.709 11 or perhaps 6.70905 E 11 and write this to 3 significant figures as 6.71×10^{11}.

EXAMPLE 7.15   **Calculating Using Scientific Notation**

Compute each of these using scientific notation to 3 significant figures.

(a) $(2.47 \times 10^{-5}) \cdot (8.15 \times 10^{-9})$
(b) $(2.47 \times 10^{-5}) \div (8.15 \times 10^{-9})$

Solution   **(a)**   Enter $\boxed{\text{ON/AC}}$ 2.47 $\boxed{\text{EXP}}$ 5 $\boxed{+ \circlearrowright -}$ $\boxed{\times}$ 8.15 $\boxed{\text{EXP}}$ 9 $\boxed{+ \circlearrowright -}$ $\boxed{=}$.
Read 2.013 -13 in the display and record 2.01×10^{-13}.

(b)   Enter $\boxed{\text{ON/AC}}$ 2.47 $\boxed{\text{EXP}}$ 5 $\boxed{+ \circlearrowright -}$ $\boxed{\div}$ 8.15 $\boxed{\text{EXP}}$ 9 $\boxed{+ \circlearrowright -}$ $\boxed{=}$.
Read 3030.6748 in the display and record 3.03×10^{3}.

Note, too, how the use of scientific notation can assist in mental approximation of calculator answers. For example, consider Example 7.15, part (a). Using only left digit approximations and rules for multiplication of exponents, think

2 times 8 = 16   times $10^{-5} \cdot 10^{-9} = 10^{-14}$ gives 1.6×10^{-13}

so the above answer is probably correct. An even closer approximation can be obtained by using a 2-digit approximation on the first number and 1-digit approximation on the second. Think

2.5 times 8 = 20   times 10^{-14} gives 2.0×10^{-13}

and the approximation is quite close. Similarly, if we use the same approximation on part (b), we think

2.4 divided by 8 = 0.3 = $3 \cdot 10^{-1}$ times $10^{-5} \cdot 10^{9} = 10^{4}$ gives 3×10^{3}

and the approximation is again quite good.

PROBLEM SET 7.2

Understanding Concepts

1. Perform these additions and subtractions by hand.
   (a) $32.174 + 371.5$ (b) $371.5 - 32.174$
   (c) $0.057 + 1.08$ (d) $0.057 - 1.08$

2. Perform these multiplications and divisions by hand.
   (a) $(37.1) \cdot (4.7)$ (b) $(3.71) \cdot (0.47)$
   (c) $138.33 \div 5.3$ (d) $1.3833 \div 0.53$

3. Estimate the result of each of these computations mentally and then perform the calculations using a calculator.
   (a) $4.112 + 31.3$ (b) $31.3 - 4.112$
   (c) $(4.112) \cdot (31.3)$ (d) $31.3 \div 4.112$

4. By long division determine the decimal expansion of each of these fractions.
   (a) $5/6$ (b) $3/11$ (c) $2/27$

5. Write each of these in scientific notation with the indicated number of significant digits.
   (a) 276543421 to 3 significant digits
   (b) 0.000005341 to 2 significant digits
   (c) 376712.543248 to 2 significant digits

6. Calculate each of these with a suitable calculator and write the answer to 3 significant digits. Note that the *Math Explorer* will simply give an error message.
   (a) $0.0000127 \times 0.000008235$
   (b) 98613428×5746312
   (c) $0.0000127 \div 98613428$
   (d) $98613428 \div 0.000008234$

7. For each of these, estimate the answer and then calculate the result to 3 significant digits on a suitable calculator.
   (a) $(7.123 \times 10^5) \cdot (2.142 \times 10^4)$
   (b) $(7.123 \times 10^5) \div (2.142 \times 10^4)$
   (c) $(7.123 \times 10^5) \cdot (2.142 \times 10^{-9})$
   (d) $(7.123 \times 10^{-2}) \div (2.142 \times 10^8)$

Thinking Critically

8. Use these numbers to make a magic square. See problem 6 in Problem Set 1.1.

   0.123, 0.246, 0.369, 0.492, 0.615, 0.738,
   0.861, 0.984, 1.107

9. Use the numbers in problem 8 to form a magic subtraction square. See problem 6 in Problem Set 1.1.

10. Use these numbers to make a magic square.

    7.02, 16.38, 11.70, 18.72, 2.34, 9.36,
    4.68, 21.06, 14.04

11. Use the numbers in problem 10 to make a magic subtraction square.

12. The sum of the numbers in any two adjacent blanks is the number immediately below and between these two numbers. Complete each of these so that the same pattern holds. The first one has been completed for you.
    (a) 2.107   1.3   4.26
            3.407   5.568
                8.967

    (b) 21.06   3.21   _____
            _____   5.00
                _____

    (c) _____   0.041   _____
            2.415   _____
                7.723

    (d) _____   1.414   _____
            _____   _____
                3.142

    (e) Can any of these be completed in more than one way? Explain.

13. Fill in the blanks so that each of these is an arithmetic progression.
    (a) 3.4, 4.3, 5.2, _____, _____, _____
    (b) -31.56, _____, -21.10, _____, _____, _____
    (c) 0.0114, _____, _____, 0.3204, _____, _____
    (d) 1.07, _____, _____, _____, 8.78, _____

14. Fill in the blanks so that each of these is a geometric progression.
    (a) 2.11, 2.321, _____, _____, _____
    (b) 35.1, _____, 2.835, _____, _____
    (c) 6.01, _____, _____, 0.75125, _____

Thinking Cooperatively

Do the next three problems with two or three other students. At each step, discuss your solution with the other members of the group and determine a consensus answer for the group.

15. The numbers 3.447, 2.821, 5.764, 3.2, 2.351, 3.001, and 4.2444 are placed in a circle in some order. Show that the sum of some three consecutive numbers must exceed 10.6. (*Hint:* Have you ever seen a similar problem before?)

16. Place numbers in the circles in these diagrams so that the numbers in the large circles are the sums of the numbers in the two adjacent smaller circles.

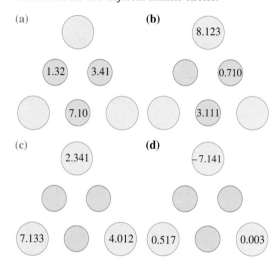

(a)

(b)   8.123
        1.32 3.41   0.710
    7.10   3.111

(c)   2.341   (d) −7.141

7.133   4.012 0.517   0.003

17. If possible, place numbers in the circles in these diagrams so that the numbers in the large circles exactly equal the sum of the numbers in the adjacent small circles.

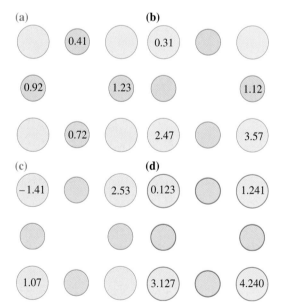

(a)   (b)
        0.41   0.31
0.92   1.23   1.12
    0.72   2.47   3.57

(c)   (d)
−1.41   2.53   0.123   1.241

1.07   3.127   4.240

(e) What must be the case for these problems to be solvable? Explain.

(f) Is there more than one solution to all or any of these?

Making Connections

18. Kristina bought pairs of gloves as Christmas presents for three of her best friends. If the gloves cost $9.72 a pair, how much did she spend for these presents?

19. Yolanda also bought identical pairs of gloves for each one of her four best friends. If her total bill was $44.92, how much did each pair of gloves cost?

20. Dante cashed a check for $74.29 and then bought a walkman for $42.91 and a special pair of ear phones for $17.02. After paying for his purchases, how much did he have left?

21. A picture frame 2.25 inches wide surrounds a picture 17.5 inches wide by 24.75 inches high.

(a) What is the area of the picture frame?

(b) What is the area of the picture?

Communicating

22. In Chapter 3 we saw how to use positional notation to bases other than ten to represent integers. The same ideas can be used to represent rational and real numbers. Write a two or three page paper explaining how this would work. Be sure to include examples.

Using a Calculator

23. Among the cryptic notes of the Indian mathematician Srinivasa Ramanujan is the equation

$$\pi^4 = 97.409091 \ldots .$$

This suggests that $\pi^4 \doteq 97.4\overline{09}$.

(a) Show that $97.4\overline{09} = 97\frac{1}{2} - \frac{1}{11}$.

(b) Use your calculator to calculate

$$\pi^4 - \left(97\frac{1}{2} - \frac{1}{11}\right)$$ and determine just

how good Ramanujan's approximation is. (If you use a *Math Explorer*, how do you interpret its display?)

24. (a) In Chapter 2 you were introduced to the process called DIFFY. Use DIFFY to complete this array. Remember that the first, second, and third circles in any row contain the differences (greatest minus least) of the numbers in the preceding row and the fourth circle contains the difference of the elements in the first and fourth circles of the preceding row.

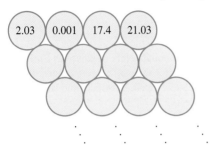

(b) Choose four more numbers and complete a second DIFFY array.

(c) Can you find four numbers that cause the process to continue for at least eight steps?

(d) Use 17.34, 31.62, 58.14, 107.1 and complete a DIFFY process. How many steps does the process continue?

(e) Do you think the process will always terminate?

25. We have found that the DIFFY process always terminated for natural numbers, integers, and rational numbers.

(a) Execute the graphing calculator program DIFFY with the irrational numbers $\sqrt{2}$, $\sqrt{3}$, π, and $\sqrt{37}$. Does DIFFY terminate for these initial entries?

(b) Execute DIFFY with the initial entries 1, 1.83928675521, 3.382975768, and 6.222262523. Does DIFFY terminate for these initial entries?

(c) How many steps did it take for DIFFY to terminate in part (b)? Considering this, do you think it might be possible to find four initial entries for which DIFFY would *never* terminate?

26. (a) For this problem use DIVVY to complete this array.

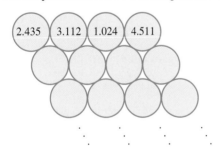

(b) Choose four positive real numbers and use DIVVY to complete the DIVVY process.

(c) Do you think the process will always terminate? Explain.

27. **(a)** Execute the graphing calculator program DIVVY with the initial irrational numbers $\sqrt{2}$, $\sqrt{3}$, π, and $\sqrt{37}$. Does DIVVY terminate for these numbers?

(b) Execute DIVVY with the initial entries 2, 3.578330778, 10.43223066, and 74.65994408. Does DIVVY terminate for these initial entries?

(c) How many steps did it take for DIVVY to terminate in part (b)? Would it be reasonable to guess that there might be four initial entries for which DIVVY would *never* terminate?

From State Student Assessments

28. (Connecticut, Grade 6)
Jenny bought three cassette tapes for $5.99 each. What was the total cost of the three tapes before tax?
A. $6.02
B. $8.99
C. $17.77
D. $17.97

29. (Massachusetts, Grade 8)
Webster Office Supply Company agrees to keep Mr. Orlando's photocopier in working condition for one year if he chooses one of these two payment plans:

Plan 1: Mr. Orlando pays $300. For the first 16,000 copies made, he pays nothing extra. For each additional copy, he pays 2.2¢.

Plan 2: Mr. Orlando pays $500. He pays nothing extra for copies, no matter how many are made.

A. Suppose Mr. Orlando makes 20,000 copies in one year. Which plan will cost him less? Explain how you found your answer.

B. How many copies would Mr. Orlando need to make so that he would pay the same amount for Plan 1 as for Plan 2? Explain how you found your answer.

For Review

30. Write each of these in Mayan notation.
(a) 231   **(b)** 15,278   **(c)** 7142

31. Write each of these (now written in Mayan notation) in base ten notation.

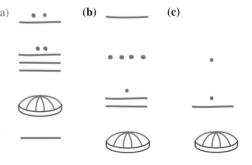

32. Write each of these using Egyptian numerals.
    (a) 547   (b) 2486   (c) 854
33. Convert each of these Egyptian numerals to their base ten equivalents.

(a)
(b)
(c)

7.3   Ratio and Proportion

At basketball practice, Caralee missed 18 free throws out of 45 attempts. Since she made 27 free throws, we say that the **ratio** of the number missed to the number made was 18 to 27. This can be expressed by the fraction 18/27 or, somewhat archaically, by the notation 18 : 27. The notation 18 : 27 is read "18 to 27" as in the statement, "The ratio of the number of free throws Caralee missed to the number she made was 18 : 27." We will always use the fraction notation in what follows.

Other ratios from Caralee's basketball practice are:

- the ratio of the number of shots made to the number attempted—27/45,
- the ratio of the number of shots missed to the number attempted—18/45,
- the ratio of the number of shots made to the number missed—27/18.

> **DEFINITON** *Ratio*
> If a and b are real numbers with $b \neq 0$, the **ratio of a to b** is the quotient a/b.

Ratios occur with great frequency in everyday life. If you use 10.4 gallons of gasoline in driving 400.4 miles, the efficiency of your car is measured in miles per gallon given by the ratio 400.4/10.4 or 38.5 miles per gallon. If Lincoln Grade School has 405 students and 15 teachers, the student-teacher ratio is the quotient 405/15. If Jose Varga got 56 hits in 181 times at bat, his batting average is the ratio 56/181. The number of examples that could be cited is almost endless.

EXAMPLE   7.16   **Determining Ratios**

Determine these ratios.

(a) The ratio of the number of boys to the number of girls in Martin Luther King High School if there are 285 boys and 228 girls.
(b) The ratio of the number of boys to the number of students in part (a).

Solution

(a) The desired ratio is 285/228.
(b) Since the total number of students is 285 + 228 (that is, 513), the desired ratio is 285/513.

The ratio of the number of boys to the number of students in Martin Luther King High School was shown to be 285/513 or 285 to 513. This is certainly correct, but it is not nearly as informative as it would be if the ratio were written in simplest form. Thus,

$$\frac{285}{513} = \frac{5}{9}$$

$$285 \div 57 = 5$$
$$513 \div 57 = 9$$

and this says that 5/9 (or a little more than 1/2) of the students in Martin Luther King High School are boys. Expressing a ratio by a fraction in simplest form is often useful and informative.

EXAMPLE   7.17

Expressing Ratios in Simplest Form

Express these ratios in simplest form.

(a)   The ratio of 385 to 440
(b)   The ratio 432/504

Solution

(a)   The ratio of 385 to 440 is the quotient 385/440. Expressing this in simplest form, we have

$$\frac{385}{440} = \frac{7}{8}.$$

Thus, in simplest form, the ratio is 7 to 8.

(b)   Expressing the quotient in simplest form,

$$\frac{432}{504} = \frac{6}{7}.$$

Thus, in simplest form, the ratio is 6/7 or 6 to 7.

EXAMPLE   7.18

Determining a Less Obvious Ratio

If one seventh of the students at Garfield High are nonswimmers, what is the ratio of nonswimmers to swimmers?

Solution

The desired ratio is the number of nonswimmers divided by the number of swimmers. Can we determine these numbers from the information given? Actually, no; but the problem can still be solved. Suppose there are n students in the school. Then $\frac{n}{7}$ are nonswimmers and $\frac{6n}{7}$ are swimmers. Thus, the desired ratio is

Use a variable.

$$\frac{\dfrac{n}{7}}{\dfrac{6n}{7}} = \frac{n}{7} \cdot \frac{7}{6n} = \frac{1}{6}.$$

Proportion

Ratios allow us to make clear comparisons when actual numbers sometimes make them more obscure. For example, at basketball practice, Caralee made 27 of 45 free throws attempted and Sonja made 24 of 40 attempts. Which player appears to be the better foul shot shooter? For Caralee, saying that the ratio of shots made to shots tried is 27/45 amounts to saying that she made 3/5 of her shots. That is,

$$\frac{27}{45} = \frac{3}{5}.$$

$\frac{27}{45}$ and $\frac{3}{5}$ are equivalent fractions.

Similarly, for Sonja the ratio of shots made to shots attempted is

$$\frac{24}{40} = \frac{3}{5},$$

$\frac{27}{45}, \frac{24}{40},$ and $\frac{3}{5}$ are all equivalent fractions.

and this suggests that the two girls are equally capable at shooting foul shots. Because of its importance in such comparisons, the equality of two ratios is called a **proportion.**

DEFINITON *Proportion*

If *a/b* and *c/d* are two ratios and

$$\frac{a}{b} = \frac{c}{d},$$

this equality is called a **proportion.**

From Chapter 6, we know that

$$\frac{a}{b} = \frac{c}{d}$$

for integers *a, b, c,* and *d,* if, and only if, *ad = bc.* But essentially the same argument holds if *a, b, c,* and *d* are real numbers. This leads to the next theorem.

THEOREM *Conditions for a Proportion*

The equality

$$\frac{a}{b} = \frac{c}{d},$$

is a proportion if, and only if, *ad = bc.*

EXAMPLE 7.19 | **Determining Proportions**

In each of these, determine x so that the equality is a proportion.

(a) $\dfrac{28}{49} = \dfrac{x}{21}$ (b) $\dfrac{2.11}{3.49} = \dfrac{1.7}{x}$

Solution

We use the preceding theorem, which amounts to multiplying both sides of the equality by the product of the denominators or "cross multiplying" as we often say.

(a) $\dfrac{28}{49} = \dfrac{x}{21}$

$28 \cdot 21 = 49x$

$\dfrac{28 \cdot 21}{49} = x$

$12 = x$

(b) $\dfrac{2.11}{3.49} = \dfrac{1.7}{x}$

$2.11x = (1.7)(3.49)$

$x = \dfrac{(1.7)(3.49)}{2.11}$

$x \doteq 2.81$

EXAMPLE 7.20 | **Obtaining a Proportion from a Proportion**

Ian made 6 and missed 9 free throws in a basketball game for a ratio of shots made to shots missed of 6/9 or 2/3. In the same game, Arlo made 4 and missed 6 shots for the same ratio of 2/3. That is, 6/9 = 4/6 is a proportion. Show that the ratios of the shots attempted to the number missed for each player also form a proportion.

Solution

Since the total number of attempts for Ian and Arlo are 6 + 9 = 15 and 4 + 6 = 10, respectively, the ratios in question are 15/9 = 5/3 and 10/6 = 5/3. Therefore, since 15/9 = 10/6, this is a proportion.

The result of the preceding example is true in general as the following example shows.

EXAMPLE 7.21 | **Proving a Property of Proportions**

If

$$\frac{a}{b} = \frac{c}{d},$$

prove that

$$\frac{a + b}{b} = \frac{c + d}{d}.$$

Solution

Understand the problem

We are given that $\dfrac{a}{b} = \dfrac{c}{d}$ is a proportion and are asked to show that $\dfrac{a+b}{b} = \dfrac{c+d}{d}$ is also a proportion.

Devise a plan

Since it is not immediately clear what to do, we ask what it means to say that $\dfrac{a}{b} = \dfrac{c}{d}$ and $\dfrac{a+b}{b} = \dfrac{c+d}{d}$ are proportions. Perhaps this will put the problem in a form that is easier to understand and to work on. By the preceding theorem.

$$\frac{a}{b} = \frac{c}{d} \text{ if, and only if, } ad = bc$$

and

$$\frac{a+b}{b} = \frac{c+d}{d}$$

if, and only if, $(a+b)d = b(c+d)$. Perhaps we can use the first of these equations to prove the second.

Carry out a plan

We want to show that $(a+b)d = b(c+d)$; that is, using the distributive property,

$$ad + bd = bc + bd.$$

But we know that

$$ad = bc$$

and adding bd to both sides of this equation gives

$$ad + bd = bc + bd$$

and hence

$$\frac{a+b}{b} = \frac{c+d}{d}$$

as was to be shown.

> Say it in a different way.

Look back

Here our principal strategy was simply to ask, "What does it mean to say that $\dfrac{a}{b} = \dfrac{c}{d}$ and $\dfrac{a+b}{b} = \dfrac{c+d}{d}$ are proportions?" Answering this question allowed us to "say it in a different way"; that is, to state an equivalent problem that proved to be quite easy to solve. The strategy, **say it in a different way,** is often very useful.

Patterns in Ratio Tables

You Will Learn

how to use ratio tables to write proportions

Vocabulary

equal ratios
ratios that give the same comparison

proportion
a statement that two ratios are equal

Learn

Softball, anyone? Courtney's and Taylor's team won a softball championship. The team often practices throwing in pairs. That's a ratio of:

$\frac{1 \text{ softball}}{2 \text{ players}}$

Courtney and Taylor play softball in Bethlehem, Pennsylvania.

Math Tip

What you know about equivalent fractions will help you work with equal ratios.

Example 1

How many softballs will be needed by 10 players? A table of equal ratios can help.

		(1×2)	(1×3)	(1×4)	(1×5)
Softballs	1	2	3	4	5
Players	2	4	6	8	10
		(2×2)	(2×3)	(2×4)	(2×5)

$\frac{1}{2} \xrightarrow[\times 5]{\times 5} \frac{5}{10}$

The ratio is 5:10. So, there are 5 softballs for 10 players.

You can also divide to find **equal ratios**.

Example 2

There are 8 teams with 72 players. Use equal ratios to find the number on 1 team.

$\frac{\text{teams}}{\text{players}} = \frac{8}{72} = \frac{1}{\blacksquare}$

		$(8 \div 2)$	$(8 \div 4)$	$(8 \div 8)$
Teams	8	4	2	1
Players	72	36	18	9
		$(72 \div 2)$	$(72 \div 4)$	$(72 \div 8)$

$\frac{8}{72} \xrightarrow[\div 8]{\div 8} \frac{1}{9}$

The ratio is 1:9. So, each team has 9 players.

A statement that two ratios are equal is called a **proportion**.

$\frac{1}{2} = \frac{5}{10}$ is a proportion. $\frac{8}{72} = \frac{1}{9}$ is a proportion.

Talk About It

How can ratio tables be used to find equal ratios?

SOURCE: *Scott Foresman–Addison Wesley Math*, Grade 5, p. 530, by Randall I. Charles et al., Copyright © 1999, Addison Wesley Longman, Inc.

Questions for the Teacher

1. How would you assist a student who found it difficult to understand that the ratios 3 : 6 and 4 : 8 are equal?

2. How would you explain to a student who does not understand, how to use division to determine if two ratios are equal as suggested above?

3. An extension of Example 2 above might be to ask how many players would be on 12 teams. How would you help a student who had trouble answering this question? By the way, is it true that most baseball teams only have 9 players? How would you respond to a student who raised this last point?

Applications of Proportions

Suppose that a car is traveling at a constant rate of 55 miles per hour. Table 7.2 gives the distances the car will travel in different time periods.

TABLE 7.2	Distance Traveled in t Hours at 55 Miles per Hour							
Time t	1	2	3	4	5	6	7	8
Distance d	55	110	165	220	275	330	385	440

The ratios d/t are all equal for the various time periods shown. That is,

$$\frac{55}{1} = \frac{110}{2} = \frac{165}{3} = \frac{220}{4} = \frac{275}{5} = \frac{330}{6}$$

and so on. Thus, each pair of ratios from the list form a proportion. Indeed, $d/t = 55$ for every pair d and t. This is also expressed by saying that the distance traveled at a constant rate is proportional to the elapsed time. In the above instance

$$d = 55t$$

for every pair d and t. The number 55 is called the **constant of proportionality.**

DEFINITON *y Proportional to x*

If the variables x and y are related by the equation

$$y = kx,$$

$$\frac{y}{x} = k$$

then **y is said to be proportional to x** and k is called the **constant of proportionality.**

This situation is extremely common in everyday life. Gasoline consumed by your car is proportional to the miles traveled. The cost of pencils purchased is proportional to the number of pencils purchased. Income from the school raffle is proportional to the number of tickets sold, and so on.

EXAMPLE 7.22 | **Income from the School Raffle**

The sixth grade class at Jefferson Middle School is raffling off a turkey as a money-making project. If the turkey cost $22 and raffle tickets are sold for 75¢ each, how many tickets will have to be sold for the class to break even? How many tickets will have to be sold if the class is to make a profit of $20?

Solution

75¢
equals
$.75

If *I* represents income in dollars and *N* represents the number of tickets sold, then *I* = 0.75*N*; that is, *I* is proportional to *N*. To break even, the class must sell enough tickets that

$$22 = 0.75N.$$

Thus,

$$N = 22 \div 0.75 = 29.\overline{3}.$$

To break even the class will have to sell at least 30 tickets. In order to make a profit of $20, enough tickets must be sold so that

$$42 = 0.75N;$$

that is,

$$N = 42 \div 0.75 = 56.$$

To make a profit of $20, 56 tickets must be sold.

Recall that in geometry, two figures are said to be similar if they are the same shape but not necessarily the same size; i.e., one is a magnification of the other.

EXAMPLE   7.23

Computing the Height of a Tree

Ms. Gulley-Pavey's fifth grade class had been studying ratio and proportion. One afternoon she took her students outside and challenged them to find the height of a tree in the school yard. After a lively discussion the students decided to measure the lengths of the shadow cast by a yardstick and that cast by the tree, arguing that these should be proportional. To help convince the class that this was so, Omari drew the picture shown. If the lengths of the shadows are 4′7″ and 18′9″, complete the calculation to determine the height of the tree.

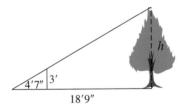
4′7″ 3′
18′9″

Solution

Since the two triangles shown in the diagram are similar, the lengths of the sides are proportional. Also, 7″ = 7/12 feet and 9″ = 9/12 feet. Therefore, we have the ratios

$$\frac{h}{3} = \frac{18\frac{9}{12}}{4\frac{7}{12}}$$

The units of both ratios must be the same.

$$= \frac{\dfrac{225}{12}}{\dfrac{55}{12}}$$

$$= \frac{225}{12} \cdot \frac{12}{55}$$

and it follows that

$$h = \frac{3 \cdot 225 \cdot 12}{12 \cdot 55} \doteq 12.27'$$

$$\doteq 12'3''$$

$0.27 \times 12 \doteq 3$

Thus, the tree was approximately 12′3″ tall.

Problem Set 7.3

Understanding Concepts

1. There are 10 girls and 14 boys in Mr. Tilden's fifth grade class. What is the ratio of
   (a) boys to girls?   (b) girls to students?
   (c) boys to students?   (d) girls to boys?
   (e) students to girls?   (f) students to boys?

2. Determine which of these are proportions.
   (a) $\dfrac{2}{3} = \dfrac{8}{12}$ (b) $\dfrac{21}{28} = \dfrac{27}{36}$
   (c) $\dfrac{7}{28} = \dfrac{8}{31}$ (d) $\dfrac{51}{85} = \dfrac{57}{95}$
   (e) $\dfrac{14}{49} = \dfrac{18}{60}$ (f) $\dfrac{20}{35} = \dfrac{28}{48}$
   (g) $\dfrac{1.5}{2.1} = \dfrac{11.5}{16.1}$ (h) $\dfrac{17.1}{6.2} = \dfrac{31.2}{9.7}$
   (i) $\dfrac{0.84}{0.96} = \dfrac{91.7}{104.8}$

3. Determine values of r and s so that each of these is a proportion.
   (a) $\dfrac{6}{14} = \dfrac{r}{21}$ (b) $\dfrac{8}{12} = \dfrac{10}{r}$ (c) $\dfrac{47}{3.2} = \dfrac{s}{7.8}$

4. Express each of these ratios as fractions in simplest form.
   (a) A ratio of 24 to 16
   (b) A ratio of 296 to 111
   (c) A ratio of 248 to 372
   (d) A ratio of 209 to 341
   (e) A ratio of 3.6 to 4.8
   (f) A ratio of 2.09 to 3.41
   (g) A ratio of 6.264 to 9.396

5. Collene had an after-school job at Taco Time at $5.50 per hour.
   (a) How much did she earn on Monday if she worked $3\frac{1}{2}$ hours?
   (b) On Tuesday she earned $27.50. How long did she work?
   (c) Show that the ratio of the time worked to the amount earned on Monday is equal to the ratio of the time worked to the amount earned on Tuesday; that is, show that these two ratios form a proportion.
   (d) Show that the ratio of the time worked on Monday to the time worked on Tuesday equals the ratio of the amount earned on Monday to the amount earned on Tuesday; that is, show that these two ratios also form a proportion.

6. David Horwitz bought four sweatshirts for $119.92. How much would it cost him to buy nine sweatshirts at the same price per sweatshirt?

7. If s is proportional to t and $s = 62.5$ when $t = 7$, what is s when $t = 10$?

8. The flag pole at Sunnyside Elementary School casts a shadow $9'8''$ long at the same time Mr. Schaal's shadow is $3'2''$ long. If Mr. Schaal is $6'3''$ tall, how tall is the flag pole to the nearest foot?

9. A kilometer is a bit more than six tenths of a mile. If the speed limit along a stretch of highway in Canada is 90 kilometers per hour, about how fast can you travel in miles per hour and still not break the speed limit?

Thinking Critically

10. If a is to b as c is to d; that is, if

$$\frac{a}{b} = \frac{c}{d},$$

   (a) show that b is to a as d is to c.
   (b) show that $a - b$ is to b as $c - d$ is to d.
   (c) show that a is to $a + b$ as c is to $c + d$.
   (d) show that $a + b$ is to $c + d$ as b is to d.

11. (a) If y is proportional to x^2 and $y = 27$ when $x = 6$, determine y when $x = 12$.
    (b) Determine the ratio of the y values in part (a).
    (c) If y and x are related as in part (a), what happens to the value of y if the value of x is doubled? Explain.

12. (a) If y is proportional to x^3 and $y = 32$ when $x = 12$, determine the value of y when $x = 6$.
    (b) Determine the ratio of the y values in part (a).
    (c) If y and x are related as in part (a), what happens to the value of y if the value of x is doubled? Tripled? Quadrupled? Explain.

13. If y is proportional to $1/x$ and $y = 3.5$ when $x = 84$, determine y when $x = 14$. (*Hint:* $y = k(1/x)$.)

Thinking Cooperatively

14. Working with two or three other students and using a rectangular mirror and a measuring tape, take needed measurements and discuss the various aspects of this problem as you seek a solution agreed upon by your entire group.
    (a) You stand in front of a mirror on a wall and can just barely see your entire reflection. If your height is h and H is the vertical dimension of the mirror, determine the ratio h to H. (*Hint:* Make a suitable drawing.)
    (b) Where should the mirror of minimum height H in part (a) be located on the wall?
    (c) Does the distance you stand from the wall make a difference in your answers to parts (a) and (b)? Explain.

Making Connections

15. Celeste Neal won a one-hundred meter race with a time of 11.6 seconds and Michelle Beese came in second with a time of 11.8 seconds. Given that each girl ran at a constant rate throughout the race, determine the ratio of Celeste's speed to Michelle's in simplest terms.

16. On a trip of 320 miles, Sunao's truck averaged 9.2 miles per gallon. At the same rate, how much gasoline would his truck use on a trip of 440 miles?

17. Which is the best buy in each case?
    (a) 32 ounces of cheese for 90¢ or 40 ounces of cheese for $1.20.
    (b) A gallon of milk for $2.21 or two half gallons at $1.11 per half gallon.
    (c) A 16-ounce box of bran flakes at $3.85 per box or a 12-ounce box at $2.94 per box.

18. The ratio of Dexter's salary to Claudine's is 4 to 5. If Claudine earns $3200 per month, how much of a raise will Dexter have to receive to make the ratio of his salary to Claudine's 5 to 6?

19. The ratio of boys to girls in Ms. Zombo's class is 3 to 2. In Mr. Stolarski's class it is 4 to 3. If there are 30 students in Ms. Zombo's class and 28 students in Mr. Stolarski's class, what is the ratio of boys to girls in the combined classes?

Communicating

20. Write a two page summary of "On Being the Right Size" by J. B. S. Haldane, on pages 952–57 of *The World of Mathematics,* James R. Newman, ed. (New York: Simon and Schuster, 1956). In particular, make clear how ratio and proportion play a role in this study.

Using a Calculator

21. If a $12''$ pepperoni pizza from Ricco's costs $9.56, what should a $14''$ pizza from Ricco's cost?

22. Suppose your car uses 8.7 gallons of gas traveling 192 miles. Determine approximately how many gallons it would use traveling a distance of 305 miles.

23. If it takes $1\frac{1}{3}$ cups of sugar to make a batch of cookies, how much sugar would be required to make four batches?

24. If three equally priced shirts cost a total of $59.97, how much would seven shirts cost at the same price per shirt?

25. If 12 erasers cost $8.04 and Mrs. Orton bought $14.07 worth of erasers, how many erasers did she buy?

26. One day Kenji Okubo took his class of sixth graders outside and challenged them to find the distance between two rocks that could easily be seen one above the other on the vertical face of a bluff near the school. After some discussion the children decided to hold a rod in a vertical position at a point 100′ from the base of the cliff.

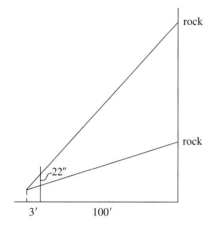

They also decided to mark the points on the rod where the lines of sight of a student standing 3′ further from the cliff and looking at the rocks cut the rod. If the marks on the rod were 22″ apart, what was the distance between the two rocks? (*Caution:* Convert all measurements to feet.)

From State Student Assessments

27. (Colorado, Grade 4)

Marcus has two different size boxes of raisins. He counts 62 raisins in the 4 ounce box.

A. Estimate how many raisins are in the 16 ounce box.

B. Explain your estimate and show your work so Marcus can see how you decided.

28. (Minnesota, Grade 5)
Use the drawing below to answer the question.

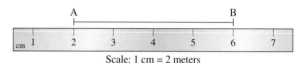

Scale: 1 cm = 2 meters

The segment AB is taken from a scale drawing. What is the actual length that this segment represents?

A. 4 meters

B. 6 meters

C. 8 meters

D. 12 meters

29. (Connecticut, Grade 6)
20 out of every 100 high school dropouts are gifted and talented students. Which of the following also describes this situation?

A. 4/25 of the dropouts are gifted and talented.

B. 1/4 of the dropouts are gifted and talented.

C. 1/5 of the dropouts are gifted and talented.

D. 5/1 of the dropouts are gifted and talented.

For Review

30. Perform these computations.

(a) $4 + (-7)$ (b) $8 - (-5)$

(c) $(-5) + (-7)$ (d) $(-8) + (-5)$

(e) $8 - (-4)$ (f) $(-3)(-5)$

(g) $12 \div (-3)$ (h) $(-28) \div 4$

(i) $(-28) \div (-4)$ (j) $(-495) \div 11$

(k) $57 \div (-19)$ (l) $[4 + (-15)] \div 11$

31. Find the prime power representation of 521,752.

32. If $a = 3^5 \cdot 5^2 \cdot 11^3$, how many divisors does a have?

33. Does $b = 3^2 \cdot 5 \cdot 11^3$ divide a of problem 31? Explain.

34. Find the smallest integer greater than b of problem 33 that is divisible by b.

35. Find the largest integer less than b of problem 33 that divides b.

7.4   Percent

It is essentially impossible to live in today's society and not be conversant with the notion of **percent.**

- What percent interest do you pay on the outstanding balance on your credit card?
- What percent interest do you pay on the amount borrowed to buy a new car? Does this amount to very much money?
- If you are required to make a down payment of 11% of the purchase price of $175,000 when buying a home, how much do you have to pay down?
- How rapidly will your retirement grow if you make periodic payments into an account paying 5% interest compounded quarterly?

Percent (from the Latin *per centum* meaning "per hundred") is one of the most important ratios in school mathematics. Thus, 50% is the ratio 50/100, and this is quickly reduced to the fraction 1/2 or written as the decimal 0.50. Thus, if I have $98 and give you 50% of what I have, I give you

$$\frac{1}{2} \cdot \$98 = \$49 \qquad \text{or} \qquad 0.5 \times \$98 = \$49.$$

The "of" in the preceding sentence translates into "times." Thus,

$$50\% \text{ of} \qquad \text{means} \qquad 50\% \times,$$

$$\frac{1}{2} \text{ of} \qquad \text{means} \qquad \frac{1}{2} \times,$$

and

$$0.5 \text{ of} \qquad \text{means} \qquad 0.5 \times.$$

DEFINITION *Percent*

If r is any nonnegative real number, then r percent, written $r\%$, is the ratio

$$\frac{r}{100}.$$

Since $r\%$ is defined as the ratio $r/100$ and the notational effect of dividing a decimal by 100 is to move the decimal point 2 places to the left, it is easy to write a given percent as a decimal. For example, 12% = 0.12, 25% = 0.25, 130% = 1.3, and so on. Conversely, $0.125 = 12.5\%$ or $12\frac{1}{2}\%$, $0.10 = 10\%$, $1.50 = 150\%$, and so on.

EXAMPLE   7.24

Expressing Decimals as Percents

Express these decimals as percents.

(a)   0.25   (b)   0.333 . . .   (c)   1.255

Solution

(a)   0.25 = 25%
(b)   0.33 . . . = 33.333 . . . % $= 33\frac{1}{3}\%$
(c)   1.255 = 125.5%

Chapter 7
Lesson
12

Understanding Percent

You Will Learn

how to use percents to name amounts less than or equal to 1

Vocabulary

percent
a way to compare a number with one hundred

Did You Know?

Percent means per 100. It comes from the Latin *per centum*.

Learn

In a recent survey, 100 students were asked which household chore they liked the least. The list shows which jobs the students mentioned.

How can you name the part of those surveyed who liked washing dishes the least?

Mia wrote a fraction to describe the part. $\frac{31}{100}$

Donnell used a **percent**. Percent means per hundred or out of 100. % is a symbol for percent. 31%

José thought of the number of students as 31 out of 100. 0.31

Chores we Like the Least
Washing dishes 31
Laundry 20
Yard work 19
Cleaning room 17
Babysitting 13

Talk About It

Look at the grid shown above. What fraction and percent name the unshaded part?

Check

Write the hundredths fraction and the percent shaded in each picture.

1.
2.
3.

4. **Reasoning** Doing laundry was the chore least liked by 20 of the 100 students. Use a grid to show the percent who named laundry.

328 Chapter 7 • Fractions and Mixed Numbers

SOURCE: *Scott Foresman–Addison Wesley Math, Grade 5*, p. 328, by Randall I. Charles et al. Copyright © 1999, Addison Wesley Longman, Inc.

Questions for the Teacher

1. This introductory lesson on percent focuses on a survey of 100 people and a rectangular array of 100. Does this seem to you a good way to begin? Explain.
2. This lesson continues with these questions. How would you help your students to answer them?

Estimation Estimate the percent of each figure that is shaded.

19. 20. 21.

3. How would you respond to a child who says that 25% is the same as 1/4? Would you welcome such an observation? Why or why not?

EXAMPLE 7.25 | **Expressing Percents as Decimals**

Express these percents as decimals.

(a)   40%   (b)   12%   (c)   127%

Solution | (a)   40% = 0.40

(b)   12% = 0.12

(c)   127% = 1.27

$$40\% = \frac{40}{100} = 0.40$$

EXAMPLE 7.26 | **Expressing Percents as Fractions**

Express these percents as fractions in lowest terms.

(a)   60%   (b) $66\frac{2}{3}\%$ (c)   125%

Solution | (a)   By definition 60% means 60/100. Therefore,

$$60\% = \frac{60}{100} = \frac{3}{5}.$$

(b) $66\frac{2}{3}\% = \dfrac{66\frac{2}{3}}{100} = \dfrac{\frac{200}{3}}{100} = \dfrac{2}{3}.$

(c) $125\% = \dfrac{125}{100} = \dfrac{5}{4} \text{ or } 1\frac{1}{4}.$

EXAMPLE 7.27 | **Expressing Fractions as Percents**

Express these fractions as percents.

(a) $\dfrac{1}{8}$ (b) $\dfrac{1}{3}$ (c) $\dfrac{16}{5}$

Solution I | *Using proportions*

Since percents are ratios, we can use variables to determine the desired percents.

(a)   Suppose $1/8 = r\% = r/100$. Then

$$r = 100 \cdot \frac{1}{8} = 12.5$$

and

$$r\% = 12.5\%$$

(b) If $1/3 = s\% = s/100$. Then

$$s = \frac{100}{3} = 33\frac{1}{3}$$

$= 33\frac{1}{3}\%$

and

$$s\% = 33\frac{1}{3}\%.$$

(c) If $16/5 = u\% = u/100$. Then

$$u = \frac{16}{5} \cdot 100 = 320$$

and

$$u\% = 320\%.$$

Solution 2 | *Using decimals*

Here we write the fractions as decimals and then as percents.

(a) By division

$$\frac{1}{8} = 0.125 = 12.5\%.$$

(b) Here

$$\frac{1}{3} = 0.333\ldots = 33.\overline{3}\% = 33\frac{1}{3}\%.$$

(c) $\dfrac{16}{5} = 3.2 = 320\%.$

Applications of Percent

Use of percents is commonplace. Three of the most common types of usages are illustrated in the next three examples.

EXAMPLE 7.28 | **Calculating a Percentage of a Number**

The Smetanas bought a house for $175,000. If a 15% down payment was required, how much was the down payment?

Solution 1 | *Using an equation*

The down payment is 15% of the cost of the house. Thus, if d is the down payment,

$$d = 15\% \times \$175,000$$
$$= 0.15 \times \$175,000$$
$$= \$26,250$$

"Of" translates into "times"

Solution 2 | *Using ratio and proportion*

The size of the down payment is proportional to the cost of the house; that is, $d/175,000$ is a ratio that is equivalent to the ratio 15%. The following diagram makes the desired proportion visually more clear. Thus,

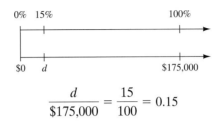

$$\frac{d}{\$175,000} = \frac{15}{100} = 0.15$$

and

$$d = 0.15 \times \$175,000$$
$$= \$26,250.$$

EXAMPLE 7.29 | **Calculating a Number of Which a Given Number Is a Given Percentage**

Soo Ling scored 92% on her last test. If she got 23 questions right, how many problems were on the test?

Solution 1 | *Using an equation*

Let n denote the number of questions on the test. Since Soo Ling got 23 questions correct for a score of 92%, we know that 23 is 92% of n; that is,

$$23 = 92\% \times n = 0.92n.$$

Hence,

$$n = \frac{23}{0.92} = 25.$$

Solution 2 | *Using ratio and proportion*

As seen in the diagram, the ratio of 23 to the number of questions on the test must be the same as the ratio 92%.

Thus,

$$\frac{23}{n} = \frac{92}{100} = 0.92.$$

Therefore,

$$23 = 0.92 \times n$$

and

$$n = 23 \div 0.92 = 25$$

as before.

EXAMPLE 7.30

Calculating What Percentage One Number Is of Another

Tara got 28 out of 35 possible points on her last math test. What percentage score did the teacher record in her grade book for Tara?

Solution I

Using the definition

Tara got twenty-eight thirty-fifths of the test right. Since

$$\frac{28}{35} = 0.80 = 80\%,$$

the teacher recorded 80% in her grade book.

Solution 2

Using ratio and proportion

Let *x* be the desired percentage. Then, as above, the diagram helps one visualize the proportion

$$\frac{x}{100} = \frac{28}{35}.$$

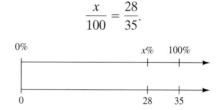

Thus,

$$x = \frac{28 \cdot 100}{35} = 80\%.$$

Compound Interest

If you keep money in a savings account at a bank, the bank pays you interest at a fixed rate (percentage) for the privilege of using your money. For example, suppose you invest $5000 for a year at 7% interest. How much is your investment worth at the end of the year? Since the interest earned is 7% of $5000, the interest earned is

$$7\% \times \$5000 = 0.07 \times \$5000 = \$350$$

and the value of your investment at the end of the year is

$$\$5000 + \$350 = \$5000 + 0.07 \times \$5000$$
$$= \$5000 \cdot (1.07)$$
$$= \$5350.$$

INTO THE CLASSROOM

Anne Lawrence Discusses Percent

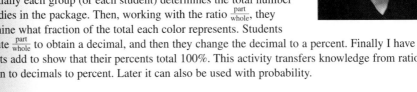

To illustrate percent in a fun way, I purchase packages of M & M's®
or Smarties®. I buy a package for each group of students, or, if the
packages are small, one package for each student.

Initially each group (or each student) determines the total number
of candies in the package. Then, working with the ratio $\frac{part}{whole}$, they
determine what fraction of the total each color represents. Students
compute $\frac{part}{whole}$ to obtain a decimal, and then they change the decimal to a percent. Finally I have
students add to show that their percents total 100%. This activity transfers knowledge from ratio to
fraction to decimals to percent. Later it can also be used with probability.

SOURCE: Scott *Foresman–Addison Wesley Middle School Math,* Course 2, p. 382D, by Randall I.
Charles et al. Copyright © 1999, Addison Wesley Longman, Inc.

If you leave the total investment in the bank, its value at the end of the second year is

$$\$5350 + 0.07 \times \$5350 = \$5350 \cdot (1.07)$$
$$= \$5000 \cdot (1.07)(1.07)$$
$$= \$5000 \cdot (1.07)^2$$
$$= \$5724.50.$$

from above

Similarly, at the end of the third year, your investment would be worth

$$\$5000 \cdot (1.07)^3 = \$6125.22$$

to the nearest penny. In general, it would be worth

$$\$5000 \cdot (1.07)^n$$

at the end of *n* years. This is an example of **compound interest,** where the term "compound" implies that each year you earn interest on all the interest earned in preceding years
as well as on the original amount invested (the **principal**).

Usually interest is compounded more than once a year. Suppose the $5000 invest-
ment just discussed was made in a bank that paid interest at the rate of 7% compounded
semi-annually; that is, twice a year. Since the rate for a year is 7%, the rate for half a year
is 3.5%. Thus, the value of the investment at the end of the year (that is, at the end of *two*
interest periods) is

$$\$5000(1.035)^2 = \$5356.13$$

and the values at the end of 2 years and 3 years respectively are

$$\$5000(1.035)^4 = \$5737.62$$

and

$$\$5000(1.035)^6 = \$6146.28.$$

These can be easily
calculated using the
$\boxed{y^x}$ key or the constant
function of your
calculator.

Compounding more and more frequently is to your advantage and, to attract customers, some banks are now compounding monthly or even daily.

The above calculations are typical, and are summarized in this theorem.

> $\frac{r}{t}$ is the rate per interest period and nt is the number of interest periods.

THEOREM *Calculating Compound Interest*

The value of an investment of P dollars at the end of n years, if interest is paid at the annual rate of $r\%$ compounded t times a year, is

$$P\left(1 + \frac{r/t}{100}\right)^{nt}.$$

EXAMPLE 7.31

Computing the Cost of Debt

Many credit card companies charge 12% interest compounded monthly on unpaid balances. Suppose your card was "maxed out" at your credit limit of $2000 and that you were unable to make any payments for two years. Aside from penalties, how much debt would you owe based on compound interest alone?

Solution

Since the interest is computed at 12% compounded monthly, the effective rate per month is 12%/12 = 1% and the number of interest periods in 2 years is 12 · 2 = 24. Thus, your debt to the nearest penny would be

$$\$2000(1.01)^{24} = \$2,539.47.$$

If the debt went unpaid for 6 years, you would owe

$$\$2000(1.01)^{72} = \$4094.20.$$

This is more than double what you originally owed! The above calculations can be made by repeatedly multiplying $2000 by 1.01 using the constant feature of your calculator. Even more easily, you can compute $\$2000(1.01)^{24}$ directly by entering the following string into your calculator.

| ON/AC | 2000 | $\times$ | 1.01 | y^x | 24 | $=$ |

The Mathematics of Growth

Population growth occurs in exactly the same way that an investment grows if it is earning compound interest. Suppose, for example, that the population in the Puget Sound region in northwest Washington is approximately 2.2 million and that it is growing at the rate of 5% per year. In one year the population will be approximately

$$2.2(1.05) = 2.3$$

million. If the growth continues unabated, in 14 years it will be approximately

$$2.2(1.05)^{14} = 4.4$$

million, twice what it is today. Given the fact that the area has already experienced several years of water shortages, these figures are cause for concern among officials in the area.

Like population growth, prices of commodities also rise with inflation as an investment grows drawing compound interest.

EXAMPLE 7.32 | **Pricing a Car**

If the economy were to experience a steady inflation rate of 2.5% per year, what would be the price of a new car in five years if the same quality car sells today for $18,400?

Solution   Using the same formula as in computing compound interest, the price of the car five years from now would be approximately

$$\$18,400(1.025)^5 \doteq \$20,818.$$

PROBLEM SET 7.4

Understanding Concepts

1. Write each of these ratios as percents.

   (a) $\dfrac{3}{16}$ (b) $\dfrac{7}{25}$ (c) $\dfrac{37}{40}$

   (d) $\dfrac{5}{6}$ (e) $\dfrac{3.24}{8.91}$ (f) $\dfrac{7.801}{23.015}$

   (g) $\dfrac{1.6}{7}$ (h) $\dfrac{\sqrt{2}}{\sqrt{6}}$

2. Write each of these as percents.

   (a) 0.19   (b) 0.015   (c) 2.15   (d) 3

3. Write each of these as fractions in simplest form.

   (a) 10%   (b) 25%   (c) 62.5%   (d) 137.5%

4. Compute each of the following.

   (a) 70% of 280   (b) 120% of 84

   (c) 38% of 751   (d) $7\dfrac{1}{2}$% of $20,000

   (e) .02% of 27,481   (f) 1.05% of 845

5. Compute each of these mentally.

   (a) 50% of 840   (b) 10% of 2480

   (c) 12.5% of 48   (d) 125% of 24

   (e) 200% of 56   (f) 110% of 180

6. What percentage of the markers in each of these arrays are Xs?

   (a) OXOXOXOXOX
       XOXOXOXOXO
       OXOXOXOXOX
       XOXOXOXOXO
       OXOXOXOXOX
       XOXOXOXOXO

   (b) XOXOXOXOXO
       OOOXXXXXXX
       XXXOOOXXXX
       XXXXXXXOXX
       OXOXOXXXXX
       XOXXOXXXOX

7. Without counting, estimate the percentage of markers in each array that are Xs.

   (a) XXXXXXXXXX
       OXXXXXXXXX
       OOXXXXXXXX
       OOOXXXXXXX
       OOOOXXXXXX
       OOOOOXXXXX

   (b) XXXXXXXXXX
       XXXXXXXXXX
       OOOOOOOOOO
       XXXXXXXXXX
       OOOOOOOOOO
       XXXXXXXXXX

8. If the 20-mm by 20-mm square shown represents 100%, draw rectangles 20 mm wide that represent each of these percentages.

   (a) 75%   (b) 125%   (c) 200%   (d) 20%

9. What percentage of each of these figures is red?

   (a)   (b)

   (c)   (d)

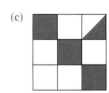 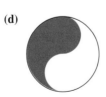

10. How many small squares must be shaded to shade the given percentages of the large square shown?

   (a) 100%   (b) 0%   (c) 25%   (d) 87%

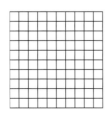

11. How many of the small rectangles must be shaded to shade the given percentages of the large rectangle shown?

   (a) 50%   (b) 25%   (c) 20%   (d) 37.5%

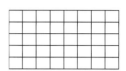

12. Mentally convert each of these to a percent.

   (a) $\dfrac{7}{28}$ (b) $\dfrac{11}{33}$

   (c) $\dfrac{72}{144}$ (d) $\dfrac{44}{66}$

13. Mentally estimate the number that should go in the blank to make each of these *true*.

   (a) 27% of _____ equals 16

   (b) 4 is _____ % of 7.5

   (c) 41% of 120 = _____

Thinking Critically

14. In a given population of men and women, 40% of the men are married and 30% of the women are married. What percentage of the adult population is married?

15. A garage advertised car repairs at 10% off the usual price—5% on parts and 5% on labor. The Consumer Protection Agency chided the garage for false advertising. Was the CPA correct? Explain.

16. After declining to do a "shady" job for Mayor Pigg for 25% of the take, Chester Slocum finally agreed to the deal when the Mayor offered him 25% of 25% of the take. What does this say about Chester's understanding of arithmetic? Explain briefly.

17. During the first half of a basketball game, the basketball team at Red Cloud High School made 60% of their 40 field goal attempts. During the second half, they scored on only 25% of 44 attempts from the field. To the nearest 1%, what was their field goal shooting percentage for the entire game?

18. During the first half of a basketball game Skeeter Thoreson missed all five of her field goal attempts. During the second half she hit 75% of her 16 attempts from the field. What was her field goal shooting percentage for the game?

Making Connections

19. Tabata's Furniture calculates the retail price of furniture they sell by marking up their cost at wholesale a full 100%.

(a) If they had a sale with all items marked down 20% from the retail price, what percentage profit did they actually make on each item sold during the sale?

(b) If they had a sale with all items marked down 50% from the retail price, what percentage profit did they make on each item sold during the sale?

20. A merchant obtains the retail price of an item by adding 20% to the wholesale price. Later he has a sale and marks every item down 20% from the retail price. Is the sale price the same as the wholesale price? Explain briefly. (*Hint:* Consider a specific item whose wholesale price is $100.)

21. Acme Electric in Boise, Idaho, purchases hot water heaters at wholesale for $185 each and sells them after marking up the wholesale price 45%. Since Idaho has a 5% sales tax, how much would you have to pay Acme for one of their water heaters?

22. Connie's Craft Corner sells its card stamping materials after marking them up 60% over their wholesale price. At a recent sale they marked their merchandise down 20%.

(a) What is the sale price of items that originally cost Connie's $46?

(b) Including sales tax of 7%, how much must a customer pay Connie's for the items in part (a)?

(c) What percentage profit does Connie's ultimately make on items sold in the sale?

23. There is $100 in the till at the start of a cashier's shift at Safeway. At the end of the shift the till contains $800. If the state has a 5% sales tax, how much of the $800 is for tax?

24. The mortgage company requires an 11% down payment on houses they finance. If the Sumis bought a house for $158,000, how much down payment did they have to make?

25. Mr. Swierkos invested $25,000 in a mutual fund. If his broker deducted a 6% commission before turning the rest of the money over to the mutual fund and the value of each share increased by 18% during the year, what percentage return on his investment did Mr. Swierkos realize at the end of the first year?

26. Kneblemann's Fine Clothes was having a sale with all merchandise marked down 20%.

(a) How much would Bethany have to pay for a dress originally priced at $78?

(b) If Natasha paid $84 for a suit at Kneblemann's sale, what was the original price of the suit?

(c) Explain a quick and easy way to calculate the sale price of items for Kneblemann's sale using a calculator.

27. Show that the sale price of items marked down 15% is the same as 85% of the original retail price.

28. Find the value of each of these investments at the end of the time period specified.

(a) $2500 invested at $5\frac{1}{4}$% interest compounded annually for 7 years.

(b) $8000 invested at 7% interest compounded semi-annually for 10 years.

Communicating

29. When asked about his performance in an upset victory in a football game, the quarterback said that he gave 110% of effort. Briefly discuss the reasonableness of this assertion.

30. In a stockholder's meeting, the chief executive officer said that the company had earned 110% of the previous year's profits. Briefly discuss the reasonableness of this assertion.

Using a Calculator

31. How much would you have to invest at 6% interest compounded annually in order to have $16,000 at the end of 5 years? (*Note:* If P is the amount invested, then $16,000 = P \cdot (1.06)^5$.)

32. Suppose you place $1000 in a bank account on January 1 of each year for nine years. If the bank pays interest on such accounts at the rate of 5.3% interest compounded annually, how much will your investment be worth on January 1 of the tenth year?

33. Successive powers of $1 + \frac{r}{100}$ are easily computed by using the constant feature of your calculator. Since the value of an investment at r% interest compounded annually for n years is $P(1 + \frac{r}{100})^n$, determine the least number of years for the value of an investment to double at each of these rates.

(a) 5%   (b) 7%   (c) 14%   (d) 20%

(e) The "rule of 72" states that you divide 72 by the interest rate to obtain the doubling time. This rule is used by many bankers to give a crude approximation to the time for the value of an investment to double at a given rate. Does it seem like a reasonable rule? Explain briefly.

34. (a) If the population of Oregon in 1999 was 3,300,000 and it is increasing at the rate of 4% per year, what will the population be in the year 2010? Give your answer correct to the nearest one hundred thousand.

(b) Using the same assumptions as in part (a), what was the population of Oregon in 1990? (*Hint:* Use the constant feature of your calculator to divide repeatedly by 1.04.)

Using a Computer

Do this problem on a spreadsheet.

35. **(a)** At age 25, Sally Saver began to contribute $1000 per year to a retirement fund that paid 8% interest compounded annually. What will be the accumulation in Sally's account when she retires at age 65? Suggestion: Enter "Year" in A1, "Sally" in B1, "$1000" in B2, "= 1000 + (1.08)*B2" in B3 and **COPY** and **PASTE** or **FILL** down to B41.

(b) Larry Livitup began his retirement savings at age 50, paying $6000 per year into an account also paying 8% interest compounded annually. What is Larry's accumulation when he retires at age 65? Suggestion: Enter "Larry" in C1 of the spreadsheet of part (a), "$6000" in C2, and "= 6000 + (1.08)*C2" in C3 and **COPY** and **PASTE** or **FILL** down to C16.

(c) Sally deposited only 40 · $1000 = $40,000 into her retirement account and Larry deposited 15 · $6000 = $90,000 into his. Who apparently has the better plan?

From State Student Assessments

36. (Oregon, Grade 5)
Richard answered 22 of the 25 questions on this week's Language Arts test correctly. About what percent of the total number of questions did he answer correctly?

A. 22 percent

B. 40 percent

C. 80 percent

D. 90 percent

37. (Massachusetts, Grade 8)
Use the advertisement below to answer the question.

ROXBURY BIKE SHOP
ONE DAY SALE – SATURDAY ONLY
All bikes must go!!

9:oo a.m. – 10% off originally-marked price

10:00 a.m. – 10% off 9:00 price

11:00 a.m. – 10% off 10:00 price

AND SO ON UNTIL
<u>ALL</u> BIKES ARE SOLD

Mr. Howard bought a bike with an originally-marked price of $400. What was the price of the bike at 12:15 P.M.?

A. $262.44

B. $240.00

C. $291.60

D. $280.00

For Review

38. Write each of these fractions in simplest form.

(a) $\dfrac{51}{69}$ **(b)** $\dfrac{143}{1001}$ **(c)** $-\dfrac{38}{57}$

39. Perform each of these additions and subtractions. Be sure to write your answer in simplest form.

(a) $\dfrac{1}{12} + \dfrac{1}{4}$ **(b)** $\dfrac{1}{5} + \dfrac{1}{12}$

(c) $\dfrac{8}{15} - \dfrac{17}{45}$ **(d)** $\dfrac{3}{143} - \dfrac{1}{91}$

(e) $\dfrac{11}{84} + \dfrac{5}{96}$ **(f)** $\dfrac{21}{60} - \dfrac{7}{75}$

40. Perform each of these multiplications and divisions leaving your answers as fractions in simplest form.

(a) $\dfrac{27}{44} \cdot \dfrac{22}{81}$ **(b)** $\dfrac{176}{247} \cdot \dfrac{95}{99}$

(c) $\dfrac{33}{35} \div \dfrac{22}{63}$ **(d)** $\dfrac{159}{286} \div \dfrac{102}{253}$

(e) $\dfrac{25}{44} \cdot \dfrac{68}{75} \cdot \dfrac{11}{16}$ **(f)** $\dfrac{169}{289} \div \dfrac{104}{221}$

41. Determine r, s, and t to make each of these equalities *true*.

(a) $\dfrac{25}{65} = \dfrac{r}{26}$ **(b)** $\dfrac{86}{99} = \dfrac{129}{s}$ **(c)** $\dfrac{4}{3} \div t = \dfrac{7}{6}$

EPILOGUE   The Number Systems of Arithmetic

With this chapter we have completed our study of the number systems of arithmetic. There is one more extension—to the complex numbers—that is needed for the study of algebra and other more advanced courses, but it is inappropriate for teaching on the elementary school level.

Table 7.3 provides a summary of the number systems we have considered and the properties that each system satisfies.

It is important to note that:

- The commutative property for neither subtraction nor division holds in any of these systems.
- Only the rational numbers, the real numbers, and the prime hour clock arithmetic have multiplicative inverses for all nonzero (nonadditive identity) elements. Hence, only these systems are closed under division except for division by zero.

TABLE 7.3   Number Systems and Their Properties

Properties	Natural numbers	Whole numbers	Integers	Rational numbers	Real numbers	n-hour clock arithmetic, n composite	n-hour clock arithmetic, n prime
Closure property for addition	•	•	•	•	•	•	•
Closure property for multiplication	•	•	•	•	•	•	•
Closure property for subtraction			•	•	•	•	•
Closure property for division except for division by zero				•	•		•
Commutative property for addition	•	•	•	•	•	•	•
Commutative property for multiplication	•	•	•	•	•	•	•
Commutative property for subtraction							
Commutative property for division							
Associative property for addition	•	•	•	•	•	•	•
Associative property for multiplication	•	•	•	•	•	•	•
Associative property for subtraction							

Properties	Natural numbers	Whole numbers	Integers	Rational numbers	Real numbers	n-hour clock arithmetic, n composite	n-hour clock arithmetic, n prime
Associative property for division							
Distributive property for multiplication over addition	•	•	•	•	•	•	•
Distributive property for multiplication over subtraction	•	•	•	•	•	•	•
Contains the additive identity; 0		•	•	•	•	•	•
Contains the multiplicative identity; 1	•	•	•	•	•	•	•
The multiplication property for 0 holds		•	•	•	•	•	•
Each element possesses an additive inverse			•	•	•	•	•
Each element except 0 possesses a multiplicative inverse				•	•		•

This table is convenient, but just knowing the properties is *not* enough. It is at least as important that teachers know conceptual and physical models appropriate to illustrate the properties and operations for each number system. They must also know how to use the systems to model and solve problems, including real-world problems. Understanding and critical thinking must be the goal of mathematical instruction—not memorizing properties and procedures by rote!

CHAPTER 7 SUMMARY

Key Concepts

The primary thrust of this chapter has been to extend the notion of decimal expansion to numbers other than integers and, thereby, to extend the number system to the system of real numbers. The rational numbers have decimal expansions that are either terminating or are nonterminating but periodic. The nonterminating and nonperiodic decimals represent numbers that are not rational; that is, irrational numbers. The set of real numbers is the set of all rational and irrational numbers. Equivalently, it is the set of all decimals—terminating, nonterminating but periodic, and nonterminating and nonperiodic.

The discussion of decimals included a review of the methods of computing with decimals. In addition to the basic arithmetic operations, this included the notions of rounding and estimation, and scientific notation and calculator computations using this notation.

From computation with decimals, the study turned to the important notions of ratio and proportion and the meaning of a phrase like "*y* is proportional to *x*." These notions are particularly important in everyday applications:

- distance traveled at a constant rate is proportional to the time of travel;
- total cost of items of the same price is proportional to the number of items purchased;
- revenue from ticket sales (at the same price per ticket) is proportional to the number of tickets sold;

and so on, with applications too numerous to mention.

Finally, the chapter closed with a study of percent—perhaps the most important ratio in everyday discourse. This discussion was extended to such applications as markups and discounts (sales) in business, compound interest, population growth, and the effects of inflation on prices.

Vocabulary and Notation

Section 7.1

Real numbers
Decimals
Negative exponents
Multiplying and dividing decimals by powers of 10
Nonterminating decimals
Terminating decimals
Repeating decimals
Ordering decimals
Irrational numbers
Real numbers

Section 7.2

Rounding decimals
Adding and subtracting decimals
Multiplying decimals
Dividing decimals
Scientific notation

Section 7.3

Ratio
Proportion
Conditions for a proportion
Proportional to
Constant of proportionality

Section 7.4

Percent
Expressing decimals as percents
Expressing percents as decimals
Expressing percents as fractions
Expressing fractions as percents
Calculating a percentage of a number
Calculating a number that is a given percent of another number
Calculating the percentage one number is of another
Compound interest
Mathematics of growth

CHAPTER REVIEW EXERCISES

Section 7.1

1. Write these decimals in expanded exponential form.
   (a) 273.425   (b) 0.000354

2. Write these fractions in decimal form.
   (a) $\dfrac{7}{125}$ (b) $\dfrac{6}{75}$ (c) $\dfrac{11}{80}$

3. Write these decimals as fractions in simplest form.
   (a) 0.315   (b) 1.206   (c) 0.2001

4. Arrange these numbers in order from least to greatest: $\dfrac{4}{12}$, 0.33, 0.3334, $\dfrac{5}{13}$, $\dfrac{2}{66}$.

5. Write these numbers as fractions in simplest form.
   (a) $10.\overline{363}$ (b) $2.1\overline{42}$

6. Suppose $a = 0.20200200020000200002\ldots$ continuing in this way with one more zero between each successive pair of 2s. Is this number rational or irrational? Explain briefly.

7. Using only mental arithmetic determine the numbers represented by these base ten numerals as fractions in simplest form.
   (a) $0.222\ldots = 0.\overline{2}$ (b) $0.363636\ldots = 0.\overline{36}$

Section 7.2

8. Perform these computations by hand.
   (a) $21.734 + 3.2145 + 71.24$
   (b) $23.471 - 2.89$
   (c) 35.4×2.37
   (d) $24.15 \div 3.45$

9. Compute the following using a calculator.
   (a) $31.47 + 3.471 + 0.0027$
   (b) $31.47 - 3.471$
   (c) 31.47×3.471
   (d) $138.87 \div 23.145$

10. Write estimates of the results of these calculations, then do the computing accurately with a calculator.
   (a) $47.25 + 13.134$
   (b) $52.914 - 13.101$
   (c) 47.25×13.134
   (d) $47.25 \div 13.134$

11. Write each of these in scientific notation using 4 significant digits.
   (a) $24,732,654$ (b) 0.000012473

12. Using an appropriate calculator and scientific notation perform each of these calculations and write the results using scientific notation with 3 significant digits.
   (a) $(2.74 \times 10^5) \cdot (3.11 \times 10^4)$
   (b) $(2.74 \times 10^5) \div (3.11 \times 10^{-4})$

13. Show that $3 - \sqrt{2}$ is irrational.

14. Show that the sum of two irrational numbers can be rational. (*Hint:* Consider problem 13.)

15. What can you say about the decimal expansion of an irrational number?

16. (a) A wall measures 8.25 feet by 112.5 feet. What is the area of the wall?
   (b) If it takes 1 quart of paint to cover 110 square feet, how many quarts of paint must be purchased to paint the wall in part (a)?

17. Give an example of a fraction whose decimal is repeating and has a period of length 4.

18. Use your calculator to determine the periodic decimal expansions of the following numbers. Remember that the calculator will necessarily round off decimals, so don't be misled by the last digit in the display if it seems to break a pattern.
$$\frac{5}{18}, \quad \frac{41}{333}, \quad \frac{11}{36}, \quad \frac{7}{45}, \quad \frac{13}{80}$$

(a) Determine where the period starts in each case.
(b) See if you can guess a rule for determining when the period of the decimal form of a fraction a/b begins.

Section 7.3

19. Maria made 11 out of 20 free throw attempts during a basketball game. What was the ratio of her successes to failures on free throws during the game?

20. Determine which of these are proportions.
   (a) $\dfrac{775}{125} = \dfrac{155}{25}$
   (b) $\dfrac{31}{64} = \dfrac{15}{32}$
   (c) $\dfrac{9}{24} = \dfrac{12}{32}$

21. If Che bought 2 pounds of candy for $3.15, how much would it cost him to buy 5 pounds of candy at the same price per pound?

22. It took Donnell 7.5 gallons of gas to drive 173 miles. Assuming that he gets the same mileage per gallon, how much gasoline will he need to travel 300 miles?

23. If y is proportional to x and $y = 7$ when $x = 3$, determine y when $x = 5$.

24. If a flag pole casts a shadow $12'$ long when a yardstick casts a shadow $10''$ long, how tall is the flag pole?

Section 7.4

25. Convert each of these to percents.
   (a) $\dfrac{5}{8}$
   (b) 2.115
   (c) 0.015

26. Convert each of these percents to decimals.
   (a) 28%
   (b) 1.05%
   (c) $33\dfrac{1}{3}\%$

27. If the sales tax is calculated at 7.2%, how much tax is due on a $49 purchase?

28. If a tax of $6.75 is charged on an $84.37 purchase, what is the sales tax rate?

29. Referring to problem 19 above, what percent of free throws attempted did Maria make during the game?

30. If you invest $3000 at 8% interest compounded every 3 months (quarterly), how much is your investment worth at the end of two years?

CHAPTER TEST

1. Write these fractions in decimal form.
   (a) $\dfrac{84}{175}$ (b) $\dfrac{24}{99}$ (c) $\dfrac{7}{11}$

2. Write each of these decimals as a fraction in simplest form.
   (a) $0.454545\ldots = 0.\overline{45}$
   (b) $31.5555\ldots = 31.\overline{5}$
   (c) $0.34999\ldots = 0.34\overline{9}$

3. Without doing the hand or calculator calculation, determine how many digits should appear to the right of the decimal point in the product 21.432×3.41.

4. Compute the product $(2.34 \times 10^{6}) \cdot (3.12 \times 10^{-19})$ using an appropriate calculator. Write your answer correct to 3 significant digits.

5. Give an example of a fraction whose decimal expansion is repeating of period 3.

6. The Pirates won 17 of their 32 hockey games.
   (a) What was the ratio of their wins to losses?
   (b) What percentage of their games did they win?

7. Mr. Spence paid $1425 down on a car selling for $9500. What percent of the purchase price did the dealer require as down payment?

8. If you invest $2000 now in a bank paying 4.2% interest compounded semi-annually, what is the least whole number of years you must leave your investment in the bank in order to withdraw at least $4000?

9. When did you invest $5000 in a bank paying $5\dfrac{3}{4}\%$ interest compounded annually if it is worth $6612.60 now?

10. Suppose that you borrow $1000 now at 9% compounded monthly. If you make no payments in the meantime, how much will you owe at the end of two years?

Statistics: The Interpretation of Data

8.1   The Graphical Representation
      of Data
8.2   Measures of Central Tendency
      and Variability
8.3   Statistical Inference

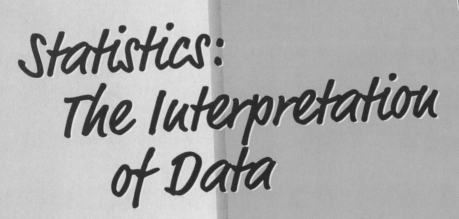

HANDS ON
How Many Are Marked?

Materials Needed

1. For each group of 10 students, a container with 100 white beans with *r* of the beans marked with a red dot where *r* is determined by the instructor.
2. A record sheet for each student as shown.

> The choice of *r* must be the same for each container and should be unknown to the students.

Name _____

1. Number of marked beans in the sample.   _____
2. Percentage of the sample consisting of marked beans.   _____
3. Estimate of the percentage of marked beans in the container. _____
4. Total number of marked beans in all samples in the class. _____
5. Percentage of marked beans in all samples (the combined sample) in the class. _____
6. Estimate of the percentage of marked beans in each container based on the result of Step 5. _____
7. Statement of your opinion of the accuracy of the estimates in Steps 3 and 6 and why you believe this to be so. _____

_____
_____
_____
_____

Directions

Step 1. In turn, each student:

- thoroughly mixes the beans in the container;
- with eyes closed, selects a sample of 10 beans from the container;
- notes the number of marked beans in his or her sample;
- returns the beans to the container and passes it on to the next student;
- completes the first three lines on his or her record sheet and records on the chalkboard the number of marked beans in his or her sample.

Step 2. When all students have completed Step 1, each should use the data on the chalkboard and complete the remainder of his or her record sheet.

Step 3. Ask the instructor what the actual percentage of marked beans in the containers was and discuss with the class the results of the activity.

CONNECTIONS   The Onslaught of Information

Every day Americans are confronted by a deluge of "facts" and figures. The public media is replete with assertions like—

"Fully 18% of Americans currently live below the poverty line."
"Studies show that 62% of teenagers in America are sexually active."

"According to the most recent Gallup poll, only 39% of Americans approve of the way the President is handling his job."
"Eight out of ten dentists surveyed prefer Whito Toothpaste."

How are such figures obtained? Are they accurate? Are they reliable? Are they misleading? Do polling organizations actually check with every American before issuing such statements? These are serious questions since the figures quoted often form the basis, not only for individual decisions, but for decisions made by government—decisions that affect us all. The fact is that many such statements are reliable while others are questionable at best.

In this chapter, we consider how assertions like these are generated and with what degree of confidence they can be believed. Without such understanding it is necessarily the case that much of what goes on in daily life must remain a mystery to be accepted or rejected on the basis of whim, or impression, or faith—a situation that is clearly less than satisfactory.

As a foundation for understanding, we must first know how data are collected, interpreted, and presented to the public.

8.1   The Graphical Representation of Data

Line Plots

In a class for prospective elementary school teachers the final examination scores for the students were as shown in Table 8.1. These are the **data** simply recorded in a list.

TABLE 8.1	Final Examination Scores in Mathematics for Elementary School Teachers, Section 1					
79	78	79	65	95	77	49
91	63	58	78	96	74	68
71	86	91	94	79	69	86
62	78	77	88	67	78	84
69	53	79	75	64	89	77

Just scanning the data gives some idea how the class did, but it is more revealing to organize the data by representing each score by an *X* placed above a number line as in Figure 8.1. Data depicted in this way is called a **line plot.** The line plot makes it possible to see at a glance that the scores ranged from 49 through 96, that most scores were between 60 and 80 with a large group between 75 and 80, and that the "typical" score was probably about 77 or 78. It also reveals that a score like 49 is quite atypical. Data organized and displayed on a line plot are much easier to interpret than raw data.

Figure 8.1
Line plot for final examination scores in Mathematics for Elementary School Teachers, Section 1

from **The NCTM Principles and Standards**

Statistics and Probability in Elementary School

A thorough grounding in statistics and probability provides tools and ways of thinking that will be useful throughout students' lives. Because some things children learn in school seem to them predetermined and rule-bound, it is critical that they also learn that some problems involve solutions that depend on assumptions and have some degree of uncertainty. The kind of reasoning used in probability and statistics is not always intuitive, and so it will not be developed in young children if it is not included in the curriculum. Students will benefit from the ability to deal intelligently with variation and uncertainty.

. . . .

In order to understand the field of statistics, students must work directly with data. This means building on the natural curiosity that young children have about their world. Questions that ask, "How many?" "How much?" "What kind?" or "Which of these?" arise quite naturally. Although these questions are not always directly about data, they do offer opportunities with which to begin the study of data. Through activities in which students collect their own data about questions of personal concern, identify attributes of things they encounter every day, and classify objects according to these attributes, students realize that data can be used to investigate phenomena, answer questions, and make predictions.

SOURCE: Reprinted with permission from *Curriculum and Evaluation Standards for School Mathematics: Discussion Draft,* copyright 1998 by the National Council of Teachers of Mathematics. All rights reserved.

Stem and Leaf Plots

Stem and leaf plots for displaying data are very similar to line plots and are particularly useful for comparison between two sets of data.

To draw a stem and leaf plot for the data in Table 8.1 we let the tens digits of the scores be the stems and let the units digits be the leaves. Thus, the scores 79, 78, and 79 are represented by

7 | 8   9   9

The completed plot appears in Figure 8.2

```
4 | 9
5 | 3  8
6 | 2  3  4  5  7  8  9  9
7 | 1  4  5  7  7  7  8  8  8  8  9  9  9  9
8 | 4  6  6  8  9
9 | 1  1  4  5  6
```

Figure 8.2
Stem and leaf plot of the final examination scores in Mathematics for Elementary School Teachers, Section 1

The stem and leaf plot gives much the same visual impression as the line plot and allows a similar interpretation.

To compare two sets of similar data, it is useful to construct stem and leaf plots on the same stems. Figure 8.3 shows such a plot for final examination scores in Sections 1 and 2 of Mathematics for Elementary School Teachers.

SECTION 2											SECTION 1														
							3		**4**		9															
					9	8	7	5	**5**		3	8														
	8	8	5	5	5	5	3	1	**6**		2	3	4	5	7	8	9	9								
			5	5	4	4	3	0	**7**		1	4	5	7	7	7	8	8	8	8	9	9	9	9		
9	7	6	4	4	2	0	0	0	**8**		4	6	6	8	9											
					6	5	5	0	**9**		1	1	4	5	6											
						0	0	0	**10**																	

Figure 8.3
Stem and leaf plots for final examination scores in Mathematics for Elementary School Teachers, Sections 1 and 2

In this figure it is easy to see that, while the two classes are quite comparable, Section 2 had a wider range of scores with one lower and several higher than those in Section 1.

Histograms

Another common tool for organizing and summarizing data is a **histogram.** A histogram for the data in Table 8.1 is shown in Figure 8.4. In a histogram, scores are grouped in intervals and the number of scores in each interval is indicated by the height of the rectangle constructed above the interval. The number of times any particular data value occurs is called its **frequency.** Similarly, the number of data values in any interval is the **frequency of the interval.** Thus, the vertical axis of a histogram indicates frequency and the horizontal axis indicates data values or ranges of data values.

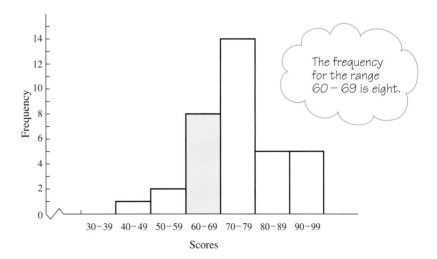

Figure 8.4
Histogram of final examination scores in Mathematics for Elementary School Teachers, Section 1

We lose some detail with the histogram. For example, the above histogram does not show how many students scored exactly 71. However, it has the advantage of giving a compact and accurate summary that is particularly useful with large collections of data that could not be conveniently represented using line or stem and leaf plots.

Histograms are useful for giving visual summaries of data that are either discrete or that vary continuously. For example, peoples' heights vary continuously. You may say that your height is 5′4″ (or 64″), but that is not exactly true. Instead, it is true only *to the nearest inch.* Consider the data in Table 8.2 that gives the heights of the 80 boys at Eisenhower High School. The heights were measured to the nearest inch so the numbers given already represent *grouped data;* that is, a measurement of 66 was recorded if a boy's height was judged to be between 65.5 and 66.5 inches. Even a height of almost exactly 66.5 inches was grouped into the 66 or 67 inch class as deemed most appropriate by the person doing the measuring.

TABLE 8.2	Heights to the Nearest Inch of Boys at Eisenhower High School Arranged in Increasing Order						
64	67	68	69	69	70	71	72
65	67	68	69	69	70	71	72
66	68	68	69	69	70	71	72
66	68	68	69	69	70	71	72
66	68	68	69	69	70	71	72
67	68	68	69	69	70	71	72
67	68	68	69	70	70	71	73
67	68	69	69	70	70	71	73
67	68	69	69	70	70	71	74
67	68	69	69	70	70	71	74

A histogram representing this data is shown in Figure 8.5. Note that, in both Figure 8.4 and Figure 8.5, the sum of the heights of the rectangles gives the number of data values.

Grouping data into classes and displaying the data in a histogram is a useful visualization of the characteristics of the data set. In drawing a histogram, the scales should be chosen so that all the data can be represented. Also, the number of classes into which the data is grouped should not be so few that it hides too much information and not so numerous that one loses the visual advantage of constructing the diagram in the first place.

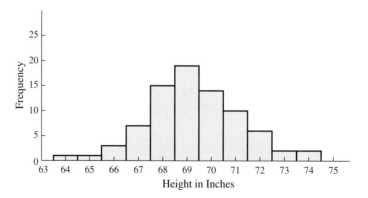

Figure 8.5
Histogram of heights of boys in Eisenhower High School

Line Graphs

A **line graph** for the data in Figure 8.5 is constructed by joining the midpoints of the tops of the rectangles in the figure by line segments (see Figure 8.6). Without the rectan-

DID YOU KNOW?

All Polls Are Not Created Equal

The news media are obsessed with polls; almost every major newspaper and television station conducts its own polls. Unfortunately, the increase in quantity has not produced better quality. In the past, media polling was criticized because simplistic and sensational tones often led to unenlightened coverage. But a new and more fundamental problem has arisen—a polling credibility gap.

The 1990 cycle was among the first with an explosion in methodologically unsound media surveys conducted by so-called pollsters without sophisticated research training or campaign expertise. Too many election-eve media polls were well beyond the margin of error, and some projected the wrong winner. The Newark *Star-Ledger,* for instance, bestowed a 17-percentage-point lead on New Jersey Sen. Bill Bradley just seven days before he barely won with 3 points. And media pollsters have had several embarrassing failures this year. In New Hampshire, most surveys exaggerated Paul Tsongas's lead over Bill Clinton and underestimated support for Pat Buchanan.

Meanwhile, campaign-conducted polling has become a highly precise science. Most voters are unfamiliar with the differences between candidate and media polling. Media polling is designed primarily to predict an outcome. Campaign polling is designed primarily to prepare a strategy to affect an outcome. As a result, sampling techniques are different, wording is different, and the analysis is different. If campaign pollsters had the same record as the average media polling outfit, they would quickly be out of business. Campaign pollsters live or die by their precision, particularly in the final days of a race. Media pollsters live by the audience they garner for their clients, not by accuracy. The more outlandish the predictions or polling result, the greater the public interest.

SOURCE: From "All polls are not created equal" from *U.S. News and World Report,* September 28, 1992, p. 24. Copyright © 1992 by U.S. News & World Report, Inc. Reprinted by permission.

gles, which would not ordinarily be drawn, the line graph appears as in Figure 8.7. Since the vertical axis represents the frequency with which measurements occur, the line graph of a set of data like this is often called a **frequency polygon.**

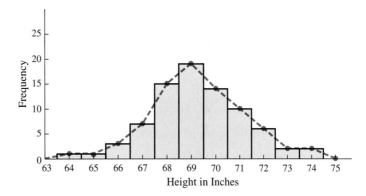

Figure 8.6

Histogram and line graph for the heights of boys at Eisenhower High School

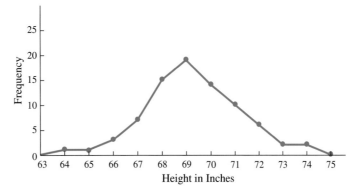

Figure 8.7

Line graph (frequency polygon) for the heights of boys at Eisenhower High School

A line graph or frequency polygon is particularly appropriate for representing data that vary continuously since this is strongly suggested by the sloping line segments. The rectangles in the histogram of Figure 8.5 tend to obscure the fact that the heights of boys represented by the rectangle centered at 67 range from 66.5" to 67.5". On the other hand, if the data really is discrete, it is probably better represented by a histogram than a frequency polygon. Since, in constructing the frequency polygon from the histogram, we added and subtracted small triangles of equal area, the area under the frequency polygon or line graph still gives the number of data values and the area under the graph and above a given interval gives the number of boys whose heights fall in that interval.

Line graphs not necessarily related to histograms are particularly effective when they are used to indicate trends over periods of years—trends in the stock market, trends in the consumption of electrical energy, and so on. For example, consider the data in Table 8.3 that gives the yearly consumer expenditure for food in the United States at five-year intervals from 1950 through 1990. This is represented visually by the line graph in Figure 8.8. In this case, the points on the graph are determined by the year and the food expenditure for that year. The points are then connected by straight line segments.

TABLE 8.3	Consumer Expenditure for Food in the United States in Billions of Dollars								
Year	1950	1955	1960	1965	1970	1975	1980	1985	1990
Expenditure	44.0	53.1	66.9	81.1	110.6	167.0	264.4	345.4	440.8

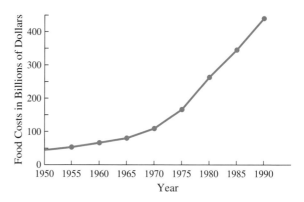

Figure 8.8
U.S. consumer expenditure for food in billions of dollars

One advantage of a line graph is that it makes it possible to estimate data values not explicitly given otherwise.

EXAMPLE 8.1 **Estimating Data Values from a Line Graph**

Using the graph in Figure 8.8, estimate the U.S. consumer expenditure for food in 1972.

Solution *Understand the problem*

The graph gives the expenditure at five-year intervals. We are asked to estimate the expenditure for 1972.

Devise a plan

Having Figure 8.8 already simplifies our task. The graph suggests that the total expenditure grows steadily each year and, while the growth is almost surely not "straight line growth" between data points as indicated by the diagram, the straight line joining the data points for 1970 and 1975 surely approximates the actual growth. If we draw a vertical line from the point representing 1972 on the horizontal axis, the height of the line segment should give us the approximate expenditure for 1972.

Carry out a plan

The point on the horizontal axis representing 1972 is two-fifths of the way from 1970 to 1975. Draw a vertical line from this point to the line graph. Then draw a horizontal line from the point where this line cuts the line graph to the vertical axis. This determines the point on the vertical axis that gives approximately $130 billion as the value of U.S. consumer expenditure for food in 1972.

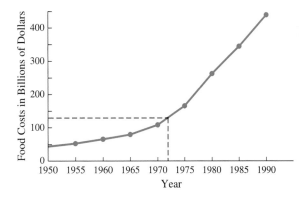

Look back

The solution was achieved by noting that the line graph, which gives the appropriate values of expenditures every five years, suggests that the expenditures steadily increase and that the actual values for intervening years no doubt lie relatively close to the straight line segments joining the given data points. Indeed, it appears that a curved line through the data points might give an even better approximation somewhat less than $130 billion. However, as an estimate, $130 billion is reasonably accurate.

Bar Graphs

SCORE	GRADE
90–100	A
80–89	B
70–79	C
60–69	D
0–59	F

Bar graphs, similar to histograms, are often useful in conveying information about so-called categorical data where the horizontal scale represents some nonnumerical attribute. For example, consider the final examination scores for Mathematics for Elementary School Teachers, Section 1, as listed in Table 8.1. Suppose that the instructor determines grades as indicated in the accompanying table. Then members of the class were awarded 5 As, 5 Bs, 14 Cs, 8 Ds, and 3 Fs. If we indicate grades on the horizontal scale and frequency on the vertical scale, we can construct the bar graph shown in Figure 8.9. In general, the rectangles in a bar graph do not abut and the horizontal scale may be

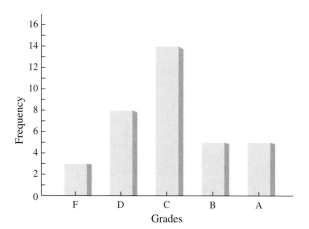

Figure 8.9
Bar graph of the final
examination grades in
Mathematics for Elementary
School Teachers, Section 1

designated by any attribute—grade in class, year, country, city, and so on. As usual, however, the vertical scale will denote frequency—the number of items in the given class.

Bar graphs are useful in displaying data concerning nonnumerical items. As the following example shows, they are also useful in comparing data concerning two or more similar groups of items.

EXAMPLE 8.2

Comparing Grades in Two Mathematics Classes by Means of a Bar Graph

Draw a suitable bar graph to make a comparison of the grades in Mathematics for Elementary School Teachers, Sections 1 and 2.

Solution

The desired bar graph can be obtained by drawing two adjacent bars (rectangles) for each letter grade with a suitable indication of which bars to associate with each section. If we use blue bars for Section 1 and pink bars for Section 2, a suitable graph might look like this. (See Figure 8.3 for the scores in Section 2. These scores merit 7 As, 9 Bs, 6 Cs, 8 Ds, and 5 Fs, using the same scale as for Section 1 above.)

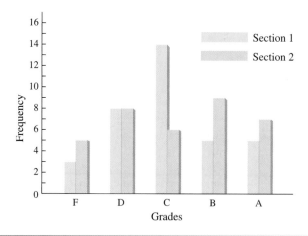

INTO THE CLASSROOM

Clem Boyer Comments on Statistics in Elementary School

In learning statistics, graphing, and probability, students are learning about the real world. When they work with tables, charts, and graphs and use the language and notation of graphing mathematics, they are developing important real-life skills in reading, interpreting, and communicating information. Working with statistics prepares students to deal with the endless number of statistics in today's world. In using probability to predict outcomes, they are learning how to cope mathematically with the uncertainties in the real world. Students should plan and carry out the collection and organization of data to satisfy their curiosity about everyday living. They need to construct, read, and interpret simple maps, tables, charts, and graphs. In doing these things, they find out how to present information about the numerical data.

In order for students to manage statistics in this age of technology, it is important for them to learn to find measures of central tendency (mean, median, and mode) and measures of dispersion (range and deviation). Further, students need to recognize the basic uses and misuses of statistical representation and inference in order for them to be wise consumers.

All of these skills in working with data improve students' ability to interpret the data they read and hear about every day. Being able to use the terminology when displaying data will help students communicate their findings.

Learning probability has applications in the real world too. Students find out how to identify situations in which immediate past experience does not affect the likelihood of future events. Their lives are enriched when they can see how mathematics is used to make predictions regarding election results, business forecasts, and sporting events.

SOURCE: From *ScottForesman Exploring Mathematics,* Grades 1–7, by L. Carey Bolster et al. Copyright © 1994 Scott, Foresman and Company. Reprinted by permission of Scott, Foresman and Company. Clem Boyer is the former Coordinator of Mathematics, K–12, for the District School Board of Seminole County in Sanford, Florida.

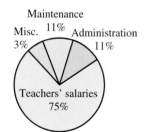

Figure 8.10
Percent of each tax dollar expended by Mile High School District by category

Pie Charts

Another pictorial method for conveying information is a **pie chart.** For example, the pie chart in Figure 8.10 shows the parts of the budget of Mile High School District used for various purposes. The number of degrees in the angular measure of each part of the chart is the appropriate fraction or percentage of 360°. Thus, the angular sector for the portion representing administration measures

$$0.11 \times 360° = 39.6°$$

and so on. As shown here, pie charts are most often used to show how a whole (total budget, total revenues, total sources of oil, and so on) is divided up.

EXAMPLE   8.3   **Making a Pie Chart**

Ajax Steel Fabricators had a gross income of $10,895,000 for the 1998–99 fiscal year. The expenses for the year were: labor—$5,120,650; materials—$4,031,150; new equipment—$326,850; and plant maintenance—$544,750; leaving $871,600 profit. Draw a pie chart illustrating how the income for Ajax was spent that year.

Solution   Draw a circle and divide it into sectors whose central angles are appropriate fractions of 360°. To the nearest degree the angles for the various classes of expenditures are:

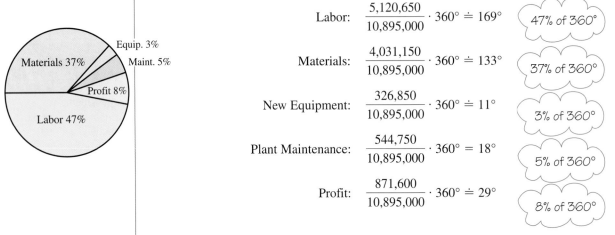

$$\text{Labor:} \quad \frac{5,120,650}{10,895,000} \cdot 360° \doteq 169°$$

47% of 360°

$$\text{Materials:} \quad \frac{4,031,150}{10,895,000} \cdot 360° \doteq 133°$$

37% of 360°

$$\text{New Equipment:} \quad \frac{326,850}{10,895,000} \cdot 360° \doteq 11°$$

3% of 360°

$$\text{Plant Maintenance:} \quad \frac{544,750}{10,895,000} \cdot 360° = 18°$$

5% of 360°

$$\text{Profit:} \quad \frac{871,600}{10,895,000} \cdot 360° \doteq 29°$$

8% of 360°

Using these as the central angles for the sectors, we obtain the pie chart shown. Such a diagram gives a quick mental image of the relative amounts of the budget spent in each category.

Increasingly, pie charts and other pictorial representations of data are drawn by computer and colored to give a more pleasing effect to the eye. If the pie chart is drawn in perspective, as if seen from an angle as in Figure 8.11, the central angles are no longer completely accurate. However, the pie chart still gives a good visual understanding of the apportionment of the whole being discussed. Also, in Figure 8.11, the pieces of the pie are separated slightly to produce a more pleasing visual effect.

Where the Income Came From:

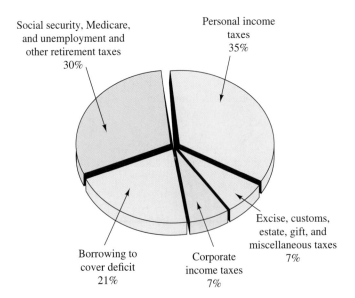

Figure 8.11
Pie chart showing U.S. government sources of revenue for fiscal year 1991.

SOURCE: 1992 IRS Form 1040 instruction booklet

Pictographs

A **pictograph** is a picture of a set of small figures or icons used to represent data and often to represent trends. Usually the icons are suggestively related to the data being represented. Consider the pictograph presentation of past and projected growth in world population in Figure 8.12. The pictograph accurately indicates that the world population more than doubled over the 40-year period from 1950 to 1990. It also suggests that, while the rate of increase is expected to diminish, the population will almost double again in the next 60 years.

To make it possible to correctly interpret a pictograph, it is necessary to include a key which indicates the value or amount each small icon represents. For example, in Figure 8.12 each icon represents one billion people. In making a pictograph, the determination of the key depends on the range of values to be represented. The key must be chosen sufficiently small that the resulting pictograph is large enough to show the desired detail but not so small that the pictograph becomes unwieldy.

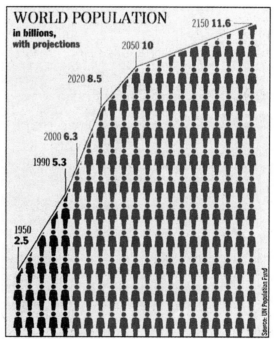

Figure 8.12
Pictograph of world population growth
SOURCE: Graph, "World Population" from *Time*, June 1, 1992, p. 54. Copyright © 1992 by Time Inc. Reprinted by permission.

Choosing Good Visualizations

Each of the graphical representations discussed is appropriate to summarize and present data so that the reader can visualize frequencies and determine trends. The various representations are more appropriate in some instances than others and most are subject to serious distortion if the intent is to mislead the reader. For example, the pictograph in

Chapter 1
Lesson
1

Reading Pictographs

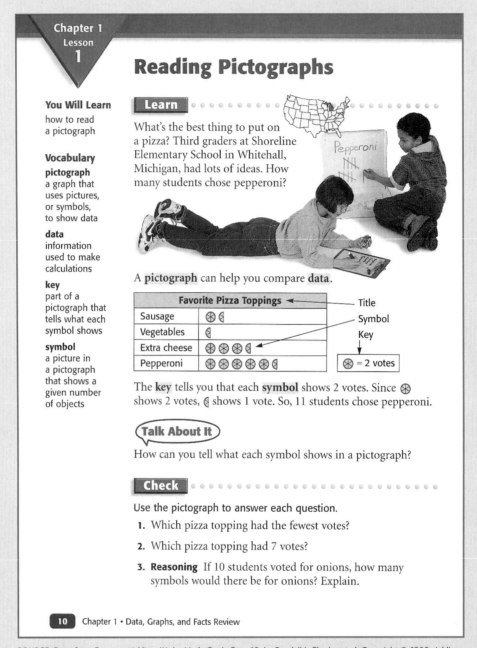

You Will Learn
how to read
a pictograph

Vocabulary

pictograph
a graph that
uses pictures,
or symbols,
to show data

data
information
used to make
calculations

key
part of a
pictograph that
tells what each
symbol shows

symbol
a picture in
a pictograph
that shows a
given number
of objects

Learn

What's the best thing to put on
a pizza? Third graders at Shoreline
Elementary School in Whitehall,
Michigan, had lots of ideas. How
many students chose pepperoni?

A **pictograph** can help you compare **data**.

Favorite Pizza Toppings	
Sausage	⊗ (
Vegetables	(
Extra cheese	⊗ ⊗ ⊗ (
Pepperoni	⊗ ⊗ ⊗ ⊗ ⊗ (

Title
Symbol
Key

⊗ = 2 votes

The **key** tells you that each **symbol** shows 2 votes. Since ⊗
shows 2 votes, (shows 1 vote. So, 11 students chose pepperoni.

Talk About It

How can you tell what each symbol shows in a pictograph?

Check

Use the pictograph to answer each question.

1. Which pizza topping had the fewest votes?

2. Which pizza topping had 7 votes?

3. **Reasoning** If 10 students voted for onions, how many
   symbols would there be for onions? Explain.

10 Chapter 1 • Data, Graphs, and Facts Review

SOURCE: From *Scott Foresman–Addison Wesley Math, Grade 3*, p. 10, by Randall I. Charles et al. Copyright © 1999, Addison
Wesley Longman, Inc.

Questions for the Teacher

1. What problem might students have in interpreting the
   above pictograph? How might you help them to achieve
   understanding?

2. What difficulties might students have in drawing a
   pictograph? What help might you need to give?

3. What is the key bit of information needed to understand
   a pictograph?

Figure 8.13 represents the oil consumption in the United States for the years 1989 and 1999.

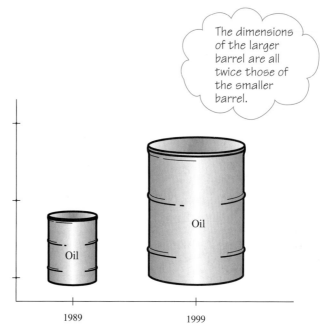

Figure 8.13
Oil consumption in the United States in 1989 and 1999

While the vertical scale honestly indicates that approximately twice as much oil was used in 1999 as in 1989, the pictograph is misleading since the volume of the larger barrel is *eight times* the volume of the smaller barrel. The casual reader is quite likely to get a badly distorted idea of the relative amount of oil used in the two years. Of course, that may be exactly what the person who constructed the pictograph intended. Have you ever seen such distortions on television? In the newspaper? In advertisements? Be observant the next time you see such a diagram.

Particularly suitable uses for the various visual representations of data described in this section are summarized here.

- Line plots: summarizing relatively small sets of data—grades in a class, heights of students in a class, birth months of students in a class, and so on.
- Stem and leaf plots: for essentially the same purposes as line plots; especially useful in comparing small data sets.
- Histograms: summarizing information in large sets of data that can be naturally grouped into intervals.
- Line graphs: summarizing trends over time.
- Pie charts: representing relative amounts of a whole.
- Pictographs: summarizing relative amounts, trends, and data sets; useful in comparing quantities.

WINDOW ON TECHNOLOGY
Statistical Plotting with a Graphing Calculator

It is still worthwhile for children to draw simple statistical plots "by hand," using squared paper and assorted drawing tools such as rulers, protractors, and colored pencils. The "hands on" approach can go far to convey a solid understanding of what it means to visualize data and what steps are required to obtain a useful visual representation. Once the basic plotting concepts are understood, however, it is instructive to see how technology can be employed. Plots drawn with a graphing calculator, spreadsheet, or other computer software offer a number of advantages.

- It becomes possible to handle large realistic data sets, such as the data gathered by a survey or the result of a scientific experiment.
- It is easy to edit and sort the data, and modify the style of plot to find the best visualization of the data set.

Plotting and charting software is now widely available, and is contained in every spreadsheet and many word processing programs. The graphing calculator also provides a statistical plotting tool, one that is especially convenient for use in the classroom. Appendix C provides a brief description of the procedures followed to create a statistical plot.

Here is a sample data set and some of the statistical plots that may be obtained with the TI-73 graphing calculator.

Insect Species

It has been estimated that there are about 751,000 insect species, including 112,000 species of moths or butterflies, 103,000 species of bees or wasps, 290,000 species of beetles, with the remaining 246,000 species falling into smaller classes. The two TI-73 screens just below show how the four insect categories and their corresponding numbers of species (in thousands) have been entered into the two lists, INSCT and SPECI. (Note: The TI-73 allows user-named lists of up to five letter or number symbols, starting with any letter.) At the right is a view of the Stat Plot editor, showing that a pie chart has been selected, with the percentages within each category to be displayed in the chart.

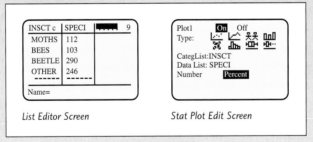

List Editor Screen   *Stat Plot Edit Screen*

The resulting pie chart of the data is shown below at the left. We could also have chosen to represent the data with a bar graph or pictograph, as shown in the middle and at the right.

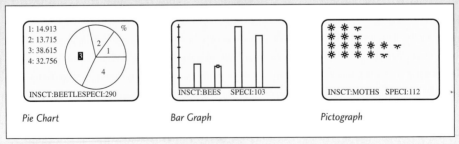

Pie Chart   *Bar Graph*   *Pictograph*

From the pie chart, we see that nearly 40% of the 751,000 different species of insects are beetles! The eminent geneticist J. B. S. Haldane once commented that "God must have loved beetles; He made so many of them."

PROBLEM SET 8.1

Understanding Concepts

1. The scores below were obtained on the final examination in an introductory mathematics class of forty students.

98	80	98	76	79	94	71	45	89	71
62	61	95	77	83	49	65	58	56	89
66	87	74	64	75	58	72	75	48	88
75	51	84	76	95	69	61	69	33	86

(a) Scanning the data, what do you think the "typical" or "average" score is?

(b) Make a line plot to organize this data.

(c) Looking at the line plot, what seems to be the "typical" score?

(d) Do you identify any scores that seem to be particularly atypical of this data set? Explain.

(e) Write a two or three sentence description of the results of the final examination.

2. Make a stem and leaf plot of the data in problem 1.

3. Make a histogram for the data in problem 1 using the ranges 20–29, 30–39, . . . , 90–99 on the horizontal scale.

4. At the same time heights of the boys at Eisenhower High School were studied, heights of the girls were also studied.

(a) Draw a histogram to summarize this data that gives the heights to the nearest inch of the 75 girls at Eisenhower High School. Use intervals one unit wide centered at the whole number values 56, 57, . . . , 74.

57	62	63	64	66
58	62	63	64	66
60	62	63	64	66
60	62	63	65	66
61	62	63	65	66
61	62	63	65	66
61	62	63	65	66
61	63	64	65	66
61	63	64	65	66
61	63	64	65	66
62	63	64	65	67
62	63	64	65	67
62	63	64	65	70
62	63	64	65	70
62	63	64	66	73

(b) Write two or three sentences describing the distribution of the heights of the girls.

5. **(a)** Draw a frequency polygon for the data in problem 4 by joining the midpoints of the tops of the rectangles of the histogram by straight line segments.

(b) What does the area under the frequency polygon and between the scores 60.5 and 64.5 represent? Explain briefly.

6. The scores on the first, second, and third hour tests given in a class in educational statistics as the term progressed are shown.

First hour test:	92, 80, 73, 74, 93, 75, 76, 68, 61, 76,
	83, 94, 63, 74, 76, 86, 82, 70, 65, 74,
	83, 87, 98, 77, 67, 64, 87, 96, 62, 64
Second hour test:	52, 65, 84, 91, 86, 76, 73, 52, 68, 79,
	88, 94, 98, 84, 53, 59, 63, 66, 77, 81,
	94, 81, 64, 56, 96, 58, 64, 57, 83, 87
Third hour test:	97, 91, 61, 67, 72, 81, 63, 56, 53, 59,
	43, 56, 64, 78, 93, 99, 84, 84, 61, 56,
	73, 77, 57, 46, 93, 87, 93, 78, 46, 87

(a) Draw three separate but parallel line plots for these three sets of scores.

(b) Write a three or four sentence analysis of these line plots suggesting what happened during the term to account for the changing distribution of scores.

7. Together the Smiths earn $64,000 per year which they spend as shown.

Taxes	$21,000
Rent	$10,800
Food	$5,000
Clothes	$2,000
Car payments	$4,800
Insurance	$5,200
Charity	$7,000
Savings	$6,000
Misc.	$2,200

Draw a pie chart to show how the Smiths spend their yearly income.

8. This pie chart indicates how the city of Metropolis allocates its revenues each year.

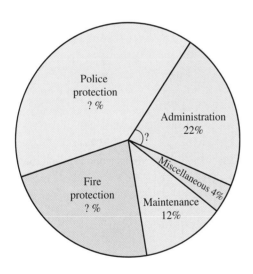

(a) What is the measurement of the central angle of the sector representing administrative expense?

(b) Using a protractor to measure the angle, determine what percent of the city budget goes for police protection.

(c) How does the city's expenditure for maintenance compare with its expenditure for police protection?

(d) How do the expenditures for administration and fire protection compare?

9. This bar graph shows the distribution of grades on the final examination in a class in English literature.

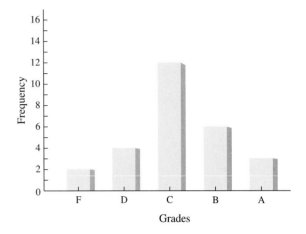

(a) From the bar graph determine how many students in the class got Cs.

(b) How many more students got Bs than Ds?

(c) What percent of the students earned As?

10. (a) Go to a busy campus parking lot and record the number of cars that are predominately white, black, red, gray, green, and "other."

(b) Make a bar graph to display and summarize your data.

(c) Based on part (a), if you were to stand on a busy street corner and watch 200 cars go by, how many would you expect to be predominately white?

11. (a) Roll two dice 50 times and record the total score for each roll. Make a bar graph with the vertical scale indicating frequency and the horizontal scale indicating the totals obtained on the various rolls.

(b) Estimate how often you would obtain each possible score if you were to repeat the experiment rolling the dice 1000 times.

12. The following is from page 11 of the teacher's edition of *Scott Foresman–Addison Wesley Math,* Grade 5, by Randall I. Charles et al. Copyright © 1999, Addison Wesley Longman, Inc.

(a) The teacher's edition shows a possible correct answer. How many small icons should the plot show for the pine category if the key is such that each icon (small tree symbol) represents 10 trees?

(b) Make your own pictograph of this data with each icon representing two trees.

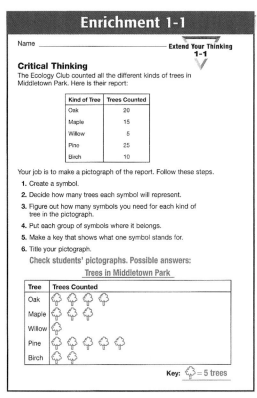

13. Buy a small package of M&Ms with mixed colors. Open the package and pour out the M&Ms.

(a) How many M&Ms of each color are in the package?

(b) Make a bar graph of the data in part (a).

(c) Make a pictograph to display the data from part (a).

(d) Would it be reasonable to guess that most packages of M&Ms contain about twice as many yellow as green candies?

Thinking Critically

Data are often presented in a way that confuses or even purposely misleads the viewer.

14. Consider these two histograms for the same data. Briefly compare the impressions they convey. Which one do you feel most accurately or clearly describes the data?

(a)

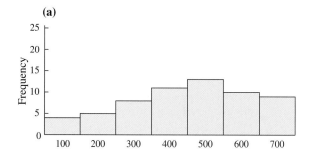

(b)

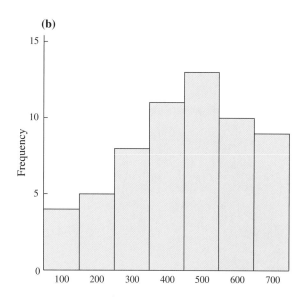

15. (a) Discuss briefly why the television evening news might show histogram (A) below rather than (B) in reporting stock market activity for the last seven days. Is one of these histograms misleading? Why or why not?

(b) What was the percentage drop in the Dow Jones average from the fourth to the fifth day as shown in the following histograms? As an investor should I worry very much about this 36 point drop in the market?

(c) Was the Dow Jones average on day five approximately half what it was on day four as suggested by histogram (A)?

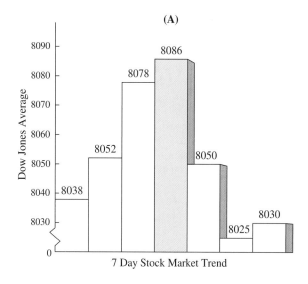

(B)

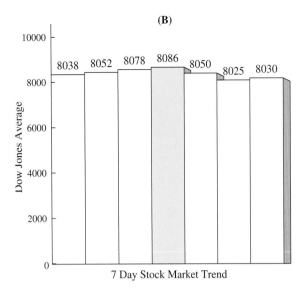

7 Day Stock Market Trend

16. Longlife Insurance Company printed a brochure with the following pictographs showing the growth in company assets over the ten year period 1990–1999.

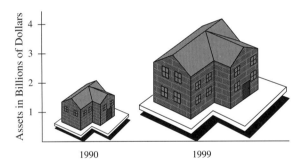

(a) Do the pictographs accurately indicate that the assets were 2 billion dollars in 1990 and 4 billion dollars in 1999, or might one assume from the pictographs that the assets were actually much greater? Explain briefly.

(b) The larger building shown is just twice the height of the smaller and the two buildings are similar as geometrical drawings. Does this accurately convey the impression that the assets of Longlife Insurance Company just doubled during the ten year period? Explain your reasoning. What is the ratio of the volume of the large building to the volume of the small building? (*Suggestion:* Suppose both buildings were rectangular boxes with the dimensions of the second just twice those of the first.)

(c) Would it have been more helpful (or honest) to print the actual asset value for each year on the front of each building?

17. Some merchandisers take advantage of optical illusions just as some pollsters, advertisers, and others do.

(a) Which of the cans depicted here seems to have the greater volume? Note that the diagrams are drawn to scale.

(b) Actually compute the volumes of the cans.

(c) Which shape of can do you see more often in the grocery store? Why do you suppose this is so?

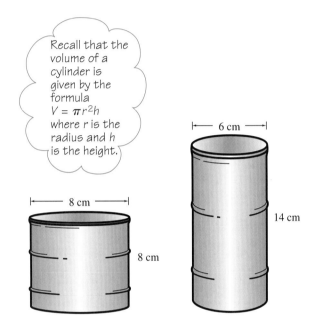

Recall that the volume of a cylinder is given by the formula $V = \pi r^2 h$ where r is the radius and h is the height.

Thinking Cooperatively

This is best done as a class activity.

18. Our measure of a "yard" was originally the length from the tip of the nose to the fingertip of the outstretched arm of an English king. Working in small groups, use a tape measure to measure this length to the nearest inch for each student in class. Record the data on the chalkboard (and for later use in Problem Set 8.2) in two sets—one set for men and one set for women. Divide the class into groups A, B, C, D, E, and F.

(a) Members of group A each make a line plot for the data in each of the two sets.

(b) Members of group B each make a double stem and leaf plot for the data in each of the two sets.

(c) Members of group C each make a histogram for the data in each of the two sets.

(d) Members of group D each make a bar graph for the data in each of the two sets.

(e) Members of group E each make a frequency polygon for the data in each of the two sets.

(f) Members of group F each make a pictograph for the data in each of the two sets.

(g) As a class, discuss the various representations of the data. Which ones seem most informative? What conclusions are suggested regarding the length of a "yard?" Discuss briefly.

Making Connections

19. **(a)** Draw a bar graph for the data in the table shown.

Wired to the World

Public schools nationwide are making steady progress in their efforts to get connected to the Internet by the year 2000.

PERCENTAGE OF SCHOOLS WIRED TO THE INTERNET

	1995	1996	1997
All schools	50%	65%	78%
Elementary	46	61	75
Secondary	65	77	89
City	47	64	74
Rural	48	60	79
Less than 6% minority	52	65	84
50% or more minority	40	56	63

SOURCE: *Newsweek,* December 14, 1998, p. 20.

(b) From the table, draw two line graphs on one diagram to show the increase in Internet access for elementary schools and secondary schools in 1995, 1996, and 1997.

(c) Could the trends of the graphs of part (b) continue until the year 2002? Why or why not?

20. This pie chart from the *Digest of Education Statistics, 1997,* shows the percentage of persons 25 years and older in 1996 that attained various levels of education.

Highest level of education attained by persons 25 years and older: March 1996

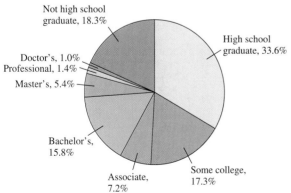

Total persons age 25 and over = 168.3 million

SOURCE: U.S. Department of Education. National Center for Education Statistics. *Digest of Education Statistics, 1997,* NCES 98-

015, by Thomas D. Snyder. Production Manager, Charlene M. Hoffman. Program Analyst, Claire M. Geddes. Washington, DC: 1997, p. 16.

(a) Assuming that these figures remain relatively constant from year to year, what percentage of high school graduates go to college but fail to earn a bachelor's degree?

(b) What percentage of high school graduates earn a bachelor's degree? (*Hint:* Assume that people who earn master's, professional, and doctor's degrees must first earn a bachelor's degree.)

(c) What percentage of the people who earn bachelor's degrees eventually earn a doctor's degree?

21. The line graph below compares salaries for elementary and secondary school teachers. Draw a double bar graph to make this same comparison for the years 1969–1970, 1974–1975, 1979–1980, 1984–1985, 1989–1990, and 1996–1997.

Average annual salary for public elementary and secondary school teachers: 1969–70 to 1996–97
[In constant 1996–97 dollars]

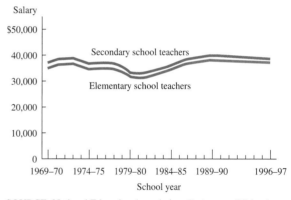

SOURCE: National Education Association, *Estimates of School Statistics,* latest edition 1996–97. Copyright 1997 by the National Education Association. (All rights reserved.)

22. Using the line graph shown:

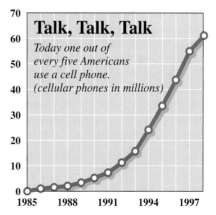

SOURCE: Cellular Telecommunications Industry Association. *Reader's Digest,* November 1998, p. 151.

(a) Estimate the number of cell phones in use in 1996.

(b) Estimate the increase *during* 1997 in the number of cell phones being used by Americans.

(c) The graph seems to indicate a definite trend in the use of cell phones. On this basis, estimate the number of cell phones that will be in use in 2002.

23. The graphs shown display projected payout and income for the Social Security fund for the years 1997 through 2032.

More Going Out Than Coming In...

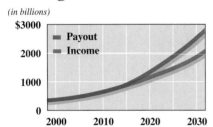

...Will Deplete Social Security Assets by 2032

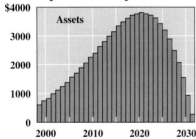

ESTIMATED OPERATIONS OF THE OASI AND DI TRUST FUNDS, EXCLUDING INTEREST EARNED. INFOGRAPHICS: © JARED SCHNEIDMAN, DESIGN

SOURCE: *Reader's Digest*, December 1998, p. 75.

(a) The payout/income line graphs show that payout and income are expected to be essentially the same for the years 1998 though 2015 and that payout should exceed income for the period 2015 through 2030. That being the case, what must be the explanation for the expected growth in assets as shown in the assets bar graph for the interval 1997 through 2020?

(b) Do the graphs make a convincing case that the present social security laws need to be changed?

💻 Using a Computer

For the following problems, use a statistical package from your computer laboratory.

24. Consider the SAT scores recorded here.

Student	Verbal Score	Math Score
Dina	502	444
Carlos	590	520
Rosette	585	621
Broz	487	493
Coleen	585	602
Deiter	481	572
Karin	605	599
Luana	547	499

(a) Make a bar graph to summarize the above data for verbal scores.

(b) Make a double bar graph to summarize the above data with one of each pair of bars for verbal scores and one for math scores.

25. For fiscal year 1998, federal expenditures were divided as follows:

Social programs—14%

Physical, human, and community development—14%

Net interest on debt—14%

Defense, veterans, and foreign affairs—24%

Social security, medicare, and other retirement—32%

Law enforcement and general government—2%

(a) Make a pie chart to reflect this data.

(b) Make a bar graph that reflects this data.

26. The numbers of successful field goals kicked by the various NFL kickers during the first 12 games of the 1998 season are as shown.

19	21	8	8	16	18
24	22	14	14	27	18
21	24	15	14	18	20
14	18	17	13	13	15
14	19	23	19	22	15

(a) Make a line plot to organize and display the data.

(b) Draw a histogram to organize and display the data.

(c) Do any of the data points seem to be largely atypical? Explain.

27. Make a line graph to graphically display this data.

Population of Washington in Millions	2.10	2.32	2.63	2.83	3.12	3.45	3.80	4.18
Year	1960	1965	1970	1975	1980	1985	1990	1995

28. Use the computer to draw a pie chart for the data from problem 7 above and measure the angles to see how it compares with your drawing for problem 7.

From State Student Assessments

29. (Minnesota, Grade 5)

Use the pie graph below to answer the question.

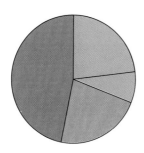

Which set of numbers would best fit this pie graph?

○ A. 54, 8, 30, 8
○ B. 47, 23, 8, 22
○ C. 51, 17, 15, 17
○ D. 27, 26, 24, 23

30. (Michigan, Grade 4)

Directions: Solve the following problem. There may be more than one way to answer correctly. Show as much of your work as possible.

    Tyler read 9 books.
    Lauren read 6 books.
    Kyle read 5 books.
    Emily read 12 books.

Use the data and make a graph. Write three questions that could be answered by using the data on this graph.

31. (Idaho, Grade 5)

The line graph shows the number of exercise books sold by Mr. Chen over 4 months. Use the graph to answer the questions which follow.

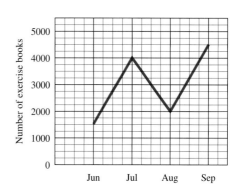

A. What was the average number of exercise books sold per month?

B. What was the increase in the number of exercise books sold from August to September?

C. If an exercise book cost $0.40, how much money did Mr. Chen receive from the sale of exercise books in July?

For Review

32. Write these fractions in decimal form.

(a) $\dfrac{1}{8}$ (b) $\dfrac{7}{40}$ (c) $\dfrac{17}{250}$ (d) $\dfrac{7}{20}$

33. Write these fractions in decimal form.

(a) $\dfrac{1}{9}$ (b) $\dfrac{3}{7}$ (c) $\dfrac{3}{14}$ (d) $\dfrac{7}{15}$

34. Write these decimals as fractions in reduced form.

(a) 0.375   (b) 0.3125   (c) 0.444   (d) 0.33

35. Write these decimals as fractions in reduced form.

(a) $3.7444\ldots = 3.7\overline{4}$ (b) $.\overline{02}$ (c) $.0\overline{2}$

(d) $31.\overline{72}$ (e) $4.7\overline{314}$ (f) $.43\overline{123}$

8.2   Measures of Central Tendency and Variability

Measures of Central Tendency

Consider the data of Table 8.1 and the corresponding line plot of Figure 8.1 (both on page 487). The line plot is a considerable improvement over the disorganized raw data for assessing the performance of the class. We can see at a glance that most of the grades lie between 62 and 96 with a large cluster between 75 and 80. We also see that the lowest grade was 49 and the highest grade was 96. But even more definitive information might be desired. For example:

- What is the "average" or "typical" grade for the class?
- How did most of the students do?
- Did many of the students perform markedly differently from the bulk of the class?

There are several different possibilities for answering these questions. First consider the following data sets, representing grades on tests, and their corresponding line plots.

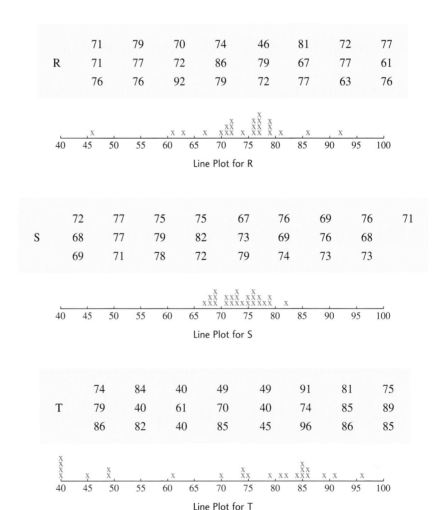

	71	79	70	74	46	81	72	77
R	71	77	72	86	79	67	77	61
	76	76	92	79	72	77	63	76

Line Plot for R

	72	77	75	75	67	76	69	76	71
S	68	77	79	82	73	69	76	68	
	69	71	78	72	79	74	73	73	

Line Plot for S

	74	84	40	49	49	91	81	75
T	79	40	61	70	40	74	85	89
	86	82	40	85	45	96	86	85

Line Plot for T

The line plots help to identify the following characteristics of the data sets.

1. The scores in data set R seem to cluster about 76 even though they range all the way from 46 to 92 and are generally rather widely spread. Apparently some of the students did very well while others did quite poorly. If we had to choose a single grade as typical of the entire class, it would probably be about 76.

2. The scores in data set S are much less spread out than those of R, ranging only from 67 to 82. Thus, all the students did reasonably well with none outstandingly good and none outstandingly poor. The grades seem to cluster about 74, and we would probably select this grade as reasonably typical of the entire class.

3. The scores in data set T are very widely spread; ranging all the way from 40 to 96. Clearly, a number of students did very poorly while a substantial number did quite well. Here, it is more difficult to select a single grade as typical. If we ignore the very poorest grades, we may want to choose 85 as typical. But there are many scores that differ widely from this.

Apparently two features naturally arise when it comes to analyzing a data set:

*   the typical or central value of the data, and
*   the dispersion or spread of the data about the central value.

We now consider various standard approaches to identifying and quantifying these features.

The Mean

The line plots just considered allow one to develop an intuitive, but not very precise, notion of the typical or central value of a set of data. One very useful and precisely defined central value is the **mean,** frequently called the **arithmetic mean** or **average.** An effective manipulative device for introducing this notion to students that is quite independent of and different from the line plots just considered is provided by a simple set of blocks. For example, consider the data 7, 5, 7, 3, 8, 6. Arrange a number of blocks in six stacks containing 7, 5, 7, 3, 8, and 6 blocks respectively as shown here and ask what is the typical or average height of all the stacks. If all the stacks were the same height, the answer would be obvious—it

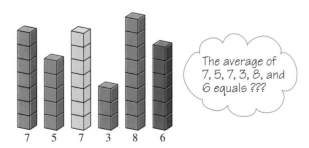

The average of 7, 5, 7, 3, 8, and 6 equals ???

7   5   7   3   8   6

would be their common height. This suggests that a reasonable approach to answer the question might be to move blocks from taller stacks to shorter ones in an effort to even them up. Indeed, the blocks can be arranged in six stacks of height 6 as shown, and this

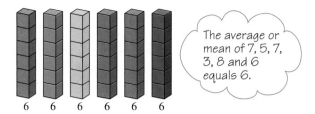

The average or mean of 7, 5, 7, 3, 8 and 6 equals 6.

6   6   6   6   6   6

suggests that the average height is 6. Arithmetically, the number of blocks in the two arrangements has not changed so that

$$6 \cdot 6 = 7 + 5 + 7 + 3 + 8 + 6 \qquad \text{and} \qquad 6 = \frac{7 + 5 + 7 + 3 + 8 + 6}{6}.$$

Thus, the average or typical height of the original stacks is found by finding the sum of their heights and dividing by the number of stacks. This naturally leads to the following definition.

> **DEFINITION**   *The Mean of a Set of Data*
> The **mean** or **average** of a collection of values is $\bar{x} = S/n$ where S is the sum of the values and n is the number of values.

For the data set R, we compute the mean by adding all scores and dividing by 24, the number of scores. Thus,

$$\bar{x} = (71 + 79 + 70 + 74 + 46 + 81 + 72 + 77 + 71 + 77 + 72 + 86$$
$$+ 79 + 67 + 77 + 61 + 76 + 76 + 92 + 79 + 72 + 77 + 63 + 76)/24$$
$$\doteq 73.8$$

This is reasonably close to our informal feeling that 76 is reasonably representative of the scores in the data set. Actually, 73.8 is somewhat smaller than expected and this shows that the mean of a data set is sensitive to atypical data values like 46. In this case, the mean of the data with 46 omitted is approximately 75—very close to our informal determination.

For the data sets S and T, we find that the means are respectively 73.6 and 70.3. For S the mean gives a very good estimate of what we intuitively felt was the typical or central value. For T, the mean of 70.3 seems unduly low and this is again a reflection of the fact that the mean can be strongly affected by the presence of extremely atypical values like 40, 40, 40, 40, 45, 49, 49, and even 61. Without these values the mean is a much more expectable 82.7. In any case, it is usually the case that, in most data sets, most data values cluster reasonably closely about the mean. This last is particularly true if we have criteria for deciding when data values are too atypical and delete them from consideration. We develop such a criterion a little later but, for now, we consider other frequently used measures of central values.

The Median

The **median** of a collection of values is the middle value in the collection arranged in order of increasing size or the average of the two middle values in case the number of values is even.

DEFINITION   *The Median of a Set of Data*

Let a collection of *n* data values be written in order of increasing size. If *n* is odd, the **median,** denoted by $\hat{x}$, is the middle value in the list. If *n* is even, $\hat{x}$ is the average of the two middle values.

EXAMPLE   8.4 | **Determining a Median**

Determine the median of the data in data set R above.

Solution | The scores in R are arranged in order in the line plot of R. Since there are 24 scores, the median is the average of the 12th and 13th scores. Thus, we see that $\hat{x} = 76$.

Note that the median in the preceding example not only closely approximates the mean, but also agrees reasonably well with our intuitive idea of the typical value of the collection of scores.

Also, it follows from the definition, that the median is a data value if the number of data values is odd and is *not* necessarily a data value if the number of values is even. Thus, the median of the 9 scores

$$24, 25, 25, 27, 29, 31, 32, 34, 37$$

is 29, the fifth score; while the median of the 10 scores

$$42, 42, 43, 44, 44, 46, 47, 47, 47, 49$$

is 45, the average of the two middle scores.

The Mode

Another value often taken as "typical" of a set of data is the value occurring most frequently. This value is called the **mode.** From the definition, it is clear that there may be more than one mode. For example, data set S has three modes, 69, 73, and 76. Even so, it may be the case that a mode gives a better indication of the typical value of the data than either the median or the mean. Moreover, unlike the mean, neither the median nor the mode is affected by the existence of extremely atypical values.

DEFINITION   *A Mode of a Set of Data*

A **mode** of a collection of values is a value that occurs the most frequently. If two or more values occur equally often and more frequently than all other values, there are two or more modes.

JUST FOR FUN

A Magic Magic Magic Square

Consider the magic magic magic square shown.

8	11	14	1
13	2	7	12
3	16	9	6
10	5	4	15

Compute the sums of the numbers indicated by the colored squares in these diagrams.

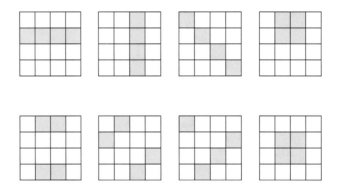

Can you find other interesting patterns of sums? Draw diagrams to show interesting patterns you find.

EXAMPLE   8.5

Determining Means, Medians, and Modes

Determine the mean, median, and mode for each of the data sets R, S, and T above and discuss which measures are most representative of the respective data sets.

Solution

Let $\bar{x}_R$, $\hat{x}_R$, $\bar{x}_S$, $\hat{x}_S$, $\bar{x}_T$, and $\hat{x}_T$ denote the means and medians of R, S, and T, respectively. We have already seen that $\bar{x}_R = 73.8$ and that $\hat{x}_R = 76$. Since the mode is the most frequently occurring score (or the several such scores if they occur equally often and more frequently than all other scores), the mode of R is 77. In this case, all three measures are reasonably representative of the scores making up the data set.

Since S has 25 scores,

$$\bar{x}_S = (72 + 77 + 75 + 75 + 67 + 76 + 69 + 76 + 71 + 68 + 77 + 79 + 82$$
$$+ 73 + 69 + 76 + 68 + 69 + 71 + 78 + 72 + 79 + 74 + 73 + 73)/25$$
$$\doteq 73.6.$$

Also, $\hat{x}_s$ is the middle or 13th score. Thus, counting on the line plot, $\bar{x}_S = 73$. Finally, S has three modes, 69, 73, and 76, since each occurs three times and more often than any other score. We observe that the mean, the median, and the middle mode all seem to reasonably represent the set of scores in S.

Finally, since T contains 24 scores,

$$\bar{x} = (74 + 84 + 40 + 49 + 49 + 91 + 81 + 75 + 79 + 40 + 61 + 70$$
$$+ 40 + 74 + 85 + 89 + 86 + 82 + 40 + 85 + 45 + 96 + 86 + 85)/24$$
$$\doteq 70.3,$$
$$\hat{x}_T = (75 + 79)/2 = 77,$$

and the mode of T is 40. As noted earlier, T is difficult to characterize. The mean, $\bar{x}_T$, is strongly affected by the several very low scores and so does not seem to fairly represent the data set. Similarly, the mode of 40 is clearly not representative. In this case the median seems to be the most representative value.

EXAMPLE 8.6 | **Determining an Average**

All 12 players on the Uni Hi basketball team played in their 78 to 65 win over Lincoln. Jon Highpockets, Uni Hi's best player, scored 23 points in the game. How many points did each of the other players average?

Solution | *Understand the problem*

The problem is to determine averages when we are not explicity given the data values. What we do know is that Uni Hi scored 78 points, that Jon Highpockets scored 23 of the points, and that 12 players are on the team.

Devise a plan

Since the average score for each of the 11 players other than Jon is the sum of their scores divided by 11, we must determine the sum of their scores.

Carry out a plan

Since Uni Hi scored a total of 78 points and Jon scored 23, the total for the rest of the team must have been $78 - 23 = 55$ points. Therefore, the average number of points for these players is $55 \div 11 = 5$.

Look back

The solution depended on knowing the definition of average. The real question was how many points were scored by all the players on Uni Hi's team other than Jon and how many such players there were. But those figures, and hence the solution to the problem, were easily obtained by subtraction.

EXAMPLE 8.7

Determining a Typical Value for a Set of Data

The owner/manager of a factory earned $850,000 last year. The assistant manager earned $48,000. Three secretaries earned $18,000 each, and the other 16 employees each earned $27,000.

(a) Prepare a line plot of the salaries of those deriving their income from the factory.

(b) Compute the mean, median, and mode of the salaries of those deriving their income from the factory.

(c) Which is most typical of the salaries of those associated with the factory—the mean, median, or mode?

Solution

(a) The line plot is shown here.

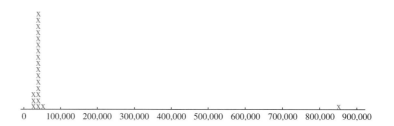

(b) The mean is

$$\overline{x} = \frac{18,000 + 18,000 + 18,000 + 27,000 + \cdots + 27,000 + 48,000 + 850,000}{21}$$

$$\doteq \$65,905.$$

The median $\hat{x}$, is the eleventh in the ordered list of salaries. Thus,

$$\hat{x} = 27,000 \text{ dollars}.$$

The mode is the most frequently occurring salary. Thus,

$$\text{mode} = 27,000 \text{ dollars}.$$

(c) The mean is clearly not typical of the salary most workers at the factory earn. The value of $\overline{x}$ is unduly affected by the huge salary earned by the owner/manager. Here the median and mode are the same and are more typical of salaries of those deriving their income from the factory since $27,000 is the salary of 16 of the 21 people. Note that this last sentence is really an argument that, in this case, the most typical value is the mode. That the mode and median here are equal is incidental.

While the mean is the most commonly used indicator of the typical value of a data set, the preceding example makes it clear that this choice can be quite misleading. As will be seen in the problem set, it is easy to construct examples where the median is the most typical value and other examples, like the preceding, where the mode is most typical.

Measures of Variability

The most useful analysis of data would reveal both the center (typical value) and the *spread,* or *variability,* of the data. We now consider how the spread of data is determined. The simplest measure is the **range,** the difference between the smallest and largest data values. This certainly tells something about how the data occurs, but it is often misleading, particularly if the data set contains a few extremely low or high values that are quite atypical of most of the other values. A better understanding is obtained by determining **quartiles.**

Somewhat imprecisely, the lower quartile, Q_L, of a set of data arranged in order of increasing size and having median $\hat{x}$ is the median value of the data values *less than* $\hat{x}$. Similarly, the upper quartile, Q_U, is the median of the data values *greater than* $\hat{x}$. The difficulty with this definition is that it is easily misunderstood. For example, for the data set

$$40, 41, 42, 42, 42, 43, 45, 46,$$

$\hat{x} = (42 + 42)/2 = 42$ and lies between the two 42s as shown. Thus, $Q_L = 41.5$ is the median of 40, 41, 42, and 42. It is *not* the median of the scores 40 and 41. Similarly, $Q_U = 44$ is the median of 42, 43, 45, and 46 and *not* the median of the scores 43, 45, and 46. More precisely, we have the following definition.

DEFINITION   *Upper and Lower Quartiles*

Consider a set of data arranged in order of increasing size. Let the number of data values, n, be written $n = 2r$ for n even or $n = 2r + 1$ for n odd for some integer r. In either case the **lower quartile,** denoted by Q_L, is the median of the first r data values. Also, the **upper quartile,** denoted by Q_U, is the median of the last r data values.*

It follows from the definition that approximately 25% of the data values are less than or equal to Q_L, approximately 25% lie between Q_L and $\hat{x}$, approximately 25% lie between $\hat{x}$ and Q_U, and approximately 25% are greater than or equal to Q_U. Thus, approximately 50% of the values in a data set lie between Q_L and Q_U and the length of this interval, called the **interquartile range** and denoted by **IQR,** provides a good measure of the spread of the data. In fact, if a data value falls below Q_L by more than $1.5 \cdot$ IQR or above Q_U by more than $1.5 \cdot$ IQR, it is called an **outlier** and is often ignored when analyzing the data set. Thus, outlier is the term applied to those values referred to earlier that are so atypical of the values in a data set that they are often ignored.

---

*The precise definition of quartiles is not entirely standardized. For example, the lower and upper quartiles for a set of $2r + 1$ data values are often taken as the medians of the first and last $r + 1$ (rather than r) values in the ordered list.

> **DEFINITION** *Outlier*
>
> An **outlier** in a set of data is a data value that is *less than* $Q_L - (1.5 \cdot IQR)$ or *greater than* $Q_U + (1.5 \cdot IQR)$.

EXAMPLE   8.8

The Median, Quartiles, the Interquartile Range, and Outliers

Determine the median, the quartiles, the interquartile range, and the outliers for data set R on page 500.

Solution

The values in R are ordered in the line plot on page 500. Since R contains 24 data values, the median is the average of the 12th and 13th data values; i.e., $\bar{x} = (76 + 76)/2 = 76$. Also, $2r = 24$, so $r = 12$ and Q_L and Q_U are the medians of the first and last 12 data values, respectively. Thus, $Q_L = (71 + 71)/2 = 71$ and $Q_U = (77 + 79)/2 = 78$. Therefore, the interquartile range is $IQR = 78 - 71 = 7$. Finally, since

$$Q_L - 1.5 \cdot IQR = 71 - (1.5 \cdot 7) = 71 - 10.5 = 60.5,$$

and

$$Q_U + 1.5 \cdot IQR = 78 + (1.5 \cdot 7) = 78 + 10.5 = 88.5,$$

it follows that 45 and 92 are outliers.

Symbolically, if the 24 points shown represent the ordered data values in R, then Q_L, $\hat{x}$, Q_U, the interquartile range, and the outliers are as shown.

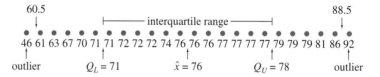

Box and Whisker Plots

The least and greatest scores, the **extremes,** along with the lower and upper quartiles and the median give a concise numerical summary, called the **5-number summary** of a set of data. Since the median of the data in Example 8.8 is 76 and the extremes are 46 and 92, the 5-number summary is $46 - 71 - 76 - 78 - 92$. Moreover, a **box and whisker plot,** often simply called a **box plot,** gives a vivid graphical representation of the 5-number summary.

> **DEFINITION** *Box and Whisker Plot*
>
> A **box and whisker plot** consists of a central box extending from the lower to the upper quartile with a line marking the median and line segments, or whiskers, extending outward from the box to the extremes.

Range, Mode, and Median

Learn

You Will Learn
how to find the range, mode, and median for a set of data

Vocabulary

range
difference between greatest number and least number

mode
number that occurs most often

median
middle number when data are in order

Suppose you wanted to buy a mountain bike. The line plot below shows the prices of different mountain bikes.

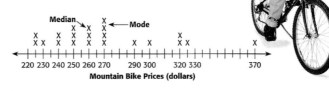

Mountain Bike Prices (dollars)

range   greatest number ($370) – least number ($225): $145

mode   number that occurs most often in a set of data: $270

median   middle number when data are ordered: $260

There can be more than one mode. If the number of data items is even, the median is halfway between the two middle numbers.

You can find the mode and median of the test scores in this line plot.

Test Scores

Problem Solving Hint
To find the median, put data items in order from least to greatest.

There are two modes: 38 and 40. There are 24 scores, so the median is halfway between the 12th and 13th scores. The median score is 39.

Talk About It

Will a set of data always have a range, a mode, and a median? Explain.

Check

Using Data Use the Data File on page 6 to answer 1–4.

1. Compare the ranges for girls' and boys' arm spans.

2. Which plot has only two modes?

3. Is the median of the girls' or boys' arm spans greater?

4. **Reasoning** Do boys or girls tend to have longer arm spans?

16   Chapter 1 • Data, Graphs, and Facts Review

SOURCE: From *Scott Foresman–Addison Wesley Math*, Grade 5, p. 16, by Randall I. Charles et al. Copyright © 1999, Addison Wesley Longman, Inc.

Questions for the Teacher

1. If you were teaching this lesson, what points would you try to bring out? Does the range accurately reflect the spread of the data for either of the two data sets shown in the line plots? Are any of the data values outliers?

2. Choose a single number for each data set that you intuitively feel is most typical of the data set. Explain the reasons for your choice.

3. Discuss how well you feel the medians and modes typify the values in the two data sets.

4. The problems at the bottom of the above page refer to an earlier activity where the students measured each other's arm spans and then analyzed the data. How do you think students would react to such an activity?

For example, the box and whisker plot for Example 8.8 is shown in Figure 8.14.

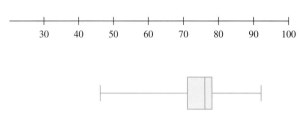

This is a pictorial representation of the 5-number summary.

Figure 8.14
Box and whisker plot for data set R.

An additional advantage of box and whisker plots is that they make it possible to make useful comparisons between data sets containing widely differing numbers of values. This is made clear in the next example.

EXAMPLE 8.9

Making Box and Whisker Plots for Comparisons

The data below are the final scores of men and women students in Calculus I. Draw box and whisker plots to compare the distribution of women's scores with the distribution of men's scores.

Women's scores: 95,   79,   53,   78,   71,   88,   77,   80,   79,   79

Men's scores: 84,   85,   53,   77,   66,   81,   79,   59,   65,   61,   81,
68,   68,   80,   76,   87,   85,   74,   92,   76,   70,   85,
55,   79,   74,   80,   73,   48,   66,   83,   48,   60,   87,
58,   64,   78,   82,   69,   76,   83,   94,   86,   73,   85,
75,   69,   49,   52,   59,   68,   65,   75,   31,   69,   73,
56,   95

Solution

To make the plots, we need the 5-number summaries. First arrange the scores in order of increasing size.

Women's scores: 53,   71,   77,   78,   79,   79,   79,   80,   88,   95

Men's scores: 31,   48,   48,   49,   52,   53,   55,   56,   58,   59,   59,
60,   61,   64,   65,   65,   66,   66,   68,   68,   68,   69,
69,   70,   73,   73,   73,   74,   74,   75,   75,   76,   76,
76,   77,   78,   79,   79,   80,   80,   81,   81,   82,   83,
83,   84,   85,   85,   85,   85,   86,   87,   87,   92,   95

For the women, the extreme scores are 53 and 95 and the median is 79, the average of the fifth and sixth scores. The lower quartile is 77, the median of the first five scores. The upper quartile is 80, the median of the last five women's scores. Thus, the 5-number summary for the women's scores is

$$53 - 77 - 79 - 80 - 95.$$

Similarly, the 5-number summary of the men's scores is

$$31 - 64 - 74 - 81 - 95.$$

These give the box plots shown.

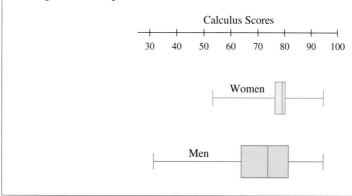

The box plots of Example 8.9 give a precise visual comparison of the performances of women and men students in calculus even though the numbers of students are quite different. One might reasonably speculate as to why the distributions of grades differ as they do. (For example, it is almost invariably the case that larger data sets have both smaller and larger extreme values as suggested here.) Nevertheless, one rather clear indication is that the women students in the class were no less able than the men.

The Standard Deviation

We have already observed that the range is one measure of the spread of a data set. It is not a very precise measure, however, since it depends only on the extreme data values which may differ markedly from the bulk of the data. This deficiency is largely remedied by the 5-number summary and its visualization by a box and whisker plot. However, an even better measure of variability is the **standard deviation.**

DEFINITION   *The Standard Deviation of a Set of Data*

Let $x_1, x_2, x_3 \ldots, x_n$ be the values in a set of data and let $\bar{x}$ denote their mean. Then

$$s = \sqrt{\frac{(\bar{x} - x_1)^2 + (\bar{x} - x_2)^2 + \cdots + (\bar{x} - x_n)^2}{n}}$$

is the **standard deviation.**

Just as the mean is an indication of the typical value of a set of data, the standard deviation* is a measure of the typical deviation of the values from the mean. If the standard deviation is large, the data are more spread out; if it is small, the data are more concentrated near the mean. This is immediately apparent from the line plots of data sets R, S, and T discussed earlier. In Figure 8.15 these line plots are reproduced again with the addition of the location of the mean as well as the spread of each data set relative to its standard deviation. A most important fact is that, for most data sets, most data values fall

---

*The **variance,** $v = s^2$, of a set of data is also a good measure of the variability of the data. However, the more commonly used measure is the standard deviation.

within one standard deviation of the mean and almost none lie as far as three standard deviations of the mean.

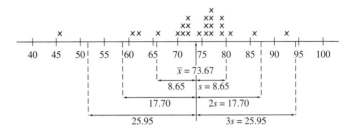

Line plot for R: All but six data points lie within one standard deviation of the mean. Only one data point lies more than three standard deviations from the mean.

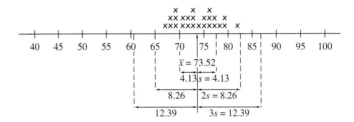

Line plot for S: All but ten data points lie within one standard deviation of the mean. None lie more than two standard deviations from the mean.

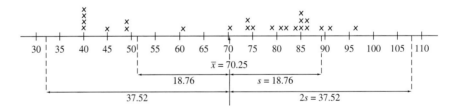

Line plot for T: All but nine data points lie within one standard deviation of the mean. None lie beyond two standard deviations of the mean.

Figure 8.15
Line plots for R, S, and T showing the location of the mean and the spread of the data relative to the standard deviation.

EXAMPLE 8.10

Computing a Standard Deviation

Compute the mean and standard deviation for this set of data.

35	42	61	29	39
47	55	54	50	41
40	34	37	51	38

Solution

$$\bar{x} = (35 + 42 + 61 + 29 + 39 + 47 + 55 + 54 + 50 + 41 + 40$$
$$+ 34 + 37 + 51 + 38)/15$$
$$\doteq 43.5$$

$$s^2 = [(43.5 - 35)^2 + (43.5 - 42)^2 + (43.5 - 61)^2 + (43.5 - 29)^2$$
$$+ (43.5 - 39)^2 + (43.5 - 47)^2 + (43.5 - 55)^2 + (43.5 - 54)^2$$
$$+ (43.5 - 50)^2 + (43.5 - 41)^2 + (43.5 - 40)^2 + (43.5 - 34)^2$$
$$+ (43.5 - 37)^2 + (43.5 - 51)^2 + (43.5 - 38)^2]/15$$
$$\doteq 76.4$$

Thus,

$$s \doteq \sqrt{76.4} \doteq 8.7.$$

The mean, $\bar{x}$, in the preceding example is easily computed on a calculator. The standard deviation, s, is also easily calculated on a machine with parentheses, $\boxed{M+}$ and $\boxed{MR}$ keys. In the present instance, on many calculators, entering the following string does the job nicely.

$\boxed{ON/AC}$ 43.5 $\boxed{M+}$ $\boxed{(}$ $\boxed{MR}$ $\boxed{-}$ 35 $\boxed{)}$ $\boxed{x^2}$ $\boxed{+}$ $\boxed{(}$ $\boxed{MR}$ $\boxed{-}$ 42 $\boxed{)}$ $\boxed{x^2}$
$\boxed{(}$ $\boxed{MR}$ $\boxed{-}$ 61 $\boxed{)}$ $\boxed{x^2}$ $\boxed{+}$ $\cdots$ $\boxed{+}$ $\boxed{(}$ $\boxed{MR}$ $\boxed{-}$ 38 $\boxed{)}$ $\boxed{x^2}$ $\boxed{=}$ $\boxed{\div}$ 15 $\boxed{=}$
$\boxed{\sqrt{}}$

Scientific and business calculators frequently have built in statistics routines that make the calculation of means and standard deviations even simpler. Alternatively, these computations can be performed automatically on a computer using a spreadsheet or other appropriate software. It is important to note that calculator and computer programs for computing standard deviations offer two alternatives that differentiate between the standard deviation of a population and the standard deviation of a sample. The standard deviation we have discussed is the standard deviation of a population. If it is not clear which one you are obtaining when you compute a standard deviation by machine, compute both

DID YOU KNOW?

A How-To Manual for Lying

"The secret language of statistics, so appealing in a fact minded culture, is employed to sensationalize, inflate, confuse, and oversimplify. Statistical methods and statistical terms are necessary in reporting the mass of data of social and economic trends, business conditions, "opinion" polls, the census. But without writers who use the words with honesty and understanding and readers who know what they mean, the result can only be semantic nonsense.

This book is a sort of primer in how to use statistics to deceive. It may seem altogether too much like a manual for swindlers. Perhaps I can justify it in the manner of the retired burglar whose published reminiscences amounted to a graduate course in how to pick a lock and muffle a footfall: The crooks already know these tricks; honest men must learn them in self defense."

Darrell Huff's book, *How to Lie With Statistics* (New York: W. W. Norton & Co., Inc., 1954) is at once a delightful and informative treatise on the art of lying with statistics.

SOURCE: Darrell Huff, *How to Lie With Statistics,* New York: W. W. Norton, Inc., 1954, pages 8 and 9.

and use the smaller of the two values obtained. For example, for the data values 1, 2, and 3, the options obtained are 1 and 0.82. For our present purpose, you should use 0.82.

EXAMPLE 8.11

Determining the Fraction of Data Values Near the Mean

Compute the fraction (expressed as a percent) of the data values in Example 8.10 that fall

(a)   within one standard deviation of the mean.

(b)   within two standard deviations of the mean.

Solution

$$43.5 - 8.7$$
$$= 34.8$$

$$43.5 + 8.7$$
$$= 52.2$$

$$43.5 - 2(8.7)$$
$$= 26.1$$

$$43.5 + 2(8.7)$$
$$= 60.9$$

(a)   In Example 8.10, $\bar{x} \doteq 43.5$ and $s \doteq 8.7$. Thus, those entries within one standard deviation of the mean lie between 34.8 and 52.2. A count reveals that 10 of the entries fall in this range and

$$\frac{10}{15} = .666 \ldots \doteq 67\%.$$

(b)   Those data values within two standard deviations of the mean must lie between 26.1 and 60.9. This includes all but one of the data values and

$$\frac{14}{15} = .9333 \ldots \doteq 93\%.$$

PROBLEM SET 8.2

Understanding Concepts

1.   Determine the mean, median, and mode for this set of data.

18	27	17	19	21	24	18	15
23	18	17	14	22	19	27	30

2.   (a) Compute the mean, median, and mode for this set of data.

69	81	77	69	64	85	81	73	79
74	70	78	86	80	71	79	77	70
67	70	79	80	71	67	69	79	81

(b) Draw a line plot for the data in part (a).

(c)   Does either the mean, median, or mode seem typical of the data in part (a)?

(d)   Might it be reasonable to suspect that the data in part (a) actually comes from two essentially different populations (say daily incomes from two entirely different companies, for example)? Explain your reasoning.

3.   (a) Compute the quartiles for the data in problem 2.

(b)   Give the 5-number summary for the data in problem 2.

(c)   Draw a box and whisker plot for the data in problem 2.

(d)   Determine the interquartile range, IQR, for the data in problem 2.

(e)   Identify any outliers in the data of problem 2.

4.   (a) Draw side-by-side box and whisker plots to compare students' performances in class A and class B if the final grades are as shown here.

Class A: 91, 63, 65, 73, 65, 86,
96, 75, 75, 79, 84, 72,
80

Class B: 87, 72, 95, 89, 69, 79,
56, 64, 66, 67, 89, 47

(b) Briefly compare the performances in the two classes on the basis of the box and whisker plots in part (a).

(c) Determine the interquartile range, IQR, for each of the classes in part (a).

(d) Identify any outliers in the classes of part (a).

5. Use the data in problem 1 to answer the following.
   (a) Compute the mean.
   (b) Compute the standard deviation.
   (c) What percent of the data are within one standard deviation of the mean?
   (d) What percent of the data are within two standard deviations of the mean?
   (e) What percent of the data are within three standard deviations of the mean?

6. (a) Choose an appropriate scale and draw a line plot for this set of measurements of the heights in centimeters of 2-year-old ponderosa pine trees.

   22.2 23.5 22.5 22.6 23.0 22.8
   22.4 22.2 23.0 23.3 23.9 22.7

   (b) Compute the mean and standard deviation for this data.
   (c) What percent of the data are within one standard deviation of the mean?
   (d) What percent of the data are within two standard deviations of the mean?
   (e) What percent of the data are within three standard deviations of the mean?

Thinking Critically

7. On June 1, 1998, the average age of the 33 employees at Acme Cement was 47 years. On June 1, 1999, three of the staff aged 65, 58, and 62 retired and were replaced by four employees aged 24, 31, 26, and 28. What was the average age of the employees at Acme Cement on June 1, 1999?

8. (a) Compute the mean and standard deviation for this data.

28   34   41   19   17   23

(b) Add 5 to each of the values in part (a) to obtain 33, 39, 46, 24, 22, and 28. Compute the mean and the standard deviation for this new set of values.

(c) What properties of the mean and standard deviation are suggested by parts (a) and (b)?

9. Compute the mean and standard deviation for the data represented by each of these two histograms.

(a)

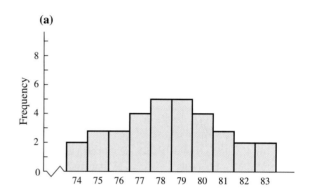

(b)

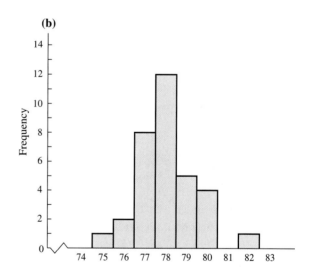

(c) Briefly explain why the standard deviation for the data of part (b) is less than that for part (a).

10. Does the mean, median, or mode seem to be the most typical value for this set of data? Explain briefly. (*Suggestion:* Draw a line plot.)

42   47   38   16   45   41   16   48   44

11. (a) Determine the mean, median, and mode of the data in the line plot shown.

(b) Does the mean, median, or mode seem to be the most typical of this data? Explain briefly.

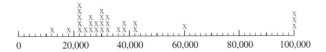

12. Produce sets of data that satisfy these conditions.

(a) mean = median < mode

(b) mean = mode < median

(c) median = mode < mean

13. (a) What can you conclude if the standard deviation of a set of data is zero? Explain.

(b) What can be said about the standard deviation of a set of data if the values all lie very near the mean? Explain.

14. Let Q_L, $\hat{x}$, and Q_U denote the lower quartile, median, and upper quartile of a set of data.

(a) Create a set of data with the property that exactly 25% of the data lie in each of these ranges.

$$x < Q_L, \; Q_L < x < \hat{x}, \; \hat{x} < x < Q_U, \; Q_U < x$$

(b) Create a set of data for which it is not true that 25% of the data lie in the ranges specified in part (a).

15. A collection of data contains 10 values consisting of a mix of ones, twos, and threes.

(a) If $\bar{x} = 3$ what is the data set?

(b) If $\bar{x} = 2$, what are the possibilities for the data set?

(c) If $\bar{x} = 1$ what is the data set?

(d) Could $\bar{x} = 1$ and $s \neq 0$ for this data set? Explain.

16. Compute the mean of each of these collections of data.

(a) A = {27, 38, 25, 29, 41}

(b) B = {27, 38, 25, 29, 41, 32}

(c) C = {27, 38, 25, 29, 41, 32, 32}

(d) D = {27, 38, 25, 29, 41, 32, 32, 32, 32, 32}

(e) What conclusion is suggested by the calculations in parts (a) through (d)?

(f) Guess the mean of this set of data and then do the calculation to see if your guess is correct.

$$E = \{27, 38, 25, 29, 41, 60, 4, 60, 4\}$$

(g) What general result does the calculation in part (f) suggest?

17. (a) The mean of each of these collections of data is 45.

R = {45, 35, 55, 25, 65, 20, 70}

S = {45, 35, 55, 25, 65, 20, 70, 45, 45}

T = {45, 35, 55, 25, 65, 20, 70, 80, 10}

Which of R and S has the smaller standard deviation? No computation is needed; justify your response with a single sentence.

(b) Like the means of R and S in part (a), the mean of T is 45. Is the standard deviation for this set the same as that for S in part (a)? Note that both these sets have the same number of entries. Explain your conclusion.

18. According to Garrison Keillor, all the children in Lake Wobegon are above average. Is this assertion just a joke or is there a sense in which it could be true?

19. If the mean of A = {$a_1, a_2, \ldots, a_{30}$} is 45 and the mean of B = {$b_1, b_2, \ldots, b_{40}$} is 65, compute the mean of the combined data set. (*Hint:* The answer is not 55.)

Thinking Cooperatively

These problems are best done as a class activity.

20. Divide the class into groups A, B, C, D, E, and F. Consider the data collected in problem 18, Problem Set 8.1.

(a) Members of groups A and B each determine the mode or modes, the mean, and the standard deviation of the data for men.

(b) Members of groups C and D each determine the mode or modes, the mean, and the standard deviation of the data for women.

(c) Members of groups E and F each determine the 5-number summaries and draw side-by-side box plots for the two sets of data.

(d) As a class, discuss the results obtained in (a), (b), and (c) and decide on a consensus opinion of the most appropriate length of a "yard" and also on a reasonable range in which the length might lie on the basis of the data considered. Do the results differ markedly for men and women?

21. In ancient times, the cubit was taken as the length of the human arm from the tip of the elbow to the tip of the middle finger (generally understood to vary from about 17 to about 21 inches). Working in groups, repeat problem 20 but for the cubit rather than the "yard."

22. Working in a group with about three other students, toss 7 pennies 30 times and record the number of heads each time.

(a) Determine the mean and standard deviation of the data obtained.

(b) Determine what percentage of the data lie within one standard deviation of the mean.

(c) What percentage of the data differs from the mean by more than two standard deviations?

23. As we have seen before, it often helps to understand a concept if it can be visualized using an appropriate manipulative. Work with about three other students to carry out the following activity.

(a) Suppose you want to demonstrate the idea of the mean of a set of data to fourth graders. Using a set of blocks, form stacks of heights 5, 1, 4, 7, 6, 7. Now move blocks from higher stacks to lower stacks in an effort to form six stacks all of the same height. Can this be done? If so, how many blocks are in each stack?

(b) Determine the mean of 5, 1, 4, 7, 6, 7.

(c) Comparing the results of parts (a) and (b), what do you conclude?

(d) How would you elaborate on the above to make the idea of the mean clear to your students? Explain carefully.

(e) How would the above idea work with this data: 5, 1, 4, 7, 11, 7? Discuss briefly.

24. **(a)** Using a metric ruler as a straightedge and for measuring, *carefully* draw a rectangle with what you deem the most aesthetically pleasing proportions (length and width). Before making your final drawing, you may want to make several free-hand sketches to help you decide which shape you prefer most. After making your final drawing, measure the length and width as accurately as possible and determine the ratio of the length of the long side to the length of the short side accurate to one decimal place. Finally, write your ratio on the chalkboard.

(b) After all the ratios are noted on the chalkboard, determine their mean and standard deviation.

(c) As a class, decide on a single number that is most representative of the data of part (a).

(d) The ancient Greeks thought that the Golden Rectangle was the most aesthetically pleasing of all. Does your class seem to agree? Note: Your instructor will know the Golden Ratio associated with the Golden Rectangle.

(e) Finally, determine what percentage of the ratios lie within one standard deviation of the mean determined in part (b).

25. **(a)** Working with a group of three or four other students, use a plastic 30-centimeter ruler to measure individual "drop distances." Working in pairs in the group, one student holds the ruler vertically by the tip and lets it drop between the thumb and forefinger of the other student. The object is to see how far the ruler drops before the second student can catch it. After a few free trials,

repeat the process five times measuring as accurately as possible the distance the ruler falls each time. Record these five measurements.

(b) Compute the mean "drop distance" for yourself and for your group, and record the latter mean on the chalkboard.

(c) Determine the mean of the means on the chalkboard as well as their standard deviation.

(d) Discuss the results of part (c) with the entire class and determine a consensus opinion of the distance that seems most typical for the members of your class. Also determine a range that encompasses the "drop distances" of most of the class.

Making Connections

26. **(a)** From the data in the bar graph shown is it possible to determine the average median income in 1995 for men 25 years old and older? Explain briefly.

(b) What legitimate conclusions can you make on the basis of the bar graph shown?

Median annual income of persons with income 25 years old and over, by highest degree attained and sex: 1995

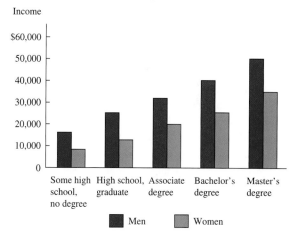

SOURCE: U.S. Department of Commerce, Bureau of the Census, *Current Population Reports,* Series P-60, "Money Income in the United States: 1995."

27. **(a)** Use the data in the pie chart shown to determine the average proceeds from the various types of lottery games in 1996.

(b) Determine the percentage of the profits from lotteries that is used to finance education.

(c) Why do you suppose the majority of the proceeds from lottery games is used to finance education?

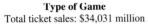

Type of Game
Total ticket sales: $34,031 million

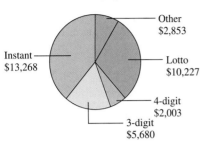

Other
$2,853

Instant
$13,268

Lotto
$10,227

4-digit
$2,003

3-digit
$5,680

Use of Profits
1964–95 cumulative total: $92,922 million

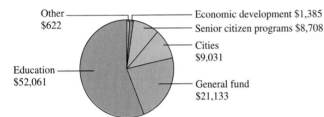

Other
$622

Economic development $1,385

Senior citizen programs $8,708

Cities
$9,031

Education
$52,061

General fund
$21,133

SOURCE: Chart prepared by U.S. Bureau of the Census. For data, see table 499. *Statistical Abstract of the United States, 1997,* 11th ed, Washington, D.C.: 1997, Figure 9.2.

 Using a Calculator or Computer

28. Use a suitable calculator or a spreadsheet or other software on a computer to determine the following for the data in Table 8.1.
   (a) $\bar{x}$ (b) $\hat{x}$ (c) the mode   (d) s
   (e) Q_L (f) Q_U (g) the box plot

29. Repeat problem 28 for the data in problem 26, Problem Set 8.1, on the success of NFL field goal kickers in 1998.

From State Student Assessments

30. (Minnesota, Grade 5)
   The members of the Spanish club sold calendars as a fund raiser. Below is a list of each person's sales.

Amy	6
Chris	9
Raul	15
Ali	9
Sonya	13
Ker	7
Maya	12
Allesandro	18
Nicky	10

   What was the mean calendar sale for a member of the Spanish club?
   ○ A. 9
   ○ B. 10
   ○ C. 11
   ○ D. 12

For Review

31. Find two rational numbers between 5/8 and 6/8.

32. Write the following real numbers in order from the least to the greatest. Be sure to identify the two numbers that are equal.

$$\frac{3}{4}, \ 0.74\overline{9}, \ 0.7\overline{49}, \ 0.74\overline{09}, \ 0.749, \ 0.74949$$

33. Given that $\sqrt{3}$ is irrational and r is rational, prove that $\sqrt{3} + r$ is irrational.

34. Given that $\sqrt{3}$ is irrational and r is rational, prove that $\sqrt{3} \div r$ is irrational.

8.3   Statistical Inference

Populations and Samples

In statistics a **population** is a particular set of things or operations about which one desires information. If the desire is to determine the average yearly income of all adults in the United States, the population is the set of *all* adults in the United States. If one is only

s voters left the voting booths on election day in 1948 they were asked by representatives of the *Chicago Tribune* if they had voted for Harry Truman or Thomas Dewey for president of the United States. On the basis of this poll, which indicated that Dewey would win by a comfortable margin, they prepared and printed a story for their morning edition with the headline, *DEWEY DEFEATS TRUMAN.* To their chagrin Truman in fact won the election and other papers gleefully printed front page stories prominently displaying a picture of Truman triumphantly holding aloft a copy of the *Tribune* with its erroneous headline.

concerned about the average yearly income of adults in Nevada, the population is the set of *all* adults in Nevada. Other examples of populations are

- all boys in Eisenhower High School in Yakima, Washington,
- all light bulbs manufactured on a given day by Acme Electric Company,
- all employees of AT&T,

and so on. One might want to determine

- the average height of boys in Eisenhower High School,
- the average life of light bulbs produced by Acme Electric company, or
- the average cost of medical care for employees of AT&T.

Since it is often impractical or impossible to check each member of a population, the idea of statistics is to study a **sample** or subset of the population, and to make inferences about the entire population on the basis of the study of the sample.

If the goal of accurate estimation of population characteristics is to be achieved, the population must be carefully identified and the sample appropriately chosen. Indeed, lack of care in identifying populations and choosing samples was precisely the source of some of the most spectacular errors of the past in the use of statistics (see Highlight from History, Dewey Wins!). When a sample does not accurately reflect the composition of the entire population, it is not surprising that attributes of the sample do not accurately indicate attributes of the population.

For example, suppose a study of the heights of boys at Eisenhower High School is desired. Instead of measuring each boy in the school, it is decided to study a sample of just 20 of the boys. If the sample were to be selected by choosing every fourth name out of an alphabetical listing of all 80 boys, would it likely be representative of the entire population? Probably, since there is likely little or no connection between last names and heights. However, a sample consisting of the members of the basketball team is clearly not representative since basketball players tend to be unusually tall. It turns out that the best approach to sampling is to use a **random sample.**

DEFINITION   *A Random Sample*
A **random sample** of size r is a subset of r individuals from the population chosen in such a way that every such subset has an equal chance of being chosen.

For example, suppose an urn contains a mixture of red and white beans and you want to estimate what fraction of the beans are red by selecting a sample of 20 beans. You proceed by mixing the beans thoroughly and then, with your eyes closed, selecting 20 beans. Since each subset of 20 beans has an equal chance of being selected, the sample is indeed random.

Other schemes also work well.

Suppose AT&T wishes to study the employees at one of its plants by selecting a random sample of 20 employees and asking them to respond to a questionnaire. One way to obtain a random sample would be to put the names of all the employees on tags, place the tags in a large container, mix the tags thoroughly, and then have someone close his or her eyes and select a sample of 20 tags. The employees whose tags are chosen constitute the random sample.

Another way to obtain the sample is to use a sequence of digits chosen in such a way that each digit is equally likely to be any one of the ten possibilities and the choice of each digit is independent of the choice of every other digit. Such a sequence would be a **random sequence of digits.** One way to select such a random sequence is to construct a simple spinner* with ten 36° sectors numbered 0, 1, 2, 3, 4, 5, 6, 7, 8, and 9 as shown in Figure 8.16. Spinning the spinner repeatedly produces a string of digits. Since the result of

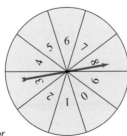

Figure 8.16
A simple random digit generator

---

*For a description of a superior and more accurate spinner, see Figure 9.2.

each spin is independent of the result of every other spin, each digit is equally likely to be selected and the digit sequence is random.

The desired sample of AT&T employees can now be obtained as follows (suppose the plant in question has 9762 employees):

1. Assign each employee a 4-digit number from among 0001, 0002, . . . , 9762.
2. Generate a random sequence of 4-digit numbers by repeatedly spinning the spinner four times. Since each digit is equally likely to appear on any spin, each 4-digit number is equally likely to appear on any four spins. If the spinning process generates 0000, a 4-digit number greater than 9762, or any number already obtained, simply ignore it and continue to generate more 4-digit numbers. When 20 appropriate numbers have been generated, they can be used to identify the 20 employees to be included in the sample.

Finally, as you might expect, many calculators have built-in statistics routines that will generate random numbers, and computer software exists for the same purpose. In Appendix C, the program for this purpose is RANDOM. RANDOM asks you to indicate the smallest and largest numbers you will allow and how many random numbers in that interval it should generate. It then proceeds to give you the desired number of random numbers, each containing ten digits, in the interval specified—one each time you press ENTER. Perhaps the easiest way to obtain a string of single random digits is to specify 0 as the minimum number allowed and 10,000,000,000 as the maximum number. Then specify 10 or 20 as the number of desired numbers and proceed to read off the digits in order in each number as it appears. This will give a sequence of random digits.

Population Means and Standard Deviations

Professional statisticians find it helpful to use different symbols for means and standard deviations for populations and for samples. For populations, the mean and standard deviation are denoted by the Greek letters μ and σ (mu and sigma). Thus, for a population of size N, the population mean and population standard deviation are given by

$$\mu = \frac{x_1 + x_2 + \cdots + x_N}{N} \text{ and } \sigma = \sqrt{\frac{(x_1 - \mu)^2 + (x_2 - \mu)^2 + \cdots + (x_N - \mu)^2}{N}}.$$

EXAMPLE 8.12

Computing a Population Mean and Standard Deviation

Consider a population that consists of the numbers shown.

64	65	68	67	59	66	63	66	64	62	65	66	63	66	66	63
63	64	62	67	63	61	60	64	64	63	63	65	64	65	66	63
65	62	63	65	61	64	63	64	62	69	65	65	64	64	63	64
66	65	64	64	63	64	66	67	69	63	65	63	64	64	64	65
67	68	64	62	66	62	64	61	65	62	65	62	65	62	66	63

Use a spreadsheet or other suitable software on your computer or the built-in statistics routine on a suitable calculator to compute μ and σ for this population.

Solution

Since there are 80 numbers in the population,

$$\mu = \frac{64 + 65 + \cdots + 63}{80} \doteq 64.2$$

and

$$\sigma = \sqrt{\frac{(64 - 64.2)^2 + (65 - 64.2)^2 + \cdots + (63 - 64.2)^2}{80}} \doteq 1.9.$$

Estimating Population Means and Standard Deviations

Suppose we wish to know the mean and standard deviation of some large or inaccessible population. Since these statistics, μ and σ, may be difficult or impossible to compute, we estimate them with the sample mean

$$\overline{x} = \frac{x_1 + x_2 + \cdots + x_n}{n}$$

and the sample standard deviation*

$$s = \sqrt{\frac{(x_1 - \overline{x})^2 + (x_2 - \overline{x})^2 + \cdots + (x_n - \overline{x})^2}{n}}$$

of a suitably chosen sample, $x_1, x_2, \ldots, x_n$, of size n.

EXAMPLE   8.13

Estimating a Population Mean and Standard Deviation

(a)   Estimate the mean and standard deviation of the population in Example 8.12 by using a spinner as illustrated in Figure 8.16 or the program RANDOM to select a random sample of size ten.

(b)   Compare the results of part (a) with the results obtained in Example 8.12.

Solution

(a)   Suppose your spinner generates the digit sequence 5, 5, 2, 9, 1, 0, 4, 5, 3, 1, 2, 4, 1, 9, 4, 6, 6, 9, 1, 7. Using these two at a time we obtain the 2-digit numbers

55	29	10	45	31
24	19	46	69	17

Since all are different, these determine the random sample shown here.

66	64	62	64	66
64	62	64	66	63

The fifty-fifth number in the ordered data set is 66, and so on.

---

*For technical reasons, statisticians replace n in the denominator by $n - 1$ in defining the standard deviation of a sample. The difference is technically important but numerically small, and we ignore it here.

Thus, the mean of the numbers in the sample is

$$\overline{x} = (66 + 64 + 62 + 64 + 66 + 64 + 62$$
$$+ 64 + 66 + 63)/10 \doteq 64.1.$$

The variance is

$$v = s^2$$
$$= [(64.1 - 66)^2 + (64.1 - 64)^2 + (64.1 - 62)^2$$
$$+ (64.1 - 64)^2 + (64.1 - 66)^2 + (64.1 - 64)^2$$
$$+ (64.1 - 62)^2 + (64.1 - 64)^2 + (64.1 - 66)^2$$
$$+ (64.1 - 63)^2]/10 \doteq 2.09,$$

and the sample standard deviation is

$$s = \sqrt{v} \doteq 1.45.$$

(b)   We observe that $\overline{x}$ and s for the sample are reasonable approximations for μ and σ for the population as determined in Example 8.12.

Suppose we were to repeat the preceding example but with a random sample of size 15. For the resulting sample, $\overline{x}$ and s should be slightly better approximations to μ and σ from Example 8.12 than obtained above. In fact, it is generally true that larger samples tend to yield better approximations to population characteristics.

Distributions

We return now to the data of Table 8.2 where the population consisted of all boys in Eisenhower High School. A histogram of the boys' heights to the nearest inch appears in Figure 8.5 and a line graph for the same data is shown in Figure 8.7.

Since the heights of the columns in the histogram represent the number or frequency of the measurements in each range (63.5–64.5, 64.5–65.5, and so on) and the width of each column is one, the total area of all the columns in the histogram is 80, the total number of boys in the population.

HIGHLIGHT FROM HISTORY
R. A. Fisher (1890–1962)

Statistics, a relative newcomer to the mathematical scene, was largely developed during the last one hundred years. One of the most influential personalities in this development was Sir Ronald A. Fisher, a British geneticist and statistician. To remove the effect of differences in soil fertility of different plots of ground used in testing the effects of various fertilizers on plant growth, Fisher introduced the idea of selecting plots by a random process and showed how to correctly compare results from such randomized experiments. Fisher also contributed other new ideas to statistics and his books and professional papers did much to shape statistics into an organized science.

The **relative frequency** of the measurements in each range in Figure 8.5 is the fraction (expressed as a decimal) of the total number of boys represented in that range. If the heights of the column in the histogram are determined by relative frequency, the diagram remains the same except for the designation on the vertical scale as shown in Figure 8.17. Also, since the width of each column is one, the *area* of each column gives the fraction of the population whose heights fall in that range. Moreover, the area of the first three columns gives the fraction of the population with heights ranging from 63.5 to 66.5 inches and the total area of the histogram is one.

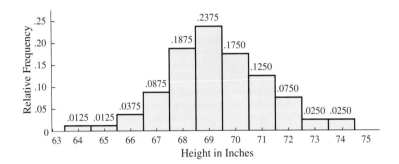

Figure 8.17

Histogram of Figure 8.15 but with the vertical scale denoting relative frequency

As noted earlier, histograms often are representations of grouped data that make it appear that all the data values in a given range are the same. As in the present case, this is frequently not so. The boys' heights are listed to the nearest inch whereas people's heights actually vary continuously. A truer representation of such data is provided by a line graph or frequency polygon as in Figure 8.7. If the vertical scale represented relative frequency rather than frequency the graph would appear unchanged as shown in Figure 8.18. Also, since such a diagram can be obtained from a histogram by deleting and adding small triangles of equal area, the area under the **relative frequency polygon** is still one and the area of that portion of the polygon from say 63.5 to 66.5 equals the fraction of the population of boys whose heights lie in this range.

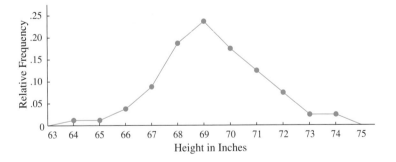

Figure 8.18

Relative frequency polygon of heights of boys in Eisenhower High School

Additionally, had the measurements been taken more and more closely and the ranges in the histogram made narrower and narrower, the tops of the columns in the histogram and also the corresponding frequency polygon would have more and more closely approximated a smooth bell-shaped curve called a **normal distribution** as shown in Figure 8.19. Here also the area under the curve and above the interval between *a* and *b* indicates the relative frequency or fraction of the boys measured having heights between *a* and *b*. This fraction indicates the *likelihood* or *probability* that a boy chosen at random from the population would have a height in the given range.

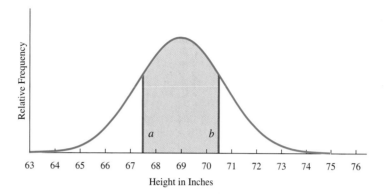

Figure 8.19
Normal distribution
of the heights of
boys in Eisenhower
High School

For many populations the distribution of the measurements of the property being considered will be a continuous (and often normal) curve as in Figure 8.19. However, in other cases the observations are not continuous, are not normal, or are discrete. If the observations are discrete the distribution "curve" is just a histogram.

> **DEFINITION**   *A Distribution Curve*
> A curve or histogram that shows the relative frequency of the measurements of a characteristic of a population that lies in any given range is a **distribution curve.** The area under such a curve or histogram is always 1.

Knowing the distribution of a population frequently allows one to say with some precision what the average value is and what percentage of the population lie within different ranges. In particular, the normal distribution has been studied in great detail and it can be shown that very nearly 68% of the data lie within one standard deviation of the mean, very nearly 95% of the data lie within two standard deviations of the mean, and very nearly 99.7% (or virtually *all*) of the data lie within three standard deviations of the mean as illustrated in Figure 8.20. Using the language of probability, we would say that the probability

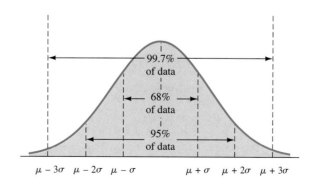

Figure 8.20
Percent of data within
one, two, and three
standard deviations of
the mean of a normal
distribution

that a given data value lies within one standard deviation of the mean is 0.68, the probability that a given data value lies within two standard deviations of the mean is 0.95, and the probability that any given data value lies within three standard deviations of the mean is 0.997 (virtually 100%). Considerations like these are what make it possible for very carefully designed polls and other studies to claim that their results are accurate to within a given tolerance, say 3%.

> **THEOREM   The 68–95–99.7 Rule for Normal Distributions**
>
> For a population that has a normal distribution, about 68% falls within one standard deviation of the mean, about 95% falls within two standard deviations of the mean, and about 99.7% falls within three standard deviations of the mean.

It turns out that many populations are normally distributed or approximately so. Thus, the 68–95–99.7 rule is approximately true for these populations and also for samples from these populations. For samples, the approximation is increasingly accurate for increasingly large sample sizes.

COOPERATIVE INVESTIGATION

Women's Hand Spans

Materials Needed

1.   A metric ruler for each cooperative group.
2.   A calculator with a built-in statistics package for each group.

Directions

1.   Divide the students in the class into groups of eight to ten students.
2.   In each group, the students measure the hand span (thumbtip to little fingertip) of each woman student in the group to the nearest millimeter, record the data, and also record the measurements on the chalkboard. (There are typically too few men in elementary education classes to sensibly do this investigation using male students.)
3.   In each group, the students compute the mean of the hand span measurements for their group.
4.   Several students now independently compute the mean, μ, and standard deviation, σ, of the data on the chalkboard (the population). If their computations do not agree, someone has made an error.
5.   Briefly conduct a class discussion on how well the means of the various groups (samples) approximate the mean of the entire class (the population).
6.   Each individual student should now compute the percentage of the population measurements that lie within one, two, and three standard deviations of the population mean.
7.   Discuss how well the results of step 6 compare with the 68–95–99.7 rule for the normal distribution. Does it seem reasonable to expect that measurements of women's hand spans are normally distributed?

PROBLEM SET 8.3

Understanding Concepts

1. Describe the population that should be sampled to determine each of these.

   (a) The percentage of freshmen in U.S. colleges and universities in 1999 who earn baccalaureate degrees within 10 years.

   (b) The percentage of U.S. college and university football players in 1999 who earn baccalaureate degrees within 10 years.

   (c) The fraction of the people in the U.S. who feel that they have adequate police protection.

   (d) The fraction of the people in Los Angeles who feel that they have adequate police protection.

   (e) Would you include children in the population you describe in parts (c) and (d)? People in mental institutions? Known criminals?

2. Polls are often conducted by telephone. Might such a technique bias the results of the poll? Explain briefly.

3. Suppose a poll is conducted by face-to-face interviews but the names of the interviewees are selected at random from names listed in the telephone book. Would such a poll yield valid results? Discuss briefly.

4. The registrar at State University wants to determine the percentages of students (a) who live at home, (b) who live in apartments, and (c) who live in dormitories. There are 25,000 students in the university and the registrar proposes to select a sample of 100 students by choosing every 250th name from the list of all students arranged in alphabetical order.

   (a) What is the population?

   (b) Is the sample random? Explain.

5. In performing a study of college and university faculty attitudes in the United States, investigators first divided the population of all colleges and universities into groups according to size—25,000 or more students, 10,000 to 24,999 students, 3000 to 9999 students, and less than 3000 students. Using their judgment they then chose two schools from each group and asked each school to identify a random sample of 100 of their faculty.

   (a) Was this a good way to obtain a statistically reliable (that is, random) sample of faculty? Why or why not?

   (b) What is the population? Are there four distinct populations? Discuss briefly.

6. To determine the average life of light bulbs they manufacture, a company chooses a sample of the bulbs produced on a given day by selecting and testing to failure every 100th bulb.

   (a) What is the population?

   (b) Is this a good way to select a sample? Why or why not?

   (c) Is the sample random? Why or why not?

7. Choose a representative sample of 20 students in your college or university and ask how many hours each person in your sample watches television each week.

   (a) Describe how you chose your sample to assure that it was representative of your entire student body.

   (b) On the basis of your sample, estimate how many hours of television most students on your campus watch each week.

   (c) Combine your data with that of all the other students in your class and determine a revised estimate of the number of hours per week each student in your college or university watches television.

8. Describe and perform a study to determine how many of the students at your college or university have seen the movie *Gone with the Wind*.

9. A container holds a large number of beans. To estimate the number of beans in the container carry out the following steps:

   Remove 25 beans and mark them with a red marker.

   Return the 25 marked beans to the container and mix the beans thoroughly.

   Now remove a handful of beans from the container and determine what fraction of the handful of beans is marked.

   (a) Using the fraction of marked beans in your sample, determine how many beans were in the container originally.

   (b) Repeat the procedure above but remove, mark, and return 50 beans to the container. Again estimate the original number of beans in the container. Compare this estimate to that of part (a). Which would you expect to be the better estimate? Explain.

(c) If the fraction of marked beans in the handful removed in part (a) is *a/b*, about how many beans were in the container originally? Explain briefly.

10. For a population with a normal distribution with mean 24.5 and standard deviation 2.7

    (a) about 68% of the population lie between what limits?

    (b) about 95% of the population lie between what limits?

    (c) about 99.7% of the population lie between what limits?

Thinking Critically

11. Suppose you generate a sequence of 0s and 1s by repeatedly rolling a die and recording a 0 each time an even number comes up and a 1 each time an odd number comes up. Is this a random sequence of 0s and 1s? Explain.

12. (a) If you repeatedly tossed a single die would this produce a random sequence of the digits 1, 2, 3, 4, 5, and 6? Why or why not?

    (b) If you repeatedly tossed a pair of dice would this produce a random sequence of the numbers 2, 3, 4, . . . , 12? Why or why not?

13. A TV ad proclaims that a study shows that eight out of ten dentists surveyed prefer Whito Toothpaste. How could they possibly make such a claim if, in fact, only 1 dentist out of 10 actually prefers Whito?

14. Two sociologists mailed out questionnaires to 20,000 high school biology teachers. On the basis of the 200 responses they received, they claimed that fully 72% of high school biology teachers in the United States believe the biblical account of creation. Is their claim justified by this survey? Explain.

15. Consider the numbers 1, 2, 4, 8, and 16.

    (a) Compute their mean, sometimes called the arithmetic mean.

    (b) Compute their **geometric mean;** that is, compute $\sqrt[5]{1 \cdot 2 \cdot 4 \cdot 8 \cdot 16}$.

    (c) Does the arithmetic mean or the geometric mean seem more typical of this sequence of numbers?

16. Katja can paddle a canoe 3 miles per hour in still water. The water in a stream flows at the rate of 1 mile per hour. Thus, going upstream in the canoe Katja's effective speed is 2 miles per hour, and going downstream it is 4 miles per hour.

    (a) What is Katja's average speed (total distance ÷ total time) if she paddles 4 miles upstream and back?

    (b) Compute the harmonic mean of 2 and 4—Katja's effective speeds upstream and downstream. The **harmonic mean** of several numbers is the reciprocal of the mean of their reciprocals.

    (c) Compute the mean or arithmetic mean of 2 and 4.

    (d) Discuss whether the arithmetic or harmonic mean seems the more appropriate "average" in this problem.

17. In the shoe business, which average of foot sizes is most important—the mean, median, or mode?

Making Connections

18. A fish biologist is studying the effect of recent management practices on the size of the cutthroat trout population in Idaho's Lochsa River. The biologist and her helpers first catch, tag, and release 200 such trout on a given day. Two weeks later, the team catches 150 cutthroat trout and determines that only three of these fish were tagged two weeks earlier. Estimate the size of the cutthroat population in the Lochsa River. (*Hint:* Determine the fraction of tagged cutthroat in the river in two different ways if there are *x* cutthroat in the river.)

Communicating

19. United States Representative, the Honorable J. J. Wacaser, recently sent a questionnaire to his constituents to determine their opinion on several bills being considered by the House of Representatives. Discuss how representative of the voters in his district the responses to his poll are likely to be.

20. Discuss how Representative Wacaser (see problem 19) might actually choose a random sample of voters in his district.

21. A large university was charged with sexual bias in admitting students to graduate school. Admissions were by departments and the figures are as shown.

    (a) Compute the percentages of men and women applicants admitted by the school as a whole.

    (b) Do the figures in part (a) suggest that sexual bias affected admission of students?

    (c) Compute the percentages of men and women applicants admitted by each department.

    (d) Do the figures in part (c) suggest that sexual bias affected admission to the various departments?

    (e) Carefully but briefly explain this apparent contradiction. (*Hint:* See the Just for Fun in Section 9.3.)

Department	MEN Number of Applicants	Number Admitted	WOMEN Number of Applicants	Number Admitted
1	373	22	341	24
2	560	353	25	17
3	325	120	593	202
4	191	53	393	94
5	417	138	375	131
6	825	512	108	89
Totals	2691	1198	1835	557

22. **(a)** Carefully describe how you might reasonably estimate, without spending a whole evening, what fraction of those attending a movie on a given night purchase popcorn.

(b) Discuss what factors might complicate your sampling procedure in part (a) and how you might deal with them.

From State Student Assessments

23. (Kentucky, Grade 5)

Which Bag Is It? Mr. Carew put the number of marbles shown below into three bags. He brought the bags to class so his students could experiment with them. Christopher and Stephanie each chose one of the bags and pulled a marble from that bag 100 times, putting the marble back into the bag each time.

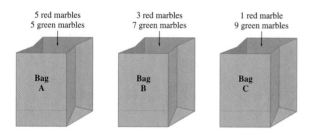

5 red marbles 5 green marbles	3 red marbles 7 green marbles	1 red marble 9 green marbles
Bag A	Bag B	Bag C

A. These are Christopher's results:

Red marble: 11 times   Green marble: 89 times

Which bag is most likely to be the one that Christopher chose? Explain why.

B. These are Stephanie's results:

Red marble: 32 times   Green marble: 68 times

Which bag is most likely to be the one that Stephanie chose? Explain why.

For Review

24. The following data are yields in pounds of hops.

3.4	4.4	4.8	4.5	5.1
4.8	5.5	4.7	3.5	3.6

(a) Compute the mean for this data.

(b) Compute the standard deviation for this data.

25. The 12 players on Uni Hi's basketball team averaged 5 points each during the first half of a game against Roosevelt. They averaged 7 points each for the entire game.

(a) How many points did Uni Hi score during the game?

(b) What was the average score for each player during the second half?

26. **(a)** What is the median of the data in problem 24?

(b) Draw a box and whisker plot for the data in problem 24.

27. Determine the mode for the data in problem 24.

28. **(a)** Compute the mean of 21, 25, 27, 20, 22.

(b) What is the mean of 21, 25, 27, 20, 22, 23?

(c) Were you sure of the answer to part (b) before doing the calculation? Explain.

(d) What is the mean of 21, 25, 27, 20, 22, 20, 26?

(e) Were you sure of the answer to part (d) before doing the calculation? Explain.

COOPERATIVE INVESTIGATION

Using Samples to Approximate Characteristics of Populations

The chart shown contains 100 integers (the population) displayed in such a way that they can be represented by a number pair (a, b). For example, entry $(2, 7)$ is the integer 24 and entry $(7, 3)$ is 26.

	0	1	2	3	4	5	6	7	8	9
0	21	22	20	24	22	29	25	21	27	17
1	25	12	28	21	22	17	28	18	18	26
2	19	17	23	29	19	16	24	24	25	19
3	22	17	26	11	31	19	14	20	23	17
4	26	13	30	26	18	23	37	24	27	28
5	14	15	25	20	24	18	20	30	35	21
6	18	30	22	20	20	23	27	26	33	13
7	24	21	23	26	28	19	28	29	31	23
8	21	27	22	25	21	16	23	27	16	25
9	23	22	24	22	16	15	19	24	25	20

For this investigation, parts (a) through (g) should be executed by each cooperative group of two or three students. Part (h) should involve the entire class.

(a) Use a spinner as in Figure 8.16 or the graphing calculator program RANDOM to generate five number pairs (a, b) to determine a sample of five numbers from the above table. Compute the mean and standard deviation of your 5-number sample.

(b) Repeat part (a) but with a sample of size 10.

(c) On the basis of parts (a) and (b) give two estimates for each of the population mean and standard deviation of the population.

(d) Record your means for parts (a) and (b) on the chalkboard.

(e) Determine $\bar{x}_5$, the mean of the means of the samples of size 5 and $\bar{x}_{10}$, the mean of the means of samples of size 10 from the chalkboard. Also compute s_5 and s_{10}, the standard deviations of the means of the samples of size 5 and size 10.

(f) Using the result of part (e) again estimate the population mean and standard deviation.

(g) Using a spreadsheet or other suitable technology, calculate the actual population mean and standard deviation for the entire population. Alternatively, these figures can be given to the class by the instructor.

(h) Briefly discuss the results of parts (a) through (g).

EPILOGUE   The Information Age

In today's world we are often confronted with masses of data that must be organized and summarized to be understood. We are also constantly bombarded with numerical information prepared by other people—pollsters, politicians, special interest groups, federal and state governments, foundations, testing agencies, and others—which we must be able to evaluate if we are to be informed citizens. As H.G. Wells once wrote, "Statistical thinking will one day be as necessary for efficient citizenship as the ability to read and write." Statistical thinking requires that we be able to read graphs and charts of all kinds, understand diagrams, and properly understand that, while sample results vary from sample to sample, a random sample of the appropriate size can yield very accurate information about a population. At the same time, it is equally important that we be able to discern how graphs, charts, and statistics can misinform, either intentionally or unintentionally.

In this chapter we have discussed many aspects of statistics—the organization, interpretation, and display of data; the meaning of the mean, median, and mode as indications of a "typical" value of a set of data; notions like the range, box and whisker plots, and the standard deviation as indications of the spread of a set of data; and the notion of a population and how samples can be used to provide information about populations. Statistics is a powerful and useful tool, but it must be used with understanding and with care.

CHAPTER 8 SUMMARY

Key Concepts

The main objectives of this chapter have been to introduce the fundamental ideas of statistics most likely to appear in elementary school texts. These central ideas include the following:

- data
- line plots
- stem and leaf plots
- histograms
- line graphs
- pie charts
- pictographs
- mean

- median
- mode
- quartiles
- box and whisker plots
- the standard deviation
- random samples
- distributions

Vocabulary and Notation

Section 8.1

Data
Line plot
Stem and leaf plot
Histogram
Frequency
Frequency polygon
Frequency of interval
Line graph
Bar graph
Pie chart
Pictograph

Section 8.2

Mean (arithmetic mean or average)
Median
Mode
Range

Quartiles
Interquartile range (IQR)
Outlier
Extremes
5-number summary
Box and whisker plot
Standard deviation
Variance

Section 8.3

Population
Sample
Random sample
Random sequence of digits
Relative frequency
Relative frequency polygon
Normal distribution
Distribution curve
The 68–95–99.7 rule

CHAPTER REVIEW EXERCISES

Section 8.1

1. The following are the numbers of hours of television watched during a given week by the students in Mrs. Karnes' fourth grade class.

17	8	17	13	16	13	8	9	17	7
8	7	14	14	11	13	11	13	11	17
12	15	11	10	12	13	9	21	19	12

   (a) Make a line plot to organize and display this data.
   (b) From the line plot estimate the average number of hours per week the students in Mrs. Karnes' class watch television.

2. Make a stem and leaf plot to organize and display the data in problem 1.

3. Choosing suitable scales, draw a histogram to summarize and display the data in problem 1.

4. The following are the numbers of hours of television watched during the same week as in problem 1 but by the students in Ms. Stevens' accelerated fourth grade class.

13	8	9	11	11	12	8	9
11	11	6	8	9	11	11	6
8	9	11	11	6	8	9	11

Prepare a double stem and leaf plot to display and compare the number of hours of television watched by Mrs. Karnes' and Ms. Stevens' classes during the given week.

5. (a) Draw a line graph to show the trend in the retail price index of farm products as shown in this table.

1960	1965	1970	1975	1980	1985	1990	1995
34	35	42	64	88	104	134	168

   (b) Using part (a), estimate the retail price index for farm products in 1972.
   (c) Using part (a), estimate what the retail price index for farm products will be in 2000.

6. Find five numbers with four of the numbers less than the mean of all five.

7. Draw a pie chart to accurately illustrate how the State Department of Highways spends its budget if the figures are as shown. Administration—12%; New Construction—36%; Repairs—48%; Miscellaneous—4%.

8. (a) Criticize this pictograph designed to suggest that the administrative expenses for Cold Steel Metal appear to be less than double in 1999 than in 1998 though, in fact, the administrative expense did double.

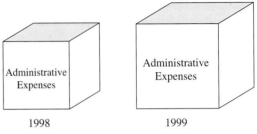

1998   1999

   (b) If the administrators are challenged by the stockholders can they honestly defend the pictographs? (*Hint:* Measure the cubes very carefully with a metric ruler and compute their volumes.)

9. What would you need to know in order to take this statement seriously? "A survey shows that the average medical doctor in the United States earns $185,000 annually."

Section 8.2

10. Compute the mean, median, mode, and standard deviation for the data in problem 1.

11. (a) Compute the quartiles for the data in problem 1.
   (b) Give the 5-number summary for the data in problem 1.
   (c) Identify any outliers in the data of problem 1.
   (d) Compute the quartiles for the data in problem 4.
   (e) Give the 5-number summary for the data in problem 4.
   (f) Identify any outliers in the data of problem 4.
   (g) Using the same scales, draw side-by-side box plots to compare the data in problems 1 and 4.

12. Compute the mean and standard deviation for the data represented in these two histograms.
   (a)

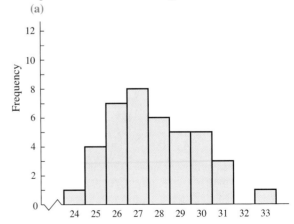

(b)

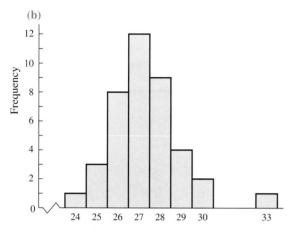

(c) Briefly explain the results of your computations in parts (a) and (b).

13. Three students were absent when the remaining 21 students took a test on which their average score was 77. When the three students took the test their scores were 69, 62, and 91. Taking these grades into account, what was the new average of all the test scores?

14. Mr. Renfro's second period Algebra I class of 27 students averaged 75 on a test and his fourth period class of 30 students averaged 78 on the same test. What was the average of all the second and fourth period test scores?

Section 8.3

15. In a study of drug use by college students in the United States, the investigators chose a sample of 200 students from State University. Was this an appropriate choice for the study? Explain.

16. Suppose you want to ascertain by a sampling procedure what percentage of the people in the United States are unemployed. How might you describe the population that should be sampled? Should every person residing in the U.S. be included in the population? Discuss briefly.

17. Discuss briefly the biases that are inherent in telephone polls.

18. Discuss briefly the biases that are inherent in samples obtained by voluntary responses to questionnaires like those sent out by members of Congress to their constituents.

19. Describe two different ways in which a random sample of 100 of the 10,000 students at State University can be obtained.

20. Suppose that only 1 dentist out of 10 actually prefers Whito Toothpaste over all other brands. By taking many random samples of size 10, might it be possible eventually to obtain a sample in which 8 out of 10 dentists in the sample preferred Whito? Explain.

CHAPTER TEST

1. Prepare a line plot to summarize and visually display this data.

42	86	80	90	74	84	86	80	63	92
93	81	95	78	70	41	66	76	87	88
75	88	87	78	89	85	77	87	81	57

2. Compute the following for the data in problem 1:
   (a) the mean   (b) the median   (c) the mode
   (d) the standard deviation.

3. Prepare a stem and leaf plot to summarize the data in problem 1.

4. (a) Sketch a box and whisker plot for the data in problem 1.
   (b) Would you say that this data contains any outliers? Explain.

5. Suppose the average American spends 40% of his or her income paying taxes. If this were to be shown with a pie chart, what should the central angle be for this portion of the chart?

6. What does it mean to say that a sample is a random sample? Be brief but lucid.

7. Suppose that Nanda obtains scores of 77%, 79%, and 72% on her first three tests in French. What total score must she earn on her last two tests in order to average at least 80% in the course?

8. The 68–95–99.7 rule does not apply to all populations but it does to a great many. What does the rule state?

9. Describe how you could choose a random sample of 200 students from your college or university.

10. In making inferences based on samples, why is it important to choose random samples?

MATHEMATICAL REASONING for ELEMENTARY TEACHERS

CHAPTER

9

Probability

9.1   Empirical Probability
9.2   Principles of Counting
9.3   Theoretical Probability

HANDS ON
Are Pennies Fair?

Materials Needed

1. One penny, preferably new, for each student.
2. Tables or level topped desks for the students to work upon.

Directions

Each student stands his or her penny on edge on the table and raps the table top sharply to cause the penny to fall. This is repeated five times, noting each time whether the penny falls heads up or tails up. When all the students have completed this task, record the data on the chalkboard and compute the fraction of heads obtained on all trials.

Is the result surprising? What does it suggest about the likelihood that a penny set on edge on a table will fall heads up if the table is rapped sufficiently hard that the penny falls?

CONNECTIONS   From Polls to Probability

In the preceding chapter we considered the idea of estimating a characteristic of a population by determining the same characteristic of a sample randomly chosen from the population. For example, suppose that a poll of 1500 randomly chosen residents of the United States shows that 61% of the sample choose blue as their favorite color. The pollster will claim that this is true of the entire population with an error of, say, $\pm 3\%$. This amounts to asserting that if you choose a person at random from the entire population, there is about a 61% chance that the person will hold the stated view. Alternatively, and perhaps more descriptively, it asserts that if you ask 100 randomly chosen residents of the United States, approximately 61 of them will choose blue as their favorite color. We could also say that the probability that a person will choose blue as his or her favorite color is about 0.61.

In this chapter, we study the notion of probability. As usual, we use concrete devices and experiences to gain an intuitive feel for the notion and to set the stage for a more mathematical approach considered later. Indeed, our approach is more than just pedagogical since there are two different but valid views of probability that correspond to the approaches taken here.

Empirical Probability

The first view of probability is that it is a measure of what happens in the long run. In the HANDS ON activity described above, unless something very unusual occurred, you discovered that pennies stood on edge on a table top do not fall heads up and tails up equally often. Rather the penny falls heads up approximately nine-tenths of the time. In terms of empirical probability we say that pennies stood on edge on a table top fall heads up with probability 9/10. This figure, based on past experience, allows us to predict that about 90 heads will appear in the next 100 repetitions of the coin experiment.

Theoretical Probability

Another view of probability is that, in many cases, the probability of an event can be defined by carefully analyzing the experiment about to be performed. For example, a quality die (*dice* is the plural of die) is made in the shape of a perfect cube with its weight evenly distributed, so that any one of its six symmetrical faces is equally likely to come up. In this case, it seems reasonable to assign the probability of 1/6 that, say, a five will be rolled. Indeed, each of the six outcomes—1, 2, 3, 4, 5, or 6—is equally likely to occur, and therefore each outcome has probability 1/6. This notion of probability is called **theoretical,** or **mathematical, probability,** or simply **probability.** Since theoretical probability is assigned before any experiments are performed, it is also call *a priori* probability, in contrast with the name *a posteriori* probability sometimes used to indicate empirical probability.

Empirical probability is examined in Section 9.1. Probabilities of events are determined on the basis of conducting experiments or examining data. Section 9.2 focuses on methods of counting, preparing the way to make the calculations needed in the concluding Section 9.3 on theoretical probability.

9.1 Empirical Probability

Suppose a penny is stood on its edge on a table, and the table is given a sharp rap to topple the coin. The experiment has two outcomes, since the coin will land either heads or tails up. If, in 100 experiments, the outcome heads occurs 91 times, we say that the empirical probability of obtaining a head is 91/100. In symbols, this will be written $P_e(H) = 0.91$, where H denotes the event that the coin lands heads upward. More generally, we have the following definition.

DEFINITION *Empirical Probability*

Suppose an experiment with a number of possible outcomes is performed repeatedly—say n times, and that a specific outcome E occurs r times. The **empirical** (or experimental or experiential) **probability,** denoted by $P_e(E)$, that E will occur on any given trial of the experiment is given by

$$P_e(E) = \frac{r}{n}.$$

If only a few experiments have been conducted, the empirical probability can vary widely and will not be a good indicator of how often to expect future outcomes of the experiment to occur. However, as the number of experiments increases, the variation decreases. This important fact, which we state without proof, is called The Law of Large Numbers. It is also known as Bernoulli's theorem, honoring the contribution of Jakob Bernoulli (1654–1705) to the theorem.

THEOREM *The Law of Large Numbers*

If an experiment is performed repeatedly, the empirical probability of a particular outcome more and more closely approximates a fixed number as the number of trials increases.

Probability in Grades 3–5

Students in grades 3–5 encounter beginning ideas about how probability can be used to describe the likelihood of events. These ideas are advanced by actively exploring familiar events in everyday contexts, particularly explorations involving chance. For instance, what is the likelihood of seeing a commercial when you turn on the television? Students can collect data about the number of minutes of commercials in an hour to estimate this probability.

Students can also experiment with probability in situations with only a few outcomes, such as game spinners with certain portions shaded. At this level, probability is linked closely to understanding important ideas involving rational numbers. Students can consider how the likelihood of an experimental event can range from impossible to certain and can denote this probability range as 0 to 1.

A striking example of the law of large numbers was provided by John Kerrich, an English mathematician imprisoned by the Germans during the Second World War. To while away the time, Kerrich decided to toss a coin 10,000 times and to recompute $P_e(H)$, the empirical probability of getting a head, after each toss. His first 10 tosses yielded 4 heads so $P_e(H)$ equalled 0.4 at that point. After 30 tosses $P_e(H)$ was 0.57, after 100 tosses it was 0.44, after 1000 tosses it was 0.49, and after that it varied up and down slightly but stayed very close to 0.5. After 10,000 tosses the number of heads obtained was 5067 for an empirical probability of $P_e(H) \doteq 0.51$. During the experiment, relatively long sequences of consecutive heads and also of consecutive tails occurred. Nevertheless, in the long run,

Highlight from History
The Mathematical Bernoullis

*L*ike talent of any kind, mathematical talent of the highest order appears in individuals with relative infrequency. This makes it most remarkable that such talent appeared in three generations of the Bernoulli family of Basel, Switzerland. Nicolaus Bernoulli (1623–1708) was a merchant and not a mathematician. However, two of his sons, four of his grandsons, and two of his great grandsons were mathematicians of the highest order. The Bernoullis were fiercely competitive and often quarreled among themselves about priority in mathematical discoveries. Nevertheless, they contributed enormously to the development of mathematics including contributions to the theory of probability by Jakob and Johann, sons of the merchant Nicolaus, and by Daniel, one of Johann's three mathematically talented sons. In particular, Jakob was the first individual to clearly conceptualize and prove the law of large numbers, the basis for the notion of empirical probability.

Jakob Bernoulli

the law of large numbers prevailed and the intuitive guess of 1/2 was borne out. The variation in $P_e(H)$ is effectively illustrated in Figure 9.1.

Figure 9.1

Ratio of the number of heads to the number of tosses in Kerrich's coin tossing experiment. (Adaptation of Figure 2 from Statistics, Second Edition by David Freedman, Robert Pisani, Roger Purves, and Ani Adhikari, p. 250. Copyright © 1991 by W.W. Norton & Company, Inc., copyright © 1978 by David Freedman, Robert Pisani, Roger Purves, and Ani Adhikari. Reprinted by permission of W.W. Norton & Company Inc.)

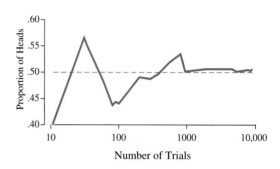

| EXAMPLE 9.1 | **Determining an Empirical Probability** |

Open a book at random and note the number of the right hand page. Do this 20 times and determine the empirical probability that the number of the right hand page is divisible by 3.

Solution

Since every third right hand page is numbered with a number that is divisible by 3, we would expect that the empirical probability should be about 1/3. Here are results obtained on checking 20 pages chosen at random.

349	69	267	407	133
395	269	123	331	373
155	235	187	273	401
297	83	852	263	303

Since a number is divisible by 3 if, and only if, the sum of its digits is divisible by 3, we determine that seven of these page numbers are divisible by 3. Hence,

$$P_e(\text{a right hand page number is divisible by 3}) = \frac{7}{20} = 0.35,$$

a very close approximation to 1/3.

Connections with Statistics

Most of what was said about statistics in Chapter 8 can be rephrased in terms of empirical probability. For example, saying that 28% of the items in a sample possess a certain property is the same as saying that the empirical probability that an item in the sample possesses a property A is $P_e(A) = 0.28$. Moreover, since population properties are estimated by properties of samples, one would go on to say that the empirical probability that an individual in the population possesses the property is also 0.28. Results of surveys, polls, summaries of data, and averages of all kinds also can be interpreted as empirical probabilities. Batting averages are empirical probabilities. Percentages of shots made in basketball are empirical probabilities. The life insurance industry is based on empirical probabilities derived from mortality tables.

EXAMPLE 9.2

Computing Empirical Probability from a Histogram

Suppose you wanted to study the heights of high school boys in the United States and decided to use Eisenhower High School as typical. Use Figure 8.17 on page 524 to determine the empirical probability that the height in inches of a high school boy is in the range $67.5 < h < 70.5$.

Solution

The percentages of boys with heights in the ranges 67.5–68.4, 68.5–69.4, and 69.5–70.5 are, respectively, 18.75%, 23.75%, and 17.5%. Thus, the total percentage of boys with heights in the range 67.5–70.5 is 18.75 + 23.75 + 17.5, or 60%. Therefore, $60\% = 0.60 = r/n$ where r is the number of boys with heights in the desired range and n is the number of boys in the high school. Since P_e also equals r/n, it follows that $P_e = 0.60$.

JUST FOR FUN

Social Security Numbers

Check and record the fifth digit of the Social Security number of 20 of your fellow students. Compute the empirical probability that this digit is even. Surprised?

Additional Examples Computing Empirical Probabilities

Empirical probabilities can be determined either from existing data or from data gathered from an experiment.

EXAMPLE 9.3

Computing Empirical Probability from Data

The final examination scores of students in a precalculus class are as shown. Compute the empirical probability that a student chosen at random from the class had a score in the 70s.

67	56	76	84	36	50	84
47	59	54	79	100	48	80
60	100	100	68	79	95	81
98	76	33	73	83	77	67

Solution

Since six of the 28 students scored in the 70s, the empirical probability that a student chosen at random had a score in the 70s is $6/28 \doteq 0.21$.

EXAMPLE   9.4

Determining Empirical Probabilities from an Experiment

Christine has 5 pennies. She is curious how often she should expect to see at most one head when all 5 coins are flipped onto the floor. To find an answer, she repeatedly flips the 5 pennies and counts the number of heads that turn up. After repeating the experiment 50 times, she obtains the following frequency table.

Number of heads	0	1	2	3	4	5
Frequency	1	7	13	16	11	2

On the basis of Christine's data, what is the empirical probability a flip of five coins results in at most one head?

Solution

The data shows that exactly 1 head appeared on 7 of the trials, and no heads (that is, all tails) appeared once. This means the outcome of at most one head occurred $1 + 7 = 8$ times in the 50 trials, giving an empirical probability of P_e(at most one head) $= 8/50 = 0.16$.

Discovering General Properties of Probability

Often an event of interest is described by coupling simpler outcomes with the word "and" or the word "or." This is called a **compound event.** The next two examples illustrate how the probability of a compound event is related to the individual probabilities of the events that have been combined to form the compound event.

EXAMPLE   9.5

Computing Empirical Probability and the Word "Or"

Roll a pair of dice 50 times and compute these empirical probabilities.

(a) $P_e(7)$ (b) $P_e(11)$ (c) $P_e(7 \text{ or } 11)$

(d)   Show that $P_e(7 \text{ or } 11) = P_e(7) + P_e(11)$

Solution

Actually performing the experiment, we obtained these results. From the data, the desired empirical probabilities are as shown.

2	3	4	5	6	7	8	9	10	11	12
l	l	lll	llll	llll llll	llll llll ll	llll lll	llll	llll	ll	ll

(a) $P_e(7) = 12/50 = 0.24$

(b) $P_e(11) = 2/50 = 0.04$

(c) $P_e(7 \text{ or } 11) = 14/50 = 0.28$

(d) $P_e(7 \text{ or } 11) = 0.28 = 0.24 + 0.04 = P_e(7) + P_e(11)$.

Example 9.5 suggests that the empirical probability of a compound event *A* or *B* is given by the formula $P_e(A \text{ or } B) = P_e(A) + P_e(B)$. However, it is important to check that no trial can result in a tally mark recorded for *both* events *A* and *B* at the same time. Two events that cannot both happen together on a single trial are called **mutually exclusive events**. This term and some others useful in probability are contained in the following list of definitions.

DEFINITIONS *The Terminology of Probability*

Outcome: a result of one trial of an experiment

Sample Space: the set of all outcomes of an experiment

Event *A*: a set *A* of some of the outcomes of an experiment (that is, a subset *A* of the sample space)

Mutually Exclusive Events *A* and *B*: two events *A* and *B* such that the occurrence of *A* precludes the occurrence of *B*, and vice versa (that is, *A* and *B* are disjoint: $A \cap B = \varnothing$).

Using these terms, the following property was illustrated in Example 9.5.

PROPERTY *Empirical Probability of Mutually Exclusive Events*

If *A* and *B* are mutually exclusive events, then $P_e(A \text{ or } B) = P_e(A) + P_e(B)$.

The next example shows how to modify the formula for non-mutually exclusive events.

EXAMPLE 9.6

Computing the Empirical Probability of Non-Mutually Exclusive Events

A penny and a dime are flipped. Determine the empirical probability that the dime shows a head or both coins land with the same side up. Use the data collected in the table, which shows the outcomes of 50 of 50 flips of the pair of coins.

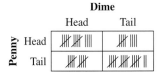

Solution

Let *A* denote the event "the dime shows a head" and let *B* denote the event "both coins land the same side up." All but the nine trials at the upper right of the table are occurrences of the event *A* or *B*, so $P_e(A \text{ or } B) = 41/50 = 0.82$. On the other hand, the empirical probability of having the dime show a head is $P_e(A) = 24/50 = 0.48$, since the 24 tallies in the left column of the table are occurrences of event *A*. Similarly, both coins showed heads 14 times and both showed tails 17 times, telling us that the empirical probability that the two coins show the same side is $P_e(B) = 31/50 = 0.62$. Then $P_e(A) + P_e(B) = 0.48 + 0.62 = 1.10$, which is 0.28 larger than $P_e(A \text{ or } B)$.

INTO THE CLASSROOM

Vera Holliday Comments on Teaching Probability in Her Classroom

Approximately one week prior to beginning our unit on probability, my students are introduced to a simple game called "Something for Nothing." I prepare a bag of 90 yellow marbles and 10 blue marbles. For three days, I have each student pick a marble from the bag. The results are recorded on a tally form provided for them, and, after each student has drawn a marble, the marbles are collected and not returned to the bag. If they pick a blue marble from the bag, they receive a specified number of extra credit points. For the next three days, the same process is followed but this time students immediately return the marble to the bag before the next student picks a marble. I continue this game through the study of probability and use it as the basis for discussing the meaning of probability.

Westlane Middle School
Indianapolis, Indiana

SOURCE: *Middle School Math,* Course 1, Volume 2 (Teacher's Edition), p. 622, Scott Foresman–Addison Wesley, 1999.

To identify the meaning of 0.28, we compute the empirical probability that both a head appeared on the dime *and* the two coins showed the same side. This compound event, *A* and *B,* corresponds to the 14 tallies in the upper left of the table, so the empirical probability is $P_e(A \text{ and } B) = 14/50 = 0.28$. This is exactly the amount $P_e(A) + P_e(B)$ exceeded $P_e(A \text{ or } B) = 0.82$, so we have the formula

$$P_e(A \text{ or } B) = P_e(A) + P_e(B) - P_e(A \text{ and } B).$$

The same reasoning can be applied to any two non-mutually exclusive events, giving the following general property of empirical probability.

PROPERTY *Empirical Probability of A or B for Non-Mutually Exclusive Events*
If *A* and *B* are any two events, then $P_e(A \text{ or } B) = P_e(A) + P_e(B) - P_e(A \text{ and } B)$.

The formula is still correct even when *A* and *B* are mutually exclusive events, since in that case $P_e(A \text{ and } B) = 0$ and the formula simplifies to

$$P_e(A \text{ or } B) = P_e(A) + P_e(B).$$

EXAMPLE 9.7

Computing Empirical Probability and the Word "And"

Determine the empirical probability of obtaining two heads on a single toss of two coins; that is, the probability of obtaining a head on the first coin **and** a head on the second coin. Does the probability turn out to be about what you would expect? So that you can tell coins apart, use a penny and a dime.

Solution   It is instructive to generate your own data, filling in a frequency table similar to the one shown here, which reproduces the data in Example 9.6. As before, let A denote the event that a head appears on the dime. This time, let B denote the event that a head appears on the penny. Using the data in the table, we find that $P_e(A) = 24/50 = 0.48$, $P_e(B) = 23/50 = 0.46$, and $P_e(A \text{ and } B) = 14/50 = 0.28$. Since $(0.48) \cdot (0.46) \approx 0.25 \approx 0.28$, we have the approximate equation

		Dime	
		Head	Tail
Penny	Head	14	9
	Tail	10	17

$$P_e(A \text{ and } B) \approx P_e(A) \cdot P_e(B).$$

In Example 9.7, it was important to understand that the outcome of one coin had no influence on the other. Events with this property are called **independent events** according to the following definition.

DEFINITION *Independent Events*

Events A and B are **independent events** if the occurrence or nonoccurrence of event A does not affect the occurrence or nonoccurrence of event B and vice versa.

For an example of *dependent* events, you might imagine flipping a dime and penny that are glued tail to tail. If A and B are the respective events that the dime and penny land with head facing upward, it is clear that the occurrence of A affects the occurrence of B.

The property of independent events that was illustrated in Example 9.7 can be stated this way.

PROPERTY *Empirical Probability of Independent Events* A *and* B

If A and B are independent events, then $P_e(A \text{ and } B) \approx P_e(A) \cdot P_e(B)$.

JUST FOR FUN

Three-Card Monte

You are shown three cards: one black on both sides, one white on both sides, and one black on one side and white on the other. One card is selected and shown to be black on one side.

(a) Considering the possibilities, what do you think is the likelihood or probability that the selected card is black on the other side as well?

(b) Conduct the experiment just described by selecting at random one of the three cards and looking at *one side only* of the card selected. If it is white, ignore it. If it is black record it and also record the color of the other side of the card. Repeat the experiment 10 times, carefully shuffling the cards between experiments. Compute the empirical probability that the second side of the card is black given that the first side is black. Does your experiment tend to confirm or refute your guess in part (a)?

COOPERATIVE INVESTIGATION

Strings and Loops

Materials

Six pieces of string per student, all pieces the same length (about 7 inches)

Procedure

Students work in pairs.

1. One student twists six lengths of the string into a loose bundle held with one hand. The student's partner then ties six knots, with three knots joining randomly selected pairs of the six strings at the top of the bundle and three other knots joining arbitrary pairs of strings at the bottom of the bundle. When the six knots have been tied, the bundle of string is put on a table.
2. The partners reverse roles, and tie six knots in another 6-string bundle.
3. The bundles are taken apart, to identify what pattern of loops have been created by the six knots. There are three possible loop patterns.

> *T:* three small 2-string loops
> *M:* one medium 4-string loop and one small 2-string loop
> *L:* one large 6-string loop

Class Project

Collect the data from all pairs of students and have each pair estimate the empirical probabilities of $P_e(T)$, $P_e(M)$, and $P_e(L)$. Which pattern seems most likely to occur? Which seems least likely? Are you surprised?

Empirical Probability and Geometry

An excellent spinner like the one shown in Figure 9.2 can be made by gluing an appropriately marked paper disc on top of a metal rimmed price tag readily obtainable at any stationery store. A round toothpick is forced through the center to act as an axle. Good results can be obtained as follows. Hold the spinner upside down and not too tightly in the left hand and up at eye level. Spin the spinner by twisting briskly between the thumb and forefinger of the right hand. Stop the spinner while it is still spinning rapidly by pinching it between the thumb and forefinger of the right hand with the forefinger on top. Before spinning the spinner, mark a vertical line on the tip of your right thumb with a pen. Then, when the spinner is pinched, let go with the left hand, turn the spinner over with the right hand, and note and record in which region the mark on your thumb lies. One can also use a standard spinner as illustrated in Figure 8.16. The "arrow" can be just a partially unbent paperclip, spun about the point of a pencil held vertically at the center of the disc.

Figure 9.2
Making a spinner

EXAMPLE   9.8

Determining Empirical Probability Geometrically

The spinner shown is spun and stopped as just described.

(a)   What do you intuitively feel the probability is that your thumb mark will fall in region A?

(b) Spin the spinner 20 times and record the number of times your thumb mark falls in each region. Then compute $P_e(A)$, $P_e(B)$ and $P_e(C)$, the empirical probabilities that the mark falls in regions A, B, and C respectively.

Solution

(a) Since the arc length associated with regions B and C is one-quarter of the circumference of the spinner and that of region A is one-half the circumference, it is reasonable to guess that $P_e(A) \doteq 1/2$ and $P_e(B) \doteq P_e(C) \doteq 1/4$.

(b) Actually spinning the spinner, denote the number of times the mark falls in A, B, and C respectively by $n(A)$, $n(B)$, and $n(C)$. Then

$$P_e(A) = \frac{n(A)}{20}, \qquad P_e(B) = \frac{n(B)}{20}, \qquad \text{and} \qquad P_e(C) = \frac{n(C)}{20}.$$

As guessed in part (a), these ratios should approximate 1/2, 1/4, and 1/4 or 0.5, 0.25, and 0.25 respectively.

Simulation

Simulation is a method for determining answers to real problems by conducting experiments whose outcomes are analogous to the outcomes of the real problem. Consider, for example, a couple with a growing family interested in understanding how many boys or girls they might anticipate. In this case, we assume

- that the birth of either a boy or a girl is equally likely, and
- that the sex of one child is completely independent of the sex of any other child.

These assumptions suggest tossing a coin since the occurrence of a head or a tail is equally likely and what happens on one toss of the coin is completely independent of what happens on any other toss.

EXAMPLE 9.9

Using Simulation to Determine Empirical Probability

Use simulation to determine the empirical probability that a family with three children contains at least one boy and at least one girl.

Solution

Using the assumptions above, we can simulate the real problem by repeatedly tossing three coins. Here are the results of such an experiment.

TTH	TTH	HHT	HHT	TTH
TTT	HTT	HTT	HHT	HHT
HHH	HHT	HHT	HHT	HHH
TTT	HHH	HTT	HHT	HHT
HHT	TTH	TTH	HHT	TTH

The empirical probability based on these results is

$$P_e = 20/25 = 0.80.$$

WINDOW ON TECHNOLOGY
Random Numbers and Simulation on a Graphing Calculator

Performing an experiment with physical objects and conducting a probabilistic study of a real-world problem may be tedious and time consuming, or even impossible or prohibitively expensive. For example, imagine the difficulties faced by a fire department that wishes to study its response times to a fire alarm. Fortunately, there is a simple and inexpensive alternative, namely using a computer or calculator to mimic the experiment. A computer model can incorporate random locations of the fire, random fire intensities, random times of day, and random traffic conditions. The computer study can help determine where a new fire station would be best located, and what equipment should be available at the station. Such a computer analysis is called a **computer model** or **simulation.** Simulations can also be carried out with a graphing calculator, providing an especially convenient tool for classroom investigations and demonstrations.

The basic random number commands on a graphing calculator are **rand** (*random*) and **randInt** (*random integer*), found under the PRB (*probability*) submenu of the MATH Menu. The **rand** command returns a random decimal number between 0 and 1, and **randInt**(*lower, upper*) returns a random integer n where *lower* $\leq n \leq$ *upper.* A new random number is obtained each time ENTER is pressed.

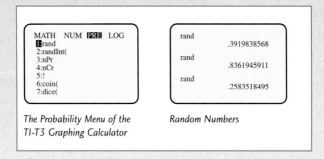

The Probability Menu of the   Random Numbers
TI-T3 Graphing Calculator

For many applications, it is necessary to modify **rand** or to use **randInt** to create a random number of the required type. For example, tossing a fair coin can be simulated with **iPart(2*rand)** or, alternatively, with **randInt(0,1).** Either command returns a 0 or a 1, which can be interpreted as a tail or a head, respectively.

To sum the total spots on a roll of a pair of dice, we could use the command **randInt(1,6) + randInt(1,6).**

The TI-73 has some built-in functions that make it especially easy to flip any number of coins and roll any number of dice. The command **coin(***n***)** will simulate flipping a coin n times by returning a random list of n 0s and 1s. The command **dice(***r,d***)** simulates r rolls of d dice, returning a list of the r sums of spots on the d dice.

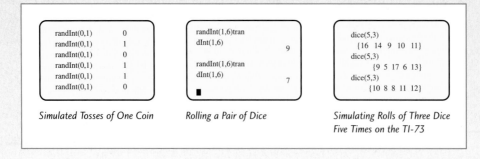

Simulated Tosses of One Coin   Rolling a Pair of Dice   Simulating Rolls of Three Dice
                                                               Five Times on the TI-73

PROBLEM SET 9.1

Understanding Concepts

1. Refer to Table 8.1 on page 479 and determine the empirical probability that a student in the class obtains a grade of 79.

2. (a) Refer to Table 8.2 on page 482 and determine the empirical probability that a boy in Eisenhower High School is between 69.5 and 70.5 inches tall.

   (b) What is the empirical probability that one of the boys in Eisenhower High School is between 70.5 and 73.5 inches tall?

3. Prepare a 3" × 5" card by writing the numbers 1, 2, 3, and 4 on it as shown. Show the card to 20 college or university students, and ask them to choose a number and tell you their choice. Record the results on the back of the card and then

   $$\boxed{1\ 2\ 3\ 4}$$

   compute $P_e(3)$, the empirical probability that a person chooses 3. Are you surprised at the result? Explain briefly.

4. (a) On a 3" × 5" card write the digits 1, 2, 3, 4, 5 as shown. Show the card to 20 different students, ask them to select a digit on the card, and then tell you which digit they selected. Record the results on the back of the card and compute the probabilities $P_e(1)$, $P_e(2)$, $P_e(3)$, $P_e(4)$, and $P_e(5)$.

   $$\boxed{1\ 2\ 3\ 4\ 5}$$

   (b) Compute $P_e(1) + P_e(2), + P_e(3), + P_e(4), + P_e(5)$.

   (c) Did you need to perform the actual calculations in part (b) to be sure what the answer would be? Explain briefly.

   (d) If you were to repeat part (a) with 100 different students, how many do you think would select the digit 4?

5. (a) Toss three coins 20 times and determine the empirical probability of obtaining three heads.

   (b) Using the data from part (a), determine the empirical probability of *not* obtaining three heads.

   (c) Using the data from part (a), determine the empirical probability of obtaining two heads and a tail.

   (d) Could part (b) of this question be easily determined from your answer to part (a)? Explain.

6. (a) Make an orderly list of all possible outcomes resulting from tossing three coins. (*Hint:* Think of tossing a penny, a nickel, and a dime.)

   (b) Does your listing in part (a) give you reason to believe that the result of problem 5(a) is about as expected? Explain briefly.

7. A computer is programmed to simulate experiments and to compute empirical probabilities. Match at least one of the computed probabilities with each of the descriptive sentences listed.

   (a) $P_e(A) = 0$ (b) $P_e(B) = 0.5$
   (c) $P_e(C) = -0.5$ (d) $P_e(D) = 1$
   (e) $P_e(E) = 1.7$ (f) $P_e(F) = 0.9$

   (i) This event occurred every time.

   (ii) There was a bug in the program.

   (iii) This event occurred often, but not every time.

   (iv) This event never occurred.

   (v) This event occurred half the time.

8. (a) Drop five thumbtacks on your desk top and determine the empirical probability that a tack dropped on a desk top will land point up.

   (b) Repeat part (a) but with 20 thumbtacks.

   (c) Give your best estimate of the number of thumbtacks that would land point up if 100 tacks were dropped on the desk top.

9. (a) Roll two dice 20 times and compute the empirical probability that you obtain a score of 8 on a single roll of two dice.

   (b) List the ways you can obtain a score of 8 on a roll of two dice. (*Hint:* Think of rolling a red die and a green die.)

   (c) Does the result of part (b) suggest that the result of part (a) is about right? (*Hint:* How many ways can a red die and a green die come up on a single roll?)

10. Construct a spinner with three regions A, B, and C as in Figure 9.2 but such that you would expect $P_e(A) \approx 1/2$, $P_e(B) \approx 1/3$, and $P_e(C) \approx 1/6$, on say 18 spins. What size angles determine the regions A, B, and C?

11. Construct a spinner as in Figure 9.2 but with the circle marked as shown here.

    (a) Spin the spinner 20 times and compute $P_e(A)$, $P_e(B)$, and $P_e(C)$.

    (b) Are the results of part (a) about as you expected? Explain briefly.

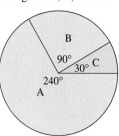

12. **(a)** A die is rolled repeatedly until a 6 is obtained. Repeat this experiment ten times and record the results. Estimate how many rolls it should take to obtain a 6.

   (b) Might it take ten rolls to obtain a 6? Explain briefly.

   (c) Might it take 100 rolls to obtain a 6? Why or why not?

13. From the data in problem 12, part (a), compute the empirical probability that a 6 first appears on the fourth roll of the die.

14. Consider a spinner similar to the one shown. The head of the spinner arrow falls in the outer ring, and the tail of the arrow falls in the inner ring. Let A be the event the head of the arrow lands in a red sector, and let B denote the event that the tail of the arrow lands in a yellow sector.

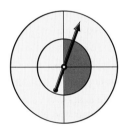

   (a) Assuming that you were to conduct a large number of spins, give estimates for each of the empirical probabilities $P_e(A)$, $P_e(B)$, $P_e(A \text{ or } B)$, $P_e(A \text{ and } B)$.

   (b) What formula can be used to check your answers to part (a)?

   (c) Are the events A and B mutually exclusive? Explain why or why not.

   (d) Are the events A and B independent? Explain why or why not.

Thinking Critically

15. Suppose that an experiment is conducted 100 times.

   (a) If event A never occurs, what is $P_e(A)$? Explain briefly.

   (b) If event A occurs every time, what is $P_e(A)$? Explain briefly.

   (c) What range of values are possible for $P_e(A)$? Explain briefly.

16. Roll a pair of dice 20 times and count the number of times you get a 7 and the number of times you get an 8.

   (a) Compute $P_e(7)$.

   (b) Compute $P_e(8)$.

   (c) Compute $P_e(7 \text{ or } 8)$.

   (d) Compute $P_e(7) + P_e(8)$.

   (e) Explain why the results of parts (c) and (d) are as they are.

17. Consider the experiment of shuffling a deck of playing cards and selecting a card at random. Repeat this experiment 20 times and note the result each time. Let $P_e(R)$ denote the empirical probability that a card is red, let $P_e(F)$ denote the empirical probability that a card is a face card, let $P_e(R \text{ or } F)$ denote the empirical probability that a card is red or is a face card, and let $P_e(R \text{ and } F)$ denote the empirical probability that a card is red and is a face card. Compute these probabilities.

   (a) $P_e(R)$ **(b)** $P_e(F)$

   (c) $P_e(R \text{ or } F)$ **(d)** $P_e(R \text{ and } F)$

   (e) $P_e(R) + P_e(F) - P_e(R \text{ and } F)$

   (f) Compare the results of parts (c) and (e). Do these results suggest a general property? Explain.

18. Consider an experiment of simultaneously tossing a single coin and rolling a single die. Repeat the experiment 20 times and compute these empirical probabilities.

   (a) $P_e(H)$, the empirical probability that a head occurs.

   (b) $P_e(5)$, the empirical probability that a 5 occurs.

   (c) $P_e(H \text{ and } 5)$, the empirical probability that a head and a 5 occur simultaneously.

   (d) $P_e(H) \cdot P_e(5)$

   (e) Should the results of parts (c) and (d) be about the same? Explain briefly.

19. Make up a three-card deck consisting of two aces and a queen. An experiment consists of shuffling the cards and inspecting the card on top and the card on the bottom. Let A denote the event that the top card is an ace, and let B denote the event that the bottom card is an ace. Repeat the experiment 30 times, keeping notes on the occurrence of the events A and B.

   (a) Use your data to compute the empirical probabilities $P_e(A)$, $P_e(B)$, $P_e(A) \cdot P_e(B)$, $P_e(A \text{ and } B)$.

   (b) Do you expect that $P_e(A \text{ and } B)$ should be approximately equal to $P_e(A) \cdot P_e(B)$? Explain why or why not.

20. Two dice are rolled 20 times. Compute $P_e(13)$, the empirical probability of obtaining a score of 13. Explain the result very briefly.

21. Two dice are rolled 20 times. Compute

$$P_e(2) + P_e(3) + P_e(4) + \cdots + P_e(12).$$

Explain the result very briefly.

Thinking Cooperatively

22. Work in a room whose floor is tiled with squares. Each student is given a thin wooden skewer (used to barbecue), cut to the length of the side of a tile. An experiment consists of throwing the skewer onto the floor and seeing whether or not the skewer crosses one of the parallel lines separating rows of floor tile. The lines separating columns of floor tiles will not be considered. Each student repeats the experiment 20 times, and computes the empirical probability $P_e(C)$ that a throw crosses one of the lines. According to a calculation of Comte de Buffon (1707–1788), $P_e(C)$ is approximately $2/\pi$, or about 0.64.

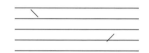

    (a) Do you expect any one student to have an empirical probability close to $2/\pi$?

    (b) Combine the data of individual students and compute a class value of $P_e(C)$. Do you expect to get better agreement with $2/\pi$?

23. Cover a large corkboard or bulletin board with a rectangular pattern of tangent circles, as shown. An experiment consists of throwing a dart, and recording whether the dart lands within a circle or not. Use circles about one inch in diameter, so while it can be certain the dart lands in the board it is uncertain if the dart lands inside any circle. If darts are inconvenient, throw small pins onto the horizontal board and determine whether the point of the pin lies directly above the interior of a circle or not.

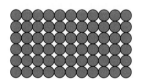

    (a) Repeat the experiment numerous times and compute the empirical probability of hitting within one of the circles on the board.

    (b) Does your empirical probability seem to be a good approximation of the ratio of the area of a circle to the area of the square that just contains the circle?

Making Connections

24. On September 8, 1998, Mark McGwire of the St. Louis Cardinals hit his 62nd home run in the 144th game of the regular season. This broke the 1961 record of 61 home runs of Roger Maris of the New York Yankees. McGwire was closely pursued by Sammy Sosa of the Chicago Cubs, who hit his 62nd home run in the 150th game of the season.

    (a) What was McGwire's empirical probability of hitting a home run during any one game, based on the first 144 games?

    (b) The major league teams each play 162 games in the regular season. On the basis of your answer to part (a), what number of home runs would you expect McGwire to hit for the season?

    (c) Answer parts (a) and (b) for Sammy Sosa, calculating his empirical probability on the basis of the first 150 games of the season.

25. The four blood types are O, A, B, and AB. These occur with the empirical probabilities $P_e(O) = 0.45$, $P_e(A) = 0.41$, $P_e(B) = 0.10$, and $P_e(AB) = 0.04$. What is the probability that, for a married couple,

    (a) both spouses are type O?

    (b) both spouses are type AB?

    (c) one spouse is type O and the other type B? (Be careful, the answer is *not* 0.045.)

26. An abbreviated mortality table is shown below. It shows, for example, that of every 10,000 people living at birth, 9806 live to see their 10th birthday.

Age	Living at Beginning of Year	Age	Living at Beginning of Year
0	10,000	50	8762
10	9806	60	7699
20	9666	70	5592
30	9480	80	2626
40	9241	90	468

Use the table to compute the empirical probability that
    (a) a newborn lives to be 10 years old
    (b) a newborn lives to be 90 years old
    (c) a person now 20 lives to be 50
    (d) a person now 30 will die before reaching age 70

Using a Calculator

The following problems can be investigated with the COINTOSS *program found in Appendix C on the graphing calculator. Alternatively, other statistical programs may be available for you to use.*

27. Flip four coins to simulate the birth of four children in a family. Use 100 repetitions to determine the empirical probability there are two boys and two girls.

28. Consider the experiment of flipping 10 coins n times. Draw line graphs showing the number of heads that appear for these values of n.

  (a) $n = 10$ (b) $n = 50$ (c) $n = 100$

  (d) If 100 coins were flipped a million times, sketch the general shape you would anticipate the histogram would take. (Don't attempt to simulate this on your calculator, since the computation time would be unreasonable.)

For Review

29. Compute the mean, median, and mode for these values.

  30 28 34 33 29 28 27 31

30. Compute the standard deviation for the data in problem 29.

31. What percent of the data in problem 29 lie within one standard deviation of the mean? Two standard deviations? Three standard deviations?

32. If a population with a normal distribution has mean 28 and standard deviation 8.4, what is the probability that an individual from the population falls in the range $11.2 \leq x \leq 44.8$?

9.2   Principles of Counting

Kerrich's experiment, discussed in the last section, showed that the empirical probability of obtaining a head on a single toss of a coin was very nearly 1/2. This is to be expected since there are only two ways a tossed coin can land and either heads or tails seems equally likely to come up. Similarly, if you repeatedly rolled a single die and computed the empirical probability of obtaining a 5 it would closely approximate $1/6 \doteq 0.17$. Again, this is expected since there are six faces on a die and these are very nearly equally likely to come up. In Example 9.7, the empirical probability of obtaining two heads on a single throw of two coins roughly approximated 1/4 and HH is one of four equally likely possibilities: HH, HT, TH, TT.

These and several of the examples and problems in the preceding section were designed to show that the empirical probability of an event could be predicted on the basis of a straightforward analysis of the possible outcomes of an experiment. Thus, if we desire the probability that two heads and a tail appear in any order when three coins are tossed, we can list the possible outcomes—

HHH	HHT	HTH	THH
HTT	THT	TTH	TTT

—and observe that in three of the eight equally likely outcomes two heads and a tail appear in some order. Hence, we would expect the empirical probability to be about $3/8 = 0.375$.

Considerations like these show that there is a close correlation between empirical and theoretical probability. Indeed, it is simply an extension of the law of large numbers to assert that the empirical probability of an event more and more closely approximates the theoretical probability provided the theoretical probability is correctly determined. In particular, it is important, as demonstrated in Example 9.7, that the equally likely outcomes of an experiment be properly identified. If this is not done successfully, the theoretical probabilities will almost surely be incorrect.

In Section 9.3 we will consider theoretical probability in some detail. First, however, it is important to develop some principles of counting. We will not want to have to list all of the equally likely outcomes each time we solve a problem. Also, since sample spaces are *sets* and events are *subsets,* much of the discussion will be stated in terms of sets and subsets. In particular, if A is any set, then $n(A)$ will denote the number of elements of A as in Chapter 2.

The words "or" and "and" play key roles in counting and a proper understanding of these roles makes solving counting problems much easier. We begin by considering the role of "or."

Counting and the Word "Or"

Consider the question, "How many diamonds or face cards are in an ordinary deck of playing cards?" Of course, we can simply count the 13 diamonds and then proceed to count the other nine face cards (kings, queens, and jacks) that are not diamonds. Thus, the answer of 22 is easily found. But there is another way to determine this sum. It seems more involved but reveals an important pattern that greatly facilitates solving more complex problems. Let D denote the set of diamonds in the deck of cards and let F denote the set of face cards. The two sets are shown in a Venn diagram in Figure 9.3, where we see there are $n(D) = 13$ diamonds, $n(F) = 12$ face cards, and $n(D \cap F) = 3$ cards that are both diamonds and face cards. The 22 cards that are diamonds or face cards is not given by $n(D) + n(F) = 13 + 12 = 25$, since the three cards in the intersection of the sets will be counted twice. To compensate, the number of cards in the intersection can be subtracted, so $n(D) + n(F) - n(D \cap F) = 13 + 12 - 3 = 22$ gives the correct count, $n(D \cup F) = 22$. Thus we have the formula $n(D \text{ or } F) = n(D) + n(F) - n(D \cap F)$, where the word "or" is used to indicate the union of the sets.

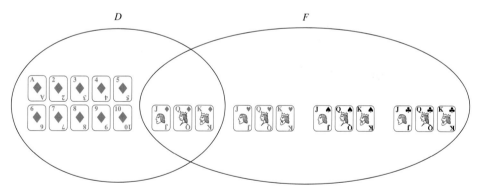

Figure 9.3
$n(D \cup F) = n(D) + n(F) - n(D \cap F)$

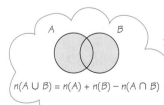

$n(A \cup B) = n(A) + n(B) - n(A \cap B)$

The same argument applies more generally to any two sets A and B and proves the following theorem.

> **THEOREM**   *The Addition Principle of Counting*
> If A and B are events, then $n(A \text{ or } B) = n(A) + n(B) - n(A \cap B)$.

EXAMPLE 9.10 | **Counting and "Or"**

In how many ways can you select a red card or an ace from an ordinary deck of play-ing cards?

Solution 1

As above, there are 26 red cards in a deck (including two aces) as well as two black aces. Thus, the desired answer is 28.

Solution 2

Let R denote the set of red cards and let A denote the set of aces. Then $n(R) = 26$, $n(A) = 4$, $n(R \cap A) = 2$, and

$$n(R \text{ or } A) = n(R) + n(A) - n(R \cap A)$$
$$= 26 + 4 - 2$$
$$= 28$$

as before.

A very important special case of the addition principle of counting is illustrated by the following example. Recall from Section 9.1 that two events A and B are **mutually exclusive** if no outcome belongs (or "is favorable") to both A and B. That is, $A \cap B = \varnothing$.

EXAMPLE 9.11 | **Counting and "Or" When Events Are Mutually Exclusive**

Determine the number of ways of obtaining a score of 7 or 11 on a single roll of two dice.

Solution 1

One way to solve this problem is simply to list all possible outcomes when rolling two dice and then to count those that are favorable. Thinking of rolling a red die and a green die makes it clear that there are 36 possible outcomes as shown below and that eight (see circled pairs) are favorable—six outcomes yield a score of 7 and two yield a score of 11. Thus,

$$n(7 \text{ or } 11) = 8 = 6 + 2 = n(7) + n(11).$$

Solution 2

Let F be the set of favorable outcomes when rolling the dice, let D be the set of out-comes yielding 7, and let E be the set of outcomes yielding 11.

Since $F = D \cup E$, we may use the addition principle of counting to obtain:

$$n(F) = n(D \cup E)$$
$$= n(D \text{ or } E)$$
$$= n(D) + n(E) - n(D \cap E).$$

But $n(D \cap E) = 0$ since $D \cap E = \varnothing$. Thus,

$$n(F) = n(D) + n(E) = 6 + 2 = 8$$

as before.

The preceding solution illustrated that

$$n(D \text{ or } F) = n(D \cup F) = n(D) + n(F)$$

when D and F are mutually exclusive events; that is, when $D \cap F = \varnothing$ and therefore $n(D \cap F) = 0$. This result is general and can be formalized as follows.

> **THEOREM**   *The Addition Principle of Counting for Mutually Exclusive Events*
> If A and B are mutually exclusive events, then $n(A \text{ or } B) = n(A) + n(B)$.

EXAMPLE   9.12

Choosing a Chocolate

A box of 40 chocolates contains 14 cremes, 16 caramels, and 10 chocolate-covered nuts. In how many ways can you select a creme or a caramel from the box?

Solution

Let C denote the set of cremes and let C^* denote the set of caramels. Then $C \cap C^* = \varnothing$ and so, by the addition principle for the mutually exclusive events C and C^*,

$$n(C \text{ or } C^*) = 14 + 16 = 30.$$

Thus, the number of ways of choosing a creme or a caramel is 30.

EXAMPLE   9.13

Determining How Many Are on an Airplane

On an airplane from Frankfurt to Paris, all the people speak only French or German. If 71 speak French, 85 speak German, and 29 speak both French and German, how many people are on the plane?

Solution 1

Let F denote the set of French speakers on the plane and let G denote the set of German speakers. Of course, a person who speaks both French and German belongs to *both* sets F and G. Since all people on the plane speak only French or German, it follows that the number of persons on the plane is $n(F \cup G)$. But, by the addition principle of counting,

$$n(F \cup G) = n(F) + n(G) - n(F \cap G)$$
$$= 71 + 85 - 29 = 127.$$

$n(F \cup G) = n(F \text{ or } G)$

Thus, 127 people are on the plane.

Solution 2

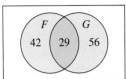

Let F and G be as above and consider the Venn diagram shown. Starting with the innermost region of the diagram, one fills in the appropriate numbers. Since 29 people fall in the set $F \cap G$, the common region of the two circles, and 71 are in the F circle, then $71 - 29 = 42$ people must fall inside the F circle but outside the common region as shown. Similarly, $85 - 29 = 56$ people must fall inside the G circle but outside the common region. Thus, finally,

$$n(F \cup G) = 42 + 29 + 56 = 127$$

as before.

Counting and the Word "And"

A bag of marbles contains three red marbles and one green one, as shown in Figure 9.4. Consider the following **two-stage experiment.**

Stage 1   Draw a marble from the bag and place it in your left hand

Stage 2   Keeping the first marble in your left hand, draw a second marble from the three remaining in the bag and place it in your right hand.

Denoting the three red marbles as r_1, r_2, and r_3, and the green one as g, one possible outcome of the two-stage experiment is r_1r_3, meaning that the red marble r_1 is placed in the left hand and the red marble r_3 is placed in the right hand. Of course, several other outcomes are also possible, and so we ask: In how many ways can this two-stage experiment be done?

One strategy is to **make an orderly list.**

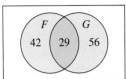

Figure 9.4

A marble bag holds three red marbles and one green marble

r_1r_2	r_1r_3	r_2r_3	r_2r_1	r_3r_1	r_3r_2
r_1g	r_2g	r_3g	gr_1	gr_2	gr_3

The list shows there are 12 outcomes. Note that outcome r_1r_2 is not the same as outcome r_2r_1.

A second strategy is to make a **possibility tree** as shown in Figure 9.5. (Curiously, trees are most often drawn sideways or upside down.) Following each "limb" from its "root" to its "leaf" corresponds to one of the 12 possible outcomes of the two-stage experiment.

Figure 9.5

A possibility tree for drawing two marbles without replacement

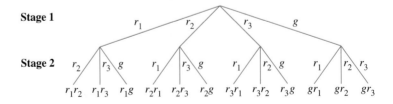

Let's next ask a somewhat different question: In how many ways will both the left hand *and* the right hand hold a red marble? In symbols, if A denotes the set of first-stage outcomes in which a red marble is put into the left hand, and B denotes the set of second-stage outcomes in which a red marble is put into the right hand, then we want to count *n*(*A* and *B*). From the list of possibilities, we see that the first row of outcomes corresponds to a red marble in each hand, so *n*(*A* and *B*) = 6. There is, however, a second way to obtain the answer by carefully examining the possibility tree in Figure 9.5. First, there are three ways to perform Stage 1 in which a red marble is placed in the left hand. That is, *n*(*A*) = 3. Next, *given* that one of the red marbles has been placed in your left hand, there are two ways to put a second red marble in your right hand. This number is symbolized by *n*(*B* | *A*) = 2, and is read as "the number of ways *B* can occur given that *A* has already occurred." Observing that *n*(*A* and *B*) = 6 = 3 · 2 = *n*(*A*)*n*(*B* | *A*), we have illustrated the following general counting principle.

> **THEOREM** *The Multiplication Principle of Counting for Dependent Events*
>
> Let *A* be a set of outcomes of Stage 1, and *B* a set of outcomes of Stage 2. Then the number of ways, *n*(*A* and *B*), that *A* and *B* can occur in a two-stage experiment is given by
>
> $$n(A \text{ and } B) = n(A)\, n(B \mid A),$$
>
> where *n*(*B* | *A*) denotes the number of ways *B* can occur given that *A* has already occurred.

It is important to notice that *n*(*B*) = 9. That is, of the 12 outcomes of the two-stage experiment, there are 9 cases where the right-hand marble is red. In three of these cases, the left-hand marble drawn first was green. Since *n*(*B*) ≠ *n*(*B* | *A*), we see that *A* and *B* are dependent events: whether or not event *A* occurs influences the number of possibilities that event *B* occurs.

In other two-stage experiments, the number of outcomes of the event *B* does not depend on whether or not event *A* has occurred. That is, *A* and *B* are *independent events* by the definition given in Section 9.1. In symbols, *n*(*B*) = *n*(*B* | *A*) for independent events. This formula gives us a special case of the multiplication principle.

> **THEOREM** *The Multiplication Principle of Counting for Independent Events*
>
> Let *A* be a set of outcomes of Stage 1, and *B* a set of outcomes of Stage 2. If *A* and *B* are independent events, then the number of ways, *n*(*A* and *B*), that *A* and *B* can occur in a two-stage experiment is given by
>
> $$n(A \text{ and } B) = n(A)\, n(B).$$

The following two examples give practice using the multiplication principles of counting.

EXAMPLE 9.14   **Counting the Number of Ways to Draw Two Aces**

How many ways, from an ordinary deck of 52 cards, can two aces be drawn in succession if

(a)   the first card drawn is replaced in the deck, the cards are reshuffled, and then the second card is drawn?

(b)   the first card is drawn but not replaced in the deck, and then the second card is drawn?

Solution   This is a two-stage experiment for which we wish to compute $n(A \text{ and } B)$, where A is the set of outcomes for which an ace is obtained on the first draw and B is the set of outcomes for which an ace is obtained on the second draw. To apply one of the multiplication principles, we must first decide if the events are dependent or independent.

(a)   Since the first card drawn is replaced in the deck, it makes no difference whether an ace was obtained or not on the first draw. For both the first and second draw, there are four aces favorable to the events A and B. Thus by the multiplication principle for independent events, $n(A \text{ and } B) = n(A)\, n(B) = 4 \cdot 4 = 16$. It should be noted that this includes the possibility that, say, the ace of hearts was drawn both times. Also, we are considering drawing, for example, the ace of hearts followed by the ace of spades as a different outcome than drawing the ace of spades first and then the ace of hearts.

(b)   If the first card drawn is an ace, then there are only three remaining aces left to choose from on the second draw. Thus drawing two cards without replacement means the events A and B are dependent. In this case, using the general multiplication principle gives $n(A \text{ and } B) = n(A)\, n(B \mid A) = 4 \cdot 3 = 12$. There are four fewer cases here than in part (a) since it is no longer possible to draw the same ace on the second draw.

EXAMPLE   9.15

Determining the Number of Code "Words"

How many 5-letter code "words" can be formed

(a)   if repetition of letters is allowed?
(b)   if repetition of letters is not allowed?

Solution   *Understand the problem*

Since we are talking about words in code, a word need not look like a word. Thus, *arefg* is a perfectly acceptable code word. Moreover, to determine a 5-letter code word, we must choose a first letter *and* a second letter *and* a third letter *and* a fourth letter *and* a fifth letter. The question then is, "in how many ways can we do all these things?"

Devise a plan

Since we have to do a first thing *and* a second thing *and* a third thing, . . . , *and* a fifth thing, the word "and" suggests that we use one of the multiplication principles of counting, extended to handle a five-stage experiment.

Carry out the plan

(a)   We must choose letters to place in these blanks.

‾‾‾‾   ‾‾‾‾   ‾‾‾‾   ‾‾‾‾   ‾‾‾‾

If repetition of letters is allowed, then the choice of any letter does not affect the choice of any other letter. Thus, the choices are independent and there are 26 ways to fill each blank so

n(5-letter code words with repetition of letters allowed)

$$= 26 \cdot 26 \cdot 26 \cdot 26 \cdot 26$$
$$= 26^5$$
$$= 11{,}881{,}376.$$

(b) If repetition is not allowed, there are still 26 choices for the first letter, but only 25 for the second, 24 for the third, 23 for the fourth, and 22 for the fifth. Thus, the number of code words in this case is

n(5-letter code words without repetition of letters)

$$= 26 \cdot 25 \cdot 24 \cdot 23 \cdot 22$$
$$= 7{,}893{,}600.$$

Look back

The key to working this problem was the use of the word "and" in describing what actually must be done to accomplish the desired task; that is, choose a first letter *and* choose a second letter, *and . . . , and* choose a fifth letter. Thus, using the multiplication principle repeatedly,

n(ways to choose a 5-letter code word) $=$

n(ways to choose 1st letter)

$\cdot\ n$(ways to choose 2nd letter | first letter)

$\cdot\ n$(ways to choose 3rd letter | first 2 letters)

$\cdot\ n$(ways to choose 4th letter | first 3 letters)

$\cdot\ n$(ways to choose 5th letter | first 4 letters).

Finally, it was necessary to decide whether the stages were independent (as in (a)) or dependent (as in (b)).

Combinations and Permutations

In Example 9.15, we were required to find the number of 5-letter code words under certain conditions. Thus, *abcde* and *acdbe* are both acceptable code words and are different since the order of the letters is different even though the sets {a, b, c, d, e} and {a, c, d, b, e} are the same. These distinctions are formalized in the following definition.

DEFINITION *Combinations and Permutations*

Let U be a set of objects. A subset of U with r objects is called a **combination of r objects of U.** An ordered sequence of r objects from U is called a **permutation of r objects of U.**

| EXAMPLE 9.16 | **Choosing a Social Committee and Officers for the Math Club** |

There are five members of the Math Club.

(a) In how many ways can the slate of officers, a president and a treasurer, be chosen?

(b) In how many ways can the two-person Social Committee be chosen?

Solution

For convenience, suppose the five members of the Math Club form the set $U = \{a, b, c, d, e\}$.

(a) Choosing the officers is the same as choosing a sequence of two members of U, first the president and then the treasurer. That is, we wish to know the number of permutations of five objects taken two at a time. By the multiplication principle of counting, there are five choices for the president and, once the president is chosen, there are four remaining members from which to choose the treasurer. Thus the number of ways to choose the two officers is 20. As a check, we can make a list of the 20 possible slates of officers, where the first person in each pair is president and the second person the treasurer:

ab	ac	ad	ae	bc	bd	be	cd	ce	de
ba	ca	da	ea	cb	bd	eb	dc	ec	ed

(b) Unlike the officer selection, the members of the Social Committee form an unordered subset of two elements. For example, a committee consisting of a and b is the same committee if b had been chosen first and then a. Thus the number of two-person committees is the number of combinations of five objects taken two at a time. Thus there are 10 committees, as shown in the following list:

$$\{a, b\} \quad \{a, c\} \quad \{a, d\} \quad \{a, e\} \quad \{b, c\} \quad \{b, d\} \quad \{b, e\} \quad \{c, d\} \quad \{c, e\} \quad \{d, e\}$$

In counting problems, the actual permutations or combinations of a set of elements taken r at a time are not important but their number is. In this context the important questions are:

- How many permutations of n things taken r at a time are there?
- How many combinations of n things taken r at a time are there?

Before answering these questions it will be helpful to introduce just a bit of new notation. As in Example 9.15, part (b), products like $26 \cdot 25 \cdot 24 \cdot 23 \cdot 22$ or $7 \cdot 6 \cdot 5 \cdot 4 \cdot 3 \cdot 2 \cdot 1$ frequently appear. Since these are somewhat tedious to write out, we use the shorthand

$$7! = 7 \cdot 6 \cdot 5 \cdot 4 \cdot 3 \cdot 2 \cdot 1$$

where $7!$ is read **"7 factorial."** Thus, for example,

$$5! = 5 \cdot 4 \cdot 3 \cdot 2 \cdot 1.$$

Moreover,

$$26 \cdot 25 \cdot 24 \cdot 23 \cdot 22 = \frac{26 \cdot 25 \cdot 24 \cdot 23 \cdot 22 \cdot (21!)}{(21!)} = \frac{26!}{21!},$$

where $21! = 21 \cdot 20 \cdot 19 \cdot \cdots \cdot 3 \cdot 2 \cdot 1$.

In general, we define $n!$ for every integer $n \geq 0$.

DEFINITION *The Factorial, n!*

Let n be a whole number. Then **n factorial,** or **$n!$,** is defined by

$$n! = n \cdot (n - 1) \cdot (n - 2) \cdots 1 \text{ for } n \geq 1$$

and

$$0! = 1.$$

That $0!$ is defined to be 1 may seem strange but we justify this part of the definition shortly.

EXAMPLE 9.17 | **Manipulating Factorials**

Compute each of these expressions.

(a) $1!, 2!, 3!, 4!$ (b) $4 \cdot 3!$ (c) $(4 \cdot 3)!$

(d) $4! + 3!$ (e) $4! - 3!$ (f) $\dfrac{8!}{5!}$

(g) $\dfrac{8!}{7!}$ (h) $\dfrac{8!}{8!}$ (i) $\dfrac{8!}{0!}$

Solution

(a) $1! = 1, 2! = 2 \cdot 1 = 2, 3! = 3 \cdot 2 \cdot 1 = 6, 4! = 4 \cdot 3 \cdot 2 \cdot 1 = 24$

(b) $4 \cdot 3! = 4 \cdot (3 \cdot 2 \cdot 1) = 4! = 24$

(c) $(4 \cdot 3)! = 12! = 479{,}001{,}600$, using a calculator

(d) $4! + 3! = 4 \cdot 3! + 3! = 5 \cdot 3! = 30$

(e) $4! - 3! = 4 \cdot 3! - 3! = 3 \cdot 3! = 18$

(f) $\dfrac{8!}{5!} = \dfrac{8 \cdot 7 \cdot 6 \cdot 5 \cdot 4 \cdot 3 \cdot 2 \cdot 1}{5 \cdot 4 . 3 \cdot 2 \cdot 1} = 8 \cdot 7 \cdot 6 = 336$

(g) $\dfrac{8!}{7!} = \dfrac{8 \cdot 7 \cdot 6 \cdot 5 \cdot 4 \cdot 3 \cdot 2 \cdot 1}{7 \cdot 6 \cdot 5 \cdot 4 \cdot 3 \cdot 2 \cdot 1} = 8$

(h) $\dfrac{8!}{8!} = 1$

(i) $\dfrac{8!}{0!} = \dfrac{8!}{1} = 8 \cdot 7 \cdot 6 \cdot 5 \cdot 4 \cdot 3 \cdot 2 \cdot 1 = 40{,}320$

With the factorial notion in hand, we now return to the problem of determining the number of permutations of n things taken r at a time and the number of combinations of n things taken r at a time. The following notation is helpful.

> **NOTATION** *P(n, r) and C(n, r)*
>
> $P(n, r)$ denotes the **number of permutations of n things taken r at a time.**
> $C(n, r)$ denotes the **number of combinations of n things taken r at a time.**

Some textbooks use the notations nPr and nCr to denote permutations and combinations. This notation is also commonly used to designate built-in functions on a graphing calculator to compute the numbers of permutations and combinations.

To derive formulas for $P(n, r)$, $P(n, n)$, and $C(n, r)$, let's reconsider the "code words" problem of Example 9.15. In part (b), we are to determine the number of different 5-letter code words with repetition not allowed. Since the order in which letters appear in a code word certainly matters, this is precisely the problem of determining the number, $P(26, 5)$. Since there are 26 choices for the first letter, 25 choices for the second letter, and so on, the answer is

$$P(26, 5) = 26 \cdot 25 \cdot 24 \cdot 23 \cdot 22.$$

five factors since we must choose five letters

Repeating the argument in general we have

$$P(n, r) = n(n - 1)(n - 2) \cdots (n - r + 1).$$

Here there are r factors since we are choosing r letters.

Note also that

$$P(n, r) = \frac{n(n-1)\cdots(n-r+1)\cdot(n-r)\cdots 1}{(n-r)(n-r-1)\cdots 1}$$

$$= \frac{n!}{(n-r)!}.$$

Setting $r = n$ in the above two formulas, we obtain

$$P(n, n) = n! \text{ and } P(n, n) = \frac{n!}{(n-n)!} = \frac{n!}{0!}.$$

Since these must be the same, it follows that we should define 0! to be 1 as above.

Suppose we wanted 26-letter code words without repetition; that is, suppose we wanted to compute $P(26, 26)$. Repeating the above argument we have that:

- the first letter can be chosen in 26 ways,
- the second letter can be chosen in 25 ways,
- the third letter can be chosen in 24 ways,

$$\vdots$$

- the last letter can be chosen in 1 way.

Since the product of these numbers gives the desired result, the number of permutations of 26 things taken all at a time is

$$P(26, 26) = 26 \cdot 25 \cdot 24 \cdots 1 = 26!$$

Repeating the argument for a general *n,* we have

$$P(n, n) = n!$$

Lastly, consider again the problem of determining the number of permutations of 26 things taken five at a time. One way to determine such a permutation is to view it as a two-stage process:

Stage 1:   choose, without regard to order, the five letters to appear in the permutation *and*

Stage 2:   determine the order in which the letters are to appear.

We can choose the five letters in $C(26, 5)$ ways and the five objects can be put in order in 5! ways. Thus, by the multiplication principle of counting,

$$P(26, 5) = C(26, 5) \cdot 5!$$

Dividing both sides of the equation by 5!, we obtain

$$C(26, 5) = \frac{P(26, 5)}{5!}$$

$$= \frac{26 \cdot 25 \cdot 24 \cdot 23 \cdot 22}{5!}.$$

five factors in both numerator and denominator, since $5! = 5 \cdot 4 \cdot 3 \cdot 2 \cdot 1$

This argument could be repeated in general to give

$$C(n, r) = \frac{n(n-1)\cdots(n-r+1)}{r!}.$$

r factors in both numerator and denominator

The formulas we have discovered can be collected to give the following important theorem.

> **THEOREM** *Formulas for P(n, r) and C(n, r)*
>
> Let n and r be natural numbers with $0 < r \le n$. Then
> $$P(n, r) = n(n - 1)(n - 2) \cdots (n - r + 1).$$
> $$P(n, n) = n!,$$
>
> and
>
> $$C(n, r) = \frac{n(n - 1)(n - 2) \cdots (n - r + 1)}{r!}.$$

EXAMPLE   9.18

Computing *P(n, r)* and *C(n, r)*

Compute each of the following.

   (a) $P(7, 2)$ **(b)** $P(8, 8)$ **(c)** $P(25, 2)$
   (d) $C(7, 2)$ **(e)** $C(8, 8)$ **(f)** $C(25, 2)$

Solution

   (a) $P(7, 2) = 7 \cdot 6 = 42$
   (b) $P(8, 8) = 8! = 40{,}320$
   (c) $P(25, 2) = 25 \cdot 24 = 600$

   (d) $C(7, 2) = \dfrac{7 \cdot 6}{2!} = 21$

   (e) $C(8, 8) = \dfrac{8!}{8!} = 1$

   (f) $C(25, 2) = \dfrac{25 \cdot 24}{1 \cdot 2} = 300$

EXAMPLE   9.19

Permutations of Four Red Flags, Three Blue Flags, and Two Green Flags

How many ways can you run four red flags, three blue flags, and two green flags up a pole if the flags are indistinguishable except for color?

Solution   *Understand the problem*

We must put four red flags, three blue flags, and two green flags in order. Since the flags are indistinguishable except for color, interchanging flags of the same color will not make any difference; that is, the arrangement

R R B G B G R B R

will not change if we interchange red flags among themselves, or blue flags among themselves, or green flags among themselves. Apparently, the only way to obtain a different arrangement is to choose different locations in which to place the red, blue, and green flags.

Devise a plan

How can we determine in how many ways we can choose the four places for red flags, the three places for blue flags, and the two places for green flags? This is just the number of ways we can choose four of the nine places to receive red flags *and* three of the remaining five places to receive blue flags *and* two of the remaining two places to receive green flags. The words "and" in the preceding sentence are the key. They suggest that we use the multiplication principle of counting.

Carry out a plan

1. The number of ways we can choose four of the nine places to receive red flags is C(9, 4), the number of combinations of nine things (spaces) taken four at a time.
2. Having chosen the four places to receive red flags, we must now choose three of the remaining five places to receive blue flags and this can be done in C(5, 3) ways.
3. This leaves two places from which we must choose the places to receive the two green flags and this can be done in C(2, 2) ways.

But we have to do step 1 *and* step 2 *and* step 3 and so, by the multiplication principle of counting, the desired answer is just the product of the number of ways we can complete each step. This is

$$C(9, 4) \cdot C(5, 3) \cdot C(2, 2) = \frac{9 \cdot 8 \cdot 7 \cdot 6}{4!} \cdot \frac{5 \cdot 4 \cdot 3}{3!} \cdot \frac{2 \cdot 1}{2!}$$

$$= \frac{9!}{4!\, 3!\, 2!}.$$

Some arithmetic shows this value is 1260.

Look back

The solution just given for the flags problem would work just as well if we had different numbers of red, blue, and green flags, or even if we also had some yellow flags. For example, suppose there are 25 flags (and a tall flag pole!), including 7 red, 9 blue, 5 green, and 4 yellow flags. Assuming the flags of any one color are indistinguishable, we could run the flags up the pole to form

$$\frac{25!}{7!\, 9!\, 5!\, 4!}$$

different color patterns. This expression can be evaluated on a scientific or graphing calculator, showing there are nearly three trillion color patterns possible with the 25 flags!

EXAMPLE   9.20   **Determining the Number of Zip Code Groups**

As seen in Section 4 of Chapter 4, the bar code commonly seen under the address on pieces of mail is the zip code in machine readable form. When broken down, it turns out that each code group consists of two long bars and three short bars; for example ıllıl . How many different code groups can be formed in this way?

Solution   This is just the number of ways one can choose the positions of the two long bars from the five positions available. By the preceding theorem, the result is

$$C(5, 2) = \frac{5!}{2!\,3!} = \frac{5 \cdot 4 \cdot 3 \cdot 2 \cdot 1}{2 \cdot 1 \cdot 3 \cdot 2 \cdot 1} = 10.$$

The result is opportune, since the ten code groups are just adequate to represent the ten digits—0, 1, 2, . . . , 9—needed to express a zip code.

PROBLEM SET 9.2

Understanding Concepts

1. Two dice are thrown. Determine the number of ways a score of 4 or 6 can be obtained. For example $4 = 3 + 1 = 1 + 3 = 2 + 2$, and so on.

2. Two dice are thrown. Determine the number of ways to obtain a score of at least 4. (*Hint:* In how many ways can you fail to obtain a score of at least 4? How many outcomes are possible all told?)

3. A coin is tossed and a die is rolled.
   (a) In how many ways can the outcome consist of a head and an even number?
   (b) In how many ways can the outcome consist of a head or an even number?

4. There are 26 students in Mrs. Pietz's fifth grade class at the International School of Tokyo. All of the students speak either English or Japanese and some speak both languages. If 18 of the students can speak English and 14 can speak Japanese,
   (a) how many speak both English and Japanese?
   (b) how many speak English but not Japanese? (*Hint:* Draw a Venn diagram.)

5. All of the 24 students in Mr. Walcott's fourth grade class at the International School of Tokyo speak either English or Japanese. If 11 of the students speak only English and nine of the students speak only Japanese, how many speak both languages?

6. In how many ways can you draw a club or a face card from an ordinary deck of playing cards?

7. In how many ways can you select a red face card or a black ace from an ordinary deck of playing cards?

8. (a) How many 4-digit natural numbers can be named using the digits 1, 2, 3, 4, 5, or 6 at most once?
   (b) How many of the numbers in part (a) begin with an odd digit? (*Hint:* Choose the first digit first.)
   (c) How many of the numbers in part (b) end with an odd digit? (*Hint:* Choose the first digit first and the last digit second.)

9. (a) If repetition of digits is not allowed, how many 3-digit numbers can be formed using the digits 1, 2, 3, 4, 5?
   (b) How many of the numbers in part (a) begin with either of the digits 2 or 3?
   (c) How many of the numbers in part (a) are even?

10. Construct a possibility tree to determine all 3-letter code words using only the letters a, b, and c without repetition.

11. If four coins are tossed, construct a possibility tree to determine in how many ways one can obtain two heads and two tails.

12. A bag contains three red marbles r_1, r_2, and r_3, and two green marbles g_1 and g_2. Two marbles are drawn in succession without replacing the marble drawn first.
   (a) Construct a possibility tree for this two-stage experiment.
   (b) Let A be the first-stage event that the marble drawn first is green, and let B be the second-stage event that the second marble drawn is red. List the outcomes of the two-stage experiment that are in the compound event A and B.
   (c) Verify that $n(A \text{ and } B) = n(A)\, n(B \mid A)$.

13. Evaluate each of these expressions.
   (a) $7!$ (b) $9! - 7!$ (c) $9! \div 7!$
   (d) $9! + 7!$ (e) $7 \cdot 7!$ (f) $0!$

14. Evaluate each of the following.
   (a) $P(13, 8)$ (b) $P(15, 15)$ (c) $P(15, 2)$
   (d) $C(13, 8)$ (e) $C(15, 15)$ (f) $C(15, 2)$

15. How many 4-letter code words can be formed using a standard 26-letter alphabet
   (a) if repetition is allowed?
   (b) if repetition is not allowed?

16. How many 5-digit numbers can be formed with the first three digits odd and the last two digits even
   (a) if repetition of digits is allowed?
   (b) if repetition of digits is not allowed?

17. The chess club has six members. In how many ways
    (a) can all six members line up for a picture?
    (b) can they choose a president and secretary?
    (c) can they choose three members to attend the regional tournament with no regard to order?

18. How many different signals can be sent up on a flag pole if each signal requires three blue and three yellow flags and the flags are identical except for color?

19. (a) How many different arrangements are there of the letters in TOOT?
    (b) How many different arrangements are there of the letters in TESTERS?

Thinking Critically

20. Two dice are thrown.
    (a) In how many ways can the score obtained be even?
    (b) In how many ways can the score be a multiple of 5?
    (c) In how many ways can the score be a multiple of 3?
    (*Hint:* All possibilities when two dice are rolled are shown in Example 9.11.)

21. In how many ways can you arrange the nine letters a, a, a, a, b, b, c, c in a row?

22. How many of the arrangements in problem 21 start with a and end with b?

23. (a) In how many of the 120 arrangements of a, b, c, d, and e does b immediately follow a? (*Hint:* Think of ab as a single symbol.)
    (b) In how many of the 120 possible arrangements of a, b, c, d, and e are a and b adjacent?
    (c) In how many arrangements of a, b, c, d, and e does a precede e?

24. Sets of six cards are selected without replacement from an ordinary deck of playing cards.
    (a) How many ways can you choose a set of 6 hearts?

(b) How many ways can you select a set of 3 hearts and 3 spades?
(c) How many ways can you select a set of 6 hearts or 6 spades?

25. How many different sequences of ten flips of a coin result in 5 heads and 5 tails?

26. The Debate Team has six girls and five boys. In how many ways can a 4-person team be selected if there are to be two boys and two girls put on the team?

27. Compute the values of $C(n, r)$ in this table and extend the table two more rows. Do you need the formula to do this last? Explain.

$$C(0, 0)$$
$$C(1, 0) \quad C(1, 1)$$
$$C(2, 0) \quad C(2, 1) \quad C(2, 2)$$
$$C(3, 0) \quad C(3, 1) \quad C(3, 2) \quad C(3, 3)$$
$$C(4, 0) \quad C(4, 1) \quad C(4, 2) \quad C(4, 3) \quad C(4, 4)$$

28. A bag contains eight marbles of assorted colors, of which just one is red. Use combinatorial symbols $C(n, r)$ to answer these questions.
    (a) In how many ways can a subset of any five marbles be chosen?
    (b) In how many ways can a subset of five marbles be chosen, none red?
    (c) In how many ways can a subset of five marbles be chosen, including the red marble?
    (d) What formula expresses the fact that your answer to part (a) is the sum of your answers to parts (b) and (c)?
    (e) Create a "marble story" to derive the formula $C(10, 4) = C(9, 4) + C(9, 3)$.

Thinking Cooperatively

29. **Making Rod Trains.** In small cooperative groups, investigate making trains with Cuisenaire rods, as described in the HANDS ON that opens Chapter 2. In particular, use the rods to form all possible trains of length five. For example, here are four ways to form a train of length five. Also notice these trains contain varying numbers of cars (that is, rods), from 1 car to 4 cars.

(a) In how many total ways can trains of length 5 be formed?
(b) How many length-5 trains contain 1 car? 2 cars? 3 cars? 4 cars? 5 cars?
(c) In the following figure, each dashed segment can either be left as is or made solid. Use this figure to explain why there are $2 \times 2 \times 2 \times 2$, or 2^4, trains of length 5.

(d) To make a 3-car train of length 5, 2 of the 4 dashed lines must be made solid to show a separation between adjacent cars. Discuss why this means there are $C(4, 2)$, or 6, trains of length 5 that each has 3 cars.

(e) Carefully explain how to find a formula giving the number of trains of length n.

(f) Carefully explain how to find a formula, in terms of $C(m, t)$ for appropriate choices of m and t, that gives the number of trains of length n that have c cars.

Making Connections

30. An electrician must connect a red, a white, and a black wire to a yellow, a blue, and a green wire in some order. How many different connections are possible?

31. (a) Mrs. Ruiz has 13 boys and 11 girls in her class. In how many ways can she select a committee to organize a class party if the committee must contain three boys and three girls?

    (b) Lourdes, a girl, and Andy always fight. How many ways can Mrs. Ruiz select the committee of part (a) if she does not want both Lourdes and Andy on the committee? Note that Lourdes can be on the committee and Andy not on the committee or vice versa.

32. In the state of Washington each automobile license plate shows three letters followed by three digits or three digits followed by three letters. How many different license plates can be made

    (a) if repetition of digits and letters is allowed?

    (b) if repetition of digits and letters is not allowed?

33. A 4-bit code "word" is any sequence of four digits, where each digit is either a zero or a one. For example, 0100 and 1011 are 4-bit words. (See the Hamming codes of Section 6 of Chapter 1.)

    (a) How many different 4-bit code words are there?

    (b) How many different 6-bit code words, such as 001011, are there?

    (c) If a vocabulary of 1000 code words is required, how long must the words be?

 ## Using a Calculator

Scientific and graphing calculators have built-in functions to compute factorials $n!$, permutations $P(n, r)$, and combinations $C(n, r)$. For example, there may be a key labeled ! or $n!$ on a scientific calculator. A graphing calculator will have functions !, nPr, and nCr under the Math and Probability menus. For example, 5 ! ENTER will give 120, 5 nPr 3 ENTER will yield 60, and 5 nCr 3 ENTER will yield 10.

34. Use a calculator to evaluate the following expressions.

    (a) 9!   (b) 11!   (c) $P(7, 5)$
    (d) $P(8, 6)$ (e) $C(7, 4)$ (f) $C(9, 5)$

35. Use a calculator to evaluate the number of ways

    (a) ten people can get in a single line for a photograph.

    (b) to place six books on a shelf, choosing from a set of ten books.

    (c) to choose a set of eight hearts from a deck of cards.

    (d) to choose your six "lucky numbers" in a lottery, choosing from the numbers 1 through 44.

Communicating

36. Write out a careful argument showing that

$$C(n, r) = C(n, n - r)$$

for whole numbers n and r with $0 \leq r \leq n$.

For Review

37. Toss two dice 20 times and determine the empirical probability of obtaining a score of 4.

38. Francine has lost 20 times in a row while playing roulette. She feels that her luck is bound to change soon and so begins to bet heavily. Briefly discuss Francine's reasoning.

39. Rashonda is 12 years old and gets a $10 allowance each week. She typically spends $5.50 for entertainment, $3.50 for snacks, and $1 for miscellaneous purchases. Draw a pie chart to show how Rashonda spends her allowance.

40. The final scores in Professor Kane's Ed Psych class were 53, 77, 82, 82, 86, 67, 77, 64, 72, 68, 60, 74, 56, 57, 82, 81, 88, and 90.

    (a) Display this data using a line plot.

    (b) Determine the mean, median, and mode for this data.

    (c) Compute the 5-number summary for this data.

    (d) Display the result of part (c) using a box and whisker plot.

9.3   Theoretical Probability

We now turn our attention to the study of **theoretical probability,** which we refer to simply as **probability.** The terminology of Section 9.1 for empirical probability—outcome, sample space, event, mutually exclusive events, and independent events—will continue to be important terms to describe the key concepts. In this section, we will make one important new assumption:

Each outcome of an experiment is as likely to occur as any other outcome.

When this can be assumed, the outcomes are said to be **equally likely.** For example, flipping a fair coin has two equally likely outcomes, a head or a tail. Drawing a card at random from a standard deck has 52 equally likely outcomes. As an example of outcomes that are not equally likely, consider flipping two fair coins. It is *not true* that two heads, two tails, and a head and a tail are the three equally likely outcomes. If the sides showing on, say a penny and a quarter, are listed as HH, HT, TH, TT, it is seen that there are four equally likely outcomes of the two-coin experiment.

When the outcomes in the sample space S of an experiment are equally likely, the probability of an event $E \subset S$ is given by the following definition.

> **DEFINITION**   *Theoretical Probability of an Event*
>
> Let S, the **sample space,** denote the set of **equally likely outcomes** of an experiment and let E, an **event,** denote a subset of outcomes of the experiment. Let $n(S)$ and $n(E)$ denote the number of outcomes in S and E respectively. The **probability** of E, denoted by $P(E)$, is given by
>
> $$P(E) = \frac{n(E)}{n(S)}.$$

Be aware that the phrase **equally likely** is of critical importance in the above definition. If the outcomes in the sample space are not equally likely, the definition of probability simply doesn't make sense. For example, suppose the experiment consists of rolling two dice. It would not do to think of the sample space as the eleven outcomes $\{2, 3, 4, \ldots, 12\}$ since these outcomes are not equally likely. The difficulty is that there is one way to obtain a 2, two ways to obtain a 3, three ways to obtain a 4, . . . , six ways to obtain a 7, . . . , and only one way to obtain a 12. Thus, the event of obtaining a 3 is twice as likely as the event of obtaining a 2, and so on. However, if we mistakenly thought of the sample space as the above set with each of 2, 3, 4, . . . , 11, and 12 equally likely, we would obtain

$$P(2) = P(3) = \cdots = P(12) = \frac{1}{11},$$

a manifest absurdity. In fact, as we have seen before, there are 36 equally likely ways two dice can come up so that

$$P(2) = \frac{1}{36}, P(3) = \frac{2}{36}, \ldots, P(12) = \frac{1}{36}.$$

Moreover, these probabilities are closely approximated by the corresponding empirical probabilities.

The definition of probability assumes that we can count outcomes. This implies that the sample space is finite. Thus, our discussion of theoretical probability will be largely restricted to the finite case. It is possible to treat the infinite case as well as with geometric probability, but the general theory is beyond the scope of this course. The needed techniques of counting are perhaps best understood by considering several examples.

EXAMPLE 9.21

Determining the Probability of Rolling Eleven with Two Dice

Compute the probability of obtaining a score of 11 on a single roll of two dice.

Solution

Here the sample space, S, is the set of all 36 equally likely outcomes illustrated in Example 9.11. Let E denote the event of rolling a score of 11. Since only two of the outcomes in the sample space result in 11,

$$P(11) = \frac{n(E)}{n(S)} = \frac{2}{36} = \frac{1}{18}.$$

EXAMPLE 9.22

Computing the Probability of 5 or 8

Determine the probability of rolling a 5 *or* an 8 on a single roll of two dice.

Solution 1

As we have just seen, the sample space, S, is the set of all 36 ways two dice can come up. The favorable outcomes are as shown here where F is the event of rolling a 5 and E is the event of rolling an 8.

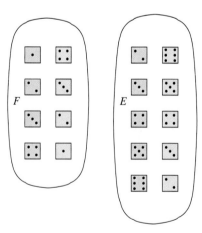

It follows that

$$P(5 \text{ or } 8) = \frac{4 + 5}{36} = \frac{1}{4}.$$

Solution 2

Note that if 5 is rolled then 8 is not and conversely. Thus, rolling 5 and rolling 8 are mutually exclusive events and the **or** in the statement of the problem reminds us that we can use the addition principle of counting mutually exclusive events. Thus,

$$P(5 \text{ or } 8) = \frac{n(5 \text{ or } 8)}{n(S)}$$

$$= \frac{n(5) + n(8)}{n(S)}$$

$$= \frac{4 + 5}{36}$$

$$= \frac{1}{4}$$

as before. Notice that

$$P(5 \text{ or } 8) = \frac{4}{36} + \frac{5}{36} = P(5) + P(8).$$

EXAMPLE 9.23

Computing the Probability of Obtaining a Face Card or a Diamond

Determine the probability of obtaining a face card *or* a diamond if a card is drawn at random from an ordinary deck of playing cards.

Solution 1

The sample space, *S*, is the set of all 52 cards in the deck. Let *D* denote the event of selecting a diamond and let *F* denote the event of selecting a face card. Since there are 13 diamonds (including face cards) and 9 nondiamond face cards,

$$P(D \text{ or } F) = \frac{13 + 9}{52} = \frac{22}{52} = \frac{11}{26}.$$

Solution 2

Using the addition principle of counting, we know that

$$P(D \text{ or } F) = \frac{n(D \text{ or } F)}{n(S)}$$

$$= \frac{n(D) + n(F) - n(D \cap F)}{n(S)}$$

$$= \frac{13 + 12 - 3}{52}$$

$$= \frac{22}{52} = \frac{11}{26}$$

as before.

Three face cards are diamonds.

JUST FOR FUN

It's a Girl!

A family has two children including at least one boy. What is the probability that the other child is a girl? The answer is not 1/2!

EXAMPLE 9.24

	Age Three	Age Four
Boys	8	3
Girls	6	7

Determining Probabilities with Restrictive Conditions

All 24 students in Mr. Henry's preschool are either three or four years old, as shown in this table. A student is selected at random.

(a)   What is the probability that the student is a three year old?

(b)   What is the probability that the student is three years old, given that a boy was selected?

Solution

Let B denote the set of boys, T the set of three year olds, and S the set of all students in the class.

(a) $P(T) = \dfrac{n(T)}{n(S)} = \dfrac{14}{24} = \dfrac{7}{12}.$

(b)   If we know that a boy was selected, then the sample space is not the set of all students in the class but *all boys in the class*. Similarly, the set of favorable outcomes is the set of all boys in the class who are three years old. Thus, the desired probability is

$$P(T \mid B) = \frac{8}{11}.$$

This is an example of so-called **conditional probability** and the standard notation $P(T \mid B)$ is read "the probability of T given that B has occurred." In this case $P(T \mid B)$ is the probability of selecting a three year old given that a boy has been selected.

EXAMPLE 9.25

Using the Multiplication Principle of Counting for Independent Events

A red die and a green die are rolled. What is the probability of obtaining an even number on the red die *and* a multiple of 3 on the green die?

Solution

The sets of favorable outcomes on the red and green dice respectively are $R = \{2, 4, 6\}$ and $G = \{3, 6\}$ and the sample space is the set of all 36 ways the two dice can come up. The word "and" is a broad hint to use one of the multiplication principles of counting. Since the dice are independent, the number of favorable outcomes is

$$n(R \text{ and } G) = n(R) \cdot n(G) = 3 \cdot 2 = 6$$

R and G are clearly independent.

Hence, the desired probability is $P = 6/36 = 1/6$. Notice that

$$P(R \text{ and } G) = \frac{6}{36} = \frac{3}{6} \cdot \frac{2}{6} = P(R) \cdot P(G).$$

JUST FOR FUN

A Probability Paradox

Consider the hats containing colored balls on the tables shown. The balls in the hats on tables *A* and *B* are combined and placed in the hats on table *C*. Let $P(R \mid G)$ denote the probability of randomly drawing a red ball from a grey hat and let $P(R \mid B)$ denote the probability of randomly drawing a red ball from a brown hat. Compute and compare $P(R \mid G)$ and $P(R \mid B)$ for each of tables *A*, *B*, and *C*. Is the result surprising?

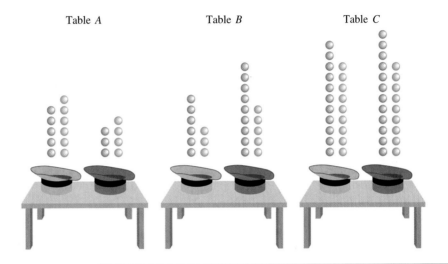

Table *A*   Table *B*   Table *C*

EXAMPLE 9.26	**Selecting Balls without Replacement**

An urn contains three identical red and two identical white balls. Two balls are drawn one after the other without replacement.

(a) What is the probability that the first ball is red?
(b) What is the probability that the second ball is red given that the first ball is red?
(c) What is the probability that both balls are red?

Solution 1

(a) Since there are initially five balls and three are red, $P(\text{1st ball is red}) = 3/5$.

(b) Having already selected a red ball on the first draw, the counts change for the selection of the second ball. For the second selection there remain four balls of which two are red. Thus,

$$P(\text{2nd ball is red} \mid \text{1st ball is red}) = \frac{2}{4} = \frac{1}{2}.$$

read as "given that"

(c) In order to select two red balls, it is necessary to select a red ball on the first draw *and* a red ball on the second draw. By the multiplication principle of counting for dependent events, the number of possible selections of two balls is $5 \cdot 4 = 20$ and the number of possible selections of two red balls is $3 \cdot 2 = 6$. Hence,

$$P(2 \text{ red balls}) = \frac{6}{20}$$

$$= \frac{3 \cdot 2}{5 \cdot 4}$$

$$= \frac{3}{5} \cdot \frac{2}{4}$$

$$= P(\text{1st ball is red}) \cdot P(\text{2nd ball is red} \mid \text{1st ball is red}).$$

Solution 2   A second way to solve this problem is to label the balls r_1, r_2, r_3, w_1, and w_2 so that we can identify the different red and white balls. With the balls identified in this way we make an orderly list of all possible selections of two balls. In this listing, for example, the entry (r_1, r_2) indicates that red ball number 1 was chosen first and red ball number 2 was chosen second.

(r_1, r_2)	(r_1, r_3)	(r_1, w_1)	(r_1, w_2)
(r_2, r_1)	(r_2, r_3)	(r_2, w_1)	(r_2, w_2)
(r_3, r_1)	(r_3, r_2)	(r_3, w_1)	(r_3, w_2)
(w_1, r_1)	(w_1, r_2)	(w_1, r_3)	(w_1, w_2)
(w_2, r_1)	(w_2, r_2)	(w_2, r_3)	(w_2, w_1)

all selections with r_1 first

all selections with r_2 first

and so on

Counting possibilities, we have

(a) $P(\text{1st ball is red}) = \dfrac{12}{20} = \dfrac{3}{5},$

(b) $P(\text{2nd ball is red} \mid \text{1st ball is red}) = \dfrac{6}{12} = \dfrac{1}{2},$ and

(c) $P(2 \text{ red balls}) = \dfrac{6}{20}$

$$= P(\text{1st ball red}) \cdot P(\text{2nd ball red} \mid \text{1st ball red})$$

as before.

EXAMPLE 9.27   **Combinations and Probability**

There are 10 boys and 13 girls in Mr. Fleck's fourth grade class and 12 boys and 11 girls in Mrs. Patero's fourth grade class. A picnic committee of six people is selected at random from the total group of students in both classes.

(a)   What is the probability that all the committee members are girls?

(b)   What is the probability that all the committee members are girls given that all come from Mr. Fleck's class?

(c)   What is the probability that the committee has three girls and three boys?

(d)   What is the probability that the committee has three girls and three boys given that Mary Akers and Ann-Marie Harborth are on the committee?

HIGHLIGHT FROM HISTORY
Srinivasa Ramanujan
(1887–1920)

*P*erhaps the most exotic and mysterious of all mathematicians was Srinivasa Ramanujan, born to a high caste family of modest means in Kumbakonam in Southern India in 1887. Largely self-taught, Ramanujan, in 1913, wrote a letter to the eminent English mathematician, G. H. Hardy, at Cambridge University in which he included a list of formulas he had discovered. Of the formulas Hardy wrote "(such formulas) defeated me completely . . . a single look at them is enough to show that they were written by a mathematician of the highest class. They must be true because, if they were not true, no one would have

had the imagination to invent them. Finally, (you must remember that I knew nothing about Ramanujan, and had to think of every possibility), the writer must be completely honest, because great mathematicians are commoner than thieves and humbugs of such incredible skill."

In any event, Hardy arranged for Ramanujan to come to England in 1914 and the two collaborated intensively for the next three years with Ramanujan using his unorthodox methods and fantastic intuition to come up with deep and totally unexpected results which Hardy, with his considerable intellectual power and formal training, then proved. Ramanujan fell ill in 1917 and returned to India where he died in 1920.

Littlewood once remarked that every positive integer was one of Ramanujan's friends. Once, during Ramanujan's illness, Hardy visited him

in the hospital in Putney. Trying to find a way to begin the conversation, Hardy remarked that he had come to the hospital in cab number 1729 and that he could not imagine a more uninteresting number. To which Ramanujan replied, "No, it is a very interesting number; it is the smallest number that can be written as the sum of two cubes in two different ways!"*

*$1729 = 9^3 + 10^3 = 1^3 + 12^3$

Solution

(a) Since there are six committee members and 46 students in all, the total number of possible committees is $C(46, 6) = 46 \cdot 45 \cdot 44 \cdot 43 \cdot 42 \cdot 41/6!$. Since there are 24 girls, the number of committees with six girls is $C(24, 6) = 24 \cdot 23 \cdot 22 \cdot 21 \cdot 20 \cdot 19/6!$. Therefore,

$$P(\text{committee has six girls}) = \frac{24 \cdot 23 \cdot 22 \cdot 21 \cdot 20 \cdot 19/6!}{46 \cdot 45 \cdot 44 \cdot 43 \cdot 42 \cdot 41/6!}$$

> Look for common factors in the numerator and denominator to simplify the fraction.

$$= \frac{24 \cdot 23 \cdot 22 \cdot 21 \cdot 20 \cdot 19}{46 \cdot 45 \cdot 44 \cdot 43 \cdot 42 \cdot 41}$$

$$= \frac{76}{5289}$$

$$\doteq 0.014.$$

(b) Here the population is the set of students in Mr. Fleck's class. Thus, P(six girls on committee | all committee members are chosen from Mr. Fleck's class)

$$= \frac{C(13, 6)}{C(23, 6)}$$

$$= \frac{13 \cdot 12 \cdot 11 \cdot 10 \cdot 9 \cdot 8/6!}{23 \cdot 22 \cdot 21 \cdot 20 \cdot 19 \cdot 18/6!}$$

$$= \frac{13 \cdot 12 \cdot 11 \cdot 10 \cdot 9 \cdot 8}{23 \cdot 22 \cdot 21 \cdot 20 \cdot 19 \cdot 18}$$

$$= \frac{52}{3059}$$

$$\doteq 0.017.$$

(c)   The committee is chosen from all the students so the sample space contains $C(46, 6)$ possible committees. Since the three boys must be chosen from among the 22 boys in both classes *and* the three girls must be chosen from among the 24 girls in both classes, we have by the multiplication principle of counting for independent events, that the number of committees with three girls *and* three boys is $C(22, 3) \cdot C(24, 3)$

Thus,

P(three girls and three boys on the committee)

$$= \frac{C(22, 3)C(24, 3)}{C(46, 6)}$$

$$= \frac{22 \cdot 21 \cdot 20}{3 \cdot 2 \cdot 1} \cdot \frac{24 \cdot 23 \cdot 22}{3 \cdot 2 \cdot 1} \cdot \frac{6 \cdot 5 \cdot 4 \cdot 3 \cdot 2 \cdot 1}{46 \cdot 45 \cdot 44 \cdot 43 \cdot 42 \cdot 41}$$

$$= \frac{1760}{5289} \doteq 0.333.$$

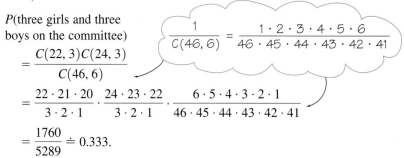

$$\frac{1}{C(46, 6)} = \frac{1 \cdot 2 \cdot 3 \cdot 4 \cdot 5 \cdot 6}{46 \cdot 45 \cdot 44 \cdot 43 \cdot 42 \cdot 41}$$

(d)   Since Ann-Marie and Mary are on the committee, choosing the committee only requires choosing four more students. Thus, the sample space consists of the $C(44, 4)$ students chosen from among the 44 children other than Ann-Marie and Mary. Also, the number of favorable cases is found by selecting one more girl from among the 22 other girls in $C(22, 1)$ ways *and* selecting the three boys in $C(22, 3)$ ways. Thus,

P(committee has three girls and three boys | Mary and Ann-Marie are on the committee)

$$= \frac{C(22, 1)C(22, 3)}{C(44, 4)}$$

$$= \frac{22}{1} \cdot \frac{22 \cdot 21 \cdot 20}{3 \cdot 2 \cdot 1} \cdot \frac{4 \cdot 3 \cdot 2 \cdot 1}{44 \cdot 43 \cdot 42 \cdot 41}$$

$$= \frac{440}{1763} \doteq 0.250.$$

$$\frac{1}{C(44, 4)} = \frac{4 \cdot 3 \cdot 2 \cdot 1}{44 \cdot 43 \cdot 42 \cdot 41}$$

Complementary Events

Suppose a card is drawn from a deck, and A is the event "draw a face card." The set of outcomes *not* in A is called the complementary event, denoted by $\overline{A}$. Since there are 12 face cards in the 52-card deck, we see that

$$n(A) = 12, \quad n(\overline{A}) = 40, \quad P(A) = \frac{12}{52}, \quad P(\overline{A}) = \frac{40}{52}.$$

More generally, if A and $\overline{A}$ are events such that $A \cup \overline{A} = S$ and $A \cap \overline{A} = \varnothing$, then A and $\overline{A}$ are called **complementary events.** Moreover, $n(A) + n(\overline{A}) = n(S)$ and this implies that

$$P(A) + P(\overline{A}) = 1.$$

$$\frac{n(A)}{n(S)} + \frac{n(\overline{A})}{n(S)} = \frac{n(S)}{n(S)}$$

$$P(A) + P(\overline{A}) = 1$$

Alternatively, this implies that

$$P(A) = 1 - P(\overline{A}).$$

In ordinary language, suppose obtaining A is considered success. Then obtaining $\overline{A}$ is failure and we have that

$$P(\text{success}) = 1 - P(\text{failure}).$$

THEOREM *Probability of Complementary Events*

Let A and $\overline{A}$ be complementary events; that is, $A \cup \overline{A} = S$ and $A \cap \overline{A} = \emptyset$. Then

$$P(A) = 1 - P(\overline{A}).$$

Equivalently, the probability of success in an experiment is 1 minus the probability of failure.

The preceding theorem is often useful as this example shows.

EXAMPLE 9.28

Using Complementary Probability

Compute the probability of obtaining a score of at least 4 on a single roll of 2 dice.

Solution

Here success is obtaining a 4 or a 5 or a 6 or . . . or a 12. The probability of doing this is the sum of all the individual probabilities and determining these requires considerable computation. However, failure occurs if we obtain either a sum of 2 or 3 and the probability of doing this is much easier to compute. Since S contains 36 equally likely outcomes and we fail by rolling two 1s, a 1 and a 2, or a 2 and a 1 in order, the probability of failure is $3/36 = 1/12$. Thus, the desired probability is $1 - 1/12 = 11/12$.

Properties of Probability

The preceding examples revealed a number of important properties of probability, which can be collected in the following theorem.

THEOREM *Properties of Probability*

1. $P(A) = 0$ if, and only if, A cannot occur.
2. $P(A) = 1$ if, and only if, A always occurs.
3. For any event A, $0 \le P(A) \le 1$.
4. For any events A and B,

    $$P(A \text{ or } B) = P(A) + P(B) - P(A \text{ and } B).$$

5. If A and B are mutually exclusive events, then

    $$P(A \text{ or } B) = P(A) + P(B).$$

6. For any events A and B,

    $$P(A \text{ and } B) = P(A)P(B \mid A).$$

7. If A and B are independent events, then

    $$P(A \text{ and } B) = P(A)P(B).$$

8. If E and $\overline{E}$ are complementary events, then $P(E) + P(\overline{E}) = 1$.

Chapter 12
Lesson
7

Exploring Fairness

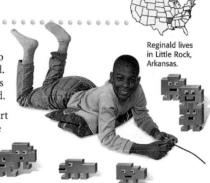

Reginald lives
in Little Rock,
Arkansas.

Problem Solving Connection

- Use Objects/ Act It Out

- Use Logical Reasoning

Materials
number cubes, labeled 1–6

Vocabulary

outcome
the result of an action or event

fair
a game is fair if each player has an equal chance of winning

equally likely
just as likely to happen as not

Explore

"What do I like to do for entertainment? Play video games!" answers Reginald. Sometimes Reginald plays video games with a friend.

In a fair game, players start out with the same chance of winning.

Work Together

1. Play a game of Match Me! with a partner. One person tosses a number cube. The partner then tosses another number cube, trying to match the number from the first toss. Repeat 10 times. Tally your scores. Change roles and play again.

Scoring
The first person gets 1 point when the cubes do not match. The partner gets 1 point when the cubes do match.

2. Play a game of Odds and Evens with a partner. Decide who will be "odds" and who will be "evens." Take turns tossing a number cube 10 times. Record each toss.

Scoring
"Odds" gets 1 point for each outcome of 1, 3, or 5. "Evens" gets 1 point for each outcome of 2, 4, or 6.

3. Which of these two games is fair to both partners? Which game is not fair? Explain your answer.

Talk About It

4. What is a "fair" game? Try to use the words *likely* or *unlikely* in your answer.

5. How could you make the unfair game more fair?

542 Chapter 12 • Dividing by 2-Digit Divisors and Probability

SOURCE: From *Scott Foresman–Addison Wesley Math, Grade 4*, p. 542, by Randall I. Charles, et al. Copyright © 1999, Addison Wesley Longman, Inc.

Questions for the Teacher

1. Kendra observes that just one number makes a match and five numbers make a mismatch. Therefore, reasons Kendra, the Match Me! game can be made fair by giving the second person five attempts to roll a matching number. How would you suggest Kendra check the fairness of this version of Match Me!?

2. Jolie and Kent have invented a new game—Checker Match Me! Six red and six black checkers are put in a bag. Each player in turn draws a checker from the bag (without replacement). The first player gets a point if the checkers have different colors. The second player gets a point if the checkers have the same color. Jolie and Kent think the game is fair, since there are equally many checkers of each color. How would you suggest that Jolie and Kent investigate the fairness of their game?

Proof   Let S be the sample space.

1. Event A cannot occur if, and only if, $n(A) = 0$. Therefore, $P(A) = n(A)/n(S) = 0$ if, and only if, A cannot occur.

2. A always occurs if, and only if, $n(A) = n(S)$. Therefore, $P(A) = n(A)/n(S) = n(S)/n(S) = 1$ if, and only if, A always occurs.

3. An event A never occurs, sometimes occurs, or always occurs. Therefore, $0 \le n(A) \le n(S)$ and, dividing by $n(S)$, we obtain

$$0 \le P(A) \le 1.$$

Divide through by $n(S)$.

4–7. These are general results from earlier representative examples.

8. Since $E \cup \overline{E} = S$ and $E \cap \overline{E} = \varnothing$, it follows that $n(S) = n(E) + n(\overline{E})$ and hence that $1 = P(E) + P(\overline{E})$.

The following example uses several of the properties of probability to reexamine the Strings and Loops Cooperative Investigation found in Section 9.1. This time our point of view is theoretical rather than empirical probability.

EXAMPLE   9.29

Determining the Theoretical Probabilities of the Strings and Loops Activity

Six pieces of string of equal length are held in a bundle in one person's hand. A second person ties three knots at each end of the bundle of strings, where each knot joins a randomly selected pair of strings. After the six knots are tied, the bundle is examined to see what pattern of loops has been formed. There are three possibilities:

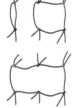

T: three small 2-string loops
M: one medium 4-string loop and one small 2-string loop
L: one large 6-string loop

What are the probabilities (a) $P(T)$, (b) $P(L)$, and (c) $P(M)$ of these events?

Solution

(a) It doesn't matter how the knots at the top of the bundle are tied, since the knots always yield the same pattern shown at the left in the figure on page 578. Event T can be viewed as a three-stage experiment— $T = A$ and B and C—where A, B, and C are the successive events that a loop is tied by the first, second, and third knot. There are six strings to choose from when tying the first knot on the bottom, so the pair to be tied can be chosen in

$$C(6, 2) = \frac{6 \cdot 5}{2} = 15 \text{ ways.}$$ Clearly three pairs result in forming a loop, so

$P(A) = \dfrac{3}{15} = \dfrac{1}{5}.$ After A has occurred, there are four strings left from which to

choose a pair. Therefore, there are $C(4, 2) = \dfrac{4 \cdot 3}{2} = 6$ pairs that can be chosen to

be tied, and two of these pairs form a loop. That is, $P(B \mid A) = \dfrac{2}{C(4,2)} = \dfrac{2}{6} = \dfrac{1}{3}.$

Since the last knot tied is certain to form a loop, we have $P(C \mid A \text{ and } B) = P(C) = 1$. It then follows from the formula on conditional probability that

$$P(T) = P(A \text{ and } B \text{ and } C) = P(A) \cdot P(B \mid A) \cdot P(C) = \frac{1}{5} \cdot \frac{1}{3} \cdot 1 = \frac{1}{15}.$$

(b) For event L to occur, only the last of the three knots tied on the bottom of the bundle can form a loop. That is, $P(L) = P(\overline{A} \text{ and } \overline{B} \text{ and } C)$. By the formula for complementary probabilities, $P(\overline{A}) = 1 - \frac{1}{5} = \frac{4}{5}$. When $\overline{A}$ has occurred there are four strings remaining from which to choose the next pair to tie. Two of these pairs form a loop, so

$$P(\overline{B} \mid \overline{A}) = 1 - P(B \mid \overline{A}) = 1 - \frac{1}{3} = \frac{2}{3}.$$

As in part (a), C is independent of the outcomes of A and B and $P(C) = 1$. Thus

$$P(L) = P(\overline{A} \text{ and } \overline{B} \text{ and } C) = P(\overline{A}) \cdot P(\overline{B} \mid \overline{A}) \cdot P(C) = \frac{4}{5} \cdot \frac{2}{3} \cdot 1 = \frac{8}{15}.$$

(c) The mutually exclusive events T, M, and L include all possible outcomes of the string experiment. Thus $S = T \cup M \cup L$, where S is the sample space. Using the results of parts (a) and (b),

$$1 = P(S) = P(T \text{ or } M \text{ or } L) = P(S) + P(M) + P(L) = \frac{1}{15} + P(M) + \frac{8}{15},$$

so

$$P(M) = 1 - \left(\frac{1}{15} + \frac{8}{15} \right) = \frac{6}{15} = \frac{2}{5}.$$

Most people are surprised to learn that obtaining three small loops is quite rare, and a bit more than half the time a single large loop is formed.

Odds

When someone speaks of the **odds** in favor of an event, E, they are comparing the likelihood that the event will happen to the likelihood that it will not happen. Consider an urn containing four blue balls and one yellow ball. If a ball is chosen at random, what are the odds that the ball is blue? Since a blue ball is four times as likely to be selected as a yellow ball, it is typical to say that the odds are 4 to 1. The odds are actually the ratio 4/1 but, when quoting odds, one usually writes 4 : 1, which is read "four to one." This is the basis for the following definition.

$$A \cup \overline{A} = S$$
$$A \cap \overline{A} = \varnothing$$

> **DEFINITION** *Odds*
> Let A be an event and let $\overline{A}$ be the complementary event. Then the **odds in favor** of A are $n(A)$ to $n(\overline{A})$ and the **odds against** A are $n(\overline{A})$ to $n(A)$.

EXAMPLE 9.30

Determining the Odds in Favor of 7 or 11

In the game of craps one wins on the first roll of the pair of dice if a 7 or 11 is thrown. What are the odds of winning on the first roll?

Solution

Let W be the set of outcomes that result in 7 or 11. Since $W = \{(1, 6), (2, 5), (3, 4), (4, 3), (5, 2), (6, 1), (5, 6), (6, 5)\}$ and there are 36 ways two dice can come up, $n(W) = 8$, and $n(\overline{W}) = 36 - 8 = 28$. Thus, the odds in favor of W are 8 to 28 or, more simply, 2 to 7.

$$\frac{8}{28} = \frac{2}{7}$$

EXAMPLE 9.31

Determining Probabilities from Odds

If the odds in favor of event E are 5 to 4, compute $P(E)$ and $P(\overline{E})$.

Solution

Since E and $\overline{E}$ are complementary, $n(S) = n(E) + n(\overline{E})$. Since the odds in favor of E are 5 to 4, $n(E) = 5k$ and $n(\overline{E}) = 4k$ for some integer k. Therefore,

$$P(E) = \frac{n(E)}{n(S)} = \frac{n(E)}{n(E) + n(\overline{E})} = \frac{5k}{5k + 4k} = \frac{5}{9}$$

and

$$P(\overline{E}) = \frac{n(\overline{E})}{n(S)} = \frac{n(\overline{E})}{n(E) + n(\overline{E})} = \frac{4k}{5k + 4k} = \frac{4}{9}.$$

$\dfrac{n(E)}{n(\overline{E})}$ in lowest terms is 5/4.

EXAMPLE 9.32

Odds from Probabilities

Given $P(E)$, determine the odds in favor of E and the odds against E.

Solution

The odds in favor of E are

$$\frac{n(E)}{n(\overline{E})} = \frac{n(E)/n(S)}{n(\overline{E})/n(S)}$$

$$= \frac{P(E)}{P(\overline{E})}$$

$P(\overline{E}) = 1 - P(E)$

$$= \frac{P(E)}{1 - P(E)}.$$

This last ratio would be expressed as a ratio of integers a/b in lowest terms and the odds quoted as a to b.

The odds against E are given by the reciprocal of the ratio giving the odds in favor of E. Thus, the odds against E are

$$\frac{1 - P(E)}{P(E)} = \frac{b}{a} \qquad \left(= \frac{P(\overline{E})}{P(E)} \right)$$

and are quoted as b to a.

Expected Value

At a carnival you are offered the chance to play a game that consists of rolling a single die just once. If you play, you win the amount in dollars shown on the die. If you play the game several times how much would you expect to win? Of course, you may be lucky and win $6 on each of a series of rolls. However, because of the law of large numbers, you would *expect* to roll a 6 only about 1/6 of the time. Since this is true for each of the numbers on the die, you should expect to win on average approximately

$$= \frac{1}{6} \cdot 1 + \frac{1}{6} \cdot 2 + \frac{1}{6} \cdot 3 + \frac{1}{6} \cdot 4 + \frac{1}{6} \cdot 5 + \frac{1}{6} \cdot 6$$

$$= \frac{1}{6} \cdot (1 + 2 + 3 + 4 + 5 + 6)$$

$$= \frac{1}{6} \cdot 21 = \$3.50$$

per roll. If it costs you $4 to play the game, the carnival confidently expects players to *lose* 50¢ per game on the average. Thus, the carnival stands to make a handsome profit if a large number of patrons play the game each night.

The preceding discussion introduces the notion of **expected value.**

> **DEFINITION**   *Expected Value of an Experiment*
> Let the outcomes of an experiment be a sequence of real numbers (values), $v_1, v_2, \ldots, v_n$, and suppose the outcomes have respective probabilities $p_1, p_2, \ldots, p_n$. Then the **expected value** of the experiment is
>
> $$e = v_1 p_1 + v_2 p_2 + \cdots + v_n p_n.$$

EXAMPLE   9.33

Winning at Roulette

An American roulette wheel has 38 compartments around its rim. Two of these are colored green and are numbered 0 and 00. The remaining compartments are numbered from 1 to 36 and are alternately colored black and red. When the wheel is spun in one direction, a small ivory ball is rolled in the opposite direction around the rim. When the wheel and the ball slow down, the ball eventually falls in any one of the compartments with equal likelihood if the wheel is fair. One way to play is to bet on whether the ball will fall in a red slot or a black slot. If you bet on red for example, you win the amount of the bet if the ball lands in a red slot; otherwise you lose. What is the expected win if you consistently bet $5 on red?

Solution   Since the probability of winning on any given try is 18/38 and the probability of losing is 20/38, your expected win is

$$\frac{18}{38} \cdot 5 + \frac{20}{38} \cdot (-5) = \frac{90 - 100}{38}$$

$$\doteq -0.26.$$

On average you should expect to lose 26¢ per play. Is it any wonder that casinos consistently make a handsome profit?

In the preceding example, it was pretty clear that you should expect to lose slightly more often than win. This next example is less clear.

EXAMPLE   9.34   **Determining the Expected Value of an Unusual Game**

Suppose you are offered the opportunity to play a game that consists of a single toss of three coins. It costs you $21 to play the game and you win $100 if you toss three heads, $20 if you toss two heads and a tail, and nothing if you toss more than one tail. Would you play the game?

Solution   Many people would play the game hoping to "get lucky" and roll HHH frequently. But is this reasonable? What is your expected return? The expected value of the game is

$$\frac{1}{8} \cdot 100 + \frac{3}{8} \cdot 20 + \frac{3}{8} \cdot 0 + \frac{1}{8} \cdot 0 = \frac{160}{8} = \$20.$$

> P(3 heads)
> P(2 heads and 1 tail)
> P(1 head and 2 tails)
> P(3 tails)

Thus, on average you expect to win $1 less than it costs you to play the game each time. Unless the excitement is worth at least $1, you should not play the game.

Geometric Probability

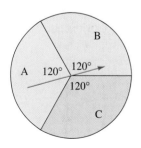

Figure 9.6
A spinner with equally likely outcomes

In Section 9.1, we considered the empirical probability of a spinner marked like that in Figure 9.6 stopping at any particular place. Here $P_e(A)$, $P_e(B)$, and $P_e(C)$ all turn out to be approximately equal to $1/3 = 0.\overline{3}$. This is not surprising since the three arcs bordering regions A, B, and C are equally long. More generally, we would define the theoretical **geometric probability** of a region on the spinner to be the ratio of its corresponding arc length to the circumference of the circle. Equivalently, the probability of stopping a spinner on a sector is the ratio of the measure of the central angle of the sector to 360°.

B.C.   **BY JOHNNY HART**

State lotteries are becoming increasingly numerous and popular. Over $20 billion worth of tickets were sold in 1990 and the figure continues to grow. The big draw is the chance to become an instant multimillionaire, but the chance of doing so is extremely small. Your expected return for each one dollar bet is only about 50 cents. In fact, your chances of winning are much better in Las Vegas or Atlantic City where the expected return on a one dollar bet is 85 to 95 cents. Indeed, the probabilities are constant in the big casinos and knowledgeable gamblers rely on the law of large numbers to predict with considerable accuracy their average winnings over the long term. But the probabilities are constantly changing in a lottery so that this calculation is quite complex. Indeed, it can be shown that, as the lottery jackpot increases and thousands of people rush to buy tickets, the probability of any ticket winning drops so much that the expected value of a dollar bet actually falls below 50 cents. State lotteries constantly produce substantial revenues and the only return for almost all players is the pleasure of imagining themselves becoming instantly wealthy.

Similarly, consider the diagram of Figure 9.7. The probability that a point chosen at random in the square (say by using a sequence of random numbers) will belong to region A should be 1/4 since one-fourth of the *area* of the region lies in A.

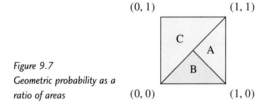

Figure 9.7
Geometric probability as a
ratio of areas

EXAMPLE   9.35 | **Determining the Geometric Probability of a Carnival Game**

At the carnival, a "double your money" game is played by tossing a quarter onto a large table that has been ruled into a grid of squares of the same size. If your quarter lands entirely within any square, you win back two quarters but if the coin touches a grid line, you lose the quarter. If a quarter is 2.5 centimeters in diameter and the squares have sides 6 centimeters long, should you play the game?

Solution | The sample space S can be considered as the points in a 6-by-6-centimeter square. To win, the center of the quarter must land at least 1.25 centimeters from each side of the large square. That is, the winning region W is a 3.5-centimeter square centered in the larger square, as shown in the diagram. The probability of a win is

$$P(W) = \frac{\text{area of small square}}{\text{area of large square}} = \frac{3.5^2}{6^2} = \frac{12.25}{36} = \frac{49}{144} \doteq 0.34.$$

We can now compute the expected value of the game, remembering that a win gives us a net gain of $0.25 (we must subtract the cost of playing from the $0.50 won) and a loss is −$0.25:

$$\text{Expected value} = \frac{49}{144} \cdot \$0.25 + \frac{95}{144} \cdot (-\$0.25) \doteq -\$0.08.$$

We expect to lose, and the operator to win, about eight cents per play.

PROBLEM SET 9.3

Understanding Concepts

1. (a) Explicitly list all the outcomes for the experiment of tossing a penny, a nickel, a dime, and a quarter.

   (b) Determine the probability, $P(\text{HHTT})$, of obtaining a head on each of the penny and nickel and a tail on each of the dime and quarter in the experiment of part (a).

   (c) Determine the probability of obtaining two heads and two tails in the experiment of part (a).

   (d) Determine the probability of obtaining at least one head in the experiment of part (a). (*Hint:* Note that the complementary event consists of obtaining four tails.)

2. Determine the probability of obtaining a total score of 3 or 4 on a single throw of two dice.

3. Acme Auto Rental has three red Fords, four white Fords, and two black Fords. Acme also has six red Hondas, two white Hondas, and five black Hondas. If a car is selected at random for rental to a customer,

   (a) what is the probability that it is a white Ford?

   (b) what is the probability that it is a Ford?

   (c) what is the probability that it is white?

   (d) what is the probability that it is white given that the customer demands a Ford?

4. Five black balls numbered 1, 2, 3, 4, and 5 and seven white balls numbered 1, 2, 3, 4, 5, 6, and 7 are placed in an urn. If one is chosen at random

   (a) what is the probability it is numbered 1 or 2?

   (b) what is the probability that it is numbered 5 or that it is white?

   (c) what is the probability that it is numbered 5 given that it is white?

5. Mrs. Ricco has seven brown-eyed and two blue-eyed brunettes in her fifth grade class. She also has eight blue-eyed and three brown-eyed blondes. A child is selected at random.

   (a) What is the probability that the child is a brown-eyed brunette?

   (b) What is the probability that the child has brown eyes or is a brunette?

   (c) What is the probability that the child has brown eyes given that it is a brunette?

6. Suppose that you randomly select a 2-digit number (that is, one of 00, 01, 02, . . . ,99) from a sequence of random numbers obtained by repeatedly spinning a spinner. What is the probability that the number selected

   (a) is greater than 80?

   (b) is less than 10?

   (c) is a multiple of 3?

   (d) is even or is less than 50?

   (e) is even and is less than 50?

   (f) is even given that it is less than 50?

7. In a certain card game, you are dealt two cards face up. You then bet on whether a third card dealt is between the other two cards. (For example, a 10 is between a 9 and a queen, and so on.) What is the probability of winning your bet if you are dealt

   (a) a 5 and a 7?

   (b) a jack and a queen?

   (c) a pair of 9s?

   (d) a 5 and a queen?

8. In playing draw poker, a flush is a hand with five cards all in one suit. You are dealt five cards and can throw away any of these and be dealt more cards to replace them. If you are dealt four hearts and a spade, what is the probability that you can discard the spade and be dealt a heart to fill out your flush?

9. You are dealt three cards at random from an ordinary deck of playing cards. What is the probability that all three are hearts? (*Hint:* How many ways can you select three cards at random from the deck? How many ways can you select three cards at random from among the hearts?)

10. Consider a spinner made as in Figure 9.2 but marked and shaded as indicated here. The spinner is spun and grasped between your thumb and forefinger while it is still spinning rapidly.

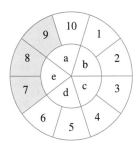

(a) What is the probability that the mark on your thumb is on the shaded area?

(b) What is the probability that your mark falls in regions 1 or 2?

(c) What is the probability that your mark falls in regions 10 or 6?

(d) What is the probability that your mark lands between the two radii that determine region e?

(e) What is the probability that the mark falls in region 8 given that it falls in the shaded area?

(f) What is the probability that it falls in a region marked by a vowel given that it falls in an odd numbered region?

(g) What is the probability that it falls in a region marked by a vowel or an odd number?

11. A dart board is marked as shown.

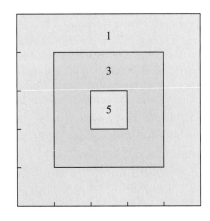

Josie is good enough that she always hits the dart board with her darts but, beyond that, the darts hit in random locations. If a single dart is thrown, compute these probabilities.

(a) $P(1)$ (b) $P(3)$ (c) $P(5)$

(d) If Josie wins the number of dollars indicated by the number of the region in which her dart falls, how much is her expected win (the expected value)?

(e) Suppose it costs Josie $2 each time she throws a dart. Should she play darts as in part (d)? Explain.

12. A dart board is marked like the spinner in problem 10. The radius of the inner circle is 1 and that of the outer circle is 2. What is the probability that a dart hitting the board at random

(a) hits in region b?

(b) misses region b, given it hits the inner circle?

(c) hits in region b given that it hits in a, b, or c?

(d) hits in region 1 given that it hits in a, 1, or 2?

13. Two dice are thrown.

(a) What are the odds in favor of getting a score of 6?

(b) What are the odds against getting a 6?

(c) What is the probability of getting a 6?

14. If $P(A) = 2/5$, compute the odds in favor of A resulting from a single trial of an experiment.

15. If $P(A) = 1/2$, $P(B) = 1/3$, $P(C) = 1/6$, and A, B, and C are mutually exclusive, compute the odds in favor of A or C resulting from a single trial of an experiment.

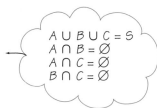

16. Compute the expected value of the score when rolling two dice.

17. A game consists of rolling a pair of dice. You win the amounts shown for rolling the score shown.

Roll	2	3	4	5	6	7	8	9	10	11	12
$ Won	4	6	8	10	20	40	20	10	8	6	4

Compute the expected value of the game.

Thinking Critically

18. Two balls are drawn at random from an urn containing six white and eight red balls.

(a) Compute the probability that both balls are white using combinations. Recall that

$$C(n, r) = \frac{n(n - 1)(n - 2) \cdots (n - r + 1)}{r!}.$$

(b) Compute the probability that both balls are red.

19. An urn contains eight red, five white, and six green balls. Four balls are drawn at random.

(a) Compute P (all four are red).

(b) Compute P (exactly two are red and exactly two are green).

(c) Compute P (exactly two are red or exactly two are green).

20. Consider the set of all 5-letter code words without repetition of letters. (Recall that

$$P(n, r) = n(n - 1)(n - 2) \cdots (n - r + 1).)$$

(a) What is the probability that a code word begins with the letter a?

(b) What is the probability that, in a code word, c is immediately followed by d?

(c) What is the probability that a code word starts with a vowel and ends with a consonant?

(d) In how many of the original set of 5-letter code words are c and d adjacent?

21. Six dice are rolled. What is the probability that all six numbers—1, 2, 3, 4, 5, 6—are obtained? (*Hint:* This can happen in more than one way. For example, 1, 2, 3, 4, 5, 6, and 6, 5, 1, 2, 3, 4 are just two of the possibilities.)

22. What is the probability that the six volumes of Churchill's *Second World War* appear in the correct order if they are randomly placed on a shelf?

23. What is the probability that a randomly dealt 5-card hand from a deck of playing cards will contain

(a) exactly two aces?

(b) at least two aces?

24. If seven dice are tossed, what is the probability that every number will appear? (*Hint:* In how many ways can the number that appears twice be chosen?)

Thinking Cooperatively

25. Modify the Strings and Loops experiment described in Example 9.29 by using eight lengths of string instead of six.

(a) How many patterns of loops can be formed by tying eight knots, four at each end, of the eight-string bundle?

(b) Perform the experiment and combine the data from the class. Use the data to estimate the empirical probabilities that four small loops are formed and one large loop is formed.

(c) Determine the theoretical probability of obtaining four small loops.

(d) Determine the theoretical probability of obtaining one large loop.

26. On a popular TV game show the contestant is asked to select one of three doors. Behind one door is a very valuable prize. Behind another door is a so-so, not very valuable prize. Behind the third door is a joke prize. After the contestant selects a door, but before the prize behind the selected door is revealed, the show host always opens a different door, which reveals one of the two lesser prizes. He then asks the contestant if he or she should like to switch from the door originally chosen and pick the other unopened door instead.

(a) Poll the class to see how many think it is better to switch or stay with the originally chosen door. Now simulate the game, first using the "don't switch" strategy and then using the "switch doors" strategy. An easy way to play the game is to use three paper cups, respectively containing a quarter, a nickel, and a penny to represent the three types of prizes. Which strategy seems to work best?

(b) In small groups, discuss the mathematical probabilities of the two strategies. For example, what is the probability that a contestant following the "don't switch" strategy will get the most valuable prize? What is the probability for a contestant following the "switch doors" strategy?

Using a Calculator

27. There are $7 \times 7 = 7^2$ ways in which two peoples' birthdays can fall on the days of the week. They will have birthdays on different days in 7×6 ways, so the probability two people have birthdays on different days of the week is $P(W_2) = \dfrac{7 \cdot 6}{7 \cdot 7} = \dfrac{6}{7}$. By complementary probabilities, the probability that two people were born on the same day of the week is (not surprisingly) $P(\overline{W}_2) = 1 - P(W_2) = 1 - \dfrac{6}{7} = \dfrac{1}{7}$.

(a) Find the probability $P(W_3)$ that three peoples' birthdays are on different days. Then find the probability $P(\overline{W}_3)$ that, in a group of three people, at least two share a birth on the same day of the week.

(b) Find the probabilities requested in part (a) but for four people.

28. Overlooking February 29th, there are 365 days on which a person's birthday can occur. In a group of five people, their birthdays can occur in 365^5 ways, and their birthdays can be on all different dates of the year in $P(365, 5) = 365 \cdot 364 \cdot 363 \cdot 362 \cdot 361$ ways. Thus, the probability that the five birthdays are distinct is

$$P(Y_5) = \frac{365 \cdot 364 \cdot 363 \cdot 362 \cdot 361}{365 \cdot 365 \cdot 365 \cdot 365 \cdot 365} = \frac{P(365, 5)}{365^5} \doteq 0.97.$$

By complementary probabilities, the probability that at least two of the five have birthdays on the same day of the year is

$$P(\overline{Y}_5) = 1 - \frac{365 \cdot 364 \cdot 363 \cdot 362 \cdot 361}{365 \cdot 365 \cdot 365 \cdot 365 \cdot 365}$$
$$= 1 - \frac{P(365, 5)}{365^5} \doteq 0.03.$$

(a) Calculate $P(Y_{23})$, the probability that there are no common birthdays in a group of 23 people. Then calculate $P(\overline{Y}_{23})$, the probability that at least two people in a group of 23 share a birthday.

(b) Make a table of values $P(\overline{Y}_n)$ for $n = 20, 21, \ldots,$ 30 that gives the probabilities, in a group of n people, that at least two people have birthdays on the same day of the year. (*Suggestion:* Define Y1 = 1 − 365 nPr X/365^X. Under $\boxed{2^{nd}}$ $\boxed{\text{TBLSET}}$ (Table Set) enter TblStart = 20 and ΔTbl = 1. View the table by pressing $\boxed{2^{nd}}$ $\boxed{\text{TABLE}}$).

Making Connections

29. In one unfortunate shipment, 10% of the portable tape players manufactured by Imperfect Electronics had defective switches, 5% had defective batteries, and 2% had both defects. If you purchased a tape player from this shipment, what is the probability that your player

(a) has a defective switch or a defective battery?

(b) has a good switch but a defective battery?

(c) has both a good switch and a good battery?

30. California originally operated a 6/49 lottery, meaning that the grand prize went to a player (or players) who picked the same six numbers that were later drawn at random from the set of numbers 1 through 49. In 1990, California went to a 6/53 lottery, but later the state went to a 6/51 lottery.

(a) Find the probability of winning a 6/49 lottery.

(b) Find the probability of winning a 6/53 lottery.

(c) Find the probability of winning a 6/51 lottery.

(d) Why do you think California changed to a 6/53 lottery?

(e) Why do you think the state went to a 6/51 lottery?

31. In the casino game Keno, the player purchases a ticket and marks eight of the "spots" numbered 1 through 80. Every 20 minutes or so, the casino randomly draws 20 balls from a drum of 80 numbered balls. If sufficiently many of the player's spots are among the 20 numbers, the player wins. Usually the player must have five winning spots to receive a prize, and a larger prize is awarded if six, seven, or all eight winning spots were marked.

(a) What is the probability of marking exactly five winning spots?

(b) What is the probability of marking exactly six winning spots?

(c) What is the probability of marking exactly seven winning spots?

(d) What is the probability of marking exactly eight winning spots?

Communicating

32. A fifth grader tells you she is certain it will rain sometime over the weekend. It seems she heard on the weather forecast that there is a 50% chance of rain both Saturday and Sunday, and of course 50% + 50% = 100%, a certainty. Write an imagined dialog with the student to convince her it may not rain after all.

From State Student Assessments

33. (Washington State, Grade 4)

Special cakes are baked for May Day in France. A small toy is dropped into the batter for each cake before baking. Whoever gets the piece of cake with the toy in it is "king" or "queen" for the day.

Which cake below would give you the best chance of finding the toy in your piece?

A.    B.   C.   D.

For Review

34. In how many ways can you choose four marbles of the same color from an urn containing seven yellow and eight blue marbles?

35. In how many ways can you choose two yellow and three blue marbles from the urn of problem 34?

36. How many 5-letter code words can be made without repetition of letters if vowels and consonants must alternate?

37. How many different permutations are there of the letters a, a, a, a, b, b, c, c, c, c, c?

EPILOGUE   Two Views of Probability

A seventeenth century Frenchman, the Chevalier de Méré, thought that the event of obtaining at least one 1 on four rolls of a die and the event of getting at least two 1s on 24 rolls of a pair of dice were equally likely. He reasoned as follows:

1st event:

- On one roll of a die, there is a 1/6 chance of getting a 1.
- Therefore, on four rolls of a die, the chance of getting at least one 1 is $4 \cdot (1/6) = 2/3$.

2nd event:

- On one roll of a pair of dice the chance of a 2 is 1/36.
- Therefore, on 24 rolls of a pair of dice the chance of at least one 2 is $24 \cdot (1/36) = 2/3$.

In each case, the chance was two-thirds. However, long experience with many trials showed that the first event was slightly more likely than the second and this difficulty became known as the Paradox of the Chevalier de Méré. De Méré asked his friend, the mathematician and philosopher Blaise Pascal, about the problem and Pascal in turn sought the help of the jurist and amateur mathematician, Pierre de Fermat. Together, Pascal and Fermat were able to solve the problem showing that the first event occurs with probability 0.518 and that the second occurs with probability 0.491.

In fact, the study of probability substantially began with the French and in direct response to questions about games of chance, even though it had been considered briefly in the sixteenth century by such mathematicians as the Italian Cardano. Today, probability and statistics play a critical role in society—in public opinion polls, in evaluating experimental data of all sorts, in quality control in manufacturing, in studying the behavior of atoms and of subatomic particles, and in countless other ways.

In this chapter we have considered the basic facts about probability. As revealed in the little vignette about the Chevalier de Méré, we have seen that there are two different but related notions of probability—empirical probability and theoretical probability. The first view of probability is that chance can be measured on the basis of long run experience. It was the experience of the Chevalier that event number one was slightly more likely than event number two even though his analysis suggested otherwise. The assertion based on experience was an expression of empirical probability—namely

$$P_e(\text{event number one}) > P_e(\text{event number two}).$$

The paradox was cleared up by Pascal and Fermat using strict mathematical principles that formed the genesis of theoretical probability. Much of the thrust of this chapter has been to show that these two notions are closely intertwined. Recall that the law of large numbers asserts that the empirical probability of an event more and more closely approaches the theoretical probability of the event as the number of trials is made larger and larger.

We have given attention to developing the ideas of probability in both senses and have seen in Chapter 8 how the interpretation of data, based on probability principles, can lead to surprisingly accurate conclusions. Without this kind of careful analysis, however, action based on collected data can lead to disastrous results.

CHAPTER 9 SUMMARY

Key Concepts

The goal of this chapter has been to develop the basic ideas of empirical probability, methods of counting, and theoretical probability.

It is convenient to think of an event as the result of an experiment:

- The empirical probability of an event is the fraction of times it occurs among a large number of trials.
- The theoretical probability of an event is the ratio of the number of times the event occurs in a sample space of equally likely outcomes to the number of outcomes in the sample space.
- The law of large numbers asserts that the empirical probability of an event more and more closely approximates the theoretical probability as the number of repetitions of the experiment becomes larger and larger.

Computing the theoretical probability of an event necessitated developing certain methods of counting:

- $n(A \text{ or } B) = n(A) + n(B) - n(A \cap B)$
  If $A \cap B = \varnothing$, $n(A \text{ or } B) = n(A) + n(B)$.
- If A is a set and B is a subset of r elements of A, then B is called a combination of r elements of A.
- If A is a set and B is an ordered sequence of r elements of A, then B is called a permutation of r elements of A.
- For $n \geq 1$, the notation $n!$, read n factorial, is defined by
  $n! = n(n-1)(n-2) \cdots 1$. Also, $0! = 1$.
- The number of combinations of n things taken r at a time is
  $$C(n, r) = \frac{n(n-1)(n-2) \cdots (n-r+1)}{r!}.$$
- The number of permutations of n things taken r at a time is
  $$P(n, r) = n(n-1)(n-2) \cdots (n-r+1).$$

The properties of theoretical probability correspond closely to the properties of counting. We consider only a finite sample space S of equally likely outcomes:

- $P(A) = 0$ if, and only if, A cannot occur.
- $P(A) = 1$ if, and only if, A must occur.
- For any A, $0 \leq P(A) \leq 1$.
- If A and $\overline{A}$ are complementary events so that $A \cup \overline{A} = S$ and $A \cap \overline{A} = \varnothing$, then
  $P(A) = 1 - P(\overline{A})$.

- $P(A \text{ or } B) = P(A) + P(B) - P(A \cap B)$. If A and B are mutually exclusive events, then $P(A \text{ or } B) = P(A) + P(B)$.
- $P(A \text{ and } B) = P(A) \cdot P(B \mid A)$. If A and B are independent events, then $P(A \text{ and } B) = P(A) \cdot P(B)$.

Vocabulary and Notation

Section 9.1

Outcome
Sample space, S
Event, $E \subseteq S$
Compound event
Mutually exclusive events
Independent events
Empirical probability of event E, $P_e(E)$
Law of large numbers
Empirical probability and geometry
Simulation

Section 9.2

Addition principle of counting
Addition principle of counting for mutually exclusive events
Two-stage experiment
Possibility tree
Multiplication principle of counting for dependent events

Multiplication principle of counting for independent events
Factorial, $n!$
Permutations
Number of permutations of n objects r at a time, $P(n, r)$
Combinations
Number of combinations of n objects r at a time, $C(n, r)$

Section 9.3

Theoretical probability or probability
Sample space, S
Outcome
Event, E
Probability of an event, $P(E)$
Equally likely
Conditional probability, $P(A \mid B)$
Complementary events, E and $\overline{E}$
Odds
Expected value
Geometric probability

CHAPTER REVIEW EXERCISES

Section 9.1

1. Toss four coins 20 times and determine the empirical probability of obtaining three heads and one tail.
2. (a) Roll three dice 20 times and determine the empirical probability of obtaining a total score of 3 or 4.
   (b) From the data in part (a) determine the empirical probability of obtaining a score of at least 5.
3. From the data of problem 2, determine

$$P_e(5 \text{ or } 6 \text{ or } 7 \mid 5 \text{ or } 6 \text{ or } 7 \text{ or } 8 \text{ or } 9).$$

4. Conduct a survey of 20 randomly chosen college students at your college or university and determine the empirical probability that chocolate is the favorite flavor of ice cream.
5. (a) Drop five thumbtacks on a table top 20 times and determine the empirical probability that precisely three of the tacks land point up.

   (b) From the data of part (a) determine the empirical probability that two or three of the five tacks in part (a) land point up.
6. (a) A die is rolled repeatedly until a 5 or a 6 appears. Perform this experiment ten times and estimate the number of rolls required.
   (b) From the data in part (a), compute the empirical probability that it takes precisely five rolls to obtain a 5 or 6 for the first time.
7. Shuffle a deck of cards and select a card at random. Return the card to the deck, shuffle, and draw again for a total of 20 trials.
   (a) Compute $P_e(\text{ace or heart})$.
   (b) Compute $P_e(\text{ace and heart})$.
   (c) Compute $P_e(\text{ace} \mid \text{heart})$.
8. Number a set of 3″ by 5″ note cards from 1 to 10. Shuffle the deck thoroughly and deal the cards face up on a table while at the same time counting the number

of cards dealt. If the number of the card is the same as the number of cards dealt, say you have a match. For example, if the sixth card dealt is the card with a 6 on it you have a match. Perform the experiment 25 times and compute the empirical probability that a match occurs.

Section 9.2

9. (a) Three coins are tossed. Make an orderly list of all possible outcomes.
   (b) In how many ways can you obtain two heads and one tail?

10. (a) How many ways can you select nine players for a baseball team from among 15 players if any player can play any position?
    (b) How many ways can you select the team in part (a) if only two players can pitch and only three others can catch? Note that these five players can also play all other positions.

11. (a) All of the 90 students in Ferry Hall speak at least one of French, English, or German. If 38 speak English, 24 speak French and English, 27 speak German and English, and 17 speak German, French, and English, how many speak German or French?
    (b) How many of the students in part (a) speak French and English but not German?

12. (a) How many ways can you select two clubs from an ordinary deck of playing cards?
    (b) How many ways can you select two face cards from an ordinary deck of playing cards?
    (c) How many ways can you select two clubs or two face cards from an ordinary deck of playing cards?

13. (a) How many 5-letter code words can be made if repetition of letters is not allowed?
    (b) How many of the 5-letter code words in part (a) start and end with vowels?
    (c) How many of the code words of part (a) contain the 3-letter sequence aef?

14. (a) In how many ways can the letters in STREETS be placed in recognizably different orders?
    (b) In how many of the orderings of part (a) are the two Es adjacent?
    (c) How many of the orderings in part (a) begin with a T?

Section 9.3

15. (a) Explicity list all elements in the sample space if two coins and a die are tossed.

(b) Compute $P(T, T, 5)$, the probability of getting two tails on the coins and 5 on the die in part (a).

16. Compute $P(5 \mid T, T)$, the probability of obtaining 5 on the die given that both coins came up tails in problem 15.

17. Compute the probability of obtaining a sum of at most 11 on a single roll of two dice.

18. An urn contains five white, six red, and four black balls. Two balls are chosen at random.
    (a) What is the probability that they are the same color?
    (b) What is the probability that both are white?
    (c) What is the probability that both are white given that they are the same color?

19. Consider a spinner made as shown in Figure 9.2 but marked as indicated here. Compute these probabilities.

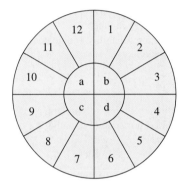

(a) $P(\text{b and } 8)$ (b) $P(\text{b or } 8)$ (c) $P(\text{b} \mid 8)$
(d) $P(\text{b and } 2)$ (e) $P(\text{b or } 2)$ (f) $P(2 \mid \text{b})$

20. Three coins are tossed.
    (a) What are the odds in favor of getting two heads and one tail?
    (b) What are the odds in favor of getting three heads?

21. (a) If $P(A) = 0.85$, what are the odds in favor of A occurring on any given trial?
    (b) If the odds in favor of A are 17 to 8, determine $P(A)$.

22. You play a game where you win the amount shown with the probability shown.

$$P(\$5) = 0.50 \qquad P(\$10) = 0.25 \qquad P(\$20) = 0.10$$

(a) What is the expected value of the game?
(b) If it costs you $10 to play the game of part (a), is it wise to play? Explain.

23. A census taker was told by a neighbor that a family of five lived in the next house—two parents and three children. When the census taker visited the house, he was greeted by a girl. What is the probability that the other two children were both boys? Explain briefly.

CHAPTER TEST

1. We claim that the probability is about 0.6 that a person shown a card with the numbers 1, 2, 3, 4 printed on it will, when asked, choose the number 3. How can such a probability be calculated? Explain briefly.

1 2 3 4

2. What kind of probability is used when an assertion like, "the probability that penicillin will cure a case of strep throat is 0.9" is made? Explain briefly.
3. Calculate each of the following.
   (a) $7!$ (b) $\frac{9!}{6!}$ (c) $\frac{8!}{(8-8)!}$ (d) $7 \cdot 6!$
   (e) $P(8, 5)$ (f) $P(8, 8)$ (g) $C(9, 3)$
   (h) $C(9, 9)$
4. In Mrs. Spangler's calculus class all of the students are also studying one or more foreign languages. If
   27 students study French,
   29 students study German,
   17 students study Chinese,
   12 students study German and French,
   3 students study German and Chinese,
   2 students study French and Chinese,
   1 student studies French, German, and Chinese
   (a) How many students are in Mrs. Spangler's class?
   (b) How many students in the class study Chinese only?
   (c) How many students study French and German but not Chinese?
5. An urn contains five distinct yellow, four distinct blue, and eight distinct green marbles. Five marbles are selected.
   (a) In how many ways can one select five green marbles?
   (b) In how many ways can one select five yellow and five green marbles?
   (c) In how many ways can one select five yellow or five green marbles?
6. If you select five marbles from the urn in problem 5, what is the probability that two are yellow given that three are green?
7. What are the odds in favor of selecting a yellow marble if a single marble is drawn from the urn described in problem 5?
8. If $P(E) = 0.35$, what are the odds of obtaining E on a single trial of an experiment?
9. How many 4-letter code words can be made using the letters a, b, c, d, e, f, and g
   (a) with repetition allowed?
   (b) with repetition not allowed?
10. How many of the code words in problem 9, part (b),
    (a) begin with a vowel?
    (b) have c and d adjacent?

CHAPTER

10

Geometric Figures

10.1   Figures in the Plane
10.2   Curves and Polygons in the Plane
10.3   Figures in Space
10.4   Networks

HANDS ON
Exploring Polygons

Materials Needed

1. Colored pencils, ruler (in millimeters), protractor, unlined paper.

2. A set of 16 equilateral triangles and squares cut from patterns photocopied onto card stock. Each set consists of two of each of the following shapes. The segments drawn on the figures meet the sides at their midpoints. A small hole is punched at the center of each shape where the lines cross.

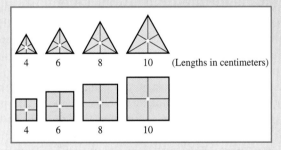

4   6   8   10   (Lengths in centimeters)

4   6   8   10

Directions

The cardstock triangles and squares will be arranged on a sheet of blank paper to form a new figure. Your goal is to discover, describe, and explore any patterns and unexpected relationships that you see in the figures.

Exploring Quadrilaterals

Choose any four card stock squares and arrange them corner to corner, as on the left below. Place pencil points at the corners *A, B, C, D,* at the midpoints *M, N, P, Q,* and at the centers *W, X, Y, Z,* of the squares. Then remove the square patterns and connect the points with line segments as shown in the figure at the right.

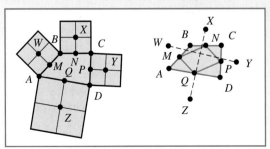

1. Does anything seem special about the quadrilateral (four-sided polygon) *MNPQ?*

2. Compare the line segment $\overline{XZ}$ (the one with endpoints *X* and *Z*) with the line segment $\overline{YW}$.

3. Suppose that the squares are chosen so that sides $\overline{AB}$ and $\overline{CD}$ are the same length, and $\overline{BC}$ and $\overline{AD}$ are the same length. What seems to be special about the quadrilateral *WXYZ?*

Exploring Triangles

Choose any three card stock triangles, place them corner to corner, and locate the points forming the right hand figure.

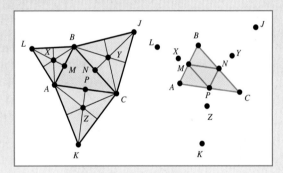

1. Compare the shapes of the triangles *ABC, AMP, BMN, CPN,* and *MNP.*

2. What is special about triangle *XYZ?*

3. Draw the line segments $\overline{AN}$, $\overline{BP}$, and $\overline{CM}$. What happens?

4. Draw the line segments $\overline{AJ}$, $\overline{BK}$, and $\overline{CL}$. What happens?

5. Draw the line segments $\overline{AY}$, $\overline{BZ}$, and $\overline{CX}$. What happens?

The Nature of Informal Geometry

This chapter is the first of five dealing with topics in geometry which have importance to the teacher of elementary school mathematics. To understand the approach in these chapters it is necessary to know what we mean by geometry—and what we do not mean. Geometry for us means the informal study of shape. The three words in this description— *informal, shape,* and *study*—warrant some discussion.

Informal. Until about 600 B.C. geometry was pursued in response to practical, artistic, and religious needs. The pyramids of ancient Egypt (c. 2500 B.C.) and the Stonehenge observatory (c. 2800 B.C.) provide evidence that complex problems of form and measurement were solved even in Neolithic times. Over the centuries people built and interacted with a variety of patterns, objects, and structures. The shapes that recurred most often were named and some of their properties were discovered. Considerable knowledge of geometry was accumulated, but mathematics was not yet an organized and independent discipline, and the ideas of proof and deduction were still absent.

In the period 600–300 B.C., Thales, Pythagoras, Zeno, Eudoxus, Euclid, and others organized this accumulated knowledge and experience, and transformed geometry into a theoretical science. Utilitarian considerations gave way to abstraction and general methods. With Euclid's *Elements,* geometry became a formal system in which geometric theorems were deduced logically from a list of statements called axioms that were accepted with no need to be proved. To many people, geometry is restricted to a Euclidean formalism in which exacting standards of proof and logical development must be met.

In this text, however, we return to learning by trusting our intuition and experience. Geometric facts are discovered by explorations with pictorial representations and physical models, with little attention given to the overall logical structure. This models the levels of learning geometry that were identified by the van Hieles' research (see Into the Classroom in Section 10.2). However, there will be many opportunities to verify patterns and conjectures by examining the consequences of properties and facts that have already been accepted.

Shape. Marjorie Senechal* points out that "shape" is an undefinable term, partly because we must leave room for new shapes as they are discovered. For example, fractals and CAT scan images are shapes of current interest and importance, made possible by a combination of mathematics and computers. For us, the shapes of interest will most often be figures such as polygons and curves, cubes and spheres, which are familiar in classical geometry.

Study. In common with geometers of ancient times, our goals are: to recognize differences and similarities among shapes; to analyze the properties of a shape or class of shapes; and to model, construct, and draw shapes in a variety of ways. These goals are inseparably intertwined, but it will be seen that the discussion follows three threads of development: *classification, analysis,* and *representation.*

Materials for Explorations

Many examples will be presented in the form of an *exploration.* First, you will represent a shape, perhaps with a drawing or physical model, that satisfies the stated conditions. You are next asked to discover, analyze, and describe the properties of the shape. Often you will not want to read further until you have followed the directions and made

---

*See "Shape," a chapter of *On the Shoulders of Giants: New Approaches to Numeracy,* L. A. Steen, ed., National Academy Press, Washington D. C., 1990.

some discoveries for yourself; only then should you read on to see if the patterns and relationships you have uncovered agree with those discussed in the text.

The following tools and materials will be useful to draw, construct, or create the shapes you will explore:

- colored pencils
- ruler (best if marked in both inches and millimeters)
- compass (be sure it is of good quality)
- tape
- glue
- protractor
- drafting triangles (30°−60°−90° and 45°−45°−90°)
- scissors
- unlined paper
- graph paper
- dot paper in both square and triangular patterns

A variety of manipulatives are available from commercial suppliers and are of great value in the study of geometry. Hopefully, you will have access to such items as:

- geoboards
- tangrams
- pattern blocks
- geometric solids (wood or plastic)
- pentominoes
- reflective drawing tool such as a Mira®

from The NCTM Principles and Standards

Geometry in Grades 3–5

Geometry includes the study of two- and three-dimensional shapes, properties and relationships of these shapes, and movement and location in space. In the primary grades students construct and examine shapes, describe their attributes, and sort them across various dimensions, such as which three-dimensional shapes roll and which do not, or which four-sided plane figures have square corners and which do not. They begin to develop and use a basic vocabulary related to these shapes but do not develop precise meanings for many of the terms they use.

The growing reasoning skills of students in grades 3–5 allow them to investigate geometrical problems of increasing complexity and to study how geometric terms relate to geometric objects. As they move from grade 3 to grade 5, they develop clarity and precision in describing properties of geometric objects and classifying objects by these properties into categories such as rectangle, triangle, pyramid, or prism. They learn about the relationships between two- and three-dimensional objects by describing the features of three-dimensional objects, representing three-dimensional objects in two dimensions, and constructing or identifying three-dimensional objects by analyzing two-dimensional representations of those objects, such as views, nets, or isometric drawings. They develop knowledge about how geometric shapes are related to each other and begin to articulate geometric arguments about the properties of these shapes. As students investigate geometric properties and relationships, their work is closely connected with other mathematical strands, especially measurement and number.

The study of geometry in grades 3–5, as in pre-K–2, should be active. It requires the use of visual images and concrete materials. Students sort, build, model, trace, measure, and construct. They make and test conjectures and justify their thinking. This exploration requires access to a variety of concrete tools such as graph paper, rulers, compasses, pattern blocks, geoboards, and geometric solids and is greatly enhanced by computer software tools that support exploration.

SOURCE: Reprinted with permission from *Curriculum and Evaluation Standards for School Mathematics: Discussion Draft,* copyright 1998 by the National Council of Teachers of Mathematics. All rights reserved.

10.1   Figures in the Plane

The shapes in the Picture Gallery of Plane Figures (page 597) and the Picture Gallery of Space Figures (page 638) are each highly complex when viewed as a whole, but underlying this complexity is an orderly arrangement of simpler parts. In this section we consider the most basic shapes of geometry: points, lines, segments, rays, and angles.

Points and Lines

A point on paper is represented by a dot. A point on a television monitor is represented by a small rectangle of phosphors called a pixel that glows when excited by a beam of electrons. Neither a dot nor a pixel is an exact representation of a geometric point. In the mind's eye, dots and pixels are decreased in size until they become ideal **points,** that is, just locations in space. On paper we still draw dots to represent points, and we label the points with uppercase letters as shown.

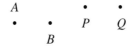

Line, like point, is undefined but its meaning is suggested by a tightly stretched thread, or a laser beam, or the edge of a ruler. We assume that any two points determine one and only one line which contains the two points. Lines will often be denoted with lower case letters such as l and m. If A and B are two points then the line through A and B is denoted by $\overleftrightarrow{AB}$. On paper, lines can be drawn with either a ruler or a **straightedge.** A straightedge is like a ruler but without any marks on it.

The arrows in the drawings and in the notation $\overleftrightarrow{AB}$ indicate that lines extend infinitely far in two directions.

A Picture Gallery of Plane Figures

Fissures in a gelatinous preparation of tin oil

Butterfly wings

M. C. Escher's sketch of a wall mosaic in the Alhambra

A snow crystal

A fractal, an example of a complex beautiful image created with the computer.

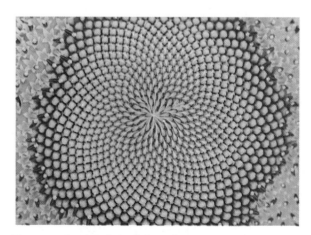

The pattern of seeds in the head of a sunflower.

WINDOW ON TECHNOLOGY
Dynamic Geometry Software

Several newly developed computer programs are now available to create geometric figures and investigate their properties. One of these programs, *The Geometer's Sketchpad,** is described in Appendix D.

Geometry programs allow the user to construct and label nearly any geometric shape. This includes points, lines, segments, and rays, and more sophisticated shapes such as circular sectors and polygon interiors. Existing elements of the figure can also be used to construct new elements of the figure. For example, given a line segment, the software can quickly construct the midpoint of the segment. Or, given a line and a point, the software will easily construct the line through the point that is parallel to the selected line. Similarly, points of intersection, perpendiculars, angle bisectors, and so on are quickly and easily constructed—certainly a welcome contrast to classical compass and ruler constructions. Moreover, once a figure has been created, its lengths, angles, area, perimeter, and other properties can be measured to high precision by the software itself.

The most exciting aspect of the new software is its dynamic nature. By clicking and dragging on a point or line of the figure, the figure can be manipulated into new shapes. For example, a line segment can be stretched or moved to new positions. If a midpoint of the segment had been constructed, the manipulation will continuously move the midpoint so that it is *always* a midpoint of the moving segment. Likewise, if a line perpendicular or parallel to the manipulated line had been constructed, these lines will automatically move to continue to be always parallel or perpendicular to the manipulated line.

The example below demonstrates the power of dynamic geometry software. First, a convex quadrilateral *ABCD* and its interior (shown lightly shaded) were constructed, as seen below at the left. Then the midpoints *E, F, G, H* of the sides were constructed, along with the segments $\overline{AF}$, $\overline{BG}$, $\overline{CH}$, and $\overline{DE}$. Finally, the intersections of these segments were constructed to form the quadrilateral *IJKL* and its interior (shown darkly shaded). The areas of the quadrilaterals *ABCD* and *IJKL* were measured and their ratio computed. As the measurements displayed in the left-hand figure show, the area of the small quadrilateral is 0.200, or one-fifth, of the area of the large quadrilateral. Was this an accident? To explore this question, we can drag a point, say *C*, to a new position as seen in the middle drawing. The areas of the shaded quadrilaterals have both changed, but not their ratio. At the right, we have manipulated the quadrilateral *ABCD* even more, but the ratio of areas has remained unchanged. We can now be confident that dynamic geometry software has revealed a general principle.

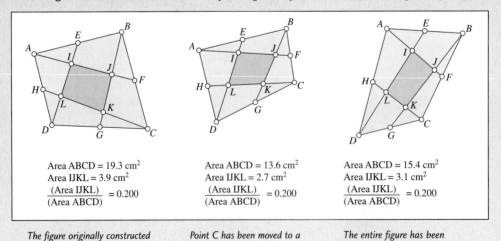

Area ABCD = 19.3 cm²
Area IJKL = 3.9 cm²
$$\frac{(\text{Area IJKL})}{(\text{Area ABCD})} = 0.200$$

Area ABCD = 13.6 cm²
Area IJKL = 2.7 cm²
$$\frac{(\text{Area IJKL})}{(\text{Area ABCD})} = 0.200$$

Area ABCD = 15.4 cm²
Area IJKL = 3.1 cm²
$$\frac{(\text{Area IJKL})}{(\text{Area ABCD})} = 0.200$$

The figure originally constructed and its measurements.

Point C has been moved to a new position.

The entire figure has been manipulated. However, the ratio of areas is unchanged.

*A free demonstration version can be downloaded from Key Curriculum Press' Web site, www.keypress.com.

Three or more points usually determine several lines, but if they lie on just one line then we say the points are **collinear** as shown in Figure 10.1.

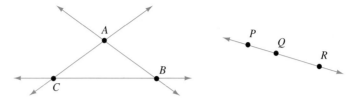

A, B, C are noncollinear points.   P, Q, R are collinear points.

Figure 10.1
Three points determine either three lines or one line.

Three noncollinear points determine a **plane,** which is yet another undefined term used to describe a set of points which idealize a flat space such as a table top. In this section we consider only sets of points which belong to a single plane. Subsets of a plane are called **plane figures** or **plane shapes.** In a later section we explore solid shapes in which not all of the points belong to a single plane.

Two lines in the plane which do not have a point in common are called **parallel.** We write $l \parallel m$ if l and m are parallel lines. Two distinct lines p and q which are not parallel must have a single point in common, called their **point of intersection,** and we write $p \nparallel q$. Three lines can intersect at 0, 1, 2, or 3 points. In the case of one point of intersection, the three lines are said to be **concurrent.** A line which intersects two other lines is called a **transversal.** The different ways in which two or three lines can be arranged in the plane are shown in Figure 10.2.

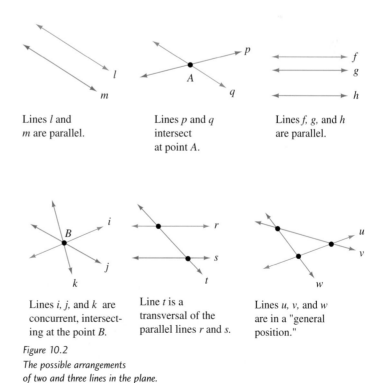

Lines l and
m are parallel.

Lines p and q
intersect
at point A.

Lines f, g, and h
are parallel.

Lines i, j, and k are
concurrent, intersect-
ing at the point B.

Line t is a
transversal of the
parallel lines r and s.

Lines u, v, and w
are in a "general
position."

Figure 10.2
The possible arrangements
of two and three lines in the plane.

EXAMPLE 10.1 | **Exploring Collinearity and Concurrency**

(a)   Draw three circles, C_1, C_2, and C_3 of different sizes, with no circle containing or intersecting another circle. Then draw two lines externally tangent to the circles C_1 and C_2 as shown, and let P denote the point of intersection.

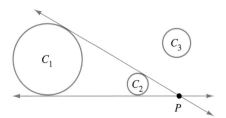

In the same way use your ruler to draw the two lines externally tangent to C_2 and C_3, and let Q be their point of intersection. Finally, draw the external tangents of C_1 and C_3, and let R be their point of intersection. What conjecture do you have concerning P, Q, and R?

(b)   Use a compass (or trace around a cup bottom) to draw an accurate circle. Then use a ruler to draw any three lines that are tangent to the circle, at points labeled X, Y, and Z, and which intersect in pairs at the points labeled A, B, and C. Finally, draw the lines $\overleftrightarrow{AX}$, $\overleftrightarrow{BY}$, and $\overleftrightarrow{CZ}$ (not shown below). What conjecture can you make about $\overleftrightarrow{AX}$, $\overleftrightarrow{BY}$, and $\overleftrightarrow{CZ}$?

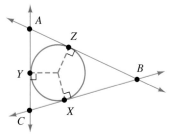

Solution

(a) P, Q, and R are collinear
(b) $\overleftrightarrow{AX}$, $\overleftrightarrow{BY}$, $\overleftrightarrow{CZ}$ are concurrent.

© 1990 CREATORS SYNDICATE, INC.

Line Segments and the Distance Between Points

Let A and B be any two points. The line $\overleftrightarrow{AB}$ will be viewed as a copy of the number line. That is, every point on $\overleftrightarrow{AB}$ corresponds to a unique real number and every real number corresponds to a unique point on $\overleftrightarrow{AB}$. If A and B correspond to the real numbers x and y respectively, then the absolute value, $|x - y|$, gives the **distance** between A and B. We denote this distance by AB.

> AB with no overbar denotes the length of segment $\overline{AB}$

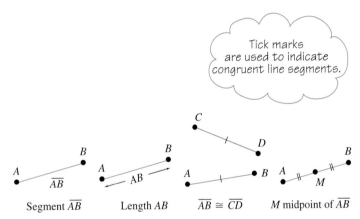

The points on the line $\overleftrightarrow{AB}$ which are between A and B, together with A and B themselves, form the **line segment** $\overline{AB}$. Points A and B are called the **endpoints** of $\overline{AB}$ and the distance AB is the **length** of $\overline{AB}$. It is important to see that the overbar used in the notation distinguishes the real number AB from the line segment $\overline{AB}$.

Two segments $\overline{AB}$ and $\overline{CD}$ are said to be **congruent** if they have the same length. This is symbolized by writing $\overline{AB} \cong \overline{CD}$. Thus, $\overline{AB} \cong \overline{CD}$ if, and only if, $AB = CD$. The point M in $\overline{AB}$ which is the same distance from A and B is called the **midpoint** of $\overline{AB}$. This is summarized in Figure 10.3.

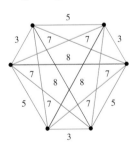
> Tick marks are used to indicate congruent line segments.

Figure 10.3
A segment $\overline{AB}$, its length AB, congruent segments, and the midpoint M of $\overline{AB}$

Rays, Angles, and Angle Measure

A **ray** is a subset of a line which contains a point P, the **endpoint** of the ray, and all points on the line lying to one side of P. If Q is any point of the ray other than P, then $\overrightarrow{PQ}$ denotes the ray. The union of two rays with a common endpoint is an **angle.** If the rays are $\overrightarrow{AB}$ and $\overrightarrow{AC}$ then the angle is denoted by $\angle BAC$. The common endpoint of the two rays is called the **vertex** of the angle and is the middle letter in the symbol for angle. The points B and C not at the vertex can be written in either order, so that $\angle CAB$ denotes the same angle as $\angle BAC$. The rays $\overrightarrow{AB}$ and $\overrightarrow{AC}$ are called the **sides** of the angle. See Figure 10.4.

An angle whose sides are not on the same line partitions the remaining points of the plane into two parts, the **interior** and the **exterior** of the angle. The points along a line segment which joins an endpoint on side $\overrightarrow{AB}$ to an endpoint on $\overrightarrow{AC}$ are all interior points of $\angle BAC$.

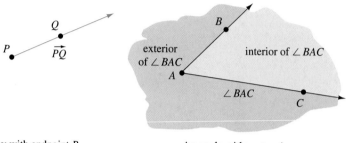

Figure 10.4
A ray $\overrightarrow{PQ}$ and an angle $\angle BAC$

A ray with endpoint P
which contains point Q.

An angle with vertex A
and sides $\overrightarrow{AB}$ and $\overrightarrow{AC}$.

If $\angle BAC$ is the only angle with its vertex at A, it is common to write $\angle A$ in place of $\angle BAC$. When more than one angle has a vertex at A, it is essential to use the full three letter symbol. Sometimes it is useful to number the angles which appear in a drawing and refer to $\angle 1$, $\angle 2$, $\angle 3$, and so on.

The size of an angle is measured by the amount of rotation required to turn one side of the angle to the other by pivoting about the vertex. The **measure of an angle** is generally given in **degrees,** where there are 360° in a full revolution. The measure of $\angle A$ is denoted by $m(\angle A)$. If the rotation is imagined to pass through the interior of the angle, the measure is a number between 0° and 180°. Unless stated otherwise, $m(\angle A)$ is the measure of $\angle A$ not larger than 180°. In some applications the measure of interest corresponds to the rotation through the exterior of the angle and is therefore a number between 180° and 360°.

An angle with measure greater than 180° but less than 360° is called a **reflex angle.** An angle of measure 180° is a **straight angle,** an angle of 90° measure is a **right angle,** and an angle of measure 0° is a **zero angle.** Angles measuring between 0° and 90° are **acute,** and angles measuring between 90° and 180° are **obtuse.** The classification of angles according to their measure is summarized in Figure 10.5.

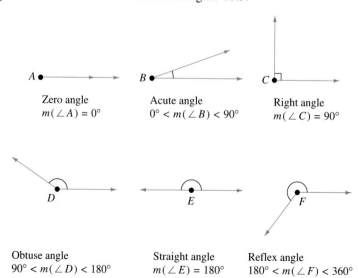

Figure 10.5
*The classification of angles by
their measure*

Zero angle
$m(\angle A) = 0°$

Acute angle
$0° < m(\angle B) < 90°$

Right angle
$m(\angle C) = 90°$

Obtuse angle
$90° < m(\angle D) < 180°$

Straight angle
$m(\angle E) = 180°$

Reflex angle
$180° < m(\angle F) < 360°$

Right angles in drawings are indicated by a small square placed at the vertex. A circular arc is required to indicate reflex angles.

Two lines *l* and *m* that intersect at right angles are called **perpendicular** lines. This is indicated in writing by $l \perp m$. Similarly, two rays, or two segments, or a segment and a ray, are perpendicular if they are contained in perpendicular lines.

Two angles are **congruent** if, and only if, they have the same measure. The symbol $\cong$ is used to denote the congruence of angles. Thus,

$$\angle P \cong \angle Q \text{ if, and only if, } m(\angle P) = m(\angle Q).$$

The **protractor** is used both to measure angles and to draw angles having a given measure. The protractor and other traditional tools useful for drawing and measuring are shown in Figure 10.6. Increasingly, these tools are being supplemented and replaced by the availability of geometry software for the computer.

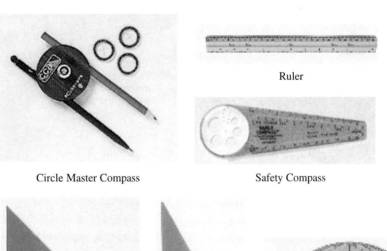

Circle Master Compass

Ruler

Safety Compass

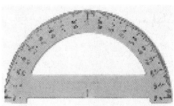

Figure 10.6
Some useful tools for measuring and drawing geometric figures

45°-45°-90°   30°-60°-90°
Drafting triangles

Protractor

EXAMPLE   10.2

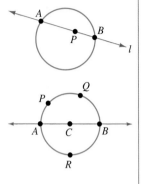

Exploring Angles and Distances in a Circle

(a) Draw a circle and choose any point *P*, other than the center, inside the circle. Any line *l* through *P* intersects the circle in two points, say *A* and *B*. Measure the distances *PA* and *PB* (to the nearest millimeter) and compute the product *PA* · *PB*. Draw several lines through *P* and measure the distances of the two segments. Which line through *P* makes the product of distances, *AP* · *PB*, as large as possible?

(b) Draw a circle with center *C*. Draw a line through *C*, and let *A* and *B* denote its intersections with the circle. Choose any three points *P*, *Q*, and *R* on the circle other than *A* or *B*. Use a protractor to measure ∠*APB*, ∠*AQB*, and ∠*ARB*. What general result does this suggest?

Solution

(a) For every choice of *l*, the product *AP* · *PB* is the same. Therefore no line through *P* gives a larger product than any other line.

(b) Each angle is a right angle. This is one of geometry's earliest theorems, attributed to Thales of Miletus (c. 600 B.C.).

Pairs of Angles and the Corresponding Angles Theorem

As shown in Figure 10.7, two angles are **complementary** if the sum of their measures is 90°. Similarly, two angles are **supplementary** if their measures sum to 180°.

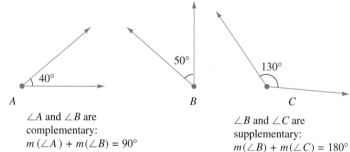

Figure 10.7
Examples of complementary and supplementary angles

∠*A* and ∠*B* are complementary:
$m(\angle A) + m(\angle B) = 90°$

∠*B* and ∠*C* are supplementary:
$m(\angle B) + m(\angle C) = 180°$

Two angles that have a common side and nonoverlapping interiors are called **adjacent** angles. Supplementary and complementary angles frequently occur as adjacent angles, as shown in Figure 10.8.

Adjacent angles

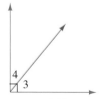

Figure 10.8
Adjacent supplementary and complementary angles

∠1 and ∠2 are adjacent supplementary angles.

∠3 and ∠4 are adjacent complementary angles.

A pair of nonadjacent angles formed by two intersecting lines are called **vertical angles,** as shown in Figure 10.9. Since $\angle 1$ and $\angle 2$ are supplementary we know that $m(\angle 1) + m(\angle 2) = 180°$. Likewise, $\angle 2$ and $\angle 3$ are supplementary and we also have $m(\angle 2) + m(\angle 3) = 180°$. Comparing these two equations shows that $m(\angle 1) = m(\angle 3)$. This proves another theorem of Thales.

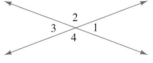

$\angle 1$ and $\angle 3$ are vertical angles
$\angle 2$ and $\angle 4$ are vertical angles

Figure 10.9
Intersecting lines form two pairs of vertical angles.

THEOREM   *Vertical Angles Theorem*
Vertical angles have the same measure.

Now consider the angles formed when two lines *l* and *m* are intersected at two points by a transversal *t*. There are eight angles formed, in four pairs of **corresponding angles.**

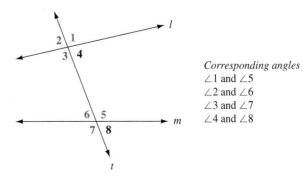

Corresponding angles
$\angle 1$ and $\angle 5$
$\angle 2$ and $\angle 6$
$\angle 3$ and $\angle 7$
$\angle 4$ and $\angle 8$

A case of special importance occurs when *l* and *m* are parallel lines, as shown in Figure 10.10. It would appear that each pair of corresponding angles is a pair of congruent angles. Conversely, if any one pair of corresponding angles is a congruent pair of angles then the lines *l* and *m* appear to be parallel. We will accept the truth of these observations, giving us the **corresponding angles property.** Many formal treatments of Euclidean geometry introduce the corresponding angles property as an axiom.

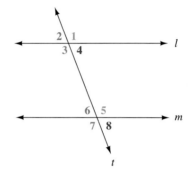

Figure 10.10
Lines l and m are parallel if, and only if, the angles in some corresponding pair have the same measure.

> **PROPERTY**   *Corresponding Angles Property*
> * If two parallel lines are cut by a transversal, then corresponding angles have the same measure.
> * If two lines in the plane are cut by a transversal and some pair of corresponding angles has the same measure, then the lines are parallel.

EXAMPLE   10.3

Using the Corresponding Angles Property

(a)   Lines *l* and *m* are parallel and $(m\angle 6) = 35°$. Find the measures of the remaining seven angles.

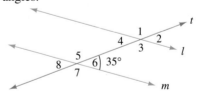

(b)   Lines *t* and *j* intersect at *P* and form an angle measuring 122°. Describe how to use a protractor and straightedge to draw a line *k* through *Q* that is parallel to line *j*.

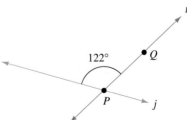

Solution

(a) Since ∠8 and ∠6 are vertical angles, $m(\angle 8) = 35°$. Also ∠5 and ∠7 are supplements of ∠6 and so $m(\angle 5) = m(\angle 7) = 180° - 35° = 145°$. By the corresponding angles property, $m(\angle 1) = m(\angle 5) = 145°$, $m(\angle 2) = m(\angle 6) = 35°$, $m(\angle 3) = m(\angle 7) = 145°$, and $m(\angle 4) = m(\angle 8) = 35°$.

(b) Use the protractor to form the corresponding angle measuring 122° at point Q.

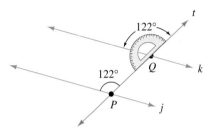

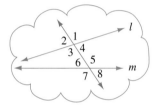

The pair of angles, ∠4 and ∠6, between l and m but on opposite sides of the transversal t are called **alternate interior angles.** Since ∠2 and ∠4 are vertical angles, they are congruent by the vertical angles theorem. Thus, the corresponding angles ∠2 and ∠6 are congruent if, and only if, the alternate interior angles ∠4 and ∠6 are congruent. This gives the following consequence of the corresponding angles property.

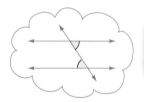

> **THEOREM** *Alternate Interior Angles Theorem*
> Two lines cut by a transversal are parallel if, and only if, a pair of alternate interior angles are congruent.

The Measure of Angles in Triangles

If a triangle ABC is cut from paper and its three corners are torn off, it is soon discovered that the three pieces will form a straight angle along a line l (see Figure 10.11). Thus $m(\angle 1) + m(\angle 2) + m(\angle 3) = 180°$ and we have a physical demonstration that the sum of the measures of the angles of a triangle is 180°.

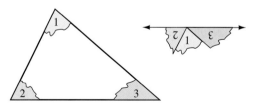

Figure 10.11
The torn corners of a triangle cut from paper can be placed along a line to show that $m(\angle 1) + m(\angle 2) + m(\angle 3) = 180°$.

The alternate interior angles theorem can be used to prove the result.

here is no doubt that degree measure, with 360 degrees comprising a full turn, had its origin in ancient Babylonia. At one time it was suggested the Babylonians thought a year was 360 days, which would mean the sun would advance one degree per day as it revolved in its circular orbit about the sun. This explanation must be dismissed however, since the early Babylonians were fully aware that a year exceeded 360 days.

A more plausible explanation has been suggested by Otto Neugebauer, an authority on Babylonian mathematics and science. In the early Sumerian period, time was often measured by how long it took to travel a Babylonian mile (a Babylonian mile was about 7 modern miles). In particular, a day turned out to be the time required to travel 12 Babylonian miles. Since the Babylonian mile, being quite long, had been subdivided into 30 equal parts for convenience, there were $(12)(30) = 360$ parts in a day's journey. The complete turn of the earth each day was therefore divided into 360 parts, giving rise to degree measure of an angle.

THEOREM   *Sum of Angle Measures in a Triangle*
The sum of the measures of the angles in a triangle is $180°$.

Proof: Consider the line l through point A that is parallel to the line $m = \overleftrightarrow{BC}$.

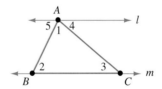

Line $\overleftrightarrow{AB}$ is a transversal to l and m for which $\angle 5$ and $\angle 2$ are alternate interior angles. Thus, $m(\angle 5) = m(\angle 2)$ by the alternate interior angles theorem. Similarly, $\angle 4$ and $\angle 3$ are alternate interior angles for the transversal $\overleftrightarrow{AC}$, so $m(\angle 4) = m(\angle 3)$. Since $\angle 5$, $\angle 1$, and $\angle 4$ form a straight angle at vertex A, we know that $m(\angle 5) + m(\angle 1) + m(\angle 4) = 180°$. Thus, by substitution, $m(\angle 2) + m(\angle 1) + m(\angle 3) = 180°$.

EXAMPLE   10.4   **Measuring an Opposite Exterior Angle of a Triangle**

In the figure below $\angle 4$ is called an **exterior angle** of triangle PQR, and $\angle 1$ and $\angle 2$ are its **opposite interior angles.** Show that the measure of the exterior angle is equal to the sum of the measures of the opposite interior angles; that is, show that $m(\angle 4) = m(\angle 1) + m(\angle 2)$.

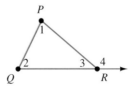

Solution   By the preceding theorem, we have $m(\angle 1) + m(\angle 2) + m(\angle 3) = 180°$. Also, $\angle 3$ and $\angle 4$ are supplementary, so that $m(\angle 3) + m(\angle 4) = 180°$. Therefore $m(\angle 1) + m(\angle 2) + m(\angle 3) = m(\angle 3) + m(\angle 4)$. Subtracting $m(\angle 3)$ from both sides of this equation gives $m(\angle 1) + m(\angle 2) = m(\angle 4)$.

Directed Angles

Until now angles have been measured without regard to the *direction*—clockwise or counterclockwise—one side rotates until it coincides with the second side. Often it is useful to specify one side as the **initial side** and the other side as the **terminal side.** Angles are then measured by specifying the number of degrees to rotate the initial side to the terminal side. Mathematicians usually assign a positive number to counterclockwise turns, and a negative number to clockwise turns. Angles which specify an initial and final side and a direction of turn are called **directed angles.** Some examples are shown in Figure 10.12, where arrows on the circular arcs indicate the direction of turn. Notice that an angle measure of $-90°$ could also be assigned the measure $+270°$.

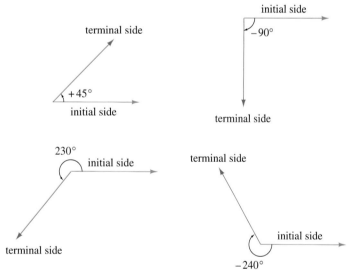

Figure 10.12
Directed angles, measured positively for counterclockwise turns

EXAMPLE   10.5   **Measuring Directed Angles**

Patty Pathfinder's trip through the woods to grandmother's house started and ended in an easterly direction, but zig-zagged through Wolf Woods to avoid trouble. The first two angles Patty turned through are $45°$ and $-60°$, as shown. Use a protractor to measure the three remaining turns. What is the sum of all five directed angles? Explain your surprise or lack of surprise.

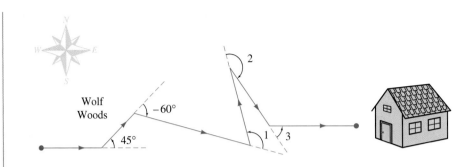

Solution

$m(\angle 1) = 120°, m(\angle 2) = -155°, m(\angle 3) = 50°$. The sum of all five directed angles is $45° - 60° + 120° - 155° + 50° = 0°$. This is not surprising since Patty's path started and stopped in the same direction and her path didn't make any loops.

PROBLEM SET 10.1

Understanding Concepts

1. Use symbols to name each of the figures shown. If more than one symbol is possible, give all possible names.

   (a) _____

   (b) _____

   (c) _____

   (d) _____

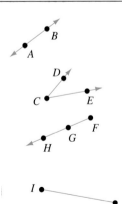

2. The points *E, U, C, L, I, D* are shown below.

   $E \bullet$ $\bullet \, U$

   $D \bullet$ $\bullet \, C$

   $I \bullet$ $\bullet \, L$

Draw the following figures:

   (a) $\overleftrightarrow{EU}$ **(b)** $\overrightarrow{CL}$ **(c)** $\overline{ID}$

3. Trace the 5 by 5 square lattice shown, and draw the line segment $\overline{AB}$.

Use colored pencils to circle all of the points *C* of the lattice that make $\angle BAC$ (a) a right angle,
   (b) an acute angle,   **(c)** an obtuse angle,
   (d) a straight angle, and   **(e)** a zero angle.

4. (a) How many nonzero angles are shown in the following figure? Give the three letter symbol, such as $\angle APB$, for each angle.

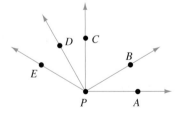

   (b) Measure each angle you identified in part (a), and classify it as acute, right, or obtuse.

5. In the figure shown, ∠BXD is a right angle and ∠AXE is a straight angle.

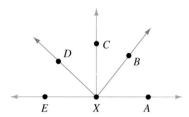

If $m(\angle BXC) = 35°$ and $m(\angle BXE) = 132°$, explain how you can determine the measures of ∠AXB, ∠CXD, and ∠DXE without using a protractor.

6. The point P shown below is the intersection of the two **external** tangent lines to a pair of circles. The point Q is the intersection of the two **internal** tangent lines to two circles.

Draw three circles, C_1, C_2, and C_3, no circle containing or intersecting either of the other circles. Let P be the intersection of the external tangent lines of C_1 and C_2, and let Q and R be the respective intersection of the internal tangent lines of the pairs of circles C_2, C_3, and C_1, C_3. What conclusion is suggested by your drawing?

7. Two intersecting circles determine a line, as shown below on the left. Draw three circles, where each circle intersects the other two circles as in the example shown on the right. Next draw the three lines determined by each pair of intersecting circles. What conclusion is suggested by your drawing?

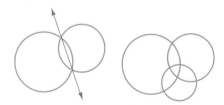

8. Use a compass (or carefully trace around a cup bottom or other circular object) to draw three circles of the same size through point A. Let B, K, and L be the other points of intersection of pairs of circles. Now draw a fourth circle of the same size as the other three that passes through B and creates points of intersection M and N as shown.

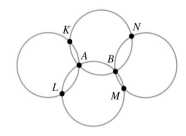

(a) Draw the lines $\overleftrightarrow{KL}$ and $\overleftrightarrow{MN}$. What can you say about these two lines?

(b) Draw the lines $\overleftrightarrow{LM}$ and $\overleftrightarrow{KN}$. What can you say about these two lines?

(c) Draw the line $\overleftrightarrow{AB}$. What connection does it seem to have to any of the lines drawn earlier?

9. Draw a circle at a point A and a second circle of the same radius at a point B, where the radius is large enough to cause the circles to intersect at two points C and D. Let M be the point of intersection of $\overline{CD}$ and $\overline{AB}$.

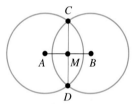

(a) Use a protractor to measure the angles at M. What can you say about how $\overline{CD}$ and $\overline{AB}$ intersect?

(b) Use a ruler to measure $\overline{MA}$ and $\overline{MB}$. What can you say about point M?

10. Draw two circles, and locate four points on each circle. Draw the segments as shown.

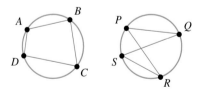

(a) Carefully measure the angles with vertices at A, B, C, and D with a protractor. What relationships do you see on the basis of your measurements?

(b) Measure the angles with vertices at P, Q, R, and S, and discuss what relationships hold between the angles in that figure.

11. Draw a circle, labeling its center as *O*. Draw an angle whose vertex is at *O* and whose sides intersect the circle at points *A* and *B*.

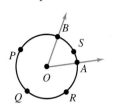
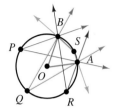

Let *P*, *Q*, and *R* be points on the circle which are in the exterior of ∠*AOB*. Let *S* be a point on the circle which is in the interior of ∠*AOB*.

(a) Use a protractor to find *m*(∠*AOB*), *m*(∠*APB*), *m*(∠*AQB*), and *m*(∠*ARB*). Describe how the angles compare to one another.

(b) Use a protractor to measure ∠*ASB* where *S* is on the smaller arc between *A* and *B*. How is ∠*ASB* related to the angles you considered in part (a)?

12. The hour and minute hands of a clock form a zero angle at noon and midnight. Between noon and midnight, how many times do the hands again form a zero angle?

13. How many degrees does the minute hand of a clock turn through   (a) in 60 minutes?   (b) in 5 minutes?   (c) in one minute? How many degrees does the hour hand of a clock turn through   (d) in 60 minutes?   (e) in 5 minutes?

14. Find the angle formed by the minute and hour hands of a clock at these times.
    (a) 3 o'clock   (b) 6 o'clock   (c) 4:30   (d) 10:20

15. The lines *l* and *m* are parallel. Find the measures of the numbered angles shown.

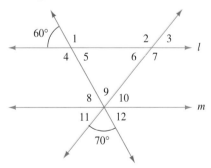

16. Determine the measure of ∠*P* if $\overrightarrow{AB}$ and $\overrightarrow{CD}$ are parallel.

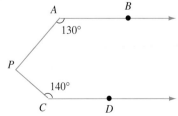

17. Find the measures of the numbered angles in the triangles shown.

(a)
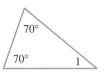

(b)

(c)

(d)
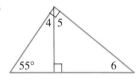

18. Find the measures of the interior angles of the following triangles.

(a)
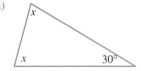

(b)

(c)

19. (a) Can a triangle have two obtuse angles? Why?
    (b) Can a triangle have two right angles? Why?
    (c) Suppose no angle of a triangle measures more than 60°. What do you know about the triangle?

20. A hiker started heading due north, then turned to the right 38°, then turned to the left 57°, and next turned right 9°. To resume heading due north, what turn must be made?

Thinking Critically

21. Five lines are drawn in the plane.
    (a) What is the smallest number of points of intersection of the five lines?

(b) What is the largest number of points of intersection?

(c) If *m* is an integer between the largest and smallest number of intersection points, can you arrange the lines to have *m* points of intersection?

22. Three noncollinear points determine three lines, as was shown in Figure 10.1.

   (a) How many lines are determined by four points, no three of which are collinear?

   (b) How many lines are determined by five points, no three of which are collinear?

   (c) How many lines are determined by *n* points? Assume that no three points are collinear.

23. What is being demonstrated in this sequence of drawings? Explain in a short paragraph.

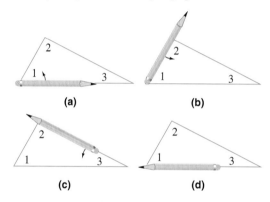

24. Use a ruler to draw a large four-sided polygon (a *quadrilateral*) such as the one shown here. Starting with a pencil laid along one side of the quadrilateral, slide the pencil to a corner, rotate it to the next side, slide the pencil to the next corner, and so on (see problem 23 above).

   (a) What direction will the pencil point to when it returns to the initial side? What does this say about the sum of the measures of the angles at the four corners of a quadrilateral?

   (b) Draw a diagonal across the quadrilateral to form two triangles. What does the sum of angle measures in the triangles tell you about the sum of angle measures in the quadrilateral?

   (c) Cut the quadrilateral out with scissors, and rip off the four corners. What angle can be covered with the four pieces?

25. In "Taxicab" geometry the "points" are the corners of a square grid of "city blocks" in the plane. In the figure below the shortest trip from *A* to *B* must cover 5 blocks and so the **taxi-distance** from *A* to *B* is 5. A

"taxi segment" is the set of points on a path of shortest taxi-distance from *A* to *B*, and so {*A, W, X, Y, Z, B*} is a taxi segment from *A* to *B*.

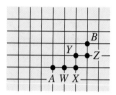

   (a) How many taxi segments join *A* and *B*?

   (b) Find all points which are at a taxi-distance of 5 from *A*. Does your "taxi circle" look like a circle drawn with a compass?

   (c) Use pencils of different colors to draw the concentric taxi circles of taxi radius 1, 2, 3, 4, 5, 6. Describe the pattern you see.

26. The incident (incoming) and reflected (outgoing) rays of a light beam make congruent angles with the flat mirror.

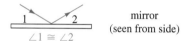

mirror
(seen from side)

Suppose two mirrors are perpendicular to one another. Show that after the second reflection the outgoing ray is parallel to the incoming ray. (*Hint:* Show that $\angle 5$ and $\angle 6$ are supplementary. Why does this imply that the rays are parallel?)

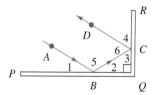

Making Connections

27. An explorer made the following trip from base camp.

   First leg: north 2 miles
   Second leg: southeast 5 miles
   Third leg: west 6 miles
   Fourth leg: south 1 mile

   (a) Make a scale drawing of the trip.

   (b) Show the angle the explorer turned through to go from one leg of the journey to the next.

   (c) Estimate the compass heading and approximate distance the explorer needs to follow to return most directly to base camp.

28. A plumb bob suspended from the center of a protractor can be used to measure the angle of elevation of a tree top. If the string crosses the protractor's scale at the

angle marked *P*, what is the measure of the angle of elevation?

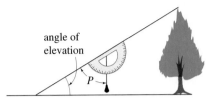

angle of elevation

P

29. **(a)** How many degrees does the earth turn in one hour?

(b) How many degrees does the earth turn in one minute?

(c) On a clear night with a full moon it can be observed that the earth's rotation makes it appear that the moon moves a diameter in 2 minutes of time. What angle does a diameter of the moon make as seen from the earth?

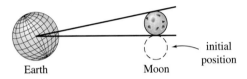

Earth   Moon   initial position

30. Suppose Polaris (the "pole star") is at an angle of elevation of 37° above the horizon. Explain how this information can be used to estimate your latitude, which is $m(\angle EOP)$ on the diagram below. *N* is the north pole, *O* is the earth's center, *E* is the point on the equator directly south of your position *P*, *H* is a point on the horizon to the north; $\overrightarrow{NS_1}$ and $\overrightarrow{PS_2}$ are parallel rays to the distant star Polaris.

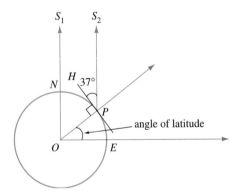

S_1 S_2

N   *H* 37°
P
O   *E*   angle of latitude

31. At the winter solstice (on or near December 21 each year), the earth's equatorial plane is tilted 23.5° away from its plane of rotation (the *ecliptic plane*) about the sun. At noon in the northern hemisphere, the angle from the horizon to the sun (the *solar altitude*) can be used to estimate the latitude of the point *P* of observation.

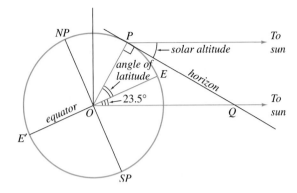

NP   *P*   To sun
solar altitude
angle of latitude *E*   horizon
equator   23.5°
O   *Q*   To sun
E′
SP

(a) Suppose the solar altitude is 42° at noon on December 21. What is the latitude?

(b) Juneau, Alaska, is approximately at latitude 58°. What is the solar altitude at noon on the winter solstice?

(c) What is the latitude of the Arctic Circle, above which the sun is below the horizon on the winter solstice?

Using a Calculator

32. Machinists, engineers, astronomers and others often require angle measurements that are accurate to a fraction of a degree. Sometimes decimal fractions are used, such as 38.24°. It is also common to follow the historic idea of first subdividing a degree into 60 equal parts called **minutes** (from the medieval Latin *pars minuta prima*, meaning first minute [mi-noot′] part) and next subdividing a minute into 60 equal parts called **seconds** (*partes minutae secundae*, meaning second minute part). For example 24°13′46″ is read 24 degrees 13 minutes and 46 seconds. The following computation shows how to convert to decimal degrees, using the facts that $1' = \dfrac{1°}{60}$ and $1'' = \dfrac{1°}{3600}$.

$$24°13'46'' = 24° + \left(\frac{13}{60}\right)° + \left(\frac{46}{3600}\right)°$$
$$\doteq (24 + 0.217 + 0.013)° = 24.230°$$

Here is how to convert to degrees-minutes-seconds from a decimal measure:

$$38.24° = 38° + (0.24)(60)' = 38° + 14.4'$$
$$= 38° + 14' + (0.4)(60)''$$
$$= 38° \ 14' \ 24''.$$

Use your calculator to convert the following angle measures from decimal to degrees-minutes-seconds, or the reverse.

(a) 58° 36′ 45″   **(b)** 141° 50′ 03″

(c) 71.32°   **(d)** 0.913°

Using a Computer

33. Use dynamic geometry software to draw any triangle *ABC*.

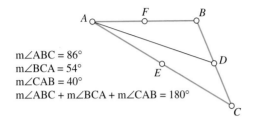

m∠ABC = 86°
m∠BCA = 54°
m∠CAB = 40°
m∠ABC + m∠BCA + m∠CAB = 180°

(a) Measure the three angles of the triangle (use the Measure Menu on Geometer's Sketchpad). Sum the three angle measures using the Measure Menu/Calculate . . . command. Click and drag a vertex or side of the triangle to manipulate the triangle to assume new shapes. What happens to the sum of the angles?

(b) Select the three sides of the triangle (hold down the shift key and click on the sides). Then use Construct Menu/Point at Midpoint to construct the midpoints of the three sides. The figure above shows the segment $\overline{AD}$, called a **median** of the triangle. Construct two medians, and construct the point *G* at which your two medians intersect. Use the Measure Menu/Distance command to measure the distances *GA* and *GD*. Then use the Measure/Calculate . . . command to compute the ratio *GA/GD*. Similarly, measure *GB* and *GA* and compute the ratio *GB/GE*. What conjecture can you make? Manipulate the triangle to lend support to your conjecture.

(c) Construct the third median of the triangle, and propose a theorem about the medians of any triangle. Manipulate the triangle to lend support to your hypothesis.

34. Draw a circle. From a point *P* outside of your circle draw three lines which each intersect the circle at two points. Let *A*, *B*, *C*, *A′*, B′, C′ be the intersection points as shown. The segments $\overline{AB'}$ and $\overline{A'B}$ intersect to determine a point *Q*. Similarly, let $\overline{BC'}$ and $\overline{B'C}$, and $\overline{AC'}$ and $\overline{A'C}$, determine the respective points *R* and *S*.

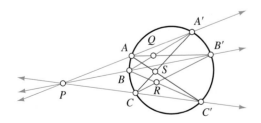

(a) What conjecture can you make concerning *Q*, *R*, and *S*? Drag *P* and the lines to investigate your conjecture.

(b) Discuss how the line $\overleftrightarrow{QR}$ can be used to construct the rays from *P* that are tangent to the circle.

35. Draw two squares that share a common vertex at *A*. Label the vertices of the squares *ABCD* and *AB′C′D′* in counterclockwise order.

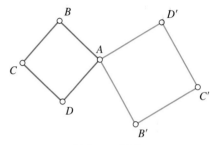

(a) Draw the lines $\overleftrightarrow{BB'}$ and $\overleftrightarrow{DD'}$ and let *P* denote their intersection point. Conjecture how the lines cross.

(b) Draw the line $\overleftrightarrow{CC'}$. Discuss how this line crosses the two lines drawn in part (a).

(c) Draw the line $\overleftrightarrow{AP}$. At what angles does it intersect the lines drawn before?

Communicating

36. The word "acute" has a nonmathematical meaning, as in *acute* appendicitis. Similarly, "obtuse" might be used to say someone's argument is "obtuse." Look these words up in a dictionary and comment on why their mathematical and nonmathematical meanings are related.

From State Student Assessments

37. (Washington State, Grade 4)

Raul is going to a friend's house. Raul remembers that his friend's house is on a street parallel to Southport. On which street does Raul's friend live?

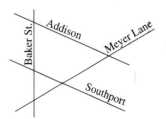

A. Addison   B. Baker Street

C. Meyer Lane

10.2   Curves and Polygons in the Plane

Curves and Regions

A **curve** in the plane can be described informally as a set of points that a pencil can trace without lifting until all points in the set are covered. A more precise definition is required for advanced mathematics but this intuitive idea of curve meets our present needs. If the pencil never touches a point more than once then the curve is **simple.** If the pencil is lifted at the same point at which it started tracing the curve then the curve is **closed.** If the common initial and final point of a closed curve is the only point touched more than once in tracing the curve then the curve is a **simple closed curve.** We require that the curve have both an initial and a final point, and so lines, rays, and angles are *not* curves for us.

Several examples of curves are shown in Figure 10.13.

(a) Simple, not closed   **(b)** Simple, closed

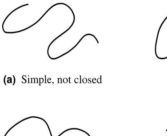

(c) Closed, not simple   **(d)** Not simple, not closed

Figure 10.13
The classification of curves

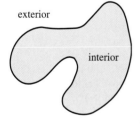

Figure 10.14
A simple closed curve and its interior and exterior

Any simple closed curve partitions the points of the plane into three disjoint pieces: the curve itself, the interior, and the exterior, as shown in Figure 10.14. This property of a simple closed curve may seem very obvious, but in fact it is an important theorem of mathematics.

> **THEOREM** *Jordan Curve Theorem*
> A simple closed plane curve partitions the plane into three disjoint subsets: the curve itself, the interior of the curve, and the exterior of the curve.

The French mathematician Camille Jordan (1838–1922) was the first to recognize that such an "obvious" result needed proof. To see why the theorem is difficult to prove (even Jordan's own proof was incorrect!) try to determine if the points *G* and *H* are inside or outside the very crinkly, but still simple, closed curve shown in Figure 10.15.

Figure 10.15
Is G in the interior or exterior of this simple closed curve? What about H?

| EXAMPLE 10.6 | **Determining the Interior Points of a Simple Closed Curve in the Plane** |

Devise a method to determine if a given point is in the interior or the exterior of a given simple closed curve.

Solution

Think of the curve as a fence. If we jump over the fence we either go from the interior to the exterior of the curve, or vice versa. Now draw any ray from the given point.

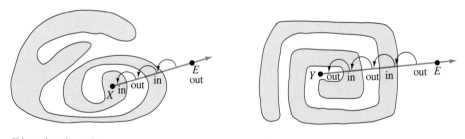

X is an interior point   Y is an exterior point

Start at an exterior point *E* on the ray and see how many times the fence is crossed as you move to the endpoint of the ray. If the curve is crossed an odd number of times to reach the point *X* from the exterior point *E*, then the given point *X* is an interior point. An even number of crossings from *E* to reach a point *Y* means that *Y* is an exterior point. It should now be simple to verify that *G* is exterior and *H* is interior to the curve in Figure 10.15.

The interior and exterior of a simple closed curve are also called **regions.** More generally the complement of some system of lines, rays, and curves will be composed of one or more regions. For example, a line partitions the plane into two regions called half planes. An angle, if not zero or straight, partitions the plane into two regions called the interior and the exterior of the angle.

EXAMPLE   10.7

Counting Regions in the Plane

Count the number of regions into which the plane is partitioned by the following shapes.

(a) a figure 8   **(b)** a segment   **(c)** two nonintersecting circles
(d) a square and its two diagonals   **(e)** a pentagram
(f) any simple nonclosed curve

Solution

(a) 3   **(b)** 1   **(c)** 3   **(d)** 5   **(e)** 7   **(f)** 1

Convex Curves and Figures

The interior of an angle has the property that the segment between any two interior points does not leave the interior. This means that the interior of an angle is a convex figure according to the following definition.

> **DEFINITION**   *Convex Figures*
> A figure is **convex** if, and only if, it contains the segment $\overline{PQ}$ for each pair of points P and Q contained in the figure.

Several convex and nonconvex shapes are shown in Figure 10.16. To show that a figure is nonconvex, it is enough to find two points P and Q within the figure whose corresponding line segment $\overline{PQ}$ contains at least one point not in the figure. A nonconvex figure is sometimes called a **concave** figure.

Convex   Nonconvex

Figure 10.16
Convex and nonconvex plane figures

Polygonal Curves and Polygons

A curve that consists of a union of finitely many line segments is called a **polygonal curve.** The endpoints of the segments are called **vertices,** and the segments are the **sides** of the polygonal curve. A **polygon** is a simple closed polygonal curve. The interior of a polygon is called a **polygonal region.** A **convex polygon** is a polygon whose interior is convex. Figure 10.17 illustrates examples of polygonal curves.

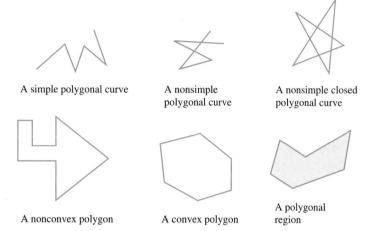

A simple polygonal curve

A nonsimple polygonal curve

A nonsimple closed polygonal curve

A nonconvex polygon

A convex polygon

A polygonal region

Figure 10.17
The classification of polygonal curves

Polygons are named according to the number of sides or vertices they have. For example a polygon of seventeen sides is sometimes called a *heptadecagon* (hepta = seven, deca = ten). With more directness it can also be called a 17-gon. The common names of polygons are shown in Table 10.1

TABLE 10.1	Names of Polygons	
Polygon	Number of Sides	Example
Triangle	3	
Quadrilateral	4	
Pentagon	5	
Hexagon	6	
Heptagon	7	
Octagon	8	
Nonagon (or enneagon)	9	
Decagon	10	
n-gon	n	

Triangle Pick-Up-Sticks

The 16 matchsticks shown below form eight triangular regions. Remove a certain number of matches and attempt to leave behind two triangular regions in each case. There can be no matches remaining that do not border one of the two triangles. Which case gives you the most trouble?

a. Remove 6 matchsticks
b. Remove 7 matchsticks
c. Remove 8 matchsticks
d. Remove 9 matchsticks
e. Remove 10 matchsticks
f. Remove 11 matchsticks

The rays containing two sides at a common vertex determine an **angle of the polygon.** For a convex polygon the interiors of these angles include the interior of the polygon. The angles are also called **interior angles,** as shown in Figure 10.18. An angle formed by replacing one of these rays with its opposite ray is an **exterior** angle of the polygon. The two exterior angles at a vertex are congruent by the vertical angles theorem. The interior angle and either of its adjacent exterior angles are supplements.

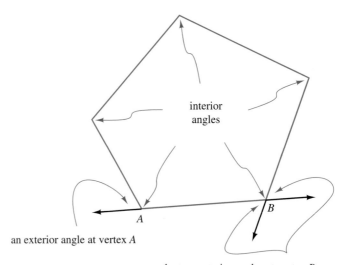

Figure 10.18
Angles in a convex polygon

In the following theorem we consider the interior angle and *one* of its supplementary exterior angles at each vertex of a convex polygon.

THEOREM   *Sums of the Angle Measures in a Convex Polygon*

(a)   The sum of the measures of the exterior angles of a convex polygon is 360°.
(b)   The sum of the measures of the interior angles of a convex n-gon is $(n - 2)180°$.

Proof:

(a) Imagine a walk completely about a polygon. At each vertex, we must turn through an exterior angle. At the conclusion of the walk we are heading in the same direction as we began, so our total turn is through $360°$. If $\angle 1'$, $\angle 2'$, ..., $\angle n'$ denote the exterior angles, this shows that $m(\angle 1') + m(\angle 2') + \cdots + m(\angle n') = 360°$.

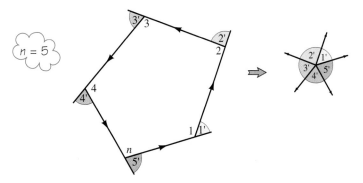

(b) Since an interior and exterior angle at a vertex are supplementary, we have the equations $m(\angle 1) = 180° - m(\angle 1')$, $m(\angle 2) = 180° - m(\angle 2')$, ..., $m(\angle n) = 180° - m(\angle n')$. Adding these n equations gives us, by part (a),

$$m(\angle 1) + m(\angle 2) + \cdots + m(\angle n)$$
$$= n \cdot 180° - [m(\angle 1') + m(\angle 2') + \cdots + m(\angle n')]$$
$$= n \cdot 180° - 360° = (n - 2) \cdot 180°,$$

where we need the result of part (a) in the second equality.

EXAMPLE 10.8 | **Finding the Angles in a Pentagonal Arch**

Find the measures $3x$, $8x$, y, and z of the interior and exterior angles of the pentagon *PENTA*.

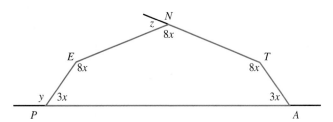

Solution

By the theorem just proved we know that the sum of the measures of the five interior angles is

$$3x + 8x + 8x + 8x + 3x = (5 - 2)180°.$$

That is, $30x = 3 \cdot 180°$ and so $x = (3 \cdot 180°/30) = 18°$. Thus, the interior angles at P and A measure $3 \cdot 18° = 54°$ and at E, N, and T measure $8 \cdot 18° = 144°$. The measures of the exterior angles are $y = 180° - 54° = 126°$ and $z = 180° - 144° = 36°$.

In a nonconvex polygon some of the interior angles are reflex angles, with measures larger than 180°. Nevertheless, it can be proved (see problem 23) that the sum of the measures of the n interior angles is still given by $(n - 2)180°$.

> **THEOREM**   *Sum of Interior Angle Measures of a General Polygon*
> The sum of the measures of the interior angles of any n-gon is $(n - 2)180°$.

An example of a nonconvex heptagon is shown in Figure 10.19.

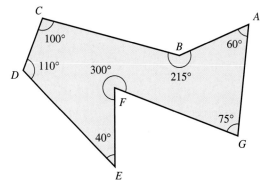

Figure 10.19
The sum of the interior angle measures of the 7-gon is $60° + 215° + 100° + 110° + 40° + 300° + 75° = 900° = (7 - 2) \cdot 180°$.

EXAMPLE   10.9   **Measuring the Angles in a Five-pointed Star**

The reflex angles at each of the five "inward" points of the star shown have three times the measure of the angles of the "outward" points. What is the measure of the angle at each point of the star?

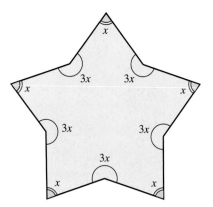

Solution   The sum of the measures of all ten interior angles of the star is $5x + 5 \cdot (3x)$, or $20x$. Since the star is a decagon (or 10-gon) the sum must equal $(10 - 2) \cdot 180° = 1440°$. This gives us the equation $20x = 1440°$. Solving for x shows that $x = 1440° \div 20 = 72°$. Thus, each acute interior angle measures 72°, and the reflex angles at the inward points each measure $3x = 216°$.

A walk about any closed curve, simple or nonsimple, which returns to the starting point and to the same heading as the walk began must have turned through some integer multiple of 360°. It is customary to measure turns to the left (counter clockwise) as positive, and turns to the right (clockwise) as negative.

> **THEOREM**   *The Total Turn Theorem*
> The total turn around any closed curve is an integral multiple of 360°.

To help determine the total turn, draw a point S at an arbitrary point along the curve and lay a pencil at that point heading in the direction of travel. Now trace the curve with the pencil, and count the net number of rotations the pencil has made when it returns to its initial position at point S. For a polygonal curve, the pencil only turns when it reaches a vertex of the curve.

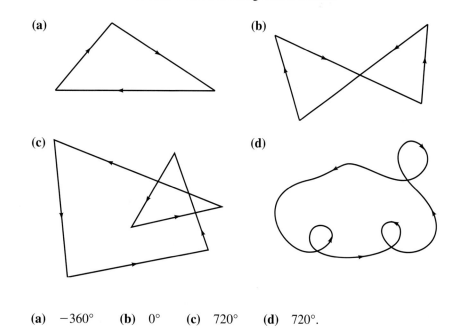

EXAMPLE   10.10   **Finding Total Turns**

Find the total turn for each of the following closed curves.

(a)

(b)

(c)

(d)

Solution   **(a)** $-360°$ **(b)** $0°$ **(c)** $720°$ **(d)** $720°$.

Triangles

Triangles are classified by the measures of their angles or sides, as shown in Table 10.2.

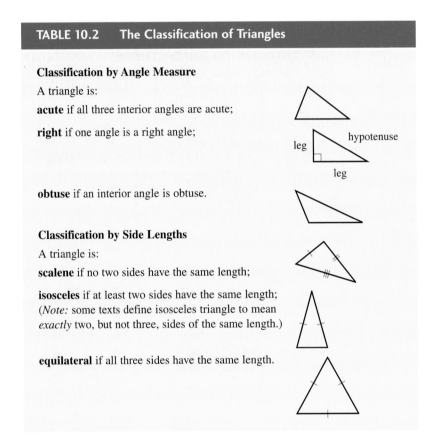

TABLE 10.2   The Classification of Triangles

Classification by Angle Measure

A triangle is:

acute if all three interior angles are acute;

right if one angle is a right angle;

obtuse if an interior angle is obtuse.

Classification by Side Lengths

A triangle is:

scalene if no two sides have the same length;

isosceles if at least two sides have the same length; (*Note:* some texts define isosceles triangle to mean *exactly* two, but not three, sides of the same length.)

equilateral if all three sides have the same length.

EXAMPLE   10.11

Classifying Triangles

There are a number of triangles in the figure shown with vertices at A, B, C, D, E, and F. Classify the triangles according to Table 10.2.

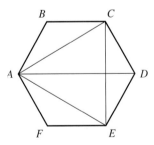

Solution

Acute: $\triangle ACE$, Right: $\triangle ACD$ and $\triangle AED$, Obtuse: $\triangle ABC$, $\triangle CDE$, and $\triangle AFE$, Scalene: $\triangle ACD$ and $\triangle AED$, Isosceles: $\triangle ABC$, $\triangle CDE$, $\triangle AFE$, and $\triangle ACE$, Equilateral: $\triangle ACE$.

Quadrilaterals

The four-sided polygons are classified as shown in Table 10.3. This classification allows a parallelogram to be described as a trapezoid, and similarly a square is a rectangle, and a rectangle is a parallelogram.

The classification hierarchy is summarized by a Venn diagram. Notice that the squares are the intersection of the rhombus and rectangle loops. Arranging figures in classes which are subsets of one another can be very useful. For example, suppose we wish

TABLE 10.3   The Classification of Convex Quadrilaterals

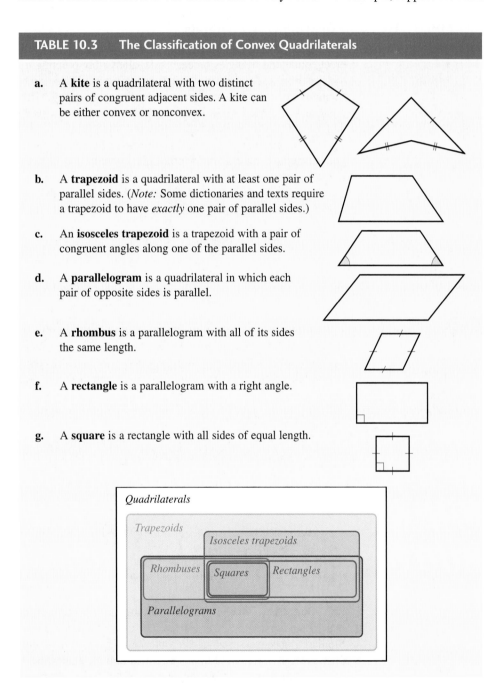

a. A **kite** is a quadrilateral with two distinct pairs of congruent adjacent sides. A kite can be either convex or nonconvex.

b. A **trapezoid** is a quadrilateral with at least one pair of parallel sides. (*Note:* Some dictionaries and texts require a trapezoid to have *exactly* one pair of parallel sides.)

c. An **isosceles trapezoid** is a trapezoid with a pair of congruent angles along one of the parallel sides.

d. A **parallelogram** is a quadrilateral in which each pair of opposite sides is parallel.

e. A **rhombus** is a parallelogram with all of its sides the same length.

f. A **rectangle** is a parallelogram with a right angle.

g. A **square** is a rectangle with all sides of equal length.

to show that the points A, B, C, D are the vertices of a square. Step 1 may be to show that one pair of sides is parallel, telling us that $ABCD$ is a trapezoid. Step 2 may show that the remaining pair of opposite sides is parallel, and now we know $ABCD$ is a parallelogram. If Step 3 shows that $ABCD$ is a kite, and Step 4 shows that $\angle A$ is a right angle, then we correctly deduce that $ABCD$ is a square.

EXAMPLE   10.12

Exploring Quadrilaterals

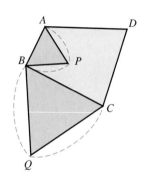

Draw a convex quadrilateral $ABCD$. Use a compass to erect equilateral triangles on each side, alternately pointing to the interior and exterior of the quadrilateral. Two such triangles are shown here, determining points P and Q. The equilateral triangles on the remaining sides determine points R and S.

What can you say about quadrilateral $PQRS$? Support your conjecture by drawing another quadrilateral and its system of equilateral triangles. Use a ruler and protractor to measure the lengths of sides and the measure of the angles of $PQRS$.

Solution

You should discover that $PQRS$ is a parallelogram.

Regular Polygons

A polygon with all of its sides congruent to one another is **equilateral** (that is, "equal sided"). Similarly, a convex polygon whose interior angles are all congruent is **equiangular** (that is, "equal angled"). A convex polygon which is both equilateral and equiangular is **regular.** Some hexagonal examples are shown in Figure 10.20.

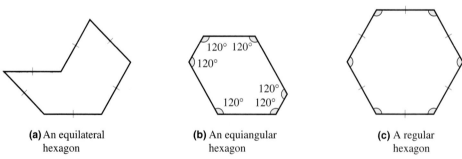

(a) An equilateral hexagon

(b) An equiangular hexagon

(c) A regular hexagon

Figure 10.20
Hexagons which are equilateral, equiangular, and regular

Since the six congruent interior angles in an equiangular hexagon have measures which add up to $(6 - 2) \cdot 180° = 720°$, each interior angle measures $720°/6 = 120°$. Similarly, the measures of the interior angles of an equiangular n-gon add up to $(n - 2) \cdot 180°$, so each of the n congruent interior angles measures $(n - 2) \cdot 180°/n$.

In a regular n-gon, any angle with vertex at the center of a regular polygon and sides containing adjacent vertices of the polygon is called a **central angle** of the polygon. The following formulas give the measures of the exterior, interior, and central angles of a regular polygon.

interior angle

exterior angle

central angle

THEOREM   *Angle Measure in a Regular n-gon*

In a regular n-gon:

- each interior angle has measure $(n - 2) \cdot 180°/n$
- each exterior angle has measure $360°/n$
- each central angle has measure $360°/n$

It is useful to observe that an interior and exterior angle are supplementary. Thus, the measure of an interior angle is also given by $180° - 360°/n$.

EXAMPLE   10.13

Working with Angles in Regular *n*-gons

(a)   The Baha'i House of Worship in Wilmette, Illinois, has the unusual floor plan shown below. What are the measures of $\angle ABC$ and $\angle AOB$?

(b)   Suppose an archeologist found a broken piece of pottery as shown on the right below. If the angle measures $160°$ and it is assumed the plate had the form of a regular polygon, how many sides would the complete plate have had?

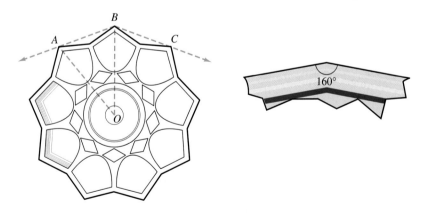

Solution

(a) $\angle ABC$ is the interior angle of a regular 9-gon and it has measure $(9 - 2) \cdot 180°/9 = 140°$. $\angle AOB$ is a central angle of a regular 9-gon, so its measure is $360°/9 = 40°$.

(b)   The corresponding exterior angle measures $20°$. Since $20° = 360°/n$ it is seen that $n = 360°/20° = 18$. Under the assumptions stated the plate would have had 18 sides.

Circles

By definition, a **circle** is the set of all points in the plane that are at a fixed distance—the **radius**—from a given point—the **center.** The **chord, diameter, tangent line, arc, sector,** and **segment** of a circle are shown in Figure 10.21. The word radius is used in two ways: it is both a segment from the center to a point on the circle and the length of such a segment. Likewise diameter is both a segment and a length. The interior of a circle is a **disc.**

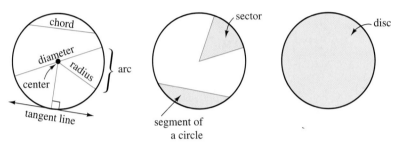

Figure 10.21
The parts of a circle

EXAMPLE   10.14

Exploring Perpendicular Chords in a Pair of Circles

Use a compass (or trace around the bottom of a cup) to draw two congruent intersecting circles. Let *A, B, C,* and *D* denote the centers and intersection points of the circles. Draw any line *m* through *C,* and denote its intersection points with the two circles as *R* and *O.* Similarly, draw the line *n* through *D* that is perpendicular to the line drawn through *C.* Let *H* and *M* denote the points at which line *n* intersects the circles.

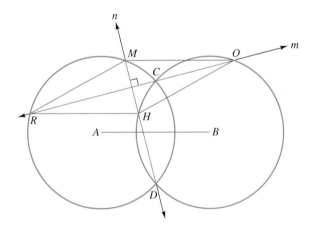

    (a)   Use measurement tools to describe the shape of the quadrilateral *RHOM.* What connection to the distance *AB* between the circles' centers do you discover?

    (b)   Use a protractor to measure the angles ∠*RAM,* ∠*MAC,* and ∠*CBO.* What relationship do you discover?

Solution

    (a)   *RHOM* is a rhombus whose sides have the same length as the distance *AB* between the centers of the circles.

    (b)   Your measurements should show that $m(\angle RAM) = m(\angle MAC) + m(\angle CBO)$.

INTO THE CLASSROOM

Activity-Based Learning and the van Hiele Levels

From kindergarten onward, geometry is learned best through hands-on activities. A successful teacher will take advantage of the enjoyment children experience when working with colored paper, straws, string, crayons, toothpicks, and other tangible materials. Children learn geometry by doing geometry as they construct two- and three-dimensional shapes, combine their shapes to create attractive patterns, and build interesting space figures using plane shapes. By its nature, informal geometry provides unlimited opportunities to construct shapes, designs, and structures that all work to capture a child's interest.

According to pioneering research of the van Hieles in the late 1950s, the knowledge children construct for themselves through hands-on activities is essential to learning geometry. Dr. Pierre van Hiele and his late wife Dr. Dina van Hiele-Geldof, both former mathematics teachers in the Netherlands, theorized that learning geometry progresses through five "levels," which can be described briefly as follows.

Level 0—Recognition of shape

Children recognize shapes "holistically." Only the overall appearance of a figure is observed, with no attention given to the component parts of the figure. For example, a figure with three curved sides would likely be identified as a triangle by a child at Level 0. Similarly, a square tilted point downward may not be recognized as a square.

Level 1—Analysis of single shapes

Children at Level 1 are cognizant of the component parts of certain figures. For example, a rectangle has four straight sides which meet at "square" corners. However, at Level 1 the interrelationships of figures and properties is not understood.

Level 2—Relationships among shapes

At Level 2 children understand how common properties create abstract relationships among figures. For example, a square is both a rhombus and a rectangle. Also, simple deductions can be made about figures, using the analytic abilities acquired at Level 1.

Level 3—Deductive reasoning

The student at Level 3 views geometry as a formal mathematical system and can write deductive proofs.

Level 4—Geometry as an axiomatic system

This is the abstract level, reached only in high level university courses. The focus is on the axiomatic foundations of a geometry, and no dependence is placed on concrete or pictorial models.

Ongoing research supports the thesis that students learn geometry by progressing through the van Hiele levels. This text—by means of hands-on activities, and examples and problems that require constructions and drawings—promotes the spirit of the van Hiele approach. However, it is the elementary classroom teacher who must bring geometry to life for his or her students, by creating interesting activities that support each child's progression through the first three van Hiele levels.

COOPERATIVE INVESTIGATION

From Paper Discs to Polygons

Materials Needed

1. Two paper discs per student, each 7 to 8 inches (or 18 to 20 centimeters) in diameter. All discs used in a group should be the same size.
2. Drawing and measuring tools (pencils, protractors, rulers).

Directions

Work in groups of four. There are two sets of explorations, each using one paper disc per student.

Explorations with the First Paper Disc

1. Make a light pencil mark on the disc that you think estimates the center of the disc. To check how close you are, lightly (do not make a heavy crease) fold the disc in half. Undo your fold and lay the disc out flat. Is your mark along the diameter you have folded? Now fold the disc in half once more in a new direction and unfold. Is your mark at the intersection of the two diameters? Clearly mark the true center of your disc, and label it O.

2. Fold across a chord of the disc so that the folded arc of the circle passes through the center O, as shown. Without unfolding the first fold, make a second fold across a chord that has the same endpoint as the first chord and again with the circular arc passing through point O. Finally, fold the remaining arc of the circle. Does it also pass through point O? What kind of a triangle seems to have been created?

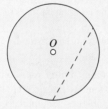  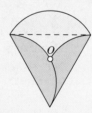

Check out your guess by measuring the three sides and the three angles of the triangle. Compare with others in your group.

3. Find the midpoints of the sides of your triangle (how can this be done with folding?) and mark them with a pencil. Fold a vertex of your triangle to the midpoint on the opposite side. What polygon have you created? Without unfolding, fold another vertex of a triangle to the marked midpoint on the opposite side. What is the polygon now? Fold the third vertex to the midpoint marked on the opposite side. What is the name of this polygon?

 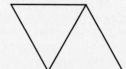

4. Unfold your disc to return to the large equilateral triangle made in Exploration 2. Now fold each vertex to the center point O. Describe the polygon you have now created.

Explorations with the Second Paper Disc

5. Mark a point well away from the center of the paper disc, and label it *H*. Fold two arcs, sharing a common endpoint, so that both arcs pass through point *H*. Next, fold the remaining arc of the disc to form a triangle. Did the third arc you folded also pass through point *H*? Compare with others in your group.

 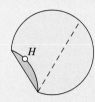

6. Unfold your triangle, and use a ruler to draw the chord that begins at a vertex of the triangle and passes through point *H*. Similarly, draw the chords through *H* from the other two vertices of the triangle. At what angle does each chord intersect the opposite side of the triangle? Use a protractor to measure the angle, and compare your answer with others in your group.

PROBLEM SET 10.2

Understanding Concepts

1. If the figure shown has the property listed, place a check in the table below.

(a)   (b)   (c)   (d)

(e)   (f)   (g)   (h)

(i)   (j)   (k)   (l)

	(a)	(b)	(c)	(d)	(e)	(f)	(g)	(h)	(i)	(j)	(k)	(l)
Simple curve												
Closed curve												
Polygonal curve												
Polygon												

2. Draw figures which satisfy the given description.

   (a) a nonsimple closed four-sided polygonal curve

   (b) a nonconvex pentagon

   (c) an equiangular quadrilateral

   (d) a convex octagon

3. Can a line cross a simple closed plane curve 99 times? Explain why or why not.

4. Classify each region as convex or nonconvex.

   (a) 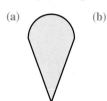 (b)   (c)

   (d) 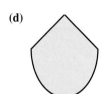 (e)

5. Imagine stretching a rubber band tightly about each figure shown. Shade the region within the band with a colored pencil. Is the shaded region always convex?

   (a)   (b)

   (c)   (d)

6. How many different regions in the plane are determined by these figures?

   (a)   (b)

   (c)   (d)

7. Determine the measures of the interior angles of this polygon.

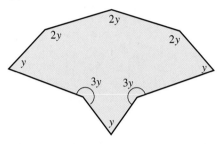

8. Calculate the measures of the angles in this nonconvex polygon.

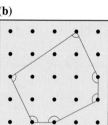

9. A **lattice polygon** is formed by a rubber band stretched over the nails of a geoboard. Find the sum of the measures of the interior angles of the following lattice polygons.

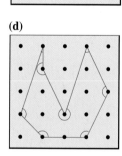

10. Draw lattice polygons (see problem 9) on squared dot paper whose interior angles have the given sum of their measures. Place arcs that indicate the interior angles, as in problem 9.

    (a) 180°   (b) 1080°   (c) 1440°   (d) 1800°

11. The interior angles of an *n*-gon have an average measure of 175°.

    (a) What is *n?*

    (b) Suppose the polygon has flexible joints at the vertices. As the polygon is flexed to take on new shapes, what happens to the average measure of the interior angles? Explain your reasoning.

12. What is the amount of total turn for the following closed curves? Assign a positive measure to counterclockwise turning.

(a)

(b)

(c)

(d)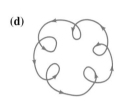

13. Suppose you walk north 10 paces, turn left through 24°, walk 10 paces, turn left through 24°, walk 10 paces, and so on.

   (a) Will you return to your starting point?

   (b) What is the shape of the path?

14. Fill in the missing vertices to give the type of triangle required, choosing vertices from *A*, *B*, *C*, *D*, *E*, *F*, *G*, and *H*. There may be more than one way to answer.

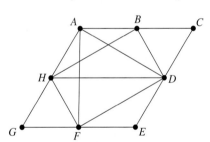

   (a) Equilateral triangle *D* __ __

   (b) Right triangle *F* __ __

   (c) Obtuse triangle *F* __ __

   (d) Isosceles triangle *E* __ __

   (e) Acute triangle *H* __ __

15. Refer to the figure shown in problem 14 to give the type of quadrilateral required, filling in vertices from *A*, *B*, *C*, *D*, *E*, *F*, *G*, and *H*.

   (a) Rhombus *A* __ __ __

   (b) Rectangle __ __ __ __

   (c) Isosceles trapezoid *A* __ __ __

   (d) Non-isosceles trapezoid *G* __ __ __

   (e) Kite *E* __ __ __

16. For each regular *n*-gon shown below, give the measures of the interior, exterior, and central angle.

(a)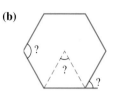

(b)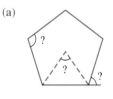

(c)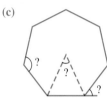

(d)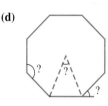

17. (a) A regular *n*-gon has exterior angles of measure 15°. What is *n*?

   (b) A regular *n*-gon has interior angles each measuring $172\frac{1}{2}°$. What is *n*?

Thinking Critically

18. A brave, but not mathematically inclined, knight at point *K* wants to rescue the princess at point *P*. The evil king has not only confined the princess to the castle tower, but has erected an enormously long impenetrable stone wall that winds and twists all over the countryside. There is also a dangerous dragon at point *D*. Looking out the one small window in the castle tower, the princess has created the map shown below. Only portions of the stone wall are visible from her window, but the mathematically knowledgeable princess knows the entire wall forms a simple closed curve.

   (a) Is the princess worried that the dragon will find the knight?

   (b) Is she hopeful the knight will come to her rescue?

19. A goat is tethered at the corner of an 80 foot by 30 foot rectangular barn. If the rope is 50 feet long, describe the region the goat can reach.

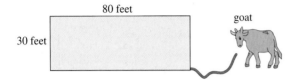

20. (a) A boat B is anchored at point A. Describe, in words and a sketch, the region where the boat can drift due to wind and currents.

(b) Suppose a second anchor at point C has been set, as shown in the next diagram. Describe, in words and a sketch, the region to which the boat is now confined.

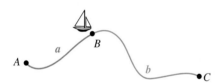

21. The segment $\overline{AB}$ is to be completed to become a side of a triangle ABC.

Describe, in words and sketches, the set of points C so that:

(a) $\triangle ABC$ is a right triangle and $\overline{AB}$ is a leg;

(b) $\triangle ABC$ is a right triangle and $\overline{AB}$ is a hypotenuse;
(*Hint:* For (b), proceed experimentally using the corner of a sheet of paper:)

(c) $\triangle ABC$ is an acute triangle;

(d) $\triangle ABC$ is an obtuse triangle.

22. If the interior angle of a polygon has measure m, then $360° - m$ is called the measure of the **conjugate**

angle at that vertex. Find a formula which gives the sum of the measures of the conjugate angles of an n-gon, and give a justification for your formula. As an example, the measures of the conjugate angles in this pentagon add up to $1260°$.

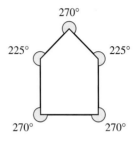

23. The heptagonal region shown on the left has been broken into five triangular regions by drawing four nonintersecting diagonals across the interior of the polygon, as shown on the right. In this way we say that the polygon is triangulated by diagonals.

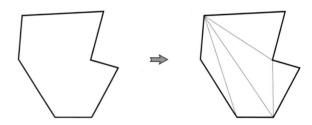

(a) Investigate how many diagonals are required to triangulate any n-gon.

(b) How many triangles are in any triangulation of an n-gon by diagonals?

(c) Explain how a triangulation by diagonals can give a new derivation of the formula $(n - 2) \cdot 180°$ for the sum of the measures of the interior angles of any n-gon.

24. The polygon below contains a point S in its interior which can be joined to any vertex by a segment which remains inside the polygon. Drawing all such segments produces a triangulation of the interior of the polygon (compare to problem 23).

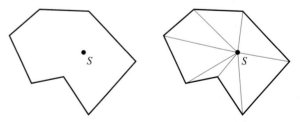

If an n-gon contains such a point S, explain how the corresponding triangulation can be used to derive the

$(n - 2) \cdot 180°$ formula for the sum of interior angle measures.

25. **(a)** Find the sum of the angle measures in the 5-pointed star shown on the left below. Explain how the Total Turn Theorem can be used to obtain your answer.

   (b) What is the measure of the angle in each point of the pentagram shown on the right?

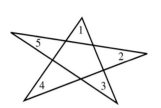

26. What is the largest number of regions you can form with a system of ten circles?

27. Regions can be formed in a circle by drawing chords, no three of which are concurrent. If C chords are drawn and they intersect in I points, determine a formula for the number of pieces, P

(that is, the regions) that are formed inside the circle.

P	C	I
3	2	0
4	2	1
5	3	1

28. Let $ABCD$ be a parallelogram.
   (a) Prove that $\angle A$ and $\angle B$ are supplementary.
   (b) Prove that $\angle A \cong \angle C$ and $\angle B \cong \angle D$.

29. Let $PQRS$ be a convex quadrilateral for which $\angle P \cong \angle R$ and $\angle Q \cong \angle S$.
   (a) Prove that $\angle P$ and $\angle Q$ are supplementary.
   (b) Prove that $PQRS$ is a parallelogram.

30. Let F and K be convex figures.
   (a) Prove that $F \cap K$ is also a convex figure.
   (b) Is $F \cup K$ necessarily a convex figure? Explain.

Thinking Cooperatively

31. Work in pairs, with one partner using a black pencil and the other partner a red pencil. Each partner draws a closed curve on his or her own clean sheet of paper. The papers are exchanged, and a second closed curve is drawn. The newly drawn curve should cross the previously drawn curve several times. However, it cannot pass through an intersection of the curve first drawn, nor can it pass through a point of intersection of the black and red curves a second time. Circle the points where the red and black curves cross one another.

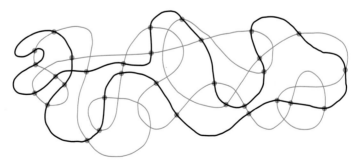

The example shows 32 points at which the red and black curves cross one another.

(a) Count the number of crossing points of the red and black curves that are circled. Compare your number with the number of crossing points counted by other partners, and redo the drawing and counting to gather more evidence. What kind of numbers seems to occur? What kinds of numbers apparently never occur?

(b) Using fresh sheets of paper, draw new closed curves. The curve will partition the plane into regions. Using the same pencil, show that each region can either be shaded or left blank to create a pattern so that regions that share a border have opposite shading. Regions that only share a point are allowed to have the same shading.

(c) Trade papers with your curves and shaded regions, and draw a new closed curve as in part (a). Is your result discovered from part (a) now more obvious? Discuss and explain.

32. Work in pairs, with one partner using a black pencil and the other partner a red pencil. Each partner draws a *simple* closed curve on his or her own clean sheet of paper. The papers are exchanged, and a second simple closed curve is drawn. The newly drawn curve should cross the previously drawn curve several times. At each intersection point, the newly drawn curve must cross from the inside to the outside of the previously drawn curve or vice versa (it cannot just touch and turn away). Each partner then classifies and marks each region of the plane by its type.

✓:Interior to both curves

×:Exterior to both curves

□:Interior to black and exterior to red curve

■:Interior to red and exterior to black curve

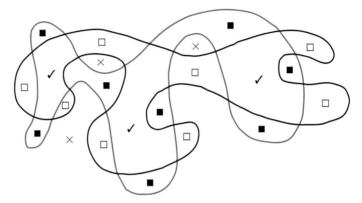

Count the number of regions of each of the four types. Compare your counts with the values obtained by other partners, and draw several additional examples to provide additional data. What connections do you see between the numbers of regions of each type in any crossing pattern created by two simple closed curves? Make a conjecture, and create additional examples to investigate your conjecture.

Making Connections

33. Access to underground utility cables, water pipes, and storm drains is usually provided by circular holes covered by heavy metal circular covers. What unsafe condition would be present if a square shape were used instead of the circular one?

34. The valve stems on fire hydrants are usually triangular or pentagonal. Fire trucks carry a special wrench with a triangular or pentagonal hole that fits over the valve stem.

(a) Why are squares and regular hexagons not used? (*Hint:* What is the shape of the jaws of ordinary adjustable wrenches?)

(b) Why are squares and regular hexagons the standard shape found in bolt heads and nuts?

🖥 Using a Computer

35. Draw two squares $ABCD$ and $AB'C'D'$ that share a common vertex at A. The labeling of the vertices is in the same direction (say counterclockwise) about the centers Q and E. Construct the midpoints R and S of $\overline{BD'}$ and $\overline{B'D}$.

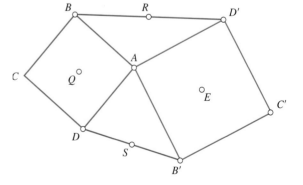

(a) What conclusion can you make about the quadrilateral *SQRE?*

(b) Does it make any difference if the squares overlap?

36. Construct a general quadrilateral *ABCD* and the midpoints *K, L, M,* and *N* of its sides. The quadrilateral *KLMN* is called the **medial quadrilateral** of *ABCD.*

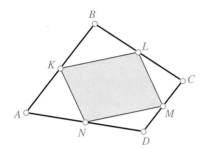

(a) What type of quadrilateral does *KLMN* appear to be? Explore with your dynamic geometry software.

(b) Construct two lines, perpendicular to one another. Next, construct a quadrilateral *ABCD* with vertices *A* and *C* on one of your lines, and vertices *B* and *D* on the other line. Finally, construct the medial quadrilateral *KLMN* of *ABCD.* What type of quadrilateral does the medial quadrilateral now appear to be? Explore with your software.

(c) Drag one of the vertices of the quadrilateral *ABCD* drawn in part (b) until the medial quadrilateral *KLMN* appears to be a square. What type of quadrilateral does *ABCD* appear to be? Explore with your software.

For Review

37. Find two triangles, one acute and one obtuse, whose interior angle measures are each an integer multiple of 36°. Give drawings of each type of triangle.

38. In the figure below ∠*APC* and ∠*BPD* are right angles. Show that ∠1 ≅ ∠3.

39. Prove that the two acute angles in a right triangle are complementary.

40. Let $\overline{PQ} \parallel \overline{AB}$ and $\overline{RQ} \parallel \overline{AC}$. Find the measures of ∠1, ∠2, . . . , ∠8. Explain how you find your answers.

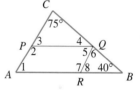

10.3   Figures in Space

The Picture Gallery of Space Figures on the next page shows several interesting examples of shapes whose points do not belong to a single plane. Intuitively, we think of space as three-dimensional. For example, the shape of a shoe box requires us to know not just width and length but height as well. In this section we classify, analyze, and represent some of the basic figures in space.

Planes and Lines in Space

There are infinitely many planes in space. Each plane partitions the points of space into three disjoint sets: the plane itself and two regions called **half-spaces.** Two planes are either **parallel** or intersect in a line, as shown in Figure 10.22.

The angle between two intersecting planes is called the **dihedral angle** (*di* = two, *hedral* = face of a geometrical form). A dihedral angle is measured by measuring an angle whose sides lie in the planes and are perpendicular to the line of intersection of the planes. Some examples of dihedral angles and their measures are shown in Figure 10.23.

A Picture Gallery of Space Figures

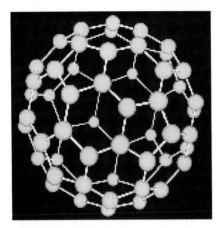

A Buckyball (named for Buckminster Fuller), the
third form of pure carbon

A seashell (left) and a computer drawn ideal representation

Leonardo da Vinci's drawings of an icosahedron
and a dodecahedron for Fra Luca Pacioli's
Di Divina Proportione

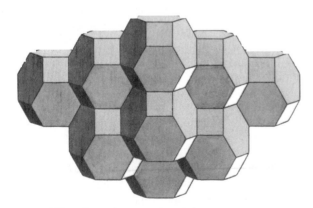

A partial filling of space by truncated octahedra

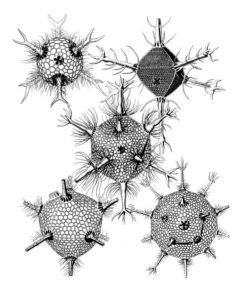

Skeletons of microscopic radiolaria

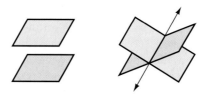

Figure 10.22
Parallel and intersecting planes

Parallel planes   Intersecting planes

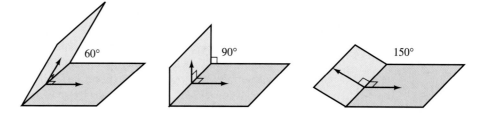

Figure 10.23
Dihedral angles and their
measures

Two nonintersecting lines in space are **parallel lines** if they belong to a common plane. Two nonintersecting lines which do not belong to a common plane are called **skew lines.** A line *l* that does not intersect a plane *P* is said to be **parallel to the plane.** A line *m* is **perpendicular to a plane** *Q* at point *A* if every line in the plane through *A* intersects *m* at a right angle. Figures illustrating these terms are shown in Figure 10.24.

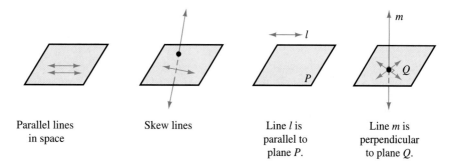

Figure 10.24
Lines and planes in space

Parallel lines   Skew lines   Line *l* is   Line *m* is
in space   parallel to   perpendicular
                                      plane *P*.   to plane *Q*.

Curves, Surfaces, and Solids

The intuitive concept of a curve can be extended from the plane to space by imagining figures drawn with a "magic" pencil whose point leaves a visible trace in the air. Two examples are shown in Figure 10.25, a helix (corkscrew) and a space octagon whose sides are 8 of the 12 edges of a cube.

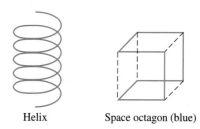

Figure 10.25
Two curves in space

Helix   Space octagon (blue)

No space curve will partition space. On the other hand, a **sphere,** which is the set of points at a constant distance from a single point called the **center,** does partition the remaining points of space into two disjoint regions, namely the points inside the sphere and the points outside the sphere. Any surface without holes and which encloses a hollow region—its interior—is called a **simple closed surface.** An easy check to see if a figure is a simple closed surface is to imagine what shape it would take if it were made of stretchy rubber: if it can be "blown up" into a sphere, then it is a simple closed surface.

The union of all points on a simple closed surface and all points in its interior form a space figure called a **solid.** For example, the shell of a hardboiled egg can be viewed, overlooking its thickness, as a simple closed surface; the shell together with the white and yolk of the egg form a solid.

A simple closed surface is **convex** if the line segment which joins any two of its points contains no point which is in the region exterior to the surface; that is, the solid bounded by the surface is a convex set in space. The sphere, soup can, and box shown in Figure 10.26 are all convex. The potato skin surface shown in the figure is not convex however, since it is possible to find two points on this surface for which the line segment contains points in the exterior region.

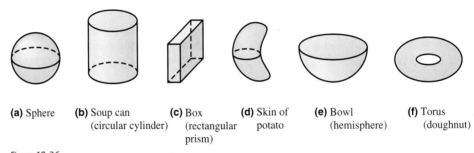

(a) Sphere   **(b)** Soup can   **(c)** Box   **(d)** Skin of   **(e)** Bowl   **(f)** Torus
(circular cylinder)   (rectangular prism)   potato   (hemisphere)   (doughnut)

Figure 10.26
(a), (b), (c), and (d) are simple closed surfaces; (e) is a nonclosed surface; and (f) is closed but not simple

Polyhedra

Joining plane polygonal regions edge-to-edge forms a simple closed surface called a **polyhedron.**

DEFINITION *Polyhedron*
A **polyhedron** is a simple closed surface formed from planar polygonal regions. Each polygonal region is called a **face** of the polyhedron. The vertices and edges of the polygonal regions are called the **vertices** and **edges** of the polyhedron.

Polyhedra (*polyhedra* is the plural of polyhedron) are named according to the number of faces. For example, a **tetrahedron** has 4 faces, a **pentahedron** has 5 faces, a **hexahedron** has 6 faces, and so on. Several polyhedra are pictured in Figure 10.27.

The most spectacular polyhedral shapes on earth are the Egyptian and Mayan pyramids. Egyptian pyramids have a square base and four congruent triangular faces which meet at a common vertex. The Mayan pyramids have a stepped form. In geometry, a **pyramid** can have any polygonal region as a base. Triangular faces rise from the base

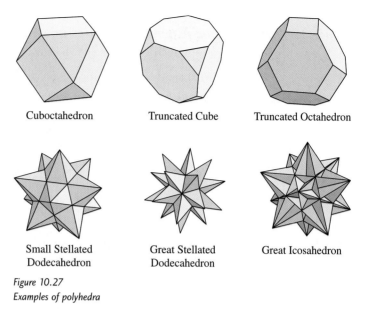

Cuboctahedron   Truncated Cube   Truncated Octahedron

Small Stellated   Great Stellated   Great Icosahedron
Dodecahedron   Dodecahedron

Figure 10.27
Examples of polyhedra

edges to meet at a common vertex, called the **apex** of the pyramid, a point that is not in the plane of the base. Examples of pyramids and their names are shown in Figure 10.28.

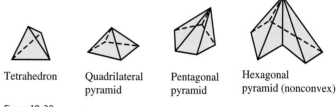

Tetrahedron   Quadrilateral   Pentagonal   Hexagonal
                pyramid   pyramid   pyramid (nonconvex)

Figure 10.28
Pyramids and their names

Another commonly occurring shape is a **prism.** A prism has two **bases** which are congruent polygonal regions lying in parallel planes; the lateral faces joining the bases are all parallelograms. If the lateral faces of a prism are all rectangles it is a **right prism;** otherwise, it is an **oblique prism** and the lateral edges are not perpendicular to the plane of the base. Examples of prisms and their names are shown in Figure 10.29.

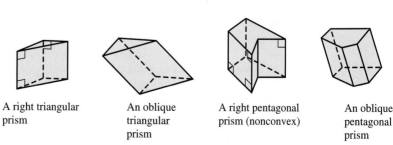

A right triangular   An oblique   A right pentagonal   An oblique
prism   triangular   prism (nonconvex)   pentagonal
                       prism   prism

Figure 10.29
Right and oblique prisms

EXAMPLE 10.15

Determining Angles and Planes in a Hexagonal Prism

The bases of the right prism shown below are regular hexagonal regions:

(a) What are the measures of the dihedral angles at which the faces intersect?

(b) How many pairs of parallel planes contain the faces of this prism?

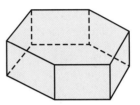

Solution

(a) Since the prism is a right prism, the dihedral angles made by either base to any lateral face measure 90°. The lateral faces meet at 120° angles, since this is the measure of the interior angles of a regular hexagon.

(b) The opposite sides of a regular hexagon are parallel, so there are three pairs of parallel planes containing the opposite lateral faces of the prism. A fourth pair of parallel planes contains the hexagonal bases of the prism.

Regular Polyhedra

> **DEFINITION** *Regular Polyhedron*
> A **regular polyhedron** is a polyhedron with these properties:
> - the surface is convex;
> - the faces are congruent regular polygonal regions;
> - the same number of faces meet at each vertex of the polyhedron.

The most common regular polyhedron is the cube: the six faces are congruent squares, and three squares meet at each of the eight vertices. The cube is the only regular polyhedron with square faces, since if we attempted to put four squares about a single vertex, their interior angle measures add up to 360°. That is, four edge-to-edge squares with a common vertex lie in a common plane and therefore cannot form a "corner" figure of a regular polyhedron.

Similar reasoning with equilateral triangles shows that corner figures in space can be formed with either 3, 4, or 5 congruent copies of the triangle. However, a convex corner cannot be formed with six or more equilateral triangles. Likewise, there is just one way to form a corner with congruent regular pentagons, and it is impossible to form a corner figure from regular n-gons for any $n \geq 6$. The possible corner figures of regular polyhedra are shown in Figure 10.30.

Surprisingly, each of the five corner figures depicted in Figure 10.30 can be completed to form a regular polyhedron. These are shown in Table 10.4, which also shows patterns called **nets**. Models of the polyhedra can be made by cutting the net from heavy paper, folding, and gluing. It helps to include flaps on every other outside edge of the net; these are then coated with glue and tucked under the adjoining face, forming a sturdy model.

JUST FOR FUN

Space Out for Success!

These five matches form two triangles. Show that six matches, touching only at their ends, can form four triangles.

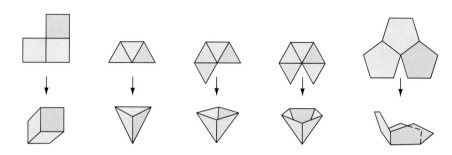

Figure 10.30
The five ways to form corner figures with congruent regular polygons

TABLE 10.4	The Five Regular Polyhedra		
Polyhedron Name	Face Polygons	Net	Model
Cube	6 squares		
Tetrahedron	4 equilateral triangles		
Octahedron	8 equilateral triangles		
Icosahedron	20 equilateral triangles		
Dodecahedron	12 regular pentagons		

The five regular polyhedra were known to the ancient Greeks. They are described in Plato's book *The Republic* and so the shapes are often referred to as the **Platonic solids.** Theaetetas (c. 415–369 B.C.), a member of the Platonic school, is credited with the first proof that there are no regular polyhedra other than the five known to Plato.

Euler's Formula for Polyhedra

The name given to a polyhedron usually indicates its number of faces. For example, an octahedron has eight faces. A more complete description of a polyhedron may include its number of vertices and edges. The following notation will be useful:

$$F = \text{the number of faces of a polyhedron}$$
$$V = \text{the number of vertices of a polyhedron}$$
$$E = \text{the number of edges of a polyhedron}$$

For a regular octahedron we have $F = 8$, $V = 6$, and $E = 12$.

COOPERATIVE INVESTIGATION

The Envelope Tetrahedron Model

Diagrams and photos of polyhedra are certainly useful, but physical models that can be seen and touched are much better. The construction of models of polyhedra is a worthwhile classroom activity; useful geometric principles are learned as students create beautiful and interesting shapes. Skeletal models are formed easily from drinking straws joined by thin string run through the straws and tied at the vertices. Paper models, in which a carefully drawn net of the polyhedron is cut, folded, and glued, can be colored in interesting ways.

Here is a quick way to construct a regular tetrahedron from an ordinary envelope.

1. Glue the flap of the envelope down.
2. Fold the envelope in half lengthwise, forming a crease $\overline{AB}$ along the centerline.
3. Fold a corner point C upward from corner D, so that C determines point E on the centerline. Once E is found, flatten out the fold.
4. Fold the envelope straight across at E, and then cut the envelope off at the height of E.
5. Make sharp folds along $\overline{DE}$ and $\overline{CE}$.
6. Open up the envelope by pulling the two sides of the envelope at E apart; a regular tetrahedron should appear!

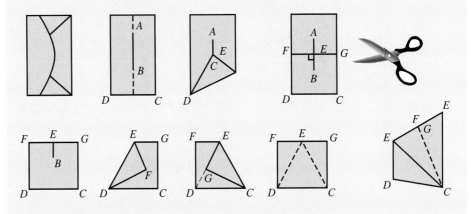

After completing your model, justify the construction procedure.

In 1752 the great Swiss mathematician Leonhard Euler discovered that the number of faces F, the number of vertices V, and the number of edges E are related to one another. Euler was unaware that he had rediscovered a formula found about 1635 by the French mathematician-philosopher Rene Descartes.

EXAMPLE 10.16 | Discovering Euler's Formula

Let V, F, and E denote the respective number of vertices, faces, and edges of a polyhedron. What relationship holds between V, F, and E?

DID YOU KNOW?

A Flexible Polyhedron

When a paper model of a polyhedron is constructed by cutting, folding, and gluing a pattern net such as shown in Table 10.4, the partially completed model is quite flexible. However, when the last face is glued in place no flexibility remains. The French mathematician Augustin-Louis Cauchy (1789–1857) conjectured that all polyhedra were rigid, and in 1813 proved that all *convex* polyhedra were indeed rigid. For over 150 years no one could show that nonconvex polyhedra must also be rigid. In 1978 the issue was resolved in an unexpected direction: Robert Connelly of Cornell University constructed a polyhedron from 18 triangular faces which is noticeably flexible! Several other flexible polyhedra are now known. The simplest one, with just 14 faces, was found by Klaus Steffen. It is pictured below, together with its pattern. All of the flexible polyhedra discovered so far share a remarkable property: as the surface flexes, the volume of the enclosed region remains the same!

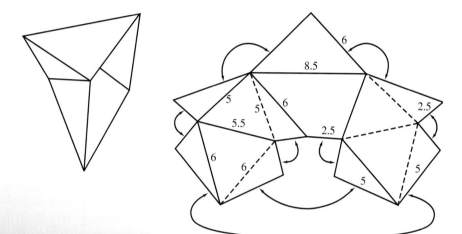

SOURCE: Figure 21 and Figure 22 from *Mathematics Magazine*, Volume 52, Number 5, November 1979, p. 281. Copyright © 1979 by the Mathematical Association of America. Reprinted by permission.

Solution

Understand the problem

The numbers V, E, and F are not independent of one another. The goal is to uncover a formula which relates the three numbers corresponding to *any* polyhedron.

Devise a plan

Formulas are often revealed by seeing a pattern in special cases. By making a table of values of V, F, and E we have a better chance to see what this pattern may be. To be confident that the pattern holds for all polyhedra, we need to examine polyhedra of varied kinds.

Carry out the plan

A pentagonal pyramid, a hexagonal prism, a "house," and a truncated icosahedron are shown below. The truncated icosahedron, formed by slicing off the corners of an icosahedron to form pentagons, may look familiar; it is a common pattern on soccer balls.

  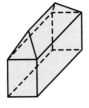

The following table lists the number of vertices, edges, and faces for these polyhedra as well as for some of the regular polyhedra depicted in Table 10.4.

Polyhedron	V	F	E
Pentagonal Pyramid	6	6	10
Hexagonal Prism	12	8	18
"House"	10	9	17
Cube	8	6	12
Tetrahedron	4	4	6
Octahedron	6	8	12
Truncated Icosahedron	60	32	90

The table reveals that the sum of the number of vertices and faces is 2 larger than the number of edges. That is, $V + F = E + 2$.

Look back

If any two values of V, F, and E are known, the remaining value can be found using Euler's formula $V + F = E + 2$. For example, the dodecahedron has $F = 12$ pentagonal faces. The product $5 \cdot 12$ counts *twice* the number of edges, since each edge borders two of the pentagonal faces. Thus, $E = 5 \cdot 12/2 = 30$ for the dodecahedron. Euler's formula can now be used to compute the number of vertices. Solving for V we get $V = E + 2 - F = 30 + 2 - 12 = 20$, so a dodecahedron has 20 vertices.

The evidence gathered in Example 10.16 supports the following theorem. A proof of the theorem is given in Section 10.4 on Networks.

THEOREM *Euler's Formula for Polyhedra*

Let V, E, F denote the respective number of vertices, edges, and faces of a polyhedron. Then

$$V + F = E + 2.$$

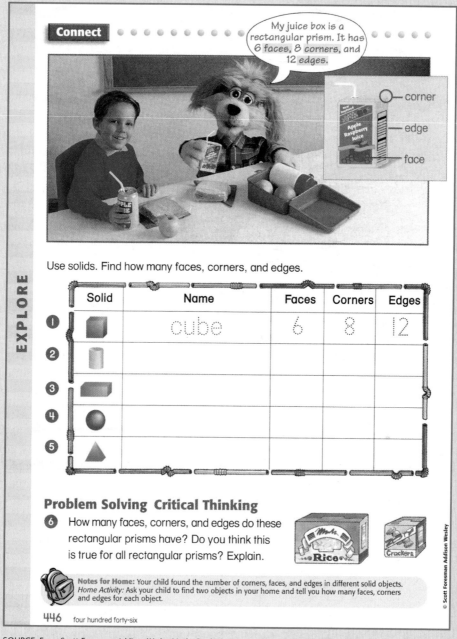

SOURCE: From *Scott Foresman–Addison Wesley Math*, Grade 2, p. 446, by Randall I. Charles et al. Copyright © 1999, Addison Wesley Longman.

Questions for the Teacher

1. All the students have identified the second solid as a cylinder, but some have filled in the respective numbers of faces, corners, and edges with 2, 0, 0 and others think it should be 3, 0, 2. Which answer is correct, and how would you explain the mistakes being made by some of the students?

2. In *Notes for Home* at the bottom of the school book page, there will be little difficulty for students to find examples of rectangular prisms in their homes. What are other objects they may look for having some of the other shapes shown on the school book page?

EXAMPLE   10.17

Searching for Polyhedra with Hexagonal Faces

The Epcot Center in Florida is the site of one of the world's largest geodesic domes. The surface of the 165 foot diameter structure is covered with both hexagons and pentagons. Similarly, the microscopic frame of the radiolarian is covered by pentagons and hexagons. These shapes suggest the following question: *Can all the faces of a polyhedron be hexagonal?* Show that this is not possible, even if the hexagons need not all be congruent and are permitted to be irregular. Assume that three hexagons meet at each vertex.

 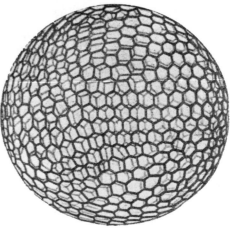

Solution

Suppose, to the contrary, that hexagonal faces can form a polyhedron. As usual, let F, E, and V denote the number of faces, edges, and vertices. Since each face is bordered by 6 edges and each edge touches 2 faces we obtain the formula $6F = 2E$. Thus, we have $E = 3F$. Similarly, three hexagons surround each of the V vertices, and each of the F hexagonal faces touches 6 vertices. This gives $3V = 6F$, which simplifies to $V = 2F$. Adding F to both sides of this equality gives $V + F = 3F$. But we have also shown that $3F = E$, so $V + F = E$. Since this contradicts Euler's formula, $V + F = E + 2$, we conclude that there is no polyhedron with each face hexagonal.

Cones and Cylinders

Cones and cylinders are simple closed surfaces which generalize pyramids and prisms respectively. A **cone** has a **base** that is any region bounded by a simple closed curve in a plane. The curved **lateral surface** is generated by the line segments which join one point—the **apex** (or **vertex**)—not in the plane of the base to the points of the curve bounding the base. A **right circular cone,** an **oblique circular cone,** and a **general cone** are shown in Figure 10.31. The line segment $\overline{AB}$ through the apex A of a cone that intersects the plane of the base perpendicularly at B is called the **altitude** of the cone.

A **cylinder** is the surface generated by translating the points of a simple closed region in one plane to a parallel plane. Examples are shown in Figure 10.32. The points joining corresponding points on the curves bounding the bases form the **lateral surface.** If the line segments joining corresponding points in the two bases are perpendicular to the planes of the bases, it is a **right cylinder.** Cylinders that are not right cylinders are **oblique cylinders.**

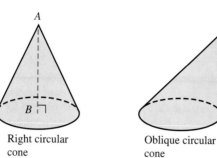

Right circular
cone

Oblique circular
cone

General cone

Figure 10.31
A right circular cone, an oblique circular cone, and a general cone

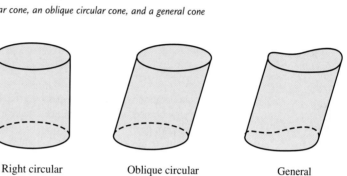

Right circular
cylinder

Oblique circular
cylinder

General
cylinder

Figure 10.32
A right circular, oblique circular, and general cylinder.

COOPERATIVE INVESTIGATION

From Paper Discs to Polyhedra

Materials Needed

Five congruent (about 4 to 5 inch diameter) paper discs per person, glue sticks

Directions

In the Cooperative Investigation *From Paper Discs to Polygons* (see Section 10.2), it was discovered that a paper disc can be folded into an equilateral triangle by folding three arcs to the center *O* of the disc.

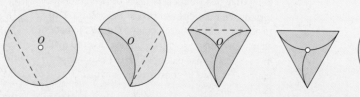

In this investigation, you will work in groups of four to fold and glue paper discs to construct polyhedra.

Activities

Each group (not individuals) will construct the polyhedra described below.

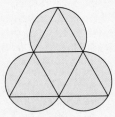

1. Glue four triangles together to form the pattern shown here. The circular segments between triangles are folded upward and glued together along their common edge. Now fold the remaining six circular segments upright, apply glue, and make a regular tetrahedron.

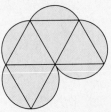

2. Use a glue stick to construct *two* copies of the 4-triangle pattern shown here. Join the two patterns to make a regular octahedron.

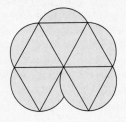

3. Work in cooperation with another 4-person group to construct an icosahedron. Each group can make a 5-disc pattern as shown here. What other pattern can each group make to complete the icosahedron?

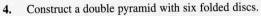

4. Construct a double pyramid with six folded discs.

5. Convex polyhedra with congruent equilateral triangular faces are called **deltahedra.** Four deltahedra have been constructed in Activities 1 through 4. There are eight deltahedra in all—see if you can find the remaining four types by constructing new deltahedra with folded discs. Compare your discoveries with other groups.

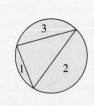

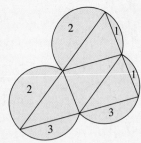

6. Fold a stack of four paper discs to form four congruent *scalene* triangles. Glue the four discs to form the pattern shown. Does this pattern form an irregular tetrahedron?

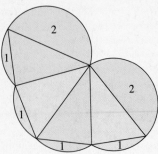

7. Fold eight congruent scalene triangles. Turn four of the discs upside down (it's helpful to make the eight triangles from paper discs of two colors, turning over the discs of one of the colors). Use two folded discs of each color to make the pattern shown, and then use the remaining discs to make an identical 4-disc pattern. Can the two 4-disc patterns be used to construct an irregular octahedron?

PROBLEM SET 10.3

Understanding Concepts

1. Which of the following figures are polyhedra?

(a)   (b)   (c)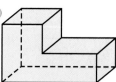

(d)   (e)   (f)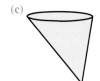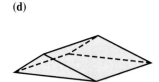

2. Name each of these surfaces.

(a)   (b)   (c)   (d)

(e) 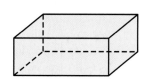   (f)   (g)

---

3. A tetrahedron is shown below.
   (a) How many planes contain its faces?
   (b) Name all of the edges.
   (c) Name all of the vertices.
   (d) Name all of the faces.

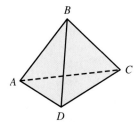

4. Draw free-hand pictures of the following figures, using dashed lines to indicate hidden edges. Don't just copy—transfer the image in your mind to paper.

(a) cube   (b) tetrahedron   (c) square pyramid
(d) pentagonal right prism
(e) oblique hexagonal prism
(f) octahedron   (g) right circular cone

5. A cube with vertices A, B, C, D, E, F, G, H is shown below. Vertices D, E, G, H are the vertices of a tetrahedron inscribed in the cube.

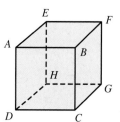

(a) Trace the cube in one color and then draw the tetrahedron *DEGH* in a different color.

(b) Three of the faces of the tetrahedron *DEGH* are subsets of the faces of the cube. Find a tetrahedron inscribed in the cube which has none of its faces in the planes of the faces of the cube. Sketch your tetrahedron and the surrounding cube.

6. The pattern shown at the left folds up to form the cube on the right.

Sketch the letter, *in its correct orientation*, that should appear on each blank face shown below, where the same pattern is used.

(a)   **(b)**   (c)

7. The apex of the pyramid shown below is at the center of the cube shown by the dashed lines. What is the dihedral angle which each lateral face of the pyramid makes **(a)** to the square base? **(b)** to an adjacent lateral face? *(Hint for (b):* It will help to imagine that the cube is filled with six congruent pyramids whose apexes coincide at the cube's center.)

8. The figure shown here is a right prism whose bases are regular pentagons.

   (a) What is the measure of the dihedral angle between each lateral face and a base?

(b) What is the measure of the dihedral angle between adjacent lateral faces?

9. Sketch a cube. Color the eight vertices either red or blue (or mark R or B at the vertices) so that no plane through any four vertices of the cube has the same color at all four vertices.

10. The numbers in the 2 by 3 grid of squares correspond to the pattern of stacked cubes shown in the **isometric drawing** at the right.

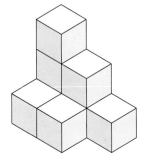

3	2	1
1	1	0

Make an isometric drawing of of these patterns.

2	3	2
2	2	1

(a)

4	2
3	0
1	1

(b)

11. Are any of the regular polyhedra **(a)** prisms? **(b)** pyramids?

12. Verify Euler's formula for

   (a) a pyramid with a hexagonal base.

   (b) a prism with octagonal bases.

   (c) the regular icosahedron. [*Suggestion:* Modify the counting method used for the regular dodecahedron in the Look Back step of Example 10.16.]

13. Complete the table below using Euler's formula. These four polyhedra are representative of a class of 13 polyhedra discovered by Archimedes.

Truncated tetrahedron   Truncated dodecahedron

Snub cube   Great rhombicosidodecahedron

| Polyhedron | Number of Vertices, Faces, and Edges | | |
	V	*F*	*E*
Truncated tetrahedron	12	8	____
Truncated dodecahedron	____	32	90
Snub cube	24	____	60
Great rhombicosidodecahedron	120	62	____

14. A **double pyramid** (or **dipyramid**) is a polyhedron with triangular faces arranged about a plane polygon and extending both upward to an upper apex and downward to a lower apex.

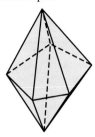

   (a) Find the number of vertices, edges, and faces for the pentagonal double pyramid shown. Then verify that Euler's formula is satisfied.

   (b) Repeat part (a), but for the double pyramid built from a polygon with 20 sides.

15. An **antiprism** has two base polygons with the same number of sides, together with triangular lateral faces.

   (a) Find the number of vertices, edges, and faces for the hexagonal antiprism shown. Then verify that Euler's formula is satisfied.

   (b) Repeat part (a), but for an antiprism whose bases are 23-gons.

16. Draw nets corresponding to the following polyhedra.

   (a) A square pyramid with equilateral triangular faces.

   (b) A truncated tetrahedron. (See the figure in problem 13.)

17. Check whether Euler's formula holds for the figures below. If not explain what assumption required for Euler's formula is not met.

   (a)   (b)   (c)

                                   (An octahedron with
                                   a square hole)

Thinking Critically

18. Let V, E, F denote the number of vertices, edges, and faces of a polyhedron.

   (a) Explain why $2E \geq 3F$. (*Hint:* Every face has at least three sides, and every edge borders two faces.)

   (b) Explain why $2E \geq 3V$. (*Hint:* Every vertex is the endpoint of at least three edges.)

   (c) Show that every polyhedron has at least six edges. (*Hint:* Add the inequalities of parts (a) and (b), and use Euler's formula.)

   (d) Use (a) and (b) to prove that no polyhedron can have seven edges. (*Hint:* Use Euler's formula.)

   (e) Show that there are polyhedra with 6, 8, 9, 10, . . . edges.

19. A convex polyhedron with five faces is called a **pentahedron.** Find and sketch two different types of pentahedra. (*Hint:* One is "easy as pie.")

20. A polyhedron with six faces is a **hexahedron.** For example, a cube is a hexahedron.

   (a) Draw a pyramid that is a hexahedron.

   (b) Draw a double pyramid (see problem 14) that is a hexahedron.

21. Suppose a skeletal model of a convex polyhedron is made, outlining just the edges of the polyhedron. If the model is viewed in perspective from a position just outside the center of a face, the edges of that face form a bounding polygon inside which the remaining edges are seen. The resulting pattern of edges is called a **Schlegel diagram,** named for the German mathematician Viktor Schlegel who invented the diagram in 1883. Schlegel diagrams for the cube and dodecahedron are shown below.

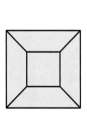   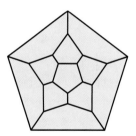

   Draw Schlegel diagrams for:

   (a) the tetrahedron, (b) the octahedron, (c) the icosahedron. (*Hint:* Start by drawing a large equilateral triangle, and keep in mind each vertex must have degree five.)

22. The dihedral angles of the regular polyhedra are given in the following table.

Regular Polyhedron	Measure of Dihedral Angle (in degrees and minutes)
Cube	90°
Tetrahedron	70° 32′
Octahedron	109° 28′
Dodecahedron	116° 34′
Icosahedron	138° 11′

(a) How many tetrahedra can be placed about a common edge without overlap? What is the size of the gap that remains?

(b) Why is the cube the only regular polyhedron that will fill space?

Thinking Cooperatively

23. Five congruent squares can be joined along edges to form 12 distinct shapes known as **pentominoes.** Pentominoes were invented by mathematician and electrical engineer Solomon Golomb in 1953 in a talk to the Harvard Mathematics Club. They are named by the letters they somewhat resemble.

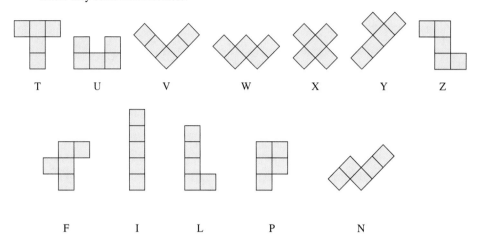

T   U   V   W   X   Y   Z

F   I   L   P   N

Source: Figure 10, "The pentominoes" from *Polyominoes* by Solomon W. Golomb, page 23. (Charles Scribner's Sons, 1965, Revised Edition, Princeton University Press, 1994.) Copyright © 1965 by Solomon W. Golomb. Reprinted with permission of the author.

(a) Which of the twelve pentominoes can be folded to form a cube-shaped box with an open top?

(b) Copy the T pentomino onto paper, cut the pattern with scissors, and construct an open topped cubical box by taping edges. Now choose a target pentomino (not the T!), and sketch it on the bottom of the box. Then, use scissors to cut the box apart to form the targeted pentomino shape.
[*Note:* This activity was created by Marion Walter of the University of Oregon, who makes the open boxes by cutting off the bottoms of clean milk cartons.]

24. A **hexomino** is formed by joining six congruent squares along edges. There are 35 different hexominoes in all, including the five shown at the right.

(a) Hexomino (i) is a net for a cube. Which of the other four hexominoes shown can be folded to form a cube?

(b) There are 11 hexominoes that can be folded to form a cube. Try to find all 11 shapes. Be careful not to repeat a shape; two congruent shapes may at first appear to be different when one is rotated or flipped over.

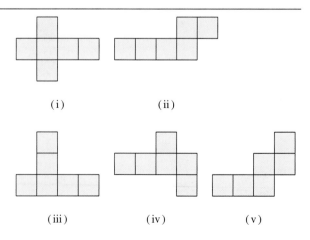

(i)   (ii)

(iii)   (iv)   (v)

25. A net for a square pyramid is shown below on the left. A net for a more general quadrilateral pyramid is shown to the right. The dot at P in each net locates the point in the plane of the base directly beneath the apex of the pyramid.

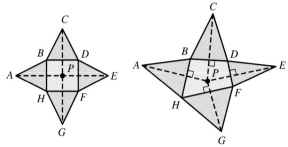

(a) Explain why $AB = BC, CD = DE, \ldots, GH = HA$ in the nets and why the dashed lines from P are perpendicular to the sides of the base polygon.

(b) Draw a convex polygon, a point P in its interior, and the rays from P that are perpendicular to the sides of the polygon. Choose a point A on one of the rays, and use a compass to draw the arc at vertex B that constructs point C as the intersection of the arc with the next ray (see the figure). Continue to draw circular arcs, completing your pattern. Finally, cut, fold, and tape your pattern to construct your paper pyramid.

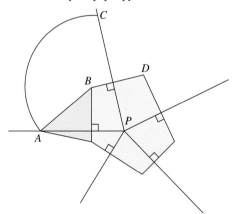

Making Connections

26. The round door shown below has a problem. What facts of space geometry create a difficulty?

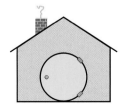

What is important about the placement of door hinges?

27. The ancient Greeks divided physical space into five parts: the universe, earth, air, fire, and water. Each of these was associated with one of the five regular polyhedra. Investigate what correspondence was made.

28. Biologists and physical scientists frequently become involved with the analysis of shape and form. For example, many viruses have an icosahedral structure and the crystalline structures of minerals are often polyhedral forms of considerable beauty. An example of a pyrite crystal is shown here.

Browse through your school library and see what three-dimensional shapes are receiving interest and attention. Report on your findings.

From State Student Assessments

29. (Washington State, Grade 4)
Look at the cube below.

Now look at figures A, B, and C.

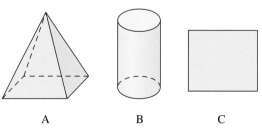

A   B   C

Choose one figure. Tell what that figure has in common with the cube. Explain your answer using words, numbers, or pictures. Now choose a different figure. Tell something it has in common with the cube. Explain your answer using words, numbers, or pictures.

For Review

30. Find the measures of x, y, and z in the following figure, where $l \parallel m$.

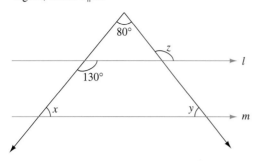

31. A triangle has no diagonals and a convex quadrilateral has two diagonals.

(a) Fill in the entries in the following table.

			n			
	3	4	5	6	7	8
Number of diagonals in convex n-gon	0	2				

(b) Describe a pattern which you see in the table.

(c) How many diagonals are in a convex dodecagon?

(d) How many diagonals are in a convex 100-gon?

32. It is easy to join the 12 points of a 3 by 4 square array by a polygon. Here is one way.

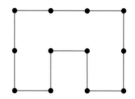

Find polygons which join all of the points of these square arrays.

(a) 4 by 6   (b) 5 by 7

10.4   Networks

The Königsberg Bridge Problem

Leonhard Euler (1707–1783) (see biography in Section 9.2) lived for a short time in the East Prussian city of Königsberg, now called Kaliningrad in the Russian Federation. The Pregel River flows through the city, forming two islands. At the time of Euler there were seven bridges connecting the islands to one another and to the two sides of the river. Euler's own drawing is reproduced in Figure 10.33. The islands are labeled A and D, the shores of the river are labeled B and C, and the bridges are labeled a, b, c, d, e, f, and g.

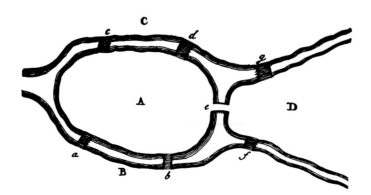

Figure 10.33
The seven bridges of Königsberg in the early 1700s

It was common for Königsbergers to take Sunday walks, and people wondered if it was possible to walk over all seven bridges without crossing any bridge more than one time. Euler solved the now famous Königsberg Bridge Problem to illustrate the ideas of what he called "the geometry of position," and what today is called topology. His most important step was to associate each of the four land masses with a point—*A, B, C,* or *D.* For each bridge joining one land mass to another he drew a curve from one point to the other corresponding point. The result, shown in Figure 10.34, is a system of points and curves known as a **network.**

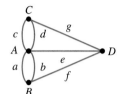

Figure 10.34
The network corresponding to the Königsberg Bridge Problem

The distances between points and the precise shape of the curves joining points are of no importance; what is important is that there are two bridges between *A* and *B,* that there is no bridge connecting *B* and *C,* and so on. Because the network contains all of the problem's relevant information, Euler was able to phrase the Königsberg Bridge Problem in a new way.

*Without lifting your pencil can you trace over **all** edges of the network exactly once?*

Euler realized that a deeper understanding of the problem would be gained if the question were asked for general networks, not just the one corresponding to the Königsberg Bridges.

DEFINITION *Network*

A **network** consists of two finite sets:

- a set of **vertices,** represented by a set of points in the plane,

and

- a set of **edges** that join some of the pairs of vertices, represented by joining the corresponding points in the plane by a curve.

Some additional examples of networks are shown in Figure 10.35. Any edge of a network must always have its endpoints at vertices of the network and there is no other vertex along the edge. In particular, a point at which two edges cross one another is not a vertex of the network. For example, network (2) of Figure 10.35 has just the six vertices shown by the large dots.

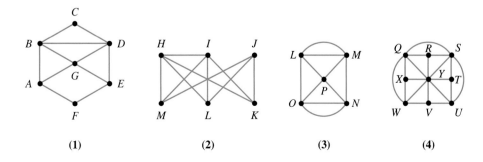

Figure 10.35
Four examples of networks

(1) (2) (3) (4)

A **path** in a network is a curve traced by following a sequence of edges in the network, where no edge is retraced but vertices can be revisited. If every pair of vertices of a network can be joined by some path, then we say that the network is **connected.** For example, each of the four networks in Figure 10.35 is connected. The Konigsberg Bridge Problem is then equivalent to asking if there is a path that covers each edge of a network once and only once.

> **DEFINITION**   *Euler Paths and Traversable Networks*
> An **Euler path** in a network is a path that traverses each edge once and only once. A network is **traversable** if, and only if, it has an Euler path.

In the next example, you will discover that classifying the vertices of a network as even or odd is most helpful in a search for an Euler path.

> **DEFINITION**   *Degree, Even, and Odd Vertices*
> * The **degree** of a vertex is the number of edges emanating from the vertex.
> * A vertex is **odd** if it has odd degree.
> * A vertex is **even** if it has even degree.

For example, vertices *A* and *E* of the network (1) of Figure 10.35 are odd since they have degree 3. The vertices *B* and *C* are even with respective degrees 4 and 2.

EXAMPLE 10.18	**When Is a Network Traversable?**

(a) Which of the networks in Figure 10.35 are traversable?
Experiment by tracing a path on a sheet of paper laid over the network.

(b) What is the number of odd vertices in each of the networks?

(c) Do you see any connection between the traversability of a network and the number of odd vertices?

Solution

(a) Network (1) is traversable; one path is *ABCDEFAGBDGE.*
Network (2) is not traversable.
Network (3) is traversable; one path is *LMNOLMPNOPL.*
Network (4) is not traversable.

(b) Network (1) has 2 odd vertices: *A* and *E.*
Network (2) has 4 odd vertices: *J, K, L, M.*
Network (3) has 0 odd vertices.
Network (4) has 6 odd vertices: *Q, R, S, T, V, X.*

(c) The networks with 0 or 2 odd vertices are traversable.
The networks with 4 or 6 odd vertices are not traversable.

Euler observed that each time a path passes through a vertex it uses two edges: one to enter the vertex and another to exit. Except for the beginning and ending vertices all of the

other vertices of a traversable network must therefore be even vertices, and it is impossible to traverse a network with more than two odd vertices. If there are two odd vertices, these are necessarily the endpoints of the Euler path. If there are no odd vertices the Euler path must terminate at the same vertex as it started, and the path forms a closed curve passing over each edge exactly one time.

This reasoning shows that if a network is traversable then it has 0 or 2 odd vertices. With more effort, the converse can also be shown: any connected network with 0 or 2 odd vertices is traversable. This is a celebrated result of Euler.

> **THEOREM** *Euler's Traversability Theorem*
> A connected network is traversable if, and only if, it has either no odd vertices or two odd vertices. If it has no odd vertices, any Euler path is a closed curve which ends at the same vertex it started from. If the network has two odd vertices, these vertices are the endpoints of any Euler path.

Since the Königsberg Bridge network has four odd vertices, there is no Euler path. Königsbergers must recross some bridge on their walk.

The Königsberg Bridge Problem and the traversability of networks may appear to have no practical importance, but in fact there are many useful applications to real problems. Here are two examples:

- What route can a telephone company inspection crew follow to check all of its lines without having to go over any section twice?
- What route can a street sweeper follow to clean all of the city streets and not have to travel over any blocks that have already been cleaned?

Counting Vertices, Edges, and Regions in Planar Networks

> **DEFINITION** *Planar Network*
> A network is **planar** if it can be drawn in the plane without any intersection points of its edges other than endpoints.

For example, the network with four vertices and edges between each pair of distinct vertices is planar, as shown in Figure 10.36. There are no intersections of the edges. The network on five vertices with edges between each pair of distinct vertices is not planar, since it is impossible to arrange all of the edges so that no two of them intersect. By removing just one edge you can arrange the remaining nine edges between five vertices to form a planar network. Try it!

Figure 10.36
A planar and nonplanar network

Planar   Nonplanar

Any connected planar network partitions the plane into disjoint regions. It is interesting to count the number of vertices V, the number of edges E, and the number of regions R which correspond to a connected network.

EXAMPLE   10.19

Counting Vertices, Edges, and Regions

The connected network below has $V = 7$ vertices, $E = 9$ edges, and partitions the plane into $R = 4$ regions (the unbounded region is counted).

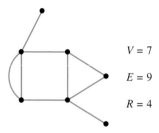

$V = 7$

$E = 9$

$R = 4$

The values 7, 4, and 9 of V, R, and E have been entered in the table. Next, count V, E, and R for each of the following networks, and enter their values in the table.

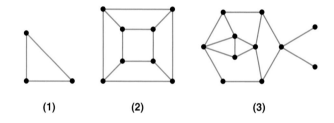

(1)   (2)   (3)

	V	R	E
	7	4	9
(1)			
(2)			
(3)			

Do you see a pattern? Draw more examples to check your conjecture.

Solution

You should discover that the sum of the number of vertices and the number of regions is 2 more than the number of edges.

The exploration in Example 10.19 leads to the conjecture that the formula $V + R = E + 2$ holds for every connected planar network. An example is shown in Figure 10.37.

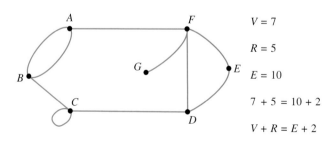

Figure 10.37
Euler's formula $V + R = E + 2$
holds for any connected planar
network with V vertices, R
regions, and E edges.

$V = 7$

$R = 5$

$E = 10$

$7 + 5 = 10 + 2$

$V + R = E + 2$

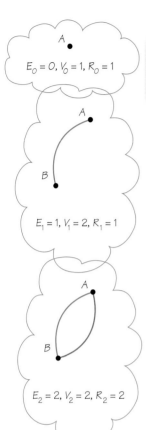

$E_0 = 0, V_0 = 1, R_0 = 1$

$E_1 = 1, V_1 = 2, R_1 = 1$

$E_2 = 2, V_2 = 2, R_2 = 2$

THEOREM   *Euler's Formula for Connected Planar Networks*

Let V be the number of vertices, R the number of regions, and E the number of edges of a connected planar network. Then V, R, and E satisfy **Euler's formula:**

$$V + R = E + 2$$

Proof*:   An informal justification for Euler's formula rests on the idea of beginning with a single point and then appending one edge at a time until any given network is completely drawn.

To keep the discussion concrete, consider drawing the network shown in Figure 10.37. Draw vertex A to start. This minimal network has one vertex ($V_0 = 1$), one region ($R_0 = 1$), and no edges ($E_0 = 0$). Thus, Euler's formula $V_0 + R_0 = E_0 + 2$ is satisfied, since $1 + 1 = 0 + 2$. Now add the vertex B and one edge joining A with B. The new network increases the number of vertices by one ($V_1 = V_0 + 1$), increases the number of edges by one ($E_1 = E_0 + 1$), and leaves the number of regions unchanged ($R_1 = R_0$). Adding 1 to each side of the equation $V_0 + R_0 = E_0 + 2$ gives us ($V_0 + 1$) $+ R_0 = (E_0 + 1) + 2$. This can be rewritten as $V_1 + R_1 = E_1 + 2$, so Euler's formula continues to hold. Next, draw the second edge from A to B. This increases both the number of edges and number of regions by one. Since adding 1 to both sides of $V_1 + R_1 = E_1 + 2$ gives ($V_1 + 1$) $+ R_1 = (E_1 + 1) + 2$, we see that Euler's formula $V_2 + R_2 = E_2 + 2$ holds for the network consisting of the vertices A and B and the two edges joining these vertices. Continuing in this way, each new edge appended to the existing network preserves the validity of Euler's formula. In particular, the formula holds when the network is completed.

EXAMPLE   10.20

Solving the Pizza Problem

Suppose C cuts are made across a circular pizza, and there are I points of intersection of pairs of cuts. Assume no two cuts intersect on the bounding circle, and no three cuts intersect at the same point inside the pizza. How many pieces, P, of pizza are there?

Solution   *Understand the problem*

It helps to examine a particular case, such as the one shown here. The cuts are drawn to satisfy the conditions of the problem. In the drawing we can see that 4 cuts and 3 intersections of cuts result in 8 pieces of pizza. Our goal is to see if we can find a formula that gives us the number P in terms of the variables C and I.

C = 4 cuts
I = 3 intersections of cuts
P = 8 pieces of pizza

*Optional

Devise a plan

The cut up pizza can be viewed as a connected planar network. If we can determine the numbers V and E of vertices and edges, Euler's formula will allow us to solve for the number R of regions of the network. Thus our plan is to relate V and E to the numbers C and I. All but the one region outside the circle correspond to a piece of pizza, so $P = R - 1$.

Carry out the plan

Each cut forms 2 vertices on the circle bounding the pizza, and each intersection of cuts gives one vertex of the network inside the circle. Altogether this gives $V = 2C + I$ vertices in the network. To count the number of edges in the network, let's first suppose that there are no intersecting cuts. Each cut then forms two edges on the circle and is itself an edge, giving $3C$ edges of the network. If we next suppose that some of the cuts intersect, it is seen that each intersection creates 2 additional edges of the network not yet counted. Altogether then, there are $E = 3C + 2I$ edges in the network. Solving for R in Euler's formula $V + R = E + 2$ we get

$$R = E - V + 2 = (3C + 2I) - (2C + I) + 2 = C + I + 2.$$

Since $P = R - 1$, we arrive at the final formula:

$$P = C + I + 1$$

Look back

In the example drawn on the previous page, there are 4 cuts intersecting in 3 points. Since $4 + 3 + 1 = 8$, we now see why we counted 8 pieces of pizza, and obtain a check that our formula is correct.

Connecting Euler's Formulas for Planar Networks and for Polyhedra

In Section 10.3, it was discovered without proof that the number of vertices, faces, and edges of a polyhedron are related by Euler's formula $V + F = E + 2$. It is natural to wonder if this formula for polyhedra is related to the very similar formula $V + R = E + 2$ for connected planar networks. To understand the connection, imagine that each edge of a polyhedron is replaced with a segment of rubber band. The rubber band skeleton of the polyhedron can then be stretched and flattened to form a connected planar network with V vertices and E edges. This is shown in the case of a cube in Figure 10.38.

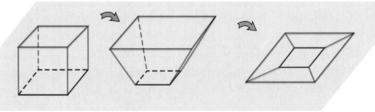

Figure 10.38
The skeleton of edges of any polyhedron, such as the cube shown, can be stretched and flattened to form a planar network.

There is a one-to-one matching between the regions of the network (including the unbounded region) and the faces of the polyhedron. Thus $R = F$, and we conclude that the two Euler formulas are equivalent to one another.

COOPERATIVE INVESTIGATION

The Game of Sprouts

The English mathematicians John Conway and Michael Paterson invented a game called Sprouts in 1967 in which two players take turns drawing new edges to an evolving network on n given initial vertices. It is permissible to draw an edge that returns to the starting vertex; such an edge is called a loop. There are just four simple rules:

1. Each new edge forms either a loop or joins two different vertices.
2. A new vertex must be created along the new edge.
3. The new edge cannot cross itself or any previously drawn edge, or pass through a vertex.
4. No vertex can have a degree larger than 3.

The first five moves of a Sprouts game on $n = 2$ initial vertices are shown below. The player who made the fifth move wins, since the other player cannot make a legal move.

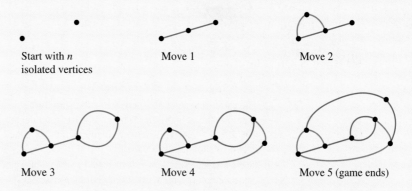

Start with n isolated vertices   Move 1   Move 2

Move 3   Move 4   Move 5 (game ends)

(a) Play several games on $n = 2$ initial vertices. At most how many moves do the games take?

(b) Play several games on $n = 3$ initial vertices. What is the largest number of moves possible before the games end?

(c) Look for a pattern on the largest number of moves possible in a Sprouts game on n initial vertices.

(d) What is the smallest number of moves to end a game on n initial vertices?

SOURCE: Sprouts is described in Martin Gardner's book *Mathematical Carnival*, New York: Knopf, 1975.

PROBLEM SET 10.4

Understanding Concepts

1. Decide which of the following networks are traversable. If it is traversable give an Euler path.

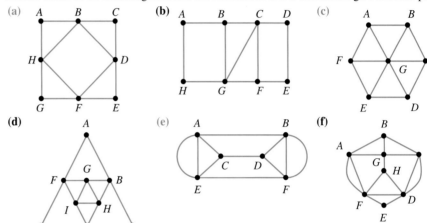

(a)   (b)   (c)
(d)   (e)   (f)

2. Find an Euler path for each of these networks.

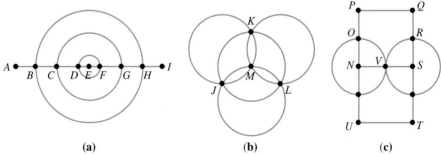

(a)   (b)   (c)

3. (a) The **total degree** D of a network is the sum of the degrees of all of the vertices. For example, the network in problem 1(a) has total degree $D = 2 + 4 + 2 + 4 + 2 + 4 + 2 + 4 = 24$. This network also has $E = 12$ edges. Find D and E for the remaining networks shown in problem 1.

   (b) Guess how the total degree D is related to the number of edges E in any network. Test your conjecture on several networks of your own choosing.

4. A connected network has the following degrees at its vertices: 2, 2, 4, 8, 3, 6, 6, 1.

   (a) Is the network traversable?

   (b) How many edges does the network have? (*Hint:* See problem 3(b).)

5. Here are two more examples from Euler's paper on the Königsberg Bridge Problem.

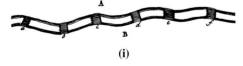

(i)

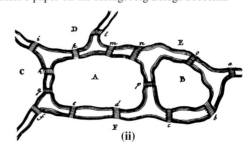

(ii)

(a) Draw the networks corresponding to (i) and (ii).

(b) Is network (i) traversable? Why?

(c) Is network (ii) traversable? Explain your reasoning.

6. (a) Draw the network that corresponds to the following system of bridges and land masses.

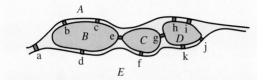

(b) Explain why the network is not traversable.

(c) What is the smallest number of new bridges required to form a traversable network? Where should the bridge(s) be placed?

7. A floor plan of a house is shown below. There are five rooms A, B, C, D, E and the outside O, connected by the doorways a, b, c, d, e, f, g.

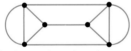

(a) Draw a network whose vertices are labeled *A, B, C, D, E, O* and whose edges correspond to the doorways.

(b) Is it possible to walk through each doorway exactly once? If so, where must you begin and end your walk?

8. A connected planar network is shown below.

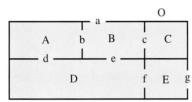

(a) What is the number of vertices *V*, regions *R*, and edges *E*?

(b) Does Euler's formula hold for this network?

9. (a) Draw a connected planar network whose 10 edges separate the plane into 6 regions.

(b) Can you draw a connected planar network with 10 edges that separates the plane into 12 regions? Explain.

Thinking Critically

10. A connected network which does not contain a closed path of distinct edges is called a **tree.**

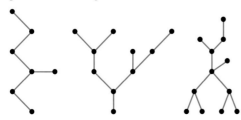

Trees

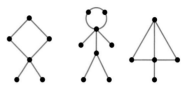

Not trees

(a) Suppose a network contains two vertices that can be joined by two different paths with no edges common to both paths. Why is it impossible for this network to be a tree?

(b) The **diameter** of a tree is the largest number of edges required in a path which joins any two vertices. For example, the leftmost tree above has diameter 5. Find the diameters of the two other trees drawn above.

(c) Let *V* and *E* denote the respective number of vertices and edges of a tree. What formula relates *V* and *E?* Prove your result.

11. What trees are traversable?

12. Let *D* represent the sum of the degrees of all of the vertices of a network and let *E* denote the number of edges in the network (*D* is the total degree of the network; see problem 3). Imagine that the network is a highway map, with the vertices representing towns and the edges representing highways connecting towns. Suppose each town puts up a city limit sign along each highway that leaves town.

(a) Show that the total number of signs is given both by *D* and by 2*E*, so that you obtain the equation *D* = 2*E*.

(b) Is it possible to construct a network whose total degree *D* is 17?

13. In problem 3 you discovered that the total degree *D* (the sum of degrees of all the vertices of the network) is given by *D* = 2*E*, where *E* is the number of edges. Suppose the degrees at the even vertices are $e_1, e_2, \ldots, e_m$, and the degrees at the odd vertices are $d_1, d_2, \ldots, d_n$. Thus $2E = D = e_1 + e_2 + \cdots + e_m + d_1 + d_2 + \cdots + d_n$.

(a) Explain why $d_1 + d_2 + \cdots + d_n$ is an even integer.

(b) Since $d_1 + d_2 + \cdots + d_n$ is even, explain why *n* is even. Since *n* is the number of odd vertices in the network, you've proved the following result:

The number of odd vertices in a network is always even.

14. Prove that the number of people at a party who have shaken hands an odd number of times is an even number. (*Hint:* See problem 13.)

15. The connected network below has 6 odd vertices, so it cannot be traced without lifting the pencil.

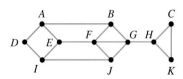

(a) Show that the network can be traced in three strokes; that is, the pencil is lifted twice and then placed at a different vertex.

(b) If a connected network has $2m$ odd vertices, with $m > 0$, explain why its edges can be traced in m strokes. (*Suggestion:* Add, temporarily, $m - 1$ new edges to the network.)

16. Suppose that you are asked to trace a connected network, without lifting your pencil, so that each edge is traced exactly twice. Is this always possible regardless of the number of odd vertices? Explain why or why not.

17. The planar network shown below on the vertices A, B, C, D, F, G, H, I, J, K, is not connected; indeed, it is made up of $P = 3$ connected pieces.

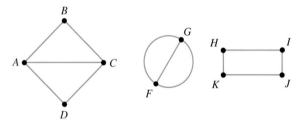

For this network $V = 10$, $E = 12$, $R = 6$ and we see that $V + R = 16$ but $E + 2 = 14$.

(a) Draw several more examples of disconnected planar networks. For each network count V, R, E, and P, where P is the number of connected pieces in your network. Can you guess an Euler formula which relates V, R, E, and P?

(b) Prove your conjecture stated in part (a). (*Suggestion:* Add new edges to connect the network.)

18. One circle separates the plane into 2 regions, 2 circles which cross one another in 2 points separate the plane into 4 regions, and 3 circles form 8 regions when each pair of circles cross at 2 points and no more than 2 circles intersect at any point.

(a) What is the number of regions determined by 4 circles? Assume that each pair of circles intersect at 2 points, and no 3 circles intersect at any one point.

(b) How many regions are formed by n intersecting circles? (*Hint:* There are $C(n,2) = \dfrac{1}{2}n(n-1)$ pairs of circles. Now use Euler's formula and mimic the solution of Example 10.20.)

Thinking Cooperatively

19. These three trees (see problem 10 for the definition of a tree) are *isomorphic* (*iso* = same, *morph* = form) to one another, since the positions of the vertices can be rearranged by bending (but not breaking) to make all three networks look exactly alike.

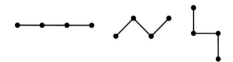

Similarly, these two trees are isomorphic:

On the other hand, each tree in the first group is *nonisomorphic* to each tree in the second group. One way to see this is to note that each tree in the first group has vertices of degrees 1, 2, 2, 1 but the lower trees each have vertices of degrees 1, 1, 1, 3. It is easy to check that any tree with 4 vertices must be isomorphic to one of the two types shown above.

Work in small groups, and compare results between groups, to carry out these investigations.

(a) Find the 3 nonisomorphic trees on 5 vertices

(b) Find the 6 nonisomorphic trees on 6 vertices

(c) Find the 11 nonisomorphic trees on 7 vertices

20. In 1958, the American mathematician David Gale invented the two-person game **Bridg-It**. The game is played on isometric dot paper, with rows alternating between two colors of dots (say red and black, as shown). The players take turn drawing horizontal or vertical edges between adjacent vertices of their color. The object of the game is to create a path from one side of the board to the other.

(a) If the red player started the game, who should be the winner of the game shown? What if black played first?

(b) Play a few games of Bridg-It.

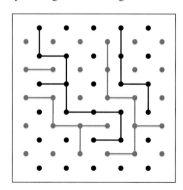

Making Connections

21. An 8 pin connecting terminal is wired as shown at the left. An electrical engineer claims that 5 of the 12 connecting wires can be eliminated. On the right-hand diagram draw 7 of the 12 original wires which provide for the same current flows as the original circuit.

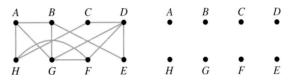

(This problem is found in *A Sourcebook of Applications of School Mathematics* by Donald Bushaw, Max Bell, Henry O. Pollak, Maynard Thompson, and Zalman Usiskin, NCTM, 1980).

22. Chemists frequently use a type of network called a *structural formula* to show the bonds linking the atoms of a molecule. For example, three-dimensional models of methane, CH_4, and ethane, C_2H_6, and their corresponding structural formulas are shown here.

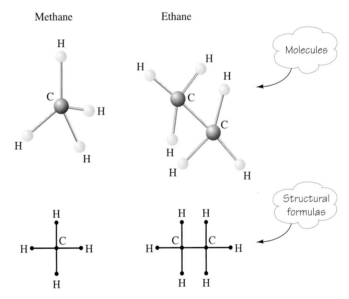

(a) What is the degree (valence) of each carbon atom? of each hydrogen atom?

(b) Sketch the structural formula of propane, C_3H_8.

(c) There are two forms of butane, C_4H_{10}. Their "skeletons," showing the four carbon atoms and the bonds between them, are:

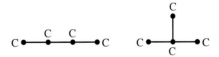

Add the hydrogen atoms and bonds to these skeletons to obtain the structural formulas for the two forms of butane.

(d) The next molecule in the series of alkanes is pentane, which has five carbon atoms. Sketch the three forms of the skeleton of pentane, and add hydrogen atoms and bonds to complete the structural formulas. Does each form have the same number of hydrogen atoms?

(e) Make reasonable guesses for the chemical formulas of hexane, heptane, and octane, the next three hydrocarbons in the alkane series.

For Review

23. Draw a parallelogram, and then draw outward facing squares along each edge of your parallelogram. What type of quadrilateral is formed by joining the successive center points of the squares?

24. The following equilateral nonagon (9-gon) is used to form the spiral pattern shown in Figure 12.26 of Chapter 12. Find the measures of all of the interior angles.

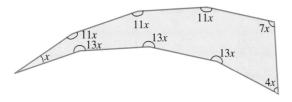

25. In the figure shown below lines l and m are parallel. Find the measures x, y, z of the indicated angles.

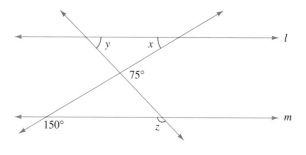

EPILOGUE   Visualization

After struggling with a difficult problem or abstract concept, a student may suddenly smile and announce "I see it now," or perhaps exclaim, "I've got the picture." Information conveyed in visual form can easily be superior to the same information described by a thousand, or even ten thousand, well-chosen words. Our ability to visualize is only partly dependent on the acuity of our eyesight: even more important is the mind's eye, which sharpens our perception by providing us with skills and abilities to identify, analyze, and classify shape.

In recent years the graphics computer has enabled us to see in directions unimaginable just a short time ago. This development is a continuation of technological advances which redefine what is observable. Nearly 400 years ago, Galileo's telescope detected the moons of Jupiter. Today, optical and radio telescopes reveal quasars at the edge of the universe. A hundred years after Galileo, the universe of the very small became observable with Leeuwenhoek's invention of the microscope. Today, tunnelling microscopes produce images in which single atoms are distinguishable.

Learning to understand and interpret new images is an exciting challenge. Fortunately, many of the concepts and experiences first encountered in elementary geometry prepare the way to meet this challenge. In this chapter we have introduced many of the basic notions of geometry: point, line, plane, curve, surface, angle, distance between points, measure of an angle, region, and space. In the chapters which follow, these basic notions are developed in more depth as we encounter the ideas of similarity, construction, measurement, isometric and similarity transformations, symmetry, and coordinate methods of geometry.

CHAPTER 10 SUMMARY

Key Concepts

This chapter introduced the basic figures of the plane and of space. Figures were represented by drawings or by physical models. Properties of figures were described and analyzed, and figures were classified according to their properties.

1. *Plane Figures*

Two points A and B lie on a unique line $\overleftrightarrow{AB}$. The distance between A and B is AB, which is also the length of the line segment $\overline{AB}$. Two rays, $\overrightarrow{AB}$ and $\overrightarrow{AC}$, with a common endpoint A form an angle, $\angle BAC$, which has measure $m(\angle BAC)$. Angles are classified by their measures as zero, acute, right, obtuse, straight, or reflex. Two angles are complementary or supplementary if their measures add up respectively to 90° or 180°. The corresponding angles property, and the alternate interior angles and vertical angles theorems, provide relationships among the angles formed when lines intersect. The measures of the interior angles of a triangle add up to 180°.

2. *Curves and Polygons in the Plane*

   Curves are classified as simple, closed, convex, and/or polygonal. A simple closed polygonal curve is a polygon. Triangles are classified as scalene, isosceles, equilateral, acute, right, and obtuse. Convex quadrilaterals are classified as trapezoids, parallelograms, rhombuses, rectangles, and squares. By the Jordan curve theorem, a simple closed curve in the plane partitions the plane into two regions, the exterior and the interior of the curve. The measures of the interior angles of an n-sided polygon add up to $(n - 2)180°$. In a regular n-gon, each interior angle has measure $(n - 2)180°/n$ and each exterior angle measures $360°/n$. The total turn about any closed plane curve is an integral multiple of 360°.

3. *Figures in Space*

   A simple closed surface is a surface without holes which encloses a region called its interior. The simple closed surfaces formed by polygonal regions are called polyhedra, and include prisms, pyramids, and the five regular polyhedra. The number of vertices, faces, and edges of any polyhedron satisfies Euler's formula $V + F = E + 2$. Spheres, cones, and cylinders are examples of curved surfaces.

4. *Networks*

   A network is a set of vertices and a set of edges joining some of the pairs of vertices. A network is connected if any two vertices are joined by a path. A network is traversable if there is an Euler path covering each edge of the network once and only once. Euler showed that a connected network is traversable if, and only if, the network has 0 or 2 vertices of odd degree. A network is planar if it can be drawn so that no two edges cross one another. Euler's formula $V + R = E + 2$ relates the number of vertices, regions, and edges of a connected planar network.

Vocabulary and Notation

Section 10.1

Point, A, B, ...
Line l, $\overleftrightarrow{AB}$
Collinear points
Plane figure
Parallel, $l \parallel m$
Concurrent lines
Distance between points, AB
Line segment, $\overline{AB}$
Congruent line segments, $\overline{AB} \cong \overline{CD}$
Measure of an angle, $m(\angle ABC)$
Ray, $\overrightarrow{AB}$
Angle, $\angle ABC$
Vertex of an angle
Zero, acute, right, obtuse, straight, reflex angles
Perpendicular, $l \perp m$
Congruent angles, $\angle A \cong \angle B$

Complementary angles
Supplementary angles
Vertical angles
Corresponding angles
Alternate interior angles
Interior and exterior angles of a triangle
Directed angle
   Initial and terminal side

Section 10.2

Curve
   Simple, closed, simple closed
Jordan curve theorem
   Interior and exterior region of a simple closed
   curve
Convex figure
Concave figure

Polygonal curve
Polygon
      Pentagon, hexagon, heptagon, octagon, nonagon
        (or enneagon), decagon, . . . , *n*-gon
Interior, exterior angles of a polygon
Triangle: acute, right, obtuse, scalene, isosceles,
    equilateral
Quadrilateral: kite, trapezoid, isosceles trapezoid,
    parallelogram, rhombus, rectangle, square
Circle
      Diameter, radius, center, chord, tangent line, arc,
        sector, segment

Cone
Cylinder
Tetrahedron
Pentahedron
Hexahedron
Apex
Base
Net of a polyhedron
Platonic solids
Lateral surface
Altitude
Right cylinder
Oblique cylinder

Section 10.3

Plane
      Parallel and intersecting planes, dihedral angle,
        half-space, skew lines, perpendicular planes
Sphere
Simple closed surface
Polyhedron
    Vertex, face, edge
    Pyramid
    Prism, right prism, oblique prism
    Regular polyhedron

Section 10.4

Network
      Vertices, edges, path, degree of a vertex, odd/even
        vertex, connected network
Traversable network
    Euler path
Planar network

CHAPTER REVIEW EXERCISES

Section 10.1

1. Let *ABCD* be the quadrilateral shown below.

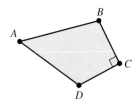

Give symbols for the following:
(a) The line containing the diagonal through *C*.
(b) The diagonal containing *B*.
(c) The length of the side containing *A* and *D*.
(d) The angle *not* containing *D*.
(e) The measure of the interior angle at *C*.
(f) The ray which has vertex at *D* and is
perpendicular to a side of the quadrilateral.

2. For the quadrilateral shown in problem 1, which
angle(s) appear to be:
(a) acute?   (b) right?   (c) obtuse?

3. An angle measures 37°. What is the measure of
(a) its supplementary angle?

(b) its complementary angle?

4. Lines *l* and *m* below are parallel. Find the measures
p, *q*, *r*, and *s* of the angles shown.

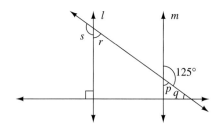

5. Find the measures *x*, *y*, and *z* of the angles in the
following figure.

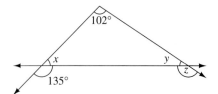

Section 10.2

6. Match each curve to one of the descriptions below.

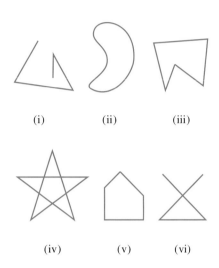

(i) (ii) (iii)

(iv) (v) (vi)

(a) nonconvex nonsimple polygonal curve

(b) nonclosed simple curve

(c) nonsimple nonclosed polygonal curve

(d) convex polygon

(e) simple closed nonconvex nonpolygonal curve

(f) nonconvex polygon

7. (a) Can a triangle have two obtuse angles?

(b) Can a convex quadrilateral have three obtuse interior angles?

(c) Is there an "acute" quadrilateral (that is, a quadrilateral whose angles are all acute)? For each part, carefully explain your reasoning.

8. Find the measures of the interior angles of this polygon.

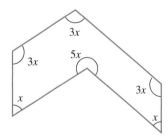

9. A turtle walks along the path *ABCDEFGA* in the direction of the arrows, returning to the starting point

and initial heading. What total angle does the turtle turn through?

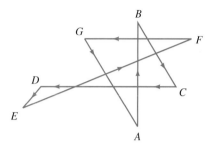

Section 10.3

10. Let *ABCDEFGH* be the vertices of a cube, as shown below.

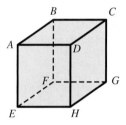

(a) How many planes are determined by the faces of the cube?

(b) Which edges of the cube are parallel to edge $\overline{AB}$?

(c) Which edges of the cube are contained in lines which are skew to the line $\overleftrightarrow{AB}$?

(d) What is the measure of the dihedral angle between the plane containing *ABCD* and the plane containing *ABGH*?

11. Name the following surfaces in space.

12. Draw the following shapes.
(a) a right circular cone
(b) a pentagonal prism
(c) a nonconvex quadrilateral pyramid

13. (a) Draw a regular octahedron.
(b) Using your drawing in part (a) count the number of vertices, faces, and edges of the octahedron, and then verify that Euler's formula holds for the octahedron.

14. A polyhedron has 14 faces and 24 edges. How many vertices does it have?

Section 10.4

15. (a) Explain why the network shown is not traversable.
    (b) Name two vertices which, if connected by a new edge, would make the resulting network traversable. Then list the vertices of an Euler path.

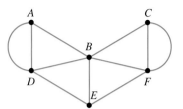

16. Is there a walk which crosses each of the bridges shown below exactly once? Explain your reasoning, using an appropriate network.

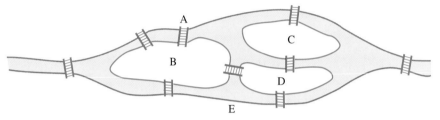

17. Count the number of vertices, regions, and edges in the following network, and then verify that Euler's formula holds.

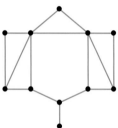

CHAPTER TEST

1. Let *P, Q, R, S, T* be the points shown. Draw and label the following figures.

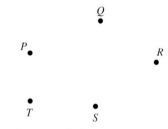

   (a) $\overrightarrow{PQ}$ (b) $\overleftrightarrow{PR}$ (c) $\overline{SQ}$ (d) $\angle PST$

2. At which vertices of the polygon does the interior angle appear to be   (a) acute?   (b) right?
   (c) obtuse?   (d) straight?   (e) reflex?

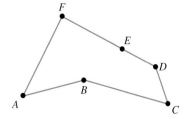

3. Sketch an example of each of the following types of curves.
   (a) a simple closed curve
   (b) a convex heptagon
   (c) a nonclosed simple polygonal curve
   (d) a closed nonsimple polygonal curve

4. Decide whether each statement below is *true* or *false*.
   (a) Every square is a rhombus.
   (b) Some right triangles are obtuse.
   (c) All equilateral triangles are isosceles.
   (d) All squares are kites.

5. For each part, name the regular polygon with the stated property.
   (a) The central angle has measure 36°.
   (b) The exterior angles each measure 45°.
   (c) The interior angles each measure 140°.

6. Find the angle measures *r*, *s*, *t* in the figure below, where lines *l* and *m* are parallel.

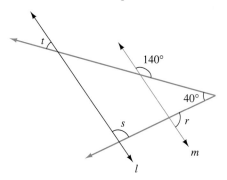

7. What is the measure of the angles in the points of this symmetric 8-pointed star? Explain how you found your answer.

8. The average interior angle measure of a convex polygon is 174°. What is the number of sides of the polygon? Explain how you found your answer.

9. A right prism has bases bounded by regular pentagons. What is the dihedral angle at which two adjacent lateral faces meet?

10. A cube octahedron has eight triangular faces and six square faces.

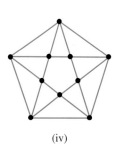

   (a) What is the number of edges of a cube octahedron? Explain how you do your counting.

   (b) What is the number of vertices of a cube octahedron? Explain how you found your answer.

11. Pyramids are erected outward to both bases of a heptagonal prism.

   (a) Sketch the surface that is described.

   (b) Directly count the number of vertices, faces, and edges of the resulting polyhedron.

   (c) Verify that Euler's formula is satisfied.

---

12. Consider the following networks.

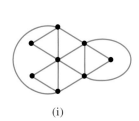
(i)

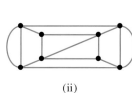
(ii)

(iii)

(iv)

   (a) Which networks are not traversable?

   (b) Which networks are traversable starting at an arbitrary vertex?

   (c) Which network is traversable starting at some, but not every, vertex?

   (d) Which network becomes traversable when only one additional edge is added to the network? Describe the new edge.

13. (a) A connected planar network with 11 edges partitions the plane into 7 regions. How many vertices does this network have?

   (b) Draw a connected planar network with 11 edges and 7 regions.

CHAPTER

11

Measurement

11.1   The Measurement Process
11.2   Area and Perimeter
11.3   The Pythagorean Theorem
11.4   Surface Area and Volume

HANDS ON
Measurements in Beanland

Materials Needed

Dry beans (small red kidney or white navy beans); enlarged copies of the figures shown in the two activities below

Directions

In Beanland, the lengths of curves are measured in *beanlengths*, abbreviated bl. Similarly, the areas of regions are measured in *beanareas*, abbreviated ba. The diagram below shows that the length of the curve is about 15 bl.

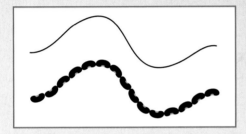

The next diagram shows a region bounded by a simple closed curve. By counting the beans, we see that the region has an area of about 55 ba.

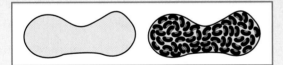

Activities

1. Consider this system of squares and circles. (Use an enlarged copy of this figure, with the larger circle about 14 to 16 beanlengths in diameter.)

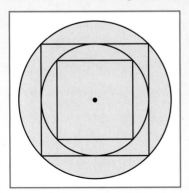

(a) Measure the area of the ring-shaped region between the two circles, using your beans.

(b) Measure the area of the smaller circle, and then compare this area to that of the ring.

(c) Measure the area of the small square and then the area of the region between the two squares. How do these areas compare?

(d) Measure the perimeter (the distance around) of the small square in beanlengths. Next measure the length of the diagonal of the large square. How do these lengths compare?

(e) Measure the circumference and the diameter of the large circle. What is the ratio of the circumference to the diameter? Compare with your classmates and determine the average ratio.

2. Consider an equilateral triangle ABC and its circumscribed and inscribed circles. (Again, use an enlargement so the larger circle has a diameter of about 14 to 16 beanlengths in diameter.)

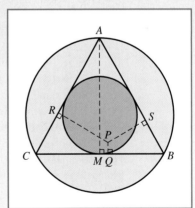

(a) Measure the area of the small circle and the area of the ring-shaped region between the two circles. What is the ratio of the area of the ring to that of the small circle?

(b) Choose an arbitrary point P inside the triangle and measure the three distances PQ, PR, and PS to the sides of the triangle. How does the sum $PQ + PR + PS$ of these three distances compare to the length AM of the altitude of the triangle?

CONNECTIONS   The Principles and Processes of Measurement

Measurement played a limited but important role in Chapter 10. Only two figures were measured: line segments, measured by the distance between their endpoints; and angles, measured by the degrees of rotation needed to turn one side to the other. In this chapter, we introduce more general notions of measurement of geometric figures. All curves, not just segments, will be given a length. Plane regions will be measured by area and perimeter. Space figures will be measured by surface area and volume.

We begin by discussing the general process of measurement and the concept of a unit of measurement. The two principal systems of measurement are then described: The U.S. Customary (English) System, used in the United States but in almost no other country; and the International System (metric), used by all countries worldwide including the United States.

11.1   The Measurement Process

The geometry of the Babylonians and ancient Egyptians always had a practical purpose, and often this purpose was dependent on having knowledge of size and capacity. It was important to know the areas of fields, the volumes of granaries, and so on. Many engineering projects gave rise to geometric problems concerned with magnitudes. To be specific, suppose a canal has a given trapezoidal cross section and a known length. Knowing how much volume of earth one worker can dig in one day, how many workers are needed to excavate the canal in a given period of time?

Determining size requires that a comparison be made to a **unit.** For example, the volume of a canal could be expressed in "worker-days," where a worker-day is the volume one person can excavate in one day's labor. The worker-day is thus a unit of volume. It is analogous to the original definition of acre, which was originally defined as the area of land that could be plowed in one day with one team of oxen.

In early times, units of measurement were defined more for convenience than accuracy. For example, many units of length correspond to parts of the human body, some of which are shown in Figure 11.1. The hand, span, foot, and cubit all appear in early records of Babylonia and Egypt.

Many of these units later became standardized and persist today. For example, horses are still measured in hands, where a hand is now 4 inches. Originally an inch was the length of 3 barleycorns placed end-to-end.

The **measurement process** can be viewed as a sequence of steps.

The Measurement Process

1. Choose the property (such as length, area, volume, capacity, temperature, time, weight) of an object or event which is to be measured.
2. Select an appropriate unit of measurement.
3. Use a measurement device to "cover," "fill," "time," or otherwise provide a comparison of the object to the unit.
4. Express the measurement as the number of units used.

Classroom Tools and Techniques for Understanding Measurement

If children's initial measurement explorations use a variety of units, nonstandard as well as standard, they will develop understanding about the nature of units and the need for standard units. For example, when students measure their height using a length of string and a meter stick and then compare uniformity of results, they build an awareness of the value of a standard unit. The same is true when different children tile an area using dominoes and unit tiles. In counting the number of objects used, the children recognize the discrepancies between measurements. Such experiences can lead to a discussion and application of standard tools. Worthwhile experiences include actually measuring with different materials, from paper clips and toothpicks to rulers.

Teachers cannot assume that children understand measurement fully, even when they can complete standard textbook exercises or worksheets involving reading a pictured ruler aligned with a pictured object. Children need hands-on experiences to develop both concepts and skills of measurement. These develop together as children place manipulative units without leaving spaces between them or compare the result of measuring with different nonstandard units. Similarly, with rulers, children learn concepts and procedures, including accurate alignment (ignoring the leading edge at the beginning of many rulers), starting at zero, and focusing on the lengths of the units rather than only the numbers on the ruler. The question, "What are you counting?" cannot be overemphasized.

Because children are operating on quantities such as lengths—comparing them, putting them together, and taking them apart—measurement activities are also strong contributors to children's development of spatial sense. Also, combining or comparing measures using addition or subtraction provides another model for these arithmetic processes and contributes to the development of number and operation sense.

SOURCE: Reprinted with permission from *Curriculum and Evaluation Standards for School Mathematics: Discussion Draft,* copyright 1998 by the National Council of Teachers of Mathematics. All rights reserved.

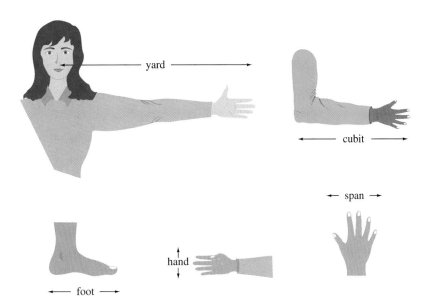

Figure 11.1
Examples of traditional units of length based on the human body

In Example 11.1 that follows, a **tangram** piece is chosen to be the unit of area measurement. Tangrams originated in ancient China and continue to be a versatile manipulative in the classroom. The instructions below show how to make a set of tangram pieces by folding and cutting a square sheet of paper. A more sturdy set of tangrams can be cut from cardboard or vinyl tile, using the paper shapes as templates.

The seven tangram pieces.

Step 1: Fold the two diagonals of the square *ABCD*. Let *E* denote its center.

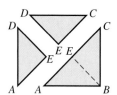

Step 2: Cut out the tangram pieces *CDE* and *ADE*, leaving triangle *ABC*.

Step 3: Fold *B* and *C* to center point *E* to create folds *FG* and *FH*.

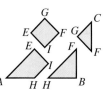

Step 4: Cut out tangram pieces *BFH*, *CFG*, and *FGEI*, leaving trapezoid *AHIE*.

Step 5: Fold *E* to *H* to create fold *IJ*.

Step 6: Cut out tangram pieces *AHIJ* and *EIJ*.

EXAMPLE   11.1

Investigating Tangram Measurements

Label the tangram pieces I, II, . . . , VII as shown. Use shape I, the small isosceles right triangle, as the unit of "one tangram area" (abbreviated 1 tga) to measure:

(a)   the area of each of the tangram pieces,

(b)   the area of the "fish,"

(c)   the area of the circle that circumscribes the square. Are your measurements exact, or only approximate?

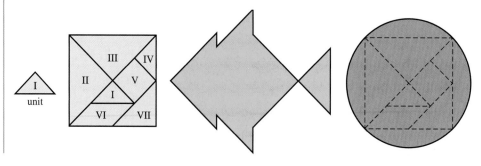

Solution

(a)   Each tangram piece can be covered by copies of the unit shape I, giving the exact measurements in the table.

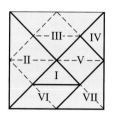

Piece	Area
I, IV	1 tga
II, III	4 tga
V, VI, VII	2 tga

(b)   The fish is covered by the seven tangram pieces, so its area is exactly (4 + 2 + 1 + 2 + 1 + 4 + 2) tga = 16 tga.

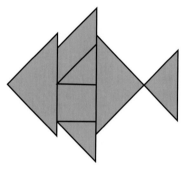

(c)   The circle can be covered by the seven tangram pieces, together with 12 additional copies of the unit shape. This shows that the circle's area is between 16 tga and 28 tga. Thus we might estimate the area at about 25 tga.

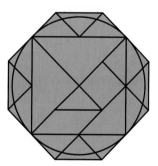

An important practical purpose of measurement is communication. By agreeing on common units of measurement, people are able to express and interpret information about size, quantity, capacity, and so on. Historically, as commerce developed and goods were traded over increasingly large distances, the need for a standard system of units became more and more apparent. In the seventeenth and eighteenth centuries, the rise of science and the beginnings of the industrial revolution gave further impetus to the development of universal systems of measurement.

The U.S. Customary, or "English," System of Measures

The English system arose from a hodgepodge of traditional informal units of measurement. Table 11.1 lists some of the units of **length** in this system. The ratios comparing one unit of length to another are clearly the result of accident, not planning.

TABLE 11.1	Units of Length in the Customary System	
Unit	Abbreviation	Equivalent Measurement in Feet
Inch	in	$\frac{1}{12}$ ft
Foot	ft	1 ft
Yard	yd	3 ft
Rod	rd	$16\frac{1}{2}$ ft
Furlong*	fur	660 ft
Mile	mi	5280 ft

*The *furlong* is a shortening of "furrow long," revealing its origin in agriculture.

Learning the customary system requires extensive memorization, and using the system involves computations with cumbersome numerical factors.

Area is a measure of the region bounded by a plane curve. Any shape that tiles the plane could be chosen as a unit, but the square is the most common shape. The size of the square is arbitrary, but it is natural to choose the length of a side to correspond to a unit measure of length. Areas are therefore usually measured in square inches, square feet, and so on. A moderate-sized house may have 1800 square feet of floor space, a living room carpet may cover 38 square yards, and a national forest may cover 642 square miles. An exception to this pattern is the acre; 640 acres have a total area of one square mile. Some common units of area are listed in Table 11.2. The notation ft^2 indicates square feet.

TABLE 11.2	Units of Area in the Customary System	
Unit	Abbreviation	Equivalent Measure in Other Units
Square inch	in^2	$\frac{1}{144}$ ft^2
Square foot	ft^2	144 in^2, or $\frac{1}{9}$ yd^2
Square yard	yd^2	9 ft^2
Acre	acre	$\frac{1}{640}$ mi^2, or 43,560 ft^2
Square mile	mi^2	640 acres, or 27,878,400 ft^2

The ratios comparing one unit of area to another can be visualized, as shown in Figure 11.2. We see that the area of a 3 ft by 3 ft square is obtained by the multiplication

3 ft × 3 ft = 3 × 3 × ft × ft = 9 ft². *In computing with dimensioned quantities it is essential to retain the units in all equations and expressions.* For example, it is correct to write 12 in = 1 ft; without the dimensions this equation would be incorrect since 12 ≠ 1. Omitting the units in expressions is a common source of errors.

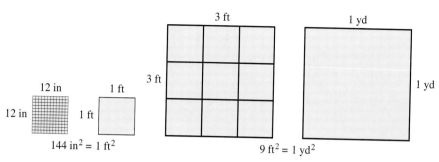

Figure 11.2
Comparing units of area measure

Volume is the measure of space taken up by a solid in three-dimensional space. The unit, as shown in Table 11.3, is the volume of a cube whose side length is one of the standard units of length. For example, the displacement of the pistons in a car engine may be 327 cubic inches, which is abbreviated 327 in³.

TABLE 11.3	Units of Volume in the Customary System	
Unit	Abbreviation	Equivalent Measure in Other Units
Cubic inch	in³	$\frac{1}{1728}$ ft³
Cubic foot	ft³	1728 in³, or $\frac{1}{27}$ yd³
Cubic yard	yd³	27 ft³

The ratios comparing units of volume are illustrated in Figure 11.3.

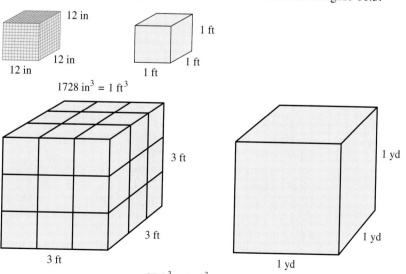

Figure 11.3
Comparing units of volume measure

Capacity is the volume which can be held in a container such as a bottle, pan, basket, tank, and so on. Capacity is often expressed in in^3, ft^3, or yd^3, but other units are also in common use, particularly for liquid measures. Examples of liquid measures include the fluid ounce, cup (8 fluid ounces), pint (2 cups), quart (2 pints), and the gallon (4 quarts). A gallon is equivalent to 231 in^3. Dry measures of capacity include the bushel (2150.42 in^3) and the peck (1/4 of a bushel).

METRIC CLOCK

Metric Units: The International System

The metric system of measurement originated in France shortly after the Revolution of 1789. The definitions of the units have been modified over succeeding years, taking advantage of scientific and technological advances. The system was codified in 1981 by the International Standardization Organization. The International System of Units, also called the **SI system** after its French name *Système Internationale,* has now achieved worldwide acceptance. The metric system has been a legal standard since 1866 in the United States; indeed the Customary units were *defined* in terms of metric units in 1893. In the 1970s a movement to replace customary units with metric units was unsuccessful. About the same time most other English-speaking countries, including Great Britain, Canada, Australia, and New Zealand, did change to metric units. Even day-to-day measurements in those countries—speed limits, distances between cities, and amounts in recipes—were replaced with metric units.

The principal advantage of the metric system—other than its universality—is the ease of comparison of units. The ratio of one unit to another is always a power of 10, which ties the metric system conveniently to the base ten numeration system. This makes it quite simple to convert a measurement in one metric unit to the equivalent measurement in another metric unit.

Each power of 10 is given a prefix which modifies the fundamental unit. For example, the factor 1000 (that is, 10^3) is expressed by the prefix *kilo*. Thus, a kilometer is 1000 meters. Similarly, the factor $\dfrac{1}{100}$ (that is, 10^{-2}) is expressed by the prefix *centi*. Therefore, a centimeter is $\dfrac{1}{100}$ of a meter. The more commonly used prefixes and their symbols are listed in Table 11.4.

TABLE 11.4	The SI Decimal Prefixes	
Prefix	Factor	Symbol
kilo	$1000 = 10^3$	k
hecto	$100 = 10^2$	h
deka	$10 = 10^1$	da
(none for basic unit)	$1 = 10^0$	(none)
deci	$0.1 = 10^{-1}$	d
centi	$0.01 = 10^{-2}$	c
milli	$0.001 = 10^{-3}$	m
micro	$0.000001 = 10^{-6}$	μ (Greek *mu*)

Length

The fundamental unit of length in the SI system is the **meter,** abbreviated by the symbol m. The unit symbol is always written last in SI, so there can be no confusion with the prefix milli, which is also given the symbol m. For example, one thousandth of a meter is a millimeter, written as 1 mm. There is no space between the first and second m, and there are no periods between or after the symbols.

The most commonly used metric units of length are listed in Table 11.5.

TABLE 11.5	Metric Units of Length	
Unit	Abbreviation	Multiple or Fraction of 1 Meter
1 kilometer	1 km	1000 m
1 hectometer	1 hm	100 m
1 dekameter	1 dam	10 m
1 meter	1 m	1 m
1 decimeter	1 dm	0.1 m
1 centimeter	1 cm	0.01 m
1 millimeter	1 mm	0.001 m
1 micrometer (or micron)	1 μm	0.000001 m

The prefix in a metric measurement can be replaced with its corresponding numerical factor. For example,

$$251 \text{ cm} = 25 \times 10^{-2} \text{ m} = 2.51 \text{ m}.$$

Similarly, a power of 10 can be replaced with the corresponding prefix, as in

$$0.179 \text{ m} = 179 \times 10^{-3} \text{ m} = 179 \text{ mm}.$$

Some metric measurements are shown in Figure 11.4.

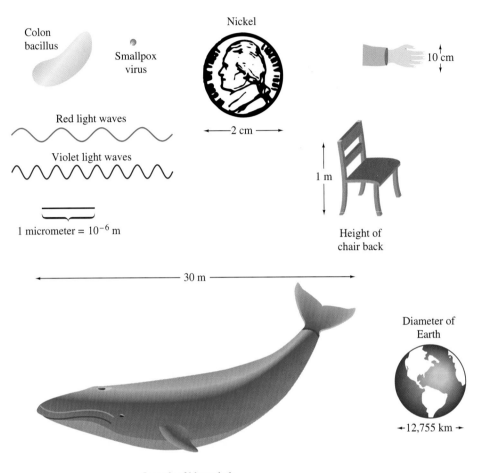

Figure 11.4
Examples of metric
measurements of length

Length of blue whale

HIGHLIGHT FROM HISTORY
Redefining the Meter

The meter was originally defined in the 1790s as one ten-millionth of the distance from the North Pole to the equator. Making the measurement, however, presented impossible difficulties. Not only was the earth quite unlike a perfect sphere, but political turmoil in revolutionary France led to the arrest of government surveyors as royalist spies, who narrowly escaped the guillotine. In 1889, the meter was fixed as the distance between two marks on a platinum-iridium bar, but scientists were unsatisfied since measurements could be no more accurate than one part in a million. In 1960 the meter was again redefined, becoming 1,650,763.73 wave lengths of the reddish-orange light emitted by krypton 86, a rare atmospheric gas. The new meter was accurate to 4 parts per billion, but still was an irritant to scientists measuring continental drift and the distance to the moon. In 1983, the meter was redefined yet again, in a way that connects length to time. The new definition specifies the meter as the distance traveled by light in space in 1/299,792,458 of a second. One second of time, which can be precisely measured with atomic clocks, is defined as the duration of 9,193,631,770 vibration cycles of the Cesium 133 atom. The definition invokes a sacred tenet of physics, that the speed of light in space is a universal constant, namely 299,792,458 meters per second.

EXAMPLE   11.2 | **Changing Units in the Metric System**

Convert these measurements to the unit shown.

(a)   1495 mm = _____ m
(b)   29.4 cm   = _____ mm
(c)   38741 m   = _____ km

Solution

(a)   1495 mm = 1495×10^{-3} m = 1.495 m
(b)   29.4 cm   = $(294 \times 10^{-1}) \times 10^{-2}$ m = 294×10^{-3} m = 294 mm
(c)   38,741 m = 38.741×10^{3} m = 38.741 km

Area

Area is usually expressed in square meters (m^2) or square kilometers (km^2). Another common unit is the hectare. A **hectare** (ha) is the area of a 100 m square; that is, 1 ha = 10,000 m^2. See Table 11.6.

The floorspace of a classroom might typically be about one **are** (pronounced "air"). A hectare is about 2.5 acres, so the area of farm land is measured in hectares in metric countries.

TABLE 11.6   Metric Units of Area

Unit	Abbreviation	Multiple or Fraction of 1 Square Meter
1 square centimeter	1 cm^2	0.0001 m^2
1 square meter	1 m^2	1 m^2
1 are (1 square dekameter)	1 a	100 m^2
1 hectare (1 square hectometer)	1 ha	10,000 m^2
1 square kilometer	1 km^2	1,000,000 m^2

Volume and Capacity

Small volumes are measured typically in cubic centimeters (abbreviated cm^3). Large volumes are often measured in cubic meters (m^3). A convenient unit of capacity is the **liter,** defined as a cubic decimeter. Thus, the liter (abbreviated either as *l* or L) is the volume of a cube whose sides each measure 1 dm = 10 cm; see Figure 11.5. Therefore, since 10 cm $\times$ 10 cm $\times$ 10 cm = 1000 cm^3, a liter is also 1000 cubic centimeters. Recalling that *milli* is the prefix for $\frac{1}{1000}$, a milliliter (ml) is the same as one cubic centimeter.

$$1 \text{ L} = 1 \text{ liter} = 1000 \text{ cm}^3$$
$$1 \text{ mL} = 1 \text{ milliliter} = 1 \text{ cm}^3$$

Large plastic bottles of soda usually contain 2 liters, while a typical soft drink can contains about 354 milliliters. A child's dose of cough medicine may be 3 mL. A recipe may call for 0.5 liters of water. In metric countries, gasoline is priced by the liter, and to fill a car's gas tank takes about 40 to 60 liters.

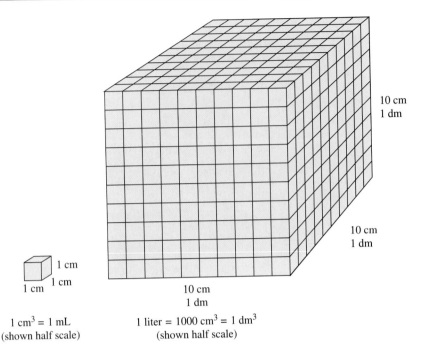

Figure 11.5
A liter is a cubic decimeter or, equivalently, 1000 cubic centimeters.

$1 \text{ cm}^3 = 1 \text{ mL}$
(shown half scale)

$1 \text{ liter} = 1000 \text{ cm}^3 = 1 \text{ dm}^3$
(shown half scale)

Weight and Mass

The **weight** of an object is the force exerted on the object by gravity. For example, a brick on the surface of the earth may weigh 6 pounds, but on the surface of the moon would only weigh about 1 pound. During the journey from earth to moon, the brick would weigh nearly nothing at all. Nevertheless, an astronaut would not care to be hit even by a weightless brick, since the brick never loses its **mass.**

In science, the distinction between mass and weight is very important: mass is the amount of matter of an object, and weight is the force of gravity on the object. But on the surface of the earth and in everyday life situations, the weight of an object is proportional to its mass. That is, the mass of an object is accurately estimated by weighing it.

The U.S. customary unit of weight is the familiar pound. Lighter weights are often given in ounces, and very heavy weights are given in tons:

$$16 \text{ ounces (oz)} = 1 \text{ pound (lb)}$$

$$2000 \text{ pounds} = 1 \text{ ton}$$

Table 11.7 lists some metric units of weight. The base unit of weight in the metric system is the **kilogram,** which is the weight of one liter of water.

TABLE 11.7	Metric Units of Weight	
Unit	Abbreviation	Multiples of Other Metric Units
1 milligram	1 mg	0.001 g
1 gram	1 g	0.001 kg
1 kilogram	1 kg	1000 g
1 metric ton	1 t	1000 kg

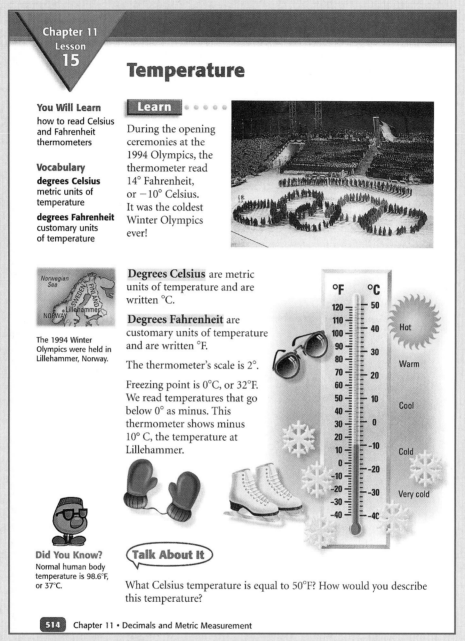

**Chapter 11
Lesson
15**

Temperature

You Will Learn
how to read Celsius and Fahrenheit thermometers

Vocabulary
degrees Celsius
metric units of temperature

degrees Fahrenheit
customary units of temperature

Learn • • • • •

During the opening ceremonies at the 1994 Olympics, the thermometer read 14° Fahrenheit, or −10° Celsius. It was the coldest Winter Olympics ever!

The 1994 Winter Olympics were held in Lillehammer, Norway.

Degrees Celsius are metric units of temperature and are written °C.

Degrees Fahrenheit are customary units of temperature and are written °F.

The thermometer's scale is 2°.

Freezing point is 0°C, or 32°F. We read temperatures that go below 0° as minus. This thermometer shows minus 10° C, the temperature at Lillehammer.

Did You Know?
Normal human body temperature is 98.6°F, or 37°C.

Talk About It

What Celsius temperature is equal to 50°F? How would you describe this temperature?

514 Chapter 11 • Decimals and Metric Measurement

SOURCE: From *Scott Foresman–Addison Wesley Math*, Grade 4, p. 514, by Randall I. Charles et al. Copyright © 1999, Addison Wesley Longman, Inc.

Questions for the Teacher

1. Since water freezes at 32° Fahrenheit and 0° Celsius, a child thinks a degree Fahrenheit is bigger than a degree Celsius. How would you respond?
2. The cold temperature in Norway at the 1994 Winter Olympics provides a context to understand 14° Fahrenheit and its metric equivalent − 10° Celsius. Give Celsius temperatures for these contexts:

(a) normal body temperature   (b) room temperature
(c) a cup of hot tea   (d) bath water   (e) Death Valley on a hot summer day   (f) cold glass of water

3. A student plans to visit her uncle in Toronto, Canada, and hopes to go sledding since the temperature is 20 degrees outside. What discussion would you suggest?

One milligram is approximately the weight of a grain of salt. It is a common measure of vitamins and medicines. A gram is approximately the weight of half a cube of sugar. Canned goods and dry packaged items at the grocery store will usually be weighed in grams. In metric countries, larger food items, such as meats, fruits, and vegetables, are priced by the kilogram. A kilogram is about 2.2 pounds.

EXAMPLE 11.3

Estimating Weights in the Metric System

Match the item in the column to the approximate weight of the item taken from the list that follows.

  (a) Nickel
  (b) Compact automobile
  (c) Two liter bottle of soda
  (d) Recommended daily allowance of vitamin B-6
  (e) Size D battery
  (f) Large watermelon

List of weights: 2 mg   2 kg,   100 g,   1200 kg,   9 kg,   5 g

Solution

  (a) 5 g   **(b)** 1200 kg   **(c)** 2 kg   **(d)** 2 mg   **(e)** 100 g
  (f) 9 kg

Temperature

There are two commonly used scales used to measure temperature. According to the **Fahrenheit scale,** 32°F represents the freezing point of water and 212° the boiling point of water. Thus, the Fahrenheit scale introduces 180 degrees of division between the freezing and boiling temperatures. The **Celsius scale** divides this temperature range into 100 degrees: the freezing point is 0° Celsius and the boiling point is 100° Celsius.

Unit Analysis

It is often of interest to express a measurement given in one unit by the equivalent measurement in a new unit. A procedure known as **unit analysis** (or **dimensional analysis**) can help arrange the calculation to make it clear if the factors comparing units are used as multipliers or divisors. The idea of unit analysis can be explained by an example. Suppose a distance has been given as 3.75 miles, and you would like the distance in yards. You recall that 1 mile = 5280 feet and 3 feet = 1 yard. These equations can also be written as $1 = \dfrac{5280 \text{ feet}}{1 \text{ mile}}$ and $1 = \dfrac{1 \text{ yard}}{3 \text{ feet}}$. Therefore,

$$3.75 \text{ mile} = 3.75 \;\cancel{\text{mile}} \times \frac{5280 \;\cancel{\text{feet}}}{1 \;\cancel{\text{mile}}} \times \frac{1 \text{ yard}}{3 \;\cancel{\text{feet}}} = \frac{3.75 \times 5280}{3} \text{ yard.}$$

Since $\dfrac{3.75 \times 5280}{3} = 6600$, we see that 3.75 miles = 6600 yards.

EXAMPLE 11.4 | Computing Speed and Capacity with Unit Analysis

(a) A cheetah can run 60 miles per hour. What is the speed in feet per second?

(b) A fish tank at the aquarium has the shape of a rectangular prism 2 m deep by 3 m wide by 3 m high. What is its capacity in liters?

Solution

(a)

$$60\frac{\text{miles}}{\text{hour}} = 60\frac{\cancel{\text{miles}}}{\cancel{\text{hour}}} \times \frac{5280 \text{ feet}}{1 \cancel{\text{mile}}} \times \frac{1 \cancel{\text{hour}}}{60 \cancel{\text{minutes}}} \times \frac{1 \cancel{\text{minute}}}{60 \text{ seconds}} = \frac{60 \times 5280}{60 \times 60}\frac{\text{feet}}{\text{second}}$$

$$= 88\frac{\text{feet}}{\text{second}}$$

(b) Recall that a liter is a cubic decimeter, and *deci* is the prefix for one tenth. Therefore, the volume of the tank is

$$(2 \text{ m}) \times (3 \text{ m}) \times (3 \text{ m}) = 18 \text{ m}^3 = 18 \text{ m}^3 \times \left(\frac{10 \text{ dm}}{1 \text{ m}}\right)^3 = 18 \times \cancel{\text{m}^3} \times 10^3 \times \frac{\text{dm}^3}{\cancel{\text{m}^3}}$$

$$= 18,000 \cancel{\text{dm}^3} \times \frac{1 \text{ liter}}{\cancel{\text{dm}^3}} = 18,000 \text{ liters}$$

PROBLEM SET 11.1

Understanding Concepts

1. For each object listed below make a list of measurable properties.
   (a) A bulletin board   (b) An extension cord
   (c) A file box   (d) A table

2. Suppose you are designing a house. Give examples of measurements you believe are important to consider. For example, the height of the house may be needed to satisfy a zoning regulation. Discuss examples of measurements of (a) length, (b) area, and (c) volume and capacity. What units are appropriate?

3. Find the area of each tangram figure shown, where a unit is the area of the small isosceles right triangle.

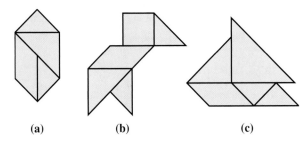

(a)   (b)   (c)

4. Let a *pen* be the area of a penny.
   (a) Estimate the area of a 4″ × 6″ card in pens.

(b) Discuss why pens are a difficult unit of area to use.

5. Arrange these solids in a list according to volume, from smallest to largest. Are there any ties?

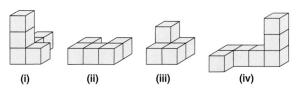

(i)   (ii)   (iii)   (iv)

6. (a) Verify that an acre contains 43,560 square feet. Show your computation.
   (b) A square lot contains 1 acre. What is the length of each side to the nearest foot?

7. (a) A football field is 120 yards long (including the end zones) and 160 feet wide. What is the area of a football field in acres?
   (b) A soccer field measures 110 meters by 70 meters. What is its area in ares? In hectares?

8. A measurement of 12.6 cm is assumed to be precise to the nearest last digit. That is, the true length is between 12.55 cm and 12.65 cm. Find the minimum and maximum true values for the following measurements.
   (a) A distance of 166 kilometers from Portland to Eugene

(b) A piece of notebook paper 27.9 centimeters long

(c) A pencil lead 0.50 millimeters in diameter

(d) A diving board 3.5 meters over the water

9. A small bottle of Perrier sparkling mineral water contains 33 cL.

(a) What is the volume in milliliters?

(b) Will three small bottles fill a 1 liter bottle?

10. Fill in the blanks.

(a) 58,728 g = _____ kg

(b) 632 mg = _____ g

(c) 0.23 kg = _____ g

(d) A cubic meter of water weighs _____ kg

11. Give the most reasonable answer listed in each part.

(a) A newborn baby weighs about: 8.3 kg, 3.5 kg, 750 g, 1625 mg

(b) A compact car weighs about: 5000 kg, 2000 g, 1200 kg, 50 kg.

(c) The recommended daily allowance of vitamin C is: 250 g, 60 mg, 0.3 kg, 0.002 mg.

12. In each of the following, select the most reasonable metric measurement.

(a) The height of the typical center in the National Basketball Association is: 6.11 m, 3 m, 95 cm, 212 cm

(b) The diameter of a coffee cup is about: 50 m, 50 mm, 500 mm, 5 km

(c) A coffee cup has a capacity of about: 8 L, 8 mL, 240 mL, 500 mL

13. Use a metric ruler to measure these items.

(a) The size of a sheet of standard notebook paper

(b) The length and width of the cover of this textbook

(c) The diameter of a nickel

(d) The perimeter of (distance around) your wrist

14. The dimensions of Noah's Ark are given in the Bible as: 300 cubits long, 50 cubits wide, and 30 cubits high. Give the dimension in (a) meters and (b) feet. Use a meter stick and ruler to measure your own cubit, as shown in Figure 11.1.

Thinking Critically

15. Pints, quarts, and gallons are part of a larger "doubling" system of capacity measure.

1 jigger = 2 mouthfuls	1 pint = 2 cups
1 jack = 2 jiggers	1 quart = 2 pints
1 jill = 2 jacks	1 bottle = 2 quarts
1 cup = 2 jills	1 gallon = 2 bottles
	1 pail = 2 gallons

(a) How many mouthfuls are in a jill? A cup? A pint?

(b) Suppose one mouthful, one jigger, one jack, . . . , and one gallon are poured into an empty pail. Does the pail overflow, is it exactly filled, or is there room for more? (*Hint:* Draw an empty pail. Put one gallon in, then one bottle, and so on.)

16. The weight of diamonds and other precious gemstones is given in *carats,* where 1 carat = 200 mg. The largest diamond discovered thus far is the Cullinan, found in 1906 at the Premier Mine in South Africa. It weighed 3106 carats. Using the conversion 2.2 kg = 1 lb, estimate the weight of the Culliman diamond in pounds.

Thinking Cooperatively

17. Nearly 4700 years ago, the Great Pyramid of Khufu was built to astonishing accuracy using the measuring unit of the cubit (see Figure 11.1). For further accuracy, the cubit was divided into seven *palms,* and each palm was further subdivided into four *digits* (finger widths). Longer distances were measured by the *hayt,* equal to 100 cubits.

(a) Use a meter stick to measure the cubit (elbow to fingertip distance, to the nearest centimeter) and palm (distance across four fingers, to the nearest millimeter) of ten classmates, and make a histogram of your data. Compute the average and standard deviation of the cubit and palm measurements. Does it seem accurate that seven palms are in a cubit?

(b) Give reasonable ancient Egyptian measurements for the height of the ceiling in your classroom, the length of a piece of notebook paper, and the length of a football field.

Using a Calculator

18. Verify that a hectare is about $2\frac{1}{2}$ acres. Use the approximate conversion 1.6 km $\doteq$ 1 mile, and show all of your steps.

19. (a) Use the conversion 1 in $\doteq$ 12.54 cm to calculate the number of cubic inches in a liter.

(b) Which volume is larger, 6.2 liters or 327 cubic inches?

20. A fortnight is 2 weeks. Convert a speed of 25 inches per minute to its equivalent in furlongs per fortnight.

21. Show there are about 30 million seconds in a year.

Making Connections

22. Here is a metric recipe for spaghetti sauce, except that the prefixes (if any) of some of the measures have been obliterated by some previous spills. Fill in the correct prefix, or indicate no prefix needed, for these ingredients in the recipe.

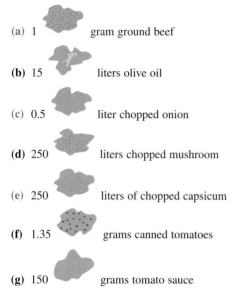

(a) 1   gram ground beef

(b) 15   liters olive oil

(c) 0.5   liter chopped onion

(d) 250   liters chopped mushroom

(e) 250   liters of chopped capsicum

(f) 1.35   grams canned tomatoes

(g) 150   grams tomato sauce

23. Metric countries rate the fuel efficiency of a car by the number of liters of gasoline required to drive 100 kilometers. If a car takes 9 liters per 100 kilometers, what is its efficiency in miles per gallon? Use the conversions 1 gal $\doteq$ 3.7854 L and 1 mile $\doteq$ 1.6 km.

24. A light-year is the distance light travels in empty space in one year.

   (a) Light travels at a speed of 186,000 miles per second. The star nearest the sun is Proxima Centauri, in the constellation Centaurus, whose distance is 4 light years. What is the distance to Proxima Centauri in miles?

   (b) In metric measurements the speed of light is 3.00×10^8 meters per second. Verify that a light year is about 10^{16} meters.

25. An herbicide is bottled in concentrated form. A working solution is mixed by adding 1 part concentrate to 80 parts water.

   (a) How many liquid ounces of concentrate should be added to 5 gallons of water?

   (b) How many liters of water should be added to 65 milliliters of concentrate?

26. Lumber is measured in board-feet, where a board-foot is the volume of a piece of lumber one foot square and one inch thick.

   (a) How many board-feet are in a two-by-four (2″ by 4″) that is 10 feet long? The volume of a rectangular solid is length times width times height.

   (b) Lumber is priced in dollars per thousand board-feet. Suppose two-by-fours 10 feet long are $690 per thousand board-feet. What is the cost of 144 two-by-fours, each 10 feet long?

27. How far did Captain Nemo's submarine *Nautilus* travel under the sea according to the title of Jules Verne's well-known novel? (*Hint:* Find the definition of "league.")

Communicating

28. Write a one paragraph report that explains why the words *ounce* and *inch* are related.

29. Write a one paragraph report that explains why the abbreviation for pound is *lb*.

30. Write a report in two or three pages that introduces and compares the Fahrenheit and Celsius scales of temperature measurement. Include sketches, examples, and several problems.

From State Student Assessments

31. (Washington State, Grade 4)
   Your class project is to build a bird feeder.

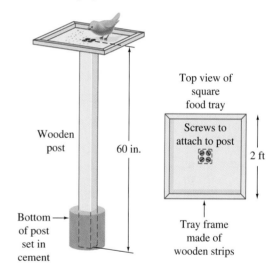

Item	Cost per Unit
wooden post	$2.50 per foot
wooden strips for tray frame	$1.00 per foot
tray bottom	$6.00
tools, screws, nails, wood glue, and cement mix	Loaned or donated by parents

Explain how you could use the information given to find the total cost of materials. Use words, numbers, or pictures.

For Review

32. What are the measures of the interior angles of this triangle?

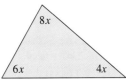

33. Prove that the measure of an exterior angle of a triangle is greater than the measure of either of the opposite interior angles: $m(\angle 3) > m(\angle 1)$ and $m(\angle 3) > m(\angle 2)$.

34. **(a)** Make a freehand (pencil only—no ruler or other drawing tools) drawing of a regular octahedron.

(b) Beside your drawing of the octahedron draw a truncated octahedron. Do this by removing the corners of the octahedron to form squares, which reduce the triangular faces of the octahedron to regular hexagonal faces.

11.2   Area and Perimeter

The number of units required to cover a region in the plane is the **area** of the region. Usually squares are chosen to define a **unit of area,** but any shape that tiles the plane (that is, covers the plane without gaps or overlaps) can serve equally well. Working with a nonstandard unit allows students to discover important general principles of the measurement process.

EXAMPLE   11.5

Making Measurements in Nonstandard Units

Find the area of each figure A, B, C, and D in terms of the unit of area shown at the right.

(a)

A   *B*   unit

(b)

C   *D*   unit

Solution

(a)   The full square A can be covered by 2 of the unit shapes, so area(A) = 2 units. Region B is covered by 6 units, so area(B) = 6 units.

(b)   The hexagon C is covered by 6 of the triangular units, so area(C) = 6 units. Region D cannot be covered directly by the triangular units, although it is evident that the area of D is between 16 and 20 units. To find the exact area, remove and then rejoin a triangular piece as shown below to form a new shape D' of the same area as D. That is, area(D') = area(D). Since D' can be covered by 18 triangular units it follows that area(D) = 18 units.

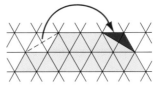

D'

The solution just given employs two useful properties of area. The following **congruence and addition properties** of area will be used repeatedly. Two figures are **congruent** if they have the same shape and size. A figure is **dissected** if it is partitioned into nonoverlapping subregions.

PROPERTIES   *The Congruence and Addition Properties of Area*

Congruence property

If region R is congruent to region S then the two regions have the same area:

$$\text{area}(R) = \text{area}(S)$$

Addition property

If a region R is dissected into nonoverlapping subregions $A, B, \ldots, F$, then the area of R is the sum of the areas of the subregions:

$$\text{area}(R) = \text{area}(A) + \text{area}(B) + \cdots + \text{area}(F).$$

These properties are illustrated in Figure 11.6.

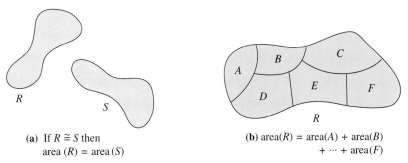

(a) If $R \cong S$ then
area (R) = area (S)

(b) area(R) = area(A) + area(B)
$+ \cdots +$ area(F)

Figure 11.6
The congruence property and the addition property of area

The congruence and addition properties show that rearranging the pieces of a figure forms a new figure with the same area as the original figure.

JUST FOR FUN

How to Cover a Long Hole with a Short Board

Can you cut the board shown into just two pieces to exactly cover the 60 cm by 12 cm hole?

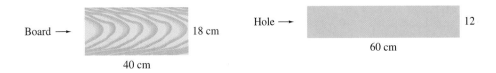

EXAMPLE   11.6

Solving Leonardo's Problems

Leonardo da Vinci (1452–1519) once became absorbed in showing how the areas of certain curvilinear (curved sided) regions could be determined and compared among themselves and to rectangular regions. The pendulum and the ax are two of the examples he included in notes for his book *De Ludo Geometrico* (roughly meaning "Fun with Geometry"), which he never completed. The dots show the centers of the circular arcs which form the boundary of the region.

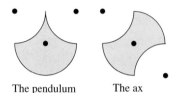

The pendulum   The ax

If the arcs forming the pendulum and the ax have radius 1, show that the areas of both figures are equal to that of a 1 by 2 rectangle.

Solution

After inscribing the figures in a square, we then use the congruence-addition property of area to rearrange the subregions to form a 1 by 2 rectangle.

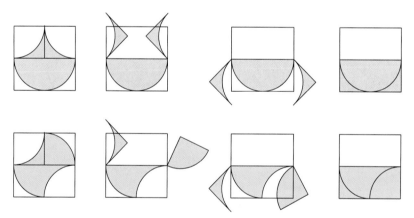

It is surprising to learn that the pendulum and ax both have an area of 2 square units. (These examples and others are described in a booklet by Herbert Wills III, *Leonardo's Dessert*, National Council of Teachers of Mathematics, Reston, Virginia, 1985.)

Unlike Examples 11.5 and 11.6, most area measurement problems are answered by giving a reasonable *estimate* of the area. Units of square shape are easy to subdivide into smaller squares to give a more precise estimation.

EXAMPLE   11.7

Investigating the Area of a Cycloidal Arch

Imagine rolling a wheel along a straight line, with a reflector at point *P* on the rim. Point *P* traces an arch-shaped curve. In the early seventeenth century Galileo investigated this curve and named it the **cycloid.** Discover for yourself the conjecture Galileo made about how the area of the cycloidal arch compares to the area of the circle used to generate the arch.

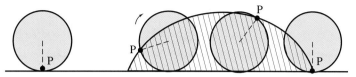

Solution   *Understand the problem*

It is visually clear that the cycloidal arch has an area that is much larger than that of the circle. Our goal is to guess the ratio area (cycloid)/area (circle) that gives the comparison between the areas.

Devise a plan

The areas of the arch and circle must both be measured in some unit of area. For example, we can use squares of size U, where the diameter of the circle is equal to the sum of four side lengths of U. For better accuracy, we can also use small square units of size u, where the side length of u is half that of U.

Carry out the plan

The circle and arch are overlaid by a square grid, with squares of unit area U.

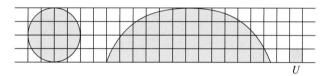

The circle is entirely within 16 squares of size U but does not entirely cover about one unit of area in each of the four corners. Thus we estimate that area (circle) $\doteq$ 12 U. Similarly, we see that area (arch) $\doteq$ 37 U is a reasonable estimate.

Better accuracy is given by the grid of squares of unit area u. The diagram below leads us to the estimates area (circle) $\doteq$ 50 u and area (arch) $\doteq$ 149 u.

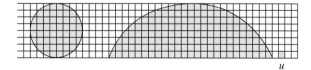

Both $\dfrac{37\,u}{12\,u}$ and $\dfrac{149\,U}{50\,U}$ are nearly 3, which in fact was Galileo's conjecture. The correctness of Galileo's conjecture was proved in 1634 by Gilles Persone de Roberval.

Look back

The finer grid of squares gave us additional precision in our measurements, but this required considerably more time and effort to obtain. The measurement process nearly always requires us to make a judgment about how to balance the conflicting needs of precision versus cost.

Areas of Polygons

Rectangles

A 3 cm by 5 cm rectangle can be covered by 15 unit squares when the unit square is 1 cm^2, as shown in Figure 11.7. Similarly a 2.5 cm by 3.5 cm rectangle can be covered by 6 whole units, 5 half unit squares and one quarter unit square, giving a total area of 8.75 square centimeters. This is also the product of the width and the length since 2.5 cm $\times$ 3.5 cm = 8.75 cm^2.

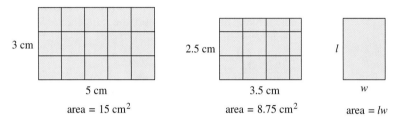

Figure 11.7
The area of a rectangle is the product of its length and width.

For any rectangle the formula for the area A is as follows.

FORMULA   *Area of a Rectangle*
A rectangle of length l and width w has area A given by the formula $A = lw$.

Parallelograms

Suppose a parallelogram has a pair of opposite sides b units long, and these sides are h units apart; an example is shown in Figure 11.8. We say that b is the **base** of the parallelogram and h is the **altitude,** or **height.** (Unless the parallelogram is a rectangle, the altitude is *not* the same as the length of the other two sides of the parallelogram.) Removing and replacing a right triangle T forms a rectangle of the same area as the parallelogram. The rectangle has length b and width h, so its area is bh. Therefore, the area of the parallelogram in Figure 11.8 is also bh.

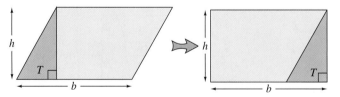

Figure 11.8
A parallelogram of base b and altitude h has the same area as a b by h rectangle.
Therefore, the area of the parallelogram is bh.

Any parallelogram with base b and altitude h can be dissected and rearranged to form a rectangle of length b and width h in a similar way to that shown in Figure 11.8. (See problem 30 in the section exercises for a more general case.) This yields the following formula.

> **FORMULA**   *Area of a Parallelogram*
>
> A parallelogram of base b and altitude h has area A given by $A = bh$.
>
>

EXAMPLE   11.8

Using the Parallelogram Area Formula

Find the area of each parallelogram, and then compute the lengths x and y.

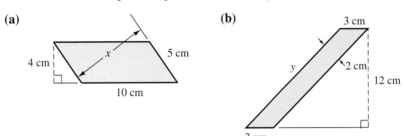

(a)

(b)

Solution

(a)   The parallelogram has base 10 cm and height 4 cm, so its area is $A = (10 \text{ cm})(4 \text{ cm}) = 40 \text{ cm}^2$. If the side of length 5 cm is considered the base, then x is the corresponding height and $A = (5 \text{ cm})x$. Since $A = 40 \text{ cm}^2$, we find $x = 40 \text{ cm}^2/5 \text{ cm} = 8 \text{ cm}$.

(b)   The procedure for (a) is followed. The area is $A = (3 \text{ cm})(12 \text{ cm}) = 36 \text{ cm}^2$. Viewing the side of length y as a base with corresponding altitude 2 cm, we have $36 \text{ cm}^2 = y(2 \text{ cm})$. Therefore $y = 36 \text{ cm}^2/2 \text{ cm} = 18 \text{ cm}$.

JUST FOR FUN

Tile and Smile

Cut a convex quadrilateral from card stock, locate the midpoints of its sides, and then cut along the segments joining successive midpoints to give four triangles T_1, T_2, T_3, T_4, and a parallelogram P.

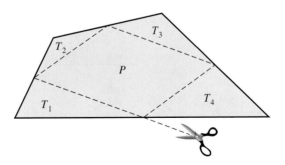

- Show that the four triangles can be arranged to cover the parallelogram.
- How does the area of the parallelogram compare to the area of the original quadrilateral?

Triangles

Figure 11.9 shows that a triangle of base b and altitude h can be dissected and rearranged to form a parallelogram of base $\dfrac{b}{2}$ and altitude h. The formula $\dfrac{1}{2}bh$ for the area of the triangle then follows from the area formula already derived for the parallelogram.

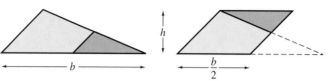

Figure 11.9
A triangle of base b and altitude h can be dissected and rearranged to form a parallelogram of base $\dfrac{b}{2}$ and altitude h.

FORMULA   *Area of a Triangle*

A triangle of base b and altitude h has area $A = \dfrac{1}{2}bh$.

Any side of a triangle can be considered as the base so there are three pairs of bases and altitudes.

EXAMPLE   11.9

Using the Triangle Area Formula

Find the area of each triangle and the distance v and w.

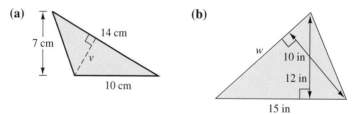

Solution

(a)   The formula $A = \dfrac{1}{2}bh$ shows the area of the triangle is $A = \dfrac{1}{2}(10 \text{ cm})(7 \text{ cm}) = 35 \text{ cm}^2$. If the side of length 14 cm is considered the base, then the corresponding altitude is v. Since $A = \dfrac{1}{2}(14 \text{ cm}) \cdot (v)$, $v = A/(7 \text{ cm}) = (35 \text{ cm}^2)/(7 \text{ cm}) = 5 \text{ cm}$.

(b) $A = \dfrac{1}{2}(15 \text{ in}) \cdot (12 \text{ in}) = 90 \text{ in}^2$ is the area of the triangle. Considering the side

of length w as the base, the corresponding altitude is 10 in and $A = \dfrac{1}{2}w(10 \text{ in})$.

Therefore, $w = (90 \text{ in}^2)/(5 \text{ in}) = 18 \text{ in}$.

Trapezoids

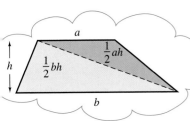

There are several ways to derive the formula for the area of a trapezoid with altitude h and bases a and b. For example, a diagonal drawn through the trapezoid dissects it into two triangles. The altitudes of both triangles are h, their bases are a and b, so the areas of the triangles are $\dfrac{1}{2}ah$ and $\dfrac{1}{2}bh$. Adding the areas gives the following formula.

> **FORMULA**   *Area of a Trapezoid*
>
> A trapezoid with bases of length a and b and altitude h has area $A = \dfrac{1}{2}(a + b)h$.

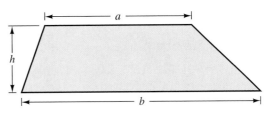

Figure 11.10

The area of a trapezoid is $\dfrac{1}{2}(a + b)\,h$.

EXAMPLE   11.10

Finding the Areas of Lattice Polygons

A polygon formed by joining the points of a square array is called a **lattice polygon.** Lattice polygons are easy to draw on dot paper, or they can be formed with rubber bands on a geoboard. Find the area of the lattice polygons shown, where the unit of area is the area of a small square of the array.

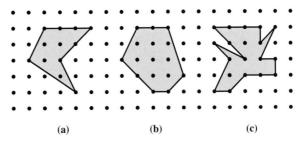

(a)   (b)   (c)

Solution

(a) A horizontal line dissects the polygon into a trapezoid A of area $\frac{1}{2}(3 + 2) \cdot (2) = 5$ and a triangle B of area $\frac{1}{2}(2)(2) = 2$. The area of the polygon is therefore 7.

(b) The lattice hexagon can be dissected into trapezoids C and D and triangle E. The total area of the hexagon is therefore

$$\frac{1}{2}(2 + 3) \cdot (2) + \frac{1}{2}(3 + 1) \cdot (2) + \frac{1}{2}(4) \cdot (1) = 11.$$

Other dissections of the hexagon can be used, but the total area will always be the same.

(c) We could solve the problem in the same way as parts (a) and (b), but there is another useful technique: construct a square about the polygon, and then subtract the areas of the regions F, G, H, I, and J. Therefore the area of the polygon is

$$16 - \left(1 + 1\frac{1}{2} + \frac{1}{2} + 1 + 1\frac{1}{2}\right) = 10\frac{1}{2}.$$

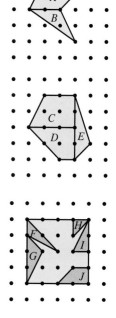

Length of a Curve

The length of a polygonal curve is obtained by summing the lengths of its sides. The length of a nonpolygonal curve is measured, or at least estimated, by calculating the length of an approximating polygonal curve with vertices on the given curve. The accuracy of the estimation is improved by using an approximating polygonal curve with more vertices, as shown in Figure 11.11.

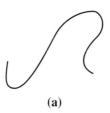   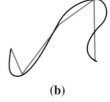   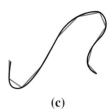

(a)   **(b)**   **(c)**

Figure 11.11
The length of a curve (a) is estimated by measuring the length of a polygonal approximation (b). Increasing the number of vertices gives an improved estimate, as in (c).

The length of a curve can also be measured by first laying a string along the curve and then straightening the string along a ruler. This is the principle that makes the flexible tape measure used for sewing so useful.

EXAMPLE 11.11

Determining the Length of a Cycloid

A circle and the cycloid it generates (see Example 11.7) are shown below. Use a marker pen and a piece of string (or thin strip of paper) to make a tape measure, where the unit of length is the diameter d of the circle.

(a)   According to your tape measure, what is the length from point A to point B along the cycloid?

(b)   What is the approximate length of the line segment $\overline{AB}$?

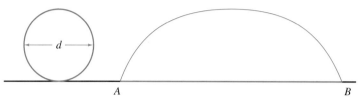

Solution

(a)   The tape measure shows that the length of the cycloid is very nearly four diameters of the circle. In 1658, Christopher Wren (1632–1723) proved that the length of a cycloid is *exactly* four diameters. Wren is perhaps best known as the architect of St. Paul's Cathedral in London.

(b)   The segment $\overline{AB}$ is a bit over 3 diameters. Because $\overline{AB}$ is covered by rolling the circle once around, AB is the length around the circle; that is, AB is the circumference.

Perimeter

The length of a simple closed plane curve is called its **perimeter.** Therefore, perimeter is a *length* measurement and is given in centimeters, inches, feet, meters, and so on. It is important that the *area* of the region enclosed by a simple closed curve not be confused with the perimeter of the figure. Area is given in cm², in², ft², m², and so on. In summary: perimeter is the measure of the distance around a region, and area is the measure of the size of the region within a boundary.

EXAMPLE   11.12   **Finding Perimeters**

The following figures have been drawn on a square grid, where each square is 1 cm on a side. Give the perimeter and area of each figure.

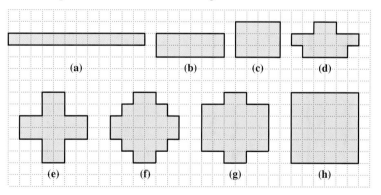

Solution

Figure	(a)	(b)	(c)	(d)	(e)	(f)	(g)	(h)	
Perimeter	26	16	14	18	24	24	24	24	centimeters
Area	12	12	12	12	20	24	28	36	square centimeters

Figures (a), (b), (c), and (d) have the same area but different perimeters. Figures (e), (f), (g), and (h) have the same perimeter but different areas.

The Circumference of a Circle

The perimeter of a circle is called its **circumference.** Using a piece of string or a tape measure, or by rolling a disc along a line (as in Example 11.11(b)), it is easy to rediscover a fact known even in ancient times: The ratio of the circumference of a circle to its diameter is the same for all circles. Two examples are shown in Figure 11.12. This ratio, which is somewhat larger than 3, is given by the symbol π, the lowercase Greek letter *pi.*

DEFINITION π

The ratio of the circumference C to the diameter d of a circle is π. Therefore,

$$\frac{C}{d} = \pi \quad \text{and} \quad C = \pi d.$$

Since the diameter d is twice the radius r of the circle, we also have the formula $C = 2\pi r$.

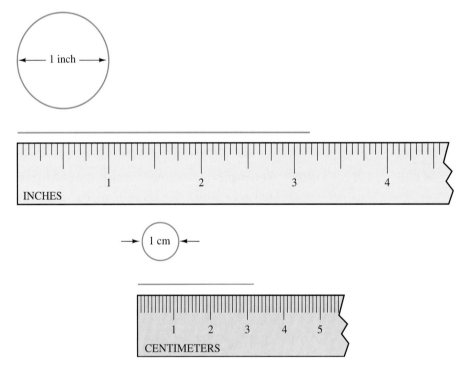

Figure 11.12
The ratio of the circumference C to the diameter d is the same for all circles: c/d = π, or C = πd.

In 1761 John Lambert proved that π is an irrational number, so it is impossible to express π exactly by a fraction or as a terminating or repeating decimal. The values $3\frac{1}{7}$ and 3.14 are useful approximate values, but precision measurements require using more decimal places in the unending decimal expansion $\pi = 3.1415927\ldots$. A circle 100 feet in diameter has an *approximate* circumference of 314 feet, but the exact circumference is 100π feet. It is acceptable to use the symbol π to express results, since this gives exact values. When an approximate numerical value is needed, an appropriate estimate of π such as 3.1416 can be used in the calculations.

| EXAMPLE   11.13 | **Calculating the Equatorial Circumference of the Earth** |

The equatorial diameter of the earth is 7926 miles. Calculate the distance around the earth at the equator using the following approximations for π: (a) 3.14   (b) 3.1416.

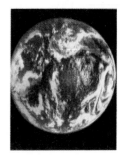

Solution

(a)   (3.14) (7926 miles) $\doteq$ 24,887.64 miles
(b)   (3.1416) (7926 miles) $\doteq$ 24,900.322 miles

The two different approximations of π account for the difference of about 12.7 miles in the answers.

The Area of a Circle

The area of a circle of radius r is given by the formula πr^2, first proved rigorously by Archimedes.

> **FORMULA**   *Area of a Circle*
> The area A enclosed by a circle of radius r is $A = \pi r^2$.

Since π is defined as a ratio of lengths, it seems surprising to find that π also occurs in the formula for the area of a circle. A convincing, but informal, derivation of the formula, $A = \pi r^2$, is shown in Figure 11.13. The circle of radius r and circumference $C = 2\pi r$ is dissected into congruent sectors which are rearranged to form a "parallelogram" of base $\frac{1}{2}C = \pi r$ and altitude r. By the formula for the area of a parallelogram, the wavy-based "parallelogram" has area $\pi r \times r = \pi r^2$. If the number of sections is made larger and larger, the thin sectors form an increasingly exact approximation to a true parallelogram of area πr^2.

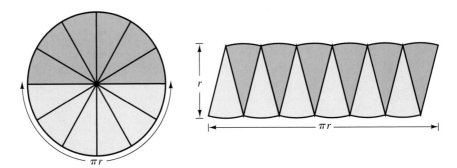

Figure 11.13
The sectors of a circle can be rearranged to approximate a parallelogram of area πr^2.

HIGHLIGHT FROM HISTORY
A Brief History of π

*I*n the third century B.C., Archimedes showed that π is approximately $3\frac{1}{7}$. To estimate π, Archimedes inscribed a regular polygon in a circle and then calculated the ratio of the polygon's perimeter to the diameter of the circle. An inscribed hexagon shows π is about 3, but by using a 96-gon Archimedes proved that $3\frac{10}{71} < \pi < 3\frac{10}{70}$. The same idea was used by the Dutch mathematician Van Ceulen (d. 1610) who used a 32,212,254,720-gon to calculate π to 20 decimals. A century later the English mathematician John Machin took advantage of the invention of calculus to calculate π to 100 decimal places. Machin's method, with some minor variations, was used well into the twentieth century. When implemented on the ENIAC in 1949, the first electronic computer spent 70 hours to calculate π to 2037 decimal places.

Recent records in the calculation of π take advantage of both the extremely high speed of super computers and the implementation of highly efficient algorithms of calculation. For example, in 1997 Yasumasa Kanada of the Computer Center at the University of Tokyo computed 51,539,600,000 (yes, over 50 billion!) decimal digits of π. The calculation took about 29 hours of computer time and used an algorithm of Borwein.

EXAMPLE   11.14

Determining the Size of a Pizza π

A 14″ pizza has the same thickness as a 10″ pizza. How many times more ingredients are there on the larger pizza?

Solution

Pizzas are measured by their diameters, so the radii of the two pizzas are 7″ and 5″. Since the thicknesses are the same, the amount of ingredients used is proportional to the areas of the pizzas. The larger pizza has area $\pi\,(7\text{ in})^2 = 49\pi\text{ in}^2$, and the smaller pizza has area $\pi\,(5\text{ in})^2 = 25\pi\text{ in}^2$. The ratio of areas is $49\pi\text{ in}^2/25\pi\text{ in}^2 = 1.96$, showing that the 14″ pizza has about twice the ingredients of the 10″ one.

PROBLEM SET 11.2

Understanding Concepts

1. Botanists often need to measure the rate at which water is lost by transpiration through the leaves of a plant. It is necessary to know the leaf area of the plant. Estimate the area of the leaf shown. It has been overlaid with a grid of squares 1 cm on a side, shown at reduced scale.

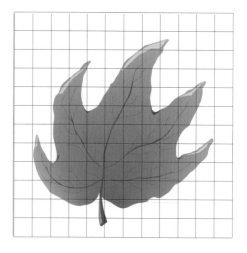

2. Measure the figure F shown below in each of the three nonstandard units of area **(a)**, **(b)**, and **(c)** shown to the right. Do so by tracing F and then tiling the region with the unit area shape.

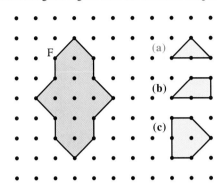

3. Find the area of each of these figures.

(a)

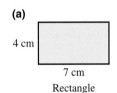

4 cm, 7 cm

Rectangle

(b)

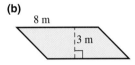

8 m, 3 m

Parallelogram

(c)

10 ft, 14 feet

Right triangle

(d)

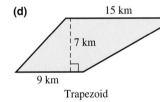

15 km, 7 km, 9 km

Trapezoid

4. Find the area of each of these figures.

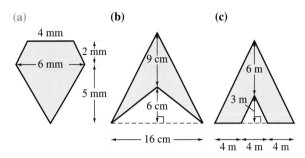

(a) 4 mm, 6 mm, 2 mm, 5 mm

(b) 9 cm, 6 cm, 16 cm

(c) 6 m, 3 m, 4 m 4 m 4 m

5. Fill in the blanks.
- **(a)** $3.45 \text{ m}^2 = $ _____ cm^2
- **(b)** $56{,}000 \text{ mm}^2 = $ _____ cm^2
- **(c)** $56{,}700 \text{ ft}^2 = $ _____ yd^2
- **(d)** $0.085 \text{ mi}^2 = $ _____ ft^2
- **(e)** $47{,}000 \text{ a} = $ _____ $\text{ha} = $ _____ m^2
- **(f)** $5{,}800{,}000 \text{ m}^2 = $ _____ $\text{ha} = $ _____ km^2

6. **(a)** A rectangle has area 36 cm^2 and width 3 cm. What is the length of the rectangle?

(b) A rectangle has area 60 cm^2 and perimeter 38 cm. Use "guess and check" to find the length and width of the rectangle.

7. Twenty-four 1 cm by 1 cm squares are used to tile a rectangle.
- **(a)** Find the dimensions of all possible rectangles.
- **(b)** Which rectangle has the smallest perimeter?
- **(c)** Which rectangle has the largest perimeter?

8. Find the areas and perimeters of the following parallelograms. Be sure to express your answer in the appropriate units of measurement.

(a)

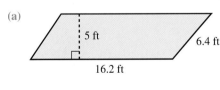

5 ft, 6.4 ft, 16.2 ft

(b)

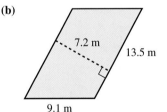

7.2 m, 13.5 m, 9.1 m

(c)

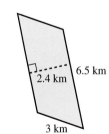

6.5 km, 2.4 km, 3 km

9. Find the areas and perimeters of these triangles.

(a)

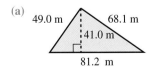

49.0 m, 68.1 m, 41.0 m, 81.2 m

(b)

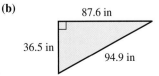

87.6 in, 36.5 in, 94.9 in

(c)

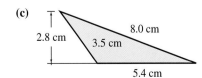

2.8 cm, 8.0 cm, 3.5 cm, 5.4 cm

10. Find the areas of these figures. Express the area in square units.

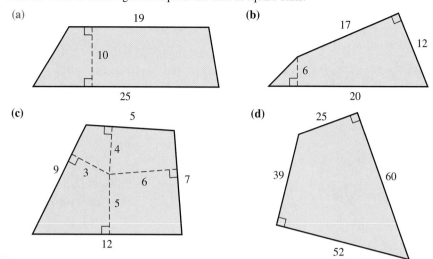

(a)

(b)

(c)

(d)

11. Lines k, l, and m are parallel to the line containing the side $\overline{AB}$ of the triangles shown here.

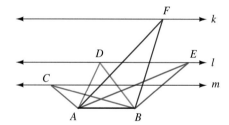

(a) What triangle has the smallest area? Why?
(b) What triangle has the largest area? Why?
(c) Which two triangles have the same area? Why?

12. Lines k, l, and m are equally spaced parallel lines. Let $ABCD$ be a parallelogram of area 12 square units.

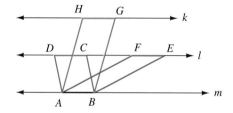

(a) What is the area of the parallelogram $ABEF$?
(b) What is the area of the parallelogram $ABGH$?
(c) If $AB = 3$ units of length, what is the distance between the parallel lines?

13. Find the area of each lattice polygon shown below.

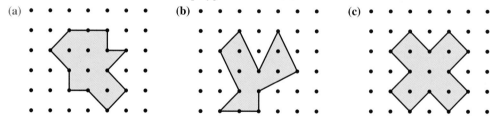

(a)

(b)

(c)

14. An oval track is made by erecting semicircles on each end of a 50 m by 100 m rectangle.

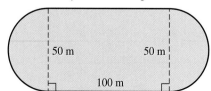

(a) What is the length of the track?
(b) What is the area of the region enclosed by the track?

15. A track has lanes 1 meter wide. The turn-radius of the inner lane is 25 meters. To make a fair race, the starting lines in each lane must be staggered so each competitor runs the same distance to the finish line. Find the distance between the starting line in one lane to the starting line in the next lane. Is the same distance used between the first and second lane and between the second and third lane?

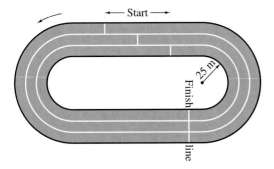

16. An **annulus** is the region bounded by two concentric circles.

(a) If the radius of the small circle is 1 and the radius of the larger circle is 2, what is the area of the annulus?

(b) A dart board has four annular rings surrounding a bull's-eye.

The circles have radii 1, 2, 3, 4, and 5. Suppose a dart is equally likely to hit any point of the board. Is the dart more likely to hit in the outermost ring (shown black) or inside the region consisting of the bull's-eye and the two innermost rings?

17. A circle is inscribed in a square. What percentage of the area of the square is inside the circle?

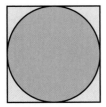

18. The meter was originally defined as one ten-millionth of the distance from the North Pole to the equator.

(a) Assuming the earth is a perfect sphere what would be the circumference of a great circle on the earth that passes through the North and South poles?

(b) The diameter of the equatorial circle of the earth is 12,755 kilometers. What is the circumference of the equator?

(c) Which is longer, the polar circle or the equator? Can you account for the difference?

Thinking Critically

19. Two regions, A and B, are cut from paper. Suppose the area of region A is 20 cm² larger than that of region B. If the regions are overlapped, by how much does the area of the nonoverlapped part of region A exceed the nonoverlapped part of region B? Explain carefully.

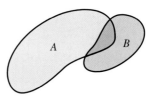

20. Four mutually tangent circles of diameter 10 cm with their centers at the vertices of a square are used to draw a vase.

(a) Use dissection and rearrangement to form a square of the same area as the vase. (Show a sequence of steps similar to the solutions in Example 11.6.)

(b) Show the vase has area 100 cm².

(c) As an extra challenge, see if you can do part (a) by cutting the vase into just 3 pieces.

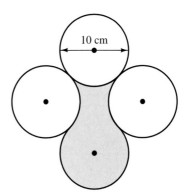

21. A square cake measures 8″ by 8″. A wedge-shaped piece is cut by two slices meeting at 90° at the cake's center. What is the area of the top of the piece? Explain your reasoning carefully.

22. For reasons lost in history, the two cornfields R and S were divided by two line segments, $\overline{AB}$ and $\overline{BC}$. The friendly owners of the fields would like to divide their adjoining fields by a single straight boundary line. Carefully describe how to divide the quadrilateral into two fields R' and S' with a single segment so the area of each new cornfield is the same as before.

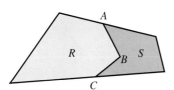

23. **(a)** The colored region shown below is formed by circular arcs drawn from two opposite corners of a 1 by 1 square. What is the area of the region?

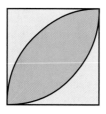

(b) Four semicircles are drawn at the midpoints of the sides of a 1 by 1 square. What is the area of the shaded region?

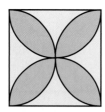

24. A sidewalk 8 feet wide surrounds the polygonally shaped garden of perimeter 300 feet as shown. The sidewalk makes circular sectors of 8 foot radius at the vertices of the polygon. Explain why the area covered by the walk is $2400 + 64\pi$ square feet.

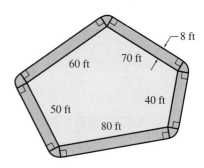

25. Problems 48 and 50 of the Rhind Papyrus suggest that the ancient Egyptians approximated π with $(16/9)^2$, which to two decimal places is the quite accurate value 3.16. Use the following sequence of figures to explain the reasoning that may have been used to derive this estimation. Notice that that area of the circle with diameter 9 is approximated with an octagon and the octagon's area is then approximated by a square of side length 8.

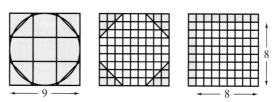

26. The commentaries of the Talmud (Tosfos Pesachim 109a, Tosfos Succah 8a, Marsha Babba Bathra 27a) present a nice approach to the formula, $A = \pi r^2$, for the area of a circle. Imagine that the interior of a circle is covered by concentric circles of yarn. Clipping the yarn circles along a vertical radius, each strand is straightened to cover an isosceles triangle. Find the area of the triangle and then explain how the area formula for a circle follows.

27. According to Jewish history, the Tabernacle of Moses was a 50 cubit by 100 cubit rectangle. The Jerusalem Talmud suggests that a square with sides of length $70\frac{2}{3}$ cubits has nearly the same area, being short by just $\frac{19}{3} - \frac{1}{9}$ square cubits. Show this is true.

28. Let P be an arbitrary point in an equilateral triangle ABC of altitude h and side s as shown. What is the sum $x + y + z$ of the distances to the sides of the triangle? (*Hint:* The areas of $\triangle ABP$, $\triangle BCP$, and $\triangle ACP$ add up to area ($\triangle ABC$).)

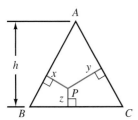

29. Joining each vertex of a triangle shown here to the midpoint of the opposite side divides the triangle into six small triangles.

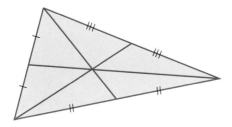

Show that all six triangles have the same area. (*Hint:* Look for pairs of triangles with the same base and height.)

Thinking Cooperatively

For the next four problems/activities, you will need several sheets of paper (including a sheet of ruled notebook paper), scissors, and a ruler.

30. The derivation of the formula for the area of a parallelogram depicted in Figure 11.8 does not apply to a tall slanted parallelogram, since more than two pieces are required to form a rectangle. Draw a parallelogram something like the one shown, where the base is, say, three vertical ruled lines long. Cut out the parallelogram, and make vertical cuts along every third ruled line. Show the pieces you obtain can be reassembled into a rectangle.

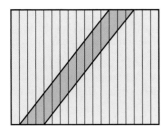

31. Fold a sheet of paper in half and cut out a pair of congruent triangles.
   (a) Show that the two triangles can be arranged to form a parallelogram.
   (b) Use the construction in part (a) to obtain a new explanation of how the formula for the area of a triangle follows from the area formula for a parallelogram.

32. Cut several triangles as illustrated from paper.

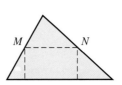 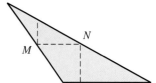

Find the midpoints, M and N, of the slanted sides (that is, the sides not the base) by folding.
   (a) Fold on the horizontal and vertical lines (shown dashed) to form a doubly covered (two layers of paper) rectangle.
   (b) If the triangle has base b and altitude h, what are the lengths of the sides of the rectangle you formed by folding? Obtain the triangle area formula $A = 1/2\,bh$.

33. The formula for the area of a trapezoid can be obtained in several ways using paper folding and cutting. Discuss how to obtain the formula by each of these methods.
   (a) Fold a sheet of paper in half and cut out, simultaneously, a pair of congruent trapezoids. Show how to arrange the two trapezoids into a parallelogram, and then explain how the area formula for a trapezoid can be derived from the area formula for a parallelogram.
   (b) Fold one of the bases of a paper trapezoid onto the other, and crease along the midline between the two bases. Now cut along the crease line to create two trapezoids. Show how to arrange them into a parallelogram, and then derive the area formula for the original trapezoid from that of the parallelogram you have formed.

Making Connections

34. Kelly has been hired to mow a large rectangular lawn, measuring 75 feet by 125 feet. The lawn mower cuts a path 21 inches wide. Estimate how far (in feet) Kelly must walk to complete the mowing job.

35. Roll-ends of carpet are on sale for six dollars per square yard. To finish the rough-cut edges, edging material costing ten cents per foot is glued in place. Compute the total cost of a roll-end measuring 8 feet by 10 feet.

36. A carpet is made by sewing a one-inch-wide braid around and around until the final shape is an oval with semicircular ends as shown. Estimate the length of braid required. (*Hint:* Estimate the area of the carpet.)

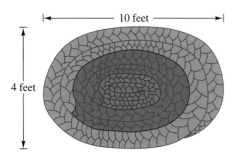

37. An L-shaped house, walkway, garage, and driveway are shown situated on a 70′ by 120′ lot. How many bags of fertilizer are needed for the lawn? Assume the bags are each 20 pounds, and one pound of fertilizer will treat 200 square feet of lawn.

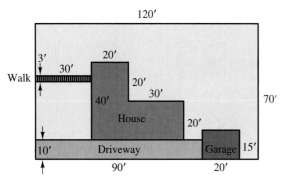

38. A 10′ by 12′ kitchen floor is to be tiled with 8″ square tiles. Estimate the number of tiles this will require.

39. **(a)** The normal-sized tires on a truck have a 14-inch radius. If oversized tires of 15-inch radius are used how much farther does the truck travel per revolution of the wheel?

   (b) If the speedometer indicates the truck is traveling at 56 miles per hour, what is the true speed when the truck is running on the oversized tires?

40. Sunaina has 600 feet of fencing. She wishes to build a corral along an existing high straight wall. She has already decided to make the corral in the shape of an isosceles triangle, with two sides each 300 feet long. What is the measure of $\angle A$ which will give Sunaina the corral of most area? (*Hint:* Consider one of the sides of length 300 feet as a base of the triangle.)

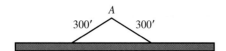

Using a Calculator

41. Let a triangle have sides of length *a*, *b*, and *c*. Also, let *s* denote half the perimeter of the triangle, so $s = \frac{1}{2}(a + b + c)$. The area of the triangle is given by **Hero's** (or **Heron's**) **formula:**

$$A = \sqrt{s(s - a)(s - b)(s - c)}.$$

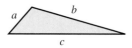

The formula is named for the Greek mathematician Hero of Alexandria, who lived about A.D 50, but the formula was discovered much earlier by Archimedes. Use Hero's formula to compute the area of these triangles.

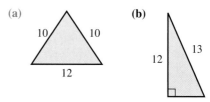

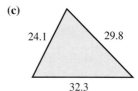

Using a Computer

42. Use dynamic geometry software to construct any convex quadrilateral. Next join the successive midpoints of the sides of the quadrilateral to form a parallelogram. Use the software to compute both the area of the quadrilateral and the area of the parallelogram. What relationship seems to exist between these areas?

43. Draw an equilateral triangle and its inscribed and circumscribed circles. How do the areas of the two circles compare? Investigate with your software.

44. Draw a regular hexagon and its inscribed and circumscribed circles. Use your software to compare the areas of the two circles.

From State Student Assessments

45. (Washington State, Grade 4)

Casey is making a quilt. Quilts are made up of quilt blocks. Each quilt block will look like the one below.

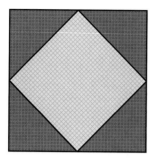

Her quilt will have 25 blocks. Casey knows how much fabric she needs to make the patterned inside squares.

Tell the steps she could take to figure out how much fabric she will need to make all of the shaded corner pieces.

Explain your thinking using words, numbers, or pictures.

46. (Washington State, Grade 4)

Which of the following is closest to the distance around the middle of an unsharpened pencil?

A. 25 millimeters

B. 25 centimeters

C. 25 meters

For Review

47. Convert these measurements to the unit shown.

(a) 1 m = _____ cm   (b) 352 mm = _____ cm

(c) 1 m^2 = _____ cm^2 (d) 1 m^3 = _____ liters

COOPERATIVE INVESTIGATION

Discovering Pick's Formula

In 1899 the German mathematician Georg Pick discovered a remarkable formula for the area of a polygon drawn on square dot paper. Polygons of this special type are also known as lattice polygons. Stretching a rubber band onto a geoboard is another easy way to form lattice polygons.

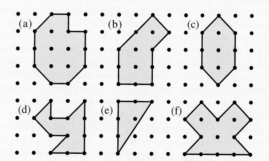

1. Complete the table of values for each polygon, where

b = number of dots on the boundary of the polygon,

i = number of dots in the interior of the polygon, and

A = area of the polygon.

The values of b, i, and A for polygon **(a)** are given as an example.

Polygon	b	i	A
(a)	11	5	$9\frac{1}{2}$
(b)			
(c)			
(d)			
(e)			
(f)			

2. Try to guess a formula for A in terms of b and i. (If you have trouble, add a column of the values of $b/2$. You may also want to obtain more data by drawing other lattice polygons.)

3. Search for an extension of Pick's formula for regions with a hole; that is, a region inside one lattice polygon but outside a second lattice polygon. Now b is the number of dots on both rubber bands, and i is the number of dots between the two rubber bands.

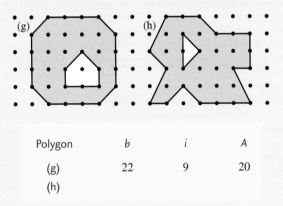

Polygon	b	i	A
(g)	22	9	20
(h)			

11.3   The Pythagorean Theorem

The Pythagorean theorem is the single most remarkable result in geometry. The theorem is aesthetically pleasing and also very useful in solving practical problems.

THEOREM *The Pythagorean Theorem*

If a right triangle has legs of length a and b and its hypotenuse has length c, then

$$a^2 + b^2 = c^2.$$

By erecting squares on the sides of a right triangle, the Pythagorean relation $a^2 + b^2 = c^2$ can be interpreted as a result about areas: *The sum of the areas of the squares on the legs of a right triangle is equal to the area of the square on the hypotenuse.* The area interpretation of the Pythagorean theorem is shown in Figure 11.14.

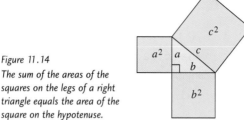

Figure 11.14
The sum of the areas of the squares on the legs of a right triangle equals the area of the square on the hypotenuse.

The area interpretation probably led to the discovery of the theorem, at least in special cases. For example, the Babylonian clay tablet shown in Figure 11.15 shows a large square subdivided by congruent isosceles right triangles. It is apparent that the area of the square on the hypotenuse equals the area in the two squares on the legs.

Figure 11.15
A Babylonian tablet suggesting a special case of the Pythagorean theorem

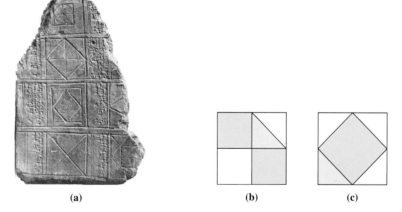

(a)   (b)   (c)

The demonstration depicted in Figure 11.15 is not a general proof of the Pythagorean theorem, because the right triangle is isosceles. However, a similar idea can be followed for arbitrary right triangles. In Figure 11.16(a) we begin with any right triangle, letting a and b denote the lengths of the legs and c the length of the hypotenuse. Next consider a square with sides of length $a + b$. Four congruent copies of the right triangle are placed inside the squares in two different ways. In Figure 11.16(b) the four triangles leave two squares uncovered, with respective areas a^2 and b^2. In Figure 11.16(c) the four triangles leave one square of area c^2 uncovered. Since the four triangles leave the same area uncovered in both arrangements, we conclude $a^2 + b^2 = c^2$.

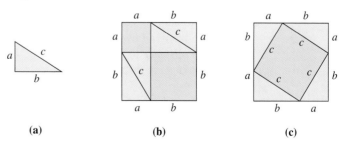

Figure 11.16
A dissection proof of the Pythagorean theorem

(a)   (b)   (c)

No records have survived to indicate what proof, if any, Pythagoras (c. 572–501 B.C.) may have offered. The dissection proof requires showing that the inner quadrilateral of Figure 11.16(c) is actually a square (why is it?), but the Pythagorean's knowledge of angles in a right triangle was sufficient to do this. Since the time of Pythagoras, a tremendous number of proofs have been devised. In the second edition of *The Pythagorean Proposition,* E. S. Loomis catalogs 370 different proofs.

EXAMPLE   11.15

Using the Pythagorean Theorem

Find the lengths x and y in the following figures.

(a)
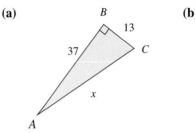

(b)
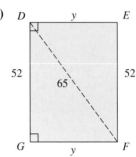

Solution

(a)   By the Pythagorean theorem, $x^2 = 13^2 + 37^2 = 169 + 1369 = 1538$. Therefore $x = \sqrt{1538} \doteq 39.2$.

(b)   The diagonal $\overline{DF}$ of rectangle $DEFG$ is the hypotenuse of the right triangle DEF. The Pythagorean theorem, applied to $\triangle DEF$, gives $y^2 + 52^2 = 65^2$. Therefore $y^2 = 65^2 - 52^2 = 4225 - 2704 = 1521$, and $y = \sqrt{1521} = 39$.

For many applications it is necessary to write and solve equations based on the Pythagorean relation. Here is an example.

EXAMPLE   11.16

Determining How Far You Can See

Imagine yourself on top of a mountain, or perhaps in an airplane, at a known altitude given in feet. Approximately how far away, in miles, is the horizon?

Solution   *Understand the problem*

Altitude is a measure of the distance above the surface of the earth. The horizon is the circle of points where our line of sight is tangent to the sphere of the earth's surface. The problem is to derive a formula that expresses, or at least approximates, the distance to the horizon as it depends on the altitude of the observer. Since the altitude is given in feet, but the distance to the horizon is to be given in miles, special care must be taken to handle the units of measure properly.

Devise a plan

The earth is very nearly a sphere. A line of sight to the horizon forms a leg of a right triangle, as the diagram shows. Since the radius, r, of the earth is about 4000 miles, and the altitude, s, is known, the Pythagorean theorem can be used to solve for the distance to the horizon. In the diagram all distances, including s, are expressed in miles; if h is the altitude in feet we can use the conversion formula $h = 5280s$ (recall that 1 mile = 5280 feet).

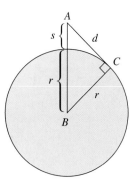

Carry out the plan

Applying the Pythagorean theorem to the right triangle ABC gives $d^2 + r^2 = (s + r)^2$. The squared term on the right can be written $s^2 + 2sr + r^2$, so $d^2 + r^2 = s^2 + 2sr + r^2$. Subtracting r^2 from both sides shows that $d^2 = s^2 + 2sr$. Therefore the exact distance d, in miles, is given by the formula

$$d = \sqrt{s^2 + 2rs}.$$

Since $r = 4000$ miles, the formula can also be written

$$d = \sqrt{s^2 + 8000s}, \quad \text{or} \quad d = \sqrt{s(s + 8000)}.$$

From the top of a mountain (say, $s = 2$), or from an airplane (say, $s = 7$), or even from the Space Shuttle (say, $s = 200$), it is evident that the altitude s is much smaller than 8000. Therefore, little accuracy is lost if the term $(s + 8000)$ in the exact formula is replaced with simply 8000. This gives us the approximate equation

$$d \doteq \sqrt{8000s}.$$

Using the equation $s = \dfrac{h}{5280}$ gives $d \doteq \sqrt{\dfrac{8000}{5280}h}$. Finally, since $\sqrt{\dfrac{8000}{5280}} \doteq 1.2$, we obtain a simple formula for the miles d to the horizon as seen from an altitude of h feet:

$$d \doteq 1.2\sqrt{h}.$$

For example, the distance to the horizon as seen from an airplane flying at 40,000 feet is about $1.2\sqrt{40,000} = (1.2)(200) = 240$ miles.

Look back

This problem involved several steps which are typical of the way the Pythagorean theorem is used:

- draw a figure and label all the distances,
- identify all the right triangles in the drawing,
- write the Pythagorean relationships for all of the right triangles, and
- solve the Pythagorean formulas to determine unknown values needed for the solution of the problem.

The Converse of the Pythagorean Theorem

The numbers 5, 12, and 13 satisfy $5^2 + 12^2 = 13^2$. Is the triangle with sides of length 5, 12, and 13 a right triangle? The answer is yes, since the Pythagorean relation $a^2 + b^2 = c^2$ holds if, *and only if, a, b,* and *c* are the side lengths of a right triangle. That is, the converse of the Pythagorean theorem is true, as stated without proof in the following theorem.

THEOREM *Converse of the Pythagorean Theorem*

Let a triangle have sides of length *a*, *b*, and *c*. If $a^2 + b^2 = c^2$, then the triangle is a right triangle and the angle opposite the side of length *c* is its right angle.

EXAMPLE   11.17 | **Checking for Right Triangles**

Determine if the three lengths given are the lengths of the sides of a right triangle.

(a)   15;   17;   8   (b)   10;   5; $5\sqrt{3}$ (c)   231;   520;   568

Solution

(a) $8^2 + 15^2 = 64 + 225 = 289 = 17^2$, so 8, 15, and 17 are the lengths of the sides of a right triangle.

(b) $5^2 + (5\sqrt{3})^2 = 25 + 25 \cdot 3 = 25 + 75 = 100 = 10^2$, so 5, $5\sqrt{3}$, and 10 are the lengths of the sides of a right triangle.

(c) $231^2 + 520^2 = 53{,}361 + 270{,}400 = 323{,}761 \neq 322{,}624 = 568^2$, so 231, 520, and 568 are not the lengths of sides of a right triangle. This would be difficult to see by measuring angles with a protractor, since this triangle closely resembles the right triangle with sides of length 231, 520, and 569. Note that $569^2 = 323{,}761$.

PROBLEM SET 11.3

Understanding Concepts

1. Find the distance *x* in each figure.

(a)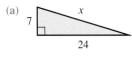

(b)

(c)

(d)

(e)

(f)

2. Find the distance x in each figure.

(a)

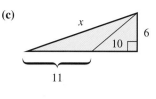

(b)

(c)

3. Find the distances x and y in the rectangular prism and the cube.

(a)

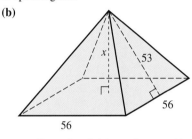

(b)

4. Find the distance x in these space figures.

(a)

(b)

(c)

Cone

Square based right regular pyramid, with sides 56 and slant height 53

Sphere cut by plane

5. Find the areas of these figures.

(a)

(b)

(c)

---

6. Francoise and Maurice cut across a 50 foot by 100 foot vacant lot on their way to school. How much distance do they save by not staying on the sidewalk?

7. A square with sides of length 2 is inscribed in a circle and circumscribed around another circle. Which is larger, the area of the region between the circles or the area inside the smaller circle?

8. At noon car A left town heading due east at 50 miles per hour. At 1 P.M. car B left the same town heading due north at 40 miles per hour. How far apart were the two cars at

(a) 2 P.M.   (b) 3:30 P.M.?

9. Find AG in this spiral of right triangles.

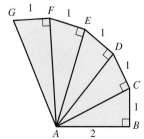

10. **(a)** What is the length of the side of a square inscribed in a circle of radius 1?

(b) What is the length of the side of a cube inscribed in a sphere of radius 1?

11. What is the distance between the centers of these circles?

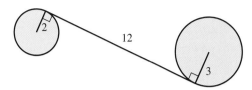

12. What is the radius of the circle shown below?

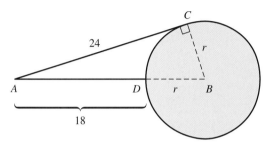

13. Which of the following can be the lengths of the sides of a right triangle?

  (a) 21, 28, 35   **(b)** 9, 40, 41

  (c) 12, 35, 37   **(d)** 14, 27, $\sqrt{533}$

  (e) $7\sqrt{2}$, $4\sqrt{7}$, $2\sqrt{77}$ **(f)** 9.5, 16.8, 19.3

14. If a, b, and c are the lengths of the sides of a right triangle, explain why $10a$, $10b$, and $10c$ are also the lengths of the sides of a right triangle.

Thinking Critically

15. **(a)** Show that the altitude h of an equilateral triangle with sides of length s is given by $h = \dfrac{\sqrt{3}}{2}\, s$.

  (b) Find a formula for the area of an equilateral triangle of side length s.

(c) Find a formula for the area of a regular hexagon of side length s.

(d) Show that the area of the inscribed circle of a regular hexagon is $\dfrac{3}{4}$ the area of the circumscribed circle.

16. There are five different lengths between pairs of nails on a 3 nail by 3 nail geoboard:

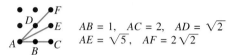

$AB = 1$, $AC = 2$, $AD = \sqrt{2}$
$AE = \sqrt{5}$, $AF = 2\sqrt{2}$

How many different lengths can you find on a 5 nail by 5 nail geoboard?

17. Find the length of the diagonals of this isosceles trapezoid.

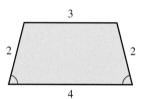

18. An ant is at corner A of a shoe box that is 9 inches long, 5 inches wide, and 3 inches high. What route should the ant follow over the surface of the box to reach the opposite corner C in the shortest distance? [*Suggestion:* It will help to tear along the vertical edges of the box and flatten the top.]

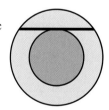

19. A chord of the large circle is tangent to the inner concentric circle. If the chord is 20 cm long, what is the area of the annulus (the region between the two circles)?

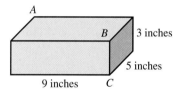

---

20. Justify why the shaded regions (which are all parallelograms) in the following sequence of diagrams have the same area. This provides a striking dynamical proof of the Pythagorean theorem.

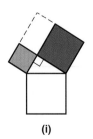

(i)

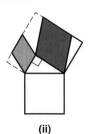

(ii)

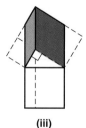

(iii)

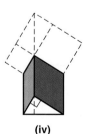

(iv)

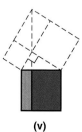

(v)

Thinking Cooperatively

For the next three problems/activities, you will need several sheets of paper and scissors. Begin by folding a sheet of paper in half twice and then cutting a diagonal to obtain four congruent right triangles. Next, use one of your triangles as a pattern to cut four paper squares whose sides match the sides a, b, $b - a$, and c of the right triangles. Be sure to cut your pieces with care and precision.

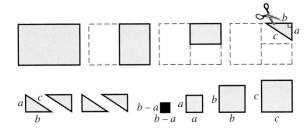

21. The twelfth century Hindu mathematician Bhaskara arranged four copies of a right triangle of side lengths a, b, c into a c by c square, filling in the center with the $b - a$ sided square.

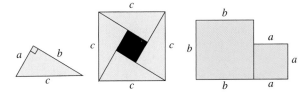

   (a) Show how the five pieces in the c by c square can be arranged to fill the "double" square region at the right.

   (b) Explain how the Pythagorean theorem follows from part (a).

22. Tile the pentagon shown below in two ways:
   (a) with two triangles and the squares of sides a and b;
   (b) with two triangles and the square of side c.

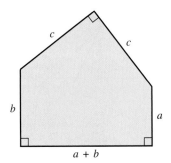

   (c) Explain why the two tilings in parts (a) and (b) prove the Pythagorean theorem.

23. In the nineteenth century, Henry Perigal, a London stockbroker and amateur astronomer, discovered a beautiful scissors-and-paper demonstration of the Pythagorean theorem. Follow these steps to complete your own demonstration. Through the center of the larger square on the leg of the right triangle, draw one line perpendicular to the hypotenuse and a second line parallel to the hypotenuse. Cut along these two lines to divide the square into four congruent pieces, and then show how to arrange these four pieces, together with the square on the shorter leg, to form a square on the hypotenuse of the right triangle.

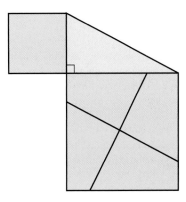

Making Connections

24. A baseball diamond is actually a square 90 feet on a side. What distance must a catcher throw the ball to pick off a runner attempting to steal second base?

25. Approximately what height can be reached from a 24-foot ladder? What assumptions have you made to arrive at your answer?

26. The ancient Egyptians squared off fields with a rope 12 units long, with knots tied to indicate each unit. Explain how such a rope could be used to form a right angle. What theorem justifies their procedure?

27. A water lily is floating in a murky pond rooted on the bottom of the pond by a stem of unknown length.

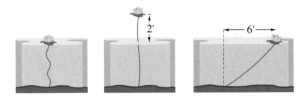

The lily can be lifted 2 feet over the water and moved 6 feet to the side. What is the depth of the pond?

28. A stop sign is to be made by cutting off triangles from the corners of a square sheet of metal 32 inches on a side. What length *x* will leave a regular octagon? Give your answer to the nearest eighth inch.

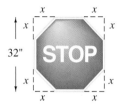

29. Any large structure made of steel must be designed to accommodate the expansion of the metal when heated. Thus pipelines, steel bridge decking, and train track rails have expansion joints. To understand why, consider a mile long steel rail built without any expansion joint. Suppose on a warm day the rail lengthens by one inch. If its ends are firmly anchored and the track bows to one side, the amount of deflection can be estimated by considering a right triangle with one leg $\frac{1}{2}$ mile long and a hypotenuse $\frac{1}{2}$ mile $+ \frac{1}{2}$ inch long. What is the deflection *x*? Convert all dimensions to feet to do your calculation.

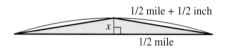

30. A **Pythagorean triple** is a triple of positive integers *a*, *b*, *c* that satisfy the Pythagorean relationship. $a^2 + b^2 = c^2$. For example, 3-4-5 is a Pythagorean triple, since $3^2 + 4^2 = 5^2$.

(a) Verify that 5-12-13, 8-15-17, and 7-24-25 are Pythagorean triples.

(b) If *a-b-c* is a Pythagorean triple, is 2*a*-2*b*-2*c* also a Pythagorean triple? Explain why or why not?

(c) If *a-b-c* is a Pythagorean triple, is the triple obtained by adding 2 to each number also a Pythagorean triple? That is, is (2 + *a*)-(2 + *b*)-(2 + *c*) also a Pythagorean triple? Explain why or why not.

(d) Let *u* and *v* be integers, with $1 \le u < v$, and set $a = v^2 - u^2$, $b = 2vu$, $c = v^2 + u^2$. Show that *a-b-c* is a Pythagorean triple.

(e) Use the formulas given in part (d) to compute the Pythagorean triples for $1 \le u < v \le 6$. [This can also be done on a spreadsheet]. Use the data to respond to investigate these questions: Which triples *a-b-c* are primitive, in the sense that *a*, *b*, and *c* have no common divisor other than 1? Is at least one of *a*, *b*, or *c* divisible by 5?

31. Use the approximate formula $d \doteq 1.2\sqrt{h}$ of Example 11.16 to answer these questions.

(a) On a cliff top 100 feet over the ocean, what is the distance to the horizon?

(b) The observation deck of the Sears Tower in Chicago is 1353 feet above ground level. How far can you see across Lake Michigan?

(c) In the Dr. Seuss book *Yertle the Turtle*, Yertle stands on the backs of other turtles and can see 40 miles. How high is Yertle?

Using a Computer

32. Use dynamic geometry software to draw any right triangle. On each side, draw outward pointing equilateral triangles. Use your software to calculate the areas of the triangles.

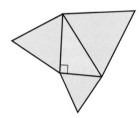

How does the sum of the areas of the triangles on the two legs compare to the area of the equilateral triangle on the hypotenuse?

33. Use a script to draw a square on an edge to construct a general triangle *ABC* with squares on its three sides, as shown here. Measure the areas of the squares and angle ∠*ABC*, and calculate the sum of the squares on sides $\overline{AB}$ and $\overline{BC}$. Manipulate the triangle until the sum of the areas of the squares closely agrees with the area of the square on side $\overline{AC}$. What is the measure of the ∠*ABC*? Write a paragraph describing your exploration.

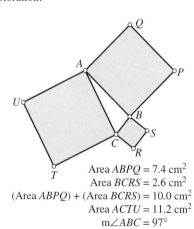

Area *ABPQ* = 7.4 cm²
Area *BCRS* = 2.6 cm²
(Area *ABPQ*) + (Area *BCRS*) = 10.0 cm²
Area *ACTU* = 11.2 cm²
m∠*ABC* = 97°

For Review

34. The length of a rectangle is increased by $33\frac{1}{3}$ percent and the width is decreased by 25 percent. By what percent does the area of the rectangle change?

35. Find the areas of these figures.

(a)

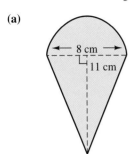

(b)

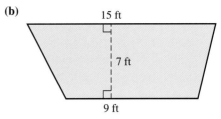

36. Two semicircular arcs, of radius 3 m and 5 m, are centered on the diameter $\overline{AB}$ of a large semicircle as shown. Which route from A to B is shorter: along the large semicircle, or along the two smaller semicircles which touch tangentially at C?

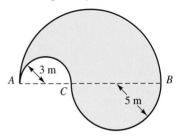

11.4   Surface Area and Volume

The **surface area,** denoted by *SA*, of any polyhedron is the sum of the areas of its faces. It's often useful to cut the faces apart and rearrange them in a single plane. In many cases the figure that is formed has an easily calculated area.

Surface Area of Right Prisms and Cylinders

Figure 11.17 on the next page shows how the surface of a right prism is cut into two congruent bases, with the lateral surfaces of the prism unfolded to form a rectangle. If the right prism has height h and the perimeter of the base is p, then the rectangle has area hp.

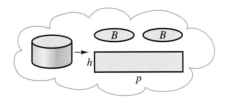

The same reasoning applies to any right cylinder, where the lateral surface is imagined to be unrolled onto the plane to form a rectangle. The formula obtained at the top of the next page, and indeed all of the formulas in this section, are of far less importance than the ideas used to derive the formulas.

In particular, it is helpful to understand that the total surface area of a three-dimensional solid is often a sum of the **base area** and the **lateral surface area** of the solid (recall that "lateral" means "side").

FORMULA *Surface Area of a Right Prism or Right Cylinder*

Let a right prism or cylinder have height h, bases of area B, and let p be the perimeter of each base. Then the surface area, SA, is given by

$$SA = 2B + ph$$

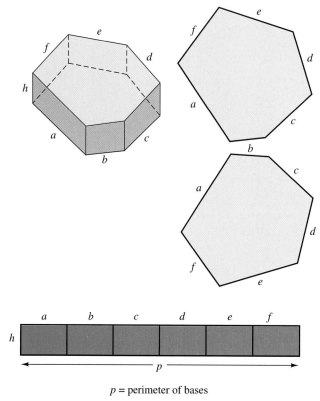

p = perimeter of bases

Figure 11.17
The surface of a right prism can be cut and unfolded to form two congruent bases and a rectangle.

EXAMPLE   11.18

Finding the Surface Area of a Prism-Shaped Gift Box

A gift box has the shape shown below. The height is 10 cm, the longer edges are 20 cm long, and the short edges of the square corner cutouts are each 5 cm long. What is the surface area of the box?

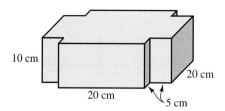

Solution

Each base has the area $B = 800$ cm^2. The lateral surface area is that of a rectangle 10 cm high and 120 cm long. That is, the lateral surface area is 1200 cm^2. Altogether the area of the box is $SA = 2 \times 800$ cm$^2 + 1200$ cm$^2 = 2800$ cm^2.

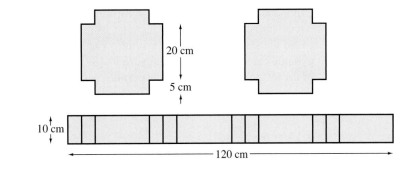

EXAMPLE   11.19

Finding the Surface Area of a Cylindrical Juice Can

A small can of frozen orange juice is about 9.5 cm tall and has a diameter of about 5.5 cm. The circular ends are metal and the rest of the can is cardboard. How much metal and how much cardboard are needed to make a juice can?

Solution

The rectangle below is 9.5 cm wide and 5.5π cm long, so the area of cardboard is $(9.5) \cdot (5.5)\pi$ cm$^2 = 52.25\pi$ cm^2, or about 164 cm^2. The circles have a radius of 2.75 cm, so each circle has area $\pi(2.75$ cm$)^2$. Twice this is 15.125π cm^2, so the area of the two metal ends is about 47.5 cm^2.

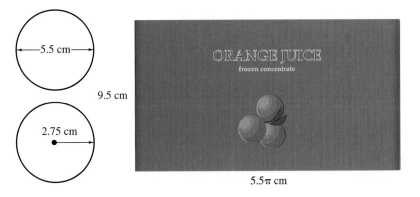

Surface Area of Pyramids

The surface area of a pyramid is computed by adding the area of the base to the sum of the areas of the triangles forming the lateral surface of the pyramid. Of special importance is the **right regular pyramid,** for which the base is a regular polygon and the lateral surface is formed by congruent isosceles triangles. The altitude of the triangles is called the **slant height** of the pyramid. The formula for the surface area of a right regular pyramid can be obtained from Figure 11.18. The triangles each have altitude s, and the sum of the lengths of the bases is the perimeter p of the base polygon. The total area of the triangles is therefore $\frac{1}{2}ps$. If the base of the pyramid has area B, then the total surface area is $SA = B + \frac{1}{2}ps$.

Figure 11.18

A right regular prism has total surface area $SA = B + \frac{1}{2}ps$.

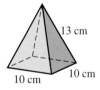

$s = \text{slant height}$

FORMULA   *Surface Area of Right Regular Pyramid*

Let a right regular pyramid have slant height s, and a base of area B and perimeter p. Then the surface area, SA, of the pyramid is given by the formula

$$SA = B + \frac{1}{2}ps$$

Once again, the reasoning that leads to the formula is much more important than the formula itself.

EXAMPLE   11.20   **Finding the Surface Area of a Right Regular Pyramid**

A pyramid has a square base 10 cm on a side. The edges that meet at the apex have length 13 cm. Find the slant height of the pyramid, and then calculate the total surface area (including the base) of the pyramid.

13 cm
10 cm
10 cm

Solution

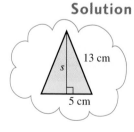

It is clear that the base of the pyramid has area $B = 100 \text{ cm}^2$ and perimeter $p = 40$ cm. The slant height can be calculated with the Pythagorean theorem, which shows that

$$s = \sqrt{13^2 - 5^2} = \sqrt{169 - 25} = \sqrt{144} = 12 \text{ cm}.$$

Thus, the surface area of the pyramid is $SA = 100 \text{ cm}^2 + \frac{1}{2} \cdot 40 \cdot 12 \text{ cm}^2 = 340 \text{ cm}^2$.

The Woven Cube

Cut three rectangular strips of paper, each strip a different color. Fold each along the dotted lines shown. Now weave the three strips into a rigid cube. The opposite faces should be the same color, and the end squares of the strips should be neatly tucked inside.

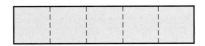

(The regular polyhedra can all be woven with suitably cut and folded paper strips. Patterns and directions may be found in *Build Your Own Polyhedra,* by Peter Hilton and Jean Pedersen, Addison-Wesley Publishing Company, 1988.)

Surface Area of Right Circular Cones

Consider a right circular cone of slant height s and with a circular base of radius r. The formula for the surface area of the cone can be derived from the surface area formula for a pyramid. To see how, imagine that the cone is closely approximated by a right regular pyramid. An example is shown in Figure 11.19, where a cone is approximated by a pyramid with a dodecagon (12-gon) as its base.

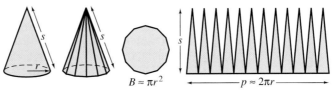

Figure 11.19
A right circular cone has total surface area $SA = \pi r^2 + \pi rs$.

The area of the circular base of the pyramid is $B \approx \pi r^2$ and the perimeter of the base is $p \approx 2\pi r$. Therefore, the surface area of the pyramid is $SA = B + \frac{1}{2}ps \approx \pi r^2 + \pi rs$.

The pyramid's approximation to the cone becomes increasingly exact as the number of sides in the base polygon is increased, giving us the following formula.

FORMULA   *Surface Area of a Right Circular Cone*
Let a right circular cone have slant height s and a base of radius r. Then the surface area, SA, of the cone is given by the formula

$$SA = \pi r^2 + \pi rs.$$

EXAMPLE   11.21

Finding the Lateral Surface Area of an Ice Cream Cone

An ice cream cone has a diameter of 2.5 inches and slant height of 6 inches. What is the lateral surface area of the cone?

Solution

Only the lateral surface area is required, so we need to compute $\pi r s$, where $r = 2.5/2$ inches $= 1.25$ inches and $s = 6$ inches. The lateral surface area is therefore $\pi(1.25 \text{ in}) \cdot (6 \text{ in}) = \pi \cdot (7.5 \text{ in}^2)$. Using 3.14 to approximate π, the lateral surface area is about 23.6 square inches.

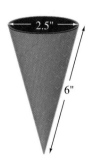

Volumes of Right Prisms and Right Cylinders

The volume of the rectangular box shown in Figure 11.20 is given by lwh, where l, w, and h are, respectively, the length, width, and height of the box. Since lw gives the area B of the base of the box, the volume can also be written in the form $V = Bh$, where B is the area of the base and h is the height.

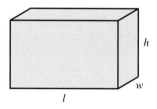

Figure 11.20

A rectangular box has volume $V = lwh$. Equivalently, $V = Bh$, where B is the area of the base and h is the height.

Figure 11.21(a) shows a solid composed of many (say n) small right rectangular prisms, all of the height h. If $B_1, B_2, \ldots, B_n$ are the areas of the bases, the total volume, V, of the prism is $B_1 h + B_2 h + \cdots + B_n h = (B_1 + B_2 + \cdots + B_n)h$. That is, the volume V is given by $V = Bh$, where $B = B_1 + B_2 + \cdots + B_n$ is the total area of the base. The right cylinder depicted in Figure 11.21(b) can be approximated to arbitrary accuracy by prisms of height h as shown at the left.

Figure 11.21

Right rectangular prisms can approximate a right prism or a right cylinder.

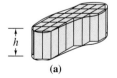

(a)   (b)

FORMULA   *Volume of a Right Prism or a Right Cylinder*

Let a right prism or right cylinder have height h and a base of area B. Then its volume, V, is given by

$$V = Bh.$$

B = area of base

EXAMPLE 11.22

Computing the Volume of a Right Prism and a Right Cylinder

Find the volume of the gift box and the juice can.

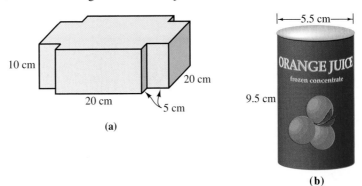

(a)

(b)

Solution

(a)   The base area, $B = 800$ cm^2, of the gift box was calculated in Example 11.18. The height is $h = 10$ cm, so the volume is $V = Bh = 8000$ cm^3. This can also be expressed as 8 liters.

(b)   The area of the circular base of the juice can is $\pi(2.75$ cm$)^2 = 7.5625\pi$ cm^2. The height is $h = 9.5$ cm, so the volume, $V = Bh$, is 71.84375π cm^3, or about 226 cm^3.

Volume of Oblique Prisms and Cylinders

A deck of neatly stacked playing cards forms a right rectangular prism as shown in Figure 11.22. The total volume of the deck is the sum of the volumes of each card. If the cards slide easily on one another, it is easy to tilt the deck to form an oblique prism of the same base area B and the same height h. The solid is still made up of the same cards, so the oblique prism still has volume Bh.

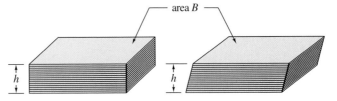

Figure 11.22
An oblique prism of base area B and height h has the same volume V = Bh as the corresponding right prism.

Any oblique prism or cylinder can be imagined as a stack of very thin cards, all shaped like the base of the solid. With no change of volume, the oblique stack can be straightened to form a right prism or right cylinder of the same height h and base area B. Both the right and oblique shapes therefore have the same volume, namely $V = Bh$. This is illustrated in Figure 11.23.

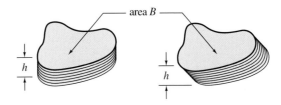

Figure 11.23
Any prism or cylinder, either right or oblique, has volume V = Bh, where B is the base area and h is the height.

Into the Classroom

Problem Solving with Measurement

Each pair of students has an orange and a sheet of centimeter squared graph paper. The challenge is then given. *Find the area of the peel of the orange.* Students well-versed in the basic principles of measurement may solve the problem in a direct yet appropriate way: the orange is peeled and then the peeling is cut or torn into small pieces to tile a region of the graph paper; the region's boundary is traced and then its area, which equals that of the orange peel, is estimated by counting the number of square centimeters covered.

Problem solving with measurement reinforces both the principles and processes of measurement. On the other hand, overemphasis on exercises which require only a routine application of a formula reduces measurement to a mechanistic level. Here are two more examples illustrating the difference between a routine exercise and a problem.

Exercise: A right triangle has legs of length 6″ and 10″. What is the area of the triangle?

Problem: Two straws, of lengths 6″ and 10″, are joined with paperclips to form a flexible hinge. At what angle should the straws meet to form the sides of a triangle of largest possible area?

Exercise: A rectangular solid has length 6 cm, width 2 cm, and height 2 cm. What is the surface area of the solid?

Problem: The Math Manipulative Supply House sells wooden centimeter cubes in sets of 24 cubes each. What shape of a box that holds one set of cubes requires the least amount of cardboard?

FORMULA   *Volume of a General Prism or Cylinder*

A prism or cylinder of height h and base area B has volume $V = Bh$.

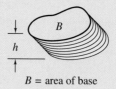

B = area of base

Volumes of Pyramids and Cones

In two-dimensional space (that is, in the plane), a diagonal dissects a square into two congruent right triangles. Thus the area of each triangle is one-half of that of the corresponding square.

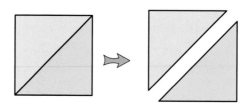

In three-dimensional space, the diagonals from one corner of a cube form the edges of three congruent pyramids that fill the cube. Therefore each pyramid has one-third the volume of the corresponding cube as shown in Figure 11.24.

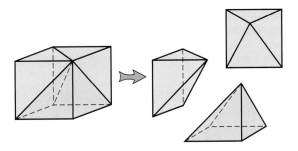

Figure 11.24
A cube can be dissected into three congruent pyramids.

Instead of a cube, consider a rectangular solid and use the diagonals from one corner to decompose the solid into three pyramids. An example is shown in Figure 11.25. In general, the three pyramids are not congruent to one another. However, it can be shown that the volumes of the three pyramids are equal. Therefore, if the prism has base area B and height h, we conclude that each pyramid has volume $\frac{1}{3}Bh$.

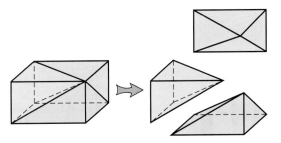

Figure 11.25
A rectangular prism can be dissected into three pyramids of equal volume.

Similar reasoning shows that *all* pyramids of base B and height h have volume $\frac{1}{3}Bh$.

The base can be any polygon and the apex can be any point at distance h to the plane of the base as shown in Figure 11.26.

Figure 11.26
A pyramid of height h and base of area B has one-third the volume of a corresponding prism of base area B and height h. Therefore the pyramid has volume $\frac{1}{3}Bh$.

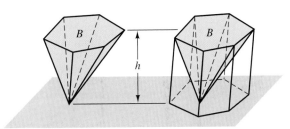

The base of a cone can be approximated to arbitrary accuracy by a polygon with sufficiently many sides, so the volume of a cone of base area B and height h is also given by the formula $\frac{1}{3}Bh$.

FORMULA   *Volume of a Pyramid or Cone*

The volume, V, of a pyramid or cone of height h and base of area B is given by

$$V = \frac{1}{3}Bh.$$

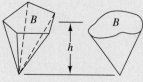

B = area of base

EXAMPLE   11.23   **Determining the Volume of an Egyptian Pyramid**

The pyramid of Khufu is 147 m high and its square base is 231 m on each side. What is the volume of the pyramid?

Solution   The area of the base is $(231 \text{ m})^2 = 53{,}361 \text{ m}^2$. Therefore, the volume is

$$\frac{1}{3}(53{,}361 \text{ m}^2) \cdot (147 \text{ m}) = 2{,}614{,}689 \text{ m}^3.$$

If the stones were stacked on a football field, a rectangular prism nearly 2000 feet high would result. For comparison, the 110 story Sears Tower in Chicago reaches 1454 feet.

The Volume of a Sphere

Suppose that a solid sphere of radius r is placed in the right circular cylinder of height $2r$ that just contains it. Filling the remaining space in the cylinder with water, it is found that removing the sphere will leave the cylinder one-third full as illustrated in Figure 11.27. This means that the sphere takes up two-thirds of the volume of the cylinder. Since the volume of the cylinder is $Bh = (\pi r^2)(2r) = 2\pi r^3$, the experiment suggests that the volume of a sphere of radius r is given by $\frac{2}{3}(2\pi r^3) = \frac{4}{3}\pi r^3$. The first rigorous proof of this remarkable formula was given by Archimedes.

Figure 11.27

A sphere fills two-thirds of the circular cylinder containing the sphere.

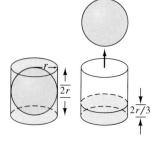

HIGHLIGHT FROM HISTORY
Sophie Germain (1776–1831)

Sophie Germain grew up in a time of social, political, and economic upheaval in France. To shield Sophie from the violence in the streets of Paris during the time of the fall of the Bastille, her wealthy parents confined their 13-year-old daughter to the family's library. Here she chanced upon J. E. Montucla's *History of Mathematics,* which recounts the legend of Archimedes' death. The story tells how a Carthaginian soldier, heedless of orders to spare the renowned mathematician, killed the unsuspecting Archimedes who remained absorbed in a geometry problem. Sophie wished to explore for herself a subject of such compelling interest.

Sophie's family initially resisted her determination to study mathematics, but eventually they gave her the freedom to follow her intellectual instincts. Since women were not permitted to enroll in the Ecole Polytechnique, which opened in Paris in 1794, Sophie resorted to collecting lecture notes from various professors at the university. The absence of a formal mathematical education was compensated by her courage to overcome strenuous challenges.

Sophie's early research was in number theory. She corresponded regularly with the great Carl Friedrich Gauss, who gave her work high praise. At the turn of the century, Sophie turned her attention increasingly to the mathematical theory of vibrating elastic surfaces. Her prize winning paper on vibrating elastic plates in 1816 placed her in the ranks of the most celebrated mathematicians of the time. Gauss recommended that she be awarded an honorary doctorate from the University of Göttingen, but unfortunately Sophie Germain's death came too soon for the awarding of the degree.

FORMULA   *Volume of a Sphere*

The volume, V, of a sphere of radius r is given by the formula

$$V = \frac{4}{3}\pi r^3.$$

EXAMPLE   11.24

Using the Sphere Volume Formula

An ice cream cone is 5 inches high and has an opening 3 inches in diameter. If filled with ice cream and given a hemispherical top, how much ice cream is there?

Solution

The hemisphere has radius 1.5 inches, so its volume is $\frac{2}{3}\pi(1.5 \text{ in})^3 = 2.25\pi \text{ in}^3$. The cone has volume $\frac{1}{3}Bh = \frac{1}{3}\pi(1.5 \text{ in})^2 \cdot (5 \text{ in}) = 3.75\pi \text{ in}^3$. Thus the total volume is $2.25\pi \text{ in}^3 + 3.75\pi \text{ in}^3 = 6\pi \text{ in}^3$, or about 19 in^3. Since a gallon is 231 in^3, we see that the cone holds very close to a third of a quart of ice cream.

The Surface Area of a Sphere

A formula for the surface area of a sphere of radius r can be discovered by dividing the sphere's surface into many (say n) tiny regions of area $B_1, B_2, B_3, \ldots, B_n$. The sum $B_1 + B_2 + B_3 + \cdots + B_n$ is the surface area, S, of the sphere. Each region can also be viewed as the "base" of a pyramid-like solid whose apex is the center of the sphere. Each of the "pyramids" has height r, so the pyramids have volumes $\frac{1}{3} B_1 r$, $\frac{1}{3} B_2 r$, $\frac{1}{3} B_3 r$, and so on. An example is shown in Figure 11.28.

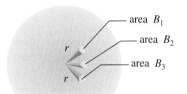

area B_1

area B_2

area B_3

$$S = B_1 + B_2 + B_3 + \cdots + B_n \qquad V = \frac{1}{3} B_1 r + \frac{1}{3} B_2 r + \frac{1}{3} B_3 r + \cdots + \frac{1}{3} B_n r$$

Figure 11.28

A solid sphere can be viewed as made up of pyramid-like pieces.

We have the following relationships:

$$S = B_1 + B_2 + B_3 + \cdots + B_n \qquad \text{(surface area of the sphere)}$$

and

$$V = \frac{1}{3} B_1 r + \frac{1}{3} B_2 r + \frac{1}{3} B_3 r + \cdots + \frac{1}{3} B_n r. \qquad \text{(volume of the sphere)}$$

Therefore,

$$V = \frac{r}{3} (B_1 + B_2 + B_3 + \cdots + B_n) = \frac{r}{3} S.$$

Since $V = \frac{4}{3} \pi r^3$, this gives us the equation

$$\frac{4}{3} \pi r^3 = \frac{r}{3} S.$$

Multiplying both sides by 3, and dividing both sides by r, we can solve for the surface area S.

FORMULA *Surface Area of a Sphere*

The surface area S of a sphere of radius r is given by the formula

$$S = 4\pi r^2.$$

EXAMPLE   11.25

Comparing Earth to Jupiter

The diameter of Jupiter is about 11 times larger than the diameter of our planet Earth. How many times greater is (a) the surface area of Jupiter? (b) the volume of Jupiter?

Solution

(a)   Let r denote the radius of Earth and R the radius of Jupiter. Therefore $R = 11r$. Using the formula for the surface area of a sphere, the ratio of the surface area of Jupiter to that of Earth is

$$\frac{4\pi R^2}{4\pi r^2} = \frac{R^2}{r^2} = \left(\frac{R}{r}\right)^2 = (11)^2.$$

That is, the surface area of Jupiter is 11^2, or 121 times the surface area of Earth.

(b)   Using the sphere volume formula, the ratio of volumes is

$$\frac{\frac{4}{3}\pi R^3}{\frac{4}{3}\pi r^3} = \frac{R^3}{r^3} = \left(\frac{R}{r}\right)^3 = (11)^3.$$

Therefore, the volume of Jupiter is about 11^3, or 1331 times the volume of Earth. Precise measurements of the two not quite spherical planets show that the volume ratio is 1323.3, which agrees closely with 1331.

Comparing Measurements of Similar Figures

Two figures are similar if they have the same shape but possibly different size. The ratio of all pairs of corresponding lengths in the two figures is a constant value called the scale factor, which we will denote by the letter k. The ratio of any *linear measurement* of the two figures—perimeter, height, diameter, slant height, and so on—is also that of the scale factor k. For example, since the diameter of Jupiter is 11 times the diameter of Earth then the scale factor is $k = 11$. We then also know that the equator of Jupiter is 11 times as long as Earth's equator.

The ratio of *areas* of similar figures is given by the *square, k^2*, of the scale factor k. The ratio of volumes is given by the *cube, k^3*, of the scale factor. This basic fact is evident for the cubes shown in Figure 11.29.

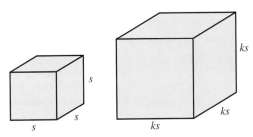

Scale factor $= k$

Figure 11.29
Area varies by the square, k^2, of the scale factor k, and volume varies by the cube, k^3, of the scale factor.

	Cube I	Cube II
Length of edge	s	$k\,s$
Area of each face	s^2	$k^2 s^2$
Volume	s^3	$k^3 s^3$

The same comparison of areas and volumes holds for any pair of similar figures, not just the cube shown in Figure 11.29. The following result is an important principle for the comparison of the measurements of similar figures.

THEOREM *The Similarity Principle of Measurement*

Let Figures I and II be similar. Suppose some length dimension of Figure II is k times the corresponding dimension of Figure I; that is, k is the scale factor. Then:

1. *any* length measurement—perimeter, diameter, height, slant height, and so on—of Figure II is k times that of the corresponding length measurement of Figure I;
2. *any* area measurement—surface area, area of a base, lateral surface area, and so on—of Figure II is k^2 times that of the corresponding area measurement of Figure I;
3. *any* volume measurement—total volume, capacity, half-full, and so on—of Figure II is k^3 times the corresponding volume measurement of Figure I.

EXAMPLE 11.26

Using the Similarity Principle

(a) Television sets are measured by the length of the diagonal of the rectangular screen. How many times larger is the screen area of a 40-inch model than a 13-inch table model?

(b) A 2″ by 4″ by 8″ rectangular brick of gold weighs about 44 pounds. What are the dimensions of a similarly shaped brick that weighs 10 pounds?

13″

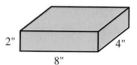

2″   4″
8″

Solution

(a) The scale factor, k, is $40/13 \doteq 3.08$. Since area varies by $k^2 \doteq (3.08)^2 \doteq 9.5$, the large screen has about 9.5 times the area of the similarly shaped small screen.

(b) The weight of a gold brick is proportional to its volume, and the volume of similarly shaped bricks varies by the factor k^3, the cube of the scale factor k. Therefore $10 = k^3 44$, so $k^3 = 10/44$ and $k \doteq (10/44)^{1/3} \doteq 0.6$. Multiplying the dimensions of the 44 pound brick by 0.6 gives the approximate dimensions of a similarly shaped 10-pound brick of gold, namely 1.2″ by 2.4″ by 4.8″.

HIGHLIGHT FROM HISTORY
Jonathan Swift (1667–1745)

*J*onathan Swift published his best known book, *Gulliver's Travels,* in England in 1726. This book has been popular for two-and-a-half centuries because it is both a delightful story about pygmies and giants and a clever satire on many eighteenth-century institutions and scholars. *Gulliver's Travels* stresses the relative contrasts of the pygmies of Lilliput and the giants of Brobdingnag. Swift points out that "nothing is great or little otherwise than by comparison." Comparisons can be fun: if a Lilliputian is 6 inches tall, about how long would his or her shoes be? What is the approximate weight of a Lilliputian?

DID YOU KNOW?

Sizing Up the Universe

We all, children and grownups alike, are inclined to live in our own little world, in our immediate surroundings, or at any rate with our attention concentrated on those things with which we are directly in touch. We tend to forget how vast are the ranges of existing reality which our eyes cannot directly see, and our attitudes may become narrow and provincial. We need to develop a wider outlook, to see ourselves in our relative position in the great and mysterious universe in which we have been born and live.

At school we are introduced to many different spheres of existence, but they are often not connected with each other, so that we are in danger of collecting a large number of images without realizing that they all join together in one great whole. It is therefore important in our education to find the means of developing a wider and more connected view of our world and a truly cosmic view of the universe and our place in it.

This book presents a series of forty pictures composed so that they may help to develop this wider view. They really give a series of views as seen during an imaginary and fantastic journey through space—a journey in one direction, straight upward from the place where it begins. Although these views are as true to reality as they can be made with our present knowledge, they portray a wonderland as full of marvels as that which Alice saw in her dreams.

Kees Boeke, a sixth grade teacher in Holland, worked with the children in his class to make a picture book that takes the reader on an imaginary journey through the universe. Going from the picture on one page to that of the next page changes the scale of view by a factor of ten, so in 40 jumps the journey moves from the gamma ray to dots representing clumps of distant galaxies. Two similar books, which more fully develop Boeke's idea, are *Powers of Ten,* by Philip and Phyllis Morrison (W. H. Freeman & Co., 1994) and *Powers of Ten Flipbook,* by Charles and Ray Eames (W. H. Freeman & Co., 1998).

SOURCE: From *Cosmic View: The Universe in 40 Jumps* by Kees Boeke, with an introduction by Arthur H. Compton. Copyright © 1957 by Kees Boeke. Reprinted by permission of Harper Collins Publishers, Inc.

PROBLEM SET 11.4

Understanding Concepts

1. Find the surface area of each of these prisms and cylinders.

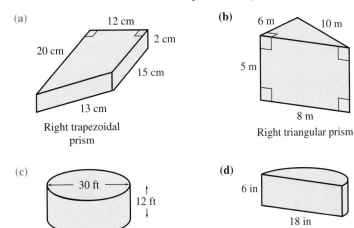

(a)
12 cm
2 cm
20 cm
15 cm
13 cm
Right trapezoidal prism

(b)
6 m
10 m
5 m
8 m
Right triangular prism

(c)
30 ft
12 ft
Right circular cylinder

(d)
6 in
18 in
Semicircular right prism

2. Find the surface area of each of these right regular pyramids and right circular cones.

(a)

40 m · 60 m · 60 m · 60 m

Right square pyramid

(b)

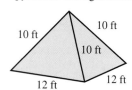

10 ft · 10 ft · 10 ft · 12 ft · 12 ft

(c)

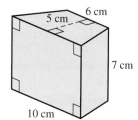

← 12 in →

15 in

Right circular cone

(d)

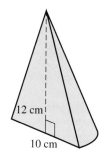

12 cm · 10 cm

Semicircular right cone

3. Find the volume of each of these prisms and cylinders.

(a)

3 cm · 4 cm · 7 cm

Oblique prism

(b)

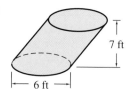

5 cm · 6 cm · 7 cm · 10 cm

Trapezoidal right prism

(c)

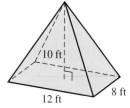

← 20 m → · 4 m

Right circular cylinder

(d)

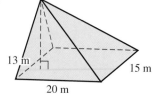

7 ft · ⊢ 6 ft ⊣

Oblique circular cylinder

4. Find the volume of each of these pyramids and cones.

(a)

10 ft · 12 ft · 8 ft

Rectangular pyramid

(b)

13 m · 15 m · 20 m

Rectangular pyramid

(c)

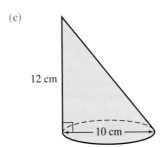

12 cm

10 cm

Oblique circular cone

(d)

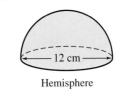

14 in

12 in

Semicircular cone

5. Find the surface area and volume of each of these solids.

(a)

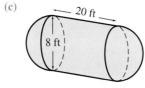

2200 km

Sphere

(b)

12 cm

Hemisphere

(c)

20 ft

8 ft

Cylindrical storage
tank with hemispherical
ends

(d)

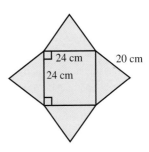

5 m

3 m

12 m

Cylindrical grain silo
with conical top

---

6. An aluminum soda pop can has a diameter of 6.5 cm and a height of about 11 cm. If there are 30 milliliters in a fluid ounce, verify that the capacity of the can is 12 fluid ounces as printed on the can's label.

7. If it takes a quart of paint to cover the base of a hemisphere, how many quarts does it take to paint the spherical part of the same hemisphere?

8. Archimedes showed that the volume of a sphere is two-thirds the volume of the right circular cylinder just containing the sphere. Show that the area of the sphere is also two-thirds the surface area of the cylinder. (Archimedes was so pleased with these discoveries that he requested that the figure shown be placed on his tombstone.)

9. A square right regular pyramid is formed by cutting, folding, and gluing the following pattern.

24 cm   20 cm

24 cm

(a) What is the slant height of the pyramid?

(b) What is the lateral surface area of the pyramid?

(c) Use the Pythagorean theorem to find the height of the pyramid.

(d) What is the volume of the pyramid?

Use the similarity principle to answer problems 10 through 15. Explain carefully how the principle is used.

10. (a) An 8″ (diameter) pizza will feed one person. How many people will a 16″ pizza feed?

    (b) Is it better to buy one 14″ pizza at $10 or two 10″ pizzas at $6 each? (*Hint:* 1.4^2 is about 2.0.)

11. (a) Eight spherical lead fishing sinkers are melted to form a single spherical sinker. If the small sinkers each have diameter of 1/4 inch, what is the diameter of the new large one?

    (b) How many small sinkers would it take to make a sinker 1 inch in diameter?

12. What fraction of the area of the large circle is shaded in each figure?

    (a) 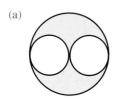   (b)

    (*Hint:* First compare each unshaded circle to the large circle.)

13. Cones I, II, and III are similar to one another. Fill in the measurements left blank in the following table.

	I	II	III	
Height	6	18		cm
Perimeter of base		30	15	cm
Lateral surface area	40			cm²
Volume			10	cm³

14. A cylindrical can holds 100 milliliters.

    (a) If the radius of the base is doubled and the height halved, what is the new volume of the can?

    (b) If the radius of the base is halved and height is doubled, what is the new volume of the can?

15. A cube 10 cm on a side holds 1 liter.

    (a) How many liters does a cube 20 cm on a side hold?

    (b) What is the length of each side of a cube that holds 2 liters?

Thinking Critically

16. A right circular cone has height r and a circular base of radius $2r$. Compare the volume of the cone to that of a sphere of radius r. Sketch both solids, using the same scale.

17. A birthday cake has been baked in a 7″ by 7″ by 2″ pan. Frosting covers the top and sides of the cake.

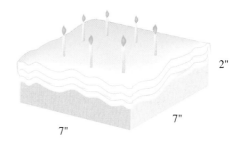

    (a) What is the volume of the cake?

    (b) What is the area covered by the frosting?

    (c) Describe how to cut the cake into eight pieces, so that each piece has the same size (measured by volume) *and* the same amount of frosting (measured by area covered with frosting).

    (d) Describe how to cut the cake in seven pieces, each with the same size and amount of frosting. (*Hint:* Consider a slice made by two vertical cuts from the center that intercepts 4 inches of the perimeter.)

18. The cube *ABCDEFGH* with edges of length s contains the tetrahedron *ACEG*.

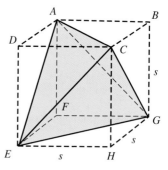

    (a) Explain why *ACEG* is a regular tetrahedron with edges of length $\sqrt{2}s$.

    (b) Show the volume of tetrahedron *ACDE* is $\frac{1}{6}s^3$.

    (c) Show that the volume of *ACEG* is $\frac{1}{3}s^3$.

    (d) Use the similarity principle to explain why a regular tetrahedron with edges of length b has volume $\sqrt{2}b^3/12$.

19. Similar figures are erected on the three sides of a right triangle. What formula relates the areas of the three figures? Explain your reasoning carefully.

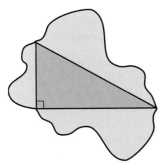

20. An ice cream soda glass is shaped like a cone of height 6 inches, and has a capacity of 16 fluid ounces when filled to the rim. Use the similarity principle to answer the following questions, using the fact that the cone of liquid is similar to the cone of the entire region inside the glass.

    (a) How high is the soda in the glass when it contains 2 fluid ounces?

    (b) How much soda is in the glass when it is filled to a level 1 inch below the rim?

Thinking Cooperatively

In these problems, you will need paper, tape, scissors, and drawing tools (ruler, compass, pencils). Work in pairs, measuring your constructed models and verifying your observations with calculations.

21. A pyramid is formed by joining a vertex of a cube of side length 8 cm to the four vertices of an opposite face.

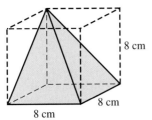

8 cm

8 cm

8 cm

(a) Use your drawing tools to accurately make a pattern that, when cut and folded, will form the pyramid. What are the lengths of each edge in your pattern? Use the Pythagorean theorem to find out. Give your answer both exactly using square roots, and as a decimal approximation.

(b) Use the lengths of the edges found in part (a) to obtain the area of the pyramid, giving both an exact answer using square roots, and as a decimal approximation.

(c) Trace your pattern onto heavy paper and cut, fold, and tape three paper models of the pyramid. Show that the three congruent copies can be arranged to form a cube. What is the volume of the cube? What is the volume of each pyramid?

22. A sheet of $8\frac{1}{2}''$ by $11''$ notebook paper can be rolled into a cylinder in either of two ways.

Which way encloses the largest volume? Make a prediction, then check it.

23. Cut out the circular sector shown, and roll it into a right circular cone in which the two 4-inch radial segments are joined.

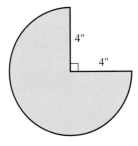

4"

4"

Find the following measurements both by exact computation and by measuring your paper model.

(a) The radius of the base of the cone.

(b) The height of the cone.

(c) Use parts (a) and (b) to compute the volume of the cone.

24. Cut out a semicircular sector, and roll it up and join the two radial segments to form a cone. Show that the diameter of the cone is equal to the slant height of the cone, both by measuring your paper model and by a calculation.

Making Connections

25. A napkin ring is being made of cast silver. It has the shape of a cylinder 1.25 inches high, with a cylindrical hole 1 inch in diameter and a thickness of 1/16 inch. How many ounces of silver are required? It will help to know that silver weighs about 6 ounces per cubic inch.

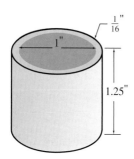

26. Give the dimensions of a rectangular aquarium 40 cm high that holds 48 liters of water.

27. A theater sells 4″ by 5″ by 8″ boxes of popcorn for $1.75. It also sells cylindrical "tubs" of popcorn for $3.50 where the tub is 10″ high and has a diameter of 6″. Is it better to buy one tub or two boxes of popcorn?

28. Small grapefruits of diameter 3 inches are on sale at five for a dollar. The large 4 inch diameter grapefruit are three for a dollar. If you are buying $5 worth of grapefruit, should you choose small ones or large ones?

29. **World Records.** *The Guiness Book of World Records,* published annually by Facts on File, New York, contains a fascinating collection of measurements.
   (a) The world's largest flawless crystal ball weighs 106.75 pounds and is 13 inches in diameter. What is the weight of a crystal ball 5 inches in diameter?
   (b) The largest pyramid is the Quetzacoatl, 63 miles southeast of Mexico City. It is 177 feet tall and covers an area of 45 acres. Estimate the volume of the pyramid. By comparison, the largest Egyptian

pyramid of Khufu (called Cheops by the Greeks) has a volume of 88.2 million ft^3. Recall that an acre is 43,560 ft^2.
   (c) The building with the largest volume in the world is the Boeing Company's main assembly plant in Everett, Washington. The building encloses 472 million ft^3 and covers 98.3 acres. What is the size of a cube of equal volume?

30. A water pipe with an inside diameter of 3/4 inches is 50 feet long in its run from the hot water tank to the faucet. How much hot water is wasted when the water inside the pipe cools down? Give your answer in gallons, where 1 gallon = 231 in^3.

31. In Jonathan Swift's satirical novel *Gulliver's Travels,* Dr. Lemuel Gulliver encounters the tiny Lilliputians. A Lilliputian is similar to Gulliver but is 6 inches tall compared to Gulliver's 6 feet.
   (a) Explain why the Lilliputians ordered 1728 rations for Gulliver's dinner.
   (b) If the material from Gulliver's shirt was cut up to make shirts for the Lilliputians, how many shirts could be made?

32. In many countries the size and shape of sheets of paper is based on the metric system. An A0 sheet is a rectangle of area 1 m^2. When cut in half across its width, it forms two A1 sheets, each of which is similar to the A0 sheet. Cutting an A1 sheet forms two A2 sheets, and so on.

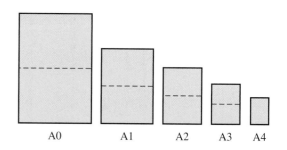

   (a) What is the scale factor by which the linear dimensions of an A0 sheet are multiplied to give the corresponding dimensions of an A1 sheet?
   (b) Find the width and length, in centimeters, of an A0 sheet.
   (c) Find the width and length of an A4 sheet.
   (d) What metric sized paper do you think is used in place of the $8\frac{1}{2}''$ by 11″ sheets in common use in the U.S.?

33. A geologist wishes to determine the density of a rock specimen: density is the weight of the rock divided by its volume. The weight is 7.34 kg, easily measured on a scale. To find the volume, the specimen is submerged

in a cylindrical water tank 16 cm in diameter, causing the level of the water to rise 5.7 cm.

(a) What is the volume of the specimen?

(b) What is the density of the specimen? Give your answer in grams per cubic centimeter.

34. A rain gauge has a funnel 6 inches in diameter at the top, tapering into a plexiglass collection cylinder whose inside diameter is 2 inches. How far apart should marks be placed on the cylinder to indicate the number of inches of rainfall? (*Hint:* Use the similarity principle.)

Communicating

35. Consider the following problem: *Which is a better buy, a 9″ pizza for $5 or a 12″ pizza for $8?*

(a) Write your own solution to the problem.

For each of the following answers, write an explanation why the reasoning is faulty.

(b) "They are equal. There are three more inches in the 12″ pizza but the price also increases by $3."

(c) "If there are eight slices per pizza then the 9″ pizza costs 62¢ per slice. The 12″ pizza costs $1 per slice. Therefore the 9″ pizza would be the better buy."

(d) "Since 9/5 = 1.8 inches per dollar and 12/8 = 1.5 inches per dollar, the 9″ pizza is the better buy."

For Review

36. Which of the following triples could be the lengths of sides of a right triangle?

(a) 30, 72, 78   **(b)** 12, 35, 37

(c) 2.0, 2.1, 2.9

37. Find formulas for the perimeter and area of a regular hexagon with sides of length b.

38. Find the perimeter and area of this lattice polygon.

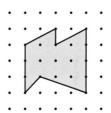

39. What is the speed equivalent to 50 inches per second when expressed in miles per hour?

40. Convert these measurements to the unit shown.

(a) 0.278 m = _____ cm

(b) 2.3 km² = _____ m²

(c) 68,532 cm³ = _____ L.

EPILOGUE   That's about the size of it!

The size of our everyday world spans about six orders of magnitude; that is, the longest distances of interest are about 10^6, or a million, times larger than the smallest sized items we deal with. At arm's length—that is, on a scale of about a meter—we find most of the objects (chairs, beachballs, and so on) and life forms (dogs, cats, horses, and so on) familiar in daily life. A thousandfold increase—to the scale of kilometers—encompasses the distances of ordinary travel, whether across town or cross country. A thousandfold decrease—to the scale of millimeters—encompasses all that can be seen easily with the unaided eye. The dot at the end of this sentence is several tenths of a millimeter across.

To a great extent, the story of science and technology is told by the increasing number of orders of magnitude required to encompass newly discovered objects and phenomena. The first major step to the measurement of the large was Eratosthenes' measurement (c. 240 B.C.) of the Earth's circumference. At noon during the summer solstice, a vertical rod at Syene (now Aswan) cast no shadow, whereas 5000 stadia to the north in Alexandria a vertical rod made an angle of "1/50 of four right angles" (that is, $7°12'$). Thus the earth's circumference is 50×5000, or 250,000 stadia, a value accurate to about 6 percent. The measurement of the solar system—the sun and its planets—was much more difficult: The Copernican model was only 1/7 of the true size, and the first accurate distances to the planets (to within 10 percent) were made in 1672 by the newly created French Academy of Science. The first accurate distance to a star was given in 1837 by Friedrich Wilhelm Bessel, who found that 61 Cygni was 619,000 times as far from earth as the sun. In 1924 Edwin Hubble proved that William Herschel's "island universes" were separate galaxies far from our own Milky Way galaxy. To measure the universe, where distant quasars are 10 billion light years away, we must measure on the astonishingly large scale of about 10^{25} meters.

Recent breakthroughs in microscopy reveal new images of the very small. At 10^{-6} m we find bacteria, at 10^{-9} m a single sodium atom, at 10^{-12} m the nucleus of the sodium atom. Current thought suggests that 10^{-16} m—the scale of quarks—may present all there is to see, at least until we reach 10^{-31} m.

This chapter has introduced the basic notions of measurement. Measurement is concerned with how size is determined and communicated. Generally measurement is an approximation, calling for appropriate judgments to be made about the selection of measurement tools and the level of precision required. For some ideal shapes—triangles, prisms, pyramids, circles, and spheres, to name a few—the measurement process is supplemented by the use of formulas. Measurement, however, is not simply a collection of formulas; often we must return to the basic principles of the measurement process.

CHAPTER 11 SUMMARY

Key Concepts

1. **The Measurement Process**

   The **measurement process** can be divided into four steps: (1) choose the property (length, area, volume, and so on) to be measured; (2) select a unit of measurement; (3) compare the object to the unit by covering, filling, and so on; (4) express the measurement as the number of units used. **Measurements are not exact,** and decisions must be made when selecting measurement tools to give appropriate accuracy and precision. A standardized system of units provides a way to communicate size and magnitude. The **metric (SI) system** is used around the world. Units are related by powers of 10 described by a **prefix system.** The most commonly used prefixes are *milli* = 1/1000, *centi* = 1/100, and *kilo* = 1000. The basic unit of length is the **meter,** so that areas are measured in square meters, m^2, and volumes in cubic meters, m^3. Areas are also measured in **hectares** (1 hectare = 10,000 m^2) and capacities are measured in **liters** (1 L = 1000 cm^3 = 1/1000 m^3). In the United States the customary system is unofficial but still in use.

2. **Area and Perimeter**

   Area is the amount of the plane covered by a plane region. The **unit of area** is arbitrary, but usually a square one unit of length on a side is chosen. To compare the area of one region to another, the **congruence** and **addition** properties are often useful. Some polygons have areas given by the following formulas:

   Rectangle of width w and length l: $A = wl$
   Parallelogram of base b and height h: $A = bh$

Triangle of base b and altitude h: $A = \dfrac{1}{2} bh$

Trapezoid of bases a and b and altitude h: $A = \dfrac{1}{2}(a + b)h$

Length is the distance along a curve, and **perimeter** is the length of a simple closed curve. In particular, the perimeter of a circle is called the **circumference** of the circle. The number π (**pi**), about 3.1416, is defined to be the ratio of the circumference to the diameter of a circle. Therefore a circle of radius r has circumference $2\pi r$. The **area of the circle** is given as πr^2.

3. **The Pythagorean Theorem**

Three numbers a, b, and c satisfy the **Pythagorean relationship** if $a^2 + b^2 = c^2$. The **Pythagorean theorem** states that the lengths of the sides of a right triangle satisfy the Pythagorean relationship. The theorem can also be viewed as a result about areas: The sum of the areas of squares on the legs equals the area of the square on the hypotenuse. The converse of the Pythagorean theorem also holds; if $a^2 + b^2 = c^2$, then a triangle with sides of length a, b, and c is a right triangle.

4. **Surface Area and Volume**

The surface area of a polyhedron is the sum of the areas of the plane faces. For some polyhedra, such as right prisms and right regular pyramids, it is useful to imagine that the surface is cut and unfolded onto the plane.

The surface area of a right prism or right cylinder of height h and bases of area B and perimeter p is given by $SA = 2B + ph$. The surface area of a right regular pyramid of slant height s and base of area B and perimeter p is $SA = B + \dfrac{1}{2} ps$. The surface area of a right circular cone of slant height s and base radius r is $SA = \pi r^2 + \pi rs$.

The volume of a prism or cylinder of base area B and height h is Bh. A pyramid or cone of base area B and height h is $\dfrac{1}{3} Bh$.

A sphere of radius r has surface area $4\pi r^2$ and volume $\dfrac{4}{3} \pi r^3$.

The **similarity principle** describes the relationship between measurements of similar figures as it depends on the scale factor k. All linear measurements are multiplied by k, all area measurements are multiplied by k^2, and all volume measurements are multiplied by k^3.

Vocabulary and Notation

Section 11.1

Measurement process
Unit of measure
U.S. Customary (English) System
    Units of length (inch, foot, yard, mile), area (in^2, ft^2, yd^2, acre, mi^2), volume and capacity (in^3, ft^3, yd^3, quart, gallon)
Metric (SI) System
    Prefixes: m = *milli* (1/1000), c = *centi* (1/100), k = *kilo* (1000)
    Units of length (meter, centimeter, kilometer), area (m^2, cm^2, km^2, hectare), volume and capacity (m^3, cm^3, km^3, liter)

Tangram
Weight
Mass
Fahrenheit temperature scale
Celsius temperature scale
Unit (dimensional) analysis

Section 11.2

Area
Unit of area
Congruence property of area
Addition property of area
Altitude and base of a parallelogram or triangle

Length of curve
Perimeter
Circumference of circle; π (pi)
Congruent
Dissected
Lattice polygon

Section 11.3

Pythagorean theorem
Converse of the Pythagorean theorem

Section 11.4

Surface area of a surface in space
Base area
Lateral surface area
Right regular pyramid
Slant height
Volume of a solid
Similarity principle of measurement

CHAPTER REVIEW EXERCISES

Section 11.1

1. Select an appropriate metric unit of measurement for each of the following.
   (a) The length of a sheet of notebook paper.
   (b) The diameter of a camera lens.
   (c) The distance from Los Angeles to Mexico City.
   (d) The height of the Washington Monument.
   (e) The area of Central Park.
   (f) The area of the state of Kentucky.
   (g) The volume of a raindrop.
   (h) The capacity of a punchbowl.
2. Give the most likely answer:
   (a) A bottle of cider contains: 30 mL,   4L,   15L
   (b) Cross-country skis have length: 190 cm,
       190 km, 190 m
   (c) The living area of a house is: 2000 cm^2,   1.2 ha,
       200 m^2
3. An aquarium is a rectangular prism 60 cm long, 40 cm wide, and 35 cm deep. What is the capacity of the aquarium in liters?

4. A sailfish off the coast of Florida took out 300 feet of line in 3 seconds. Estimate the speed of the fish in miles per hour.

Section 11.2

5. Let M be the midpoint of side $\overline{AD}$ of the trapezoid $ABCD$. What is the ratio of the area of triangle MBC to the area of the trapezoid? (*Hint:* Dissect the parallelogram by a horizontal line through M, and rearrange the two pieces to form a parallelogram.)

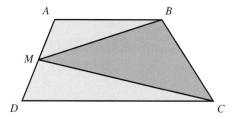

6. Find the areas of these figures.

(a)
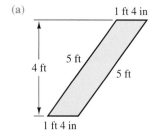

(b)
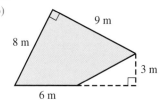

(c)
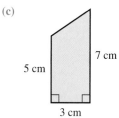

7. Find the area of each lattice polygon.

(a)
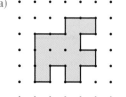

(b)
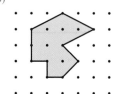

(c)

8. Find the areas and perimeters of these figures.

(a)

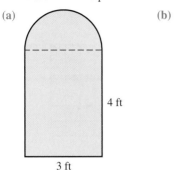

4 ft

3 ft

(b)

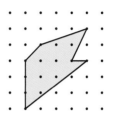

3 m

3 m

Section 11.3

9. Solve for *x* and *y* in the figure.

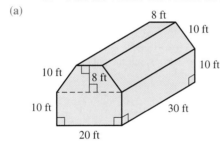

$\sqrt{6}$

y

$\sqrt{30}$

x

10. A right circular cone has slant height 35 cm and a base of diameter 20 cm. What is the height of the cone?

11. A rectangular box has sides of length 4 inches, 10 inches, and 12 inches. What are the lengths of each of the four diagonals of the box?

12. Find the perimeter of the following lattice polygon.

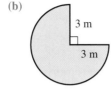

Section 11.4

13. Find the volume and surface area of these figures.

(a)

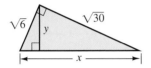

8 ft

10 ft

10 ft

10 ft

8 ft

10 ft

30 ft

20 ft

(b)

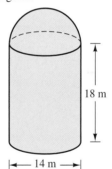

18 m

14 m

(c)

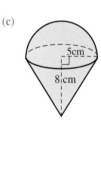

5cm

8 cm

14. Which has the largest volume, a sphere of radius 10 meters or four cubes with sides of length 10 meters?

15. Heather's garden has a similar shape as Johan's, but is 75 feet long whereas Johan's is 50 feet long.

(a) Johan needed 180 feet of fencing to enclose his garden. How much fencing does Heather need?

(b) Heather used 45 pounds of fertilizer. How much will Johan use, assuming it is applied at the same number of pounds per square foot?

CHAPTER TEST

1. Fill in the blank with the metric unit of measurement that makes the statement reasonable.
   (a) The haze filter on Donna's camera has a diameter of 52 _____.
   (b) A gray whale has length 18 _____.
   (c) In the 1968 Olympics Bob Beaman had a long jump of 8.90 _____.
   (d) The Mississippi River has a length of 1450 _____.
   (e) A cup of coffee contains about 250 _____.
   (f) A fill-up at the gas station took 46 _____.

2. Fill in the blanks:
    (a) 2161 mm = _____ cm
    (b) 1.682 km = _____ cm
    (c) 0.5 m^2 = _____ cm^2
    (d) 1 ha = _____ m^2
    (e) 4719 mL = _____ L
    (f) 3.2 L = _____ cm^3

3. Complete the conversions of the measurements in the U.S. Customary system, using your calculator when convenient.
    (a) 1147 in = _____ yd
    (b) 7942 ft = _____ mi
    (c) 32.4 yd^2 = _____ ft^2
    (d) 9402 acres = _____ mi^2
    (e) 7.6 yd^3 = _____ ft^3
    (f) 5961 in^3 = _____ ft^3

4. (Washington State Student Assessment, Grade 4)
    Jim says that the area of shape A is equal to the area of shape B.

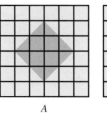

□ = 1 sq. unit

    A B

    Explain why Jim's thinking is *wrong* using words, numbers, or pictures.

5. Explain how the formula for the area of a triangle can be derived from that of a parallelogram by cutting the triangle along the segment joining the midpoints of the sides opposite the base.

6. Find the area of each geoboard polygon. The nails are 1 cm apart.

    (a)   (b)   (c)

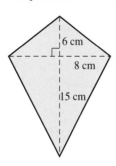

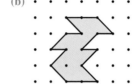

7. Find the area and perimeter of the following kite.

    6 cm
    8 cm
    15 cm

8. Find the area and perimeter of the following figure.

    4 ft
    12 ft
    9 ft

9. Find the area of each figure.

    (a)   (b)   (c)

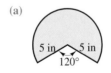

    5 in   5 in
    120°

    2.6 m   1.4 m
          3 m

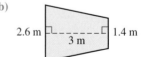

    24 cm
    30°

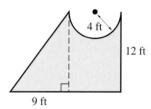

10. What is the ratio of the area of the inscribed square to the area of the square circumscribed about the same circle?

11. A lens is made by cutting a section from a sphere. If the lens has diameter 10 mm and height 4 mm, what is the radius of the sphere from which it was cut?

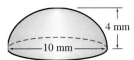

4 mm

10 mm

12. A ladder 15 feet long rests against a vertical wall. If the bottom of the ladder is 6 feet from the base of the wall, how high does the ladder reach?

13. (a) Find the perimeter of the geoboard triangle PQR.

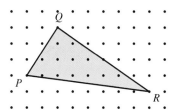

Q

P

R

(b) Is $\triangle PQR$ a right triangle?

14. Find the surface area and volume of these figures.

(a)

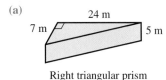

24 m

7 m   5 m

Right triangular prism

(b)

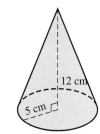

6 in

8 in

Cylinder with semicircular base

(c)

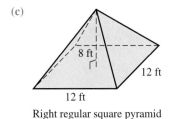

8 ft

12 ft

12 ft

Right regular square pyramid

(d)

12 cm

5 cm

Right circular cone

15. Find the surface area and volume of each figure.

(a)

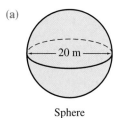

20 m

Sphere

(b)

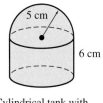

5 cm

6 cm

Cylindrical tank with hemispherical top

16. Papa Bear, Mama Bear, and Baby Bear have similar shapes, except Papa Bear is 5 ft tall, Mama Bear is 4 ft tall, and Baby Bear is 2 ft tall. Fill in the values left blank in the following chart.

	Papa Bear	Mama Bear	Baby Bear
Length of suspenders		40 in	
Weight			30 lb
Number of fleas	6000		

17. A grapefruit has an outside diameter of 5 inches. When cut open it is discovered that the peel is 3/4 inches thick. What percentage of the grapefruit's volume is peel?

CHAPTER

12

Transformations, Symmetries, and Tilings

12.1   Rigid Motions and Similarity
Transformations

12.2   Patterns and Symmetries

12.3   Tilings and Escher-like
Designs

HANDS ON
Exploring Reflection and Rotation Symmetry

Materials Needed

Clear acetate sheets, overhead transparency pens, tissues to clean acetate sheets for reuse, Mira (if available)

How to Check for Reflection and Rotation Symmetry

A figure has **reflection (or line) symmetry** if there is a mirror line which reflects the figure onto itself. For example, the parafoil kite below has a vertical line of symmetry. The wheel cover at the right does not have reflection symmetry but it does have **rotation symmetry** since the figure turns onto itself when rotated through 72° about the center point.

Reflection symmetry can be verified by the "trace-and-flip" test. The figure and its line of symmetry are traced on an acetate sheet. The acetate is then flipped across the proposed symmetry line, turning the sheet upside down, to check that the points of the traced figure coincide with the original figure. Alternatively, reflection symmetry can be investigated by placing the drawing line of a Mira over a proposed line of symmetry of a figure.

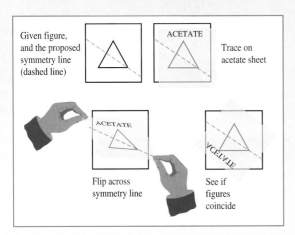

Rotation symmetry can be investigated by the "trace-and-turn" test, illustrated below. The point held fixed is the **center of rotation.** Since the tracing coincides with the original figure after a 120° turn, the "trace-and-turn" test shows that an equilateral triangle has 120° rotation symmetry.

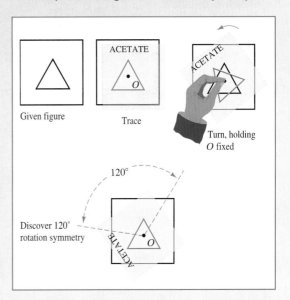

Activities

1. Use either a Mira or the "trace-and-flip" test to find all lines of symmetry of the following figures. Use dashed lines to draw the symmetry lines.

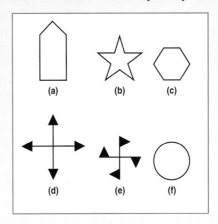

2. Use the "trace-and-turn" test to describe the rotation symmetries of the figures in Activity 1. Indicate the center of rotation and the angle measure of the rotation.

3. Sketch all lines of symmetry and describe all rotation symmetries for the following polygons.
   (a) Triangles: equilateral, isosceles, scalene
   (b) Quadrilaterals: square, rhombus, rectangle, parallelogram, trapezoid, isosceles trapezoid, kite

CONNECTIONS   Transformational Geometry, the Mathematics of Patterns and Symmetries

The Northwest Coast Indians occupy a narrow band of land along the western coasts of Washington, Canada, and southeast Alaska. The tribal groups of this region are renowned for their striking graphic art depicting whales, seals, eagles, bears, and other animal forms. Often the design is highly symmetric, such as the example of Haida art shown in Figure 12.1.

Figure 12.1
Sea lions on a Haida dance tunic

A trip to your local museum will show that symmetry is a common element found in the decorations and artwork created by all the world's cultures. Moreover, while a design from China is easily distinguished from a design from Central America, it is often evident that the two designs are based on the same underlying pattern of symmetry.

Most people, including school children, have an intuitive sense of symmetry, but usually the sense is too vague for precise classification and understanding. In this chapter we will see that the concept of a geometric transformation makes it possible to give a precise meaning to symmetry.

Section 1 of this chapter defines and investigates the rigid motions. It is discovered that any rigid motion of the plane is one of four basic types—slides, turns, flips, and glide reflections. Slides, turns, and flips are also called translations, rotations, and reflections, respectively. Dilations are also considered, leading to the concept of a similarity transformation.

Rigid motions are used as a tool to explore symmetry in Section 2. Of special interest are the patterns in the plane, created by endlessly repeating a single motif.

Section 3 investigates the patterns in the plane formed with polygonal tiles. Escher-like designs are then created by modifying polygonal tiles to assume more general shapes.

12.1   Rigid Motions and Similarity Transformations

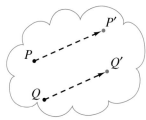

Imagine that each point P of the plane is "moved" to a new position P' in the same plane. Call P' the **image** of P, and call P the **preimage** of P'. If distinct points P and Q have distinct images P' and Q', and every point has a unique preimage point, then the association $P \leftrightarrow P'$ defines a one-to-one correspondence of the plane onto itself. Such a correspondence is called a **transformation of the plane.**

> **DEFINITION**   *Transformation of the Plane*
>
> A one-to-one correspondence of the set of points in the plane to itself is a **transformation of the plane.** If point P corresponds to point P', then P' is called the **image** of P under the transformation. Point P is called the **preimage** of P'.

In this section we investigate a special type of transformation called a **rigid motion.** As the name implies, a rigid motion does not allow stretching or shrinking.

> **DEFINITION**   *Rigid Motion of the Plane*
>
> A transformation of the plane is a **rigid motion** if, and only if, the distance between any two points P and Q equals the distance between their image points P' and Q'. That is, $PQ = P'Q'$ for all points P and Q.

A rigid motion is also called an **isometry,** meaning "same measure" (*iso* = same, *metry* = measure).

   A useful physical model of a rigid motion of the plane can be realized with a sheet of clear acetate and a sheet of paper on which figures with points labeled $A, B, C, \ldots$ are drawn. The figures are traced onto the transparency and a rigid motion is modeled by moving the transparency to a new position in the plane of the paper. An example is shown in Figure 12.2, where primed letters $A', B', C', \ldots$ indicate the points in the image figure which correspond to the respective points $A, B, C, \ldots$ in the original figure. A rigid motion actually maps *all* of the points of the plane, but usually it is enough to show how a simple figure such as a triangle is moved to describe the motion. It is allowable to turn the transparency upside down before it is returned to the plane of the paper, since the definition of rigid motion is still satisfied.

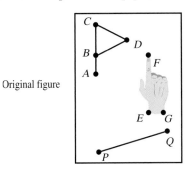

Original figure

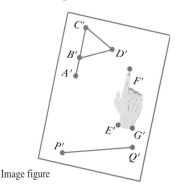

Image figure

Figure 12.2
Illustrating a rigid motion of the plane

   It needs to be emphasized that only the initial and final positions of a transformation are of interest. The transparency could have been taken for a roller coaster ride before

WINDOW ON TECHNOLOGY
Geometric Transformations with Dynamic Geometry Software

Accurate drawings of the rigid motions are not easy to create, especially for youngsters. The following three suggestions may be helpful:

- use squared paper or square dot paper (or a triangular grid of lines or dots)
- use a "tile" of a basic figure (say cut from cardstock or made from snap cubes) which can be traced to show its new positions under a motion or sequence of motions
- use a reflective drawing tool such as a Mira™

Transform
Translate…
Rotate…
Dilate…
Reflect
Mark Center
Mark Mirror
Mark Vector
Mark Distance
Mark Angle
Mark Ratio
Define Transform…

These techniques and tools continue to be valuable in the classroom. However, dynamic geometry software (see Appendix D) offers an exciting new way to explore rigid motions and other transformations of the plane. For example, the Transform Menu in *The Geometer's Sketchpad* shown at the left shows the commands to translate, rotate, dilate, or reflect a selected figure. Even quite young children will quickly understand how to use these commands to perform the basic motions.

As an example, suppose that a flag, *FLAG*, has been drawn, as well as points *P* and *Q* used to define a translation. To translate the flag with the slide arrow from *P* to *Q*, select points *P* and *Q* (in that order) and execute the **Mark Vector** command. Now select the flag figure, and execute **Translate . . . By Marked Vector** to obtain the image, $F'L'A'G'$ of the flag.

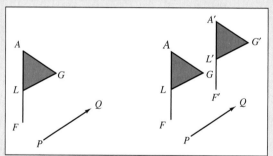

To perform a rotation, first select a point *C* and mark it as the center of rotation. A selected figure can then be rotated by an angle given either in degrees or as a marked angle. In the same way, a flip is performed by marking a line segment such as $\overline{MN}$ as the mirror line and then reflecting a selected figure across the line.

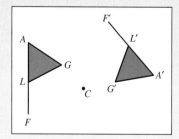

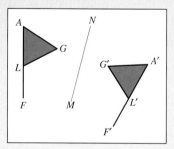

Once the basic motions are understood, it is fun for students to create more complex figures to demonstrate both their geometric understanding and their skills with the software. For example, the "smiley face" figure is constructed by drawing first the left side of the face and then reflecting across a vertical centerline.

reaching its final position. When the net outcomes of two motions are the same, the transformations are said to be **equivalent.**

Four transformations of the plane have special importance. They are the four **basic rigid motions of the plane:** translations, rotations, reflections, and glide reflections.

Translations

A **translation,** also known as a **slide,** is the rigid motion in which all points of the plane are moved in the same direction and by the same distance. A translation is illustrated by the "trace-and-slide" model in Figure 12.3. An arrow drawn from a point P to its image point P' completely specifies the two pieces of information required to define a translation: the direction of the slide is the direction of the arrow and the distance moved is the length of the arrow. The arrow is called the **slide arrow** or **translation vector.**

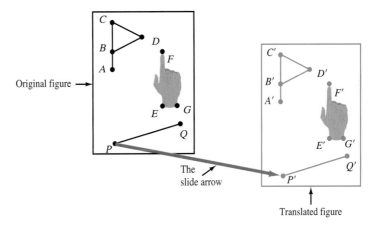

Figure 12.3
A slide, or translation, moves each point of the plane in the same direction and through the same distance.

EXAMPLE   12.1

Finding the Image Under a Translation

Find the image of the pentagon $ABCDE$ under the slide that takes the point C to C'.

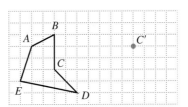

Solution

The slide arrow from C to C' is 7 units to the right and 2 units up. Therefore A' is found by moving 7 units to the right of A and then 2 units up. The remaining points are found in the same way, always using the same slide arrow.

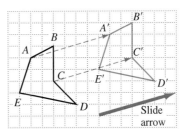

JUST FOR FUN

Inverting the Tetractys

Ten pennies can be tightly packed to form an equilateral triangle. This pattern was called the "tetractys" by the ancient Pythagoreans, and is still familiar today in ten pin bowling alleys. The problem is to turn the tetractys upside down by sliding one penny at a time to a new position in which it touches two other pennies. It's easy to do moving four pennies, but you should be able to find a three-move solution.

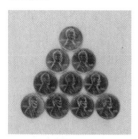

A three-coin triangle can be inverted in one move, a six-coin triangle in two moves, and, as noted above, a ten-coin triangle takes three moves. It would be reasonable to guess that a 15-coin triangle can be inverted in four moves, but it actually takes five moves. Try it!

Rotations

The **rotation,** also called a **turn,** is another basic rigid motion. One point of the plane—called the **turn center** or the **center of rotation**—is held fixed and the remaining points are turned about the center of rotation through the same number of degrees—the **turn angle.** A counterclockwise turn about point O through $120°$ is shown in Figure 12.4. Note that the right hand EFG is taken to the right hand $E'F'G'$.

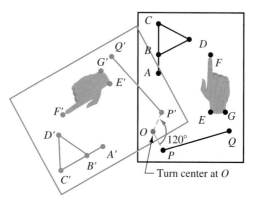

Figure 12.4
A turn, or rotation, rotates each point of the plane about a fixed point O—the turn center—through the same number of degrees and in the same direction of rotation.

A rotation is determined by giving the turn center and the directed angle corresponding to the turn angle. This information can be pictured by a **turn arrow,** as shown in Figure 12.5.

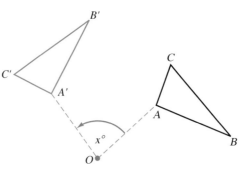

Figure 12.5
The rotation about center O by x° can be indicated by a turn arrow.

Usually counterclockwise turn angles are assigned positive degree measures, whereas negative measures indicate that the rotation is clockwise. In this way a $-120°$ turn is equivalent to a $240°$ turn about the same center. Remember that only the initial and final positions are considered, not the actual physical motion.

EXAMPLE   12.2   **Finding Images Under Rotations**

Find the image of each figure under the indicated turn.

(a)   90° rotation about P **(b)**   180° rotation about Q **(c)**   −90° rotation about R

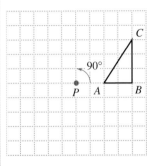 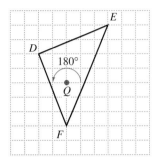 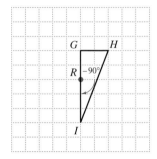

Solution   **(a)**   **(b)**   **(c)**

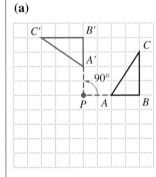 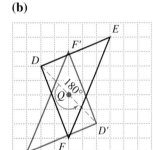 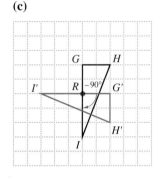

Reflections

The third basic rigid motion is a **reflection,** which is also called a **flip** or a **mirror reflection.** A reflection is determined by a line in the plane called the **line of reflection** or the **mirror line.** Each point P of the plane is transformed to the point P' on the opposite side of the mirror line m and at the same distance from m, as shown in Figure 12.6. Note that P' is located so that m is the perpendicular bisector of $\overline{PP'}$. Every point Q on m is transformed to itself; that is, $Q' = Q$ if Q is any point on m. Note that a right hand is reflected to a left hand, and vice versa.

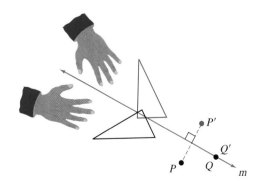

Figure 12.6

A flip, or reflection, about a line m transforms each point of the plane to its mirror image on the opposite side of m.

Reflections can be performed with a "trace-and-flip" procedure using an acetate transparency. First, the original figure is traced, including the line of reflection and a reference point (such as *Q* in Figure 12.6). The transparency is then turned over to perform the flip, and the points along the line of reflection are placed over their original position. The alignment of the reference point ensures that no sliding along the reflection line occurred.

The Mira™ is ideally suited to draw reflections. As shown in Figure 12.7, the plastic surface of a Mira both reflects a figure in front and still allows points behind the surface to be seen. This makes it simple to draw the reflected image of a given figure, with the bottom edge of the Mira acting as the line of reflection.

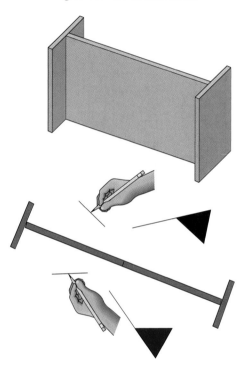

Figure 12.7
The Mira™ on the top can be used to draw reflections, as shown on the bottom.

EXAMPLE 12.3	**Finding Images Under Reflections**

Sketch the image of the "flag" under a flip across line *m*.

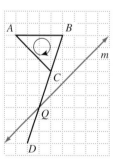

Solution

We can follow the "trace-and-flip" method if an acetate sheet or tracing paper is available, or we can use a Mira. Alternatively, the point *A′* which is the mirror point of *A* across line *m* can be plotted. Similarly *B′*, *C′*, and so on, can be plotted, until the entire image can be sketched accurately.

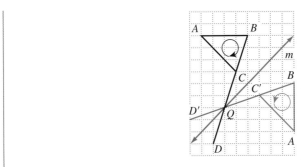

It's important to notice that a reflection reverses left-handed and right-handed orientations. For example, the left-pointing flag in Example 12.3 is transformed to a right-pointing flag, and the clockwise-pointing arrow on the circle becomes a counter-clockwise-pointing arrow in the image. A rigid motion which interchanges "handedness" is called **orientation reversing.** Thus, a reflection is orientation reversing. Translations and rotations, since they do not reverse handedness, are **orientation preserving** transformations.

Glide Reflections

The fourth and last basic rigid motion is the **glide reflection.** As the name suggests, a glide reflection combines both a slide and a reflection. The example most easily recalled is the motion which transforms a left footprint to a right footprint, as depicted in Figure 12.8. It is required that the line of reflection be parallel to the direction of the slide. In Figure 12.8 the slide came before the reflection, but if the reflection had preceded the slide the net outcome would have been the same.

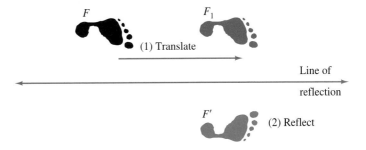

Figure 12.8
A glide reflection combines (1) a slide and (2) a reflection, where the line of reflection is parallel to the direction of the slide.

A glide reflection changes handedness, so it is an orientation reversing rigid motion. This is due to the reflection part of the motion.

To determine a glide reflection, it is useful to observe from Figure 12.9 that the midpoint M of the segment $\overline{PP'}$ lies on the mirror line of the reflection. This information is the key to solving the problem in the next example.

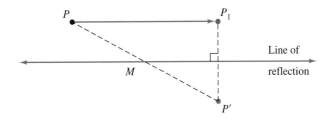

Figure 12.9
If points P and P′ correspond under a glide reflection, then the midpoint M of PP′ lies on the line of reflection.

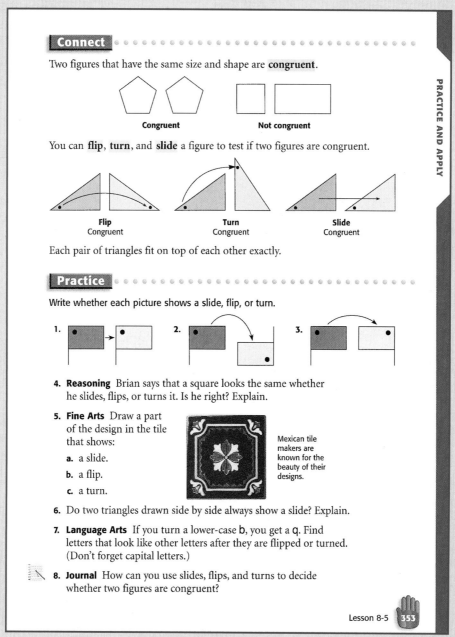

Connect

Two figures that have the same size and shape are **congruent**.

Congruent   Not congruent

You can **flip**, **turn**, and **slide** a figure to test if two figures are congruent.

Flip
Congruent

Turn
Congruent

Slide
Congruent

Each pair of triangles fit on top of each other exactly.

Practice

Write whether each picture shows a slide, flip, or turn.

1.

2.

3.

4. **Reasoning** Brian says that a square looks the same whether he slides, flips, or turns it. Is he right? Explain.

5. **Fine Arts** Draw a part of the design in the tile that shows:

   a. a slide.

   b. a flip.

   c. a turn.

Mexican tile makers are known for the beauty of their designs.

6. Do two triangles drawn side by side always show a slide? Explain.

7. **Language Arts** If you turn a lower-case **b**, you get a **q**. Find letters that look like other letters after they are flipped or turned. (Don't forget capital letters.)

8. **Journal** How can you use slides, flips, and turns to decide whether two figures are congruent?

Lesson 8-5   353

SOURCE: From *Scott Foresman–Addison Wesley Math*, Grade 4, p. 353, by Randall I. Charles et al. Copyright © 1999, Addison Wesley Longman, Inc.

Questions for the Teacher

1. Flips, turns, and slides are illustrated with scalene triangles, and flags *with flag poles* are shown in Practice Questions 1, 2, and 3. Why are these shapes preferred to either an equilateral triangle or a rectangle?

2. The Teacher's Edition claims that the answer to Practice Question 4 is "Not always true; a square has equal sides and angles, so it looks the same when you slide it or flip it. It could look like a rhombus if it were turned." Comment on the accuracy of this answer.

3. A student asks you if it is possible to flip the flag with the pole downward so the image pole points upward. What's a good response to this student?

4. Another student asks if it is possible to flip the green flag with the pole pointing downward so the image pole is horizontal. How should you respond?

EXAMPLE   12.4   **Determining a Glide Reflection**

A glide reflection has taken points A and B of triangle ABC to the points A' and B', as shown below. Find the line of reflection and the slide arrow of the glide reflection, and then sketch the image triangle $A'B'C'$ under the glide.

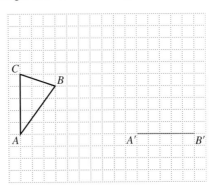

Solution

The square grid makes it easy to draw the respective midpoints M and N of the line segments $\overline{AA'}$ and $\overline{BB'}$. Since both M and N lie on the mirror line, $m = \overleftrightarrow{MN}$ is the line of reflection of the glide. Reflecting A' across m determines the point A_1, and the slide arrow of the glide is drawn by connecting A to A_1. The slide arrow is 8 units to the right and 4 units up, which allows us to find C_1. Reflecting C_1 across the line of reflection locates C', and therefore $\triangle A'B'C'$ can be completed.

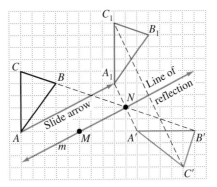

The four basic rigid motions are summarized in Table 12.1 on the next page.

The Net Outcome of Two Successive Reflections

Recall that any two rigid motions which have the same net outcome are called equivalent. For example, rotations of $-120°$ and $+240°$ about the same center O are equivalent. Similarly the motion consisting of two consecutive 180° rotations about a point O is equivalent to the **identity transformation,** which is the rigid "motion" that leaves all points of the plane fixed.

Two consecutive reflections across the same line of reflection also bring each point back to its original position, so any "double flip" is also equivalent to the identity transformation. Suppose, however, that two flips are taken in succession across two *different* lines of reflection, say first over m_1 and next over m_2. There are two cases to consider, where m_1 and m_2 are parallel and where m_1 and m_2 intersect.

Table 12.1 summarizes useful information about the four basic rigid motions.

TABLE 12.1 The Four Basic Rigid Motions			
Name (alternate name) and Sketch	Information Needed	Description	Orientation Property
Translation (slide)	Slide arrow, indicating distance and direction.	Every point of the plane is moved the same distance in the same direction.	Orientation is preserved.
Rotation (turn)	Turn arrow, indicating turn center and turn angle.	Every point of the plane is rotated through the same directed angle about the turn center.	Orientation is preserved.
Reflection (flip)	Line of reflection.	Every point of the plane is moved to its mirror image on the opposite side of the line of reflection.	Orientation is reversed.
Glide reflection (glide)	Slide arrow and a line of reflection parallel to the slide direction.	Every point of the plane is moved by the same translation and reflected across the same line parallel to the slide direction.	Orientation is reversed.

EXAMPLE 12.5   Exploring Consecutive Reflections Across Parallel Lines

Let m_1 and m_2 be parallel lines of reflection.

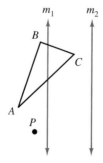

(a)   Sketch the image of $\triangle ABC$ and point P under the reflection across m_1; let the image be labeled as $\triangle A_1 B_1 C_1$ and P_1.

(b)   Sketch the image of $\triangle A_1 B_1 C_1$ and P_1 under reflection across line m_2; let the image be labeled $\triangle A'B'C'$ and P'.

(c)   Describe the net outcome of the rigid motion consisting of the two successive reflections, first across m_1 and next across m_2.

Solution

(a)   **and (b)**   Each reflection can be drawn with a Mira, by the "trace-and-flip" method with an acetate sheet, or, easiest of all, using dynamic geometry software. Whatever method is used will result in the images shown below.

(c)   If d is the directed distance from line m_1 to line m_2, we see that point P is moved a distance $2d$ in the direction perpendicular to m_1 and m_2 and pointing from m_1 toward m_2. In fact *all* points of the plane are moved in this direction through the same distance $2d$ and so the net outcome of two successive reflections across a pair of parallel lines is equivalent to the translation shown at the right below.

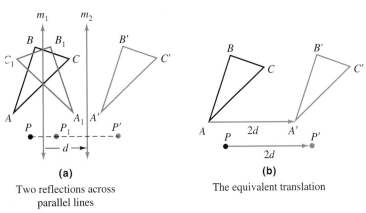

(a)
Two reflections across
parallel lines

(b)
The equivalent translation

A similar investigation can be carried out for the motion consisting of two successive reflections across lines m_1 and m_2 which intersect at a point O. Most people find the result very surprising: *the net outcome of the two reflections across intersecting lines is equivalent to a rotation about the point O of intersection of m_1 and m_2. The angle of rotation is twice the measure of the directed angle that turns line m_1 onto line m_2.* This is illustrated in Figure 12.10.

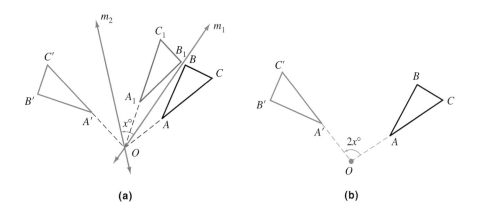

Figure 12.10
*Two reflections across
intersecting lines are equivalent
to a rotation about the point
of intersection of the two lines.*

(a)

(b)

The following theorem summarizes the two possible net outcomes of a pair of successive reflections.

THEOREM *The Net Outcome of Two Reflections*

The net outcome of two successive reflections is either a translation, if the lines of reflection are parallel, or a rotation, if the lines of reflection intersect.

The Net Outcome of Three Successive Reflections

Three lines can be arranged in several ways in the plane. For example, the lines m_1, m_2, and m_3 in Figure 12.11(a) are parallel to one another. The successive images of $\triangle ABC$ across the lines are shown, with $\triangle A'B'C'$ the image at the completion of all three reflections. In Figure 12.11(b), we see that $\triangle ABC$ can be taken to $\triangle A'B'C'$ by a *single* reflection over the line l. Line l is the image of line m_1 under the translation that takes m_2 to m_3. Thus, successive reflections across three parallel lines is equivalent to a single reflection.

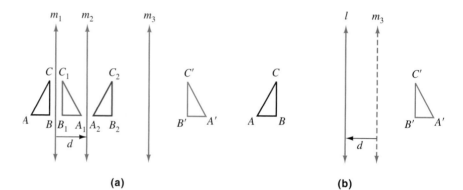

Figure 12.11

Three reflections across parallel lines m_1, m_2, m_3, is equivalent to a reflection across one line, l.

(a)   **(b)**

Three reflections across concurrent lines m_1, m_2, and m_3 can also be discovered to be equivalent to a single reflection across a certain line l which passes through the point O of concurrence. (See problem 22 in the section exercises.) In all other cases, where the three lines are neither parallel nor concurrent, it can be shown that the net outcome of three successive reflections is equivalent to a glide reflection. (See problem 23 in the section exercises.)

In summary, we have the following result.

THEOREM *The Net Outcomes of Three Reflections*

The net outcome of three successive reflections across lines m_1, m_2, and m_3 is equivalent to either:

- a reflection, if m_1, m_2, and m_3 are parallel or concurrent;

or

- a glide reflection, if m_1, m_2, and m_3 are neither parallel nor concurrent.

Classification of General Rigid Motions

Any rigid motion can be modeled by moving an acetate sheet to a new position in the same plane. If the rigid motion takes $\triangle ABC$ to $\triangle A'B'C'$, the final position of the acetate sheet is uniquely determined by aligning point A with A', point B with B', and point C with C'. Let's now see how the three points can be aligned by a sequence of at most three reflections, as illustrated in Figure 12.12. Beginning with $\triangle ABC$ and its image $\triangle A'B'C'$, the first reflection across the perpendicular bisector of $\overline{AA'}$ maps $\triangle ABC$ to $\triangle A'B_1C_1$. The second reflection across the perpendicular bisector of $\overline{B_1B'}$ maps $\triangle A'B_1C_1$ to $\triangle A'B'C_2$. The third and last reflection across the perpendicular bisector $\overline{C_2C'}$ maps $\triangle A'B'C_2$ to $\triangle A'B'C'$.

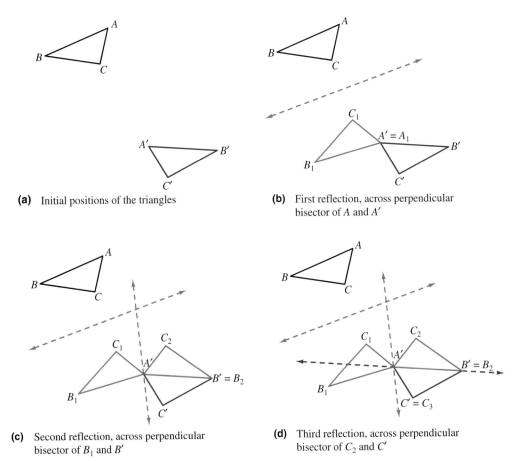

(a) Initial positions of the triangles

(b) First reflection, across perpendicular bisector of A and A'

(c) Second reflection, across perpendicular bisector of B_1 and B'

(d) Third reflection, across perpendicular bisector of C_2 and C'

Figure 12.12
Any rigid motion is equivalent to a sequence of at most three reflections.

If it happens that $A = A'$, the first reflection is omitted. Similarly, if $B_1 = B'$ the second reflection is omitted, and the third reflection is omitted if $C_2 = C'$.

Since two reflections are equivalent to a translation or rotation, and three reflections are equivalent to a single reflection or a glide reflection, we have proved the following remarkable theorem.

> **THEOREM**　*Classification of General Rigid Motions*
> Any rigid motion of the plane is equivalent to one of the four basic rigid motions: a translation, a rotation, a reflection, or a glide reflection.

Rigid motions have many applications in geometry. For example, the informal definition of congruence to mean "same size and shape" can now be made precise.

> **DEFINITION**　*Congruent Figures*
> Two figures are **congruent** if, and only if, one figure is the image of the other under a rigid motion.

The periodic drawings and block prints of M. C. Escher show how the plane can be tiled by congruent figures. Figure 12.13 illustrates a two-motif pattern of fish of two types.

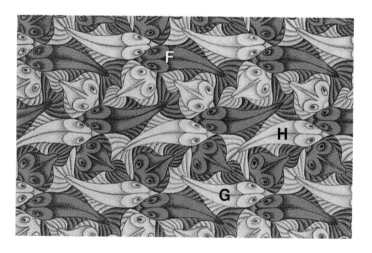

Figure 12.13
A two-motif tiling of the plane by M. C. Escher

EXAMPLE　12.6　Classifying Rigid Motions

Examine the tiling of M. C. Escher shown in Figure 12.13. Three of the large fish are labeled F, G, and H.

(a) What type of rigid motion takes F onto G?
(b) What type of rigid motion takes F onto H?
(c) What type of rigid motion takes G onto H?

Solution

(a) Since F and G have the same orientation (both bend the tail to the left), they are related by an orientation preserving transformation. Since the fish face in opposite directions, the motion is not a translation and so it must be a rotation. (Can you identify the turn center and the size of the angle of rotation?)

(b) F and H have opposite orientation, so either a reflection or glide reflection takes F onto H. H is not a reflection of F, so it must be a glide reflection. (Can you determine the line of reflection of the glide?)

(c) A glide reflection takes G onto H. The slide is horizontal to the right.

Dilations and Similarity Motions

A rigid motion takes any two points P and Q to the image points P' and Q' without changing their distance apart. That is, $PQ = P'Q'$. Therefore, any figure mapped by a rigid motion is unchanged in both size and shape. Suppose, however, we wish to find transformations of the plane that preserve shape but change the size of any figure. Transformations with this property are quite common: consider making an enlargement or reduction on a photocopy machine, or using the zoom command from the View Menu of a computer program.

The simplest transformation to change the size of a figure, but not its shape or orientation, is a **dilation** (also called a **size transformation**). A point O is chosen as the center and the points of the plane are all moved toward ($k < 1$) or away ($k > 1$) from the center O by the same proportional factor k. More precisely, we have the following definition.

> **DEFINITION**   *Dilation, or Size Transformation*
>
> Let O be a point in the plane and k a positive real number. A **dilation, or size transformation,** with **center O** and **scale factor k** is the transformation that takes each point $P \neq O$ of the plane to the point P' on the ray $\overrightarrow{OP}$ for which $OP' = k \cdot OP$, and takes the point O to itself.

Two examples of dilations are shown in Figure 12.14.

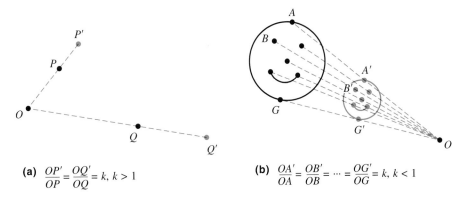

(a) $\dfrac{OP'}{OP} = \dfrac{OQ'}{OQ} = k, k > 1$

(b) $\dfrac{OA'}{OA} = \dfrac{OB'}{OB} = \cdots = \dfrac{OG'}{OG} = k, k < 1$

Figure 12.14
Two dilations, or size transformations

When the scale factor k is larger than 1, the image of a figure is larger than the original and the dilation is an **expansion.** If $k < 1$ the dilation is a **contraction.** If $k = 1$ then all points are left unmoved—that is, $P = P'$ for all P—and the dilation is the identity transformation.

The most important fact about dilations is contained in the following theorem. Recall that if a point P is taken to the image point P', we say that P is the preimage of P'.

> **THEOREM**   *Distance Change Under a Dilation*
>
> Under a dilation with scale factor k, the distance between any two image points is k times the distance between their preimages. That is, for all points P and Q, $P'Q' = k \cdot PQ$.

A sequence of dilations and rigid motions, performed in succession, will be called a **similarity transformation.**

> **DEFINITION**   *Similarity Transformation*
>
> A transformation is a **similarity transformation** if, and only if, it is a sequence of dilations and rigid motions.

We can now give a precise definition of similarity of figures.

> **DEFINITION**   *Similar Figures*
>
> Two figures F and G are **similar,** written $F \sim G$, if, and only if, there is a similarity transformation that takes one figure onto the other figure.

DID YOU KNOW?
You Can't Listen for Congruence

In 1966 Mark Kac of Rockefeller University asked an apparently simple question, "Can you hear the shape of a drum?" A drum, for Kac, can have any shape. All that's required is that it be a two-dimensional figure having an interior (the drumhead) and a boundary (the rim). The shape of the boundary determines an infinite set of characteristic frequencies at which the interior "drum head" will vibrate. Two drums of the same shape generate the same set of frequencies, but Kac wanted to know if the converse is true: If you hear the same set of frequencies from two drums, are the drums necessarily the same shape?

In 1991 Carolyn Gordon and David Webb, formerly at Washington University in St. Louis, and Scott Wolpert at the University of Maryland showed that you cannot hear the shape of a drum. They did so by finding two noncongruent shapes which, if made into drums with drumheads of the same material stretched at the same tension, would vibrate at exactly the same frequencies.

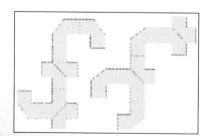

SOURCE: Adapted from Barry Cipra, "You Can't Hear the Shape of a Drum," *Science,*
Vol. 255 (March 27, 1992): 1642.

The fish *F* and *G* in Figure 12.15 are similar to one another. A dilation centered at point *O* maps *F* to *F'* and a reflection maps *F'* to *G*.

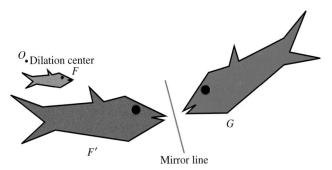

Figure 12.15
A dilation centered at O followed by a reflection define a similarity transformation taking figure F to figure G. Therefore, figures F and G are similar.

| EXAMPLE   12.7 | **Verifying Similarity** |

Show that the small letter *F* and the larger letter *F* are similar by describing a similarity transformation that takes the smaller figure onto the larger one.

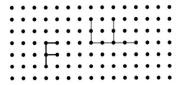

Solution

We need a sequence of dilations and rigid motions that rotate, stretch, and position the smaller letter onto the larger. This can be done in three steps: (a) make a 90° rotation, (b) do a dilation with scale factor $k = 2$, and (c) perform a translation.

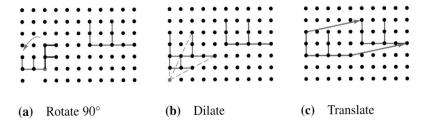

(a)   Rotate 90°   **(b)**   Dilate   **(c)**   Translate

These three steps are not unique. For example, a translation could have been taken first, then a 90° rotation, and finally a dilation with a properly chosen center. Showing that *some* similarity transformation takes one figure to the other is all that is required.

Dɪᴅ Yᴏᴜ Kɴᴏᴡ?

Self-similarity and Fractals

A line is one-dimensional, and a plane is two-dimensional. But what if someone asks for a geometric figure whose dimension is *between* one and two? The question may seem unanswerable. However, beginning in the late nineteenth century, mathematicians have created numerous objects of uncertain dimension. The Koch curve is an example, named after the Swedish mathematician, Helge von Koch, who first described it in 1904. To construct the Koch curve, begin with a line segment. Next replace the middle third by an equilateral triangular bump, resulting in a 4-segment polygonal curve. In the third step, a triangular bump is added to

each side of the curve, yielding a curve with 16 sides.

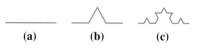

(a)   (b)   (c)

Repeating the process infinitely often gives the Koch curve.

The Koch curve has many interesting properties, but of special interest is its self-similarity: if fragments of the curve are viewed with microscopes of 100 power, or 1000 power, or any power whatever, the enlargements all appear identical. This unlimited "roughness" of the Koch curve suggests that its dimension is larger than one. In 1975, Benoit B. Mandelbrot, a Fellow at IBM's Thomas

J. Watson Research Center, published the first comprehensive study of the geometry of self-similar shapes such as the Koch curve, the Sierpinski gasket, and the Menger sponge. According to Mandelbrot's definition, the Koch curve has dimension D given by the equation $4 = 3^D$. That is, $D = 1.2619 \ldots$. Since self-similar objects may have nonintegral dimension, Mandelbrot called such objects fractals, from the same verb *frangere* (to break) that is the source of our word fraction.

Fractals are not simply abstract creations of mathematicians. Indeed, intense ongoing scientific research suggests that many, and possibly most, of the physical and life processes are what can be described as chaotic, and the geometric shapes of chaos are fractals. (For a nontechnical introduction to self-similarity, fractals, and chaos consult James Gleick's *Chaos: Making a New Science*, Penguin Books, New York, 1987.)

Pʀᴏʙʟᴇᴍ Sᴇᴛ 12.1

Understanding Concepts

1. Which of the following "transformations" correspond to a rigid motion? Explain the reasoning you have used to give your answer.

    (a) A deck of cards is shuffled.

    (b) A completed jigsaw puzzle is taken apart and then put back together.

    (c) A jigsaw puzzle is taken from the box, assembled, and then replaced in its box.

    (d) A painting is moved to a new position on the same wall.

    (e) Bread dough is allowed to "rise."

2. For each figure shown, find its image under the translation which takes P to P'.

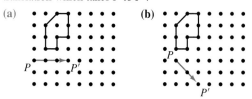

3. The translation that takes point P to P' has transformed triangle ABC (not shown) to its image $A'B'C'$ (shown below).

    (a) Draw triangle ABC.

    (b) Describe the rigid motion that transforms $\triangle A'B'C'$ to $\triangle ABC$, and compare it to the translation that takes $\triangle ABC$ to $\triangle A'B'C'$.

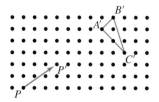

4. In each of the following give an equivalent answer between 0° and 360°.

    (a) A clockwise rotation of 60° is equivalent to a counterclockwise rotation of _____.

    (b) A clockwise rotation of 433° is equivalent to a clockwise rotation of _____.

(c) A clockwise rotation of 3643° is equivalent to a clockwise rotation of _____.

(d) A sequence of two consecutive clockwise rotations, first of 280° and next of 120°, is equivalent to a single clockwise rotation of _____.

(e) A rotation of −260° is equivalent to a rotation of _____.

5. Sketch the image of △*ABC* under the given rotations.

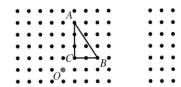

(a) 90° counterclockwise about *O*

(b) 180° about *P*

6. A rotation has sent *A* to *A'* and *B* to *B'*, as shown below.

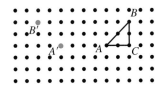

(a) Find the center of rotation.

(b) Find the turn angle.

(c) Sketch the image triangle *A'B'C'*.

7. Trace the following figure, which shows △*ABC* and its image under a rotation. Use any drawing tools you wish (Mira, compass, and straightedge) to construct the center of rotation. (*Hint:* Why is the center of rotation on the perpendicular bisector of $\overline{AA'}$?)

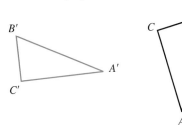

8. Redraw the figure below on squared graph paper. Then sketch the reflection of △*ABC* across the mirror line *m*.

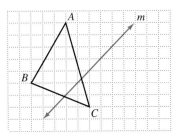

9. A reflection has sent *P* to *P'*.

(a) Find the line of reflection.

(b) Find the image of the polygon *PQRST* under the reflection that takes *P* to *P'*.

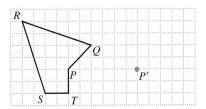

10. (a) A reflection across line *m* leaves point *A* fixed, so that *A'* = *A*. What can be said about *A*'s relationship to *m*?

(b) A reflection across line *m* leaves two points *A* and *B* fixed, so that *A'* = *A* and *B'* = *B*. What can you say about *A*, *B*, and *m*?

(c) A reflection takes point *C* to point *D*. Where does the reflection take point *D*?

11. A glide reflection is defined by the slide arrow and line of reflection *m* shown. Draw the following images of the polygon *ABCDE*.

(a) The image $A_1B_1C_1D_1E_1$ under the slide.

(b) The image *A'B'C'D'E'* under the glide reflection.

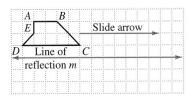

12. A glide reflection has taken *B* to *B'* and *E* to *E'*. Find

(a) the line of reflection of the glide.

(b) the slide arrow.

(c) the image *A'B'C'D'E'* of the polygon *ABCDE*.

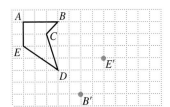

13. In each part below, draw a line m_2 so that the net outcome of successive reflections about m_1 and then m_2 is equivalent to the translation specified by the slide arrow shown.

(a)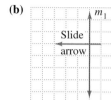

(b)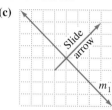

(c)

14. A reflection across line j followed by a reflection across line k shown below is equivalent to the translation by 4 units to the right, as shown in the table.

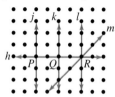

Fill in the missing entries (a) through (f) in the table.

REFLECTION LINES

First	Second	Equivalent transformation
j	k	Translate right 4 units
l	m	Rotate clockwise 90° around point R
j	l	(a)
k	(b)	Translate left 4 units
(c)	k	Translate left 4 units
h	m	(d)
m	(e)	Rotate 180° about point P
k	(f)	Identity transformation (all points fixed)

15. Use dot or graph paper to copy $\triangle ABC$ and points O and P. Then draw the image of $\triangle ABC$ for:

(a) the dilation with center O and scale factor 2;

(b) the dilation with center P and scale factor 1/2.

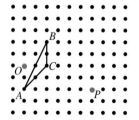

16. In the figure shown below, $\triangle DEF$ is the image of $\triangle ABC$ under the dilation with center O and scale factor 2.

(a) Describe the size transformation that takes $\triangle DEF$ onto $\triangle GHI$. Show the center of the transformation on a sketch and give the scale factor.

(b) Describe the dilation that takes $\triangle ABC$ onto $\triangle GHI$ by locating the center and giving the scale factor.

(c) The Pythagorean theorem shows that $AB = \sqrt{5}$, so the perimeter of $\triangle ABC$ is $3 + \sqrt{5}$. Explain how to use the scale factors determined in parts (a) and (b) to obtain the perimeters of $\triangle DEF$ and $\triangle GHI$.

(d) A dilation with scale factor 4 takes $\triangle ABC$ onto $\triangle JKL$. What is the perimeter of $\triangle JKL$?

(e) Find the areas of the three triangles. Explain how the areas are related to the scale factors.

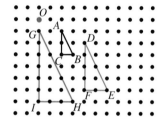

17. Sketch the image of $\triangle JKL$ under the similarity transformation composed of a dilation centered at point P with scale factor 2/3 followed by a reflection across line m.

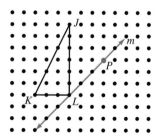

18. Describe a similarity transformation that takes quadrilateral *ABCD* onto quadrilateral *A'B'C'D'* as shown. Sketch the intermediate images of the dilation and rigid motions that compose the similarity transformation.

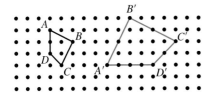

Thinking Critically

19. A rigid motion takes points *A*, *B*, *C*, and *P* to the respective image points *A'*, *B'*, *C'* and *P'*, where $AB = 3$ cm, $AC = 4$ cm, $AP = 2$ cm, $BC = 2$ cm, $BP = 4$ cm, and $CP = 4$ cm. In each part use a compass and ruler to draw the smallest set of points which you know must contain the point *P'* when you are given:

   (a) only point *A'*. (*Hint:* The answer is a circle.)

   (b) points *A'* and *B'*.

   (c) points *A'*, *B'*, and *C'*.

20. Two successive 90° rotations are taken, first about center O_1 and then about center O_2, where $O_1O_2 = 2$ cm. Describe the basic rigid motion that is equivalent to the successive rotations. Explain carefully, using words and sketches.

21. Suppose that the 90° rotations in problem 20 are each replaced with a 120° rotation. What basic rigid motion is equivalent to the net outcome of the two rotations? Explain with words and sketches.

22. (a) Find the image △*A'B'C'* of △*ABC* under the rigid motion consisting of three consecutive reflections across the concurrent lines m_1, m_2, and m_3.

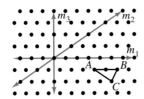

   (b) Find a line *l* so that △*ABC* is taken onto △*A'B'C'* by one reflection across *l*.

23. (a) Find the image △*A'B'C'* of △*ABC* under the rigid motion consisting of three consecutive reflections across lines m_1, m_2, and m_3.

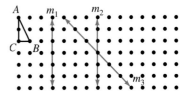

   (b) Find the image of △*ABC* under the glide reflection whose slide arrow extends from *P* to *P'* and whose line of reflection is line *l*.

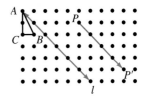

   (c) What conclusion can you make about the two rigid motions described in (a) and (b)?

24. Trace the figure below, where △*ABC* is congruent to △*A'B'C'*.

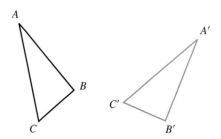

   (a) Use a Mira (or other drawing tools) to draw the line m_1 across which *A* is reflected to *A'*. Also, draw the images of *B* and *C* and label them B_1 and C_1.

   (b) Draw the line m_2 across which B_1 reflects to *B'*. What is the image of C_1 across m_2?

   (c) Use the lines m_1 and m_2 to describe the basic rigid motion that takes △*ABC* to △*A'B'C'*.

25. Trace the figure below, where △*ABC* is congruent to △*A'B'C'*.

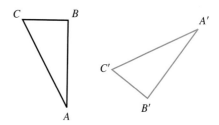

   (a) Use a Mira (or other drawing tools) to draw three lines of reflection—m_1, m_2, and m_3—so that:

     (i) reflection across m_1 takes *A* to *A'* (and *B*, *C* are taken to B_1, C_1);

(ii) reflection across m_2 takes B_1 to B' (and C_1 is taken to C_2);

(iii) reflection across m_3 takes C_2 to C'.

(b) Describe the type of basic rigid motion that takes $\triangle ABC$ to $\triangle A'B'C'$.

26. In each of the following parts, a complicated sequence of rigid motions is described. Explain how you know what type of basic rigid motion is equivalent to the net outcome of the motion described.

(a) Reflections are taken across six lines and no point is taken back to its original position.

(b) Reflections are taken across eleven lines and there are points which are taken back to their original positions.

(c) Two different glide reflections are taken in succession, with the net outcome taking some point back to its original location.

27. Let C and D be the two circles on the same side of mirror m. Construct a tangent line to circle C which, after reflection, is also tangent to circle D. How many solutions can you find?

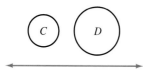

28. A tiling by M. C. Escher is shown below.

(a) What rigid motion takes figure A onto figure B?

(b) What rigid motion takes figure A onto figure C?

(c) What rigid motion takes figure C onto figure D?

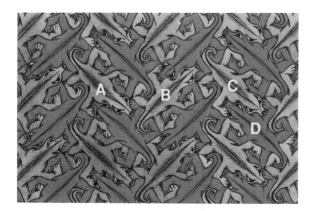

29. A size transformation centered at some point O of line l has taken point P to P'. Explain how to draw (a) the center O of the transformation, and (b) the image Q' of the point Q, where Q lies on l.

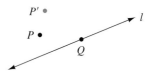

30. A size transformation takes P to P' and Q to Q', where the four points P, P', Q, Q' are collinear as shown here. Explain (a) how to draw the image R' of point R, and (b) how to locate the center O of the size transformation. (*Hint:* What line through P' must contain R'?)

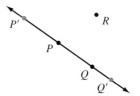

Making Connections

31. Estelle wants to install a "full-length" mirror on her closet door. She is 5′2″ tall, and her eyes are 6″ below the top of her head. How tall must the mirror be for Estelle to see her entire reflection? How high should the top of the mirror be off the floor? (*Hint:* Draw a stick-figure picture, showing Estelle and her mirror image behind the plane of the mirror.)

32. **Fermat's Principle.** Suppose that a ray of light emanating from point P is reflected from a mirror at point R toward point S. It was known even in ancient times that the incident and reflected rays of light make congruent angles to the line m of the mirror. Pierre de Fermat (1601–1665) proposed an important principle to explain why this is so: *light follows the path of shortest distance.* According to Fermat's principle, if Q is some point on the mirror other than R, then the distance $PQ + QS$ must exceed the distance $PR + RS$ traveled by the light.

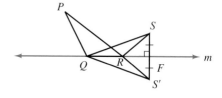

Answer the following questions to verify that $PQ + QS > PR + RS$. Let S' be the image of S under reflection across line m.

(a) Why are $RS' = RS$ and $QS' = QS$? (*Hint:* The reflection across m is a *rigid* motion which preserves distances.)

(b) Why is $PQ + QS' > PS'$?

(c) How does the inequality of part (b) give the desired result that $PQ + QS > PR + RS$?

33. Let P and S be two points on the same side of mirror m. If S' is the point of reflection of point S across m, then the line drawn from P to S' intersects m at the point R of reflection (see the figure in problem 32). Suppose P and S are between *two* mirrors, m and l, as shown below.

(a) Construct a doubly reflected light path $PQRS$ which is reflected off mirror m at Q and then off mirror l at R.

(b) Construct another doubly reflected path $PABS$ which first reflects off l at A and then off mirror m at B.

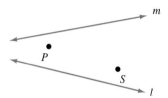

34. A **corner mirror** is formed by placing two mirrors together at a right angle. Explain why looking at yourself in a corner mirror is quite different than seeing yourself in an ordinary mirror. Use sketches to make your ideas clear.

35. A billiard ball is located at a point P along an edge of a rectangular billiard table. Show that there is a billiard shot which strikes the cushions on the other three rails (sides) of the table and then returns to bounce at P.

(*Hint:* Suppose the table T is reflected across its sides successively, forming the images T', T'', and T'''.) Explain how a billiard path $PQRSP$ can be found by drawing the line segment $\overline{PP'''}$. Sketch the path $PQRSP$ on the original table T.

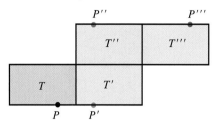

36. A **pantograph** is a mechanical device used to draw enlargements. A simple version can be constructed from cardboard strips that are hinged with brass fasteners.

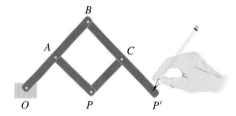

The pivot point at O is held fixed as P is moved over the figure. The pencil point at point P' traces out an enlargement.

(a) Explain why the pantograph mechanically gives a size transformation.

(b) What is the scale factor of the size transformation? Assume that all of the adjacent points along a strip are the same distance apart.

🖳 Using a Computer

37. Draw any convex quadrilateral $ABCD$ with dynamic geometry software, and construct the midpoint M of side $\overline{AB}$. Mark point M as the center of rotation, and rotate the quadrilateral $180°$ about M to form the hexagon $AC'D'BCD$. Show that translations of the hexagon will fit together to tile the plane.

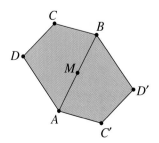

38. Use geometry software to construct a triangle ABC and the outward-pointing equilateral triangles with centers X, Y, and Z, as shown.

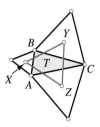

(a) Construct the triangle XYZ. Use your software to investigate the properties of $\triangle XYZ$.

(b) Mark X as a rotation center, and rotate the entire figure shown above by $120°$. Similarly, rotate the figure $120°$ about the centers of the other equilateral triangles. What pattern is formed by the centers X, Y, Z of all the equilateral triangles and their rotations?

39. Use geometry software to construct a parallelogram $ABCD$ and the outward squares with centers X, Y, Z, and W, as shown below.

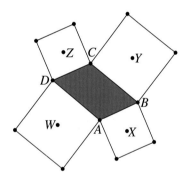

(a) Construct the quadrilateral $XYZW$. Use your software to investigate the properties of $XYZW$.

(b) Mark X as a rotation center, and rotate the entire figure shown by $90°$. Similarly, rotate the figure $90°$ about the centers of the other squares. What pattern is formed by the centers of all the squares and their rotations?

Communicating

40. Explore what happens when translations are taken in succession, writing a report on your conclusions. Give

both specific examples and state any general principles you find. In particular, include answers to the following questions:

(a) Why is the net outcome of two successive translations equivalent to another translation?

(b) If the first translation takes A to A_1 and the second translation takes A_1 to A', why is the arrow from A to A' the slide arrow of the combined motion of the two translations?

(c) What happens to the net outcome if the order in which the two translations are taken is reversed?

From State Student Assessments

41. (Oregon, Grade 5)
Which two of these figures are congruent?

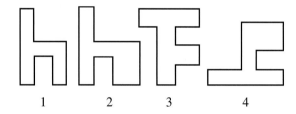

1   2   3   4

A. 1 and 3

B. 1 and 2

C. 2 and 3

D. 2 and 4

For Review

42. The measures of the three angles in a triangle are $2x°$, $3x°$, and $4x°$. What are the three angle measures?

43. A triangle RST has area 87 cm^2 and $RS = 3$ cm. What is the distance from T to the line containing RS?

44. Give a counterexample that shows that the following conjecture is false: *the midpoints of the sides of a rhombus are the vertices of a square.*

45. If the word "square" in the conjecture stated in problem 44 is replaced with "rectangle" do you think the conjecture is true? Give a proof or provide a counterexample.

12.2   Patterns and Symmetries

Symmetry is a universal principle of organization and form. The circular arc of a rainbow and the hexagonal symmetry of an ice crystal are visible expressions of the symmetry of many, indeed most, of the physical processes of the universe. A sea shell and the fanned tail of the peacock are spectacular examples of biological symmetry. Symmetry is the norm of nature and natural law, not the exception.

In the human domain, all cultures of the world, even those in prehistoric times, developed a useful intuitive understanding of the basic concepts of symmetry. Decorations on pottery, walls, tools, weapons, musical instruments, and clothing are most often highly symmetric. Buildings, temples, tombs, and other structures are usually designed with an eye to symmetry and balance. Music, poetry, and dance frequently incorporate symmetry in their underlying structure.

While people have long had an informal understanding of symmetry, it is only more recently that mathematics has provided a deeper understanding of what symmetry means and how different kinds of symmetry can be described and classified. In the classroom, youngsters are drawn to this artistic and aesthetic aspect of mathematics.

What Is Symmetry?

The concept of a rigid motion, which we defined and explored in the last section, makes it possible to give a precise definition of a symmetry of a geometric figure in the plane.

> **DEFINITION**   *A Symmetry of a Plane Figure*
> A **symmetry** of a plane figure is any rigid motion of the plane that moves all the points of the figure back to points of the figure.

Thus, all points P of the figure are taken by the symmetry motion to points P' that also are points of the figure. The identity motion is a symmetry of any figure, but of more interest are figures that have symmetries other than the identity. Under a nonidentity symmetry some points in the figure move to new positions in the figure, even though the figure as a whole appears unchanged by the motion.

The classification theorem of the preceding section tells us that there are just four basic rigid motions. Therefore, any symmetry of a figure is one of these four basic types, and the symmetry properties of a figure can be fully described by listing all of the symmetries of each type.

from **The NCTM Principles and Standards**

Transformations and Symmetry

Young children move shapes intuitively, as when they solve a tangram puzzle. They turn tangram pieces, flip them over, and experiment with new arrangements. These actions are explorations with transformations, and they are an important part of spatial learning. Young children can learn substantial mathematics through guided explorations. For example, working with structured geometric materials such as pattern blocks, children create designs with linear and rotational symmetry. A teacher may challenge students to recognize, describe, and informally prove the symmetric characteristics of their designs.

At this age, children naturally use their own physical experiences and the geometric patterns they create while playing with shapes to learn about symmetries and transformations such as slides, turns, and flips. Folding paper cutouts or using mirrors to investigate lines and planes of symmetry are other ways for children to observe figures in a variety of positions, become aware of their important properties, and compare and contrast them.

SOURCE: Reprinted with permission from *Curriculum and Evaluation Standards for School Mathematics: Discussion Draft*, copyright 1998 by the National Council of Teachers of Mathematics. All rights reserved.

Reflection Symmetry

A figure has **reflection symmetry** if a reflection across some line is a symmetry of the figure. The line of reflection is called a **line of symmetry** or a **mirror line** of the figure. Each point P of the figure on one side of the line of symmetry is matched to a point P' of the figure on the opposite side of the line of symmetry. Some figures and their lines of symmetry (shown dashed) are shown in Figure 12.16.

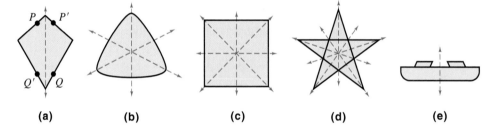

Figure 12.16
Plane figures and their lines of symmetry

(a)   (b)   (c)   (d)   (e)

Reflection symmetry is also called **line symmetry** or **bilateral symmetry.** Bilateral symmetry is also used to describe figures in space that have a plane of symmetry. For example, ferries (as suggested in Figure 12.16(e)) are often bilaterally symmetric across midships to simplify loading and unloading their cargo of cars and trucks. Infrequent passengers on such ferries can find it very disorienting when the bow and stern are indistinguishable.

EXAMPLE   12.8   **Identifying Lines of Symmetry**

How many lines of symmetry does each letter shown below have?

(a)   (b)   (c)   (d)

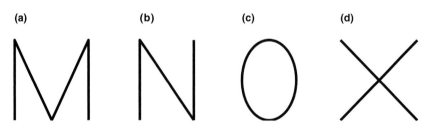

Solution   **(a)** 1   **(b)** 0   **(c)** 2   **(d)** 4, since the segments are congruent and intersect at right angles.

George W. Brainerd, a North American archeologist, was the first person to use the principles of symmetry as a tool for anthropological study. His analysis of the designs on pottery of the prehistoric Anasazi of Monument Valley, Arizona, and of the Maya of the Yucatan Peninsula, led him to formulate a number of principles for the use of symmetry classifications in pattern analysis. Brainerd published his ideas in the article "Symmetry in Primitive Conventional Design," which appeared in 1942 in *American Antiquity,* the leading journal of North American anthropology. Unfortunately, Brainerd's work was almost completely neglected, although it did attract the attention of Anna O. Shepherd, a geologist at the Carnegie Institution in Washington, D.C. In her monograph *The Symmetry of Abstract Design with Special Reference to Ceramic Decoration,* published in 1948, Shepherd discusses how certain symmetries predominate within a specific culture, and how changes within a culture can be identified by symmetry. Shepherd's work, like that of Brainerd, had to wait until the mid-1970s to be fully appreciated. Today, the anthropological significance of symmetry analysis is well established.

Rotation Symmetry

A figure has **rotation symmetry,** or **turn symmetry,** if the figure comes back to itself when it is rotated through a certain angle between 0° and 360°. The center of the turn is called the **center of rotation.** Some examples of figures with rotation symmetry are shown in Figure 12.17.

(a) 90° symmetry

(b) 72° symmetry

(c) 45° symmetry

(d) 180° symmetry

Figure 12.17
Figures with rotation symmetry

A figure with 90° rotation symmetry automatically has 180° and 270° rotation symmetry. For this reason it is customary to give just the *smallest* positive angle measure which turns the figure back to itself. The only exception is for figures composed of concentric circles, which turn back to themselves after *any* turn about their center. Such figures have **circular symmetry.**

EXAMPLE   12.9

Finding Angles of Rotation Symmetry

Determine the measures of the angles of rotation symmetry of these figures.

(a)   (b)   (c)   (d)

Solution

(a)   The smallest positive angle of rotation of a regular hexagon measures 60°, so the turn angles of all of the rotation symmetries are 60°, 120°, 180°, 240°, and 300°.

(b)   The only rotation angle measures 180°.

(c)   The smallest amount of turn of a regular 9-gon is 360°/9 = 40°, so the turn angles are 40°, 80°, 120°, 160°, 200°, 240°, 280°, and 320°.

(d)   This figure has circular symmetry.

Point Symmetry

A figure has **point symmetry** if it has 180° rotation symmetry about some point O as shown in Figure 12.18. This means that a half-turn takes the figure back to itself, and every point P of the figure has a corresponding point P' of the figure that is directly opposite the turn center O with $OP = OP'$.

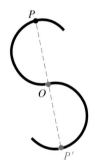

Figure 12.18
The letter S has point symmetry.

EXAMPLE   12.10

Identifying Point Symmetry

What letters, in uppercase block form, can be drawn to have point symmetry?

Solution

H, I, N, O, S, X, Z.

Patterns: Figures with Translation Symmetries

A **pattern** is a figure with a translation symmetry. To avoid considering the whole plane as a pattern, or even just some set of horizontal lines, it is assumed that there is some minimum positive distance required to translate a pattern back onto itself. Thus a pattern must be an infinite figure (why?) with motifs repeated infinitely often. Patterns are common on wallpaper, decorative brick walls, printed and woven fabrics, ribbons, and friezes (ceiling border decorations in older buildings). Enough of the pattern must be shown to make it clear how to extend the pattern indefinitely.

INTO THE CLASSROOM

Mathematics in Motion

The words "transformation" and "symmetry" often suggest advanced topics best left for gifted middle school students or postponed to the high school curriculum. Quite the opposite is true, however, since there are activities, games, artistic constructions, and problems—all exploring "motion geometry"—that are suitable for students at every grade level. If available, primary children can work with Miras, pattern blocks, and geoboards to create and investigate symmetric patterns. For example, each student can create a "half" figure with rubber bands on the upper half of a geoboard. Boards are then exchanged, and the student is challenged to complete a mirror image figure in the lower half of the geoboard. Older children could replace the geoboard with squared paper or dot paper, and investigate rotations and point symmetry as well as reflections and line symmetry. Dynamic geometry software also offers exciting possibilities for investigations in transformation geometry.

Here are three more ideas, suggesting how patterns and motions can be approached in the classroom.

- *Follow the leader.* Draw a line with a ruler down a blank sheet of paper. In pairs of students, the "leader" slowly draws a curve and simultaneously the "follower" draws the reflected curve across the line of symmetry. The students can interchange roles of leader and follower. To explore point symmetry, a prominent dot can be drawn at the center of the sheet. Some students, with a pencil in each hand, might like to attempt a solitaire game.

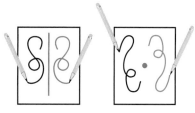

- *Punchy puzzles.* If the square shown at the far left is folded along the dashed lines, then the pattern of holes can be seen to be created with just one punch. How can a square of paper be folded and punched *one time only* to create the other hole patterns shown?

- *Stained glass window search.* Eight congruent isosceles right triangles, with four of each color, will form a square window. Three windows are shown here, but a reflection and rotation show that the first two windows are really the same. How many different window patterns are there, each with four panes of each of two colors? (You should be able to find 13 distinct patterns with no two patterns the same under either a rotation or a reflection.)

There are two types of patterns in the plane, **border patterns** and **wallpaper patterns.** As their names suggest, a border pattern has a repeated motif that has been translated in just one direction to create a strip design, whereas a wallpaper pattern has a motif translated in two non-parallel directions to create a wall design.

Border Patterns and Their Classification

Seven examples of border patterns from a variety of cultures are shown in Figure 12.19.

DRAGON AND PHOENIX CARPET, ASIA MINOR

GREEK FRET

MASONRY FRET, TEMPLE AT MITLA, MEXICO

POMPEIAN MOSAIC

GREEK FRET FROM A VASE

CHINESE ORNAMENT PAINTED ON PORCELAIN

MODERN RUG

Figure 12.19
Border patterns from around the world

Some border patterns may have other symmetries in addition to their translation symmetries. However, the possibilities are limited. For example, the only possible rotation symmetry is a half-turn. A careful study has shown that every border pattern has the same symmetries as one of the seven types shown in Figure 12.20.

The two-symbol name assigned by the International Crystallographic Union is shown at the left of each pattern in Figure 12.20. To find the classification symbol of any border, follow these steps.

First Symbol: *m,* if there is a vertical line of symmetry.
                        1, otherwise.

Second Symbol: *m,* if there is a horizontal line of symmetry.
                        g, if there is a glide reflection (but no horizontal line of symmetry)
                        2, if there is a half-turn symmetry (but no horizontal line of symmetry or glide symmetry)
                        1, otherwise.

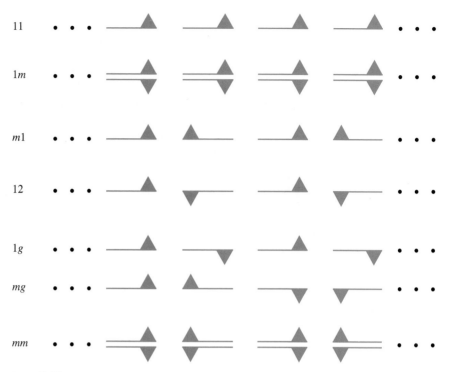

Figure 12.20
The seven symmetry types of border patterns

EXAMPLE 12.11

Classifying Border Patterns

Classify the symmetry type of the following border patterns by assigning the appropriate two-symbol notation.

(a)   **(b)**   **(c)**

Solution

It is helpful to view the patterns upside down, in a mirror, with a Mira, and so forth, since this will help you discover and verify what symmetry motions are present. A transparency copy of the pattern, if available, is an almost ideal tool to explore and classify patterns of symmetry.

(a) This border has both a vertical and horizontal line of reflection, so the symmetry is of type *mm*.

(b) There is no vertical symmetry line, so the first symbol is 1. There is no horizontal symmetry line but there is a glide symmetry, so the second symbol is *g*. Altogether, the symmetry is type 1*g*.

(c) There are no lines of reflection, nor is there a glide reflection symmetry. However, there is half-turn symmetry, so the symbol is 12.

Wallpaper Patterns

Two examples of wallpaper patterns are shown in Figure 12.21.

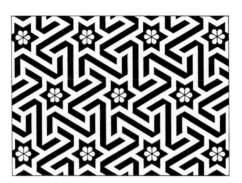 

Figure 12.21
Examples of wallpaper patterns

The Arabian pattern on the left has centers of both 60° and 120° rotational symmetry. This pattern also has a 180° rotational symmetry at the center of each of the Z-shaped black bars. The Egyptian pattern has centers of 90° rotational symmetry. It can be shown that 60°, 90°, 120°, and 180° are the only possible angle measures of rotational symmetry of any wallpaper pattern, a result called the *crystallographic restriction*. This and other restrictions limit the number of symmetry types to be found in a wallpaper pattern. Indeed, it has been shown that any wallpaper pattern is one of just 17 distinct types.

In the next section, several wallpaper patterns will be created by covering the plane with tiles.

HIGHLIGHT FROM HISTORY
Classifying Symmetry

In the years 1230 to 1354, the Moors constructed the magnificent Alhambra, a group of palatial buildings in the hills overlooking Granada. The walls and ceilings are decorated with striking patterns formed by regularly repeated motifs. Thirteen of the 17 types of plane symmetry can be found. It is thought that the Islamic ban on human and animal motifs gave rise to the creation of such intricate abstract geometric decoration.

Similarly, artisans from other world cultures have discovered and used repeated motif designs. Indeed numerous examples representing all 17 symmetry types have been identified. It took mathematical methods, however, to *prove* that no more than 17 patterns of plane symmetry exist.

The first step toward classification was made by the Russian crystallographer Evgraf Federov in 1891. His work was made more widely available in 1924 through the work of P. Niggli and George Pólya. Fedorov, as a crystallographer, was also interested in patterns of symmetry of space figures. He was able to show that 230 patterns of symmetry exist in three-dimensional space.

Other generalizations have been investigated. For example, colors may be used in a systematic way, such as the red-and-black coloration of a checkerboard. The two-colored patterns were classified by a mathematically knowledgeable textile worker in the 1930s. He discovered that there are 17 two-colored border patterns and 46 two-colored wallpaper patterns.

DID YOU KNOW?

Symmetries of Culture

*I*n this book we demonstrate how to use the geometric principles of crystallography to develop a descriptive classification of patterned design. Just as specific chemical assays permit objective analysis and comparison of objects, so too the description of designs by their geometric symmetries makes possible systematic study of their function and meaning within cultural contexts.

This particular type of analysis classifies the underlying structure of decorated forms; that is, the way the parts (elements, motifs, design units) are arranged in the whole design by the geometrical symmetries which repeat them. The classification

emphasizes the way the design elements are repeated, not the nature of the elements themselves. The symmetry classes which this method yields, also called motion classes, can be used to describe any design whose parts are repeated in a regular fashion. On most decorated forms such repeated design, properly called pattern, is either planar or can be flattened (e.g., unrolled), so that these repeated designs can be described either as bands or strips (one-dimensional infinite) or as overall patterns (two-dimensional infinite) in a plane.

These excerpts are from the introduction to *Symmetries of Culture: Theory and Practice of Plane Pattern Analysis,* by Dorothy K. Washburn and Donald W. Crow. Nearly every page of *Symmetries of Culture* is graced by beautiful photographs and drawings that illustrate the principles of

symmetry discovered and utilized by contemporary and historic cultures from around the world.

SOURCE: From *Symmetries of Culture: Theory and Practice of Plane Pattern Analysis* by Dorothy K. Washburn and Donald W. Crow, page ix. Copyright © 1988 by The University of Washington Press. Reprinted by permission.

PROBLEM SET 12.2

Understanding Concepts

1. Carefully trace each figure and draw all of its lines of symmetry.

    (a)   (b)   (c)   (d)   (e)

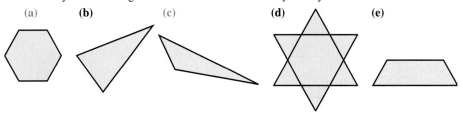

2. Carefully trace each figure and draw all of its lines of symmetry.

    (a)   (b)   (c)   (d)   (e)

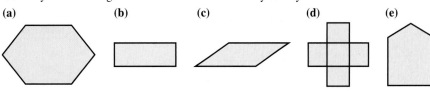

3. Draw polygons with the following symmetries, if possible.

   (a) One line of symmetry but no rotation symmetry.

   (b) Rotation symmetry but no reflection symmetry.

   (c) One line of symmetry and rotation symmetry.

4. Complete each figure to give it reflection symmetry about line *m*.

   (a)   (b)

   (c)   (d)

5. Complete each of these figures to give it point symmetry about point *O*.

   (a)   (b)

   (c)   (d)

6. Copy the following figures onto graph paper. Then complete each figure to give it reflection symmetry across the dashed line.

   (a)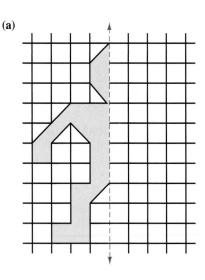

(b)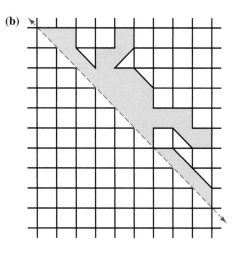

7. A valentine heart is easy to make symmetric: Cut it from a piece of construction paper folded once in half.

   (a) Suppose the paper is folded in half twice. Sketch the shape you obtain when you unfold the cut pattern.

   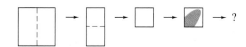

   (b) Describe how to make a 6-fold symmetric snowflake by folding and cutting a sheet of paper.

8. Describe all symmetries of each of the following company logos.

   (a)    (b)

(c)

(d)

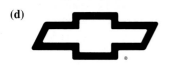

(e)

9. Describe the symmetries of the wheel covers shown.

(a)   (b)

(c)   (d)

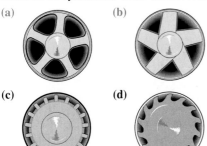

10. (a) Complete the figure shown to give it 90° rotation symmetry about point *O*.

•*O*

  (b) Repeat part (a), but giving the resulting figure 60° symmetry.

11. Identify the regular *n*-gons in each part that have the given symmetries.
  (a) There are exactly three lines of symmetry.
  (b) There are exactly four lines of symmetry.
  (c) There are exactly 19 lines of symmetry.
  (d) The polygon has 10° rotation symmetry.

  (e) The polygon has both 6° and 15° rotation symmetry.

12. List all the digits 0, 1, 2, 3, 4, 5, 6, 7, 8, 9 that have:
  (a) vertical reflection symmetry.
  (b) horizontal reflection symmetry.
  (c) vertical and horizontal reflection symmetry.
  (d) point symmetry.
  Write the digits in the most symmetric way you can.

13. Repeat problem 12, but for uppercase capital letters A, B, . . . , Z, written as symmetrically as possible.

14. Repeat problem 12 for the lowercase letters a, b, . . . , z, written as symmetrically as possible.

15. Describe all the symmetries of each border pattern, and classify it by the two-symbol notation used in crystallography.
  (a) . . . **A A A A A A** . . .
  (b) . . . **B B B B B B** . . .
  (c) . . . **N N N N N N** . . .

16. Describe all the symmetries of each border pattern, and give its two-symbol classification used by crystallographers.
  (a) . . . **H O H O H O** . . .
  (b) . . . **M W M W M W** . . .
  (c) . . . **9 6 9 6 9 6** . . .

Thinking Critically

17. A **palindrome** is a word, phrase, sentence, or numeral that is the same read either forward or backward. Examples are WOW, NOON, and TOOT.
  (a) If a word written in all capital letters has a vertical line of symmetry, why must it be a palindrome?
  (b) NOON does not have a line of symmetry. Find another palindrome with no line of symmetry.
  (c) What symmetry do you see in the word "pod"?

18. Describe what symmetries you see in these statements.
  (a) "Sums are not set as a test on Erasmus"
  (b) "Is it odd how asymmetrical
          is 'symmetry'?
      'Symmetry' is asymmetrical.
          How odd it is."
  (c) "Able was I ere I saw Elba." (attributed to Napoleon)

19. Carefully explain why no border pattern has the symbol "*m*2." (*Hint:* If a border pattern has a vertical line of symmetry and 180° rotation symmetry, what other symmetry must it also have?)

20. Give the two-symbol classification of each of the seven border patterns shown in Figure 12.19.

21. Classify the following Maori rafter patterns. The Maori, the indigenous people of New Zealand, used principles of symmetry to express their belief system. Disregard the color scheme when you classify the symmetry type of the pattern.

(a)   (b)

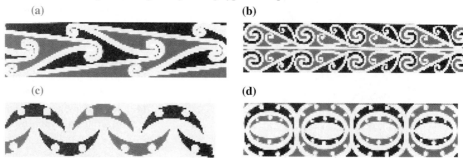

(c)   (d)

22. Classify the following Inca border patterns.

(a)

(b)

23. In each strip of rectangles shown below, a certain rigid motion applied to the left-most rectangle takes the figure to the next rectangle. Apply the same motion, but to the second rectangle, to draw the image of the second rectangle in the third rectangle. Continue to use the same motion to fill in the successive rectangles, and then classify the border pattern which is produced.

(a) | p | p | p | | | |

(b) | p | q | | | | |

(c) | p | d | | | | |

(d) | p | b | | | | |

24. The following border is of type 11. For each of the other six types of border symmetry, complete the pattern to give it the corresponding symmetry type by adding as little as possible.

| | | p | | | | p | | | | p | | |
| | | | | | | | | | | | | |

25. These drawings were made by George Pólya for his 1924 paper classifying the 17 wallpaper pattern types.

(a)   (b)

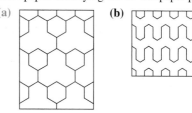

(c)

For each pattern, give

(i)   the number of directions of reflection symmetry.

(ii) the number of directions of glide symmetry.

(iii) the sizes of angles of rotation symmetry.

26. A three-dimensional figure has **bilateral symmetry** if there is a plane for which every point P of the figure has a mirror image P' of the figure on the opposite side of the plane. For example, a right prism with an equilateral triangular base has four planes of symmetry. Find the number of planes of symmetry of these space figures:

(a) a 1 by 2 by 3 rectangular prism.

(b) a $1 \times 2 \times 2$ rectangular prism.

(c) a cube.

(d) a square-based right regular pyramid (the apex is equidistant from the vertices of the base).

Making Connections

27. Describe what symmetries, or lack of symmetry, you see in the following forms and objects.

(a) a pair of scissors

(b) a tee shirt

(c) a dress shirt

(d) a golf club

(e) a tennis racket

(f) a crossword puzzle

28. Describe the symmetry you find in

   (a) an addition table.

   (b) a multiplication table.

   (c) Pascal's triangle.

29. The figures below result from a famous experiment in physics, the Chladni plate. A square metal plate is supported horizontally at its center, sprinkled with fine dry sand, and then vibrated at different frequencies. The sand migrates to the *nodal lines,* where there is no movement of the plate. In the dark regions between the nodal lines, the plate is in vertical vibrational motion.

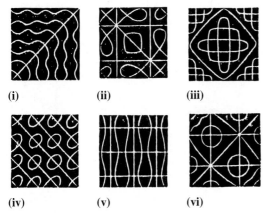

(i)   **(ii)**   **(iii)**

(iv)   **(v)**   **(vi)**

   (a) Describe the symmetries of each of the six Chladni plates shown.

   (b) The apparatus of the experiment has the symmetries of a square. Do the nodal lines always have the symmetries of a square, or can the vibrational pattern "break" square symmetry? (The Chladni plates shown were published in 1834 in *Of the Connexion of the Physical Sciences* by Mary Somerville, one of the great women mathematicians of the nineteenth century.)

Thinking Cooperatively

30. *Mu Torere.* The Maori people of New Zealand play the two-person game *mu torere* on a board shaped in a regular 8-pointed star. The points of the star are the *kawai,* and the center the *putahi.* Each player has 4 counters, say red beans and white beans, arranged initially so the red beans of one player are in the four upper positions and the opponent's white beans are in the lower positions. Players alternate moving one of their beans either into an empty adjacent *kawai* or into

(or out of) the *putahi.* A bean can move into the *putahi* only if the bean is adjacent to an opponent's bean. If not, the move is *tapu* (not allowed). The object of the game is to move your beans to a position where the opponent is blocked: any move of the opponent is *tapu.*

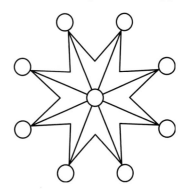

Work in pairs to make, play, and investigate *mu torere.*

   (a) Describe how to make a *mu torere* board by folding and cutting a sheet of paper.

   (b) What is the reason a bean cannot be moved to the center unless it is adjacent to an opponent's bean?

   (c) Play several games of *mu torere.* Describe the formation that wins the game.

   (d) Make a list of games that use a symmetric board. Describe the type of symmetry found in the board.

31. Cut out an interesting shape from cardboard or heavy paper. A border pattern can be drawn on a strip of paper by repeatedly tracing around the template.

Template   Border Pattern Drawn on Paper Strip

   (a) Use the shape to create seven border patterns, drawing one pattern of each symmetry type on a separate strip of paper. Do not write the symmetry symbol on the strip.

   (b) Pair up with another student. Match each of your strips to the corresponding strip of your partner having the same symmetry type.

Communicating

32. Write an illustrated short report entitled "Examples of Symmetry in _____" where the blank is filled in with your choice of topic. For example, you might choose "Sports," "Board Games," "Jewelry," "Musical Forms," "Navaho Blankets," "Native American Art," "Flowers." Use your imagination and draw on your outside interests and hobbies to be creative. You should include drawings, photocopies, pictures cut from discarded magazines, and so on. Be sure to identify and classify the type of symmetry found in each example.

33. Go on a symmetry hunt across campus, looking for striking examples of symmetry in buildings, decorative brickwork, sculptures, gardens, or wherever you may find it. Provide photos or drawings of three or four examples that you find especially interesting. Describe and classify the types of symmetry found in your examples. Include a border pattern and a wallpaper pattern.

 Using a Computer

34. Use dynamic geometry software to create a bilaterally symmetric "funny face." An example was shown in the Window on Technology in Section 12.1.

35. Use dynamic geometry software to create wheel cover patterns (see problem 9) having the required properties.
   (a) 45° rotational symmetry only
   (b) 60° rotational symmetry *and* bilateral symmetry

From State Student Assessments

36. (Minnesota, Grade 3)

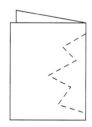

The piece of paper above is folded in half. Then a piece is cut out of it along the dotted lines. How will the piece look when it is unfolded?

37. (Minnesota, Grade 5)
Ken folded a piece of paper in half and then folded it in half again. He cut out a shape and threw it away. This is how the paper looked when he unfolded it.

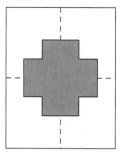

Which drawing below shows how his paper looked **before** he unfolded it?

For Review

38. Fill in the blanks in the two statements below.
   (a) A counterclockwise rotation of size 130° about point O followed by a counterclockwise rotation of 220° also about O is equivalent to a single counterclockwise rotation of _____° about O.
   (b) The net outcome of the two rotations described in (a) is equivalent to a clockwise rotation of _____° about O.

39. **(a)** Triangle ABC is equilateral with sides of length 2 units. Find the images of points A, B, and C under reflection across the three successive lines m_1, m_2, and m_3 shown. Label the respective image points A', B', and C'.

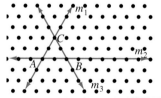

   (b) Describe the basic rigid motion that takes $\triangle ABC$ onto $\triangle A'B'C'$.

12.3   Tilings and Escher-like Designs

This section explores patterns in the plane which are formed by combining repeated shapes. The art of tiling has a history as old as civilization itself. In virtually every ancient culture the artisan's choices of color and shape were guided as strongly by aesthetic urges as by structural or functional requirements. Imaginative and intricate patterns decorated baskets, pottery, fabrics, wall coverings, and weapons. Some examples of ornamental patterns from different cultures are shown in Figure 12.22 on page 790.

In recent times the interest in tiling patterns has gone beyond their decorative value. For example, metallurgists and crystallographers wish to know how atoms can arrange themselves in a periodic array. Similarly, architects hope to know how simple structural components can be combined to create large building complexes, and computer engineers hope to integrate simple circuit patterns into powerful processors called neural networks. The mathematical analysis of tiling patterns is a response to these contemporary needs. At the same time the creation and exploration of tilings provides an inherently interesting setting for geometric discovery and problem solving in the elementary and middle school classroom. In particular, children enjoy learning how to create their own periodic drawings in the style of the pioneering Dutch artist M. C. Escher.

Tiles and Tilings

The precise meaning of a tile and a tiling is given in the following definition.

> **DEFINITION**   *Tiles and Tiling*
>
> A simple closed curve, together with its interior, is a **tile.** A set of tiles forms a **tiling** of a figure if the figure is completely covered by the tiles without overlapping any interior points of the tiles.

Since all points in the figure are covered there can be no gaps between tiles. Tilings are also known as **tessellations,** since the small square tiles in ancient Roman mosaics were called *tessella* in Latin.

Regular Tilings of the Plane

Each tiling shown in Figure 12.23 on page 791 is a **regular tiling:** the tiles are regular polygons of one shape and they are joined edge-to-edge.

Any arrangement of nonoverlapping polygonal tiles surrounding a common vertex is called the **vertex figure.** Thus, four squares form each vertex figure of the regular square tiling, and three regular hexagons form each vertex figure of the hexagonal tiling. The measures of the interior angles meeting at a vertex figure must add to 360°. For example, in the square tiling 90° + 90° + 90° + 90° = 360°.

Pre-Inca fabric from Peru

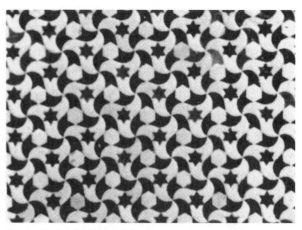

Detail of tiled wall in the Alhambra

Window of a fourteenth century mosque in Cairo

Mosaic floor of the fourteenth and fifteenth century in the Basilica of Saint Marks Cathedral, Venice

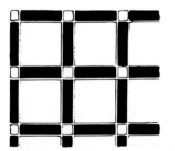

Tilings from Portugal, fifteenth to sixteenth centuries

Figure 12.22
Tiling patterns from varied cultures

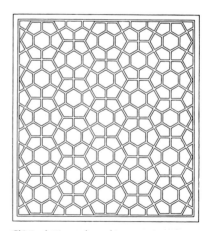

Chinese lattice work, used to support paper windows

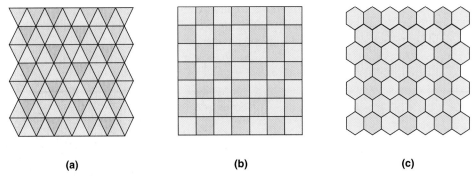

(a) **(b)** **(c)**

Figure 12.23
The three regular tilings of the plane

Suppose we attempt to form a vertex figure with regular pentagons as shown in Figure 12.24. The interior angles of a regular pentagon each measure $(5 - 2) \cdot 180°/5 = 108°$. Thus, three regular pentagons fill in $3 \cdot 108° = 324°$ and leave a $36°$ gap. On the other hand four regular pentagons create an overlap since $4 \cdot 108° = 432° > 360°$. Since a vertex figure cannot be formed, no tiling of the plane by regular pentagons is possible.

Three pentagons leave a gap.   Four pentagons overlap.

Figure 12.24
Regular pentagons do not tile the plane.

Similarly a regular polygon of seven or more sides has an interior angle larger than $120°$. Thus two such polygons leave a gap but three overlap. We have the following result.

> **THEOREM** *The Regular Tilings of the Plane*
> There are exactly three regular tilings of the plane: (a) by equilateral triangles, (b) by squares, and (c) by regular hexagons.

Semiregular Tilings of the Plane

A regular tiling uses congruent polygons of one type to tile the plane. What if regular polygons of several types are allowed? An edge-to-edge tiling of the plane with more than one type of regular polygon *and* with identical vertex figures is called a **semiregular tiling.** It is important to understand the restriction made about the vertex figures—*the same types of polygons must surround each vertex, and they must occur in the same order.* The two vertex figures in Figure 12.25 are not identical since the two triangles and the two hexagons on the left figure are adjacent but on the right side the triangles and the hexagons alternate with one another.

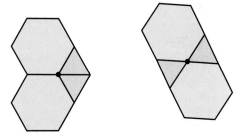

Figure 12.25
There are two distinct types of vertex figures formed by two equilateral triangles and two regular hexagons.

To see if the vertex figures in Figure 12.25 can be extended to form a semiregular tiling we must check to see if the pattern can be completed to make *all* of the vertex figures match the one shown. It is soon discovered that the pattern with adjacent triangles cannot be extended (try it!). On the other hand, the vertex figure of alternating triangles and hexagons extends to a semiregular tiling. You should be able to find it in Figure 12.26.

It can be shown that there are 18 ways to form a vertex figure with regular polygons of two or more types. Of these, eight extend to a semiregular tiling, shown in Figure 12.26.

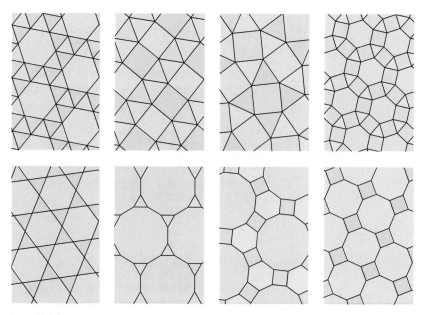

Figure 12.26
The eight semiregular tilings

HIGHLIGHT FROM HISTORY
Johannes Kepler and Tiling Patterns

*T*he astronomer Johannes Kepler (1571–1630) is celebrated in scientific history for his identification of the elliptical shape of the orbits of the planets about the sun. Less known is Kepler's contribution to the theory of tiling. Here are some drawings from Kepler's book *Harmonice Mundi,* which he published in 1619.

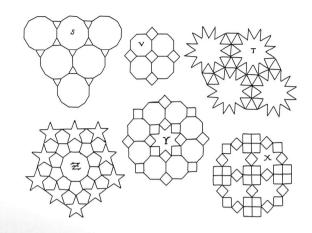

SOURCE: Illustration from *Tilings and Patterns* by Branko Grünbaum and G. C. Shephard. Copyright © 1987 by W. H. Freeman and Company. Reprinted by permission.

Tilings with Irregular Polygons

In the following example it is helpful to cut tile patterns from cardboard or heavy card stock. You can then trace around them to form, if possible, a tiling of the plane. Better yet, create and explore tilings with dynamic geometry software.

EXAMPLE   12.12

Exploring Tilings with Irregular Polygons

Which of the polygons below tile the plane?

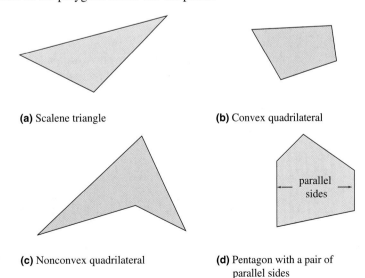

(a) Scalene triangle

(b) Convex quadrilateral

(c) Nonconvex quadrilateral

(d) Pentagon with a pair of parallel sides

Solution

(a) Two triangles of identical size and shape can be joined along a corresponding edge to form a parallelogram. Since it is evident that parallelograms tile the plane, it follows that *any triangle will tile the plane.*

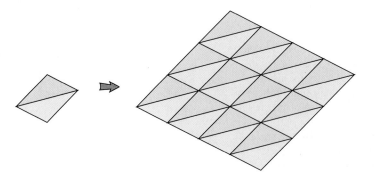

(b) (c) As illustrated below, any quadrilateral will tile the plane. A 180° turn about the midpoint of a side rotates the quadrilateral from one position to an adjacent position. Notice that each vertex of the tiling is surrounded by angles congruent to the four angles of the quadrilateral, whose measures add up to 360°.

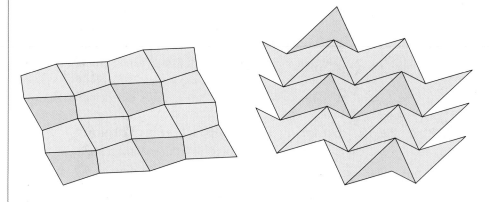

(d) A pentagonal tile with two parallel sides can always tile the plane. If the parallel edges are congruent the tiling will be edge-to-edge.

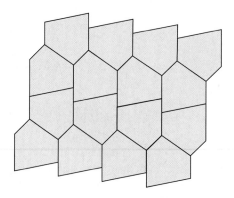

Much like the quadrilateral tiling shown on the previous page, a hexagon will tile the plane if it has a pair of opposite sides which are parallel and of the same length (see problem 10). If all three pairs of opposite sides are congruent and parallel, it is not even necessary to rotate the tile from one position to any other (see problem 9). It has been shown that no convex polygon with seven or more sides can tile the plane. The following theorem summarizes these discoveries.

> **THEOREM**   *Tiling the Plane with Congruent Polygonal Tiles*
> The plane can be tiled by:
>
> - any triangular tile;
> - any quadrangular tile, convex or not;
> - certain pentagonal tiles (for example, those with two parallel sides);
> - certain hexagonal tiles (for example, those with two opposite parallel sides of the same length).
>
> The plane cannot be tiled by any convex tile with seven or more sides.

Quadrilateral + Quadrilateral = Parallelogram?

Fold a sheet of paper in half, and then use scissors to cut a pair of congruent convex quadrilaterals. Cut one of the quadrilaterals along one of the diagonals, and cut the second quadrilateral along

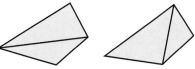

the other diagonal. Show that the four triangles can be arranged to form a parallelogram. (This brainteaser of V. Proizvolov appeared in *Quantum, The Student Magazine of Math and Science,* September/October 1992, p. 31.)

Although no convex polygon of seven or more sides can tile the plane, there are many interesting examples of nonconvex polygons that tile. Figure 12.27 shows a striking example of a spiral tiling by 9-gons (nonagons) created by Heinz Voderberg in 1936.

Figure 12.27
Heinz Voderberg's spiral tiling with nonagons

Tilings of Escher Type

The Dutch artist Maurits Cornelius Escher (1898–1972) has created a large number of artistic tilings. His designs have great appeal to artists and the general public, and have also captured the interest of professional geometers. Escher's graphic work is most often based on modifications of known tiling patterns. However, he also discovered new principles of pattern formation which mathematicians had overlooked.

To see how Escher created his print of the birds on the left side of Figure 12.28, we begin by identifying the underlying grid of parallelograms shown on the right.

Figure 12.28
M. C. Escher's birds and its grid of parallelograms

The concept of a translation, discussed in Section 12.1 of this chapter, helps us understand how the parallelogram has been modified to become the bird-shaped motif of the tiling. First, imagine replacing the upper edge of the parallelogram with the V-shape separating the wings. The V-shape is then translated to replace the opposite edge of the parallelogram. Similarly, one of the two remaining straight edges of the parallelogram is modified to form the leading edge of the forward wing, and this curve is then translated to replace the opposite edge of the parallelogram. Finally, the outline is filled in with details such as feathers and an eye to complete the bird motif. The steps modifying the parallelogram into the bird motif are shown in Figure 12.29.

Figure 12.29
Modifying a parallelogram with two translations

Similar procedures will transform any polygonal tiling to an Escher-like tiling. For example, sixth grade teacher Nancy Putnam used translations to modify each of three pairs of opposite parallel congruent sides of hexagon *ABCDEF*. Her whale tiling is shown in Figure 12.30.

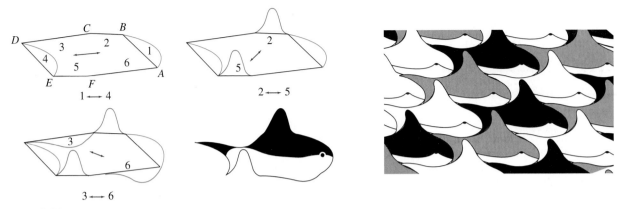

Figure 12.30

Sixth grade teacher Nancy Putnam modified a hexagon with opposite parallel congruent sides to create an Escher-type tiling.

Rotations can also be used to create **Escher-like designs** with interesting symmetries. Here is an example of how a lizard tile can be created by modifying a regular hexagon *ABCDEF*. Side $\overline{AB}$ is first modified and then rotated about vertex *B* to modify side $\overline{BC}$. The remaining two pairs of sides are modified similarly, resulting in the outline of the lizard tile. The steps used to form the tile and the resulting tiling are shown in Figure 12.31.

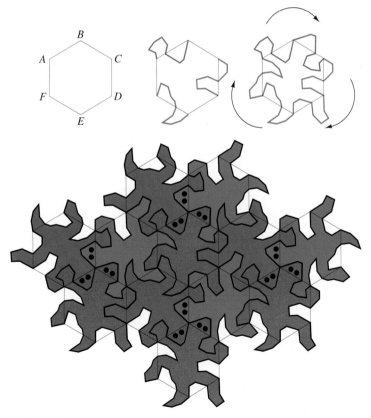

Figure 12.31

Modifying a regular hexagon with rotations to create a lizard tiling

DID YOU KNOW?

Escher's Method of Artistic Tilings

"How did he do it?"

The work of M. C. Escher provokes that irrepressible question. A recurring theme as well as a device in his work from 1937 onward was, in his words, the "regular division of the plane." We see the jigsaw puzzle-like interlocking of birds, fish, lizards, or other creatures in his work; their rigid paving is usually just a fragment, a pause in a transition from two to three dimensions, a springboard from lockstep order to freedom. Escher confesses that the subject is for him a passion.

In his 1958 book *Regelmatige Vlakverdeling (Regular Division of the Plane)*, he tells us much about why he uses regular division, explains some of the geometric elements of regular division, addresses the central question of figure and ground, and leads us through the development of a metamorphosis of form. But when we persist in asking "How did he do it?"—that is, how did he make those interlocking creatures—we do not find answers. We do find a few tantalizing hints in the book that Escher did study some technical papers and that he worked out his own theory:

> At first I had no idea at all of the possibility of systematically building up my figures. I did not know any "ground rules" and tried, almost without knowing what I was doing,

to fit together congruent shapes that I attempted to give the form of animals. Gradually, designing new motifs became easier as a result of my study of literature on the subject, as far as this was possible for someone untrained in mathematics, and especially through the formulation of my own layman's theory, which forced me to think through the possibilities. It remains an extremely absorbing activity, a real mania to which I have become addicted, and from which I sometimes find it hard to tear myself away.

Professor Schattschneider's book is an account of Escher's discovery of the world of geometry and how he used his knowledge to create his intriguing interlocking figures.

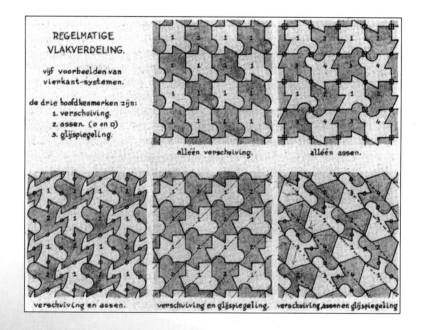

OPERATIVE INVESTIGATION

Creating an Escher-like Design

Materials Needed

1. Note cards, 3″ × 5″ (or other cardstock)
2. Scissors
3. Pencils and colored markers
4. Blank sheets of paper

Directions

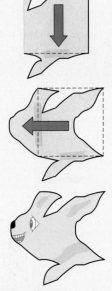

Step 1. Cut a small (say 2 1/2″ by 3″) rectangle from a note card or cardstock.

Step 2. Cut out one side of the rectangle. Translate the cutout piece to the opposite side and tape it in place.

Step 3. Repeat Step 2 for the remaining two parallel sides of the rectangle, as shown.

Step 4. Do an "ink blot" test. Is your shape a frog, a bird, a face, a _____? Brainstorm with a partner. It may help to rotate your shape or flip it over. Add eyes, mouth, nose, ears, feet, beaks, horns, clothing, scales, fur, and other imaginative details to make your tiling template recognizable and interesting.

Step 5. Trace around the template to create your Escher-like design on a blank sheet of paper. Use colored markers to fill in the details and make your design attractive.

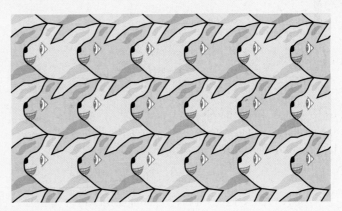

Extensions

Instead of a rectangle, start with any parallelogram and follow the directions given above. It is also possible to adapt this method to create templates based on other tilings of the plane. Several suggestions are described in problems 11–14 of Problem Set 12.3.

PROBLEM SET 12.3

Understanding Concepts

1. On dot paper arranged in a square grid show that the given shape will tile the plane.

    (a)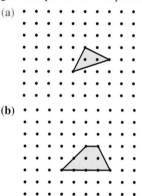

    (b)

2. On "isometric" dot paper (arranged in a grid of equilateral triangles) show that the given shape will tile the plane.

    (a)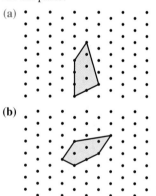

    (b)

3. Branko Grünbaum and G. C. Shephard (*Tilings and Patterns*, W. H. Freeman and Co., 1987) discovered the tiling shown here in the children's coloring book *Altair Design* (E. Holiday, London: Pantheon, 1970).

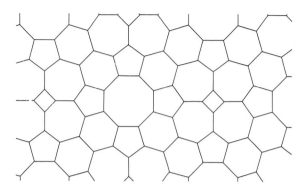

   (a) What kinds of polygons appear?

   (b) Grünbaum and Shephard claim this is a "fake" tiling by regular polygons. Explain why.

4. A vertex figure of regular polygons is shown.

   (a) Find the angle measures of each polygon and directly verify that they add up to 360°.

   (b) Explain why the vertex figure does not extend to form a semiregular tiling. [*Suggestion:* Attempt to form the vertex figure at the other two vertices of the triangle.]

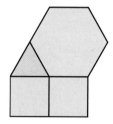

5. Consider the vertex figure formed by a square, a regular pentagon, and a regular 20-gon. Find the measures of the interior angle of each polygon and show that these three measures add up to 360°.

6. Some "letters" of the alphabet will tile the plane. For each letter shown, create an interesting tiling on square dot paper. Look for different patterns which use the same tile.

    (a)   (b)   (c)   (d)   (e)

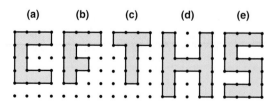

7. A tetromino is a tile formed by joining four congruent squares edge to edge, where adjacent squares must share a common edge. Two tetrominoes and two non-tetrominoes are shown below.

Two tetrominoes   Two non-tetrominoes

(a) There are five noncongruent tetrominoes altogether. Find the other three.

(b) Which tetrominoes tile the plane, using unlimited congruent copies of one tetromino?

(c) The five noncongruent tetrominoes have a total area of 20 square units. Can the five shapes tile a 4 by 5 rectangle? [*Suggestion:* Imagine that the rectangle is colored in a red and black checkerboard pattern of unit squares. How many red and how many black squares are covered by each tetromino?]

---

8. Tiles formed by joining five congruent squares edge-to-edge are called **pentominoes.** The twelve pentominoes are shown in problem 23 of Problem Set 10.3. Use square paper (or dot paper) to decide which pentominoes tile the plane.

9. Fold a 3″ by 5″ note card in half, and then use scissors to cut (simultaneously) two general quadrilaterals. Rotate one quadrilateral a half-turn and tape the two quadrilaterals together along their corresponding edges to form a hexagonal tile.

Fold   Cut quadrilaterals   Rotate and tape

Show, using the paper model as a template, that the hexagon tiles the plane. Must the tile be rotated?

10. Cut a hexagon *ABCDEF* from a rectangular piece of card stock, using a ruler to ensure that the opposite sides $\overline{AB}$ and $\overline{DE}$ have the same length. No restriction is placed on the position of points *C* or *F*. Use the paper template to illustrate that a hexagon with a congruent and parallel pair of opposite sides can tile the plane. [*Suggestion:* Half-turns of the template will be required.]

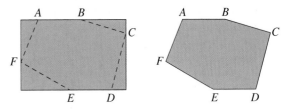

Thinking Critically

11. Construct a paper hexagonal tile with each pair of opposite sides parallel and congruent. The template can be cut from a note card following the method described in problem 9. Make cutouts on three adjacent sides. Translate each cutout to the opposite side and tape along the corresponding edges to form a template (see the instructions in the Cooperative Investigation *Creating an Escher-like Design*). Create a design with your template, adding details such as eyes, mouths, and so forth, to give added interest to your design.

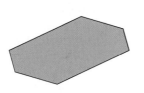 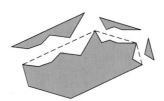 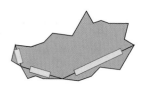

12. Cut an accurate square from a note card. Make cutouts on opposite sides. Rotate each cutout 90° and tape as shown. Use the paper template to create an Escher-like design.

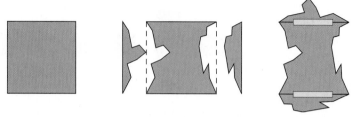

13. Cut an arbitrary triangle from a note card, and lightly fold (do not make a heavy crease) one vertex to another to determine the midpoint of the side between the vertices. The side can be modified by making a cutout on one side of the midpoint, rotating it 180° about the midpoint, and taping it in place. The steps to modify one side of a triangle are shown below.

Midpoint of side

Modify the remaining two sides of the triangle, and use the resulting template to create an Escher-like design.

14. Cut a convex quadrilateral from a note card. Make midpoint modifications, as described in problem 13, to each of the four sides. Use the resulting template to create an Escher-like design.

15. For any integer *n, n* ≥ 3, show that there is some *n*-gon that tiles the plane. [*Suggestion:* Consider the midpoint modification described in problems 13 and 14.]

16. Suppose a vertex figure of regular polygons includes a regular octagon. Show that the figure must include another octagon and a square.

17. An equilateral triangle and a parallelogram are each examples of "reptiles," short for "repeating tile." In each case copies of the tile can be arranged to form its own similar shape.

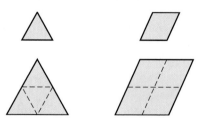

Use square dot paper to show that each of these shapes is a "reptile."

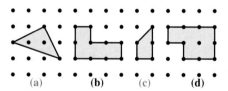

(a)   (b)   (c)   (d)

18. A hexiamond is formed from six congruent equilateral triangles. There are 12 different hexiamonds, including the Sphinx, Chevron, and Lobster shown below. Find the remaining nine hexiamonds and see if you can match their shape to their names: Hexagon, Crook, Crown, Hook, Snake, Yacht, Bar, Signpost, Butterfly.

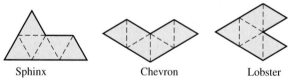

Sphinx   Chevron   Lobster

19. (a) Show that the Sphinx is a reptile. (See problems 17 and 18 for the definition of a reptile and a diagram of the Sphinx.)

(b) It requires four copies of the Sphinx to form a second generation Sphinx. How many copies of the original Sphinx are required to form a third generation Sphinx? Explain your reasoning and provide a sketch.

(c) Explain why any reptile provides a tiling of the plane.

Thinking Cooperatively

20. The seven **tangram** pieces originated in ancient China. As shown below, there are five triangles, a square, and a parallelogram. A serviceable set can be cut from a square of cardboard (see Section 11.1), although plastic and wooden sets are easy to buy or make.

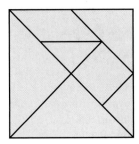

(a) The most common activity is the Chinese *tangram puzzle.* A figure is shown in outline, and the challenge is to tile the figure using *all* seven tangram pieces. Form the following animals (taken from the Multicultural Poster Set, National Council of Teachers of Mathematics, 1984), working in pairs.

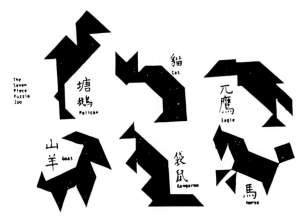

(b) Use the seven tangram pieces to form other recognizable shapes. Use a marker to draw only the outline. Then trade the tangram puzzles between groups and solve the puzzles.

21. Work in groups to find all of the different convex figures which can be tiled by tangrams (see problem 20). Be sure to use all seven tangram pieces in each of the convex figures. There are 13 noncongruent figures in all, and most of the figures can be tiled in several ways.

⌨ Using a Computer

22. *The Geometer's Sketchpad* dynamic geometry software includes scripts that enable the user to quickly construct a variety of polygons. In particular, the regular polygons of sides 3, 4, 5, 6, and 8 are easily constructed by selecting two points to be adjacent vertices. [Details are found in the *User Guide and Reference Manual* that accompanies the software; also see Appendix D.]

(a) Use the software to create examples of some of the semiregular tilings of the plane.

(b) Write a brief report that shows your tiling examples and discusses what steps you discovered to make your tilings.

23. Use dynamic geometry software to create an Escher-like design based on the tiling of the plane by equilateral triangles, following these steps. Begin by constructing an equilateral triangle. Next, modify one side of the triangle and rotate it 60° about an endpoint vertex to modify a second side of the triangle. Alter the remaining side of the triangle by constructing the midpoint and doing a midpoint modification (see problem 13 and the figure below). Hide unwanted lines and add decorations to complete the tile. To use the tile to make your design, first use rotations to form a six-tile arrangement as shown below. Translations of the six-tile arrangement will complete your design.

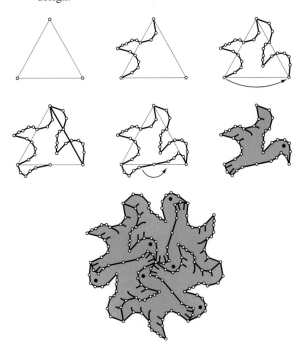

For Review

24. What rule is used to separate the letters of the alphabet in the following arrangement?

A   EF HI KLMN   T VWXYZ
———————————————————————————————————
   BCD   G   J   OPQRS U

25. Find four points, *A*, *B*, *C*, *D*, in the plane that satisfy these conditions: $\overline{AD} \perp \overline{BC}$, $\overline{CD} \perp \overline{AB}$, $\overline{AC} \perp \overline{BD}$.

26. Show how to draw this closed polygonal curve in such a way that no side is retraced and the pencil is not lifted until the drawing is completed.

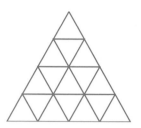

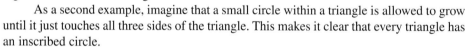

EPILOGUE   The Dynamical View of Geometry

Geometry in Euclid's time presented a static view of shape, as if only still pictures of figures were to be seen in the mind's eye. The concept of a geometric transformation, introduced in the latter part of the nineteenth century, has provided a dynamic view of geometry. Figures are allowed, and even invited, to move and perhaps even change size. The mind's eye sees an animated world of shapes in action.

The dynamic viewpoint is a useful tool for problem solving and discovery. Here's an example: *Show that any finite set of points in the plane is contained inside (or on) some circle of smallest radius.* To see why, first imagine surrounding the points with a very large circle. Now let the circle shrink around the set of points as tightly as possible, allowing the center of the moving circle to move as well.

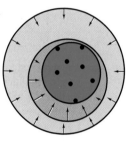

As a second example, imagine that a small circle within a triangle is allowed to grow until it just touches all three sides of the triangle. This makes it clear that every triangle has an inscribed circle.

Recent developments in computer graphics, both hardware and software, provide new opportunities to explore which properties change, and which remain invariant, as a figure is altered.

CHAPTER 12 SUMMARY

Key Concepts

1. **Rigid Motions and Similarity Transformations**
   (a) A **transformation of the plane** is a one-to-one correspondence of the points of the plane. If point *P* corresponds to point *P'*, *P'* is the **image** of *P* and *P* is the **preimage** of *P'*.
   (b) A **rigid motion,** also called an **isometry,** is a transformation of the plane that preserves distance: $PQ = P'Q'$ for all points *P*, *Q* and corresponding image points *P'*, *Q'*.
   (c) There are four **basic rigid motions: translations, rotations, reflections,** and **glide reflections.** These are also called **slides, turns, flips,** and **glides.**
   (d) The **identity transformation** is the rigid motion for which each point corresponds to itself: $P = P'$ for all points *P*.

(e) Two transformations are **equivalent** if both transformations take each point P to the same image point P'.

(f) A sequence of two reflections across parallel lines is equivalent to a translation. A sequence of two reflections across intersecting lines is equivalent to a rotation.

(g) A sequence of three reflections across parallel or concurrent lines is equivalent to a reflection. Otherwise a sequence of three reflections is equivalent to a glide reflection.

(h) Every rigid motion is equivalent to one of the basic motions: a translation, a rotation, a reflection, or a glide reflection.

(i) Two figures are **congruent** if, and only if, one figure is the image of the other under a rigid motion.

(j) A **dilation**, or **size transformation**, with **center O scale factor** k takes point P, $P \neq O$ to the point P' on ray $\overrightarrow{OP}$ for which $OP' = k \cdot OP$, and leaves O fixed.

(k) A dilation multiplies all distances by the scale factor k, so $P'Q' = k \cdot PQ$ for all P, Q.

(l) A **similarity transformation** is a sequence of dilations and rigid motions.

(m) Two figures are **similar** if, and only if, there is a similarity transformation that takes one figure onto the other.

2. Patterns and Symmetries

(a) A **symmetry** of a figure is a rigid motion which takes every point of the figure to an image point that is also a point of the figure.

(b) A figure has **reflection symmetry** if reflection across some line—called a **line of symmetry**—takes a figure onto itself.

(c) A figure has **rotation symmetry** if rotation about some center O takes the figure to itself.

(d) A figure has **point symmetry** about point O if it has half-turn ($180°$) symmetry about O.

(e) A **pattern** is a plane figure with translation symmetries, including some translation of smallest positive distance.

(f) A pattern with translations in one direction only is a **border pattern.** There are seven symmetry types of border patterns.

(g) A pattern with translations in more than one direction is a **wallpaper pattern.** There are 17 symmetry types of wallpaper patterns.

(h) The **crystallographic restriction:** Any rotation symmetry of a wallpaper has size $60°$, $90°$, $120°$, or $180°$.

3. Tilings and Escher-like Designs

(a) A **tile** is a simple closed curve in the plane together with its interior. A covering of a figure with tiles, with neither gaps nor overlaps, is a **tiling** of the figure.

(b) There are three **regular tilings** of the plane—by equilateral triangles, squares, and regular hexagons—and eight **semiregular tilings.**

(c) Arbitrary triangles and quadrilaterals, and certain pentagons and hexagons, tile the plane. No convex n-gon with $n \geq 7$ tiles the plane.

(d) Escher-like designs are created by modifying the straight sides of a polygonal tile to assume more general curves, following rules that preserve the tiling property of the resulting shape.

Vocabulary and Notation

Section 12.1

Transformation of the plane
Preimage, image
Rigid motion, or isometry
Basic rigid motion: translation (slide), rotation (turn),
    reflection (flip), glide reflection (glide)
Slide arrow (or translation vector)
Center of rotation
Turn angle, turn arrow
Line of reflection (mirror line)
Orientation reversing/preserving transformation
Equivalent transformations
Identity transformation
Congruent figures, $F \cong G$
Dilation, or size transformation
    Center, O
    Scale factor k ($0 < k < 1$: contraction,
        $k > 1$: expansion)
Similarity transformation
Similar figures

Section 12.2

Symmetry of a figure
Reflection symmetry (line symmetry, bilateral
    symmetry)
    Line of symmetry (mirror line)
    Rotation symmetry (turn symmetry)
Center of rotation
Circular symmetry
Point symmetry
Pattern
    Border pattern
    Wallpaper pattern

Section 12.3

Tile
Tiling, or tessellation
Regular tiling of the plane
Vertex figure
Semiregular tiling of the plane
Escher-like design

CHAPTER REVIEW EXERCISES

Section 12.1

1. Draw the image of *ABCDE* under the translation that takes *A* to *A'*.

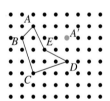

2. Determine the center and turn angle of the rotation that takes *A* to *A'* and *B* to *B'*. Use a protractor, Mira, ruler, or whatever drawing tools you wish.

3. Describe the basic rigid motion that takes *A*, *B*, *C* to *A'*, *B'*, *C'*. Use any drawing tools you wish.

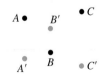

4. A glide reflection has a horizontal line *l* as its line of reflection and translates 4 inches to the right. Draw three lines of reflection—m_1, m_2, and m_3—so that

successive reflections across m_1, m_2, and m_3 result in a motion equivalent to the glide reflection.

5. Sketch the image of the square *ABCD* under each of these transformations:
    (a) the dilation centered at *O* with scale factor 2
    (b) the dilation centered at *A* with scale factor 1/3.

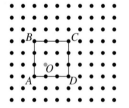

6. Describe the similarity transformation that takes the square *ABCD* to the square *JKLM*, where *J*, *K*, *L*, and *M* are the midpoints of square *ABCD* as shown.

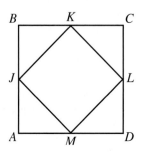

Section 12.2

7. The geometric forms shown are from African art. How many lines of symmetry does each figure have?

(a)

(b)

(c)

(d)

(e)

(f)

8. For each of the figures shown in problem 7, give all of the angles of rotation symmetry.

9. Describe the symmetries of each of these border patterns.

(a)

FRENCH RENAISSANCE ORNAMENT FROM CASKET

(b)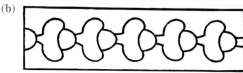

STAINED GLASS, CATHEDRAL OF BOURGES

Section 12.3

10. Four regular polygons form a vertex figure in a tiling of the plane. Three of the polygons are a triangle, a square, and a hexagon. What is the fourth polygon?

11. Draw two different vertex figures which each incorporate three equilateral triangles and two squares.

12. Show that the shape below will tile the plane.

CHAPTER TEST

1. A translation takes points A, B, C to A′, B′, C′. Show the location of C′ and B.

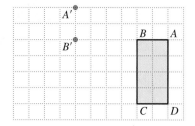

2. Copy the rectangle ABCD and points A′ and B′ onto squared paper.
   (a) Show that A′ and B′ are the image of A and B under a rotation. Give the center of rotation and the size of the rotation angle.
   (b) Draw the image rectangle A′B′C′D′.

3. Trace the drawing of ∠A. Suppose A′ is the image of A under a reflection. Explain how to draw the image of ∠A under the reflection.

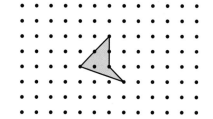

4. Find the line of reflection and slide arrow of the glide reflection that takes rectangle ABCD onto A′B′C′D′.

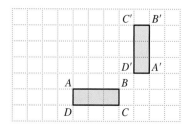

5. Draw two parallel lines, m_1 and m_2, so that the sequence of reflections across m_1 and m_2 will map point P to point P'.

6. Draw two lines, l_1 and l_2, so that a sequence of reflections across l_1 and l_2 will rotate point Q to point Q' about the turn center O.

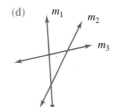

7. Three lines—m_1, m_2, and m_3 are shown in each part. What type of rigid motion is equivalent to a sequence of reflections across m_1, m_2, and m_3?

(a)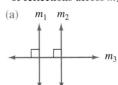

(b) Parallel lines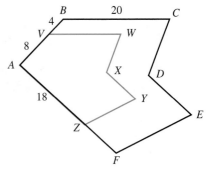

(c)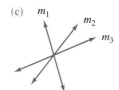

(d)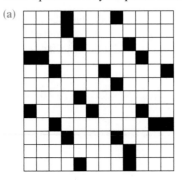

8. A dilation has taken $ABCDEF$ onto $AVWXYZ$ as shown, where $AV = 8$, $VB = 4$, $BC = 20$, and $AZ = 18$.

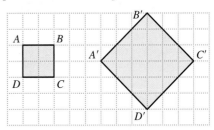

(a) What is the center of the dilation?
(b) What is the scale factor?
(c) What is the distance VW?
(d) What is the distance ZF?

9. Describe a similarity transformation that takes the square $ABCD$ onto the square $A'B'C'D'$.

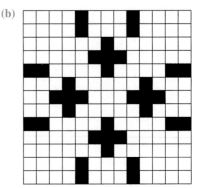

10. Draw all of the lines of symmetry for these figures.

(a)   (b)   (c)

11. What is the size of the smallest positive angle of rotation symmetry in each figure shown in problem 10?

12. Two blank crossword puzzles are shown. What symmetries are found in the grid of black and white squares used by the puzzle maker?

(a)   (b)

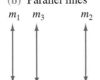

13. List the symmetries found in each of the border patterns shown.

(a)

INDIAN PAINTED LACQUER WORK

(b)

MALTESE LACE

(c)

ANCIENT GREEK SCROLL BORDER

(d)

ITALIAN DAMASK OF THE RENAISSANCE

14. Which of the following shapes will tile the plane?

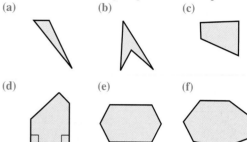

(a)   (b)   (c)

(d)   (e)   (f)

15. Sketch a portion of the semiregular tiling of the plane which uses square and octagonal tiles with a common side length.

16. In the Escher tiling shown, what type of rigid motion
 (a) takes figure A onto figure B?
 (b) takes figure B onto figure C?

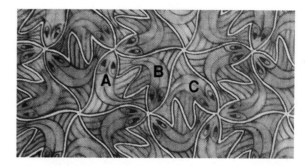

CHAPTER

13

Congruence, Constructions, and Similarity

13.1   Congruent Triangles
13.2   Constructing Geometric Figures
13.3   Similar Triangles

HANDS ON

Exploring Toothpick Triangles

Materials Needed

Toothpicks of equal length (20 per person)

Directions

Three toothpicks, placed end-to-end, form a triangle in one way—an equilateral triangle. Four toothpicks do not form a triangle. Five and six toothpicks each form just one triangle. Two different (that is, noncongruent) triangles can be formed with seven toothpicks.

Triangles	△	△	△	▷
Number of toothpicks, n	3	4	5	6	7
Number of triangles, $T(n)$	1	0	1	1	2

Explore how many different triangles you can form with 8, 9, 10, 11, or 12 toothpicks. Extend the table above to include your results.

Questions for Consideration

1. How many isosceles toothpick triangles are there for which the two sides of equal length each use four toothpicks?

2. One side of a toothpick triangle uses three toothpicks and a second side uses five toothpicks. What are the possible numbers of toothpicks in the third side?

3. If two sides of a toothpick triangle together use 11 toothpicks, what is the largest number of toothpicks that can be used in the third side?

4. Suppose toothpicks form a triangle with p, q, and r toothpicks on its three sides. What can you say about the integer r in terms of the numbers p and q?

5. In your table of the number of triangles, suppose $T(n)$ is the number of different toothpick triangles formed from n toothpicks. For n odd, compare $T(n)$ to $T(n + 3)$. For example, compare $T(3)$ to $T(6)$, and compare $T(5)$ to $T(8)$. What pattern do you observe?

CONNECTIONS   Creating and Relating Geometric Figures

This chapter investigates three topics—congruent triangles, geometric constructions, and similar triangles.

Two triangles are **congruent** if they have the same size and shape. In Section 13.1, we investigate what measurements for two triangles are sufficient to guarantee they are congruent to one another. A constructive approach is taken, using the traditional tools of the compass and straightedge introduced by Euclid.

Additional constructions using compass and straightedge are taken up in Section 13.2. This section also introduces new tools and methods of construction, including paper-folding, reflective drawing tools such as the Mira® and Image Reflector™, and geometry software for the computer.

The concluding Section 13.3 investigates **similar triangles**—triangles with the same shape but not necessarily the same size.

The topics of this chapter—congruence, constructions, and similarity—have increasingly many connections to our modern technological world. For example, a company strives to manufacture a product that is uniform in quality, performance, and reliability—each item should replicate the same design. Modern industry's ability to produce congruence makes it possible to manufacture affordable automobiles, computers, household appliances, and other sophisticated devices. Congruence and similarity are also a part of our personal lives. Some familiar examples related to congruence are cookie cutters, rubber stamps, and clothing patterns. Examples in daily life dependent on similarity are maps, scale models, floor plans, and the enlargement feature of a photocopy machine.

13.1   Congruent Triangles

Before considering triangles, it is helpful to investigate line segments. Given two line segments, it is enough to know their lengths to decide if they are congruent: two line segments are congruent if, and only if, they have the same length. We can also take a constructive approach. Construction 1 shows how a compass and straightedge are used to construct a line segment that is congruent to a given segment.

Construct a Congruent Line Segment

Construction 1

Construct a line segment that is congruent to a given line segment $\overline{AB}$.   A ———— B

Procedure

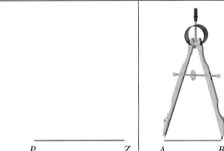

P ———— Z	A ———— B	P ——/Q— Z
Step 1. Draw segment $\overline{PZ}$, longer than AB.	**Step 2**. Put the point of the compass at A, and the pencil point on B.	**Step 3**. Without changing the opening of the compass, move the point of the compass to P and draw a circular arc. The point of intersection determines the point Q for which $\overline{PQ} \cong \overline{AB}$.

With this prolog, the investigation of congruent triangles will consider these questions:

- What measurements of a triangle completely describe its size and shape?
- Given two triangles, what subsets of measurements are sufficient to decide if the triangles are congruent to one another?
- Given certain measurements of a triangle ABC, how can a compass and straightedge be used to construct a triangle $\triangle PQR$ that is congruent to $\triangle ABC$?

The size and shape of a triangle are described completely if we specify the **six parts of a triangle,** namely the three sides $\overline{AB}$, $\overline{BC}$, $\overline{CA}$ and the three angles $\angle A$, $\angle B$, and $\angle C$. A second triangle, *PQR*, is congruent to triangle *ABC* if there is a matching of vertices $A \leftrightarrow P$, $B \leftrightarrow Q$, $C \leftrightarrow R$ under which *all six* parts of triangle *ABC* are congruent to the corresponding six parts of triangle *PQR*. This is illustrated in Figure 13.1.

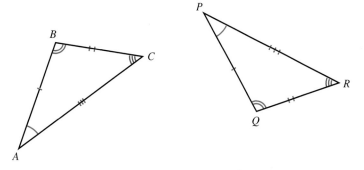

Figure 13.1
Triangles ABC and PQR are congruent under the vertex correspondence $A \leftrightarrow P$, $B \leftrightarrow Q$, $C \leftrightarrow R$ if, and only if, $\overline{AB} \cong \overline{PQ}$, $\overline{BC} \cong \overline{QR}$, $\overline{CA} \cong \overline{RP}$, and $\angle A \cong \angle P$, $\angle B \cong \angle Q$, and $\angle C \cong \angle R$.

> **DEFINITION**   *Congruent Triangles*
>
> Two triangles are **congruent** if, and only if, there is a correspondence of vertices of the triangles such that the corresponding sides and corresponding angles are congruent.

The notation $\triangle ABC \cong \triangle PQR$ is read "triangle *ABC* is congruent to triangle *PQR*," and conveys the following information:

- The vertex correspondence is $A \leftrightarrow P$, $B \leftrightarrow Q$, $C \leftrightarrow R$.
- The corresponding sides are congruent: $\overline{AB} \cong \overline{PQ}$, $\overline{BC} \cong \overline{QR}$, $\overline{CA} \cong \overline{RP}$.
- The corresponding angles are congruent: $\angle A \cong \angle P$, $\angle B \cong \angle Q$, $\angle C \cong \angle R$.

It is important to notice that the order in which the vertices are listed specifies the vertex correspondence. For the triangles depicted in Figure 13.1, we see that $\triangle ABC \ncong \triangle QRP$ ($\ncong$ is read "is not congruent to"). However, it is correct to say that $\triangle BCA \cong \triangle QRP$.

EXAMPLE   13.1

Exploring the Congruence Relation

Use a ruler and protractor to find the two pairs of congruent triangles among the six triangles shown. State the two congruences in the symbolic form $\triangle \underline{\hspace{1cm}} \cong \triangle \underline{\hspace{1cm}}$.

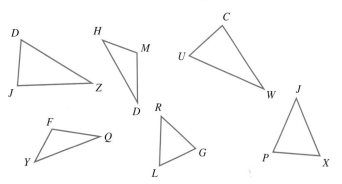

Solution

$\triangle DJZ \cong \triangle UCW$ and $\triangle HMD \cong \triangle YFQ$. The order of the vertices can be permuted in each statement. For example, it would also be correct to express the first congruence as $\triangle ZDJ \cong \triangle WUC$.

Suppose that we have only some of the measurements of a triangle *ABC*. For example, suppose that we know the lengths *AB*, *BC*, and *CA* of the three sides, but we are not given any information about the angles. Or, suppose we are given a length *AB* and the measurement of two angles, $\angle A$ and $\angle B$. Is the information we have sufficient to construct a triangle *PQR* that is necessarily congruent to $\triangle ABC$? These questions will be explored constructively; that is, we will attempt to use a compass and straightedge to construct a triangle *PQR* that is congruent to $\triangle ABC$.

The Side-Side-Side (SSS) Property

EXAMPLE   13.2

Exploring the Side-Side-Side Property

The three sides of triangle *ABC* are given as shown. Construct a triangle *PQR* that is congruent to $\triangle ABC$.

$$A \overset{x}{\rule{2cm}{0.4pt}} B \quad B \overset{y}{\rule{1.2cm}{0.4pt}} C \quad A \overset{z}{\rule{1.5cm}{0.4pt}} C$$

Solution

Step 1   Construct a segment $\overline{PQ}$ of length $x = AB$ using Construction 1.

$$P \overset{x}{\rule{3cm}{0.4pt}} Q$$

Step 2   Set the compass to radius $y = BC$ and draw a circle of radius y centered at Q.

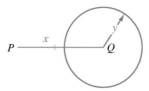

Step 3   Set the compass to radius $z = AC$ and draw a circular arc of radius z centered at P. Let R be either point of intersection with the circle drawn in Step 2.

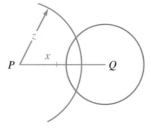

Step 4 Draw the segments $\overline{PR}$ and $\overline{RQ}$. Then $\triangle PQR \cong \triangle ABC$.

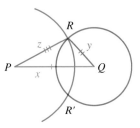

The size and shape of $\triangle PQR$ are uniquely determined. Even if we had chosen the second point of intersection R', we see that $\triangle PQR'$ has the same size and shape as $\triangle PQR$. Therefore we are led to the following basic property.

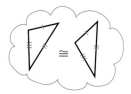

> **PROPERTY** *Side-Side-Side (SSS)*
>
> If the three sides of one triangle are respectively congruent to three sides of another triangle, then the two triangles are congruent.

In most formal treatments of Euclidean geometry, the SSS property is adopted as a postulate. That is, SSS is true by assumption, not by proof.

EXAMPLE 13.3 | **Using the SSS Property**

Let $ABCD$ be a quadrilateral with opposite sides of equal length: $AB = CD$ and $AD = BC$. Show that $ABCD$ is a parallelogram.

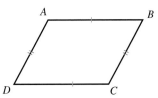

Solution Many problems in geometry are solved by constructing additional lines or arcs to reveal features of the original figure that would otherwise remain hidden. In this case we construct the diagonal $\overline{AC}$.

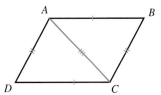

Since $\overline{AC}$ is congruent to itself we see that $\triangle ABC \cong \triangle CDA$ by the SSS property. Thus the corresponding angles $\angle BAC$ and $\angle DCA$ are congruent. By the alternate interior angles theorem of Chapter 10, we conclude that $\overline{AB} \parallel \overline{DC}$. Similarly, the congruence $\angle BCA \cong \angle DAC$ shows that $\overline{AD} \parallel \overline{BC}$.

An important consequence of the SSS property is the following construction of a congruent angle.

Construct a Congruent Angle

Construction **2**

Construct an angle that is congruent to a given angle, ∠D as shown.

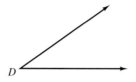

Procedure

Step 1	Step 2	Step 3	Step 4
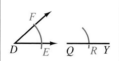 Use the straightedge to draw a line segment $\overline{QY}$.	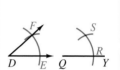 Draw arcs of the same radius centered at D and Q; let E and F be the points at which the arc intersects the sides of the given angle, and let R be the point at which the arc intersects $\overline{QY}$.	Place the point of the compass at E and adjust it to draw an arc through F. Draw an arc of the same radius centered at R to locate S.	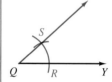 Use the straightedge to draw a line segment from Q through S; then ∠Q ≅ ∠D.

The construction procedure shows that $DE = QR$, $DF = QS$, and $EF = RS$. Therefore $\triangle DEF \cong \triangle QRS$ by the SSS property, and we see that the corresponding angles, ∠D and ∠Q, are congruent.

The Triangle Inequality

The SSS property guarantees that two triangles are congruent if they have corresponding sides of the same length. However, not every triple of given lengths corresponds to a triangle, since the length of any side must be less than the sum of the lengths of the other two sides. An example is shown in Figure 13.2.

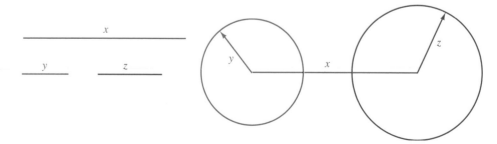

Figure 13.2
If $x \geq y + z$ there is no triangle with sides of length x, y, and z.

The lengths of the sides of a triangle must satisfy the following property.

> **PROPERTY**   *Triangle Inequality*
> The sum of the lengths of any two sides of a triangle must be greater than the length of the third side.

A triangle gives rise to three inequalities, as shown in Figure 13.3

Figure 13.3

The lengths of the sides of any triangle satisfy the triangle inequalities.

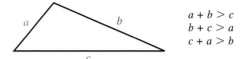

$$a + b > c$$
$$b + c > a$$
$$c + a > b$$

EXAMPLE 13.4

Applying the Triangle Inequality

The four towns of Abbott, Brownsville, Connell, and Davis are building a new power generating plant that will serve all four communities. To keep the costs of the power lines at a minimum, the plant is to be located so that the sum of the distances from the plant to the four towns is as small as possible. An engineer recommended locating the plant at point E. A mathematician, seeing that the four towns formed a convex quadrilateral as shown, recommended that the plant be built at the point M at which the diagonals of the quadrilateral intersect. Why is location M better than E?

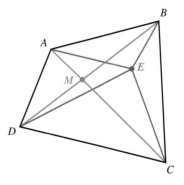

Solution

The triangle inequality, applied to $\triangle ACE$, gives $EA + EC > AC$. Since M is on the diagonal $\overline{AC}$ we also know $AC = MA + MC$, and therefore

$$EA + EC > MA + MC.$$

If we apply the triangle inequality to $\triangle BDE$, the same reasoning gives us the inequality

$$EB + ED > MB + MD.$$

Adding these two inequalities gives us

$$EA + EB + EC + ED > MA + MB + MC + MD.$$

This shows that the sum of the distances to the towns from point E is greater than the sum of the distances to the towns from point M.

COOPERATIVE INVESTIGATION

Random Spaghetti Triangles

Materials Needed

Uncooked spaghetti, two strands per student
Calculator with random number generator
Metric rulers
Pencils or marking pens

Directions

Use the calculator to generate pairs of random numbers x and y in the interval $0 < x, y < L$, where L is the length of the spaghetti in centimeters. Mark the distances x and y from one end on each strand of spaghetti. Break the strand at these two points, and (if possible) form a triangle from the three lengths of broken spaghetti.

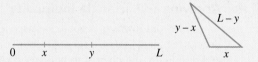

Repeat with the second strand, using another pair of random distances. Gather data from the class in a table.

Number of students	Number of triangles	Number of acute triangles	Number of obtuse triangles

Work in small collaborative groups to answer these questions.

Questions

1. What fraction of the broken spaghetti strands formed a triangle?
2. Assume that x and y are ordered so $0 < x < y < L$. Then the lengths of the three pieces of spaghetti are $x, y - x, L - y$. What inequalities must be satisfied for the pieces to form a triangle with sides $x, y - x, L - y$?
3. Among the triangles that are formed with the broken spaghetti, which type of triangle seems to be most likely—acute or obtuse?

The Side-Angle-Side (SAS) Property

The next example explores how to construct a triangle with two given sides and the angle included between the given sides.

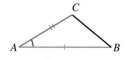

**Christine Ladd-Franklin
(1847–1930)**

The "Metaphysical Club" of the Johns Hopkins University met for the first time in October 1879. The Club's founder, the great logician C. S. Pierce, read the paper "Non-Euclidean Space." What was unusual was that the paper's author, seated in the audience, was a newly admitted graduate student named Christine Ladd—and Johns Hopkins University did not admit women! Some earlier background explains why an exception was made.

Following her 1869 B.A. from Vassar, Christine had hoped to continue studies in physics but was denied access to laboratories largely because of her gender. She therefore turned to mathematics, which she studied on her own as she took a succession of positions teaching science. Shortly after the founding of Johns Hopkins University in 1876, Christine's application to admission to graduate studies was given a favorable report by Fabian Franklin, a young member of the mathematics department who was impressed by several articles and problem solutions she had published in some English periodicals.

Admitted "on a special status" in 1879, Christine Ladd studied mathematics, philosophy, and psychology, and wrote papers in logic, algebra, geometry, and other subjects. By 1882 she had married Fabian Franklin and completed the requirements for a Ph.D. but, as a woman, could not be given the degree (this was finally rectified in 1924, when she received the degree at age 76).

Christine Ladd-Franklin continued to write papers in logic throughout her life, but after 1882 turned her attention again to experimental science, especially the psychology of vision. Her lifetime work includes about twenty papers in mathematics, another twenty in logic, and about fifty papers and a book on the theory of vision. Near the end of her life she was described as "the most distinguished woman scientist America had produced."

EXAMPLE   13.5

Exploring the Side-Angle-Side Condition

Two sides, $\overline{AB}$ and $\overline{AC}$, and the angle $\angle A$ included by these sides, are given for $\triangle ABC$ as shown. Show that a triangle PQR can be constructed for which $\triangle PQR \cong \triangle ABC$.

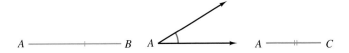

Solution

Step 1   Follow the steps of Construction 2 to construct an angle congruent to $\angle A$; let P denote its vertex.

Step 2   Use Construction 1 to construct segments $\overline{PQ}$ and $\overline{PR}$ along the sides of $\angle P$ which are, respectively, of length AB and AC.

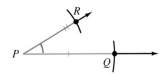

Step 3   Draw segment $\overline{QR}$; then $\triangle PQR \cong \triangle ABC$.

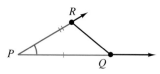

The procedure described in Example 13.5 uniquely determines the size and shape of $\triangle PQR$ when we are given the three parts, side-angle-side, of $\triangle ABC$. The angle had to be the **included angle,** the angle between the given sides. This property is often abbreviated as **SAS (side-angle-side).**

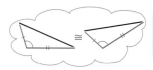

> **PROPERTY**   *Side-Angle-Side (SAS)*
>
> If two sides and the included angle of one triangle are congruent to two sides and the included angle of another triangle, then the two triangles are congruent.

EXAMPLE   13.6

Using the SAS Property

Two line segments, $\overline{AB}$ and $\overline{CD}$, intersect at their common midpoint M. Show that $\overline{AD}$ and $\overline{BC}$ are parallel and have the same length.

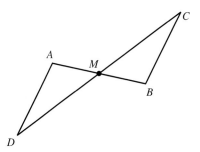

Solution

It is useful to add tick marks and arcs to your drawing to summarize the given information. In this problem, M is the midpoint of $\overline{AB}$, so $AM = BM$. We indicate this on the drawing by putting a single tick mark on each of the segments $\overline{AM}$ and $\overline{MB}$. Similarly $CM = DM$ and we put double tick marks on each of the segments $\overline{CM}$ and $\overline{MD}$. We also use single arcs to indicate the congruence of the vertical angles at M formed by the intersecting segments.

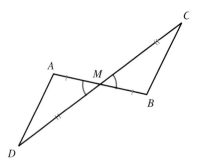

It is now apparent that the SAS property gives us the congruence $\triangle AMD \cong \triangle BMC$. It follows that the corresponding sides $\overline{AD}$ and $\overline{BC}$ are congruent, so that $AD = BC$. We also have that $\angle A \cong \angle B$, so the alternate interior angles theorem of Chapter 10 guarantees that $\overline{AD}$ and $\overline{CB}$ are parallel.

The following theorem about isosceles triangles is an important consequence of the SAS property.

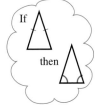

THEOREM *Isosceles Triangle Theorem*
The angles opposite the congruent sides of an isosceles triangle are congruent.

Proof   Let $\triangle ABC$ be isosceles, with $\overline{AB}$ and $\overline{AC}$ congruent. Consider the vertex correspondence $A \leftrightarrow A, B \leftrightarrow C, C \leftrightarrow B$, (which amounts to looking at the same triangle from the back!).

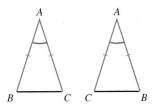

Since $\overline{AB} \cong \overline{AC}$ and $\angle A \cong \angle A$ it follows from the SAS property that $\triangle ABC \cong \triangle ACB$. But then all six corresponding parts of $\triangle ABC$ and $\triangle ACB$ are congruent, including $\angle B \cong \angle C$.

The isosceles triangle theorem has many uses. In particular it gives a simple way to prove **Thales' theorem.**

THEOREM *Thales' Theorem*
Any triangle ABC inscribed in a semi-circle with diameter $\overline{AB}$ has a right angle at point C.

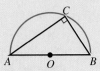

Proof   Draw the radius $\overline{OC}$. This divides $\triangle ABC$ into two isosceles triangles, $\triangle AOC$ and $\triangle COB$. The isosceles triangle theorem tells us that the measures of the base angles of $\triangle AOC$ are equal, say x. Likewise, the base angles of $\triangle COB$ are equal, say y. Since the sum of the measures of the interior angles of $\triangle ABC$ is $180°$, we have that $x + y + (x + y) = 180°$. But this equation tells us that $m(\angle C) = x + y = 90°$.

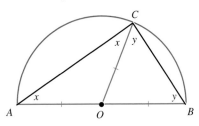

The Angle-Side-Angle (ASA) Property

In the next example, we suppose that two angles of a triangle, and the side included between these angles, are given. Is this information sufficient to be able to construct a congruent triangle?

EXAMPLE   13.7

Exploring the Angle-Side-Angle Property

Two angles and their **included side** are given for △*ABC*, as shown. Construct a triangle *PQR* that is congruent to triangle *ABC*.

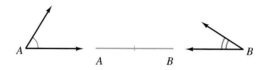

Solution

Step 1   Use Construction 2 to construct ∠*P* ≅ ∠*A*.

Step 2   Use Construction 1 to construct segment $\overline{PQ}$ on a side of ∠*P* so that *PQ* = *AB*.

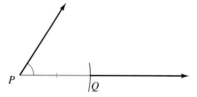

Step 3   Construct an angle congruent to ∠*B* at vertex *Q*, with one side containing *P* and the other side intersecting ∠*P* to determine point *R*. Then △*PQR* ≅ △*ABC*.

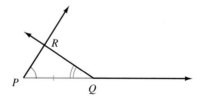

The construction just shown illustrates the **angle-side-angle property**, abbreviated as **ASA.**

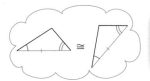

PROPERTY *Angle-Side-Angle (ASA)*

If two angles and the included side of one triangle are congruent to the two angles and the included side of another triangle, then the two triangles are congruent.

The ASA property allows us to prove that any triangle with two angles of the same measure is isosceles.

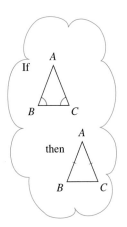

THEOREM *Converse of the Isosceles Triangle Theorem*

If two angles of a triangle are congruent, then the sides opposite them are congruent; that is, the triangle is isosceles.

Proof   Let $\triangle ABC$ have two congruent angles, say $\angle B \cong \angle C$. We know that $\overline{BC} \cong \overline{CB}$, since a line segment is congruent to itself. By the ASA property it follows that $\triangle ABC \cong \triangle ACB$. This means that the corresponding sides of $\triangle ABC$ and $\triangle ACB$ are congruent, so $\overline{AB} \cong \overline{AC}$.

The Angle-Angle-Side (AAS) Property

The side in the ASA theorem is the one included by the two angles. However, if *any* two angles of one triangle are congruent to two angles of a second triangle, then all three pairs of corresponding angles are congruent. This follows from the fact that the measures of the three angles of a triangle add up to 180°, so the third angle is uniquely determined by the other two angles. This gives us the **angle-angle-side property,** abbreviated as **AAS.**

PROPERTY *Angle-Angle-Side (AAS)*

If two angles and a nonincluded side of one triangle are congruent respectively to two angles and the corresponding nonincluded side of a second triangle, then the two triangles are congruent.

JUST FOR FUN   Twice Around a Triangle

Draw any triangle ABC and let P be any point on side $\overline{AB}$. Draw an arc centered at B to determine the point Q on side $\overline{BC}$ for which $BP = BQ$. In the same way, draw an arc at C to locate point R on $\overline{CA}$, and then draw an arc centered at A to determine point P' on $\overline{AB}$. In three more steps, go around the triangle a second time, constructing Q', R', and finally P'' on $\overline{AB}$. What do you find interesting about P''?

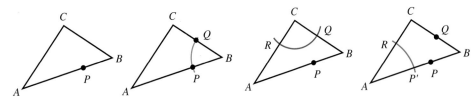

Are There SSA and AAA Congruence Properties?

There is no "SSA" congruence property since it is possible for two noncongruent triangles to have two pairs of congruent sides and a congruent nonincluded angle. An example is shown in Figure 13.4.

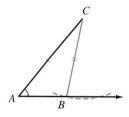
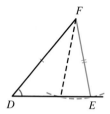

Figure 13.4
Triangles ABC and DEF are not congruent even though
AC = DF, BC = EF, and ∠A ≅ ∠D.

Similarly, there is no "AAA" congruence property. For example, Figure 13.5 shows two triangles with three pairs of congruent angles. However, the triangles are not congruent since they are of different size. On the other hand, the shapes of the two triangles are the same, so they are called similar triangles. The properties and applications of similar triangles will be discussed in Section 13.3 of this chapter.

Figure 13.5
The AAA condition guarantees
similarity but not congruence

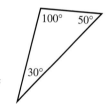

PROBLEM SET 13.1

Understanding Concepts

1. The two triangles shown below are congruent.

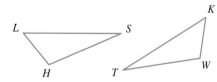

   Determine the following:
   (a) Corresponding vertices
       L ↔ _____ , H ↔ _____ , S ↔ _____
   (b) Corresponding sides
       $\overline{LH}$ ↔ _____ , $\overline{HS}$ ↔ _____ , $\overline{SL}$ ↔ _____

   (c) Corresponding angles
       ∠L ↔ _____ , ∠H ↔ _____ , ∠S ↔ _____
   (d) △LHS ≅ △ _____ .

2. Suppose △JKL ≅ △ABC, where △ABC is shown below.

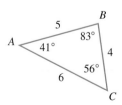

   Find the following:
   (a) KL   (b) LJ   (c) m(∠L)   (d) m(∠J)

3. Segments of length *x* and *y* are shown below.

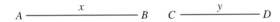

Describe procedures, using only a straightedge and a compass, to construct:

(a) a line segment $\overline{EF}$ of length $x + y$;

(b) a line segment of length $x - y$.

4. Trace the angle, $\angle D$, shown below. Then use a compass and straightedge to construct an angle, $\angle Q$, congruent to $\angle D$. Use a protractor to measure each angle, and report on how closely the measurements of the two angles agree.

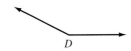

5. Two angles, $\angle A$ and $\angle B$, are shown below.

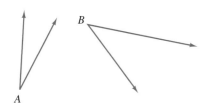

Describe procedures, using only a straightedge and a compass, to construct

(a) $\angle C$, so that $m(\angle C) = m(\angle A) + m(\angle B)$.

(b) $\angle D$, so that $m(\angle D) = m(\angle B) - m(\angle A)$.

(c) $\angle E$, so that $m(\angle E) + m(\angle A) + m(\angle B) = 180°$.

6. Use a ruler, protractor, and compass to construct, when possible, a triangle with the stated properties. If such a triangle cannot be drawn, explain why. Decide if there can be two or more noncongruent triangles with the stated properties.

(a) an isosceles triangle with two sides of length 5 cm and an apex angle of measure 28°

(b) an equilateral triangle with sides of length 6 cm

(c) a triangle with sides of length 8 cm, 2 cm, and 5 cm

(d) a triangle with angles measuring 30° and 110° and a nonincluded side of length 5 cm

(e) a right triangle with legs (the sides including the right angle) of length 6 cm and 4 cm

(f) a triangle with sides of length 10 cm and 6 cm and a nonincluded angle of 45°

(g) a triangle with sides of length 5 cm and 3 cm and an angle of 20°

7. Each part below shows two triangles, with arcs and tick marks identifying congruent parts. If it is possible

to conclude that the triangles are congruent, describe what property or theorem you use. If you cannot be sure the triangles are congruent, state "no conclusion possible." The first one is done for you.

(a)

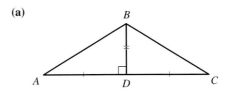

Answer $\triangle ABD \cong \triangle CBD$ by SAS.

(b)

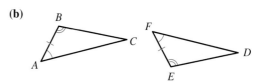

(c)

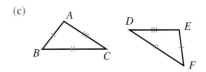

(d)

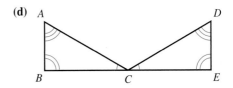

(e)

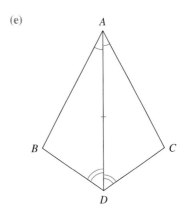

(f)

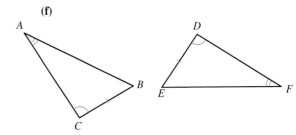

(g)

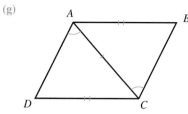

(h)

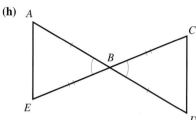

(i)

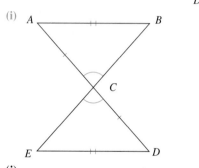

(j)

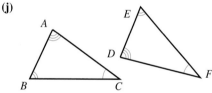

8. Prove that an equilateral triangle is equiangular.

9. Prove that an equiangular triangle is equilateral.

10. Draw an angle $\angle BAC$ and use a protractor to measure the angle. Next construct an arc at A to determine points D and E. Finally, draw arcs of equal radius centered at D and E, denoting the point of intersection of the arcs as F.

   (a) Measure angles 1 and 2. How do they compare to the measure of $\angle BAC$?

   (b) Prove that $\triangle AFD$ is congruent to $\triangle AFE$.

   (c) Explain why angles 1 and 2 are congruent, using the result of part (b).

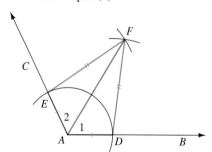

11. Draw a line m and a point P not on the line. Construct an arc centered at P that intersects the line in two points, Q and S. Next, draw two arcs of equal radius centered at Q and S, labeling their intersection as point T. Finally, construct the segment from P to T and let V be its intersection with the line m.

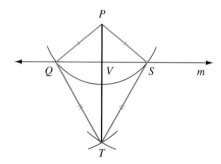

Give reasons why these relationships hold.

   (a) $\triangle QPT \cong \triangle SPT$

   (b) $\angle QPT \cong \angle SPT$

   (c) $\triangle QPV \cong \triangle SPV$

   (d) $\angle QVP$ is a right angle

Therefore, the construction gives a line $\overleftrightarrow{PT}$ perpendicular to m that passes through point P.

12. Let $ABCD$ be a parallelogram.

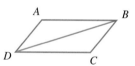

   (a) Prove that $\triangle ABD \cong \triangle CDB$. (*Hint:* Use the ASA property.)

   (b) Prove that opposite sides of a parallelogram have the same length.

   (c) Prove that opposite angles of a parallelogram have the same measure.

13. Let the two diagonals of parallelogram $ABCD$ intersect at point M.

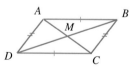

   (a) Use the fact that $AB = CD$ (shown in problem 12(b)) to prove that $\triangle ABM \cong \triangle CDM$.

   (b) Use part (a) to explain why M is the midpoint of both diagonals of the parallelogram.

14. Let the two diagonals of a rhombus *ABCD* intersect at *M*.

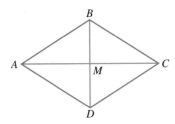

   (a) Show that the triangles *ABM*, *CBM*, *CDM*, and *ADM* are congruent to one another.

   (b) Use part (a) to explain why the diagonals of a rhombus bisect the interior angles of the rhombus, and intersect at a right angle at *M*.

15. Let *ABC* be a right triangle with hypotenuse $\overline{AB}$ and right angle at vertex *C*. Explain why the circle centered at the midpoint *O* of the hypotenuse that passes through point *C* also passes through points *A* and *B*. This gives the

   Converse of Thales' Theorem: The hypotenuse of a right triangle inscribed in a circle is a diameter of the circle.

   (*Suggestion:* Imagine the right triangle *ABC* is created by constructing the diagonal $\overline{AB}$ of a rectangle *ACBD*.)

16. Suppose you drew a circle by tracing around a bowl. Explain how you can locate the center of the circle with a piece of notebook paper. (*Hint:* Use the converse to Thales' theorem stated in Problem 15.

17. A triangle has sides of length 4 cm and 9 cm. What can you say about the length of the third side?

18. **(a)** A quadrilateral has sides of length 2 cm, 7 cm, and 5 cm. What inequality does the length of the fourth side satisfy?

   (b) Let *A*, *B*, *C*, and *D* be any four points in the plane. Explain why $AD \leq AB + BC + CD$.

Thinking Critically

19. Two angles and a *nonincluded* side of △*ABC* are drawn below.

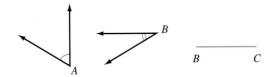

   Describe and show the steps of a straightedge and compass construction of a triangle *PQR* that is congruent to △*ABC*.

20. In the figure below, *AB* = *AE* and *AC* = *AD*.

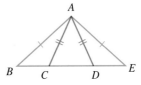

   (a) Why is ∠*B* ≅ ∠*E*?

   (b) Why is ∠*ACD* ≅ ∠*ADC*?

   (c) Use the AAS property to prove that △*ABC* ≅ △*AED*.

   (d) Prove that *BC* = *DE*.

21. Recall that a trapezoid with a pair of congruent angles adjacent to one of its bases is called an isosceles trapezoid.

   (a) Prove that the sides joining the bases of an isosceles trapezoid are congruent. The following figure may help you show that *AD* = *BC*.

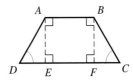

   (b) Prove that the diagonals of an isosceles trapezoid are congruent.

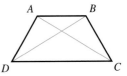

22. For each part, decide if the given conditions are sufficient to conclude that △*ABC* ≅ △*ADE*. If so, give a proof; if not, draw a figure which satisfies the information but shows that △*ABC* is not congruent to △*ADE*.

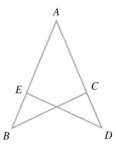

   (a) *AB* = *AD* and m(∠*B*) = m(∠*D*)

   (b) *AB* = *AD* and *BC* = *DE*

   (c) *AB* = *AD* and *AE* = *AC*

   (d) *EB* = *CD* and *BC* = *DE*

23. Each edge of a tetrahedron is congruent to its opposite edge. For example, $\overline{AB} \cong \overline{CD}$. Prove that the faces of the tetrahedron are congruent to one another.

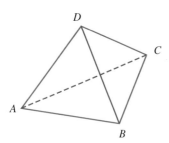

24. (a) Let T be a point on the side $\overline{QR}$ of triangle PQR. Use the triangle inequality to explain why $QP + QR > TP + TR$.

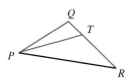

(b) Let S be a point in the interior of triangle PQR. Use part (a) to explain why $QP + QR > SP + SR$. This shows that the sum of distances from a vertex Q to the endpoints of the opposite side $\overline{PR}$ is larger than the sum of distances to the same two points from a point S within the triangle.

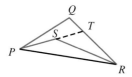

25. In Example 13.4, the four towns formed a convex quadrilateral. Suppose instead that Davis is in the interior of the triangle formed by the other three towns, as shown in the figure below. Show that the power station serving the four towns is best located at Davis, instead of an alternative point such as point E, by answering these questions.

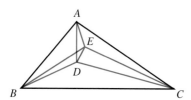

(a) Why is $EA + ED > DA$?

(b) Why is $EB + EC > DB + DC$? (*Suggestion:* Use the result of problem 24(b).)

(c) Why is $EA + ED + EB + EC > DA + DB + DC$?

26. Six towns are located at the vertices A, B, C, D, E, F of a regular hexagon. A power station located at Q would require $QA + QB + QC + QD + QE + QF$ miles of transmission line to serve the six communities. Describe a better location, P, for the station, and prove it has the least possible sum of distances to A, B, C, D, E, and F.

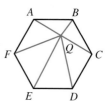

Making Connections

27. A bicycle rack is made from three pieces of metal box tubing. There are bolts at A, B, C, and D that join the tubing and attach the rack to the bumper of a car.

(a) Why is the top of the rack likely to shift sideways?

(b) If a fourth piece of tubing is available, where can it be attached to make the rack rigid? Explain why this works.

(c) Would a rope from A to C make the rack rigid? How about two pieces of rope, from A to C and from B to D?

28. Carpenters construct a wall by nailing studs to a top and bottom plate, as shown below.

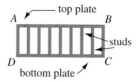

The studs are cut to the same length, and the top and bottom plates are the same length.

(a) If the pieces are properly cut and nailed, is $ABCD$ necessarily rectangular, or are there other shapes the framework can take?

(b) Carpenters frequently "square up" a stud wall by adjusting it so that it has diagonals of equal length. Prove that a parallelogram with congruent diagonals is a rectangle.

(c) Once the wall is "squared up" a diagonal brace is nailed across the frame. Why is this? What geometric principle is involved?

29. The two frameworks shown below are constructed with drinking straws and pins. The triangle is a rigid framework by the SSS property, but the quadrilateral is flexible.

Decide if the straw-and-pin frameworks below are rigid or flexible. It may be helpful to build the frameworks to check your reasoning.

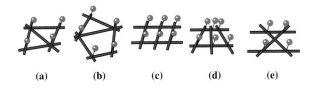

   (a)   **(b)**   **(c)**   **(d)**   **(e)**

▣ Using a Computer

30. In the power plant location problem of Example 13.4, suppose the town at D (Davis) drops out. This leaves three towns, at A, B, and C, who wish to jointly build a power plant at some location P serving the three communities. To minimize the cost of power lines, P should be situated so the total length $PA + PB + PC$ is as small as possible. Use dynamic software to duplicate the figure shown below. Use the **Calculate . . .** command found under the Measure Menu to compute $PA + PB + PC$. Drag point P, watching the sum, to determine what seems to be the best position for point P.

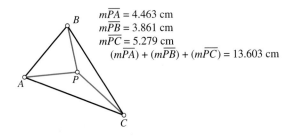

$m\overline{PA} = 4.463$ cm
$m\overline{PB} = 3.861$ cm
$m\overline{PC} = 5.279$ cm
$(m\overline{PA}) + (m\overline{PB}) + (m\overline{PC}) = 13.603$ cm

Describe the optimal location of P by considering two types of triangles.

(a) $\triangle ABC$ has an angle at one of its vertices measuring at least $120°$.

(b) No angle of $\triangle ABC$ has measure larger than $120°$. In this case, describe the location of P by measuring the three angles at P made by the segments joining P to A, B, and C.

(c) (*For more advanced software users*) Construct an outward pointing equilateral triangle on each of the three sides of $\triangle ABC$ considered in part (b). Next, construct the center of each equilateral triangle, and the circle through the endpoints of the corresponding side of $\triangle ABC$. In the figure below, all three equilateral triangles are constructed but just two of the circles. After constructing the third circle, see if you now know how to locate the power plant serving the towns at A, B, and C.

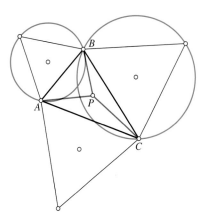

31. Construct a circle, and label its center O. Next construct three points A, B, and P on the circle and draw two angles, $\angle AOB$ and $\angle APB$, that both intercept the arc of the circle between A and B.

(a) Measure $\angle AOB$ and $\angle APB$. What relationship do you observe? Move P around the circle and investigate what happens to the measure of $\angle APB$.

(b) Make a conjecture that relates the measures of $\angle AOB$ and $\angle APB$.

(c) Justify your conjecture. (*Hint:* Draw the diameter through P and then mimic the proof of Thales' theorem.)

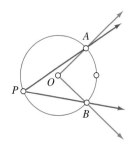

32. Draw a circle. Next construct four points *A*, *B*, *C*, and *D* on the circle, which are joined by line segments to form the inscribed quadrilateral *ABCD*.

    (a) Measure ∠*A* and ∠*C*. What relationship do you observe? Move some of the points of your quadrilateral and see if the relationship between ∠*A* and ∠*C* is preserved.

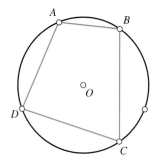

    (b) Make a conjecture concerning the relationship of opposite angles of an inscribed quadrilateral.

    (c) Justify your conjecture. (*Hint:* Draw the radii $\overline{OA}$, $\overline{OB}$, $\overline{OC}$, and $\overline{OD}$. This creates four isosceles triangles.)

From State Student Assessments

33. (Colorado, Grade 5) Your teacher told you in class today that the square shown is divided into 8 congruent triangles. After you got home your best friend called and said he did not know what that meant. What would you say to your friend to help him out?

For Review

34. A partially completed jigsaw puzzle and the remaining pieces are on a table. Each remaining piece can be imagined to be put into its correct position by one of the four basic rigid motions in the plane: a translation, a reflection, a rotation, or a glide reflection.

    (a) Which motions will properly position a right side up piece of the puzzle?

    (b) Which motions will properly position an upside down remaining piece?

35. **(a)** Show that translations of the numeral 4 shown below can tile the plane.

    (b) Show that translations and rotations of the numeral 5 shown below can tile the plane.

    Sketch each tiling on squared graph or dot paper.

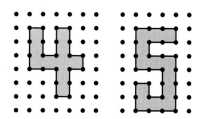

36. For each whole number *n* = 0, 1, 2, 3, . . . draw (if possible) a hexagon with exactly *n* lines of symmetry.

13.2   Constructing Geometric Figures

In the last section two basic constructions were described:

    • Construction 1   Construct a congruent line segment
    • Construction 2   Construct a congruent angle

Since only the straightedge and compass were used, these are examples of Euclidean constructions. In this section we describe a number of other Euclidean constructions and explore some related applications and theorems. We also investigate constructions with the Mira and by paper folding. The constructions shown in the examples and called for in the problems can also be done with dynamic geometry software.

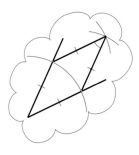

To be certain that a construction results in a figure that has a desired property, a proof of the validity of the construction must be given. For example, Construction 2 of a congruent angle is a consequence of the SSS property. Many constructions can be verified by appealing to the properties of a rhombus listed in Figure 13.6. A rhombus is easily constructed by drawing intersecting arcs of circles of the same radius.

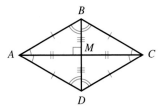

Figure 13.6
The rhombus ABCD has many useful properties:
- *The diagonals are angle bisectors.*
- *The diagonals are perpendicular.*
- *The diagonals intersect at their common midpoint M.*
- *The sides are all congruent to one another.*
- *The opposite sides are parallel.*

Constructing Parallel and Perpendicular Lines

If l is a given line and P is a given point not on l, it is useful to know how to construct the line through P that is either parallel or perpendicular to l. There are several procedures that can be devised and it is interesting to invent some of your own. The following constructions each take advantage of the properties of a rhombus.

Construct a Parallel Line

Construction 3

Given P and l as shown, construct a line through P that is parallel to l.

P

$\longleftrightarrow l$

Procedure

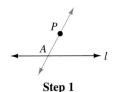	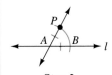	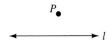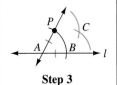	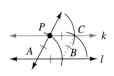
Step 1	**Step 2**	**Step 3**	**Step 4**
Draw a line through P that intersects l at a point labeled A.	Draw an arc centered at A through P, and let B denote its intersection with l.	With the same radius AB, draw arcs with centers at P and B; let C be the intersection of the two arcs.	Draw the line $k = \overleftrightarrow{PC}$; since $ABCP$ is a rhombus its opposite sides are parallel, and so $k \parallel l$.

INTO THE CLASSROOM
Constructions in Space

Constructions using a compass and a straightedge lead to pictorial figures, confined to a sheet of paper. Interest and excitement can also be generated by constructing figures in space, using sticks, brass fasteners, paper clips, string, cut paper, multilink cubes, or indeed whatever is available. Such figures can be held and felt, literally giving students a feel for shape. In some cases the shapes can be bent or flexed to give a dynamic liveliness to figures which would remain of lesser interest when only drawn on a sheet of paper.

Books, pamphlets, and journals published by the National Council of Teachers of Mathematics and other publishing companies provide the teacher with a wide variety of ideas and resources of three-dimensional constructions and related activities. Every teacher will want to gather a personal collection of favorite hands-on constructions suitable for his or her own classroom. Here are three suggestions for constructions to do in the classroom:

- *Hinged polygons.* Strips of cardstock can be joined with brass fasteners through holes at the ends of each strip. Any triangle is rigid, demonstrating the SSS congruence property. Any quadrilateral, however, is flexible. As the quadrilateral flexes the sum of the angle measures remains at 360°, as can be checked with a protractor.

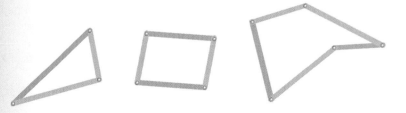

- *Space polygons and polyhedra.* Thin wooden sticks, say from a "Pick-Up-Sticks" game, can be cut to differing lengths and joined by short pieces of rubber tubing at their endpoints. More than two sticks can meet at a single vertex by inserting a length (or several lengths) of tubing through a hole punched sideways through another section of tubing. It is easy to form quadrilaterals that flex in space, and joining the midpoints of the four sides by elastic bands shows that a parallelogram is always formed. Properties of cubes, tetrahedra, and other polyhedra can also be explored with easily constructed skeletal models.

- *Geodesic domes.* Even primary grade children will enjoy constructing simple geodesic dome models with toothpicks and mini-marshmallows. The pattern for a small model is shown in its flattened position. The framework is then positioned vertically and wrapped around to insert toothpicks b and c into marshmallow A, toothpick a into marshmallow B, and the four upward pointing toothpicks into marshmallow C. The photograph shows first-graders with the domes they've made. A full discussion is found in the article "Marshmallows, Toothpicks, and Geodesic Domes" by Stacy Wahl (in *Geometry for Grades K-6: Readings from the Arithmetic Teacher*, National Council of Teachers of Mathematics, 1987).

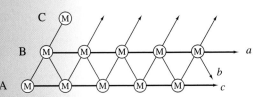

Basic Pattern, 1 *v.* 5/8 geodesic dome.

Construction 4

Construct a Perpendicular Line Through a Point Not on the Given Line

Given line *l* and point *P* not on *l* as shown, construct a line through *P* that is perpendicular to *l*.

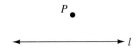

Procedure

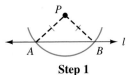	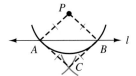	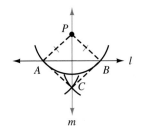
Step 1 Draw an arc at *P* that intersects *l* at two points, *A* and *B*.	**Step 2** With the compass still at radius *AP*, draw arcs at *A* and *B*, and let *C* be their point of intersection.	**Step 3** Draw the line $\overleftrightarrow{PC}$; since $\overline{PC}$ is a diagonal of rhombus *APBC* it is perpendicular to $\overline{AB}$.

The construction of perpendicular lines has several applications, as shown in Figure 13.7. The point *F* at which the perpendicular intersects the line is called the **foot of the perpendicular through *P***. The length of $\overline{PF}$ is the **distance from the point *P* to the line *l*.**

The point P' on the opposite side of l from P for which $PF = P'F$ is called the **point of reflection** of P across l. In a triangle, the perpendicular line segment from a vertex to the line containing the opposite side is an **altitude of the triangle.**

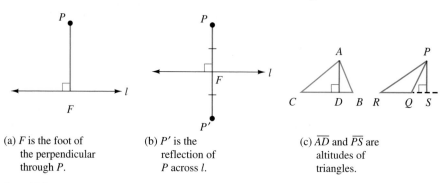

(a) F is the foot of the perpendicular through P.

(b) P' is the reflection of P across l.

(c) $\overline{AD}$ and $\overline{PS}$ are altitudes of triangles.

Figure 13.7
Applications of perpendicular lines

If point P lies on line l, a small modification in the second step of the procedure above is required to construct the line perpendicular to l at P.

Construction 5

Construct the Perpendicular Line Through a Point on a Given Line

Given line l and point P on l as shown, construct the line through P perpendicular to l.

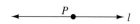

Procedure

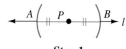 **Step 1** Draw two arcs of equal radius centered at P; let A and B be their points of intersection with l.	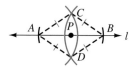 **Step 2** Draw arcs centered at A and B with a radius *greater* than AP; let C and D be their points of intersection.	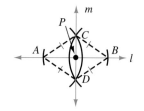 **Step 3** Draw line $m = \overleftrightarrow{CD}$; since $\overline{CD}$ is a diagonal of the rhombus $ABCD$ and P is the midpoint of diagonal $\overline{AB}$, m passes through P and is perpendicular to $l = \overleftrightarrow{AB}$; that is, m is perpendicular to l.

Constructing the Midpoint and Perpendicular Bisector of a Line Segment

The line perpendicular to a segment at its midpoint is called the **perpendicular bisector** of the segment. The following construction is also justified by properties of the rhombus.

Construct the Midpoint and Perpendicular Bisector of a Line Segment

Construction **6**

Construct the midpoint and perpendicular bisector of the segment $\overline{AB}$ shown.

$$A \text{ —————————— } B$$

Procedure

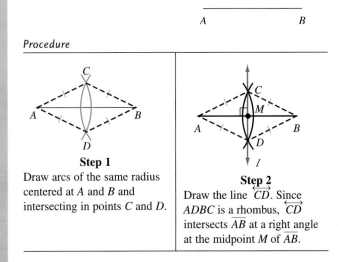

Step 1
Draw arcs of the same radius centered at A and B and intersecting in points C and D.

Step 2
Draw the line $\overleftrightarrow{CD}$. Since $ADBC$ is a rhombus, $\overleftrightarrow{CD}$ intersects $\overline{AB}$ at a right angle at the midpoint M of $\overline{AB}$.

The midpoint of a line segment M is the same distance from A and B. Indeed, every point P of the perpendicular bisector of a segment $\overline{AB}$ is equidistant from the end points of the segment. That is, $PA = PB$.

> **THEOREM** *Equidistance Property of the Perpendicular Bisector*
> A point lies on the perpendicular bisector of a line segment if, and only if, the point is equidistant from the endpoints of the segment.

Proof Let l be the perpendicular bisector of segment $\overline{AB}$. Thus, l intersects $\overline{AB}$ at right angles at the midpoint M, as shown in the left side of the diagram below. Let P be any point of l. By the SAS property, $\triangle PMA \cong \triangle PMB$. This means that the corresponding sides $\overline{PA}$ and $\overline{PB}$ are congruent. Hence, $PA = PB$ as claimed.

The proof that equidistant points from A and B lie on the perpendicular bisector is similar. (See problem 23.)

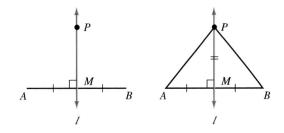

EXAMPLE 13.8

Locating an Airport

The Tri-Cities Airport Authority wishes to locate a new airport to serve their three cities, located at A, B, and C as shown. If possible, they would like a site, P, that is the same distance from A, B, and C. How can P be located?

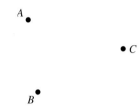

Solution

To be equidistant from A and B, P must be on the perpendicular bisector of the segment $\overline{AB}$. Similarly, P must be on the perpendicular bisector of $\overline{BC}$. Since A, B, and C are not collinear, the perpendicular bisectors to $\overline{AB}$ and $\overline{BC}$ are not parallel and we can choose P as their point of intersection. Since $PA = PB$ and $PB = PC$ we have that $PA = PC$. Therefore, P is also equidistant from A and C, so P is also on the perpendicular bisector of $\overline{AC}$. Therefore P is equidistant from A, B, and C, as desired.

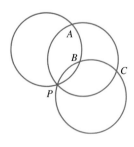
Point P is the center of a unique circle containing A, B, and C as shown in Figure 13.8. The circle is called the **circumscribing circle** of $\triangle ABC$, and P is called the **circumcenter** of $\triangle ABC$. Frequently the circumscribing circle is called the **circumcircle** of the triangle.

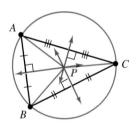

Figure 13.8
The perpendicular bisectors of the sides of △ABC are concurrent at a point P equidistant from A, B, and C. Point P is the center of the circumscribing circle of △ABC.

Constructing the Angle Bisector

Given $\angle ABC$ (see Figure 13.9) we wish to construct the ray $\overrightarrow{BD}$ that forms congruent angles with the sides $\overrightarrow{BA}$ and $\overrightarrow{BC}$. If $\angle ABD \cong \angle CBD$ then $\overrightarrow{BD}$ is the **angle bisector** of $\angle ABC$.

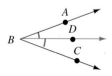

Figure 13.9
$\overrightarrow{BD}$ is the angle bisector of $\angle ABC$ if $\angle ABD \cong \angle DBC$.

Once again the properties of a rhombus justify the following construction.

Construct the Angle Bisector

Construct the angle bisector of $\angle E$ shown.

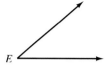

Procedure

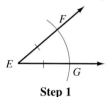	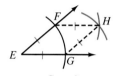	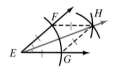
Step 1	**Step 2**	**Step 3**
Draw an arc centered at *E*; let *F* and *G* denote the points at which the arc intersects the sides of $\angle E$.	Draw arcs, centered at *F* and *G*, of radius *EF*. Let *H* be the point of intersection of the two arcs.	Draw the ray $\overrightarrow{EH}$. Since the diagonal $\overline{EH}$ forms congruent angles to the sides $\overline{EG}$ and $\overline{EF}$ of the rhombus *EGHF*, $\overrightarrow{EH}$ is the angle bisector of $\angle E$.

The following theorem tells how far the points on the angle bisector are from the sides of an angle.

> **THEOREM** *Equidistance Property of the Angle Bisector*
> A point lies on the bisector of an angle if, and only if, the point is equidistant from the sides of the angle.

Proof   Let *P* be any point on the bisector of $\angle A$ as shown. Let *F* and *F'* be the feet of the perpendiculars from *P* to the sides of $\angle A$.

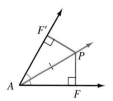

By the AAS congruence property, $\triangle PAF \cong \triangle PAF'$. Therefore, $PF = PF'$. The proof of the converse is similar and left to the reader.

By mimicking the solution of the airport problem of Example 13.8 it can be shown that the bisectors of the interior angles of a triangle are concurrent at the point *I* which is equidistant to three sides of the triangle (see Figure 13.10). Point *I*, called the **incenter** of $\triangle ABC$, is the center of the **inscribed circle,** or **incircle,** of $\triangle ABC$.

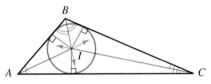

Figure 13.10
The bisectors of the interior angles of a triangle are concurrent at a point I equidistant from the sides of the triangle. I is the center of the inscribed circle of the triangle.

Constructing Regular Polygons

A square is easily constructed with compass and straightedge. For example, construct two perpendicular lines and a circle centered at the point of intersection, as shown in Figure 13.11(a).

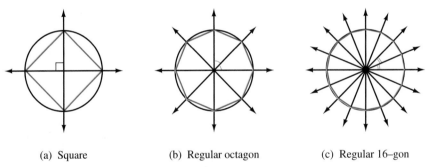

(a) Square   (b) Regular octagon   (c) Regular 16–gon

Figure 13.11
Constructing angle bisectors doubles the number of sides of a regular polygon inscribed in a circle.

By constructing angle bisectors, the eight vertices of a regular octagon are constructed. Angle bisectors can then be constructed to the octagon of Figure 13.11(b) to yield the regular 16-gon of part (c) of the figure. When the vertices of a polygon are all points of a given circle, the polygon is called an **inscribed polygon.**

A regular hexagon is particularly easy to inscribe in a given circle with a compass and straightedge: pick any point *A* on the circumference of the circle centered at *O* and then successively strike arcs of radius *OA* around the circle to locate *B*, *C*, *D*, *E*, and *F*. The hexagon *ABCDEF* is regular since joining the sides to the center *O* forms six congruent equilateral triangles *OAB*, *OBC*, . . . , *OFA*. As shown in Figure 13.12, connecting every other vertex gives a construction of the inscribed equilateral triangle *ACE*. On the other hand, constructing angle bisectors of the central angles of the hexagon produces an inscribed regular dodecagon.

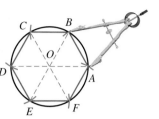

Figure 13.12

The regular 3-, 6-, and 12-gons can be inscribed with compass and straightedge in a given circle.

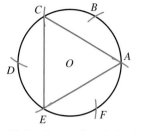

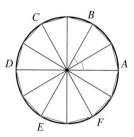

(a) Inscribed regular hexagon

(b) Inscribed equilateral triangle

(c) Inscribed regular dodecagon

A compass and straightedge construction of the regular pentagon requires more ingenuity. (One method is outlined in problem 19 at the end of this section.)

The ancient Greek geometers knew how to construct the regular polygons shown so far. They also knew that the regular 15-gon can be constructed with compass and straightedge. (The construction is outlined in problem 26 at the end of this section.) For over 2000 years, the only regular polygons known to be constructible with compass and straightedge were the ones contained in Book IV of Euclid's *Elements:* the regular 3-, 4-, 5- and 15-gons and, by angle bisection, the regular polygons obtained by successively doubling the number of sides.

On March 30, 1796, one month before his nineteenth birthday, Carl Friedrich Gauss (1777–1855) entered into a notebook his discovery that a number of other regular polygons were constructible, including the 17-gon, the 257-gon, and the 65,537-gon. The numbers 3, 5, 17, 257, and 65,537 are prime numbers of the special form $F_k = 2^{2^k} + 1$, where k is a nonnegative integer. For example, $F_0 = 2^{2^0} + 1 = 2^1 + 1 = 3$, $F_1 = 2^{2^1} + 1 = 2^2 + 1 = 4 + 1 = 5$, and so on. Numbers of this form had been studied earlier by Pierre de Fermat (1601–1665), and prime numbers of the form $2^{2^k} + 1$ are known as **Fermat primes.**

Here is the remarkable theorem of Gauss. The proof of the "only if" part of the theorem is due to Pierre Wantzel (1814–1848).

THEOREM   *The Gauss-Wantzel Constructibility Theorem*

A regular polygon of n sides is constructible with compass and straightedge if, and only if, n is

1.   4;
2.   a Fermat prime;
3.   a product of distinct Fermat primes;
4.   a power-of-two multiple of a number that is one of the types from 1., 2., or 3. above.

For example, the regular heptagon is not constructible since 7 is not a prime number of the form $2^{2^k} + 1$. A regular nonagon (9-gon) is also not constructible since 9 has two factors of 3. On the other hand, a regular polygon of $1020 = 2^2 \cdot 3 \cdot 5 \cdot 17$ sides is constructible since its odd prime factors are distinct Fermat primes.

Fermat believed that all numbers of the form $F_k = 2^{2^k} + 1$ were prime, but Euler proved this assertion to be false by showing that $F_5 = 2^{2^5} + 1$ is composite; in fact, $F_5 = 4{,}294{,}967{,}297 = (641) \cdot (6{,}700{,}417)$. Likewise, $F_6, F_7, \ldots, F_{21}$ are now known to be composite. It is generally believed that there are only five Fermat primes, namely 3, 5, 17, 257, and 65,537.

Mira and Paper Folding Constructions

Figure 13.13 shows a Mira, which was used in Chapter 12 to draw images under reflection and to investigate lines of symmetry. The Mira can also be used to construct perpendicular lines, midpoints, angle bisectors, and so on. With a little practice, constructions with a Mira are quick and yet very accurate.

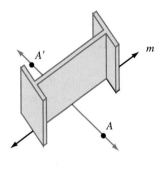

(a) The Mira

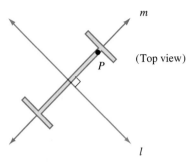

(Top view)

(b) Pivot the Mira about *P* until line *l* coincides with its reflection to construct the line *m* through *P* that is perpendicular to *l*.

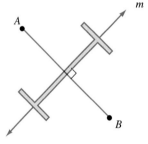

(c) When the reflection of *B* coincides with *A*, the drawing edge of the Mira determines the perpendicular bisector of $\overline{AB}$.

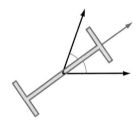

(d) Pivot the Mira about the vertex until the reflection of the near side coincides with the far side to construct the angle bisector.

Figure 13.13
The Mira and its use in three basic constructions

Mira constructions can usually be converted to equivalent paper folding procedures. The drawing line of the Mira is replaced by the crease line of a fold. It is helpful to draw lines and points very dark, so they can be seen from the reverse side of the paper. A folding construction of the perpendicular bisector is shown in Figure 13.14.

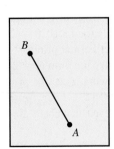
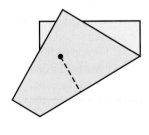
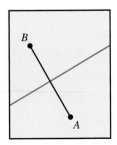

Figure 13.14
Folding point A onto point B forms a crease on the perpendicular bisector of $\overline{AB}$.

HIGHLIGHT FROM HISTORY
Three Impossible Construction Problems

*T*he straightedge allows us to draw a line of indefinite length through any two given points, and the compass* allows us to draw a circle with a given point as its center and passing through any given distinct second point. It then becomes a challenge to find procedures to construct a figure using only these simple tools. Many important contributions to geometry were inspired by attempts to solve the following famous problems, each of which arose in antiquity.

1. *The trisection of an angle:* Divide an arbitrary given angle into three congruent angles.

2. *The duplication of the cube:* Given a cube, construct a cube with twice the volume.

3. *The squaring of the circle:* Given a circle, construct a square of the same area as the circle.

Extensive efforts for over 2000 years failed to solve any of these problems. It was not until the early 1800s that it was shown that these problems were impossible to solve when only the straightedge and compass were allowed. It is interesting to note that methods of algebra were used to prove the impossibility of these geometric construction problems.

*The usage "the compass" is common, but some texts and authors still prefer "compasses" or even "a pair of compasses."

Constructions with Dynamic Geometry Software

Constructions made with tangible materials—paper, dowels, rubber bands, and so on—continue to have an important role to play in teaching and learning the principles of geometry. However, increasingly many classrooms are also taking advantage of the computer. Dynamic geometry software, as described in Appendix D, allows figures to be constructed on the screen, colored, manipulated, explored with measurement tools, and printed out for display and further investigation. The spirally tiled regular hexagon shown in Figure 13.15 is tedious with compass and straightedge, but enjoyable to create with *The Geometer's Sketchpad.*

Figure 13.15
A figure constructed with dynamic geometry software.

COOPERATIVE INVESTIGATION

Exploring Quadrilaterals and Circles

Every triangle has both an inscribed circle and a circumscribed circle, but most quadrilaterals have neither an inscribed nor circumscribed circle. Let's investigate how to construct some quadrilaterals that have at least one of these special circles. Work in pairs to discuss and compare your discoveries.

Materials Needed

Spaghetti noodles (uncooked), $3'' \times 5''$ cards, scissors, drawing and measuring tools (ruler, compass, Mira, and so on)

Exploring Spaghetti Quadrilaterals

Break each of two equally long spaghetti noodles into two pieces. Form a quadrilateral with the four lengths of spaghetti, with opposite sides coming from the same noodle. Put points at A, B, C, and D, and then remove the noodles and draw the quadrilateral $ABCD$.

1. Assuming that the quadrilateral $ABCD$ has an inscribed circle, discuss how you can construct its center and radius. Carry out your procedure: does it appear that $ABCD$ has an inscribed circle?
2. Make another quadrilateral of a different shape but using the same pieces of spaghetti. Does it have an inscribed circle?

Exploring Notecard Quadrilaterals

Cut a $3'' \times 5''$ note card diagonally into two pieces. Arrange the pieces as shown and use your ruler to extend the sides to form a quadrilateral $APBQ$.

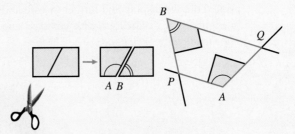

3. Assuming that the quadrilateral $APBQ$ has a circumscribed circle, discuss how you can construct its center. Carry out your procedure: does it appear that there is a circle through all the vertices of $APBQ$?
4. Rearrange the two pieces of notecard to form another quadrilateral of a different shape. Does it have a circumscribed circle?

A Further Investigation

5. Draw a quadrilateral that has both an inscribed and a circumscribed circle. Describe your method, and draw the two circles.

Constructing and Investigating Geometric Shapes in Grades 3–5

Students in grades 3–5 should be reasoning about geometric relationships within and between shapes. Students should investigate the properties of shapes and make conjectures about these properties. For example, a fourth-grade classroom might consider the following problem:

> Start with any two congruent triangles. Join them along sides of equal length. What kinds of figures can result?

Students might experiment by drawing various triangles, then tracing or cutting out two copies of each to form figures. This may lead them to the conjecture that parallelograms are made up of two congruent triangles, or perhaps that the opposite sides of parallelograms are congruent. However, if one of the triangles is "flipped over," then a kite will be formed instead of a parallelogram.

In fifth grade, students make frequent use of drawings and concrete shapes to investigate and demonstrate their ideas, but they will also be developing mental models of shapes and their properties. By fifth grade students should be working to develop clear mathematical arguments about why a geometric relationship is true, for example: "You can't possibly make a triangle with two right angles because if you start with one side of the triangle across the bottom, the other two sides go straight up. They're parallel, so they can't possibly ever meet, so you can't get it to be a triangle."

SOURCE: Reprinted with permission from *Curriculum and Evaluation Standards for School Mathematics: Discussion Draft,* copyright 1998 by the National Council of Teachers of Mathematics. All rights reserved.

PROBLEM SET 13.2

Understanding Concepts

1. The sequence of steps shown below outline the "corresponding angles" construction to draw a line k that is parallel to a line l and passes through the point P not on l.

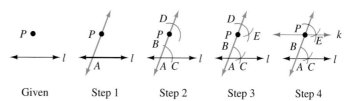

Given	Step 1	Step 2	Step 3	Step 4

   (a) Give a written description of each of the four steps.

   (b) Explain why the construction gives the desired line k.

2. (a) Describe, in words and drawings, a Mira construction which gives the line k parallel to a line l and through a point P not on l.

   (b) Answer (a), but use paper folding instead of the Mira.

3. The drafting triangle and straightedge can be used to construct parallel lines, as shown below.

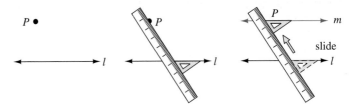

(a) What geometric principle justifies this construction?

(b) Describe, in words and drawings, a procedure using a straightedge and drafting triangle to construct the line *m* perpendicular to a given line *l* and passing through a given point *P*.

---

4. Use compass and straightedge to construct the following:

(a) Line perpendicular to *l* through *P*

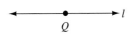

(b) Line perpendicular to *l* through *Q*

(c) Perpendicular bisector to $\overline{ST}$

$$S \text{——————} T$$

(d) Bisector of $\angle A$

5. Repeat the constructions in problem 4 with a Mira (if available).

6. Repeat the constructions in problem 4 with paper folding.

7. Construct the circumcenters and circumscribing circles of triangles of the three types shown. Use any tools you wish to draw the perpendicular bisectors of the sides of the triangles.

(a) Acute triangle

(b) Right triangle

(c) Obtuse triangle

(d) Make a conjecture about where—inside, on, or outside the triangle—the circumcenter of a triangle will be located.

8. Construct the incenters and inscribed circles of the three types of triangles shown in problem 7, using

(a) a compass and straightedge.

(b) a Mira (if available) and compass.

(c) paper folding (copy and cut the triangles from paper with scissors, then fold) and compass.

9. A point *P* is exterior to a circle centered at *Q*. Use Thales' theorem to justify why drawing the circle with diameter $\overline{PQ}$ gives a construction of the two lines $\overleftrightarrow{PS}$ and $\overleftrightarrow{PT}$ that are tangent to the circle centered at *Q*.

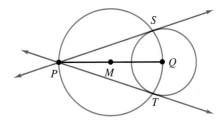

10. Draw any triangle *ABC*. Using any tools you wish, draw both the inscribed and the circumscribed circles of your triangle. Now choose an arbitrary point *X* on the larger circle and draw the chords $\overline{XY}$ and $\overline{XZ}$ that are tangent to the smaller circle. Finally, draw chord $\overline{YZ}$ of the larger circle. Start with a new point *X'* and again draw a triangle *X'Y'Z'* (colored pencils are helpful). Make a conjecture about all such triangles.

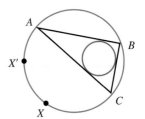

11. **(a)** Use any drawing tools you wish to construct the altitudes of the three types of triangles in problem 7.

(b) Make a conjecture about the three altitudes of an acute triangle.

(c) Make a conjecture about the three altitudes of a right triangle.

(d) Make a conjecture about the three lines containing the altitudes of an obtuse triangle.

---

12. Justify the following construction of an equilateral triangle inscribed in a given circle.

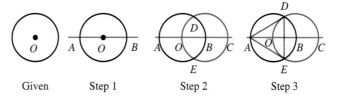

Given   Step 1   Step 2   Step 3

---

13. A **median** of a triangle is a line segment from a vertex to the midpoint of the opposite side. Using any drawing tools you wish, draw the three medians in each of several triangles. Give a statement that describes what you observe.

14. Let the lines k and l intersect to form two pairs of vertical angles. Prove that the lines m and n that bisect the vertical angles are perpendicular.

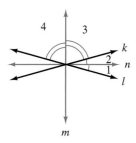

15. **(a)** Prove that the perpendicular bisector of any chord of a circle contains the center of the circle.

(b) Trace partway around a cup bottom to draw a circular arc. Then explain how to construct the center of the arc. (*Hint:* Use part (a), twice!)

(c) The three congruent circles below are centered at points A, B, and C on the large circular arc, and the circles at centers A and C contain point B. Where do the dashed lines intersect? Explain why.

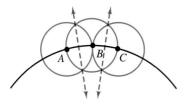

16. Prove that the angle bisectors of a triangle are concurrent, using the equidistance property of the angle bisector. The discussion in Example 13.8 can be used as a model for your proof.

17. The diagram shows how to erect an equilateral triangle ABC on a given line segment $\overline{AB}$ using a compass and straightedge.

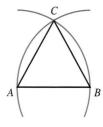

Give careful step-by-step instructions to construct these polygons erected on a given side $\overline{AB}$.

(a) a square   **(b)** a regular hexagon

18. Reflecting point B to fall on the perpendicular bisector of $\overline{AB}$ shows how a Mira can be used to draw an equilateral triangle ABC on a given side $\overline{AB}$.

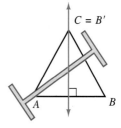

Give careful step-by-step instructions to construct these polygons on a given side with a Mira.

(a) a square   **(b)** a regular hexagon

19. **(a)** Construct a regular pentagon inscribed in a circle by following the steps outlined.

(b) Use a ruler and protractor to check that *PENTA* is regular.

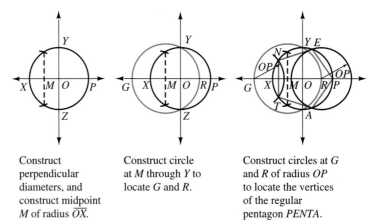

Construct perpendicular diameters, and construct midpoint *M* of radius $\overline{OX}$.

Construct circle at *M* through *Y* to locate *G* and *R*.

Construct circles at *G* and *R* of radius *OP* to locate the vertices of the regular pentagon *PENTA*.

20. **(a)** Construct a heptagon inscribed in a given circle by following the steps outlined below.

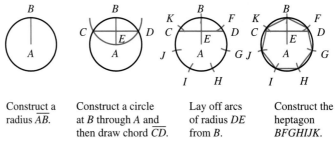

Construct a radius $\overline{AB}$.

Construct a circle at *B* through *A* and then draw chord $\overline{CD}$.

Lay off arcs of radius *DE* from *B*.

Construct the heptagon *BFGHIJK*.

(b) Is it possible for *BFGHIJK* to be a regular heptagon, or is it just a close approximation?

21. List the constructible regular *n*-gons up to *n* = 100, using the Gauss-Wantzel theorem.

22. Someone claims that trisecting the chord $\overline{BC}$ of an arc centered at *A* gives a compass and straightedge trisection of ∠*A*. How would you respond to this assertion? How well does the method appear to work on an angle of measure 150°? Make a drawing and use a protractor to measure the angles.

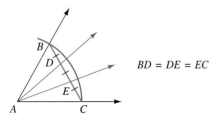

BD = DE = EC

Thinking Critically

23. Complete the proof of the equidistance property of the perpendicular bisector. Do so by showing that if *P* is equidistant from *A* and *B*, then the line $\overleftrightarrow{PM}$

containing *P* and the midpoint *M* of $\overline{AB}$ is the perpendicular bisector of $\overline{AB}$.

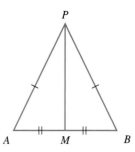

24. An **altitude** of a triangle is a line through a vertex of the triangle that is perpendicular to the line containing the opposite side of the triangle. The altitude through vertex *A* has been constructed in this figure:

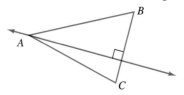

(a) Construct any triangle *ABC* and all three of its altitudes. What property do you discover about the altitudes of a triangle?

(b) Append three congruent copies of △*ABC* to form △*PQR*, as shown. It becomes apparent that the altitudes of △*ABC* are simultaneously the perpendicular bisectors of the sides of △*PQR*. Use this fact to explain why the altitudes of any triangle are concurrent. The common point of intersection of altitudes is called the **orthocenter** of the triangle.

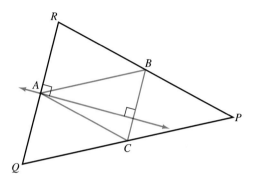

25. Draw any triangle *ABC*. Using any tools you wish, draw its orthocenter (that is, the point of concurrence of the three altitudes of △*ABC*; see problem 24). Label the orthocenter *D*. Now trace the four points *A*, *B*, *C*, and *D* on a clean sheet of paper, and draw the orthocenter of △*BCD*. Are you surprised? Guess, and then check what the orthocenters of △*ACD* and △*ABD* are.

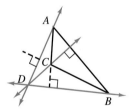

26. A regular pentagon *PENTA* and an equilateral triangle *PQR* are both inscribed in the same circle centered at *O*, with *P* a common vertex. Calculate *m*(∠*NOQ*) and explain why laying off segments of length *QN* about the circle constructs a regular inscribed 15-gon.

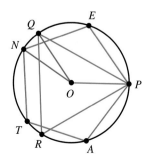

Thinking Cooperatively

The following paper folding constructions are enjoyable group activities. Each collaborative group needs several sheets of blank paper (origami squares or patty paper work well), scissors, ruler, protractor, and colored pencils.

27. **Folding an Angle Trisection.** Construct an angle *ABC*, using the lower edge of a piece of rectangular notebook paper as the side $\overline{AB}$. Fold the lower edge to create two equally spaced folds parallel to $\overline{AB}$, and let *D* and *E* denote the fold points along the left edge of the paper. Now fold the lower corner *B* so that it lies along the lower horizontal fold and, at the same time, point *E* lies along the side $\overrightarrow{BC}$ of ∠*ABC*. Mark the points *B'* and *D'* as shown. Finally, unfold the paper and construct the two rays from *B* that pass through *B'* and *D'*. Measure ∠*ABC*, ∠*ABB'*, ∠*B'BD'*, and ∠*D'BC*. Your group should discover that the smaller angles trisect ∠*ABC*. Report your measurements and compare the success of your folded angle trisection with other groups.

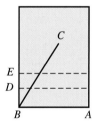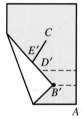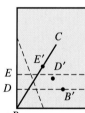

28. **Folding Special Points in a Triangle.** Cut out several paper triangles with scissors. Discuss procedures to use folding to construct the following points and segments.

(a) The midpoints of the sides of the triangle.

(b) The medians (the segments connecting a vertex to the midpoint of the opposite side). What property do you observe is satisfied by the three medians?

(c) The angle bisectors of a triangle. What special point of the triangle is constructed with the folds?

(d) The perpendicular bisectors of the sides of an acute triangle. What special point is constructed with these folds?

(e) The altitudes (an altitude is a line through a vertex that is perpendicular to the opposite side) of an acute triangle. What special point is constructed with these folds?

29. **Folding Regular Polygons.** A square can be folded from a rectangular sheet of paper by following the procedures illustrated in this sequence of steps.

Discuss procedures and give demonstrations to construct these regular polygons with paper folding.

(a) An equilateral triangle. Carefully describe the sequence of folds you make.

(b) A regular hexagon, starting with the equilateral triangle cut from your construction in part (a). (*Suggestion:* First, use folding to construct the center of the equilateral triangle.)

(c) A regular octagon, starting with a square. Carefully describe the folds you make.

Using a Calculator

 30. Verify that $F_3 = 2^{2^3} + 1$ and $F_4 = 2^{2^4} + 1$ are given decimally by 257 and 65,537.

 31. **(a)** Verify that the Fermat number $F_5 = 2^{2^5} + 1$ is 4,294,967,297.

(b) Verify that the Fermat number $F_5 = 4{,}294{,}967{,}297$ is composite by computing $(641)(6700417)$.

Using a Computer

32. Draw any triangle *ABC*. Construct the following three points:

G, the **centroid** (intersection of the medians, see problem 13);

H, the orthocenter (intersection of the altitudes, see problem 24); and
P, the circumcenter (intersection of the perpendicular bisectors of the sides).

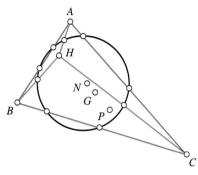

(a) Euler discovered an interesting fact about *G*, *H*, and *P*. What do you suppose the "Euler line" might be?

(b) Measure the distances *PG* and *GH*, and then make a conjecture concerning the ratio of these distances.

(c) Find the midpoint *N* of the segment $\overline{PH}$, and draw the circle centered at *N* which passes through the midpoint of a side of your triangle. Where does it intersect the other sides of the triangle?

(d) Describe how the circle at *N* intersects the segments $\overline{HA}$, $\overline{HB}$, and $\overline{HC}$.

33. Draw any triangle *ABC*. On each side construct outward pointing equilateral triangles *BCR*, *CAS*, and *ABT*. Also construct the incenters *X*, *Y*, and *Z* of the equilateral triangles.

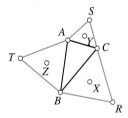

(a) What kind of triangle is *XYZ*? Measure lengths and angles to support your guess.

(b) Construct the segments $\overline{AR}$, $\overline{BS}$, and $\overline{CT}$, showing they are concurrent at a point *F*. (*F* is called the **Fermat point,** and in an acute triangle *ABC* it is the point with the smallest sum *FA* + *FB* + *FC* of distances to the vertices of $\triangle ABC$).

(c) At what angles do the lines drawn in part (b) intersect at *F*? Measure to verify your guess.

(d) Draw the segments $\overline{AX}$, $\overline{BY}$, $\overline{CZ}$, showing they are concurrent at a point *N*. (*N* is called the **Napoleon point;** supposedly it was Napoleon who discovered the theorem that you likely discovered in answering part (a).)

(e) Construct the circumcenter *P* of △*ABC*. What can you conjecture about the three points *F, N,* and *P*?

34. Construct three equilateral triangles that share a common vertex *A*. Let the triangles, labeled counterclockwise around their respective interiors, be △*ABC,* △*AB'C',* and △*AB"C"*. Draw the midpoint *T* of $\overline{BC''}$, as shown below. Similarly, draw the midpoint *R* of $\overline{B'C}$ and the midpoint *I* of $\overline{C'B''}$. Finally, draw the triangle *TRI*. What kind of a triangle does *TRI* seem to be? Measure *TRI* to check your conjecture.

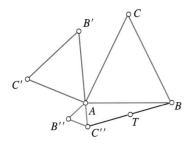

35. Construct a circle and the radii to four points *A, B, C,* and *D* on the circle. Then construct tangent lines to the circle at *A, B, C,* and *D*. Let *Q, R, S,* and *T* denote the points at which successive pairs of tangent lines intersect, to give a quadrilateral *QRST* that is circumscribed about the circle.

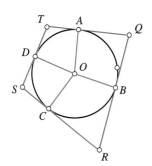

(a) Investigate how the sums of opposite lengths of the sides of *QRST* compare. Make a conjecture about *QR* + *ST* and *RS* + *QT*.

(b) Prove your conjecture. (*Hint:* Notice that *QA* = *QB, RB* = *RC, SC* = *SD,* and *TD* = *TA*.)

For Review

36. Consider the two triangles shown below.

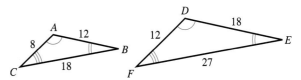

Are the following assertions *true* or *false*? Explain your answer.

(a) Five parts of △*ABC* are congruent to five parts of △*DEF*.

(b) △*ABC* is congruent to △*DEF*.

37. The Girl Scout troop needed to determine the width of the river. Alicia followed this plan. First she paced off equally spaced markers at *A, B,* and *C,* where *A* is across the river from a tree at point *T*. Then Alicia walked 126 feet directly away from the river until she reached point *D*, at which the tree at *T* was in line with the stake at *B*. What is the width of the river, and what geometric property is Alicia relying on?

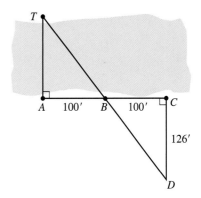

38. Two segments, $\overline{AB}$ and $\overline{CD}$, are congruent, parallel, and not on the same line. Prove that the endpoints of the segments are the vertices of a parallelogram.

13.3   Similar Triangles

Two figures are **similar** if they have the same shape but not necessarily the same size. For example, an overhead projector forms an image on the screen that is similar to the figure on the transparency. The same is true of a photocopy made on a machine at the enlarge or reduce setting. Figures in space can also be similar to one another. Design engineers often build small scale models of buildings, airplanes, or ships and then make tests and measurements on the model to predict whether or not the design objectives will be met in the full scale structure.

A map or model will indicate how its size compares to actual size by giving a **scale factor.** For example, a ship model may be scaled at 1:100, meaning that two points at a distance x on the model correspond to points on the real ship at a distance $100x$. Conversely, any length on the actual ship divided by 100 gives the corresponding length for the model.

The following definition gives an exact description of similarity for triangles.

DEFINITION   *Similar Triangles and the Scale Factor*

Triangle *ABC* is **similar** to triangle *DEF*, written $\triangle ABC \sim \triangle DEF$, if, and only if, corresponding angles are congruent and the lengths of corresponding sides have the same ratio. That is, $\triangle ABC \sim \triangle DEF$ if, and only if, $\angle A \cong \angle D$, $\angle B \cong \angle E$, $\angle C \cong \angle F$ and

$$\frac{DE}{AB} = \frac{EF}{BC} = \frac{DF}{AC}.$$

The common ratio of lengths of corresponding sides is called the **scale factor** from $\triangle ABC$ to $\triangle DEF$.

The scale factor from $\triangle DEF$ to $\triangle ABC$ is the reciprocal of the scale factor from $\triangle ABC$ to $\triangle DEF$. For example, if the sides of $\triangle DEF$ are three times the length of the sides of the similar triangle ABC, then the sides of $\triangle ABC$ are one-third the length of the sides of $\triangle DEF$.

Two examples of similar triangles and their scale factors are shown in Figure 13.16.

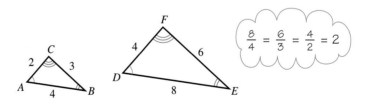

$$\frac{8}{4} = \frac{6}{3} = \frac{4}{2} = 2$$

$\triangle ABC \sim \triangle DEF$
Scale factor from $\triangle ABC$ to $\triangle DEF = 2$

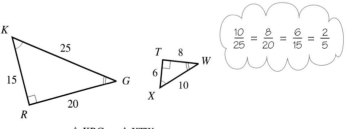

$$\frac{10}{25} = \frac{8}{20} = \frac{6}{15} = \frac{2}{5}$$

$\triangle KRG \sim \triangle XTW$
Scale factor from $\triangle KRG$ to $\triangle XTW = 2/5$

Figure 13.16
Two pairs of similar triangles

It is possible to conclude that two triangles are similar even when we have incomplete information about the sides and angles of the triangles. The most commonly used criteria for similarity are the angle-angle (AA), side-side-side (SSS), and side-angle-side (SAS) properties.*

The Angle-Angle-Angle (AAA) and Angle-Angle (AA) Similarity Properties

In Figure 13.17, $\triangle ABC$ and $\triangle DEF$ have corresponding angles measuring 110°, 40°, and 30°. We see that $\triangle ABC \sim \triangle DEF$. The scale factor can be determined by measuring the lengths of two corresponding sides and forming their ratio. For example, the scale factor is DE/AB.

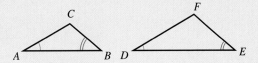

Figure 13.17
Two triangles with three congruent angles are similar by the AAA Similarity Property.

In general, two triangles with three pairs of congruent angles are similar, an observation known as the **angle-angle-angle (AAA) property** of similar triangles. However all three angles of a triangle are determined once we know two of its angles, since the three measures of the angles add up to 180°. Therefore, the more general property is called the **angle-angle (AA) property of similarity.**

> **PROPERTY** *The AA Similarity Property*
> If two angles of one triangle are congruent respectively to two angles of a second triangle, then the triangles are similar.

| EXAMPLE 13.9 | **Making an Indirect Measurement with Similarity** |

A tree at point T is in line with a stake at point L when viewed from point N. Use the information in the diagram to measure the distance across the river.

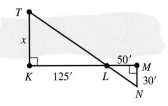

---

*In some books, some or even all of these properties are proved on the basis of other assumptions, making the properties theorems. In other texts, the properties are adopted as postulates. In this text, in keeping with an informal treatment of Euclidean geometry, we will refer to the AA, SSS, and SAS criteria for similarity as *properties*.

Solution

By the vertical angles theorem, $\angle TLK \cong \angle NLM$. Also $\angle K \cong \angle M$ since both are right angles. By the AA similarity property, $\triangle TLK \sim \triangle NLM$. Thus $\dfrac{TK}{NM} = \dfrac{KL}{ML}$, since the lengths of corresponding sides have the same ratio. Since $TK = x$, $NM = 30'$, $KL = 125'$, and $ML = 50'$ this gives the proportion $\dfrac{x}{30'} = \dfrac{125'}{50'}$. Therefore, $x = \dfrac{30' \cdot 125'}{50'} = 75'$. We have found the distance across the river by an indirect measurement using similar triangles.

The Side-Side-Side (SSS) Similarity Property

PROPERTY *The SSS Similarity Property*

If the three sides of one triangle are proportional to the three sides of a second triangle, then the triangles are similar. That is, if $\dfrac{DE}{AB} = \dfrac{EF}{BC} = \dfrac{DF}{AC}$ then $\triangle ABC \sim \triangle DEF$.

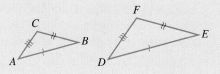

"Wavy" tick marks are helpful to identify corresponding proportional sides of similar figures, as shown above.

EXAMPLE   13.10

Applying the SSS Similarity Property

A contractor wishes to build an L-shaped concrete footing for a brick wall, with a 12 foot leg of the wall meeting a 10 foot leg of the wall at a right angle. The contractor knows that a 3 by 4 by 5 foot triangle has a right angle opposite the 5 foot side. How can the contractor place stakes at points X, Y, and Z to form a right angle at point Y? The wall will be built along string lines stretched from X to Y and from Y to Z.

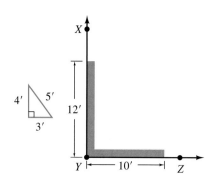

Solution   By the SSS similarity property, the 3–4–5 foot right triangle can be magnified by a convenient scale factor to give an accurate right triangle. A scale factor of 4 gives a 12–16–20 foot right triangle. The contractor can place a stake at *X* that is 16 feet from the corner point *Y*. Using two measuring tapes, a stake is placed at the point *Z* where the 20 foot mark on the tape from *X* crosses the 12 foot mark on the tape from *Y*.

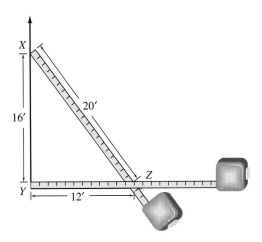

DID YOU KNOW?

The Navajo's Organization of Space and Time

The Navajo believe in a dynamic universe. Rather than consisting of objects and situations, the universe is made up of processes. Central to our Western mode of thought is the idea that things are separable entities that can be subdivided into smaller discrete units. For us, things that change through time do so by going from one specific state to another specific state. While we believe time to be continuous, we often even break it into discrete units or freeze it and talk about an instant or point in time. Or, we often just ignore time. For example, when we speak of a boundary line dividing a surface into two parts or a line being divided by a point, we are describing a static situation, that is, one in which time plays no role whatever. Among the Navajo, where the focus is on process, change is everpresent; interrelationship and motion are of primary significance. These incorporate and subsume space and time.

. . . To us, the significant aspect of a boundary is that it is a spatial divider; to the Navajo, the significance is the processes of which the boundary is a part and how it affects and is being affected by those processes. The Navajo react quite negatively when fences are placed upon their reservation land. One major reason is their belief that space should *not* be segmented in an arbitrary and static way.

These excerpts, contrasting Western and Navajo organization of space and time, are from Marcia Ascher's book *Ethnomathematics: A Multicultural View of Mathematical Ideas.* The book gives a fascinating introduction to multicultural mathematical ideas from peoples such as the Inuit, Navajo, and Iroquois of North America; the Incas of South America; the Malekula, Warlpiri, Maori, and Caroline Islanders from Oceania; and the Tshokwe, Bushoong, and Kpelle of Africa.

SOURCE: Marcia Ascher, *Ethnomathematics: A Multicultural View of Mathematical Ideas.*
Pacific Grove, CA: Brooks/Cole Publishing Company, 1991, pp. 128–29.

Thales' Puzzle

Thales is reputed to have calculated the height of the pyramids in Egypt by comparing the shadow cast by the pyramid to the shadow cast by a vertical stick. By similar right triangles $H/h = y/x$, where H is the height of the pyramid, h is the height of the stick, x is the length of the shadow of the stick, and $y = PB$ is the length of the shadow of the pyramid from a point P on the ground to the point B directly beneath apex A. Thus, the height of the pyramid is given by the formula $H = yh/x$. Unfortunately, Thales still has a difficulty: he can easily measure h and x, but y is not simple to measure since point B is somewhere *inside* the pyramid!

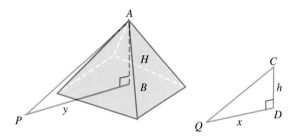

After marking points P and Q one morning. Thales returned a few hours later and realized he could now calculate the height of the pyramid. How did Thales solve his problem?

The Side-Angle-Side (SAS) Property

PROPERTY *The SAS Similarity Property*

If, in two triangles, the ratios of any two pairs of corresponding sides are equal and the included angles are congruent, then the two triangles are similar. That is, if $\dfrac{DE}{AB} = \dfrac{DF}{AC}$ and $\angle A \cong \angle D$ then $\triangle ABC \sim \triangle DEF$.

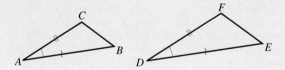

EXAMPLE   13.11

Applying the SAS Similarity Property

The sun is about 93 million miles from Earth and the moon is about 240,000 miles distant. If the diameter of the moon is 2200 miles, what is the approximate diameter of the sun? (*Hint:* From the earth, the sun and moon appear to have the same diameter.)

Solution

Because the moon (M) appears to have the same diameter as the sun (S) during an eclipse, they form nearly congruent angles when viewed from Earth (E). This

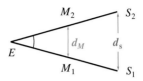

illustration is far from a true scale drawing, but it does show that $\triangle EM_1M_2 \sim \triangle ES_1S_2$ by the SAS similarity property. Thus, $\dfrac{S_1S_2}{M_1M_2} = \dfrac{ES_1}{EM_1}$, so $S_1S_2 = \dfrac{ES_1}{EM_1} \cdot M_1M_2 = \dfrac{93,000,000}{240,000} \cdot 2200$ miles $= 852,500$ miles. This estimate compares well with the sun's actual diameter of 864,000 miles given by more accurate methods.

Geometric Problem Solving Using Similar Triangles

The following sequence of examples illustrates how similar triangles can be used to explore the properties of geometric figures. These examples are unified by exploring figures constructed by joining the midpoints of sides of triangles or quadrilaterals.

EXAMPLE   13.12

Exploring the Medial Triangle

If X, Y, and Z are the midpoints of the sides of $\triangle ABC$, then $\triangle XYZ$ is called the **medial triangle** of $\triangle ABC$.

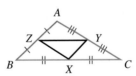

Show that $\triangle ABC \sim \triangle XYZ$, with a scale factor of $\dfrac{1}{2}$, and each side of the medial triangle is parallel to the corresponding side of $\triangle ABC$. For example, $\overline{XY} \parallel \overline{AB}$ and $\dfrac{XY}{AB} = \dfrac{1}{2}$.

Solution

From the figure shown above, it is seen that $\dfrac{CY}{CA} = \dfrac{CX}{CB} = \dfrac{1}{2}$. Therefore, by the SAS similarity property, $\triangle ACB \sim \triangle YCX$, with a scale factor of $\dfrac{1}{2}$. In particular, $\dfrac{XY}{BA} = \dfrac{1}{2}$. Moreover, $\angle CAB \cong \angle CYX$ so $\overline{XY} \parallel \overline{AB}$ by the corresponding angles property. By the same reasoning, the remaining two sides of $\triangle XYZ$ are also parallel and half of the length of the corresponding sides of $\triangle ABC$. Since the sides of $\triangle XYZ$ are half the length of the corresponding sides of $\triangle ABC$, the two triangles are similar by the SSS similarity property.

Similar Figures

10-7

▶ **Lesson Link** You've learned about geometric figures. Now you'll explore a class of figures whose dimensions are proportional. ◀

Explore Similar Figures

The Same ... But Different!

Materials: Centimeter ruler, Protractor

1. Draw a large triangle, △A, with three unequal sides. Measure and label the length of each side and the width of each angle.

2. Draw a smaller triangle whose angles have the same measures as the angles of △A. Call the new triangle △B. Measure and label the length of each side.

3. Find these ratios:

a. $\dfrac{\text{longest side of } \triangle A}{\text{longest side of } \triangle B}$ **b.** $\dfrac{\text{mid-length side of } \triangle A}{\text{mid-length side of } \triangle B}$

c. $\dfrac{\text{shortest side of } \triangle A}{\text{shortest side of } \triangle B}$

4. Are the longest sides proportional to the shortest sides? Explain.

5. Are the longest sides proportional to the mid-length sides? Explain.

6. Are the mid-length sides proportional to the shortest sides? Explain.

You'll Learn ...
■ what similar figures are
■ to use proportions to find lengths in a similar figure

... How It's Used

Drivers use similar figures when calculating the actual distance between two locations on a road map.

Vocabulary
similar

Learn Similar Figures

Recall that figures with the same size and shape are *congruent*. The symbol ≅ means "is congruent to."

Figures that have the same shape but not necessarily the same size are **similar** figures. The symbol ~ means "is similar to."

The objects pictured are similar because their shapes are the same, even though their sizes are different.

10-7 • Similar Figures **543**

SOURCE: From *Scott Foresman–Addison Wesley Middle School Math*, Grade 6, Course 1, p. 543, by Randall I. Charles et al. Copyright © 1999 Addison Wesley Longman, Inc.

Questions for the Teacher

1. What similarity property is being explored in the sequence of six instructions and questions on the school book page?

2. Design a similar sequence of instructions and questions that explore the SAS similarity property.

EXAMPLE 13.13

Classifying the Midpoint Figure of a Quadrilateral

Two quadrilaterals are shown. It appears that joining successive midpoints of the sides of these quadrilaterals forms a parallelogram. Prove that this is indeed the case.

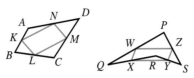

Solution

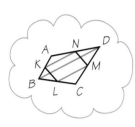

Let *KLMN* be the midpoint figure of the quadrilateral *ABCD*. Draw the diagonal $\overline{BD}$ and consider $\triangle ABD$ and $\triangle CBD$. By Example 13.12 we know $\overline{KN}$ and $\overline{LM}$ are both parallel to $\overline{BD}$ and have length *BD*/2. But then $\overline{KN}$ and $\overline{LM}$ are congruent and parallel segments. The same reasoning shows $\overline{KL}$ and $\overline{NM}$ are congruent and parallel, since both segments are parallel to $\overline{AC}$ and have length *AC*/2. By definition, *KLMN* is a parallelogram.

The proof just given remains valid for *space* quadrilaterals, for which the four vertices are not necessarily in the same plane. For example, the quadrilateral *PQRS* shown above may be easily visualized as a nonplanar quadrilateral. However, the midpoint quadrilateral *WXYZ* is a parallelogram, so it lies in a plane. It's interesting to confirm this result with a quadrilateral made of sticks whose midpoints are joined by elastic bands to form the midpoint parallelogram.

EXAMPLE 13.14

Discovering the Centroid of a Triangle

A **median** of a triangle is a line segment joining a vertex to the midpoint of the opposite side as shown. Prove that the three medians of a triangle are concurrent at a point *G* which is 2/3 of the distance along each median from the vertex toward the midpoint. *G* is the **centroid** or **center of gravity** of the triangle.

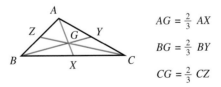

$$AG = \tfrac{2}{3}\, AX$$
$$BG = \tfrac{2}{3}\, BY$$
$$CG = \tfrac{2}{3}\, CZ$$

Solution

Understand the problem

There are really *two* problems to be solved. First, there is a *distance* problem: if *G* is the point where the two medians $\overline{BY}$ and $\overline{CZ}$ intersect, then we must show that $BG = 2/3\ BY$, or equivalently $BG = 2GY$. Second, there is a *concurrence* problem: if *G* is the point of intersection of $\overline{BY}$ and $\overline{CZ}$, then we must show that the third median $\overline{AX}$ also passes through *G*.

Devise a plan

Since we hope to show $BG = 2GY$ and $CG = 2GZ$, it may be useful to consider the midpoints *M* of $\overline{BG}$ and *N* of $\overline{CG}$. The distance problem for medians $\overline{BY}$ and $\overline{CZ}$ will be solved if it can be shown that *M* and *G* trisect $\overline{BY}$, and *N* and *G* trisect $\overline{CZ}$. Since *Z*, *M*, *N*, and Y are the successive midpoints of the quadrilateral $ABGC$, we should gain important information by constructing the midpoint figure $ZMNY$, which we know is a parallelogram by Example 13.13.

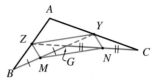

Carry out the plan

Because $ZMNY$ is a parallelogram, the point G at which the diagonals intersect is the midpoint of the diagonal $\overline{MY}$ of the parallelogram. Thus $MG = GY$. But M is the midpoint of $\overline{BG}$, so $BM = MG$. This shows that G is 2/3 of the distance from B to Y along the median $\overline{BY}$. The same reasoning shows that G and N trisect the median $\overline{CZ}$. The concurrence problem is now solved by symmetry: if G' is the point of intersection of the medians $\overline{BY}$ and $\overline{AX}$, then G' is 2/3 of the distance from a vertex along either median; therefore, $G = G'$.

Look back

The problem-solving strategies used in this example are likely to be helpful for other problems:

- *Divide the problem into simpler parts:* we solved a distance problem and a concurrence problem.
- *Consider a simpler problem first:* G was defined as the intersection of *two* medians, and it was to be shown G was 2/3 of the distances along the two medians from the vertices.
- *Use a related result:* the previous example, showing that the midpoints of sides of any quadrilateral formed a parallelogram, was a key idea in the solution.

COOPERATIVE INVESTIGATION

Explorations with Centers of Gravity

The **center of gravity,** or **centroid,** of a figure is its point of balance. A plane figure, cut from cardboard, will hang horizontally when it is suspended by a string pinned at the centroid. If pushed slowly over the edge of a table, the figure will begin to teeter just as the centroid reaches the table's edge.

Materials Needed

Heavy cardboard, scissors, ruler, pins, and strings

Directions

1. Cut a large (sides ranging from 6″ to 12″) triangle from cardboard. Hang the triangle from string pinned at some point of the triangle (alternatively, balance the figure on the upright point of a pin). Move the pin to new points to determine the centroid experimentally. Balance the triangle on the edge of a table, and see if the point you found experimentally lies directly over the table's edge.

2. Draw the medians on the triangle, and see if they intersect at the point found experimentally.

3. Cut a large convex quadrilateral from cardboard, and find its centroid experimentally with both the string and table edge methods.

4. Devise a method to *draw* the centroid of a convex quadrilateral. (*Hint:* Each diagonal of the quadrilateral forms two triangles.)

5. Use the method you've devised to draw the centroids of the cardboard quadrilaterals. Do your points coincide with the experimentally found centroids?

Archimedes made many discoveries about the center of gravity for both plane and solid figures. He was well aware that the medians of a triangle intersected at the centroid.

PROBLEM SET 13.3

Understanding Concepts

1. Which of the following pairs of triangles are similar? If they are similar, explain why, express the similarity with the ~ notation, and give the scale factor.

(a)

(b)

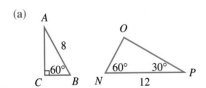

(c)

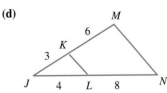

(d)

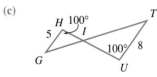

(e)

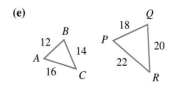

2. Are the following figures necessarily similar? If so, explain why. If not, draw an example to show why not.

(a) Any two equilateral triangles.

(b) Any two isosceles triangles.

(c) Any two right triangles having an acute angle of measure 36°.

(d) Any two isosceles right triangles.

(e) Any two congruent triangles.

(f) A triangle with sides of lengths 3 and 4 and an angle of 30° and a triangle with sides of lengths 6 and 8 and an angle of 30°.

3. A pair of similar triangles is shown in each part. Find the measures of the segments marked with a letter a, b, c, or d.

(a)

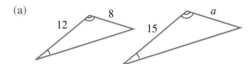

(b)

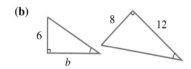

(c)

(d)

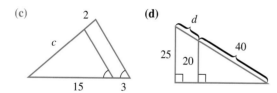

4. (a) Two convex quadrilaterals, *ABCD* and *EFGH*, have congruent angles at their corresponding vertices: $\angle A \cong \angle E$, $\angle B \cong \angle F$, $\angle C \cong \angle G$, $\angle D \cong \angle H$. Can you conclude that the two convex quadrilaterals are similar? Explain.

(b) Two convex quadrilaterals have corresponding sides in the same ratio. Are the quadrilaterals necessarily similar? Explain.

5. Suppose $\triangle ABC \sim \triangle DEF$, where only points *D* and *E* are shown. Find all possible locations for *F*, and draw the corresponding triangles *DEF*.

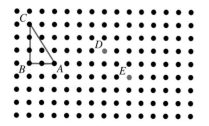

6. The diagonals of the trapezoid *ABCD* shown below intersect at *E*, where $\overline{AB} \parallel \overline{CD}$.

(a) Explain why $\triangle ABE \sim \triangle CDE$.

(b) Determine *x* and *y*.

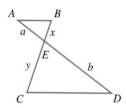

7. Let $\overline{AB}$ and $\overline{CD}$ be parallel, and let $\overline{AD}$ and $\overline{BC}$ intersect at *E*. Prove that $a \cdot y = x \cdot b$.

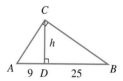

8. $\triangle ABC$ is a right triangle with altitude $\overline{CD}$.

(a) Explain why $\triangle ADC \sim \triangle CDB$.

(b) Find an equation for *h* and solve it to show that $h = \sqrt{9 \cdot 25} = 3 \cdot 5 = 15$.

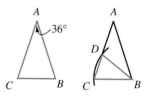

9. An isosceles triangle whose apex angle measures 36° is sometimes called a **golden triangle.**

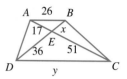

(a) Draw an arc centered at *B* and passing through *C*. If *D* is the point at which the arc intersects $\overline{AC}$, prove that $\triangle BCD$ is also a golden triangle. (*Hint:* What is $m(\angle C)$?)

(b) Construct three more golden triangles *CDE*, *DEF*, and *EFG*, where each contains the next.

10. $\triangle ABC$ is an isosceles triangle with apex *C*. It has the unusual property that the circular arc centered at *A* intersects the opposite side at a point *D* for which

$\triangle ABC \sim \triangle BCD$. Use this property to find the measures of the base and apex angles of $\triangle ABC$.

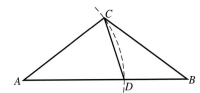

11. Suppose $\triangle ABC \sim \triangle BCA$. What more can you say about $\triangle ABC$?

12. Lined notebook paper provides a convenient way to subdivide a line segment into a specified number of congruent subsegments. The diagram shows how swinging an arc of radius AB subdivides the segment into five congruent parts: $\overline{AX} \cong \overline{XY} \cong \overline{YZ} \cong \overline{ZW} \cong \overline{WB}$.

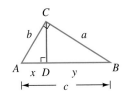

(a) Show how to subdivide a segment $\overline{AB}$ into seven congruent segments.

(b) Carefully explain why the procedure is valid.

Thinking Critically

13. Let $\overline{CD}$ be the altitude drawn to the hypotenuse of the right triangle ABC shown.

$$a = BC, \quad b = AC, \quad c = AB$$
$$x = AD, \quad y = DB$$

(a) Explain why $\triangle ABC \sim \triangle ACD$ and $\triangle ABC \sim \triangle CBD$.

(b) Explain why $\dfrac{x}{b} = \dfrac{b}{c}$ and $\dfrac{y}{a} = \dfrac{a}{c}$.

(c) Use part (b) to show that $c^2 = a^2 + b^2$. (This gives a proof of the Pythagorean theorem.)

14. Prove that the square shown inscribed in a right triangle has sides of length $x = \dfrac{ab}{a+b}$, where a and b are the lengths of the legs of the triangle.

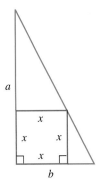

15. The square $ABCD$ has sides of unit length and midpoints at J, K, L, and M. The four segments that join vertices of the square to the midpoints of opposite sides form a smaller inner square $PQRS$.

(a) Use the Pythagorean theorem to show that $DJ = \dfrac{1}{2}\sqrt{5}$.

(b) Observe that the segment $\overline{ST}$ has length $\dfrac{1}{2}$ and creates $\triangle STP$ that is similar to $\triangle DJA$. Use this fact to compute the length PS.

(c) What is the area of the inner square?

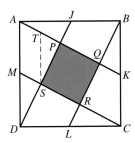

16. The square $ABCD$ has sides of unit length and "one-third" points at J, K, L, and M. Join the vertices of the square to successive "one-third" points to form the smaller inner square $PQRS$. Follow the steps in problem 15 to show that the inner square formed with "one-third" points has 40% of the area of the larger square $ABCD$.

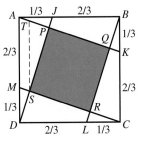

17. Let three arbitrary perpendiculars to the sides of $\triangle ABC$ of the diagram be drawn, meeting in pairs at the points P, Q, and R. Prove that $\triangle PQR \sim \triangle ABC$.

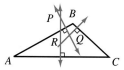

18. Let $PQRS$ be a space quadrilateral, and let W, X, Y, Z be the midpoints of successive sides. Explain why $\overline{WY}$ and $\overline{XZ}$ intersect at their common midpoint M.

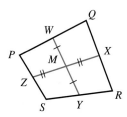

19. Let $ABCD$ be a trapezoid as illustrated, with bases of length $a = AB$ and $b = CD$. Let the diagonals $\overline{AC}$ and $\overline{BD}$ intersect at P, and suppose $\overline{EF}$ is the segment parallel to the bases that passes through P.

Show that $EP = FP = \dfrac{ab}{a+b}$. (Thus $EF = \dfrac{2ab}{a+b}$, which is called the **harmonic mean** of a and b.)

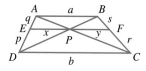

(*Hint:* Explain why $x/a = p/(p+q)$ and $x/b = q/(q+p)$. What happens when these equations are added?)

20. Let M and N be the midpoints of the sides of parallelogram $ABCD$ opposite A as shown. Show that $\overline{AM}$ and $\overline{AN}$ divide the diagonal $\overline{BD}$ into 3 congruent segments: $BP = PQ = QD$. (*Hint:* Construct $\overline{AC}$, and see Example 13.14.)

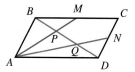

21. Use similarity to find the distances AP, BP, CP, and DP in the figure shown. The squares on the lattice have sides of unit length.

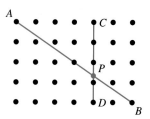

Making Connections

22. Mingxi is standing 75 feet from the base of a tree. The shadow from the top of Mingxi's head coincides with the shadow from the top of the tree. If Mingxi is 5'9″ tall and his shadow is 7′ long, how tall is the tree?

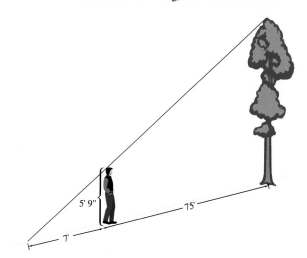

23. Mohini laid a mirror on the level ground 15 feet from the base of a pole as shown. Standing 4 feet from the mirror, she can see the top of the pole reflected in the mirror. If Mohini is 5'5″ tall, how can she estimate the height of the pole? What must she allow for in her calculation?

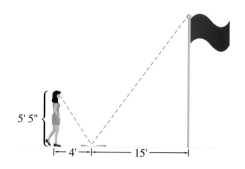

24. By holding a ruler 2 feet in front of her eyes as illustrated in the diagram, Ginny sees that the top and bottom points of a vertical cliff face line up with marks separated by 3.5″ on the ruler. According to the map, Ginny is about a half mile from the cliff. What is the approximate height of the cliff? Recall that a mile is 5280 feet.

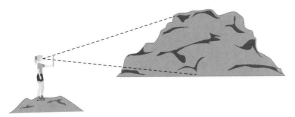

25. A vertical wall 18 feet high casts a shadow 6 feet wide on level ground. If Lisa is 5′3″ tall, how far away from the wall can she stand and still be entirely in the shade?

26. A drive from Prineville to Queenstown currently requires passing through Renton, due to a steep intervening hill. This is shown on the rough map drawn below. The two roads are level and straight, and meet at 55° at Renton.

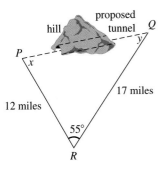

(a) How many miles would be saved by boring a tunnel through the hill? Make an accurate scale drawing, and take measurements off of your drawing.

(b) Two construction crews will dig the tunnel from opposite sides of the hill. What angle measures, *x* and *y*, will ensure that the two crews meet properly at the center of the hill? Take measurements from your scale drawing to give accurate estimates.

27. A sloping ramp is to be built with vertical supports placed at points *B*, *C*, and *D* as shown. The supports at *A* and *E* are 8 and 12 feet high, respectively. How high must the supports be at the points *B*, *C*, and *D*?

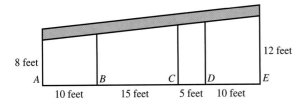

Using a Computer

28. Construct a circle and two chords, $\overline{AB}$ and $\overline{CD}$, that intersect at a point *P*. Measure the angles in the triangles *BCP* and *DAP*.

(a) What conclusion about $\triangle BCP$ and $\triangle DAP$ is suggested by your measurements?

(b) Measure the lengths of $\overline{PA}$, $\overline{PB}$, $\overline{PC}$, and $\overline{PD}$, and then compare $PA \cdot PB$ with $PC \cdot PD$. Does your answer to part (a) justify your observation about the two products?

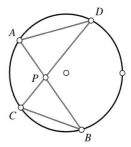

29. Construct a circle and a point *P* that is outside of the circle as shown. Next, draw two rays from *P* that intersect the circle at the points *A*, *B*, *C*, and *D*. Measure the angles in $\triangle BCP$ and $\triangle DAP$.

(a) What conclusion about $\triangle BCP$ and $\triangle DAP$ is suggested by your measurements?

(b) Measure the lengths of $\overline{PA}$, $\overline{PB}$, $\overline{PC}$, and $\overline{PD}$, and then compare $PA \cdot PB$ with $PC \cdot PD$. Does your answer to part (a) justify your observation about the two products?

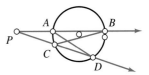

Communicating

30. (a) In Example 13.13 it was shown that joining the successive midpoints of a quadrilateral formed a parallelogram. Explore what you find by *reversing* the construction. That is given a parallelogram *KLMN*, can you construct a quadrilateral *ABCD* for which *KLMN* is the midpoint figure? Is *ABCD* unique?

(b) Write a report discussing your results of part (a).

For Review

31. Find three pairs of congruent triangles in this figure.

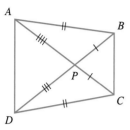

32. Find the measures of the interior angles of △RST.

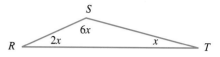

33. Determine the measures of the interior, exterior, and central angles of this regular polygon.

EPILOGUE   From Compasses to Computers

Euclid allowed just two instruments to construct a geometric figure—the straightedge and the compass. Within the strict limitations of the Euclidean rules of construction, it is still possible to draw a large number of useful figures, such as angle bisectors, parallel and perpendicular lines, midpoints, and perpendicular bisectors. In this chapter we have used compass and straightedge constructions to motivate the properties of congruent and similar triangles. We have also seen practical applications of congruence and similarity, such as to the indirect measurement of angles and distances.

In the early nineteenth century the limitations of the compass and straightedge were made clear with the results of Gauss, Wantzel, and others. It is easy to trisect any line segment, but not all angles can be trisected by Euclidean methods. Any procedure which claims otherwise is flawed: either the construction is not Euclidean, or else it is an approximation.

Using tools other than the compass and straightedge, such as rulers and protractors, widens the scope of figures which can be drawn and investigated. For example, the angle trisectors of any triangle meet in pairs to form the most special triangle of all, the equilateral triangle. Since Euclid was not able to construct angle trisectors with compass and straightedge, it is not too surprising that he missed this remarkable theorem discovered in 1911 by Frank Morley (see Figure 13.18).

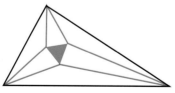

Figure 13.18
Morley's theorem: The adjacent angle trisectors of any triangle intersect at the vertices of an equilateral triangle.

At the dawn of the twenty-first century, traditional drawing instruments such as the ruler and protractor play an increasingly minor role in the construction of figures and images. Industries now turn to methods of computer-aided design (CAD). Astronomers and astrophysicists depend on radio telescopes and sophisticated optical telescopes to study the large scale structure of the universe. In the opposite direction, the force tunnelling microscope forms images in which single atoms are discernible. Ultrasound and CAT scan images have become invaluable in diagnostic procedures. The construction and study of shape are increasingly dependent on computers and other modern technology. Nevertheless the geometric principles involved are not entirely outside the K–12 curriculum. Indeed, it has become clear that the construction and study of geometric shape should be an integral part of the mathematics classroom beginning with the earliest grades.

CHAPTER 13 SUMMARY

Key Concepts

1. **Congruent Triangles**
   - (a) Two figures are **congruent** if, and only if, they have the same size and shape. In particular, two triangles are congruent if, and only if, the angles and sides of one triangle are congruent to the corresponding angles and sides of the second triangle.
   - (b) Two triangles are congruent if they satisfy one of the following properties:
     1. SSS (Side-Side-Side)
     2. SAS (Side-Angle-Side)
     3. ASA (Angle-Side-Angle)
     4. AAS (Angle-Angle-Side)
   - (c) The **triangle inequality:** The length of the side of a triangle is less than the sum of the lengths of the other two sides.
   - (d) The **isosceles triangle theorem and its converse:** Two angles of a triangle are congruent if, and only if, their opposite sides are congruent.
   - (e) **Thales' theorem:** A triangle inscribed in a semicircle is a right triangle with the diameter the hypotenuse.

2. **Constructing Geometric Figures**
   - (a) With compass and straightedge it is possible to copy a line segment; copy an angle; construct a parallel to a line through a point not on the line; construct a perpendicular from a point to a line; construct a perpendicular to a line through a point on the line; construct a perpendicular bisector; and construct an angle bisector.
   - (b) **Equidistance property of the perpendicular bisector:** A point is on the perpendicular bisector of a segment if, and only if, the point is equidistant from the endpoints of the segment.
   - (c) **Equidistance property of the angle bisector:** A point in the interior of an angle is on the angle bisector if, and only if, it is equidistant from the sides of the angle.
   - (d) The **Gauss-Wantzel theorem** describes which regular n-gons have compass and straightedge constructions.

3. **Similar Triangles**
   - (a) Two triangles are **similar** if corresponding angles are congruent and corresponding sides have the same ratio of lengths of sides. The common ratio of lengths of corresponding sides is the **scale factor.**
   - (b) Two triangles are similar if they satisfy one of the following properties:
     1. AA (Angle-Angle) similarity (two pairs of congruent angles)
     2. SSS (Side-Side-Side) similarity (three proportional sides)
     3. SAS (Side-Angle-Side) similarity (two proportional pairs of sides include congruent angles)

Vocabulary and Notation

Section 13.1

Congruent
Parts of a triangle
Congruent triangles, $\triangle ABC \cong \triangle DEF$
Congruence properties of triangles: SSS, SAS, ASA, AAS

Section 13.2

Constructions: compass and straightedge, Mira, paper folding, dynamic geometry software
Foot of the perpendicular
Circumscribing circle, or circumcircle

Circumcenter
Incenter
Inscribed circle, or incircle
Altitude of a triangle
Perpendicular bisector
Angle bisector
Fermat prime

Section 13.3

Similar figures
Similar triangles, $\triangle ABC \sim \triangle DEF$
Scale factor (ratio of similitude)
Similarity properties of triangles: AA, SSS, SAS

CHAPTER REVIEW EXERCISES

Section 13.1

1. In each figure, find at least one pair of congruent triangles. Express the congruence using the $\cong$ symbol, and justify why the triangles are congruent.

(a)
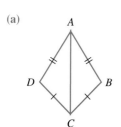

(b)
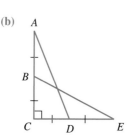

(c)
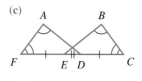

(d)
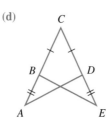

(e)
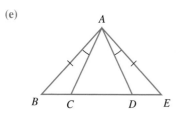

(f)
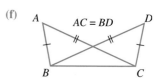

2. Without measuring, fill in the blanks below these figures.

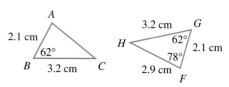

(a) $AC =$ _____   (b) $m(\angle H) =$ _____
(c) $m(\angle A) =$ _____   (d) $m(\angle C) =$ _____

3. Let D be any point of the base $\overline{BC}$ of an isosceles triangle ABC. Locate E on $\overline{AC}$ and F on $\overline{AB}$ so that $EC = BD$ and $BF = DC$. Draw the figure as it is described and then prove that $DE = DF$.

Section 13.2

4. Construct the following with a compass and a straightedge. Show and describe all of your steps.

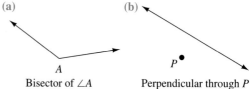

(a)   (b)
Bisector of $\angle A$ Perpendicular through P

(c)

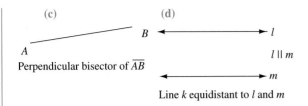

Perpendicular bisector of $\overline{AB}$

(d)

$l \parallel m$

Line k equidistant to l and m

5. Show and describe the position of a Mira which performs each of the constructions of problem 4 in one step.

6. (a) Construct $\triangle ABC$, where $\angle A$, $\overline{AB}$, and $\overline{BC}$ are the parts shown below. Is the shape of $\triangle ABC$ uniquely determined?

   (b) Is the shape of $\triangle ABC$ uniquely determined if $\angle C$ is obtuse?

7. Construct a regular hexagon $ABCDEF$, where diagonal AD is given below.

A D

Section 13.3

8. (a) If only a ruler is available, is it possible to determine if two triangles are similar?

   (b) If only a protractor is available, is it possible to determine if two triangles are similar?

9. Triangle ABC is given below. Construct a triangle DEF for which $\triangle ABC \sim \triangle DEF$ and $DE = (3/2)AB$, using a compass and a straightedge.

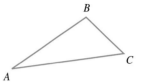

10. Explain why each pair of triangles is similar. State the similarity using the $\sim$ symbol and give the scale factor.

(a)   (b)

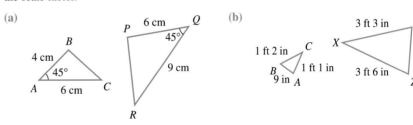

(c)   (d)

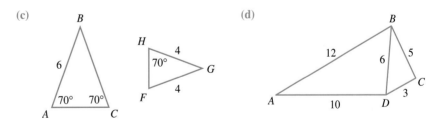

11. Lines k, l, and m are parallel. Find the distances x and y using similar triangles.

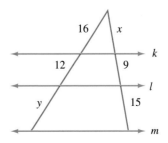

CHAPTER TEST

1. In each figure find a pair of congruent triangles. State what congruence property justifies your conclusion, and write the congruence using the congruence symbol $\cong$.

(a)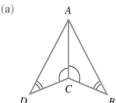

(b)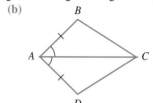

(c)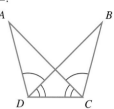

(d)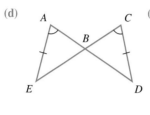

(e)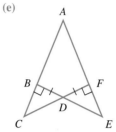

(f)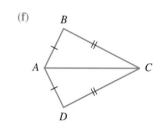

2. A triangle has sides of length 10 feet and 16 feet. What is the range of lengths of the third side?

3. Construct a triangle DEF so that $\triangle DEF \cong \triangle ABC$ and $\angle A$, $\overline{AB}$, and $\angle B$ are given as shown below. List the steps you follow.

4. Decide if the following pairs of triangles are necessarily congruent. If so state why, and give the vertex correspondence. If not give a counterexample.

(a)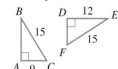

(b)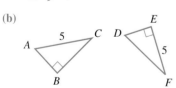

(c)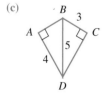

(d)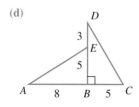

5. Let $ABCDE$ be a regular pentagon. Let $PQRST$ be inscribed so that $AP = BQ = CR = DS = ET$. Prove that $PQRST$ is a regular pentagon.

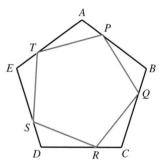

6. In $\triangle FGH$, $\angle F \cong \angle G$ and $FG = FH$. What can you conclude about the triangle?

7. Let $\overline{PQ}$ be perpendicular to line l.

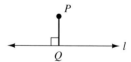

(a) Use a compass and a straightedge to construct two equilateral triangles, $\triangle PQR$ and $\triangle PQS$, each with $\overline{PQ}$ as a side.

(b) Use a compass and a straightedge to construct an equilateral triangle PTU for which $\overline{PQ}$ is an altitude. Describe your procedure.

8. Explain why each pair of triangles is similar. Express the similarity with the ~ notation.

(a)
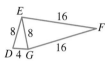

(b)
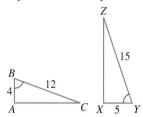

(c)
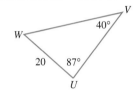

(d)
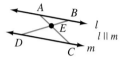

9. Fill in the blanks below, where △*KLM* ~ △*UVW*.

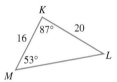

(a) $m(\angle W) = $ _____
(b) Scale factor = _____
(c) $UV = $ _____

10. A person 6 feet tall casts a shadow 7 feet long, and a tree casts a shadow 56 feet long.

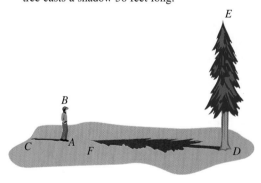

(a) What assumption can you make about the sun's rays?
(b) What other assumption can you make to conclude that △*ABC* ~ △*DEF*?
(c) How tall is the tree?

11. If $AB = 12$ and $AD = 2DC$ find AE and EB.

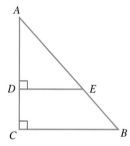

Explain how you found your answer.

12. In △*ABC* the midpoint *M* of side $\overline{AB}$ satisfies $MC = MA$. Prove that △*ABC* is a right triangle.

CHAPTER

14

Coordinate Geometry

14.1 The Cartesian Coordinate System
14.2 Lines and Their Graphs
14.3 Solving Geometric Problems Using Coordinates
14.4 Graphing Functions

HANDS ON
Joining Lattice Points

Materials Needed

Two sheets of graph paper (preferably quarter-inch)

Directions

Step 1. Draw two intersecting number lines—one vertical and one horizontal as shown. Number each number line starting with 0 at the point of intersection. Any point where the grid lines intersect is called a lattice point and can be identified uniquely by an ordered pair of integers (a, b). For example, the lattice point 3 units to the right and 4 units up from the

point of intersection of the number lines is identified by the pair (3, 4) and conversely. Marking a point like (3, 4) on the grid is called plotting the point.

Step 2. Plot four lattice points on a grid so that none of the six line segments determined by the four points contains a lattice point other than its end points. For example, the line segment joining (3, 4) and (1, 7) is such a segment. However, the segment joining (3, 4) and (7, 2) also contains the lattice point (5, 3). Repeat this process of plotting four such sets of points several times and on a different grid each time (about four such grids can be drawn conveniently on a single sheet of quarter-inch graph paper).

Step 3. Return to each of the examples produced in Step 2. See if you can add a fifth lattice point to any of these configurations without creating a situation where at least one of the ten line segments determined by the five lattice points contains a lattice point other than its end points. If a line segment is created that contains a lattice point other than its end points, carefully identify and describe the lattice point. Make a conjecture based on your investigations in this part of the activity.

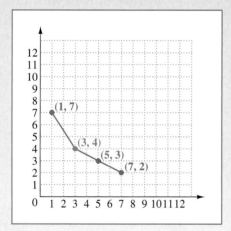

CONNECTIONS   Synthetic and Analytic Geometry

In Chapters 10, 11, 12, and 13 we considered various aspects of geometry involving points, lines, planes, angles, lengths, and areas. We discovered many interesting and surprising geometric properties and these were "proved" or justified most frequently using notions like similarity, congruence, and measurement. Such arguments are usually called *synthetic* because they depend on the synthesis of ideas and results obtained earlier. In this chapter we consider geometry from a different point of view using numbers and equations to establish geometric properties. Geometry from this perspective is called *coordinate geometry* and is developed by a powerful blending of synthetic and algebraic methods. This approach makes it possible to discover and verify geometric properties algebraically. Conversely, we can use geometric insight to understand and visualize algebraic phenomena. Historically, this blending of algebra and geometry breathed new life into both subjects, and is carried on in such subjects as analytic geometry, linear algebra, calculus, differential equations, and much of the rest of mathematics. Coordinate geometry provides an important method to solve geometric problems.

14.1   The Cartesian Coordinate System

Consider the two perpendicular number lines illustrated in Figure 14.1. Any point in the plane can be uniquely located by giving its distance to the right or left of the vertical number line and its distance above or below the horizontal number line. In Figure 14.1, the point P is 5 units to the right of the vertical number line and 3 units above the horizontal number line, and there is only one such point. Thus, P is identified by the ordered number pair $(5, 3)$ and we sometimes write $P(5, 3)$ as shown. Other times we will just write $(5, 3)$.

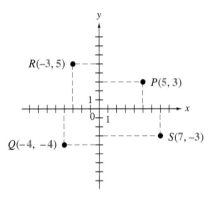

Figure 14.1
The Cartesian coordinate system

The two number lines are called **coordinate axes** or just **axes.** Typically the horizontal number line is called the **x-axis** and the vertical number line is called the **y-axis.** The two numbers in the number pair (a, b) that locate a point are called the **coordinates** of the point. The first number in the pair is called the **x-coordinate** and gives the distance of the point to the right or left of the vertical axis; that is, in the direction of the x-axis. The second number in the ordered pair is called the **y-coordinate** and gives the distance of the point above or below the horizontal axis; that is, in the direction of the y-axis. The axes divide the plane into four regions or **quadrants** numbered I, II, III, and IV counterclockwise from the upper right-hand quadrant. A point:

- lies in quadrant I if both its coordinates are positive,
- lies in quadrant II if the first coordinate is negative and the second coordinate is positive,
- lies in quadrant III if both coordinates are negative, and
- lies in quadrant IV if the first coordinate is positive and the second is negative.

The point $(0, 0)$ where the axes intersect is called the **origin** of the coordinate system. These notions are summarized in Figure 14.2

*I*t is often difficult to ascribe the development of any particular body of mathematics to its originator. The fact is that mathematics is the cumulative result of the efforts of numerous individuals working over hundreds or even thousands of years. The invention of coordinate geometry is customarily ascribed to René Descartes (1596–1650), one of the leading seventeenth century mathematicians, who did indeed make

great strides in commingling the ideas of geometry and algebra as explained in a book titled *La géométrie*. However, Descartes never thought of an ordered pair (*a*, *b*) as the coordinates of a point in the plane. Thus, the terminology, "Cartesian product" and "Cartesian coordinate system," ascribing these ideas to Descartes, is largely misplaced. The idea of coordinates goes back at least as far as the Greek, Apollonius of Perga, in the third century B.C., and was utilized by Nicole Oresme (1323?–1382), the French Bishop of Lisieux, and by others. The idea was also known to the amateur but inspired Pierre de Fermat, a contemporary of

Descartes, and was certainly popularized by the Dutch mathematician, Frans van Schooten (1615–1700) in his *Geometria a Renato Des Cartes* (*Geometry by René Descartes*) in 1649. It is probably not unreasonable to say that our modern ideas of coordinate geometry were inspired by Descartes but organized and popularized by Schooten.

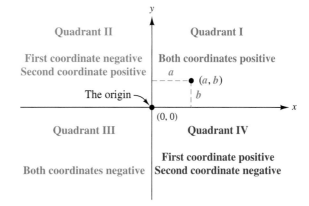

Figure 14.2
Salient features of the
Cartesian coordinate system

EXAMPLE   14.1   **Plotting Points**

The diagram below shows the partial outline of a house.

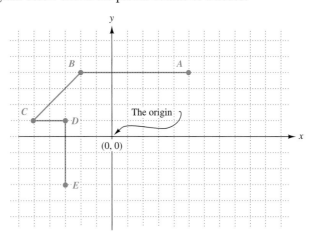

(a) Give the coordinates; that is, the ordered pair naming each of *A*, *B*, *C*, *D*, and *E*.

(b) Plot the points *F*(8, −3), *G*(8, 1), *H*(10, 1), *I*(7, 4), *J*(6, 4), *K*(6, 5), and *L*(5, 5).

(c) Draw the segments $\overline{EF}$, $\overline{FG}$, $\overline{GH}$, $\overline{HI}$, $\overline{IJ}$, $\overline{JK}$, $\overline{KL}$, and $\overline{LA}$.

Solution

(a) *A* is 5 units to the right of (0, 0) (that is, in the *x*-direction from the origin) and 4 units above (0, 0) (that is, in the *y*-direction from the origin). Thus, *A* is the point (5, 4). The *x*-coordinate of *A* is 5 and the *y*-coordinate of *A* is 4. Similarly, we determine that the coordinates of the other points are *B*(−2, 4), *C*(−5, 1), *D*(−3, 1), and *E*(−3, −3).

(b) The point *F*(8, −3) is 8 units to the right of (0, 0) and 3 units *below* (0, 0). Similarly, the other points are located as shown.

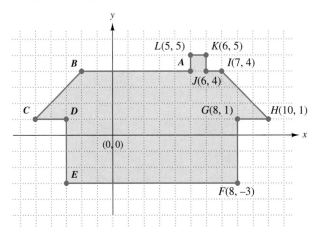

(c) Drawing the designated line segments, the completed figure forms the outline of a house.

The Midpoint Formula

Suppose *M* is the midpoint of the line segment $\overline{PQ}$. If the coordinates of *P* and *Q* are known, can we calculate the coordinates of *M*? Let's begin with a particular example.

EXAMPLE   14.2

Determining the Midpoint of a Line Segment

Compute the coordinates of the midpoint, *M*, of the line segment joining *P*(3, 6) and *Q*(7, 11).

Solution   *Understand the problem*

We are given the coordinates of the endpoints *P* and *Q*. We must find the coordinates of the midpoint, *M*.

Devise a plan

A diagram will allow us to see how *P*, *Q*, and *M* are related on a coordinate plane. If horizontal and vertical distances can be identified, we should be able to determine the coordinates of *M*.

Carry out the plan

If we draw a coordinate system and plot the points P and Q as shown here, we certainly get a better feeling for the problem.

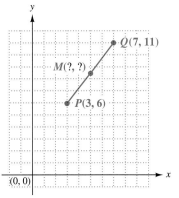

Perhaps we can add to the picture and use some of the geometric facts from Chapter 11. Draw the horizontal segments $\overline{PS}$ and $\overline{MT}$ and the vertical segments $\overline{MR}$ and $\overline{QS}$ as shown.

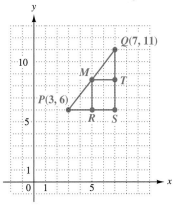

Then, since $\overline{MT}$ and $\overline{PS}$ are parallel as are $\overline{RM}$ and $\overline{SQ}$, and $\overline{PM} \cong \overline{MQ}$, it follows that $\triangle PMR \cong \triangle MQT$. But then R is the midpoint of $\overline{PS}$ and must have coordinates $(r, 6)$ where

$$r = 3 + \frac{1}{2}PS$$

$$= 3 + \frac{1}{2}(7 - 3)$$

$$= 5.$$

Also, T is the midpoint of $\overline{SQ}$ and must have coordinates $(7, s)$ where

$$s = 6 + \frac{1}{2}SQ$$

$$= 6 + \frac{1}{2}(11 - 6)$$

$$= 8.5.$$

Thus, M has coordinates $(r, s) = (5, 8.5)$ as was to be determined.

Look back

The key to this solution was drawing a picture on a coordinate plane. This made it possible to determine the coordinates of key points and, finally, the desired coordinates of the midpoint, M.

Observe that

$$5 = 3 + \frac{1}{2}(7 - 3)$$

$$= 3 + \frac{1}{2} \cdot 7 - \frac{1}{2} \cdot 3$$

$$= \frac{1}{2} \cdot 3 + \frac{1}{2} \cdot 7$$

$$= \frac{3 + 7}{2}$$

The average of 3 and 7 is 5.

and,

$$8.5 = \frac{6 + 11}{2}.$$

The average of 6 and 11 is 8.5.

Thus, the coordinates of the midpoint of $\overline{PQ}$ are the *average* of the x-coordinates of P and Q and the average of the y-coordinates of P and Q.

The preceding example is typical of the general case which is stated here as a theorem.

THEOREM   *The Midpoint Formula*

Consider points $P(a, b)$ and $Q(c, d)$. The midpoint of the segment $\overline{PQ}$ is the point

$$M\left(\frac{a + c}{2}, \frac{b + d}{2}\right).$$

A useful notational device when working with midpoints is to write a number as twice or even four times another number. For example, we can write 3 as $2 \cdot (1.5)$, -4.5 as $2 \cdot (-2.25)$, 7 as $4 \cdot (1.75)$, and -3 as $4 \cdot (-0.75)$. In general, we can write any number in the form $2a$ or $4b$ or $3c$, and so on. This device helps avoid fractions. For example, the midpoint of the segment joining $P(2r, 2s)$ and $Q(2u, 2v)$ is

$$M\left(\frac{2r + 2u}{2}, \frac{2s + 2v}{2}\right) = M(r + u, s + v).$$

JUST FOR FUN

The Greek Cross—I

A Greek cross is formed by adjoining five squares as shown here. Cut out a Greek cross and then cut it into four pieces along the dotted lines determined by the midpoints P, Q, R, and S of their respective segments as illustrated. Show how to reassemble the pieces into a single square.

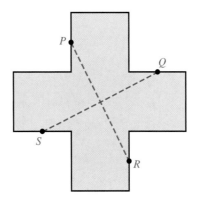

EXAMPLE   14.3

Proving that the Diagonals of a Rectangle Bisect Each Other

Show that the diagonals of a rectangle bisect each other.

Solution

Any rectangle $ABCD$ can be placed on a coordinate system with $\overline{AB}$ along the positive y-axis and $\overline{AD}$ along the positive x-axis as shown. Then A is the point $(0, 0)$, B is $(0, 2b)$, and D is $(2d, 0)$ for some positive real numbers b and d. Also C is the point $(2d, 2b)$. By the preceding theorem the midpoint of $\overline{AC}$ is

$$\left(\frac{0 + 2d}{2}, \frac{0 + 2b}{2} \right) = (d, b)$$

and the midpoint of $\overline{BD}$ is

$$\left(\frac{0 + 2d}{2}, \frac{2b + 0}{2} \right) = (d, b)$$

But this shows that the two diagonals meet at the point M which is the midpoint of each diagonal.

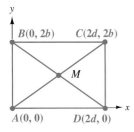

Dividing a Line Segment

We just determined the coordinates of the midpoint of a line segment. Suppose we wanted to determine M so that M is 1/3 of the way from A to B; that is, so that

$$\frac{AM}{AB} = \frac{1}{3}.$$

Consider Figure 14.3 with *B* above and to the right of *A*.

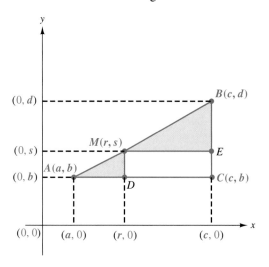

Figure 14.3
The point 1/3 of the way from
A to B

Draw horizontal segments $\overline{ME}$ and $\overline{AC}$ and vertical segments $\overline{MD}$ and $\overline{BC}$. It follows that $\triangle AMD$ and $\triangle ABC$ are similar so that corresponding sides are of proportional length. Since

$$AM = \frac{1}{3}AB,$$

it follows that

$$AD = \frac{1}{3}AC \quad \text{and} \quad CE = \frac{1}{3}CB.$$

Thus,

$$r = a + \frac{1}{3}(c - a)$$

$$= a + \frac{1}{3}c - \frac{1}{3}a$$

$$= \frac{2}{3}a + \frac{1}{3}c$$

and similarly

$$s = \frac{2}{3}b + \frac{1}{3}d.$$

The argument when *B* is to the right and below *A* is similar and the final result is the same.

The preceding argument can be repeated exactly with 1/3 replaced by *t* to obtain the following result concerning division of a line segment.

THEOREM *Division of a Line Segment*
The point the fraction *t* of the distance from $A(a, b)$ to $B(c, d)$ is

$$M((1 - t)a + tc, \quad (1 - t)b + td).$$

EXAMPLE 14.4

Determining the Point 1/3 of the Way from (3, 6) to (12, −6)

Determine the coordinates of the point 1/3 of the way from $A(3, 6)$ to $B(12, -6)$.

Solution

Let $M(r, s)$ be the desired point. Then,

$$r = \frac{2}{3}(3) + \frac{1}{3}(12) = 6$$

and

$$s = \frac{2}{3}(6) + \frac{1}{3}(-6) = 2.$$

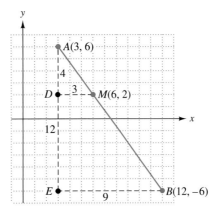

The point M is (6, 2). As a check we compute the distances AM and AB using the Pythagorean theorem from Chapter 12.

$$AM = \sqrt{3^2 + 4^2} = \sqrt{9 + 16} = 5$$
$$AB = \sqrt{9^2 + 12^2} = \sqrt{81 + 144} = 15$$

> Triangles *AMD* and *ABE* are right triangles.

Thus, $AM/AB = 1/3$ as desired.

The Distance Formula

We have just discovered how to divide a line segment in a given ratio. We can also determine its length. Consider this example.

EXAMPLE 14.5

Determining the Length of a Line Segment

Compute the length of the line segment $\overline{PQ}$ where P is the point (2, 5) and Q is (7, 8).

Solution

Drawing the line segment $\overline{PQ}$, we construct the right triangle PQR where $\overline{PR}$ and $\overline{QR}$ are parallel to the *x*- and *y*-axes, respectively. Since $\triangle PQR$ is a right triangle, the Pythagorean theorem applies. Thus,

$$PQ^2 = PR^2 + RQ^2.$$

Hence,

$$PQ = \sqrt{PR^2 + RQ^2}$$
$$= \sqrt{(7 - 2)^2 + (8 - 5)^2}$$
$$= \sqrt{25 + 9} = \sqrt{34} \doteq 5.8$$

as required.

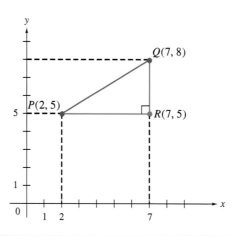

The preceding example suggests a formula for finding the distance between two points whose coordinates are known. As before, the proof is an exact translation of the preceding solution where we replace $P(2, 5)$ and $Q(7, 8)$ by $P(a, b)$ and $Q(c, d)$, respectively. Since the translation is exact, the proof is omitted.

THEOREM   *The Distance Formula*

Let P and Q be the points (a, b) and (c, d). Then the distance between P and Q is

$$PQ = \sqrt{(c - a)^2 + (d - b)^2}.$$

Since the square of the negative of a number is the same as the square of the number,

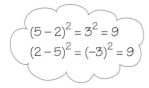

$$(c - a)^2 = (a - c)^2 \quad \text{and} \quad (d - b)^2 = (b - d)^2.$$

Thus, in the distance formula, it does not make any difference which point is chosen for P and which is chosen for Q. For example, the distance between $(4, 7)$ and $(1, 3)$ is given by both

$$\sqrt{(4 - 1)^2 + (7 - 3)^2} = \sqrt{3^2 + 4^2}$$
$$= \sqrt{9 + 16} = \sqrt{25} = 5$$

and

$$\sqrt{(1 - 4)^2 + (3 - 7)^2} = \sqrt{(-3)^2 + (-4)^2}$$
$$= \sqrt{9 + 16} = \sqrt{25} = 5.$$

EXAMPLE 14.6 | **Proving that a Triangle Is Isosceles**

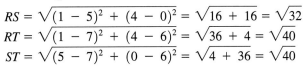

Prove that the triangle with vertices $R(1, 4)$, $S(5, 0)$, and $T(7, 6)$ is isosceles.

Solution

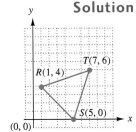

We compute the length of the three sides.

$$RS = \sqrt{(1 - 5)^2 + (4 - 0)^2} = \sqrt{16 + 16} = \sqrt{32}$$
$$RT = \sqrt{(1 - 7)^2 + (4 - 6)^2} = \sqrt{36 + 4} = \sqrt{40}$$
$$ST = \sqrt{(5 - 7)^2 + (0 - 6)^2} = \sqrt{4 + 36} = \sqrt{40}$$

Since $RT = ST$, it follows that $\triangle RST$ is isosceles.

PROBLEM SET 14.1

Understanding Concepts

1. What can be said about the coordinates of a point P if
   (a) P lies on the x-axis?
   (b) P lies in the second quadrant?
   (c) P lies in the fourth quadrant?
   (d) P lies on the y-axis?
   (e) P is at the origin?

2. Plot and label the following points on a Cartesian coordinate system drawn on a sheet of graph paper.
   (a) $P(5, 7)$ (b) $Q(5, -7)$ (c) $R(-5, 7)$
   (d) $S(-5, -7)$ (e) $T(0, 5)$ (f) $U(7.5, 0)$
   (g) $V(0, -5.2)$ (h) $W(-7, 0)$ (i) $X(0, 0)$

3. Plot these points and connect them in order with line segments: (1, 1), (1, 11), (4, 13), (5, 15), (6, 13), (7, 12), (10, 11), (9, 10), (6, 9), (4, 7), (1, 1).

4. (a) Plot the points (5, 0), (4, 3), (3, 4), (0, 5), (−3, 4), (−4, 3), (−5, 0), (−4, −3), (−3, −4), (0, −5), (3, −4), and (4, −3).
   (b) What do you observe about the points in part (a)?

5. Let $A(0, 0)$, $B(2, 3)$, $C(r, s)$, and $D(5, 0)$ be the vertices of parallelogram $ABCD$ reading clockwise around from A. Determine r and s. (*Hint:* Draw a diagram.)

6. Let $M(r, s)$ be the midpoint of $\overline{PQ}$. Determine $M(r, s)$ for these choices of P and Q. Also, plot P, Q, and M on graph paper in each case.
   (a) $P(2, 7)$, $Q(6, 1)$ (b) $P(-1, 1)$, $Q(3, 5)$
   (c) $P(0, 7)$, $Q(-4, 1)$ (d) $P(-2, -5)$, $Q(4, 1)$
   (e) $P(2, 3)$, $Q(7, -3)$ (f) $P(3, 4)$, $Q(-1, -5)$

7. Consider the points $A(1, -7)$ and $B(-7, 9)$. Determine the coordinates of the point P
   (a) one-fourth of the way from A to B.
   (b) three-fourths of the way from A to B.
   (c) five-fourths of the way from A to B.
   (d) Plot the points in parts (a), (b), and (c) on a Cartesian coordinate system.

8. Consider the convex quadrilateral $A(-2, -1)$, $B(4, 3)$, $C(6, 1)$, and $D(0, -7)$.
   (a) Determine the midpoints P, Q, R, and S of $\overline{AB}$, $\overline{BC}$, $\overline{CD}$, and $\overline{DA}$ respectively.
   (b) Show that $\overline{PR}$ and $\overline{QS}$ from part (a) bisect each other.
   (c) On graph paper, draw the quadrilaterals $ABCD$ and $PQRS$.

9. Compute the distance between these pairs of points.
   (a) $(-2, 5)$ and $(4, 13)$ (b) $(3, -4)$ and $(8, 8)$
   (c) $(0, 7)$ and $(8, -8)$ (d) $(3, 5)$ and $(2, -4.3)$

10. (a) Prove that $R(1, 2)$, $S(7, 10)$, and $T(5, -1)$ are the vertices of a right triangle.
    (b) Draw the triangle RST of part (a) on graph paper.

11. Consider the quadrilateral with vertices $A(2, 4)$, $B(12, 0)$, $C(10, -5)$, and $D(0, -1)$.
    (a) Show that $ABCD$ is a rectangle.
    (b) Show that $\overline{AC}$ and $\overline{BD}$ bisect one another.
    (c) Draw $ABCD$ and the line segments $\overline{AC}$ and $\overline{BD}$ on a coordinate system.

12. Classify the triangles with these vertices as one or more of right, acute, obtuse, equilateral, isosceles, or scalene.

(a) $(1, 1), (1, -4), (6, -4)$

(b) $(-5, -4), (-1, -1), (3, -4)$

(c) $(-1, 3), (2, 5), (7, -3)$

(d) $(0, 2), (3, 7), (8, 2)$

Thinking Critically

13. (a) Plot the set of points $P(a, b)$ with a and b integers, $a + b = 6$, and $-5 \le a \le 5$.

(b) What do you observe about the points in part (a)?

14. (a) Plot the set of points $Q(r, s)$ with r and s being real numbers, $r - s = 6$ and $-5 \le r \le 5$.

(b) What do you observe about the points in part (a)?

15. (a) Plot the set of points $(a, 5)$ with a being an integer and $-6 \le a \le 6$.

(b) What can you say about the points in part (a)?

16. (a) Plot the set of points $(-2, b)$ with b being a real number and $-4 \le b \le 4$.

(b) What seems to be true about the points in part (a)?

17. (a) Plot the set of points (x, y) with x and y being integers, $2x + 3y = 6$, and $-12 \le x \le 12$. (*Hint:* Give x integer values in the prescribed range, compute the corresponding values of y, and plot the resulting point (x, y) if y is an integer.)

(b) Carefully describe the set of points in part (a).

(c) The set of plotted points in part (a) is called the **graph** of the equation $2x + 3y = 6$ subject to the given conditions. Conjecture what the graph would look like if the conditions that x and y be integers and $-12 \le x \le 12$ were removed.

18. Determine the point Q such that $\overline{PQ}$ is symmetric about the y-axis for each of the following choices for P. Also, plot P and Q and draw $\overline{PQ}$ in each case but the last.

(a) $P(3, 5)$ (b) $P(-2, 4)$ (c) $P(-3, -5)$

(d) $P(0, 5)$ (e) $P(5, 0)$ (f) $P(a, b)$

19. Determine the point T such that the segment $\overline{ST}$ is symmetric about the x-axis for all of these choices for S. Also, plot S and T and draw $\overline{ST}$ in each case but the last.

(a) $S(2, 7)$ (b) $S(-2, -4)$ (c) $S(3, 0)$

(d) $S(0, 4)$ (e) $S(-3, 5)$ (f) $S(u, v)$

20. Determine the point D that is the image of C under the indicated rotation about the origin in each case. Plot C and D in each case.

(a) $C(2, 4)$,   90° counterclockwise rotation.

(b) $C(3, -5)$,   90° clockwise rotation.

(c) $C(3, -5)$,   270° counterclockwise rotation.

(d) $C(2, 0)$,   60° counterclockwise rotation.

(e) $C(0, -2)$,   45° clockwise rotation.

21. Determine the point F that is the image of E under the indicated slides. Plot E and F in each case except the last.

(a) $E(3, 4)$,   slide 2 to the right and 3 up.

(b) $E(-1, -3)$,   slide 3 to the left and 4 up.

(c) $E(a, b)$,   slide c to the right and d down, $c > 0$ and $d > 0$.

22. Determine the point H such that the segment $\overline{GH}$ is symmetric about the origin. Plot G, H, and draw $\overline{GH}$ in each case but the last.

(a) $G(3, -5)$ (b) $G(-2, -4)$ (c) $G(0, 3)$

(d) $G(-4, 0)$ (e) $G(-2, 7)$ (f) $G(a, b)$

23. (a) If $A(0, 0)$, $B(3, 5)$, $C(r, s)$, and $D(7, 0)$ are the vertices of a parallelogram, determine r and s.

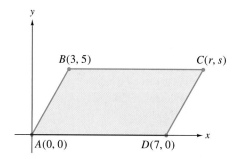

(b) Using the result of part (a), show that the diagonals of the parallelogram bisect each other.

24. (a) Consider the quadrilateral $A(0, 0)$, $B(2, 5)$, $C(6, 9)$, and $D(8, 0)$. Let P, Q, R, and S be the midpoints of $\overline{AB}$, $\overline{BC}$, $\overline{CD}$, and $\overline{DA}$, respectively. Show that the segments $\overline{PR}$ and $\overline{QS}$ bisect each other.

(b) Draw the quadrilateral $ABCD$ and the segments $\overline{PR}$ and $\overline{QS}$ on a coordinate system.

Thinking Cooperatively

Do the next two problems in cooperation with two or three other students. Discuss the problems with your collaborators and agree on group responses to all the questions.

25. (a) Consider the diagram shown with P above and to the left of Q. Determine an expression for the area of the triangle in terms a, b, c, and d. (*Hint:* Draw vertical lines from P and Q to the x-axis.)

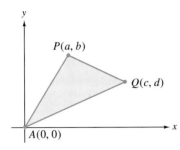

y

$P(a, b)$

$Q(c, d)$

$A(0, 0)$

x

(b) Repeat part (a) with Q above and to the left of P.

(c) Express the results of (a) and (b) in a single formula using absolute value.

(d) Use your answer to (c) to compute the area of the triangle with vertices $A(0, 0)$, $B(0, b)$, and $C(c, 0)$ with $b > 0$ and $c > 0$.

26. **(a)** On a full sheet of graph paper with a reasonably large grid (say, squares 0.5 cm on a side) draw a pair of coordinate axes centered about 15 units above and to the right of the lower left-hand corner of the sheet. Using this coordinate system, plot the points $A(2, 3)$ and $B(14, 19)$.

(b) Consider the point $T = (2(1 - t) + 14t,$ $3(1 - t) + 19t)$. Let C denote the point T when $t = 1/4$. Let D denote the point T when $t = 1/2$. Let E denote the point T when $t = 3/4$. Let F denote the point T when $t = 5/4$. And let G denote the point when $t = -5/4$. Compute the coordinates of C, D, E, F, and G and plot these points on the coordinate system of part (a).

(c) Compute AB, AD, AE, AF, BF, and AG.

(d) What do you observe about the points in part (b)?

(e) On the basis of your observation in part (c), conjecture what the set of plotted points would look like if t were allowed to assume all real values without exception. Explain briefly.

Using a Calculator

27. **(a)** Reading in order and clockwise around a polygon, its vertices are $A(3, 2)$, $B(1, 6)$, $C(4, 9)$, $D(4, 7)$, $E(7, 7)$, $F(11, 4)$, and $A(3, 2)$. Determine the perimeter of this polygon to the nearest tenth.

(b) Using graph paper, carefully draw the polygon of part (a) and determine its area using Pick's formula $A = \dfrac{b}{2} + i - 1$ (see page 711).

(c) The formula for the area of a polygon with vertices (x_1, y_1), (x_2, y_2), (x_3, y_3), . . . , (x_n, y_n) is

$$A = \frac{1}{2} \left| x_1y_2 + x_2y_3 + x_3y_4 + \cdots + x_{n-1}y_n \right.$$
$$+ x_ny_1 - x_2y_1 - x_3y_2 - x_4y_3 - \cdots$$
$$\left. - x_ny_{n-1} - x_1y_n \right|.$$

Use this formula to check the result of part (b). (*Note:* Here $n = 6$ and $(x_1, y_1) = (3, 2)$, $(x_2, y_2) = (1, 6)$, $(x_3, y_3) = (4, 9)$, $(x_4, y_4) = (4, 7)$, $(x_5, y_5) = (7, 7)$, and $(x_6, y_6) = (11, 4)$.)

Making Connections

28. **(a)** Write an equation using x and y that states that the point $P(x, y)$ is 3 units from the origin.

(b) Carefully describe what the graph of the set of points in part (a) looks like.

(c) Compute the perimeter of the figure of part (a) correct to the nearest tenth.

(d) Compute the area of the figure in part (a) correct to the nearest tenth.

29. A cross-country course is laid out as shown. Determine the length of the course correct to the nearest meter.

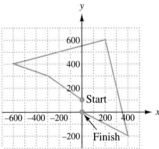

Distances are in meters.

From State Student Assessments

30. (Colorado, Grade 4)
This is a game board.

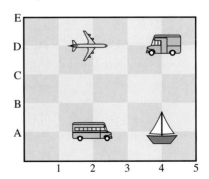

Which object is located at (2, D)?

A. The plane   C. The bus

B. The truck   D. The boat

31. (Colorado, Grade 4)
Look at the grid below. Point X is identified by the
ordered pair (7, 6).

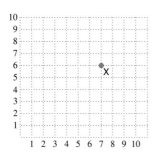

Which set of ordered pairs identifies three points that
will form a straight line when connected?

A. (2, 1), (5, 5), and (8, 7)

B. (2, 7), (4, 5), and (7, 4)

C. (3, 2), (6, 5), and (9, 8)

32. (Massachusetts, Grade 8)
Use the figure below to answer the question.

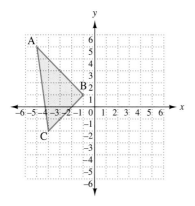

If the triangle shown above is reflected across the
y-axis, what will be the coordinates of the image of
point C?

A. $(-4, 2)$

B. $(-4, -2)$

C. $(4, -2)$

D. $(4, 2)$

For Review

33. In the figure shown, $\overline{AB}$ and $\overline{DE}$ are parallel. Prove
that $\triangle ABC \sim \triangle EDC$.

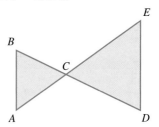

34. Determine *x* in the diagram shown given that $\overline{AB}$ is
parallel to $\overline{CD}$.

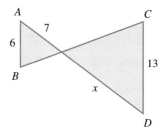

35. Determine *y* in the diagram shown given that $\overline{CD}$ is
parallel to $\overline{AB}$.

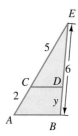

36. Determine *z* in the diagram shown.

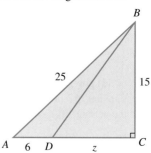

COOPERATIVE INVESTIGATION
Locating Centers of Gravity

Materials Needed

1. Tagboard or cardboard and a sheet of graph paper
2. Scissors

Directions

Step 1. Paste a sheet of graph paper onto a piece of tagboard.

Step 2. Cut out a tagboard triangle and note the coordinates of its vertices.

Step 3. Find the center of gravity of the triangle by balancing it on the edge of a table. Carefully draw a line on the triangle by holding it tight and by using the table edge as a straight edge. Rotate the triangle and, repeating the balancing procedure, draw a second line. Where the two lines intersect is the *center of gravity;* that is, the triangle would hang horizontally if hung by a thread from this point.

Step 4. Determine the coordinates of the center of gravity.

Step 5. Using the data from Steps 2, 3, and 4, conjecture a formula for the coordinates of the center of gravity in terms of the coordinates of the vertices of any triangle.

14.2   Lines and Their Graphs

Slope

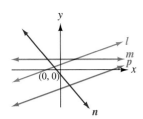

Figure 14.4
Lines in the plane

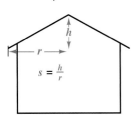

Figure 14.5
Slope on a roof

Consider the lines *l*, *m*, *n*, and *p* in Figure 14.4. The properties that distinguish between two lines are their location on the coordinate system and their direction or steepness. The direction or steepness of a line is the same as that of any segment of the line and this leads to the notion of **slope.**

Carpenters use the ratio

$$s = \frac{h}{r},$$

where *h* is the vertical distance a roof rises and *r* is the horizontal distance over which the rise takes place, to compute the slope of a roof as shown in Figure 14.5. This is sometimes expressed by saying that the slope of a roof is "the rise over the run." Surveyors use the same idea when calculating the slope of a road. If a road rises five feet while moving forward horizontally 100 feet, the road has a slope of 0.05. In surveying, slopes are usually expressed as percents. Thus, a grade with a slope of 0.05 is said to be a 5% grade.

We also use the idea *rise over run* to determine the slope of a line segment. Consider the points $P(3, 5)$ and $Q(9, 7)$ shown in Figure 14.6 on the next page. In moving from *P* to *Q* one moves up 2 units while moving to the right 6 units. The rise over the run gives a slope of 1/3 indicated by the letter *m*. In this case,

$$m = \frac{7 - 5}{9 - 3} = \frac{2}{6} = \frac{1}{3}.$$

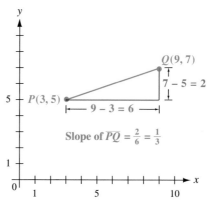

Figure 14.6
Slope of a segment

In general, the reasoning is similar and leads to this definition of slope.

> **DEFINITION**   *Slope of a Line Segment*
> Let $P(x_1, y_1)$ and $Q(x_2, y_2)$ with $x_1 \neq x_2$ be two points. Then the **slope of the line segment** PQ is given by
>
> $$m = \frac{y_2 - y_1}{x_2 - x_1}.$$

If $x_1 = x_2$ in the preceding definition, then $x_2 - x_1 = 0$ and $\overline{PQ}$ is vertical. Since division by zero is undefined, we must say that *a vertical segment has no slope* or, equivalently, that *the slope of a vertical segment is undefined.*

If $y_1 = y_2$ in the preceding definition, then $\overline{PQ}$ is horizontal and $m = 0$. Thus, saying that a line segment is horizontal is the same as saying that it has zero slope.

In computing the slope of a segment, it makes no difference which point is chosen as P and which is chosen as Q. However, once the choice is made, one must stick with it and always subtract *in the same direction* in both numerator and denominator. For example, in computing the slope of the segment in Figure 14.6, we identified P and Q as $(3, 5)$ and $(9, 7)$, respectively. But this could have been reversed to obtain

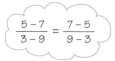

$$m = \frac{5 - 7}{3 - 9} = \frac{-2}{-6} = \frac{1}{3}$$

as before.

Finally, in Figure 14.6 the slope was positive and the segment sloped upward to the right. This is always the case for segments with positive slopes. (Why?) If $y_1 = y_2$ in the definition of slope then the slope is 0 and the segment $\overline{PQ}$ is necessarily horizontal. If the slope of a segment is negative, the segment slopes *downward to the right* as illustrated in the next example.

EXAMPLE   14.7

Determining a Negative Slope

Compute the slope of the line segment determined by $R(-3, 7)$ and $S(5, -2)$.

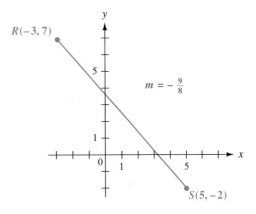

Solution

As seen in the diagram, the segment slopes downward to the right. Also, from the definition,

$$m = \frac{7 - (-2)}{-3 - 5}$$

$$= \frac{9}{-8} = -\frac{9}{8}.$$

Subtracting in the other direction, we obtain

$$m = \frac{-2 - 7}{5 - (-3)}$$

$$= \frac{-9}{8} = -\frac{9}{8}$$

as well.

The **slope of a line** is the slope of any segment on the line as in the following definition.

DEFINITION   *Slope of a Line*
The **slope of a line** is the slope of any segment on the line.

It makes no difference which segment (that is, which two points on the line) are used to determine the slope. Indeed, this follows immediately from what we already know about similar triangles.

Consider the segments $\overline{AB}$ and $\overline{CD}$ on the line of Figure 14.7 on the next page. If we choose P and Q so that $\overline{AP}$ and $\overline{CQ}$ are parallel to the x-axis and $\overline{BP}$ and $\overline{DQ}$ are parallel to the y-axis, then $\triangle ABP \sim \triangle CDQ$. (Why?) But corresponding sides of similar triangles are of proportional lengths. Thus,

$$\frac{CQ}{AP} = \frac{DQ}{BP} = k$$

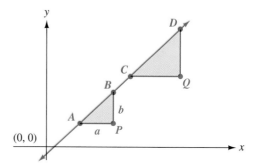

Figure 14.7
Slope of a line from different segments

for some scale factor k. It follows that if $AP = a$ and $BP = b$, then

$$CQ = k \cdot AP = ka \qquad \text{and} \qquad DQ = k \cdot BP = kb.$$

But then

$$\text{slope } \overline{AB} = \frac{BP}{AP} = \frac{b}{a} = \frac{kb}{ka} = \frac{DQ}{CQ} = \text{slope } \overline{CD}.$$

Hence, the slope of the line can be computed using either segment.

Slopes of Parallel Lines

As noted earlier, the slope of a line is a measure of its steepness on a coordinate system. Thus, if lines are equally steep, they are parallel and, if they are parallel then they are equally steep. In terms of slopes, we have the following theorem.

> **THEOREM** *Condition for Parallelism*
> Two segments (lines) are parallel if, and only if, they have same slope.

EXAMPLE 14.8

Showing that Line Segments Are Parallel

Let P, Q, R, and S be the points $(-7, -1), (-1, 3), (-1, -3)$, and $(8, 3)$, respectively. Show that $\overline{PQ}$ is parallel to $\overline{RS}$.

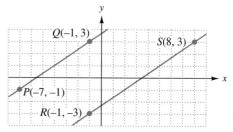

Solution

By the preceding theorem, line segments are parallel if, and only if, they have the same slope. Since

$$\text{slope } \overline{PQ} = \frac{3 - (-1)}{-1 - (-7)} = \frac{4}{6} = \frac{2}{3}$$

and

$$\text{slope } \overline{RS} = \frac{3 - (-3)}{8 - (-1)} = \frac{6}{9} = \frac{2}{3},$$

it follows that the two segments are parallel.

JUST FOR FUN

Square Inch Mysteries

From a sheet of graph paper cut an 8 by 8 square into the four pieces *A*, *B*, *C*, and *D* as shown.

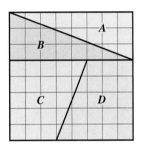

Now rearrange the four pieces into a rectangle as shown here. Does the rectangle have the same area as the square?

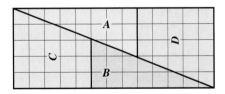

Before you run out to buy 8 by 8 bricks of gold, rearrange the four pieces into a "propeller." Can you account for the changes in area?

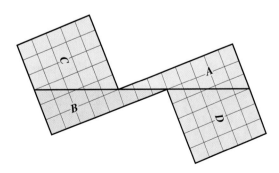

EXAMPLE 14.9

Determining a Segment with a Given Slope

Let P be the point $(3, -4)$. Determine a point Q so that $\overline{PQ}$ has slope $-2/3$.

Solution

Locate the point $(3, -4)$ on a coordinate system as shown. Since $\overline{PQ}$ must have slope $-2/3$, the segment slopes downward to the right. Also, the "rise" is -2 and the run is 3. Thus, we can find Q by counting down 2 units from $(3, -4)$ and to the right 3 units. Thus, Q is the point $(6, -6)$. Moreover, since the slope is a ratio, we could count down 4 units and to the right 6 units to determine $R(9, -8)$, such that $\overline{PR}$ also has slope $-2/3$. Similarly, counting backwards, we determine points, S, T, and V such that $\overline{PS}$, $\overline{PT}$, and $\overline{PV}$ all have slope $-2/3$. (Check these.) Apparently there are infinitely many points that satisfy the condition of the problem.

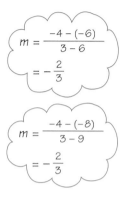

$$m = \frac{-4 - (-6)}{3 - 6}$$

$$= -\frac{2}{3}$$

$$m = \frac{-4 - (-8)}{3 - 9}$$

$$= -\frac{2}{3}$$

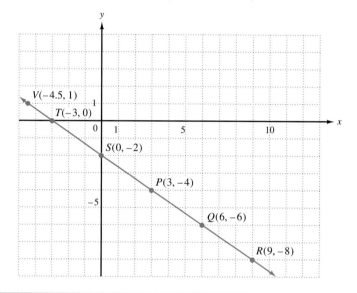

Slopes of Perpendicular Lines

Two lines are parallel if, and only if, they have the same slope. What is the case when lines are perpendicular? Since parallel lines have the same slope, we can restrict our attention to perpendicular lines that meet at the origin.

Consider the diagram of Figure 14.8. Lines r and s are perpendicular and meet at the origin. Let $P(a, b)$ be a point in the first quadrant and on r, and let $\overline{PQ}$ be parallel to

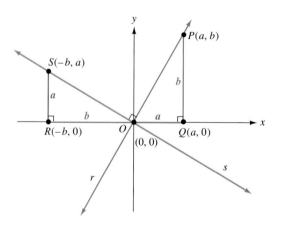

Figure 14.8
Slopes of perpendicular line segments

HIGHLIGHT FROM HISTORY
Maria Agnesi (1718–1799)

Maria Gaetana Agnesi was a child prodigy. Her father Pietro Gaetana, who was a professor of mathematics at the University of Bologna in Italy, recognized his daughter's talent and encouraged her studies. Before she was 13, Agnesi spoke many languages including Greek, Hebrew, and Latin. As a young woman, she gave talks on mathematics and philosophy to adult friends of her parents during parties at their home.

Agnesi's famous two-volume book, *Analytical Institutions,* took her ten years to write. It includes discussions of algebra, geometry, and calculus. In it, she describes the *Witch of Agnesi,* a curve first proposed by the French mathematician Fermat and studied extensively by Agnesi herself. Because *Analytical Institutions* was so clearly written, it was translated into French and English and used as a textbook. It is the first work of such stature that has survived that was written by a woman.

According to some accounts, Pope Benedict XIV appointed Agnesi to teach at the University of Bologna around 1750; however, it is possible that she never actually taught there. It is certain that Agnesi retired from mathematics just as her intellectual powers were at their peak. When in her forties, she decided to devote the remaining years of her life to helping the sick and poor. Maria Gaetana Agnesi died at the age of 81, leaving the world a rich scholastic and humanitarian legacy.

SOURCE: From *Portraits for Classroom Bulletin Boards: Women Mathematicians,* text by Virginia Slachman. Copyright © 1990 by Dale Seymour Publications, Palo Alto, CA 94303. Reprinted by permission.

the *y*-axis. Place *R* on the *x*-axis to the left of 0 so that $\overline{RO} \cong \overline{QP}$. Thus, *R* has coordinates $(-b, 0)$. Let $\overline{RS}$ be vertical and intersect *s* at *S*. It follows that $\triangle OPQ \cong \triangle OSR$. (Why?) Hence, *S* has coordinates $(-b, a)$ as shown. But then

$$\text{slope } \overline{OP} = \frac{b - 0}{a - 0} = \frac{b}{a}$$

and

$$\text{slope } \overline{OS} = \frac{a - 0}{-b - 0} = -\frac{a}{b}.$$

This shows that the slopes of perpendicular lines have the property that one is the negative of the reciprocal of the other. Equivalently, the product of the slopes of perpendicular lines is -1 since

$$\frac{b}{a} \cdot \left(-\frac{a}{b}\right) = -1.$$

The converse of these last assertions is also true but we omit the proof. In any case, the condition for perpendicularity can be formalized as a theorem.

> **THEOREM**   *Condition for Perpendicularity*
>
> Let two line segments (or lines) that are neither vertical nor horizontal have slopes m_1 and m_2. Then the segments (lines) are perpendicular if, and only if, $m_1 m_2 = -1$ or, equivalently,
>
> $$m_1 = -\frac{1}{m_2}.$$
>
> If a line segment (or line) is vertical, it has no slope and any line segment (line) perpendicular to it must be horizontal with slope 0 and conversely.

EXAMPLE   14.10

Showing that the Diagonals of a Rhombus Are Perpendicular

Consider the quadrilateral $A(0, 0)$, $B(1, \sqrt{3})$, $C(3, \sqrt{3})$, and $D(2, 0)$.

(a)   Show that the figure $ABCD$ is a rhombus.

(b)   Show that the diagonals $\overline{AC}$ and $\overline{BD}$ are perpendicular.

Solution

It is helpful to make a sketch to assist in the analysis of the problem.

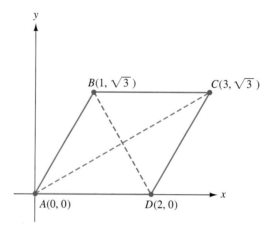

(a)   To show that the figure is a rhombus, we must show that the sides have equal lengths. Clearly, $AD = BC = 2$. Moreover, by the distance formula,

$$AB = \sqrt{(1 - 0)^2 + (\sqrt{3} - 0)^2} = \sqrt{1 + 3} = 2$$

and

$$DC = \sqrt{(3 - 2)^2 + (\sqrt{3} - 0)^2} = \sqrt{1 + 3} = 2.$$

(b)   Using the formula that defines the slope of a line segment

$$\text{slope } \overline{AC} = \frac{\sqrt{3} - 0}{3 - 0} = \frac{\sqrt{3}}{3}$$

and

$$\text{slope } \overline{BD} = \frac{\sqrt{3} - 0}{1 - 2} = \frac{\sqrt{3}}{-1} = -\sqrt{3}.$$

Since

$$\frac{\sqrt{3}}{3} \cdot (-\sqrt{3}) = \frac{-3}{3} = -1.$$

it follows from the preceding theorem that $\overline{AC}$ and $\overline{BD}$ are perpendicular.

Equations of Lines

Using the tools of coordinate geometry it is now possible to write equations whose graphs are lines. Then, just as we could use coordinates alone to prove geometric results as above, we can use algebra and the equations of lines to obtain other geometric results. Conversely, we can use geometric ideas to clarify and/or demonstrate results in algebra.

We begin by considering a particular example.

EXAMPLE 14.11   **Determining the Equation of a Line Through (2, 3) with Slope 4/3**

Derive an equation of the line through point $P(2, 3)$ and having slope 4/3.

Solution   *Understand the problem*

There is one, and only one, line through the point (2, 3) and having slope 4/3. One can draw the line by plotting the point $P(2, 3)$ and then plotting the point $Q(5, 7)$ 3 units to the right and 4 units above P. The line segment through these points must have slope 4/3, so the line through these points must be the desired line. Suppose $R(x, y)$ is *any* point on the line. We must find an equation involving x and y that is satisfied by those, and only those, points that lie on the line.

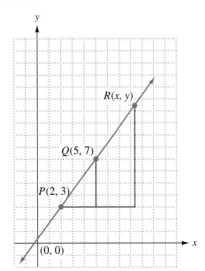

Devise a plan

Since the slope of a line can be determined by *any* two points on the line, $R(x, y)$ is on the line if, and only if,

$$\text{slope } \overline{PR} = \frac{4}{3}.$$

Perhaps we can use this fact to derive the desired equation.

Carry out the plan

Since

$$\text{slope } \overline{PR} = \frac{y - 3}{x - 2},$$

it follows that R is on the line in question if, and only if,

$$\frac{y - 3}{x - 2} = \frac{4}{3}$$

or, alternatively,

$$y - 3 = \frac{4}{3}(x - 2).$$

Hence, this must be the desired equation.

Look back

Since there is one, and only one, line through a given point and having a given slope, $R(x, y)$ is on the desired line if, and only if, slope $\overline{PR} = 4/3$. By expressing slope $\overline{PR}$ in terms of x and y, we obtained the desired equation.

The preceding example is typical and the result can be stated as a theorem which would be proved by exactly the same argument as that of Example 14.11.

> **THEOREM** *Point-Slope Form of the Equation of a Line*
> The equation of the line through $P(a, b)$ and having slope m is
> $$y - b = m(x - a).$$
> This is called the **point-slope form** of the equation of a line.

As this theorem suggests, there are several forms of the equation of a line. Another particularly useful form is stated in the next theorem. First we note that if a line crosses the y-axis at the point $(0, b)$, b is called the **y-intercept** of the line.

> **THEOREM**   *Slope-Intercept Form of the Equation of a Line*
> The **slope-intercept form of the equation of a line** is
> $$y = mx + b$$
> where m is the slope and b is the y-intercept.

Proof   Since b is the y-intercept, the line passes through the point $(0, b)$. Also, it has slope m. Therefore, by the point-slope form of the equation of a line, the desired equation is

$$y - b = m(x - 0)$$

or, equivalently,

$$y = mx + b$$

as claimed.

EXAMPLE   14.12   **Using the Slope-Intercept Form of the Equation of a Line**

Write the equations of the following lines with the slope and y-intercept as indicated. Also, draw each line on a coordinate system.

(a) $m = -3,\quad b = 5$ **(b)** $m = 0,\quad b = -4$

Solution

(a)   Using the above theorem, we obtain the equation $y = -3x + 5$. To draw the line, we plot the point $(0, 5)$ and the point $(1, 2)$ which is 3 units *below* and 1 unit to the right of $(0, 5)$. Then draw the line through these 2 points.

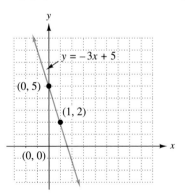

(b)   This line goes through the point $(0, -4)$ and has slope 0. Therefore, using the slope-intercept form, we obtain the equation

$$y = 0x + (-4)$$

or just

$$y = -4.$$

This says that the line is horizontal and that a point is on this line if, and only if, its y-coordinate is -4. The x-coordinates of these points are unrestricted. The line is as shown.

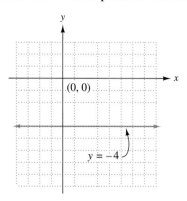

The preceding example suggests that *every* horizontal line has an equation of the form $y = b$; the slope is 0 and the x values of points on the lines are left unrestricted. By analogy, *every* vertical line has an equation of the form $x = a$; there is *no* slope and the y values of points on the lines are left unrestricted.

EXAMPLE 14.13   Determining the Equation of a Line Through Two Points

(a)   Determine the equation of the line through $P(3, 5)$ and $Q(-2, 1)$.

(b)   Determine the equation of the line through $P(3, 5)$ and perpendicular to the line in part (a).

Solution

(a)   The slope of the desired line is the slope of the segment $\overline{PQ}$;

$$\text{slope } \overline{PQ} = \frac{5 - 1}{3 - (-2)} = \frac{4}{5}.$$

We now use the point-slope form of the equation of the line using either P or Q. Using P we have

$$y - 5 = \frac{4}{5}(x - 3),$$

$$5y - 25 = 4x - 12,$$

$$4x - 5y + 13 = 0.$$

> Multiply both sides by 5 and use the distributive property.

> Subract 5y − 25 from both sides.

Or, using Q as the point, we have

$$y - 1 = \frac{4}{5}(x - (-2))$$

which can be simplified to

$$4x - 5y + 13 = 0$$

as before. It makes no difference which of the two points is used.

(b)   Since the slopes of perpendicular lines are negative reciprocals of one another, the slope of the line through P and perpendicular to the line of part (a) is $-5/4$.

Hence, the desired equation is

$$y - 5 = -\frac{5}{4}(x - 3)$$

which can be simplified to

$$5x + 4y - 35 = 0.$$

Lastly, we observe that all equations of lines considered so far can be written in the form

$$Ax + By + C = 0$$

where A, B, and C are real numbers and not both A and B are zero. Such an equation is called a **linear equation** and every such equation is the equation of a line.

- If $A = 0$ and $B \neq 0$, the line is horizontal and crosses the y-axis at the point $(0, -C/B)$.
- If $A \neq 0$ and $B = 0$, the line is vertical and crosses the x-axis at $(-C/A, 0)$.
- If $A \neq 0$ and $B \neq 0$, the line has slope $-A/B$, which is positive if A and B have opposite signs and negative if A and B have the same sign.

Intersections of Lines

By definition and as illustrated in Figure 14.9, two distinct lines must either be parallel or they must intersect in a single point. Since the graph of a line consists of all points whose coordinates satisfy the equation of the line, if two lines intersect at a common point (a, b) that point is said to be a **simultaneous solution of the two linear equations** corresponding to the two lines. Thus, from the geometry:

- two linear equations have precisely one simultaneous solution, or
- two linear equations have no simultaneous solution, or
- two linear equations actually represent the same line and so have infinitely many simultaneous solutions.

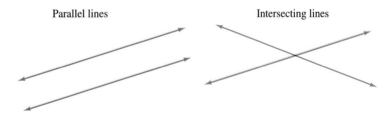

Parallel lines   Intersecting lines

Figure 14.9
Two distinct lines must be parallel or they must intersect in a single point.

EXAMPLE   14.14

Determining Simultaneous Solutions of Linear Equations

(a)   Show that the lines $2x + 5y = -11$ and $3x - 2y = 12$ are not parallel.
(b)   Find the simultaneous solution to the equations in part (a).

Solution

(a)   Solving for y in terms of x to obtain the slope-intercept forms of the equations of the lines in question, we obtain

$$y = -\frac{2}{5}x - \frac{11}{5} \quad \text{and} \quad y = \frac{3}{2}x - 6.$$

Thus, the slopes of the lines are $-2/5$ and $3/2$ and the lines are not parallel.

(b)   Since the x and y values of the point of intersection of the lines must be the same, it follows from part (a) that, at this point,

$$-\frac{2}{5}x - \frac{11}{5} = \frac{3}{2}x - 6.$$

$$10 = \text{LCM}(5, 2)$$

Multiplying through by 10 to eliminate fractions we have

$$-4x - 22 = 15x - 60,$$
$$-19x - 22 = -60,$$
$$-19x = -38,$$

and

$$x = 2.$$

Now, substituting 2 for x in either equation in part (a), we obtain

$$y = -\frac{2}{5} \cdot 2 - \frac{11}{5} = -\frac{4}{5} - \frac{11}{5} = \frac{-15}{5} = -3.$$

Even more easily, from the other equation,

$$y = \frac{3}{2} \cdot 2 - 6 = 3 - 6 = -3.$$

Thus, the simultaneous solution is the point $(2, -3)$.

The solution can be visualized by drawing the lines and reading off the coordinates of the point of intersection as shown here.

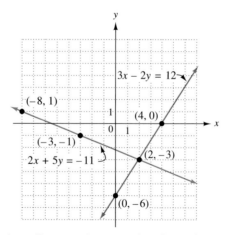

Since two points determine a line, we plot two points for each equation. For the first equation, if $y = 1$, then $x = -8$, and if $y = -1$, then $x = -3$. Therefore, $(-8, 1)$ and $(-3, -1)$ determine the first line. Similarly $(4, 0)$ and $(0, -6)$ determine the second line. We read off $(2, -3)$ as the simultaneous solution as shown.

Chapter 12
Lesson
3

Exploring Equal Ratios

Liz is from Marcus, Iowa.

Problem Solving Connection

■ Make a Table

■ Look for a Pattern

Materials
grid paper

Vocabulary
coordinates
an ordered number pair used in graphing

Explore

Liz keeps herself busy. She enjoys making porcelain dolls and their clothes. She also swims each week.

Work Together

Liz swims one day a week. She works on her dolls three days a week.

1. What is the ratio of doll-making days to swimming days in one week?

2. Copy and complete the ratio table that shows this ratio up to 6 weeks. Show each ratio as an ordered pair.

Ratio of Doll-Making Days to Swimming Days						
Week	1	2	3	4	5	6
Doll-Making	3	6		12		
Swimming	1					
Ordered Pairs	(3,1)					

3. Create a graph and plot the **coordinates** in the ratio table. What will you label each axis on this graph?

Did You Know?
Fred Newton swam the longest distance on record in 1930. He swam 1,826 mi down the Mississippi River.

Talk About It

4. What happens when ordered pairs for equal ratios are graphed? What kind of pattern do you see?

5. Explain why the ratios $\frac{3}{2}$, $\frac{6}{4}$, $\frac{9}{6}$, $\frac{12}{8}$, and $\frac{15}{10}$ would lie on the same line if they were graphed.

532 Chapter 12 • Ratio, Percent, and Probability

SOURCE: *Scott Foresman–Addison Wesley Math*, Grade 5, p. 532, by Randall I. Charles et al. Copyright © 1999 Addison Wesley Longman, Inc.

Questions for the Teacher

1. This lesson emphasizes an important relationship between equal ratios and graphing. Describe the graph the students will obtain in response to item 3 above. What would be the case if all these points were connected by line segments. If (x, y) were a number pair associated in the table, determine an equation relating x and y.

2. This lesson can be connected to the game Guess My Rule (see problem 5, Problem Set 1.3). Max is it and, in the following set of ordered pairs, the first entries are the numbers the students chose and the second entries are the corresponding numbers Max gave back: (1, 5), (4, 14), (0, 2), (3, 11), and (5, 17). Graph the ordered pairs and give Max's rule. Explain the connection between Max's rule, the graph, and the above lesson.

PROBLEM SET 14.2

Understanding Concepts

1. Compute the slopes of the line segments determined by these pairs of points. In each case tell whether the segment is vertical, horizontal, slopes upward to the right, or slopes downward to the right.

   (a) $P(1, 4)$, $Q(3, 8)$ (b) $R(-2, 5)$, $S(-2, -6)$

   (c) $U(-2, -3)$, $V(-4, -7)$

   (d) $C(3, 5)$, $D(-3, 5)$

   (e) $E(1, -2)$, $F(-2, -5)$

   (f) $G(-2, -2)$, $H(4, -5)$

2. Determine b so that the slope of $\overline{PQ}$ is 2 where P and Q are the points $(b, 3)$ and $(4, 7)$, respectively.

3. Determine d so that the slope of $\overline{CD}$ is undefined if C and D are the points $(d, 3)$ and $(-5, 5)$, respectively.

4. Determine e so that $\overline{EF}$ is horizontal if E and F are the points $(-3, -5)$ and $(2, e)$, respectively.

5. Determine a if the point $(a, 3)$ is on the line $2x + 3y = 18$.

6. (a) Determine two different points on the line $3x + 5y + 15 = 0$.

   (b) Draw the graph of the line in part (a) on a coordinate system.

7. Graph each of these lines on a single coordinate system and label each line.

   (a) $3x + 5y = 12$ (b) $6x = -10y + 12$

   (c) $5y - 3x = 15$ (d) $6x + 10y = 24$

   (e) What do you conclude about the lines of parts (a) and (d)?

8. Graph each of these lines on a coordinate system.

   (a) $2y - 16 = 0$ (b) $x = -7$ (c) $x + y = 2$

   (d) $x - y = 4$ (e) $y = 3x + 4$

   (f) $y = -2x + 6$

9. (a) Determine two points on the line $4x + 2y = 6$.

   (b) Use the points determined in part (a) to compute the slope of the line.

   (c) Solve the equation in part (a) for y in terms of x and so again determine the slope of the line and also the y-intercept. (*Hint:* Solving for y in terms of x gives the slope-intercept form of the equation of a line.)

10. In each case determine k so that the line is parallel to the line $3x - 5y + 45 = 0$.

    (a) $7x + ky = 21$ (b) $kx - 8y - 24 = 0$

    (c) $y = kx + 5$ (d) $x = ky + 5$

11. Determine the slope and y-intercept of each of these lines.

    (a) $3x - 7y + 21 = 0$ (b) $2x + 5y = 20$

    (c) $y = 6$ (d) $y = 0.3x + 15$

    (e) $x = -5$ (f) $2x = 3y - 18$

12. Determine whether these pairs of lines are parallel, perpendicular, or neither parallel nor perpendicular.

    (a) $3x + 7y + 15 = 0$, $6x + 15y + 31 = 0$

    (b) $2x - 5y = 7$, $4x = 10y + 20$

    (c) $x + 4y + 6 = 0$, $8x = 2y + 13$

    (d) $7x + 3y + 21 = 0$, $3x - 7y + 21 = 0$

    (e) $y = 3x + 15$, $6x - 2y + 12 = 0$

13. Determine k so that $2x + ky + 6 = 0$ is

    (a) parallel to $3x - 5y = 15$.

    (b) perpendicular to $3x - 5y = 15$.

14. Determine if these are equations of lines that intersect. If the lines intersect, determine the coordinates of the point of intersection; that is, determine the simultaneous solution to the pair of equations.

    (a) $2x - 3y = 9$, $4x - 4y = 16$

    (b) $3x + 5y = 15$, $6x + 10y = 30$

    (c) $4x - 3y = 12$, $8x - 6y = 0$

15. (a) Write the equation of the line perpendicular to the line $5x - 2y = 10$ and which passes through the point $(-1, 7)$.

    (b) Determine the point where the two lines of part (a) intersect.

Thinking Critically

16. (a) Compute the midpoint of the segment $\overline{PQ}$ where P and Q are $(3, -5)$ and $(5, 9)$, respectively.

    (b) Compute the slope of $\overline{PQ}$ from part (a).

    (c) Use the results of (a) and (b) and determine the equation of the perpendicular bisector of $\overline{PQ}$.

17. A point is on the perpendicular bisector of a segment if, and only if, it is equidistant from the end points of

the segment. Use this fact and the distance formula to determine the perpendicular bisector of the segment $\overline{PQ}$ in problem 16. (*Hint:* $(r - s)^2 = r^2 - 2rs + s^2$.)

18. Determine the equation of the perpendicular bisectors of the segments determined by these pairs of points.

    (a) $P(3, 5)$, $Q(-1, 7)$ (b) $R(4, -6)$, $S(8, -4)$
    (c) $C(3, -2)$, $D(4, 6)$ (d) $E(3, 7)$, $F(3, -4)$
    (e) $G(-1, 5)$, $H(5, 5)$ (f) $I(2, 2)$, $J(-3, 5)$

19. (a) Determine the equations of the three altitudes of the triangle with vertices $A(0, 0)$, $B(3, 6)$, and $C(9, 0)$.

    (b) Show that the three altitudes of part (a) meet at a common point. (*Hint:* Determine the point of intersection of each pair of equations in part (a).)

    (c) Draw the triangle and graph the equations of part (a) on a coordinate system.

20. Show that the three perpendicular bisectors of the sides of the triangle in problem 19 meet at a common point.

21. Show that the medians of the triangle in problem 19 meet at a common point.

22. Show that the point where the three medians in problem 21 meet is two-thirds of the way from each vertex to the midpoint of the opposite side.

23. Show that the three points determined in problems 19, 20, and 21 are collinear. The line on which they lie is called the **Euler line.** (*Hint:* If P, Q, and R are collinear, what must be true about slope $\overline{PQ}$ and slope $\overline{PR}$?)

24. Determine the shortest distance from the point $(1, 5)$ to the line $3x - 2y = 6$.

Communicating

25. (a) On four separate coordinate systems sketch these lines.

    (i) $\dfrac{x}{2} + \dfrac{y}{5} = 1$ (ii) $\dfrac{x}{4} + \dfrac{y}{-3} = 1$

    (iii) $\dfrac{x}{-4} + \dfrac{y}{-3} = 1$ (iv) $\dfrac{x}{-5} + \dfrac{y}{2} = 1$

    (b) On the basis of your graphs in part (a), carefully discuss the significance of a and b for the graph of $\dfrac{x}{a} + \dfrac{y}{b} = 1$.

26. If $a \neq 0$ and $b \neq 0$, discuss what can be said about the lines

    $$ax + by = c \qquad \text{and} \qquad bx - ay = d.$$

    (*Hint:* Compute the slope in each case.)

Making Connections

27. (a) The maximum allowable slope for a ramp for disabled persons using a wheelchair is 1/20. If the sill of the door to a building is 3.5 feet above the level of the sidewalk, at least how far from the building must a ramp for wheelchair users begin?

3.5′

    (b) How long is the shortest allowable ramp in part (a)?

28. It is customary to design highways so that the grade (slope) never exceeds 6%. If it is necessary to exceed this limit, truckers are always warned by a sign indicating how long the stretch of highway is with the grade exceeding 6%.

    (a) If it is 9 miles from Lenore to Pierce and the elevation of Pierce is 3000 feet greater than that of Lenore, what is the slope of the straight line connecting the two towns? There are 5280 feet in a mile.

    (b) Is it possible to build a highway from Lenore to Pierce without exceeding the 6% restriction on the grade? Explain.

29. Scientists often need to determine the relationship between two quantities, say x and y. This is often done by determining corresponding values of the quantities, plotting the points determined by these number pairs on a coordinate system, then drawing a line that seems to fit the plotted points most closely, and finally determining the equation of this line. The line described is called the **line of best fit** and there is a technical method for determining it. Here we do it "by eye." For example, the data points and the "line of best fit" might appear as shown.

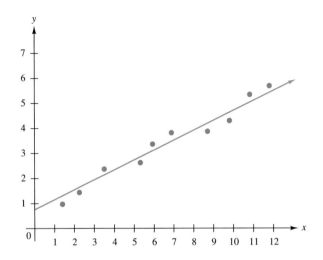

Since the points (1, 1.1) and (10, 5) appear to lie on the line, the equation of the line of best fit is approximately

$$y - 5 \doteq \frac{5 - 1.1}{10 - 1}(x - 10)$$

which simplifies to

$$y \doteq 0.43x + 0.67.$$

Using this equation, we could predict that, when $x = 20$, $y \doteq 9.27$. By eye, draw the line of best fit for each of the data sets illustrated, determine the equation of the line, and predict the value of y when $x = 15$.

(a)

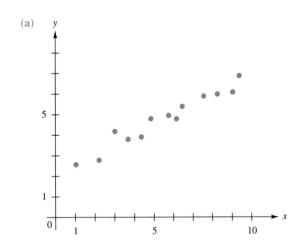

(b)

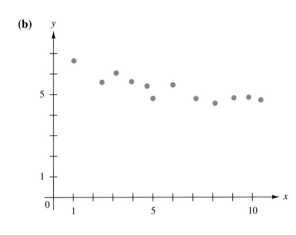

From State Student Assessments

30. (Oregon, Grade 8)

Loni is opening a mail order house. For the clothes she sells, she wants to charge twice what they cost her plus a $5.00 shipping and handling charge. Which chart shows her pricing plan?

A.

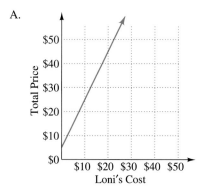

C.

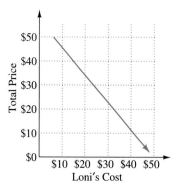

B.

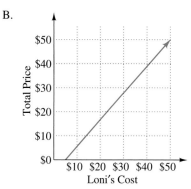

D.

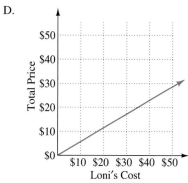

31. (Oregon, Grade 8)

Jolene and Jake are in charge of hiring the Disc Jockey (DJ) for the Spring Dance. The DJ from radio station KDOT charges $150 plus $2 per person. The DJ from radio station KBOP charges $250 plus $1 per person. Since most of the students like the DJ from KBOP better, show how many students would need to attend the dance to make KBOP cost the same as KDOT. The following is a solution by one of the students. How would you rate this student's performance? Discuss briefly.

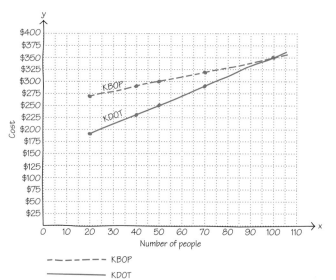

For Review

32. Consider the figures shown here.

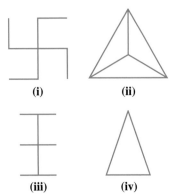

(i)   (ii)

(iii)   (iv)

(a) Which of the figures has precisely one line of symmetry?

(b) Which of the figures has precisely two lines of symmetry?

(c) Do any of the figures have more than two lines of symmetry?

(d) Which of the figures is symmetric about a point?

(e) List those figures that have rotational symmetry and indicate the angle or angles of rotation in each case.

33. If a geometrical figure is symmetric about a point, must it have rotational symmetry? Explain briefly.

34. If a plane geometric figure has one or more rotational symmetries, must it also have symmetry about a point? Explain briefly.

35. Using graph paper, copy the figure shown and draw its reflection in the given line.

(a)

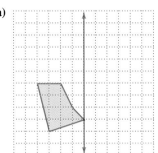

(b)

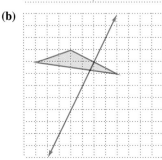

36. Using graph paper, copy the figure shown and draw the figure that results from rotating the given figure through an angle of 90° counterclockwise about the point *P*.

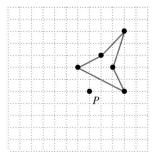

OPERATIVE INVESTIGATION

Stretching a Spring

Materials Needed

1. A screen door spring about 20″ long.
2. Several objects weighing between 0.5 and 2 pounds.
3. A tin can that can be suspended from the spring.
4. A scale.
5. A meter stick.

Directions

1. Attach the spring to a support as indicated in the diagram and attach the can to the spring.
2. Weigh each object and record its weight, *w*.
3. Place each object in the can on the spring and measure the amount, *s*, the weight *stretches* the spring.
4. Plot the points (*w*, *s*) on an appropriate coordinate system.
5. Draw the line of best fit and determine its equation in terms of *w* and *s*.
6. Use the equation of the line of best fit to predict *s* when *w* = 3 lbs.
7. Actually measure *s* when *w* = 3 lbs. and see how close your approximation is.

COOPERATIVE INVESTIGATION

Swinging a Pendulum

Materials Needed

1. A pendulum made by tying three or four heavy washers together on the end of a string about 150 centimeters long.
2. A stopwatch.
3. Graph paper for each student.
4. A calculator for each student or pair of students.

The Problem

The problem is to determine the relationship between the length, *l*, of the pendulum and the time, *t*, required for the pendulum to complete 10 complete swings back and forth.

Directions

Step 1.   Mark the string at 10-centimeter intervals starting where it ties onto the washers.

Step 2.   Hold the pendulum at length *l* = 10 centimeters on a solid support (say a coat rack) and carefully note the time in seconds for 10 complete swings.

Step 3.   Repeat Step 2 for *l* = 20, 30, 40, 50, and 60 centimeters.

Step 4.   Let $x = \sqrt{l}$ and plot the points (*t*, *x*) for the measurements in Steps 2 and 3.

Step 5.   Draw a line of best fit for the points in Step 4 and determine an equation relating *t* and *x* and hence *t* and $\sqrt{l}$.

Step 6.   Use the formula in Step 5 to predict how long it will take for 10 swings of the pendulum if *l* = 100 centimeters.

Step 7.   Actually time 10 swings of the pendulum when *l* = 100 to check the accuracy of your prediction in Step 6.

14.3   Solving Geometric Problems Using Coordinates

Proofs Using Coordinates

The problems and examples in sections 14.1 and 14.2 suggest that many of the general theorems of geometry can be obtained using the techniques of coordinate geometry and methods of algebra. Suppose, for example, that you are asked to show that the line segment joining the midpoints of two sides of a triangle is parallel to the third side. This does not mean we are to show that the property holds for a particular triangle, or even for a certain type of triangle—equilateral, isosceles, scalene, right, or acute. We are asked to show that this is a general result, true for all triangles. This means that the argument we use must be completely general and must not depend on special properties of some particular

INTO THE CLASSROOM

Using Activities to Introduce Coordinates

As with other mathematical notions, in teaching students about ordered pairs as coordinates of points, it is useful to use manipulatives and activities. For example, tell the students that they are SECRET AGENTS and will be identified by a number pair like (2, 3)—meaning the student in the third seat from the front in the second row from the left. Calling on students by number pairs quickly makes clear the idea of coordinates and how they are related to locations.

To introduce the idea of equations of lines

- ask all those students to stand whose first number (coordinate) is four.
- ask all those students to stand whose sum of coordinates is five.
- ask all those students to stand if the first of their coordinates minus the second is two.
- ask all those students to stand whose second coordinate is three.
- ask all those students to stand if the ratio of their second coordinate to their first coordinate is two.

The activity is interesting to students and they will be surprised to note that, in each case, those students standing form a straight line across the room. Discussing these and similar situations leads to the concepts of linear equations and graphing.

For a cross-curricular activity that not only teaches about ordered pairs as coordinates but also develops an awareness of the geography of the United States, create a bulletin board using a wall-sized map of the United States. Make a grid across the map by stapling colored yarn to the board. Label the vertical and horizontal pieces of yarn with consecutive integers starting at the lower left-hand corner of the grid. Cities can then be associated with ordered pairs. For example, (1, 6) might locate Seattle, (2, 5) might locate San Francisco, (4, 4) might locate Minneapolis, and so on. This allows for a variety of activities: locating state capitals, locating the ten largest cities in the United States, locating cities that have professional football teams (basketball teams, baseball teams), and so on. Divide the class into two teams and have a contest where one team calls out ordered pairs and the other responds with the proper location and vice versa. To introduce the notion of lines and graphing, ask one team to place red-headed pins or thumbtacks on all points whose sum of coordinates is five. Ask the other team to place blue-headed pins on all points where the first coordinate minus the second equals one, and so on. The possibilities are limited only by your imagination. From beginnings like these, it is not difficult to move on to coordinate axes on graph paper and the use of coordinates to identify points, to graphs, and to all that follows from these ideas.

triangle. Consider any triangle—say the one shown in Figure 14.10. This is not any particular triangle, just one that we drew to assist our thought processes. To continue our analysis using coordinate geometry, we add axes to the drawing as in Figure 14.11 with A at the origin, C on the positive x-axis, and B above the x-axis as shown.

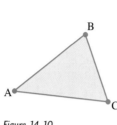

Figure 14.10

Triangle ABC

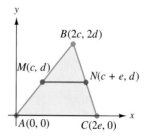

Figure 14.11

Triangle ABC on a coordinate system

Then A has coordinates $(0, 0)$, B has coordinates $(2c, 2d)$, and C has coordinates $(2e, 0)$ for suitable real numbers c, d, and e. Since this could be done for *any* triangle and c, d, and e are not further specified, the argument will apply to *any* triangle; it is completely general. Let M and N be the midpoints of $\overline{AB}$ and $\overline{BC}$, respectively. Then, M and N have coordinates (c, d) and $(c + e, d)$, respectively, and

$$\text{slope } \overline{MN} = \frac{d - d}{c - (c + e)}$$

$$= 0.$$

Since

$$\text{slope } \overline{AC} = \frac{0 - 0}{2e - 0}$$

$$= 0,$$

it follows that $\overline{MN}$ is parallel to $\overline{AC}$ as we were to show.

To illustrate the method further, we consider two more examples.

EXAMPLE 14.15 | **Proving a Result via Coordinates**

Show that the line segments joining the midpoints of the sides of a quadrilateral form a parallelogram.

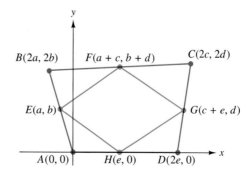

Solution   Any quadrilateral can be placed on a coordinate system with one vertex at the origin, one vertex on the positive x-axis, and the other two vertices above the x-axis. Let quadrilateral $ABCD$ be so placed as shown. Then, for suitable numbers, a, b, c, d, and e, with $e \neq a$, the coordinates of the vertices are $A(0, 0)$, $B(2a, 2b)$, $C(2c, 2d)$, and $D(2e, 0)$. By the midpoint formula, the midpoints of $\overline{AB}$, $\overline{BC}$, $\overline{CD}$, and $\overline{DA}$ are, respectively, $E(a, b)$, $F(a + c, b + d)$, $G(c + e, d)$ and $H(e, 0)$. Therefore,

$$\text{slope } \overline{EF} = \frac{(b + d) - b}{(a + c) - a} = \frac{d}{c},$$

$$\text{slope } \overline{FG} = \frac{(b + d) - d}{(a + c) - (c + e)} = \frac{b}{a - e},$$

$$\text{slope } \overline{GH} = \frac{d - 0}{(c + e) - e} = \frac{d}{c},$$

and

$$\text{slope } \overline{HE} = \frac{b - 0}{a - e} = \frac{b}{a - e}.$$

This shows that $\overline{EF}$ is parallel to $\overline{GH}$ and $\overline{FG}$ is parallel to $\overline{HE}$. Thus, $EFGH$ is a parallelogram as was to be shown.

EXAMPLE   14.16

Proving that the Diagonals of a Rhombus Are Perpendicular

Show that the diagonals of a rhombus are perpendicular.

Solution   Any rhombus can be placed on a coordinate system so that one vertex is at the origin, one vertex is on the positive x-axis, and the other two vertices are in quadrant I as shown. Let $A(0, 0)$, $B(a, b)$, $C(r, s)$, and $D(c, 0)$ be the vertices of the rhombus as shown. Since a rhombus is a parallelogram, $\overline{BC}$ is parallel to $\overline{AD}$ and so is horizontal. Thus, $s = b$. Also, the sides of a rhombus are the same length so

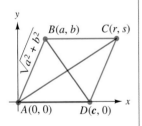

$$r = a + c \quad \text{and} \quad c = \sqrt{a^2 + b^2}.$$

This implies that

$$c^2 = a^2 + b^2$$

or, equivalently, that

$$-b^2 = a^2 - c^2.$$

To show that $\overline{AC}$ and $\overline{BD}$ are perpendicular, we consider their slopes.

$$\text{slope } \overline{AC} = \frac{s - 0}{r - 0}$$

since $s = b$ and $r = a + c$ from above

$$= \frac{b}{a + c}$$

$$\text{slope } \overline{BD} = \frac{b}{a - c}$$

But then

$$\text{slope } \overline{AC} \cdot \text{slope } \overline{BD} = \frac{b}{a+c} \cdot \frac{b}{a-c}$$

$$= \frac{b^2}{a^2 - c^2}$$

$$= \frac{b^2}{-b^2}$$

$$= -1.$$

Remember,
$(a + c)(a - c)$
$= a^2 - c^2$.

since $-b^2 = a^2 - c^2$

This shows that the diagonals of the rhombus are perpendicular as claimed.

The idea in each of the preceding examples was that any plane geometrical figure can be placed on a coordinate system. Moreover, this was done in such a way that the coordinates of certain key points were kept general and yet as simple as possible to facilitate later computation. Thus, the proofs were completely general and showed that the results claimed held for *all* such figures.

Proofs Using Equations and Coordinates

The preceding proofs only depended on the use of coordinates, the midpoint formula, and the notion of slope. Algebraic methods, however, make it possible to use equations of lines as well.

EXAMPLE   14.17

Showing that the Altitudes of a Triangle Are Concurrent

Show that the altitudes of a triangle are concurrent.

Solution

We orient the triangle on a coordinate system with one vertex at the origin, one vertex on the positive *x*-axis, and one vertex in the upper half plane. Let $A(0, 0)$, $B(c, d)$, and $C(e, 0)$, with $c \neq e$, be these vertices.

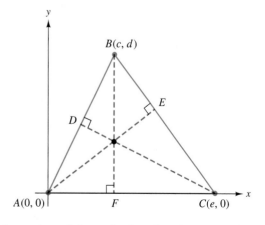

We now use the notion of slope, the fact that the slopes of perpendicular lines are negative reciprocals of one another, and the point-slope form of the equation of a line. Let $\overline{AE}$, $\overline{BF}$, and $\overline{CD}$ be the altitudes of the triangle.

Then

$$\text{slope } \overline{BC} = \frac{d}{c - e} \quad \text{so slope } \overline{AE} = \frac{e - c}{d}.$$

Therefore, the equation of $\overleftrightarrow{AE}$ is

$$y - 0 = \frac{e - c}{d}(x - 0)$$

or simply

$$dy = ex - cx.$$

Similarly,

$$\text{slope } \overline{AB} = \frac{d}{c} \quad \text{so slope } \overline{DC} = -\frac{c}{d}.$$

Therefore, the equation of $\overleftrightarrow{DC}$ is

$$y - 0 = -\frac{c}{d}(x - e)$$

or simply

$$dy = -cx + ce.$$

To find where $\overleftrightarrow{AE}$ and $\overleftrightarrow{DC}$ intersect, we determine the simultaneous solution of the equations of these two lines. Subtracting the equation for $\overleftrightarrow{DC}$ from the equation for $\overleftrightarrow{AE}$, we obtain

$$0 = ex - ec.$$

Therefore, the x-coordinate of the point of intersection is

$$x = \frac{ec}{e} = c.$$

Hence, without even determining the y-coordinate of the point of intersection of $\overleftrightarrow{AE}$ and $\overleftrightarrow{DC}$, it follows that the point of intersection lies on $\overleftrightarrow{BF}$ since $\overleftrightarrow{BF}$ is vertical, passes through the point $B(c, d)$, and so has equation $x = c$. Thus, the three altitudes are concurrent as was to be shown.

Equations of Circles

Since circles possess many interesting properties that can be treated by methods of coordinate geometry, we now consider equations of circles.

EXAMPLE 14.18 | **Determining Points Equidistant from a Fixed Point**

(a) In words, describe the set of all points in a coordinate plane that are at distance 2 from the point (2, 3).

(b) Derive a formula that expresses the condition that $P(x, y)$ be one of the points in part (a).

Solution

(a)   The set of all points at distance 2 from the point (2, 3) is a circle of radius 2 with (2, 3) as its center as shown.

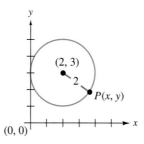

(b)   The point P is on the circle if, and only if, its distance from (2, 3) is 2. Thus, using the distance formula,

$$\sqrt{(x - 2)^2 + (y - 3)^2} = 2$$

or, equivalently,

$$(x - 2)^2 + (y - 3)^2 = 4.$$

Since $P(x, y)$ lies on this curve if, and only if, its coordinates satisfy the equation, this equation is the equation of the circle described.

The preceding example is typical of the general case stated here as a theorem.

> **THEOREM**   *Equation of a Circle*
> The equation of a circle of radius r with center $C(a, b)$ is
> $$(x - a)^2 + (y - b)^2 = r^2.$$
> In the special case where the center is the origin, the equation is $x^2 + y^2 = r^2$.

EXAMPLE   14.19

Finding the Circle with a Given Center and Passing Through a Given Point

Find the equation of the circle with center (5, 12) and which passes through the origin.

Solution

If the center of the circle is (5, 12) and the circle passes through the origin, then the radius of the circle is the distance from (0, 0) to (5, 12). Thus,

$$r = \sqrt{(5 - 0)^2 + (12 - 0)^2} = \sqrt{169} = 13.$$

By the theorem, the desired equation is

$$(x - 5)^2 + (y - 12)^2 = 169.$$

The Greek Cross—II

In the earlier Greek cross puzzle you were asked to cut the cross into four pieces that could be reassembled into a single square. Show how to cut the cross into four pieces, different from the first time, that can still be reassembled into a single square. (*Hint:* How long must the side of the square be?)

EXAMPLE 14.20 | **Finding the Center of a Circle**

    (a)   Write the equation of the circle of radius 5 and center $C(1, 2)$.
    (b)   Show that the points $A(-3, -1)$ and $B(4, 6)$ both lie on the circle.
    (c)   Determine the equation of the perpendicular bisector of chord $\overline{AB}$.
    (d)   Show that the center of the circle lies on the perpendicular bisector of $\overline{AB}$.

Solution   **(a)**   By the theorem, the desired equation is

$$(x - 1)^2 + (y - 2)^2 = 25.$$

    (b)   Since

$$(-3 - 1)^2 + (-1 - 2)^2 = (-4)^2 + (-3)^2 = 25$$

        and

$$(4 - 1)^2 + (6 - 2)^2 = 3^2 + 4^2 = 25,$$

        $(-3, -1)$ and $(4, 6)$ both satisfy the equation of part (a) and so lie on the circle. Thus, $\overline{AB}$ is a chord of the circle.
    (c)   Let $M(c, d)$ be the midpoint of $\overline{AB}$. By the midpoint formula,

$$c = \frac{-3 + 4}{2} = \frac{1}{2} \quad \text{and} \quad d = \frac{-1 + 6}{2} = \frac{5}{2}.$$

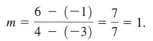

Also, the slope of $\overline{AB}$ is

$$m = \frac{6 - (-1)}{4 - (-3)} = \frac{7}{7} = 1.$$

It follows that the slope of the perpendicular bisector is -1 and its equation is

$$y - \frac{5}{2} = -1\left(x - \frac{1}{2}\right)$$

which simplifies to

$$x + y = 3.$$

(d) Since $1 + 2 = 3$, it follows that the center, $C(1, 2)$, of the circle lies on the perpendicular bisector of the chord.

PROBLEM SET 14.3

Understanding Concepts

1. **(a)** Let $A(0, 0)$, $B(a, 0)$, $C(r, s)$, and $D(0, c)$ with $a > 0$ and $c > 0$ be the vertices of a square. Determine r, s, and c in terms of a.

    (b) Draw the figure of part (a) on a Cartesian coordinate system.

2. **(a)** Let $A(0, 0)$, $B(a, 0)$, $C(r, s)$, and $D(0, c)$ with $a > 0$ and $c > 0$ be the vertices of a rectangle that is not a square. Determine r and s in terms of a and c.

    (b) Draw the figure of part (a) on a Cartesian coordinate system.

3. **(a)** Let $A(0, 0)$, $B(a, b)$, $C(r, s)$, and $D(c, 0)$ with $a > 0$, $b > 0$, and $c > 0$ be the vertices of a parallelogram that is not a rectangle. Determine r and s in terms of a, b, and c.

    (b) Draw the figure of part (a) on a Cartesian coordinate system.

4. **(a)** Let $A(0, 0)$, $B(a, b)$, and $C(2c, 0)$ with a, b, and c positive be the vertices of an equilateral triangle. Determine a and b in terms of c.

    (b) Sketch the figure of part (a) on a Cartesian coordinate system.

5. In words, describe the set of points satisfying each of these equations.

    (a) $x^2 + y^2 = 81$ **(b)** $(x - 2)^2 + y^2 = 4$

    (c) $x^2 + (y + 5)^2 = 0$

    (d) $(x - 3)^2 + (y - 5)^2 = 36$

6. Plot the set of all points satisfying each of these equations.

    (a) $(x - 2)^2 + (y + 3)^2 = 49$

    (b) $(x - 3)^2 + (y - 5)^2 = -9$

7. Write the equations of the circles satisfying these conditions.

    (a) Center at $(2, 5)$,   radius 3

    (b) Center at $(3, -4)$,   radius 1

    (c) Center at $(-1, 2)$ and just touching the x-axis

    (d) Center at $(2, b)$ and just touching the y-axis

8. **(a)** Show that the point $A(6, 2)$ lies on the circle $(x - 1)^2 + (y - 2)^2 = 25$.

    (b) The points $B(1, -3)$ and $A(6, 2)$ both lie on the circle of part (a). Determine the equation of the perpendicular bisector of the chord joining $B(1, -3)$ and $A(6, 2)$.

    (c) Show that the center of the circle lies on the perpendicular bisector of the chord determined in part (b).

9. One, and only one, circle can be drawn through any three noncollinear points.

    (a) Determine the center of the circle through the points $(7, 7)$, $(-1, 1)$, and $(6, 0)$. (*Hint:* Use the idea of problem 8, part (b).)

    (b) Determine the radius of the circle in part (a).

    (c) Determine the equation of the circle in part (a).

    (d) Plot the circle of part (b) on a Cartesian coordinate system.

Thinking Critically

10. Use coordinate geometry to show that the diagonals of a parallelogram bisect each other.

11. **(a)** Let $A(0, 0)$, $B(4a, 4b)$, $C(4c, 4d)$, and $D(4e, 0)$ with $b > 0$, $d > 0$, and $e > 0$ be the vertices of a quadrilateral. Let P, Q, R, and S be the midpoints of $\overline{AB}$, $\overline{BC}$, $\overline{CD}$, and $\overline{DA}$, respectively. Show that $\overline{PR}$ and $\overline{QS}$ bisect each other.

    (b) Draw a sketch to illustrate part (a).

12. Using the results of problem 4, show that the medians of an equilateral triangle are also the altitudes of the triangle.

13. **(a)** Any triangle can be placed on a coordinate system so that one point is at the origin, one point is on the positive x-axis, and one point is in the first quadrant. Thus, without loss of generality, we can take $A = A(0, 0)$, $B = B(2a, 2b)$, and $C = C(2c, 0)$. Show that the three medians of the triangle meet at the point.

$$G\left(\frac{2a + 2c}{3}, \frac{2b}{3}\right).$$

    (b) Show that the centroid of a triangle is two-thirds of the way from each vertex to the midpoint of the opposite side.

14. Show that the perpendicular bisectors of the sides of a triangle are concurrent using methods of coordinate geometry.

15. Use coordinate methods to show that the sum of the squares of the lengths of the diagonals equals the sum of the squares of the lengths of the sides of a parallelogram. (*Hint:* Any parallelogram can be placed on a coordinate system as shown. Let P be the point (a, b) and R the point $(c, 0)$.)

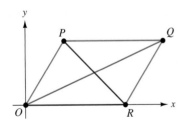

16. Consider the squares shown in this diagram. Let P, Q, R, and S be the centers of the squares as shown.

    (a) Using coordinate geometry, show that $\overline{PR} \cong \overline{QS}$.

    (b) Show that $\overline{PR}$ is perpendicular to $\overline{QS}$.

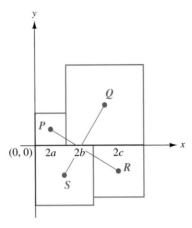

17. Consider the triangle SPQ inscribed in a semicircle as shown. Use coordinate methods to prove Thales' theorem; that is, show that $\overline{PQ}$ is perpendicular to $\overline{PS}$. (*Hint:* Recall that $x^2 + y^2 = r^2$ and $(x + r)(x - r) = x^2 - r^2$.)

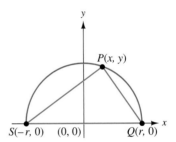

Making Connections

18. **(a)** Consider a ladder 12 feet long standing vertically against a wall. Let $M(x, y)$ be the midpoint of the ladder.

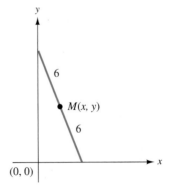

Determine the equation of the path described by M as the ladder is pulled away from the wall until it is lying flat on the ground but with the top and bottom of the ladder touching the wall and the ground, respectively, at all times.

(b) Copy the sketch in part (a) and draw the path described by *M*.

▣ Using a Computer/Using an Automatic Drawer

19. **(a)** Draw a triangle with vertices at *A*, *B*, and *C* and erect squares on $\overline{AB}$, $\overline{BC}$, and $\overline{AC}$ (on the outside of the triangle).

(b) Plot *D*, the center of the square on $\overline{AB}$; plot *E*, the center of the square on $\overline{BC}$; and plot *F*, the center of the square on $\overline{AC}$.

(c) Draw and measure $\overline{AE}$ and $\overline{DF}$. What conjecture does this result suggest? Explain.

(d) Measure the angle between the lines $\overleftrightarrow{AE}$ and $\overleftrightarrow{DF}$. What conjecture does this result suggest?

(e) Does dragging *A*, *B*, or *C* alter your conjectures in parts (c) and (d)?

20. **(a)** Plot two points *A* and *B*; draw $\overline{AB}$; and plot a (any) point *C* on $\overline{AB}$.

(b) Erect squares on $\overline{AC}$ and $\overline{CB}$ on one side of $\overline{AB}$ and a square on $\overline{AB}$ on the other side. Plot *D*, the center of the square on $\overline{AC}$; plot *E*, the center of the square on $\overline{CB}$; and plot *F*, the center of the square on $\overline{AB}$.

(c) Draw and measure $\overline{DE}$ and $\overline{CF}$, and measure the angles between $\overleftrightarrow{DE}$ and $\overleftrightarrow{CF}$. What conjectures do these measurements suggest?

(d) Let $A = A(0, 0)$, $B = B(2b, 0)$ and $C = C(2c, 0)$ with $c < b$, and proceed to prove your conjectures of part (c).

(e) Is the proof of part (d) completely general? Explain.

For Review

21. Determine the sum of the interior angles of a convex decagon.

22. Determine the sum of the exterior angles of a convex decagon.

23. Determine the measure of each interior angle of a regular decagon.

24. Determine the measure of each exterior angle of a regular decagon.

---

25. Determine if the point *P* is in the interior or the exterior of the region formed by the closed curve shown.

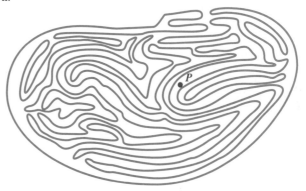

14.4   Graphing Functions

Graphing Functions

Suppose you invest $1000 at 7% interest compounded annually. How much will your investment be worth in one year? In two years? In twenty years? In *n* years? The answer to these questions can be found by using the compound interest formula

$$A = 1000(1.07)^n$$

A(n) is a function of n.

developed in Section 7.4. This formula gives the value of the investment at the end of *n* years; that is, *A* is a *function* of *n* and, to emphasize this fact, we sometimes write

$$A(n) = 1000(1.07)^n.$$

$A(1)$ is the value of the investment at the end of the first year, $A(1.5)$ is the value of the investment at the end of a year and a half, and so on.

The function $A(n)$ certainly enables one to answer the questions at the beginning of the preceding paragraph.* However, just looking at the function does not give most people good understanding of the way an investment grows at compound interest. A table like Table 14.1 certainly helps, but even the table does not suggest how rapidly the investment grows in later years.

TABLE 14.1	The Value at the End of Each Year of $1000 Invested at 7% Compounded Annually						
n	$A(n)$	n	$A(n)$	n	$A(n)$	n	$A(n)$
1	1070.00	6	1500.73	11	2104.85	16	2952.16
2	1144.90	7	1605.78	12	2252.19	17	3158.82
3	1225.04	8	1718.19	13	2409.85	18	3379.93
4	1310.80	9	1838.46	14	2578.53	19	3616.53
5	1402.55	10	1967.15	15	2759.03	20	3869.68

This can perhaps best be conveyed by the visual impact of a graph as in Figure 14.12. The points on the graph are those with coordinates $(n, A(n))$ determined by the formula.

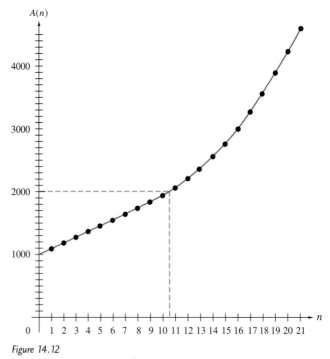

Figure 14.12
Graph of A(n) = 1000(1.07)^n

---

*To compute $1000(1.07)^2$ enter this string into a calculator: [ON/AC] 1.07 [y^x] 2 [×] 1000 [=]

Actually, we plotted only the points from the data in Table 14.1, but if these points are joined by a smooth curve, we can read from the graph the values of $A(n)$ for other values of n. Thus, from the graph, $A(10.5) \doteq 2030$ and, by direct computation, $A(10.5) \doteq 2034.84$. Note, in particular, that the graph shows that the investment grows steadily but modestly at first (the first half dozen points lie almost on a straight line), but that the growth is much more dramatic in later years. In fact, at the end of 40 years the investment is worth an astonishing \$14,974.46! (Show this by using the $\boxed{y^x}$ key on a calculator.)

The following definition makes the notion of the graph of a function more precise.

> **DEFINITION** *The Graph of a Function*
> The **graph of the function $f(x)$** is the set of points (x, y) whose coordinates satisfy the equation $y = f(x)$.

EXAMPLE 14.21

Drawing the Graph of a Function
Graph the function $y = \sqrt{16 - x^2}$.

Solution

Since the graph is the set of all points (x, y) that satisfy the equation, we use a calculator to prepare a table of values of x and corresponding values of y as shown. However, since we can do this for only a finite set of points, we do it only for a representative set of values of x, plot the points, and then connect them with a smooth curve. Note, by the way, that the domain of this function is $\{x: -4 \le x \le 4\}$. For values of x outside this range $16 - x^2$ is negative and so has no real number as its square root.* The graph of the function is the semicircle of radius 4 as shown.

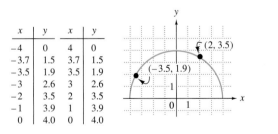

x	y	x	y
−4	0	4	0
−3.7	1.5	3.7	1.5
−3.5	1.9	3.5	1.9
−3	2.6	3	2.6
−2	3.5	2	3.5
−1	3.9	1	3.9
0	4.0	0	4.0

Note that by $\sqrt{n}$ we *always* mean the positive number a such that $a^2 = n$.

It is important to note that any vertical line cuts the graph in Example 14.21 in at most one point. This is the visual counterpart of the requirement in the definition of a function that to each x in the domain of the function there corresponds precisely one y in the range. Thus, one can tell at a glance if a graph is or is not the graph of a function.

> **THEOREM** *The Vertical Line Test*
> A graph is the graph of a function if, and only if, every vertical line cuts the graph in at most one point.

---

*Negative numbers do have square roots but they are complex numbers, inappropriate for this course and also for the elementary school curriculum.

EXAMPLE 14.22

Using the Vertical Line Test

In each of the following indicate if the graph is the graph of a function. If it is not the graph of a function, tell why.

(a) (b) (c)

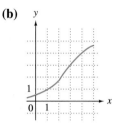

Solution

(a) This graph is not the graph of a function since the line $x = 1$ cuts the graph in a whole interval of values of y.

(b) This is the graph of a function since each vertical line cuts the graph just once.

(c) This is not the graph of a function since some vertical lines cut the graph more than once. In particular, this is true of the line $x = 1$.

Graphs of functions can be symmetric with respect to the y-axis and also with respect to the origin. Can the graph of a function be symmetric with respect to the x-axis? Unless $f(x) = 0$ for all x, the answer is *no* since, as is apparent from Figure 14.13, any such graph necessarily fails the vertical line test.

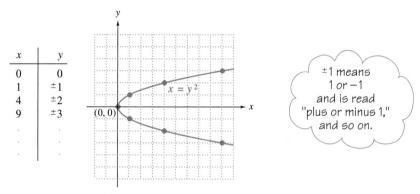

x	y
0	0
1	±1
4	±2
9	±3
.	.
.	.
.	.

$x = y^2$

$(0, 0)$

±1 means
1 or −1
and is read
"plus or minus 1,"
and so on.

Figure 14.13
The graph of $y^2 = x$. Here y is not a function of x.

Maximum and Minimum Values of Functions

Companies desire to maximize profit and to minimize cost. Traffic engineers want to design systems that maximize traffic flow and minimize travel time. Telephone companies want to design networks that maximize the number of calls that can be handled. Such desires may require finding the maximum or minimum value of a function. A number of methods can be used to determine maxima and minima but, for elementary school students, one accessible way is to use a graph.

EXAMPLE   14.23 | **Determining the Minimum Value of $f(x) = x^2 + 4x$**

Draw the graph of $f(x) = x^2 + 4x$ and determine the minimum value of the function.

Solution | The desired graph is the set of points satisfying the equation

$$y = x^2 + 4x.$$

Make a table of corresponding values (x, y), plot the points, and join these with a smooth curve. The resulting graph is as shown. The minimum value of the function is the least of the y-coordinates of the points on the graph. Since the graph is symmetric about the line $x = -2$, it is apparent that the minimum value is -4 and that it occurs when $x = -2$.

x	y
0	0
1	5
-1	-3
-2	-4
-3	-3
-4	0
-5	5

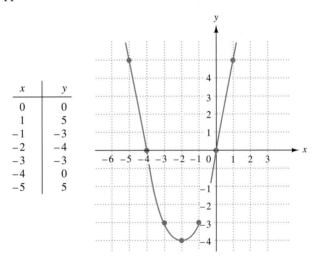

EXAMPLE   14.24 | **Solving a Practical Problem**

A farmer has 100 yards of fencing with which to enclose a rectangular garden to be located along an existing straight fence as shown. What should the dimensions of the new garden be if it is to have the largest possible area?

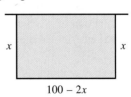

$100 - 2x$

Solution | *Understand the problem*

We are given the length of fence available to enclose the new garden. Some of the fence must be used to reach straight out from the existing fence and the remainder will run parallel to the existing fence. If the garden were to extend 50 yards out from the existing fence, it would be zero yards wide and would enclose no area. Similarly, if it were to extend 100 yards along the existing fence no area would be enclosed. For gardens between these two extremes, area *is* enclosed, and we must determine the dimensions so that this area is as large as possible.

Use a variable.

Devise a plan

Since the desired dimensions are unknown, perhaps part of our strategy should be to represent the dimensions using a variable. Since the area of a rectangle is length times width, we can then represent the area of the new garden as a function of the variable. Since we desire the maximum area, we may then be able to proceed along the lines of the preceding example.

Carry out the plan

Let x represent the length of the two portions of fence extending out at right angles to the existing fence. Then, since the farmer has only 100 yards of fencing, the length of the fence parallel to the existing fence must be $100 - 2x$. Then the area is given by the function $A(x) = x(100 - 2x) = 100x - 2x^2$.

In the last example, we discovered the minimum of a function by graphing; perhaps the same idea will work here. Consider the table of corresponding values of x and y and the graph obtained by plotting the points (x, y) as shown below. Since this graph is symmetric about the line $x = 25$, it is apparent that the maximum y value, and hence the maximum value of the function, occurs when $x = 25$. Thus, the maximum area is 1250 yd^2 and it occurs when the field measures 25 yards by 50 yards with the long side of the garden along the existing fence.

x	y
0	0
5	450
10	800
15	1050
20	1200
25	1250
30	1200
35	1050
40	800
45	450
50	0

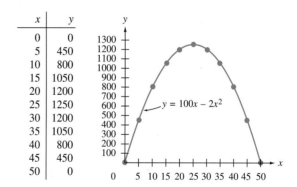

Look back

The key to solving this problem was to use a variable to express the area of the garden as a function of x. Then, drawing a graph, we were able to determine the dimensions of the field that yielded maximum area.

JUST FOR FUN

Watering a Playfield

The principal of Elmwood Elementary school hired a plumber to install underground sprinklers to water the school's playfield. The plumber decided to install one large sprinkler at the middle of each side of the field—adjusting the sprinkler so that it will just reach the two adjacent corners. He shows the principal his sketch.

The principal is not convinced that the plumber's sketch is right and draws his own sketch that indicates that the middle of the field will not be watered.

Who is right—the plumber or the principal?

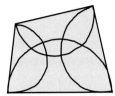 

Plumber's sketch   Principal's sketch

PROBLEM SET 14.4

Understanding Concepts

1. Draw the graphs of each of these linear functions.
   (a) $y = 2x - 3$ (b) $y = 0.5x + 2$
   (c) $y = -3x$

2. (a) On the same coordinate system draw the graphs of these three linear functions: $y = 4x$, $y = 4x + 5$, and $y = 4x - 3$.
   (b) Briefly discuss the graphs in part (a).

3. (a) Draw the graph of $3x + 2y + 6 = 0$.
   (b) Does the equation of part (a) define y as a function of x? If so, identify the function.
   (c) Draw the graph of the equation $5x - 3y - 15 = 0$.
   (d) Does the equation of part (c) define y as a function of x? If so, identify the function.
   (e) Does the equation of part (c) define x as a function of y? If so, define the function.

4. (a) On a single set of axes, draw the graphs of $y = 2x + 3$, $y = 2(x - 3) + 3$, and $y = 2(x + 4) + 3$.
   (b) Compare the graphs of part (a).

5. Use the vertical line test to decide which of these are graphs of functions.

(a)   (b)

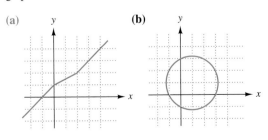

(c)   (d)

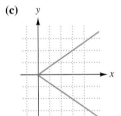 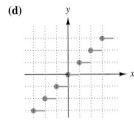

6. Graph each of these functions.
   (a) $y = x^2$ (b) $y = (x - 2)^2$ (c) $y = (x + 3)^2$
   (d) Discuss the relationship between the graphs of parts (a), (b), and (c).

7. Graph each of these functions.
   (a) $y = x^2 - 4x + 4$
   (b) $y = x^2 + 6x + 9$ (c) $y = x^2 + 4x + 4$
   (d) Could you write each of these functions in a different, more concise form? (*Hint:* Consider problem 6.)

8. (a) On a single set of axes, graph the equations $y = x^2$, $y = x^2 + 4$, and $y = x^2 - 3$.
   (b) Compare the graphs of part (a).

9. Use graphing techniques to find
   (a) the minimum value of the quantity $x^2 + 10x$ and the value of x at which it occurs.
   (b) the maximum value of $8x - 2x^2$ and the value of x at which it occurs.
   (c) the minimum value of $2x^2 - 4x + 10$ and the value of x for which it occurs.

Thinking Critically

10. (a) Graph $y = x^2 + 2x$.

    (b) If the graph of part (a) has a line of symmetry, identify it.

11. (a) Graph the set of points that satisfy $y^2 = x + 4$.

    (b) If the graph of part (a) has a line of symmetry, identify it.

    (c) Does the equation of part (a) define y as a function of x? Explain.

12. (a) Graph $y = \sqrt{x + 4}$. Recall that $\sqrt{n}$ is the *positive* number a such that $a^2 = n$.

    (b) Compare the graph of part (a) to that of problem 11, part (a). Explain.

    (c) Does the equation of part (a) define y as a function of x?

    (d) Discuss the graph of $y = -\sqrt{x + 4}$.

13. (a) Graph the function $f(x) = 1/x$. (*Hint:* Along with other values, be sure to plot points for positive and negative x values near 0.)

    (b) What is $f(0)$ in part (a)?

14. Graph the function $y = 1/x^2$. Be sure to consider positive and negative values of x near zero.

15. (a) Graph the function $y = |x - 1|$. Recall that $|a|$ means the absolute value of a.

    (b) If the function in part (a) has a line of symmetry, identify it.

16. The notation $\lfloor x \rfloor$ indicates the largest integer less than or equal to x. Thus, $\lfloor 3 \rfloor = 3, \lfloor \pi \rfloor = 3, \lfloor -\pi \rfloor = -4$, and so on. Graph the function $y = \lfloor x \rfloor$.

17. Graph the equation $|y| + |x| = 1$ for $-1 \le x \le 1$ and $-1 \le y \le 1$. (*Hint:* Recall that $|a| = a$ if $a \ge 0$ and $|a| = -a$ if $a < 0$ and consider the four cases (i) $x \ge 0$, $y \ge 0$, (ii) $x \ge 0$, $y < 0$, (iii) $x < 0$, $y \ge 0$, and (iv) $x < 0$, $y < 0$.)

18. The graph in problem 17 is not the graph of a function. Describe how to break it up into two functions and draw their graphs. (*Hint:* Consider problem 12 again.)

Making Connections

19. Acme Athletic Manufacturing Company has discovered that the number of running shoes they can sell per week is given by the function $s(x) = 400 + 80x - x^2$ where x is the price in dollars of a pair of shoes.

    (a) What is the maximum number of shoes Acme can sell per week?

    (b) What price should Acme charge in order to achieve maximum sales each week?

20. The height in feet of a ball shot upward from the ground with a velocity of 640 feet per second is given by the function $h(t)$ where $h(t) = -16t^2 + 640t$ and t is the time in seconds after the ball is shot upward.

    (a) What is the height of the ball when $t = 0$?

    (b) What is the height of the ball when $t = 40$?

    (c) What is the maximum height reached by the ball?

    (d) At what time t does the ball reach its maximum height?

21. Populations of bacteria grow because, after a suitable interval, each cell divides into two identical cells. A certain type of cell divides once every minute.

    (a) If one such cell is placed in an agar dish at time $t = 0$, what function, $p(t)$, gives the population size at the end of t minutes?

    (b) Graph the function $p(t)$ of part (a) using suitable scales on the vertical and horizontal axes.

Communicating

22. One of the cells described in problem 21 is placed in a bottle at 11:00 A.M. and the bottle is exactly full at noon.

    (a) When is the bottle half-full?

    (b) When is the bottle 1/4 full?

    (c) When is the bottle 1/16 full?

    (d) If you were one of the bacterium in the bottle when it was 1/16 full, do you think you would worry about having space to live? Should you worry? Explain briefly.

Using a Calculator

23. Populations grow in the same way that investments accrue at compound interest. Thus, if N is the present population of Seattle and it is growing at the rate of 5% per year, the future population is given by the formula $P(t) = N(1.05)^t$ where time t is in years.

    (a) Using the $\boxed{y^x}$ key on your calculator or using the constant function to repeatedly multiply by 1.05, graph the function $P = N(1.05)^t$ for $0 \le t \le 30$ with the horizontal axis representing time in years scaled in units of one year and the vertical axis representing population P scaled in units of $0.2N$ where N is the population of Seattle now.

    (b) From the graph, determine the population of Seattle in terms of N in 14 years if this rate of growth continues.

    (c) If N is the population of Seattle now, what will it be in 28 years if the present growth rate continues?

(d) Discuss in some detail what problems the growth in parts (a) and (b) poses for Seattlites in the next 40 years. For example, it is worth noting that Seattle suffered water shortages in several recent years.

For Review

24. Use the methods of coordinate geometry to show that the diagonals of a rhombus

(a) bisect each other.　**(b)** are perpendicular.

25. Determine the slopes of these lines.
(a) $y = -3x + 17$　**(b)** $x = 5y + 2$
(c) $3x + 5y = 15$

26. Write the equation of the line with slope 4 that passes through the point $(3, -2)$.

27. Write the equation of the line parallel to the line $2x - 7y = 14$ and which passes through the point $(-2, -3)$.

28. Write the equation of the line perpendicular to the line $4x - 5y = 14$ and which passes through the point $(4, 2)$.

EPILOGUE　The Themes of Geometry

In this chapter we have considered geometry from an algebraic point of view. That is, we have considered coordinate or analytic geometry.

In brief summary, we have seen:

- how to represent points by ordered pairs of numbers using a Cartesian coordinate system;
- how to determine the distance between two points;
- how to determine the midpoint of a line and, more generally, how to determine the coordinates of a point M on segment $\overline{PQ}$ such that $PM/PQ = t$;
- how to determine the slope of a line;
- how to write the equation of a line in various forms;
- how to find the simultaneous solution to two linear equations;
- how to write equations of circles;
- how to use these tools to prove general results about geometric figures;
- how to graph equations; and
- how to use graphs to determine the maxima and minima of functions.

The methods of coordinate geometry are pervasive in most of mathematics that students will study after elementary school.

This concludes our study of informal geometry. Several themes have cut across these geometry chapters. These themes, which could properly form the basis for the geometry portion of the elementary school curriculum, are as follows:

- *Invariance*

    Invariance involves the idea that, while many properties of geometric figures change from figure to figure, some, often surprisingly, do not. Indeed, much of the interest in, and utility of, geometry derives from this fact. For example, the ratio of the circumference of a circle to the diameter is always $\pi = 3.1415\ldots$; the volume of any cone is always one-third the volume of the corresponding cylinder; the sum of the exterior angles of any convex polygon is always $360°$; and so on. Geometry is replete with remarkable and useful invariances.

- *Symmetry*

    There are many kinds of symmetry in geometry. There is the repetitive symmetry that manifests itself in tilings and tessellations; the symmetry of an object as if it were reflected in a mirror (that is, symmetry with respect to a line);

symmetry of an object through a point; and rotational symmetry. There is also a sort of symmetry in many of the formulas of geometry. For example, the Pythagorean expression $c^2 = a^2 + b^2$ is unchanged if a and b are interchanged and similar symmetries are exhibited by the distance and slope formulas in coordinate geometry.

- *Congruence*

    The notion of congruence (that is, that one figure is exactly the same size and shape as another) is of great importance.

- *Similarity*

    This embodies the idea that two figures are the same *shape* but of different size, as if one figure is simply a magnification of the other. Perhaps the most important consequence of similarity is that corresponding lengths in similar figures are proportional.

- *Locuses*

    Though we have not used the word locus, the idea is to consider sets of points that satisfy certain conditions. For example, a circle is the set of all points in a plane that are equidistant from a fixed point O. Similarly, the set of points $P(x, y)$ that satisfy an equation like $3x - 4y = 17$ is a straight line.

- *Maxima and minima*

    Of all triangles of fixed perimeter, the equilateral triangle has maximum area. Of all rectangles of fixed area, the square has least perimeter. Such maximum and minimum questions often arise in informal geometry.

- *Homeomorphism*

    We have not previously used the word, but homeomorphism embodies the idea that objects, configurations, and so on, may look quite different but are nevertheless essentially the same. For example, the networks shown here appear quite different. However, they are actually the same in the sense that vertices of the networks can be identified so that the same vertices are connected by edges in each case.

- *Limit*

    As an example of the notion of limit, as n gets larger and larger a regular n-gon more and more closely approximates a circle. Indeed, we would say that the limit of a regular n-gon as n tends to infinity *is* a circle. This notion was used in developing the formula for the area of a circle.

- *Measurement*

    This notion needs no comment. The ability to measure and communicate information concerning size and amount is basic to geometric thinking and applications of geometry in the real world.

- *Coordinates*

    This theme stresses the idea that geometric objects can be viewed as sets of points determined by ordered pairs of numbers that satisfy certain conditions.

This powerful notion makes it possible to use methods of arithmetic and algebra to obtain geometric results.

- *Logical structure*

    As in the rest of mathematics, geometric ideas do not stand alone. Even in informal geometry it is important for students to see how some results follow from others and to realize that guessing or conjecturing alone is not enough.

CHAPTER 14 SUMMARY

Key Concepts

The main idea of this chapter has been to introduce the idea of the Cartesian coordinate system and to show how points in the plane can be represented by ordered pairs of real numbers. In particular:

- $P(a_1, b_1)$ is the point a_1 units to the right or left of the y-axis and b_1 units above or below the x-axis, depending on the signs of a and b.
- The midpoint of the segment $\overline{PQ}$, where P and Q are, respectively, the points (a, b) and (c, d), is

$$M\left(\frac{a + c}{2}, \frac{b + d}{2}\right).$$

- Let $P(a, b)$ and $Q(c, d)$ be any two points and $0 < t < 1$. The point

$$M((1 - t)a + tc, (1 - t)b + td)$$

is such that M is on $\overleftrightarrow{PQ}$ and

$$\frac{PM}{PQ} = t.$$

- The distance between $P(x_1, y_1)$ and $Q(x_2, y_2)$ is given by

$$PQ = \sqrt{(x_1 - x_2)^2 + (y_1 - y_2)^2}.$$

- The slope of $\overline{PQ}$ with P and Q as above and $x_1 \neq x_2$ is m, where

$$m = \frac{y_2 - y_1}{x_2 - x_1} = \frac{y_1 - y_2}{x_1 - x_2}.$$

- A segment with positive slope slopes upward to the right and one with negative slope slopes downward to the right. A segment with zero slope is horizontal and a vertical segment has no slope (it is undefined).
- The slope of a line is the slope of any segment on the line.
- Two lines are parallel if, and only if, they have the same slope.
- Two lines are perpendicular if, and only if, the product of their slopes is -1.
- The equation of the line with slope m and through the point (a, b) is

$$y - b = m(x - a).$$

This is the point-slope form of the equation of a line.

- The equation of a line with slope m through the point $(0, b)$ is

$$y = mx + b.$$

This is the slope-intercept form of the equation of a line. The number b is called the y-intercept of the line.

- A line is horizontal if, and only if, it has an equation of the form $y = b$. A line is vertical if, and only if, it has an equation of the form $x = a$.
- If two distinct lines are not parallel they must intersect and the coordinates (r, s) of their point of intersection satisfy the equation of each line and are called the simultaneous solution of the two equations.
- Every circle has an equation of the form

$$(x - a)^2 + (y - b)^2 = r^2$$

  where (a, b) is the center of the circle and r is its radius.
- The preceding facts can be used to prove results about geometric figures.

Vocabulary and Notation

Section 14.1

The Cartesian coordinate system
Coordinate axes
    x-axis
    y-axis
Coordinates
    x-coordinate
    y-coordinate
    Quadrant
Origin, $(0, 0)$
The midpoint formula
Dividing a line segment
The distance formula

Section 14.2

Slope
    Of a line segment
    Of a line

Condition for parallelism
Condition for perpendicularity
Equations of lines
    Point-slope form
    Slope-intercept form
Linear equation
Simultaneous solution of two linear equations

Section 14.3

Proofs using coordinates
Proofs using equations and coordinates
Equation of a circle

Section 14.4

The graph of a function
The vertical line test
Maximum and minimum values of functions

CHAPTER REVIEW EXERCISES

Section 14.1

1. Plot each of these points on a Cartesian coordinate system.
   (a) $(5, -2)$ (b) $(1.4, 1.7)$
   (c) $(-3, -4.5)$ (d) $(-3, 1.5)$
2. In what quadrant does $P(a, b)$ lie
   (a) if $a > 0$ and $b < 0$?
   (b) if $a < 0$ and $b > 0$?
   (c) if $ab > 0$?
   (d) if $ab < 0$?
3. Determine a and b if $M(a, b)$ is the midpoint of the segment $\overline{PQ}$ where P and Q are the points given.
   (a) $(1, 5)$, $(3, -1)$ (b) $(3.2, 1.7)$, $(1.4, -1.5)$
   (c) $(0, 3)$, $(-5, -4)$ (d) $(0, 0)$, $(-2, -9)$
4. Determine PQ for each of the pairs of points in problem 3.

5. Show that the triangle with vertices $A(-3, 1)$, $B(0, 5)$, and $C(1, -2)$ is a right triangle.
6. Show that the triangle with vertices $R\left(-7, \dfrac{9}{2}\right)$, $S(3, 0)$, and $T(1, -3)$ is isosceles.

Section 14.2

7. If possible determine the slope of each of the segments with the indicated endpoints.
   (a) $M(3, -2)$, $N(2, -3)$
   (b) $P(3, -7)$, $Q(3, 5)$
   (c) $R(-2, -5)$, $S(1, -7)$
   (d) $A(2, 5)$, $B(2, -3)$
8. Determine c so that $\overline{PQ}$ has slope 5 where P and Q are respectively $(c, -2)$ and $(-2, 7)$.

9. Consider the points $C(3, 5)$, $D(2, b)$, $E(-1, 2)$, and $F(2, -7)$.
   (a) Determine b so that $\overleftrightarrow{CD}$ is parallel to $\overleftrightarrow{EF}$.
   (b) Determine b so that $\overleftrightarrow{CD}$ is perpendicular to $\overleftrightarrow{EF}$.

10. Determine if $(-4, 5)$ is on the perpendicular bisector of $\overline{PQ}$ where P and Q are, respectively, $(0, 5)$ and $(-3, 1)$.

11. Determine b so that the point $(3, b)$ satisfies the equation $3x - 5y = 17$.

12. Write the equation of the line through $P(3, -2)$ and $Q(-4, 7)$.

13. Write the equation of the line with slope 3/2 and y-intercept 10.

14. Determine the slope of the line $3x - 4y = 15$.

15. Determine the equation of the line through the point $(5, 1.5)$ and perpendicular to the line of problem 14.

16. Find the simultaneous solution to the equations $3x - 5y = 19$ and $2x + 3y = 0$.

Section 14.3

17. Consider the right triangle shown, where M is the midpoint of the hypotenuse. Let D be the midpoint of the square in the second quadrant with one side $\overline{AB}$ and let E be the midpoint of the square in the fourth quadrant with one side $\overline{AC}$.
   (a) Show that $\triangle EMD$ is a right triangle.
   (b) Show that E, A, and D are colinear. (*Hint:* What must be true about the slopes of $\overline{EA}$ and $\overline{ED}$ if, and only if, E, A, and D are collinear?)

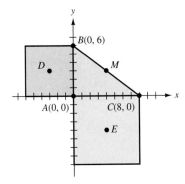

18. Consider the three squares drawn on the coordinate system as shown. Let E, G, and H be the centers of the three squares and let F be the point $(6, 0)$.
   (a) Show that $\overline{EG} \cong \overline{FH}$.
   (b) Show that the line $\overleftrightarrow{EG}$ is perpendicular to the line $\overleftrightarrow{FH}$.

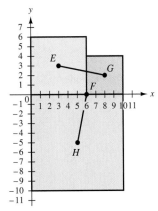

19. Consider the four squares drawn on the coordinate system as shown. Let E, F, G, and H be the midpoints of the squares.
   (a) Show that $\overline{EG} \cong \overline{FH}$.
   (b) Show that the line $\overleftrightarrow{EG}$ is perpendicular to the line $\overleftrightarrow{FH}$.

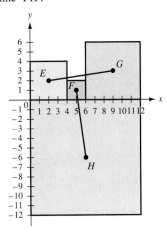

20. Consider the right triangle shown where M is the midpoint of the hypotenuse. Let D be the midpoint of the square in the second quadrant with one side $\overline{AB}$ and let E be the midpoint of the square in the fourth quadrant with one side $\overline{AC}$.
   (a) Show that $\triangle EMD$ is a right triangle.
   (b) Show that E, A, and D are collinear.

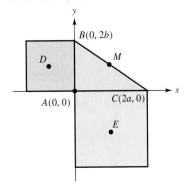

21. Consider the three squares drawn on the coordinate system. Let E, G, and H be the centers of the three squares and let F be the point $(2a, 0)$.

(a) Prove that $\overline{EG} \cong \overline{FH}$.

(b) Prove that the line $\overleftrightarrow{EG}$ is perpendicular to the line $\overleftrightarrow{FH}$.

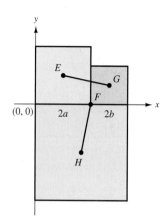

CHAPTER TEST

1. If $A(0, 0)$, $B(3, 5)$, $C(r, s)$, and $D(7, 0)$ are the vertices of a parallelogram, determine r and s.

2. Determine the point 1/4 of the way from $A(-8, 0)$ to $B(4, 12)$.

3. Determine the equation of the perpendicular bisector of $\overline{AB}$ where A and B are the points $(2, 5)$ and $(7, 4)$.

4. Show that the triangle with vertices $R(-3, 2)$, $S(7, 10)$, and $T(1, -3)$ is a right triangle.

5. Determine r so that the segments $\overline{PQ}$ and $\overline{RS}$ are parallel where P, Q, R, and S are the points $(2, -5)$, $(-3, 4)$, $(2, r)$, and $(4, 1)$, respectively.

6. Determine the equation of the line through $P(4, 2)$ and $Q(-1, 5)$.

7. Determine the slope of the line whose equation is $5x + 2y = 19$.

8. Determine the equation of the circle with center $(-2, 5)$ and radius 4.

9. Determine the simultaneous solution to the equations $2x - 3y = 9$ and $3x - 5y = 14$.

10. Give a general proof that the diagonals of a parallelogram bisect each other.

11. Compute the value of an investment of $5000 at the end of 5 years if interest is computed at the rate of 7% compounded annually.

12. Consider the function $y = 2x^2 + 4x$.

(a) Graph the function.

(b) Determine the minimum value of the function and the value of x for which it occurs.

APPENDIX A

*Manipulatives in the Mathematics Classroom**

What Are Manipulatives?

More and more we are hearing calls for greater use of manipulatives in elementary mathematics teaching. Manipulatives are concrete materials that are used for "modeling" or representing mathematical operations or concepts. In much the same way that children make models of airplanes or clipper ships so that they can study and learn about them, your students can make and learn from models of two-digit numbers or division. The difference between the two situations is that while the airplane and boat models are smaller versions of actual concrete things, the number models or division models are concrete models of abstract concepts.

When children use bundles of Popsicle™ sticks and single sticks to represent tens and ones, or stretch rubber bands around nails on a geoboard to show squares and triangles, they are using manipulatives to "model" mathematical ideas. Technically, even when young children count on their fingers, they are concretely modeling numbers!

It is important to note that some frequently used "manipulatives" materials fail to fit this definition of manipulatives. Flashcards, for instance, even though they are certainly manipulated, are never used to model mathematical ideas. Other objects like checkers in a checker game also are manipulated but are not used to directly represent mathematical ideas.

What Kinds of Things Can Be Used as Manipulatives?

Good teachers use a great variety of things as manipulatives. Popsicle™ sticks, dried beans, smooth stones, egg cartons, and poker chips are all inexpensive and effective materials. Some teachers even like to use the students in their classes themselves as models for sets and numbers.

There are also, however, commercial materials that serve more specific modeling purposes. Some of these are base-ten blocks, geoboards, fraction strips or pieces, and algebra tiles. What's important about the materials you select is not their cost, but that they accurately represent the concept or operation that your students are ready to learn about.

---

*By Warren Crown, associate professor of mathematics education, Rutgers, The State University of New Jersey. Used by permission of ScottForesman Marketing Department.

What Does Research Say About Using Manipulatives?

For the last twenty years, research support for using manipulatives in elementary math teaching has been growing. In 1977, Suydam and Higgins were able to identify and review 23 research studies that addressed the question of the effectiveness of manipulative materials for instruction. They concluded that instruction using manipulative materials had a higher probability of producing greater mathematics achievement than nonmanipulative instruction (Suydam & Higgins, 1977).

Twelve years later, Sowell (1989) had 60 studies to work with in a similar review. These studies were conducted at all educational levels, from kindergarten to college, and focused on many different mathematical topics. After using a sophisticated statistical procedure called meta-analysis, Sowell was able to offer a much stronger conclusion than Suydam and Higgins: that manipulative materials do, indeed, have a significant positive effect on achievement, especially when they are used over a long period of time (Sowell, 1989). In addition, Sowell found that the use of concrete materials for instruction was effective in improving students' attitudes toward mathematics.

What Do the Professional Organizations Say?

Because of the growing research support, professional organizations and leading educators have been urging increased use of concrete materials in teaching. Manipulatives play a very prominent role in the National Council of Teachers of Mathematics *Curriculum and Evaluation Standards for School Mathematics.* Even though there is no single standard which says that manipulatives should be used more frequently, their use is supported for many different topics at all levels, from kindergarten through twelfth grade. In the area of Number Sense and Numeration, for example, the *Standards* suggest that:

> *Students should be able to construct number meaning through real-world experiences and the use of physical materials. (Standards, p. 38)*

In Fractions and Decimals,

> *Students should be able to use models to relate fractions to decimals and to find equivalent fractions, and to explore operations on fractions and decimals. (Standards, p. 57)*

Although manipulatives have traditionally been used more in the lower elementary grades than the upper grades, the *Standards* also make a clear statement about their applicability and desirability in grades 5–8:

> *Implementation of the 5–8 standards should consider the unique characteristics of middle school students. As vast changes occur in their intellectual, psychological, social, and physical development, students in grades 5–8 begin to develop their abilities to think and reason more abstractly. Throughout this period, however, concrete experiences should continue to provide the means by which they construct knowledge. From these experiences, they abstract more complex meanings and ideas. (Standards, p. 68)*

How Does Concrete Modeling Help Children Learn Mathematics?

The mechanism by which concrete modeling promotes the learning process is still somewhat of a mystery to us, but the fact that it does is becoming more certain all the time. Most research shows that the best instructional sequence to follow for the presentation of elementary mathematical material is concrete-pictorial-symbolic. Activities with concrete materials should precede those which show pictured relationships and those should, in turn, precede formal operations with symbols. Ultimately, students need to reach that final level of symbolic proficiency with many of the mathematical skills that they master, but the meanings of those symbols and abstract operations must be firmly rooted in experiences with real objects. Otherwise, their performance of the symbolic operations will simply be rote repetitions of meaningless, memorized procedures.

Concrete and pictorial models are, at best, imperfect representations of abstract mathematical ideas and concepts. Not every characteristic of the concrete model is important mathematically. For example, many teachers use a yellow, wooden rod to represent the number "5," but "yellowness" certainly has nothing to do with the "fiveness." To prevent the child from abstracting inappropriate characteristics of the model as characteristics of the mathematical idea, multiple models should be used for important concepts. Multiple models of the same idea which are perceptually very different from each other direct the student to abstract from them only what they have in common—the mathematical concept. This abstraction is what leads to meaningful mathematics learning.

When Should Manipulatives Be Used?

Manipulatives and concrete models can be used almost anywhere in the elementary mathematics curriculum and should be used with all students. The most frequent occurrence of modeling in the curriculum will probably be at the point of introduction of new topics. The use of concrete materials while introducing a new topic allows students to gain that necessary foundational experience before trying to demonstrate their understandings symbolically. But intelligent use of manipulatives can also provide the most effective form of remediation. Engaging students in concrete activities related to the mathematics that they are struggling with will frequently help them to identify exactly which part of the process is causing the confusion, and then to work through it.

Manipulative use is also not just important for younger children. As stated in the NCTM *Standards,* older children can benefit just as much from appropriate concrete activity. The skills and concepts that they are asked to deal with are increasingly complex, and concrete introductions can frequently pave the way toward true understanding. Good concrete and pictorial models are available to help students deal with percent, ratio, geometric formulas, integers, and even solving algebraic equations.

Manipulative *Do's* and *Don'ts*

Elementary teachers who have been using manipulatives for many years have learned some rules which make their use in classrooms more effective. Don't use the materials exclusively for demonstrations and teacher explanations. The most effective way to use manipulatives is to have the children work directly with the materials. It is through touching and moving that the learning takes place. Watching the teacher do the manipulation is much less successful.

Discuss appropriate behavior before distributing the materials and allow plenty of free exploration time after. Children need to have time to do what they want with the materials before they will do what you want with them. This exploration time is also learning time. The more familiar they are with the materials, the more effective will be their later use of them.

Have children work with the materials in small groups and explain their thinking to each other as they do so. Asking children to verbalize their thoughts for others gives them the opportunity to clarify their own thinking. By listening to the discussions, you can make judgments about how well they understand the concepts.

How Can I Get More Information About Using Manipulatives?

This list of references is a good place to start. The first two citations will be helpful for the practitioner, while the second two are the research reviews mentioned earlier.

National Council of Teachers of Mathematics. *Curriculum and Evaluation Standards for School Mathematics.* Reston, Virginia: NCTM, 1989.

Reys, Robert E., Suydam, Marilyn N., and Lindquist, Mary Montgomery. *Helping Children Learn Mathematics,* Second Edition. Englewood Cliffs, New Jersey: Prentice Hall, Inc., 1989.

Sowell, Evelyn, J. "Effects of Manipulative Materials in Mathematics Instruction." *Journal for Research in Mathematics Education,* vol 20, no. 5 (November 1989), pp. 498–505.

Suydam, Marily N., and Higgins, Jon L. *Activity-Based Learning in Elementary School Mathematics: Recommendations from Research.* Columbus, Ohio: ERIC Center for Science, Mathematics, and Environmental Education, 1977.

APPENDIX B

Spreadsheets

Spreadsheet Basics

Spreadsheets are computer programs* that allow you to organize and analyze information arranged in a rectangular table. A spreadsheet document, as shown in Figure B.1, is arranged in **columns** that are lettered A, B, C, . . . , from left to right, and **rows** that are numbered downward 1, 2, 3, ... The rectangular box at the intersection of a row and a column is called a **cell.** Each cell is uniquely identified by its **cell address.** For example, the cell in column D and row 3 has the cell address D3. In Figure B.1, the cursor has been clicked on cell D3, turning it into the **active cell.** The active cell is outlined by a heavy border and its address is displayed at the left of the formula bar.

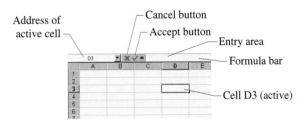

Figure B.1
The spreadsheet screen

Two types of data can be entered into the active cell:

- A **constant value** can be either text or a numerical value such as a fraction, monetary value, time, and so on. A constant value is either typed directly into the cell, or can be entered by positioning the cursor in the entry area of the formula bar and typing. When the typing is completed, click on the Accept button on the formula bar. Alternatively, you can press Enter, Tab, or an arrow key to enter the typed value into the cell.
- A **formula** is an expression that creates a value in the active cell that depends on the current values of one or more other cells in the spreadsheet. Formulas always begin by typing in an equal sign, =, followed by the expression that defines the

---

*The screens and commands in this appendix refer most directly to *Microsoft Excel;* however, only minor changes, and often none at all, are necessary for users of other spreadsheets.

function. For example, if cell D3 is to be the sum of the values in cells A3, B3, and C3, type in either "= A3 + B3 + C3" or use the SUM function and type in "= SUM(A3:C3)" to indicate the sum over the range of cells from A3 to C3. (*Note:* type what is between the quotes, not the quotation marks.) After typing the formula, click the Accept button or press Enter, Tab, or an arrow key to accept the formula. Changes or corrections in a value or formula can be made by selecting the cell and typing the changes in the entry area of the formula bar.

EXAMPLE B.1	**Setting Up a Spreadsheet Grade Book**

Mr. Akmal will be giving 100 possible points for homework, a 25-point quiz, a 50-point project, and a 150-point final exam. He wants to record the scores of his students, total their individual scores, and convert their scores to percents to help him assign grades. Design an electronic grade sheet to record and process the grades.

Solution

The students' names are entered in column A, and the graded items and their total possible points are entered in rows 1 and 2 of columns B, C, D, and E. To allow the longer names to show, the width of a column can be adjusted by dragging the boundary on the right side of the column heading until the column is the width you want. The scores are entered into the corresponding array of cells, as shown below. The total points available are placed in cell F2 by entering the formula "= SUM(B2:E2)". When the Accept button is clicked, the total point value of 325 points will show in cell F2. The sum of Akiko's scores could be entered by typing "= SUM(B3:E3)" into cell F3, and similar formulas entered in the cells F4, F5, and F6. However, it is much easier to use a cut and paste procedure. First, select cell F2 and do **Copy.** Next, select *all* of the cells in the range F3 to F6 and do **Paste.** Another method to copy values or formulas is to use the **Fill** command:* first, use the mouse to drag from cell F2 downward to cell F6, thereby selecting a range of cells; then, execute the **Edit/Fill ▶ Down** command.

G3	▼	**=**	=F3/F$2			
	A	B	C	D	E	F	G
1		Homewor	Quiz	Project	inal Exa	otal Point	Percent
2	Points	100	25	50	150	325	100%
3	Akiko	85	22	45	136	288	89%
4	Chad	78	19	46	122	265	82%
5	Maia	93	24	44	150	311	96%
6	Tariq	91	20	41	146	298	92%
7							

---

*In *Excel,* it is even easier to drag the copy handle at the lower right corner of a cell to fill downward or across.

The final task is to set up column G to compute the overall percent scores. Since the numerical values within this column are percents, select the column by clicking on the G at the top of the column and then click the Percent Style button found on the format toolbar. Next, select cell G2 and enter the formula "= F2/F$2". A "100%" now appears in cell G2. The $ symbol was typed in front of the row number of the divisor to fix the row number. Now, select and copy cell G2, and paste (or use **Fill/Down**) to enter the desired formulas into the cell range G3:G6. Each student's total points are divided by the value given in cell F2, and the result is written as a percent. If the $ symbol had been omitted, Akiko's percentage would be given by the incorrect formula "= F3/F3" rather than the correct formula "= F3/F$2", and similar errors would occur for Chad, Maia, and Tariq.

Spreadsheet Functions

Spreadsheets have a variety of built-in functions that can be inserted into formulas. These include the arithmetic operations, using the familiar symbols $+$, $-$, $*$, $/$, $\wedge$ for addition, subtraction, multiplication, division, and power, respectively. A few more frequently used functions are shown in Table B.1.

TABLE B.1 Some Commonly Used Spreadsheet Functions	
Function	Outcome
ABS(*number*)	absolute value of the number
SQRT(*number*)	square root of the number
SUM(*number 1, number 2, . . .*)	sum of the numbers
PI()	value of π
FACT(*number*)	factorial of the number
COMBIN(*n, r*)	number of combinations of n objects r at a time
PERMUT(*n, r*)	number of permutations of n objects r at a time
GCD(*number 1, number 2, . . .*)	greatest common divisor of the numbers
LCM(*number 1, number 2, . . .*)	least common multiple of the numbers
MIN(*number 1, number 2, . . .*)	minimum of the numbers
MAX(*number 1, number 2, . . .*)	maximum of the numbers
AVERAGE(*number 1, number 2, . . .*)	average (mean) of the numbers
MEDIAN(*number 1, number 2, . . .*)	median of the numbers
MODE(*number 1, number 2, . . .*)	mode of the numbers
STDEVP(*number 1, number 2, . . .*)	standard deviation of the population
STDEV(*number 1, number 2, . . .*)	standard deviation of the sample
QUARTILE(*array, k*)	kth quartile of the numbers in the array, $k = 0, 1, 2, 3,$ or 4

EXAMPLE   B.2

Setting Up DIFFY on a Spreadsheet

In DIFFY, one begins with a row of four numbers, say, for example, 2, 23, 14, and 12. The next row of numbers is created by taking each successive difference of the numbers in the first row, always subtracting the smaller number from the larger. Thus the first three numbers in the second row are $21 = 23 - 2$, $9 = 23 - 14$, and $2 = 14 - 12$. The last number of the row is obtained by using the first and last number of the first row, to give $10 = 12 - 2$. The third row is obtained from the second row in the same way that the second row was obtained from the first row, and additional rows are formed using the same pattern until something interesting happens. Set up a spreadsheet to enable you to explore DIFFY for many different choices of the first row.

Solution

The four starting numbers are entered in columns A, B, C, and D of row 1. To ensure that the result of a subtraction is entered as a positive value, the absolute value of the difference is taken. For, example, cell A2 contains the formula "=ABS(A1−B1)". Copying cell A2 and pasting into B2, C2, and D2 will enter the correct formulas in cells B2 and C2 but cell D2 will incorrectly read "=ABS(E1−D1)". To correct the error, select cell D2 and edit the formula in the entry area of the formula bar so that it reads "=ABS(D1−A1)". To enter subsequent rows, select and copy the range A2:D2, and paste into a rectangular range of selected cells with A3 at the upper left corner and a cell in column D (say D10) at the lower right corner (or use the **Fill/Down** command).

D2	▼	=	=ABS(D1-A1)

	A	B	C	D
1	2	23	14	12
2	21	9	2	10
3	12	7	8	11
4	5	1	3	1
5				

Once your spreadsheet has been set up, you are ready to explore DIFFY with ease. Try replacing the initial row with other starting values. Don't be afraid to insert some really wild choices, with negative numbers or numbers up in the millions or billions that even require you to widen the columns. If necessary, extend the formulas into new rows to see what eventually happens. Are you surprised at the results? In particular, try the beginning entries 31, 57, 105, and 193.

Other Spreadsheet Features

There are a large number of additional capabilities of a spreadsheet, including many that are useful in the classroom. For example, a spreadsheet can be used as a handy calculator, with the added advantages of being able to display and arrange the calculations and even save and print them.

A spreadsheet can also make some interesting graphs. For example, as shown in Figure B.2, the constant value 1 is entered into both cells A1 and A2. The formula "= A1 + A2" is entered in cell A3, and the formula is then copied down column A. This creates the Fibonacci number sequence 1, 1, 2, 3, 5, 8, 13, 21, in column A. Next, enter the formula "= A2/A1" in cell B2 and copy the formula downward into the rest of column B. It appears that the values in column B are becoming increasingly close to a limit value of about 1.61. This is shown visually by the line graph in the figure, which also reveals that the values in column B alternate between values greater and less than the limit value. To create the line graph, select the cell range B2:B10, click the chart wizard button, and follow the on-screen instructions.

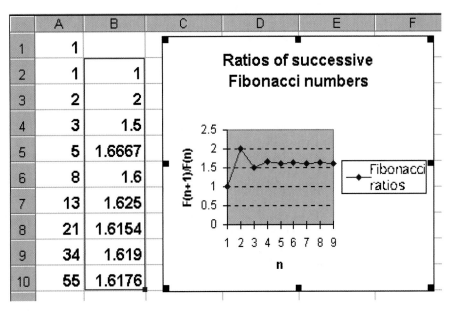

Figure B.2
A line graph created on a spreadsheet

Conclusion

Just a few spreadsheet features have been discussed in this appendix. Even so, we have been able to set up a useful electronic grade book and provide a tool to investigate number patterns. With a little instruction and encouragement, students in the upper elementary grades can quickly become proficient in spreadsheet basics. It is not surprising that more and more teachers are incorporating the spreadsheet as a valuable tool for teaching and learning.

PROBLEM SET B

1. **Tracking Expenses.** Arik, Kaia, and Lena went to a teachers' conference for which they were to be reimbursed for their travel expenses by their school district. Arik traveled 252 miles, and had meals and lodging expenses of $57 and $89, respectively. Kaia's expenses were 382 miles, $72, and $66, and Lena's expenses were 124 miles, $48, and $56. Mileage was reimbursed at 31.5 cents per mile.

   (a) Set up a spreadsheet for the three teachers' expenses. Compute each teacher's total dollar amount and the total amount of expense to the district.

   (b) Suppose Lena's mileage was mistakenly reported as one way, when in fact she should have reported round trip mileage of 248 miles. Make this correction, and find Lena's correct total expense and total expense to the district.

2. **Exploring Number Sequences.** Place a 1 in cell A1, the formula "= 1 + A1" in cell A2, and copy the formula into the range A3 through A15. This will place the sequence 1, 2, 3, . . . , 15 in column A.

   (a) Enter the formula "=SUM(A$1:A1)" in cell B1 and copy the formula downward into column B. Describe the number sequence you obtain.

   (b) Enter a 1 in cell C1, the formula "=C1 + A2" in cell C2, and copy the formula into column C. How does column C compare with column B?

   (c) Enter a 1 in cell D1, enter the formula "=C1 + C2" in cell D2, and copy the formula into column D below D2. What sequence of numbers is obtained? Describe how the same sequence can be generated in column E by referring to the values of column A.

3. **The Lucas Sequence.** Set up the spreadsheet shown in Figure B.2, giving the Fibonacci numbers and their ratios in columns A and B. To reproduce the line graph, select the range B2:B10 and click the Chart button (or use **Insert . . ./Chart**). Follow the on-screen instructions to finish the plot.

   (a) Replace the 1 in cell A2 with a 3, so that the **Lucas sequence** 1, 3, 4, 7, 11, . . . appears in column A. What is the tenth Lucas number? What is the ratio of the tenth to the ninth Lucas number? Does the sequence of ratios of successive Lucas numbers seem to have a limit value? How does it compare to the sequence of ratios of successive Fibonacci numbers shown in Figure B.2?

   (b) Replace the values in cells A1 and A2 with any two numbers of your choice. Does this appear to affect the limit value of the ratios?

4. **Fibonacci Fractions.** Select column A of a new spreadsheet document, and under **Format/Cells . . .** select the Custom category under the Number tab. In the box labeled Type, enter the code ??????/?????? to allow fractions with up to six digits in both numerator and denominator. Click the OK button to return to the main screen. Now place a 1 in cell A1, enter the formula "=1+1/A1" in cell A2, and copy the formula down the column. Describe the number sequence that you observe in the numerators and denominators of the values in column A.

5. **Fibonacci Identities.** Create a spreadsheet that contains the Fibonacci numbers 1, 1, 2, 3, 5, 8, . . . in column A.

   (a) In column B, calculate the sums, 1, 1 + 1, 1 + 1 + 2, . . . of successive Fibonacci numbers. (*Suggestion:* use the formula "=SUM(A$1:A1)" in cell B1.) What connection to the Fibonacci numbers in column A do you observe?

   (b) In column C, calculate the squares of the Fibonacci numbers, 1, 1, 4, 9, 25, . . . Similarly, in column D calculate the sequence of sums of the squares, 1, 1 + 1, 1 + 1 + 4, 1 + 1 + 4 + 9, . . . , and in column E calculate the sequence of products of successive pairs of Fibonacci numbers, 1*1, 1*2, 2*3, 3*5, 5*8, ... Describe how columns D and E are related, and use your observations to state a Fibonacci number identity.

6. **Statistical Computations.** Consider the data, 3, 15, 37, 22, 5, 35, 19, 53, 44, 22, 45, 26, 37. Use a spreadsheet to find

   (a) the mean and population standard deviation

   (b) the lower and upper quartiles, and the median of the data.

7. **Problem Solving with a Spreadsheet.** Use a spreadsheet to answer the following problem: *What is the shape of the rectangular field of largest area that can be enclosed with 40 ten-foot long sections of fence?* Take advantage of several spreadsheet features, including graphing (see problem 3), to give a thorough analysis of the problem's solution.

APPENDIX C

Graphing Calculators

Introduction

In this appendix, some of the most useful features of the graphing calculator are discussed and used to solve problems. By following along with a graphing calculator, and perhaps consulting its user's manual occasionally, you will learn some basic graphing calculator skills. We hope you will be enticed to continue to develop your skills, enabling you to use the graphing calculator effectively both as a tool for solving mathematical problems and as an adjunct to mathematics instruction.

The graphing calculator is easily identified by its large screen, which can display multiple lines of text, graphs of equations, and statistical plots. In this appendix we will refer most directly to the *Texas Instruments* TI-73, a calculator expressly designed for use in upper elementary and middle school mathematics and science classrooms. Users of other graphing calculators, such as the TI-82 or TI-83, or even calculators from other manufacturers, should not find it too difficult to modify the procedures described here to apply to their particular model. The TI-73 is shown in Figure C.1.

Figure C.1
The TI-73 Graphing Calculator

Entering, Evaluating, and Editing Expressions

The primary screen is called the **Home screen.** To return to the Home screen from a menu or application, press $\boxed{2^{nd}}$ $\boxed{\text{QUIT}}$. Press $\boxed{\text{CLEAR}}$ to show a blank screen. From the Home screen, expressions can be entered and evaluated as on any calculator. As a specific example, suppose that we wish to work with the expression $1.2\sqrt{(X)}$, finding its value for various choices of X. This expression is interesting, since it gives the approximate distance to the horizon in miles as observed from a height of X feet. For example, to estimate the distance to a ship on the horizon when observed from a 400-foot-high cliff, we can key in*

$$1.2 \boxed{\times} \boxed{2^{nd}} \boxed{\sqrt{}} 400 \boxed{\text{ENTER}}.$$

The output shows us that the ship is about 24 miles away. Unlike a simple calculator, the input expression remains in view on a graphing calculator. Better yet, the expression can be edited and reused. For example, suppose you hike to a higher point at an elevation of 600 feet and want to know how far you can now see to the horizon. Press $\boxed{2^{nd}}$ $\boxed{\text{ENTRY}}$, use the left arrow key to move the cursor over the 4, and then type "6" to replace the 4 with a 6. Pressing $\boxed{\text{ENTER}}$ now gives the output 29.39387691. This answer contains more decimals than reasonable for an approximate value, so you may find it useful to open the $\boxed{\text{MODE}}$ menu and select, say, 1 decimal place. Return to the home screen by pressing $\boxed{2^{nd}}$ $\boxed{\text{QUIT}}$, and then redo your calculation by pressing the keys $\boxed{2^{nd}}$ $\boxed{\text{ENTRY}}$ $\boxed{\text{ENTER}}$ to get the value 29.4. That is, you can see 29.4 miles to the horizon from a height of 600 feet.

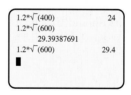

Expressions can be edited by using the arrow keys to position the cursor at the point of the desired change and typing over unwanted symbols. You can use the $\boxed{\text{DEL}}$ (*delete*) key to remove unwanted symbols, and use $\boxed{2^{nd}}$ $\boxed{\text{INS}}$ (*insert*) to insert new symbols between symbols that you want to remain in place.

Entering and Using Lists in the Home Screen

A **list** is an ordered sequence of numerical values. For example, suppose that we wish to create a list of the altitudes 100, 400, and 900 feet above sea level. The following entry string will create the list from the home screen. On the TI-73, press $\boxed{2^{nd}}$ $\boxed{\text{TEXT}}$ to obtain the required curly braces { and } from the text editor. (On the TI-82/83, press $\boxed{2^{nd}}$ $\boxed{\{}$ and $\boxed{2^{nd}}$ $\boxed{\}}$ to enter left and right braces.)

---

*On the TI-73, the square root appears with a left parenthesis automatically in place. A right parenthesis should be keyed in to enclose the expression whose square root is desired.

$$\{\ 100\ ,\ 400\ ,\ 900\ \}$$

The list can be stored to one of the six built-in list names:* L1, L2, L3, L4, L5, L6. On the TI-73, use the commands STO▶ 2ⁿᵈ STAT 1 ENTER. (On the TI-82/83, use STO▶ 2ⁿᵈ L1 ENTER.) The part of the list that has scrolled off the screen to the right may be viewed by pressing the right arrow key.

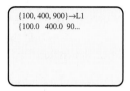

Now we can evaluate the function $1.2\sqrt{(X)}$ with X replaced by the list L1. This is shown on the next screen, where we have entered

$$1.2\ \times\ 2^{nd}\ \sqrt{\ }\ 2^{nd}\ STAT\ 1\ )\ ENTER$$

on the TI-73. (On a TI-82/83, use $1.2\ \times\ 2^{nd}\ \sqrt{\ }\ 2^{nd}\ L1\ ENTER$.)

```
{100, 400, 900}→L1
{100.0  400.0  90...
1.2*√(L1)
{12.0  24.0  36.0}
```

We see that the distances are 12.0, 24.0, and 36.0 miles to the horizon, as viewed from the respective heights of 100, 400, and 900 feet.

Lists are a convenient way to generate a sequence of function values with little more effort than generating just a single value of the function. Lists are also used to store and manipulate data for statistical analyses and plots.

Entering and Graphing Equations

As its name suggests, a graphing calculator can graph equations. There are three essential steps to follow:

Step 1 **Enter the function.** Press Y= to enter, edit, and select (or deselect) functions in the Y= editor. (*Note:* To select or deselect a function in the Y= editor, position the cursor over the = sign and press ENTER. Selected functions have a dark box containing the = sign, to look like ▣.)

Step 2 **Set windows values.** Press WINDOW to set the range of desired *x* and *y* values to show in your graph.

Step 3 **Display the graph.** Press GRAPH to see the selected function's graph.

---

*On the TI-73, you can also type in a list name of your own choice.

EXAMPLE C.1

Graphing the Distance to the Horizon Function

Graph the distance to the horizon function, $y = 1.2\sqrt{X}$, for $0 < X < 1000$.

Solution

Step 1   Press the $\boxed{Y=}$ key in the top row of your calculator. This opens the $\boxed{Y=}$ editor, showing a list $Y1 = , Y2 = , \ldots$ (On a TI-82/83 you may need to press $\boxed{MODE}$ and select Func (*function*) mode.) A function of the variable X can then be entered into the space to the right of each of the equal signs. Use the arrow keys to move the cursor around the screen. The function $1.2\sqrt{X}$ has been entered on the first line shown here.

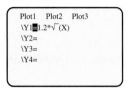

The variable X is entered in the formula using the $\boxed{x}$ key (see Figure C.1 for the TI-73). (Use the $\boxed{X,T,\theta}$ key on the TI-82/83.) The dark box containing the equal sign indicates that the Y1 function is selected.

Step 2   Press the $\boxed{WINDOW}$ key and enter appropriate minimum and maximum values of both x and y, as shown on the next screen. The spacing of tick marks along the x- and y-axes is set by choosing respective values of Xscl (*x scale*) and Yscl (*y scale*). (Note: ΔX will not appear on the TI-82/83.*)

Step 3   Press $\boxed{GRAPH}$ to display the graph. If another graph appears on the screen, it is necessary to deselect (turn off) any unwanted active functions in the $\boxed{Y=}$ editor or statistical plots in the $\boxed{2^{nd}}$ $\boxed{PLOT}$ editor (or $\boxed{2^{nd}}$ $\boxed{STAT\ PLOT}$ editor on the TI-82/83).

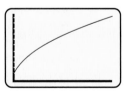

---

*On the TI-73, setting Xmin and Xmax will automatically set the value of ΔX according to the formula $\Delta X = (Xmax - Xmin)/94$. The value of ΔX determines the x-coordinates of a trace, as described below.

Exploring a Function Graph with TRACE

To move the cursor along points of the graph, press the TRACE key and use the left and right arrows to move the blinking cursor along the graph of the function. The coordinates of the cursor are displayed at the bottom of the screen. Continuing with Example C.1, the following screen shows that to see 30 miles to the horizon you need a height of about 630 feet.

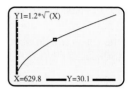

The next example will review and extend your graphing skills.

EXAMPLE C.2	**Graphing the Achilles versus the Tortoise Race**

Achilles and the Tortoise have agreed to compete in a 1000-yard race. At the starting signal, the tortoise lumbers off at a steady 3.8 feet per second (which is actually extremely fast for a tortoise!). Achilles, who knows he runs much faster than the tortoise, grandstands in front of the crowd, and finally, after horsing around for 10 minutes, takes off for the finish line at a steady 14.7 feet per second. Does Achilles win the race, or has he been overconfident?

Solution

The tortoise will have traveled Y1 = 3.8*X feet at a time of X seconds into the race. Achilles, however, doesn't start the race for 10 minutes (that is, for 600 seconds), so his distance toward the finish line is* Y2 = 14.7*(X − 600) for $X > 600$. The distance to the finish line is Y3 = 3000 feet. All three functions are entered and selected as shown on the left screen below. The window editor is shown in the center screen, and the three graphs are shown at the right. It's a tight race!

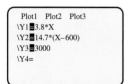 

To get a closer look, use ZOOM and TRACE . First, press ZOOM and choose Zbox, as shown at the left below. To draw the small rectangular zoom box shown in the center screen below, use the arrow keys to position the cursor at a corner of the box and press ENTER . Then move the cursor with the arrow keys to the opposite corner of the box and press ENTER once more. This will give you the expanded graph shown in the rightmost screen.

Better yet, enter Y2 = 14.7(X − 600) (X > 600). Including the parenthetic condition ($X > 600$) restricts the domain of Y2 to $X > 600$.

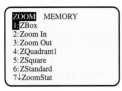 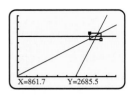 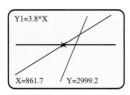

We now see clearly that Achilles has been overconfident. Pressing $\boxed{\text{TRACE}}$, we can position the cursor along the Y1 graph to show that the tortoise crossed the finish line at about 790 seconds. Pressing the down arrow puts the cursor on the graph of the Y2 function, and moving the cursor to the finish line with the right arrow key we see that Achilles crossed the finish line at about 804 seconds.

Entering and Editing Data in the $\boxed{\text{LIST}}$ Editor

There are five steps to define a list:

Step 1 Open the list editor by pressing $\boxed{\text{LIST}}$. (Use $\boxed{\text{STAT}}$ **Edit . . .** on the TI-82/83.)

Step 2 Use arrow keys to position the cursor at a list, one of L1 through L6. To clear a list, select the list name at the top and press $\boxed{\text{CLEAR}}$ $\boxed{\text{ENTER}}$.

Step 3 Enter the list values. Press $\boxed{\text{ENTER}}$ or the down arrow to go to the next value.

Step 4 Edit the list as necessary, using $\boxed{2^{\text{nd}}}$ $\boxed{\text{INS}}$, $\boxed{\text{DEL}}$, or $\boxed{\text{CLEAR}}$.

Step 5 Exit the list editor by pressing $\boxed{2^{\text{nd}}}$ $\boxed{\text{QUIT}}$.

EXAMPLE C.3

Creating Lists of Student Grades

Professor Garza wants to analyze how her students' performances on the 100-point quiz taken early in the semester compares to the overall percents received at the end of the semester. Help her enter the grade book data of her 13 students into a graphing calculator.

Student	1	2	3	4	5	6	7	8	9	10	11	12	13
Quiz	88	58	92	82	84	60	94	100	74	40	78	96	94
Overall	85	71	98	80	89	74	82	90	77	74	69	83	98

Solution

To analyze grades it is enough to round values to the nearest integer, so first set the number of decimals to 0 in the $\boxed{\text{MODE}}$ menu. Next, press $\boxed{\text{LIST}}$ (or $\boxed{\text{STAT}}$ **Edit . . .** on the TI-82/83) to open the list editor, as shown at the left of the figure on the next page. The highlighted first line of the list also appears at the bottom of the screen, where we see that the first entry of list L1 is denoted by L1(1) and has the value of 100.0. List L1 was defined earlier and is no longer needed, so delete it by first using the up arrow to highlight the list name L1 on the top line. Next press $\boxed{\text{CLEAR}}$ $\boxed{\text{ENTER}}$. This will clear the list L1, as shown at the right.

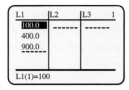 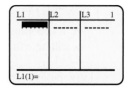

Now enter the quiz scores into list L1. When finished with list L1, use the right arrow to move to the position L2(1). Now type in the corresponding percent values. If you make a typing error, it can be corrected using the $\boxed{\text{DEL}}$, $\boxed{2^{nd}}$ $\boxed{\text{INS}}$, and $\boxed{\text{CLEAR}}$ editing keys. Your lists should appear as shown below.

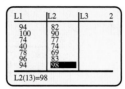

Creating Statistical Plots

A large number of statistical plots are easily created with a graphing calculator. Here we'll demonstrate two types, the scatter plot and the box plot, using the data entered in the lists shown in Example C.3. Pie charts, bar graphs, and histograms can also be plotted with a graphing calculator.

Scatter Plot

Press $\boxed{2^{nd}}$ $\boxed{\text{PLOT}}$ (use $\boxed{\text{STAT PLOT}}$ on the TI-82/83) to open the Stat Plot Menu screen shown at the left. Press 1 to open the Stat Plot Editor of Plot 1, as shown at the right.

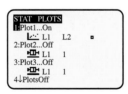 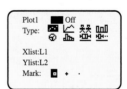

In the Stat Plot Editor, we have selected (turned on) Plot 1, selected a scatter plot from among the types of plots available, used $\boxed{2^{nd}}$ $\boxed{\text{STAT}}$ 1 on the TI-73 ($\boxed{2^{nd}}$ $\boxed{\text{L1}}$ on the TI-82/83) to specify L1 as the Xlist, specified L2 as the Ylist, and have chosen small open squares to mark the points in the plot.

There are three remaining steps:

- Turn off (deselect) any selected functions in the $\boxed{\text{Y=}}$ editor
- Set the parameters in the $\boxed{\text{WINDOW}}$ values screen
- Press $\boxed{\text{GRAPH}}$ to display the scatter plot

The window values screen is shown at the left, and the scatter plot is shown at the right.

 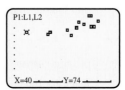

The $\boxed{\text{TRACE}}$ key and arrow keys were used to identify the leftmost point in the plot. Its coordinates show that the student starting out with a 40% score on the first quiz was still able to achieve an overall 74% in the course.

Box Plots

Press $\boxed{2^{\text{nd}}}$ $\boxed{\text{PLOT}}$ 1 and turn off Plot 1. To look at Plot 1 again at a later time, we could turn Plot 1 back on. Next press $\boxed{2^{\text{nd}}}$ $\boxed{\text{PLOT}}$ 2 and turn on Plot 2. The leftmost screen below shows our choices to give us a box plot of the quiz scores contained in list L1. Similarly, set Plot 3 to show a box plot of the list L2. To enter the list name, highlight the list name shown by default and press $\boxed{2^{\text{nd}}}$ $\boxed{\text{STAT}}$ 2 to insert the list name L2, as shown at the right below.

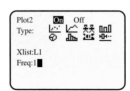   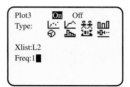

To show the two box plots, press $\boxed{\text{WINDOW}}$ and select appropriate Xmin, Xmax, and Xscl values (the y values are not used). Then press $\boxed{\text{GRAPH}}$. We have also pressed $\boxed{\text{TRACE}}$, so we can read off the maximum, minimum, median, and upper and lower quartile values, using the arrow keys. We see that the overall course median is 82%, just slightly lower than the quiz median of 84%. We also see how the minimum and lower quartiles improved from the first quiz to the final overall percentages earned.

   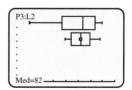

Programming the Graphing Calculator

A **program** is a sequence of commands to be executed by the calculator. The procedures to create, edit, and execute programs can be found in the user's guide accompanying your calculator.

EXAMPLE C.4	**Writing a Program to Calculate the Volume of a Right Circular Cylinder**

Write a program named CYLINDER that computes the volume of a right circular cylinder. The program will ask for the radius R and height H of the cylinder to be input, and the program will return the volume of the cylinder using the formula $\pi R^2 H$.

Solution

To name and enter the program, press $\boxed{\text{PRGRM}}$ **NEW/Create New.** Type in the program name "CYLINDER", and then press $\boxed{\text{ENTER}}$. The cursor will now be positioned just after the colon at the first line of the program.

```
PROGRAM:CYLINDER
:Input "RADIUS
",R
:Input "HEIGHT
",H
:Disp "VOLUME",π
R²*H
:Pause
```

To enter the first line, press $\boxed{\text{PRGRM}}$ **I/O** (*input/output*) **Input.** You are now returned to the program editor, where "Input" now appears on the first line. Complete the first line by typing "RADIUS",R where the quotation marks designate a text entry. Then press $\boxed{\text{ENTER}}$ to take you to the next line of the program. Enter the second line, **Input** "HEIGHT" *H*, the same way as the first line. The third line is entered by pressing $\boxed{\text{PRGRM}}$ $\boxed{\text{I/O}}$ **Disp** (*display*), then typing the text "VOLUME", and finally pressing $\boxed{,}$ $\boxed{2^{nd}}$ $\boxed{\pi}$ $\boxed{\times}$ R $\boxed{2^{nd}}$ $\boxed{x^2}$ $\boxed{\times}$ H $\boxed{\text{ENTER}}$ to enter the expression $\pi R^2 H$ that computes the volume of a cylinder. The last line is entered by pressing $\boxed{\text{PRGRM}}$ $\boxed{\text{CTL}}$ (*control*) **Pause.** The **Pause** command gives you an opportunity to see the display before the program ends. The program is now complete, so exit the program editor by pressing $\boxed{2^{nd}}$ $\boxed{\text{QUIT}}$.

To execute your program, press $\boxed{\text{PRGRM}}$ $\boxed{\text{EXEC}}$, use the down arrow key to select the program CYLINDER, and then press $\boxed{\text{ENTER}}$. Press $\boxed{\text{ENTER}}$ once more to start the program. The program will soon pause, giving you the opportunity to input the value of the radius of the cylinder followed by $\boxed{\text{ENTER}}$. You will next enter the cylinder's height, again followed by $\boxed{\text{ENTER}}$. The program then displays the volume of the cylinder of the radius and height you have entered. To run the program again, press $\boxed{\text{ENTER}}$. To quit a program at any time, press $\boxed{\text{ON}}$ $\boxed{\text{QUIT}}$. The result of running CYLINDER for a cylinder with a radius of 5 and a height of 10 is shown below.

```
RADIUS  5              ⋮
HEIGHT 10
VOLUME
                785.3981634
```

Programs for the Graphing Calculator

The programs for the TI-73 listed below can be typed into your calculator. You may also copy programs from one calculator to another with the unit-to-unit link cable that accompanies your calculator. Users of other TI graphing calculators (or even other brands) will require only minor changes of syntax to adapt these programs to their machine. For example, the **Clear Home** command of the TI-73 must be replaced with the **ClrHome** command on the TI-82/83. When the calculator pauses, say to let you enter a value or view a displayed value or graph, you must press $\boxed{\text{ENTER}}$ to execute the next step of the program. To quit a program press the $\boxed{\text{ON}}$ key and then press 1 or $\boxed{\text{ENTER}}$ (or, on the TI-82/83, press 2 or $\boxed{\text{ENTER}}$). You can also use the **Goto** command to edit the program you are quitting.

Program	Inputs Required	Output of Program
COINTOSS	Number of coins N and number of tosses T	How often x heads appeared in the T tosses, for $x = 0, 1, 2, \ldots, N$
COLLATZ	Initial positive integer	See Problem Set 1.1
DICE	Number of dice N and number of tosses T	How often the sum x appeared in the T tosses, for x between N and 6N. The values are displayed in a line graph. Use $\boxed{\text{TRACE}}$ to read values on the plot.
DIFFY	Four numbers	See Cooperative Investigation in Section 2.3
DIVISORS	Two positive integers, A and B	The divisors of A and B are given in side-by-side lists.
DIVVY	Four positive numbers	See Problem 27, Problem Set 6.2
EUCLID	Two positive integers, A and B	Steps in Euclidean algorithm, leading to computation of GCD(A, B) and LCM(A, B)
FACTOR	Positive integer N	Prime power factorization of N.
KAPREKAR	Initial positive integer	See Problem Set 1.1.
MULTIPLS	Two positive integers, A and B	The multiples of A and B are given in side-by-side lists.
PALINDRM	Positive integer	See Problem Set 1.1.
RANDOM	A, B, N	N random numbers between A and B.
SQDIGSUM	Positive integer	See Problem Set 1.1.

COINTOSS

```
Input "NUMBER OF COINS",N
Input "NUMBER OF TOSSES",T
ClrList L1
N + 1 → dim(L1)
For(X,1,T)
sum(seq(iPart(2*rand),X,1,N)) → H
1 + L1(H + 1) → L1(H + 1)
End
ClrScreen
For(X,1,N + 1)
Output(2,1,X − 1)
Output(2,5,"HEADS")
Output(3,1,"CAME UP")
Output(4,1,L1(X))
Output(4,5,"TIMES")
Output(7,5,"PRESS ENTER")
Pause
ClrScreen
End
```

COLLATZ

```
0 → C
Repeat N > 0 and fPart(N = 0)
Clear Home
Disp "ENTER INITIAL"
```

```
Disp "POSITIVE INTEGER"
Prompt N
Disp "PRESS ENTER"
Disp "FOR EACH"
Disp "NEW STEP"
End
Repeat N = 1
Disp N
If fPart(N/2) = 0
Then
(N/2) → N
Else
(N*3 + 1) → N
End
Pause
C + 1 → C
End
Disp N
Disp "TOTAL STEPS",C
Pause
```

DICE

```
Input "NUMBER OF DICE",A
Input "NUMBER OF TOSSES",T
ClrList L1
6*A → dim(L1)
```

```
For(K,1,T)
sum(seq(iPart(6*rand + 1),X,1,A))
    → H
L1(H) + 1 → L1(H)
End
ClrScreen
For(X,A,6*A)
Output(2,1,"TOTAL")
Output(2,7,X)
Output(4,1,"OCCURRED")
Output(4,11,L1(X))
Output(5,1,"TIMES")
End
PlotsOff
seq(X,X,1,6*A) → L2
Plot1(xyLine,L2,L1)
ZoomStat
DispGraph
Pause
```

DIFFY

```
Clear Home
Disp "ENTER FOUR"
Disp "NUMBERS"
Input A
Input B
```

Input C
Input D
0 → I
Clear Home
Disp A,B,C,D
Repeat A = 0 and B = 0 and C = 0
  and D = 0
Pause
Clear Home
abs(A − B) → W
abs(B − C) → X
abs(C − D) → Y
abs(D − A) → Z
W → A
X → B
Y → C
Z → D
Disp A,B,C,D
I + 1 → I
End
Disp "TOTAL STEPS"
Disp I
Pause

DIVISORS

Repeat A > 0 and B > 0 and
  fPart(A) = 0 and fPart(B) = 0
Clear Home
Disp "ENTER TWO"
Disp "POSITIVE"
Disp "INTEGERS"
Input A
Input B
End
1 → C
0 → dim(L1)
0 → dim(L2)
For(I,1,A/2,1)
If fPart(A/I) = 0
Then
I → L1(C)
C + 1 → C
End
End
A → L1(C)
1 → C
For(I,1,B/2,1)
If fPart(B/I) = 0
Then
I → L2(C)
C + 1 → C
End
End
B → L2(C)
Clear Home
Output(1,1,"DIVISORS OF")
Output(2,1,A)
Output(3,1,"AND")
Output(4,1,B)
Pause
Clear Home

If dim(L1) > dim(L2)
Then
dim(L1) → K
Else
dim(L2) → K
End
0 → I
While(I < K)
For(C,1,8,1)
If I ≤ dim(L1) − 1
Then
Output(C,1,L1(I + 1))
End
If I ≤ dim(L2) − 1
Then
Output(C,9,L2(I + 1))
End
I + 1 → I
End
Pause
Clear Home
End

DIVVY

Float
Clear Home
Disp "ENTER FOUR"
Disp "NUMBERS"
Input A
Input B
Input C
Input D
0 → I
Clear Home
Disp A,B,C,D
Repeat abs(A − 1) < 10^ −9 and
  abs(B − 1) < 10^ −9 and
  abs(C − 1) < 10^ −9 and
  abs(D − 1) < 10^ −9
Pause
Clear Home
If A ≥ B
Then
(A/B) → W
Else
(B/A) → W
End
If B ≥ C
Then
(B/C) → X
Else
(C/B) → X
End
If C ≥ D
Then
(C/D) → Y
Else
(D/C) → Y
End
If A ≥ D
Then

(A/D) → Z
Else
(D/A) → Z
End
W → A
X → B
Y → C
Z → D
Disp A,B,C,D
I + 1 → I
End
Disp "TOTAL STEPS"
Disp I
Pause

EUCLID

Repeat A > 0 and B > 0 and
  fPart(A) = 0 and fPart(B) = 0
Clear Home
Disp "INPUT TWO"
Disp "POSITIVE INTS"
Input A
Input B
End
If B > A
Then
A → C
B → A
C → B
End
A → X
B → Y
While 1
iPart(A/B) → Q
round(B*fPart(A/B)) → R
Clear Home
Output(1,1,A)
Output(1,iPart(log(A) + 3),"=")
Output(2,1,Q)
Output(2,iPart(log(Q) + 3),"*")
Output(2,iPart(log(Q) + 5),B)
Output(3,1,"+")
Output(3,3,R)
Pause
B → T
B → A
R → B
If R < .1
Then
Clear Home
Output(1,1,"A =")
Output(1,3,X)
Output(2,1,"B =")
Output(2,3,Y)
Output(3,1,"GCD(A,B) =")
Output(4,3,T)
Output(5,1,"LCM(A,B) =")
Output(6,1,"A*B/GCD(A,B) =")
Output(7,3,(X*Y/T))
Pause
Stop

End
End

FACTOR

Prompt N
ClrList(L1,L2)
1 → S
2 → P
0 → E
√(N) → M
While P ≤ M
While fPart(N/P) = 0
E + 1 → E
N/P → N
End
If E > 0
Then
P → L1(S)
E → L2(S)
0 → E
S + 1 → S
√(N) → M
End
If P = 2
Then
3 → P
Else
P + 2 → P
End
End
If N ≠ 1
Then
N → L1(S)
1 → L2(S)
End
Disp "PRIME FACTORS",L1
Disp "POWERS",L2
Pause

KAPREKAR

Repeat N > 0 and fPart(N) = 0
Clear Home
Disp "ENTER A"
Disp "POSITIVE"
Disp "INTEGER"
Prompt N
End
While N ≠ 0
0 → A
0 → D
0 → dim(L1)
For(C,1,iPart(log(N)) + 1,1)
round(10*fPart((N/10)) → L1(C)
iPart(N/10) → N
End
SortA(L1)
For(C,1,dim(L1),1)
D + L1(C)*10^ (C − 1) → D
A + L1(C)*10^ (dim(L1) − C) → A
End
Clear Home

Output(1,3,D)
Output(2,1,"−")
Output(2,3,A)
Output(3,3,D − A)
Pause
D − A → N
End

MULTIPLS

Repeat A > 0 and B > 0 and
   fPart(A) = 0 and fPart(B) = 0
Clear Home
Disp "ENTER TWO"
Disp "POSITIVE"
Disp "INTEGERS"
Input A
Input B
End
0 → dim(L1)
0 → dim(L2)
If B > A
Then
For(I,1,B,1)
A*I → L1(I)
B*I → L2(I)
End
Else
For(I,1,A,1)
A*I → L1(I)
B*I → L2(I)
End
End
Clear Home
Output(1,1,"POSITIVE")
Output(2,1,"MULTIPLES OF")
Output(3,1,A)
Output(4,1,"AND")
Output(5,1,B)
Pause
Clear Home
1 → I
While(I ≤ dim(L1))
For(C,1,8,1)
If I ≤ dim(L1)
Then
Output(C,1,L1(I))
End
If I ≤ dim(L2)
Then
Output(C,9,L2(I))
End
I + 1 → I
End
Pause
Clear Home
End

PALINDRM

Repeat N > 0 and fPart(N) = 0
Clear Home
Disp "ENTER A"

Disp "POSITIVE"
Disp "INTEGER"
Prompt N
End
0 → R
N → T
While 1
For(C,iPart(log(N)),0, −1)
R + (round(10*fPart(T/10))*10^
   C) → R
iPart(T/10) → T
End
If N = R
Then
Clear Home
Output(1,1,N)
Output(2,1,"IS A
   PALINDROME")
Pause
Stop
End
Clear Home
Output(3,12 − iPart(log(N)),N)
Output(4,12 −
   (iPart(log(R)) + 2),"+")
Output(4,12 − iPart(log(R)),R)
Output(5,12 −
   iPart(log(N + R)),N + R)
N + R → N
N → T
0 → R
Pause
End

RANDOM

Clear Home
Disp "RANGE MIN"
Input A
Disp "RANGE MAX"
Input B
Disp "HOW MANY"
Disp "NUMBERS?"
Input N
For(X,1,N,1)
Disp((B − A)*rand + A)
Pause
End

SQDIGSUM

0 → T
1 → L
1 → C
Repeat A > 0 and A < 10000
   and fPart(A) = 0
Clear Home
Disp "ENTER A"
Disp "POSITIVE INT"
Disp "LESS THAN 10000"
Prompt A
End
Clear Home

```
While 1                    Output(L,C,"+")              If L = 9
While A ≠ 0                C + 1 → C                    Then
10*(fPart(A/10)) → Z       End                          1 → L
iPart(A/10) → A            T + Z² → T                   Clear Home
Output(L,C,Z)              End                          End
C + 1 → C                  Output(L,C,"=")              1 → C
Output(L,C,"²")            C + 1 → C                    T → A
C + 1 → C                  Output(L,C,T)                0 → T
If A ≠ 0                   Pause                        End
Then                       L + 1 → L
```

PROBLEM SET C

1. **Calculating Values.** According to Newton's Inverse Square Law of Gravity, an object's weight varies inversely proportionally to the square of the distance from the center of the earth. Assuming the earth's radius is 4000 miles, this means that a person who weighs 150 pounds on the surface of the earth will weigh $150\left(\dfrac{4000}{4000 + X}\right)^2$ at an altitude of X miles above the earth's surface. The function giving the person's weight is therefore Y1 = 150 * $(4000/(4000 + X))^2$, as written in the form entered into a calculator.

    (a) Find the person's weight at an altitude of 500 miles.

    (b) Find the weights of the person at the heights 1000, 2000, and 3000 miles, using a list to replace the single numerical value.

    (c) Use guess and check to estimate the altitude at which the person's weight is 75 pounds.

2. **Making a Table.** Enter the function Y1 = 150 * $(4000/(4000 + X))^2$ introduced in problem 1, using the $\boxed{Y=}$ editor. Press $\boxed{2^{nd}}$ $\boxed{TBLSET}$ (*table setup*) and define TblStart = 0 and ΔTbl = 500. To see the table of Y1 values this creates, press $\boxed{2^{nd}}$ $\boxed{TABLE}$. Use the arrow keys to find a value in the table that estimates the altitude at which the person's weight is just 15 pounds, 10% of that on the earth's surface.

3. **Making a Graph.** Consider again the weight function of problem 1.

    (a) Graph the function Y1 = 150 * $(4000/(4000 + X))^2$.

    (b) Use $\boxed{TRACE}$ to estimate that altitude at which the person weighs 25 pounds.

    (c) Use $\boxed{TRACE}$ to estimate the person's weight at an altitude of 4000 miles.

4. **Making a Piecewise Graph.** Imagine a deep well, so deep it extends clear to the center of the earth. The weight of a 150-pound person lowered into the well is given by Y2 = 150 * (4000/X) (X < 4000), where X is the distance from the center of the earth. For values of X larger than the 4000-mile radius of the earth, the person's weight varies by the more familiar Inverse Square Law. That is, a person's weight is given by the function Y3 = 150 * $(4000/X)^2$(X > 4000). (Note: The conditions (X < 4000) and (X > 4000) listed in parentheses limit the definitions of Y2 and Y3 to their respective domains.)

    (a) Enter the two functions Y2 and Y3 given above and obtain their graphs. (The symbols < and > are found in the text editor, $\boxed{2nd}$ $\boxed{TEXT}$ on the TI-73, and under $\boxed{2nd}$ $\boxed{TEST}$ on the TI-82/83.)

    (b) Use $\boxed{TRACE}$ to find the two distances from the earth's center where the person's weight is about 32 pounds.

5. A ball is thrown upward (and slightly outward) from the roof of a 100-foot-high building with an initial upward velocity of 135 feet per second. Its height above the ground after X seconds is given by the function Y1 = 100 + 135 * X − 16 * X^2. Use the graphing calculator to

    (a) graph the time versus height function of the ball's motion,

    (b) estimate the maximum height reached by the ball and the number of seconds into the motion when this height is reached, and

    (c) estimate the time into the motion, to the nearest second, when the ball strikes the ground.

6. Graph the following four functions:

    $$Y1 = X \qquad Y2 = 2 * X \qquad Y3 = (1/2) * X \qquad Y4 = -X$$

    To see the true shape of the graphs, use $\boxed{ZOOM}$ **ZSquare** so the scales of both the x- and y-axes are the same. Consider Y1 as the basic function and Y2, Y3, and Y4 as modifications of the basic function.

(a) Carefully describe what is similar about the graphs of the modified functions compared to the graph of the basic function.

(b) How are the graphs of the modified functions different from that of the basic function?

(c) Predict the appearance of the graphs of the following functions, and then check the accuracy of your predictions by editing the functions in your calculator and redrawing the graphs.

$$Y2 = 5 * X \qquad Y3 = (1/5) * X \qquad Y4 = -5 * X$$

7. Graph the function $Y1 = \{1, 5, 1/5, -1\} * X^2$. Using the list $\{1, 5, 1/5, -1\}$ as the coefficient of x^2 gives a simple way to simultaneously graph the four functions $y = x^2, y = 5x^2, y = (1/5)x^2, y = -x^2$. Sketch the four parabolic graphs, and associate each with a corresponding parameter 1, 5, 1/5, or -1. Give reasons for your choices.

8. **Making a Pie Chart on the TI-73.** Mr. Hsu's fifth-grade class took a poll of their favorite ice cream flavors. They discovered that vanilla was the favorite of 9 students, chocolate was favored by 15 students, strawberry by 4 students, and raspberry was 8 of the children's favorite flavor. Enter the categories in list L1, either by number 1, 2, 3, 4 or (using the text editor) by name, say "VAN", "CHO", "STRA", and "RAS" (the quotes distinguish a text entry from a numerical entry). In list L2, enter the corresponding sequence of numbers 9, 15, 4, and 8. Now press $\boxed{2^{nd}}$ $\boxed{\text{PLOT}}$ 1 and turn on Plot 1, set the plot type as a pie chart, set CategList to L1, set Data List to L2, and choose either **Number** or **Percent**. Press $\boxed{\text{GRAPH}}$ to see your pie chart. What percent of the children favor chocolate?

9. **Making a Bar Chart on the TI-73.** Mrs. O'Leary's class has 4, 12, 9, and 10 students whose respective favorite flavors of ice cream are vanilla, chocolate, strawberry, and raspberry. Mr. Hsu's class has the corresponding numbers 9, 15, 4, and 8 (see problem 8). Enter the values 9, 15, 4, 8 into list L2 and 4, 12, 9, 10 into list L3. Use the Stat Plot editor to make a bar chart to compare the two classes. Set CategList to L1, DataList1 to L2, DataList2 to L3, and the number of datalists to 2 so that the choice of DataList3 is not required. Do both classes have the same most common favorite flavor? The same least common favorite flavor?

10. **Making a Histogram.** The table below shows the grades for Mr. Hsu's fifth-grade class project. Two students received 100, one student had a 97, three students received a 94, and so on, as shown by the frequency list. Scores 90–100 will receive an A, 80–89 a B, 70–79 a C, 60–69 a D, and 0–59 an F. Make a histogram of the grade distribution by entering the scores in list L1 and the corresponding frequencies in list L2. Turn off all plots except Plot 1, and choose list L1 as the Xlist and list L2 as the Freq list in the plot editor. To group the scores by the grade intervals, set the window values to Xmin = 40, Xmax = 100, Xscl = 10, Ymin = -5, Ymax = 15, Yscl = 1. The number of values within any interval can be displayed by tracing the histogram. Which letter grade is most common on the project? How many A grades are given?

Score	100	97	94	92	91	88	87	84	83	82	80	77	74	71	69	62	53	47
Frequency	2	1	3	2	2	1	4	2	3	1	2	3	4	2	1	1	1	1

APPENDIX D

A Brief Guide to The Geometer's Sketchpad

Exciting new possibilities for exploring geometric concepts on the computer are available with dynamic geometry software. This software allows the user to construct geometric figures with both speed and precision. The software will also give the measures of angles, lengths of segments, and areas of regions. Once a figure is constructed, it can be manipulated to a continuum of new shapes which preserve the geometric relationships used to construct the original figure. In this way the geometric properties of the configuration can be explored in a dynamic environment not possible with traditional paper and pencil sketches.

Several geometry programs are currently available, including the following:

Cabri (Brooks/Cole Publishing Co.)
The Geometry Inventor (Sunburst Communications, Inc.)
The Geometer's Sketchpad (Key Curriculum Press, Inc.)

This appendix provides a short introduction to *The Geometer's Sketchpad.* More advanced features of *Sketchpad* are described in the *User Guide and Reference Manual* which accompanies the software. Users of other programs will need to refer to the manual pertinent to their own software. Even so, there is much common ground, and it should not be difficult to modify the procedures in the examples below to accommodate the software being used.

The Sketch Window

- **Menu bar**   Dragging downward accesses a list of commands available to create and investigate figures.
- **Toolbox**   Clicking the icon activates the corresponding tool.
- **Sketch plane**   The area where drawings appear.
- **Tool status box** Shows which tool is active.

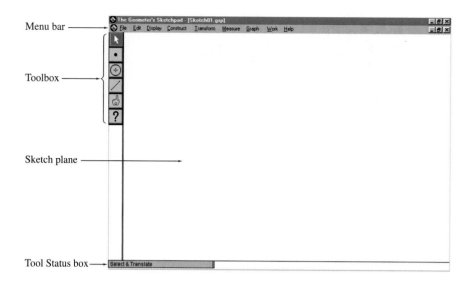

Menu bar

Toolbox

Sketch plane

Tool Status box

Using the Toolbox

The names of the tools and their specific functions are discussed below. To activate a tool, point and click on the tool icon. You will notice that the icon becomes highlighted. The rotation and dilation tools are hidden beneath the selection tool, and similarly the ray and line tools are beneath the segment tool. To choose a hidden tool, point at the tool they are concealed under and then press and hold down the mouse button. The other tools are revealed. While holding down the mouse button, drag your pointer to the tool you wish to use and release the mouse button. Your tool can now be used. You will notice that the icon of the new tool now appears in the toolbox.

Selection Arrow Tool, Translate Tool, Rotate Tool, and Dilate Tool

There are actually three different tools represented here: the Translation, Rotation, and Dilation tools. All of them can also be used to select objects in the sketch window. The **Translate tool** is used to move an object from one position in the sketch window to another position. The **Rotate tool** is used to rotate the position of an object, and the **Dilate tool** is used to enlarge or shrink an object's size. The center of the dilation or rotation is made by selecting the desired point and using the **Mark Center** command in the Transform Menu.

Point Tool

This tool creates points at the cursor position in the sketch plane; each click creates a new point.

Compass Tool

This tool constructs a circle by dragging the cursor from the center to a point on the circle.

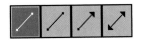

Straightedge Tools

There are three different tools concealed here: the Segment, Ray, and Line tools. They respectively create a segment, ray, or line by clicking on one point and dragging to a second point on the object.

Text Tool

This tool enables you to label and create captions for your objects and sketches.

Object Information Tool

This tool will give you information about objects in your sketch.

EXAMPLE D.1

Constructing a Triangle with the Toolbox

Construct a triangle and investigate how it can be labeled and manipulated.

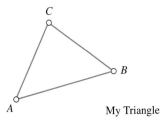

Solution

Begin with a clear sketch plane. (*Note:* The **New Sketch** command in the File Menu will create a new sketch window with a blank sketch plane.) Select the Segment tool, and move the cursor back to the sketch plane. Now click and drag from *A* to *B*, click, then drag from *B* to *C*, click, and finally drag from *C* back to *A*. This will construct triangle *ABC*. Next return to the toolbox, and click on the Selection tool. Click on points and segments of your triangle to see how selected objects become highlighted. Notice that a click on another object will deselect the first object. By holding down the Shift key, a sequence of objects can be selected or deselected. Also see that dragging the Select arrow creates a box in which all objects are selected, and clicking at a point outside your figure deselects all objects. Finally, return to the toolbox and highlight the Text tool icon to create a label. Clicking the pointer hand, when it turns black, provides a label of the vertex or side of your triangle. A second click will hide the label. Double-clicking a label allows you to edit the label. With the Text tool still active, drag to create a box in which text can be typed.

> Hold down the Shift key and click on objects to select or deselect the objects.

The use of the toolbox can be explored in "free play" experimentation. You will quickly discover how to construct circles, rays, line segments, and polygons. However, for more sophisticated constructions you will want to use commands from the Construct and Transform Menus.

Using the Menus

Construct
Point On Object
Point At Intersection
Point At Midpoint
Segment
Perpendicular Line
Parallel Line
Angle Bisector
Circle By Center+Point
Circle By Center+Radius
Arc On Circle
Arc Through 3 Points
Interior
Locus
Construction Help...

The Construct Menu

An alternative method to construct a line segment is to first select the desired end-points of the segment in the sketch plane. The **Segment** command will draw the segment between the selected points. A line is constructed similarly, but you must first highlight the Line tool in the toolbox before going to the Construct Menu. Each command in the Construct Menu requires certain objects in your sketch be selected in advance. If the command appears a light gray color in the menu, it tells you that you do not have the proper objects selected to execute that command. Clicking on the **Construction Help . . .** command at the bottom of the menu gives a list of the required selections for each Construct Menu command.

EXAMPLE   D.2

Constructing an Equilateral Triangle, the Medians, and the Centroid with the Construct Menu

Construct any two points *A* and *B*. Then draw an equilateral triangle *ABC*, and construct the midpoints of the sides. Draw each segment from the vertex of the triangle to the midpoint of the opposite side. These three segments, the medians, are concurrent at the centroid, *G*, of the triangle.

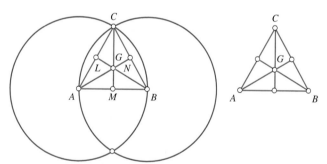

Solution

Select the Point tool from the toolbox and draw two points, *A* and *B*, in the sketch plane. Choose the Select tool from the toolbox and, holding down the Shift key, select *A* and then *B*. Use the **Circle By Center + Point** command to construct the circle centered at *A* that passes through *B*. In the same way, select point *B* and then point *A* to construct the circle centered at *B* that passes through point *A*. Next, select the two circles and use the **Point At Intersection** command. The two points at which the circles intersect will be constructed. Select one of these to be point *C*. While holding down the Shift key, also select *A* and *B*. Executing the **Segment** command from the Construct Menu will construct the sides of the desired equilateral triangle *ABC*. The three sides just drawn are automatically selected, so the **Point At Midpoint** command will construct the midpoints *L*, *M*, and *N* of the sides of the triangle. The centroid *G* of the triangle is now easy to construct: draw $\overline{AN}$ and $\overline{BL}$ and then construct the point, *G*, at which these two segments intersect. Selecting the circles and executing the **Hide** command from the Display Menu will hide the circles from view.

The Difference Between a Construction and a Drawing

The triangle constructed in Example D.1 has no special property other than being a triangle. By dragging any vertex or side, the triangle can be manipulated to assume any triangular shape (including the "degenerate" case where the three vertices lie on the same line). It is possible to drag point C so that $\triangle ABC$ appears to be an equilateral triangle. In this way, you will have *drawn* an "equilateral" triangle. However, dragging a vertex quickly changes the triangle to become non-equilateral, so you can easily check that you have not constructed a true equilateral triangle. On the other hand, the triangle created in Example D.2 is equilateral by *construction*. Once points A and B were given, the point C was *constructed* to make $\triangle ABC$ equilateral. You can still drag either point A or B, but point C will always move so that $\triangle ABC$ remains equilateral. It is often best to use commands from the Construct Menu to construct a figure, since figures created with the Toolbox are frequently just drawings.

> **Important Tip:** *Construct Your Figure, Don't Just Draw It*
>
> Determine if you have made a construction or a drawing by dragging several different test points in your figure.
>
> - If the correct geometric relationships are retained in the figure throughout the manipulation, you likely have constructed the figure.
> - If incorrect geometric relationships become apparent (for example, a "right angle" changes size), you know that you have made a drawing.

The Transform Menu

Transform

Translate...
Rotate...
Dilate...
Reflect

Mark Center
Mark Mirror

Mark Vector
Mark Distance
Mark Angle
Mark Ratio

Define Transform...

The Transform Menu allows objects to be translated, rotated, dilated, and reflected. For example, to perform a reflection select the desired line of reflection and execute the **Mark Mirror** command. Next, back in the sketch plane, select all of the objects that you wish to reflect. Now execute the **Reflect** command. This will construct the reflection of the selected objects across the mirror line. Translations, rotations, and dilations are performed in a similar way, and again some free play experimentation will quickly make it clear how the commands in the Transform Menu are used in constructions and investigations.

EXAMPLE D.3   Creating a Hexagonal Tiling with the Transform Menu

Draw a hexagon $ABCDEF$ with a pair of opposite sides, $\overline{AB}$ and $\overline{DE}$, that are parallel and congruent. Construct the midpoint, M, of $\overline{BC}$ and rotate the hexagon by $180°$ about the midpoint to create a ten-sided polygonal tile. Then show that translations of the decagon will tile the plane.

Solution   Use the Segment tool to construct three sides, $\overline{AB}$, $\overline{BC}$, and $\overline{CD}$. With the Shift key held down, select points B and D, in that order, and execute the **Mark Vector** command in the Transform Menu. Next, select point A and segment $\overline{AB}$ and then execute the **Translate . . . By Marked Vector** command in the Transform Menu. This will extend $ABCD$ to become $ABCDE$, where $\overline{DE}$ is parallel to and the same length as $\overline{AB}$. Now complete the hexagon by constructing point F and segments $\overline{EF}$ and $\overline{FA}$. Construct the midpoint M by selecting the segment $\overline{BC}$ and executing the **Point At Midpoint** command from the Construct Menu. Now select M and execute the **Mark Center** command to choose M as the center of rotation. Next, select the hexagon (all six sides and all six vertices) and execute the **Rotate . . . By Fixed Angle** (namely by 180°) command. This creates the desired ten-sided tile. Selecting the tile and repeatedly executing the **Translate . . . By Marked Vector** command will quickly produce a partial tiling of the plane.

The Measure Menu

Measure
Distance
Length
Slope
Radius
Circumference
Area
Perimeter
Angle
Arc Angle
Arc Length
Ratio
Coordinates
Equation
Calculate...
Tabulate
Add Entry

Distances, lengths, areas, perimeters, angles, and so forth, can be measured by executing commands in the Measure Menu. For example, selecting three points A, B, and C (in that order) and executing the **Angle** command will display the measure of $\angle ABC$ in the sketch plane. The measurement caption can be dragged to any convenient position in the sketch plane.

Once you have displayed measurements in the sketch plane, you can select a set of measurements that you wish to include in a table. To create a table, use the **Tabulate** command. The current measurements of the selected objects are now displayed in the table. These entries are permanent, and will not change if the figure under investigation is manipulated. The new measurements of a manipulated figure can be added to the table by executing the **Add Entry** command in the Measure Menu. (Alternatively, double-click on the table to add a new set of measurements to the table).

Algebraic and trigonometric expressions in terms of measurements of the figure under investigation can be formed by selecting the relevant measures and then invoking the **Calculate . . .** command of the Measure Menu. The expression and its value are then displayed in the sketch plane.

EXAMPLE   D.4   **Exploring the Converse of the Pythagorean Theorem with the Measure Menu**

Draw any triangle ABC, and use the Text tool to label the three sides as a, b, c. Measure the lengths a, b, and c of the three sides and measure $\angle ACB$. Use the **Calculate . . .** command to display $a^2 + b^2 - c^2$. Select the $a^2 + b^2 - c^2$ and $\angle ACB$ measures and display these in a table by using the **Tabulate** command. What kind of a triangle is *ABC* when $a^2 + b^2 - c^2$ is zero? positive? negative?

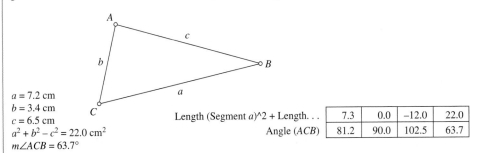

| Length (Segment a)^2 + Length. . . | 7.3 | 0.0 | −12.0 | 22.0 |
| Angle (*ACB*) | 81.2 | 90.0 | 102.5 | 63.7 |

a = 7.2 cm
b = 3.4 cm
c = 6.5 cm
$a^2 + b^2 - c^2 = 22.0$ cm^2
$m\angle ACB = 63.7°$

Solution

We have already described how a triangle can be drawn. The length and angle measurements are displayed in a table by following the procedures just above which described the use of the Measurement Menu. Manipulating the triangle and adding additional entries to the table should reveal that $\angle ACB$ is a right angle precisely when the expression $a^2 + b^2 - c^2$ is zero. If $a^2 + b^2 - c^2 > 0$ the angle measure is less than 90° and triangle *ABC* is an acute triangle. On the other hand, if $a^2 + b^2 - c^2 < 0$ then the angle measure is greater than 90° and *ABC* is an obtuse triangle.

The Graph Menu

Graph
Create Axes
Show Grid
Snap To Grid
Grid Form ▶
Plot Measurement ...
Plot Points ...
Coordinate Form ▶
Equation Form ▶

The **Create Axes** command turns the sketch plane into a coordinate plane with origin *A*:(0, 0) at the screen center and point *B*:(1, 0) one unit away from *A* on the positive *x*-axis. Dragging point *A* allows you to reposition the origin, and dragging point *B* allows you to change the scale of the plane. **Plot Points . . .** opens a dialog box in which you enter the *x* and *y* coordinates of a list of points you wish to plot. **Equation Form . . .** allows you to choose the form of equations you wish to work with: lines can be given in slope-intercept form $y = mx + b$, or in general form $Ax + By + C = 0$; circles can be given in center/radius form $(x - x_1)^2 + (y - y_1)^2 = R^2$, or in general form $x^2 + y^2 + Dx + Ex + F = 0$. To obtain the equation of any line or circle, select the line or circle and use the **Equation** command found in the Measure Menu.

EXAMPLE D.5 | Plotting Points and Finding Equations

Plot the points *C*:(3, 4), *D*:(9, 1), *E*:(−1, 1), *F*:(2, 7), and then construct the lines $\overleftrightarrow{CD}$ and $\overleftrightarrow{EF}$ and the point *G* where the lines intersect. Find the equations and slopes of the two lines, and show that the product of the slopes is −1. Next, plot the point *H*:(4, 1) and construct the circle centered at *H* that passes through *G*. Find the equation of the circle to verify that the radius is 5 to check that the circle also passes through *D* and *E*.

Solution

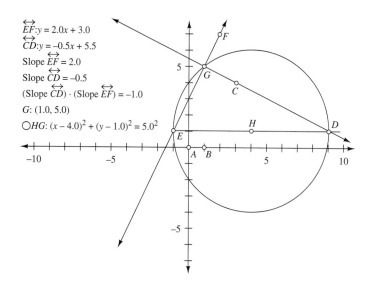

$$\overset{\leftrightarrow}{EF}: y = 2.0x + 3.0$$
$$\overset{\leftrightarrow}{CD}: y = -0.5x + 5.5$$
Slope $\overset{\leftrightarrow}{EF} = 2.0$
Slope $\overset{\leftrightarrow}{CD} = -0.5$
$(\text{Slope } \overset{\leftrightarrow}{CD}) \cdot (\text{Slope } \overset{\leftrightarrow}{EF}) = -1.0$
$G: (1.0, 5.0)$
$\bigcirc HG: (x - 4.0)^2 + (y - 1.0)^2 = 5.0^2$

The points can be plotted by opening the **Plot Points . . .** dialog box. Alternatively, with the grid points shown using the **Show Grid** setting, the points can be plotted directly with the Point tool from the toolbox. The lines and their intersection at point G are readily constructed. Select both of the lines and use the **Equation** and **Slope** commands from the Measure Menu to display the equations and slopes of the lines. Use **Calculate . . .** to verify that the product of the slopes is -1. This checks that the two lines are perpendicular to one another. Select point G and use the **Coordinates** command from the Measure Menu to display the coordinates of G. Use the Compass tool from the toolbox to construct the circle at point F through G. With the circle selected, again use the **Equation** command to display the equation of the circle. The radius is seen to be 5. Since both D and E are 5 units from H, we see that the circle has diameter DE.

The File, Edit, Display, and Work Menus

The File Menu allows you to create new sketch windows and will open a saved sketch. Newly created sketches, or those that have been edited, can be saved for future use. Completed sketches can be printed.

The Edit Menu allows you to undo and redo steps in your constructions, allows you to cut, copy, and paste selected objects within or between sketch windows, and has a variety of commands that are helpful to selecting objects in the sketch window.

The Display Menu allows you to control the thickness and color of lines, the shading density and color of regions, and the size and style of the type font.

The Work Menu is a convenient way to move from one sketch window to another, or to view script windows. A **script** is a recorded sequence of steps to be followed to complete a construction. For example, by selecting the equilateral triangle constructed in Example D.2 and using the **Make Script** command, you will create the script to construct an equilateral triangle on two given vertices. Now you can construct additional equilateral triangles without having to repeat all of your construction steps. To use a script, first select the *Given* objects in the sketch window that are required by the script (for example, the two points that play the role of A and B are the givens for the equilateral triangle script). Next, open the script window in the Work Menu. Finally, click the Play button to have

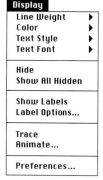

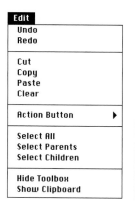

Sketchpad automatically complete the construction steps for you. A large number of useful scripts are found in the *Sample Scripts* file that accompanies *The Geometer's Sketchpad* application software.

Advanced Features

The construction methods described and illustrated in the examples above will enable the user of *The Geometer's Sketchpad* to create a wide variety of interesting figures to investigate. However, *Sketchpad* has other features that more experienced users will find valuable. For example, *Sketchpad* can add an exciting dynamic dimension to a sketch by incorporating animation, movement, hide/show buttons, and so on. The user's manuals for the software describe these features and how they are used.

PROBLEM SET D

1. **Drawing Figures.** Construct a general quadrilateral, and perform the following manipulations.

   (a) Drag the vertices of the quadrilateral until your quadrilateral appears to be a rhombus. See how close you've come by measuring the lengths of the four sides. Why is the rhombus a drawing and not a construction?

   (b) Drag the vertices of the quadrilateral until your quadrilateral appears to be a rectangle. What measurements can be made to see how close your drawing comes to a true rectangle?

2. **Constructing Figures.** Construct each figure listed below, using commands from the Construct Menu. In words, describe the construction steps that you followed. Hide any midpoints, perpendicular bisectors, parallel lines, circles, and so on that you used to construct your figure. Check that your figure is a construction by dragging various points and observing if the figure retains all of the necessary properties that define the type of figure. Look for alternative constructions of the figures.

   (a) isosceles triangle (given base $\overline{AB}$)

   (b) kite *KITE* (given *K* and *T*)

   (c) isosceles trapezoid *ABCD* (given base $\overline{AB}$)

   (d) parallelogram *ABCD* (given *A*, *B*, *C*)

   (e) rhombus *ABCD* (given *A* and *C*)

   (f) square *ABCD* (given *A* and *B*)

3. **A Hexagonal Tiling.** Construct any quadrilateral and construct the midpoint of one of its sides. Mark the midpoint as a rotation center (alternatively, just double-click the desired rotation center). Select the

entire quadrilateral and use **Transform/Rotate . . .** (by 180° about the marked center) to create a 6-sided polygonal tile. Finally, translate the hexagonal tile repeatedly to create a tiling of the plane. Does your quadrilateral still tile the plane if you drag one of its vertices to form a nonconvex quadrilateral?

4. **Measuring and Calculating.** Construct a general quadrilateral *ABCD* and the inscribed quadrilateral *JKLM*, where *J*, *K*, *L*, and *M* are the respective midpoints of the sides of *ABCD*. Use the Measure Menu, including **Calculate . . .** , to answer these questions.

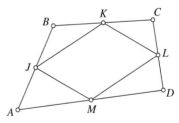

   (a) What is the sum of the measures of the interior angles of *ABCD*?

   (b) What relationships hold for the measures of the interior angles of the quadrilateral *JKLM*?

   (c) What relation exists between the lengths of the sides of *JKLM* and the diagonal distances *AC* and *BD* across the quadrilateral?

   (d) Select (in order) the vertices of *ABCD* and use **Construct/Polygon Interior** to construct the interior of the quadrilateral. Similarly, construct the interior of *JKLM*. Select the interiors of both

ABCD and *JKLM* and measure their respective areas with **Measure/Area.** What relationship do you observe between the areas?

5. **Constructing Figures with Coordinates.** To keep the points visible in the plots requested below, select centimeter measure under **Preferences . . .** in the Display Menu. Also select **Create Axes** and **Snap to Grid** under the Graph Menu.

(a) Plot the points $(0, 6)$, $(-3, 0)$, and $(9, -6)$, and show these are the vertices of a right triangle.

(b) Show that $(6, 3)$, $(-3, 0)$, $(-5, -4)$, and $(4, -1)$ are the vertices of a parallelogram.

(c) Show that $(13, 1)$, $(-3, 9)$, and $(0, -12)$ are the vertices of a triangle inscribed in a circle centered at $(2, -1)$.

Answers to Selected Problems

Chapter 1

Problem Set 1.1   (page 6)

1. (a) $9 \times 9 = 81$
$79 \times 9 = 711$
$679 \times 9 = 6111$
$5679 \times 9 = 51{,}111$
$45{,}679 \times 9 = 411{,}111$
$345{,}679 \times 9 = 3{,}111{,}111$
$2{,}345{,}679 \times 9 = 21{,}111{,}111$
$12{,}345{,}679 \times 9 = 111{,}111{,}111$

3. (a) $1 \times 8 + 1 = 9$
$12 \times 8 + 2 = 98$
$123 \times 8 + 3 = 987$

5. (a) $67 \times 67 = 4489$
$667 \times 667 = 444{,}889$
$6667 \times 6667 = 44{,}448{,}889$

6. (b)

10. (a) $1 \times 142{,}857 = 142{,}857$
$2 \times 142{,}857 = 285{,}714$
$3 \times 142{,}857 = 428{,}571$
$4 \times 142{,}857 = 571{,}428$
$5 \times 142{,}857 = 714{,}285$

12. (a) *P, Q,* and *R* appear to be collinear.
14. $\overline{AD}$, $\overline{BE}$, and $\overline{CF}$ appear to be concurrent.
18. (a) Results will vary. It very likely always stops.

JUST FOR FUN   For Careful Readers   (page 12)

1. The second engineer was the first engineer's daughter.
2. There was no smoke since the train was electric.
3. The 12th rung down since the ladder rises with the ship.

Problem Set 1.2   (page 15)

1. (a) 21 bikes, 6 trikes **4. (a)**   **5.** 12

9. (a)

11. (d) There are no solutions. **12. (a)** 1, 2, 3, 5, 8, 13, 21
(c) 3, 5, 8, 13, 21, 34, 55 **(e)** 2, 1, 3, 4, 7, 11

Problem Set 1.3   (page 25)

1. No. When 10 is multiplied by 5 and 13 is added, the result is 63, not 48. **3.** 3
5. (a) Yes. Yes. The rules are really the same.
6. (a)   **(c)**   **8.** 49

10. 1357, 1375, 1537, 1573, 1735, 1753, 3157, 3175, 3517, 3571, 3715, 3751, 5137, 5173, 5317, 5371, 5713, 5731, 7135, 7153, 7315, 7351, 7513, 7531 **12.** Assuming that the bags are identical, the possibilities are as shown.

Bag 1	Bag 2	Bag 3
23	1	1
21	3	1
19	3	3
19	5	1
17	3	5
17	7	1
15	5	5
15	3	7
15	1	9
13	9	3
13	7	5
13	11	1
11	7	7
11	9	5
11	11	3
9	9	7

14. 4 and 24, 6 and 16, 8 and 12 **16.** 9 minutes
19. Dawkins, Chalmers, Ertl, Albright, Badgett
21. 46 square meters

Problem Set 1.4   (page 42)

1. (a) 14, 17, 20 **(c)** 10, 15, 15 **(e)** 162, 486, 1458
2. (a) • • • •   • • • • •   • • • • • •
• • • •   • • • • •   • • • • • •
(d) The *n*th even number **(f)** 1,443,602
4. (a) 16 **5. (a)** 320 **(c)** 595
7. (a) $1 + 2 + 3 + 4 + 5 + 4 + 3 + 2 + 1 = 25$
$1 + 2 + 3 + 4 + 5 + 6 + 5 + 4 + 3 + 2 + 1 = 36$

10. (a) 86 **(d)** 42

12. (a) $1 - 4 + 9 - 16 + 25 = 15$
$1 - 4 + 9 - 16 + 25 - 36 = -21$
(b) $1 - 4 + 9 - 16 + 25 - 36 + 49 = 28$
$1 - 4 + 9 - 16 + 25 - 36 + 49 - 64 = -36$
(c) For even n, $1 - 4 + 9 - \cdots - n^2 = -\dfrac{n(n+1)}{2}$. For

odd n, $1 - 4 + 9 - \cdots + n^2 = \dfrac{n(n+1)}{2}$.

18. (a) 6 **(c)** 4950

22. (a)

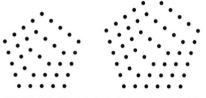

(b) 1, 5, 12, 22, 35, 51 **(c)** $1 + 4 + 7 + 10 + 13 = 35$,
$1 + 4 + 7 + 10 + 13 + 16 = 51$ **(d)** 28 **(e)** 145
(f) $3n - 2$ **(g)** $p_n = \dfrac{n(3n-1)}{2}$ **26. (a)** 30, 2100, 29400

**JUST FOR FUN   How Many Pages in the Book?
(page 50)**

To number pages 1 through 9 takes $9 \cdot 1 = 9$ digits. To
number pages 10 through 99 takes $90 \cdot 2 = 180$ digits. This
leaves $867 - 180 - 9 = 678$ digits to number 3-digit pages.
Thus, there are $678 \div 3 = 226$ 3-digit pages and
$226 + 90 + 9 = 325$ pages in the book.

Problem Set 1.5   (page 55)

1. Yes. Answers will vary. The second player can add
enough tallies to make a multiple of five at each step,
forcing the first player to be the one to exceed 30.
3. (a) $28   **6.** Moe was wearing Hiram's coat and Joe's
hat; Hiram was wearing Joe's coat and Moe's hat.
7. (a) 25. Not all of the information was needed.
8. Beth is the center; Jane is the guard; Mitzi is the forward.
11. (a) 3 **13.** Since there are only 10 digits (0, 1, 2, . . . ,
9) in any collection of 11 natural numbers there must be two
which have the same units digit. The difference of these two
numbers must have a zero as its units digit and is thus
divisible by 10. **15.** If five points are chosen in a square
with diagonal of length $\sqrt{2}$. Then, by the Pigeonhole
Principle, at least two of the points must be in or on the
boundary of one of the four smaller squares shown. The
farthest these two points can be from each other is $\sqrt{2}/2$
units if they are on opposite corners of the small square.

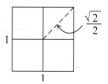

17. If the cups of marbles are arranged as described, each
cup will be part of three different groups of three adjacent
cups. The sum of all marbles in all groups of three adjacent
cups is $3 \cdot (10 \cdot 11/2) = 165$ since each cup of marbles is
counted three times. With the marble count of 165 and ten
possible groups of three adjacent cups, by the Pigeonhole
Principle at least one group of three adjacent cups must have
17 or more marbles since $165 \div 10 = 16.5 > 16$.
19. (i) Since there are 20 people at the party, if each person
has at least one friend at the party, each must have either 1
or 2 or so on up to 19 friends at the party. Since $20 > 19$, it
follows from the Pigeonhole Principle that at least two of the
20 people must have the same number of friends at the party.

Problem Set 1.6   (page 67)

1. 17 min, NENNEE or NENENE or NENEEN
4. Sara should get the racket, and pay Ken $11.25.
8. (a)   **(c)** Correct **9. (a)**

(b) Since all three circles are bad, the error must be in the
intersection of all three circles. **12. (a)** $36

Chapter 1   Review Exercises   (page 74)

1. (a) 8; 168; 2568; 34,568; 434,568; 5,234,568;
61,234,568; 701,234,568; 7,901,234,568 **(b)** No, there is a
recognizable pattern. **(c)** Yes. **(d)** No. It suggests that
examples only *hint at* a pattern or result. A proof is really
needed to be sure. **2. (a)** The result is a 7-digit number
with all digits your favorite. **(b)** 1,111,111 **(c)** 1,111,111 =
$239 \cdot 4649$ and 239 and 4649 are both primes.
3. (a)   **(b)**   **4.** 4884 **5.** 28

67	1	43
13	37	61
31	73	7

7	1	31
13	37	61
43	73	67

6. (a) Answers will vary. One solution is as follows:

$$\begin{array}{r} 179 \\ 368 \\ +\ 452 \\ \hline 999 \end{array}$$

(b) Yes. The digits in any column can be arranged in any
order. **(c)** No. The hundreds column digits must add up
to 8 to allow for a carry from the tens column. If the digit
1 is not in the hundreds column, the smallest this sum
can be is $2 + 3 + 4 = 9$. Thus, the digit 1 must be in the
hundreds column. **7.** 9 **8.** 60 **9.** 88 square feet **10.** 9
11. (a) Multiply by 5, then subtract 2. **(b)** Answers will
vary. A good strategy is to give Chanty consecutive integers
starting with 0. **12. (a)** 3, 6, 12, 24, 48, 96 **(b)** 4, 8, 16,
32, 64, 128 **(c)** 1, 6, 36, 216, 1296, 7776 **(d)** 2, 10, 50,
250, 1250, 6250 **(e)** 7, 7, 7, 7, 7, 7 **13.** Kimberly is the

lawyer and the painter; Terry is the engineer and the doctor; Otis is the teacher and the writer.

14. (a) $14 + 16 + 18 + 20 = 4^3 + 4$
$22 + 24 + 26 + 28 + 30 = 5^3 + 5$
$32 + 34 + 36 + 38 + 40 + 42 = 6^3 + 6$
(b) $92 + 94 + 96 + 98 + 100 + 102 + 104 + 106 + 108 + 110 = 10^3 + 10$ **15. (a)** 25 **(b)** 1075
16. (a) 11th **(b)** 6141 **(c)** Duly observed.
(d) $6141 = (6 + 12 + \cdots + 3072 + 6144) - (3 + 6 + \cdots + 3072) = 6144 - 3 = 6141$. **17.** 442,865
18. (a) $\dfrac{n(n + 1)}{2} + 1$ **(b)** $\dfrac{n(n - 1)}{2}$ **(c)** n^2
19. The product of the squared entries appears to be equal to the product of the circled entries. **20. (a)** 3 **(b)** 9 **(c)** 27
(d) $P_0 + P_1 \cdot 2^1 + P_2 \cdot 2^2 + \cdots + P_n \cdot 2^n = 3^n$, where P_k is the kth element of the nth row of Pascal's triangle. **(e)** 4, 16, 64 **(f)** $P_0 + P_1 \cdot r^1 + P_2 \cdot r^2 + \cdots + P_n r^n = (r + 1)^n$
21. (a) 5 **(b)** 9 **(c)** 50 **22.** 17 **23. (a)** 2500 dollars
(b) A B G I M or A B C D F J M
24. Judy gets the house; Joshua gets the motor home and the painting; JoAnn gets the automobile. Joshua should give $94,500 to Judy, $308,000 to John, and $267,500 to JoAnn.
25. (a) 1101000 **(b)** 1000101 **(c)** 1010010
26. (a) 0110001 **(b)** correct **(c)** 1010010

Chapter 1 Test   (page 77)

1. 21,111,111; 12,111,111; 11,211,111; 11,121,111; 11,112,111; 11,111,211; 11,111,121; 11,111,112
2. (a) $17 + 18 + 19 + 20 + 21 + 22 + 23 + 24 + 25 = 64 + 125 = 225 - 36$
$26 + 27 + 28 + 29 + 30 + 31 + 32 + 33 + 34 + 35 + 36 = 125 + 216 = 441 - 100$
(b) $82 + 83 + 84 + \cdots + 98 + 99 + 100 = 729 + 1000 = 3025 - 1296$
(c) $[(n - 1)^2 + 1] + [(n - 1)^2 + 2] + \cdots + n^2 = (n - 1)^3 + n^3 = \left(\dfrac{n(n + 1)}{2}\right)^2 - \left(\dfrac{(n - 1)(n - 2)}{2}\right)^2$
3. 36 **4.** 3 **5. (a)**

57	2	37
12	32	52
27	62	7

(b)

7	2	27
12	32	52
37	62	57

6. 10 days **7. (a)** $2 + 5 + 8 + 11 + 8 + 5 + 2 = 41 = 3^2 + 2 \cdot 4^2$
$2 + 5 + 8 + 11 + 14 + 11 + 8 + 5 + 2 = 66 = 4^2 + 2 \cdot 5^2$
(b) $2 + 5 + 8 + \cdots + 26 + 29 + 26 + \cdots + 8 + 5 + 2 = 281 = 9^2 + 2 \cdot 10^2$
8. (a) $S_{20} = -110$, $S_{21} = 121$ **(b)** For n odd,
$S_n = \left(\dfrac{n + 1}{2}\right)^2$. For n even, $S_n = -\left(\dfrac{n}{2}\right)\left(\dfrac{n}{2} + 1\right)$.
9. (a) 1101000 **(b)** 0101101 **10.** 20, EENNEEN

Chapter 2
Problem Set 2.1   (page 88)

1. (a) {Arizona, California, Idaho, Oregon, Utah}
2. (a) {1, i, s, t, h, e, m, n, a, o, y, c} **3. (a)** {8, 9, 10, 11, 12} **(c)** {3, 6, 9, 12, 15, 18} **4.** Answers will vary.
(a) $\{x \in U \mid 11 \le x \le 14\}$ or $\{x \in U \mid 10 < x < 15\}$
(c) $\{x \in U \mid x = 4n \text{ and } n \in N\}$ **5.** Answers may vary.
(a) $\{x \in N \mid x \text{ is even and } x > 12\}$ or $\{x \in N \mid x = 2n \text{ for some } n \in N \text{ and } n > 6\}$ **6. (a)** No, it is not clear which cities with these names are meant. **(b)** Yes, it is clear which four cities are included in the set. **7. (a)** True **(c)** True
(e) True **8.**

(a) $B \cup C = \{a, b, c, h\}$

(c) $B \cap C = \{a, b\}$ **(e)** $\overline{A} = \{f, g, h\}$ **9. (a)** $M = \{45, 90, 135, 180, 225, 270, 315, \ldots\}$ **(b)** $L \cap M = \{90, 180, 270, \ldots\}$ = the set of simultaneous multiples of 6 and 45 = the set of multiples of 90. **(c)** 90
11. (a)

(c)

(e)

12. (a)

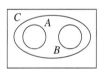

13. No, it is possible that there are elements of A that are also elements of B but not C, or C but not B. For example, let $A = \{1, 2\}$, $B = \{2, 3\}$, $C = \{3\}$.
14. (a) $\overline{A \cap B} = \{1, 2, 3, 4, 5, 7, 8, 9, 10, 11, 13, 14, 15, 16, 17, 19, 20\}$
$\overline{A} \cup \overline{B} = \{1, 2, 3, 4, 5, 7, 8, 9, 10, 11, 13, 14, 15, 16, 17, 19, 20\}$
$\overline{A \cup B} = \{1, 5, 7, 11, 13, 17, 19\}$
$\overline{A} \cap \overline{B} = \{1, 5, 7, 11, 13, 17, 19\}$
(b) $\overline{A \cap B} = \overline{A} \cup \overline{B}$ and $\overline{A \cup B} = \overline{A} \cap \overline{B}$
15. (a)

red circles

(c)

triangles and hexagons

(e)

blue figures not circles

16. (a) $L \cap T$ **(c)** $S \cup T$

17. (a) $8; \varnothing, \{a\}, \{b\}, \{c\}, \{a, b\}, \{a, c\}, \{b, c\}, \{a, b, c\}$
(c) 8, 8 **(e)** $2^{26} = 67,108,864$

18. (a)

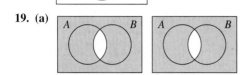

(c) $\overline{A} \cap B \cap C \cap \overline{D}$

19. (a)

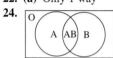

21. (a) $6 \cdot 2 \cdot 3 = 36$
22. (a) Only 1 way
24.

26. Answers will vary. **29.** *Understand the problem* The squares are $1^2 = 1$, $2^2 = 4$, $3^2 = 9$, and so on. The problem is to arrange the numbers 1, 2, . . . , 15 in a list so that pairs of adjacent numbers have sums that are squares. *Devise a plan* 1 can be added to 15 or 8 to give a square; 2 can be added to 14 or 7, 3 can be added to 13 or 6; and so on. However, 8 can only be added to 1 and 9 can only be added to 7. Thus, there are two possible sums for each number except for 8 and 9. Using this information, we should be able to order the list as required. *Carry out the plan* Since only one sum can contain 8 and similarly for 9, these numbers must be on the ends of our list. We start with 8 and then 1. Then the only possibility for the successor to 1 is 15, and so on. This yields the following list: 8, 1, 15, 10, 6, 3, 13, 12, 4, 5, 11, 14, 2, 7, 9 *Look back* The successful plan arose from looking at numbers in the list whose sums were squares. For all but two numbers, there were two numbers that could be added to the number being considered that would result in a square. However, there was only one possibility for 8 (and also 9) so 8 had to go on one end of the list and this determined all the remaining choices.

JUST FOR FUN Red and Green Jelly Beans (page 96)

They are the same. After the first move the jar labeled G contains 20 red jelly beans. Let r red and g green, with $r + g = 20$, be the number of red and green jelly beans moved back from jar G to jar R. Then jar R contains g green jelly beans and jar G contains $20 - r$ red jelly beans, but $g = 20 - r$ since $r + g = 20$.

Problem Set 2.2 (page 99)

1. (a) 13: ordinal
    first: ordinal
2. (a) Equivalent, since there are five elements in $\{A, B, M, N, P\}$. **3.** Apparently, the cardinality of the set of seats in the auditorium is less than the cardinality of the set of potential audience members. **5. (a)** 15 **(c)** 2

7. (a) The correspondence $0 \leftrightarrow 1$, $1 \leftrightarrow 2$, $2 \leftrightarrow 3$, . . . , $w \leftrightarrow w + 1$ . . . shows $W \leftrightarrow N$. **8. (a)** Finite
9. (a) For example, $Q_1 \leftrightarrow Q_2$, $Q_3 \leftrightarrow Q_4$, and so on.

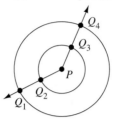

(c) For example $Q_1 \leftrightarrow Q_2$, and so on.

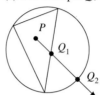

10. (a) True **(c)** True
11. (a) $n(A \cap B) \leq n(A)$. The set $A \cap B$ contains only the elements of A that are also elements of B. Thus, $A \cap B$ cannot have more elements than A.
13.

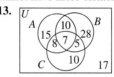

15. (a)

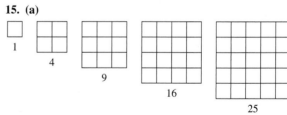

16. (a) 37, 61 **17. (a)** No. Since he lives forever, Joe will eventually earn enough to pay all his bills through any given week though he falls further and further behind.
(b) 1000 weeks. The bills for week 100 are paid at the end of week $10 \times 100 = 1000$. **18. (a)** Coconuts 3 and 4 are in the barrel on day 2; coconuts 4, 5, and 6 on day 3; coconuts 101 through 200 on day 100. At the "end of time" there are no coconuts left in the barrel, since coconut n was tossed into the ocean on day n and n can be any natural number. **19. (a)** Let each element $a \in A$ be matched to itself: $a \leftrightarrow a$. This gives a one-to-one correspondence from A to itself, so $A \sim A$. **(b)** If $A \sim B$, there is a one-to-one correspondence that matches each element $a \in A$ to an element $b \in B$: $a \leftrightarrow b$. Since each element of B is matched exactly once, the correspondence can be reversed: $b \leftrightarrow a$. This shows that $B \sim A$, and therefore set equivalence is symmetric. **(c)** If $A \sim B$ and $B \sim C$, then there are two one-

to-one correspondences: $a \leftrightarrow b$ and $b \leftrightarrow c$. Combining these correspondences gives us a one-to-one correspondence $a \leftrightarrow c$ from A to C. Thus $A \sim C$, and so set equivalence is transitive. **23.** Using a Venn diagram and guess and check, we discover that **(a)** four students have visited all three countries. **(b)** 14 students have been only to Canada. **24. (a)** Making an orderly list, we obtain the following:

$$a \leftrightarrow 1, \quad b \leftrightarrow 2, \quad c \leftrightarrow 3$$
$$a \leftrightarrow 1, \quad b \leftrightarrow 3, \quad c \leftrightarrow 2$$
$$a \leftrightarrow 2, \quad b \leftrightarrow 1, \quad c \leftrightarrow 3$$
$$a \leftrightarrow 2, \quad b \leftrightarrow 3, \quad c \leftrightarrow 1$$
$$a \leftrightarrow 3, \quad b \leftrightarrow 1, \quad c \leftrightarrow 2$$
$$a \leftrightarrow 3, \quad b \leftrightarrow 2, \quad c \leftrightarrow 1$$

25. (a) Row 0: 1   Row 1: 1 1   Row 2: 1 2 1
Row 3: 1 3 3 1   Row 4: 1 4 6 4 1
26. Since we are given that $k < l$ and $l < m$, we can choose sets K, L, and M satisfying $K \subset L \subset M$ and $n(K) = k$, $n(L) = l$, and $n(M) = m$. By the transitive property of set inclusion (see Section 1, or just look at a Venn diagram) we know that $K \subset M$ and so $k < m$. **28.** As the Venn diagram shows, four people have type AB blood.

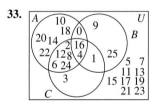

33.

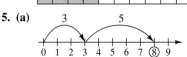

34. (a) $\overline{A} = \{b, c, f, g\}$ **(c)** $A \cup \overline{B} = \{a, b, d, e\}$
(e) $\overline{A} \cap \overline{B} = \{b\}$ **(g)** $\overline{A \cap B} = \{a, b, c, d, f, g\}$
35. (a)

JUST FOR FUN   Paper Clip Comparison   (page 109)

Many people will say just one more and will be surprised when shown that the answer is two more.

Problem Set 2.3   (page 113)

1. (a) (i) 5 (ii) 5 (iii) 4 **(b)** (ii) and (iii)
3. (a) 4, 5, 6, 7, or 8 **(b)** 4
4. (a)

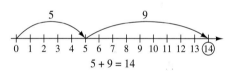

5. (a)

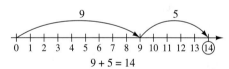

(c)

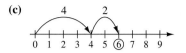

(e)

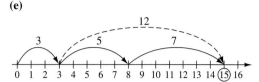

8. (a) Closed **(c)** Closed **(f)** Closed **9. (a)** Commutative property of addition **(c)** Additive identity property of zero **10.** The parentheses may be overlooked and the addends rearranged because the associative and commutative properties of addition allow the addends to be added in any order.

12. (a)

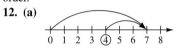

(c)

13. (a) $5 + 7 = 12$ $\qquad 12 - 7 = 5$
$\qquad\quad 7 + 5 = 12$ $\qquad 12 - 5 = 7$
(b) $4 + 8 = 12$ $\qquad 12 - 8 = 4$
$\qquad\quad 8 + 4 = 12$ $\qquad 12 - 4 = 8$

14. (a)

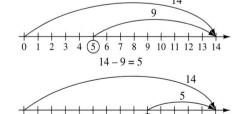

15. (a) Comparison **(b)** Missing addend **(c)** Take-away **(d)** Comparison **17.** $257 - 240 = 17$ pages
18. (a) $(8 - 5) - (2 - 1) = 2$ **(c)** $((8 - 5) - 2) - 1 = 0$

19. (a)

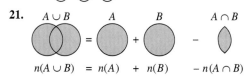

20. (a)

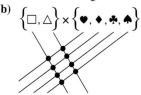

21.

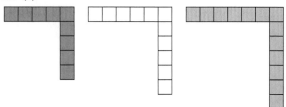

$$n(A \cup B) = n(A) + n(B) - n(A \cap B)$$

23. (a) The number of circles on the 45° diagonals are 1, 2, 3, 2, and 1.

24. (a)

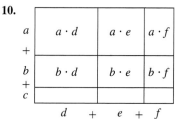

(c) $100^2 = 10{,}000$ **25. (a)** 98 **26.** {0}

28. (a)

n	1	2	3	4	5	6	7	8
t_n	1	3	6	10	15	21	28	36

9	10	11	12	13	14	15
45	55	66	78	91	105	120

(b) $11 = 10 + 1, 12 = 6 + 6, 13 = 10 + 3,$
$14 = 10 + 3 + 1, 15 = 15, 16 = 15 + 1,$
$17 = 15 + 1 + 1, 18 = 15 + 3, 19 = 10 + 6 + 3,$
$20 = 10 + 10, 21 = 21, 22 = 21 + 1, 23 = 10 + 10 + 3,$
$24 = 21 + 3, 25 = 15 + 10$

29.

+	5	4	1	6	9	2	0	8	7	3
3	8	7	4	9	12	5	3	11	10	6
9	14	13	10	15	18	11	9	17	16	12
6	11	10	7	12	15	8	6	14	13	9
4	9	8	5	10	13	6	4	12	11	7
0	5	4	1	6	9	2	0	8	7	3
7	12	11	8	13	16	9	7	15	14	10
5	10	9	6	11	14	7	5	13	12	8
2	7	6	3	8	11	4	2	10	9	5
1	6	5	2	7	10	3	1	9	8	4
8	13	12	9	14	17	10	8	16	15	11

31. (a) $0 = 5 - (1 + 4), 1 = 5 - 4, 2 = (1 + 5) - 4,$
$3 = 4 - 1, 4 = 5 - 1, 5 = 1 + 4, 6 = 1 + 5$
34. (a) 2 **(c)** 10 **(e)** 5 **35.** 50 students take only geometry

and 80 students are not enrolled in any of these three courses.

Problem Set 2.4   (page 132)

1. (a) $3 \times 5 = 15$ **(c)** $4 \times 10 = 40$ **(e)** $3 \times 6 = 18$
2. (a) Array model **(c)** Measurement model
4. (a) Each of the a lines coming from set A intersects each of the b lines coming from set B.

(b)

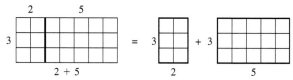

5. (a) Not closed. $2 \times 2 = 4$ and 4 is not in the set.
(c) Not closed. $2 \times 4 = 8$ and 8 is not in the set.
(e) Closed. The product of any two odd whole numbers is always another odd whole number. **(g)** Closed. $2^m \times 2^n = 2^{m+n}$ for any whole numbers m and n.
7. (a) Commutative property of multiplication
(c) Multiplication by zero property **(e)** Associative property of multiplication **8. (a)** Commutative property of multiplication: $5 \times 3 = 3 \times 5$
9. (a)

$$3 \begin{array}{|c|c|} \hline & \\ \hline \end{array} \; \begin{array}{c} 2 \quad\quad 5 \\ \end{array}$$

10.

	d +	e +	f
a +	$a \cdot d$	$a \cdot e$	$a \cdot f$
b +	$b \cdot d$	$b \cdot e$	$b \cdot f$
c			

$(a + b + c) \cdot (d + e + f) = a \cdot d + a \cdot e + a \cdot f + b \cdot d + b \cdot e + b \cdot f + c \cdot d + c \cdot e + c \cdot f$
12. $18 \times 0.86 + 18 \times 0.14 = 18 \times (0.86 + 0.14) = 18 \times 1 = 18.00$ **13. (a)** Distributive property
14. (a) $18 \div 6 = 3$ **15. (a)** $4 \times 8 = 32, 8 \times 4 = 32,$
$32 \div 4 = 8, 32 \div 8 = 4$ **16. (a)** Repeated subtraction
17. (a) 6 **(c)** 6 R 12 **18.** Answers will vary. For example, **(a)** $3 \div 2$ is not a whole number. **19. (a)** If a/b and d/b are defined, then there exist whole numbers r and s such that $a/b = r$ and $d/b = s$. But then $a = br$ and $d = bs$ so that $a + d = br + bs = b(r + s)$. This implies that $(a + d)/b$ is defined, and also that

$$\frac{a + d}{b} = r + s = \frac{a}{b} + \frac{d}{b}.$$

20. (a) 29 **21. (a)** 3^{35} **(c)** 3^{10} **(e)** $(yz)^3$ **22. (a)** 2^3
(c) 2^{10} **23. (a)** $4^2 = (2^2)^2 = 2^{(2 \cdot 2)} = 2^4$. The power operation is not commutative, since $2^3 = 8$ and $3^2 = 9$ so $2^3 \neq 3^2$. **24. (a)** 4 **(c)** 10 **25.** The large square has side length $a + b$ so its area is $(a + b)^2$. But the square is divided into four regions with areas a^2, ab, ab, and b^2, showing that the total area can also be expressed by $a^2 + 2ab + b^2$.
27. (a) "How many tickets must still be sold?"
29. (a) $4 \cdot (5 - 2) = 4 \cdot 3 = 12, 4 \cdot 5 - 4 \cdot 2 = 20 - 8 = 12$. Therefore, $4 \cdot (5 - 2) = 4 \cdot 5 - 4 \cdot 2$.
(b) The diagram below makes it clear that

$a(b - c)$ $=$ ab $-$ ac

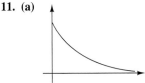

31. $2(1 + 2 + 3 + 4 + 5 + 6 + 7 + 8 + 9 + 10 + 11 + 12) = 2 \cdot \dfrac{12 \cdot 13}{2} = 156$ times
34. $0 = 2 \times (3 - 3), 1 = 2^{(3 - 3)}, 2 = 2 + (3 - 3)$,
$3 = 3^{(3 - 2)}, 4 = 3 + (3 - 2), 5 = 2^3 - 3, 6 = 3^2 - 3$,
$7 = 3 \times 3 - 2, 8 = 3 + 3 + 2, 9 = ?, 10 = ?, 11 = 2^3 + 3$
or $(3 \times 3) + 2, 12 = 3^2 + 3, 13 = ?, 14 = ?$,
$15 = 3 \times (3 + 2), 16 = ?, 17 = ?, 18 = 2 \times 3 \times 3$
39. $2 + 7 = 9, 7 + 2 = 9, 9 - 7 = 2, 9 - 2 = 7$
41. $2 \times 3 = 6, 3 \times 2 = 6$

Problem Set 2.5 (page 144)

1. (a) Not a function in general, since many students take more than one class. **(c)** This is a function. **3. (a)** Not a function, since element c is associated with more than one element of set B and element d is not associated with any element of set B. **(b)** Is a function, with range $\{p, q, r\} \subset B$. **4. (a)** Not the graph of a function: for example, there are three y values associated with the value $x = 3$. **(c)** This is the graph of a function defined on the domain $\{1, 2, 3, 4\}$ and with range $\{1, 2, 3, 4\}$.
7. (a) $g(0) = 5, g(1) = 4, g(2) = 5, g(3) = 8, g(4) = 13$
(b) $\{4, 5, 8, 13\}$ **9. (a)** 12:45 **(b)** 1:00 **10. (a)** G3
11. (a)

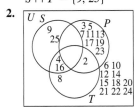

12. (a) $A = 2x^2$ **(b)** $P = 6x$ **(c)** $D = \sqrt{5} \cdot x$
13. (a) Add 5: $y = x + 5$ **16. (a)** 6, 8, 10, 12
17. (a) $F = 10 M$ **18. (a)** $S_5 = 1^2 + 2^2 + 3^2 + 4^2 + 5^2 = 55 = 10 \cdot 11 \cdot 12/24$
$S_6 = 1^2 + 2^2 + 3^2 + 4^2 + 5^2 + 6^2 = 91 = 12 \cdot 13 \cdot 14/24$
(b) $S_n = 2n(2n + 1)(2n + 2)/24$

19. (a)

Size of the Array	Number of Squares of Size					Total Number of Squares
	1×1	2×2	3×3	4×4	5×5	
1×1	1					1
2×2	4	1				5
3×3	9	4	1			14
4×4	16	9	4	1		30
5×5	25	16	9	4	1	55

21. $m = 2, b = 10$ **23.** $4.58\overline{3}$ sec. **25.** $d = \dfrac{760t}{60 \cdot 60} \doteq \dfrac{t}{5}$
26. (a) \$7.15 **27. (a)** $g = 2w + 2h$ **28. (a)** 55 cents
29. (a) \$8234 **(b)** $\$8234 - \$8206 = \$28$
30. (a) $\$3802.50 + 0.28 \times (\$41,162 - \$25,350) = \$3802.50 + \$4427.36 = \$8229.86$
31. (a) The function is $(1.44)^n$, where n is the number of copies made. **35. (a)** The calculator shows 5 which corresponds to Friday. **(b)** Sunday **(c)** Tuesday
36. 7501 boxes **38. (a)** 6 **(b)** 2 **(c)** 9 **(d)** 3

Chapter 2 Review Exercises (page 153)

1. (a) $S = \{4, 9, 16, 25\}$
$P = \{2, 3, 5, 7, 11, 13, 17, 19, 23\}$
$T = \{2, 4, 8, 16\}$
(b) $\overline{P} = \{4, 6, 8, 9, 10, 12, 14, 15, 16, 18, 20, 21, 22, 24, 25\}$
$S \cap T = \{4, 16\}$
$S \cup T = \{2, 4, 8, 9, 16, 25\}$
$S \cap \overline{T} = \{9, 25\}$
2.

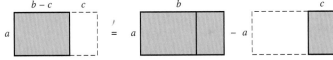

3. (a) $\subseteq$ **(b)** $\subset$ **(c)** $\cap$ **(d)** $\cup$
4. $n(S) = 3, n(T) = 6, n(S \cup T) = 7, n(S \cap T) = 2$,
$n(S \cap \overline{T}) = 1, n(T \cap \overline{S}) = 4$
5. 1 4 9 16 25 36 49 64 81 100
$\updownarrow$ $\updownarrow$ $\updownarrow$ $\updownarrow$ $\updownarrow$ $\updownarrow$ $\updownarrow$ $\updownarrow$ $\updownarrow$ $\updownarrow$
 a b c d e f g h i j
6. There is a one-to-one correspondence between the set of cubes and a proper subset. For example,

1 8 27 64 125 ... k^3 ...
$\updownarrow$ $\updownarrow$ $\updownarrow$ $\updownarrow$ $\updownarrow$ $\updownarrow$
1 2 3 4 5 ... k ...

7. (a) Suppose $A = \{a, b, c, d, e\}$ and $B = \{\blacksquare, \bigstar\}$. Then $n(A) = 5$, $n(B) = 2$, $A \cap B = \varnothing$ and $n(A \cup B) = 5 + 2 = 7$. **(b)**

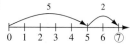

8. (a) Commutative property for addition: $7 + 3 = 3 + 7$ **(b)** Additive identity property of zero: $7 + 0 = 7$
9. (a)   **(b)**

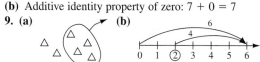

10. $6'' \times 6'' \times 8''$ **11.** Eight rows, with seven full rows and eight soldiers in the back row
12. (a)

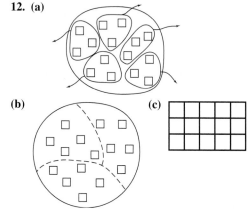

(b)   **(c)**

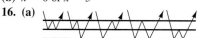

13. (a) Not a function, since two y values are assigned to $x = 3$ **(b)** Function, with domain $\{3, 4, 6, 7, 8\}$ and range $\{1, 2, 3, 4, 5\}$ **(c)** Function, with domain $\{3, 4, 6, 7, 8\}$ and range $\{3, 4\}$ **14. (a)** $y = 3x + 2$ **(b)** $y = x(x + 1)$, or $y = x^2 + x$ **15. (a)** $f(3) = 0, f(0.5) = -2.5, f(-2) = 20$ **(b)** $x = 0$ or $x = 3$
16. (a)

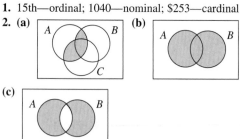

(b) Number of paths with n reflections = number of paths with $n - 1$ reflections + number of paths with $n - 2$ reflections. That is, the number of paths with n reflections is the Fibonacci number $F_{n + 2}$.

Chapter 2   Test   (page 154)

1. 15th—ordinal; 1040—nominal; $253—cardinal
2. (a)   **(b)**

(c)

3. $A \cap \overline{B} = \varnothing$ **4. (a)** 10 **(b)** 4 **(c)** 2 **(d)** 20
5. (a) Associative property of addition **(b)** Distributive

property of multiplication over addition **(c)** Additive identity property of zero **(d)** Associative property of multiplication **6. (a)** 64 bottles **(b)** Grouping
7. $n(A \cap B) = 5$ $n(\overline{A \cap B}) = 21$ **8.** 1, 3, 7, or 21
9. (a) $4 \times 2 = 8$ **(b)** $12 \div 3 = 4$ **(c)** $5 \cdot (9 + 2) = 5 \cdot 9 + 5 \cdot 2$ **(d)** $10 - 4 = 6$ **10. (a)** Yes **(b)** No
11. (a)

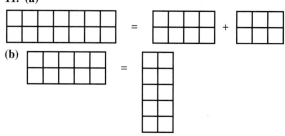

(b)

12. (a) Number line **(b)** Comparison **(c)** Missing addend
13. (a) G3 **(b)** G1 **(c)** G2 **14.** $\{1, 2, 5, 10\}$ **15. (a)** 5
(b) The bee can enter cell $n + 2$ from either cell $n + 1$ or cell n. If there are $F(n + 1)$ ways to get to cell $n + 1$ and $F(n)$ ways to get to cell n, then the number of ways to get to cell $n + 2$ is $F(n + 1) + F(n)$. **(c)** 144

Chapter 3

JUST FOR FUN   For Careful Readers   (page 166)

1. None: it's a hole! **2.** Three inches, the difference between the radii of the two circles. **3.** A quarter and a penny. One was not a quarter but the other was.

Problem Set 3.1   (page 174)

1. (a) 2137 **(c)** 120,310 **(e)** 697 **(g)** 60 **(i)** 152
(k) 16,920 **2. (a)** ⌒| **3. (a)** IX

4. (a) ▼▼▼▼⟨▼ **5. (a)**

11. (a) MIM, MM, MMI
13. (a) 3795 **(c)** 6048 **14. (a)** ═ 𝕋 ⊥ ∥∥

(c) 𝕋 ∥∥∥ **15. (a)** 𝕋 ≡ ∥∥∥ $374 + 281 = 655$

(c) ≡ ∥∥∥ ≡ ∥ $6224 - 732 = 5492$

16.

20. 10 units will be traded for 1 strip, and 20 strips will be traded for 2 mats giving 5 mats, 5 strips, and 3 units.
23. (a) 14 **(c)** 13 **(e)** 217 **25. (b)** 413
27. (a)   **(c)**

(e)   **(g)**

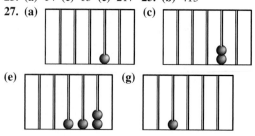

28. (a) The "fives" wire **30. (a)** Yes. No matter what number is represented, one can always be added by bringing over one more bead on the right-most wire and following the rule: If there are 5 beads showing on any wire, then they shall be moved to the back and one bead brought forward on the wire immediately to the left. **32. (a)** $\{1, 2, 3, 4, 5, 7, 9\}$ **(c)** $\{2, 4, 6, 8\}$ **(e)** $\{1, 3\}$ **(g)** $n(A) = 5, n(C) = 4$, $n(A \cup C) = 9$ **(i)** Since A and C are disjoint $(A \cap C = \varnothing)$, $n(A \cup C) = n(A) + n(C)$. However, A and B have two elements in common $(n(A \cup B) = 2)$ so the sum $n(A) + n(B)$ counts those elements twice; by subtracting $n(A \cap B)$ we get $n(A \cup B)$. **33. (a)** Distributive property of multiplication over addition **(c)** Commutative property of addition **34. (a)** $10 - 3 = 7, 10 - 7 = 3$

Problem Set 3.2   (page 180)

1.   0   **5. (a)** 108 **(c)** 5 **(e)** 125 **6. (a)** 153 **(c)** 6
1   **(e)** 216 **7. (a)** 591 **(c)** 12 **(e)** 1728
2   **8. (a)** 2422_{five} **(c)** 10_{five} **9. (a)** 1330_{six} **(c)** 10_{six}
3   **10. (a)** 1707_{twelve} **(c)** 100_{twelve}
4   **11. (a)**
10
11
12
13
14
20
21
22
23
24
30
31
32
33
34
40
41
42
43
44   **(c) (i)** 11000_{two} **(ii)** 10010_{two} **(iii)** 10_{two} **(iv)** 1000_{two}
100 **13. (a)** $100{,}000{,}000_{\text{two}}$ **14. (a)** $7_{\text{ten}} = 111_{\text{two}}$,
$2^3 = 8$, and row $n = 7$ has eight odd entries.
15. (a) 000, 100, 010, 110, 001, 101, 011, 111 Append a 0 onto the end of the four 2-digit sequences, then append a 1 onto the end of the four 2-digit sequences. **(c)** 32
16. (a) 0, 1, 2, 3, 4, 5, 6, 7 **(c)** The whole numbers from 0 to $2^n - 1$. There are 2^n of these whole numbers, each with a different n-digit base two representation corresponding to one of the n-digit sequences of 0s and 1s.
17. (a) $2 \cdot 2 \cdot 2 = 2^3 = 8$ **(b)** 8

One Thousand Twenty-Fours	Five Hundred Twelves	Two Hundred Fifty-Sixes		
1024	512	256		
2^{10}	2^9	2^8		
One Hundred Twenty-Eights	Sixty-Fours	Thirty-Twos		
128	64	32		
2^7	2^6	2^5		
Sixteens	Eights	Fours	Twos	Units
16	8	4	2	1
2^4	2^3	2^2	2^1	2^0

18. (a) 000,   a purple rod

001,   a light green rod followed by a white rod

010,   two red rods

011,   a red rod followed by two white rods

100,   a white rod followed by a light green rod

101,   a white rod, followed by a red rod, followed by a white rod

110,   two white rods followed by a red rod

111,   three white rods

As shown here , there are three places a 4-train may or may not be broken into separate cars. A particular train is formed by deciding to remove a dotted line (choose 0) or make the dotted line solid (choose 1). Since there are two choices for each dotted line, there are $2 \cdot 2 \cdot 2 = 2^3 = 8$ possible different trains.
21. (a) $51 \div 3 = 17, 51 \div 17 = 3$
22. (a) $11 \times 31 = 341, 341 \div 31 = 11$ **24. (a)** $n + 6$

JUST FOR FUN   What's the Difference?   (page 193)

91	95	42	62	74
$-\ 19$	$-\ 59$	$-\ 24$	$-\ 26$	$-\ 47$
72	36	18	36	27
61	82	81	32	54
$-\ 16$	$-\ 28$	$-\ 18$	$-\ 23$	$-\ 45$
45	54	63	9	9

(a) All answers are evenly divisible by 9. **(b)** Yes. The tens digit in the answer is 1 less than the difference between the digits in the subtrahend (the top number) in each subtraction problem and the units digit is 9 minus the tens digit. **(c)** In each case the sum of the digits is 9.

Problem Set 3.3   (page 193)

1. (a)

$36 + 75 = 111$

2. (a)   23
$+ 44$
7
60
67

5. (b)

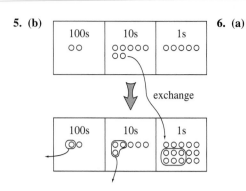

$275 - 136 = 139$

9. In these problems, we must exchange 60 seconds for one minute and 60 minutes for one hour or vice versa.

(a)   3 hours, 24 minutes, 54 seconds
+ 2 hours, 47 minutes, 38 seconds
5 hours, 71 minutes, 92 seconds = 5 hours,
72 minutes,
32 seconds
= 6 hours,
12 minutes,
32 seconds

(c)   5 hours, 24 minutes, 54 seconds
− 2 hours, 47 minutes, 38 seconds
4 hours, 84 minutes, 54 seconds
− 2 hours, 47 minutes, 38 seconds
2 hours, 37 minutes, 16 seconds

11. (a)   3′ 8″
4′ 2″
6′10″
+ 5′11″
18′31″ = 20′7″

13. (a)   0
1
2
3
10
11
12
13
20
21
22
23
30
31
32
33

15. (a) 1012 **(c)** 2120 **(e)** 111 **(g)** 113

16. (a)   6763 **(c)**   881 **(e)**   4002
+ 5519   + 362   − 1843
12,282   1243   2159

17. (a)   2437 **(c)**   3891
281   2493
+ 3476   + 5125
6194   11,509

18. (a)   835 **(c)**   7342
− 241   − 6534
594   808

19. (a) five **(c)** seven or greater **(e)** seven
(g) twelve

22. (a) $1 \cdot s = 19{,}998$ $6 \cdot s = 119{,}988$
$2 \cdot s = 39{,}996$ $7 \cdot s = 139{,}986$
$3 \cdot s = 59{,}994$ $8 \cdot s = 159{,}984$
$4 \cdot s = 79{,}992$ $9 \cdot s = 179{,}982$
$5 \cdot s = 99{,}990$ $10 \cdot s = 199{,}980$
(d) $14 \cdot s = 279{,}972$ **(f)** Arithmetic
$23 \cdot s = 459{,}954$
$32 \cdot s = 639{,}936$

6. (a)   7 8
− 3 5
4 3

24. (a) $1001 \div 91 = 11$, $1001 \div 11 = 91$, $91 \times 11 = 1001$
25. (a) $143 \times 7 = 1001$, $1001 \div 143 = 7$
27. (a) $A \cup B \cup C = \{1, 2, 3, 4, 5, 6, 7, 8\}$
$A \cap B = \{2, 4\}$
$A \cap C = \{3, 4, 5\}$
$B \cap C = \{4, 6\}$
$A \cap B \cap C = \{4\}$

JUST FOR FUN   What's the Sum?   (page 205)

91	95	42	62	74
19	59	24	26	47
110	154	66	88	121

61	82	81	32	54
16	28	18	23	45
77	110	99	55	99

(a) All the divisions come out even. **(b)** Yes. If the sum of the digits of the top number is d and $d < 10$, then the decimal representation of the sum in question is dd; that is 66, or 55, or whatever. If the sum of the two digits of the top number is the 2-digit number st, then the sum in question is $s(s + t)t$; that is $1(1 + 4)4 = 154$, $1(1 + 1)1 = 121$, and so on.

Problem Set 3.4   (page 206)

1. (a)

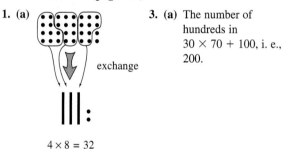

$4 \times 8 = 32$

3. (a) The number of hundreds in $30 \times 70 + 100$, i. e., 200.

5. (a) Distributive property of multiplication over addition
(c) Associative property of addition

6.

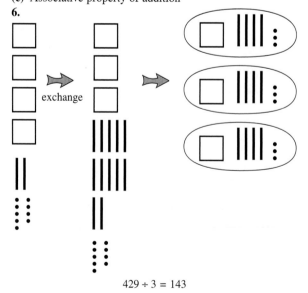

$429 \div 3 = 143$

9. (a) $27 = 4 \cdot 6 + 3$

10. (a)
$$
\begin{array}{r}
21 \\
1 \\
20 \\
351\overline{)7425} \\
7020 \\
\hline
405 \\
351 \\
\hline
54
\end{array}
$$
$7425 = 351 \cdot 21 + 54$

11. (a) $\dfrac{1\ 7\ 4 \text{ R } 3}{5\overline{)8\ ^3 7\ ^2 3}}$ **14. (a)** $\begin{array}{r} 23 \\ \times\ 3 \\ \hline 124 \end{array}$

15. (a)
$$
\begin{array}{r}
31 \quad \text{R } 2 \\
4\overline{)231} \\
22 \\
\hline
11 \\
4 \\
\hline
2
\end{array}
$$

17. (a) $34 \cdot 54 = (17 \cdot 2) \cdot 54 = 17 \cdot (2 \cdot 54) = 17 \cdot 108$ since 2 evenly divides 34. **19. (a)** Yes. This is simply a rearrangement of the rows in the usual algorithm. Thus, we usually write

$$
\begin{array}{r}
374 \\
23 \\
\hline
1122 \\
748 \\
\hline
8602
\end{array}
$$

Here we multiply by 20 first and then 3 to obtain

$$
\begin{array}{r}
374 \\
\times\ 23 \\
\hline
748 \\
1122 \\
\hline
8602
\end{array}
$$

(b)
$$
\begin{array}{r}
285 \\
\times\ 362 \\
\hline
855 \\
1710 \\
570 \\
\hline
103{,}170
\end{array}
$$

20. (a) $1256_{\text{seven}}, 1 \cdot 7^3 + 2 \cdot 7^2 + 5 \cdot 7 + 6 = 482_{\text{ten}}$
(c) $111100010_{\text{two}}, 1 \cdot 2^8 + 1 \cdot 2^7 + 1 \cdot 2^6 + 1 \cdot 2^5 + 1 \cdot 2 = 482_{\text{ten}}$ **21. (a)** $\begin{array}{r} 7531 \\ \times\ 9 \\ \hline 67{,}779 \end{array}$ **25. (a)** 912,000

27. (a) Without clearing the calculator and reentering the numbers after the equals signs we obtain the following results.

$\boxed{\text{ON/AC}}\ 276{,}523\ \boxed{\div}\ 511\ \boxed{=}\ 541.1409\ \boxed{-}\ 541\ \boxed{=}$
$0.1409002\ \boxed{\times}\ 511\ \boxed{=}\ 71.999997.$

Therefore, $q = 541$ and $r = 72$. To check, note that $541 \cdot 511 + 72 = 276{,}523$. **28. (a)** $141{,}111_{\text{five}}$
(c) 3419_{twelve}

Actually, with the *Math Explorer,* all you have to enter is
$\boxed{\text{ON/AC}}\ 5781\ \boxed{\text{INT}\div}\ 5\ \boxed{=}\ \boxed{=}\ \boxed{=}\ \boxed{=}\ \boxed{=}\ \boxed{=}$ to write 5781_{ten} in base five and similarly for other bases. You should repeatedly press the $\boxed{=}$ key until you obtain a quotient of 0.

30. (a)
$$
\begin{array}{rl}
634 = & 6 \text{ hundreds} + 3 \text{ tens} + 4 \text{ ones} \\
+\ 163 = & 1 \text{ hundred } + 6 \text{ tens} + 3 \text{ ones} \\
\hline
= & 7 \text{ hundreds} + 9 \text{ tens} + 7 \text{ ones} \\
= & 797
\end{array}
$$

(c)
$$
\begin{array}{rl}
363 = & 3 \text{ hundreds} + 6 \text{ tens} + 3 \text{ ones} \\
+\ 532 = & 5 \text{ hundreds} + 3 \text{ tens} + 2 \text{ ones} \\
\hline
= & 8 \text{ hundreds} + 9 \text{ tens} + 5 \text{ ones} \\
= & 895
\end{array}
$$

(e)
$$
\begin{array}{rl}
725 = & 7 \text{ hundreds} + 2 \text{ tens} + 5 \text{ ones} \\
-\ 413 = & -(4 \text{ hundreds} + 1 \text{ ten } + 3 \text{ ones}) \\
\hline
= & 3 \text{ hundreds} + 1 \text{ ten } + 2 \text{ ones} \\
= & 312
\end{array}
$$

31. (a)
$$
\begin{array}{rl}
374 = & 3 \text{ hundreds} + \ 7 \text{ tens} + 4 \text{ ones} \\
+\ 483 = & 4 \text{ hundreds} + \ 8 \text{ tens} + 3 \text{ ones} \\
\hline
= & 7 \text{ hundreds} + 15 \text{ tens} + 7 \text{ ones} \\
= & 8 \text{ hundreds} + \ 5 \text{ tens} + 7 \text{ ones} \\
= & 857
\end{array}
$$

(c)
$$
\begin{array}{rl}
724 = & 7 \text{ hundreds } + 2 \text{ tens} + \ 4 \text{ ones} \\
+\ 532 = & 5 \text{ hundreds } + 3 \text{ tens} + \ 2 \text{ ones} \\
\hline
= & 12 \text{ hundreds } + 5 \text{ tens} + \ 6 \text{ ones} \\
= & 1 \text{ thousand } + 2 \text{ hundreds} + 5 \text{ tens} + 6 \text{ ones} \\
= & 1256
\end{array}
$$

(e)
$$
\begin{array}{rl}
367 = & 3 \text{ hundreds} + 6 \text{ tens} + 7 \text{ ones} \\
-\ 249 = & -(2 \text{ hundreds} + 4 \text{ tens} + 9 \text{ ones}) \\
\hline
367 = & 3 \text{ hundreds} + 5 \text{ tens} + 17 \text{ ones} \\
-\ 249 = & -(2 \text{ hundreds} + 4 \text{ tens} + \ 9 \text{ ones}) \\
\hline
= & 1 \text{ hundred } + 1 \text{ ten } + \ 8 \text{ ones} \\
= & 118
\end{array}
$$

32. (a)
$$
\begin{array}{rl}
213 = & 2 \text{ twenty-fives} + 1 \text{ five } + 3 \text{ ones} \\
+\ 131 = & 1 \text{ twenty-five } + 3 \text{ fives} + 1 \text{ one} \\
\hline
= & 3 \text{ twenty-fives} + 4 \text{ fives} + 4 \text{ ones} \\
= & 344_{\text{five}}
\end{array}
$$

(c)
$$
\begin{array}{rl}
142 = & 1 \text{ twenty-five } + 4 \text{ fives} + \ 2 \text{ ones} \\
+\ 123 = & 1 \text{ twenty-five } + 2 \text{ fives} + \ 3 \text{ ones} \\
\hline
= & 2 \text{ twenty-fives} + 6 \text{ fives} + \ 5 \text{ ones} \\
= & 2 \text{ twenty-fives} + 1 \text{ twenty-five} + 1 \text{ five} + \\
& 1 \text{ five} + 0 \text{ ones} \\
= & 3 \text{ twenty-fives} + 2 \text{ fives} + 0 \text{ ones} \\
= & 320_{\text{five}}
\end{array}
$$

(e)
$$
\begin{array}{rl}
344 = & 3 \text{ twenty-fives} + 4 \text{ fives} + 4 \text{ ones} \\
-\ 232 = & -(2 \text{ twenty-fives} + 3 \text{ fives} + 2 \text{ ones}) \\
\hline
= & 1 \text{ twenty-five } + 1 \text{ five } + 2 \text{ ones} \\
= & 112_{\text{five}}
\end{array}
$$

34. (a) 112 **(c)** 241 **(e)** 233 **(g)** 12 R 13

Problem Set 3.5   (page 221)

1. (c) 92 **(e)** 240 **2. (c)** 138 **(e)** 576 **3. (a)** 787
(e) 1026 **4. (a)** 240,000 **5. (a)** 900 **(c)** 27,000,000
8. (a) 52,000 **(c)** 49,000 **(e)** 13,000 **9. (a)** 90,000
10. (a) 750 **12. (a)** 3 **13. (a)** 27,451
15. (a) $(24) \cdot (678) = 16{,}272$ **(c)** $(2467) \cdot (8) = 19{,}736$
16. (a) $(88) + 8 + 8 + 8 + 8 + 8 + 8 = 136$
(c) $(888) + 8 + 8 + 8 + 8 + 8 = 928$
17. (a) $(844{,}422) \div 1 = 844{,}422$
(c) $(84) \div (44 \div (22 \div 1)) = 42$

24. (a)
```
    2742
    415
    6943
  + 2718
   12,818
```
25. (a)
```
    2734
  − 2643
      91
```
26. (a)
```
    347
     42
    694
   1388
  14,574
```

Problem Set 3.6   (page 237)

1. (a) 641 **(c)** 101,388 **(e)** 770 **(g)** 770 **(i)** 237
2. (a) 98,915 **(c)** 32 **3. (a)** 49 **(c)** 13 **4. (a)** 841 **(c)** 33
5. (a) $\boxed{\text{ON/AC}}$ $\boxed{(}$ 784 $\boxed{\sqrt{\ }}$ $\boxed{-}$ 91 $\boxed{\div}$ 13 $\boxed{)}$ $\boxed{\div}$
$\boxed{(}$ 8 $\boxed{\times}$ 49 $\boxed{-}$ 11 $\boxed{\times}$ 35 $\boxed{)}$ $\boxed{=}$
7. (a)
$1831 - (17 \times 28) + 34$ **13.** 390
16. (a) The following algorithm generates the Lucas
numbers. We show at each step the Entry, the value of x in
the display, and the value, M, in the memory. The Lucas

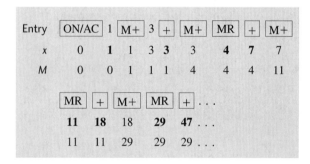

Entry	$\boxed{\text{ON/AC}}$	1	$\boxed{\text{M+}}$	3	$\boxed{+}$	$\boxed{\text{M+}}$	$\boxed{\text{MR}}$	$\boxed{+}$	$\boxed{\text{M+}}$
x	0	**1**	1	**3**	**3**	3	**4**	**7**	7
M	0	0	1	1	1	4	4	4	11

	$\boxed{\text{MR}}$	$\boxed{+}$	$\boxed{\text{M+}}$	$\boxed{\text{MR}}$	$\boxed{+}$	...
	11	**18**	18	**29**	**47**	...
	11	11	29	29	29	...

numbers are printed in bold.
17. (a) $(1 + \sqrt{5})/2$ The computed number is located in
both the display and the memory.
20. (a) To compute $y = \sqrt{5 \cdot 2^2 - 4}$, for example, we
enter the string $\boxed{\text{ON/AC}}$ 5 $\boxed{\times}$ 2 $\boxed{x^2}$ $\boxed{-}$ 4 $\boxed{=}$ $\boxed{\sqrt{\ }}$ to
obtain 4. Since this is a whole number, we enter it in the
table below the x-value 2. Completing the table, we obtain
the results shown.

x	1	2	3	4	5	6	7	8
y	1	4			11			

23. $17 + 18 = 35; 35 - 17 = 18; 35 - 18 = 17$
25. $11 \cdot 27 = 297; 297 \div 27 = 11; 297 \div 11 = 27$

27.

5 · 7 = 35

Chapter 3 Review Exercises   (page 241)

1. (a) 2353 **(b)** 58,331 **(c)** 1998 **2.**

3. Exchange 30 units for 3 strips, then exchange all 30 strips
for 3 mats. The result is 8 mats, 0 strips, and 2 units.
4. (a) 45_{ten} **(b)** 181_{ten} **(c)** 417_{ten}
5. (a) 2122_{five} **(b)** 100011111_{two} **(c)** 560_{seven}
6.

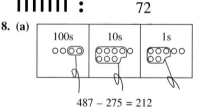

7. (a)
```
   42
 + 54
    6
   90
   96
```
(b)
```
   47
 + 35
   12
   70
   82
```
(c)
```
   59
 + 63
   12
  110
  122
```

8. (a)

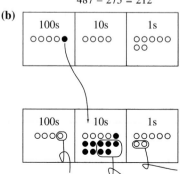

$487 - 275 = 212$

(b)

$547 - 152 = 395$

9. (a)
```
    2433
 +   141
    3124
```
(b)
```
    2433
 -   141
    2242
```
(c)
```
      243
  ×    42
     1041
    21320
   22,411
```

10. (a)
```
     357
  ×    4
      28
     200
    1200
    1428
```
(b)
```
     642
  ×   27
      14
     280
    4200
      40
     800
   12000
   17,334
```
11. (a)
```
      127
        7
       20
      100
  7)895
      700
      195
      140
       55
       49
        6
```
(b)
```
          79
           9
          70
  347)27,483
       24,290
        3193
        3123
          70
```

12. (a)
```
    5487 R 1
  5)27,436
```
(b)
```
    4948 R 0
  8)39,584
```

13. (a) 2121_{five} **(b)** 2023221_{five} **14.**
```
  42     35
  21     70
  10    140
   5    280
   2    560
   1   1120
       1470
```

15. (a) 300,000 **(b)** 270,000 **(c)** 275,000

16. 657 rounds to 700, 439 rounds to 400, 1657 rounds to 2000 and 23 rounds to 20. Thus,

(a) $657 + 439$ is approximately $700 + 400 = 1100$. The actual sum is 1096.

(b) $657 - 439$ is approximately $700 - 400 = 300$. The actual answer is 218.

(c) $657 \cdot 439$ is approximately $700 \cdot 400 = 280,000$. The actual answer is 288,423.

(d) $1657 \div 23$ is approximately $2000 \div 20 = 100$. The actual answer to the nearest hundredth is 72.04.

17. 2 **18. (a)** 8088 **(b)** 49,149 **19. (a)** 11, 18, 29, 47 **(b)** The integer nearest $[(1 + \sqrt{5})/2] \cdot L_n$ is L_{n+1} for all integers n. **(c)** No. It does not hold for $L_1, L_2,$ and L_3. **(d)** The nearest integer to $[(1 + \sqrt{5})/2] \cdot L_n$ is L_{n+1} for $n \geq 4$.

Chapter 3 Test   (page 242)

1. (a) 197_{ten} **(b)** 207_{ten} **(c)** 558_{ten}
2. (a) 2111_{five} **(b)** 100011001_{two} **(c)** $1E5_{\text{twelve}}$
3. (a) 340 **(b)** 144 **(c)** 23111

4.

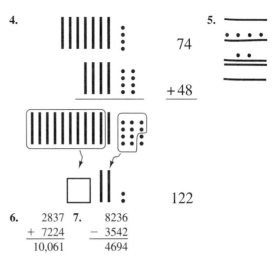

74
+48
122

5.

6.
```
    2837
 +  7224
   10,061
```
7.
```
    8236
 -  3542
    4694
```

8. (a) 3,000,000 **(b)** 3,400,000 **(c)** 3,380,000 **(d)** 3,377,000 **9.** 4800 **10.**
```
    751
  ×  93
  69,843
```
11.
```
    468
  ×  20
   9360
```

12. (a) 1, 2, 5, 12 **(b)** 29, 70 **(c)** $f_n = 2f_{n-1} + f_{n-2}$ for $n \geq 3$.

13. (a) 1 and 1
9 and 9
36 and 36
100 and 100

(b) 1, 3, 6, 10 **(c)** $\left(\dfrac{n(n + 1)}{2}\right)^2$ **14.** 1575 **15.** 1,464,843

16. Answers may vary. One possibility is as follows:

| ON/AC | 2 | M+ | 5 | M+ | $x \circlearrowright M$ | M+ |
$x \circlearrowright M$ | M+ | . . .

Chapter 4

JUST FOR FUN   The Chinese Remainder Problem (page 256)

Use the constant function of your calculator to find the following arithmetic sequences. Positive integers having remainder 2 when divided by 5:

2, 7, 12, 17, 22, 27, 32, 37, 42, 47, 52, 57, 62, 67, 72, 77, 82, 87, 92, 97, 102, 107, 112, 117, 122, 127, 132, 137, 142, 147, 152, 157, 162, . . .

Positive integers having remainder 3 when divided by 7:

3, 10, 17, 24, 31, 38, 45, 52, 59, 66, 73, 80, 87, 94, 101, 108, 115, 122, 129, 136, 143, 150, 157, 164, 171, . . .

Positive integers having remainder 4 when divided by 9:

4, 13, 22, 31, 40, 49, 58, 67, 76, 85, 94, 103, 112, 121, 130, 139, 148, 157, 166, 175, . . .

The first number appearing in all three lists is 157. The second least integer having this property is 472.

Problem Set 4.1 (page 258)

1. (a)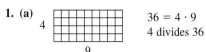
$36 = 4 \cdot 9$
4 divides 36

3. (a) 0, 8, 16, 24, 32, 40, 48, 56, 64, 72

5. (a) 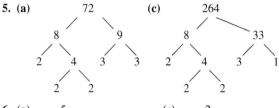 **(c)**

6. (a)
$$5\overline{)25}$$
$$2\overline{)50}$$
$$2\overline{)100}$$
$$7\overline{)700}$$
$700 = 7 \cdot 2 \cdot 2 \cdot 5 \cdot 5$

(c)
$$3\overline{)6}$$
$$3\overline{)18}$$
$$5\overline{)90}$$
$$5\overline{)450}$$
$450 = 5 \cdot 5 \cdot 3 \cdot 3 \cdot 2$

7. (a) 1, 2, 3, 4, 6, 8, 12, 16, 24, 48
8. (a) $136 = 2^3 \cdot 17^1$, $102 = 2^1 \cdot 3^1 \cdot 17^1$
(b) The divisors of 136 are
$2^0 \cdot 17^0 = 1, 2^1 \cdot 17^0 = 2, 2^2 \cdot 17^0 = 4, 2^3 \cdot 17^0 = 8$
$2^0 \cdot 17^1 = 17, 2^1 \cdot 17^1 = 34, 2^2 \cdot 17^1 = 68, 2^3 \cdot 17^1 = 136$
9. (a) $48 = 2^4 \cdot 3^1$ **(c)** $2250 = 2^1 \cdot 3^2 \cdot 5^3$
10. (a) Yes, because $28 = 2^2 \cdot 7^1$ so all the prime factors of 28 appear in a and to at least as high a power. **(c)** $2^1 \cdot 7^2$
13. No. For example, $10 = 2 \cdot 5$ with 2 and 5 both primes. Yet $5 > 3.162 \cdots = \sqrt{10}$.
14. (a) $1, 3, 3^2 = 9$ **15. (a)** $496 = 2^4 \cdot 31^1$
(b) $1 + 2 + 4 + 8 + 16 + 31 + 62 + 124 + 248 = 496$
16. (a) deficient **(b)** abundant
19. (a) True. $n \cdot 0 = 0$ for every natural number n.
(c) True. $1 \cdot n = n$ for every natural number n.
(e) False. $0 \div 0 = q$ if, and only if, $0 \cdot q = 0$ for a unique integer q. However, this is true for *every* integer q.
21. Yes. If $p \mid bc$ then p must appear in the prime factorization of the product bc and hence in the prime factorization of b or c. But then $p \mid b$ or $p \mid c$ as claimed.
24. (a) $N_4 = N_2 \cdot 101, N_6 = N_2 \cdot 10101, N_8 = 11 \cdot 1010101$
26. (a) No. **(c)** Yes. **30. (a)** $2^2 \cdot 137^1$ **(c)** $2^1 \cdot 137^1$
(e) $(2^1 \cdot 137^1)$ divides $(2^2 \cdot 137^1)$ and $(2^3 \cdot 3^2 \cdot 13^1)$ divides $(2^3 \cdot 3^2 \cdot 7^2 \cdot 13^1)$ **31. (a)** $2^2 \cdot 3^3 \cdot 7^2 \cdot 13^2$ **(c)** $3^4 \cdot 5^6$
(e) The exponents in the prime power representation are even. **32. (a)** False. The sum of two odd natural numbers is an even natural number. **(c)** True. $a + b = b + a$ if a and b are any natural numbers. **(e)** True. $a + (b + c) = (a + b) + c$ if a, b, and c are any natural numbers.
(g) True. $a(b + c) = ab + ac$ if a, b, and c are any natural numbers. **(i)** True. 1 is an element of S.
33. (a) 299 **34. (a)** 19, 23, 27 **(c)** 15, 21, 28
(e) 48, 96, 192 **35. (a)** 4082

Problem Set 4.2 (page 268)

1. (a) Divisible by 2 and 3 **(c)** Divisible by 5
2. (a) 1554 **(c)** None **3. (a)** Divisible by 7 and 13
(c) Divisible by 7 **4. (a)** None **(c)** None
9. (a) For any palindrome with an even number of digits, the digits in the odd positions are the same as the digits in the even positions, but with the order reversed. Thus, the difference of the sums of the digits in the even and odd position is zero which is divisible by 11. **10.** When testing for divisibility by 7, 11, and 13 the digits of the number are broken up into 3-digit groups. If a number has form $abc,abc,$ then the difference in the sums of the 3-digit numbers in odd positions and even positions will be zero, which is divisible by each of 7, 11, and 13. **13.** No. He or she could have made other kinds of errors that by chance resulted in the record being out of balance by an amount that is a multiple of 9. **14. (e)** No. **16. (a)** $2^7 \cdot 3^2 \cdot 7^1$
17. (a) 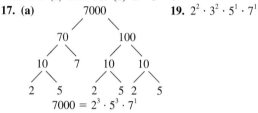 **19.** $2^2 \cdot 3^2 \cdot 5^1 \cdot 7^1$

JUST FOR FUN Making a Chain (page 270)

Four. Open all four of the links in one section of chain. These can then be used to connect the remaining five sections of chain into a single chain of 24 links.

JUST FOR FUN A Weighty Matter (page 271)

If the basketball weighs 21 ounces plus half its own weight, then 21 ounces must be half the weight of the ball. Therefore, the basketball weighs 42 ounces.

Problem Set 4.3 (page 279)

1. (a) 3 **2. (a)** 216 **3. (a)** $GCD(24, 27) \cdot LCM(24, 27) = 3 \cdot 216 = 648 = 24 \cdot 27$
4. (a) $GCD(r, s) = 2^1 \cdot 3^1 \cdot 5^2 = 150$, $LCM(r, s) = 2^2 \cdot 3^3 \cdot 5^3 = 13,500$
7. (a) $GCD(a, b, c) = 2^0 \cdot 3^1 \cdot 5^1 \cdot 7^0 = 15$, $LCM(a, b, c) = 2^2 \cdot 3^3 \cdot 5^3 \cdot 7^1 = 94,500$
8. (a) $D_{18} = \{1, 2, 3, 6, 18\}$
$D_{24} = \{1, 2, 3, 4, 6, 8, 12, 24\}$
$D_{12} = \{1, 2, 3, 4, 6, 12\}$
$GCD (18, 24, 12) = 6$
$M_{18} = \{18, 36, 54, 72, 90, \ldots\}$
$M_{24} = \{24, 48, 72, 96, \ldots\}$
$M_{12} = \{12, 24, 36, 48, 60, 72, 84, \ldots\}$
$LCM (18, 24, 12) = 72$
10. (a) $GCD(24, 18) = 6$, $GCD(GCD(24, 18), 12) = GCD(6, 12) = 6$
$LCM(24, 18) = 72$, $LCM(LCM(24, 18), 12) = LCM(72, 12) = 72$
The final results are the same.

11. (a) The 1, 3, and 9 rods **(d)** The 1, 2, 3, 6, 9, and 18 trains. **12. (a)** 12 **(b)** 12 **16. (a)** 18; 76; 1364 **(c)** No. $F_{19} = 4181 = 37 \cdot 113$ **(h)** If $GCD(F_{16}, F_{20}) = 4$, then the conjecture must be false.
18. (a) 1224 sec, 1224 = LCM(72, 68)
20. (a) LCM(220, 264) = 1320; LCM(220, 275) = 1100; LCM(264, 275) = 6600 **(c)** GCD(220, 264) = 44; GCD(220, 275) = 55; GCD(264, 275) = 11
21. (a) 3 **22. (a)** 720 **23. (a)** $205,800 = 2^3 \cdot 3^1 \cdot 5^2 \cdot 7^3$, $31,460 = 2^2 \cdot 5^1 \cdot 11^2 \cdot 13^1$, $25,840 = 2^4 \cdot 5^1 \cdot 17^1 \cdot 19^1$
25. (a)

n	$n^2 - 81n + 1681$	Prime?
1	1601	yes
2	1523	yes
3	1447	yes
4	1373	yes
5	1301	yes

(c) No. If a conjecture is true for several cases, it does not mean it is true for *every* case. **(e)** The conjecture may seem more probable, but we still cannot say if it is *always* true.
26. (a) No. If $p \mid a$ and $p \nmid b$ then $p \nmid (a + b)$.
27. (a) No. If $p \mid a$ and $p \nmid b$ then $p \nmid (a + b)$.

Problem Set 4.4   (page 293)

1. (a) 2 **(c)** 0 **(e)** 8 **2. (a)** 2 **(c)** 9 **(e)** 6
3. (a) 2 **(c)** 8 **(e)** 3 **4. (a)** 5 **(c)** 3
5. (a) $9 -_{12} 7 = 9 +_{12} 5 = 2$ **(c)** $5 -_{12} 9 = 5 +_{12} 3 = 8$
(e) $2 -_{12} 11 = 2 +_{12} 1 = 3$ **6. (a)** 11 **(c)** 0 **(e)** 0
7. (a) 11 **(c)** undefined **(e)** 9 **8. (a)** 1, 5, 7, 11
10. (a) 2 **(c)** 3 **(e)** 1 **(g)** 4 **(i)** 0 **(k)** 4
11. (a) $0; n +_5 0 = n$ for $n = 0, 1, 2, 3, 4$.
12. (a) 4, 3, 2, 1, 0 **13. (a)** 1, 2, 3, 4
14. (a) $4 \div_{12} 7 = 4$ **(c)** $3 \div_5 2 = 4$ **(e)** $2 \div_5 4 = 3$
(g) $4 \times_{12} 7^{-1} = 4 \times_{12} 7 = 4$ **(i)** $3 \times_5 2^{-1} = 3 \times_5 3 = 4$
(k) $2 \times_5 4^{-1} = 2 \times_5 4 = 3$
15. (c) $y +_{12} 2 = 3 \times_{12} 11$
$\qquad y +_{12} 2 = 9$
$\qquad\qquad y = 9 -_{12} 2$
$\qquad\qquad y = 7$

16. (a)

17. (a) The bar code gives the digits: 1057486537. This code is incorrect because the sum of the digits is 46—not a multiple of 10. **18. (a)** 3 **(c)** 3 **(e)** 4 **(g)** 4

19. (a)

n	$2^n - 2$	$2^n - 2$ in n-hour clock arithmetic
2	2	0
3	6	0
4	14	2
5	30	0
6	62	2
7	126	0
8	254	6
9	510	6
10	1022	2
11	2046	0
12	4094	2
13	8190	0

25. (a) (i) is incorrect. (ii) is correct. **26. (a)** 1
30. (a) $D_{60} = \{1, 2, 3, 4, 5, 6, 10, 12, 15, 20, 30, 60\}$
$D_{150} = \{1, 2, 3, 5, 6, 10, 15, 25, 30, 50, 75, 150\}$
So GCD(60, 150) = 30.
31. (a)

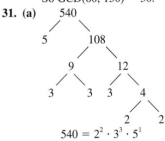

$540 = 2^2 \cdot 3^3 \cdot 5^1$
32. (a) $540 = 2^2 \cdot 3^3 \cdot 5^1, 600 = 2^3 \cdot 3^1 \cdot 5^2$

Chapter 4 Review Exercises   (page 298)

1.

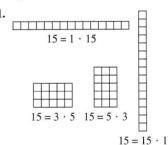

$15 = 1 \cdot 15$
$15 = 3 \cdot 5$ $15 = 5 \cdot 3$
$15 = 15 \cdot 1$

2.

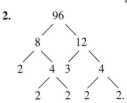

3. (a) $D_{60} = \{1, 2, 3, 4, 5, 6, 10, 12, 15, 20, 30, 60\}$
(b) $D_{72} = \{1, 2, 3, 4, 6, 8, 9, 12, 18, 24, 36, 72\}$
(c) $D_{60} \cap D_{72} = \{1, 2, 3, 4, 6, 12\}$, so GCD(60, 72) = 12.
4. (a) $1200 = 2^4 \cdot 3^1 \cdot 5^2$ **(b)** $2940 = 2^2 \cdot 3^1 \cdot 5^1 \cdot 7^2$
(c) GCD(1200, 2940) = $2^2 \cdot 3^1 \cdot 5^1 \cdot 7^0 = 60$
LCM(1200, 2940) = $2^4 \cdot 3^1 \cdot 5^2 \cdot 7^2 = 58,800$
5. Composite; $847 = 11 \times 77$. **6. (a)** Answers will vary.
For example, $15 = 3 \cdot 5$; $5 > \sqrt{15}$. **(b)** Yes. $3 \le \sqrt{15}$.
7. Answers will vary. For example, 8 divides 16 and 4
divides 16 but 32 does not divide 16. **8.** Since $n = 2536$,
the prime, 2, divides $3 \cdot 5 \cdot 7 + 11 \cdot 13 \cdot 17$.
9. (a) Divisible by 2, 5 **(b)** Divisible by 3, 11
(c) Divisible by 5 **(d)** Divisible by 5, 11
10. (a) Divisible by 11 **(b)** Divisible by 7, 13
(c) Divisible by 11, 13 **11. (a)** False **(b)** True **(c)** False
(d) True **12. (a)** $(1 + 4)(1 + 2) = 15$ **(b)** 1, 3, 7, 9, 21,
27, 49, 63, 81, 147, 189, 441, 567, 1323, 3969
13. $d = 5$ **14. (a)** $2^3 \cdot 3^5 \cdot 7^3 \cdot 11^3 \cdot 13^1 = 11,537,501,976$
(b) $2^2 \cdot 3^5 \cdot 7^2 \cdot 11^1 = 523,908$
15. (a) $D_{63} = \{1, 3, 7, 9, 21, 63\}$
     $D_{91} = \{1, 7, 13, 91\}$
     $D_{63} \cap D_{91} = \{1, 7\}$, so GCD(91, 63) = 7.
(b) $M_{63} = \{63, 126, 189, 252, 315, 378, 441, 504, 567, 630,$
                $693, 756, 819, 882, 945, 1008. \ldots\}$
$M_{91} = \{91, 182, 273, 364, 455, 546, 637, 728, 819,$
                                          $910, \ldots\}$
$M_{63} \cap M_{91} = \{819, 1638, \ldots\}$, so LCM(63, 91) = 819.
(c) $7 \cdot 819 = 5733 = 63 \cdot 91$ **16. (a)** $2 \cdot 11^2 = 242$
(b) $2^3 \cdot 3^2 \cdot 5^2 \cdot 7^1 \cdot 11^3 = 16,770,600$
17. (a) $12,100 \overline{)119,790}$ 9 R 10,890

$10,890 \overline{)12,100}$ 1 R 1210 $1210 \overline{)10,890}$ 9 R 0
Thus, GCD(119,790, 12,100) = 1210.
(b) LCM(119,790, 12,100) = 119,790 · 12,100/1210 =
1,197,900.
18. 2192 **19. (a)** 1 **(b)** 5 **(c)** 12 **(d)** Undefined
(e) 5 **(f)** 12 **(g)** Undefined **(h)** 3 **(i)** 3
20. (a) 4 **(b)** 1 **(c)** 2 **(d)** 4 **21.** 2, 4, 5, 6, 8, 10
22. (a) 9 **(b)** 3 **23. (a)** 80321 − 1589 **(b)** 60648 − 9960

Chapter 4 Test (page 299)

1. (a) F **(b)** T **(c)** T **(d)** F
2. (a)
                    8532
              /   \
          12   711
        /   \   /   \
       3   4   9   79
             / \   / \
            2   2   3   3

(b) $8532 = 2^2 \cdot 3^3 \cdot 79^1$ **(c)** 4266 **(d)** 17,064
3. (a) Divisible by 2, 3 **(b)** Divisible by 3
4. (a) 73 R 9494   1 R 4040
$13,534 \overline{)997,476}$ $9494 \overline{)13,534}$

---

     2 R 1414   2 R 1212
$4040 \overline{)9494}$ $1414 \overline{)4040}$

     1 R 202   6 R 0
$1212 \overline{)1414}$ $202 \overline{)1212}$

GCD(997,476, 13,534) = 202
(b) LCM(997,476, 13,534) = 997,476 · 13,534/202
                = 66,830,892
5. (a) No. The prime power representation of r contains two
7s, but the prime power representation of m contains only
one 7, so r does not divide m. **(b)** $(3 + 1)(2 + 1)(1 + 1)$
$(4 + 1) = 120$ **(c)** $2^2 \cdot 5^0 \cdot 7^1 \cdot 11^3 = 37,268$ **(d)** $2^3 \cdot 5^2 \cdot$
$7^2 \cdot 11^4 = 143,481,800$
6.

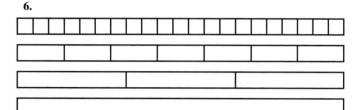

7. (a) 4 **(b)** 12 **(c)** 5 **(d)** 3 **(e)** 3 **(f)** 7
8. (a) $0 +_{10} 6 +_{10} 9 +_{10} 9 +_{10} 2 +_{10} 7 +_{10} 5 +_{10} 4 +_{10} 8 = 0$,
so the zip code is correct. **(b)** $8 +_{10} 4 +_{10} 2 +_{10} 3 +_{10} 2 +_{10}$
$7 +_{10} 6 +_{10} 1 +_{10} 2 = 5$, so the zip code is incorrect.
9. Since $533 = 3 \cdot 154 + 91$, $154 = 1 \cdot 91 + 63$,
$91 = 1 \cdot 63 + 28$, $63 = 2 \cdot 28 + 7$, and $28 = 4 \cdot 7$,
it follows that GCD(154, 553) = 7 and LCM(154, 553) =
$(154 \times 553) \div 7 = 12,166$. **10.** Since $\sqrt{281} \doteq 16.7$, we
must check for divisibility by 2, 3, 5, 7, 11, and 13. Standard
divisibility tests immediately rule out divisibility by 2, 3,
and 5. Also, $281 = 40 \cdot 7 + 1$, $281 = 11 \cdot 25 + 6$, and
$281 = 13 \cdot 21 + 8$. Therefore, 281 is a prime.

Chapter 5

Problem Set 5.1 (page 311)

1. Answers will vary. Two possibilities are shown in each
case. **(a)**   **(c)**

2. (a) ● ● **(c)** (no counters) **3. (a)**

(c) opp17 **4. (a)** At mailtime, you are delivered a check
for \$14. **6. (a)** −15
7. (a), (c), (e)

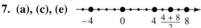

8. (a) 4 **(c)** 6 **9. (a)**

(c)

12. (a) 34 **(c)** 76   **13. (a)** 13, −13
15. (a) 4 red counters
16. (a) −12, −10, −8, −6, −4, −2, 0, 2, 4, 6, 8, 10, 12
18. (a) $\{n \mid n$ is an integer and $-12 \le n \le 12\}$
20. (a) 2^{20} **21. (a)** 100 black, 110 red **23. (a)** $2^5 = 32$
24. (a) 90 **(c)** 3,402,000
25. (a) No. The prime power representation of c contains
more 3s than the prime power representation of a.
26. (a) $1400 = 2^3 \cdot 5^2 \cdot 7^1$
27. (a)

$$
4554\overline{)5445} \quad 1\text{ R }891
$$

$$
891\overline{)4554} \quad 5\text{ R }99
$$

$$
99\overline{)891} \quad 9\text{ R }0
$$

GCD(4554, 5445) = 99

JUST FOR FUN   Choosing the Right Box   (page 321)

Note that there is a symmetry in the problem between apples
and oranges. Thus, it probably does not make sense to select
the piece of fruit from the box labeled "apples" or the box
labeled "oranges." We select from the box labeled "apples
and oranges." Since the box is mislabeled, if we obtain an
apple it contains only apples and should be so labeled. The
remaining boxes contain oranges only and a mixture of
apples and oranges. But each box is mislabeled. Thus, the
box labeled "oranges" should be relabeled "apples and
oranges" and the box labeled "apples and oranges" should
be relabeled "oranges." A similar analysis holds if on our
first selection we obtain an orange. Then the boxes should be
relabeled as shown.

apples and oranges → oranges
apples → apples and oranges
apples and oranges → apples

Problem Set 5.2   (page 330)

1. (a)

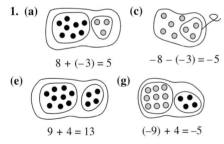

(c)

$8 + (-3) = 5$

$-8 - (-3) = -5$

(e)

$9 + 4 = 13$

(g)

$(-9) + 4 = -5$

2. (a) At mailtime you receive a bill for $27 and a bill for
$13. $(-27) + (-13) = -40$ **(c)** The mail carrier brings
you a check for $27 and a check for $13. $27 + 13 = 40.$
(e) At mailtime you receive a bill for $41 and a check for
$13. $(-41) + 13 = -28$ **(g)** At mailtime you receive a bill
for $13 and a check for $41. $(-13) + 41 = 28$
3. (a)

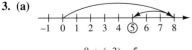

$8 + (-3) = 5$

(c)

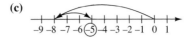

$-8 + 3 = -5$

(e)

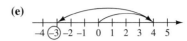

$4 + (-7) = -3$

(g)

$(-4) + 7 = 3$

4. (a) $13 + (-7)$ **(c)** $(-13) + (-7)$ **(e)** $3 + (-8)$
(g) $(-8) + (-13)$ **5. (a)** 40 **(c)** −27 **(e)** −135
(g) −135 **9. (a)** More; by $106. **11. (a)** $-117 < -24$
(c) $18 > 12$ **(e)** $-5 < 1$ **13. (a)** True **(c)** True
15. No. If $a \ge b$, then it is possible that $a = b$ and so $a > b$
is false. **17.** −6, −5, −4, −3, −2, −1, 0, 1, 2, 3, 4, 5, 6
19. (a) (i) 6 **(iii)** 15 **(b) (i)**

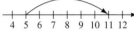

distance is 6

(iii)

distance is 15

20. (a) (i) $|7 + 2| = 9, |7| + |2| = 9$
(iii) $|7 + (-6)| = 1, |7| + |-6| = 13$
(v) $|6 + 0| = 6, |6| + |0| = 6$
22. (a)

3	−4	1
−2	0	2
−1	4	−3

23. (a)

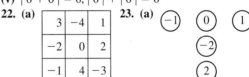

24. (a) $7 - (-3) = 10, (-3) - 7 = -10$
28. (a) $F_1 + F_3 + F_5 + F_7 = 1 + 2 + 5 + 13 = 21 = F_8$
$F_1 + F_3 + F_5 + F_7 + F_9 = 1 + 2 + 5 + 13 + 34 = 55 = F_{10}$
31. (a) Yes. $F_0 + F_1 = 0 + 1 = 1 = F_2$
32. (a) $101 + 3 = 104$
35. (a)

t	h
0	0
1	80
2	128
3	144
4	128
5	80
6	0
7	−112

38. (a) 50 **39. (a)** 1575 **(c)** −5909 **(e)** 2053
42. (a) Divisible by 3 **43. (a)** Divisible by 7, 13

JUST FOR FUN   Three on a Bike?   (page 337)

The problem is that 27 + 2 should *not* add to 30. Of the
$30, $25 is in the till, $2 is in the helper's pocket, and $3 has
been returned to the bikers. Alternatively, of the $27, $25 is
in the till and $2 is in the helper's pocket.

Problem Set 5.3   (page 341)

1. (a) 77 **(c)** −77 **(e)** 108 **(g)** −108 **(i)** 0
2. (a) 4 **(c)** −4 **(e)** −13 **(g)** 16 **(i)** 36
3. $(-25,753) \cdot (-11) = 283,283$
$283,283 \div (-11) = -25,753$
$283,283 \div (-25,753) = -11$
5. (a) Richer by $78; $6 \cdot 13 = 78$. **6. (a)** $6 \cdot 3 = 18$
8. (a) Multiplicative property of zero; Distributive property
of multiplication over addition; Definition of the additive
inverse.
9. (a)   **(c)**

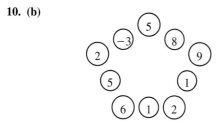

10. (b)

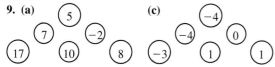

16. (a) $7 **(b)** $(-105) \div 15 = -7$. A loss of $105 shared
among 15 people results in each person losing $7.
18. (b) 59 **19. (a), (b)** The sequence of entries

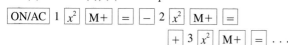

successively computes $s_1, s_2, s_3, \ldots$ and $a_1, a_2, a_3, \ldots$. After
each $\boxed{=}$ entry, the calculator will show the appropriate
entry in the a-sequence and will have the appropriate entry
in the s-sequence in memory. To see the s entry press
$\boxed{x \circ M}$ right after $\boxed{=}$. Then, to get on with the
calculation, press $\boxed{x \circ M}$ again and continue as before.
We thus compute the a and s entries in the following table.
The $3s \div a$ entries are computed separately afterward.

n	a_n	s_n	$3s_n \div a_n$
1	1	1	3
2	−3	5	−5
3	6	14	7
4	−10	30	−9
5	15	55	11
6	−21	91	−13

21. (b) 2,621,440 **22. (a)** 5, 12, 29, 70

Chapter 5 Review Exercises   (page 348)

1. (a) −1 **(b)** 5 **(c)** − 15, −13, −11, . . . , 11, 13, 15
2. (a) Richer by $12; 12 **(b)** Poorer by $37; −37
3. (a) 12 **(b)** −24 **4. (a)** Answers will vary. Any "drop"
that shows 5 more red counters than black counters
represents the integer −5. **(b)** Any "drop" that shows 6
more black counters than red counters represents the
integer 6. **5.** Answers will vary. **(a)** At mailtime you
receive a bill for $114 and a check for $29. **(b)** The mail
carrier brings you a bill for $19 and a check for $66.
6. (a) −44 **(b)** 61 **7.** $2 + (-4) = -2$
8. $(-1) - (-3) = 2$ **9. (a)** $45 + (-68) = -23$
(b) $45 - (-68) = 113$ **10. (a)** $6 + 3 = 9$
(b) $8 + (-4) = 4$ **(c)** $7 - 5 = 2$ **(d)** $3 - 9 = -6$
(e) $(-3) + (-4) = -7$ **(f)** $(-3) - (-7) = 4$
(g) $(-5) - 6 = -11$ **11. (a)** −2 **(b)** −22 **(c)** −32
(d) 12 **(e)** 20 **(f)** −4 **12. (a)** 27° below zero
(b) $(-15) - 12 = -27$ **13. (a)** $25
(b) $(-12) + 37 = 25$
14. (a)

(b) −9, −5, −2, 0, 2, 7 **(c)** $-9 + 4 = -5, -5 + 3 = -2$,
$-2 + 2 = 0, 0 + 2 = 2, 2 + 5 = 7$
15. (a) $3 \cdot 4 = 12$ **(b)** $3 \cdot (-4) = -12$
(c) $(-3) \cdot 4 = -12$ **(d)** $(-3) \cdot (-4) = 12$
16. (a)

$3 \cdot 0 = 0$	by the multiplicative property of 0
$3 \cdot [5 + (-5)] = 0$	since $5 + (-5) = 0$
$3 \cdot 5 + 3 \cdot (-5) = 0$	by the distributive property

(b)

$3 \cdot (-5) = -(3 \cdot 5)$	by the definition of the additive inverse

(c)

$0 \cdot (-5) = 0$	by the multiplicative property of 0
$[3 + (-3)] \cdot (-5) = 0$	since $3 + (-3) = 0$
$3 \cdot (-5) + (-3) \cdot (-5) = 0$	by the distributive property
$-(3 \cdot 5) + (-3) \cdot (-5) = 0$	since $3 \cdot (-5) = -(3 \cdot 5)$ by part (b)

(d) $(-3) \cdot (-5) = -[-(3 \cdot 5)] = 3 \cdot 5$ by the definition of the additive inverse since $-[-(3 \cdot 5)] = 3 \cdot 5$
17. (a) 56 **(b)** -56 **(c)** -56 **(d)** -7 **(e)** -12 **(f)** 12
18. (a) At mailtime you receive 7 checks, each for $12.
(b) The mail carrier takes away 7 checks, each for $13.
(c) The mail carrier takes away 7 bills, each for $13.
19. If d divides n, there is an integer c such that $dc = n$. But then $d \cdot (-c) = -n, (-d) \cdot (-c) = dc = n$, and $(-d) \cdot c = -dc = -n$. Thus, d divides $-n$, $-d$ divides n, and $-d$ divides $-n$. **20. (a)** 3 **(b)** 11 **21.** By the division algorithm, n must be of one of these forms: $6q$, $6q + 1$, $6q + 2$, $6q + 3$, $6q + 4$, or $6q + 5$. If n is not divisible by 2, however, then n cannot be of any of the forms $6q$, $6q + 2$ or $6q + 4$. Likewise, if n is not divisible by 3, n cannot be of the form $6q + 3$ either. Thus, there must be an integer q such that either $n = 6q + 1$ or $n = 6q + 5$.
Case 1 $n = 6q + 1$
$$n^2 - 1 = (6q + 1)^2 - 1$$
$$= (36q^2 + 12q + 1) - 1$$
$$= 36q^2 + 12q$$
$$= 12q(3q + 1)$$
If q is even, then 24 divides $12q$ and $n^2 - 1$ is divisible by 24. If q is odd, then $3q + 1$ is even, so again 24 divides $12q(3q + 1)$ and hence $n^2 - 1$ is divisible by 24.
Case 2 $n = 6q + 5$
$$n^2 - 1 = (6q + 5)^2 - 1$$
$$= (36q^2 + 60q + 25) - 1$$
$$= 36q^2 + 60q + 24$$
$$= 12(3q^2 + 5q + 2)$$
$$= 12(3q + 2)(q + 1)$$
If q is even, $3q + 2$ is even. If q is odd, $q + 1$ is even. In either case, it follows that $n^2 - 1$ is divisible by 24.

Chapter 5 Test   (page 350)

1. (a) -26 **(b)** 12 **(c)** 26 **(d)** -12 **(e)** -361 **(f)** -408
(g) -864 **(h)** 105 **(i)** 0
2. 2160, the same as LCM(240,54) **3.** Richer by $135; $(-5) \cdot (-27) = 135$
4. (a)

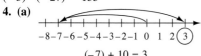

$(-7) + 10 = 3$

(b)

$10 - (-7) = 17$

(c)

$7 \cdot (-5) = -35$

5. At mailtime the mail carrier delivers a check for $7 and takes away a bill for $4. You are $11 richer.
6. $381; $129 + 341 - 13 - 47 - 29 = 381$
7. Poorer by $9; $(-27) \div 3 = -9$
8. (a) $-5, -3, -8, -11, -19, -30$ **(b)** $7, -5, 2, -3, -1, -4$ **(c)** $6, -8, -2, -10, -12, -22$
9. (a)
$$1 = 1$$
$$1 - 4 = -3$$
$$1 - 4 + 9 = 6$$
$$1 - 4 + 9 - 16 = -10$$
$$1 - 4 + 9 - 16 + 25 = 15$$
(b) $1 - 4 + \cdots + n^2 = t_n$ if n is odd.
$1 - 4 + \cdots - n^2 = -t_n$ if n is even.
10. (a) $-18, -17, -16, \ldots, -3, -2, -1, 0, 1, 2, 3, \ldots, 16, 17, 18.$ **(b)** Yes.

Chapter 6

JUST FOR FUN   Playing Card Fractions   (page 362)

The fractions are equal. To see this, note that $r + b = 26$ and $r + r' = 26$ so that $b = r'$. Similarly, $b' + b = 26$, and it follows that $b' = r$.

Problem Set 6.1   (page 366)

1. (a) $\dfrac{1}{6}$ **(c)** $\dfrac{0}{1}$ **(e)** $\dfrac{2}{6}$
2. (a)   **(c)**

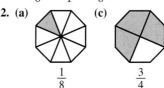

$\dfrac{1}{8}$ $\dfrac{3}{4}$

3. (a) $A: \dfrac{1}{4}, B: \dfrac{3}{4}, C: \dfrac{3}{2}$ or $\dfrac{6}{4}$ **(c)** $G: \dfrac{0}{5}, H: \dfrac{2}{5}, I: \dfrac{8}{5}$
4. (a)

5. (a) $\dfrac{1}{3}$ **(c)** $\dfrac{5}{7}$ **(e)** $\dfrac{1}{4}$ **(g)** $\dfrac{2}{3}$ **7. (a)** $\dfrac{3}{6} = \dfrac{1}{2}$
9. (a)   **10. (a)** 24 **(c)** -140

11. (a) Equivalent **(c)** Not Equivalent
12. (a) Equivalent **13. (a)** Yes **(c)** Yes
14. (a) $\dfrac{7}{12}$ **(c)** $\dfrac{-31}{43}$ **15. (a)** $\dfrac{96}{288} = \dfrac{2^5 \cdot 3^1}{2^5 \cdot 3^2} = \dfrac{1}{3}$
16. Answers will vary. Possible answers are shown.
(a) $\dfrac{15}{55}$ and $\dfrac{22}{55}$ **(c)** $\dfrac{32}{24}, \dfrac{15}{24}$, and $\dfrac{4}{24}$
17. (a) $\dfrac{9}{24}$ and $\dfrac{20}{24}$ **(c)** $\dfrac{136}{96}$ and $\dfrac{21}{96}$

18. (a) $\dfrac{7}{12}, \dfrac{2}{3}$ **(c)** $\dfrac{29}{36}, \dfrac{5}{6}$

19. (a) True. Given two fractions, two equivalent fractions with a common denominator may be found by finding a common multiple of the two original denominators. Once these fractions, say $\dfrac{a}{c}$ and $\dfrac{b}{c}$ are found, infinitely many more pairs of equivalent fractions can be found; namely, $\dfrac{a \cdot n}{c \cdot n}$ and $\dfrac{b \cdot n}{c \cdot n}$ for any integer n other than 0. **(c)** False. Given any positive fraction, a smaller positive fraction may be found by multiplying the denominator by 2. So there cannot be a least positive fraction.

20. (a) $\left\{ \dfrac{a}{b} \,\middle|\, a = 3n, b = 5n \text{ for any integer } n \neq 0 \right\}$

(c) $\left\{ \dfrac{0}{n} \,\middle|\, n \text{ is any integer, } n \neq 0 \right\}$

22. (a)

$\dfrac{4}{8}$

(d)

$\dfrac{1}{5}$

(f)

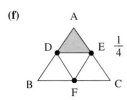

$\dfrac{1}{4}$

23. (a)

Each new Fibonacci fraction is between the last two placed on the number line: between $\dfrac{8}{5}$ and $\dfrac{5}{3}$. **(b)** Add, noticing that 58, 87, and 232 are all multiples of 29.

26. (a) $\dfrac{1}{2}, \dfrac{1}{6}, \dfrac{1}{3}$ **28. (a)** 18 gal **29. (a)** 3/5 **(c)** 1/4

30. Yes. Lakeside won $\dfrac{19}{25}$ of their games while Shorecrest won $\dfrac{16}{21}$ of their games, and $\dfrac{16}{21} > \dfrac{19}{25}$. **31. (a)** Carol; Carol

32. (a) $\dfrac{1}{2}$ **(c)** $\dfrac{3}{6}$ **36. (a)** 5, −8, 13, −21, 34, −55, 89, −144, 233, −377 **37. (a)** $m = 7, n = 5$ **38.** $d = 5$

JUST FOR FUN   The Sultan's Estate   (page 372)

Since $(1/2) + (1/3) + (1/9) = 17/18$, the canny old Sultan did not leave all his horses to his sons. The uncle, realizing this, saw that if he included his horse before the division, the sons could each receive a whole number of horses and the uncle could then take back his own horse.

JUST FOR FUN   Bookworm Math   (page 376)

The bookworm only needs to eat through the front cover of Volume 1 and the back cover of Volume 2 for a total of $1/8 + 1/8 = 1/4$ inch.

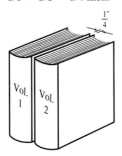

Problem Set 6.2   (page 386)

1. (a) $\dfrac{1}{3} + \dfrac{1}{2} = \dfrac{5}{6}$

2. (a)

$\dfrac{2}{5}$ + $\dfrac{6}{5}$ = $\dfrac{8}{5}$

3. (a)

4. (a)

$\dfrac{3}{4} + \dfrac{-2}{4} = \dfrac{1}{4}$

5. (a) $\dfrac{5}{7}$ **(c)** $\dfrac{5}{6}$ **(e)** $\dfrac{19}{15}$ **(g)** $\dfrac{73}{100}$ **6. (a)** $2\dfrac{1}{4}$ **(c)** $4\dfrac{19}{23}$

7. (a) $\dfrac{19}{8}$ **(c)** $\dfrac{557}{5}$ **8. (a)** $\dfrac{5}{6} - \dfrac{1}{4} = \dfrac{7}{12}$

9. (a) $\dfrac{3}{8}$ **(c)** $\dfrac{4}{3}$ **(e)** $\dfrac{1}{3}$ **(g)** $\dfrac{625}{642}$ **10. (a)** $3 \times \dfrac{5}{2} = \dfrac{15}{2}$

11. (a)

$2 \times \dfrac{3}{5} = \dfrac{6}{5}$

13. (a) $\dfrac{8}{3}$ **(c)** $\dfrac{4}{9}$ **(e)** $\dfrac{1}{5}$

14. (a) $\dfrac{8}{15}$ **(c)** $\dfrac{10}{11}$ **(e)** $\dfrac{4}{7}$ **15. (a)** 1

16. (a) $2\dfrac{1}{2} \times 3\dfrac{3}{4} = \dfrac{5}{2} \times \dfrac{15}{4} = \dfrac{75}{8} = 9\dfrac{3}{8}$ miles

17. (a) $\dfrac{3}{4} - \dfrac{2}{3} = \dfrac{9}{12} - \dfrac{8}{12} = \dfrac{1}{12} > 0$

18. $\frac{17}{18}$, since 17 of the total of 18 horses are given to the sons.

19. (a)

$\frac{1}{2}$	$\frac{1}{12}$	$\frac{5}{12}$
$\frac{1}{4}$	$\frac{1}{3}$	$\frac{5}{12}$
$\frac{1}{4}$	$\frac{7}{12}$	$\frac{1}{6}$

20. (a) $3\frac{1}{2} + 1\frac{2}{5} = \frac{7}{2} + \frac{7}{5} = \frac{35}{10} + \frac{14}{10} = \frac{49}{10}$ and

$3\frac{1}{2} \times 1\frac{2}{5} = \frac{7}{2} \times \frac{7}{5} = \frac{49}{10}$ **23. (a)** Simply add.

24. (a) $\frac{1}{5} + \frac{1}{45} = \frac{9}{45} + \frac{1}{45} = \frac{10}{45} = \frac{5 \cdot 2}{5 \cdot 9} = \frac{2}{9}$

26. (a) It terminates.

27. (a) The process terminates when one row consists of all ones.

28. 3, 3, 4, 5, 6, 6 **31.** 23 bows **33.** $42.00

38. (a) $\frac{7}{2}$ **40.** 180, $\frac{203}{180}$

Problem Set 6.3 (page 401)

1. Commutative and associative properties for addition:

$(3 + 2 + 8) + \left(\frac{1}{5} + \frac{2}{5} + \frac{1}{5} \right)$

3. (a) $\frac{-4}{5}$

(c) $\frac{8}{3}$

4. (a) $\frac{-1}{2}$ **(c)** $\frac{11}{8}$ The most useful property here is equivalence of fractions.

5. (a) $\frac{-7}{20}$ **(c)** $\frac{7}{24}$ **(e)** $\frac{-41}{12}$ The most useful property here is equivalence of fractions.

6. (a) $\frac{7}{8}$ **(c)** $\frac{1}{2}$ **(e)** 8 The most useful property here is equivalence of fractions.

7. (a) $\frac{2}{3}$

(c) $\frac{11}{4}$

(e) $\frac{-1}{2}$

8. (a) $\frac{2}{3}$ **(c)** 0 **9. (a)** Addition of rational numbers— definition.

10. $\frac{7}{6}$, since $\frac{a}{b} = \frac{2}{3} \div \frac{4}{7} = \frac{2}{3} \cdot \frac{7}{4} = \frac{14}{12} = \frac{7}{6}$.

11. (a) $x = \frac{-3}{4}$ **(c)** $x = \frac{-6}{5}$

12. (a) Closure property for subtraction and the existence of a multiplicative inverse.

13. (a) $\frac{-1}{5}, \frac{2}{5}, \frac{4}{5}$

(c) $\frac{3}{8}, \frac{1}{2}, \frac{3}{4}$

14. (a) $-4 \cdot 4 = -16 < -15 = 5(-3)$

15. (a) $x + \frac{2}{3} > -\frac{1}{3}$ **(c)** $\frac{3}{4}x < -\frac{1}{2}$

$x > -\frac{1}{3} - \frac{2}{3} = -1$ $x < -\frac{1}{2} \div \frac{3}{4}$

$x < -\frac{1}{2} \cdot \frac{4}{3}$

$x < -\frac{2}{3}$

16. (a) Answers can vary. One answer is $\frac{1}{2}$, since $\frac{4}{9} < \frac{1}{2} < \frac{6}{11}$. **(c)** Answers can vary. Since $\frac{7}{12} = \frac{14}{24} = \frac{28}{48}$ and $\frac{14}{23} = \frac{28}{46}$, one answer is $\frac{28}{47}$. **18. (a)** $\frac{1}{4}$ **(c)** -1

19. (a) 9 **20. (a)** $\frac{3}{2}$ **(c)** $\frac{3}{5}$ **(e)** 40 **(g)** $-2\frac{1}{8}$

21. (a) How many acres does Hal own after his new purchase? **22.** Answers will vary. Possible answers include: **(a)** Two pizzas were ordered. $\frac{3}{4}$ of one pizza and $\frac{1}{2}$ of another were eaten. How much pizza was eaten in all?

25. $\dfrac{1260}{250} = 5\dfrac{1}{25}$ **26.** (a) 8 (c) $\dfrac{3}{5}$ (e) $\dfrac{56}{9}$

29. (a) 4, since $\dfrac{1}{2} + \dfrac{2}{8} + \dfrac{1}{4} = \dfrac{2}{4} + \dfrac{1}{4} + \dfrac{1}{4} = \dfrac{4}{4}$

30. (a) Change $= \dfrac{-3}{4}$ (c) Wednesday close $= 61$

33. Cut the 8 inch side in half and the 10 inch side in thirds
to get six $3\dfrac{1}{3}$ by 4 inch rectangles.

35. (a) $-\dfrac{3}{125}$ **36.** (a) The replacement rule gives

$\dfrac{7 + 2 \cdot 5}{7 + 5} = \dfrac{17}{12}$. This is a good approximation to $\sqrt{2}$ since

$\left(\dfrac{17}{12}\right)^2 = \dfrac{289}{144} = 2 + \dfrac{1}{144}$.

38. (a) 2 yd^2 **39.** \$230 to \$345

Chapter 6 Review Exercises   (page 409)

1. (a) $\dfrac{2}{4}$ (b) $\dfrac{6}{6}$ (c) $\dfrac{0}{4}$ (d) $\dfrac{5}{3}$

2.

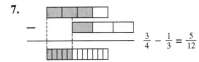

3. (a) $\dfrac{1}{3}$ (b) $\dfrac{4}{33}$ (c) $\dfrac{21}{4}$ (d) $\dfrac{297}{7}$ **4.** $\dfrac{13}{30}, \dfrac{13}{27}, \dfrac{1}{2}, \dfrac{25}{49}, \dfrac{26}{49}$

5. (a) 36 (b) 18 **6.**

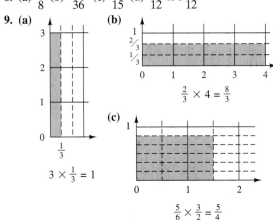

7.

$\dfrac{3}{4} - \dfrac{1}{3} = \dfrac{5}{12}$

8. (a) $\dfrac{5}{8}$ (b) $\dfrac{-7}{36}$ (c) $\dfrac{2}{15}$ (d) $\dfrac{41}{12}$ or $3\dfrac{5}{12}$

9. (a)

(b)

$\dfrac{2}{3} \times 4 = \dfrac{8}{3}$

(c)

$3 \times \dfrac{1}{3} = 1$

$\dfrac{5}{6} \times \dfrac{3}{2} = \dfrac{5}{4}$

10. $\dfrac{57}{10}$ miles $= 5\dfrac{7}{10}$ miles

11. (a) $\dfrac{-1}{8}$ (b) $\dfrac{3}{2}$ (c) $\dfrac{-1}{2}$ (d) $\dfrac{-7}{10}$

12. (a) $x = 2$ (b) $x = \dfrac{-1}{6}$ (c) $x = \dfrac{5}{18}$ (d) $x = \dfrac{9}{16}$

13. Write $\dfrac{5}{6} = \dfrac{55}{66}$ and $\dfrac{10}{11} = \dfrac{60}{66}$. Then $\dfrac{56}{66}$ and $\dfrac{57}{66}$ are

between $\dfrac{5}{6}$ and $\dfrac{10}{11}$. Other answers may be given.

14. (a) 4 (b) 5 (c) 20

Chapter 6 Test   (page 410)

1. (a)

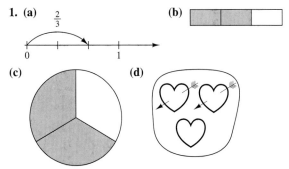

(b)

(c)

(d)

2. Answers will vary. Possibilities include $\dfrac{-6}{8}, \dfrac{-9}{12}, \dfrac{-12}{16}$.

3. $-3, \ -1\dfrac{1}{2}, 0, \dfrac{5}{8}, \dfrac{2}{3}, 3, \dfrac{16}{5}$ **4.** (a) $\dfrac{1}{8}$ (b) $\dfrac{-7}{9}$ (c) 3 (d) 1

5. (a) If $\dfrac{a}{b}$ and $\dfrac{c}{d}$ are rational numbers with $\dfrac{c}{d} \ne 0$, then

$\dfrac{a}{b} \div \dfrac{c}{d} = \dfrac{e}{f}$ if, and only if, $\dfrac{a}{b} = \dfrac{c}{d} \cdot \dfrac{e}{f}$. (b) If $\dfrac{a}{b} \div \dfrac{c}{d} = \dfrac{e}{f}$,

then $\dfrac{a}{b} = \dfrac{c}{d} \cdot \dfrac{e}{f} = \dfrac{e}{f} \cdot \dfrac{c}{d}$. So $\dfrac{a}{b} \cdot \dfrac{d}{c} = \dfrac{e}{f} \cdot \dfrac{c}{d} \cdot \dfrac{d}{c} = \dfrac{e}{f}$.

Thus, $\dfrac{a}{b} \div \dfrac{c}{d} = \dfrac{a}{b} \cdot \dfrac{d}{c}$.

6. (a) Answers will vary. (b) Answers will vary.

7. (a) $x > \dfrac{-3}{2}$ (b) $x = \dfrac{-2}{9}$ (c) $x > \dfrac{-4}{15}$ (d) $x > \dfrac{-1}{12}$

8. $\dfrac{a + b}{b} = \dfrac{c + d}{d}$ if, and only if, $(a + b)d = b(c + d)$;

that is, if, and only if, $ad + bd = bc + bd$. But this is so if,

and only if, $ad = bc$. And this is so if, and only if, $\dfrac{a}{b} = \dfrac{c}{d}$.

9. (a) 40 acres (b) $\dfrac{1}{4}$ mile **10.** (a) If $\dfrac{a}{b}$ and $\dfrac{c}{d}$ are two

rational numbers with $\dfrac{a}{b} < \dfrac{c}{d}$, then there is a rational number

$\dfrac{e}{f}$ such that $\dfrac{a}{b} < \dfrac{e}{f} < \dfrac{c}{d}$. (b) Write $\dfrac{3}{5} = \dfrac{18}{30}$ and $\dfrac{2}{3} = \dfrac{20}{30}$ to see that $\frac{19}{30}$ is between $\frac{3}{5}$ and $\frac{2}{3}$. **11. (a)** $11\frac{1}{2}$ **(b)** 48 **(c)** 23

12. (a) If $\frac{a}{b}$ is a rational number, then its additive inverse is

the rational number $\frac{-a}{b}$. **(b)** $\frac{-3}{4}, \frac{7}{4}, \frac{8}{2}$ **13. (a)** If $\frac{a}{b}$ is a

rational number with $a \neq 0$, then its multiplicative inverse is

the rational number $\frac{b}{a}$. **(b)** $\frac{2}{3}, -\frac{5}{4}, \frac{-1}{5}$

14. (a) 0, since $\frac{2}{3} + \frac{-4}{6} = 0$. **(b)** 2, since $\frac{5}{6} \cdot \frac{36}{15} =$

$\frac{5}{15} \cdot \frac{36}{6} = \frac{1}{3} \cdot 6 = 2$. **(c)** 1, since $\frac{9}{5} - \frac{1}{5} = \frac{8}{5}$ is the

reciprocal of $\frac{5}{8}$. **(d)** $\frac{1}{3}$, since $\frac{2}{3} \cdot \frac{3}{4} \cdot \frac{4}{5} \cdot \frac{5}{6} = \frac{2}{6} = \frac{1}{3}$.

Chapter 7
Problem Set 7.1 (page 433)

1. (a) $273.412 = 200 + 70 + 3 + \frac{4}{10} + \frac{1}{100} + \frac{2}{1000}$;

$273.412 = 2 \cdot 10^2 + 7 \cdot 10^1 + 3 \cdot 10^0 + 4 \cdot 10^{-1} + 1 \cdot 10^{-2} + 2 \cdot 10^{-3}$

2. (a) $\frac{81}{250}$; $250 = 2^1 \cdot 5^3$ **3. (a)** 0.35 **(c)** 0.04

4. (a) $\frac{107}{333}$ **(d)** 1 **(e)** $\frac{1}{4}$ **(g)** $\frac{1}{7}$ **5. (a)** Answers will vary.

For example, $113/999 = 0.113113\ldots$ **6. (a)** 0.007, 0.017,

$0.01\overline{7}$, 0.027 **(c)** $0.35, 0.3\overline{5}, 0.36 = \frac{9}{25}, \frac{10}{25}$

8. Assume $3 - \sqrt{2}$ is rational, then $3 - \sqrt{2} = q$ where q is rational. This implies that $\sqrt{2} = 3 - q$. But $3 - q$ is rational since the rational numbers are closed under subtraction. This can't be true since we know $\sqrt{2}$ is irrational. Thus, the assumption that $3 - \sqrt{2}$ is rational must be false. So $3 - \sqrt{2}$ is irrational.

10. (a) $0.1 = 1/10$ **11. (a)** $0.\overline{09}$ **(c)** $0.\overline{0009}$

12. (a) $\frac{74}{99}$ **13. (a)** $0.\overline{5}$ **(d)** $0.\overline{51}$ **14.** Answers will vary.

(a) One example is $\sqrt{2} + (3 - \sqrt{2}) = 3$ since $\sqrt{2}$ and $(3 - \sqrt{2})$ are both irrational. **(b)** One example is $\sqrt{3} + \sqrt{3} = 2\sqrt{3}$ since $\sqrt{3}$ and $2\sqrt{3}$ are both irrational.

17. Answers will vary. For example, $\frac{\sqrt{2}}{2\sqrt{2}} = \frac{1}{2}$ and $\frac{1}{2}$ is

rational.

28. (a) $\frac{0}{1}, \frac{1}{4}, \frac{1}{3}, \frac{2}{5}, \frac{1}{2}, \frac{3}{5}, \frac{2}{3}, \frac{3}{4}, \frac{1}{1}$

$\frac{0}{1}, \frac{1}{5}, \frac{1}{4}, \frac{2}{7}, \frac{1}{3}, \frac{3}{8}, \frac{2}{5}, \frac{3}{7}, \frac{1}{2}, \frac{4}{7}, \frac{3}{5}, \frac{5}{8}, \frac{2}{3}, \frac{5}{7}, \frac{3}{4}, \frac{4}{5}, \frac{1}{1}$

29. (a) $\frac{7}{6}$ **(c)** $\frac{1}{3}$ **(e)** $\frac{6}{5}$

Problem Set 7.2 (page 446)

1. (a) 403.674 **(c)** 1.137 **2. (a)** 174.37 **(c)** 26.1
3. (a) 35.412 **(c)** 128.7056 **4. (a)** $0.8\overline{3}$
5. (a) 2.77×10^8 **6. (a)** 1.05×10^{-10} **(c)** 1.29×10^{-13}
7. (a) 1.53×10^{10} **8.**

0.984	0.123	0.738
0.369	0.615	0.861
0.492	1.107	0.246

12. (c)

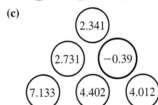

$$\underline{2.374} \quad \underline{0.041} \quad \underline{5.267}$$
$$\underline{2.415} \quad \underline{5.308}$$
$$\underline{7.723}$$

13. (a) 3.4, 4.3, 5.2, 6.1, 7.0, 7.9 **(c)** 0.0114, 0.1144, 0.2174, 0.3204, 0.4234, 0.5264
14. (a) 2.11, 2.321, 2.5531, 2.80841, 3.089251
16. (a)

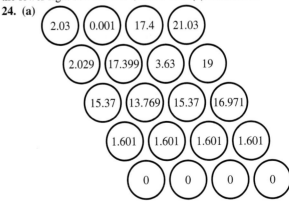

(c) 5, 9, 17, 31

(c) Answers vary. However, all solutions must have 5.01 in the lower right corner. **18.** $29.16 **21. (a)** 210.375 in^2

26. (a) Working to nine decimal places, this yields 1, 1, 1, 1 after four steps.

30. (a)  **31. (a)** 56,525

32. (a)

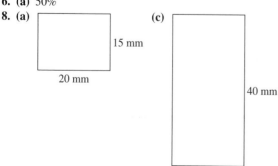

33. (a) 2303

JUST FOR FUN   Who Shaves Francisco?   (page 455)

This is a logical paradox. If Francisco doesn't shave himself, then he must shave himself. However, if he shaves himself then he does not shave himself. This type of self-reference often leads to a paradox and has had to be ruled out in logical discourse.

Problem Set 7.3   (page 457)

1. (a) $\dfrac{7}{5}$ **(c)** $\dfrac{7}{12}$ **(e)** $\dfrac{12}{5}$ **2. (a)** Yes **(c)** No **(e)** No

(g) Yes **3. (a)** $r = 9$ **4. (a)** $\dfrac{3}{2}$ **(c)** $\dfrac{2}{3}$

5. (a) \$19.25 **(c)** $\dfrac{3.5}{19.25} = 0.\overline{18}, \dfrac{5}{27.5} = 0.\overline{18}$ **8.** 19 ft

10. (a) $\dfrac{a}{b} = \dfrac{c}{d}$ **(c)** $\dfrac{a}{b} = \dfrac{c}{d}$

$ad = bc$ $ad = bc$

$da = cb$ $ac + ad = ac + bc$

$\dfrac{d}{c} = \dfrac{b}{a}$ $a(c + d) = (a + b)c$

          $\dfrac{a}{a + b} = \dfrac{c}{c + d}$

11. (a) $y = 108$ **12. (a)** $y = 4$ **15.** 59 to 58
17. (a) 32 ounces of cheese for 90¢ **21.** \$13.01
24. \$139.93 **30. (a)** −3 **(c)** −12 **(e)** 12 **(g)** −4
(i) 7 **(k)** −3 **32.** 72 **34.** $2b = 2^1 \cdot 3^2 \cdot 5^1 \cdot 11^3$

Problem Set 7.4   (page 468)

1. (a) 18.75% **(c)** 92.5% **(e)** $36.\overline{36}\%$ **(g)** 22.86%

2. (a) 19% **(c)** 215% **3. (a)** $\dfrac{1}{10}$ **(c)** $\dfrac{5}{8}$ **4. (a)** 196

(c) 285.38 **(e)** 5.4962 **5. (a)** 420 **(c)** 6 **(e)** 112
6. (a) 50%
8. (a)

9. (a) $\dfrac{1}{8} = 0.125 = 12.5\%$ **(c)** $\dfrac{7}{18} = 0.3888 \cdots \doteq 39\%$

10. (a) 100 **(c)** 25 **11. (a)** 20 **(c)** 8
12. (a) 25% **(c)** 50% **14.** 34.29% **17.** 42%
19. (a) 60% **24.** \$17,380 **26. (a)** \$62.40
28. (a) \$3576.80 **31.** \$11,956.13 **33. (a)** 15 **(c)** 6
34. (a) 5,100,000 **38. (a)** $\dfrac{17}{23}$ **39. (a)** $\dfrac{1}{3}$ **(c)** $\dfrac{7}{45}$ **(e)** $\dfrac{41}{224}$

40. (a) $\dfrac{1}{6}$ **(c)** $\dfrac{27}{10}$ **(e)** $\dfrac{17}{48}$ **41. (a)** $r = 10$

Chapter 7 Review Exercises   (page 474)

1. (a) $2 \cdot 10^2 + 7 \cdot 10^1 + 3 \cdot 10^0 + 4 \cdot 10^{-1} + 2 \cdot 10^{-2} + 5 \cdot 10^{-3}$ **(b)** $3 \cdot 10^{-4} + 5 \cdot 10^{-5} + 4 \cdot 10^{-6}$

2. (a) 0.056 **(b)** 0.08 **(c)** 0.1375 **3. (a)** $\dfrac{63}{200}$ **(b)** $\dfrac{603}{500}$

(c) $\dfrac{2001}{10,000}$ **4.** $\dfrac{2}{66}, 0.33, \dfrac{4}{12}, 0.3334, \dfrac{5}{13}$ **5. (a)** $\dfrac{3451}{333}$

(b) $\dfrac{707}{330}$ **6.** Irrational. The decimal expansion of a does not have a repeating sequence of digits and it does not terminate.

7. (a) $\dfrac{2}{9}$ **(b)** $\dfrac{36}{99}$ **8. (a)** 96.1885 **(b)** 20.581 **(c)** 83.898

(d) 7.0 **9. (a)** 34.9437 **(b)** 27.999 **(c)** 109.23237 **(d)** 6.0
10. (a) About 60,   60.384 **(b)** About 40,   39.813
(c) About 500,   620.5815 **(d)** About 3,   3.5975
11. (a) 2.473×10^7 **(b)** 1.247×10^{-5}
12. (a) 8.52×10^9 **(b)** 8.81×10^8
13. Suppose $3 - \sqrt{2} = r$ where r is rational. Then $3 - r = \sqrt{2}$. But this implies that $\sqrt{2}$ is rational since the rationals are closed under subtraction. This is a contradiction since $\sqrt{2}$ is irrational. Therefore, by contradiction, $3 - \sqrt{2}$ is irrational. **14.** $(3 - \sqrt{2}) + \sqrt{2} = 3$
15. The decimal expansion of an irrational number has no repeating sequence of digits and is nonterminating.
16. (a) 928.125 ft² **(b)** 8.4375 qts **17.** Answers will vary. For example, 4123/9999 is such a fraction.
18. (a) $5/18 = 0.2\overline{7}$; the period starts in the second decimal place. $41/333 = 0.\overline{123}$; the period starts right after the decimal point. $11/36 = 0.30\overline{5}$; the period starts in the third decimal place. $7/45 = 0.1\overline{5}$; the period starts in the second decimal place. $13/80 = 0.1625$; this decimal is terminating.
(b) Consider the prime factor representation of the denominator in each of the above. If the highest power of 2 and/or 5 appearing in this prime factor representation is r, the period begins in the $r + 1$ decimal place.
19. 11 to 9 **20. (a)** Yes **(b)** No **(c)** Yes **21.** \$7.88

22. 13 gal **23.** $y = \dfrac{35}{3}$ **24.** 43.2 feet **25. (a)** 62.5%

(b) 211.5% **(c)** 1.5% **26. (a)** 0.28 **(b)** 0.0105 **(c)** $0.\overline{3}$
27. \$3.53 **28.** 8% **29.** 55% **30.** \$3514.98

Chapter 7 Test   (page 476)

1. (a) 0.48 (b) $0.\overline{24}$ (c) $0.6\overline{3}$ **2.** (a) $\dfrac{5}{11}$ (b) $\dfrac{284}{9}$ (c) $\dfrac{7}{20}$
3. 5 **4.** 7.30×10^{-13} **5.** Answers will vary. A suitable choice is 125/999. **6.** (a) 17 to 15 (b) 53.125%
7. 15% **8.** 17 yrs **9.** 5 years ago **10.** $1196.41

Chapter 8

JUST FOR FUN   A Matter of Speed   (page 482)

To drive 300 miles at an average speed of 60 miles per hour requires $300 \div 60 = 5$ hours. Since it takes 5 hours to drive the first 250 miles at 50 miles per hour, it is impossible to average 60 miles per hour for the entire trip.

Problem Set 8.1   (page 493)

3.

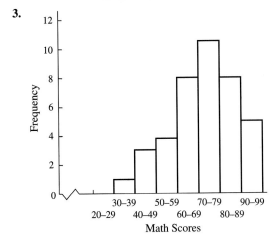

7.

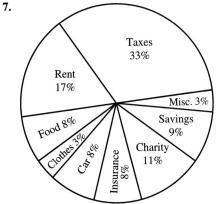

9. (a) 12 **15.** (a) Histogram (A) overemphasizes the changes in the daily Dow Jones average by its choice of vertical scale and by ignoring the bottom part of the diagram. The changes appear to be large in histogram (A) thus exaggerating the report of stock activity on the evening news. Histogram (B) makes it clear that the changes are minimal. (b) $\left(\dfrac{36}{8086}\right) \cdot (100\%) \doteq 0.45\%$ which an investor probably would not worry about.

17. (b) First can: $V \doteq \pi(4\text{ cm})^2 (8\text{ cm}) \doteq 402\text{ cm}^3$
Second can: $V \doteq \pi(3\text{ cm})^2 (14\text{ cm}) \doteq 396\text{ cm}^3$
20. (a) The percentage of individuals that go to college is $17.3 + 7.2 + 15.8 + 5.4 + 1.4 + 1.0 = 48.1$ percent. The percentage not obtaining a bachelor's degree is $17.3 + 7.2 = 24.5$ percent. Therefore, the desired percentage is $24.5/48.1 \doteq 51\%$. **22.** (a) A horizontal line through the dot on the graph above 1996 intersects the vertical axis at about 44. Therefore, we estimate that there were about 44 million cell phones in use in 1996.
24. (a)

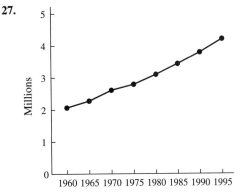

25. (a)

Physical, human, and community development 14%
Social programs 14%
Net interest on debt 14%
Social Security, Medicare, and other retirement 32%
Defense, veterans, and foreign affairs 24%
Law enforcement and general government 2%

27.

32. (a) 0.125 (c) 0.068 **33.** (a) $0.\overline{1}$ (c) $0.2\overline{142857}$
34. (a) $\dfrac{3}{8}$ (c) $\dfrac{111}{250}$ **35.** (a) $\dfrac{337}{90}$ (c) $\dfrac{1}{45}$ (e) $\dfrac{47,267}{9990}$

JUST FOR FUN   A Magic Magic Magic Square
(page 504)

There are many patterns that all add to 34. Some not already shown include the following.

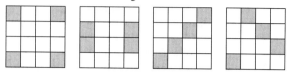

Problem Set 8.2   (page 514)

1. $\bar{x} = 20.6$, $\hat{x} = 19$,   mode $= 18$
3. (a) $Q_L = 70$, $Q_U = 80$ **(b)** $64 - 70 - 77 - 80 - 86$
5. (a) 20.56 **(b)** 4.44 **(c)** 69% **(d)** 94% **(e)** 100%
8. (a) $\bar{x} = 27$, $s \doteq 8.4$ **(b)** $\bar{x} = 32$, $s \doteq 8.4$
11. (a) $\bar{x} \doteq 36{,}900$, $\hat{x} = 30{,}000$,   mode $= 22{,}000$
12. Many examples satisfy these conditions. **(a)** 5, 7, 10, 14, 14; $\bar{x} = 10$, $\hat{x} = 10$,   mode $= 14$
13. (a) If $s = 0$, then all the data values are equal.
15. (a) All 3s **16. (a)** 32 **(c)** 32 **19.** The total of data values in A is $30 \cdot 45 = 1350$. The total of data values in B is $40 \cdot 65 = 2600$. For the combined data,
$$\bar{x} = \frac{1350 + 2600}{30 + 40} \doteq 56.4.$$ **28. (a)** $\bar{x} = 76.17$ **(b)** $\hat{x} = 78$
(c) 78 and 79 **(d)** $s \doteq 11.53$
(e,g) $Q_L = Q_1 = 68$ shown on the box plot in this printout.

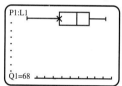

(f,g) $Q_U = Q_3 = 86$ shown on the box plot in this printout.

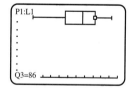

31. There are many possible answers. One pair would be $\frac{11}{16}$ and $\frac{21}{32}$. **33.** Assume that $\sqrt{3} + r = s$ where s is rational. Then $\sqrt{3} = s - r$, and $s - r$ is rational since the rational numbers are closed under subtraction. But this says $\sqrt{3}$ is rational and is a contradiction. Therefore, $\sqrt{3} + r$ is irrational.

Problem Set 8.3   (page 527)

1. (a) All freshmen in U.S. colleges and universities in 1999 **(c)** All people in the U.S. **2.** Yes. Many poorer people cannot afford telephones, many people are irritated by telephone surveys and sales pitches, and so on. These factors could certainly bias a sample. **5. (a)** This is surely

a poor sampling procedure. The sample is clearly not random. The selection of the colleges or universities could easily reflect biases of the investigators. The choices of the faculty to be included in the study almost surely also reflects the bias of the administrators of the chosen schools. **(b)** Presumably the population is all college and university faculty. But the opinions of faculty at large research universities are surely vastly different from those of their colleagues at small liberal arts colleges. Indeed, there are almost surely four distinct populations here.
9. (a) Suppose the container contains n beans. Then the number of marked beans is $25/n$. This fraction would be approximated by the fraction a/b of marked beans in the handful. Thus, approximately,
$$\frac{25}{n} = \frac{a}{b} \quad \text{and} \quad n = \frac{25b}{a}$$
is approximately the number of beans in the container.
10. (a) Between 21.8 and 27.2 **11.** Yes, since all sides of the die are equally likely to come up, all sequences of 0s and 1s are equally likely to appear. **15. (b)** 4 **16. (a)** Her time going upstream is $4 \div 2 = 2$ and her time going downstream is $4 \div 4 = 1$. Thus, the average speed is $8 \div 3 = 2.\overline{6}$ miles per hour. **(b)** $\dfrac{2}{\frac{1}{4} + \frac{1}{2}} = \dfrac{8}{3}$ **24. (a)** $\bar{x} = 4.43$ **(b)** $s \doteq 0.68$
28. (a) 23 **(b)** 23

Chapter 8 Review Exercises   (page 532)

1. (a)

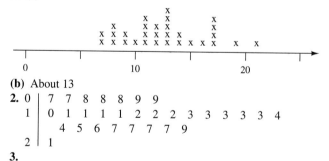

(b) About 13
2.
```
0 | 7  7  8  8  8  9  9  9
1 | 0  1  1  1  1  2  2  2  2  3  3  3  3  3  4
  |    4  5  6  7  7  7  7  9
2 | 1
```
3.

4.

Mrs. Karnes		Ms. Stevens
9 9 8 8 8 7 7	0	6 6 6 8 8 8 8
		8 9 9 9 9 9
2 2 1 1 1 1 0	1	1 1 1 1 1 1 1
3 3 3 3 3 2		1 1 2 3
7 7 6 5 4 4		
9 7 7		
1	2	

5. (a)

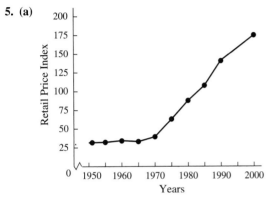

(b) 50 **(c)** About 200
6. Many examples exist. One example is 1, 2, 3, 4, 90 with a mean of 20. **7.**

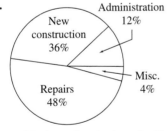

8. (a) The volume of the larger box is about double that of the smaller box. But the length of a side of the larger box is less than double the length of a side of the smaller box, suggesting that the change was less than doubling. **(b)** The volume of the larger is about twice that of the smaller, which defends the pictograph. **9.** How is medical doctor defined? Does this include all specialists? osteopaths? naturopaths? chiropractors? acupuncturists? How was the sampling done to determine the stated average?
10. $\bar{x} \doteq 12.6$, $\hat{x} = 12.5$, mode $= 13$, $s \doteq 3.6$
11. (a) $Q_L = 10$, $Q_U = 15$ **(b)** $7 - 10 - 12.5 - 15 - 21$
(c) There are no outliers. **(d)** $\hat{x} = 9$, $Q_L = 8$, $Q_U = 11$
(e) $6 - 8 - 9 - 11 - 13$ **(f)** There are no outliers.
(g)

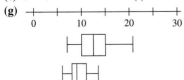

12. (a) $\bar{x} \doteq 27.8$, $s \doteq 2.0$ **(b)** $\bar{x} = 27.3$, $s \doteq 1.6$
(c) The means are about the same for the two sets of data, but the standard deviation is smaller for the second histogram since the data is less spread out from the mean.
13. There are $21 \cdot 77 = 1617$ points for the 21 students. So there are 1839 points for all 24 students. Thus, the average is $1839 \div 24 \doteq 76.6$. **14.** There are $27 \cdot 75 = 2025$ points for the second period students and $30 \cdot 78 = 2340$ points for the fourth period students. Thus, the average for all students is $(2340 + 2025)/57 \doteq 76.6$. **15.** No. The sample only represents the population of students at State University, not university students nationwide. **16.** You might want to limit your sample to persons 20 years old and older who want to work. Alternatively, you might want to define several populations and determine figures for each: persons 20 years old and older who want to work, teenagers who want full-time employment, teenagers who want part-time employment, adults 20 years old and older who want part-time employment, and so on. **17.** Telephone polls sample only persons sufficiently affluent to own a telephone. They are also biased by the fact that many people do not like telephone polls or telephone commercial solicitations and so refuse to respond or respond inaccurately because of anger.
18. Voluntary responses to mailed questionnaires tend to come primarily from those who feel strongly (either positively or negatively) about an issue or who represent narrow special interest groups. They are rarely representative of the population as a whole. **19.** One way is to number the students in alphabetical order and select the sample using a spinner or a random number generator on a computer. Alternatively, one might print the names of all students on slips of paper, place them in a container, mix them well, and have someone close their eyes and select from the container the names of those to be in the sample. **20.** Yes. Just continue taking samples until one finally shows up with eight out of the ten in the sample preferring WHITO toothpaste.

Chapter 8 Test   (page 533)

1.

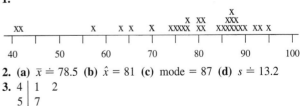

2. (a) $\bar{x} \doteq 78.5$ **(b)** $\hat{x} = 81$ **(c)** mode $= 87$ **(d)** $s \doteq 13.2$
3.

4	1 2
5	7
6	3 6
7	0 4 5 6 7 8 8
8	0 0 1 1 4 5 6 6 7 7 7 8 8 9
9	0 2 3 5

4. (a) $41 - 75 - 81 - 87 - 95$ **(b)** 41 and 42 are outliers, since they are less than $Q_L - 1.5 \cdot IQR = 57$.

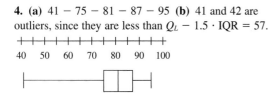

5. $(0.40) \cdot (360°) = 144°$ **6.** A random sample is one chosen in such a way that every subset of the population has an equal chance of being included. **7.** To average 80% on all five tests, she must score at least 400. Thus, the total score for her last two tests should be $400 - (77 + 79 + 72) = 172$. **8.** With a normal distribution, 68% of the data will be within one standard deviation of the mean, 95% of the data will be within two standard deviations of the mean, and 99.7% of the data will be within three standard deviations of the mean. **9.** One way would be to number the students and select 200 using random numbers from a random number generator to determine which students are included in the sample. **10.** If the sample is not chosen at random it is quite likely to reflect bias—bias of the sampler, bias reflecting the group from which the sample was actually chosen (views of teamsters, or AARP members), and so on.

Chapter 9

JUST FOR FUN   Social Security Numbers   (page 539)

Over 90 percent of the numbers will have an even digit in this position.

JUST FOR FUN   Three-Card Monte   (page 543)

(a) There are three possibilities for the three cards: BB, BW, and WW. If a card is dealt at random and a black side comes up, then the card is either the BB card or the BW card. Thus, it might appear that the probability that the other side is black is 1/2. However, the BB card can come up either way and still show B. Thus, in two out of three cases, a card showing B is B on the other side as well. Thus, the probability in question is 2/3. **(b)** We did 15 trials, obtaining 11 black on the second side for a probability of $P_e = 0.73$. This tends to confirm the above guess.

Problem Set 9.1   (page 547)

1. $P_e = 4/35 \doteq 0.11$ **4. (b)** 1 **7. (a)** iv **(c)** ii **(e)** ii
9. (b) $2 + 6, 3 + 5, 4 + 4, 5 + 3, 6 + 2$. **11. (a)** Answers will vary. We got $P_e(A) = 12/20 = 0.6$, $P_e(B) = 6/20 = 0.3$, and $P_e(C) = 2/20 = 0.1$. **(b)** About right since there are $360°$ in a complete revolution and $240/360 = 0.67$, $90/360 = 0.25$, and $30/360 = .08\overline{3}$. **13.** Answers will vary. We obtained P_e (first 6 on fourth roll) $\doteq 0.2$.
17. Answers will vary. When we did the experiment, we obtained four hearts including one face card, seven diamonds including three face cards, five spades including two face cards, and four clubs with no face cards. This

yielded the following results. **(a)** $P_e(R) = 11/20 = 0.55$ **(b)** $P_e(F) = 6/20 = 0.3$ **(c)** $P_e(R \text{ or } F) = 13/20 = 0.65$ **(d)** $P_e(R \text{ and } F) = 4/20 = 0.2$ **(e)** $P_e(R) + P_e(F) - P_e(R \text{ and } F) = 0.55 + 0.3 - 0.2 = 0.65$ **(f)** This suggests that $P_e(R \text{ or } F) = P_e(R) + P_e(F) - P_e(R \text{ and } F)$ unlike the result suggested by problem 15. **18.** Answers will vary. When we did the experiment, H occurred all told 12 times, 5 occurred all told three times, and 5 and H occurred together two times. This yielded the following results. **(a)** $P_e(H) = 12/20 = 0.6$ **(b)** $P_e(5) = 3/20 = 0.15$ **(c)** $P_e(H \text{ and } 5) = 2/20 = 0.1$ **(d)** $P_e(H) \cdot P_e(5) = (0.6)(0.15) = 0.09$ **(e)** Yes. Since the events H and 5 are independent, the number of simultaneous occurrences of H and 5 should be about $P_e(H) \cdot$ (the number of occurrences of 5). But then

$$P_e(H \text{ and } 5) \approx \frac{P_e(H) \cdot \text{(the number of occurrences of 5)}}{20}$$

$$= P_e(H) \cdot P_e(5).$$

24. (a) $62/144 \doteq 0.43$ **(b)** If HR denotes the total homeruns, then $(0.43) = HR/162$. So $HR = (0.43) \times 162 \doteq 70$. Thus McGwire would hit about 70 homeruns for the season, which is exactly what he did.
25. (a) $(0.45) \times (0.45) = 0.2025$ or about 20% of all couples. **26. (a)** $9806/10,000 = 0.9806$ **28.** Answers will vary. The following line graph is representative. The point with coordinate (x, y) shows x heads occurred y times, for $x = 0, 1, 2, \ldots, 10$.
(a) $n = 10$

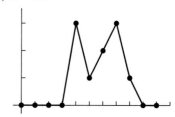

30. $s \doteq 2.3$ **32.** Since this range extends two standard deviations on either side of the mean,

$$P(\text{an individual falls in the range}) = 0.95.$$

Problem Set 9.2 (page 564)

1. $4 = 1 + 3 = 2 + 2 = 3 + 1$
$6 = 1 + 5 = 2 + 4 = 3 + 3 = 4 + 2 = 5 + 1$
So there are 8 ways to score 4 or 6.
3. (a) 3 ways; H and 2, H and 4, H and 6 **5.** The Venn diagram shows that four students speak both English and Japanese.

7. Let R be the set of red face cards and let A be the set of black aces. Since $R \cap A = \varnothing$, the addition principle of counting for mutually exclusive events applies and $n(R$ or $A) = n(R) + n(A) = 6 + 2 = 8$. **8. (a)** $6 \cdot 5 \cdot 4 \cdot 3 = 360$ **(b)** $3 \cdot 5 \cdot 4 \cdot 3 = 180$ **(c)** $3 \cdot 2 \cdot 4 \cdot 3 = 72$

10.

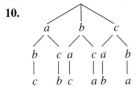

The code words are *abc*, *acb*, *bac*, *bca*, *cab*, and *cba*.
13. (a) 5040 **(c)** 72 **(e)** 35,280 **14. (a)** $13 \cdot 12 \cdot 11 \cdot 10 \cdot 9 \cdot 8 \cdot 7 \cdot 6 = 51,891,840$ **(c)** $15 \cdot 14 = 210$
(e) $\dfrac{15!}{15!} = 1$ **16. (a)** $5 \cdot 5 \cdot 5 \cdot 5 \cdot 5 = 3125$
17. (a) $P(6, 6) = 6! = 720$ **19. (a)** $\dfrac{4!}{2! \, 2!} = 6$
20. (a) To obtain an even sum, two odd faces or two even faces must come up. This can happen in $3 \cdot 3 + 3 \cdot 3 = 18$ ways. **23. (a)** If we think of *ab* as a single entity, then there are four things to put in order. This can be done in $4! = 24$ ways. **(b)** There are 24 with *b* immediately following *a* and, by the same reasoning as in part (a), 24 with *a* immediately following *b*. Therefore, there are 48 with *a* and *b* adjacent. **(c)** By symmetry, in half the possible arrangements *a* would precede *e* and in half *e* would precede *a*. Therefore, *a* precedes *e* in $5!/2 = 60$ arrangements. Alternatively, if *a* is first, *a* precedes *e* in $4! = 24$ arrangements. If *a* is second, *a* precedes *e* in $3 \cdot 3! = 18$ arrangements. If *a* is third, *a* precedes *e* in $2 \cdot 3! = 12$ arrangements and if *a* is fourth, it precedes *e* in $3! = 6$ arrangements. Adding, we again obtain 60 as before. **26.** The girls can be picked in $C(6, 2) = (6 \cdot 5)/(2 \cdot 1) = 15$ ways, and the boys can be picked in $C(5, 2) = (5 \cdot 4)/(2 \cdot 1) = 10$ ways. By the multiplication principle for independent events, the 3 committees can be formed in $15 \cdot 10 = 150$ ways. **28. (a)** $C(8, 5)$ **(b)** $C(7, 5)$, since there are 7 marbles that are not red. **29. (a)** There are 16 trains of length 5. **(b)** There is 1 one-car, 4 two-car, 6 three-car, 4 four-car, and 1 five-car trains of length 5. **31. (a)** $C(13, 3) \cdot C(11, 3) = \dfrac{13 \cdot 12 \cdot 11}{3 \cdot 2 \cdot 1} \cdot \dfrac{11 \cdot 10 \cdot 9}{3 \cdot 2 \cdot 1} = 47{,}190$ ways
33. (a) 2^4, or 16 words. **34. (a)** 362,880 **(c)** 2520 **(d)** 20.160 **(e)** 35 **35. (a)** $10! = 3{,}628{,}800$ **(c)** $C(13, 8) = 1287$ **38.** It is incorrect since the trials are completely independent. What happens on one trial has no effect on any other trial. She may continue to lose all evening!
40. (a)

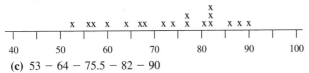

(c) $53 - 64 - 75.5 - 82 - 90$

JUST FOR FUN   It's a Girl!   (page 569)

The possibilities in order of age are boy, boy; boy, girl; girl, boy; girl, girl. In three cases there is at least one boy and in two of these the other child is a girl. Thus, the desired probability is 2/3.

JUST FOR FUN   A Probability Paradox   (page 571)

For the three tables the probabilities are as follows:

Table A: $P(R \mid G) = 5/11 \doteq 0.45$, $P(R \mid B) = 3/7 \doteq 0.43$
Table B: $P(R \mid G) = 6/9 \doteq 0.67$, $P(R \mid B) = 9/14 \doteq 0.64$
Table C: $P(R \mid G) = 11/20 = 0.55$, $P(R \mid B) = 12/21 \doteq 0.57$

This is quite surprising since $P(R \mid G) > P(R \mid B)$ on each of tables A and B, but $P(R \mid G) < P(R \mid B)$ on table C where the balls in the hats were obtained by combining the balls in the hats on tables A and B. This is another example of Simpson's paradox.

Problem Set 9.3   (page 583)

1. (a) Listed in the order penny, nickel, dime, quarter, the possibilities are:

HHHH	HTHH	THHH	TTHH
HHHT	HTHT	THHT	TTHT
HHTH	HTTH	THTH	TTTH
HHTT	HTTT	THTT	TTTT

(c) $P(2$ heads and 2 tails$) = 6/16 = 0.375$
3. (a) $4/22 \doteq 0.18$ **(c)** $6/22 \doteq 0.27$ **4. (a)** $4/12 \doteq 0.33$
5. (a) $7/20 = 0.35$ **6. (a)** 0.19 **(c)** 0.33 **(e)** 0.25
7. (a) $4/50 = 0.08$ **(c)** $0/50 = 0$ **9.** $P(3\text{H}) =$
$C(13, 3)/C(52, 3) = \dfrac{13 \cdot 12 \cdot 11}{3 \cdot 2 \cdot 1} \div \dfrac{52 \cdot 51 \cdot 50}{3 \cdot 2 \cdot 1} \doteq 0.013$.
10. These answers are determined by ratios of angular measures of appropriate regions. **(a)** $P(\text{shaded area}) = 3/10 = 0.30$ **(c)** $P(10$ or $6) = 2/10 = 0.20$
(e) $P(8 \mid \text{shaded area}) = 1/3$ **(g)** $P(\text{vowel or an odd numbered region}) = 7/10 = 0.70$ **11.** Here the probabilities are ratios of areas. **(a)** $P(1) = 16/25 = 0.64$
(c) $P(5) = 1/25 = 0.04$ **12. (a)** $P(b) = 1/20$
(b) $P(a$ or c or d or $e \mid a$ or b or c or d or $e) = 4/5$
13. (a) $5 : 31$ or, equivalently, $5/31$ **15.** $P(A$ or $C) = P(A) + P(C) = \dfrac{1}{2} + \dfrac{1}{6} = \dfrac{4}{6} = \dfrac{2}{3}$. Thus, the odds in favor of A or C are $\dfrac{\dfrac{2}{3}}{1 - \dfrac{2}{3}} = \dfrac{2}{1}$ or $2 : 1$. **17.** $E = \$4 \cdot \dfrac{1}{36} +$
$\$6 \cdot \dfrac{2}{36} + \$8 \cdot \dfrac{3}{36} + \$10 \cdot \dfrac{4}{36} + \$20 \cdot \dfrac{5}{36} + \$40 \cdot \dfrac{6}{36} +$
$\$20 \cdot \dfrac{5}{36} + \$10 \cdot \dfrac{4}{36} + \$8 \cdot \dfrac{3}{36} + \$6 \cdot \dfrac{2}{36} + \$4 \cdot \dfrac{1}{36} =$
$\dfrac{\$600}{36} = \$16.67$ to the nearest penny.

18. (a) $P(\text{both white}) = \dfrac{C(6, 2)}{C(14, 2)} = \dfrac{\dfrac{6 \cdot 5}{2 \cdot 1}}{\dfrac{14 \cdot 13}{2 \cdot 1}} \doteq 0.16$

19. (a) $P(\text{all four red}) = \dfrac{C(8, 4)}{C(19, 4)} = \dfrac{\dfrac{8 \cdot 7 \cdot 6 \cdot 5}{4 \cdot 3 \cdot 2 \cdot 1}}{\dfrac{19 \cdot 18 \cdot 17 \cdot 16}{4 \cdot 3 \cdot 2 \cdot 1}}$

$\doteq 0.02$ **20. (a)** $P(\text{a code word begins with a}) =$

$\dfrac{25 \cdot 24 \cdot 23 \cdot 22}{26 \cdot 25 \cdot 24 \cdot 23 \cdot 22} \doteq 0.04$ **23. (a)** $P(\text{a five card hand}$ contains exactly two aces)

$$= \dfrac{C(4, 2) \cdot C(48, 3)}{C(52, 5)}$$

$$= \dfrac{\dfrac{4 \cdot 3}{2 \cdot 1} \cdot \dfrac{48 \cdot 47 \cdot 46}{3 \cdot 2 \cdot 1}}{\dfrac{52 \cdot 51 \cdot 50 \cdot 49 \cdot 48}{5 \cdot 4 \cdot 3 \cdot 2 \cdot 1}}$$

$$\doteq 0.04$$

24. The seven numbers with two alike in a fixed order appear with probability $(1/6)^7$. To compute the number of ways seven such numbers can appear note that we can choose the number to appear twice in six ways *and* each of the other numbers in only one way *and* we can then order these numbers in 7!/2! ways. Thus, the desired probability is

$$6 \cdot \dfrac{7!}{2!} \cdot \left(\dfrac{1}{6}\right)^7 \doteq 0.05.$$

25. (a) There are five patterns: four 2-loops (that is, the small loops formed by two strings), two 2-loops and a 4-loop, one 2-loop and a 6-loop, two 4-loops, one 8-loop. **(c)** There are $C(8, 2) = 8 \cdot 7/2 = 28$ ways to choose the pair of 8 strings to be tied. Four of these pairs give a small loop. Thus, the first knot yields a small 2-loop with probability $4/28 = 1/7$. In Example 9.29, it was shown that the next three knots each give small loops with probability 1/15. The probability of 4 small loops is therefore $(1/7) \cdot (1/15) = 1/105$. **27. (a)** $P(W_3) =$ $\dfrac{7 \cdot 6 \cdot 5}{7 \cdot 7 \cdot 7} = \dfrac{30}{49}, P(\overline{W}_3) = 1 - P(W_3) = 1 - \dfrac{30}{49} = \dfrac{19}{49}.$ **28. (a)** $P(Y_{23}) = 0.493, P(\overline{Y}_{23}) = 1 - P(Y_{23}) = 0.507.$ In a group of 23 people, it is more likely than not that two or more share a birthday. **30. (a)** $1/C(49, 6) =$ $1/13,983,816$, or about 1 in almost 14 million **31. (a)** $\dfrac{C(8, 5) \cdot C(72, 15)}{C(80, 20)} \doteq 0.0183$

34. $C(7, 4) + C(8, 4) = \dfrac{7 \cdot 6 \cdot 5 \cdot 4}{4 \cdot 3 \cdot 2 \cdot 1} + \dfrac{8 \cdot 7 \cdot 6 \cdot 5}{4 \cdot 3 \cdot 2 \cdot 1} = 105$

36. $5 \cdot 21 \cdot 4 \cdot 20 \cdot 3 + 21 \cdot 5 \cdot 20 \cdot 4 \cdot 19 = 184,800$

Chapter 9 Review Exercises   (page 589)

1. Answers will vary. When we did the experiment, three heads and a tail occurred five times so that $P_e = 5/20$ $= 0.25$. **2.** Answers will vary. When we did the experiment we obtained the following:

2	3	4	5	6	7	8	9	10	11	12
I	I	II	II	III	III	IIII	I	II	I	

Using this data **(a)** $P_e(3 \text{ or } 4) = 3/20 = 0.15$ **(b)** $P_e(\text{score at least } 5) = 16/20 = 0.80$ **3.** Answers will vary. Using the above data, we obtain $P_e(5 \text{ or } 6 \text{ or } 7 \mid 5 \text{ or } 6$ or 7 or 8 or 9) $= 8/13 \doteq 0.6$ **4.** Answers will vary. In our study, seven out of 20 chose chocolate so that $P_e = 7/20 = 0.35$ **5.** Answers will vary. When we did the experiment we obtained the data shown below.

Point up	5	4	3	5	2	4	3	2	2	3	2	3
Head up	0	1	2	0	3	1	2	3	3	2	3	2

Point up	3	1	2	0	4	4	3	2
Head up	2	4	3	5	1	1	2	3

Using this data **(a)** $P_e(3 \text{ tacks land point up}) = 6/20 = 0.30$ **(b)** $P_e(2 \text{ or } 3 \text{ tacks land point up}) = 12/20 = 0.60$ **6.** Answers will vary. Doing the experiment, we obtain the following data with the results indicated in (a) and (b).

Number of trials to get a 5 or 6	1	2	3	4	5	6	7
		II	IIII	III		I	

(a) Average number of rolls required is

$$\dfrac{3 + 3 + 4 + 4 + 4 + 4 + 5 + 5 + 5 + 7}{10} = 4.4$$

We guess that it should take 4 or 5 rolls to get a 5 or 6. **(b)** $P_e(\text{it takes precisely five rolls to obtain 5 or 6}) = 3/10 = 0.30$ **7.** Answers will vary. Doing the experiment, we obtained the following data yielding the results in (a), (b), and (c).

	Heart	Nonheart
Ace	I	II
Nonace	JHT III	JHT IIII

(a) $P_e(\text{ace or heart}) = 11/20 = 0.55$ **(b)** $P_e(\text{ace and heart}) = 1/20 = 0.05$ **(c)** $P_e(\text{ace} \mid \text{heart}) = 1/9 \doteq 0.11$

8. A match will occur with a probability of about 0.63. Thus, you will usually get around 15 or 16 matches in 25 trials.

9. (a) HHH   HTT **(b)** 3
HHT   THT
HTH   TTH
THH   TTT

10. (a) $C(15, 9) = \dfrac{15 \cdot 14 \cdot 13 \cdot 12 \cdot 11 \cdot 10 \cdot 9 \cdot 8 \cdot 7}{9 \cdot 8 \cdot 7 \cdot 6 \cdot 5 \cdot 4 \cdot 3 \cdot 2 \cdot 1} =$

5005 **(b)** $C(2, 1) \cdot C(3, 1) \cdot C(13 \cdot 7) =$

$\dfrac{2}{1} \cdot \dfrac{3}{1} \cdot \dfrac{13 \cdot 12 \cdot 11 \cdot 10 \cdot 9 \cdot 8 \cdot 7}{7 \cdot 6 \cdot 5 \cdot 4 \cdot 3 \cdot 2 \cdot 1} = 10{,}296$

11. Fill in the Venn diagram from the inside out.

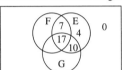

(a) $90 - 4 = 86$ **(b)** 7

12. (a) $C(13, 2) = \dfrac{13 \cdot 12}{2 \cdot 1} = 78$ **(b)** $C(12, 2) =$

$\dfrac{12 \cdot 11}{2 \cdot 1} = 66$ **(c)** $C(13, 2) + C(12, 2) - C(3, 2) =$

$78 + 66 - 3 = 141$ **13. (a)** $26 \cdot 25 \cdot 24 \cdot 23 \cdot 22 = 7{,}893{,}600$ **(b)** $5 \cdot 4 \cdot 24 \cdot 23 \cdot 22 = 242{,}880$

(c) $3 \cdot 23 \cdot 22 = 1518$ **14. (a)** $\dfrac{7!}{2! \, 2! \, 2! \, 1!} = 630$

(b) $\dfrac{6!}{2! \, 2! \, 1! \, 1!} = 180$ **(c)** $\dfrac{6!}{2! \, 2! \, 1! \, 1!} = 180$

15. (a) HH1, HH2, HH3, HH4, HH5, HH6
HT1, HT2, HT3, HT4, HT5, HT6
TH1, TH2, TH3, TH4, TH5, TH6
TT1, TT2, TT3, TT4, TT5, TT6

(b) $P(\text{TT5}) = 1/24 \doteq 0.04$ **16.** $P(5 \mid \text{TT}) = 1/6 \doteq 0.17$

17. $P(\text{sum at most } 11) = 1 - P(\text{sum is } 12) = 1 - \dfrac{1}{36} \doteq 0.97$

18. (a) $[C(5, 2) + C(6, 2) + C(4, 2)]/C(15, 2) =$

$\left(\dfrac{5 \cdot 4}{2 \cdot 1} + \dfrac{6 \cdot 5}{2 \cdot 1} + \dfrac{4 \cdot 3}{2 \cdot 1}\right)\Big/\dfrac{15 \cdot 14}{2 \cdot 1} \doteq 0.30$

(b) $P(\text{both white}) = \dfrac{C(5, 2)}{C(15, 2)} = \dfrac{\frac{5 \cdot 4}{2 \cdot 1}}{\frac{15 \cdot 14}{2 \cdot 1}} \doteq 0.10$

(c) $P(\text{both white} \mid \text{both the same}) = \dfrac{C(5, 2)}{C(5, 2) + C(6, 2) + C(4, 2)}$

$= \dfrac{10}{10 + 15 + 6}$

$\doteq 0.32$

19. (a) $P(\text{b and } 8) = 0$ **(b)** $P(\text{b or } 8) = P(\text{b}) + P(8) =$

$\dfrac{90}{360} + \dfrac{30}{360} = \dfrac{1}{3} \doteq 0.33$ **(c)** $P(\text{b} \mid 8) = 0$

(d) $P(\text{b and } 2) = \dfrac{30}{360} \doteq 0.08$

(e) $P(\text{b or } 2) = P(\text{b}) + P(2) - P(\text{b and } 2)$

$= \dfrac{90}{360} + \dfrac{30}{360} - \dfrac{30}{360}$

$= 0.25$

(f) $P(2 \mid \text{b}) = 30/90 \doteq 0.33$ **20. (a)** 3 : 5 or 3/5
(b) 1 : 7 or 1/7 **21. (a)** $P(A)/[1 - P(A)]$; that is,

$\dfrac{0.85}{1 - 0.85} = \dfrac{0.85}{0.15} = \dfrac{17}{3}$ or 17 : 3

(b) $P(A) = 17/25 = 0.68$ **22. (a)** E = $5 \cdot (.50) +$ $10 \cdot (.25) + $20 \cdot (.10) = 7 **(b)** No. On average you expect to lose $3 per game. **23.** Since the sexes of children are independent, $P(\text{other two children are}$

boys$) = \dfrac{1}{2} \cdot \dfrac{1}{2} = 0.25.$

Chapter 9 Test (page 591)

1. Prepare a card as shown and ask a number of people to choose a number. Calculate the empirical probability of choosing 3 as the number of times 3 is chosen divided by the number of people questioned. **2.** This would be an empirical probability obtained by keeping records for a large number of trials of treating strep throat with penicillin. **3. (a)** 5040 **(b)** 504 **(c)** 40,320 **(d)** 5040 **(e)** 6720 **(f)** 40,320 **(g)** 84 **(h)** 1 **4. (a)** Fill in the regions in the Venn diagram starting with the innermost region.

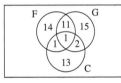

Adding all the counts, there are 57 students in all.
(b) 13 students **(c)** 11 students
5. (a) $C(8, 5) = \dfrac{8 \cdot 7 \cdot 6 \cdot 5 \cdot 4}{5 \cdot 4 \cdot 3 \cdot 2 \cdot 1} = 56$ **(b)** 0 ways. Only 5 balls are being selected. **(c)** $C(5, 5) + C(8, 5) =$

$\dfrac{5 \cdot 4 \cdot 3 \cdot 2 \cdot 1}{5 \cdot 4 \cdot 3 \cdot 2 \cdot 1} + \dfrac{8 \cdot 7 \cdot 6 \cdot 5 \cdot 4}{5 \cdot 4 \cdot 3 \cdot 2 \cdot 1} = 57$

6. $P(2 \text{ yellow balls} \mid 3 \text{ green balls}) =$ $C(5, 2)/C(14, 2) \doteq 0.11$ **7.** 5 to 12 **8.** 7 to 13
9. (a) $7^4 = 2401$ **(b)** $7 \cdot 6 \cdot 5 \cdot 4 = 840$
10. (a) $2 \cdot 6 \cdot 5 \cdot 4 = 240$ **(b)** Choose cd as a single unit in 1 way, and choose two more letters in $C(5, 2) = 10$ ways, and arrange these three items in order in $3! = 6$ ways. Similarly for dc. Therefore, the desired number is $2 \cdot 1 \cdot 10 \cdot 6 = 120.$

Chapter 10

JUST FOR FUN   Arranging Points at Integer Distances (page 601)

The isosceles trapezoid with bases 3″ and 4″ has 2″ sides and 4″ diagonals.

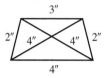

Problem Set 10.1   (page 610)

1. (a) $\overleftrightarrow{AB}$, or $\overleftrightarrow{BA}$

2. (a)

$$\xrightarrow{\hspace{1cm}} \quad E \qquad U \quad \xrightarrow{\hspace{1cm}}$$

3. (a)

4. (a) 10 angles. $\angle APB$, $\angle APC$, $\angle APD$, $\angle APE$, $\angle BPC$, $\angle BPD$, $\angle BPE$, $\angle CPD$, $\angle CPE$, $\angle DPE$.

5.

$m(\angle AXB) = m(\angle AXE) - m(\angle BXE) = 180° - 132° = 48°$
$m(\angle CXD) = m(\angle BXD) - m(\angle BXC) = 90° - 35° = 55°$
$m(\angle DXE) = m(\angle BXE) - m(\angle BXD) = 132° - 90° = 42°$

7. The three lines are concurrent.   **10. (a)** Opposite angles are supplementary: $m(\angle A) + m(\angle C) = 180°$, $m(\angle B) + m(\angle D) = 180°$.   **11. (a)** Angle measurements will be different for different drawings. You should find $m(\angle APB) = m(\angle AQB) = m(\angle ARB)$ and this measure is half the measure of $\angle AOB$.   **12.** Ten times; once between 1 and 2, once between 2 and 3, . . . , and once between 10 and 11.   **13. (a)** 360°   **(d)** 30°   **14. (a)** 90°   **(c)** The minute hand is on the 6 and the hour hand is halfway between the 4 and the 5. The angle between two consecutive numbers is $\frac{1}{12}$ of a revolution, or 30°. So the angle is $(1.5)(30°) = 45°$.   **16.** Draw a horizontal ray $\overrightarrow{PQ}$ at P, in the opposite direction of $\overrightarrow{AB}$ and $\overrightarrow{CD}$. The opposite interior angles theorem then gives $m(\angle APQ) = 130°$, $m(\angle CPQ) = 140°$. Thus $m(\angle P) = 360° - 130° - 140° = 90°$.   **17. (a)** 40°, since the interior angles of a triangle add up to 180°   **(c)** 49°, since the interior angles of a triangle add up to 180° and a right angle has measure 90°   **18. (a)** $x + x + 30° = 180°$ so $x = 75°$. The interior angles measure 75°, 75°, and 30°.   **19. (a)** No, because an obtuse angle has measure greater than 90° and adding two such measures would exceed 180° which is the sum of all three interior angle measures for any triangle.   **21. (a)** Zero intersection points if the five lines are parallel to each other.   **22. (a)** 6 lines   **23.** The pencil turns through each interior angle of the triangle. Since the pencil faces the opposite

direction when it returns to the starting side, it has turned a total of 180°. This demonstrates that the sum of measures of the interior angles of a triangle is 180°.   **25. (a)** By trial and error, ten taxi segments. Alternatively, this is the number of sequences of 3 E(east) and 2 N(north) segments, and there are ten ways to form such sequences: NNEEE, NENEE, . . . , EEENN.

27. (a)

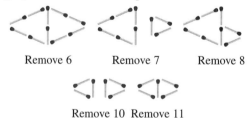

29. (a) A full revolution takes 24 hours, so the earth turns $\frac{1}{24}$ of a revolution, or 15°, in one hour.   **30.** The angle of latitude is equal to the angle of elevation to Polaris.

32. (a) $58° \ 36' \ 45'' = 58° + \left(\frac{36}{60}\right)° + \left(\frac{45}{3600}\right)° = 58.6125°$ **(c)** $71.32° = 71° + (0.32)(60') = 71° + 19.2' = 71° + 19' + (0.2)(60'') = 71° \ 19' \ 12''$

34. (a) Q, R, and S are collinear   **35. (a)** The lines $\overleftrightarrow{BB}'$ and $\overleftrightarrow{DD}'$ intersect at a right angle at P.

JUST FOR FUN   Triangle Pick-Up-Sticks   (page 620)

It is not possible to remove nine matchsticks and leave two triangles, but the other cases are possible.

Remove 6   Remove 7   Remove 8

Remove 10 Remove 11

Problem Set 10.2   (page 631)

1.

	(a)	(b)	(c)	(d)
Simple curve		✓		
Closed curve		✓	✓	✓
Polygonal curve	✓	✓		
Polygon		✓		

2. (a) An example is

(c) An example is

4. (a) Convex **(b)** Nonconvex

5. (a) 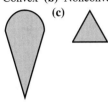 **(c)**

6. (a) 6 **(c)** 8 **7.** $2x + 5x + 5x + 5x + 5x + 2x = (6 - 2)(180°)$ or $24x = 720°$, so $x = 30°$. The angles measure 60°, 150°, 150°, 150°, 150°, and 60°.

9. (a) $(5 - 2)(180°) = 540°$ **(c)** $(6 - 2)(180°) = 720°$

10. Pictures will vary. **(a)** Triangle **(c)** Decagon

12. (a) 360° **(c)** 0° **14. (a)** DAF and DBC

16.

	(a)	**(c)**
Interior angle	108°	$128\frac{4}{7}°$
Exterior angle	72°	$51\frac{3}{7}°$
Central angle	72°	$51\frac{3}{7}°$

17. (a) $\dfrac{360°}{n} = 15°$ so $n = 24$.

18. (a) Any curve from K to D "crosses" the wall an odd number of times, so the dragon is on the opposite side of the wall from the knight and therefore presents no danger.

20. (a) The boat can drift to any position inside the circle centered at A, where the radius of the circle is the length of the anchor rope.

21. (a)

C could be any point (other than A or B) on either of the two lines drawn through A and through B which are perpendicular to $\overline{AB}$.

(b)

C could be any point (other than A or B) on the circle with $\overline{AB}$ as diameter.

22. At a vertex, the interior angle and the conjugate angle add up to 360°. For an n-gon, the sum of all interior and all conjugate angles is $n \cdot 360°$. All the interior angles add up to

$(n - 2) \cdot 180°$, so all the conjugate angles add up to $360°n - (n - 2)180° = 360°n - 180°n + 360° = 180°n + 360° = (n + 2) \cdot 180°$.

24. Such a point S allows for n triangles to be formed, all with the vertex S. The sum of all the interior angles of these n triangles is $n \cdot 180°$ which is equal to the sum of all the interior angles of the n-gon plus 360° for the angles that surround the point S. Thus the sum of the interior angles of the n-gon is $n \cdot 180° - 360° = (n - 2) \cdot 180°$.

26. Each new circle creates a new region each time it intersects a previously drawn circle. Since the new circle intersects each of the old circles in two points, this creates the following pattern:

NUMBER OF		NUMBER OF	
Circles	Regions	Circles	Regions
1	$2 \qquad = 2$	6	$22 + 2 \cdot 5 = 32$
2	$2 + 2 \cdot 1 = 4$	7	$32 + 2 \cdot 6 = 44$
3	$4 + 2 \cdot 2 = 8$	8	$44 + 2 \cdot 7 = 58$
4	$8 + 2 \cdot 3 = 14$	9	$58 + 2 \cdot 8 = 74$
5	$14 + 2 \cdot 4 = 22$	10	$74 + 2 \cdot 9 = 92$

29. (a) The sum of the interior angles is $360° = m(\angle P) + m(\angle Q) + m(\angle R) + m(\angle S)$. We also know $m(\angle P) = m(\angle R)$ and $m(\angle Q) = m(\angle S)$, so $360° = m(\angle P) + m(\angle Q) + m(\angle P) + m(\angle Q)$, giving us $180° = m(\angle P) + m(\angle Q)$. **(b)** $m(\angle Q) + m(\angle q) = 180°$ and $m(\angle P) + m(\angle Q) = 180°$ so $m(\angle q) = m(\angle P)$. $\angle q$ and $\angle P$ are corresponding angles, so segments $\overline{PS}$ and $\overline{QR}$ are parallel. $m(\angle q) = m(\angle P)$ and $m(\angle P) = m(\angle R)$ so $m(\angle q) = m(\angle R)$. $\angle q$ and $\angle R$ are alternate interior angles, so their congruence gives $\overline{PQ}$ parallel to $\overline{SR}$. Hence the figure is a parallelogram.

$$\begin{array}{l} P \qquad\qquad Q \\ \hline \angle P \quad \angle Q \,/\, \angle q \\ \angle S \quad \angle R \\ \hline S \qquad\qquad R \end{array}$$

31. (a) Drawings will vary. **(b)** After drawing the black curve, various regions are determined. The colored curve will begin in some region and cut through the black curve into another region and then into another region and so on, eventually returning to the starting place to close off the curve. Each crossing switches the colored curve from the interior to the exterior region formed by the black curve, or vice versa. So the crossings must be even in number since the colored curve gets back to where it started.

33. The square cover could fall through the hole if it were on edge and slightly rotated from its position when in place.

35. (a) $SQRE$ is a square **(b)** No

37.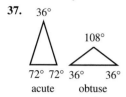

72° 72°   36°   36°
acute   obtuse

39. One angle is 90°; call the other two angles A and B. The interior angles of a triangle add up to 180°, so 90° + $m(\angle A) + m(\angle B) = 180°$, or $m(\angle A) + m(\angle B) = 90°$.

JUST FOR FUN   Space Out for Success!   (page 642)

Form a tetrahedron with the six matches.

Problem Set 10.3   (page 651)

1. (a) Polyhedron **(c)** Polyhedron **(e)** Not a polyhedron
2. (a) Pentagonal prism **(c)** Oblique circular cone
(e) Right rectangular prism **3. (a)** 4 **(c)** A, B, C, D
5. (a)   **6. (a)**

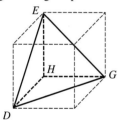

7. (a) 45° since the dihedral angle between the adjacent sides of the cube is 90° and another pyramid would fit into the gap between the original pyramid and a vertical side of the cube. **(b)** Filling the cube with six such pyramids, one sees that three pyramids surround the edge between the cube's center and any corner. Thus three copies of the dihedral angle give a full revolution of 360° around this edge, so the dihedral angle measures 120° **11. (a)** A cube is a prism. **(b)** A tetrahedron is a pyramid. **14. (a)** $F = 10$, $V = 7, E = 15$, so $V + F = E + 2$ since $7 + 10 = 15 + 2$
16. (a)

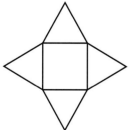

17. (a) $V = 10, E = 20, F = 12$. $V + F = 22$ and $E + 2 = 22$. Euler's formula holds. **18. (a)** Suppose the

faces of a polyhedron consist of a p-gon, a q-gon, an r-gon, and so on. Since each edge of the polyhedron borders two faces, the sum $p + q + r + \cdots$ is twice the number of edges. That is, $p + q + r + \cdots = 2E$. Since there are F faces and $p, q, r, \ldots$ are all three or greater, we get $2E \geq 3 + 3 + \cdots = 3F$. **(b)** Each of the V vertices of a polyhedron is the endpoint of three or more edges that meet at the vertex. Thus, $3V$ is less than or equal to the total number of ends of the edges. But each of the E edges has two ends, so there are $2E$ ends of edges. We see that $3V \leq 2E$. **(c)** Adding $3V \leq 2E$ and $3F \leq 2E$ shows that $3V + 3F \leq 4E$. But $V + F = E + 2$ (Euler's formula), so $3V + 3F = 3E + 6$. Comparing this to the inequality, we see that $3E + 6 \leq 4E$. Subtracting $3E$ from both sides shows that $6 \leq E$. **(d)** Suppose $E = 7$. Since $3F \leq 2E = 14$, we see that F is no larger than 4 ($F \geq 5$ would give $3F \geq 15$). Similarly, $3V \leq 2E = 14$ means that $V \leq 4$. Since both $V \leq 4$ and $F \leq 4$, then $V + F \leq 8$. But $V + F = E + 2$ (Euler's formula), and $E = 7$, so $V + F = 9$. This contradicts $V + F \leq 8$, so our assumption $E = 7$ is not possible. **(e)** A pyramid with a base of $3, 4, 5, \ldots, n, \ldots$ sides has $6, 8, 10 \ldots, 2n, \ldots$ edges, respectively. Slicing off a tiny corner at one vertex somewhere on the base of the pyramid adds three new edges, giving us polyhedra with $9, 11, 13, \ldots, 2n + 3, \ldots$ edges. Altogether, the pyramids and pyramids with a truncated base corner give us polyhedra with $6, 8, 9, 10, 11, \ldots$ edges.
20. (a) The base is a pentagon.

(b) The center polygon is a triangle.

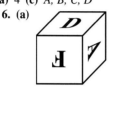

21. (a)   (b)

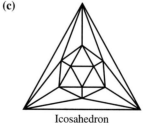

Tetrahedron   Octahedron

(c)

Icosahedron

25. (a) When folded, these edges coincide and so must be the same length in the net. The dashed segment $\overline{AP}$ is

perpendicular to edge $\overline{BH}$ because folding along $\overline{BH}$ moves point A along a circle that is in a plane perpendicular to the axis $\overline{BH}$ of the fold. **26.** The axis of all the hinges on a door must be along the intersection of the planes of the wall and the plane of the opened door. Since planes meet in a line, the axes of the hinges must be along a single line. **30.** $m(\angle x) = 50°$, $m(\angle z) = 130°$, $m(\angle y) = 50°$
31. (a)

n	3	4	5	6	7	8
Diagonals	0	2	5	9	14	20

(c) 54 **32. (a)** Many polygons are possible.

Problem Set 10.4   (page 664)

1. (a) Yes. *AHGFEDCBHFDBA* is one Euler path.
(c) No **(e)** Yes. *CEAEFBFDBACD* **3. (a)** $D = 22$, $E = 11$ for (b); $D = 24$, $E = 12$ for (c); $D = 30$, $E = 15$ for (d); $D = 22$, $E = 11$ for (e); $D = 30$, $E = 15$ for (f)
4. (a) Yes, since exactly two vertices are odd.
(b) $D = 2 + 2 + 4 + 8 + 3 + 6 + 6 + 1 = 32$, so $E = 16$.
6. (a)

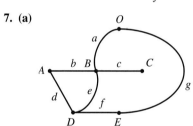

7. (a)

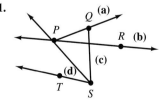

8. (a) $V = 6$, $R = 7$, $E = 11$ **10. (a)** Combining these two paths gives a closed path with distinct edges. **11.** The trees with no branches. **14.** Consider a network with a vertex for each person and an edge between two vertices for each time the corresponding persons have shaken hands. By the result stated in problem 12, there are an even number of people with odd numbers of handshakes. **16.** Requiring that each edge is traced exactly twice is equivalent to duplicating each edge in the network and asking if the new "doubled edge" network is traceable. Since doubling the edges at each vertex always creates an even vertex, the "doubled edge" network is always traceable. **18. (a)** 14, as can be counted from a diagram.
19. (a) 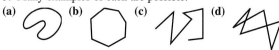 **21.** One collection of edges

is *HA, AB, BG, GF, FD, DC, DE.* **23.** A square.
25. $x = 30°$, $y = 45°$, $z = 135°$

Chapter 10 Review Exercises   (page 670)

1. (a) $\overleftrightarrow{AC}$ **(b)** $\overline{BD}$ **(c)** AD **(d)** $\angle ABC$ or $\angle CBA$
(e) $90°$ **(f)** $\overrightarrow{DC}$ **2. (a)** $\angle BAD$ **(b)** $\angle BCD$
(c) $\angle ABC$, $\angle ADC$ **3. (a)** $143°$ **(b)** $53°$ **4.** $p = 55°$,
$r = 55°$, $s = 125°$, $q = 35°$ **5.** $x = 45°$, $y = 33°$, $z = 147°$
6. (a) (iv) **(b)** (i) **(c)** (vi) **(d)** (v) **(e)** (ii) **(f)** (iii)
7. (a). No, because obtuse angles have measure greater than $90°$ and the sum of the three interior angles of a triangle is $180°$. **(b)** Yes, try angles of $100°$, $100°$, $100°$, and $60°$.
(c) No, because acute angles have measure less than $90°$ and the sum of the interior angles must be $360°$. **8.** The interior angles add up to $(6 - 2)(180)° = 720°$. So $16x = 720°$ and $x = 45°$. The angles are $135°$, $135°$, $135°$, $45°$, $225°$, $45°$.
9. $360°$ **10. (a)** 6 **(b)** $\overline{CD}$, $\overline{EF}$, $\overline{GH}$ **(c)** $\overline{DH}$, $\overline{GC}$, $\overline{EH}$, $\overline{FG}$
(d) $45°$ **11.** Square right prism; triangular pyramid or tetrahedron; oblique circular cylinder; sphere; hexagonal right prism.
12. (a)   **(b)**

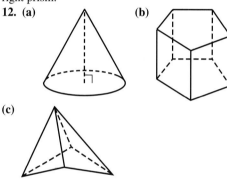

(c)

13. (a) See Table 10.4. **(b)** $V = 6$, $F = 8$, $E = 12$. Thus $V + F = 14$ and $E + 2 = 14$, so Euler's formula holds.
14. By Euler's formula, $V + 14 = 24 + 2$, so $V = 12$.
15. (a) It has four odd vertices. **(b)** An edge between any two of the vertices A, B, C, and E. Many Euler paths are possible. **16.** Construct a network with vertices A, B, C, D, and E and edges corresponding to bridges. Since just two vertices, A and D, have odd degree, there is an Euler path. The Euler path corresponds to a walking path which crosses each bridge exactly once. **17.** $V = 11$, $R = 7$, $E = 16$. $V + R = 18$ and $E + 2 = 18$, so $V + R = E + 2$ holds.

Chapter 10 Test   (page 672)

1.

2. (a) C, A **(b)** F **(c)** D **(d)** E **(e)** B
3. Many examples of each are possible.
(a)   **(b)**   **(c)**   **(d)**

4. (a) True **(b)** False **(c)** True **(d)** True **5. (a)** Decagon **(b)** Octagon **(c)** Nonagon **6.** $t = 40°$, $r = 80°$, $s = 100°$ **7.** The total turn angle is 1080°, so the turn at each of the seven vertices is 1080°/8 = 135°. This means that the interior angle at each point is $180° - 135° = 45°$. **8.** The average interior angle measure for an n-gon is $\dfrac{(n - 2)(180°)}{n}$. We want this value to be 174°, so $\dfrac{180(n - 2)}{n} = 174$. This gives $n = 60$. **9.** The same as an interior angle of a regular pentagon, which is $\dfrac{3 \cdot 180°}{5} = 108°$. **10. (a)** 24. Each edge borders a square face and a triangular face. So just count the edges of all the square faces (or all the edges of the triangular faces). **(b)** 12. Either count in the diagram or use Euler's formula. **11. (a)** Diagrams will vary. **(b)** $V = 16$, $F = 21$, $E = 35$ **(c)** $V + F = 37$ and $E + 2 = 37$, so Euler's formula holds. **12. (a)** (iii) **(b)** (iv) **(c)** (i), (ii) **(d)** (iii) add an edge between any two of the four odd vertices. **13. (a)** By Euler's formula, $V + 7 = 11 + 2$, so $V = 6$. **(b)** Many such networks can be drawn.

Chapter 11

Problem Set 11.1   (page 689)

1. (a) Height, length, thickness, area, diagonal, weight **(c)** Height, length, depth **4. (a)** Answers will vary, anywhere from 40 to 54 **(b)** The circular portions of area don't fit well together, but leave gaps between them. **6. (a)** 1 acre = $\dfrac{1}{640}$ mi², so 1 acre = $\left(\dfrac{1}{640}\text{mi}^2\right)\left(\dfrac{5280\text{ ft}}{\text{mi}}\right)^2 = 43{,}560 \text{ ft}^2$. **8. (a)** Between 165.5 km and 166.5 km **(c)** Between 0.495 mm and 0.505 mm **9. (a)** 33 cL = $33 \cdot 10^{-2}$ L = 0.33 L = $330 \cdot 10^{-3}$ L = 330 mL. **(b)** Not quite, since 1 liter = 1000 mL and 3 · 33 cL = 990 mL. **10. (a)** 58.728 kg **(c)** 230 g **11. (a)** 3.5 kg **13. (a)** About 28 cm by 22 cm **(c)** About 2 cm **15. (a)** 8, 16, 32 **18.** 1 ha = (10,000 m²) $\left(\dfrac{1\text{ km}}{1000\text{ m}}\right)^2\left(\dfrac{1\text{ mi}}{1.6\text{ km}}\right)^2\left(\dfrac{640\text{ acres}}{1\text{ mi}^2}\right) \doteq 2.5$ acres **20.** $\dfrac{25\text{ in}}{1\text{ min}} \cdot \dfrac{60\text{ min}}{1\text{ hr}} \cdot \dfrac{24\text{ hr}}{1\text{ day}} \cdot \dfrac{14\text{ day}}{\text{fortnight}} \cdot \dfrac{1\text{ ft}}{12\text{ in}} \cdot \dfrac{1\text{ furlong}}{660\text{ ft}} \doteq$ 63.6 furlong/fortnight **22. (a)** kilo **(c)** no prefix **(e)** milli **23.** $\dfrac{100\text{ km}}{9\text{ L}} \cdot \dfrac{3.7854\text{ L}}{1\text{ gal}} \cdot \dfrac{1\text{ mi}}{1.6\text{ km}} \doteq 26.3 \dfrac{\text{mi}}{\text{gal}}$ **25. (a)** 5 gal $\cdot \dfrac{4\text{ qt}}{1\text{ gal}} \cdot \dfrac{32\text{ ounces}}{1\text{ qt}} = 640$ ounces. Since $640 \div 80 = 8$, add 8 liquid ounces of concentrate. **(b)** Add 80 $\times$ 65 mL = 5200 mL = 5.2 L of water. **27.** A league varied from time to time in history, but was usually close to 3 miles. Thus the Nautilus traveled about

60,000 miles. **32.** Interior angle measures of a triangle add up to 180°, so $8x + 6x + 4x = 180°$, and $x = 10°$. Angles are of measure 80°, 60°, and 40°. **33.** Since $m(\angle 3) = m(\angle 1) + m(\angle 2)$, we see that $m(\angle 3) > m(\angle 1)$ and $m(\angle 3) > m(\angle 2)$.

JUST FOR FUN   How to Cover a Long Hole with a Short Board   (page 693)

JUST FOR FUN   Tile and Smile   (page 697)

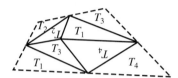

The parallelogram has one-half of the area of the quadrilateral.

Problem Set 11.2   (page 704)

2. (a) 12 units

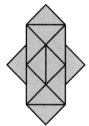

4. (a) $\dfrac{1}{2}$ (4 mm + 6 mm)(2 mm) + $\dfrac{1}{2}$ (6 mm)(5 mm) = 25 mm². **6. (a)** 12 cm **7. (a)** 1 cm by 24 cm; 2 cm by 12 cm; 3 cm by 8 cm; 4 cm by 6 cm. The dimensions can also be given in the opposite order. **8. (a)** 81 ft², 45.2 ft **9 (a)** 1664.6 m², 198.3 m **10. (a)** 220 square units **11. (a)** $\triangle ABC$. All triangles have the same base and $\triangle ABC$ has the smallest height and therefore the smallest area. **(b)** $\triangle ABF$. It has the largest height. **(c)** $\triangle ABD$ and $\triangle ABE$. They have equal heights and the same base. **13. (a)** 9 square units **14. (a)** 100 m + 100 m + $\pi \cdot$ 50 m = (200 + 50π) m $\doteq$ 357 m **(b)** (50 m)(100 m) + π(25 m)² = (5000 + 625π) m² $\doteq$ 6963 m² **16. (a)** $\pi(2)^2 - \pi(1)^2 = 3\pi$ square units $\doteq$ 9.4 square units **18. (a)** 40,000,000 m **(b)** 12,755π km $\doteq$ 40,071,000 m **(c)** Equator is longer, since the earth bulges slightly at the equator and is slightly flattened at the poles. **19.** 20 cm². The common overlap reduces the area of both regions by the same amount, so the difference in area is unchanged.

23. (a)

The unshaded region at the left has area $1^2 - \frac{1}{4}\pi(1^2) = 1 - \pi/4$.

The shaded region at the left has area $1 - (1 - \pi/4) - (1 - \pi/4) = (\pi/2) - 1$.

24. The areas of the rectangular portions of sidewalk total 2400 ft^2. The pieces formed with circular areas have total turning of $360°$, so when placed together form a circle with radius 8 ft of area $\pi(8$ ft$)^2 = 64\pi$ ft^2. Total area is $(2400 + 64\pi)$ ft^2.

28. Draw $\overline{AP}, \overline{BP}, \overline{CP}$. Then area $(\triangle ABC) = \frac{1}{2}sh =$ area

$(\triangle ABP) +$ area $(\triangle BPC) +$ area $(\triangle CPA) = \frac{1}{2}sx + \frac{1}{2}sz +$

$\frac{1}{2}sy = \frac{1}{2}s(x + y + z)$. Therefore, $\frac{1}{2}sh = \frac{1}{2}s(x + y + z)$, and $h = x + y + z$. *Alternate visual proof:*

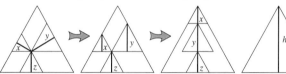

34. The lawn has area 75 ft $\times$ 125 ft $= 9375$ ft^2. Since 21 in $= 7/4$ ft, the lawn area is equivalent to a rectangle 21 in wide and $9375 \div 7/4 = 5357.14 \ldots$ ft long. That is, Kelly will walk about 5375 feet, a bit over a mile (1 mile $= 5280$ ft).

36. Consider the carpet as a 6 ft by 4 ft rectangle with semicircular ends of radius 2'. Then the carpet's area is $(6$ ft$)(4$ ft$) + \pi(2$ ft$)^2 = 36.57$ ft$^2 \doteq 5266$ in^2. The carpet contains about 5266 inches of braid, or about 439 ft.

38. Area $= 120$ ft$^2 = 17,280$ in^2, so $\dfrac{17,280 \text{ in}^2}{64 \text{ in}^2} = 270$ tiles are needed. Some extra tiles should also be ordered to account for mistakes, wastage, and so on. **40.** $90°$, since viewing one side of length $300'$ as the base, the altitude of the triangle is greatest if the angle is $90°$. **41. (a)** 48 square units. **43.** The circumscribed circle has four times the area of the inscribed circle. **47. (a)** 100 cm **(c)** 10,000 cm^2

Problem Set 11.3   (page 716)

1. (a) $x^2 = 7^2 + 24^2 = 625$, so $x = 25$. **(c)** $x^2 + 5^2 = 22^2$, so $x = \sqrt{459}$. **(e)** $x^2 = 1^2 + 1^2 = 2$, so $x = \sqrt{2}$.
2. (a) $x^2 + (2x)^2 = 25^2$, $5x^2 = 625$, $x = \sqrt{125} = 5\sqrt{5}$.
3. (a) $x^2 = 10^2 + 15^2 = 325$, so $x = \sqrt{325}$; $y^2 = x^2 + 7^2 = 325 + 49 = 374$, so $y = \sqrt{374}$. **4. (a)** $x = \sqrt{13^2 - 12^2} = 5$ **5. (a)** Height $= \sqrt{15^2 - 9^2} = 12$, so

area $= (20)(12) = 240$ square units. **7.** The areas are equal. The small circle of radius 1 has area π, and the large circle of radius $\sqrt{2}$ has area $\pi(\sqrt{2})^2 = 2\pi$, so the area between the circles is $2\pi - \pi = \pi$. **9.** $AG = 3$, since $AC = \sqrt{5}$, $AD = \sqrt{6}, AE = \sqrt{7}, AF = \sqrt{8}$, and $AG = \sqrt{9}$.
11.

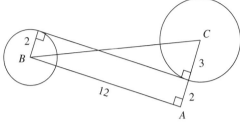

The distance between centers, B and C, is $\sqrt{12^2 + 5^2} = 13$.
13. (a) $(21)^2 + (28)^2 = 1225 = (35)^2$, yes **(c)** $(12)^2 + (35)^2 = 1369 = (37)^2$, yes **(e)** $(7\sqrt{2})^2 + (4\sqrt{7})^2 = 210 \neq 308 = (2\sqrt{77})^2$, no
15. (a)

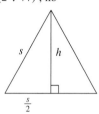

$\left(\dfrac{s}{2}\right)^2 + (h)^2 = s^2$, by the Pythagorean theorem. Therefore $h = \dfrac{\sqrt{3}}{2}s$. **18.** Flattening the top of the box as suggested gives the diagram shown. By the Pythagorean theorem, $AC' = \sqrt{12^2 + 5^2} = \sqrt{169} = 13$ and $AC'' = \sqrt{9^2 + 8^2} = \sqrt{145} = 12.04. \ldots$ The shortest distance is therefore about 12 inches, crossing over the 9 inch edge.

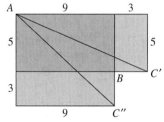

21. (a)

(b) Since the square and "double square" are covered by the same five shapes, their areas are equal. The respective areas are c^2 and $a^2 + b^2$, so $c^2 = a^2 + b^2$.

23.

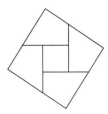

25. Answers will vary, but your ladder cannot be vertical, so the height is less than 24 feet. If the base is 7 feet from the wall the top of the ladder is still nearly 23 feet off of the ground. **27.** Let d be the depth of the pond. The stem length is $d + 2$ (in feet). Held to the side, a right triangle is formed with legs of length 6 and d and hypotenuse of length $(d + 2)$. Then $6^2 + d^2 = (d + 2)^2$, so $d = 8$ feet.
31. (a) $d \doteq 1.2\sqrt{100} = 12$ miles. **32.** The sum of the areas of the equilateral triangles on the legs equals the area of the equilateral triangle on the hypotenuse. **34.** Let the original dimensions be l and w. The changed dimensions are $\frac{4}{3}l$ and $\frac{3}{4}w$. Therefore, area $= \left(\frac{4}{3}l\right)\left(\frac{3}{4}w\right) = lw$, the same as the original area. **36.** Along large semicircle:
$\frac{1}{2}(2 \cdot \pi \cdot 8 \text{ m}) = 8\pi$ m. Along the two smaller semicircles:
$\frac{1}{2}(2 \cdot \pi \cdot 3 \text{ m}) + \frac{1}{2}(2 \cdot \pi \cdot 5 \text{ m}) = 8\pi$ m. The distances are the same.

Problem Set 11.4   (page 735)

1. (a) $SA = 2 \cdot \frac{1}{2}(20 \text{ cm} + 15 \text{ cm})(12 \text{ cm}) + (2 \text{ cm}) \cdot$
$(60 \text{ cm}) = 540 \text{ cm}^2$ **(c)** $SA = 2 \cdot \pi(15 \text{ ft})^2 + 2\pi \cdot (15 \text{ ft}) \cdot$
$(12 \text{ ft}) = 810\pi \text{ ft}^2 \doteq 2545 \text{ ft}^2$
2. (a) slant height $= \sqrt{(40 \text{ m})^2 + (30 \text{ m})^2} = 50$ m,
$SA = (60 \text{ m})^2 + 4 \cdot \frac{1}{2} \cdot (60 \text{ m}) \cdot (50 \text{ m}) = 9600 \text{ m}^2$
(c) $SA = \pi(6 \text{ in})^2 + \pi(6 \text{ in}) \cdot (15 \text{ in}) = 126 \pi \text{ in}^2 \doteq 396 \text{ in}^2$
3. (a) $V = Bh = (7 \text{ cm})(4 \text{ cm})(3 \text{ cm}) = 84 \text{ cm}^3$
(c) $\pi(10 \text{ m})^2 (4 \text{ m}) = 400\pi \text{ m}^3 \doteq 1257 \text{ m}^3$
4. (a) $\frac{1}{3}(8 \text{ ft})(12 \text{ ft})(10 \text{ ft}) = 320 \text{ ft}^3$
(c) $\frac{1}{3}\pi(5 \text{ cm})^2 (12 \text{ cm}) = 100\pi \text{ cm}^3 \doteq 314 \text{ cm}^3$
5. (a) $SA = 4\pi(2200 \text{ km})^2 = 19,360,000\pi \text{ km}^2 \doteq$
$6.08 \times 10^7 \text{ km}^2$,
$V = \frac{4}{3}\pi(2200 \text{ km})^3 \doteq 4.46 \times 10^{10} \text{ km}^3$
(c) $SA = 4\pi(4 \text{ ft})^2 + 2\pi(4 \text{ ft}) (20 \text{ ft}) = 224 \pi \text{ ft}^2 \doteq 704 \text{ ft}^2$,
$V = \frac{4}{3}\pi(4 \text{ ft})^3 + \pi(4 \text{ ft})^2(20 \text{ ft}) \doteq 1273 \text{ ft}^3$
8. Area (sphere) $= 4\pi r^2$ square units. Area (cylinder) $=$
$2 \cdot \pi \cdot r^2 + 2\pi r \cdot (2r) = 6 \pi r^2$ square units. Thus,
$4 \pi r^2/6 \pi r^2 = 2/3$. **9. (a)** 16 cm **10. (a)** 4, considering

area **(b)** One 14" pizza is nearly the same amount of pizza, but will save \$2. **12. (a)** $1 - \frac{1}{4} - \frac{1}{4} = \frac{1}{2}$ (the small circles have one-half the diameter, so 1/4 the area) **14. (a)** 200 ml (doubling the radius increases volume by factor of 4; halving height halves the volume) **19.** Suppose the area of the similar figure with straight side of length 1 is A. By the similarity principle, the areas of the figures erected on the sides of the triangle are then a^2A, b^2A, and c^2A, since a, b, and c are the respective scale factors. Since $a^2 + b^2 = c^2$ (Pythagorean theorem), we get $a^2A + b^2A = c^2A$, showing that the sum of the areas of the figures erected on the legs is equal to the area of the figure erected on the hypotenuse.
20. (a) 3 in, since $2/16 = 1/8 = (1/2)^3$ and $\frac{1}{2} \cdot 6" = 3"$.
21. (a)

(diagram with measurements $8\sqrt{2}$, 8, $8\sqrt{2}$, 8, 8, 8, $8\sqrt{2}$, $8\sqrt{3}$, $8\sqrt{2}$, $8\sqrt{3}$)

23. (a) Circumference of the cone is $\frac{3}{4} \cdot 2 \cdot \pi(4 \text{ in}) = 6 \pi$ in, so the radius is 3 in. **24.** Let s be the radius of the semicircle. Then the slant height of the cone is s. Let d be the diameter of the cone. Then $\pi d = \frac{1}{2}(2\pi)(s)$, so $d = s$.

25. $V(\text{ring}) = \pi\left(\frac{9}{16}\text{ in}\right)^2\left(\frac{5}{4}\text{ in}\right) - \pi\left(\frac{1}{2}\text{ in}\right)^2\left(\frac{5}{4}\text{ in}\right) \doteq$
0.26 in^3, so about 1.56 ounces. **27.** $V(\text{box}) = 160 \text{ in}^3$ and $V(\text{tub}) = \pi(3 \text{ in})^2(10 \text{ in}) \doteq 283 \text{ in}^3$. Two boxes is a better buy. **29. (a)** $\left(\frac{5 \text{ in}}{13 \text{ in}}\right)^3 (106.75 \text{ pounds}) \doteq 6.07$ pounds
31. (a) The scale factor is 12 and volume would be increased by the factor $12^3 = 1728$.
32. (a) $s = 1/\sqrt{2}$, since then $s^2 = 1/2$ showing that the area of an A1 sheet is half that of an A0 sheet.
(b)

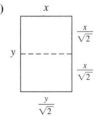

Using part (a), we see that the width x of an A0 sheet is $y/\sqrt{2}$, where y is the length. Then $xy = y^2/\sqrt{2} = 1 \text{ m}^2$, so $y = 2^{1/4}$ m $\doteq 1.2$ m and $x = 1/2^{1/4}$ m $\doteq 0.84$ m. **34.** The circular cross sections are related by a scale factor of 3, so 9 inches of water in the cylinder corresponds to 1 inch of rainfall. **35. (b)** The 3" and \$3 are not scale factors. The reasoning seems to suggest that a 6" pizza should cost $2, and a 3" pizza is given away together with $1. **36. (a)** Yes, since $30^2 + 72^2 = 6084 = 78^2$ **38.** $P \doteq 8 + 2\sqrt{5} + \sqrt{2} + \sqrt{10} \doteq 17.$ $A = 12$ square units. **39.** $\dfrac{50 \text{ in}}{\text{sec}} \cdot \dfrac{1 \text{ ft}}{12 \text{ in}} \cdot \dfrac{1 \text{ mile}}{5280 \text{ ft}} \cdot \dfrac{60 \text{ sec}}{1 \text{ min}} \cdot \dfrac{60 \text{ min}}{1 \text{ hr}} \doteq 2.84$ miles per hour.

40. (a) 27.8 cm

Chapter 11 Review Exercises   (page 744)

1. (a) Centimeters **(b)** Millimeters **(c)** Kilometers **(d)** Meters **(e)** Hectares **(f)** Square kilometers **(g)** Milliliters **(h)** Liters
2. (a) 4 L **(b)** 190 cm **(c)** 200 m^2 **3.** 84 L
4. $\dfrac{300 \text{ ft}}{3 \text{ sec}} \cdot \dfrac{1 \text{ mile}}{5280 \text{ ft}} \cdot \dfrac{60 \text{ sec}}{1 \text{ min}} \cdot \dfrac{60 \text{ min}}{1 \text{ hr}} \doteq 68$ miles per hour
5.

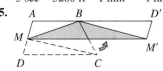

The triangle has half the area of the parallelogram $AD'M'M$, so it also has half the area of the trapezoid $ABCD$.

6. (a) $768 \text{ in}^2 = 5\dfrac{1}{3} \text{ ft}^2$ **(b)** $\dfrac{1}{2}(8 \text{ m})(9 \text{ m}) + \dfrac{1}{2}(3 \text{ m}) \cdot$

$(6 \text{ m}) = 45 \text{ m}^2$ **(c)** $\dfrac{1}{2}(5 \text{ cm} + 7 \text{ cm})(3 \text{ cm}) = 18 \text{ cm}^2$

7. (a) 11 square units **(b)** 9 square units **(c)** $9\dfrac{1}{2}$ square

units **8. (a)** $A = (3 \text{ ft})(4 \text{ ft}) + \dfrac{1}{2}\pi(1.5 \text{ ft})^2 \doteq 15.5 \text{ ft}^2,$

$P = 11 \text{ ft} + \pi(1.5 \text{ ft}) \doteq 15.7 \text{ ft}$ **(b)** $A = \dfrac{3}{4}\pi(3 \text{ m})^2 \doteq$

$21.2 \text{ m}^2, P = \dfrac{3}{4} \cdot 2\pi(3 \text{ m}) + 6 \text{ m} \doteq 20.1 \text{ m}$ **9.** $x = 6,$

$y = \sqrt{5}$ (*Methods to solve:* Find the area two ways, or use similar triangles.) **10.** $\sqrt{1125} \text{ cm} \doteq 33.5 \text{ cm}$
11. $\sqrt{116} \text{ in}, \sqrt{160} \text{ in}, \sqrt{244} \text{ in}, \sqrt{260} \text{ in}$
12. $9 + \sqrt{2} + \sqrt{10} + \sqrt{5} \doteq 15.8$ units

13. (a) $V = [(10 \text{ ft})(20 \text{ ft}) + \dfrac{1}{2}(8 \text{ ft} + 20 \text{ ft})(8 \text{ ft})](30 \text{ ft}) =$

9360 ft^3

$SA = 2 \cdot \dfrac{1}{2}(8 \text{ ft} + 20 \text{ ft})(8 \text{ ft}) + 2 \cdot (10 \text{ ft})(20 \text{ ft}) +$
$2 \cdot (10 \text{ ft})(30 \text{ ft}) + 2 \cdot (10 \text{ ft})(30 \text{ ft}) +$
$(8 \text{ ft})(30 \text{ ft}) + (20 \text{ ft})(30 \text{ ft}) = 2664 \text{ ft}^2$

(b) $V = \pi(7 \text{ m})^2(18 \text{ m}) + \dfrac{1}{2} \cdot \dfrac{4}{3}\pi(7 \text{ m})^3 \doteq 3489 \text{ m}^3$

$SA = \dfrac{1}{2} \cdot 4\pi(7 \text{ m})^2 + 2\pi(7 \text{ m})(18 \text{ m}) + \pi(7 \text{ m})^2 \doteq$

1253 m^2

(c) $V = \dfrac{1}{3}\pi(5 \text{ cm})^2(8 \text{ cm}) + \dfrac{1}{2} \cdot \dfrac{4}{3}\pi(5 \text{ cm})^3 \doteq 471 \text{ cm}^3$

$SA = \dfrac{1}{2} \cdot 4\pi(5 \text{ cm})^2 + \pi(5 \text{ cm})(\sqrt{25 + 64} \text{ cm}) =$

$(50 + 5\sqrt{89})\pi \text{ cm}^2 \doteq 305 \text{ cm}^2$

14. $V(\text{sphere}) = \dfrac{4}{3}\pi(10 \text{ m})^3$ and $V(\text{four cubes}) = 4(10 \text{ m})^3.$

Since $\pi > 3$, then $\dfrac{4}{3}\pi > 4$, showing that the sphere has

larger volume. **15. (a)** $(180 \text{ ft})(1.5) = 270 \text{ ft}$, since $k = 1.5$

is the scale factor. **(b)** $\dfrac{45 \text{ pounds}}{(1.5)^2} = 20$ pounds, since

Johan's garden area is $(1/1.5)^2$ times that of Heather's.

Chapter 11 Test   (page 745)

1. (a) mm **(b)** m **(c)** m **(d)** km **(e)** mL **(f)** liters
2. (a) 216.1 cm **(b)** 168,200 cm **(c)** 5000 cm^2
(d) 10,000 m^2 **(e)** 4.719 L **(f)** 3200 cm^3
3. (a) Approximately 31.86 yd **(b)** Approximately 1.5 mi
(c) 291.6 ft^2 **(d)** Approximately 14.69 mi^2 **(e)** 205.2 ft^3
(f) Approximately 3.45 ft^3 **4.** Each figure contains four full units of area. Figure A contains an additional eight half-units of area, and figure B contains an additional four half-units of area. Jim should conclude that Figure A is four half-units, or two units, of area larger than B.
5.

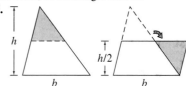

area (triangle) = area (parallelogram) = $(b)(h/2) = \dfrac{1}{2}bh.$

6. (a) 8 cm^2 **(b)** 8 cm^2 **(c)** 8.5 cm^2 **7.** $A = \dfrac{1}{2} \cdot (6 \text{ cm}) \cdot$

$(16 \text{ cm}) + \dfrac{1}{2}(15 \text{ cm})(16 \text{ cm}) = 168 \text{ cm}^2.$ Sides are 10 cm

and 17 cm by the Pythagorean theorem, so $P = 54 \text{ cm}.$

8. $A = \dfrac{1}{2}(9 \text{ ft})(12 \text{ ft}) + (8 \text{ ft})(12 \text{ ft}) - \dfrac{1}{2}\pi(4 \text{ ft})^2 \doteq 125 \text{ ft}^2$

$P = 15 \text{ ft} + 9 \text{ ft} + 8 \text{ ft} + 12 \text{ft} + \dfrac{1}{2} \cdot 2\pi(4 \text{ ft}) \doteq 56.6 \text{ ft}$

9. (a) $\dfrac{2}{3}\pi(5 \text{ in})^2 \doteq 52.4 \text{ in}^2$ **(b)** $\dfrac{1}{2}(2.6 \text{ m} + 1.4 \text{ m})(3 \text{ m}) =$

6.0 m^2 **(c)** $\dfrac{1}{12} \cdot \pi(24 \text{ cm})^2 \doteq 151 \text{ cm}^2$

10. Let the radius of the circle be r. Then the circumscribed square has sides of length $2r$ and the inscribed square has sides of length $\sqrt{2}\,r.$

$$\dfrac{\text{area (inscribed)}}{\text{area (circumscribed)}} = \dfrac{(\sqrt{2}r)^2}{(2r)^2} = \dfrac{2r^2}{4r^2} = \dfrac{1}{2}.$$

Alternate solution: The scale factor of the large to the small square is $1/\sqrt{2}$, so the small square has $(1/\sqrt{2})^2 = 1/2$ the area of the large square.

11. Cross-sectional view:

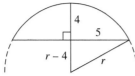

$(r - 4)^2 + (5)^2 = r^2$, or $r^2 - 8r + 16 + 25 = r^2$. Then $r = (16 + 25)/8$ mm $= 5.125$ mm.

12. $\sqrt{189}$ ft $\doteq 13.7$ ft, by the Pythagorean theorem.

13. (a) $P = \sqrt{52} + \sqrt{13} + \sqrt{65} \doteq 18.9$ units

(b) Yes, $(\sqrt{52})^2 + (\sqrt{13})^2 = 65 = (\sqrt{65})^2$.

14. (a) $SA = 2 \cdot \dfrac{1}{2}(7 \text{ m})(24 \text{ m}) + (7 \text{ m} + 24 \text{ m} + 25 \text{ m}) \cdot$

$(5 \text{ m}) = 448 \text{ m}^2$, since the diagonal is 25 m.

$V = \dfrac{1}{2}(7 \text{ m})(24 \text{ m})(5 \text{ m}) = 420 \text{ m}^3$

(b) $SA = 2 \cdot \dfrac{1}{2}\pi(4")^2 + \dfrac{1}{2} \cdot 2\pi(4")(6") + (6")(8") \doteq 173.7 \text{ in}^2$

$V = \dfrac{1}{2}\pi(4")^2(6") \doteq 150.8 \text{ in}^3$

(c) Slant height is 10 ft. $SA = 4 \cdot \dfrac{1}{2}(12 \text{ ft})(10 \text{ ft}) +$

$(144 \text{ ft})^2 = 384 \text{ ft}^2$

$V = \dfrac{1}{3}(12 \text{ ft})^2(8 \text{ ft}) = 384 \text{ ft}^3$

(d) Slant height is 13 cm. $SA = \pi(5 \text{ cm})^2 +$

$\pi(5 \text{ cm})(13 \text{ cm}) = 90\ \pi \text{ cm}^2 \doteq 283 \text{ cm}^2$

$V = \dfrac{1}{3}\pi(5 \text{ cm})^2(12 \text{ cm}) = 100\ \pi \text{ cm}^3 \doteq 314 \text{ cm}^3$

15. (a) $SA = 4\pi(10 \text{ m})^2 = 400\pi \text{ m}^2 \doteq 1257 \text{ m}^2$

$V = \dfrac{4}{3}\pi(10 \text{ m})^3 \doteq 4189 \text{ m}^3$

(b) $SA = \pi(5 \text{ cm})^2 + 2\pi(5 \text{ cm})(6 \text{ cm}) +$

$\dfrac{1}{2} \cdot 4\ \pi(5 \text{ cm})^2 = 135\pi \text{ cm}^2 \doteq 424 \text{ cm}^2$

$V = \pi(5 \text{ cm})^2(6 \text{ cm}) + \dfrac{1}{2} \cdot \dfrac{4}{3}\pi(5 \text{ cm})^3 \doteq 733 \text{ cm}^3$

16.

	Papa	Mama	Baby
Length of suspenders	50	40	20
Weight	468.75	240	30
Number of fleas	6000	3840	960

Scale Factors	
PB to MB	4/5
MB to BB	1/2

17. $V(\text{peel}) = \dfrac{4}{3}\pi(2.5 \text{ in})^3 - \dfrac{4}{3}\pi(1.75 \text{ in})^3 \doteq 43.0 \text{ in}^3$,

and $V(\text{grapefruit}) = \dfrac{4}{3}\pi(2.5 \text{ in})^3 \doteq 65.4 \text{ in}^3$. About 66 percent is peel. *Alternate solution:* The scale factor is

$\left(2\dfrac{1}{2} - 3/4\right) \Big/ 2\dfrac{1}{2} = 0.7$. Since $(0.7)^3 = 0.343$, it follows that 34.3 percent of the grapefruit is not peel, and 65.7 percent is peel.

Chapter 12

JUST FOR FUN   Inverting the Tetractys   (page 754)

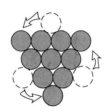

Problem Set 12.1   (page 768)

1. (a) Not a rigid motion. Distances between particular cards will change. **(c)** No, distances between particular pieces almost certainly will have changed.

2. (a)

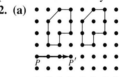

4. (a) 300° **(c)** 43° **5. (a)**

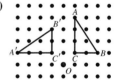

6. (a) Center O is the intersection of $\overleftrightarrow{AB}$ and $\overleftrightarrow{A'B'}$.

9. (a) Draw the vertical line through the midpoint of PP'.

11. (a), (b)

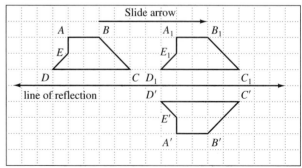

13. (a)

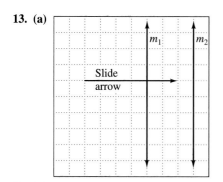

15. (a)

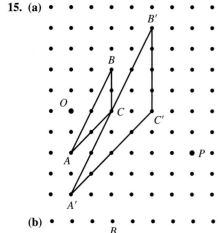

(b)

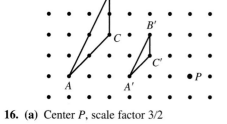

16. (a) Center P, scale factor 3/2

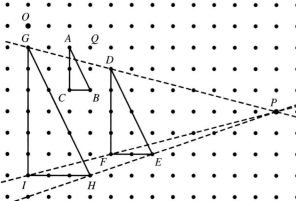

18. Rotate 90° counterclockwise about B. Then perform a dilation centered at P with scale factor 2. (Other sequences will also work.)

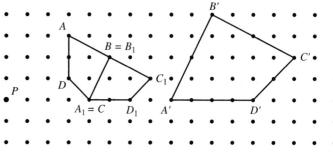

19. (a)

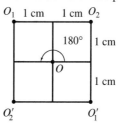

P' is some point of the circle at A' of radius 2 cm.

20. On a 1 cm square grid, the two 90° rotations take O_1 to O'_1 and O_2 to O'_2 as shown. This motion is equivalent to the 180° rotation about the point O.

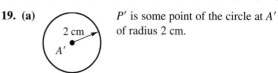

22. (a), (b)

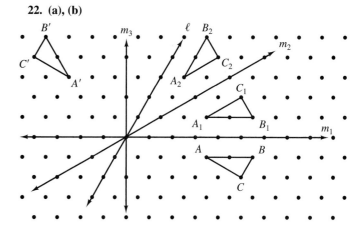

24. (a)

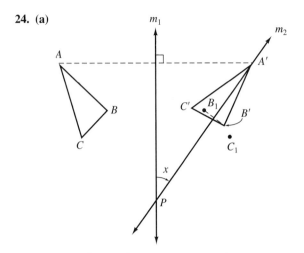

(b) C' **(c)** Reflection first across line m_1 and then across line m_2 is equivalent to a rotation about the point P of intersection of m_1 and m_2, through an angle twice the measure x of the directed angle from line m_1 toward line m_2.
26. (a) A translation. Six reflections give an orientation preserving rigid motion, so it is either a rotation or a translation. Since a rotation has a fixed point (namely the rotation center), the motion is a translation.
28. (a) A glide reflection **29.** The line $\overleftrightarrow{PP'}$ passes through O, so constructing this line determines point O. $\overline{PQ}$ and $\overline{P'Q'}$ are parallel, so the line through P' that is parallel to $\overline{PQ}$ will determine Q'.

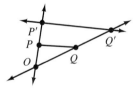

31. The mirror only needs to be 31" tall, half of Estelle's height of 62". The top of the mirror must be 3" lower than the top of Estelle's head; that is, the top is 59" off the floor. It does not matter how far away Estelle stands; her reflection is always twice the distance she stands from the mirror.

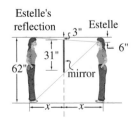

32. (a) $\overline{RS'}$ is the reflection of $\overline{RS}$ across m, so $RS' = RS$ since a reflection preserves all distances. Similarly, $QS' = QS$. **34.** A single mirror reverses orientation, so the double reflection seen in a corner mirror preserves

orientation. The corner mirror reflection of your right hand will appear as a right hand.

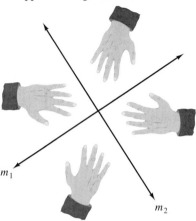

38. (a) Measurements show $\triangle XYZ$ is equilateral. **(b)** The centers of the rotated equilateral triangles form an equilateral triangular grid. **42.** $2x + 3x + 4x = 180$, so $x = 20$, giving angles of measure 40°, 60°, and 80°. **44.** Midpoints form a nonsquare rectangle in this example.

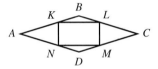

JUST FOR FUN   The Penny Game   (page 780)

Lynn can always place a penny at the position that is point symmetric to Kelly's last move. Since Lynn can always make a move, Kelly will be the first player unable to find space for an additional penny on the table.

Problem Set 12.2   (page 783)

1. (a)   **(c)**

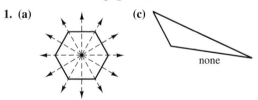

3. (a) Many figures are possible.

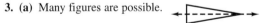

4. (a) m **(c)** m

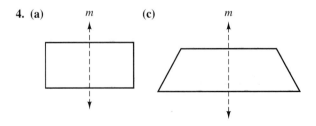

7. (a)

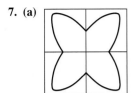

8. (a) One line of symmetry **9. (a)** Five lines of symmetry and 72° rotation symmetry **(b)** 72° rotation symmetry
10. (a)

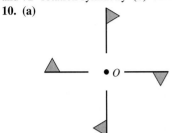

11. (a) Equilateral triangle **(b)** Square **12. (a)** 0, 8
(b) 0, 3, 8 **(c)** 0, 8 **(d)** 0, 8 **15. (a)** m1
16. (a) There are vertical lines of symmetry through the centers of each letter, and there is a horizontal line of symmetry. The symbol type is *mm*. **17. (a)** No letter or digit reflects vertically into a different letter or digit, so it must reflect into itself. **19.** The pattern must also have a horizontal line of symmetry, so it would be an mm pattern.
21. (a) lg **(c)** mg
23. (a) 11

p	p	p	p	p	p

(c) 12

.p	d	p	d	p	d

25. (a) Three directions of reflection symmetry; three directions of glide symmetry; 120° rotation symmetry.
26. (a) 3 **27. (a)** As left-handed people know well, scissors are not symmetric. **(c)** A man's dress shirt is not quite symmetric, since it buttons right handed. **(e)** Tennis rackets have two planes of bilateral symmetry.
28. (a) Across the line of diagonal entries **38. (a)** 350°
39. (a)

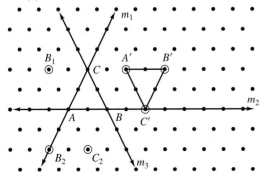

(b) Glide reflection, 3 units right and reflect across the line *l* parallel to $\overline{AB}$ and midway between *C* and $\overline{AB}$.

JUST FOR FUN   Quadrilateral + Quadrilateral = Parallelogram?   (page 795)

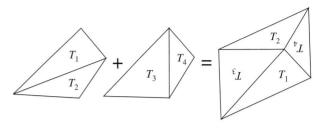

Problem Set 12.3   (page 800)

1. Many different tilings can be formed. For example:
(a)

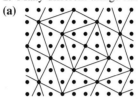

2. Yes, tilings are possible. For example:
(a)

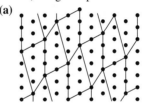

3. (a) Squares, pentagons, hexagons, heptagons, octagons **(b)** Many vertex figures that appear in the tiling cannot correspond to regular polygons. For example, regular 5-, 6-, and 8-gons have interior angles of measure 108°, 120°, and 135°. These add up to 108° + 120° + 135° = 363° ≠ 360°.
5. The interior angle of a square is 90° and for a pentagon is
$$\frac{(5 - 2)(180°)}{5} = 108°$$ and for a 20-gon is
$$\frac{(20 - 2)(180°)}{20} = 162°.$$ Then, 90° + 108° + 162° = 360°.
15. Here's one way to make a tiling 12-gon, by modifying a square tile.

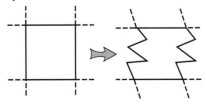

Similarly, modifying an equilateral triangle by a midpoint modification with opposite parallel congruent sides will form a 11-gon that tiles as shown.

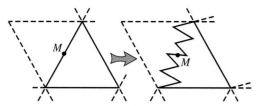

The same idea can be used for any $n \geq 6$, using a modified square for even n, and a modified equilateral triangle for odd n.

17. (a) 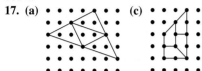 **(c)**

19. (a)

24. Letters above the line are formed with straight pen strokes while letters below the line involved curved pen strokes. **25.** Let A, B, and C be the vertices of an equilateral triangle, and D the center (centroid) of the triangle.

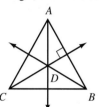

Chapter 12 Review Exercises   (page 806)

1.

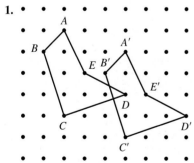

2. Find the perpendicular bisectors of segments $\overline{AA'}$ and $\overline{BB'}$. Their intersection is the turn center O, and the measure of $\angle AOA'$ is the turn angle.
3. Reflection across line l.

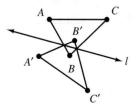

4. Draw any two vertical lines two inches apart. There are then three ways to choose the successive lines of reflection.

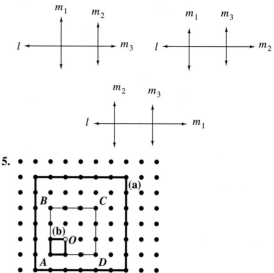

5.

6. Rotate $ABCD$ 45° about the center, P, of the square. Then do a dilation about P with scale factor $\dfrac{\sqrt{2}}{2}$. **7. (a)** 1 **(b)** 2 **(c)** 0 **(d)** 0 **(e)** 3 **(f)** All lines through the center point, since the figure has circular symmetry. **8. (a)** none **(b)** 180° **(c)** 180° **(d)** 72°, 144°, 216°, 288° **(e)** 120°, 240° **(f)** Any angle **9. (a)** Vertical line of symmetry **(b)** Horizontal line of symmetry **10.** The angles are 60° for the triangle, 90° for the square, and 120° for the hexagon. The angles of the four polygons must add up to 360°, so the fourth angle is 90°, and therefore the fourth polygon is a square. **11.**

12. Use 180° rotations of the tile about the midpoints of the sides.

Chapter 12 Test   (page 807)

1. C' is 2 units right of B'; B is 2 units left of C.
2. (a) Center P and rotation angle 90°
(b)

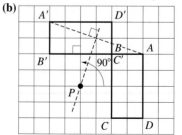

3. Construct the perpendicular bisector of $\overline{AA'}$, and suppose it intersects the sides of $\angle A$ at points labeled B and C. Then $\angle BA'C$ is the desired angle.

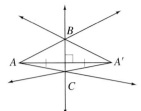

4.

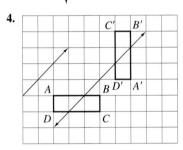

5. Various pairs of lines are possible. The distance between the lines must be half the distance between P and P'.

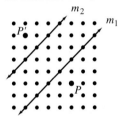

6. Many pairs of lines are possible. The two lines need to intersect at point O and the directed angle between the lines should be half the measure of $\angle QOQ'$.

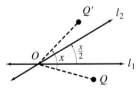

7. (a) Glide reflection **(b)** Reflection **(c)** Reflection **(d)** Glide reflection

8. (a) A **(b)** $\dfrac{2}{3}$ **(c)** $\dfrac{40}{3}$ **(d)** 9

9. Many transformations are possible. Here is one sequence: translate the square so A is taken to A'; rotate about A' by 45°; perform a dilation about A' with scale factor $3\sqrt{2}/2$ (since $A'B' = 3\sqrt{2}$ and $AB = 2$).

10. (a)

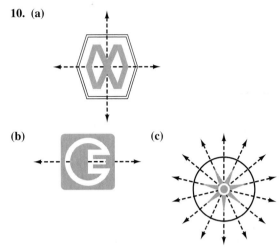

(b)   **(c)**

11. (a) 180° **(b)** none **(c)** 360°/7 **12. (a)** Point (180° rotation) symmetry, and two diagonal lines of symmetry **(b)** Four lines of symmetry, and 90° rotation symmetry **13. (a)** Glide reflection (1g) **(b)** Vertical and horizontal lines of symmetry (mm), and glide and half-turn symmetries **(c)** Half-turn symmetry (12) **(d)** Half-turn symmetry, vertical line of symmetry, glide reflection (mg) **14.** *(a), (b), (c), (d),* and *(e)* tile the plane. **15.** A vertex figure uses two octagons and one square. **16. (a)** Rotation **(b)** Rotation

Chapter 13

JUST FOR FUN   Twice Around a Triangle (page 823)

P'' coincides with the original point P.

Problem Set 13.1   (page 824)

1. (a) $L \leftrightarrow K, H \leftrightarrow W, S \leftrightarrow T$ **(b)** $\overline{KW}, \overline{WT}, \overline{TK}$ **(c)** $\angle K, \angle W, \angle T$ **(d)** $\triangle KWT$
3. (a) Draw a line l and mark any point as E. Set your compass to AB and determine a point G on your line segment with an arc centered at E. Set your compass to distance CD and draw an arc centered at G to determine F on l, away from E. **(b)** Begin as in (a). Set compass to CD and draw an arc centered at G to determine on l F, back toward E.
6. (a) One such triangle. **(c)** Impossible by the triangle inequality, since $2 + 5 < 8$. **(e)** One such triangle.
7. (c) $\triangle ABC \cong \triangle EFD$ by SSS **(e)** $\triangle ABD \cong \triangle ACD$ by ASA **(g)** No conclusion possible. **(i)** No conclusion possible. **8.** Let $\triangle ABC$ be equilateral. Since $AB = BC$, it follows from the isosceles triangle theorem that $\angle A \cong \angle C$. In the same way, since $BC = CA$ it follows that $\angle B \cong \angle A$. Thus all three angles are congruent. **11. (a)** $\triangle QPT \cong \triangle SPT$ by the SSS congruence property. **12. (a)** $\angle ABD \cong \angle CDB$, as alternate interior angles between parallel lines. Likewise, $\angle ADB \cong \angle CBD$, and $DB = BD$. By ASA, $\angle ABD \cong \angle CDB$.
16. Place a corner of the rectangular sheet of paper at a point C on the circle and mark the points A and B where the

edges of the paper cross the circle. By the converse of Thales' theorem, $\overline{AB}$ is a diameter of the circle. Repeating the procedure at a second point C' will allow you to construct a second diameter $\overline{A'B'}$. The center of the circle is where the two diameters intersect.

17. It is longer than 5 cm and shorter than 13 cm (remember the triangle inequality). **18. (a)** $0 < s < 14$ cm, where s is the length of the fourth side. **20. (a)** $\triangle ABE$ is isosceles, with $AB = BE$, so the base angles are congruent by the isosceles triangle theorem. **(b)** $\triangle ACD$ is isosceles, so its base angles are congruent. **(c)** $\angle ACB$ and $\angle ACD$ are supplementary, as are $\angle ADC$ and $\angle ADE$. Since $\angle ACD \cong \angle ADC$, then we get $\angle ACB \cong \angle ADE$. Using $\angle B \cong \angle E$ and $AC = AD$, the AAS property gives $\triangle ABC \cong \triangle AED$. **(d)** From part (c), $\overline{BC} \cong \overline{ED}$. **22. (a)** Yes, using ASA. **(c)** Yes, using SAS. **23.** If $AB = CD = a$, $BC = AD = b$, and $AC = BD = c$, then each face of the tetrahedron is a triangle with sides of length a, b, and c. By the SSS property, the triangles are congruent to one another. **24. (a)** By the triangle inequality, $QP + QT > TP$. Therefore, $QP + QT + TR > TP + TR$. But $QT + TR = QR$, so $QP + QR > TP + TR$. **25. (a)** $EA + ED > DA$ by the triangle inequality. **27. (a)** The angles at the vertices of a quadrilateral can change even though the lengths of the sides are fixed. (There is no "SSSS congruence property" for a quadrilateral). **28. (a)** The framework forms a parallelogram, but not necessarily a rectangle.
31. (a), (b) The measure of $\angle APB$ is a constant, always satisfying the equation $m(\angle AOB) = 2\, m(\angle APB)$ **(c)** Draw the diameter $\overline{PQ}$. There are two cases to consider.

Case 1:

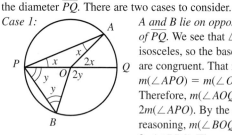

A and B lie on opposite sides of $\overline{PQ}$. We see that $\triangle POA$ is isosceles, so the base angles are congruent. That is, $m(\angle APO) = m(\angle OAP) = x$. Therefore, $m(\angle AOQ) = 2x = 2m(\angle APO)$. By the same reasoning, $m(\angle BOQ) = 2y = 2m(\angle BPO)$. Thus, $m(\angle AOB) = 2x + 2y = 2m(\angle APB)$.

Case 2:

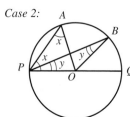

A and B are on the same side of $\overline{PQ}$. Nearly the same analysis holds, but now $m(\angle AOB) = 2x - 2y = 2m(\angle APB)$.

34. (a) The motion is either a translation or a rotation, since only these motions keep the picture side of the piece facing upward. **(b)** The motion must flip the puzzle piece over so it is either a reflection or a glide reflection.

JUST FOR FUN   Circle Amazement   (page 836)

The jar lid will also give the circle through A, B, and C. When it is drawn, each of the four points A, B, C, and P is the intersection of three of the circles.

Problem Set 13.2   (page 843)

1. (a) Step 1: Draw a line through P that intersects l. Label the intersection point A. Step 2: Draw arcs of equal radius at A and P. Label, with B and C, the intersection points of the arc at A, and label as D the intersection of the arc at P with $\overleftrightarrow{AP}$. Step 3: Set the compass to radius BC, and draw an arc at D. Let E denote the intersection with the arc drawn at P. Step 4: Construct the line k through P and E. **(b)** The construction gives the congruence of the corresponding angles, $\angle PAC \cong \angle DPE$. Therefore $k \parallel l$ by the corresponding angles property. **3. (a)** The corresponding angles property guarantees that k is parallel to l. **(b)** Align the ruler with the line; slide the drafting triangle, with one leg of the right triangle on the ruler, until the second leg of the triangle meets point P. **7. (a)** The circumcenter will be inside the acute triangle. **(b)** The circumcenter will be at the midpoint of the hypotenuse of a right triangle. **(c)** The circumcenter will be outside an obtuse triangle. **(d)** The circumcenter is inside, on, or outside a triangle if, and only if, the triangle is acute, right, or obtuse, respectively. **9.** Since $\triangle PQS$ is inscribed in the circle with diameter $\overline{PQ}$, it has a right angle at S by Thales' theorem. Thus $\overline{PS} \perp \overline{SQ}$. Similarly, $\overline{PT} \perp \overline{TQ}$. **12.** By Thales' theorem, $\angle ADB$ is a right angle. We also see that $\triangle ODB$ is an equilateral triangle, since all sides have the length of the radius. Moreover, $ODBE$ is a rhombus, so the side $\overline{DE}$ is a bisector of the $60°$ angle $\angle ODB$. Thus $m(\angle ADE) = m(\angle ADB) - m(\angle EDB) = 90° - 30° = 60°$. Similarly, $m(\angle AED) = 60°$. Therefore all angles of $\triangle ADE$ have measure $60°$, so $\triangle ADE$ is equilateral. **14.** Since $m(\angle 1) + m(\angle 2) + m(\angle 3) + m(\angle 4) = 180°$, $m(\angle 1) = m(\angle 2)$, and $m(\angle 3) = m(\angle 4)$, it follows that $m(\angle 2) + m(\angle 3) = 180°/2 = 90°$. **15. (a)** Suppose the perpendicular bisector of chord $\overline{AB}$ intersects the circle at a point C. Then the circle is the circumscribing circle of $\triangle ABC$. The center of the circumscribing circle is the point of concurrence of the perpendicular bisectors of all three sides of $\triangle ABC$. In particular, the perpendicular bisector of side $\overline{AB}$ contains the center of the circle. **17. (a)** Extend $\overline{AB}$, and construct the line at A that is perpendicular to $\overline{AB}$. Set the compass to radius AB and mark off this distance on the perpendicular line to determine a point C for which $AC = AB$. Similarly, construct a perpendicular line at B to $\overline{AB}$, and determine a point D (on the same side of $\overline{AB}$ as C) on this perpendicular so $BD = AB$. $ABDC$ is a square with given side $\overline{AB}$. (Other constructions also work.) **18. (a)** Extend $\overline{AB}$ to a longer segment. Erect perpendicular rays to $\overline{AB}$ at both A and B, to the same side of $\overline{AB}$. Bisect the right angle at A, and let its intersection with the ray at B determine point C. Erect the perpendicular at C to $\overline{BC}$, and let D be the intersection with the ray constructed at A. Then $ABCD$ is a square erected on the given side $\overline{AB}$. **21.** Constructible: 3, 4, 5, 6, 8, 10, 12, 15, 16, 17, 20, 24, 30, 32, 34, 40, 48, 51, 60, 64, 68, 80, 85, 96. **24. (a)** The three altitudes of a triangle are concurrent (pass through a single point). **(b)** The perpendicular bisectors of $\triangle PQR$ are concurrent since they intersect at the center of the circle that circumscribes $\triangle PQR$. Since the perpendicular bisectors of $\triangle PQR$ are also the altitudes of $\triangle ABC$, the three altitudes are concurrent. **26.** $m(\angle NOQ) = m(\angle PON) - m(\angle POQ) = 144° - 120° = 24°$, since a central angle for a regular pentagon is 72° and is 120° for an equilateral triangle. A regular 15-gon has central angle $\dfrac{360°}{15} = 24°$, so laying off segments of length QN would give 15 equally spaced points around the circle. **31. (a)** $F_5 = 2^{2^5} + 1 = 2^{32} + 1 = 4{,}294{,}967{,}296 + 1 = 4{,}294{,}967{,}297$. **32. (a)** G, H, and P are collinear. The Euler line passes through G, H, and P. **(b)** $GH/GP = 2$. Thus G is one-third of the distance from P to H along the Euler line. **(c)** The circle intersects all sides of $\triangle ABC$ at their midpoints. **(d)** The circle bisects each of the segments $\overline{AH}$, $\overline{BH}$, and $\overline{CH}$. **34.** $\triangle TRI$ is equilateral. **36. (a)** True. Three pairs of angles and two pairs of sides are congruent. **(b)** False. After pairing up congruent angles, the sides with equal lengths are not corresponding sides in the triangles, so the two triangles are not congruent.

JUST FOR FUN   Thales' Puzzle   (page 854)

Later in the day, the points A and C will cast new shadows, say at P' and Q'. Since both P and P' are away from the pyramid, Thales can easily measure PP' and QQ', and calculate the scale factor $PP'/QQ' = s$. The height of the pyramid is therefore sh, where h is the height of the vertical stick.

Problem Set 13.3   (page 859)

1. (a) First notice that $m(\angle O) = 180° - 60° - 30° = 90°$. Therefore, by the AA similarity property, $\triangle ABC \sim \triangle PNO$. The scale factor from $\triangle ABC$ to $\triangle PNO$ is $\dfrac{12}{8} = \dfrac{3}{2}$. **(c)** By the AA similarity property, $\triangle GHI \sim \triangle TUI$, with scale factor 8/5. **2. (a)** Yes, by AA: all angles are the same, 60°. **(c)** Yes, by the AA similarity property. **(e)** Yes, by the SSS similarity property, or AA, or SAS. **3. (a)** $\dfrac{12}{15} = \dfrac{8}{a}$, so $a = 10$. **(c)** $\dfrac{c}{15} = \dfrac{c+2}{18}$; $18c = 15c + 30$; $c = 10$.

4. (a) No. A square and a nonsquare rectangle are convex quadrilaterals with congruent angles, yet are not similar quadrilaterals. **6. (a)** $\overline{AB}$ is parallel to $\overline{CD}$ so, by alternate interior angles, $\angle BAE \cong \angle DCE$. Also, $\angle AEB \cong \angle CED$, being vertical angles, so the AA similarity property gives $\triangle ABE \sim \triangle CDE$. **(b)** By similarity, $\dfrac{x}{36} = \dfrac{17}{51}$, so $x = 12$. Also, $\dfrac{26}{y} = \dfrac{17}{51}$, so $y = 78$. **8. (a)** $\angle CAD \cong \angle BAC$, since they are the same angle, and $m(\angle ADC) = m(\angle ACB) = 90°$. By the AA similarity property, $\triangle ADC \sim \triangle ACB$. Likewise, $\triangle CDB \sim \triangle ACB$. Thus, $\triangle ADC \sim \triangle CDB$. **12. (a)** Draw an arc of large enough radius so that point B is on the seventh line above the line with point A. **13. (a)** Use the AA similarity property. **(b)** Using $\triangle ACD \sim \triangle ABC$, then $\dfrac{AD}{AC} = \dfrac{AC}{AB}$ or $\dfrac{x}{b} = \dfrac{b}{c}$. Similarly, $\triangle CBD \sim \triangle ABC$ gives $\dfrac{BD}{BC} = \dfrac{CB}{AB}$ or $\dfrac{y}{a} = \dfrac{a}{c}$. **(c)** $x = \dfrac{b^2}{c}$ and $y = \dfrac{a^2}{c}$. Also, $x + y = c$, so $c = \dfrac{b^2}{c} + \dfrac{a^2}{c}$, or $c^2 = a^2 + b^2$.

15. (a) $DJ = \sqrt{1^2 + \left(\dfrac{1}{2}\right)^2} = \sqrt{\dfrac{5}{4}} = \dfrac{1}{2}\sqrt{5}$ **(b)** By similarity, $\dfrac{PS}{AD} = \dfrac{TS}{JD}$. Therefore, using part (a), $PS = AD \cdot \dfrac{TS}{JD} = 1 \cdot \dfrac{\frac{1}{2}}{\frac{\sqrt{5}}{2}} = \dfrac{1}{\sqrt{5}}$. **(c)** area $(PQRS) = PS^2 = \dfrac{1}{5}$. That is, the inner small square has 20% of the area of the large square $ABCD$. **18.** The midpoints W, X, Y, and Z are the vertices of a parallelogram, and we know that the diagonals of any parallelogram intersect at their common midpoints. **20.** Let L denote the midpoint of $\overline{AC}$, which is also the midpoint of $\overline{BD}$. By Example 13.14, P is the centroid of $\triangle ABC$ and $BP = \dfrac{2}{3} BL$. Since $BL = \dfrac{1}{2} BD$, this shows $BP = \dfrac{2}{3} \cdot \dfrac{1}{2} BD = \dfrac{1}{3} BD$. By the same reasoning, Q is the centroid of $\triangle ADC$ and $QD = \dfrac{1}{3} BD$. Finally, $PQ = BD - BP - QD = \left(1 - \dfrac{1}{3} - \dfrac{1}{3}\right) BD = \dfrac{1}{3} BD$. **21.** The right triangles, $\triangle ACP$ and $\triangle BDP$, have congruent vertical angles at P. Thus, $\triangle ACP \sim \triangle BDP$ by AA similarity. Since $AC/BD = 4/2$, the scale factor is 2. Therefore $CP = 2DP$. Since $CD = 4$ and $CD = CP + DP$, we see that $CP = \dfrac{2}{3}(4) = 8/3$ and $DP = \dfrac{1}{3}(4) = 4/3$. By the Pythagorean theorem, $AP = \sqrt{4^2 + (8/3)^2} = (4/3)\sqrt{13}$ and so $BP = (2/3)\sqrt{13}$. **23.** The right triangles also have a

congruent angle at the vertex at the mirror, so the triangles are similar by the AA property. Assuming Mohini's eyes are 5" beneath the top of her head, this gives the proportion $h/5' = 15'/4'$, making the pole $h = (5')(15'/4') = 18'\,9''$.
25. By similar triangles, $(6 - x)/6 = 5.25'/18'$. Therefore, $x = 6'(1 - 5.25'/18') = 4.25' = 4'3''$.

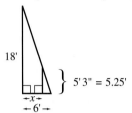

$5'\,3'' = 5.25'$

28. (a) $\triangle BCP \sim \triangle DAP$ **(b)** $PA/PC = PD/PB$, so $PA \cdot PB = PC \cdot PD$
31. $\triangle APB \cong \triangle DPC$; $\triangle ABC \cong \triangle DCB$; $\triangle ABD \cong \triangle DCA$

Chapter 13 Review Exercises (page 866)

1. (a) $\triangle ACD \cong \triangle ACB$ by SSS. **(b)** $\triangle ACD \cong \triangle ECB$ by SAS. **(c)** $\triangle ADF \cong \triangle BEC$ by AAS. **(d)** $\triangle ACD \cong \triangle ECB$ by SAS. **(e)** $\angle B \cong \angle E$ since $\triangle ABE$ is isosceles. Therefore, $\triangle ABC \cong \triangle AED$ by ASA and $\triangle ABD \cong \triangle AEC$ by ASA. **(f)** $\triangle ABC \cong \triangle DCB$ by SSS. **2. (a)** 2.9 cm **(b)** 40° **(c)** 78° **(d)** 40° **3.** $\angle B = \angle C$ since $\triangle ABC$ is isosceles. By construction, $BF = DC$ and $BD = EC$. Therefore, $\triangle BDF \cong \triangle CED$ by SAS, so $DE = DF$. **4. (a), (b), (c)** Standard constructions as in Section 13.2. **(d)** Draw a circle at any point A on line m, and let it intersect line l at B and C. Construct $\overline{AB}$ and $\overline{AC}$. Draw circles of the same radius at B and C to determine the respective midpoints M and N of $\overline{AB}$ and $\overline{AC}$. Then $k = \overleftrightarrow{MN}$ is the desired line. Alternatively, construct a perpendicular line to l at a point on l. This determines a perpendicular segment between l and m. The perpendicular bisector of the segment is the desired line k.

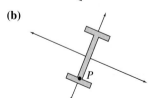

5. (a)

Reflect one side of $\angle A$ to the other.

(b)

Pivot Mira about P until the line reflects to itself.

(c)

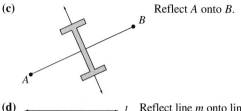

Reflect A onto B.

(d)

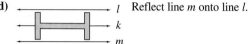

Reflect line m onto line l.

6. (a) Construct $\angle A$, lay off length AB, and draw a circle at B of radius BC. The circle intersects the other ray from A at two points, C_1 and C_2, giving two triangles $\triangle ABC_1$ and $\triangle ABC_2$.

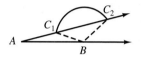

(b) Only $\triangle ABC_1$ has $\angle C = \angle C_1$ obtuse.
7. Find the midpoint M of $\overline{AD}$. Then draw circles of radius AM centered at A, D, and M.

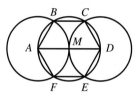

8. (a) Yes, using the SSS similarity property. **(b)** Yes, using the AA similarity property. **9.** Bisect sides $\overline{AB}$ and $\overline{AC}$ to determine their midpoints, M and N. Extend $\overline{AB}$ beyond B and draw the circle at B through M. Let E be the intersection with the extension. Similarly, extend $\overline{AC}$ beyond C, draw the circle at C through N, and let F be the intersection of this circle with the extension. Choosing $D = A$, the SAS similarity property guarantees that $\triangle ABC \sim \triangle DEF$. **10. (a)** $\triangle BAC \sim \triangle PQR$ by SAS similarity. The scale factor is 6 cm/4 cm $= 3/2$. **(b)** $\triangle ABC \sim \triangle YZX$ by SSS similarity. The scale factor is $42''/14'' = 3$. **(c)** $\triangle ABC \sim \triangle HGF$ by AA similarity. The scale factor is $4/6 = 2/3$. **(d)** $\triangle ADB \sim \triangle BCD$ by SSS similarity. The scale factor is $5/10 = 1/2$.
11. Draw additional line segments parallel to the given transversals. This creates similar triangles from which it follows that $x/9 = 16/12$, so $x = 9(16/12) = 12$ and $y/12 = 15/9$, so $y = 12 \cdot (15/9) = 20$.

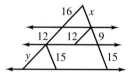

Chapter 13 Test   (page 868)

1. (a) $\triangle ADC \cong \triangle ABC$ by AAS. **(b)** $\triangle ABC \cong \triangle ADC$ by SAS. **(c)** $\triangle ADC \cong \triangle BCD$ by ASA. **(d)** $\triangle ABE \cong \triangle CBD$ by AAS. **(e)** $\triangle BDC \cong \triangle FDE$ by ASA and $\triangle ABE \cong \triangle AFC$ by ASA. **(f)** $\triangle ABC \cong \triangle ADC$ by SSS. **2.** The third side is greater than 6 feet and less than 26 feet by the triangle inequality. **3.** Construct a segment $\overline{DE}$ that is congruent to $\overline{AB}$. Construct rays at D and E to form angles that are respectively congruent to $\angle A$ and $\angle B$. Let F be a point of intersection of the rays. Then $\triangle DEF \cong \triangle ABC$.
4. (a) The Pythagorean theorem shows $AB = 12$ and $DF = 9$. Therefore, $\triangle ABC \cong \triangle DEF$ by SSS or SAS.
(b) Not congruent. The hypotenuse of $\triangle ABC$ is 5. Since $EF = 5$, the hypotenuse of $\triangle DEF$ is larger than 5, so the hypotenuses cannot correspond. **(c)** The Pythagorean theorem shows $AB = 3$ and $CD = 4$. Therefore, $\triangle ABD \cong \triangle CBD$ by SSS or SAS. **(d)** $\triangle ABE \cong \triangle DBC$ by SAS.
5. The small triangles are congruent to one another by the SAS congruence property, so $PQRST$ is equilateral. Let x and y be the measures of the acute angles in $\triangle APT$. Then each interior angle of $PQRST$ has measure $180° - x - y$, so $PQRST$ is equiangular. Altogether, $PQRST$ is regular.
6. $\triangle FGH$ is equilateral. **7. (a)** Draw circles of radius PQ, one centered at P and one centered at Q. The circles intersect at points R and S for which $\triangle PQR$ and $\triangle PQS$ are equilateral. **(b)** Construct the angle bisectors of $\angle QPR$ and $\angle QPS$, and denote their intersection with line l as T and U. $\triangle PTU$ is the desired equilateral triangle.
8. (a) $\triangle ADE \sim \triangle ACB$ by the AA similarity property, since both triangles contain $\angle A$ and a right angle.
(b) $\triangle ABC \sim \triangle XYZ$ by the SAS similarity property since $\dfrac{5}{4} = \dfrac{15}{12}$. **(c)** $\triangle DEG \sim \triangle EFG$ by the SSS similarity property, since $\dfrac{16}{8} = \dfrac{16}{8} = \dfrac{8}{4}$. **(d)** $\triangle AEB \sim \triangle CED$ by the AA similarity property since $\angle AEB \cong \angle CED$ being vertical angles and $\angle EBA \cong \angle EDC$ being alternate interior angles between parallel lines.
9. (a) $m(\angle W) = 180° - 87° - 40° = 53°$. **(b)** $\dfrac{20}{16} = \dfrac{5}{4}$
(c) $UV = \dfrac{5}{4} KL = \dfrac{5}{4}(20) = 25$.
10. (a) That they form the same angle relative to the ground, namely the angle of elevation, since the distant sun's rays are parallel. **(b)** That the person and the tree stand at the same angle with the ground; for example, both vertical. Then $\triangle ABC \sim \triangle DEF$ by the AA similarity property.
(c) $\dfrac{DE}{6'} = \dfrac{56'}{7'}$, so $DE = 48'$. **11.** $\triangle ADE \sim \triangle ACB$ by the AA similarity property, since both triangles contain $\angle A$ and a right angle. Thus $AE/AB = AD/AC = AD/(AD + DC) = 2DC/(2DC + DC) = 2/3$. Then $AE = \dfrac{2}{3}(AB) = \dfrac{2}{3}(12) = 8$ and $EB = AB - AE = 12 - 8 = 4$. **12.** Draw the circle

with radius MC centered at M. The circle passes through A, B, and C. Thus, by Thales' theorem, $\triangle ABC$ is a right triangle because it is inscribed in a semicircle of diameter $\overline{AB}$.

Chapter 14

JUST FOR FUN   The Greek Cross-I   (page 877)

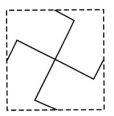

Problem Set 14.1   (page 881)

1. (a) The second coordinate is 0. **(c)** The first coordinate is positive and the second coordinate is negative.
2. (a), (c), (e), (g), (i)

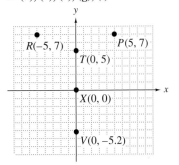

6. (a)

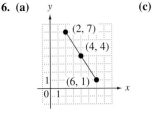

(c)

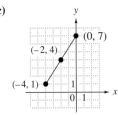

(e)

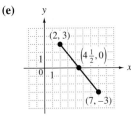

7.

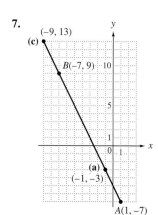

9. (a) $\sqrt{(4 - (-2))^2 + (13 - 5)^2} = \sqrt{36 + 64} = \sqrt{100} = 10$ **(c)** $\sqrt{(8 - 0)^2 + (-8 - 7)^2} = \sqrt{64 + 225} = \sqrt{289} = 17$

10. (a) $(RS)^2 = (\sqrt{(7 - 1)^2 + (10 - 2)^2})^2 = (\sqrt{36 + 64})^2 = (\sqrt{100})^2 = 100$

$(RT)^2 = (\sqrt{(5 - 1)^2 + (-1 - 2)^2})^2 = (\sqrt{16 + 9})^2 = (\sqrt{25})^2 = 25$

$(ST)^2 = (\sqrt{(7 - 5)^2 + (10 - (-1))^2})^2 = (\sqrt{4 + 121})^2 = (\sqrt{125})^2 = 125$

Since $(RS)^2 + (RT)^2 = (ST)^2$, by the Pythagorean theorem $\triangle RST$ is a right triangle. **12.** By plotting vertices and calculating the lengths of sides we determine the following. **(a)** Right, isosceles **(c)** Acute, scalene

13. (a)

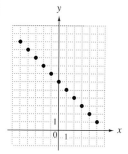

15. (a)

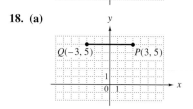

18. (a)

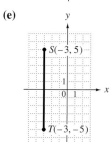

(c)

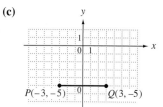

(e)

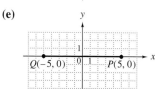

19. (a)

(c)

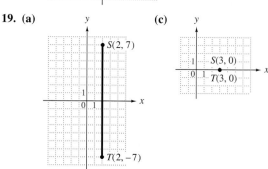

(e)

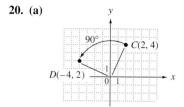

20. (a)

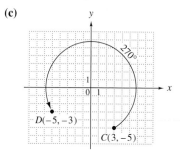

(c)

22. (a)

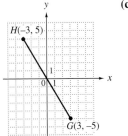

(c)

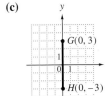

(e)

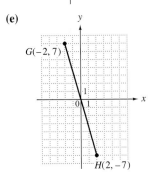

23. (a) $r = 10$, $s = 5$ **(b)** The midpoint of $\overline{AC}$ is
$\left(\dfrac{10 + 0}{2}, \dfrac{5 + 0}{2}\right) = \left(5, \dfrac{5}{2}\right)$. The midpoint of $\overline{BD}$ is
$\left(\dfrac{3 + 7}{2}, \dfrac{5 + 0}{2}\right) = \left(5, \dfrac{5}{2}\right)$. Therefore, the diagonals
bisect each other. **28. (a)** $x^2 + y^2 = 9$ **(b)** A circle of
radius 3 and center at the origin. **33.** $\angle BCA \cong \angle ECD$ as
vertical angles. $\angle ABC \cong \angle CDE$ as alternate interior angles
when parallel lines are cut by a third line. Similarly,
$\angle BAC \cong \angle CED$. So, by the AA similarity property,
$\triangle ABC \sim \triangle EDC$. **35.** $\angle CED \cong \angle AEB$. Since $\overline{CD}$ is
parallel to $\overline{AB}$, the corresponding angles, $\angle CDE$ and $\angle ABE$,
are congruent. Hence, by the AA similarity property,
$\triangle CDE \sim \triangle ABE$. Since corresponding sides are
proportional, we have:

$$\frac{5}{7} = \frac{6 - y}{6}$$
$$30 = 42 - 7y$$
$$-12 = -7y$$
$$\frac{12}{7} = y$$

Just For Fun   Square Inch Mysteries   (page 889)

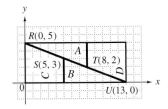

Place the rectangle on a coordinate system and label the
points $R(0, 5)$, $S(5, 3)$, $T(8, 2)$, and $U(13, 0)$ as shown. Since

$$\text{slope } \overline{RS} = \frac{3 - 5}{5 - 0} = \frac{-2}{5} = -0.40$$

and

$$\text{slope } \overline{SU} = \frac{0 - 3}{13 - 5} = \frac{-3}{8} = -0.375,$$

R, S, and U do *not* lie on a straight line. Similarly,

$$\text{slope } \overline{RT} = \frac{2 - 5}{8 - 5} = \frac{3}{8} = -0.375$$

and

$$\text{slope } \overline{TU} = \frac{0 - 2}{13 - 8} = \frac{-2}{5} = -0.40,$$

so R, T, and U do *not* lie on a straight line. Indeed, as the
slopes show, $RTUS$ is a very thin parallelogram—a fact
obscured by the heavy lines used in the diagram. It turns out
that this parallelogram has area one and this accounts for the
extra unit of area.

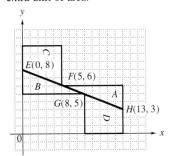

Now place the "propeller" on a coordinate system and
label the points $E(0, 8)$, $F(5, 6)$, $G(8, 5)$, and $H(13, 3)$ as
shown. Here

$$\text{slope } \overline{EF} = \frac{6 - 8}{5 - 0} = -\frac{2}{5} = -0.40$$

and

$$\text{slope } \overline{FH} = \frac{3 - 6}{13 - 5} = \frac{-3}{8} = -0.375,$$

so E, F, and H do not lie on a straight line. Similarly,

$$\text{slope } \overline{EG} = \frac{5 - 8}{8 - 0} = \frac{-3}{8} = -0.375$$

and

$$\text{slope } \overline{GH} = \frac{3 - 5}{13 - 8} = \frac{-2}{5} = -0.40,$$

so E, G, and H also do not lie on a straight line. Indeed, as
the slopes show, $EFHG$ forms a small parallelogram where
the pieces of the puzzle overlap—a fact again obscured
by the heavy lines used in making the drawing. It turns out

that this parallelogram has area one, and this accounts for the missing one unit of area.

Problem Set 14.2   (page 900)

1. **(a)** 2, upward **(c)** 2, upward **(e)** 1, upward

2. 2 **5.** $a = \dfrac{9}{2}$

7. **(a)**

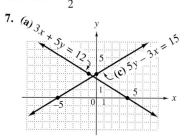

8.

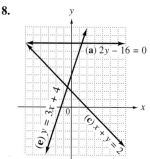

10. **(a)** $\dfrac{-35}{3}$ **(c)** $\dfrac{3}{5}$ **11.** **(a)** $m = \dfrac{3}{7}, b = 3$ **(c)** $m = 0,$

$b = 6$ **(e)** Slope undefined, no y-intercept

12. **(a)** Neither **(c)** Perpendicular **13.** **(a)** $\dfrac{-10}{3}$

14. **(a)** $(3, -1)$ **16.** **(a)** $(4, 2)$ **18.** **(a)** $y - 6 = 2(x - 1)$

(c) $y - 2 = -\dfrac{1}{8}\left(x - \dfrac{7}{2}\right)$ **(e)** $x = 2$ **24.** The shortest

distance is along the line $y - 5 = -\dfrac{2}{3}(x - 1)$ through $(1, 5)$

and perpendicular to $3x - 2y = 6$. These two lines meet at $(4, 3)$ so the shortest distance is $\sqrt{(1 - 4)^2 + (5 - 3)^2} = \sqrt{13}$. **29.** **(a)** Many lines are possible. One line is

$y - 6 = \dfrac{1}{2}(x - 8)$ or $y = \dfrac{1}{2}x + 2$. When $x = 15$,

$y = \dfrac{1}{2}(15) + 2 = \dfrac{19}{2}$. **32.** **(a)** iv **(c)** Yes, ii has three lines

of symmetry. **34.** No. The figure shown has $120°$ rotation symmetry, but no symmetry about a point.

JUST FOR FUN **The Greek Cross—II** **(page 912)**

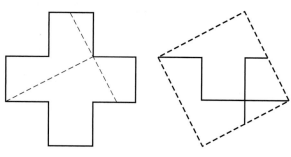

Problem Set 14.3   (page 913)

1. **(a)** $r = a, s = a, c = a$ **3.** **(a)** $r = a + c, s = b$
5. **(a)** Circle centered at $(0, 0)$ with radius 9 **(c)** The single point $(0, -5)$
6. **(a)**

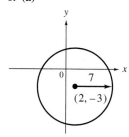

7. **(a)** $(x - 2)^2 + (y - 5)^2 = 9$ **(c)** $(x + 1)^2 + (y - 2)^2 = 4$
9. **(a)** Find the equations of the perpendicular bisectors of two chords. Their point of intersection is the center of the circle. The three perpendicular bisectors are $y - 4 = \dfrac{-4}{3}(x - 3), y - \dfrac{1}{2} = 7\left(x - \dfrac{5}{2}\right)$, and $y - \dfrac{7}{2} = \dfrac{-1}{7}\left(x - \dfrac{13}{2}\right)$. The center is $(3, 4)$.
10. A general parallelogram can be drawn as shown.

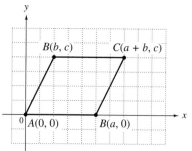

The midpoint of $\overline{AC}$ is $\left(\dfrac{a + b}{2}, \dfrac{c}{2}\right)$ and the midpoint of $\overline{BD}$ is $\left(\dfrac{a + b}{2}, \dfrac{c}{2}\right)$ so the diagonals bisect each other.

13. (a) The medians are

$$y - b = \frac{b}{a - 2c}(x - a),$$

$$y = \frac{2b}{2a - c}(x - c),$$

and

$$y = \frac{b}{a + c}x.$$

Each pair of medians intersect in the point

$$G\left(\frac{2a + 2c}{3}, \frac{2b}{3}\right).$$

16. (a) The points are $P(a, a)$, $Q(2a + b + c, b + c)$, $R(2a + 2b + c, -c)$ and $S(a + b, -(a + b))$. Thus,

$$PR = \sqrt{(a + 2b + c)^2 + (-c - a)^2} = \sqrt{(a + 2b + c)^2 + (c + a)^2}$$

and

$$SQ = \sqrt{((2a + b + c) - (a + b))^2 + ((b + c) - (-(a + b)))^2} = \sqrt{(a + c)^2 + (a + 2b + c)^2}.$$

Therefore, $\overline{PR} \cong \overline{SQ}$.

(b) Slope $\overline{PR} = \dfrac{-c - a}{(2a + 2b + c) - a} = -\dfrac{a + c}{a + 2b + c}$

Slope $\overline{SQ} = \dfrac{(b + c) - (-(a + b))}{(2a + b + c) - (a + b)}$

$\qquad = \dfrac{a + 2b + c}{a + c}$

Since the slope of $\overline{SQ}$ is the negative of the reciprocal of the slope of $\overline{PR}$, $\overline{PR} \perp \overline{SQ}$. **21.** $1440°$ **23.** $360°$

JUST FOR FUN   Watering a Playfield   (page 920)

The plumber is right. Is he ever just *barely* right?

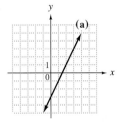

Problem Set 14.4   (page 921)

1.

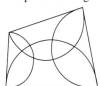

3. (a)

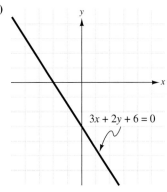

(b) Yes. The function is $y = -\dfrac{3}{2}x - 3$.

(d) Yes. The function is $y = \dfrac{5}{3}x - 5$.

5. (a) Yes, this is a graph of a function.

6.

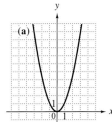

7.

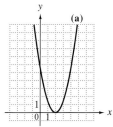

9. (a) From the graph, the minimum of $x^2 + 10x$ is -25.

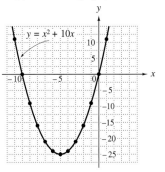

10. (a)

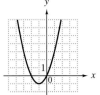

(b) $x = -1$

11. (a)

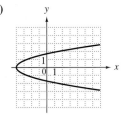

15. (a)

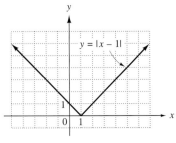

19. (a) 2000 **22. (a)** 11:59 A.M. **24. (a)** In the diagram below D is a units from A. If D has coordinates (b, c), then by the Pythagorean theorem, $b^2 + c^2 = a^2$. Hence, $c^2 = b^2 - a^2$ and $c = \sqrt{a^2 - b^2}$. Since $DC = a$, C has coordinates $(a + b, \sqrt{a^2 - b^2})$. Thus, the midpoint of AC is

$$\left(\frac{a + b}{2}, \frac{\sqrt{a^2 - b^2}}{2} \right)$$

and the midpoint of $\overline{BD}$ is also

$$\left(\frac{a + b}{2}, \frac{\sqrt{a^2 - b^2}}{2} \right).$$

Thus, the diagonals bisect each other.

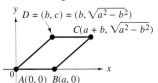

25. (a) -3 **27.** $y + 3 = \dfrac{2}{7}(x + 2)$

Chapter 14 Review Exercises   (page 926)

1.

y

(−3, 1.5)   **(b)** (1.4, 1.7)
(d) 1
0 1 x
(−3, −4.5)   • **(a)**
    (5, −2)
(c)

2. (a) IV **(b)** II **(c)** I or III **(d)** II or IV **3. (a)** $a = 2$, $b = 2$ **(b)** $a = 2.3$, $b = 0.1$ **(c)** $a = -2.5$, $b = -0.5$ **(d)** $a = -1$, $b = -4.5$ **4. (a)** $\sqrt{40} = 2\sqrt{10}$ **(b)** $\sqrt{13.48} \doteq 3.67$ **(c)** $\sqrt{74}$ **(d)** $\sqrt{85}$ **5.** $AB = 5$, $BC = \sqrt{50}$, $AC = 5$. $(AB)^2 + (AC)^2 = 5^2 + 5^2 = 50 = (\sqrt{50})^2 = BC^2$. Thus, by the Pythagorean theorem, the triangle is a right triangle. **6.** $RS = \sqrt{\dfrac{481}{4}} = RT$ so the triangle is isosceles. **7. (a)** 1 **(b)** Undefined **(c)** $-2/3$

(d) Undefined **8.** $-19/5$ **9. (a)** $b = 8$ **(b)** $b = 14/3$ **10.** $R(-4, 5)$ is on the perpendicular bisector of $\overline{PQ}$ if, and only if, it is equidistant from P and Q. Since

$$RP = \sqrt{(-4 - 0)^2 + (5 - 5)^2} = 4$$

and

$$RQ = \sqrt{(-4 - (-3))^2 + (1 - 5)^2} = \sqrt{17} \doteq 4.12,$$

R is *not* on the perpendicular bisector of $\overline{PQ}$. **11.** $b = -8/5$ **12.** Since the slope $\overline{PQ} = -9/7$, the equation of the line is

$$y + 2 = -\frac{9}{7}(x - 3) \text{ or, equivalently, } y - 7 = -\frac{9}{7}(x + 4).$$

13. $y = \dfrac{3}{2}x + 10$ **14.** Solving for y in terms of x, we obtain $y = (3/4)x - 15/4$. Thus, the slope is $3/4$.
15. $y - 1.5 = (-4/3)(x - 5)$ **16.** $(3, -2)$
17. (a) The coordinates of M, D, and E are $M(4, 3)$, $D(-3, 3)$, and $E(4, -4)$. Thus, $\overline{DM}$ is horizontal, $\overline{ME}$ is vertical and $\angle DME$ is a right angle. **(b)** slope $\overline{EA} = \dfrac{0 - (-4)}{0 - 4} = -1$, slope $\overline{ED} = \dfrac{3 - (-4)}{-3 - 4} = -1$. Since the slopes are the same, E, A, and D are collinear.
18. (a) Since the coordinates of E, G, and H are $E(3, 3)$, $G(8, 2)$, and $H(5, -5)$, $EG = \sqrt{26} = FH$ and $\overline{EG} \cong \overline{FH}$. **(b)** Since the slope of $\overline{EG}$ is $-1/5$ and the slope of $\overline{FH}$ is 5, it follows that $\overline{EG}$ and $\overline{FH}$ are perpendicular. **19. (a)** Since the coordinates of E, F, G, and H are $E(2, 2)$, $F(5, 1)$, $G(9, 3)$, and $H(6, -6)$, $EG = \sqrt{50} = FH$ and $\overline{EG} \cong \overline{FH}$. **(b)** Since the slope of $\overline{EG}$ is $1/7$ and the slope of $\overline{FH}$ is -7, it follows that $\overline{EG}$ and $\overline{FH}$ are perpendicular.
20. (a) Since the coordinates of M, D, and E are $M(a, a)$, $D(-b, b)$, and $E(a, -a)$, $\overline{MD}$ is horizontal and $\overline{ME}$ is vertical. Thus, $\angle EMD$ is a right angle and $\triangle EMD$ is a right triangle. **(b)** Since slope $\overline{EA} = -1 = $ slope $\overline{ED}$, it follows that E, A, and D are collinear. **21. (a)** The coordinates of E, F, G, and H are $E(a, a)$, $F(2a, 0)$, $G(2a + b, b)$, and $H(a + b, -a - b)$. Therefore,

$$EG = \sqrt{(a + b)^2 + (b - a)^2} = \sqrt{2a^2 + 2b^2}$$

and

$$FH = \sqrt{(b - a)^2 + (-a - b)^2} = \sqrt{2a^2 + 2b^2}$$

so $\overline{EG} \cong \overline{FH}$. **(b)** Since

$$(\text{slope } \overline{EG}) \cdot (\text{slope } \overline{FH}) = \frac{b - a}{a + b} \cdot \frac{a + b}{a - b} = -1,$$

$\overline{EG}$ and $\overline{FH}$ are perpendicular.

Chapter 14 Test   (page 928)

1. $r = 10$, $s = 5$ **2.** The desired point is

$$\left(\left(1 - \frac{1}{4} \right) \cdot (-8) + \frac{1}{4} \cdot 4, \left(1 - \frac{1}{4} \right) \cdot 0 + \frac{1}{4} \cdot 12 \right) = (-5, 3).$$

3. The midpoint of $\overline{AB}$ is (9/2, 9/2) and the slope is $-1/5$. Therefore, the equation of the perpendicular bisector is

$$y - \frac{9}{2} = 5\left(x - \frac{9}{2}\right).$$

4. $RS = \sqrt{164}$, $ST = \sqrt{205}$, and $RT = \sqrt{41}$. Therefore, $(RS)^2 + (RT)^2 = 164 + 41 = 205 = (ST)^2$ and so $\triangle RST$ is a right triangle. **5.** $r = 23/5$ **6.** Slope $\overline{PQ} = \dfrac{2 - 5}{4 - (-1)} = \dfrac{-3}{5}$, equation is $y - 2 = -\dfrac{3}{5}(x - 4)$ or, equivalently, $y - 5 = -\dfrac{3}{5}(x + 1)$. **7.** $-5/2$ **8.** $(x + 2)^2 + (y - 5)^2 = 16$

9. $(3, -1)$

10.

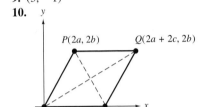

Any parallelogram can be placed on coordinate axes as shown and with vertices with coordinates as indicated with a, b, and c all positive. The midpoint of $\overline{PR}$ is $((2a + 2c)/2,$ $(2b + 0)/2) = (a + c, b)$ and the midpoint of $\overline{OQ}$ is $((2a + 2c)/2, (2b + 0)/2) = (a + c, b)$ also. Thus, the diagonals bisect one another. **11.** $\$5000 \cdot (1.07)^5 \doteq \$7012.76$

12. (a)

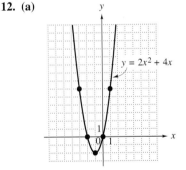

(b) Minimum value is -2 when $x = -1$.

Appendix B   (page 938)

1. (a) Arik: $\$225.38$; Kaia: $\$258.33$; Lena: $\$143.06$; district: $\$626.77$. (b) Lena corrected: $\$182.12$; district corrected: $\$665.83$. **3.** (a) $L(10) = 123$. $L(10)/L(9) = 123/76 = 1.61842 \ldots$. The ratio of Lucas numbers appears to approach the same limit value as the ratio of Fibonacci numbers. **5.** (a) The value of cell Bn is one less than the Fibonacci number in cell A$(n + 2)$. This demonstrates the identity $1 + 1 + 2 + 3 + 5 + \cdots + F(n) = F(n + 2) - 1$. **6.** (a) mean $= 27.9$, population standard deviation $= 14.3$ (b) lower quartile $= 19$, median $= 26$, upper quartile $= 37$

Appendix C   (page 951)

1. (a) 119 pounds **2.** 8500 miles **3.** (b) 5745 miles **4.** (b) 851 and 8723 miles from the earth's center **6.** (a) All graphs are straight lines through the origin. (b) The y-values of Y_2 are twice that of the basic function at the same x-coordinate, giving Y_2 a steeper positive slope than Y_1. The function Y_3 has half the y-values, giving it a more shallow slope. The function Y_4 is the reflection of the basic function across the horizontal x-axis. **9.** Chocolate is the favorite flavor of both classes. Vanilla is the least most frequent favorite in Mrs. O'Leary's class, but it is strawberry in Mr. Hsu's class.

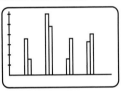

10. The most common grade is a B, earned by 13 students. The trace also shows that 8 students earned between 90 and 99, so together with the 2 students earning 100 there are a total of 10 A grades.

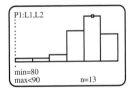

Appendix D   (page 961)

1. (a) The sides are only approximately, not exactly, all the same length. **2.** (a) Construct the midpoint M of the segment $\overline{AB}$. Construct the perpendicular to the segment through M. Construct a point C on the perpendicular bisector. The triangle ABC is equilateral. (c) Construct any point M on the perpendicular bisector of segment $\overline{AB}$. Construct the parallel to $\overline{AB}$ through point M and construct any circle centered at M. If the circle intersects the parallel at points C and D then $ABCD$ is an isosceles trapezoid. (e) Construct the segment $\overline{AC}$ and the perpendicular bisector of the segment. Construct a point B on the perpendicular bisector. Construct the circle centered at A through B. If the circle intersects the perpendicular bisector at D, then $ABCD$ is a rhombus with opposite vertices at A and C. **4.** (a) The angle measures sum to $360°$. **5.** (a) Let the respective points be C, D, and E. There are several methods to show that triangle CDE is a right triangle with the right angle at vertex D. *Method One:* Use **Length** to measure the lengths CD, DE, and CE, and use the **Calculate . . .** to show that $CD^2 + DE^2 = CE^2$. Triangle CDE is a right triangle by the converse of the Pythagorean theorem. *Method Two:* Measure the slopes of $\overline{CD}$ and $\overline{DE}$ and show that the product of the slopes is -1. This shows the segments are perpendicular to one another. *Method Three:* Measure $\angle CDE$ and see that it is $90°$.

ACKNOWLEDGMENTS

Chapter 1

Page 8, Garfield cartoon. GARFIELD © 1989 Paws, Inc. Reprinted with permission of Universal Press Syndicate. All Rights Reserved. Page 24, photo of auto race. Focus on Sports. Page 30, photo of George Polya. Stanford University News Service. Page 34, Carl Friedrich Gauss. Culver Pictures. Page 53, photo of pigeons. ANIMALS ANIMALS/OSF/G.I. Bernard. Page 58, photo of man working with scientific equipment. © 1999 Jeff Guerrant Photography. Page 61, photo of Henri Poincare. Library of Congress.

Chapter 2

Page 80, photo of Incan quipu. Museo Nacional De Arqueologia, Antropologia E Historia Del Peru. Page 81, photo of Georg Cantor. Baveria-Verlag. Pages 86, 90, reprinted with permission of Cuisenaire, an imprint of Pearson Learning. Page 148, photo of packages. Comstock.

Chapter 3

Page 177, photo of Benjamin Banneker stamp. U.S. Postal Service. Page 212, Calvin and Hobbes cartoon. CALVIN AND HOBBES © 1990 Watterson. Reprinted with permission of Universal Press Syndicate. All rights reserved. Page 219, photo of Emily Noether. Professor Gottfried E. Noether. Page 225, photo of Math Explorer calculator. Texas Instruments.

Chapter 4

Page 249, cartoon of "Hold on there Mr. Webster . . .". © 1999 by Sydney Harris. Page 274, photo of Julia Robinson. Photo courtesy of the American Mathematical Society. Reprinted with permission. Page 276, photo of Dr. Andrew Wiles. Copyright Denise Applewhite/ Sygma.

Chapter 5

Page 336, photo of Charlotte Angas Scott. Bryn Mawr College Archives.

Chapter 6

Page 355, Hagar the Horrible cartoon by Dik Browne. © 1995. Reprinted with permission of King Features Syndicate.

Chapter 7

Page 427, "I thought it was a breakthrough, but it was only a misplaced decimal" cartoon. © 1999 by Sydney Harris. Page 430, photo of Pythagoras bust. Corbis.

Chapter 8

Page 489, pictograph of world population growth. © 1992 Time Inc. Page 497, "Wired to the World." from Newsweek, 12/14/98 © 1998 Newsweek, Inc. All rights reserved. Reprinted by permission. Page 497, graph of "Talk, talk, talk." READER'S DIGEST, November 1998. Reprinted with permission. Page 498, 2 graphs. "More going out than coming in . . ." and ". . . Will deplete Social Security Assets by 2032." READER'S DIGEST, December 1998. Reprinted with permission. Page 519, photo of Harry Truman. Corbis. Page 520, cartoon showing bizarre sequence of computer-generated numbers. © 1999 by Sydney Harris.

Chapter 9

Page 582, B.C. cartoon. © 1989. By permission of Johnny Hart and Creators Syndicate, Inc. Page 571, Illustration of A Probability of Paradox. Adapted from "Mathematical Games" by Martin Gardner, SCIENTIFIC AMERICAN, March 1976. Copyright © 1976 by Scientific American, Inc. All rights reserved. Page 538, Ratio of the number of heads to the number of tosses in Kerrich's coin-tossing experiment. Adapted from Figure 2 in STATISTICS, Second Edition by David Freedman, Robert Pisani, Roger Purves, and Ani Adhikari. Reprinted by permission of W.W. Norton & Company, Inc. Page 537, photo of Jakob Bernoulli. Museum fur Volkskunde von Schweizerriches. Page 580, photo of roulette wheel. Arthur Tilley/ Tony Stone Images.

Chapter 10

Page 597, photo of butterfly wings. John Bove/Photo Researchers. Page 597, photo of a snow crystal. SS/Photo Researchers. Page 597, photo of sunflower. Ray E. Ellis/Photo Researchers. Page 597, A fractal, "Tail of the Seahorse," Mandlebrot set from H.O. Pietgen and P.H. Richter, THE BEAUTY OF FRACTALS, Heidelberg, Springer-Verlag, 1986. Page 597, M.C. Escher's "Wall Mosaic in the Alhambra," © 1999 Cordon Art B.V.-Baarn-Holland. All rights reserved. Page 597, photo of fissures in a gelatinous preparation of tin foil. Manfred P. Kage/Peter Arnold, Inc. Page 600, B.C. cartoon. © 1990. By permission of Johnny Hart and Creators Syndicate, Inc. Page 603, reprinted with permission of Cuisenaire, an imprint of Pearson Learning. Page 627, photo of Baha'i House of Worship in Wilmette, Illinois. National Baha'i Headquarters. Page 638, skeletons of microscopic radiolara. ERNST HAECKEL, CHALLENGER, Monograph, 1887. Page 638, photo of Buckyball. S. Camazine/Photo Researchers. Page 638, A partial filing of space by truncated octahedra. D'Arcy W. Thompson, ON GROWTH AND FORM, New

Edition, Cambridge University Press, Cambridge and New York, 1948. Page 638, daVinci's drawings of an icosahedron and a dodecahedron. Rare Book Room, New York Public Library. Astor, Lenox, and Tilden Foundations. Page 638, Seashell and computer-drawn ideal representation. Dr. Guiseppe Mazza. Page 645, A Flexible Polyhedron. Figures 21 and 22 from MATHEMATICS MAGAZINE, Volume 52, Number 5, November 1979, p. 281. Copyright © 1979 by The Mathematical Association of America. Reprinted by permission. Page 648, photo of Epcot. Murray & Assoc./Tony Stone Images. Page 648, Polyhedron. D'Arcy W. Thompson, ON GROWTH AND FORM, New Edition, Cambridge University Press, Cambridge and New York, 1948. Page 654, Pentominoes. Figure 10, "The pentominoes" from POLYOMINOES by Solomon W. Golomb, page 23. (Charles Scribner's Sons, 1965, Revised Edition, Princeton University Press, 1994). Copyright © 1965 by Solomon W. Golomb. Reprinted with permission of the author. Page 655, photo of pyrite crystal. H. Chaumeton/Photo Researchers.

Chapter 11

Page 682, Metric Clock Cartoon. © 1999 Sydney Harris. Page 703, photo of the earth. NASA. Page 713, photo of Babylonian tablet. The British Museum. Page 730, photo of Egyptian pyramid. Catherine Koehler. Page 731, photo of Sophie Germain. Ecole Sophie Germain, Paris. Page 734, portrait of Jonathan Swift. National Portrait Gallery, London.

Chapter 12

Page 750, sea lions on a Haida dance tunic. Thomas Burke Memorial/Washington State Museum. Page 764, M.C. Escher's "Two-motif tiling of the plane," © 1999 Cordon Art B.V.-Baarn-Holland. All rights reserved. Page 766, photo of Carolyn Gordon and David Webb. Washington University of St. Louis. Page 772, Escher tiling. M.C. Escher's "Symmetry Drawing," © 1999 Cordon Art B.V.-Baarn-Holland. All rights reserved. Page 777, photo of George W. Brainerd. Southwest Museum, Los Angeles. Page 777, photo of Anna O. Shepherd. Carnegie Institute of Washington D.C. Page 780, border patterns from around the world. From AESTHETIC MEASURE by George D. Birkoff, © 1933/Harvard University Press, Cambridge, MA. Page 783, Pfembe maternity statue. © Musee Royale de l'Afrique Centrale, Belgium. Page 784, Mercedes-Benz emblem, courtesy Mercedes-Benz (now DaimlerChrysler) of North America, Inc. Page 785, "The Chevrolet Bow Tie emblem and the Oldsmobile Rocket emblem are trade marks of the Chevrolet Motor Division and Oldsmobile Motor Division, respectively, General Motors Corporation, used with permission. General Motors Corporation, however, does not endorse or assume any responsibility for the test, errors, or omissions of Addison Wesley Longman Publishers, its officers, agents, employees or other representatives." Page 785, Sterling logo, Sterling Savings Association. Colfax, Washington. Page 787, problem 12.2.29 illustration, 6 Chladni Plates from FEARFUL SYMMETRY © 1992 Ian Stewart and Martin Golubitsky. Printed by Blackwell Publishers. Page 790, Tilings from Portugal, fifteenth to sixteenth centuries. SIMOES. Page 790, Pre-Inca fabric from Peru. ISUMI. Page 790, Chinese lattice work. Daniel Sheets Dye, A GRAMMAR OF CHINESE LATTICE, Figures C9b, S12a, Harvard-Yenching Institute Monograph V, Cambridge, MA. 1937. Page 790, Window of a fourteenth century mosque in Cairo. Israel National Museum, Jerusalem. Page 790, Mosaic floor of the fourteenth and fifteenth century in the Basilica of Saint Marks Cathedral. Saint Marks Cathedral, Venice. Page 795, Heinz Voderberg's spiral tiling. From Martin Gardner's PENROSE TILES TO TRAPDOOR CIPHERS, W.H. Freeman, 1989. Page 796, M.C. Escher's "Birds and its grid of parallelograms," © 1999 Cordon Art B.V.-Baarn-Holland. All rights reserved. Page 798, M.C. Escher's "Regular divisions of the plane (5 examples)," © 1999 Cordon Art B.V.-Baarn-Holland. All rights reserved. Page 800, Fake tiling by regular polygons. from TILINGS AND PATTERNS by Branko Grunbaum and G.C. Shepard. © 1987 W.H. Freeman and Company. Used by permission. Page 803, Chinese tangram puzzle. Reprinted with permission from CURRICULUM AND EVALUATION STANDARDS FOR SCHOOL MATHEMATICS, copyright 1989 by the National Council of Teachers of Mathematics. All rights reserved. Page 807, Chapter review problem #9 a and b. From AESTHETIC MEASURE by George D. Birkoff, © 1933/Harvard University Press, Cambridge, MA. Page 809, Chapter test problem #13 a-d. From AESTHETIC MEASURE by George D. Birkoff, © 1933/Harvard University Press, Cambridge, MA. Page 809, Chapter test problem #16. Copyright 1999, M.C. Escher/Cordon Art—Baarn—Holland. Private Collection.

Chapter 13

Page 819, photo of Christine Ladd-Franklin. National Cyclopedia of American Biography.

Chapter 14

Page 891, Maria Agnesi. Corbis.

MATHEMATICAL LEXICON

Many of the words, prefixes, and suffixes forming the vocabulary of mathematics are derived from words and word roots from Latin, Greek, and other languages. Some of the most common terms are listed below, to serve as an aid to learning and understanding the terminology of mathematics.

acute from Latin *acus* "needle" by way of *acutus* "pointed, sharp"

algorithm distortion of Arabic name *al-Khowarazmi* "the man from Khwarazm," whose book on the use of Indo-Arabic numeration was translated into Latin as *Liber Algorismi* meaning "Book of al-Khowarazmi"

angle from Latin *angulus* "corner, angle"

apex from Latin word meaning "tip, peak"

area Latin *area* "vacant piece of ground, plot of ground, open court"

associative from Latin *ad* "to" and *socius* "partner, companion"

axis from Latin word meaning "axle, pivot"

bi- from Latin prefix derived from *dui-* "two"; *bi*nary, *bi*nomial, *bi*sect

calculate from Latin *calc* "chalk, limestone" and diminutive suffix *-ulus* [a *calculus* was a small pebble; *calculare* meant "to use pebbles" = to do arithmetic]

cent- from Latin *centum* "hundred"; *cent*imeter, per*cent*

circum- from Latin *circum* "around"; *circum*ference, *circum*scribe

co-, col-, com-, con- from Old Latin *com* "together with, beside, near"; *com*mutative, *col*linear, *com*plement, *con*gruent

commutative from Latin *co-* "together with" and *mutare* "to move"

concurrent from Latin *co-,* "together with" and *currere* "to run"

conjecture from Latin *co-* "together with" and *iactus* "to throw" [conjecture = throw (ideas) together]

cylinder from Greek *kulindros* "a roller"

de- Latin preposition *de* "from, down from, away from, out of"; *de*nominator, *de*duction

deca-, deka- from Greek deka- "ten"; *deca*gon, do*deca*hedron, *deka*meter

deci- from Latin *decimus* "tenth"; *deci*mal, *deci*meter

diagonal from Greek *dia-* "through, across" and *gon-* "angle"

diameter from Greek *dia-* "through, across" and *metron* "measure"

digit from Latin *digitus* "a finger"

distribute from Latin prefix *dis-* "apart, away" and Latin *tribu* "a tribe [of Romans]"

empirical from Latin *empiricus* "a physician whose art is founded solely on practice"

equal from Latin *æquus,* "even, level"

equilateral from Latin *æquus,* "even, level" and *latus* "side"

equivalent from Latin *æquus,* "even, level" and *valere* "to have value"

exponent from Latin *ex* "away" and *ponent-* = present participial stem of *ponere* "to put"

figure from Latin *figura* "shape, form, figure"

fraction from Latin *fractus,* past participle of *frangere* "to break"

geometry from Greek *geo-* "earth" and *metron* "measure"

-gon   from Greek *gonia* "angle, corner"; poly*gon,* penta*gon*

-hedron   from Greek *hedra* "base, seat"; poly*hedron,* tetra*hedron*

hept-, sept-   Greek *hept,* from prehistoric Greek *sept,* meaning "seven"; *hepta*gon

heuristic   from Greek *heuriskein* "to find, discover"

hex-   from Greek *hex* (prehistoric Greek *sex*) "six"; *hex*agon, *hex*omino

icosahedron   from Greek *eikosi* "twenty" and *hedra* "bases, seat"

inch   from Latin *uncia,* a unit of weight equal to one twelfth of the *libra,* or Roman pound

inscribe   from Latin *in* "in" and *scribere* "to scratch" hence "to write"

integer   from Latin *in-* "not" and Indo-European root *tag-* "to touch" [an integer is untouched, hence "whole"]

inverse   from Latin *in* "in" and *versus,* past participle of *vertere* "to turn"

isosceles   from Greek *isos* "equal" and *skelos* "leg"

kilo-   from Greek *khiloi* "thousand"; *kilo*gram, *kilo*meter

lateral   from Latin *latus* "side"

lb.   abbreviation for pound, from *libra,* the Roman unit of weight

line   from Latin *linum* "flax" [The Romans made *linea,* linen thread, from flax.]

median   from Latin *medius* "in the middle"

meter   from Greek *metron* "measure, length"

milli-   from Latin *mille* "one thousand"

multiply   from Latin *multi* "many" and Indo-European *pel* "to fold"

nonagon   from Latin *nonus* "ninth" and Greek *gon* "angle"

number   from Latin *numerus* "number"

obtuse   from Latin *ob* "against, near, at" and *tusus* "to strike, to beat" [*obtusus* = beaten down to the point of being dull]

oct-   from Greek *octo* "eight"; *oct*agon, *oct*ahedron

parallel   from Greek *para* "alongside" and *allenon* "one another"

pent-   Greek *pent* "five"; *pent*agon, *pent*agram, *pent*omino

percent   from Latin *per* "for" and *centum* "hundred" [percent = for (each) hundred]

peri-   from Greek *peri* "around"; *peri*meter

plane   from Latin *planus "flat"*

poly-   from Greek *polus* "many"; *poly*gon, *poly*hedra, *poly*omino

prism   from Greek *prisma* "something that has been sawed"

quadr-   Latin *quadr-* "four"; *quadr*ant, *quadr*ilateral

rectangle   from Latin *rectangulus* "right-angled"

-sect   from Latin *sectus,* past participle of *secui* "to cut"; bi*sect,* inter*sect*

surface   from Latin *super* "over" and *facies* "form, shape"

symmetric   from Greek *sun-* "together with" and *metron* "measure"

tetra-   Greek *tetra-* "four"; *tetra*hedron, *tetr*omino

trans-   Latin *trans* "across"; *trans*itive, *trans*lation, *trans*versal

tri-   from Latin *tri* "three"; *tri*angle, *tri*sect

vertex   from Latin verb *vertere* "to turn"

zero   from Arabic *çifr* "empty"

a	act, bat	j	just, fudge	œ	as in German schön or in French feu
ā	cape, way	k	keep, token	R	rolled r as in French rouge or in German rot
â	dare, Mary	KH	as in Scottish loch, or in German ich		
ä	alms, calm	N	as in French bon or un	sh	shoe, fish
ch	child, beach	o	ox, wasp	th	thin, path
e	set, merry	ō	over, no	u	up, love
ē	equal, bee	o͝o	book, poor	û	urge, burn
ə	like a in alone or e in system	oo	ooze, fool	y	yes, onion
g	give, beg	ô	ought, raw	z	zeal. lazy
i	if, big	oi	oil, joy	zh	treasure, mirage
ī	ice, bite	ou	out, cow		

Abacus, 169–171
Abbott, Edwin, 603
Absolute value, of integer, 308–309
Accumulator, 142
Acute angles, 602
Acute triangles, 624
Adams, Clifford W., 134
Adams' magic hexagon, 134
Addition
  clock, 283–285, 287, 288
  of decimals, 437–438
  in Egyptian system, 161
  explanation of, 103
  of integers, 313–320, 329–330
  measurement model of, 105
  properties of whole number, 105–108
  of rational numbers, 371–375, 390–392
  set model of, 104–105
  of whole numbers, 103–108
Addition algorithm
  in base five, 194–195
  developing, 186–187
  exchanging and, 188–189
  explanation of, 184
Addition property
  of area, 693, 694
  of rational numbers, 394
Additive identity property
  of addition of integers, 315
  of zero, 105–107, 391
Additive inverse
  of addition of integers, 315

  of addition of rational numbers, 391
  explanation of, 288
  rational numbers and, 391
Adjacent angles, 604
Adjustment, in mental calculation, 215–216
Agnesi, Maria Gaetana, 891
Aha! Insight (Gardner), 42
Ahmes, 80
Algebraic logic, 225, 226
Algorithmic thinking, 234–235
Algorithms
  addition, 184–189, 194–195
  in bases, 193–196
  division, 127, 203–206, 383, 388
  duplation, 208
  Egyptian, 208
  Euclidean, 274–275, 278
  explanation of, 158
  on graphic calculators, 236
  lattice, 208
  multiplication, 199–203
  origin of term, 186
  Russian peasant, 208
  subtraction, 190–193, 195–196
Alternate interior angles, 607
Altitude
  of parallelograms, 696
  of triangle, 846, 909–910
Analytical Institutions (Agnesi), 891
Ancient Egyptians
  algorithms and, 208
  fractions and, 377

  hieroglyphics and, 159, 377
  numeration system and, 159–162
  steepness measurement and, 403
Angle bisectors, 836–838
Angle-angle (AA) property, of similar triangles, 851–852
Angle–angle–angle (AAA) property, of similar triangles, 851–852
Angle–angle–side (AAS) property, of congruent triangles, 823
Angles
  acute, 602
  adjacent, 604
  alternate interior, 607
  complementary, 604
  congruent, 603
  conjugate, 634
  corresponding, 606–607
  degrees of, 602, 608, 614
  dihedral, 637, 639
  directed, 609–610
  explanation of, 601–602
  exterior, 608–609, 617, 620
  interior, 617, 620–622
  measurement of, 603
  obtuse, 602
  pairs of, 604–607
  of polygon, 620
  right, 602, 603
  straight, 602
  in triangles, 607–609
  trisection of, 841, 847, 864

Angles (*continued*)
  types of, 602–603
  vertical, 605
  zero, 602
Angle-side-angle (ASA) property, of
    congruent triangles, 822–823
Anthropology, 777
Antiprisms, 653
Apex, of pyramids, 641
Apollonius of Perga, 873
Approximation, 219, 221
Arago, Francois, 558
Archimedes, 403, 704, 730
Area
  of circle, 703–704
  in customary system, 680, 681
  explanation of, 680
  metric units of, 685
  of polygons, 696–701
  properties of, 693–695
  surface, 721–726, 732–733 (*See also*
        Surface area)
  unit of, 692
Area models, 355–356
Arguments, from a special case, 40
Arithmetic
  clock, 283–293, 472
  mental, 213–218
  of rational numbers, 371–386
Arithmetic logic, 225
Arithmetic mean. *See* Mean
Arithmetica (Diophantus), 346
Array model, 118
Ascher, Marcia, 853
Asimov, Isaac, 603
Association of Women in Mathematics
    (AWM), 274
Associative property
  of addition, 106
  of addition of integers, 315
  of addition of rational numbers, 391
  of intersection, 86
  of multiplication, 120, 121
  of multiplication of integers, 337
  of multiplication of rational numbers, 393
  of union, 86
Average. *See* Mean
Ax, 694
Axes, coordinate, 872

Babylonians
  calendars and, 70
  degree measure and, 608
  numeration system of, 164–165
Banneker, Benjamin, 177
Bar codes, 290–293
Bar graphs, 485–487
Base
  algorithms in other, 193–196
  explanation of, 129

five, 179, 193–196
six, 203
ten, 168, 169, 179, 193
three, 183, 212–213
utility of, 180
Base ten blocks, 171, 172, 417–418
Basketball math, 369–370
Bell, Eric Temple, 219
Bellman, Richard, 60
Bernoulli, Daniel, 537
Bernoulli, Jakob, 536, 537
Bernoulli, Johann, 537
Bernoulli, Nicolaus, 537
Bessel, Friedrich Wilhelm, 742
Bhaskara, 719
Bilateral symmetry, 776, 786
Binary codes, 65
Binary digits, 65
Binary operations, 103
Binomials, 122–123
Bits, 65
Black-red game, 301
Blood typing, 91
Boeke, Kees, 735
Border patterns, 780–781
Bouchet, Edward A., 307
Box, 640
Box and whisker plots
  for comparisons, 510–511
  explanation of, 508, 510
Boyer, Clem, 487
Brain, mathematics and, 142
Brainerd, George W., 777
Bridg-It, 666
Buckyball, 638

Cabri, 953
Calculators. *See also* Graphing calculators
  adding and subtracting integers with, 329
  algorithmic thinking and, 234–236
  automating algorithms on graphing, 236
  built-in constant function on, 233
  to compute tax rate, 148–149
  computing quotients and remainders on,
        210–211
  constant function on, 32
  day of week function and, 149–150
  functions on graphing, 143
  graphical representations on, 492
  integer divide capability on, 210, 211,
        232–233
  least common multiple and greatest com-
        mon divisor using graphing, 279
  logic determining operation of, 225
  mean and standard deviation and, 513
  NCTM Principles and Standards for use
        of, 225–226
  order of operations and, 227–228
  prime power factorizations with graphing,
        257

priority of operations and, 226–227, 229
rational numbers and, 399
scientific notation and, 443–445
statistics routines on, 521
sum of arithmetic progression on, 233
sum of geographic progression on,
        233–234
use of fraction, 361, 386
use of specific keys on, 228–232
Cantor, Georg, 80, 81
Cap, 84
Capacity
  computing, 688
  explanation of, 682
  metric units of, 685–686
Cardinal numbers, 92
Cartesian coordinate system
  dividing line segment and, 877–881
  explanation of, 872–874
  midpoint formula and, 874–877
Cartesian product
  multiplication and, 118–120
  origin of term, 873
  of sets, 119
CAT scans, 864–865
Cathode ray tubes (CRT), 85
Cauchy, Augustin-Louis, 645
Cavanaugh, Mary, 171
Celsius temperature scale, 402, 688
Center of gravity
  explorations with, 858–859
  locating, 885
  of triangle, 857
Central angle, of polygons, 626–627
Central tendency
  determining an average and, 505
  determining typical value for set of data
        and, 506
  mean and, 501–502, 504–505
  measures of, 500–501
  median and, 502–503
  mode and, 503–505
Centroid
  explanation of, 848, 858
  of triangle, 857, 859
Ceulen, Van, 704
Chimpanzees, problem-solving, 42
Chinese remainder problem, 256
Circles
  angles and distances in, 604
  area of, 703–704
  circumscribing, 836
  equations of, 910–913
  explanation of, 628–629
  finding center of, 912–913
  inscribed, 838
  perpendicular chords in pair of, 629
  squaring of, 841
Circular cylinders, 640
Circular symmetry, 777

Circumcircle, of triangles, 836
Circumference, 702–703
Circumscribing circles, 836
Clock arithmetic
  addition and, 283–285, 287, 288
  applications of, 290
  bar codes on envelopes and postal cards
    and, 290–293
  in classroom, 289
  division and, 288
  multiplication and, 285
  power in *n*-hour, 294
  properties of, 472–473
  subtraction and, 286–288
Closed curves, 616, 617, 623
Closure property
  of addition, 105, 106
  of addition of integers, 315
  of addition of rational numbers, 391
  of multiplication, 121
  of multiplication of integers, 337
  of multiplication of rational numbers, 393
  of subtraction of integers, 325
The Clouds (Aristophanes), 605
Collatz's problem, 11
Collinear points, 599, 600
Color monitors, 85
Colored counters
  addition of integers using, 313–315
  representing integers by "drops" of,
    302–303, 305–306
  subtraction of integers using, 321–325
Colored regions, as models for fractions,
  355–356
Combinations, 557–560
Common denominators
  examples of finding, 363–364
  explanation of, 362
Common multiple, 275
Commutative property
  of addition, 106, 107
  of addition of integers, 315
  of addition of rational numbers, 391
  of intersection, 86
  of multiplication, 120, 121
  of multiplication of integers, 337
  of multiplication of rational numbers,
    393
  of union, 86
Comparison model, 109, 110
Compasses, 603, 864
Complementary angles, 604
Complements, set, 82, 83
Composite numbers, 249, 255
Composition, 146
Compound events, 540–541
Compound interest
  calculation of, 467
  example of, 468
  explanation of, 465–467

Computer software, *The Geometer's
  Sketchpad,* 598, 615, 752, 803, 841,
  953–958
Computer-aided design (CAD), 864
Concrete modeling, 931
Concurrent lines, 599, 600
Cones
  explanation of, 648
  illustrations of, 649
  volume of, 728–730
Congruence property, 693, 694
Congruent
  explanation of, 601, 924
  figures as, 764
Congruent angles, 603, 816
Congruent line segments, 812
Congruent triangles
  additional properties and, 824
  angle-angle-side property and, 823
  angle-side-angle property and, 822–823
  explanation of, 813–814
  side-angle-side property and, 818–821
  side-side-side property and, 814–815
  triangle inequality and, 816–817
Conjugate angle, 634
Connelly, Robert, 645
Consider special cases
  example of, 38–40
  explanation of, 35
  Pascal's triangle and, 35–38
Constant of proportionality, 455
Construction
  of angle bisector, 836–838
  of circles, 842
  of congruent angle, 816
  with dynamic geometry software, 598,
    615, 752, 803, 841
  in grades 3–5, 843
  historical background of, 864–865
  of line segment, 812
  of midpoint and perpendicular bisector of
    line segment, 834–836
  Mira and paper folding, 840
  overview of, 830–831
  of parallel lines, 831
  of perpendicular lines, 833, 834
  of quadrilaterals, 842
  of regular polygon, 838–839
  of rhombus, 831
  in space, 832–833
Convex curves, 618
Convex polygons, 618, 620
Convex simple closed surface, 640
Conway, John, 663
Coordinate axes, 872
Coordinate geometry
  activities to introduce, 906
  Cartesian coordinate system and, 872–881
  equations of circles and, 910–913
  explanation of, 871–872

  graphing functions and, 915–921
  historical background of, 873
  lines and graphs and, 885–899
  proofs using, 906–910
Coordinate system, 872
Coordinates, 924–925
Corner mirror, 773
Corresponding angles, 606–607
Counterexamples, 87
Counting
  addition principle of, 551–553
  combinations and permutations and,
    557–564
  mathematically, 79–80
  overview of, 550–551
  value of, 150, 158
  word "and" and, 554–557
  word "or" and, 551–554
Counting boards, 169
Counting numbers. *See* Natural numbers
Cox, Elbert, 307
Crow, Donald W., 783
Cubes, 96, 642, 643, 841
Cuboctahedron, 641
Cuisenaire rods, 96
Cup, 84
*Curriculum and Evaluation Standards for
  School Mathematics* (National
  Council of Teachers of
  Mathematics)
  calculation skills and, 184
  calculator use and, 226
  manipulatives and, 930
  Standard 1, 3
Curves
  closed, 616, 617, 623
  convex, 618
  explanation of, 616
  polygonal, 618, 619, 700–701
  simple, 616, 617, 623
  in space, 639–640
Customary system, 680–682
Cycloid
  explanation of, 694
  length of, 700–701
Cycloidal arch, 694–695
Cylinders
  explanation of, 648
  general, 649, 728
  illustrations of, 649
  oblique, 648, 727–728
  right, 648, 721–723

Data
  computing empirical probability from,
    539
  graphical representation of, 487–492 (*See
    also* Graphical representations)
  third grade and analysis of, 490
Davis, Robert, 4

De Méré, Chevalier, 587–588
Decagons, 619
Decimal point, 417
Decimals
    addition and subtraction of, 437–438
    comparing and ordering, 427
    converting fractions to, 424
    explanation of, 168–169, 415–416
    expressed as percent, 460
    multiplication of, 439–440
    multiplied or divided by powers of 10,
        421–422
    NCTM Principles and Standards and,
        420
    negative exponents and expanded
        exponential form and, 420–421
    nontermination repeating, 423–427, 429
    ordering, 427–429
    percent expressed as, 462
    positional values and, 420
    repeating, 423–427
    representations of, 416–418
    rounding of, 444–445
    scientific notation and, 443–445
    using money to represent, 426
Degenerate triangle, 34
Degrees, of angle, 602, 608, 614
Deltahedra, 650
Denominators
    common, 362–364
    explanation of, 354, 355
Density property, of rational numbers,
    394–395
Dependent events, 543, 555
Descartes, René, 119, 128, 129, 644, 873
Diameter, of tree, 665
Difference, 108
DIFFY game, 112, 388–389, 936
Digits, 168
Dihedral angles, 637
Dilations, 765–766
Dimensional analysis. See Unit analysis
Diophantus, 346
Dipyramids, 653
Directed angles, 609–610
Disjoint sets, 84
Distance formula, 880
Distribution curve, 525
Distributions
    explanation of, 523–525
    normal, 525–526
Distributive property
    of intersection, 86
    of multiplication, 120, 121
    of multiplication of integers, 337
    of multiplication of rational numbers,
        393
    of union, 86
    verifying, 87
Dividend, 124

Divisibility tests
    by 10, 262
    by 11, 265–266
    by 2, 3, 5, 9, and 10, 264
    by 7, 11, and 13, 266, 267
    by 2 and 5, 262
    by 3 and 9, 263
    by 4 and 8, 268
    explanation of, 261–262
    by powers of 2, 267–268
    by products, 262–263
Division
    clock, 288
    in Egyptian system, 162
    explanation of, 420–421
    by grouping, 123
    of integers, 339–340
    missing-factor model of, 124–125
    modeled for fourth grade, 126
    partition model of, 123–124
    of rational numbers, 381–386, 392–394
    with remainders, 125, 127, 128
    repeated subtraction model of, 123
    by sharing, 123
    symbols for, 129
    by zero, 125
Division algorithm
    example using, 128
    explanation of, 127, 203
    greatest common divisor and, 274
    long, 204–205
    short, 206
Division patterns, 265
Divisors
    of 6, 248
    explanation of, 124, 247
    greatest common, 270–275
    of natural numbers, 251–252
    proper, 247
DIVVY, 389
Dodecahedron, 638, 641, 643
Domain, of function, 136
Double pyramids, 653
Drafting triangles, 603
Draw a picture/diagram
    example of, 24–25
    explanation of, 12, 13, 24
Duplation algorithm, 208
Dynamic geometry software, 598, 615, 752,
    803, 841

Earth, circumference of, 703
Easy combinations, 214–215
Edges
    in networks, 657
    in planar networks, 659–663
Egyptians. See Ancient Egyptians
Einstein, Albert, 219
Element, of set, 81
Elements (Euclid), 253, 273, 594

Eliminate possibilities strategy
    example of, 50–51
    explanation of, 50
Empirical probability. See also Probability
    of compound events, 540–541
    computing, 539, 540, 542–543
    determining, 538, 540
    explanation of, 536–538
    geometry and, 543–545
    of mutually exclusive events, 541
    of non-mutually exclusive events,
        541–542
    simulation and, 545–546
Empty sets, 84, 86
Encryption, 285
Endpoint, 601
Enneagons, 619
Envelope tetrahedron model, 644
Epcot Center, 648
Equality symbol, 98
Equations
    of circles, 910–913
    of lines, 893–897
    proofs using, 909–910
    simultaneous solution of two linear,
        897–898
Equiangular polygons, 626
Equidistance property, 837
Equilateral polygons, 626
Equilateral triangles, 624
Equivalent fractions
    examples of, 359–360
    explanation of, 358–359
Equivalent sets, 93
Eratosthenes of Cyrene, 254, 255, 265,
    741–742
Error-correcting code, 65, 66
Error-correcting problems, 63, 65–67
Escher, Maurits Cornelius, 796, 798
Escher-like tiling, 796–799
Estimation. See also Mental arithmetic
    elements of, 219
    example of, 220
    rational numbers and, 396
    rounding and, 219, 221
Ethnomathematics, A Multicultural View of
        Mathematical Ideas (Ascher), 853
Euclid, 70, 253, 273, 594, 864
Euclidean algorithm, 274–275, 278
Eudoxus, 594
Euler, Leonhard, 558, 644, 656, 658
Euler's formula
    for connected planar networks, 661–663
    for polyhedra, 643–646, 648
Events
    complementary, 574–575
    dependent, 543
    explanation of, 541
    independent, 543
    mutually exclusive, 541

Exchanging
  adding with, 188–189
  multiplying with, 201
  subtracting with, 192–193
  subtracting without, 190
Expanded exponential form, 420–421
Expanded form, 415–416
Expected value, 580–581
Exponentials
  explanation of, 129
  multiplication rules of, 130
  rules for division of, 131
Exponents
  explanation of, 129
  negative, 421
  power operation and, 128–129
  working with, 129–131
  zero as, 130, 421
Exterior angles, 608–609

Fact family, 124
Factor tree, 250
Factorials, 559–560
Factors
  divisors and, 270
  explanation of, 118, 247
Fahrenheit temperature scale, 402, 688
Fair division problems
  examples of, 61–63
  spreadsheets and, 64
Fascinating Fibonaccis: Mystery and Magic
    in Numbers (Garland), 287
Federov, Evgraf, 782
Fermat, Pierre de, 276, 587, 873
Fermat point, 848
Fermat primes, 839
Fermat's principle, 772
Fibonacci (Leonardo of Pisa), 29, 71, 170,
    377
Fibonacci numbers, 28–29, 287, 442
Fibonacci sequence
  algorithmic generation of, 234–235
  explanation of, 28, 141, 170
Fibonacci Sum record sheet, 260–261
Fifth grade
  geometric shapes in, 843
  graphing in, 899
  problem solving in, 52
  statistics in, 509
  understanding percent in, 469
Finite sets, 94
First class postage, 148
Fisher, Sir Ronald A., 523
  5-number summary, 508
  5-up rule, 218
Flatland: A Romance of Many Dimensions
    (Abbott), 603
Flip. *See* Reflection
Force tunneling microscope, 864–865
Formulas, 139–140

Fourth grade
  geometric shapes in, 843
  modeling division in, 126
  probability in, 584
  rigid motions in, 766
  temperature measurement in, 687
Fractals, 597, 768
Fraction squares, 370
Fraction strips, 356, 372
Fractions
  in ancient Egypt, 377
  converted to decimals, 424
  equivalent, 358–360
  explanation of, 354–355
  expressed as percent, 462–463
  fundamental law of, 358
  hands-on activity for, 352–353
  mixed numbers and proper, 374–375
  models for, 355–357
  music and, 404
  NCTM Principles and Standards and,
    357
  nontermination repeating decimals as,
    423–424
  ordering, 365
  percent expressed as, 462
  in probability, 370
  simplest form of, 272, 360–364
  technology and, 406–407
Franklin, Fabian, 819
Frequency, 481
Frequency of interval, 481
Frequency polygon
  explanation of, 483, 484
  relative, 524
Functions
  application of, 141–142
  explanation of, 136–137
  as formulas, 139–140
  on graphing calculators, 143
  graphs of, 140–141, 915–921
  Guess My Rule game to introduce,
    138–139
  linear, 147–148
  as machines, 140
  minimum and maximum values of,
    918–921
  range of, 137
  as tables, 140
Fundamental theorem of arithmetic
  prime power form of, 251
  simple product form of, 250

Gaetana, Pietro, 891
Galileo, 668, 694, 695
Gardner, Martin, 42
Garland, Trudi Hammel, 287
Gauss, Carl Friedrich, 33, 34, 219, 296,
    731, 839, 864
Gauss's trick, 33

Gauss-Wantzel constructibility theorem,
    839
General cones, 648, 649
General cylinders, 649, 728
General prisms, 728
Generalization, 397
Geodesic domes, 833
The Geometer's Sketchpad, 598, 615, 752,
    803, 841, 953–958
Geometric probability
  of carnival game, 582–583
  explanation of, 581–582
Geometry. *See also* Coordinate geometry
  curves and polygons in plane, 616–631
    (*See also* Planes)
  dynamical view of, 804
  empirical probability and, 543–545
  explanation of, 594
  figures in plane, 596–610 (*See also*
    Planes)
  figures in space, 637–650 (*See also*
    Space)
  materials for exploring, 594–595
  motion, 779
  nature of informal, 594
  NCTM Principles and Standards and,
    595–596
  networks, 656–663
  of self-similar shapes, 768
  shapes in, 597
  synthetic, 871
  themes of, 923–924
  transformational, 750
  van Heile levels and, 627
  visualization and, 668
The Geometry Inventor, 953
Germain, Sophie, 731
Glide reflection, 757, 759
Gold coin game, 48–50
Gordon, Carolyn, 765
Graphical representations
  bar graphs, 485–487
  choosing good visualizations for, 489,
    491
  graphing calculators and, 492
  histograms, 481–482, 491
  line graphs, 482–485, 491
  line plots, 479, 491
  pictographs, 489–491
  pie charts, 487–488, 491
  stem and leaf plots, 480–481, 491
Graphing calculators. *See also* Calculators
  automating algorithms on, 236
  creating statistical plots on, 945–946
  day of week function and, 149–150
  entering, evaluating, and editing expres-
    sions on, 940
  entering and editing data on, 944–945
  entering and graphing equations on, 941,
    942

Graphing calculators *(continued)*
  entering and using lists in home screen
    on, 940–941
  explanation of, 939
  exploring function graph with, 943–944
  finding least common multiple and
    greatest common divisor using, 279
  functions on, 143
  graphical representations on, 492
  operations with integers and, 304
  prime power factorizations with, 257
  programming of, 946–947
  programs for, 947–951
  random numbers and simulation on, 546
Graphs
  application of, 141–142
  bar, 485–487
  in fifth grade, 899
  of functions, 140–141, 915–921
  line, 482–485
Gravity. *See* Center of gravity
Greater than or equal to, 319
Greatest common divisor machine, 280
Greatest common divisors
  Euclidean algorithm and, 274–275
  explanation of, 270
  by intersection of sets, 271
  from prime power representations, 271,
    273, 277–278
  using technology to find, 279
Greek cross, 877
Guess and check strategy
  examples of, 13–14, 19–22
  explanation of, 11–12
Guess My Rule game, 25–26, 28, 138–139
Gulliver's Travels (Swift), 734

Half planes, 617
Half-spaces, 637
Hamming, Richard, 65
Hamming code, 65
Hands On. *See also* Manipulatives
  are pennies fair?, 535
  black-red game, 301
  counting cars and trains, 79
  exploring polygons, 593
  folded fractions, 352–353
  how many are marked?, 478
  lattice points, 871
  measurements in Beanland, 675
  numbers from rectangles, 157
  one-sided paper, 2–3
  reflection and rotation symmetry, 749
  representing integers as sums, 245
  toothpick triangles, 811
  triangles and squares, 413
Hardy, G. H., 573
Harmonic mean, 528
Harriot, Thomas, 98, 129
Hectare, 685

Helix, 639
Heptadecagons, 619
Hero of Alexandria, 710
Hero's formula, 710
Herschel, William, 742
Hexagonal pyramids, 641
Hexagons, 619
Hexahedron, 640, 653
Hexiamond, 802
Hexomino, 654
Hieroglyphics, 159, 377
Hilbert, David, 81, 274
Hippasus, 430
Histograms
  computing empirical probability from,
    539
  explanation of, 481–482, 491
  function of, 523, 524
  on graphing calculator, 952
History of of Mathematics (Montucla), 731
Hoecke, Vander, 111
Holliday, Vera, 542
Homeomorphism, 924
Hooke's law, 147
How to Lie with Statistics (Huff), 513
How to Solve It (Pólya), 16, 18
Hubble, Edward, 742
Hypatia, 138, 274

Icosahedron, 638, 641, 643
Identification numbers, 92
Image, 136, 751
Incas, 80
Incenter, 838
Incircle, 838
Independent events
  explanation of, 543
  multiplication principle of counting for,
    555, 570
Indo-Arabic numeration system, 168, 169,
  417
Inequality
  operating with, 320–321
  of rational numbers, 365
  symbol for, 98
Infinite sets, 94
Information age, 530–531
Initial side, 609
Innumeracy, 137
Inscribed circle, 838
Inscribed polygons, 838
Integers
  absolute value of, 308–309
  addition of, 313–320, 329–330
  colored counters and, 302–303, 305–306
  division of, 339–340
  explanation of, 301–302
  function of, 415
  mail-time representations of, 306
  multiplication of, 334–339

NCTM Principles and Standards and, 304
  negative, 303–305
  the negative of the negative of, 308
  notation and, 303–304
  number line representations of, 306–308
  positive, 303–305
  properties of, 472–473
  to represent quantities, 310
  subtraction of, 321–330
International Standardization Organization,
  682
International System of Units (SI system),
  682–683
Interquartile range (IQR), 507, 508
Intersection
  associative property of, 86
  commutative property of, 86
  distributive property of, 86
  of lines, 897–898
  point of, 599
Intersection of sets
  explanation of, 84, 271, 276
  greatest common divisors of, 271
  least common multiple of, 276
Invariance, 923
Irrational numbers
  explanation of, 429
  irrationality of ÷2 and, 429–431
  proof for, 431–432
  Pythagoras and, 430
Isometric drawings, 652
Isometry, 751. *See also* Rigid motions
Isosceles trapezoids, 625
Isosceles triangle theorem, 821, 823
Isosceles triangles, 624, 821, 881

Jenkins, Charlotte, 383
Jordan curve theorem, 616

Kac, Mark, 765
Kanada, Yasumasa, 704
Kaprekar's number, 10
Kepler, Johannes, 793
Kerrich, John, 537, 550
al-Khowarizmi, 186
Kilogram, 686
Kite, 625
Koch, Helge von, 768
Koch curve, 768
Königsberg Bridge Problem, 656–659
Kronecker, Leopold, 81
Krypto game, 131

Ladd-Franklin, Christine, 819
Lambert, John, 702
Landsteiner, Karl, 91
Lateral surface
  of cone, 648
  of cylinders, 648
  of prism, 722

Lattice algorithm, 208
Lattice points, 871
Lattice polygons, 632, 699–700, 711–712
Law of large numbers, 536–538
Law of the lever, 403
Lawrence, Anne, 466
Leap year, 404
Least common multiple
    explanation of, 275
    by intersection of sets, 276
    from prime power representations,
        277–278
    from use of Euclidean algorithm, 278
    use of technology to find, 279
Left to right method for mental calculation,
    216–217
Leibniz, Gottfried, 129
Length
    in customary system, 680
    explanation of, 601
    metric units of, 683–685
Length of the period, 425
Leonardo da Vinci, 694
Leonardo of Pisa (Fibonacci). *See* Fibonacci
    (Leonardo of Pisa)
Less than or equal to, 319
Liber Abaci (Leonardo of Pisa (Fibonacci)),
    71, 170
Lightning distance function, 148
Limit, 924
Line graphs, 482–485, 491
Line of best fit, 901
Line of reflection, 755
Line of symmetry, 776
Line plots, 479, 491
Line segments
    congruent, 812
    construction of, 812
    construction of midpoint and perpendicular
        bisector, 834–836
    determining length of, 879–880
    division of, 877–878
    explanation of, 601
    slope of, 885–887
Linear functions, 147–148
Lines
    concurrent, 599
    equations of, 893–897
    explanation of, 596, 599
    intersections of, 897–898
    parallel, 599, 639, 760–761, 831,
        888–889
    perpendicular, 603, 833, 834
    skew, 639
    slope of, 885, 887–888
    in space, 637, 639
    transversal, 599
Lists. *See* Make a table/list strategy
Liter, 685, 686
Locuses, 924

Look for a pattern strategy
    explanation of, 12, 13, 27
    in numerical sequence, 28–29
Lotteries, 590
Lower quartiles, 507

Machin, John, 704
Machines, 140
Magic addition square, 135
Magic in Base Three trick, 212–213
Mail-time stories
    addition of integers using, 315
    integers and, 306
    multiplication of integers using, 337–338
    subtraction of integers using, 325–326
Make a table/list strategy
    examples of, 23, 29, 31–32
    explanation of, 12, 13, 22
Mandelbrot, Benoit B., 768
Manipulatives. *See also* Hands On; *specific*
        manipulatives
    for addition algorithms, 184–189
    classroom use of, 171
    for clock arithmetic, 284
    concrete modeling and, 931
    for decimals, 416–418
    do's and don'ts regarding, 931–932
    explanation of, 929
    for geometry, 595
    information sources for, 932
    for measurement, 678–679
    for multiplication algorithms, 200–202
    for positional systems, 169–173
    professional organizations' views of, 930
    research on, 930
    for subtraction algorithms, 190–192,
        195–196
    types of, 929
    when to use, 931
Math Explorer (Texas Instruments). *See also*
        Calculators
    explanation of, 225
    fractions on, 361, 386
    integer divide on, 210, 211, 232–233
    memory in, 230–231
Mathematical Discovery (Pólya), 18
Mathematical probability. *See* Probability
Mathematics
    brain and, 142
    fascination with, 70–72
    of optimization, 58
    origins of, 80
    real-world applications of, 58–67
Mathematics and Plausible Reasoning
        (Pólya), 18
Mathematics instruction. *See also* NCTM
        Principles and Standards; *specific*
        grades
    of comparing and ordering integers, 319
    effects of inadequate, 137

efforts to reform and revitalize, 3
    manipulative use in (*See* Manipulatives)
    on sets, 86
Mats. *See also* Manipulatives
    learning algorithms using, 184–190,
        192
    learning decimals using, 416
    use of, 171, 172
Maxima, 924
Mayan numeration system, 165–168
Mean
    calculator use and, 513
    determining, 504–505
    explanation of, 501–502
    fraction of data values near, 514
    harmonic, 528
    population, 521–523
Measurement
    of area, 685, 692–704 (*See also* Area)
    bean activity for, 675
    of capacity, 685–686, 689
    explanation of, 676, 678, 742, 924
    of length, 683–685
    NCTM Principles and Standards and,
        677
    in nonstandard units, 692
    overview of, 676
    problem solving with, 728
    Pythagorean theorem and, 712–716
    of similar figures, 733–734
    steps in process of, 676
    of surface area, 721–726, 732–733
    tangram, 678–679
    of temperature, 688, 695
    of volume, 685–686, 689, 726–731
    of weight and mass, 686, 688
Measurement model
    of addition, 105
    division of rational numbers and,
        381–382
    explanation of, 109
    illustration of, 376
Measurement systems
    English or customary, 680–682
    metric system of, 682–683
Medial triangles, 855
Median
    determining, 503–506, 508
    explanation of, 502–503
    of triangle, 845, 857
Mediant, of fractions, 368
Member, of set, 81
Mental arithmetic. *See also* Estimation
    adjustment in, 215–216
    easy combinations and, 214–215
    importance of, 213–214
    one-digit facts and, 214
    rational numbers and, 396, 397, 399
    rounding and, 218
    working from left to right in, 216–217

Mersenne, Father Marin, 256
Mersenne Numbers, 256
Meter, 683, 684
Metric system
    changing units in, 685
    estimating weights in, 688
    explanation of, 682–684
Midpoint
    explanation of, 601
    of line segment, 834–836, 874–876
    in quadrilaterals, 857
Midpoint formula, 876
Millay, Edna St. Vincent, 253
Minima, 924
Minimum-time routing problems, 58–61
Minuend, 108
Minutes (degree), 614
Mira, 752, 756, 840
Mirror line, 755, 776
Mirror reflection. *See* Reflection
Missing-addend model
    explanation of, 109, 110
    illustration of, 376
Missing-factor model
    example of, 385–386
    explanation of, 124–125
Mode
    determining, 504–506
    explanation of, 503–504
Money, learning decimals using, 418
Morley, Frank, 864
Mu torere game, 787
Multilink Cubes, 96
Multiplication
    array model for, 118
    of binomials, 122–123
    Cartesian product model of, 118–120
    clock, 285
    of decimals, 420–421, 439–440
    in Egyptian system, 162
    exponents and, 128–131
    of integers, 334–339
    NCTM principles and standards, 122
    properties of whole number, 120–121
    of rational numbers, 378–381,
        392–394
    as repeated addition, 117–118
    symbols for, 118, 129
    by zero property, 121
Multiplication algorithm
    developing, 200–202
    examples using, 201–202
    explanation of, 199–200
    in other bases, 202–203
Multiplication principle of counting, 555,
    570
Multiplication property of rational numbers,
    394
Multiplication table, 12-hour clock, 289
Multiplication tic-tac-toe, 224–225

Multiplicative identity
    explanation of, 120, 121, 125
    multiplication of rational numbers and,
        393
Multiplicative inverse
    explanation of, 294, 384
    rational numbers and, 393–394
Music, fractions in, 404
Musical notes, 282
Musical scale, Pythagorean, 398
Mutually exclusive events
    addition principle of counting and,
        552–553
    empirical probability of, 541

Napoleon point, 848
National Council of Teachers of
    Mathematics, 930
Natural numbers
    development of, 346, 414
    divisibility of, 247–256
    divisors of, 251–252
    function of, 415
    primes as, 249–250
    properties of, 472–473
    set of, 81–82
    as sum of consecutive integers, 245
Navajos, 853
NCTM Principles and Standards
    calculator use, 225–226
    fractions and decimals, 420
    geometric shapes, 843
    geometry, 595–596
    integers, 304
    meaning and relationships of operations,
        122
    measurement, 677
    number theory, 246
    probability, 537
    problem solving, 3–4
    reasoning with fractions, 357
    statistics and probability, 225–226; 480
    transformations and symmetry, 775–776
Negative exponents, 420–421
Negative integers, 303
Negative inverse, 391
Negative numbers, 346
Nets, 642
Networks
    Euler's formula and, 661–663
    examples of, 657
    explanation of, 657–658
    Königsberg bridge problem and,
        656–659
    planar, 659–663
    structural formula, 667
    traversable, 658, 659
    vertices, edges, and regions in planar
        networks, 659–662
Neugebauer, Otto, 608

n-gon, 619, 628
Niggi, P., 782
Noether, Emmy, 219
Nominal numbers, 92
Nonagons, 619, 795
Nontermination repeating decimals
    as fractions, 423–424
    rational numbers and, 425–427
Normal distributions
    explanation of, 524–525
    rule for, 526
Northwest Coast Indians, 750
Notation
    integers and, 303–304
    for sets, 81
Number lines
    addition of integers using, 317–318
    addition properties on, 108
    explanation of, 96–97
    fractions on, 357
    multiplication of integers using, 338–339
    real numbers and, 432
    representing integers on, 306–308
    subtraction of integers using, 326–327,
        329
    use of, 109, 110
Number rods, 96
Number strips, 96
Number theory
    importance of, 296–297
    NCTM Principles and Standards and,
        246
    study of, 285
Numbers. *See also* Natural numbers;
        Rational numbers; Real numbers;
        Whole numbers
    composite, 249, 255
    Mersenne, 256
    mixed, 374–375
    patterns in sequences of, 28–29
    perfect, 246–247, 253
    prime, 249
    types of, 91
Numerals, 158
Numeration systems. *See also* Standard
        notation
    of Babylonians, 164–165
    Egyptian, 159–162
    Indo-Arabic, 168, 169, 417
    Mayan, 165–168
    nondecimal positional, 176–180
    overview of, 158–159, 414–415
    physical models for positional, 169–173
    Roman, 162–164
Numerators, 354, 355

Oblique circular cones, 648, 649
Oblique cylinders, 648, 727–728
Oblique prisms, 641, 727–728
Obtuse angles, 602

Obtuse triangles, 624
Octagons, 619, 639
Octahedron, 638, 641, 643
Odd numbers, 29
Odds, 578–580
One-to-one correspondence, 92–93
Opposite exterior angles, 608–609
Optimization, mathematics of, 58
Order relation properties, 394
Ordered pair, 118–119
Ordinal numbers, 92
Oresme, Nicole, 873
Orientation preserving transformations, 757
Orientation reversing, 757
Oughtred, William, 129
Outcome, 541, 567
Outliers, 508

Palindromes, 10, 785
Paper clip comparison, 109
Paper folding constructions, 840, 847–848
Parallel lines
   construction of, 831
   explanation of, 599
   exploring consecutive reflections across, 760–761
   slope of, 888–889
   in space, 639
Parallelograms
   area of, 696–697
   explanation of, 625, 626
   tiling and, 796
Partition model, 123, 125
Pascal, Blaise, 37, 587
Pascal's triangle
   explanation of, 37–38
   finding pattern in row sums of, 38–40
   problem-solving strategy with, 35–38
   on spreadsheet, 41
Paths, in networks, 658
Patterns
   border, 780–781
   classroom instruction and, 779
   in row sums of Pascal's triangle, 38–40
   on spreadsheet, 41
   strategy for finding, 12, 13, 27–29
   translation symmetry and, 778, 780–782
   wallpaper, 782
Patterson, Michael, 663
Paulos, John Allen, 137
Pendulums, 694, 905
Pentagonal arch, 621
Pentagonal pyramids, 641
Pentagons, 619
Pentahedron, 640, 653
Pentominoes, 653, 801
Percent
   applications of, 463–465
   explanation of, 460

expressed as decimals, 462
expressed as fractions, 462
expressing decimals as, 460
expressing fractions as, 462–463
fifth grade and understanding, 469
Perfect numbers
   explanation of, 246–247
   formula for even, 253
Perigal, Henry, 719
Perimeter
   of circle, 702–703
   explanation of, 701
Periodic decimals. *See* Repeating decimals
Permutations, 557–564
Perpendicular bisectors, 834
Perpendicular lines
   construction of, 833, 834
   explanation of, 603
   slope of, 890–893
Pi (π)
   ancient Egyptians and, 708
   explanation of, 702–703
   historical background of, 704
   pizza size and, 704
Pick, Georg, 711
Pick's formula, 711–712
Pictographs, 489–491
Pie charts, 487–488, 491
Pierce, C. S., 819
Pigeonhole principle, 53–54
Pizza problem, 661–662
Place value
   abacus use and, 171
   decimals and, 427
   explanation of, 164
Place value cards, 187, 189, 190, 192–196, 200, 201
Plane shapes, 599
Planes
   curves and polygons in
      circles and, 628–631
      convex curves and figures, 618
      curves and regions, 616–618
      polygon curves and polygons and, 618–623
      quadrilaterials, 625–626
      regular polygons, 626, 628
      triangles and, 624
   explanation of, 599
   figures in
      angles in triangles, 607–609
      collinearity and concurrency, 600
      directed angles, 609–610
      line segments and distance between points, 601
      pairs of angles and angles theorem, 604–607
      points and lines, 596, 599
      rays, angles, and angle measures, 601–604

parallel and intersecting, 637, 639
   in space, 637–639
   transformation of, 751
Plato, 643
Platonic solids, 643
Poincaré, Henri, 18, 61
Point of intersection, 599
Point symmetry, 778
Points
   collinear, 599
   distance between, 601
   explanation of, 596
Point-slope form, of equation of line, 894
Polls, 483, 535
Pólya, George, 16, 18, 782
Polygonal curves
   explanation of, 618
   illustrations of, 619
   length of, 700–701
Polygonal region, 618
Polygons. *See also* Quadrilaterals; *specific polygons*
   activity for exploring, 593
   angle of, 620
   area of, 696–701
   central angle of, 626–627
   congruent, 791
   conjugate angle of, 634
   convex, 620
   equiangular, 626
   equilateral, 626
   explanation of, 618–620
   explorations using, 593, 630–631
   hinged, 832
   inscribed, 838
   interior and exterior angles in, 620–622
   lattice, 632, 699–700, 711–712
   names of, 619
   paper folding activities for, 848
   regular, 626–628
   space, 832
   tiling with irregular, 793–795
Polyhedra
   cooperative investigation with, 649–650
   Euler's formula and, 643–646, 648, 662–663
   explanation of, 640
   flexible, 645
   hands-on activities with, 725
   with hexagonal faces, 648
   regular, 642–643
   space, 832
   surface area of, 721
   types of, 640–642
Population
   distribution of, 523, 525
   explanation of, 518–519
   samples to approximate characteristics of, 538

Population growth, 467–468
Population mean, 521–523
Population standard deviation, 521–523
Positional systems
    Mayan, 166, 167
    nondecimal, 176–180
    physical models for, 169–173
Positive integers, 303
Possibility tree, 554
Post office applications
    bar codes on envelopes and postal cards,
        290–293
    first class postage, 148
Postage, 148
Power, 129
Power of Ten (Morrison & Morrison), 735
Power operation for whole numbers,
    128–129
Powers of Ten Flip Book (Eames & Eames),
    735
Preimage, 751
Prime numbers
    determining if given integer is,
        254–256
    explanation of, 249–250, 255
    largest, 256
    number of, 253
    twin, 94
Prime power form of fundamental theorem
    of arithmetic, 251
Prime power representations
    finding least common multiple and
        greatest common divisor using,
        277–278
    greatest common divisor from, 271, 273
Principal, 466
*Principles and Standards for School
    Mathematics* (National Council of
    Teachers of Mathematics), 3
Prisms
    angles and planes in hexagonal, 642
    explanation of, 641
    oblique, 641, 721–723
    right, 641, 721–723
Probability
    combinations and, 557–564, 572–574
    complementary events and, 574–575
    conditional, 570
    empirical, 535–545
    equally likely outcomes and, 567
    examples of, 568–572
    expected value and, 580–581
    fractions in, 370
    general properties of, 540–541
    geometric, 581–583
    multiplication principle of counting for
        independent events and, 555,
        570
    NCTM Principles and Standards and,
        480, 537

odds and, 578–580
origins of, 587–588
permutations and, 557–564
polls and, 535
properties of, 575, 577
with restrictive conditions, 570
simulation and, 545–546
statistics and, 538–539
strings and loops activity and, 577–578
terminology of, 541
theoretical, 536
Probability Paradox, 571
Problem solving
    in fifth grade, 52
    guidelines to teaching, 70
    introduction to, 11–12
    looking back in, 73
    Pólya's principles of, 16–19
    in real world, 58–67 (*See also* Real-world
        problem solving)
    Standard 6, NCTM Principles and
        Standards, 3–4
    in third grade, 30
    with whole numbers and Venn
        diagrams, 95
Problem-solving strategies
    argue from special case, 40
    consider special case, 35–40
    draw a picture/diagram, 12, 13
    eliminate possibilities, 50–51
    guess and check, 11–14, 19–22
    look for a pattern, 12, 13, 27–29
    make a table/list, 12, 13, 22–23, 29,
        31–32
    pigeonhole principle, 53–54
    solve an easier similar problem, 36, 40
    solve an equivalent problem, 36, 40
    working backward, 48–50
Proper divisors, 247
Proper fractions, 374–375
Proper subsets, 84
Proportion
    applications of, 455–457
    conditions for, 451
    determining, 452
    explanation of, 451
    obtaining proportion from, 452
    proving property of, 452–453
Protractors, 603, 864
Ptolemy, Claudius, 375
Public key encryption, 285
Putnam, Nancy, 796
Pyramids
    double, 653
    explanation of, 640–641
    hexagonal, 641
    pentagonal, 641
    quadrilateral, 641
    surface area of, 724–725
    volume of, 728–730

Pythagoras, 70, 430, 594
Pythagorean comma, 398
Pythagorean musical scale, 398
Pythagorean theorem
    converse of, 716
    explanation of, 430, 712–714
    use of, 714–716
Pythagorean triple, 720

Quadrants, 872
Quadrilateral pyramids, 641
Quadrilaterals. *See also* Polygons
    activity for exploring, 593
    classification of, 625–626
    explanation of, 619
    exploration of, 842
    midpoint in, 857
    space, 857
Quartiles, 507, 508
Quipus, 80
Quotients, 127

Radiolaria, 638
Ramanujan, Srinivasa, 573
Rand, 546
Randlnt, 546
Random numbers, on graphing calculator,
    546
Random sample, 519–520
Random sequence of digits, 520–521
Random spaghetti triangles, 818
Range, 137, 507
Rational numbers
    addition and subtraction properties and,
        390–392
    addition of, 371–375
    application of, 399–400
    on calculators, 399
    comparing, 365–366
    computations with, 396, 397, 399
    density property of, 394–396
    division of, 381–386
    explanation of, 353, 364
    function of, 415
    inequality of, 365
    mental arithmetic and, 396, 397
    multiplication and division properties
        and, 392–394
    multiplication of, 378–381
    nontermination decimals and, 425
    order relation properties and, 394
    ordering fractions and, 365–366
    properties of, 472–473
    Pythagorean musical scale and, 398
    reciprocal of, 383–384
    representing, 364
    subtraction of, 375–378
    terminating decimals and, 423, 424
Ratios
    determining, 449–450

explanation of, 449
in simplest form, 450
tables of, 454
Rays, 601
Real numbers
explanation of, 415
number line and, 432
properties of, 472–473
set of, 429
Real-world problem solving
correcting errors problems, 63, 65–67
fair division problems, 61–63
minimum-time routing problems,
58–61
overview of, 58
with rational numbers, 399–400
Reason, Charles, 307
Recorde, Robert, 98
Rectangles
area of, 696
explanation of, 625
Hands On using, 157
Rectangular prism, 640
Reflection
explanation of, 755–756
finding images under, 756–757
glide, 757, 759
outcome of three successive, 762
outcome of two successive, 759–762
Reflection symmetry, 749
Reflex angles, 602, 603
Regions
in planar networks, 659–663
of simple closed curve, 617
Regular polygons
construction of, 838–839
explanation of, 626–628
Regular polyhedra, 642–643
Regular tilings, 789, 791
Relative frequency, 524
Remainders
division with, 125, 127, 128
explanation of, 127
Repeated-subtraction model
example of, 385
explanation of, 123, 125
Repeating decimals
decimal expansion and, 441–443
explanation of, 425
nontermination, 423–425
as rational numbers, 426, 427
The Republic (Plato), 643
Reverse Polish notation, 225
Rhind, Henry, 70
Rhind papyrus, 70–71, 80, 388
Rhombus
construction of, 831
diagonals of, 892–893, 908
explanation of, 625
Right angles, 602, 603

Right circular cones
explanation of, 648, 649
surface area of, 725–726
Right cylinders
explanation of, 648
surface area of, 721–723
Right prisms
explanation of, 641
volume of, 726–727
Right regular pyramids, 724
Right triangles, 624
Rigid motions
classification of general, 763–765
explanation of, 751, 753, 760
in fourth grade, 766
geometry software to create, 752
glide reflection and, 757, 759, 760
reflection and, 755–757, 760–762
rotation and, 754–755, 760
similarity motions and, 765–768
translation and, 753, 760
Robinson, Julia Bowman, 274
Robinson, Raphael, 274
Rohn, J. H., 129
Rolsen, Nancy, 319
Roman numerals, 162
Roman numeration systems, 162–164
Rotation
center of, 754
Escher-like tiling and, 797
explanation of, 754
finding images under, 755
Rotation symmetry, 749, 777–778
Roulette, 580–581
Rounding, 218
Rule of signs, 336, 340
Rulers, 596, 603, 864
Russian peasant algorithm, 208

Sample space, 541
Samples
to approximate population characteristics,
538
explanation of, 519–521
random, 519–520
Sarton, George, 80
Scale factor, similar triangles and, 850
Scalene triangles, 624
Schattschneider, Doris, 798
Schlegel, Viktor, 653
Schlegel diagrams, 653
Schooten, Frans van, 873
Scientific notation, 443–445
Scott, Charlotte Angas, 336
Scratch method, 198
Second grade, exploring solids in, 647
Seconds (degree), 614
Self-similar objects, 768
Semiregular tilings, 791–792
Senechal, Marjorie, 594

Sequences
explanation of, 140
Fibonacci, 28
patterns in numerical, 28–29
Set model, of addition, 104–105
Set operations
explanation of, 80, 86
properties of, 86, 87
Sets
Cartesian product of, 119
describing, 82
disjoint, 84
empty, 84
equivalent, 93
explanation of, 81
finite, 94
function of, 80–81
infinite, 94
intersection of, 84, 271, 276
one-to-one correspondence between,
92–93
performing operations on, 85
problem solving using, 85–87
relationships and operations on, 83–85
union of, 84
Venn diagrams and, 82–87, 91
verifying properties of, 87
well-defined, 81
Shepherd, Anna O., 777
SI system, 682–683
Side-angle-side (SAS) property
of congruent triangles, 818–821
of similar triangles, 854–855
Sides, of polygonal curves, 618
Side-side-side (SSS) property
of congruent triangles, 814–815
of similar triangles, 852–853
Sieve of Eratosthenes, 254, 255
Significant digits, 443–444
Similar triangles
angle-angle-angle and angle-angle
similarity properties and,
851–852
explanation of, 849–850
geometric problem solving using, 855,
857–858
scale factor and, 850
side-angle-side property and, 854–855
side-side-side similarity property and,
852–853
Similarity, 924
Similarity principle of measurement, 734
Similarity transformations, 766–768
Simple closed surface, 640
Simple product form of fundamental
theorem of arithmetic, 250
Simulation
to determine empirical probability, 545
explanation of, 545, 546
on graphing calculator, 546

The Sixth Book of Mathematical Games from Scientific American (Gardner), 280
Sixth grade, similar figures in, 856
Size transformation, 765
Skew lines, 639
Slide arrow, 753
Slope
  of line segments, 885–887, 890
  of lines, 885, 887–888
  of parallel lines, 888–889
  of perpendicular lines, 890–893
Slope-intercept form of equation of line, 895
Solar system, 742
Solar year, 404
Space
  cones and cylinders in, 648, 649
  construction of figures in, 832–833
  curves, surfaces and solids in, 639–642
  Euler's formula for polyhedra in, 643–646, 648
  explanation of, 637–639
  illustrations of figures in, 638
  Navajo's organization of, 853
  quadrilaterals in, 857
  regular polyhedra in, 642–643
Space octagon, 639
Speed, 148, 688
Spheres
  explanation of, 640
  surface area of, 732–733
  volume of, 730–731
Spreadsheets
  additional features of, 937
  estate division on, 64
  explanation of, 933–934
  exploring number patterns on, 41
  functions of, 935
  grade book using, 934–935
  setting up DIFFY on, 936
Sprouts game, 663
Square inch mysteries, 889
Square numbers, 29
Squares, 413, 625
Standard 1, *Curriculum and Evaluation Standards for School Mathematics* (National Council of Teachers of Mathematics), 3
Standard 6, *Principles and Standards for School Mathematics* (National Council of Teachers of Mathematics), 3–4
Standard deviation
  calculator use and, 513
  computing, 512–514
  explanation of, 511–512
  population, 521–523
Standard notation
  converting from Babylonian to, 165

converting from Egyptian to, 160
converting from Mayan to, 167
converting from Roman to, 164
Stars, 622
State lotteries, 590
Statistical inference
  distributions and, 523–526
  population means and standard deviations and, 521–523
  populations and samples and, 518–521
Statistics
  deception and, 513
  development of, 523
  in fifth grade, 509
  graphical representation of data and, 479–492
  measures of central tendency and variability and, 500–514
  NCTM Principles and Standards and, 480
  use of, 530–531
Steffen, Klaus, 645
Stellated dodecahedron, 641
Stem and leaf plots, 480–481, 491
Stevin, Simon, 433
Sticks in bundles, 171–172
Straight angles, 602
Straight line depreciation, 148
Straightedges, 596, 841, 864
Strings and loops activity, 544, 577–578
Strips. *See also* Manipulatives
  fraction, 356, 372
  learning algorithms using, 184–190, 192
  learning decimals using, 416
  number, 96
  use of, 171, 172
Structural formula, 667
Subsets, 83, 84
Subtraction
  clock, 286–288
  of decimals, 438
  in Egyptian system, 161
  identifying conceptual models of, 111
  of integers, 321–330
  of rational numbers, 375–378, 390–392
  of whole numbers, 108–111
Subtraction algorithm
  in base five, 195–196
  with exchanging, 192–193
  explanation of, 190
  using manipulatives to learn, 191–192, 195–196
  without exchanging, 190
Subtrahend, 108
Supplementary angles, 604
Surface, simple closed, 640
Surface area
  explanation of, 721
  measurement of, 721–726, 732–733

of polyhedra, 721
of prisms, 721–723
of pyramids, 724–725
of right circular cones, 725–726
of right cylinders, 721–723
of similar figures, 733–734
of sphere, 732–733
Swift, Jonathan, 734
Symbols
  equality and inequality, 98
  for multiplication, division, and power, 129
  origin of + and −, 111
Symmetries of Culture: Theory and Practice of Plane Pattern Analysis (Washburn & Crow), 783
Symmetry
  anthropology and, 777
  bilateral, 786
  circular, 777
  classifying, 782
  classroom instruction and, 779
  of culture, 783
  explanation of, 775, 923–924
  identifying lines of, 776
  line of, 776
  NCTM Principles and Standards, 775–776
  patterns with translation, 778, 780–782
  point, 778
  reflection, 749, 776
  rotation, 749, 777–778

Tables, 140. *See also* Make a table/list strategy
Take-away model
  explanation of, 109, 110
  illustration of, 376
Tallies, 158
Talmud, 708
Tangrams
  explanation of, 678, 803
  measurement using, 678–679
Tax rate schedules, 148–149
Tax tables, 148, 149
Taxi fare, 148
Technology. *See also* Calculators; Graphing calculators; Window on Technology
  fractions and, 406–407
  geometry software and, 598, 615, 752, 803, 841
Temperature, 687, 688
Temperature conversion, 148
Terminal side, 609
Terminating decimals, 425
Tessellations, 789. *See also* Tilings
Tetractys, 754
Tetrahedron, 640, 641, 643, 644
Tetromino, 801
Thales of Miletus, 594, 613, 854

Thales' puzzle, 854
Thales' theorem, 821
Theaetetas, 643
Theano, 138
Theoretical probability, 536. *See also* Probability
Third grade
analyzing data in, 498
geometric shapes in, 843
problem solving in, 30
Thomson, Sir William (Lord Kelvin), 79
Three-card Monte, 544
TI-73 (Texas Instruments), 304. *See also* Graphing calculators
TI-82 (Texas Instruments). *See* Graphing calculators
TI-83 (Texas Instruments). *See* Graphing calculators
Tic-tac-toe, multiplication, 224–225
Tiles
computing quotients with, 125
explanation of, 96, 789
Tilings
Escher-type, 796–799
examples of, 790
explanation of, 789
historical background of, 789
with irregular polygons, 793–795
regular, 789, 791
semiregular, 791–792
Time, Navajo's organization of, 853
Toothpick triangles, 811
Toolbox, 954–955
Torus, 640
Total turn theorem, 623
Transformations
NCTM Principles and Standards on, 775–776
of plane, 751
similarity, 766–768
size, 765
Transitive property
of inclusion, 86
of rational numbers, 394
Translation symmetry, 778, 780–782
Translation vector, 753
Translations
Escher-like tiling and, 796
explanation of, 753
finding images under, 753
Transversal lines, 599
Trapezoids, 625, 699
Traversability theorem, 659
Triangle inequality, 816–817
Triangle pick-up sticks, 620
Triangles
activity for exploring, 593
acute, 624
altitude of, 846, 909–910
angles in, 607–609

area of, 698–699
centroid of, 857–858
circumcircle of, 836
classification of, 624
congruent, 811–824 (*See also* Congruent triangles)
degenerate, 34
equilateral, 624
explanation of, 619
explorations with, 413, 811, 818
hands-on activities using, 413
isosceles, 624, 821, 881
medial, 855
median of, 845, 857
obtuse, 624
paper folding activities for, 847
Pascal's, 35–41
right, 624
scalene, 624
similar, 811, 849–859 (*See also* Similar triangles)
Triangular numbers, 34
Trichotomy property, 319, 394
Trisections, of angle, 841, 847, 864
Truncated cubes, 641
Truncated octahedron, 641
Turn. *See* Rotation
Turn angle, 754
Turn arrow, 754
Turn center, 754
Turn symmetry. *See* Rotation symmetry
Twin primes, 94
Two-stage experiments, 554, 556

Ultrasound, 864–865
Unifix™ cubes, 172
Unit analysis, 688
Units. *See also* Manipulatives
of area, 692
learning algorithms using, 184–191
learning decimals using, 416
use of, 171, 172
Universe, of objects, 81
Upper quartiles, 507

Value, 136
van Hiele, Pierre, 635
van Hiele-Geldof, Dina, 635
Variability
measures of, 507–508, 510–511
standard deviation and, 511–514
Variables
to determine general formula, 34–35
explanation of, 33
problem–solving strategy using, 33
Variance, 511*n*
Venn, John, 82
Venn diagrams
examples of, 84, 91
explanation of, 82–83

problem solving with, 95
use of, 84–86
verifying properties with, 87
Vertex figure, 789
Vertical angles, 605
Vertical angles theorem, 605
Vertical line test, 917–918
Vertices
of angles, 601–602
degree of, 658
explanation of, 618
in networks, 657
odd and even, 658
in planar networks, 659–663
of traversable network, 658–659
Vigesimal system, 166
Visualization
choosing good representations for, 489, 491
geometry instruction and, 668
Voderberg, Heinz, 795
Volume
of cones, 728–730
in customary system, 681–682
of cylinders, 727–728
explanation of, 681
measurement of, 685–686, 689, 726–731
metric units of, 685–686
of prisms, 727–728
of pyramids, 728–730
of right prisms, 726–727
of spheres, 730–731

Wallis, John, 129
Wallpaper patterns, 782
Wantzel, Pierre, 839, 864
Washburn, Dorothy K., 783
Webb, David, 765
Weight, 686, 688
Wells, H. G., 531
Weyl, Hermann, 219
Whole numbers
addition of, 103–108, 184–189
determining, 94
division of, 123–128
explanation of, 80, 93–94, 157
function of, 415
multiplication of, 117–123, 129–130
order of, 97, 98
physical and pictorial representations for, 95–97
power operation for, 128–129
problem solving with, 95
properties of, 472–473
rounding of, 218
subtraction of, 108–111, 190–193, 195–196
Widman, Johannes, 111
Wiener, Alexander, 91
Wiles, Andrew, 276

Windchill index, 149
Window on Technology
    automating algorithms, 236
    estate division on a spreadsheet, 64
    functions with graphing calculator, 143
    geometry software, 598, 752
    number patterns on spreadsheet, 41
    prime power factorizations, 257
    random numbers and simulation, 546
    statistical plotting, 492
Witch of Agnesi, 891
Wolpert, Scott, 765

Women's hand spans, 526
Wood stairs design, 399–400
Work backward strategy, 48–50
World population, 149
Wren, Christopher, 701

x-axis, 872
x-coordinate, 872

y-axis, 872
y-coordinate, 872
y-intercept, 894

Zavrotsky, Andres, 280
Zeno, 594
Zero
    as additive identity, 105
    Babylonian system and, 164–165
    development of notion of, 346
    division by, 125
    as exponent, 130, 421
    in Mayan numeration system, 166
    origin of, 95
Zero angles, 602